W9-BIG-812

WITHDRAWN

SCCCC - LIBRARY
4601 Mid Rivers Mall Drive
St. Peters, MO 63376

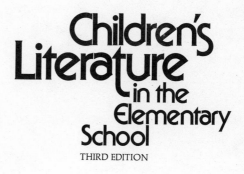

Children's Literature in the Elementary School

THIRD EDITION

76-501

628.5
H 88

Charlotte S. Huck

Children's Literature in the Elementary School

THIRD EDITION

SCCCC - LIBRARY
4601 Mid Rivers Mall Drive
St. Peters, MO 63376

Holt, Rinehart and Winston

New York   Chicago   San Francisco   Atlanta
Dallas   Montreal   Toronto   London   Sydney

MARY'S COLLEGE OF O'FALLON
200 NORTH MAIN STREET
O'FALLON, MISSOURI 63366

Cover design: Fred Pusterla
Book design: Art Ritter
Library of Congress Cataloging in Publication Data
Huck, Charlotte S.
 Children's Literature in the elementary school.
Includes bibliographical references and indexes.
1. Children's literature—Study and teaching.
I. Title.
LB1575.H8   1976   372.6'4   75-29281

ISBN: 0-03-010051-8

Copyright © 1961, 1968 by Holt, Rinehart and Winston, Inc.
Copyright © 1976 by Charlotte S. Huck
All rights reserved.
Printed in the United States of America
6 7 8 9   032   9 8 7 6 5 4 3 2 1

ACKNOWLEDGMENTS

Grateful acknowledgement is made to the following authors, publishers, and agencies for permission to reprint poetry selections from copyrighted material.

Two verses from "Abraham Lincoln" from *A Book of Americans* by Rosemary and Stephen Vincent Benét (Holt, Rinehart and Winston, Inc.). Copyright, 1933, by Stephen Vincent Benét. Copyright renewed © 1961, by Rosemary Carr Benét. Reprinted by permission of Brandt & Brandt. "The Adventures of Isabel" by Ogden Nash, Copyright 1936 by Ogden Nash. From *The Face Is Familiar* by Ogden Nash, by permission of Little, Brown and Co. "Apartment House" by Gerald Raftery, by permission of Gerald Raftery. "April" by Marcia Lee Masters. From her book *Intent on Earth*, originally from the magazine *Contemporary Poetry*. Used by permission of the author. "Ashes my burnt hut," permission granted by The Peter Pauper Press, Inc., Mount Vernon, New York. "Asleep," from the poem "Asleep," which appears in *The Sparrow Bush* by Elizabeth Coatsworth. Text copyright © 1966 by Grosset and Dunlap, Inc. Published by Grosset and Dunlap, Inc. "At the edge of the world" from *Singing for Power* by Ruth Underhill. Originally published by The University of California Press; reprinted by permission of the Regents of the University of California.

From "The Ballad of William Sycamore" from *Ballads and Poems* by Stephen Vincent Benét. Copyright 1931 by Stephen Vincent Benét. Copyright © 1959 by Rosemary Carr Benét. Reprinted by permission of Holt, Rinehart and Winston, Inc. "Blue" by Mary Joyce Pritchard, in *Elementary English*, vol. 40 (May 1963), p. 543. Reprinted by permission of the National Council of Teachers of English. "Boys Don't Cry" from *What's Happening Magazine*. By permission of the Director, Horace Mann-Lincoln Institute. "Brother" by Mary Ann Hoberman, reprinted by permission of Russell and Volkening, Inc., as agents for the author. Copyright © 1959 by Mary Ann Hoberman. "Buildings" by Myra Cohn Livingston, from *Whispers and Other Poems* by Myra Cohn Livingston. Copyright © 1958 by Myra Cohn Livingston. By permission of the author.

"The cabin is small' by Carol Bartlett, 6th grade student of Allaire Stuart, Boulder, Colorado. Reprinted by permission of *Woman's Day Magazine*. Copyright © 1961 by Fawcett Publications, Inc. "The Cat Heard the Cat-Bird" by John Ciardi from *I Met a Man*. Copyright © 1961 by John Ciardi. Reprinted by permission of the publisher Houghton Mifflin Company. "Song of an Unlucky Man" from the book *A Crocodile Has Me by the Leg: African Poems* by Leonard W. Doob, published by Walker & Company, Inc., New York, N.Y., © 1966, 1967 by Leonard W. Doob. "Children When They're Very Sweet" from *The Man Who Sang the Sillies* by John Ciardi. Copyright © 1961

by John Ciardi. Reprinted by permission of J. B. Lippincott Company. "Circles" from *The People, Yes* by Carl Sandburg, copyright 1936, by Harcourt Brace Jovanovich, Inc.; renewed, 1964, by Carl Sandburg. Reprinted by permission of the publishers. "City" by Langston Hughes, reprinted by permission of Harold Ober Associates Incorporated. Copyright © 1958 by Langston Hughes. "City, City" by Marci Ridlon from *That Was Summer*. Text copyright © 1969 by Marci Ridlon. Used by permission of the author. "Conversation with Myself" by Eve Merriam, Copyright © 1964 by Eve Merriam. From *It Doesn't Always Have to Rhyme*. Used by permission of Atheneum Publishers. "Cow" by Valerie Worth, reprinted with the permission of Farrar, Straus & Giroux, Inc., from *Small Poems* by Valerie Worth, Copyright © 1972 by Valerie Worth. "Cows" by James Reeves, published by the Oxford University Press in *The Blackbird in the Lilac*. Used by permission of the author.

"December Leaves" from *Don't Ever Cross a Crocodile* by Kaye Starbird. Copyright © 1963 by Kaye Starbird. Reprinted by permission of J. B. Lippincott Company. Portion of the poem "Dinky," copyright 1953 by Beatrice Roethke, Administratrix of the Estate of Theodor Roethke, from the book *The Collected Poems of Theodor Roethke*. Reprinted by permission of Doubleday & Company, Inc. "Discovery" from *The Golden Hive*, copyright, 1962, 1967, by Harry Behn. Reprinted by permission of Harcourt Brace Jovanovich, Inc. "The Doors", COPYRIGHT © 1966, by Richard Lewis. Reprinted by permission of Simon and Schuster. "Dreams" by Langston Hughes, Copyright 1932 by Alfred A. Knopf, Inc., and renewed 1960 by Langston Hughes. Reprinted from *Don't You Turn Back*, by Langston Hughes, by permission of Alfred A. Knopf, Inc. "Dunkirk," Copyright 1941 and renewed 1969 by Robert Nathan. Reprinted from *The Green Leaf*, by Robert Nathan, by permission of Alfred A. Knopf, Inc.

"Everybody Says," reprinted by permission of G. P. Putnam's Sons from *All Together* by Dorothy Aldis. Copyright 1925–1928, 1934, 1939, 1952 by Dorothy Aldis.

"Far and Near" from *The Wizard in the Well*, © 1956 by Harry Behn. Reprinted by permission of Harcourt Brace Jovanovich, Inc. "A few flies/ and I," Copyright © 1969, by Jean Merrill, from *A Few Flies and I: Haiku by Issa*, selected by Jean Merrill and Ronni Solbert, published by Pantheon Books. "First Snow" from *A Pocketful of Poems* by Marie Louise Allen. Text copyright © 1957 by Marie Allen Howarth. By permission of Harper & Row, Publishers, Inc. "Foghorns," text copyright © 1969 by Lilian Moore. From *I Thought I Heard the City*. Used by permission of Atheneum Publishers. "Fueled," from *Serve Me a Slice of Moon*, © 1965, by Marcie Hans. Reprinted by permission of Harcourt Brace Jovanovich, Inc.

"The Grasshopper," Copyright 1952 by David McCord. From *Every Time I Climb a Tree* by David McCord, by permission of Little, Brown and Co.

"Hello and Good-by" by Mary Ann Hoberman. Reprinted by permission of Russell and Volkening, Inc., as agents for the author. Copyright © 1959 by Mary Ann Hoberman. "Homesick" from . . . *I Never Saw Another Butterfly. . .* edited by H. Volavkova. 1964. McGraw-Hill Book Company. Used with permission of the publisher. From "Homework" in *Egg Thoughts and Other Frances Songs* by Russell Hoban. Text copyright © 1972 by Russell Hoban. Reprinted by permission of Harper & Row, Publishers, Inc. "Hughbert and the Glue" from *The Rose on My Cake* by Karla Kuskin. Copyright © 1964 by Karla Kuskin. Reprinted by permission of Harper and Row, Publishers, Inc.

"I Like It When It's Mizzly" from *I Like Weather* by Aileen Fisher. Text Copyright © 1963 by Aileen Fisher, with permission of Thomas Y. Crowell Company, Inc., publisher. "'I,' says the poem," Copyright © 1964 by Eve Merriam. From *It Doesn't Always Have to Rhyme.* Used by permission of Atheneum Publishers. Excerpt from *Independent Voices,* Copyright © 1968 by Eve Merriam. From *Independent Voices.* Used by permission of Atheneum Publishers. Eight lines from "Indian" from *A Book of Americans* by Rosemary and Stephen Vincent Benét (Holt, Rinehart and Winston, Inc.). Copyright, 1933, by Stephen Vincent Benét. Copyright renewed © 1961, by Rosemary Carr Benét. Reprinted by permission of Brandt & Brandt. "Inside a Poem," Copyright © 1964 by Eve Merriam. From *It Doesn't Always Have to Rhyme.* Used by permission of Atheneum Publishers. "It Happened," Copyright © 1972 by Myra Cohn Livingston. From *The Malibu and Other Poems* by Myra Cohn Livingston (A Margaret K. McElderry Book). Used by permission of Atheneum Publishers.

"Keep a poem in your pocket" and other lines from *Something Special* by Beatrice Schenk de Regniers, © 1958. By permission of Harcourt Brace Jovanovich, Inc.

"Lemons," Copyright © 1963 by Patricia Hubbell. From *The Apple Vendor's Fair.* Used by permission of Atheneum Publishers. "Lengths of Time" from *Wonderful Time* by Phyllis McGinley. Copyright © 1965, 1966 by Phyllis McGinley. Reprinted by permission of J. B. Lippincott Company. "The limerick's lively to write," Copyright © 1961, 1962 by David McCord. From *Take Sky* by David McCord, by permission of Little, Brown and Co. "Little Miss Muffet" by Paul Dehn—© Punch, London. Reprinted by permission of Rothco Cartoons, Inc. "The Lizard," copyright © 1961 by Theodor Roethke from the book *The Collected Poems of Theodor Roethke.* Reprinted by permission of Doubleday & Company, Inc. "The Lone Dog" from *Songs to Save a Soul* by Irene Rutherford McLeod. All rights reserved. Reprinted by permission of The Viking Press, Inc.

"maggie and milly and molly and may" © 1958 by e. e. cummings. Reprinted from his volume *Complete Poems, 1913–1962* by permission of Harcourt Brace Jovanovich, Inc. "March" from *Summer Green* by Elizabeth Coatsworth (Copyright 1948 by Macmillan Publishing Co., Inc.) From "Mother to Son," © 1926, 1954, from *Selected Poems* by Langston Hughes, published by Alfred A. Knopf, Inc. "Motor Cars" from *Songs Around a Toadstool Table* by Rowena Bennett. Copyright © 1967 by Rowena Bennett. Used by permission of Follett Publishing Company, a division of Follett Corporation. "The Mountain" from *Chrysalis.* Reprinted by permission of Curtis Brown, Ltd. Copyright © 1949, 1952, 1953, 1956, 1957, 1960, 1963, 1964, 1966, 1967, 1968 by Harry Behn. "Mrs. Peck-Pigeon," Copyright 1933, © renewed 1961 by Eleanor Farjeon. From *Poems for Children* by Eleanor Farjeon. Copyright 1951 by Eleanor Farjeon. Reprinted by permission of J. B. Lippincott Company. Also reprinted by permission of Harold Ober Associates Incorporated, Copyright 1933, 1961 by Eleanor Farjeon. "My Parents Kept Me from Children Who Were Rough," Copyright 1934 and renewed 1962 by Stephen Spender. Reprinted from *Collected Poems, 1928–1953,* by Stephen Spender, by permission of Random House, Inc. Also reprinted by permission of Faber and Faber Ltd. from *Collected Poems.*

"New Shoes," Copyright © 1932, by The John Day Company, Inc. Reprinted from *The Golden Flute* by Alice Hubbard and Adeline Babbit by permission of The John Day Company, Inc., an Intext publisher.

"The Old House" by Walter de la Mare, by permission of The Literary Trustees of Walter de la Mare, and The Society of Authors as their representative. "An old silent pond," Basho. From *Cricket Songs: Japanese Haiku* translated and © 1964 by Harry Behn. Reprinted by permission of Harcourt Brace Jovanovich, Inc. "Otto" from *Bronzeville Boys and Girls* by Gwendolyn Books. Copyright © 1956 by Gwendolyn Brooks Blakely. Reprinted by permission of Harper & Row, Publishers, Inc.

"The Pickety Fence," Copyright 1952 by David McCord. From *Every Time I Climb a Tree* by David McCord, by permission of Little, Brown and Co. "Poem," Copyright 1932 by Alfred A. Knopf, Inc., and renewed 1960 by Langston Hughes. Reprinted from *Don't You Turn Back,* by Langston Hughes, by permission of Alfred A. Knopf, Inc. "Poem of Praise" from *Poems* by Elizabeth Coatsworth (Copyright 1934 by Macmillan Publishing Co., Inc., renewed 1962 by Elizabeth Coatsworth Beston). "Poem to Mud," text copyrighted © 1969 by Zilpha Keatley Snyder from *Today Is Saturday.* Used by permission of Atheneum Publishers. "The Prayer of the Cock" from *Prayers from the Ark* by Carmen Bernos de Gasztold, translated by Rumer Godden. English text copyright © 1962 by Rumer Godden. All rights reserved. Reprinted by permission of The Viking Press, Inc. "Primer Lesson" from *Slabs of the Sunburnt West* by Carl Sandburg, copyright, 1922, by Harcourt Brace Jovanovich, Inc.; renewed, 1950, by Carl Sandburg. Reprinted by permission of the publishers. "Pussy Willows" is reprinted by permission of Charles Scribner's Sons from *In the Woods, In the Meadow, In the Sky* by Aileen Fisher. Text copyright © 1965 by Aileen Fisher.

"Questions" by Marci Ridlon from *That Was Summer.* Text copyright © 1969 by Marci Ridlon. Used by permission of the author.

"Satellite, Satellite," Copyright © 1962 by Eve Merriam. From *There Is No Rhyme for Silver.* Used by permission of Atheneum Publishers. "The Sea" from *The Wandering Moon* by James Reeves. By permission of William Heinemann Ltd., Publishers. "The Sea Gull" from *Summer Green* by Elizabeth Coatsworth (Copyright 1947 by Macmillan Publishing Co., Inc.). "Skins" by Aileen Fisher. By permission of the author. "The Snare" from *Collected Poems* of James Stephens (Copyright 1915 by Macmillan Publishing Co., Inc., renewed 1943 by James Stephens.) Also, from *Collected Poems* by James Stephens, reprinted by permission of Mrs. Iris Wise; Macmillan London & Basingstoke; and The Macmillan Company of Canada Limited. "Solitude" from the book *Now We Are Six* by A. A. Milne. Decorations by E. H. Shepard. Copyright, 1927, by E. P. Dutton & Co., Inc. Renewal, 1955, by A. A. Milne. Published by E. P. Dutton & Co., Inc. and used with their permission. Also reprinted by permission of the Canadian Publishers, McClelland and Stewart Limited, Toronto. "Song of the Open Road," Copyright 1932 by Ogden Nash. From *Verses from 1929 On* by Ogden Nash, by permission of Little, Brown and Co. "Song to Night," reprinted by permission of Coward, McCann & Geoghegan, Inc., from *The Creaking Stair* by Elizabeth Coatsworth. Copyright 1923 by Elizabeth Coatsworth; 1929, 1949 by Coward-McCann, Inc. "A spark in the sun," © 1964 by Harry Behn. Reprinted from his volume *Cricket Songs; Japanese Haiku* by permission of Harcourt Brace Jovanovich, Inc. "Steam Shovel" from *Upper Pasture:*

76501

Poems by Charles Malam. Copyright 1930, © 1958 by Charles Malam. Reprinted by permission of Holt, Rinehart and Winston, Inc. "The Storm," by Adrien Stoutenberg, reprinted from *The Things that Are,* copyright 1964 by the Reilly and Lee Company, a division of Henry Regnery Company, Chicago. "Summons," reprinted by permission of Robert Francis and the University of Massachusetts Press from *Come Out Into the Sun: New & Selected Poems* by Robert Francis, © Copyright 1965.

"Tea Party" from *Windy Morning,* copyright, 1953, by Harry Behn. Reprinted by permission of Harcourt Brace Jovanovich, Inc. "There is joy in," reprinted by permission of William Collins + World Publishing, Co., Inc., from *Beyond the High Hills* by Knud Rasmussen, Copyright © 1961 The World Publishing Company. "There Isn't Time!," Copyright 1933, © renewed 1961 by Eleanor Farjeon. From *Poems for Children* by Eleanor Farjeon. Copyright 1951 by Eleanor Farjeon. Reprinted by permission of J. B. Lippincott Company. Also reprinted by permission of Harold Ober Associates, Inc. Copyright 1933, 1961 by Eleanor Farjeon. "This Is My Rock," Copyright 1929 by David McCord. From *Every Time I Climb a Tree* by David McCord, be permission of Little, Brown and Co. "To Look at Any Thing" © 1961 by John Moffitt. Reprinted from his volume, *The Living Seed,* by permission of Harcourt Brace Jovanovich, Inc. "Tractor," reprinted with the permission of Farrar, Straus & Giroux, Inc., from *Small Poems* by Valerie Worth. Copyright © 1972 by Valerie Worth. "Tree," text copyright © 1969 by Zilpha Keatley Snyder. From *Today Is Saturday.*

Additional acknowledgments are made as follows: Copyright © 1969 by Miska Miles. From *Apricot ABC* by Miska Miles, by permission of Little, Brown and Co., in association with the Atlantic Monthly Press. Lines from "Buckingham Palace" from *When We Were Very Young* by A. A. Milne. Copyright 1924 by E. P. Dutton & Co., Inc.; renewal, 1952, by A. A. Milne. Reprinted by permission of the publishers, E. P. Dutton & Co., Inc., and The Canadian Publishers, McClelland and Stewart Limited, Toronto. From "Catalog" by Rosalie Moore. Reprinted by permission. *The New Yorker* Magazine; copyright 1940, 1968. Lines from "Choosing Shoes" by Ffrida Wolfe from her book *The Very Thing.* With permission of Sidgwick & Jackson Ltd, Publishers. Lines from "The Coin" from *Collected Poems* of Sara Teasdale (Copyright 1920 by Macmillan Publishing Co., Inc., renewed 1948 by Mamie T. Wheless). Used by permission of Macmillan Publishing Company. "Crocus" from *All That Sunlight* by Charlotte Zolotow. Text copyright © 1967 by Charlotte Zolotow. Reprinted by permission of Harper & Row, Publishers, Inc. From "Cynthia in the Snow" in *Bronzeville Boys and Girls* by Gwendolyn Brooks. Copyright © 1956 by Gwendolyn Brooks Blakely. Reprinted by permission of Harper & Row, Publishers, Inc. From "The Deer" by Mary Austin in *The Children Sing in the Far West,* by permission of Houghton Mifflin Company. Lines from "The Dinner Party" by Dorothy Aldis from *All Together.* Copyright 1925, 1926, 1927, 1928, 1934, 1939, 1952, by Dorothy Aldis. By permission of the publisher, G. P. Putnam's Sons. From *English Fairy Tales* by Flora Annie Steel (Copyright 1918 by Macmillan Publishing Co., Inc., renewed 1946 by Mabel H. Webster). Used by permission of Macmillan Publishing Company. Lines from "The House of the Mouse" from *Another Here and Now Story Book* by Lucy Sprague Mitchell. Copyright 1937 by E. P. Dutton & Co., Inc.; renewal © 1965 by Lucy Sprague Mitchell. Reprinted by permission of the publishers, E. P. Dutton & Co., Inc. From "I Woke Up This Morning" in *The Rose on My Cake* by Karla Kuskin. Copyright © 1964 by Karla Kuskin. Reprinted by permission of Harper & Row, Publishers, Inc. Lines from "An Irish Airman Foresees His Death" from *Collected Poems* of William Butler Yeats (Copyright 1919 by Macmillan Publishing Co., Inc., renewed 1947 by Bertha Georgie

Used by permission of Atheneum Publishers. "Triolet Against Sisters" from *Times Three* by Phyllis McGinley. Copyright © 1959 by Phyllis McGinley. Originally appeared in *The New Yorker.* Reprinted by permission of The Viking Press, Inc.

"Well, Yes" from *Street Poems* by Robert Froman. Copyright, © 1971 by Robert Froman. Reprinted by permission of the publishers, Saturday Review Press/E. P. Dutton & Co., Inc. "Whispers" from *Whispers and Other Poems* by Myra Cohn Livingston. Copyright © 1958 by Myra Cohn Livingston. By permission of the author. "White Season" by Frances Frost from *Pool in the Meadow.* Copyright 1933 by Frances M. Frost. Reprinted by permission of the publisher, Houghton Mifflin Company. "Whose Are This Pond and House," Copyright © Robert Kotewell and Norman L. Smith, 1962. Reprinted by permission of Penguin Books, Ltd. "Wind Song," text copyright © 1967 by Lilian Moore. From *I Feel the Same Way.* Used by permission of Atheneum Publishers. "Winter and Summer" from *Whispers and Other Poems* by Myra Cohn Livingston. By permission of the author. "Word Poem," reprinted by permission of William Morrow & Co., Inc., from *Black Feeling, Black Talk, Black Judgment* by Nikki Giovanni. Copyright © 1968, 1970 by Nikki Giovanni. "Write a limerick now," excerpted from "Write Me a Verse," Copyright 1961, 1962 by David McCord. From *Take Sky* by David McCord, by permission of Little, Brown and Co.

Special thanks are due to Mr. and Mrs. Robert Johnson for permission to use the photograph that introduces Part I.

Yeats). Used by permission of Macmillan Publishing Company. Lines from "Just Me" from *Farther Than Far* by Margaret Hillert (© Follett 1969). Used by permission of the author. From "Little Fox Lost" from *The Little Whistler* by Frances Frost. Copyright 1949 by Frances Frost. Used with permission of McGraw-Hill Book Company. Lines from "Lullaby" by Robert Hillyer from *Collected Poems.* Copyright 1933 by Robert Hillyer. By permission of the publisher, Alfred A. Knopf, Inc. Lines from "Morning in Winter" by Harry Behn from *Windy Morning.* By permission of Harcourt Brace Jovanovich, Inc. Data of "Hierarchy of Needs" from *Motivation and Personality,* 2nd ed., by Abraham H. Maslow (Harper & Row, 1970). Used with permission. Lines from "New Little Boy" by Harry Behn from *Windy Morning.* By permission of Harcourt Brace Jovanovich, Inc. Lines from "A New Song to Sing about Jonathan Bing" from *Jonathan Bing* by Beatrice Brown. Used with permission of the publisher, Lothrop, Lee & Shepard. Lines from "Night" from *Collected Poems* of Sara Teasdale (Copyright 1930 by Sara Teasdale Filsinger, renewed 1958 by Guaranty Trust Company of New York, Executor). Used by permission of Macmillan Publishing Company. From "Night of Wind" by Frances Frost in *Pool in the Meadow,* by permission of Houghton Mifflin Company. Lines from "Poetry," Copyright 1938 by Eleanor Farjeon. Copyright © renewed 1966 by Gervase Farjeon. From *Poems for Children* by Eleanor Farjeon. Copyright 1951 by Eleanor Farjeon. Reprinted by permission of J. B. Lippincott Company. Lines from "A Recollection" by Frances Cornford from *Collected Poems.* Used by permission of Barrie & Jenkins, Publishers. Lines from *Red Riding Hood.* Text Copyright © 1972 by Beatrice de Regniers. From *Red Riding Hood Retold in Verse* by Beatrice de Regniers. Used by permission of Atheneum Publishers. Lines from "The Secret Place" by Dorothy Aldis from *All Together.* Copyright 1925, 1926, 1927, 1928, 1934, 1939, 1952, by Dorothy Aldis. By permission of the publisher, G. P. Putnam's Sons. Lines from "Some One" by Walter de la Mare, used with permission of The Literary Trustees of Walter de la Mare and The Society of Authors as their representative. From "Sunning" in *Crickety Cricket! The Best-Loved Poems of James S. Tippett.* Text copyright © 1973 by Martha K. Tippett. Reprinted by permission of Harper & Row, Publishers, Inc.

In memory of
Doris Young Kuhn
1920–1969

POEM

I loved my friend
He went away from me
There's nothing more to say.
The poem ends,
Soft as it began—
I loved my friend.

LANGSTON HUGHES

Preface

In writing this third edition of *Children's Literature in the Elementary School* my primary purpose was to share my knowledge and enthusiasm for the literature of childhood with students, teachers, and librarians, hoping that they in turn would communicate their excitement about books to the children they teach. As a nation we have become so concerned with teaching the skills of reading that we have neglected to help children discover the joys of reading. I believe that children become readers only by reading many books of their own choosing and by hearing someone reading literature of quality aloud with obvious delight and enthusiasm. It is my hope that the students, teachers, and librarians who read this text will be able to create in children a joy and love of good books.

The field of children's literature has grown tremendously in the past ten years. While the publishing of juvenile books is currently on the decline, there are still nearly 45,000 children's books in print! How can prospective teachers and librarians learn to select that which is best from this huge number? How can they help children learn to be discriminating readers? Another constant purpose of this book, then, is to help each person reading it to begin to build a frame of reference about children's literature; developing criteria for evaluation of the various kinds or genre of literature, discovering favorite books of children at various developmental levels, knowing the quality of writing of various authors, building a personal list of favorite books to share with children, and being able to recommend the right book for the right child.

I also wanted to show how books can become an integral part of the curriculum. The new chart in Chapter 4, "A Cultural Study of Folktales," for example suggests many ways that the study of any country may be enriched by the knowledge of its folklore and its traditional literature; while the contemporary realistic fiction that is the subject of Chapter 7 could lead to a lively discussion of the social and moral issues which face our changing society. Chapters 8 ("Historical Fiction") and 9 ("Informational Books and Biography") present many books which will help children become more thoughtful evaluators of the past and

more critical thinkers through comparing various informational books and determining their accuracy and authenticity. Most importantly, Chapter 12 ("The Literature Program") details the unique contribution of literature for children and suggests its rightful place in the curriculum.

Over 80 percent of this edition has been rewritten, while every chapter has been updated and expanded. In Part I a greater emphasis has been placed upon child development and the research showing the importance of literature to the child's language growth, reading achievement, and cognitive and affective development. The chart, "Books for Ages and Stages," has been expanded to include some Piagetian principles of developmental levels. Emphasis is placed not only upon what books can do for children but also on what students, teachers, and librarians can learn about children through their response to books.

In Part II the chapters have been rearranged and reorganized. Chapter 5 ("Modern Fantasy"), which has its very roots in folklore and myth, seemed more logically to follow the chapter on traditional literature. Biography, which was formerly with historical fiction, has been combined with other nonfiction books in Chapter 9 ("Informational Books and Biography"). In order to maintain consistency in presenting books by genre, the chapter, "Books for Special Interests," which appeared in the second edition, has been eliminated; but these books—including animal stories, sports stories, humorous books, and mysteries—have been incorporated in Chapter 7 of this edition.

The chapter on traditional literature has been expanded to include a discussion of the motifs in folktales as well as the folktales of various cultures. Four new charts have been added to this chapter. Over one hundred poems, half of which are new to this edition, have been included in the poetry chapter. Recent research on children's poetry preferences has also been cited. Because poetry seems the most neglected of all literature in the elementary school, special teaching activities relating to poetry have been included.

Concern for racism and discrimination and sex-role stereotyping has been considered in relation to "Picture Books," "Historical Fiction," "Informational Books," and "Realistic Fiction." Both poor and good examples have been compared. Issues relating to the new freedoms and changing criteria for evaluating contemporary literature are discussed in Chapter 7. Concrete examples of books that present such social problems as divorce, alternative life styles, drugs, aging, and death have been included in this chapter, as well. Guidelines for evaluating minority literature are also presented in Chapter 7 in the section, "Living in a Pluralistic Society."

The three chapters which make up Part III suggest the necessary steps for developing a literature program in an elementary school. Chapter 10 ("Creating the Learning Environment") stresses the importance of developing classroom environments and school library media centers, which open up the possibilities for growth and enrichment of children through many rich experiences and exposure to a wide variety of books and media. The role of the media specialist in the school library has been expanded, and more attention has been given to some of the unique contributions of the public library and other community agencies in bringing books and children together. In Chapter 11 ("Extending Literature through Creative Activities"), emphasis is placed on the child's involvement and interpretation of literature through art, drama, creative writing, making of books, puppets, games, and other worthwhile activities which can make books more memorable. Chapter 12 ("The Literature Program") stresses both wide reading and in-depth discussions of books. Teaching strategies, which include charts on how to "web a book" and ways to develop good questioning techniques are provided. Some sample literature lessons are included, along with some actual transcripts showing children's responses to books. Another new feature of Part III is a color section showing fine learning environments and pictures of children's interpretations of various books.

While this is a text about children's literature, it is also a book about teaching children's literature. It is impossible in writing such a text not to reveal one's personal philosophy about what constitutes good teaching. This I have done openly in both text and pictures. For the past five years I have been involved in an alternative program of teaching at The Ohio State University. I have had the opportunity of working closely with master teachers and great students.

Not a week goes by that I do not visit an elementary school classroom. I know how exciting teaching and learning can be when teachers release the potential within each child, rather than impose the same subject matter on all. Throughout this text I have recommended the importance of giving children choices of the books they wish to read and in finding a variety of ways for children to respond to books. I have suggested that school should be a place where children have real experiences of living and learning, and I have tried to show how books may enrich these experiences and how literature of quality can provide vicarious experiences of its own. I know this can be done, for I have been fortunate in working with teachers who do make books an integral and authentic part of all that children do. I know, too, that how we teach is almost as important as what we teach; that it is possible to teach a child to read and to hate reading at the same time; that it is just as easy to teach children to read and develop a love of reading. I believe that schools can be joyful places where the quality of living is equal to the quality of learning.

In writing this edition I have missed the fine insights and wise counsel of my co-author of the first two editions, Doris Young Kuhn, who was killed in a tragic accident in 1969. Knowing Doris as long and as well as I did, I take some consolation in thinking that she would have approved the direction of this third edition.

No one writes a text of this magnitude alone, however, even if my name is listed as the only author. I am deeply indebted to many persons: the teachers, librarians, and children in the schools where I have always been welcomed; the students in my children's literature classes; the EPIC program and my Ph.D. students—all of whom have taught me more than I have taught them. These persons have shared their insights of children's responses and interpretations of literature with me; they have sent me pictures or allowed me to take pictures in their schools. I thank them all and hope they will continue to share their enthusiasm and excitement about children and books.

Specifically, I wish to express my appreciation to Mary Karrer, Media Specialist in the Worthington Public Schools for her research on Chapter 9 ("Informational Books and Biography"). I am particularly grateful to Gay Dunn, Ph.D. student at The Ohio State University, for her care and research in the initial updating of Appendix B ("Book Selection Aids"). Harold G. Shane, Patricia Cianciolo, and Anne Izard read the manuscript and wrote most helpful criticism, which was incorporated into the text whenever possible. I also wish to acknowledge my enormous debt to Louise Waller, Developmental Editor at Holt, Rinehart and Winston, whose care, concern, and attention to detail are seen throughout this text, and whose gentle proddings were essential for its final production.

Everything always happens in threes in fairy tales, and so it seems appropriate that I have had three persons who were my good companions in the writing of this text. Without their constant and able support the journey could never have been made. Barbara Fincher typed both the rough and final drafts of this manuscript and gave me good advice along the way. Barbara Friedberg always arrived just when I needed her most, to begin another chapter, to try out particu-

lar activities in her classroom, and to convey her enthusiasm for the book. She has a way of making the mountains look like hills. Janet Hickman, a published author of children's books, interrupted her own writing to give me hours of her time in research; writing the rough draft of Chapter 9; and doing the arduous task of making the author, illustrator, and title index. Even when progress slowed to a snail's pace she never doubted that we would reach our destination. There is no way to adequately thank these companions except to wonder at the glory of being fortunate enough to have had their company and support. Without them this edition could never have been published, and I shall be forever grateful.

—C.S.H.

Columbus, Ohio
December 1975

CONTENTS

PART 1
Learning about Children and Books

1 Understanding Children and Literature

Was there ever a child who did not respond to the game of "Pat a Cake, Pat a Cake, Baker's Man"; march to the rhythm of "They're changing guards at Buckingham Palace/Christopher Robin went down with Alice"; or join in the timeless refrain of "Hundreds of cats, thousands of cats, millions and billions and trillions of cats"? I hope not. For the literature experience begins with the child's response to these well-loved favorites. It continues with the spontaneous delight of discovering a pathetic Eeyore and a lovable Pooh; it wells up in tears over the death of a spider in *Charlotte's Web* or the shooting of a faithful dog in *Old Yeller.*

The child begins to learn who he is as he sees his behavior mirrored by that of a disobedient rabbit who nearly meets with disaster in Mr. MacGregor's garden. He recognizes the same harsh feelings of jealousy that beset a demanding badger named Frances who must learn to accept her baby sister, Gloria. The value of cooperative effort is seen in the story of *The Great Big Enormous Turnip;* while the devastating effect of ridicule is revealed in *The Hundred Dresses.*

The growing child experiences loneliness and fear as he imagines what it would be like to live as Karana did, alone on her *Island of the Blue Dolphins* for some eighteen years. Or he can relive the exciting moments of the year 1773 when *Johnny Tremain* was an apprentice to a silversmith named Paul Revere. He can read of the injustice inflicted upon the Indians in *Sing Down the Moon,* and realize that humans do not always learn from the past, as he reads of the same kind of injustice imposed upon the Japanese-Americans in *Journey to Topaz.* He can experience man's inhumanity to man in the story of *Sounder;* and he can learn of the horrors of war by reading *The Man in the Box, A Story from Vietnam.* A better future can be imagined as he projects himself into space and views the world from the perspective of Elana, *Enchantress from the Stars,* a member of a more highly developed culture devoted to the service of others.

All that people have ever thought, done, or dreamed lies waiting to be discovered in a book. Literature begins with Mother Goose. It includes Sendak as well as Shakespeare, Milne as much as Milton, and Carroll before Camus. For children's literature is a part of the mainstream of all literature, whose source is life itself.

Knowing Children's Literature

LITERATURE DEFINED

Today, there is an abundance of literature for children that has never existed before in the history of the world. Different kinds of books, vastly increased production of books, and widespread distribution techniques make thousands of books available to children. Revolving racks in drugstores, supermarkets, bus depots, and airports display brightly illustrated books designed to attract young readers. Parents select books as they pile groceries into the cart. Encyclopedias are found next to frozen foods. Children's paperbacks are becoming as popular as adult ones. Following adult patterns, selections from children's book-of-the-month clubs and children's magazines find their way into thousands of homes. Begun with the assistance of the federal government, most schools have recognized the importance of a library media center and trained librarian for every elementary school. Thousands of children also visit attractive rooms in public libraries each week where trained librarians give them assistance.

From the over forty thousand books now available for boys and girls, how shall teachers, librarians, and parents select that which is literature? How can one distinguish the trees from the forest? In this plethora of books, there is the great danger of overlooking really fine literature. The number of books published each year increases the difficulty of book selection and, at the same time, emphasizes its need. Two questions need to be considered: (1) What is literature? and (2) What literature is appropriate for children?

Literature is the imaginative shaping of life and thought into the forms and structures of language. The province of literature is the human condition; life with all its feelings, thoughts, and insights. The experience of literature is always two dimensional, for it involves both the book and the reader. Some critics consider Carroll's *Alice in Wonderland* the greatest book ever written for children. However, if the child has no background in fantasy, cannot comprehend the complexity of the plot, nor tolerate the logic of its illogic, he will not be able to interact with the book and so experience literature. We need then to consider the function of the words and pic-

tures. How do the symbols produce an aesthetic experience; in other words, how do the symbols help the reader perceive pattern, relationships, feelings that produce an inner experience of art? This aesthetic experience may be a vivid reconstruction of past experience, an extension of experience, or creation of a new experience.

> We all have, in our experience, memories of certain books which changed us in some way—by disturbing us, or by a glorious affirmation of some emotion we knew but could never shape in words, or by some revelation of human nature. Virginia Woolf calls such times "moments of being," and James Joyce titles them "epiphanies."[1]

W. H. Auden differentiates between first-rate literature and second-rate literature, writing that the reader responds to second-rate literature by saying:

> "That's just the way I always felt." But first-rate literature makes one say: "Until now, I never knew how I felt. Thanks to this experience, I shall never feel the same way again."[2]

The graphic symbols of literature consist of language and illustrations presented in such a way that the reader is made aware of an order, a unity, a balance, or a new frame of reference. For order is that beautiful harmony of relationships that makes a truly significant book. Good writing, or effective use of language, on any subject may produce aesthetic experiences. The imaginative use of language produces both intellectual and emotional responses. It will cause the reader to perceive characters, conflicts, elements in a setting, and universal problems of mankind; it will help the reader to experience the delight of beauty, wonder, and humor; or the despair of sorrow, injustice, and ugliness. Vicariously, he will experience other places, other times, and other life styles; he may identify with others, or find his own self-identity; he may observe nature more closely or from a different perspective; he will encounter the thrill of taking risks and meeting mystery; he will endure suffering; he will enjoy a sense of achievement, and feel he belongs

[1] Frances Clarke Sayers, *Summoned by Books* (New York: Viking, 1965), p. 16.
[2] W. H. Auden, as quoted by Robert B. Heilman in "Literature and Growing Up," *English Journal*, Vol. 45 (September 1956), p. 307.

to one segment or all of humanity. He will be challenged to dream dreams, to ponder, and to ask questions of himself.

What Is Children's Literature?

It might be said that a child's book is a book a child is reading, and an adult book is a book occupying the attention of an adult. Before the nineteenth century only a few books were written for the specific readership of children. Children read books written for adults, taking from them what they could understand. Today, children continue to read some books intended for adults; for example, Eric Segal's *Love Story* and *Manchild in the Promised Land* by Claude Brown. And yet some books first written for children—such as *The Velveteen Rabbit, Winnie the Pooh,* and *The Hobbit*—have been claimed as their own by college students. *Watership Down* by Richard Adams was published as a children's book in England and as an adult book in the United States. Soon after its publication in the U.S., it was listed as a best seller for adults, young people, and children. Obviously the line between children's literature and adult literature is blurred.

Children today are more sophisticated and knowledgeable than any other generation of their age has been. They spend more time viewing television than they spend in school. The evening news has shown them actual views of war while they ate their dinners. They have witnessed the Watergate scandal, the shootings of Martin Luther King and George Wallace, the starving of Biafran children. While the modern child is separated from first-hand knowledge of birth, death, and senility, the mass media has brought him the vicarious and daily experiences of crime, poverty, war, sex, divorce, and murder.

Such exposure has forced adults to reconsider what seems appropriate for children's literature. It seems unbelievable that a few years ago L'Engle's *Meet the Austins* was rejected by several publishers because it began with a death; or that some reviewers were shocked by a mild "damn" in *Harriet the Spy* by Fitzhugh. Such taboos have long since disappeared. Children's books are reflecting the problems of today, the ones children read about in the newspapers and see on television.

However, the content of children's literature is limited by the experience and understanding

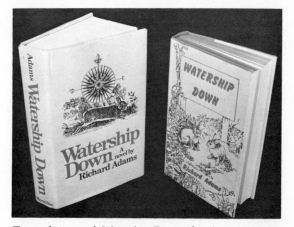

Two editions of *Watership Down*; the American one for adults; the English one for children.

From *Watership Down* by Richard Adams. Jacket illustration copyright © 1974 by Macmillan Publishing Co., Inc. Used by permission of the publisher. From *Watership Down* by Richard Adams. Jacket design by Hazel Underwood. Used with permission of Rex Collings Limited, Publishers.

of children. Certain emotional and psychological responses seem outside the realm of childhood. For example, the feeling of nostalgia is an adult emotion that is foreign to most boys and girls. Children seldom look back on their childhood, but always forward. Such a sentimental, nostalgic book as *Childhood Is a Time of Innocence* by Joan Walsh Anglund is not for children but is about childhood. One also wonders what frame of reference a child brings to understanding the old nostalgic engravings which were used to illustrate the book *The Slightly Irregular Fire Engine* by Barthelme. The young child does not revere the past or his own childhood; he is too busy living in the present.

Cynicism and despair are not childlike emotions. The cynic is bitter, angry, frustrated about the loss of values he once believed in. Some books, such as *Don't Play Dead Before You Have To* by Wojciechowska, are destructive of values before children have had time to develop them. Few children have known despair. They may have endured pain, sorrow, or horror; they may be in what we would consider hopeless situations, but they are not without hope. The truth of the Russian folktale by Reyher, *My Mother Is the Most Beautiful Woman in the World*, shines clear. Children see beauty where there is ugliness; they are hopeful when adults have given up. This is not to suggest that all stories for children must have happy endings; many today do not. It is only to say that when you close the door on hope, you have left the realm of childhood. The only limitations, then, that seem binding on literature for children are those that appropriately reflect the emotions and experiences of children today.

Writing for Children

The skilled author does not write differently or less carefully for children just because he thinks they will not be aware of style or language. In the introduction to *Hakon of Rogen's Saga*, author Haugaard wrote, "It was not written for 'youth' in the sense that I have blunted my pen before I started."[3] Just as a pediatrician must know the essentials of medicine and then apply this knowledge to child patients, so the author of children's literature must know the essentials of fine writing and apply this knowledge to children's books. The surgeon and the pediatrician are equally honored. (Likewise, no one would think of calling a pediatrician a "Kiddy doctor"; it seems too bad to demean the literature of childhood by calling it "Kiddy–lit.") Authors of children's literature and those who write for adults should receive equal approbation. C. S. Lewis[4] maintained that he wrote a children's story because a children's story was the best art form for what he had to say. Lewis wrote both for adults and children, as have Rumer Godden, Elizabeth Yates, Pearl Buck, E. B. White, Isaac Bashevis Singer, and many other well-known authors. They do not "blunt their pens" when they write for boys and girls.

The uniqueness of children's literature, then, lies in the audience that it addresses. Authors of children's books are circumscribed only by the experiences of childhood, but these are vast and complex. For children think and feel; they wonder and they dream. Their lives may be filled with love or terror. Much is known, but little is explained. The child is curious about life and adult activities. He lives in the midst of tensions, of balances of love and hate within the family and the neighborhood. The author who can fill these experiences with imagination and insight,

and communicate them to children is writing children's literature.

EVALUATING CHILDREN'S BOOKS

A young child's initial response to a book, story, or poem is emotional; the child will tell you how he feels about it and what it means to him. Once a child begins to deal with the "whys" of his feelings he will discover the ways in which the author builds plot, develops characters, and uses language to create meaning and feeling. While teachers and librarians will begin at the affective level of response, they will want to extend children's discriminatory powers to help them discover what constitutes a well-written book. This means that teachers and librarians must know something of the structures and forms of literature; at the same time, they will want to learn much about the structure of children's thought, language acquisition, social and emotional development, and changing interests. For only when teachers and librarians are knowledgeable about both children and books can they ever hope to bring the two together for a meaningful experience of literature.

The traditional criteria by which we evaluate a work of fiction include such elements as plot, setting, theme, characterization, style, and format. Specialized criteria need to be applied to different types of literature, such as picture books, biographies, and informational books. Additional criteria are also needed to evaluate certain forms of fiction. For example, criteria for a realistic story would not be the same as those used for modern fantasy. Historical fiction requires the added criteria of authenticity of setting and mood. Perhaps the first task of both the teacher and the children is to identify the kind of book they are reading in order to apply the appropriate criteria for evaluation. In evaluating fiction, we usually begin with these criteria:

Plot

Of prime importance in any work of fiction is the plot. Children ask first, "Does the book tell a good story?" The plot is the plan of action; it tells what the characters do and what happens to them. It is the thread that holds the fabric of the story together and makes the reader want to continue reading.

[3]Erik Christian Haugaard, *Hakon of Rogen's Saga* (Boston: Houghton Mifflin, 1963).
[4]C. S. Lewis, "On Three Ways of Writing for Children," *The Horn Book Magazine*, Vol. 39 (October 1963), p. 460.

A well-constructed plot is organic and inter-related. It grows logically and naturally from the actions and the decisions of the characters in given situations. The plot should be credible and ring true rather than depend on coincidence and contrivance. It should be original and fresh rather than trite, tired, and predictable.

The appeal of the series books is based com-pletely on action and happenings. Their stories are always predictable; Nancy Drew never fails to solve a mystery and Tom Swift accomplishes one major feat after another. These books move rapidly from one improbable happening to an-other. The action is beyond the capabilities of the characters and becomes contrived and sensa-tional.

In books that have substance, obstacles are not quickly overcome, and choices are not always clearcut. In *The Wild Heart* by Helen Griffiths a boy must make a cruel decision in order to save the horse he loves. This is not the typical horse story in which the hero finally tames the wild stallion or wins a race, but one that is compel-lingly different and original.

Books may be exciting, fast-moving, and well-written. Sperry's *Call It Courage* gains increasing momentum with each of Mafatu's courageous feats until the climax is reached at the close of the book. Suspense is maintained with the rising action of the story. The climax of a story should be easily identifiable and develop naturally from the story. Children prefer a swift conclusion fol-lowing the climax, but the denouement should knit together the loose ends of the story.

Most of the plots in children's literature are presented in a linear fashion. Usually children do not have the maturity to follow several plots or many flashbacks in time or place. However, sev-eral excellent books for middle-graders do make use of these devices. The Newbery Award book, *Julie of the Wolves* by Jean George, begins at the point at which the thirteen-year-old Eskimo girl realizes she is lost without food on the North Slope of Alaska. The middle section is a flash-back to her earlier life and the reason she ran away, while the last part relates her tortuous trek back to civilization. The flashback accounts for her desperate predicament and creates suspense and interest as the reader worries about the out-come. In *Ash Road,* Ivan Southall skillfully por-trays the actions of some five families in a roaring bushfire in Australia. The plot is complex, as it shifts from one group of children to another, but individuals are sharply delineated as they react to the searing horror of the fire. The effectiveness of the structure, then, depends upon the clarity of the author's presentation and the child's ability to comprehend complexity.

Plot is but one element of good writing. If a book does not have a substantial plot, it will not hold children's interest long. But well-loved books contain indefinable qualities and are mem-orable for more than plot alone.

Setting

The structure of the story pertains to both the construction of the plot and its setting. The set-ting may be in the past, the present, or the future. The story may take place in a specific locale, or the setting may be deliberately vague to convey the universal feeling of all small towns, all large cities, or all rural communities.

Both the time and place of the story should affect the action, the characters, and the theme. The setting for the haunting tale of *Sounder* by William Armstrong is the rural South sometime near the turn of the century. The story portrays the injustices and cruelties inflicted on a black sharecropper because he had stolen a ham for his hungry family. While the story has a specific setting in time and place, for many it represents the plight of all blacks in the rural South before Selma. The filmed version of *Sounder* changed the locale from Virginia to Louisiana and the time from the early nineteen hundreds to the depres-sion year of 1933, with little loss in the impact of the story. Such a change suggests the univer-sality of this story and its setting.

Whenever a specific period of time or locale is presented, it should be authentic and true to what the author knows of that period, place, or people. Part of the challenge of writing accurate historical fiction is believable reconstruction of the time and place of the action. *The Valley of the Shadow* by Hickman chronicles a grim massacre of the Christianized Indians at Gnadenhutten in what is now Ohio. Based upon careful research into the diaries of the early missionaries, even an accurate accounting of the weather and its influence on the action of the story is recorded.

In an award-winning biography by Elizabeth Yates, the setting both reflects, and helps to create, the strength and quiet dignity of *Amos Fortune, Free Man*. The physical and symbolic presence of Monadnock Mountain looms large in the story of this remarkable man. Always, Amos looks to "his" mountain for fortitude and courage. In return, it is as if the strength of the hills were his also. The setting of a story can do much to create the mood and theme of a book.

The imaginary settings of fantasy must be carefully detailed in order to create a believable story. In *Charlotte's Web*, E. B. White has made us see and smell Wilbur's barnyard home so clearly that it takes little stretch of the imagination to listen in to the animals' conversations. The microcosm that is the world of *Winnie the Pooh* by A. A. Milne has been detailed in a map by Ernest Shepard. It pictures the "100 Aker Wood," "Eeyore's Gloomy Place," "Pooh's Trap for Heffalumps" and "Where the Woozle Wasn't"—all familiar places to a *Winnie the Pooh* buff. In *A Wizard of Earthsea*, a more serious fantasy by Ursula Le Guin, the tale of wizards, dragons, and shadows is played out in an archipelago of imagined islands. Ruth Robbins has provided a map of Earthsea, for its geography is as exact as the laws and limits of magic used by the wizards of the isles.

Blackbriar, a mysterious old English house secluded in the woods, provides the setting and the action of a story by William Sleator. The old gray house exerts an influence on Danny from the moment he sees it:

> It was desolate, it was lonely, it was almost forbidding. Yet it did not seem derelict. There was a feeling of life about the place, as if it had *not* been left for centuries to crumble and decay. Something, Danny felt was waiting there; and suddenly he had the uncanny sensation that it was waiting for him.[5]

The mystery and eerie influence of Blackbriar permeate this exciting and well-written book.

The setting of a story, then, is important in creating mood, authenticity, and credibility. The accident of place and time in a person's life may be as significant as the accident of birth. For the places life sets us down can be tremendously important in a person's life and story.

Theme

The third point for the evaluation of any story is its *overarching theme*. The theme of a book reveals the author's purpose in writing the story. Most well-written books may be read for several layers of meaning—plot, theme, or metaphor. On one level the story of *Charlotte's Web* by E. B. White is simply an absurd but amusing story of how a spider saves the life of a pig; on another level, it reveals the meaning of loneliness and the obligations of friendship. A third layer of significance can be seen in White's tongue-in-cheek commentary on the irony of awarding a prize to a pig for words spelled out by a spider. How often society ignores the deserving! The story of *The Yearling* may appear to be the story of a boy and his pet deer; in reality, Marjorie Kinnan Rawlings has described the painful experience of achieving manhood. The theme of Lynd Ward's picture book, *The Biggest Bear*, is similar to *The Yearling*, although its ending is more appropriate for younger children.

Theme provides a dimension to the story that goes beyond the action of the plot. The theme of a book might be the acceptance of self or others, growing up, the overcoming of fear or prejudice. The theme of a story should be worth imparting to young people and be based upon justice and integrity. Sound moral and ethical principles should prevail. Paul Hazard, writing in *Books Children and Men*, made these comments concerning the kind of children's books that he felt were good:

> . . . and books that awaken in them not maudlin sentimentality, but sensibility; that enable them to share in great human emotions; that give them respect for universal life—that of animals, of plants; that teach them not to despise everything that is mysterious in creation and in man. . . . I like books that set in action truths worthy of lasting forever, and inspiring one's whole inner life. . . .
>
> In short, I like books that have the integrity to perpetuate their own faith in truth and justice. . . .[6]

[5] William Sleator, *Blackbriar* (New York: Dutton, 1972), p. 32.

[6] Paul Hazard, *Books Children and Men* (Boston: Horn Book, 1944), pp. 42–44.

One danger in writing books for children particularly is that the theme will override the plot. Authors may be so intent on conveying a message that story or characterization may be neglected. Didacticism is still alive and well in the twentieth century. It may hide behind the façade of ecology, drug abuse, or alienation, but it destroys fine writing. Despite the value of its message about the danger of drugs, such books as *The Grass Pipe* by Robert Coles could be more honestly presented as informational books than as thinly disguised fiction. These books in which the theme overpowers the story are the social tracts of the twentieth century.

Characterization

True characterization is another hallmark of fine writing. The people portrayed in children's books should be as convincingly real and lifelike as our next-door neighbors. Many of the animal characters in modern fantasy have real personalities, also. The credibility of characters will depend upon the author's ability to show their true natures, their strengths, and their weaknesses.

Just as it takes time to know a new friend in all his various dimensions, so, too, does an author try to present many facets of a character. In revealing character an author may simply (1) tell about the person through narration, (2) record the character's conversation with others, (3) describe the thoughts of the character, (4) show the thoughts of others about the character, or (5) show the character in action. While children prefer action in their stories, and dislike too much introspection, a character that is revealed in only one way is apt to lack depth. In many series books the characters are stock characters, not realistic human beings. If only one dimension of a character is presented, or one trait overemphasized, the result is likely to be stereotyped and wooden. In the Tom Swift stories the reader is always told *how* the hero performs his daring exploits rather than letting the actions and the feelings grow out of the circumstance of the story. Children do not need to be told that Mafatu overcomes his fear of the sea in Sperry's *Call It Courage;* he shows his bravery by his actions. Fine writing does not have to tell; it lets the character reveal.

In addition to realism in characterization, there should be consistency in character portrayal. This consistency should not conform to a pattern but to the true nature of the character as the author has presented him. The characters should be depicted so that everything they do, think, and say will seem natural and inevitable. It is as appropriate for Robert to use a black dialect when he is speaking in the first person to tell about *Stevie* (in the book of that title by Steptoe), as it is for Obadiah and his family to use the plain talk of the Quakers in the book *Obadiah the Bold* by Turkle. For *Stevie* takes place in Harlem today, while Old Nantucket provides the setting for Obadiah. Characters should act and speak in accordance with their age, culture, and educational background.

Another aspect of sound characterization is growth and development. Do the characters change in the course of the story, or do they remain the undaunted and self-sufficient personalities that they were in the beginning of the tale? Not all characters will change, of course, but many are memorable for their personality development. No girl will ever forget the struggle of headstrong, self-centered Jo of *Little Women* in taming her rebellious ways. Marguerite de Angeli has created a vivid character study of Robin in her oustanding book, *The Door in the Wall.* Robin, crippled son of a great lord, must learn to accept his infirmity and find a useful place in life. The gradual development of his character is made clear as he solves these problems. In today's more enlightened world it is easy to empathize with the tomboy, *Caddie Woodlawn,* in her struggle against the far-reaching demands of the mid-nineteenth century that she become a lady even in the wilds of Wisconsin. When Caddie has finally put away her tomboy ways, she says: "How far I've come! I'm the same girl and yet not the same. I wonder if it's always like this? Folks keep growing from one person into another all of their lives. . . ."[7]

In all these books, and many more, the characters seem real and alive. To be truly human they must grow and change before the reader's eyes. In keeping with life itself, that change is

---

[7]Carol Ryrie Brink, *Caddie Woodlawn* (New York: Macmillan, 1936), p. 27.

Parade of characters.

Reprinted by permission of William Collins & World Publishing Co., Inc., from *The Wind in the Willows* by Kenneth Grahame, illustration by Tasha Tudor. Copyright © 1966.

Illustration by Mary Shepard from *Mary Poppins,* copyright 1934, 1962, by P.L. Travers, reproduced by permission of Harcourt Brace Jovanovitch, Inc.

Illustration from *Peter's Chair* by Ezra Jack Keats. Copyright © 1967 by Ezra Jack Keats. Reprinted by permission of Harper & Row, Publishers, Inc.

usually gradual and convincing, rather than mercurial and unrealistic.

A character may be three-dimensional, stand out in sharp relief, and still not change. It is as though the character were frozen in a particular time period of his life. Such characters may be very interesting with many facets of their personalities clearly delineated. Homer Price, Henry Huggins, and Pippi Longstocking show little development of character, yet they remain consistent to their natures in all their adventures. There is a difference, then, between character delineation and character development.

Long after we have forgotten their stories, we can recall some of the personalities of children's literature. We recognize them as they turn the corner of our memories, and we are glad for their friendship. The line is long; it includes animals and people. It is hard to tell where it begins, and we are happy there is no end. In our mind's eye we see the three loyal friends, Mole, Toad, and Rat returning from their adventures on the open road; Mary Poppins flies by holding tightly to her large black umbrella with one hand and carrying her carpet bag in the other; there's the Potts family and their wonderful magical car, Chitty-Chitty-Bang-Bang; Georgie hops down the road looking for "New folks coming" and nearly interrupts Pooh and Piglet in their search for a Woozle. In the barnyard Wilbur has just discovered a wonderful new friend, Charlotte A. Cavatica, much to the amusement of the wise geese and the sly rat, Templeton. If one looks closely, he can see tiny Arrietty and Pod, out for a Borrowers holiday; Stuart Little paddles his souvenir canoe along the drainage ditch; and our favorite Hobbit, Bilbo Baggins, outwits the terrifying Gollum. School appears to be out, for here come Henry Huggins and Ribsy followed by Beezus and Ramona. They meet Peter and his dog, Willie. Queenie Peavy walks by herself, a stone tightly clenched in one hand. Pippi Longstocking has completed her first and only day of school; and Harriet, with flashlight and notebook, is beginning her spy route. It goes directly by the Bellini's newsstand where Chester Cricket, under the auspices of Harry the Cat and Tucker the Mouse, is preparing to give his evening concert of Mozart.

The line is long in this procession of real personages in children's literature. It reaches

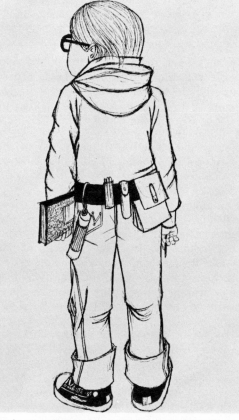

Illustration from *Harriet the Spy* by Louise Fitzhugh. Copyright © 1964. Reprinted by permission of Harper & Row, Publishers, Inc.

ways in which DeJong and O'Dell have described characters who have been left alone:

> The dog had no name. For a dog to have a name, someone must have him and someone must love him, and a dog must have someone. The dog had no one, and no one had the dog. . . . The dog had only himself, so the dog had nothing, and he was afraid.[8]

> The thought of being alone on the island while so many suns rose from the sea and went slowly back into the sea filled my heart with loneliness. . . . Now I was really alone. I could not eat much, nor could I sleep without dreaming terrible dreams.[9]

DeJong presents layered dimensions of aloneness and increases the reader's empathy for the little lost dog. O'Dell, on the other hand, uses economy of expression as Karana, the Indian girl, states quite simply how she feels after her brother has been killed by the wild dogs and she

[8]Meindert DeJong, *Hurry Home, Candy* (New York: Harper & Row, 1953), p. 1.
[9]Scott O'Dell, *Island of the Blue Dolphins* (Boston: Houghton Mifflin, 1960), p. 60.

back in our memories to include Beth, Jo, Amy, and Meg; it stands outside a Secret Garden and listens to the laughing voices of Mary, Colin, and Dickon; and with Laura, it delights in the warm coziness of the fire and the sound of Pa's fiddling in *Little House in the Big Woods*. We know all these characters well because their authors created them and blew the breath of life into each one of them. They have come alive in the pages of books; and they will live forever in our memories.

Style

An author's style of writing is simply his selection and arrangement of words in presenting the story. Good writing style is appropriate to the plot, theme, and characters, both creating and reflecting the mood of the story. An author's style is individual and unique. Compare the different

From *Winnie-the-Pooh* by A.A. Milne. Illustrated by Ernest H. Shepard. Copyright, 1926, by E.P. Dutton & Co. Renewal copyright 1954, by A.A. Milne. Reprinted by permission of the publishers, E.P. Dutton & Co., Inc.

is left all alone on the island. The simplicity of style reflects the basic stoicism of the Indian of her day.

The style of writing should mirror the setting of the story and the background of the characters. In *The Valley of the Shadow*, Hickman skillfully describes emotions in metaphors that reflect the woodland Indians' knowledge of nature:

> For the Long Knives owned this valley now, and when Tobias looked into their determined eyes he learned how the deer feels facing the bow, and the beaver in the trap.[10]

In retelling an Hawaiian legend, Marcia Brown uses figurative language that is appropriate to the island setting of this ancient tale:

> The big wave swamps even the strong canoe, Pakaa felt his heart almost go under in the flood of aloha for the boy and relief at his words. He held his son to him and wept.[11]

Children do not enjoy a story that is too descriptive, but they can appreciate figurative language, provided the comparisons are within their background of understanding.

Children in the middle grades can also comprehend symbolic meanings. Literary symbols are recurring concrete objects or events that represent an abstract idea. Eight- and nine-year-olds, for example, were able to understand DeJong's use of a broom as a symbol of all that had frightened the little dog in *Hurry Home, Candy*. The significance of the title, *The Cabin Faced West* by Fritz was clearly grasped by another group of middle graders. Children as young as seven and eight understand the importance of the cloak that Sarah Noble's mother had given her to wear when she went into the wilderness with her father. Its symbolic meaning is obvious when Sarah and her family are once more together in their new log cabin:

> That night Sarah slept warm under the quilts. On a peg near by hung her cloak—and she did not need it. She had kept up her courage and it was

something that would be always with her. Always— even when the cloak was all worn out.[12]

Frequently, the language pattern utilized by the author will reflect the action or setting of the story. In *Backbone of the King*, Marcia Brown has captured the rhythmical pattern of the ancient chants of the Hawaiians by her skilled use of parallel construction:

> It was too late to regret the untrue word said and the true word unsaid, the cruel deed done and the kind deed undone.[13]

Sometimes, language patterns will change to help create the action of the story. Short, staccato sentences will increase the feelings of mounting excitement. The language patterns of *Time of Wonder* change from long, lazy sentences describing the childhood joys of summer living to short, jerky sentences that relate the onslaught of the storm:

> . . . in the afternoon, when the tide is out, they build a castle out of the rocks and driftwood below the spot where they had belly-whopped and dog-paddled during the morning. . . . Suddenly the wind whips the water into sharp, choppy waves. It tears off the sharp tops and slashes them in ribbons of smoky spray. And the rain comes slamming down. The wind comes in stronger and stronger gusts. A branch snaps from a tree.[14]

The author's choice of the point of view of the story will necessarily influence the style. Is the story told in the first person, the third person, or from a standpoint of an omniscient narrator who knows the thoughts of all the characters involved? *Island of the Blue Dolphins* is told in the first person, which increases the reader's awareness of the isolation of Karana. *The Valley of the Shadow* and *The Courage of Sarah Noble* are both told in the third person. *Time of Wonder* is one of the few children's books told in the second person. In the story *Claudia, Where Are You?* by

---

[10] Janet Hickman, *The Valley of the Shadow* (New York: Macmillan, 1974), pp. 188–189.

[11] Marcia Brown, *Backbone of the King* (New York: Scribner, 1966), p. 149.

[12] Alice Dalgliesh, *The Courage of Sarah Noble* (New York: Scribner, 1954), p. 54.

[13] Brown, p. 121.

[14] Robert McCloskey, *Time of Wonder* (New York: Viking, 1957), pp. 24, 44.

Hila Colman the point of view alternates with each chapter from the third person of Claudia's mother to the first person of runaway Claudia. In evaluating these books we need to ask why the author chose the particular point of view, how this choice influenced the style of writing, and how the story might have been different if another point of view had been used.

The tastes of children place some demands on the writer's style. Children tend to want action in their stories and prefer a style that has movement rather than too much description or introspection. Children also demand conversation in their stories. They feel as Alice did when she looked into her sister's book and said, "What's the use of a book without pictures or conversation?" Master craftsmen at writing dialogue that sounds natural and amusing are A. A. Milne in *Winnie the Pooh* and E. B. White in *Charlotte's Web.* Writing dialogue that is contemporary is difficult indeed, for current expressions and slang quickly become dated. The dialogue in *Freaky Friday* by Mary Rodgers is witty and believable. Both E. L. Konigsburg and Judy Blume have captured the sound of today's idiom in their popular stories.

The best test of an author's style is through oral reading. Did it read smoothly and effortlessly? Was the conversation stilted, or did it really sound like people talking? Did the author introduce variety in the sentence patterns and use of words? Several years ago the expression "Tom Swifties" was coined to characterize the kind of writing in series books in which every verb was modified by a descriptive adverb—for example: "Tom said earnestly," or "Tom fought gallantly." In one recent children's book the author used the word "said" some eighty times in just one chapter. Read aloud, this book seems very repetitious and dull.

Although it is difficult for children to analyze a particular author's style, they do react to it. Children are quick to detect the patronizing air of an author who talks down to them in little asides, for example. They dislike a story that is too sentimental; and they see through the disguise of the too moralistic tales of the past. Adults respond to the cute, the clever, the slyly written, and the sarcastic; children do not. Frequently, a child is better able to identify what he dislikes about an author's style than to identify what he likes. However, the matter of style is important when adults evaluate books for children.

Format

The format of a book includes its size, shape, the design of pages, illustrations, typography, quality of paper, and binding. Frequently, some small aspect of the format, such as the book jacket, will be an important factor in a child's decision to read a story. Books today are more attractive than ever before. A new point of view in art and technical progress in printing and picture reproduction have produced some startling results in book illustrating.

Not only do we have beautiful picture books for young children but books for older boys and girls are becoming increasingly well designed and attractive. While illustrations are not essential in books for older children, they may enrich the interpretation of the story, and should be carefully planned and integrated with the text. Beth and Joe Krush have made the miniature world of *The Borrowers* series seem quite believable with their captivating illustrations. The black-and-white sketches are detailed and intricate. Frequently, Pod, Homily, and Arrietty are almost camouflaged by leaves, curtains, or bric-a-brac. The artists have skillfully portrayed some of the perils and delights of being six inches high in our "normal"-sized world. Mary Norton has written a charming, humorous fantasy; the illustrations give it an added dimension of enchantment.

The total format of Marguerite de Angeli's *The Door in the Wall* complements the medieval background of this well-written historical fiction. Her many black-and-white pictures realistically portray the castle, churches, and people of that period. Three illustrations are as rich in color and detail as an original illuminated manuscript. The design of the title and dedication pages remind the reader that fine books can be works of artistic as well as literary merit.

The design and decorations by Maurice Sendak reflect and extend the theme of Randall Jarrell's haunting fantasy, *The Animal Family.* Based upon man's need for a family, no matter how

In this book, which celebrates the meaning of home and family, a picture of the habitat of each character appropriately introduces the story.

Copyright © 1965 by Maurice Sendak. Reprinted from *The Animal Family*, by Randall Jarrell, illustrated by Maurice Sendak, by permission of Pantheon Books, a Division of Random House, Inc.

bizarre, this is the story of a boy growing to manhood on a deserted island and the family that he gradually acquires. Preceding each chapter that describes the members of the family is a picture of their former habitat; the home of the hunter, the sea for the mermaid, the cave of the bear cub, the rocky cliffs of the lynx, and the drifting canoe of the boy. Only the scenes of their origins are portrayed; the family is left to your imagination. The book itself seems to be almost the shape of a little rectangular house put together with thick binder's board covered in blue homespun. Wide margins appear to make a home for the print. The impact of the total format of this book is one of complete harmony with its theme of man's need for home and family.

There are factors other than illustrations that need to be considered in the format of a book. Typography is very important. The type should be large enough for easy reading by the age level for which it was intended. At the same time, if the type face is too large, children will consider the book "babyish." The space between the lines (leading) should be sufficient to make the text clear.

The quality of the paper must also be considered. A cream-tinted, dull-finished paper that is thick enough to prevent any penetration of ink is most desirable. The binding should be durable and practical, one that can withstand the use of many interested, but frequently grimy, hands. For library and classroom use, books that are bound in cloth, with soil-resistant washable covers are recommended. However, a book should never be selected on the basis of format alone, without an accompanying evaluation of its content. No book is better than its text.

Additional Considerations

A book should not be considered in isolation but as a part of the larger body of literature. Books need to be compared with other books on the same subject or theme. Is this just another horse story, or does it make a distinctive contribution? Every teacher and librarian should know some books so well that each has developed a personal list of books of excellence that can serve as models for comparison. How does this adventure story compare with Sperry's *Call It Courage*, this fantasy with *A Wrinkle in Time* by L'Engle, or this historical fiction with Forbes' *Johnny Tremain?* These reference points of outstanding books will help to sharpen evaluations.

An author's new book should be compared with his previous works. Contributions by the same author may be uneven and inconsistent in quality. What is the best book DeJong has written? Is *The Almost All White Rabbity Cat* as good as *Hurry Home, Candy?* How does *Shadrach* compare with *Far Out the Long Canal?* Too frequently, books are evaluated on the basis of the author's reputation rather than for their inherent worth.

Many informational and biographical series are written by different authors. The quality of the book will vary with the ability of the writer, despite similarities in approach and format. Rather than condemning or approving an entire series, each book should be evaluated on its own merits.

A book needs to be compared with outstanding prototypes, with other books written by the same author, and with other books in the same series. What have reputable reviewers said about this book? Where have they placed it in relation to others of its type? A comparison of reviews of one book would probably reveal more similarities than differences, but the elusive factor of personal preference of both adults and children should be respected.

In summary, the basic considerations for the evaluation of fiction for children are a well-constructed plot that moves, a significant theme, authentic setting, convincing characterization, appropriate style, and attractive format. Not all books will achieve excellence in each of these areas. Some books are remembered for their fine characterizations, others for their exciting plots, and in others the quality of the setting looms large. The following list of questions may help the reader evaluate a book more carefully. However, not all questions will be appropriate for each book.

CLASSICS IN CHILDREN'S LITERATURE

Knowledge of children's classics, those books that have stood the test of time, may provide further guidance for evaluating children's books. What makes a book endure from one generation to another? Jordan states: "Until a book has weathered at least one generation and is accepted in the next, it can hardly be given the rank of a classic. . . ."[15]

Many books and poems have achieved an honored position among the best of children's literature through a combination of adult adoration, parent perpetuation, and teacher assignments. Most adults remember with nostalgia the books they read as children. They tend to think that what they read was best, and ignore the possibility of the production of any better books. It is easy to forget that every "classic" was once a new book; that some of today's new books will be the classics of tomorrow. Times have changed, but some adults seem unaware of the change in children's reading interests. Teachers and librarians should begin with the modern child and his

interests, not his parents' interests when they were children.

Certain books became classics when there were very few books from which children could choose. In fact, many classics were not children's books at all, but were written for adults. In their desire to read, children claimed these adult books, struggled through the difficult parts, and disregarded that which they did not understand. They had no other choice. Today's child is not so persevering because he sees no reason for it. The introductory sentence of *Robinson Crusoe* runs the length of the entire first page and contains difficult vocabulary and syntax. Defoe wrote this story in 1719 for adult readers, but children quickly discovered its excitement and plunged into it. Some children may still enjoy this story of shipwreck and adventure. However, they can find the same tingling excitement and more readable prose in Sperry's *Call It Courage* or Steele's *Winter Danger*.

The classics should not be excused from re-evaluation by virtue of their past veneration. They should be able to compete favorably with modern-day books. Unimpressed with vintage or lineage, children seldom read a book because they think they should. They read more for enjoyment than edification. Some books have been kept alive from one generation to the next by common consent; these are the true classics of children's literature. No teacher or parent has to cajole a child into reading them. These books can hold their own amid the ever-increasing number of new and beautiful books of today.

What is the continuing appeal of these well-loved books for the contemporary child? First and foremost they are magnificent stories. There are adventure and suspense in *Treasure Island, Robinson Crusoe, Swiss Family Robinson, The Adventures of Tom Sawyer,* and *The Adventures of Huckleberry Finn.* Mystery and excitement fill the stories of *Hans Brinker, or The Silver Skates* and *The Secret Garden.* The characterization in most of the classics is outstanding. There is very little plot in the story of *Little Women,* but what reader can forget the March sisters? They could have been your next-door neighbors. This is also true of Tom and Aunt Polly and Huck. The animal personalities of Christopher Robin's stuffed toys are unmistakable. Even adults have known a Bear of Little

[15] Alice M. Jordan, *Children's Classics* (Boston: Horn Book, 1947), p. 4.

Brain and a gloomy Eeyore! And anyone, young or old, who has weathered the disappointments of friendship, can admire the enduring loyalty of Ratty and Mole for the rich conceited Toad who drags them away from their beloved riverbank on one wild escapade after another.

The appeal of many of the classics is based upon the type of story they represent. Family chronicles such as *Little Women* and "The Little House" books give the reader a sense of warmth and security. A feeling of place and atmosphere is skillfully developed in the well-loved *Heidi*.

Animal stories are represented by *Black Beauty, The Jungle Book,* and *Bambi. Black Beauty* is a sentimental tale filled with short essays on the prevention of cruelty to animals. The theme was timely in 1877 when Anna Sewell wrote this story. However, the genuine emotion in *Black Beauty* appears to be timeless, for it remains popular despite its Victorian airs. Boys and girls still enjoy the beautifully written story of Mowgli who was adopted by the wolf pack when he was a baby and taught the law of the jungle by Bagheera, the panther, and Baloo, the bear. Other

---

GUIDES FOR EVALUATING CHILDREN'S LITERATURE

Before Reading

What kind of book is this?
What does the reader anticipate from the:
    Title?
    Dust jacket illustration?
    Size of print?
    Illustrations?
    Chapter headings?
    Opening page?
For what age range is this book appropriate?

Plot

Does the book tell a good story? Will children enjoy it?
Is there action? Does the story move?
Is the plot original and fresh?
Is it plausible and credible?
    Is there preparation for the events?
    Is there a logical series of happenings?
    Is there a basis of cause and effect in the happenings?
Is there an identifiable climax?
How do events build to a climax?
Is the plot well constructed?

Setting

Where does the story take place?
How does the author indicate the time?
How does the setting affect the action, characters, or theme?
Does the story transcend the setting and have universal implications?

Theme

Does the story have a theme?
Is the theme worth imparting to children?
Does the theme emerge naturally from the story, or is it stated too obviously?
Does the theme overpower the story?
Does it avoid moralizing?

favorites in Kipling's *The Jungle Book* include "Rikki-Tikki-Tavi," the story of a mongoose, and "Toomai of the Elephants." Most children respond favorably to Felix Salten's sensitively written, if somewhat sentimental, life story of *Bambi*, a deer of the Danube forest.

Many classics are fantasies. Children's reactions to fantasy are like those of many adults who seem to thoroughly enjoy or completely reject them. For some people, *Alice in Wonderland, Peter Pan, The Wind in the Willows, Winnie the Pooh,* and *The Wizard of Oz* have never been surpassed in the field of children's literature. Others actively dislike these books. Many readers do not "discover" these fantasies until they are adults, and then they applaud them as excellent fare for children! True classics appeal to both children and adults. As one father reported: "I've learned one important thing in three years. It's possible to read to a young child without boring either child or parent. I think parent's boredom is just as important as the child's."[16]

[16]Edward Eager, "A Father's Minority Report," reprinted in *A Horn Book Sampler* (Boston: Horn Book, 1959), p. 166.

GUIDES FOR EVALUATING CHILDREN'S LITERATURE (*Continued*)

Characterization

How does the author reveal characters?
    Through narration?
    In conversation?
    By thoughts of others?
    By thoughts of the character?
    Through action?
Are the characters convincing and credible?
Do we see their strengths and their weaknesses?
Does the author avoid stereotyping?
Is the behavior of the characters consistent with their ages and background?
Is there any character development or growth?
Has the author shown the causes of character behavior or development?

Style

Is the style of writing appropriate to the subject?
Is the style straightforward or figurative?
Is the dialogue natural and suited to the characters?
Does the author balance narration and dialogue?
How did the author create a mood? Is the overall impression one of mystery, gloom, evil, joy, security?
What symbols has the author used to intensify meaning?
Is the point of view from which the story is told appropriate to the purpose of the book?

Format

Do the illustrations enhance or extend the story?
Are the illustrations consistent with the story?
How is the format of the book related to the text?
What is the quality of the paper?
How sturdy is the binding?

Other Considerations

How does the book compare with other books on the same subject?
How does the book compare with other books written by the same author?
How have other reviewers evaluated this book?

Some cautions need to be observed when presenting classics to children. It should be remembered that so-called classics are not fare for all children and frequently appeal most to the exceptional child. Many classics are more thoroughly appreciated if they are read aloud and shared with an adult rather than read by the child alone. It is important that timing be considered if children are to enjoy these books. Frequently, the classics are introduced before children are ready for them; most five-years-olds are not ready for the whimsy of *Winnie the Pooh,* nor are eight-year-olds ready for *Treasure Island.* There is a readiness in appreciation that needs to be developed. Before reading *The Wind in the Willows,* introduce children to Lawson's *Rabbit Hill* and White's *Charlotte's Web.* Today's child needs to know Cleary's *Henry Huggins,* McCloskey's *Homer Price,* and Robertson's *Henry Reed Inc.* before he is ready for *The Adventures of Tom Sawyer.* Young readers should be introduced to *James and the Giant Peach* by Dahl and *The Phantom Tollbooth* by Juster before meeting the complex *Alice in Wonderland.* Students who have been intrigued with such survival stories as *Island of the Blue Dolphins* by O'Dell and *My Side of the Mountain* and *Julie of the Wolves* by George are more likely to be interested in *Robinson Crusoe.* Adults should reread the "wonderful books we read as children" to see if they are as fine as we once thought. Finally, the practice of requiring children to read certain books should be questioned. Children's literature should provide enjoyment and lead to a deeper understanding of life. These purposes are not served by "forced feeding" of classics. Boys and girls should enjoy reading; they should be exposed to the fine writing that may be found in both the classics and the new books. Today, with over 40,000 juvenile books in print, we have no right to confine children's reading to a list of so-called classics.

THE AWARD BOOKS

Teachers and librarians will find it helpful to be familiar with books that have won awards. These awards have been established for various purposes and provide criteria for what experts consider to be the best in children's literature. Such awards have helped to counteract the judgment of the market place by focusing attention on beautiful and worthwhile books. In an age of mass production, they have stimulated artists, authors, and publishers to produce books of distinction and have helped children's literature achieve a worthy status.

Occasionally, one hears the criticism that the award books are not popular with children. This is true of some of them. However, most of the awards are not based on popularity but upon recognized excellence. They were never intended to rubber stamp the tastes of children, but to raise them. Children's reactions to books are significant, but it is important to remember that they are not the final test of distinction. Likewise, adult praise of a book is no assurance of popularity among children.

Newbery and Caldecott Awards[17]

The two most coveted awards in children's literature are the Newbery and Caldecott awards, determined every year by a committee of twenty-three members of the Children's Services Division of the American Library Association. A candidate for either of the awards must be a citizen or resident of the United States. The book must have been first published in the United States.

The John Newbery Medal is the oldest award for children's books, having been established in 1922. It is named for John Newbery, a British publisher and bookseller of the eighteenth century. Appropriately called the "father of children's literature," he was the first to conceive the idea of publishing books expressly for children. The Newbery Medal is awarded to the author of the most distinguished contribution to American literature for children published the preceding year.

The Randolph J. Caldecott Medal is named in honor of the great English illustrator of the nineteenth century, Randolph Caldecott. Caldecott was well known for his sprightly picture books depicting the country life of England. The Caldecott Medal was established in 1938, and is awarded to the most distinguished American picture book for children chosen from those first published in the United States during the previ-

---

[17]A list of various children's book awards, criteria, conditions, and winners is given in Appendix A.

ous year. The text should be worthy of the illustrations, but the award is made primarily for the art work.

Students of children's literature would do well to acquaint themselves with these award-winning books and their authors and illustrators. It is also interesting to review the Honor Books for these awards. In 1939 the Newbery Award was given to *Thimble Summer,* a story that has limited appeal for girls only. However, an Honor Book for that year was the still popular and dearly loved *Mr. Popper's Penguins.* Likewise, the highly praised *Charlotte's Web* was an Honor Book in 1953; the winner was *Secret of the Andes,* a beautifully written and sensitive story that, unfortunately, is not popular. It is interesting to see the number of times a particular author has been nominated and still has failed to win. Books by Laura Ingalls Wilder were honored for five different years, but never received the Award. Final restitution was made, perhaps, by the establishment of the Laura Ingalls Wilder Award, which serves a different purpose (see "Lifetime Contributions" below).

Since the selection for the Newbery Award must be limited to books published in one year, the quality of the Award books varies, for certain years produce a richer harvest than others. The selection in 1957 must have been very difficult, for committee members had to choose from among *Old Yeller, House of Sixty Fathers, Mr. Justice Holmes,* and *Miracles on Maple Hill.* Again, in 1971 it must have been frustrating to have to make a choice from among *Summer of the Swans, Kneeknock Rise, Enchantress from the Stars,* and *Sing Down the Moon.* In the majority of cases, the years have shown the choices to have been wise ones. Many age ranges are represented, but most of the Newbery books are for able, mature readers. Frequently, these books have to be read aloud and discussed with an adult before children develop a taste for their excellence.

There has been less controversy over the choices for the Caldecott Award. The list again shows variety as to type of art work, media used, age appeal, and subject matter. The range of art work includes the realistic paintings of Weisgard, the childlike primitive work of Leo Politi, the stylized patterns of Ed Emberley, the comic almost cartoon style of William Steig, and the compassionate well-designed pictures of Evaline

Ness. Various media are represented among the winners, including collage, woodcut, watercolor, opaque paints, and various combinations of pen and ink and paint. Robert McCloskey, Marcia Brown, and Nonny Hogrogian have won the Caldecott Award twice. Joseph Krumgold and Elizabeth Speare have received two Newbery Awards, while Robert Lawson is the only person to have won both the Newbery and Caldecott awards.

National Book Award

In March 1969 the National Book awards included for the first time in its twenty-year history an award in the category of children's books. The award is given to the juvenile title that a panel of judges considers the most distinguished for that year. The book must be written by an American citizen and published in the U.S. Meindert DeJong was the first recipient of the award for *Journey from Peppermint Street.* Unfortunately, in 1975 the children's category was eliminated for economic reasons. It is hoped that it will be restored soon.

International Book Award

The Hans Christian Andersen Medal was established in 1956 as the first international children's book award. It is given by the International Board on Books for Young People every two years to a living author and an illustrator (since 1966) in recognition of his entire body of work. Meindert DeJong, Maurice Sendak, and Scott O'Dell are the only Americans to have received a medal so far.

Lifetime Contributions

To honor an author or illustrator for a substantial and lasting contribution to children's literature, The Laura Ingalls Wilder Award was established in 1954 by the Children's Services Division of the American Library Association. It was presented first to Laura Ingalls Wilder herself, for her "Little House" books. Given every five years, the award makes no requirement concerning the number of books that must be produced, but a body of work is implied and the books must be published in the United States. The Award was presented posthumously to Clara Ingram Judson in 1960. In 1965 Ruth Sawyer received this distinctive honor. E. B. White was

The Hans Christian Andersen Award was given to Carigiet for his total contribution as a Swiss illustrator of children's books.

Illustration from *The Pear Tree, the Birch Tree and the Barberry Bush* by Alois Carigiet. Copyright © 1967 by Schweizer Spiegel Verlag. Used by permission of Henry Z. Walck, Inc., publishers.

the recipient in 1970, while Beverly Cleary was honored in 1975.

In 1959 The Catholic Library Association established a somewhat similar award to be presented annually for "continued distinguished contribution to children's literature." The Regina Medal "is not limited to one creed, nor one country, or to one criterion, other than excellence." It may be given to writers, illustrators, editors, and others who have given unstintingly of their creative genius to the field.

No one but the most interested follower of children's literature would want to remember all the awards that are given for children's books. Like the coveted "Oscars" of the motion picture industry and the "Emmys" of television the awards in children's literature focus attention not only on the winners of the year but also on the entire field of endeavor. They recognize and honor the best and also point the way to improved writing, illustrating, and producing of worthwhile and attractive books for children.

Understanding Children and How They Learn

Fostering enjoyment and appreciation for literature comes from knowing the age and psychological disposition of children, those dispositions that cause a child to like a particular book. Child development has contributed knowledge about children that provides certain guideposts for selecting books. Exciting new developments have occurred in the research in children's cognitive and language growth which have direct application for the choice of appropriate books for boys and girls. While this text can only highlight some of these recent findings, it can serve to alert the student of children's literature to the importance of finding the right match between stories and the child's level of development.

DIMENSIONS OF GROWTH

Parents, teachers, and librarians need to be aware of the dimensions of growth of each child as they guide his selection of books and his reading. In the early decades of child study emphasis was placed upon discovery of "normal" behavior patterns for each age. Growth studies revealed similarities in patterns of physical, mental, and emotional growth. More recently, longitudinal studies have shown wide variables in individual rates of growth. Within one child growth may be uneven, and a spurt in one aspect of development may precede a spurt in another. Age trends continue to be important in understanding the child, but recent research has been more concerned with the interaction of biological, cultural, and life experience forces. We know, for example, that development does not result as a process of the maturation of neural cells but evolves as new experience reshapes existing structures. Experience affects the age at which development may appear. The child-development point of view begins with the recognition and the acceptance of the uniqueness of childhood. Children are not miniature adults but individuals with their own rights, needs, interests, and capacities. This concept suggests a need for literature that captures the wonders, humor, and disappointments of childhood.

Physical Development

Graded school organization falsely appears to provide homogeneous classroom groups. Not only may there be a two-to-three-year chronological age range within one class but children of the same age will reflect wide and varied levels of development. Increasingly, many of our schools are developing multi-age units or family groupings which further increase diversity of interest and ability. In order to provide appropriate literature experiences for these children, the teacher needs to know each of them as individuals—their level of development, their rate of development, and their varying interests. To meet these needs, the school must provide an extensive collection of books and media covering a wide range of topics at various interest and reading levels.

Children's attention span increases with age and interest. Frequently, young children cannot sit quietly for even a twenty-minute story. It is better to have several short story times for these children than to demand their attention for longer periods and so lose their interest. Some kindergarten and primary teachers in informal classrooms have given children the option of listening to a story or doing quiet work on their own. These same classrooms also provide many opportunities for children to listen to stories in small groups of two or three by using the listening center or asking parent aides or student-teachers to read to as few as one or two children.

Children's physical development not only influences their attention span but also their interests. American society places a premium on achievement in sports, particularly for boys. Unfortunately, only the most physically mature and well-coordinated can be successful in highly complex team sports. Books about sports and sports figures are in demand by both those who play and those who must do their winning vicariously through stories.

American children are growing up both physically and psychologically faster than they ever have before.[18] Many children, especially girls, reach puberty during the elementary school years. They have been fascinated by Judy Blume's *Are You There God? It's Me, Margaret*, not because it is a religious story but because it accurately reflects the heroine's concerns about menstruation and when she will begin her pe-

[18] W. Sullivan, "Boys and Girls Are Now Maturing Earlier," in the *New York Times*, January 24, 1971, pp. 1, 36. (This article is based on research by H. Bakwin, A. Darum, S. F. Daw, F. Falkner, Rose E. Frisch, J. McClung, M. Schatzoff, H. C. Stuard, J. M. Tanner, A. E. Treloar, Isabelle Valadian, R. J. Wurtman, and Lenora Zacharias.)

riod. Margaret has frequent chats with God which include such hilarious pleas as:

> "Are you there God? It's me, Margaret. I just told my mother I want a bra. Please help me grow God. You know where. . ."[19]

> "Are you there God? It's me, Margaret. I can't wait until two o'clock, God. Thats when our dance starts. Do you think I'll get Philip Leroy for a partner? It's not so much that I like him, God, but as a boy he's very handsome."[20]

Both physical maturity and social forces have led to younger heterosexual interests. Sophisticated seven-year-olds are teased about their "boy friends" or "girl friends," and the "Margarets" who are worrying about dance partners are eleven. It is somehow as if childhood were something to be transcended rather than enjoyed. One result of this shortened childhood is a decrease in the length of time in which boys and girls are interested in reading children's literature. Many of them turn to reading teenage novels or adult fiction before they have read such fine books as *Enchantress from the Stars* by Engdahl, *One Is One* by Barbara Picard, or Hautzig's *The Endless Steppe*—all well-written complex stories about young adolescents.

Cognitive Development

Recent years have seen renewed interest in the work of the great Swiss psychologist, Jean Piaget.[21] His research has cast a new light on our understanding of children's intellectual development. One important idea proposed by Piaget is that intelligence develops as a result of the interaction of environment and the maturation of the child. Piaget's findings suggest distinct stages in the development of logical thinking. All children go through these stages of intellectual development in the same progression, but not necessarily at the same age. Each stage is incorporated into the next stage as new thinking structures are developed.

The sensory-motor period is the earliest period of cognitive development, according to Piaget, and is characteristic of the learning of infants to toddlers of about two years. The child learns during this period through co-ordinating sensory perceptions and motor activity. By $1\frac{1}{2}$ to 2 years children enjoy many of the action or game rhymes of Mother Goose. They pay little attention to the words of "This Little Pig Went to Market" or "Pat a Cake, Pat a Cake," but they delight in the anticipation of the pinching and patting that accompany these rhymes. Tactile books such as *Pat the Bunny* by Dorothy Kunhardt appeal to their sensory perceptions by encouraging them to pat a flannel bunny, or feel Daddy's sand-papered cheek, or play peek-a-boo with a tiny handkerchief pasted on the page. Such an introduction to books incorporates what the young child responds to best—sensory-motor play and participation with a loving adult.

The child in the *preoperational period* (ages 2–7 years) learns to represent his world symbolically through the medium of language, play, and drawing. His thinking is still egocentric and is based upon immediate perception and direct experience. He has not yet learned to conserve. (A child who conserves can hold an idea or image constant in his mind regardless of how much it is changed in form. A cup of milk is a cup, despite the shape of the glass that it is in.) This explains why young children so enjoy such cumulative stories as "The House that Jack Built," "The Gingerbread Boy" or *Mr. Gumpy's Outing* by Burningham. The repetition in these tales carries the sequence of the story along for them. Older children, who have learned to conserve, can remember the sequence of events and frequently reject the slowness and repetition of such cumulative stories.

As children's ideas of seriation develop, they are intrigued with such stories as "The Three Bears" or "The Three Billy Goats Gruff" with their emphasis on the concept of gradation of size. The structure of many folk tales is based upon the relating of three events with rising action. Thus, young children can anticipate the climax of the "Three Billy Goats" and the final overthrow of the troll.

---

[19] Judy Blume, *Are You There God? It's Me, Margaret* (Englewood Cliffs, N.J.: Bradbury Press, 1970), p. 37.
[20] Blume, p. 65.
[21] Barbel Inhelder and Jean Piaget, *The Growth of Logical Thinking* (New York: Basic Books, 1962); John Flavell, *The Developmental Psychology of Jean Piaget* (Princeton, N.J.: Van Nostrand, 1963); Hans G. Furth, *Piaget for Teachers* (Englewood Cliffs, N.J.: Prentice-Hall, 1970).

Characteristic of the cognitive growth of the child during the preoperational stage is the tremendous increase in language development and concept formation. In *One Morning in Maine*, McCloskey gives us a beautiful example of a child attempting to conceptualize the notion of "toothness." Young Sal wakes one morning to find she has her first loose tooth. She shows her loose tooth to everyone she meets including her parents, a fish hawk, loon, seal, sea gull, clam, and the men at the general store. She wonders for the first time if each of these creatures have teeth that come loose. When Sal finally does lose her tooth on the beach and can't find it, she substitutes a gull's feather to put under her pillow. Sal again applies the notion of a tooth to the worn-out spark plug that must be replaced in the motor of the family's boat. Such overgeneralized attempts at conceptualization are characteristic of the thinking of this period.

Sal's behavior is also illustrative of what Piaget calls the *assimilation process*, in which the child assimilates what he hears, sees, and feels by accepting new ideas into an already existing set of schema. By watching the loon swallow a herring whole without chewing, Sal decides he doesn't have teeth. Her father tells her that clams don't have any teeth. She learns from her mother that her sister Jane doesn't even have all of her baby teeth yet. And so Sal constantly assimilates knowledge about teeth and *accommodates* to the notion that there are creatures who do not need to chew.

Another story that well illustrates the processes of assimilation and accommodation is *Evan's Corner* by Hill. Evan longs for a place to call his own in a crowded two-room apartment that must provide a home for his mother, father, three sisters, and two brothers. Evan's mother points out that there are eight corners in the apartment, one for each member of the family. Overjoyed, Evan immediately picks the best corner for himself, the one with the window, and begins to fix it up. At school he realizes he could paint a picture for his corner; he sees a flower in a pot and decides his corner needs a flower; he remembers a canary he had seen and decides to earn money to buy a pet turtle. Each of these things which he had seen in his neighborhood now takes on new importance in relation to his project. He has assimilated them. When Evan's corner is completed and he is still not happy, his mother says:

> "Well, . . . just fixing up your own corner isn't enough." She smiled into his eyes. "Maybe you need to step out now, and help somebody else."[22]

Notice that Evan's mother doesn't tell Evan that he has to help his little brother; she lets him make that discovery for himself. This is the essence of fine teaching! Evan does decide to help his younger brother, Adam, fix up his corner, and they are both happy. At this point we could say that Evan has accommodated to the needs of his brother, and his egocentrism begins to decline. Books provide one very real source for assimilation of knowledge. Literature may give rise to the accommodating process as children see themselves or their world in a new light. When new insights are developed, the child is accommodating.

[22]Elizabeth Starr Hill, *Evan's Corner,* illustrated by Nancy Grossman (New York: Holt, Rinehart and Winston, 1967), unpaged.

After Evan made his special corner, he was eager to help his young brother create his own place.

From *Evan's Corner* by Elizabeth Starr Hill. Illustrated by Nancy Grossman. Copyright © 1967 by Elizabeth Starr Hill. Copyright © 1967 by Nancy Grossman. Reproduced by permission of Holt, Rinehart and Winston, Inc.

Egocentrism is characteristic of the thinking of children during the preoperational period. Egocentricity, in this sense, does not imply selfishness or putting one's own desires ahead of others. It simply means that the young child is not capable of assuming another person's point of view. He sees everything from his own perception. A book which clearly demonstrates this kind of egocentrism is *Fish Is Fish* by Leo Lionni. In this picture book a tadpole and a fish are inseparable friends. When the tadpole becomes a frog he crawls out of the pond and discovers the wonders of a new world. He splashes back into the pond and describes these extraordinary things to the fish. As he describes birds with wings and legs, the fish imagines large feathered fish with wings. He sees a cow as a "fish cow," people as "fish people." In fact, he sees everything from his own fishy point of view. So, too, the young child responds best to stories in which he can identify with the major character, and in which the plot or theme closely resembles his own actions and feelings. The appeal of *Bedtime for Frances* by Hoban lies in the fact that although Frances is a badger, she always behaves as a rather typical 4- or 5-year-old. The young child has no difficulty in identifying with her.

As children move from the preoperational to the *concrete-operational* level of thought (ages 7–11), their response to literature and poetry changes. Characterized by thought that is flexible and reversible, children in the concrete-operational stage can accept stories within a story as represented by such books as Yashima's *Seashore Story* or *The Biggest House in the World* by Lionni. Flashbacks and shifts in time periods as seen in *Julie of the Wolves* by George or *Tom's Midnight Garden* by Pearce are understood, as children begin to develop a time sense and can project themselves into the future or past. Shifting from an egocentric pattern of thought, children in the concrete-operational period can more easily identify with different points of view.

One research study[23] asked children of various ages to retell the "Story of the Three Bears" from the point of view of Baby Bear. A little girl

of 6, who was still at the preoperational level of thinking, was simply unable to assume another point of view. She said: "I'm not used to being anybody but me!" A 7-year-old confidently said he could do it, but then promptly told the story in the third person with the exception of one sentence when he referred to himself as "I, the little bear, found out that somebody had been laying in *his* bed and she was still there." While he made the attempt, he could not sustain the role throughout one sentence. A 9-year-old, however, easily assumed the role of either Baby Bear or Goldilocks. Her thinking showed the flexibility that is characteristic of the concrete-operational period. No longer egocentric in her thought pattern, she could readily put herself into the position of another person. Stories may help children in this decentering process as they begin to see that other people have points of view different from theirs. The ability (or lack of it) to tell a story from another point of view would provide the teacher with a clue to the child's stage of development.

The last period of cognitive development is described by Piaget as the period of *formal operations* and appears in early adolescence at age 11 or 12 years and on. The youngster is now capable of abstract theoretical thought, reasoning from hypothesis to logical conclusions. He can hold several plots or sub-plots in his mind and see the interrelations among them as developed by Southall in *Ash Road,* for example. While he has understood the use of such obvious symbols as Sarah Noble's cloak or the broom in *Hurry Home Candy,* the child can now interpret the many symbols and layers of meaning found in some poetry and in such complex books as Garner's *The Owl Service.* He can think about the form and pattern of reasoning, as well as its content, which is why it is referred to as the period of formal thought. This would appear to be the time, then, when literary criticism would be most appropriately introduced. While teachers would have been steadily building some knowledge and appreciation of literature at all levels, detailed analysis of a work would probably not be undertaken prior to this period of intellectual development. Even then, teachers would want such a discussion to arise from the child's personal response to the book.

[23]Ruth Moline, "Relationship between Children's Understanding of Point of View in Literature and Certain Piagetian Tasks" (Dissertation in progress, Ohio State University, Columbus, Ohio).

Language Development

Characteristic of the development of all children is the phenomenal growth of language which occurs during the pre-school years. Chukovsky,[24] a Russian poet, refers to the tremendous "speech-giftedness of the pre-school child" and maintains that "beginning with the age of two, every child becomes for a short period of time a linguistic genius."

While there are different points of view concerning how children acquire language, most language theorists would subscribe to the importance of providing a rich language environment for the young child. Cazden maintains that the child's oral language develops "when a richly supplied cafeteria [of language] is available from the beginning. . . ."[25] While it is not the purpose of this text to give a detailed description of language acquisition, it is appropriate to discuss the role literature plays in developing the language power of children. Recent research has highlighted this function of literature.

One study by Irwin[26] indicates that the systematic reading of stories to infants over an eighteen-month period will increase the spontaneous vocalizations of $2\frac{1}{2}$-year-old children. Mothers of the experimental group spent fifteen to twenty minutes daily reading and talking about the story and pictures with the child. Few differences were noted during the first four months of the experiment, then the differences became significant in favor of the experimental group. Cazden[27] contrasted two methods of providing young children with adult language input. One treatment was to expand the child's short telegraphic utterance into a complete sentence. For example, when he said "Dog bark," the mother replied "Yes, the dog is barking." The other treatment focused on the idea of the child and extended it through discussion and reading stories. A third group of children in the experiment received no treatment. Contrary to Cazden's expectations, the second group of nursery-school-age children gained the most on all six measures of language development. Cazden points out the value of reading to the young child in a review of her study:

> Reading to an individual child may be a potent form of language stimulation for two reasons. First, the physical contact with the child and second, such reading seems inevitably to stimulate interpolated conversation about the pictures which both adult and child are attending to.[28]

Cohen's study[29] showed the positive effect that reading aloud had on twenty classes of 7-year-olds in Harlem in New York City. In this study the ten teachers in the experimental classes read for twenty minutes daily from a carefully selected list of children's books. Following the reading of the story, the children were asked to do something with the book to make it a memorable experience for them. This involved discussing it, dramatizing it, or interpreting it through art or music. At the end of the year the experimental classes had gained significantly in their vocabulary and reading comprehension scores. A group of researchers from New York University[30] extended the Cohen study to include five hundred black children from kindergarten through third grade in four New York City schools. The experimental group participated in a literature-based oral language program which included the daily story followed by creative dramatics, role-playing, story-telling, puppetry, or discussion. The control groups participated in the literature program, but not in the language activities. The conclusions of the study were that the use of literature did expand the language skills of both groups significantly, but the experi-

[24]Kornei Chukovsky, *From Two to Five*, translated by Miriam Morton (Berkeley, Calif.: University of California Press, 1963), pp. 7, 9.

[25]Courtney B. Cazden, *Child Language and Education* (New York: Holt, Rinehart and Winston, 1972), p. 138.

[26]O. C. Irwin, "Infant Speech: Effect of Systematic Reading of Stories," *Journal of Speech and Hearing Research*, Vol. 3 (June 1960), pp. 187–190.

[27]Courtney B. Cazden, "Environmental Assistance to the Child's Acquisition of Grammar" (Unpublished Ph.D. dissertation, Harvard University, 1965).

[28]Courtney B. Cazden, "Some Implications of Research on Language Development for Preschool Education," paper prepared for Social Science Research Council Conference on Preschool Education, Chicago, Illinois, February 7–9, 1966 (ERIC, Ed. 011 329), p. 9.

[29]Dorothy Cohen, "The Effect of Literature on Vocabulary and Reading Achievement," *Elementary English*, Vol. 45 (February 1968), pp. 209–213, 217.

[30]Bernice E. Cullinan, Angela Jaggar, and Dorothy Strickland, "Language Expansion for Black Children in the Primary Grades: A Research Report," *Young Children*, Vol. 29 (January 1974), pp. 98–112.

mental group made the larger gains. Also, the greatest gain was evident among the kindergarten group, suggesting that such a program should start at as early an age as possible.

In Durkin's studies[31] of children who learned to read before entering school, family respect for reading was found to be a significant factor. This was evidenced by the fact that all her early readers had been read to from the age of 3 or before.

All of these studies show the effect of planned exposure to literature on improving language or reading facility in children. Chomsky[32] measured the language acquisition of thirty-six children between the ages of 6 and 10 and found a high positive correlation between their linguistic stages of development and their previous exposure to literature, as measured by a simple inventory of their literary backgrounds.[33] She concluded that a valid relation between reading exposure and linguistic stages exists.

This study confirms the findings of the others; evidently reading to children increases their language development, while those children who have a high linguistic competence are the ones who have been exposed to much literature. On the basis of these research studies alone, all teachers and librarians should feel a responsibility to read aloud to the children in their schools every day. For literature offers the child creative and qualitative opportunities to extend and enrich his language development.

Personality Development

It is well known that every aspect of growth is intertwined with every other. All learning is a meshing of cognitive dimensions, affective or emotional responses, social relationships, and value orientation. The process of "becoming" is a highly complex one indeed. To become a "fully functioning" person the child's basic needs must be met. He needs to feel he is loved and understood; he must feel he is a member of a group

BASED ON MASLOW'S HIERARCHY OF NEEDS[34]

significant to him; he has to feel he is achieving and growing toward independence. Behavior is consistent with the child's perception of the environment at the moment and with his continuing purpose of enhancing the self. Maslow's research suggests that a person develops through a "hierarchy of needs" from basic animal-survival necessities to the "higher," more uniquely human and spiritual needs. While some higher-level animals, such as the apes, appear to have needs of belongingness and even esteem, only humans seek to reach their greatest potential in the self-actualizing process in which they are at last free to be themselves. In the 1970 revision of his book *Motivation and Personality,* Maslow added the needs to "know and understand" and "aesthetic needs" as higher need states after discovering that many persons were motivated by them as a part of self-actualization. The search for self-actualization may take a lifetime, or it may never be achieved. But the concept that the individual is continually "becoming" is a more positive view than the notion that little change can take place in personality.

Erikson[35] has noted eight stages in this process of becoming: a sense of *trust* must be gained during the first year; a sense of *autonomy* should be realized from 12 to 15 months; between 4 and 5 years the sense of *initiative* is needed; and a

[31] Dolores Durkin, "Children Who Read Before Grade One," *The Reading Teacher,* Vol. 14 (January 1961), pp. 163–166.
[32] Carol Chomsky, "Stages in Language Development and Reading Exposure," *Harvard Educational Review,* Vol. 42 (February 1972), pp. 1–33.
[33] Charlotte S. Huck, *Taking Inventory of Children's Literary Background* (Glenview, Ill.: Scott Foresman, 1966).

[34] Abraham H. Maslow, *Motivation and Personality,* rev. ed. (New York: Harper and Row, 1970), pp. 35–58.
[35] Erik H. Erikson, *Childhood and Society,* rev. ed. (New York: Norton, 1964).

sense of *duty and accomplishment* occupies the period of childhood from 6 to 12 years. In adolescence a sense of *identity* is built; while a sense of *intimacy*, a parental sense or *productivity*, and a sense of *integrity* are among the tasks of adulthood.

Havighurst[36] has identified certain developmental tasks for growing up in the American culture. Some of the developmental tasks with which the elementary-school child needs assistance are:

Developing a satisfactory self-concept.
Learning to get along with peers.
Learning his appropriate sex role.
Developing skills in reading, communicating, and using numbers.
Developing scientific and social concepts necessary for effective everyday living.
Developing values, attitudes, and conscience.
Developing self-direction.

Books alone cannot bring about the satisfaction of basic needs. Literature may provide opportunities for identification and for understanding the self and others. Books may contribute to feelings of success as children satisfy their desires for new experiences, gain new insights into their behavior and that of others, or "try on" new roles as they identify with various characters.

FACILITATING LEARNING

Investigations of the learning process have yielded general agreements on conditions that facilitate learning. The following guides will aid teachers and librarians in planning the literature program in the elementary school:

The child is an active participant in his own learning.
Children learn best through first-hand experiencing, active contact with a stimulating environment.
The learner reacts as a whole. Anxiety and interest are involved in learning.
A single experience may result in multiple learnings, including development of values and attitudes.

Learning and behavior result as the behaver perceives the situation. Total development, including level of aspiration, influences learning.
Readiness for learning involves finding the right "match" for the child's developmental level.
Readiness is influenced by the child's perception of the value and meaning of the task, as well as the interplay of biological and environmental factors. Instruction can foster readiness.
Rewards include the satisfactions of new experiences and feelings of accomplishment.
Learning through intrinsic motivation is preferable to learning through extrinsic motivation.
Learning is facilitated as the learner is clued into the structure of the content and the learning process itself.
Participation in selecting and planning the learning activity increases interest.
Each learner is unique in his perception. He interprets experience according to his own "set."
Achievement is an interaction between the inner growth potential of the child and the experiences, learning, or nurture he has been given.

CHILDREN'S READING INTERESTS

Literature can both develop and extend children's interests. Teachers and librarians need to know what are the current interests of the children they serve, so that they might better provide books to meet these immediate needs. It is also useful to know what children of a particular age level generally like, recognizing, however, the danger of stereotyping children's interests without regard to their backgrounds, reading abilities, or personal needs.

Children have decided reading interests, and in many instances they can articulate them. The following letters were written to the author by children from a class of 8-, 9-, and 10-year-olds in response to the question, "What are your favorite books and why?"[37]

[36] Robert J. Havighurst, *Developmental Tasks and Education* (New York: McKay, 1955).

[37] Barbara Friedberg, Teacher, Martin Luther King, Jr., Laboratory School, Evanston, Illinois Public Schools.

I really can't say I have any favorite book, but here are some that are what I could call "favorite."

1. *The Big Joke Game.* I like it because no matter how many times I read it, it always seems different.
2. I like Laura Ingalls Wilder books because they are quiet and if I read them when I am sad, they make me feel better. If I read them when I feel bored, they seem to open up a whole new world.
3. I like *Old Yeller* because when I read it I feel I am living right then and there with the characters.

—KATY SULLIVAN

My favorite book is *Miss Osborne the Mop.* The reason why I like it is because it is funny. And it has magic in it. I like magic books. But I don't read magic books all of the time. The book is very funny.

Picking a book is not hard for me. I read the title first, then I open it and find out what the first chapter is about. I like to read a lot, but I only like books that are kind of fat.

—KRISTY YOUNG

My favorite book is *The World of Model Trains.* I like it because it has neat pictures and it gives you pointers on how to prevent railroad decay and making scenery. And it gives you price ranges for turn tables and bumpers, switches and other kind of track, and shows you layouts. It gives you good ideas for your layout if you are going to build one. It's a neat book!

—ANDREW ZWICK

Obviously these three children, all in one class, have different interests and different purposes for reading. Andrew has found a book that gives him information about his major interest, model-railroading. Kristy, on the other hand, derives entertainment from her reading and some self-esteem in being able to read "fat books." Interestingly, the format of the book is important to her. Katy has learned that books have the power to change the way she is feeling and to give her new, vicarious experiences. She has found that a good book deserves to be read again.

Children's reading interests reflect the pattern of their general interests. Stories of animals, real-istic fiction, adventure and exploration, biographies, and stories of the past—all have appeal for children. Humor, make-believe, suspense, and action are the qualities that children enjoy most in their reading. Nonfiction books are becoming increasingly popular; children seek specific information about every imaginable subject from astronauts to pioneers, from auto-racing to scuba-diving, from tie-dying to wildcrafting.

Factors Influencing Reading Interests

AGE AND SEX

There have been many investigations of children's reading preferences and the elements that attract children to books. Huus reviewed the literature on children's reading interests and found rather consistent results in some eight studies reported over a period of twenty years. She listed seven conclusions that point up age and sex differences in children's preferences for books:

Interests of children vary according to age and grade level.
Few differences between the interests of boys and girls are apparent before age 9.
Notable differences in the interests of boys and girls appear between ages 10 and 13.
Girls read more than boys, but boys have a wider interest range and read a greater variety.
Girls show an earlier interest in adult fiction of a romantic type than do boys.
Boys like chiefly adventure and girls like fiction, but mystery stories appeal to both.
Boys seldom show preference for a "girl's" book, but girls will read "boys'" books to a greater degree.[38]

An extensive review of the research of reading interests at all age levels by Purves and Beach[39] substantiates these conclusions with the exception that sex differences are appearing at a slightly earlier age. Robinson and Weintraub also note that sex differences are appearing in

[38] Helen Huus, "Interpreting Research in Children's Literature," in *Children, Books and Reading* (Newark, Del.: The International Reading Association, 1964), p. 125.
[39] Alan C. Purves and Richard Beach, *Literature and the Reader* (Urbana, Ill.: National Council of Teachers of English), 1972.

early primary grades and becoming increasingly prominent through the elementary school. These reviewers maintain that individual differences are so marked that group studies of reading interests are of little value in helping teachers meet the needs of a particular class.[40]

MENTAL AGE

Besides sex and age, reading interests have also been linked to mental ability. Russell came to three major conclusions after comparing the studies of reading interests and intelligence:

Bright children like books that dull children two to three years older like.

Bright children read three or four times as many books as do average children and do not taper off in reading at 13 as most children do.

There is little variation in the reading interests of bright, average, and dull children, except bright children have a wider range of interests.[41]

FORMAT OF BOOK

Illustrations, color, format, type of print, and style are all factors that influence children's choice of books. In a study of 2,500 kindergarten children, Cappa[42] found that illustrations were the most important source (34 percent) of appeal for these children. Story content (30 percent) was second, followed by information in content, humor, the surprise element, and refrain.

Children in the middle grades may decide a book is too babyish because of the size of the print. Boys frequently will not choose a book if a girl is pictured on the cover or if a girl's name is in the title. Foreign words in a title may discourage both boys and girls from selecting the book.

Brown[43] compared two methods for determining fifth-grade children's choices of books; actual handling of the book as contrasted with an annotation of the book. She found boys chose books about science and health more frequently when they could examine the books, whereas realistic fiction was chosen less frequently upon examination. Contrary to earlier studies, paperback books were not chosen any more frequently than hardback books. The cover and illustrations within the book did make a difference in the children's choices.

ENVIRONMENT

Environmental factors—such as availability and accessibility of reading materials in the home, classroom, public, and school libraries— determine and affect the development of reading interests. Children's reading interests do not seem to vary greatly according to their geographical location. Rural, urban, and metropolitan children have somewhat similar tastes in reading. Johns[44] studied the reading preferences of inner-city children in grades four, five, and six to see if they preferred stories that dealt with inner city life. He found that their preferences were for stories that depicted middle-class settings and characters with positive self-concepts.

Cultural expectations are influential factors in determining individual interests. For example, girls may be interested in dolls, but have not been expected to express interest in mechanics. The child acquires interests that bring approval through conformity to social expectations. A fourth-grade girl may not be "interested" in horses or horse stories, but if most of the girls in her group express these interests, she will also ask for books related to this theme. Boys in the group may reject horse stories because "those are just for girls." It is too early to see what impact the women's liberation groups will have on the cultural expectations of children. It is hoped that as more opportunities are given to girls and more books published that portray women in a wide variety of roles, there will be less "sex-typing" of books as either "boys' stories" or "girls' stories."

[40]Helen M. Robinson and Samuel Weintraub, "Research Related to Children's Interests and to Developmental Values of Reading," *Library Trends,* Vol. 22 (October 1973), pp. 81–108.

[41]David Russell, *Children Learn to Read* (Boston: Ginn, 1961), pp. 394–395.

[42]Dan Cappa, "Sources of Appeal in Kindergarten Books," *Elementary English,* Vol. 34 (April 1957), p. 259.

[43]Carol Lynch Brown, "A Study of Procedures for Determining Fifth Grade Children's Book Choices" (unpublished dissertation, The Ohio State University, Columbus, Ohio, 1971).

[44]Jerry L. Johns, "Expressed Reading Preferences of Intermediate Grade Students in Urban Settings" (unpublished dissertation, Michigan State University, East Lansing, 1970).

As the child identifies with parents and teachers who are enthusiastic readers, he develops his own interests. Getzels[45] pointed out that: "One cannot so much *teach* interests as *offer appropriate models* for *identification* [sic]."

The child cannot be interested in something that does not exist for him; therefore, the school, home, and community must provide opportunities for children to have many first-hand, multi-sensory experiences. Through a background of meaningful experience he can build interests. As Smith so ably pointed out:

> The reading interests with which pupils come to school are the teacher's opportunity—the reading interests with which children leave school are the teacher's responsibility.[46]

Guides for Ages and Stages

Adults who are responsible for children's reading need to be aware of the guides from child development, learning theory, and children's interests. They must also recognize characteristics and needs of children at different ages and stages of development. At the same time, it is important to remember that each child has his unique pattern of growth. The following charts describe some characteristic growth patterns, suggest implications for selection and use of books, and provide examples of suitable books for a particular stage of development.

OBSERVING CHILDREN

The teacher or librarian may be very familiar with the general characteristics and interest patterns of children at various age levels and understand the basic principles of learning. Such knowledge is of value only if it is applied to guiding each child as a unique individual. It is important to know that most 6-year-olds enjoy simple folk tales and that many 10-to-12-year-olds are interested in career books. However, the teacher will find wide individual variations from the norms established for particular age groups.

Only after studying each child can the teacher say, "David loved L'Engle's *A Wrinkle in Time.* I must tell him about the sequel, *A Wind in the Door.* Beth has started doing macrame—I wonder if she has seen this new book on it. Peter is somewhat slow in reading, but he enjoyed *A Snake-Lover's Diary;* he might like to try to make a terrarium for his snake. I saw one in that new book on terrariums." And so the teacher plans for the extension of children's reading interests with care. This information can be shared with the school librarian who is in a unique position to study the child over a period of years.

Understanding of the child and the accumulated effect of past experiences is gained through observing him in many situations. The teacher or librarian observes the child as he studies or reads alone, as he reacts to others in work and play situations, and as he meets problems. The teacher will note what he does not do or say, as well as his active behavioral responses. The teacher seeks to understand the child's perception of himself, for this self-concept influences his behavior and his choices as well as his achievement.

Observation provides many clues regarding the reading interests and habits of children. Watching the child as he selects a book will help adults determine what his interests in books are. Does he go directly to a specific book section? Does he know where to find science books, poetry, biography, or fiction? Does he look at the chapter headings or illustrations before selecting a book? Does he ask for help in locating books? Does the child seem to follow the leadership of one or two other children, selecting in accordance with their choice? Is he really browsing and getting to know books, or is he engaged in aimless wandering? Does he select books that are too difficult to read in order to gain status?

Observing the child as he begins to read reveals other helpful information. Does he begin quickly? Can you sense his appreciation of the illustrations? Does the position of his body reflect relaxation and interest in the book? How long does he spend in actual reading?

[45]Jacob W. Getzels, "Psychological Aspects," in *Developing Permanent Interest in Reading,* Helen Robinson, ed., Supplementary Educational Monographs No. 84 (Chicago, Ill.: University of Chicago Press, 1956), p. 9.

[46]Dora V. Smith, "Current Issues Relating to Development of Reading Interests and Tastes," in *Recent Trends in Reading,* W. S. Gray, ed. (Chicago, Ill.: University of Chicago Press, 1939), p. 300.

BOOKS FOR AGES AND STAGES

Preschool and Kindergarten—Ages 3, 4, and 5

Characteristics	Implications	Examples
Rapid development of language.	Interest in words, enjoyment of rhymes, nonsense, and repetition and cumulative tales. Enjoys retelling folktales and stories from books without words.	*Mother Goose* Burningham, *Mr. Gumpy's Outing* Gág, *Millions of Cats* Hutchins, *Rosie's Walk* Spier, *Crash! Bang! Boom!* Watson, *Father Fox's Pennyrhymes* Wezel, *The Good Bird* *The Gingerbread Boy* *The Three Bears*
Very active, short attention span.	Requires books that can be completed "in one sitting." Enjoys participation through naming, touching, and pointing. Should have the opportunity to hear stories several times each day.	Carle, *Do You Want to Be My Friend?* Carle, *The Very Hungry Caterpillar* Dunn, *Things* Kunhardt, *Pat the Bunny* Munari, *Who's There? Open the Door!* Wildsmith, *Puzzles*
Child is the center of his world. Interest, behavior and thinking are egocentric.	Likes characters with which he can clearly identify. Can only see one point of view.	Buckley, *Grandfather and I* Hoban, *Bedtime for Frances* Keats, *The Snowy Day* Massie, *Walter Was a Frog*
Curious about *his* world.	Stories about everyday experiences, pets, playthings, home, people in his immediate environment are enjoyed.	Cohen, *Will I Have a Friend?* Hoban, *Best Friends for Frances* Keats, *Peter's Chair* Zolotow, *William's Doll*
Building concepts through many first-hand experiences.	Books extend and reinforce child's developing concepts.	Brown, *The Important Book* Hoban, *Count and See* Hoban, *Push Pull, Empty Full* Showers, *The Listening Walk* Udry, *A Tree Is Nice*
Child has little sense of time. Time is "before now," "now," and "not yet."	Books can help children begin to understand the sequence of time.	Buckley, *Too Many Crackers* Burningham, *Seasons* Tresselt, *It's Time Now* Zolotow, *Over and Over*
Child learns through imaginative play.	Enjoys stories that involve imaginative play. Likes personification of toys and animals.	Burton, *Mike Mulligan and His Steam Shovel* DeRegniers, *May I Bring a Friend?* Ets, *Just Me* Lexau, *Every Day a Dragon* Skorpen, *Charles*
Seeks warmth and security in relationships with adults.	Likes to be close to the teacher or parent during storytime. The ritual of the bedtime story begins literature experiences at home.	Brown, *Goodnight Moon* Ehrlich, *Zeek Silver Moon* Flack, *Ask Mr. Bear* Hutchins, *Good-Night, Owl!* Krauss, *The Bundle Book* Minarik, *Little Bear*

Preschool and Kindergarten—Ages 3, 4, and 5

Characteristics	Implications	Examples
Beginning to assert his independence. Takes delight in *his* accomplishments.	Books can reflect emotions.	Brown, *The Runaway Bunny* Krauss, *The Carrot Seed* Lexau, *Benjie* Mayer, *Mine!* Myller, *No! No!* Preston, *The Temper Tantrum Book*
Beginning to make value judgments about what is fair and what should be punished.	Requires poetic justice and happy endings in the stories.	Hutchins, *Titch* Massie, *Dazzle* Piper, *The Little Engine that Could* Potter, *The Tale of Peter Rabbit* Potter, *The Tale of Benjamin Bunny*

Primary—Ages 6 and 7

Characteristics	Implications	Examples
Continued development and expansion of language.	Daily story hour provides opportunity to hear qualitative and creative language of literature.	McCloskey, *Time of Wonder* Steig, *Amos and Boris* Tresselt, *A Thousand Lights and Fireflies* Poetry of Aileen Fisher, Karla Kuskin, David McCord, Stevenson, and others.
Attention span increasing.	Prefers short stories, or may enjoy a continued story provided each chapter is a complete incident.	Flack, *Walter the Lazy Mouse* Lobel, *Frog and Toad Together* Parish, *Amelia Bedelia*
Striving to accomplish skills demanded by adults.	Child is expected to learn the skills of reading and writing. Needs to accomplish this at his own rate and feel successful. First reading experiences should be enjoyable.	Conford, *Impossible, Possum* Duvoisin, *Petunia* Guilfoile, *Nobody Listens to Andrew* Kraus, *Leo the Late Bloomer* Lobel, *Mouse Tales*
Learning still based upon immediate perception and direct experiences.	Uses informational books to verify experience. Watches guinea pigs, or records changes in a tadpole *prior* to using a book.	Adkins, *How a House Happens* Hoban, *Look Again!* Rockwell, *Olly's Polliwogs* Silverstein, *Guinea Pigs, All about Them*
Continued interest in the world around him—eager and curious. Still sees world from his egocentric point of view.	Needs wide variety of books. TV has expanded his interests beyond his home and neighborhood.	Aliki, *Green Grass and White Milk* Fuchs, *Journey to the Moon* Koren, *Behind the Wheel* Lionni, *Fish Is Fish* Swinton, *Digging for Dinosaurs*
Vague concepts of time.	Simple biographies and historical fiction may give a feeling for the past, but accurate understanding of chronology is beyond this age group.	Aliki, *A Weed Is a Flower* Dalgliesh, *The Bears on Hemlock Mountain* Hutchins, *Clocks and More Clocks* Turkle, *Obadiah the Bold*
More able to separate fantasy from reality. Developing greater imagination.	Enjoys fantasy. Likes to dramatize simple stories.	Ness, *Sam Bangs and Moonshine* Sendak, *Where the Wild Things Are* Slobodkina, *Caps for Sale* Tolstoy, *The Great Big Enormous Turnip*
Beginning to develop empathy and understanding for others.	Adults can ask such questions as, "What would you have done?" "How do you think Stevie felt about Robert?"	Hill, *Evan's Corner* Steptoe, *Stevie* Yashima, *Crow Boy* Zolotow, *Do You Know What I'll Do?*

Primary—Ages 6 and 7

Characteristics	Implications	Examples
Has a growing sense of justice. Demands applications of rules, regardless of circumstances.	Expects poetic justice in books.	Bishop, *The Five Chinese Brothers* Freeman, *Dandelion* Hutchins, *The Surprise Party* Udry, *Let's Be Enemies* Zemach, *The Judge*
Humor is developing; enjoys incongruous situations, misfortune of others, and slapstick.	Encourage appreciation of humor in literature. Reading aloud for pure fun has its place in the classroom. Enjoys books that have surprise endings, play on words, and broad comedy.	Aruego, *Look What I Can Do* Barrett, *Animals Should Definitely Not Wear Clothing* DuBois, *Lazy Tommy Pumpkinhead* Kuskin, *Just Like Everyone Else* Segal, *Tell Me a Mitzi*
Beginning sexual curiosity.	Teachers need to accept and be ready to answer children's questions about sex.	Andry, *How Babies Are Made* Gruenberg, *The Wonderful Story of How You Were Born* Sheffield, *Where Do Babies Come From?*
Physical contour of the body is changing. Permanent teeth appear. Learning to whistle and develop other fine motor skills.	Books can help the child accept physical changes in himself and differences in others.	Keats, *Whistle for Willie* McCloskey, *One Morning in Maine*
Continues to seek independence from adults.	Needs opportunities to select books of his own choice. Should be encouraged to go to the library on his own.	Ardizzone, *Tim to the Rescue* Petrides, *Hans and Peter* Steptoe, *Train Ride* Taylor, *Henry the Explorer*
Continues to need warmth and security in adult relationships.	Books may emphasize universal human characteristics in a variety of life styles.	Clark, *In My Mother's House* Gill, *Hush, Jon* Reyher, *My Mother Is the Most Beautiful Woman in the World* Scott, *Sam* Zolotow, *Mr. Rabbit and the Lovely Present*

Middle Elementary—Ages 8 and 9

Characteristics	Implications	Examples
Attaining independence in reading skill, may read with complete absorption. Others may still be having difficulty in learning to read. Wide variation in ability and interest. Research indicates boys and girls developing different reading interests during this time.	Discovers reading as an enjoyable activity. Prefers an uninterrupted block of time for independent reading. During this period, many children become avid readers.	Butterworth, *The Enormous Egg* Colver, *Bread-and-Butter Indian* Enright, *Gone-Away Lake* Fox, *Maurice's Room* Heide, *Sound of Sunshine, Sound of Rain* Konigsburg, *From the Mixed-Up Files of Mrs. Basil E. Frankweiler* McKee, *Mr. Benn-Red Knight* Murray, *Nellie Cameron* Schulz, *Snoopy and His Sopwith Camel* Selden, *The Cricket in Times Square* Steele, *Winter Danger*

Middle Elementary—Ages 8 and 9

Characteristics	*Implications*	*Examples*
Reading level may still be below appreciation level.	Essential to read aloud to children each day in order to extend interests, develop appreciation, and provide a balance in children's reading choices.	Bulla, *The White Bird* Dahl, *James and the Giant Peach* DeJong, *Hurry Home, Candy* Grimm, *Snow-White and the Seven Dwarfs* Lexau, *Striped Ice Cream* Peare, *The Helen Keller Story* White, *Charlotte's Web*
Peer group acceptance becomes increasingly important.	Children need opportunities to recommend and discuss books. Book choices may be influenced by leaders in the peer group. Reading certain books may provide status.	Burch, *Queenie Peavy* Estes, *The Hundred Dresses* Fitzhugh, *Harriet the Spy* Fox, *How Many Miles to Babylon?* Greene, *The Unmaking of Rabbit* Lionni, *Swimmy*
Developing standards of right and wrong. Begins to see viewpoints of others.	Books provide opportunities to relate to several points of view.	Brown, *Once a Mouse* Keeping, *Through the Window* McDermott, *Anansi the Spider* Stolz, *The Bully of Barkham Street* Stolz, *A Dog on Barkham Street* Turkle, *The Fiddler of High Lonesome*
Less egocentric, developing empathy for others. Questioning death.	Enjoys some sad stories or likes to read about handicapped persons.	Hunter, *Child of the Silent Night* Little, *Take Wing* Miles, *Annie and the Old One* Slobodkin, *Sarah Somebody* Warburg, *Growing Time*
Time concepts and spatial relationships are developing. This age level is characterized by thought that is flexible and reversible.	Interested in biographies; life in the past, in other lands, and the future. Prefers fast-moving, exciting stories.	Coatsworth, *Jon the Unlucky* DeJong, *Far Out the Long Canal* Fritz, *The Cabin Faced West* Key, *The Forgotten Door* McGovern, *Runaway Slave: The Story of Harriet Tubman* O'Brien, *Mrs. Frisby and the Rats of NIMH*
Enjoys slapstick humor in everyday situations. Appreciates imaginary adventure.	Teachers need to recognize the importance of books for releasing tension and providing enjoyment.	Beatty, *Bob Fulton's Amazing Soda Pop Stretcher* Blume, *Tales of a Fourth Grade Nothing* Lindgren, *Pippi Longstocking* Milne, *Winnie the Pooh* Viorst, *Alexander and the Terrible, Horrible, No Good, Very Bad Day*
Likes the challenge of solving puzzles and mysteries. Enjoys secret codes and languages.	High interest in mysteries and creating secret codes.	Corbett, *The Big Joke Game* Epstein, *First Book of Codes and Ciphers* Hicks, *Alvin's Secret Code* Sobol, *Encyclopedia Brown Takes the Case*
Improved coordination makes proficiency in games possible. Success in team sports becomes a developmental task of this age.	Interest in sports books. Wants specific knowledge about sports.	Christopher, *The Year Mom Won the Pennant* Coombs, *Be a Winner in Baseball* Hollander, *The Modern Encyclopedia of Basketball* Lord, *Mystery Guest at Left End*

Middle Elementary—Ages 8 and 9

Characteristics	Implications	Examples
Interest in hobbies and collections is high.	Enjoys how-to-do it books and series books. Likes to collect and trade paperback books. Begins to look for books of one author.	Bond, *A Bear Called Paddington* Cleary, *Henry Huggins* Hautzig, *Cool Cooking* Simon, *The Paper Airplane Book* Wilder, "Little House" series
Seeks specific information to answer his questions. May go to books that are beyond his reading ability to search out answers.	Requires guidance in locating information. Needs help in use of library, card catalogue, and reference books.	Cousteau, *Oasis in Space* Gallob, *City Leaves, City Trees* McWhirter, *The Guinness Book of World Records* Sarnoff, *A Great Bicycle Book*

Later Elementary—Ages 10, 11, and 12

Characteristics	Implications	Examples
Rate of physical development varies widely. Rapid growth precedes beginning of puberty. Girls about two years ahead of boys in development and reaching puberty. Boys and girls increasingly curious about all aspects of sex.	Continued sex differentiation in reading preferences. Guide understanding of growth process and help children meet personal problems.	Blume, *Are You There God? It's Me, Margaret* Blume, *Then Again, Maybe I Won't* DeSchweinitz, *Growing Up* Donovan, *I'll Get There, It Better Be Worth the Trip* Ravielli, *Wonders of the Human Body*
Understanding and accepting the sex role is a developmental task of this period. Boys and girls develop a sense of each other's identity.	Books may provide impetus for discussion and identification with others meeting this task.	George, *Julie of the Wolves* Greene, *A Girl Called Al* Jones, *Edge of Two Worlds* L'Engle, *The Moon by Night* Wier, *The Loner*
Increased emphasis on peer group and sense of belonging. Deliberate exclusion of others. Expressions of prejudice.	Emphasize unique contribution of all. In a healthy classroom atmosphere discussion of books can be used for values clarification.	Armstrong, *Sounder* Farmer, *The Summer Birds* Neville, *Berries Goodman* Southall, *Josh*
Family patterns changing. Highly critical of siblings. By end of period may challenge parents' authority.	Books may provide some insight into these changing relationships.	Clymer, *My Brother Stevie* Mann, *My Dad Lives in a Downtown Hotel* Neville, *It's Like This, Cat* Rodgers, *Freaky Friday* Wersba, *The Dream Watcher*
Begins to have models other than parents. May draw them from TV, movies, sports figures, and books. Beginning interest in future vocation.	Biographies may provide appropriate models. Career books may open up new vocations and provide useful information.	Carruth, *She Wanted to Read: The Story of Mary McLeod Bethune* Franchere, *Willa: The Story of Willa Cather's Growing Up* Goldreich, *What Can She Be? A Lawyer* Lee, *Boy's Life of John F. Kennedy* Robinson, *Breakthrough to the Big League*
Sustained, intense interest in specific activities.	Children spend more time in reading at this age than any other. Tend to select books related to one topic; for example, horses, sports, or a special hobby.	Graham, *Great No-Hit Games of the Major Leagues* Henry, *Black Gold* Kidder, *Illustrated Chess for Children* Lightbody, *Let's Knot, A Macrame Book* Ross, *Racing Cars and Great Races*

BOOKS FOR AGES AND STAGES (*Continued*)

Later Elementary—Ages 10, 11, and 12

Characteristics	Implications	Examples
Reflecting current adult interest in the mysterious, occult, and supernatural.	Enjoys mysteries, science fiction, and books about witchcraft.	Hitchcock, *Alfred Hitchcock's Daring Detectives* Hunter, *The 13th Member* L'Engle, *Wrinkle in Time* McHargue, *Funny Bananas* Sleator, *Blackbriar*
Highly developed sense of justice and concern for others. Innate sympathy for weak and downtrodden.	Likes "sad stories" about handicapped persons, sickness, or death.	Byars, *Summer of the Swans* Picard, *One Is One* Robinson, *David in Silence* Smith, *A Taste of Blackberries*
Increased understanding of the chronology of past events. Beginning sense of his place in time. Able to see many dimensions of a problem.	Literature provides the opportunity to examine issues from different viewpoints. Needs guidance in being critical of biased presentations.	Frank, *Anne Frank: The Diary of a Young Girl* Hickman, *The Valley of the Shadow* Hunt, *Across Five Aprils* Lester, *To Be a Slave* Tunis, *His Enemy, His Friend* Uchida, *Journey to Topaz*
Search for values. Interested in problems of the world. Can deal with abstract relationships; becoming more analytical.	Valuable discussions may grow out of teacher's reading aloud prose and poetry to this age group. Questions may help students gain insight into both the content and literary structure of a book.	Cunningham, *Dorp Dead* Dunning, *Reflections on a Gift of Watermelon Pickle and Other Modern Verse* Engdahl, *Enchantress from the Stars* Hirsch, *The Living Community: A Venture into Ecology* Kroeber, *Ishi, Last of His Tribe* Neufeld, *Edgar Allen* Steele, *Journey Outside* Wojciechowska, *Shadow of a Bull*

If a child becomes absorbed in the book, he is not distracted by ordinary movements or sounds in the library or classroom. The teacher may find it helpful to record these brief observations for a part of the continuous anecdotal record.

A record of each child's reading should be kept and added to his personalized reading file. It is as important for the teacher to know what a child is reading as it is to know how well he is reading. In fact, knowledge of the books a child has read and enjoyed is usually a good indication of his reading ability.

There are various ways in which children may help to keep their own records. They may want to make and bind their own special books to record their reading for the year. A gaily painted or covered box can hold the children's file folders. As a book is read, the child may record the author, title, and date of completion, and file it in his own folder. A plan for individual reading records can be arranged so that competition is avoided and the child's privacy respected. The number of books read is not as important as the child's growing delight in what he reads. A "star chart" is never necessary in a classroom in which the teacher knows what each of the children is reading and can share his enthusiasm for books with them.

Teachers will want to have individual conferences with each child and chat about the books each has read. This will give the teacher another opportunity to talk with children about their favorite books, see if there is a discernible pattern in their reading, and recommend further reading.

Children can evaluate their reading also, as each one answers such questions as, "What kind of books do I enjoy most? Am I reading different kinds of books? How much time do I really spend in reading? Do I want to set any goals for my reading?"

Observing how children select books, noting what they choose, talking with them about their favorites will be far more helpful than attempting to determine interests by the somewhat artificial device of an interest inventory. It is a poor teacher who has to be told what the children's interests are. It does take skill and knowledge, however, to link children's interests to the books they will enjoy.

Guidelines for Selection of Materials

THE NEED FOR SELECTION

Evaluation of a single book involves literary criticism. Evaluation of a particular book for a particular child entails an understanding of literature and the background of the individual child. Evaluation of many books, films, filmstrips, tapes, and media for many children who will use them for a variety of purposes requires the establishment of criteria for selection.

While the subject of this text is primarily confined to children's literature, the author fully approves the concept of a school library media center for each school. (*See* Chapter 10 for a description of a functioning media center.) The explosion of knowledge is part of the reality of the twentieth century. It has been estimated that beginning with the year 1 A.D., knowledge doubled in 1750, again in 1900, the third time in 1950, the fourth time in 1960, and has continued to double every eight to ten years since.[47] Children should have the opportunity to obtain information on any subject within their comprehension, regardless of format or "packaging" of the source. Davies[48] suggests that: "Library re-

sources can no longer be limited to printed materials; a school library program designed to implement a quality education program must provide all types and kinds of instructional resources regardless of media format." Today there is an abundance of materials in a diversity of formats covering all areas of human knowledge. Obviously, school and public library budgets require selection from this vast array of material.

Since the subject matter of contemporary children's books is changing, the need for written criteria of selection has increased. The new realism in children's books and young teenage novels simply reflects the new freedom that can be seen on TV, at the movies, and in books for adults. It makes no sense "to protect" children from well-written or well-presented materials on such controversial subjects as abortion, narcotics, or sexual deviations, yet allow them to see sensational stories on the same subjects on TV. Increased sensitivity to sexism, racism, and bias in books and nonbook materials is another area of recent concern that points up the need for a clear statement on selection policies.

The period of childhood is decreasing; our children are growing up faster today than twenty years go. In the limited time in which children have to be a child, we want to give them the very best books available. The adage of "the right book at the right time" still holds true. Most children's books have to be read at the appropriate age and stage in the development of a child or they will *never be read*. The 8-year-old does not read *The Tale of Peter Rabbit;* the 12-year-old doesn't want to be seen reading *Little House in the Big Woods;* and the junior high student has outgrown Lawson's *Rabbit Hill.* Introduced at the right time, each of these books would have provided a rich, satisfying experience of literature.

The number of books that any one child can read is limited, also. Assuming that a child reads one book every two weeks from the time he is 7 (when he may begin to read independently) until he is 13 or 14 (when he starts reading adult books), he will read about twenty-five books a year, or some 200 books during this period of childhood. Currently, there are over 40,000 children's books in print. It is possible that a child may have read widely and *never have read a significant book*. Under these circumstances, the need for good book selection is imperative.

---

[47]National Education Association, *Schools for the Sixties* (New York: McGraw-Hill), p. 50.
[48]Ruth Ann Davies, *The School Library a Force for Educational Excellence* (New York: Bowker, 1969), p. 21.

PRINCIPLES OF SELECTION

The American Association of School Librarians has reaffirmed its belief in the Library Bill of Rights of the American Library Association, and has created its own School Library Bill of Rights which asserts that the responsibility of the school library media center is:

To provide a comprehensive collection of instructional materials selected in compliance with basic, written selection principles, and to provide maximum accessibility to these materials.

To provide materials that will support the curriculum, taking into consideration the individual's needs, and the varied interests, abilities, socio-economic backgrounds, and maturity levels of the students served.

To provide materials for teachers and students that will encourage growth in knowledge, and that will develop literary, cultural and aesthetic appreciation, and ethical standards.

To provide materials which reflect the ideas and beliefs of religious, social, political, historical, and ethnic groups and their contribution to the American and world heritage and culture, thereby enabling students to develop an intellectual integrity in forming judgments.

To provide a written statement, approved by the local Boards of Education, of the procedures for meeting the challenge of censorship of materials in school library media centers.

To provide qualified professional personnel to serve teachers and students.[49]

It is important that each school district develop a written statement of the policy which governs its selection of materials. Factors to be considered in such a policy would include:

1. Who selects the materials?
2. The quality of material.
3. Appropriate content.
4. Needs and interests of the children.
5. School curriculum needs.
6. Providing for balance in the collection.

7. Re-evaluation of library materials.
8. Censorship and challenged materials.

Ideally, such statements should be developed cooperatively by library personnel, administrators, teachers, parents, and representatives of the school board or board of trustees. Such policy statements, including a plan for considering complaints, should be established prior to any selection of materials or criticism of books.

Who Selects the Materials?

Teachers and students may recommend particular titles, but the final selection of materials for the school library media center should be determined by professionally trained personnel. Frequently, librarians will appoint interested teachers and, occasionally, a parent to serve on a book selection committee, but the final responsibility should rest with the professionally trained staff of the school library media center.

In schools where there is no librarian, a teacher committee with an interested chairperson appointed by the principal could make the selections. Every effort should be made, however, to consult with a trained librarian either at the state department or public library.

QUALITY OF MATERIAL

Criteria for evaluation and selection of all types of instructional materials should be established.[50] Such criteria should be available in written form. Books for the collection should meet the criteria of fine writing described earlier in this chapter. More detailed criteria for each genre is given in the chapters in Part II of this text.

The content of the materials to be selected must be evaluated in terms of the quality of the writing or presentation. Almost any subject can be written about for children depending upon the honesty and sensitivity of its treatment by the author. In order to be specific, two examples are given. The first book is recommended; the second is not.

The story of the growing up of 13-year-old Davy Ross is sensitively told by Donovan in the book, *I'll Get There, It Better Be Worth the Trip.*

---

[49]Reprinted in *Policies and Procedures for Selection of Instructional Materials* (Chicago, Ill.: American Library Association, 1970).

[50]See Chapter 10 for a discussion of films, filmstrips, and tapes.

Following the death of a loved grandmother, Davy is sent to live in a New York City apartment with a mother he hardly knows, a mother who drinks too much. Davy adjusts to his new life and school, but he is desperately lonely until he finds a real friend in Douglass Altschuler. While the boys are on the floor roughhousing with their dog, an incident of open sexuality between them occurs. Davy's mother makes much more of the incident than either of the boys felt, but this adds to Davy's feelings of fear and guilt. The problem is resolved, and Davy develops a better sense of who he is as he moves toward maturity. The incidence of sex in the story is essential to its theme. It grows naturally out of the characters' backgrounds and present situation. The author's point of view is one of sympathy and compassion for an adolescent who feels very alone in his world.

A brief encounter with sex is also part of the story of *Gone and Back* by Benchley. Obadiah, a 13-year-old boy, and his family join the race for new lands in the West. During their trek Obadiah meets Lennie, a girl about his age. Talking in a barn one day Lennie asks Obadiah if he knows what it is to mate and if he would like to learn. He does; he would; so they do. And that's the end of the scene. It could be removed from the story and never missed in much the same way as the obligatory sex scenes of some adult fiction. Such writing may have shock value, but it does not constitute quality literature.

APPROPRIATE CONTENT

Content of materials selected should be evaluated not only in terms of quality but in terms of appropriateness for the group or individual who will use them. Determining the appropriateness of a particular book or film for a certain group or age of children is difficult indeed. For example, the content of both of the books mentioned above is appropriate for some 13-year-olds who are discovering their sexuality at this age. However, as we have seen, it is the total effect of the book that determines its appropriateness. If these elements are necessary to the theme of the book and grow naturally from the situations and characters, they are acceptable.

Controversy about the inappropriateness of violence in books for young children has long been a subject for discussion. After protests by some psychologists, fairy tales were rewritten to temper the grim details that were once included. However, folk tales represent the plight of the human condition and are symbolic of good and evil. The horror may serve as catharsis for fears and anxieties that may be larger than those depicted in the stories. In Grimm's story of *The Seven Ravens* the little girl must cut off her finger in order to enter the crystal palace and save her brothers. Neither pain nor blood is described. In the broad context of the story the action represents the sacrifice of the girl who was partially responsible for the original curse placed upon her brothers. The rewards of the fairy tale are not easily won, and something must be given for each favor received. The monsters in *Where the Wild Things Are* by Sendak have been criticized for being too grotesque and frightening to children. Yet children do not seem frightened of them at all. And the important theme of that story is that Max does return home where he finds the reality of warmth and love.

In some instances, books may be the very instruments by which children first encounter death or the horrors of war. How many countless children have wept over the death of Beth in *Little Women,* the necessary destruction of the faithful dog in *Old Yeller,* and even the end of a loyal spider in *Charlotte's Web?* Hopefully our children will not know the unbelievable horrors of war that Chau Li, the Montagnard boy who saved *The Man in the Box,* had to face all alone. This book, with its starkly vivid writing, contains a message that attacks the very roots of survival in the twentieth century. It may not be a book that all children are fortified to withstand. But there is no reason to overprotect or coddle the child's mind. There is no reason either to shock or deliberately frighten the child until such time as he may have developed the maturity and inner strength to face the tragedies of life, even vicariously. This is a matter of age and experience, and points up the importance of teachers and librarians knowing the children in their classrooms well.

NEEDS AND INTERESTS OF CHILDREN

Materials should always be purchased in terms of the children who will be using them.

The chart on pages 31–36 showing needs of children at various stages of their growth should guide book selection. Particular groups of children in an elementary school may have special needs; for example, a partially sighted class will require library books with large type. The background and abilities of the school population should be considered when selecting books. Children from educationally disadvantaged backgrounds may need more easy reading books and audiovisual materials than children with more educational advantages who may be demanding young adult materials. It is a mistake, however, to assume that city children need books with urban settings and multi-ethnic characters any more than suburban children do. All children need books that will give them insight into their own lives, but they should also have books to take them out of those lives to help them see the world in its many dimensions. Suburban children need to read of life in the ghetto—it may be their only contact with it. And slum children must be introduced to the best literature we have. We cannot tolerate the notion that somehow it is all right to give poor children poor books. Regardless of their backgrounds, a good selection policy should provide a wide range of quality books and diversity of materials for all children.

SCHOOL CURRICULUM NEEDS

Librarians will want to consider the particular needs of the school curriculum when ordering materials. Particular units in social studies—such as "The Role of Women in History," or a science unit on ecology and pollution, or a study of African folklore in literature—may require special books, films, filmstrips, or artifacts. Intensive study of the local region will require additional copies of books about the particular state, industries, and people of the region. Children may want to go out and tape record interviews of persons in the neighborhood, or they could film sites of local interest. Teachers and librarians will want to have the equipment ready for children's first-hand research. Many teachers may have changing classroom libraries of paperback books. These are best ordered and kept in the school library media center, where teachers can select them. Such arrangements must be made jointly with the personnel of the center and the rest of the faculty. The function of the school library media center is to provide a wide range of materials specially chosen to meet the demands of the school curriculum.

BALANCE IN THE COLLECTION

Every school library media center will want to maintain a balanced collection. Keeping in mind the total needs of the school, the librarian will consider the following balances: book and nonbook material (including tapes, records, films, filmstrips, and other materials), hardback and paperback books, reference books and trade books, fiction and nonfiction, poetry and prose, classics (both old and "new"), realistic and fanciful stories, books for younger and older children, books for poor and superior readers at each grade level, and books for teachers to read to students and use for enrichment purposes, and professional books for teachers and parents.

The librarian must always select materials in terms of the present library collection. What are the voids and needs in the collection now? What replacements should be considered? How many duplicate copies of a particularly popular book should be ordered? Every book added to a collection should make some distinct contribution to it. Just because children are interested in magnets does not mean that all new books on magnets should be ordered. What is unique about a particular book? Perhaps, it presents new information; perhaps the experiments are more clearly written than in similar books; or it may be for a different age group than the one already in the library. Only the person who knows the total collection can make these book-buying decisions.

Many elementary school library media centers do not begin to meet the new standards established jointly by the American Library Association, the American Association of School Librarians, and the Association for Educational Communications and Technology.[51] For a detailed discussion of these standards see Chapter 10.

CONTINUOUS RE-EVALUATION OF
LIBRARY MATERIALS

Re-evaluation of a collection is as important as the basic selection of new materials. Children's

---

[51] The American Library Association and the Association for Educational Communication and Technology. *Media Programs* (Chicago, Ill.: The American Library Association, 1975), pp. 70–80.

librarians and school media specialists are constantly assessing their current collections, discarding out-of-date science books and geography books.

The Children's Service Division of ALA has drawn up a policy statement in which they maintain that it is equally important to re-evaluate *fictional* materials. Their rationale states:

> Because most materials reflect the social climate of the era in which they are produced, it is often difficult to evaluate some aspects of a work at the time of purchase. But social climate and man's state of knowledge are constantly changing and librarians should therefore continuously re-evaluate their old materials in light of growing knowledge and broadening perspectives.[52]

Such a policy seems only sensible. Certainly, the old *Nicodemus* stories that are derogatory to blacks and perpetuate stereotyped images of "pickaninnies" and Aunt Jemima characters should have been removed from library shelves years ago. There is an inherent danger in such a policy, however: in our zeal to present accurate pictures of minorities—be they blacks, Chicanos, or women—we may attempt to rewrite history in terms of today's standards. *Amos Fortune*, a Newbery Award winning book by Yates, has been criticized for being an "Uncle Tom" book. And yet Amos Fortune was a real person who was bound into slavery and had the patience and persistence to buy his own freedom and that of four other persons. By today's standards he may have been an Uncle Tom, but he could not have been a militant and survived in the year 1725. By any standards his life is a glorious testament to the courage and dignity of an individual. Likewise, *Caddie Woodlawn* was a tomboy who would please the hearts of any supporter of women's liberation, except that she finally succumbed to the Victorian standards of the day and became a lady. In the period in which she lived, she had no other choice. We do need to be cognizant of racism, sexism, and prejudice in contemporary books. We have a right to question modern-day encyclopedias that picture only men in professional occupations such as dentists, anthropolo-

gists, psychologists, and so on. But we must not allow our zeal for unbiased materials to demand that what was written in the past conform to today's standards. Children need to know what "has been," as well as "what is."

CENSORSHIP AND CHALLENGED MATERIALS

There is a fine line between careful selection of books for children and censorship. Selection is made on the basis of quality of writing and appropriateness for children. Censorship, however, would curtail the purchase of books that represent conflicting religious, political, or social points of view. The "Library Bill of Rights," first adopted in 1948 and amended in 1961 and again in 1967 by the American Library Association, states six basic policies which should govern the services of all libraries. The first four of these policies relate to matters of censorship and are reproduced below; the last two relate to free access to the library for all individuals or groups.

1. As a responsibility of library service, books and other library materials selected should be chosen for values of interest, information and enlightenment of all the people of the community. In no case should library materials be excluded because of the race or nationality or the social, political, or religious views of the authors.

2. Libraries should provide books and other materials presenting all points of view concerning the problems and issues of our times; no library materials should be proscribed or removed from libraries because of partisan or doctrinal disapproval.

3. Censorship should be challenged by libraries in the maintenance of their responsibility to provide public information and enlightenment.

4. Libraries should cooperate with all persons and groups concerned with resisting abridgment of free expression and free access to ideas.[53]

Almost every school or children's librarian in a public library has faced some criticism of the books in the children's collection. Although re-

[52]"Statement on Reevaluation of Library Materials for Children's Collection," *Top of the News*, Vol. 29 (April 1973), pp. 190–191.

[53]*Library Bill of Rights*, adopted June 18, 1948, amended February 2, 1961, and June 27, 1967, by the American Library Council (Chicago, Ill.: American Library Association.)

cent years have seen an increase in the number of attacks, there have always been some groups who wished to protect children from certain books. Some twenty years ago, during the "cold war" with the USSR, certain groups took exception to an innocent, homey Russian folk tale titled *My Mother Is the Most Beautiful Woman in the World.*[54] In typical folktale style, the story described Russia's wheat as "the most nourishing," her vegetables as the "most delicious," her apples as the "crunchiest"; and so on. In no way did this story represent Communist propaganda, only the literary hyperbole of folklore. *Finders Keepers,* another simple picture book and winner of the Caldecott Award in 1952, was construed as subversive.

In recent years law enforcement groups have censored the 1970 Caldecott Award winning book, *Sylvester and the Magic Pebble* by William Steig, because it portrayed policemen as pigs. All the characters in the book are animals; Sylvester and his family are donkeys and other characters appear as pigs. Steig obviously enjoys telling about and drawing pigs; his first book for children was titled *Roland, The Minstrel Pig.* Librarians themselves in Caldwell Parish, Louisiana, censored Sendak's *In The Night Kitchen* by painting black tempera diapers on the naked hero, Mickey. No book is really safe from censors. Almost all censors feel they are really acting for "the children's best interests."

Contemporary fiction for older children has come under increasing attack as these books began to show the influence of the new freedom allowed in books and films for adults. Such titles as Holland's *The Man Without a Face,* which deals sensitively with a homosexual relationship, Klein's *Mom, the Wolf Man, and Me,* which openly accepts alternative family patterns, or Blume's *Deenie,* which includes several references to masturbation, have all received criticism and censorship. Criteria for these books will be thoroughly discussed in Chapter 7.

Every school should be ready for such an attack *before* it happens. Complainants should be asked to file a written report[55] citing specific objections to the books in question. A panel that might include outside experts, as well as local parent and teacher representatives, should be selected to deal with the criticism. Adequate time should be allowed for reviewing the problem and making recommendations. Frequently, the objection is dropped when such a procedure is calmly suggested.

A more subtle and frightening kind of censorship is that which is practiced voluntarily by librarians and teachers. If a book has come under negative scrutiny in a nearby town, it is carefully placed under the librarian's desk until the controversy dies down. Or, perhaps the librarians and the teachers just do not order controversial books. "Why stir up trouble when there are so many other good books available?" they falsely reason. One teacher feared the possibilities of a frank discussion of restricted real-estate sales that might accompany reading Neville's book, *Berries Goodman.* Although sensitive to community feeling, this teacher denied children the opportunity to evaluate a social problem.

It is not always easy to stand firm in the face of pressure and publicity. But careful preparation for book selection with the assistance of the administration should strengthen the professional position of the librarian. A very large principle is at stake—the principle of freedom to read, to inquire, to know all sides. The student has this right; the librarian and teacher must guarantee it.

SELECTION AIDS[56]

Teachers and librarians are faced with an enormous problem in finding materials for special topics or units, keeping up with the new books and other media, and ordering new materials for the classroom and the school library media center. The number of books published every year makes it increasingly difficult to read all books before ordering, and teachers cannot know all of the materials available on every topic of study. In order to make wise decisions about these problems, teachers and librarians need to know about the excellent selection aids that are available.

[54] Becky Reyher, *My Mother Is the Most Beautiful Woman in the World* (New York: Lothrop, 1945), unpaged.

[55] *See* Kenneth L. Donelson, *The Student's Right to Read,* for a sample form (Urbana, Ill.: The National Council of Teachers of English, 1972).

[56] *See* Appendix B for an extended and annotated list of selection aids.

REFERENCE TOOLS

Students, teachers, and librarians will find certain reference tools indispensable in locating materials. Two companion books, *Subject Guide to Children's Books in Print* and *Children's Books in Print* are both published annually by the R. R. Bowker Company. Let's assume you wanted to do a unit on Appalachia; by using the subject guide you could find a listing of both fiction and nonfiction books about Appalachia. Perhaps you are writing a paper on Sendak and you need to know the names of all of the books which he has illustrated. By checking the illustrators index provided in *Children's Books in Print* you can find the information you need. If you wish to order a certain book for your library the price, available editions (library binding, paperback, and so on), publisher, author, illustrator, date of publication, and grade level (when suggested by the publisher) are included in each of these references. Some 7,000 subject headings are listed in the subject guide.

A somewhat similar reference book for poetry is the *Index to Poetry for Children and Young People 1964–1969* by Brewton, *et al.*, published by the H. W. Wilson Company in 1972. Earlier volumes were simply titled *Index to Poetry*. The most recent book indexes 117 poetry collections. The title of the poem, author, subject, and first line are listed in a single alphabetical index. Certain subjects such as "winter" have many more entries than "pollution," for instance, but poets no doubt preferred the first topic over the second! For a teacher who wants to prepare an integrated unit on a particular topic, this tool and the *Subject Guide to Children's Books* would prove most helpful.

A unique reference tool is *Reading Ladders for Human Relations,* edited by Virginia Reid for the National Council of Teachers of English. This publication gives annotated reviews of books around four themes: the individual's concept of himself; his relationship with his family, peers, and others; his appreciation of different cultures; and his ability to cope with change. Five different maturity levels are given, ranging from picture books for primary readers to books for the mature reader. The annotations give enough detail to really describe the problem situation. A primary teacher wishing to find books in which children must cope with sibling rivalry could read the annotations for primary readers under the category "Coping with Change" and discover several book titles.

Many other specialized lists of materials— including bibliographies on the American Indian, *The Black Experience in Children's Books,* Ecology, and so on—are included in Appendix B in this book.

BOOK SELECTION GUIDES

Two indispensable guides to book collections are the *Children's Catalog* published by the H. W. Wilson Company and *The Elementary School Library Collection* edited by Mary V. Gaver for Bro-Dart. Most school libraries own both of these. Both works provide annotations on each of the books listed. Author, title, and subject indexes make them extremely useful. *The Elementary School Library Collection* provides listings for such non-print materials as films, filmstrips, and records. Both these works are revised periodically. They are extremely useful in setting up a new library, providing balance for an older collection, and as a reference tool.

BOOK REVIEWS

Four major library periodicals review new books and materials for children and will be very useful for helping you keep up in the field. These include *The Booklist, The Bulletin of the Center for Children's Books, The Horn Book Magazine,* and *School Library Journal.*

The Booklist is published twice a month from September through July, with one issue in August, by the American Library Association, and contains reviews of recommended books, films, filmstrips, and recordings. School and children's librarians assist the children's reviewer by giving their opinions of the books considered for review. *The Booklist* is widely used by librarians and media specialists.

The Bulletin for the Center of Children's Books is published monthly except August, and reviews books for children and young people including books they consider marginal and those titles not recommended. An advisory committee meets weekly to discuss books and reviews with the staff of the Center for Children's Books at the University of Chicago.

The Horn Book Magazine publishes discriminating reviews of books for children and young adults, along with articles on children's literature.

It is a magazine of literary criticism of children's books. The reviews are written and signed by the magazine's juvenile editors. It is published six times a year and has its editorial office in Boston.

School Library Journal is published monthly from September through May by the Bowker Company. It provides signed reviews of books and audiovisual materials recommended and not recommended for grades K–12. Reviews are written by over 250 volunteer librarian-reviewers. Articles of interest to teachers and librarians are included. Subscribers to *School Library Journal* may obtain *Previews* at a special rate. This magazine has the same policy as *School Library Journal*, but reviews only nonprint media.

There is no shortage of tools for the selection of materials for children. Faithful and consistent reading of one of the publications that reviews books for children will lead interested persons to those titles they will want to read and appraise for themselves. The experts cannot give a complete presentation of any book in a six-line review. They can only help the teacher or librarian decide if this is a book he or she would like to consider. Book selection aids should help eliminate the *number* of books that most librarians and teachers must read, but they should not eliminate reading. Whether it is for a 7-year-old or a 70-year-old, there is no substitute for the personal reading of a book you recommend.

SUGGESTED LEARNING EXPERIENCES

1. Write an autobiographical account of the development of your reading interests. What factors facilitated your interests; what were the inhibiting factors? What were your favorite books?

2. If possible, interview one child concerning his reading habits, likes, and dislikes. Also interview one of his parents to determine the reading environment in the home. What relationship can you identify?

3. Ask three children of various ages (5, 7, 9) to retell the story of "Goldilocks and the Three Bears" from the point of view of Baby Bear. Or have a group of college students retell it from Father Bear's viewpoint. Where might he be telling it? To whom? How does this second viewpont change the story?

4. Choose one of the many books without words, and share it with a 4-year-old, asking the child to tell you the story from the pictures. Repeat the procedure with a 6-year-old, and with an 8-year-old. What differences do you note in response to the story?

5. If you can meet with a class of children, ask them to submit the names of their ten favorite books. How do their choices reflect their particular ages and stages of development?

6. Visit the children's room of a public or school library to watch children in the process of choosing books. Keep a list, if you can, of the books examined and rejected, as well as those finally chosen. What factors seem to influence the children's choices?

7. Can you think of any one book that you read and reread as a child? What particular qualities of the story appealed to you? Reread it and evaluate it according to the criteria established in this chapter. Would you still recommend it for children?

8. Read one of the series books: the Bobbsey Twins, the Hardy Boys, the Sue Barton, or Nancy Drew series. Look closely at the literary craftsmanship of this book. How many contrived incidents can you find? Do the characters have real strengths *and* weaknesses? If you read this book aloud, would the language be a delight to the ear?

9. Form a mock Newbery Award Committee and review the winners and Honor Books for one year. Do you agree with the opinions of the actual judges? Be prepared to state your reasons why or why not.

10. Read a recently published book; then find reviews from two or more sources. Compare the reviews with your own reaction. Do the reviewers seem to use the same criteria as you do in judging this book?

11. Using at least three of the selection aids described in this chapter, or in Appendix B, make a list of appropriate poems, books, and materials that you would want to use to explore a particular topic with a selected age grouping. You might choose "mice," "night,"

or "friends" for primary grades; "the role of women," "pollution," or "beauty" might be topics for older children.

RELATED READINGS

1. Almy, Millie. *Ways of Studying Children.* New York: Bureau of Publications, Teachers College, Columbia University, 1959.

    The author presents many suggestions for collecting evidence for child study through observation, discussion, interviews, and records. Chapter 5, "Study the Ways Children Express Themselves," is particularly related to the use of literature in studying children.

2. Arbuthnot, May Hill, and Zena Sutherland. *Children and Books,* 4th ed. Glenview, Ill.: Scott Foresman, 1972.

    A comprehensive and detailed study of books for children. Chapter 1 presents children's needs that are satisfied through books, while Chapter 2 discusses criteria for selection.

3. Cameron, Eleanor. *The Green and Burning Tree.* Boston: Little, Brown, 1969.

    A collection of critical essays on the writing and enjoyment of children's books by a well-known author of children's science fiction. The essays that discuss style, characterization, and sense of place extend the criteria established in this chapter.

4. *Children's Books: Awards and Prizes.* New York: The Children's Book Council, 1972.

    A complete listing of all awards and prizes given to children's books. Updated frequently.

5. Chukovsky, Kornei. *From Two to Five,* translated and edited by Miriam Morton. Berkeley, Col.: University of California Press, 1963.

    A fascinating discussion by a Russian children's poet on the child's growth in language, his linguistic creativity, and his love of poetry and fantasy.

6. Cullinan, Bernice E. *Literature for Children: Its Discipline and Content.* Dubuque, Iowa: W. C. Brown, 1970.

    A scholarly presentation of the literary criteria for evaluating children's books. The final chapter suggests a sound approach to literary study in the classroom.

7. Egoff, Sheila, G. T. Stubbs, and L. F. Ashley. *Only Connect: Readings on Children's Literature.* Toronto: Oxford University Press, 1969.

    An excellent collection of forty essays on children's literature encompassing literary criticism, standards, changing tastes, child's responses to books, and writing and illustrating books. Many well-known contributors including Rumer Godden, Nat Hentoff, C. S. Lewis, John Rowe Townsend, and others.

8. Furth, Hans G. *Piaget for Teachers.* Englewood Cliffs, N.J.: Prentice-Hall, 1970.

    Discusses the educational implications of Piaget's theory in a readable, thoughtful way.

9. Hazard, Paul. *Books Children and Men.* Boston: Horn Book, 1947.

    Glowing prose illuminates the relationship of literature to life, and stresses the values of providing opportunities of bringing literature to children. Criteria for good books for children are established.

10. Kingman, Lee, ed. *Newbery and Caldecott Medal Books: 1956–1965,* with Acceptance Papers, Biographies, and Related Material chiefly from *The Horn Book Magazine.* Boston: Horn Book, 1964.

    The origin of the medals, an analysis of the themes of the medal books, and critical appraisals of the Newbery and Caldecott books are included with the information outlined in the title. Reproductions of illustrations from the Caldecott books help the student contrast the styles of picture books.

11. Miller, Bertha Mahony, and Elinor Whitney Field, eds. *Newbery Medal Books: 1922–1955.* Horn Book Papers, Vol. I. Boston: Horn Book, 1955.

    A brief history of the Newbery Award and a biographical sketch of John Newbery.

A book note, excerpt from the book, biographical note, and acceptance speech of each award winner from the inception of the award are included. The winning books are presented in chronological arrangement. Some illustrations from the award books are included.

12. Sayers, Frances Clarke. *Summoned by Books.* New York: Viking, 1965.

A collection of speeches and essays by an outstanding critic of children's literature. "Lose Not the Nightingale" and "Books that Enchant: What Makes a Classic?" are particularly appropriate reading for this chapter.

13. Smith, Irene. *A History of the Newbery and Caldecott Medals.* New York: Viking, 1957.

The author reviews the events that led to the founding of the awards, describes the selection proceedings, appraises the winning books, and points out the far-reaching influence of the awards. Chapter 9 is one of the most interesting—it discusses the popularity of the award books.

14. Smith, Lillian. *The Unreluctant Years: A Critical Approach to Children's Literature.* Chicago, Ill.: American Library Association, 1953.

"The Case for Children's Literature" discusses the qualities of literature that satisfy children's needs and places children's literature in the body of literature. In "An Approach to Criticism," the author establishes standards for good writing and gives an excellent analysis of the process of literary criticism.

15. Townsend, John Rowe. *A Sense of Story, Essays on Contemporary Writers for Children.* Boston, Mass: The Horn Book, 1971.

Townsend, a distinguished English author of books for children, has written critical reviews of some nineteen leading writers for children. Americans who are included in these in-depth studies include Meindert De Jong, Eleanor Estes, Paula Fox, Madeleine L'Engle, and Andre Norton.

RECOMMENDED REFERENCES[57]

Adkins, Jan. *How a House Happens.* Walker, 1972.

Alcott, Louisa. *Little Women,* illustrated by Barbara Cooney. Crowell, 1955 (1868).

Aliki, pseud. (Aliki Brandenberg). *Green Grass and White Milk.* Crowell, 1974.

———. *A Weed Is a Flower: The Life of George Washington Carver.* Prentice-Hall, 1965.

Andry, Andrew C., and Steven Schepp. *How Babies Are Made,* illustrated by Blake Hampton. Time-Life, 1968.

Ardizzone, Edward. *Tim to the Rescue.* Walck, 1949.

Armstrong, William H. *Sounder,* illustrated by James Barkley. Harper & Row, 1969.

Aruego, Jose. *Look What I Can Do.* Scribner, 1971.

Atwater, Richard, and Florence Atwater. *Mr. Popper's Penguins,* illustrated by Robert Lawson. Little, Brown, 1938.

Babbitt, Natalie. *Kneeknock Rise.* Farrar, Straus, 1970.

Barrett, Judi. *Animals Should Definitely Not Wear Clothing,* illustrated by Ron Barrett. Atheneum, 1970.

Barrie, James M. *Peter Pan,* illustrated by Nora S. Unwin. Scribner, 1949 (1911).

Baum, L. Frank. *The Wizard of Oz.* World Publishing, 1972 (1900).

Beatty, Jerome. *Bob Fulton's Amazing Soda Pop Stretcher.* Young Scott, 1963.

Bishop, Claire Huchet. *The Five Chinese Brothers,* illustrated by Kurt Wiese. Coward-McCann, 1938.

Blume, Judy. *Are You There God? It's Me, Margaret.* Bradbury, 1970.

———. *Deenie.* Bradbury, 1973.

———. *Tales of a Fourth Grade Nothing,* illustrated by Dale Roy. Dutton, 1972.

———. *Then Again, Maybe I Won't.* Bradbury, 1971.

[57] All books listed at the end of this chapter are recommended, subject to the qualifications noted in the text. See Appendix D for publishers' complete address. In the case of new editions the original publication date of the text sometimes appears in parentheses.

Bond, Michael. *A Bear Called Paddington,* illustrated by Peggy Fortnum. Houghton Mifflin, 1960.

Brenner, Barbara. *A Snake-Lover's Diary.* Young Scott, 1970.

Brink, Carol Ryrie. *Caddie Woodlawn.* Macmillan, 1936.

Brown, Marcia. *Backbone of the King.* Scribner, 1966.

———. *Once a Mouse.* Scribner, 1961.

Brown, Margaret Wise. *Goodnight Moon,* illustrated by Clement Hurd. Harper & Row, 1947.

———. *The Important Book,* illustrated by Leonard Weisgard. Harper & Row, 1949.

———. *The Runaway Bunny,* illustrated by Clement Hurd. Harper & Row, 1972 (1942).

Buckley, Helen E. *Grandfather and I,* illustrated by Paul Galdone. Lothrop, 1959.

———. *Too Many Crackers,* illustrated by Evaline Ness. Lothrop, 1966.

Bulla, Clyde R. *The White Bird,* illustrated by Leonard Weisgard. Crowell, 1966.

Burch, Robert. *Queenie Peavy,* illustrated by Jerry Lazare. Viking, 1966.

Burnett, Frances Hodgson. *The Secret Garden,* illustrated by Tasha Tudor. Lippincott, 1962 (1910).

Burningham, John. *Mr. Gumpy's Outing.* Holt, Rinehart and Winston, 1971.

———. *Seasons.* Bobbs-Merrill, 1970.

Burton, Virginia Lee. *Mike Mulligan and His Steam Shovel.* Houghton Mifflin, 1939.

Butterworth, Oliver. *The Enormous Egg,* illustrated by Louis Darling. Little, Brown, 1956.

Byars, Betsy. *Summer of the Swans,* illustrated by Ted CoConis. Viking, 1970.

Carle, Eric. *Do You Want to Be My Friend?* Crowell, 1971.

———. *The Very Hungry Caterpillar.* World Publishing, 1969.

Carroll, Lewis, pseud. (Charles L. Dodgson). *Alice's Adventures in Wonderland and Through the Looking Glass,* illustrated by John Tenniel. Macmillan, 1963 (first published separately, 1866 and 1872).

Carruth, Ella K. *She Wanted to Read: The Story of Mary McLeod Bethune,* illustrated by Herbert McClure. Abingdon, 1966.

Christopher, Matt. *The Year Mom Won the Pennant.* Little, Brown, 1968.

Clark, Ann Nolan. *In My Mother's House,* illustrated by Velino Herrera. Viking, 1941.

———. *Secret of the Andes,* illustrated by Jean Charlot. Viking, 1952.

Cleary, Beverly. *Beezus and Ramona,* illustrated by Louis Darling. Morrow, 1955.

———. *Henry Huggins,* illustrated by Louis Darling. Morrow, 1950.

———. *Ribsy,* illustrated by Louis Darling. Morrow, 1964.

Clymer, Eleanor. *My Brother Stevie.* Holt, Rinehart and Winston, 1967.

Coatsworth, Elizabeth. *Jon the Unlucky,* illustrated by Esta Nesbitt. Holt, Rinehart and Winston, 1964.

Cohen, Miriam. *Will I Have a Friend?,* illustrated by Lillian Hoban. Macmillan, 1967.

Colman, Hila. *Claudia, Where Are You?.* Morrow, 1969.

Colver, Anne. *Bread-and-Butter Indian,* illustrated by Garth Williams. Holt, Rinehart and Winston, 1964.

Conford, Ellen. *Impossible, Possum,* illustrated by Rosemary Wells. Little, Brown, 1971.

Coombs, Charles. *Be a Winner in Baseball.* Morrow, 1973.

Corbett, Scott. *The Big Joke Game,* illustrated by Mircea Vasiliu. Dutton, 1972.

Cousteau, Jacques. *Oasis in Space.* World Publishing, 1972.

Cunningham, Julia. *Dorp Dead,* illustrated by James Spanfeller. Pantheon, 1965.

Dahl, Roald. *James and the Giant Peach,* illustrated by Nancy Burkert. Knopf, 1961.

Dalgliesh, Alice. *The Bears on Hemlock Mountain,* illustrated by Helen Sewell. Scribner, 1952.

———. *The Courage of Sarah Noble,* illustrated by Leonard Weisgard. Scribner, 1954.

De Angeli, Marguerite. *The Door in the Wall.* Doubleday, 1949.

Defoe, Daniel. *Robinson Crusoe,* illustrated by N. C. Wyeth. Scribner, 1920 (1719).

DeJong, Meindert. *The Almost All-white Rabbity Cat,* illustrated by H. B. Vestal. Macmillan, 1972.

———. *Far Out the Long Canal,* illustrated by Nancy Grossman. Harper & Row, 1964.

———. *The House of Sixty Fathers,* illustrated by Maurice Sendak. Harper & Row, 1956.

———. *Hurry Home, Candy,* illustrated by Maurice Sendak. Harper & Row, 1953.

————. *Journey from Peppermint Street,* illustrated by Emily McCully. Harper & Row, 1968.

————. *Shadrach,* illustrated by Maurice Sendak. Harper & Row, 1963.

De Regniers, Beatrice Schenk. *May I Bring a Friend?,* illustrated by Beni Montresor. Atheneum, 1964.

De Schweinitz, Karl. *Growing Up,* rev. ed. Macmillan, 1967.

Dodge, Mary Mapes. *Hans Brinker, or The Silver Skates,* illustrated by George Wharton Edwards. Scribner, 1915 (1865).

Donovan, John. *I'll Get There, It Better Be Worth the Trip.* Harper & Row, 1969.

DuBois, William Pène. *Lazy Tommy Pumpkinhead.* Harper & Row, 1966.

Dunn, Judy. *Things,* photographs by Phoebe and Tris Dunn. Doubleday, 1968.

Dunn, Mary L. *The Man in the Box: A Story from Vietnam.* McGraw-Hill, 1968.

Dunning, Stephen, *et al. Reflections on a Gift of Watermelon Pickle and Other Modern Verse.* Lothrop, 1967.

Duvoisin, Roger. *Petunia.* Knopf, 1950.

Ehrlich, Amy. *Zeek Silver Moon,* illustrated by Robert Andrew Parker. Dial, 1972.

Engdahl, Sylvia Louise. *Enchantress from the Stars,* illustrated by Rodney Shackell. Atheneum, 1970.

Enright, Elizabeth. *Gone-Away Lake,* illustrated by Beth and Joe Krush. Harcourt Brace Jovanovich, 1957.

————. *Thimble Summer.* Holt, Rinehart and Winston, 1938.

Epstein, Sam, and Beryl Epstein. *First Book of Codes and Ciphers,* illustrated by Laszlo Roth. F. Watts, 1956.

Estes, Eleanor. *The Hundred Dresses,* illustrated by Louis Slobodkin. Harcourt Brace Jovanovich, 1944.

Ets, Marie Hall. *Just Me.* Viking, 1965.

Farmer, Penelope. *The Summer Birds,* illustrated by James Spanfeller. Harcourt Brace Jovanovich, 1962.

Fitzhugh, Louise. *Harriet the Spy.* Harper & Row, 1964.

Flack, Marjorie. *Ask Mr. Bear.* Macmillan, 1932.

————. *Walter the Lazy Mouse,* illustrated by Cyndy Szekeres. Doubleday, 1963 (1937).

Fleming, Ian. *Chitty-Chitty-Bang-Bang,* illustrated by John Burningham. Random House, 1964.

Forbes, Esther. *Johnny Tremain,* illustrated by Lynd Ward. Houghton Mifflin, 1946.

Fox, Paula. *How Many Miles to Babylon?,* illustrated by Paul Giovanopoulos. D. White, 1967.

————. *Maurice's Room,* illustrated by Ingrid Fetz. Macmillan, 1966.

Franchere, Ruth. *Willa: The Story of Willa Cather's Growing Up,* illustrated by Leonard Weisgard. Crowell, 1958.

Frank, Anne. *Anne Frank: The Diary of a Young Girl,* translated by B. M. Mooyart. Doubleday, 1967.

Freeman, Don. *Dandelion.* Viking, 1964.

Fritz, Jean. *The Cabin Faced West,* illustrated by Feodor Rojankovsky. Coward-McCann, 1958.

Fuchs, Erich. *Journey to the Moon.* Delacorte, 1970.

Gág, Wanda. *Millions of Cats.* Coward-McCann, 1928.

Gage, Wilson. *Miss Osborne-the-Mop,* illustrated by Paul Galdone. World Publishing, 1963.

Gallob, Edward. *City Leaves, City Trees.* Scribner, 1972.

Garner, Alan. *The Owl Service.* Walck, 1968.

George, Jean. *Julie of the Wolves,* illustrated by John Schoenherr. Harper & Row, 1972.

————. *My Side of the Mountain.* Dutton, 1959.

Gill, Joan. *Hush, Jon!,* illustrated by Tracy Sugarman. Doubleday, 1968.

Gipson, Fred. *Old Yeller,* illustrated by Carl Burger. Harper & Row, 1956.

Goldreich, Gloria, and Esther Goldreich. *What Can She Be? A Lawyer,* photographs by Robert Ipcar. Lothrop, 1973.

Graham, Frank. *Great No-Hit Games of the Major Leagues.* Random House, 1968.

Grahame, Kenneth. *The Wind in the Willows,* illustrated by E. H. Shepard. Scribner, 1908.

Greene, Constance C. *A Girl Called Al,* illustrated by Byron Barton. Viking, 1969.

————. *The Unmaking of Rabbit.* Viking, 1972.

Griffiths, Helen. *The Wild Heart,* illustrated by Victor Ambrus. Doubleday, 1963.

Grimm, the Brothers. *The Seven Ravens,* illustrated by Felix Hoffmann. Harcourt Brace Jovanovich, 1963.

———. *Snow-White and the Seven Dwarfs,* translated by Randall Jarrell, illustrated by Nancy Ekholm Burkert. Farrar, Straus, 1972.

Gruenberg, Sidonie M. *The Wonderful Story of How You Were Born,* rev. ed., illustrated by Symeon Shimin. Doubleday, 1970.

Guilfoile, Elizabeth. *Nobody Listens to Andrew.* Follett, 1957.

Haugaard, Erik Christian. *Hakon of Rogen's Saga,* illustrated by Leo Dillon and Diane Dillon. Houghton Mifflin, 1963.

Hautzig, Esther. *Cool Cooking,* illustrated by Jan Pyk. Lothrop, 1973.

———. *The Endless Steppe.* Crowell, 1968.

Heide, Florence P. *Sound of Sunshine, Sound of Rain.* Parents', 1970.

Henry, Marguerite. *Black Gold,* illustrated by Wesley Dennis. Rand McNally, 1957.

Hickman, Janet. *The Valley of the Shadow.* Macmillan, 1974.

Hicks, Clifford B. *Alvin's Secret Code,* illustrated by Bill Sokol. Holt, Rinehart and Winston, 1963.

Hill, Elizabeth Starr. *Evan's Corner,* illustrated by Nancy Grossman. Holt, Rinehart and Winston, 1967.

Hirsch, S. Carl. *The Living Community: A Venture into Ecology,* illustrated by William Steinel. Viking, 1966.

Hitchcock, Alfred, ed. *Alfred Hitchcock's Daring Detectives,* illustrated by Arthur Shilstone. Random House, 1969.

Hoban, Russell. *Bedtime for Frances,* illustrated by Garth Williams. Harper & Row, 1960.

———. *Best Friends for Frances,* illustrated by Lillian Hoban. Harper & Row, 1969.

Hoban, Tana. *Count and See.* Macmillan, 1972.

———. *Look Again!* Macmillan, 1971.

———. *Push Pull, Empty Full.* Macmillan, 1972.

Holland, Isabelle. *The Man Without a Face.* Lippincott, 1972.

Hollander, Zander, ed. *The Modern Encyclopedia of Basketball.* Four Winds, 1969.

Hunt, Irene. *Across Five Aprils.* Follett, 1964.

Hunter, Edith F. *Child of the Silent Night,* illustrated by Bea Holmes. Houghton Mifflin, 1963.

Hunter, Mollie, pseud. (Maureen McIlwraith). *The 13th Member.* Harper & Row, 1971.

Hutchins, Pat. *Clocks and More Clocks.* Macmillan, 1970.

———. *Good-Night, Owl!* Macmillan, 1972.

———. *Rosie's Walk.* Macmillan, 1968.

———. *The Surprise Party.* Macmillan, 1969.

———. *Titch.* Macmillan, 1971.

Jarrell, Randall. *The Animal Family,* illustrated by Maurice Sendak. Pantheon, 1965.

Jones, Weyman. *Edge of Two Worlds,* illustrated by J. C. Kocsis. Dial, 1968.

Judson, Clara Ingram. *Mr. Justice Holmes,* illustrated by Robert Todd. Follett, 1956.

Juster, Norton. *The Phantom Tollbooth.* Random House, 1961.

Keats, Ezra Jack. *Peter's Chair.* Harper & Row, 1967.

———. *The Snowy Day.* Viking, 1962.

———. *Whistle for Willie.* Viking, 1964.

Keeping, Charles. *Through the Window.* F. Watts, 1970.

Key, Alexander. *The Forgotten Door.* Westminster, 1965.

Kidder, Harvey. *Illustrated Chess for Children.* Doubleday, 1970.

Kipling, Rudyard. *The Jungle Books,* illustrated by Robert Shore. Macmillan, 1964 (1894).

Klein, Norma. *Mom, the Wolf Man and Me.* Pantheon, 1972.

Konigsburg, E. L. *From the Mixed-Up Files of Mrs. Basil E. Frankweiler.* Atheneum, 1967.

Koren, Edward. *Behind the Wheel.* Holt, Rinehart and Winston, 1972.

Kraus, Robert. *Leo the Late Bloomer,* illustrated by Jose Aruego. Windmill, 1971.

Krauss, Ruth. *The Bundle Book,* illustrated by Helen Stone. Harper & Row, 1951.

———. *The Carrot Seed,* illustrated by Crockett Johnson. Harper & Row, 1945.

Kroeber, Theodora. *Ishi, Last of His Tribe,* illustrated by Ruth Robbins. Parnassus, 1964.

Kunhardt, Dorothy. *Pat the Bunny.* Golden Press, 1962 (1940).

Kuskin, Karla. *Just Like Everyone Else.* Harper & Row, 1959.

Lawson, Robert. *Rabbit Hill.* Viking, 1944.

Lee, Bruce. *Boy's Life of John F. Kennedy.* Sterling, 1964.

LeGuin, Ursula K. *A Wizard of Earthsea,* illustrated by Ruth Robbins. Parnassus, 1968.

L'Engle, Madeleine. *Meet the Austins.* Vanguard, 1960.

——. *The Moon by Night.* Farrar, Straus, 1963.

——. *A Wind in the Door.* Farrar, Straus, 1973.

——. *A Wrinkle in Time.* Farrar, Straus, 1962.

Lester, Julius. *To Be a Slave,* illustrated by Tom Feelings. Dial, 1968.

Lexau, Joan. *Benjie,* illustrated by Don Bolognese. Dial, 1964.

——. *Every Day a Dragon,* illustrated by Ben Shecter. Harper & Row, 1967.

——. *Striped Ice Cream,* illustrated by John Wilson. Lippincott, 1968.

Lightbody, Donna. *Let's Knot, A Macrame Book.* Lothrop, 1972.

Lindgren, Astrid. *Pippi Longstocking,* illustrated by Louis Glanzman. Viking, 1950.

Lionni, Leo. *The Biggest House in the World.* Pantheon, 1968.

——. *Fish Is Fish.* Pantheon, 1970.

——. *Swimmy.* Pantheon, 1963.

Little, Jean. *Take Wing.* Little, Brown, 1968.

Lobel, Arnold. *Frog and Toad Together.* Harper & Row, 1972.

——. *Mouse Tales.* Harper & Row, 1972.

Lord, Beman. *Mystery Guest at Left End,* illustrated by Arnold Spilka. Walck, 1964.

McCloskey, Robert. *Homer Price.* Viking, 1943.

——. *One Morning in Maine.* Viking, 1952.

——. *Time of Wonder.* Viking, 1957.

McDermott, Gerald. *Anansi the Spider.* Holt, Rinehart and Winston, 1972.

McGovern, Ann. *Runaway Slave: The Story of Harriet Tubman,* illustrated by R. M. Powers. Four Winds, 1965.

McHargue, Georgess. *Funny Bananas,* illustrated by Heidi Palmer. Holt, Rinehart and Winston, 1975.

McKee, David. *Mr. Benn-Red Knight.* McGraw-Hill, 1968.

McWhirter, Norris, and Ross McWhirter. *The Guinness Book of World Records.* Sterling, 1971.

Mann, Peggy. *My Dad Lives in a Downtown Hotel,* illustrated by Richard Cuffari. Doubleday, 1973.

Massie, Diane Redfield. *Dazzle.* Parents', 1969.

——. *Walter Was a Frog.* Scribner, 1970.

Mayer, Mercer, and Marianna Mayer. *Mine!* Simon & Schuster, 1970.

Miles, Miska. *Annie and the Old One,* illustrated by Peter Parnall. Little, Brown, 1971.

Milne, A. A. *When We Were Very Young,* illustrated by E. H. Shepard. Dutton, 1924.

——. *Winnie the Pooh,* illustrated by E. H. Shepard. Dutton, 1926.

Minarik, Else Holmelund. *Little Bear,* illustrated by Maurice Sendak. Harper & Row, 1957.

Munari, Bruno. *Who's There? Open the Door!* World Publishing, 1957.

Murray, Michele. *Nellie Cameron,* illustrated by Leonora E. Prince. Seabury, 1971.

Myller, Lois. *No! No!,* illustrated by Cyndy Szekeres. Simon & Schuster, 1971.

Ness, Evaline. *Sam, Bangs and Moonshine.* Holt, Rinehart and Winston, 1966.

Neufeld, John. *Edgar Allen,* illustrated by Loren Dunlap. S. G. Phillips, 1968.

Neville, Emily C. *Berries Goodman.* Harper & Row, 1965.

——. *It's Like This, Cat,* illustrated by Emil Weiss. Harper & Row, 1963.

Norton, Mary. *The Borrowers,* illustrated by Beth and Joe Krush. Harcourt Brace Jovanovich, 1953.

O'Brien, Robert C. *Mrs. Frisby and the Rats of NIMH,* illustrated by Zena Bernstein. Atheneum, 1971.

O'Dell, Scott. *Island of the Blue Dolphins.* Houghton Mifflin, 1960.

——. *Sing Down the Moon.* Houghton Mifflin, 1970.

Parish, Peggy. *Amelia Bedelia,* illustrated by Fritz Siebel. Harper & Row, 1963.

Pearce, Philippa. *Tom's Midnight Garden,* illustrated by Susan Einzig. Lippincott, 1959.

Peare, Catherine O. *The Helen Keller Story.* Crowell, 1959.

Petrides, Heidrun. *Hans and Peter.* Harcourt Brace Jovanovich, 1963.

Picard, Barbara. *One Is One.* Holt, Rinehart and Winston, 1966.

Piper, Watty. *The Little Engine that Could,* illustrated by George and Doris Hauman. Platt & Munk, 1954 (1930).

Potter, Beatrix. *The Tale of Benjamin Bunny.* Warne, 1904.

———. *The Tale of Peter Rabbit.* Warne, n.d.

Preston, Edna Mitchell. *The Temper Tantrum Book,* illustrated by Rainey Bennett. Viking, 1969.

Ravielli, Anthony. *Wonders of the Human Body.* Viking, 1954.

Rawlings, Marjorie Kinnan. *The Yearling,* illustrated by Edward Shenton. Scribner, 1938.

Reyher, Becky. *My Mother Is the Most Beautiful Woman in the World,* illustrated by Ruth Gannett. Lothrop, 1945.

Robertson, Keith. *Henry Reed, Inc.,* illustrated by Robert McCloskey. Viking, 1958.

Robinson, Jackie, and Alfred Duckett. *Breakthrough to the Big League.* Harper & Row, 1965.

Robinson, Veronica. *David in Silence,* illustrated by Victor Ambrus. Lippincott, 1965.

Rockwell, Anne. *Olly's Polliwogs,* illustrated by Harlow Rockwell. Doubleday, 1970.

Rodgers, Mary. *Freaky Friday.* Harper & Row, 1972.

Ross, Frank. *Racing Cars and Great Races,* Lothrop, 1972.

Salten, Felix. *Bambi,* illustrated by Barbara Cooney. Simon & Schuster, 1970 (1929).

Sarnoff, Jane, and Reynold Ruffins. *A Great Bicycle Book.* Scribner, 1973.

Schulz, Charles. *Snoopy and His Sopwith Camel.* Holt, Rinehart and Winston, 1969.

Scott, Ann Herbert. *Sam,* illustrated by Symeon Shimin. McGraw-Hill, 1967.

Segal, Lore. *Tell Me a Mitzi,* illustrated by Harriet Pincus. Farrar, Straus, 1970.

Selden, George. *The Cricket in Times Square,* illustrated by Garth Williams. Farrar, Straus, 1960.

Sendak, Maurice. *In the Night Kitchen.* Harper & Row, 1970.

———. *Where the Wild Things Are.* Harper & Row, 1963.

Sewell, Anna. *Black Beauty,* illustrated by John Groth. Macmillan, 1962 (1877).

Sheffield, Margaret. *Where Do Babies Come From?,* illustrated by Sheila Bewley. Knopf, 1973.

Showers, Paul. *The Listening Walk,* illustrated by Aliki. Crowell, 1961.

Silverstein, Alvin, and Virginia Silverstein. *Guinea Pigs, All about Them.* Lothrop, 1972.

Simon, Seymour. *The Paper Airplane Book,* illustrated by Byron Barton. Viking, 1971.

Skorpen, Liesel. *Charles,* illustrated by Martha Alexander. Harper & Row, 1971.

Sleator, William. *Blackbriar.* Dutton, 1972.

Slobodkin, Florence, and Louis Slobodkin. *Sarah Somebody.* Vanguard, 1969.

Slobodkina, Esphyr. *Caps for Sale.* W. R. Scott, 1947.

Smith, Doris Buchanan. *A Taste of Blackberries,* illustrated by Charles Robinson. Crowell, 1973.

Sobol, Donald J. *Encyclopedia Brown Takes a Case,* illustrated by Leonard Shortall. Nelson, 1973.

Sorensen, Virginia. *Miracles on Maple Hill,* illustrated by Beth and Joe Krush. Harcourt Brace Jovanovich, 1956.

Southall, Ivan. *Ash Road,* illustrated by Clem Seale. St. Martin, 1965.

———. *Josh.* Macmillan, 1972.

Sperry, Armstrong. *Call It Courage.* Macmillan, 1940.

Spier, Peter. *Crash! Bang! Boom!* Doubleday, 1972.

Spyri, Johanna. *Heidi,* illustrated by Greta Elgaard. Macmillan, 1962 (1884).

Steele, Mary Q. *Journey Outside,* illustrated by Rocco Negri. Viking, 1969.

Steele, William O. *Winter Danger,* illustrated by Paul Galdone. Harcourt Brace Jovanovich, 1954.

Steig, William. *Amos and Boris.* Farrar, Straus, 1971.

———. *Roland, the Minstrel Pig.* Harper & Row, 1968.

———. *Sylvester and the Magic Pebble.* Windmill, 1969.

Steptoe, John. *Stevie.* Harper & Row, 1969.

————. *Train Ride.* Harper & Row, 1971.

Stevenson, Robert Louis. *Treasure Island,* illustrated by N. C. Wyeth. Scribner, 1911 (1883).

Stolz, Mary. *The Bully of Barkham Street,* illustrated by Leonard Shortall. Harper & Row, 1963.

————, *A Dog on Barkham Street,* illustrated by Leonard Shortall. Harper & Row, 1960.

Swinton, William E. *Digging for Dinosaurs,* illustrated by B. Driscoll. Doubleday, 1962.

Taylor, Mark. *Henry the Explorer,* illustrated by Graham Booth. Atheneum, 1966.

Tolkien, J. R. R. *The Hobbit.* Houghton Mifflin, 1938.

Tolstoy, Alexei. *The Great Big Enormous Turnip,* illustrated by Helen Oxenbury. F. Watts, 1969.

Travers, Pamela L. *Mary Poppins,* illustrated by Mary Shepard. Harcourt Brace Jovanovich, 1934.

Tresselt, Alvin. *It's Time Now,* illustrated by Roger Duvoisin. Harper & Row, 1969.

————. *A Thousand Lights and Fireflies,* illustrated by John Moodie. Parents', 1965.

Tunis, John R. *His Enemy, His Friend.* Morrow, 1967.

Turkle, Brinton. *The Fiddler of High Lonesome.* Viking, 1968.

————. *Obadiah the Bold.* Viking, 1965.

Twain, Mark, pseud. (Samuel Clemens). *The Adventures of Huckleberry Finn.* Harper & Row, 1884.

————. *The Adventures of Tom Sawyer.* Harper & Row, 1876.

Uchida, Yoshiko. *Journey to Topaz,* illustrated by Donald Carrick. Scribner, 1971.

Udry, Janice May. *Let's Be Enemies,* illustrated by Maurice Sendak. Harper & Row, 1961.

————. *A Tree is Nice,* illustrated by Marc Simont. Harper & Row, 1956.

Viorst, Judith. *Alexander and the Terrible, Horrible, No Good, Very Bad Day,* illustrated by Ray Cruz. Atheneum, 1972.

Warburg, Sandol S. *Growing Time,* illustrated by Leonard Weisgard. Houghton Mifflin, 1969.

Ward, Lynd. *The Biggest Bear.* Houghton Mifflin, 1952.

Watson, Clyde. *Father Fox's Pennyrhymes,* illustrated by Wendy Watson. Crowell, 1971.

Wersba, Barbara. *The Dream Watcher.* Atheneum, 1968.

Wezel, Peter. *The Good Bird.* Harper & Row, 1964.

White, E. B. *Charlotte's Web,* illustrated by Garth Williams. Harper & Row, 1952.

————. *Stuart Little,* illustrated by Garth Williams. Harper & Row, 1945.

Wier, Ester. *The Loner,* illustrated by Christine Price. McKay, 1963.

Wilder, Laura Ingalls. The *Little House* Series, illustrated by Garth Williams. Harper & Row, 1953.

 On the Banks of Plum Creek, 1937.
 Little House in the Big Woods, 1932.
 Little House on the Prairie, 1935.
 Little Town on the Prairie, 1941.
 The Long Winter, 1940.
 By the Shores of Silver Lake, 1939.
 These Happy Golden Years, 1943.

Wildsmith, Brian. *Brian Wildsmith's Puzzles.* F. Watts, 1971.

Will and Nicolas, pseud. (William Lipkind and Nicolas Mordvinoff). *Finders Keepers.* Harcourt Brace Jovanovich, 1951.

Williams, Margery. *The Velveteen Rabbit,* illustrated by William Nicholson. Doubleday, 1958 (1922).

Wojciechowska, Maia. *Shadow of a Bull,* illustrated by Alvin Smith. Atheneum, 1964.

Wyss, Johann. *Swiss Family Robinson,* illustrated by Lynd Ward. Grosset & Dunlap, 1949 (1814).

Yashima, Taro, pseud. (Jun Iwamatsu). *Crow Boy.* Viking, 1955.

————. *Seashore Story.* Viking, 1967.

Yates, Elizabeth. *Amos Fortune, Free Man,* illustrated by Nora Unwin. Dutton, 1950.

Zemach, Harve. *The Judge,* illustrated by Margot Zemach. Farrar, Straus, 1969.

Zolotow, Charlotte. *Do You Know What I'll Do?,* illustrated by Garth Williams. Harper & Row, 1958.

————. *Mr. Rabbit and the Lovely Present,* illustrated by Maurice Sendak. Harper & Row, 1962.

————. *Over and Over,* illustrated by Garth Williams. Harper & Row, 1951.

————. *William's Doll,* illustrated by William Pène DuBois. Harper & Row, 1972.

2 Children's Books of Yesterday and Today

The history of children's literature reveals the changing attitude of society toward children and changing cultural values. Compare the language, the content, and the illustrations of the following two stories written nearly one hundred years apart.

"Cruel Boys."

From *Sunnybank Stories: My Teacher's Gem.* Boston, Mass.: Lee and Shepard, 1863.

"GOOD-BYE!"
"GOOD-BYE!"

Let's Be Enemies by Janice May Udry.

Illustration by Maurice Sendak from *Let's Be Enemies* by Janice May Udry. Pictures copyright © 1961 by Maurice Sendak. Reprinted by permission of Harper & Row, Publishers, Inc.

Cruel Boys

"O, what a shame!" a kind child may be ready to say on looking at this picture. You see these boys, little as they are, have hard and cruel hearts. They have been robbing a happy little bird family of one of the young ones; and now they will so hurt it that it will die, or they will let it starve to death. And they have robbed another pair of birds of their nest and eggs. How unhappy must all these birds now be! and how wicked it is to give such needless pain to any of God's creatures! No kind child can think of hurting a dear, innocent little bird. But those who delight in such sport will very likely grow up to be capable of injuring their fellow-men in the various ways of which we so often hear and read. Let us be kind to every thing that lives.

And this isn't the whole story about these wicked boys. Don't you see they are in a *quarrel*, how they shall divide what they have so cruelly stolen from the poor birds? Ah, that is the way in doing wrong—one wrong step leads on to another; and robbing birds' nests does not usually go alone—a quarrel, or some other wickedness, usually follows it. Beware, then of the *beginnings* of cruelty and wickedness.[1]

[1] Asa Bullard, *Sunnybank Stories: My Teacher's Gem* (Boston: Lee and Shepard, 1863), pp. 22–24.

Excerpt from *Let's Be Enemies*

James used to be my friend.
But today he is my enemy.
James always wants to be the boss.
James carries the flag.
James takes all the crayons.
He grabs the best digging spoon
and he throws sand. . . .
I'm going right over to James' house and tell him. . . .
"Hullo, James."
"Hullo, John."
"I came to tell you that I'm not your friend any more."
"Well then, I'm not *your* friend either."
"We're enemies."
"All right!"
"GOOD-BYE!"
"GOOD-BYE!"
"Hey, James!"
"What?"
"Let's roller skate."
"O.K. Have a pretzel, John."
"Thank you, James."[2]

[2] Excerpt from *Let's Be Enemies* by Janice May Udry. Text copyright © 1961 by Janice May Udry. Reprinted by permission of Harper & Row, Publishers, Inc.

SCCCC - LIBRARY
4500 Mid Rivers Mall Drive
St. Peters, MO 63376
WITHDRAWN

"Cruel Boys" is taken from *My Teacher's Gem,* a collection of moralistic stories printed in 1863. Its purpose was to instruct the young by first describing a horrible example of misbehavior and then warning of the dire consequences of, in this instance, stealing. It is told in the third person from the point of view of an adult admonishing all children. The moral of the story is explicitly stated. "Cruel Boys" is illustrated with only one black-and-white print, a picture that was used in many different books at that time. The "pirating" of pictures and stories from other books was a common practice.

Let's Be Enemies (1961), on the other hand, captures the experience, the feelings, and the language of the modern child. The story is told in the first person from the point of view of the child protagonist, and the young listener can quite easily identify with the growing anger of John. But five-year-olds' quarrels are as fleeting as the brief showers that Sendak includes in his childlike illustrations. The sun soon comes out; and true to the nature of young children, John and James are fast friends at the end of the story.

By contrasting these two stories, it is easy to see how literature for children has changed. Today's child is allowed his childhood. He can be himself in literature. He has a right to his feelings and thoughts. Literature does not have to instruct; it can entertain.

The elementary school teacher can better appreciate the richness of children's literature today by tracing the development of books for children. Meigs states:

> To be aware of the greatness of a literature is not always to understand it fully, since to have interest and regard for it does not imply entire knowledge of what it is and how it came to be. But if thinking people are to have any part in shaping the literature of the present and the future, they should have a fuller understanding of it as a whole and of its past.[3]

The literature available for children reflects the attitudes of society in that period. Books for children have always been viewed as instruments for transmitting the mores of the culture and for inculcating attitudes and values. For example, colonial children were treated as miniature adults, not as developing personalities important in their own right. When Joseph Downing published the first catalogue of books for children and young people, *The Young Christians Library* (1710), he stressed the idea that the purpose of such books was to foster the health of the child's soul. Children were admonished to avoid "books, ballads, songs, sonettes, and ditties of dalliance."

Today, as in the past, adults write the books; adults print the books; teachers, librarians, parents, and gift-givers review and select most of the books children read. Hazard says children defend themselves, ". . . when they have singled out a work that they like and have decided to take possession of it, nothing can make them change their minds. . . . It is that book there that they want, that very one and not its neighbor."[4] Children *are* the final arbiters of books they will read, but Sloane reminds us that: "It is impossible to determine precisely how much of the change that occurred in children's literature was due to increasing sagacity of adults and how much was due to increasing demands of children."[5] As society changed its attitude toward children, the didactic and dour became the fanciful and "precious." Adults became more aware of children's demands for informational books and adventure. In addition, the changing attitudes, values, philosophies, and concepts of man and the universe are reflected in children's books.

[4]Paul Hazard, *Books Children and Men* (Boston: Horn Book, 1947), p. 51.
[5]William Sloane, *Children's Books in England and America in the Seventeenth Century* (New York: Kings Crown, 1955), p. 17.

[3]Cornelia Meigs, ed. *A Critical History of Children's Literature* (New York: Macmillan, 1953), p. 3.

An understanding of the growth of children's literature as part of a developing culture will enable the classroom teacher to better evaluate children's books of today.

Children's Books: Seventeenth and Eighteenth Centuries

BACKGROUND

To that "stern and rock-bound coast" the early colonists brought old-world concepts and philosophies that would yield to new-world pressures and needs. Traditional Christian theism held that children were born in sin, that eternal salvation could come only to the elect, and that eternal punishment would be meted out to the sinner. Voting rights and office-holding privileges were reserved for members of the church. Children were viewed as miniature adults who learned obedience to authority through fear.

By the middle of the eighteenth century there was a shift from knowledge based upon religious sanctions to knowledge derived from human investigation. Newton, Bacon, Copernicus, Kepler, and Galileo had challenged the divine laws and authoritarian reasoning, and had shown the way toward a method of science. Apparent natural laws suggested the study of nature and human nature. Locke stated that human nature was at least partially the result of the environment; Rousseau emphasized the natural unfolding of a child nature which he believed to be inherently good.

Concurrently, an agrarian feudalism was changing to commercial capitalism. There was a growing middle class; the emphasis on trade led to new educational needs. Some of the religious sects introduced social reform and emphasized teaching children through love. Colonial government had been based upon the view that only the few "godly" men should rule; the changing eighteenth-century view held that government should be based upon the natural rights of all men.

By the end of the century the idea of the individual rights of the child was being recognized. Life was often uncomfortable and rigorous in this new land, and there were few books for adults or children to relieve the drabness of living.

BOOKS OF THE AMERICAN COLONIAL PERIOD

What books were packed in the chests that came across the Atlantic with the early colonists? The Bible was a treasured book of those who could afford to have one. Perhaps a copy of William Caxton's 1497 book, *The Book of Courtesye* was owned by some colonists. This was a description of the typical day of the well-bred English child. Another book of manners was *Youth's Behavior*, translated from the French in 1636. Here, one could read how to dress properly, how to walk, how to remove fleas tactfully, how to dispose of bones neatly, and other niceties of life. *Properties of Things*, printed by Wynken de Worde in 1495, gave the names of parts of the body, plants, mountains, and diseases. Caxton also printed *Aesop's Fables* in 1484, using many woodcuts.

Probably some of the colonists owned at least one of the bestiaries, animal tales that combined elements of fable and scripture. Topsel's *The History of Four-Footed Beasts* (1658) is an example of these books about dragons, unicorns, and other strange creatures. The first picture book planned for children was written by Comenius in 1657. Perhaps a few colonists brought the 1658 English translation of this book, *Orbus Pictus*, with its woodcuts illustrating everyday objects.

Just before sailing, a colonist might have purchased a chapbook from a peddler. These were very small, inexpensive paper booklets sold by peddlers or chapmen. "A ballad of a most strange wedding of the froggee and the mouse" had been licensed in 1580. In a collection published in the 1680s, may be found *Tom Thumb, Guy of Warwick*, and accounts of crimes and executions, descriptions of the art of making love, and riddles. The earliest known edition of *Jack the Giant Killer* seems to be a chapbook printed in 1711.

The religious leaders could give approval to the moral and religious instruction in John Bunyan's *Pilgrim's Progress*, first printed in 1678. No doubt children skipped the long theological dialogues as they found adventure by traveling with the clearly defined characters.

Early writers and educators often thought that

All illustrations on this page are from "The History of Sir Richard Whittington," published about 1770.

A forerunner of cartoon style is seen in a woodcut used to illustrate a popular chapbook.

From *Pictures and Stories from Forgotten Children's Books* by Arnold Arnold, Dover Publications, Inc., 1969.

words of wisdom and lectures instilling good manners and a righteous way of life could best be given children in verse form. Their recognition of the child's delight in rhythm and rhyme was a step toward a literature for children. This trend was exemplified by the eight pages of rhymed couplets describing the wares of the peddler-author, Thomas Newbery, entitled, *A Booke in Englysh Metre, of the great Marchante Man called Dives Pragmaticus, very preaty for children to reade* (1563). John Bunyan gave emblematic lessons in his verses about everyday objects and nature, *A Book for Boys and Girls or Country Rhymes for Children* (1696). The emblem books provided examples of the good and dutiful life through symbols:

This bee an Emblem truly is of Sin,
Whose Sweet unto many a Death hath been.

A 1679 title reflects the purpose of such books, *The Prodigal Son Sifted, or the lewd life and lamentable end of extravagant persons emblematically set forth, for a warning to unexperienced youth.*

MOTHER GOOSE

There is reassurance in the knowledge that children who experienced the hardships of the seventeenth and eighteenth centuries had access to the nonsense and gaiety of Mother Goose. The Mother Goose verses apparently originated in the spoken language of the common folk and royalty. Some have been traced as far back as the pre-Christian era. A few writers hold the theory that "Jack and Jill" refers to the waxing and waning of the moon. It is believed that many of the verses were written as political satires or told of royal tragedy. "Pussycat, Pussycat," for example, was based upon an incident in Queen Elizabeth's court. "Three Wise Men of Gotham" reflects stories of the foolish inhabitants of Gotham before the days of King John. Thomas cites the account of a deed in the possession of a Horner family signed by Henry VIII that was a "plum" pulled out of the pie—the King's collection of deeds.[6] However, other scholars have found little evidence of these relationships.[7]

The name of Mother Goose was first associated with folk tales rather than the verses known today. In 1697 Charles Perrault published in France a collection of nursery tales that included "Cinderella," "Red Riding Hood," "Puss in Boots," and "Sleeping Beauty." The frontispiece of the book showed an old woman spinning and telling stories to children. The caption read, "Contes de ma Mere l'Oye" (Tales of Mother Goose). These tales were brought to England and translated about 1729.[8] According to French legends, two Berthas may have been Mother Goose. One, called goose-footed, was known to tell stories to children. Another was rumored to have borne a child with the head of a goose.

While the Revolutionary War was in progress,

[6] Katherine Elwes Thomas, *The Real Personages of Mother Goose* (New York: Lothrop, 1930).
[7] Iona and Peter Opie, *The Oxford Nursery Rhyme Book* (London: Oxford University Press, 1952). William S. Baring-Gould and Ceil Baring-Gould, *The Annotated Mother Goose* (New York: Charles N. Potter, 1962).
[8] Baring-Gould, p. 149.

Old Mother Hubbard and Her Wonderful Dog

London: J. Catnach, Printer and Publisher, 2 Monmouth Court, Seven Dials, circa 1800

Venerable Mother Goose has delighted many generations.

Woodcut from *Pictures and Stories from Forgotten Children's Books* by Arnold Arnold, Dover Publications, Inc., 1969.

an American publisher, Isaiah Thomas, somehow obtained Newbery's books for children. These smuggled books were reprinted with few changes; thus, *Mother Goose, The History of Little Goody Two Shoes,* and *Robinson Crusoe* became available for children of the new country. No copies of this 1785 edition of Mother Goose are now extant, but a reproduction by W. H. Whitmore was published in 1889.

The legend that Dame Goose is buried in Boston is kept alive for tourists and children who visit the Boston burying ground, but it has created confusion regarding the origin of the verses. Even the publication of *Songs for the Nursery; or Mother Goose's Melodies* by the son-in-law of Dame Goose has become a legend. According to the story, Thomas Fleet tired of the good woman's frequent renditions of the ditties as she cared for his children, so he decided to collect and publish them. There has been no actual evidence of this 1719 edition.

The Comic Adventures of Old Mother Hubbard and

Her Dog, by Sarah Martin, first appeared in 1805. In the same year *Songs from the Nursery Collected by the Most Renowned Poets* was published. For the first time, "Little Miss Muffet" and "One, Two, Buckle My Shoe" appeared in print.

FOLK TALES AND ADVENTURE

Handed down by word of mouth for centuries, folk tales were among the first types of literature to be printed. It is difficult to find the point at which they were considered suitable *only* for the young. In France, Charles Perrault recorded eight fairy tales for adults at court. "Puss in Boots," "Sleeping Beauty," "Cinderella," and "Little Red Riding Hood" were included. For the first time, tales were written so children, too, could hear them over and over in exactly the same words. *The Arabian Nights* is another collection of old tales that came from India, Persia, and North Africa. Galland published these tales in 1704; and it appears they were available in English translation in 1712. Ridley also published a series of tales modeled after the Arabian Nights under the title, *The Tales of the Genii* (1766).

In the first half of the seventeenth century stories of St. George, St. Patrick, and other knights were roughly printed on 12-by-18-inch sheets. Also, small gilt books were popular with children and adults. For example, *The History of Cajanus, The Swedish Giant,* was printed in 1742 on $3\frac{1}{4}$-by-$2\frac{1}{4}$-inch sheets and bound in floral Dutch gilt boards.

Defoe did not write his account of the eighteenth-century hero, Robinson Crusoe, for children, but they made his story part of their literature. *The Life and Strange and Surprising Adventures of Robinson Crusoe* (1719) was later printed in an abridged and pocket-sized volume that became a "classic" of children's literature. *Gulliver's Travels* was a scathing satire of high society, yet young and old alike enjoyed this tale published in 1726. Perhaps children recognized or wished themselves to be dwarfs or giants. The forerunner of the modern superman may be identified in the stories of *Tommy Trip* written by John Newbery in 1759. In one story Tommy Trip, the size of Tom Thumb, challenges and defeats a giant who tormented a child.

NEWBERY PUBLISHES FOR CHILDREN

Although there was strong emphasis upon religious literature, it is apparent that the colonists and their children enjoyed the chapbooks. These little books of sixteen, thirty-two, or sixty-four pages were small, folded booklets that might be compared to modern comics. Ballads about Guy of Warwick, Bevis of Southhampton, and Robin Hood brought adventure to drab lives. Although children took these books for their own, it was not until 1744 in England that John Newbery published a book especially designed for children. The title page notes, *A Little Pretty Pocketbook,* "Intended for the Instruction and Amusement of Little Master Tommy and Pretty Miss Polly, with an agreeable Letter to read from Jack the Giant Killer, as also a Ball and a Pincushion, the use of which will infallibly make Tommy a good Boy, and Polly a good Girl." The advertisement in Newbery's shop, The Bible and Sun, said: "The books are to be given away, only the binding is to be paid for." For parents, the book included Locke's advice on children.

No documentary evidence is available to determine whether John Newbery or Oliver Goldsmith wrote *The History of Little Goody Two Shoes,* published by Newbery in 1766. Records do show that Newbery gave Goldsmith lodging above his shop, and it is probable that Goldsmith was the author of some of the two hundred books published by Newbery. In this story of righteousness Margery Meanwell, turned out of her own home by a grasping villain, became a teacher who moralized as she taught children to read. Eventually, she married a rich gentleman and carried on her good works.

Newbery's books emphasized love rather than the wrath and punishment of God. The gilt-paper covers of his small books were gay, but the moral lessons were still plain to the young readers who came to this first juvenile bookstore operated by Newbery from 1745 to 1767.

BOOKS OF INSTRUCTION

With the invention of the Horn book, English and colonial children were able to handle their own books. A sheet of paper printed with the alphabet, vowels, the Lord's Prayer, and Roman numerals was fastened to a small board about 2¾ by 5 inches. The parchment was covered with transparent horn and bound with strips of brass. Sometimes a hole in the handle made it possible for the child to carry the book on a cord around his neck or waist. Colonial children learned to read from the Horn book.

Shortly after the middle of the eighteenth century the battledore was developed. This consisted of a cardboard folded with three leaves. There were no religious teachings, but alphabets, numerals, easy reading lessons, and woodcuts of animals were included. Probably these were the first books of pictures that could be handled by children themselves. Battledores were still being used in the nineteenth century.

Children were expected to memorize John Cotton's catechism, *Spiritual Milk for Boston Babes in either England, drawn from the Breasts of both Testaments for their Souls' nourishment*. Originally published in England in 1646, it was revised for American children, and was the first book written and printed for children in America. Later books followed its question-and-answer approach with such questions as, "How did God make you?" The accompanying answer, "I was conceived in sin and born in iniquity" was memorized by the child. Even alphabet rhymes for the youngest emphasized the sinful nature of humans. For example, the *New England Primer*, first recorded in 1683, includes, "In Adam's fall We sinned all." The rhyming alphabet did change with the times. For example, "The Judgment made *Felix* afraid" was used instead of "The idle *Fool* is whipt at school." This primer also provided a catechism, the Ten Commandments, and verses about death. The 1781 edition included the prayer, "Now I Lay Me Down to Sleep." Approximately three million copies of this primer were sold.

Early in the eighteenth century James Janeway's book, *A Token for Children, Being an Exact Account of the Conversion, Holy, and Exemplary Lives and Joyful Deaths of Several Young Children*, was published in England. Before it was printed in America, Cotton Mather added life histories of New England children.

In the latter half of the seventeenth century, informational books were published. One of the first geographies appeared in 1665. The author,

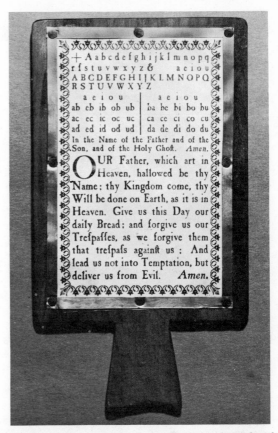

This facsimile of a colonial horn book may be ordered from The Horn Book, Inc. (585 Boylston Street, Boston, Massachusetts 02116).

Henry Winstanly, considered California a South Sea island and noted that Virginia lay directly south of New England; but his book, titled *All the Principal Nations of the World Presented in their Habits of Fashions of Dressing . . .* , was a milestone leading to modern travel and informational books.

In the first part of the eighteenth century several "science" books were published. Isaac Watts presented *The Knowledge of the Heavens and the Earth Made Easy, or the First Principles of Geography and Astronomy Explained* (1726). Ten years later, Thomas Breman introduced the idea that learning should be fun, in his title, *A Description of a Great Variety of Animals and Vegetables . . . especially for the Entertainment of Youth*. In America, Isaiah

Facsimilies of cardboard battledores.

Thomas reprinted books pirated from England, including *Jack Dandy's Delight: or the History of Birds and Beasts,* a juvenile natural history. *The Circle of the Sciences* (1745), *Tommy Trip's History of Beasts and Birds* (1779), and *Juvenile Rambles* (1786) were some of the informational books published by John Newbery.

Religious history had been part of the fare for children before the eighteenth century—many read descriptions of the horrors in John Foxe's *Book of Martyrs* written in 1563. Nathaniel Crouch edited *The Young Man's Calling,* a collection of stories for youth that included engravings of beheadings, burnings of martyrs, and information about proper behavior.

After the American Revolution, several distinctly American histories appeared. In the 1795 book, *The History of America,* six woodcuts were used over and over (the same woodcut was used for Christopher Columbus and General Montgomery). *Cooper's History of America abridged for the Use of Children of All Denominations* appeared in 1795.

Textbooks for subject matter areas were introduced to American schools near the end of the eighteenth century. Noah Webster's *Blue Backed Speller, Simplified and Standardized American Spelling,* published in 1783, was used widely for spelling bees. Webster's *Third Part* of the series, published in 1785, was the first secular reader. In 1789, Jedediah Morse introduced the first American geography with his *American Universal Geography.* Nicholas Pike's *Arithmetic* (1793) and Root's *Introduction to Arithmetic* (1796) were two of the first arithmetic texts. The influence of the rising commercial classes made such textbooks necessary.

Consequently, these textbooks constituted a major portion of the books available for children during the period.

DIDACTIC TALES

In the last half of the eighteenth century women writers entered the field of juvenile literature with the purpose of teaching through stories. In *Mrs. Teachem's School for Girls,* Sarah Fielding published stories that emphasized character development. *Easy Lessons for Children,* published in 1760 by Mrs. Barbauld, presented lessons for children of different ages. Mrs. Sarah Trimmer apparently agreed with Locke, who had approved of fables for children, for she created a family of robins who could talk of problems in day-to-day family life. She gave some information about nature by weaving facts into conversations in her *Fabulous Histories* (1786). Meigs quotes a sample of the conversation: "I am delighted, my dear children, with your humane behavior toward the animal creation . . . but though it is a most commendable propensity, it requires regulation."[9] One wonders what meaning children derived from such difficult and unnatural vocabulary.

As the eighteenth century drew to a close, the influence of Rousseau was felt in children's literature. Following Rousseau's theory of accompanying the child in his natural search for knowledge, parents, relatives, or teachers were always at hand to seize upon every comment made by a child or to call attention to objects of interest so that the incident might be used as a means of instruction. Books frequently contained dialogues and conversations. Instead of long lists of rules, the lessons were now concealed in didactic tales and juvenile biographies.

Thomas Day utilized the conversational approach in *The History of Sandford and Merton,* a didactic tale that appeared in three sections (1783, 1786, 1789). Harry Sandford and Tommy Merton were 6-year-old boys who were tutored together, although Harry was the son of a farmer. It was Harry who exemplified the just and righteous for the spoiled Tommy Merton. Day after day, lecture after lecture, the tutor presented long lessons that interrupted the narrative. These priggish children served as models of behavior for nearly one hundred years.

[9]Meigs, p. 78.

He that ne er learns his **A, B, C,**
For ever will a Blockhead be :

Woodcuts illustrate an alphabet page in the *New England Primer.*

POETRY

In this period poetry for children also emphasized religion and instruction. Although Isaac Watts spent most of his time writing hymns, he did devote some of his energy to writing poetry for children. *Divine Songs Attempted in Easy Language for the use of Children* (1715) made religious instruction more pleasant for children.

Play was still seen as an occasion for mischief and a time when children might come under the influence of Satan. In 1785 children were told to use play as a time for introspection. The verses in *A Present to Children* suggested thoughts for play:

> Now on the Ice I shape the Slide,
> And smoothly O'er the Surface glide,
> I learn amidst the slipp'ry Play
> Most dangerous is the easiest way.

John Newbery printed *Pretty Poems for Children Three Feet High* and added the inscription: "To all those who are good this book is dedicated by their best friend."

An engraver and artist, William Blake, wrote poetry that children enjoyed, but the poems of

Songs of Innocence, 1789, were not specifically written for children. The poetry was filled with imagination and joy, and made the reader aware of beauty without preaching. One artist emerged during this period as an illustrator of books for boys and girls. Thomas Bewick's white-line wood engravings for *A Pretty Book of Pictures for Little Masters and Misses: or Tommy Trip's History of Beasts and Birds* (1767) were interesting and of excellent workmanship.

As the century terminated, most of the stories for children were about how to live the "good life." Information about the natural world was peddled in didactic lectures sugar-coated with conversational style. Little prigs were models for young people to follow. However, there was now a literature for children. Authors and publishers were aware of a new market for books. Parents and teachers were beginning to recognize the importance of literature for children.

Children's Literature: Nineteenth Century

BACKGROUND

The nineteenth century brought tremendous changes to the Western world as powerful nations arose. The Industrial Revolution, use of agricultural machinery, and improved communication and transportation, brought technological changes that influenced men's values and attitudes. In America, the Westward Movement led to emphasis upon individualism, and a growing nationalism emphasized freedom and enlightenment for all peoples. Education came to be viewed as a *natural right* for all children. With the influx of immigrants, the school became the institution in which to mold new Americans. In science there was emphasis upon fact-finding and classified knowledge. Psychology was beginning to be considered a science, as Wilhelm Wundt, William James, and G. Stanley Hall observed and recorded human behavior. This led to more emphasis on life in the present. With Darwin's work in biological evolution and the findings of La-Place and other astronomers, the world and its life were increasingly viewed as products of natural forces. However, the basic school texts continued to reflect the view of God's will influencing all

of life. Transcendentalism pushed even further the idea of nonsectarian religion; it was now deemed possible to be a good citizen yet not a member of a religious sect.

In the last three decades of the nineteenth century, teaching children through objects in nature was emphasized. Experimental schools were based on the idea of the child as the center of the school curriculum. Near the end of the century the pragmatists—Peirce, James, and Dewey—asserted that knowledge arises out of experience and theories must be tested. Dewey's new philosophy held that education was a social process; the child's interests were significant and should be channeled; thinking was viewed as problem-solving. These ideas were in the growing stages; neither schools nor books actually changed very much, but there was an optimistic, expanding feeling—a young nation progressing. Art and music reflected classical traditions. Realism in art was emphasized, although the Impressionists were beginning to create new styles of painting.

These changes of the nineteenth century were slowly reflected in books for children. Libraries were established; the Sunday School Movement led to distribution of tracts and books. The didactic stories that preached good behavior continued to be of major importance during this period, but some books were written with a child audience in mind. The school curriculum was broadened to include natural science, history, geography, and citizenship training. Science and technology made possible travel to far places, and realistic accounts of these journeys became popular. A growing nationalism led to books of American history and geography. Pioneer adventures and stories of the War of 1812 and the Civil War provided exciting plots for boys.

The emphasis upon individual rights and freedom for all seemed to influence attitudes toward children. Conditions created a climate in which a son's opinions were as valid as his father's. Children were considered individuals with unique rights. The attitudes toward religion gave way to secularism and to recognition of play as an acceptable part of child life. Each type of book reflected these social, political, and economic changes. By the end of the century there was a growing body of literature expressly written for children.

BOOKS OF RELIGION AND MORALS

In the first half of the nineteenth century the didactic school of writing for children flourished, as women writers wielded influential pens. They condemned fairy stories and relentlessly dispensed information in lengthy dialogues between parent and child. Martha Sherwood, a prolific writer, produced about 350 moralizing books and tracts. While living in India, she wrote *The History of Little Henry and His Bearer* (1814). The story of little Henry's conversion illustrates her missionary theme. St. John notes that the advertisement of a later edition read: "Upwards of two hundred and fifty thousand copies have been sold . . ."[10]

Mrs. Mary Sherwood wrote a series of stories about *The Fairchild Family*, beginning in 1812. The first book opens with a funeral, as many of the tales of that period were wont to begin. The religious tone is still present, and moral lessons are provided through stilted dialogue. For example, one evening Papa tells about the globe. After a long discourse Lucy asks, "Papa may we have some verses about mankind having evil hearts?" Each child then quotes scripture.

The horrible-example technique was also employed by some writers for children. In one book, published near the end of the eighteenth century, children were given animal bodies, as "Jacky Idle turned into the body of an Ass," "Master Greedy-guts into a Pig," and "Miss Dorthy Chatterfast became a Magpie."

John Locke's essays on education had wide influence on children's literature. He suggested combining learning and pleasure, recommended the use of fables, and encouraged the use of illustrations. At the same time he urged educators and parents to set a good example for children. These influences may be seen in Maria Edgeworth's *Easy Lessons*, which contained examples of children who always obeyed their parents. Maria Edgeworth was determined to educate young readers, but she did add suspense to her stories. Usually a gracious lady or nobleman appeared to make an award or point out a moral. *The Parent's Assistant: or Stories for Children* (1796) included "The Purple Jar," "Waste Not, Want Not," and "Lazy Lawrence." In this series of essays the author incorporated the story of *Rosa-*

[10]Judith St. John, *The Osborne Collection of Early Children's Books 1566–1910* (Toronto, Canada: Toronto Public Library, 1958).

A VISIT TO THE BLIND ASYLUM.

In order "to awaken a love and regard for truth and create sentiments of gratitude, obedience and humanity," children were exposed to the realism of insane and blind asylums, prison, and the death of parents. From *The Good Child's Reward* (1828) by Henry Sharpe Horsley.

As reprinted in *Flowers of Delight* edited by Leonard de Vries. Copyright © 1965 by Leonard de Vries. Used with permission of Pantheon Books, a Division of Random House, Inc., and with the permission of Dobson Books Ltd.

mund and the Purple Jar. Little Rosamund learned that a purple jar she desired instead of new shoes was only a clear glass bottle colored by a bad smelling liquid.

BOOKS OF INSTRUCTION

By 1800 the *New England Primer* reflected the changing social purposes and interests of the new nation. The alphabet became less pious:

A was an angler and fished with a hook
B was a Blockhead and ne'er learned his book.

A picture of George Washington was substituted for the woodcut of George III. Adaptations of the *Primer* were made by several educators. "A

Religion and manners were emphasized in the early 1800s. *The Good Girl's Soliloquy Containing Her Parent's Instructions, Relative to Her Disposition and Manners.*

From *Pictures and Stories from Forgotten Children's Books* by Arnold Arnold, Dover Publications, Inc., 1969.

Mother" added space and large print for *Lessons for Children from Two to Four Years Old.* Another revision included such little stories as:

Bring the tea things. Bring the boy's milk. Where is the bread and butter? Little boys do not eat butter. Sop the bread in your tea.

The illustrations were crude, and size relationships were of little importance. In Mathew Carey's 1813 edition of *The American Primer,* for example, the illustration of a mouse was the same size as that of a horse.

Rhymes to help children learn the multiplication tables were presented in *Marmaduke Multiply's Merry Method of Making Minor Mathematicians* by Harris in 1816. *The Multiplication Table,* in verse, printed in 1819, included:

Twice one are two sweet little cats
One black, the other gray.

Twice two are four as pretty mice
That from them ran away.[11]

Nonsense about parts of speech and punctuation was the basis for *Punctuation Personified.* Mr. Stop, who was shown in accompanying illustrations, told the reader how to use punctuation marks.

Reading for patriotism, good citizenship, and industry was the purpose of the well-loved *Eclectic Readers* by William H. McGuffey. They were used so widely from 1834 to 1900 one could almost say these readers comprised the elementary curriculum in literature. A glance at the *Fifth Reader* reflects the type of material included in these readers: speeches by Daniel Webster, essays by Washington Irving, selections from Shakespeare (although the play is often not identified), narrative, sentimental and patriotic poetry, and many didactic essays with such titles as "Advantages of a Well-educated Mind," "Impeachment of Warren Hastings," and "Eulogy on Candlelight."

Although compulsory education was being extended, and the publicly supported common school was being established, parents were also expected to teach children at home. The parent's role was established through stories in which mothers embroidered, sipped tea, and dispensed information to *sweet* children. The following conversation was in *A Key to Knowledge,* published in 1822:

Louisa—By the by, when I come to think of it, what a dirty thing honey is; first swallowed by bees, and then by us.
Mother—Your description is certainly not very inviting. Suppose rather that we should call the honey, the syrup of flowers, drawn from the opened buds by the trunk, or proboscis, of the industrious bee.
Louisa—Now I like honey again. . . .[12]

In the early nineteenth century nature study and contemplation of the universe was encouraged to develop an admiration of God's works. In this period Samuel Goodrich was chiefly responsible for eliminating the British background in books for American children. History, geogra-

[11]St. John, p. 131.
[12]"19th Century Juvenilia," *Times Educational Supplement,* 2262:1412 (September 26, 1958).

phy, and science were included in his *Tales of Peter Parley about America* (1827). As Goodrich tried to satisfy children's curiosity, in an 1839 edition of *Peter Parley's Farewell*, the idea of a series of informative books was initiated. Peter Parley told tales of Europe and Africa and of the sun, moon, and stars. Isaac Taylor wrote a series of *Scenes* "for little tarry-at-home travellers." *Scenes in Africa* was printed in 1820, while *Scenes of Commerce, by Land or Sea; or, "Where Does It Come from?" answered* was published ten years later. Jacob Abbott also followed this plan as he wrote about *Little Rollo* learning to talk, Rollo learning to read, and of Rollo's travels to Europe. In the first books of the series, published in 1834, Rollo was a natural little boy, but as he became older and traveled about the world he became another little prig.

The Bodley Family, conceived by Horace Scudder, explored New England, Holland, and other countries (1857). In *Seven Little Sisters Who Live on the Big Round Ball that Floats in the Air* (1861), Jane Andrews told of little girls who lived in the far north, in the desert, in China, and in Switzerland. Through a dramatic family story, *Hans Brinker: or The Silver Skates*, Mary Mapes Dodge gave accurate glimpses of Dutch life in 1865. The skating race is actually less important than the daring brain surgery performed on Father Brinker, who had been nearly an idiot for several years after an accident. The bravery and courage of Hans and his sister in facing poverty, scorn, and their father's illness provided further examples for child behavior. To make another country seem real, Johanna Spyri wrote *Heidi* in 1884. Not only did readers share the joys and sorrow in Heidi's life, they "breathed" the clear mountain air and "lived" in Switzerland.

Problems of war, temperance, and slavery were topics in histories in the first half of the nineteenth century. Samuel Wood discussed the miseries of the world as he gave information in *The Seven Wonders of the World* (1814). Biographies of churchmen published by the American Tract Society gave children some historical background. Thomas Higginson's *A Young Folk's History of the United States* (1875) marks the beginning of history-writing for American children. Famous battles were described by Charles Coffin in *Boys of '76* and *Boys of '61*. In 1880 George Henty wrote

a military history for boys, *The Young Buglers*. This book was only one of his many stories of adventure and war. History in the form of biographies was written by George Towle in an 1883 publication, *Young Folk's Heroes of History. Ten Boys Who Lived on the Road from Long Ago to Now* by Jane Andrews gave young readers information about Puritans, Horatius, and other heroes (1886).

Most of the science books were about flowers and gardens. Mrs. Margaret Gatty's *Parables from Nature, Worlds Not Realized*, gave accurate information as well as moral instruction. One writer who did not "write down" to children was Mrs. Ewing, who published a series of nature lessons under the title *Mary's Meadow* (1886). The science of astronomy was presented to children in an 1805 publication, *The Wonders of the Telescope*.

Only a few writers and publishers seemed to realize that children want to learn about their world. Children had to plod through pages of tiresome conversations with moralistic overtones to gain the information they sought. It was not until much later that informational books on almost every subject were placed on bookshelves for boys and girls.

FOLK-TALE COLLECTIONS

Early in the nineteenth century two German brothers went about asking servants and peasants to recall stories they had heard. In 1812 Jacob and Wilhelm Grimm published the first volume of *Kinder und Hausmarchen* (Household Stories). These serious scholars tried to preserve the form as well as the content of the old tales that were translated and published in England by Edgar Taylor in 1823–1826. "The Elves and the Shoemaker," "Rumplestiltskin," and "Snow White," in addition to many others, became part of the literature of childhood.

In America, Washington Irving included "Rip Van Winkle" and "The Legend of Sleepy Hollow" in the 1819 *Sketch Book*. These tales, written mainly for adults, were also enjoyed by older children.

The origin of *The Three Bears* has been questioned by various authorities. Meigs[13] noted it was published in Robert Southey's *Doctor*, 1834–1837. Muir reported there was some evi-

[13]Meigs, p. 157.

dence that it was written by an anonymous author in 1831 and retold by Southey. Lexau identified this author as Eleanor Mure, whose 1831 manuscript was located by Edgar Osborne, English collector of children's books.[14] Mure's story was written in verse. In the early version of the story a wicked old woman comes to visit the bears who are pictured as wee, middle-sized, and huge. Through many retellings the story has been changed to the more familiar fair-haired child visiting a bear family.

In 1846 Mary Howitt translated a book of tales called *Wonderful Stories for Children*. Hans Christian Andersen's stories came to England and America, and children were enthralled by "The Tinder Box," "The Princess and the Pea," and "The Ugly Duckling." In these stories inanimate objects and animals come alive. The values and foibles of human life are presented in stories with action and rich language.

In the last half of the nineteenth century folk tales and fairy tales were given new importance as well-known authors contributed their versions. John Ruskin retold *The King of the Golden River* in 1851, and Charles Dickens' *The Magic Fishbone* was written as a serial in 1868. *The Wonderbook for Boys and Girls* was published by Nathaniel Hawthorne in 1852, and was followed by *Tanglewood Tales* in 1853. Sir George Dasent translated *Popular Tales from the North* in 1859, making it possible for children to enjoy more tales from Scandinavia. *The Nürnberg Stove* was another favorite, first published by Louise de la Ramee in a collection of children's stories in 1882. Joel Chandler Harris collected stories from the South for *Uncle Remus, His Songs and Sayings* (1881).

Collections of folk tales were made by Andrew Lang in his famous series beginning with *The Blue Fairy Book*. The *Red, Green,* and the *Yellow* fairy books followed the 1889 publication of the first volume of folklore. Joseph Jacobs was also interested in retelling folk tales for children. *English Fairy Tales* (1892), *Celtic Fairy Tales* (1893), and

[14]Joan Lexau, "The Story of the Three Bears and the Man Who Didn't Write It," *The Horn Book Magazine,* Vol. 40 (February 1964), pp. 88–94. Lexau suggests comparing versions in *English Fairy Tales* by Joseph Jacobs, *The Green Fairy Book* by Andrew Lang, Leslie Brooke's *The Story of the Three Bears,* and "Scrapefoot" in *Told under the Green Umbrella* by the Association for Childhood Education.

Indian Fairy Tales (1892) were important contributions to the realm of folklore. As the merits of folklore were recognized everywhere, there was increasing interest in such volumes as Howard Pyle's *Pepper and Salt* (1886) and *The Wonder Clock* (1888).

STORIES OF FAMILY LIFE

Some authors felt that the joys of realistic children should be portrayed in lifelike situations. In England, Charlotte Yonge's *The Daisy Chain* (1856) described the daily life and learning of a family of eleven children. Somewhat later, series books about families appeared. The *Dotty Dimple* series and the *Little Prudy* series were written by Rebecca Clarke under the name of Sophie May. *Little Prudy's Captain Horace* centered on the Clifford family during the Civil War. Eight-year-old Horace is described as a very naughty boy; yet the reader sympathizes with him. Horace's sister Grace keeps a record of all his misdeeds and such bad words as "shucks," "gallus," and "by George." Cousin Prudy exerts a good influence on the boy, who pretends to be a captain after his father joins the Union Army. There is great sorrow and pages of grief when they receive news that Horace's father is killed. An interesting advertisement appears on the last page; it shows Red Riding Hood meeting the wolf, and a doggerel verse tells how she tames the beast by sharing her Jello.

Harriet Lathrop (under the pseudonym Margaret Sidney) presented a lively family in the *Five Little Peppers* in a series starting in 1880. Popular through the years, a new edition appeared as late as 1962. Under the name of Farquharson, Martha Finley initiated the *Elsie Dinsmore* series in 1867. Pools of tears were shed over the life of this character. By 1894 Elsie had become a grandmother and accompanied her growing family to the World's Fair. Several chapters included long discussions of the Bible.

The most familiar and well-loved family described in series books is probably the March family. Written by the irrepressible Jo, Louisa May Alcott, this series about a warm, human family remains an American classic. *Little Women* (1868) and *Little Men* (1871) are still the favorites of the series.

Frances Hodgson Burnett described family conflict within the English aristocracy in *Little*

Lord Fauntleroy (1886). Her second book, *Sara Crewe* (1888), told of the pitiful plight of a wealthy pupil who is orphaned and reduced to servitude in a boarding school. Mrs. Burnett's best-known book is *The Secret Garden* (1910), which presents an exciting plot in a mysterious setting.

STORIES OF ADVENTURE

The pioneer spirit sought stories of adventure. *Swiss Family Robinson* by J. H. Wyss was translated in 1814, bringing excitement to many children. In America daily life was full of adventure, as conceived by children today. A few writers recognized the value of recording some of the incidents and also realized the growing demand for such literature. Although written for adults, *The Last of the Mohicans* by James Fenimore Cooper interested children when it was published in 1826. Its bloody incidents and tragedy gave a sense of tingling adventure. Captain Frederick Marryat began a series of sea adventures with *Adventures of a Naval Officer; or Frank Mildmay* in 1829. *Mr. Midshipman Easy* and *Masterman Ready* were juvenile adventures that followed in 1836 and 1844. In 1856 Robert Ballantyne began his series of nearly eighty books, with an account of his fur-trading experiences, *The Young Fur Trader.* Ballantyne was a writer for boys who related exciting stories based upon events in the world. *The Battery and the Boiler; or Adventures in the Laying of Submarine Electric Cables* would have been of great interest to boys in 1883. Boy readers also found adventure in W. H. G. Kingston's *Peter the Whaler* and in the short stories in *Kingston's Magazine for Boys.*

Ragged Dick (1867) was the first of the series of stories by Horatio Alger. Over one hundred of these stories of triumph over difficulties in the climb from rags to riches were published by this American writer. The final paragraph of *Struggling Upwards* presents the theme.

So closes an eventful passage in the life of Luke Larkin. He has struggled upward from a boyhood of privation and self-denial into a youth and manhood of prosperity and honor. There has been some luck about it, I admit, but after all he is indebted for most of his good fortune to his own good qualities.[15]

[15]Horatio Alger, Jr., *Struggling Upwards; or Luke Larkin's Luck* (New York: Superior Printing, n.d.), p. 280.

Oliver Optic was the pen name of William Adams, a teacher who wrote such series as *The Boat Club Series* (1855), *The Army and Navy Series,* and *The Starry Flag Series.* There were many scenes of excitement and adventure, but Oliver's readers also learned some geography as they traveled with the heroes. *Outward Bound* told of reckless boy sailors, but stilted speeches and the incidents of drinking and gambling led librarians to eliminate these books from their shelves.

In 1860 the first dime novel was published by Beadle and Adams, beginning the tremendous business of cheap books for the 10- to 16-year-old. Ann S. W. Stephens *Malaeska, the Indian Wife of the White Hunter* was the first of the avalanche to be written by hacks. William S. Patten created the red-blooded Frank Merriwell in 1896. Travel, rescue of helpless women, and success were the ingredients in more than 800 books of this stereotyped character.

In the latter half of the century there appeared the first great school story, *Tom Brown's School Days* (1885) by Thomas Hughes. In this book sports were of great interest to the pupils, and excitement was provided in accounts of team events.

Many of the series books provided adventure, but the characters tended to be rather superficial. In 1882 a serial intended for boys was acclaimed by adults as well. Robert Louis Stevenson published it as *Treasure Island* in 1883. Not only were there tense, thrilling moments, the characters were convincingly and consistently drawn.

Mark Twain combined realism, humor, and adventure in his classic accounts of the Missouri boys, Tom Sawyer and Huckleberry Finn. *Adventures of Tom Sawyer,* published in 1876, was followed by *Adventures of Huckleberry Finn* in 1884. The author's imagination and understanding made possible this realistic portrayal of American boyhood.

The beginning of science fiction and adventure can surely be found in Jules Verne's *Twenty Thousand Leagues under the Sea* (1870) and *Around the World in Eighty Days* (1872). Modern readers may be surprised to note the early date of these books.

ANIMAL STORIES

A Dog of Flanders (1872) by Louise de la Ramee has been considered the first modern dog story. *Black Beauty* appeared in 1877 as a protest against cruel treatment of horses. Some children today continue to enjoy Anna Sewell's rather over-drawn and sentimental tale. Kipling's *The Jungle Books* (1894–1895) were exciting animal stories. Many children know the story of Mowgli, a child raised by a wolf family, a bear, and a panther.

Ernest Thompson Seton's sketches added much to children's enjoyment of *Wild Animals I Have Known* (1898). This book, with "personal" histories of animals, was a forerunner of the modern books written about one animal.

BOOKS OF HUMOR AND FANTASY

Although many of the early titles of books for children included the word "amusing," the main purpose was to instruct or moralize. Undoubtedly, children enjoyed the broad humor in some of the folk tales and the nonsense in Mother Goose, but few books used humor or nonsense before the middle of the nineteenth century.

The early steps toward a literature for children's enjoyment led naturally to the development of fantasy. Charles Kingsley's story of Tom's adventures with the sea creatures in *The Water-Babies* (1863) represents the beginning of modern fantasy. This story of a chimney sweep who became a water baby with gills might have amused adults, but children would find it difficult to understand some of the hidden meanings. Mrs. Bedonebyasyoudid teaches her lessons:

> . . . for you must know and believe that people's souls make their bodies just as a snail makes its shell (I am not joking, my little man; I am in serious solemn earnest). And therefore, when Tom's soul grew all prickly with naughty tempers, his body could not help growing prickly too, so that nobody would cuddle him or play with him, or even like to look at him.[16]

On a summer day in 1862 a professor of mathematics, Charles Dodgson, told a story to three little girls at a picnic. In response to their request that he record the story, Dodgson wrote *Alice's Adventures Underground* and presented it to his young friends as a Christmas gift in 1864. At the insistence of others, he decided to have it

[16]Charles Kingsley, *The Water-Babies* (New York: Platt & Munk, 1900), p. 149.

The Mad Tea Party as depicted by John Tenniel.
From *Alice in Wonderland* by Lewis Carroll, Macmillan, 1866, illustrated by Tenniel.

Arthur Rackham paints a more elegant tea party.
From *Alice's Adventures in Wonderland* by Lewis Carroll, illustrated by Arthur Rackham. Reproduced by permission of Doubleday & Company, Inc.

published. By 1865 the artist, Tenniel, completed the drawings, and *Alice's Adventures in Wonderland* was ready for the host of readers to come. The scenes at the Mad Hatter's tea party, the croquet game, and the court scene are enjoyed more by adults than children for their nonsense and play on words. For example, the phrase "was immediately suppressed by the court" is explained to Alice when the guinea pig who cheered in court was stuffed into a bag. Now she "understood" that phrase! Her second adventure occurs as she goes through the looking glass to fairyland. Children who are beginning to play chess may enjoy hearing some of these incidents.

Other well-known fantasies were published near the end of the century. *At the Back of the North Wind,* George MacDonald's fantasy, appeared in 1871. From Italy came *The Adventures of Pinocchio* (1892) by Carlo Lorenzini (pseudonym, C. Collodi). While she was in India and homesick for her children, Helen Bannerman wrote *The Story of Little Black Sambo* (1899). In this fantasy one absurd incident after another occurs, excitement is high, and the ending is satisfying.

In the category of books for fun, the books with movable parts might also be included. Harlequinades, or turnups, first appeared in 1766. They consisted of a page of pictures covered with flaps that could be raised or lowered to create other scenes. Doggerel verse on each section told a simple story. In 1810 stories in rhyme were printed on sheets with slots, and pockets were fastened to the reverse side. Cutout figures could be slipped through the slot and were held in the pocket. A hero or heroine could appear in a number of different costumes in this way. From 1840 until about 1900 a variety of books with flaps and movable parts was published. By pulling tabs, various pictures appeared to illustrate the verse or story.

BOOKS OF GAMES AND SPORTS

Essays on proper conversation, manners, drawing, and music were included with games in Lydia Child's 1858 edition of *The Girl's Own Book: A Course of Geography, by means of instructive games . . .* published in 1829. It included maps and counters for locating the places. Craft books, too, were available. *Papyroplastics, or The art of modelling in paper; being an instructive amusement for*

Movable parts give a venetian-blind effect in this early book for children.

From *Pleasant Surprises: A Novel Mechanical Book for Little Ones* (*circa* 1880). Courtesy of P. K. Thomajon Collection of Animated Juvenilia.

young persons of both sexes was translated from the German by D. Boileau, and printed in 1825. Another title that suggested fun for children appeared about 1800, *The Whim Wham; or Evening Amusement for All Ages and Sizes. . . .*

POETRY

In the nineteenth century a wide variety of poetry was written for children. The Taylor sisters, Ann and Jane, emphasized polite behavior in their volume published in 1804, *Original Poems for Infant Minds.* Their poems about lifelike young people in everyday life were translated and published on the continent. Morals, death, and justice were emphasized in the poems, as in this example:

> You are not so healthy and gay
> So young, so active and bright,
> That death cannot snatch you away,
> Or some dread accident smite.
>
> Here lie both the young and the old,
> Confined in the coffin so small
> The earth covers over them cold,
> The grave-worms devour them all.

Jane Taylor wrote the oft-parodied, "Twinkle Twinkle Little Star" for this collection. The entire poem, with its original illustrations, is reproduced in *Flowers of Delight* by De Vries.

Fantastic verse and brightly colored pictures were introduced in 1807 with *The Butterfly's Ball and the Grasshopper's Feast* by William Roscoe.

Clement Moore, a professor who wrote to please his own children, gave the world the Christmas classic, *A Visit from St. Nicholas.* One of the first American contributions to a joyous literature for children, it was published with this title in 1822, but is now known as *The Night before Christmas.* In 1846 an author appeared who wrote verse solely to entertain. Edward Lear's nonsense poems brought joy to both children and adults as they met fantastic Pobbles and Quangle Wangles. In the 1872 volume, *More Nonsense*, the owl and the pussy cat went out to sea in their pea-green boat, and other impossibles appeared to delight young and old alike.

Christina Rossetti's poetry for children is reminiscent of Mother Goose, but she also wrote verse that brought to children vivid descriptions of the beauty around them. *Sing Song* (1872) continues to delight young children with such verses as:

Mix a pancake
Stir a pancake,
Pop it in the pan;
Fry the pancake,
Toss the pancake,
Catch it if you can.

In the latter half of the nineteenth century young people were also enjoying William Allingham's *Ballad Book* (1865). John Greenleaf Whittier wrote many of the fine poems of the period in *Child Life, A Collection of Poems* (1871). Kate Greenaway is known as an illustrator, but her verses were enjoyed as much as the drawings in *Under the Window* (1878) and *Marigold Garden* (1885).

The century ended with the appearance of a volume of poetry for children that told of everyday life and the child's own world as he views it. This volume by Robert Louis Stevenson was originally titled *Penny Whistles* (1885) and later changed to *A Child's Garden of Verses.* Stevenson was a poet who could recapture a child's imaginings for all to enjoy. "My Shadow," "My Bed Is a Boat," "Windy Nights," and "Good

Play" tell of fun and bring rhythm to the child's world.

The close of the nineteenth century found two American poets writing for children. Eugene Field's *Poems of Childhood* (1896) included "The Sugar Plum Tree" and "The Duel." In *Rhymes of Childhood* (1891), James Whitcomb Riley employed dialect as he described local incidents and Indiana farm life. His "Little Orphant Annie" and "The Raggedy Man" continue to be favorites.

MAGAZINES

Magazines formed a significant part of the literature for children in the last half of the nineteenth century. In keeping with the philosophy of the times, a French teacher, Madame Beaumont, published a magazine titled *Magasin des infants.* Madame Beaumont also wrote seventy books, including *Beauty and the Beast.* The chapbooks sold by peddlers in England might be considered forerunners of magazines, but they were really books. The comic hero and adventurer, Jack Harkaway, of one of the chapbooks, closely resembled the modern comic-book figure.

The first true magazine for English children appeared in 1852 under the title *The Charm.* It was not until the 1860s that children's magazines gained importance. Many of the best stories for children first appeared in such form. Charlotte Yonge's own stories appeared in her magazine, *The Monthly Packet.* Mrs. Gatty and Mrs. Ewing were among the early writers who contributed to *Aunt Judy's Magazine*, initiated in 1868.

The first magazine planned for children in America, *The Juvenile Miscellany*, 1827, emphasized American history and biography. Other magazines resulted from the Sunday School Movement. Horace Scudder, editor of *The Riverside Magazine*, published several of Hans Christian Andersen's stories. He was also one of the earliest editors to discuss selection of books for children. *The Youth's Companion*, 1827–1941, engaged such writers as Tennyson, Gladstone, Kipling, Oliver Wendell Holmes, and Mark Twain.

In 1873 Mary Mapes Dodge became editor of one of the most famous magazines for children, *St. Nicholas.* Meigs writes of the editorial policy: "With the advent of St. Nicholas didacticism as the chief element in reading for children fled away forever."[17] Stories, verse, a "How to Do and Make" section, and letters from children were included in the magazine. Such well-known writers for children as Alcott, Stevenson, Kipling, Burnett, Lucretia Hale, and Laura E. Richards wrote for this magazine which guided children's reading for over half a century.

Magazines provided new outlets for children's authors and illustrators. It was now respectable for children to read purely for pleasure. Juvenile magazines of the nineteenth century made a significant contribution to the total development of a literature for children.

IMPROVEMENTS IN BOOK PRINTING

The printing process dates back to the seventh century in China when paper was rubbed over inked wood blocks. Today, ink is still rubbed from varied surfaces onto paper. During the nineteenth century, improvements in the printing process made possible publication of a larger quantity of books, and books of a better quality. In 1803 a method for making paper by machinery was invented, and the process of making paper from wood pulp was developed in 1840. Type had been set by hand; each block was cut and fastened in place, until the linotype was patented in 1884. In mid-century the cylinder type of press and steam power made printing large quantities of books much easier.

The student of children's literature should be familiar with the three basic methods of printing. *Relief printing* is done by moving the ink roller over the plate that has blocks with letters or illustrations raised above the surface. Only the high ridge receives ink that can then be transferred to paper. *Intaglio printing* results when designs are scratched below the surface by using an engraving tool or etching with acid. The ink is rolled on the plate, sinking into the low areas; another roller wipes it off the higher surface. As the paper is pressed against the plate, it absorbs the ink. The *planographic method* uses a repellent on areas that are not to be printed. Lithography is an example of the planographic method of printing. The artist draws directly on a porous limestone with a grease pencil. Water is added to the other areas. When the ink is rolled over

the stone it adheres only to the grease. A method developed later uses zinc or aluminum plates. Today, the plate prints the design on a rubber roller that applies the ink to the paper. This offset method makes quantity printing possible. Photo-offset printing has come to be termed lithography, but it does not refer to the original process of printing with stone.

Another significant development in the latter part of the nineteenth century was the halftone process. By taking a photograph of an illustration through a fine screen, a series of tiny dots is created. This negative is used to etch the plates, with lighter areas having smaller dots and darker areas having larger dots.

Early illustrations were made by relief designs in woodcuts. To withstand the pressure of steam presses, copper plates were used. In the early part of the century groups of children or families colored the sheets by hand. Later, one color could be added on the copper plate. Today, three- and four-color processes make possible the lovely illustrations in children's books.

Technological developments of the nineteenth century were the basis for the vast improvements in the process of printing in the century ahead.

ILLUSTRATORS OF THE NINETEENTH CENTURY

In the nineteenth century several outstanding artists emerged as illustrators of children's books. George Cruikshank was an engraver who illustrated *Grimm's Fairy Tales* in 1820 with gay, cheerful people, instead of the solemn prigs children had known earlier. A cartoonist, his work appeared in newspapers and journals as well as the children's periodical, *Aunt Judy's Magazine.* His elves and fairies were especially appealing.

Walter Crane used flat, bright colors and bold outlines in his first picture books, *The House that Jack Built,* and *History of Cock Robin and Jenny Wren.* Delicate, fairylike pencil drawings illustrated *The First of May.* He especially enjoyed drawing animals and outdoor scenes, and his pages were decorated with elaborate borders.

The picture books by Randolph Caldecott established new standards of illustration for children's books. His drawings were filled with action, joy of living, and good fun. His love of animals and the English countryside is reflected in the illustrations that seem to convey much meaning through a few lines. On the Caldecott medal there is a reproduction of John Gilpin's famous ride, a reminder of this famous illustrator of the nineteenth century.

Kate Greenaway's name brings visions of English gardens; delicate, prim figures; and the special style of costume on her rather fragile children. Her flowers in *The Language of Flowers* and *Marigold Garden* (1885) were beautifully drawn.

Crane, Caldecott, and Greenaway created a happy world and reflected the English countryside, but they expressed little individuality or emotion in the faces of their children. Crane and Greenaway seemed to decorate rather than to extend the text through visual images.

Howard Pyle created *real* people for his collection of folk tales and legends. His characters from the Middle Ages were strong; the life of the times was portrayed with interesting, clear detail. Pyle also illustrated for the popular magazines of his day, *St. Nicholas* and *Scribner's Monthly*. He made a further contribution by establishing classes for illustrators of children's books.

CLOSE OF THE NINETEENTH CENTURY

With the steady decline of Puritanism, there came a gradual realization that the morbid tone of many books for children was actually harmful. Make-believe accounts of impossible children and perfect parents were no longer being written. Imaginary characters, such as fairies were finally accepted, and by the end of the century literature was expressly designed for children to give them happiness rather than moral lectures.

Children's Literature: Twentieth Century

BACKGROUND

In the rapidly changing world of the twentieth century the child became an important individual in the family, school, and community. The importance of early childhood was emphasized by Freudian psychologists and others, social anthropologists, and students of child development. The emerging concepts of child development emphasized continuous growth; uniqueness of the individual; and the interrelationship of physical, emotional, and social growth. Kindergartens became an accepted part of many school systems. Needs for love, affection, and belonging were stressed in many books and articles for parents and teachers. Television producers and advertisers became aware of a vast new market, as the infant population boomed in the 1940s. The "world of childhood" was recognized as a unique and significant world.

Art of the twentieth century was now experimental. After the 1919 Armory Show in New York, there was an awareness of new styles of painting. Freedom, light, and color marked the abstract designs of cubism, surrealism, and other new art forms. This influence was seen in the art of such picture books as the Rands' *I Know a Lot of Things* (1956), or Wildsmith's use of brilliant geometric design in *Puzzles* (1971), or his Mother Goose book, or the abstract symbolism found in Charles Keeping's *Joseph's Yard* (1969) and *Through the Window* (1970). In the 1960s Op art and Pop art influenced design, while the 1970s saw a revival of interest in art deco and the romantic art of Arthur Rackham. Early in the century jazz reflected distinctly American rhythms, only to be joined by modern folk songs, protest ballads, rock music, and the phenomenon known as Woodstock. A new realism in literature was followed eventually by starkly realistic film portrayals of human problems. The philosophy of existentialism led to re-examination of age-old questions regarding the meaning of life. To some, there was no purpose; life was an absurdity. From the influences of such writers as Sartre and Camus came the literature of despair, reflected to some degree in children's books by such titles as Weik's *The Jazz Man* (1966), Donovan's *Wild in the World* (1971), and Mohr's *Nilda* (1973).

In the United States of the 1950s and 1960s the federal government played an increasing role in education. Curriculum reform movements emphasized the structures of the disciplines and developed new materials for math, science, and English. The Center for Curriculum Studies at the University of Nebraska and the Hawaiian Curriculum Project produced materials for the teaching of literature beginning at the kindergarten level. Pre-school programs were established with federal funds as part of the attack on poverty. Under the Elementary and Secondary Education Act of 1965, federal financial assistance became available for experimental programs, new materials, and school media centers.

New programs included a new emphasis on black studies, the teaching of English as a second language, and such experiments as the Teachers and Writers Collaborative, which placed professional writers in classrooms to work on a regular basis with teachers and children. All these programs influenced the production of more and different types of trade books. For the first time in many elementary schools, monies were made available under Title II of The Elementary and Secondary Education Act (ESEA) for materials for school library media centers. The full impact of the role of the federal government can be seen in the growth of media centers in elementary schools. Between 1964 and 1968 the number of elementary schools having centralized media centers nearly doubled. Today, some 81 percent[18] of the elementary schools having enrollments of 300 or more have school library media centers, while only 19 percent do not. This tremendous increase must be attributed to the role of the federal government.

The federal government's "Right To Read Program" was begun in 1969 with the challenge that illiteracy in our nation be eradicated by 1980. While this program made a slow start, it has provided materials, demonstration centers, and in-service education for many schools that could not afford them otherwise.

The cutback in federal assistance to education in the 1970s brought many of these new programs to a grinding halt. However, the influence of Silberman's book *Crisis in the Classroom,* which described American schools as "grim, joyless places"[19] in contrast to the more humane primary schools of England, was tremendous. The concept of open education with its emphasis upon the individual child and freedom of choice grew rapidly in the U.S. While there are many variations of the so-called "open schools"—as advocated by Silberman, Featherstone, Barth, Holt, Kozol, and others—almost all of these commentators adhere to the principle of providing children with many trade books (rather than textbooks or basic readers), and ample time for reading. This approach to teaching and learning holds great promise for developing children who will enjoy literature and see it as an exciting part of their lives in school.

The types of literature published for the child's expanding world reflected the changes and challenges of life in the twentieth century. Just as adult literature has reflected the disillusionment of depression, wars, and materialism by becoming more sordid, sensational, and psychological, children's literature has become more realistic and honest, portraying such concerns of young people today as war, drugs, divorce, abortion, sex, and homosexuality. Children's books are now more sophisticated than they were ten years ago, and authors who used to write for adults are now writing for young people.

TECHNICAL IMPROVEMENTS

The printing improvements initiated in the nineteenth century were fully realized in the next four decades. Photo-offset lithography made it possible to print many more books at a lower cost. Bindings were more durable, often washable, and bright and gay. It was possible to create beautiful, fine books for children and just as easy to mass produce shoddy, cheap editions. Paperback editions of good books for children became available early in the latter half of the twentieth century.

Technological improvements of the twentieth century have made possible such exciting innovations as the use of computers, copy machines, videotapes, cassettes, film loops, and cable TV. These recent inventions are just coming into their own in school library media programs. They hold the tremendous promise of instant information in almost any form the reader wants it.

FICTION FACTORIES

The dime novel had been initiated in the nineteenth century, and the series books of George Henty, Oliver Optic, Sophie May, and Horatio Alger had introduced the repetitive incident plot

[18] Mary Helen Mahar, *An Evaluative Survey Report on ESEA Title II: Fiscal Years 1966–68, Part II Tables* (Washington, D.C.: Department of Health, Education and Welfare, Office of Education, 1972), p. 109.

[19] Charles E. Silberman, *Crisis in the Classroom* (New York: Random House, 1970), p. 10.

and stereotyped character.[20] "Fiction factories" were developed by Edward Stratemeyer, who wrote literally hundreds of books under a variety of pseudonyms.[21] *The Motor Boys, Tom Swift,* and *Nancy Drew* all came from this manufacturer of plots. Stratemeyer would give a three-page outline of characters and plot to hack writers to complete. In the biography of Howard Garis, *My Father Was Uncle Wiggly,* Roger Garis tells how his father worked for the Stratemeyer syndicate. Garis wrote *The Motor Boys* under the name of Clarence Young, *Tom Swift* books as Victor Appleton, and, with Mrs. Garis, created *The Bobbsey Twins.* Garis could produce a book every eight or ten days. *Tom Swift* (1910), *The Rover Boys* (1899), *The Bobbsey Twins* (1904), and *Nancy Drew* continue to be "best sellers." The plots and characters have remained the same, although modern versions deal with nuclear war, space flights, and submarines. The hero remains a child or adolescent, but partakes of adult adventure and acts with adult wisdom. A representative of good, he triumphs over all obstacles—unaided, undaunted, undefeated.

RECOGNITION OF CHILDREN'S LITERATURE

Disturbed by the influence of the fifty-cent juvenile, Franklin K. Mathiews, Chief Scout Librarian, sought to raise the level of reading for children. His suggestion for establishing a Children's Book Week was promoted in 1919 by Frederick Melcher as a project of the American Booksellers Association. Schools, libraries, newspapers, and bookstores supported the event that became a significant stimulant to the development of children's literature. In 1945 the Children's Book Council was established to promote Book Week and to distribute information on children's books throughout the year.

Melcher also promoted another event that has encouraged the development of children's literature. He proposed the presentation of an annual award for the most distinguished book for chil-

[20]"The Grinch & Co.," *Time,* Vol. 70 (December 23, 1957), pp. 74–76.
[21]"For It Was Indeed He," *Fortune Magazine,* Vol. 9 (April 1934), pp. 86–89. Reprinted in *Only Connect: Readings on Children's Literature,* edited by Sheila Egoff, *et al.* (New York: Oxford University Press, 1969).

dren. Since 1922 the Newbery Award and the Caldecott Medal for picture books, awarded first in 1938, have had great influence in raising the standards of writing and illustrating in children's books. An international award, the Hans Christian Andersen Award was established in 1956 and is given every two years to a living author for his complete body of work. Since 1966 an artist's medal has also been given. Beginning in 1969 the National Book awards included a prize for children's literature (*see* Chapter 1). Recently this has been cancelled for lack of funds.

The addition of children's departments to publishing firms indicated the growing importance of literature for the young. In 1919 Macmillan made Louise Seaman children's editor, and other companies were soon to follow this innovation. May Massee became editor of children's books at Doubleday in 1922. The first critical reviews of children's books appeared in *The Bookman* in 1918. Anne Carroll Moore continued this influential work in her *New York Herald Tribune* column, "The Three Owls." *The Horn Book Magazine,* a publication solely devoted to children's literature, was first published in 1924 under the editorship of Bertha Mahony.

Public libraries instituted children's rooms and many elementary schools had libraries. By 1915 the American Library Association had established a School Library division. However, it was not until the enactment of The Elementary and Secondary Education Act of 1965 that the concept of school library media centers for every elementary school seemed a viable possibility.

The Junior Literary Guild was established in 1929 and was the first to send children selected books each month. In the late 1950s paperback book clubs made it possible for more children to own books and increased their enthusiasm for reading. Currently, many book clubs offer selections of children's literature.

RISE OF THE PICTURE BOOK

The importance of early childhood made it imperative that books be designed for young children. Technological progress made it possible to produce picture books for preschoolers and picture storybooks for children in primary grades. C. B. Falls' *ABC Book* of 1923 presented woodcuts of high quality. *Clever Bill,* written and illustrated by William Nicholson, was published in England in 1926. Wanda Gág's delightful tale, *Millions of Cats,* published in 1928, has been called the first American picture storybook. In that same year Boris Artzybasheff illustrated *The Fairy Shoemaker and Other Poems,* beginning his outstanding work. In England, Arthur Rackham was drawing his grotesque people and almost human trees, often evoking an eerie atmosphere with his skilled lines. His illustrations of *Aesop's Fables, Gulliver's Travels,* and *Mother Goose* show fine detail, imaginative elves and gnomes, and excellent use of color. Leslie Brooke's animals in *Johnny Crow's Garden* were costumed and personified with facial expressions conveying feeling, humor, and charm.

The production of American picture books not only benefited from improved techniques in the field of graphic arts but also from the influx of many fine European artists who, for one reason or another, sought refuge in this country. These artists found a legitimate outlet for their creative talents in the field of children's literature. Picture books were greatly enriched through their unique contributions. A glance at a roster of some of the names of well-known illustrators will indicate the international character of their backgrounds: Aichinger, d'Aulaire, Duvoisin, Eichenberg, Mordvinoff, Petersham, Rojankovsky, Simont, Shulevitz, Slobodkin, Yashima, and many more. The variety of their national backgrounds has added a cosmopolitan flavor to our picture books that is unprecedented both in time and place. American children have become the beneficiaries of an inheritance from the whole artistic world.

GROWTH OF INFORMATIONAL BOOKS

Lucy Sprague Mitchell utilized knowledge of child development in her *Here and Now Story Book* first published in 1921. She pointed out the young child's preoccupation with himself and his interest in daily experiences. Other writers recognized that such simple themes as taking a walk, planting a carrot, or listening to night sounds represented adventure for the 3- to 5-year-old. Books helped the pre-school child interpret experience; they were not designed to funnel information into his head. E. Boyd Smith's *The Farm Book* and *The Chicken World,* published in 1910, were among the first illustrative informational books.

The child's natural curiosity was extended through realistic stories or through straightforward texts. The Lucy Fitch Perkins *Twins* series, beginning in 1911, gave information through stories. In *The Japanese Twins,* for example, Taro and Take are always "nice" children having a "nice" time in the series of incidents described. The inferior place of woman symbolized in the scene in which the new male baby's foot is placed on his big sister's neck was realistic. Most children would miss the meaning of this incident that ends as the mother sighs and turns her face to the wall. Unfortunately, stereotyped characters prevailed.

Maud and Miska Petersham, who used rich colors to illustrate informational books about oil, wheat, food, clothing, and other products were the first to give children in the early 1930s information about such processes. Reed's *The Earth for Sam* and Fenton's *Along the Hill* (1935) exemplify the beginning of accurate informational books.

Since the 1940s quantities of informational books have rolled from the presses to give children facts on almost every conceivable subject. Series books in the areas of science and social studies were important developments in this period. The *First Books, All About Books,* and the *True Books* series are examples of the trend. Many books of experiments by such authors as the Schneiders and Freemans stimulated children's science activities. Developments in the fields of atomic energy and exploration of space have been reflected in books for children. In the 1950s factual books about rockets, satellites, and space almost seemed to be fantasy, but by the 1960s such books were an accepted fact of daily life. Accounts of space flights and detailed descriptions of the work of the astronauts have helped children understand the technology of the new age. Concurrently, science books have pointed up problems of modern life, including a flood of books on ecology—ranging from Gabel's *Sparrows Don't Drop Candy Wrappers* (1971) to Perry's *Our Polluted World: Can Man Survive?* (1972).

Biographies appeared to satisfy children's interest in national heroes. Daugherty's *Daniel Boone*, published in 1939, was outstanding for its time. The *Childhood of Famous Americans* series initiated the trend of publishing biographies for boys and girls in series form. By the 1960s biographies gave less emphasis to the early years of great men and women. More biographies for young children became available, including such lively and authentic books as Fritz's *And Then What Happened, Paul Revere?* (1973) and *Poor Richard in France* (1973) by F. N. Monjo. Biographies of Civil Rights leaders honored such well-known persons as Martin Luther King, Jr., and lesser-known participants such as Rosa Parks, the woman who refused to give up her seat on a bus in Montgomery, Alabama, in 1955. More concern was evidenced for publishing biographies about women, and Crowell began their series on Women in America, which includes titles on Gertrude Stein, Fanny Kimble, and others.

Early in the twentieth century, historical fiction was written for children. Laura Richards quoted from diaries and letters as she wrote *Abigail Adams and Her Times* (1909). *The Horsemen of the Plains* (1910) by Altsheler related exciting frontier stories. The legendary approach to history was utilized by MacGregor in *Story of Greece* (1914). *When Knights Were Bold* brought another period of history to life when Tappan published this book in 1911. The sweep of history was shown in Van Loon's *The Story of Mankind* (1921). Coatsworth's historical fiction about America was initiated with *Away Goes Sally* in 1934. Long selections from original diaries and journals were presented in the historical accounts of Smith's *Pilgrim Courage* (1962) and *The Coming of the Pilgrims* (1964).

Bealer's *Only the Names Remain: The Cherokees and the Trail of Tears* (1972) is representative of a new emphasis on readable, carefully documented history. It also attempts to balance the record of history by presenting the American Indian point of view. The Newbery Award winner for 1974, *The Slave Dancer* by Paula Fox, realistically faces up to the wrongs of the past. Celebration of the Bicentennial has spurred publication of many attractive and authentic books on eighteenth-century America.

There is no accurate accounting of the number of nonfiction children's titles that are published in contrast to fiction, but a survey of the new titles would suggest that nearly two-thirds of the books published today could be classified as informational. Informational books and biographies are discussed in detail in Chapter 9 of this book.

FOLK TALES

A famous storyteller, Gudrun Thorne-Thomsen, recorded stories from Norway in *East O' the Sun and West O' the Moon* in 1912. Kate Douglas Wiggin edited tales from the *Arabian Nights* and Ellen Babbitt brought forth a collection of *Jataka Tales* from India. From 1900 to 1920 many collections of folk tales were purchased. Serious scholars recognized the value of these tales, and story-tellers in schools and libraries brought them into the lives of children. Padraic Colum, Kate Douglas Wiggin, Parker Fillmore, and others contributed significant collections. Tales from the Far East and Africa were also added in the 1940s and 1950s. Wanda Gàg illustrated single tales, but it was Marcia Brown who developed the trend of illustrating single tales by the publication of *Stone Soup* (1947). *Cinderella* (1954) and *Once a Mouse* (1961) won Caldecott Medals, while her other fairy tales, *Puss in Boots, Dick Whittington and His Cat*, and *The Steadfast Tin Soldier* were honor books for the award. Greater emphasis was placed upon African folk tales, Jewish folk tales, and legends of native Americans during the decade of the sixties and on into the seventies. Gail Haley won the Caldecott Award (1971) for *A Story, A Story*, an African tale of Anansi; while *Anansi the Spider* by McDermott was a Caldecott Honor Book (1973). *Arrow to the Sun*, a Pueblo Indian tale by McDermott won the award in 1975.

HUMOR AND FANTASY

Fantasy for children in the first half of the twentieth century seemed to come mainly from English writers. The *Just So Stories* (1902) stimulated children's imaginations as Kipling gave delightful accounts of the origin of animal characteristics. The boy who refused to grow up and lose the beauties of Never Never Land, Peter Pan, appeared in a London play in 1904 by J. M. Barrie, who made the play into a story titled *Peter Pan and Wendy* in 1911.

Another storyteller, Kenneth Grahame, wrote installments of the adventures of a water rat, a mole, and a toad for his small son, who was on a vacation. *The Wind in the Willows* was written and published in 1908.

Selma Lagerlöff had been commissioned to write a geographical reader on Sweden. She decided to present the information in the form of fantasy in which a boy is changed into an elf who flies over Sweden on a gander's back. *The Wonderful Adventures of Nils* appeared in 1907.

E. Nesbit's fantasies of magic rings, wishes, and invisible children mix humor, the real, and the unreal. Written in the early 1900s, *The Story of the Treasure Seekers* tells of the Bastable family which tries to recover a fortune. These magic tales were forerunners of the Mary Poppins stories.

In 1900 the Cowardly Lion and the Tin Woodsman met Dorothy in the Land of Oz. Although its merits have been debated by librarians and teachers, *The Wizard of Oz* by Baum has been enjoyed by thousands of children and adults. The first book of the series might well have sufficed, for the others in the series are repetitious and not as well written.

One of the most delightful books of humor appeared in 1926. A. A. Milne created such believable characters as Eeyore, Piglet, and Pooh for young Christopher Robin, his son. The stuffed animals in *Winnie the Pooh* have many adventures that are true fantasy.

Perhaps the books of humor and fantasy reflected the need for escape from the shadows of world tensions and war. New theories of child development recognized the rights of children to be themselves; the mental-health movement pointed up the values of recreation and fun for wholesome personality development. McCloskey's *Homer Price* (1943), Cleary's *Henry Huggins* (1950), and the Atwaters' *Mr. Popper's Penguins* (1938) brought humor to realistic stories. Certainly the most well-loved animal fantasy to be written by an American appeared in 1952: E. B. White's *Charlotte's Web*. The late 1960s and 1970s saw Americans writing such high fantasy as Lloyd Alexander's Prydain Series and Ursula Le Guin's superb tales of Earthsea. Susan Cooper, an English author living in the United States, created *The Dark Is Rising* sequence, five stories

about the age-old conflict between the dark and the light. No longer is it possible to say that all the best fantasy comes from England.

ANIMAL ADVENTURE

One of the most famous animals in literature is Peter Rabbit, who appeared in Mr. MacGregor's garden at the turn of the century. Two privately published editions preceded the book that was published by Warne in 1902 as *The Tale of Peter Rabbit*. Beatrix Potter introduced other animals, *Jemima Puddleduck* and *Benjamin Bunny*, but the cottontail family is best known and loved. While younger children were enjoying Peter Rabbit, older boys and girls turned to Jack London's *The Call of the Wild* (1903).

Although many teachers would place Hugh Lofting's *The Story of Doctor Dolittle* (1920) with books of fantasy, children usually think of it as an animal story. Boys and girls read and reread Terhune's story of the faithful collie, *Lad: A Dog* (1919). *Smoky the Cowhorse* (1926) by Will James was an exciting story of the early decades of the century. This moving story of an intelligent horse who was mistreated by a series of owners brought a new realism to younger readers.

In the 1940s Anderson wrote the Blaze stories, Henry delighted children with Misty and Brighty, and Farley's *Black Stallion* series gained popularity.

Many realistic, informational books about specific animals appeared in the 1950s, representing a new type of literature to meet children's interests.

During the early sixties three animal stories written for adults became favorites of boys and girls in the middle grades. These were Sterling North's *Rascal* (1963), an autobiographical story of an 11-year-old and his pet raccoon; Maxwell's *Ring of Bright Water* (1961), which described the author's friendship with two otters; and *Born Free* (1960) by Adamson, the story of a lioness raised among people and then retrained so that she could return to the wild. All three of these books were either filmed or televised, which helps to account for their popularity.

REALISTIC FICTION

Realistic fiction often reflected war, depression, and social problems in the contemporary scene. Just as in the past, children's books continued to mirror adult concerns and interests. Intercultural education took on new significance. Lois Lenski pioneered in presenting authentic, detailed descriptions of life in specific regions of the United States. By living in the community, observing the customs of the people, and listening to their stories, she was able to produce a significant record of American life from the 1930s into the 1960s. Problems of the migratory worker were dramatized by Gates in *Blue Willow* (1940). Eleanor Estes was one of the first to write about poverty and children's interrelationships in their closed society. Her book, *The Hundred Dresses* (1944), enabled teachers to undertake and guide frank discussions of the problem of being "different."

Very few books dealt with racial problems. Books that portrayed Negroes, for example, showed stereotypes of the bandana-covered, fat mammy and the kinky-haired, thick-lipped "funny" boy. This stereotype was epitomized in the Nicodemus series written by Hogan in the late 1930s with such titles as *Nicodemus and the Gang* (1939). The jacket of this book quotes part of a *New York Herald Tribune* review that said: "A story that will get itself remembered when some longer and louder ones are forgotten." Fortunately, Nicodemus with his gang—who have such stereotyped names as Rastus, Obadiah, and Petunia—have been forgotten. "I'se a comin'," "Yas'm Mammy," and "nex' time, I spec you better stan' on de groun' fo' speech makin'" exemplified the "black-face" dialect used in this series. The segregation of Negroes was clearly shown in *Araminta* (1935) by Evans and the photographic essay, *Tobe* (1939), by Sharpe. It was nearly ten years later that Negroes and whites were shown participating in activities together. The theme of *Two Is a Team* (1945) by the Beims is revealed in both the title and the action as a Negro boy and a white boy play together. Prejudice was openly discussed for the first time in Jackson's *Call Me Charley* (1945) and Marguerite de Angeli's *Bright April* (1946).

Mary Jane (1959) by Sterling, *The Empty Schoolhouse* (1965) by Carlson, and *Patricia Crosses Town* (1965) by Baum discussed the new social problems caused by school integration. By the mid-1960s, a few books showed black characters in the illustrations, but this was not mentioned in the text. Examples included *The Snowy Day* (1962) by Keats, *Mississippi Possum* (1965) by Miles, and Shotwell's *Roosevelt Grady*, (1963). In the seventies such books were criticized for "whitewashing" the blacks and attempting to make everyone the same. Books such as *Zeely* (1967) by Hamilton and *Stevie* (1969) by Steptoe, both written by black authors, captured something of the special pride of the black experience in children's literature.

The "new realism" in children's literature can probably be dated from the publication of *Harriet the Spy* (1964) by Fitzhugh. Harriet is a precocious 11-year-old who keeps a notebook in which she records with brutal honesty her impressions of her family, friends, and neighborhood characters. The sequel to this story, *The Long Secret* (1965), contains a frank discussion of menstruation by Harriet and her friend Beth Ellen. Following *Harriet*'s breakthrough, the long-standing taboos in children's literature came tumbling down. The Cleavers wrote about death and suicide in *Where the Lilies Bloom* (1969) and *Grover* (1970); alcoholism and homosexuality are described in *I'll Get There, It Better Be Worth the Trip* (1969) by Donovan; and *(George)* (1970) by Konigsburg includes divorced parents, a psychologically disturbed child, and LSD. *Mom, The Wolf Man and Me* (1972) by Norma Klein is the candid story of a young girl's fear that her single mother will get married. *Deenie* (1973) by Judy Blume is primarily the story of a beautiful girl who discovers she must wear a back brace for four years. The story contains several references to masturbation. Even picture books have reflected the impact of this new freedom. Mickey fell out of bed and out of his clothes in Sendak's *In the Night Kitchen* (1970). In *My Special Best Words* (1974) by Steptoe, bodily functions are discussed naturally, as a slightly older sister tries to toilet train her younger brother.

All these problems are legitimate concerns of childhood. They have always existed, but only in the last ten years have they been openly and honestly written about in books for children. Further discussion of realism in children's literature is presented in Chapter 7.

POETRY

"Liquid liveliness," "rare charm," "exquisite mastery of words"—these phrases have been used to describe the beauty in the poems of and for children by Walter de la Mare. *Songs for Childhood* appeared in 1902, beginning the new century with a work that helped young and old alike perceive infinite beauty and enchantment. Eleven years later *Peacock Pie* brought readers new melodies, nursery rhymes, and poems about imaginary beings.

The fun and gaiety of the child's everyday world was interpreted by such poets as A. A. Milne, Rachel Field, Dorothy Aldis, and Aileen Fisher. The transition in children's poetry from the didactic to the descriptive, from moralizing to poems of fun and nonsense had at last been achieved.

New interests in poetry were seen in the 1960s with the increasing number of books on haiku and the many books of poetry written by children. Richard Lewis published his first volume of children's writing from around the world, *Miracles* (1964). In the late 1960s and 1970s more strident voices were heard in the poetry of cynicism and protest. *Young Voices* (1971) is an anthology of poems written by fourth-, fifth-, and sixth-grade children in response to a 1969 Poetry Search by the Center for Urban Education in New York City. Nancy Larrick published a collection of poems written by American youth titled *I Heard a Scream in the Street* (1970). Eve Merriam's *Inner-city Mother Goose* (1969), first written for adults, is a devastating commentary on the injustices of the ghetto. The spotlight has been focused on poems about girls in Hopkins' *Girls Can Too* (1972) and *Amelia Mixed the Mustard* (1975) by Evaline Ness.

An International Literature for Children

An exciting development in children's literature was the rise of international interest in children's books during the years after World War II. This was indicated by an increased flow of children's books between countries. In 1950 *Pippi Longstocking* by the Swedish author, Lindgren,

arrived in our country and was an immediate success. This was the beginning of many such exchanges.

The Mildred L. Batchelder Award for the most outstanding translated children's book originally published abroad and then published in the United States was established in 1966 by the Children's Services Division of the American Library Association to honor their retiring executive secretary who had worked tirelessly for the exchange of books. This award has served as an impetus in promoting the translation of fine children's books from abroad. Such excellent books as *Don't Take Teddy* (1967) by the Norwegian writer Friis-Baastad; *Friedrich* (1970) by Richter of Germany; and two books from Greece, *Wildcat under Glass* (1968) and *Petro's War* (1972) by Alki Zei, have been the recipients of this award.

Another indicator of the growing internationalism of children's literature during the 1950s was the number of congresses, book fairs, and exhibitions of children's books that were held around the world. The first general assembly of The International Board of Books for Young People (IBBY) was held in 1953. Jella Lepman, founder of IBBY, maintained that the organization should serve as a world conscience for international children's books and call attention to the best in the field by awarding international prizes. Consequently, IBBY awarded its first Hans Christian Andersen Medal to Eleanor Farjeon in 1956. In 1966 IBBY decided to extend the award to include a medal for the most outstanding artist as well as author of children's books. Alois Carigiet was the first artist to receive this award. Then, in 1967, Jella Lepman created the annual International Children's Book Day, which was appropriately established on April 2nd, the birthday of Hans Christian Andersen. The IBBY congresses meet every other year.

In 1967 the Biennale of Illustrations in Bratislava, Czechoslovakia (BIB), held its first exhibition. It is now scheduled to meet in the odd-numbered years, alternating with the IBBY congress. Other international displays include the annual Frankfurt Book Fair in September of each year and the Bologna Children's Book Fair in April. Not everyone can attend these international meetings, but *Bookbird*, an international magazine concerned with children's literature, was first published in 1963 and provides a wide audience with information on activities in the world of children's books. The fifties and the sixties, then, saw the formation of international organizations for the exchange and appreciation of children's books throughout the world. These developments paved the way for UNESCO to designate 1972 as International Book Year.

Children's Books Today

At the present time the publication and distribution of juvenile books comprises a big business—producing a $150 million children's book market! The number of juveniles published in 1970 was nearly ten times the number published in 1880. These statistics show the increased rate of growth for each decade of publication of juveniles over a ninety-year period.

The largest number of juvenile titles published was in 1965, when some 2,895 titles were offered. This increase reflected the influence of federal funds for the support of library materials. While the number of juveniles published has declined slightly in the last few years, this may be partially accounted for by the increase of paperback editions in the juvenile field. Unfortunately, statistics on paperback children's books are not kept separately from adult paperback figures. However, recent years have seen a dramatic increase in quality paperbacks for children as individual publishing houses have selected some of the best of their previously published titles for reissue in

paperback form. Increasingly, publishers are bringing out new titles in hardcover and paperback simultaneously.

Another indicator of the state of the children's book market lies in the growing number of books that can be classified as best sellers. *Stuart Little* and *Charlotte's Web* by E. B. White together have sold more than two million copies in hardcover editions; *Charlotte's Web* alone has sold well over three million in paperback.[22] *Caps for Sale* by Slobodkina had sold over a million copies by 1973; and Henry's *Misty of Chincoteague* sold more than half a million. Other titles that were reported above the quarter-million mark for hardcover sales included *Little House in the Big Woods* by Wilder, *The Biggest Bear* by Ward, and Sendak's *Where the Wild Things Are.*[23]

A visit to the juvenile book section of a large department store illustrates the wide variety of literature available for children today. On the shelves are books of all sizes and shapes, from Sendak's diminutive *Nutshell Library* to the oversized book of D'Aulaires' *Trolls.* Beautifully designed picture books may be on the same table as the slick "flats" of the latest Disney production. Books of poetry, nonsense, history, science, biography, and fiction are displayed. The new freedom of adult books is reflected in the content of books for children and teenagers. Judy Blume's book about divorce, *It's Not the End of the World,* may be next to a new edition of *Little Women.* Classics such as *The Wind in the Willows* and *Winnie the Pooh* may be shelved next to row upon row of series books. There are books for adults to read to children, books with controlled vocabularies for the beginning reader, and books for the skilled reader.

A visit to a child's home may reveal the same confusing array of books or, what is even sadder, no books at all. Many parents pride themselves on providing their children with personal libraries, but unfortunately, purchase all their books at the supermarket or at drugstores. A child may have a bookcase full of books, and not have one good book among them. Or the child may be fortunate enough to come from a book-loving

Juveniles Published*	
1880	270
1890	408
1900	527
1910	1,010
1920	477
1930	933
1940	984
1950	1,059
1960	1,725
1970	2,640

* *The Bowker Annual of Library and Book Trade Information* (New York: Bowker, 1972).

[22] Ursula Nordstrom, "Stuart, Wilbur, Charlotte: A Tale of Tales," *New York Times Book Review* (May 12, 1974), p. 8.
[23] Jean Spealman Kujoth, *Best-selling Children's Books* (Metuchen, N.J.: The Scarecrow Press, 1973), pp. 251–255.

family that reads to him, takes him to the library, provides such fine magazines as *The National Geographic* or one for the child himself, *Cricket.* There is no dearth of books and materials for children today; selecting from the vast array that is available is the challenging task for parents, teachers, and librarians.

Emphasis upon individualization of instruction and increased awareness of the need for many materials for learning have been major factors in the trend toward the use of trade books and audiovisual materials in the basic school curriculum. At long last, teachers are accepting the idea of using many materials instead of a single text.

Trade books are increasingly used for instruction, as reading programs become more individualized. Educators recommend a minimum of four to six different books for each child in the classroom for individualized reading instruction. It is assumed that this collection would be changed frequently. The science and social studies curricula also draw upon many trade books, as children demand more information and more up-to-date material than can be found in a single textbook. It is difficult for revisions of a textbook series to keep pace with new science information,

whereas a single trade book containing the most recent material can be easily published. For example, *Skylab* by Coombs was published *before* the astronauts had launched the first one.

Increased use of listening centers in both the classroom and the library allows children to enjoy literature or seek information through listening to records, cassettes, and tapes, or seeing filmstrips and films. Children make overhead transparencies for their reports; they may use the tape-recorder for telling stories or conducting interviews; and they make their own 8-millimeter films. Increasingly, instructional materials centers are including facsimile documents and artifacts in their collections. While all these materials have become significant tools for learning, books continue to be the major source of information and enjoyment.

Literature for children has come of age—it has been recognized nationally and internationally. Most of our schools have, or have hopes of beginning, a school library media center staffed by trained personnel. Teachers and librarians have learned the value of providing children with many materials and the time to use them. All of us now have the opportunity of bringing children and books together.

SUGGESTED LEARNING EXPERIENCES

1. Interview five adults of different ages. Inquire about their favorite books and childhood reading interests.
2. Prepare a display of early children's books; note the printing and binding, the illustrations, the subject matter. Display a varied selection of recent books as well. What contrasts do you see, and what similarities?
3. Identify adult purposes in several recent books for children. Can you find any examples of didactic stories written in the last ten years? Be sure to look at several books dealing with current social problems.
4. Read and compare two books of realistic fiction with blacks as major characters—one published within the last five years, the other published before 1960. How does each book specifically reflect the time in which it was written?
5. If possible, read two books aloud to a group of children. Choose one old book and one new, but on a similar theme, such as the books about quarreling in the introduction to this chapter. Elicit the children's responses. What do they see as differences. Which book do they prefer?

RELATED READINGS

1. Arnold, Arnold. *Pictures and Stories from Forgotten Children's Books.* New York: Dover Publications, 1969.
    A paperback publication containing some 485 illustrations and complete stories from early children's books. Inexpensive, it would be an interesting publication for a teacher to share with students.

2. Baring-Gould, William S., and Ceil Baring-Gould. *The Annotated Mother Goose,* illustrated by Walter Crane, Randolph Caldecott, Kate Greenaway, and others. New York: Bramhale House (Clarkson Potter), 1962.

   Annotations for each rhyme suggest the source (if known) and interpret the meanings of many of the obsolete words. Interesting for the scholar of Mother Goose rhymes.

3. De Vries, Leonard. *Flowers of Delight: An Agreeable Garland of Prose and Poetry 1765–1830.* New York: Pantheon, 1965.

   The editor selected books and poems from the Osborne collection of early children's books, and has published them with the original illustrations. It is an especially valuable collection because the story or poem is printed in its entirety. Reproductions of illustrations are excellent.

4. Folmsbee, Beulah. *A Little History of the Horn Book.* Boston, Mass. Horn Book, 1942.

   A tiny volume, the size of the early hornbooks, gives the recipe for making sheets of horn and tells how the hornbook was constructed.

5. Haviland, Virginia, ed. *Children and Literature, Views and Reviews.* Glenview, Ill.: Scott, Foresman, 1972.

   Chapters One and Two of this fine book of readings contain many articles related to the history of children's literature. Chapter Ten presents a comprehensive study of children's literature in eight major foreign countries.

6. Haviland, Virginia, ed. *Children's Books of International Interest: A Selection from Four Decades of American Publishing.* Chicago, Ill.: American Library Association, 1973.

   A carefully selected annotated list of books judged by the editor and past members of the International Relations Committee of the Children's Services Division of ALA as being the most enduring American books with continued interest for teachers, librarians, and publishers abroad. Prepared as a project for IBBY and the International Book Year of 1972.

7. Haviland, Virginia. *Children's Literature, A Guide to Reference Sources.* Washington, D.C.: Library of Congress, 1966. Also *First Supplement* to the above, issued in 1972.

   The first volume was an annotated bibliography of the expanding body of literature, both national and international, devoted to children. The supplement covers the period from 1966–1969. It includes a large number of entries on minorities and two new sections on "Publishing and Promotion" and "Teaching Children's Literature."

8. Jordan, Alice M. *From Rollo to Tom Sawyer.* Boston, Mass.: Horn Book, 1948.

   Biographies of authors of children's books of the latter half of the nineteenth century help the teacher understand the books of this period.

9. Kiefer, Monica. *American Children through Their Books 1700–1835.* Philadelphia, Pa.: University of Philadelphia Press, 1948.

   The significance of the changing status of children in the development of literature is clearly delineated. Influences of educational philosophers are illustrated in this reference. Description of children's clothing and customs are also interesting.

10. Kujoth, Jean Spealman. *Best-selling Children's Books.* Metuchen, N.J.: The Scarecrow Press, 1973.

    Although the completeness of this report is marred by the lack of statistics from some of the major publishers, it is nevertheless a fascinating look at books which have sold more than 100,000 copies. Most helpful for comparison purposes are the six separate listings of best sellers: by author, with annotation; by title; by illustrator; by year of original publication; by number of copies sold; by type, subject, and age level.

11. McKendry, John J., ed. *Aesop: Five Centuries of Illustrated Fables.* The Metropolitan Museum of Art. Greenwich, Conn.: New York Graphic Society, 1964.

    Through the pages of this book a reader can trace the development of many types of illustrations, from German woodcuts of the fifteenth century to engravings of the nineteenth and modern woodcuts of the twentieth century. The introduction provides a good summary of the development of fables and their varied illustrations.

12. Meigs, Cornelia, *et al. A Critical History of Children's Literature: A Survey of Children's Books in English, Prepared in Four Parts under the Editorship of Cornelia Meigs.* Rev. ed. New York: Macmillan, 1969.

An interesting survey of books for children from earliest times to the present. The organization by chronological periods emphasizes influences upon children's literature and trends. The title of Part 4 in the revised edition has been changed from "The Golden Age" to "Golden Years and Time of Tumult."

13. Muir, Percy. *English Children's Books 1600 to 1900.* London, England: Batsford, 1954. Reissued, New York: Praeger, 1973.

The development of literature for children in England is outlined in detail. The section describing the work of early illustrators of children's books is particularly useful.

14. Pellowski, Anne. *The World of Children's Literature.* New York: Bowker, 1968.

A comprehensive volume which pictures the development of literature in every country. A commentary for each country discusses the political or educational influences on the development of literature and the present state of the art. Annotated bibliographies of books and articles follow each commentary.

15. Pitz, Henry C. *Illustrating Children's Books.* New York: Watson-Guptill, 1963.

Technical aspects of illustrating are emphasized in this book that includes information about illustration for books in England, Europe, and America. Many examples of modern illustration are included to show techniques and influences of artists from many countries.

16. St. John, Judith. *The Osborne Collection of Early Children's Books 1566–1919: A Catalogue.* Toronto, Canada: Toronto Public Library, 1958.

This catalogue describes approximately 3,000 books in the Osborne Collection. The books are classified according to interests such as nursery and fairy tales, poetry, instruction, and stories. The reproductions from these early books are excellent.

17. Smith, Dora V. *Fifty Years of Children's Books 1910–1960: Trends, Backgrounds, Influences.* Urbana, Ill.: National Council of Teachers of English, 1963.

The author's choices of best books in the fifty-year period of the title. The book recognizes the influence of foreign writers and illustrators and awards and organizations, as well as social concerns and changes in educational practice.

18. Smith, Elva S. *The History of Children's Literature.* Chicago, Ill.: American Library Association, 1937.

An outline of influences and types of books of each period from 1659–1900. The list of representative writers of each period would be useful to the serious student of the history of children's literature.

19. Thwaite, Mary. *From Primer to Pleasure in Reading,* 2nd ed. Boston, Mass.: Horn Book, 1973.

An introduction to the history of children's books in England from the invention of printing until 1914. The last section, "Children's Books Abroad," has been extended to cover children's books in Australia, North America, and Western Europe.

CHAPTER REFERENCES[24]

Adamson, Joy. *Born Free: A Lioness of Two Worlds.* Pantheon, 1960.

Aesop's Fables, illustrated by Arthur Rackham. F. Watts, 1967.

Alcott, Louisa May. *Little Men,* illustrated by Paul Hogarth. Macmillan, 1963 (1871).

———. *Little Women: Or Meg, Jo, Beth and Amy.* Little, Brown, 1868.

Alexander, Lloyd. *The Black Cauldron.* Holt, Rinehart and Winston, 1965.

———. *The Book of Three.* Holt, Rinehart and Winston, 1964.

———. *The Castle of Llyr.* Holt, Rinehart and Winston, 1966.

———. *The High King.* Holt, Rinehart and Winston, 1968.

———. *Taran Wanderer.* Holt, Rinehart and Winston, 1967.

All About . . . Series. Random House.

Altsheler, Joseph A. *The Horsemen of the Plains.* Macmillan, 1967 (1910).

[24] The references for this chapter include only those titles which remain in print. Where multiple editions exist, only one has been listed. In the case of new editions the original publication date of the text (where available) appears in parentheses. *Note:* The titles in this list are included on the basis of historical significance and are not necessarily recommended.

Andersen, Hans Christian. *Hans Christian Andersen: The Complete Fairy Tales and Stories,* translated by Erik Christian Haugaard. Doubleday, 1974 (1874).

———. *The Steadfast Tin Soldier,* translated by M. R. James, illustrated by Marcia Brown. Scribner, 1953.

Anderson, Clarence W. *Blaze and the Forest Fire.* Macmillan, 1962 (1938).

Appleton, Victor, pseud. (Howard Garis). *Tom Swift* Series. Grosset & Dunlap.

Arabian Nights. Retold by Padraic Colum, illustrated by Lynd Ward. Macmillan, 1964 (1704).

Atwater, Richard, and Florence Atwater. *Mr. Popper's Penguins,* illustrated by Robert Lawson. Little, Brown, 1938.

d'Aulaire, Ingri, and Edgar P. d'Aulaire. *D'Aulaires' Trolls.* Doubleday, 1972.

Bannerman, Helen. *The Story of Little Black Sambo.* Lippincott, 1923 (1899).

Barrie, J. M. *Peter Pan,* edited by Eleanor Graham, illustrated by Nora Unwin. Scribner, 1950 (1904).

Baum, Betty. *Patricia Crosses Town,* illustrated by Nancy Grossman. Knopf, 1965.

Baum, L. Frank. *The Wizard of Oz.* World Publishing, 1972 (1900).

Bealer, Alex. *Only the Names Remain,* illustrated by William Bock. Little, Brown, 1972.

Beim, Lorraine, and Jerrold Beim. *Two Is a Team,* illustrated by Ernest Crichlow. Harcourt Brace Jovanovich, 1945.

Blake, William. *Songs of Innocence,* illustrated by Ellen Raskin. Doubleday, 1966 (1789).

Blume, Judy. *Deenie.* Bradbury, 1973.

———. *It's Not the End of the World.* Bradbury, 1972.

Brooke, Leslie. *Johnny Crow's Garden.* Warne, 1903.

Brown, Marcia. *Cinderella.* Scribner, 1954.

———. *Dick Whittington and His Cat.* Scribner, 1950.

———. *Once a Mouse.* Scribner, 1961.

———. *Stone Soup.* Scribner, 1947.

Bunyan, John. *Pilgrim's Progress.* Dodd, 1967 (1678).

Burnett, Frances H. *Little Lord Fauntleroy,* illustrated by Harry Toothill. Dutton (1886).

———. *Sara Crewe.* Scholastic (1888).

———. *The Secret Garden,* illustrated by Tasha Tudor. Lippincott, 1962 (1910).

Carlson, Natalie Savage. *The Empty Schoolhouse,* illustrated by John Kaufmann. Harper & Row, 1965.

Carroll, Lewis, pseud. (Charles L. Dodgson). *Alice's Adventures in Wonderland and Through the Looking Glass,* illustrated by John Tenniel. Macmillan, 1963 (1865 and 1872).

Childhood of Famous Americans Series. Bobbs-Merrill.

Cleary, Beverly. *Henry Huggins,* illustrated by Louis Darling. Morrow, 1950.

Cleaver, Vera, and Bill Cleaver. *Grover,* illustrated by Frederic Marvin. Lippincott, 1970.

———. *Where the Lilies Bloom,* illustrated by Jim Spanfeller. Lippincott, 1969.

Coatsworth, Elizabeth. *Away Goes Sally,* illustrated by Helen Sewell. Macmillan, 1934.

Collodi, C., pseud. (Carlo Lorenzini). *The Adventures of Pinocchio,* illustrated by Naiad Einsel. Macmillan, 1963 (1892).

Coombs, Charles. *Skylab.* Morrow, 1972.

Cooper, James Fenimore. *The Last of the Mohicans,* illustrated by N. C. Wyeth. Scribner, 1919 (1826).

Cooper, Susan. *The Dark Is Rising,* illustrated by Alan E. Cober. Atheneum, 1973.

———. *Greenwitch.* Atheneum, 1974.

———. *Over Sea, Under Stone,* illustrated by Marjorie Gill. Harcourt Brace Jovanovich, 1966.

Daugherty, James. *Daniel Boone.* Viking, 1939.

De Angeli, Marguerite. *Bright April.* Doubleday, 1946.

Defoe, Daniel. *Robinson Crusoe,* illustrated by N. C. Wyeth. Scribner, 1920 (1719).

De la Mare, Walter. *Peacock Pie,* illustrated by Barbara Cooney. Knopf, 1961 (1913).

De la Ramee, Louise. *A Dog of Flanders, and Other Stories,* illustrated by M. Leone. Grosset & Dunlap (1872).

Dickens, Charles. *The Magic Fishbone,* illustrated by Louis Slobodkin. Vanguard, 1953 (1868).

Dodge, Mary Mapes. *Hans Brinker, or The Silver Skates,* illustrated by George Wharton Edwards. Scribner, 1915 (1865).

Donovan, John. *I'll Get There, It Better Be Worth the Trip.* Harper & Row, 1969.
————. *Wild in the World.* Harper & Row, 1971.
Estes, Eleanor. *The Hundred Dresses,* illustrated by Louis Slobodkin. Harcourt Brace Jovanovich, 1944.
Falls, C. B. *ABC Book.* Doubleday, 1957 (1923).
Farley, Walter. *The Black Stallion* Series. Random House.
Field, Eugene. *Poems of Childhood,* illustrated by M. Parrish. Scribner, 1904 (1896).
First Book of . . . Series. F. Watts.
Fitzhugh, Louise. *Harriet the Spy.* Harper & Row, 1964.
————. *The Long Secret.* Harper & Row, 1965.
Fox, Paula. *The Slave Dancer,* illustrated by Eros Keith. Bradbury, 1973.
Friis-Baastad, Babbis. *Don't Take Teddy,* translated from the Norwegian by Lise S. McKinnon. Scribner, 1967.
Fritz, Jean. *And Then What Happened, Paul Revere?,* illustrated by Margot Tomes. Coward-McCann, 1973.
Gabel, Margaret. *Sparrows Don't Drop Candy Wrappers,* illustrated by Susan Perl. Dodd, 1971.
Gág, Wanda. *Millions of Cats.* Coward-McCann, 1928.
Gates, Doris. *Blue Willow,* illustrated by Paul Lantz. Viking, 1940.
Grahame, Kenneth. *The Wind in the Willows,* illustrated by E. H. Shepard. Scribner, 1908.
Greenaway, Kate. *Marigold Garden.* Warne, 1885.
————. *Under the Window.* Warne, 1879.
Grimm Brothers. *Household Stories,* translated by Lucy Crane, illustrated by Walter Crane. McGraw-Hill, 1966 (1886) (*Kinder und Hausmarchen,* 1812).
Haley, Gail E. *A Story, A Story.* Atheneum, 1970.
Hamilton, Virginia. *Zeely,* illustrated by Symeon Shimin. Macmillan, 1967.
Harris, Joel Chandler. *Uncle Remus, His Songs & Sayings,* rev. ed., illustrated by A. B. Frost. Hawthorn, 1921 (1881).
Hawthorne, Nathaniel. *The Wonderbook and Tanglewood Tales,* illustrated by Maxfield Parrish. Dodd, 1934 (1852 and 1853).
Henry, Marguerite. *Misty of Chincoteaque,* illustrated by Wesley Dennis. Rand McNally, 1947.
Hope, Laura Lee, pseud. *The Bobbsey Twins* Series. Grosset & Dunlap.
Hopkins, Lee Bennett. *Girls Can Too! A Book of Poems,* illustrated by Emily McCully. F. Watts, 1972.
Hughes, Thomas. *Tom Brown's School Days,* illustrated by S. Van Abbe. Dutton (1885).
Irving, Washington. *Rip Van Winkle and The Legend of Sleepy Hollow,* illustrated by David Levine. Macmillan (*The Sketch Book,* 1819).
Jackson, Jesse. *Call Me Charley,* illustrated by Doris Spiegel. Harper & Row, 1945.
Jacobs, Joseph. *Celtic Folk and Fairy Tales,* illustrated by John D. Batten. Putnam, 1905 (1893).
————. *English Fairy Tales,* 3rd rev. ed., illustrated by John D. Batten. Putnam (1892).
————. *Indian Folk and Fairy Tales,* illustrated by John D. Batten. Putnam, 1925 (1892).
James, Will. *Smoky, the Cowhorse.* Scribner, 1926.
Keats, Ezra Jack. *The Snowy Day.* Viking, 1962.
Keene, Carolyn, pseud. The *Nancy Drew* Series. Grosset & Dunlap.
Keeping, Charles. *Joseph's Yard.* F. Watts, 1969.
————. *Through the Window.* F. Watts, 1970.
Kingsley, Charles. *The Water-Babies,* illustrated by Harold Jones. F. Watts, 1961 (1863).
Kipling, Rudyard. *The Jungle Books,* illustrated by Robert Shore. Macmillan, 1964 (1894–1895).
————. *Just So Stories,* illustrated by Etienne Delessert. Doubleday, 1972 (1902).
Klein, Norma. *Mom, The Wolf Man and Me.* Pantheon, 1972.
Konigsburg, E. L. (*George*). Atheneum, 1970.
Lagerlöff, Selma. *The Wonderful Adventures of Nils,* translated by Richard E. Oldenburg, photos by Hans Malmberg. Doubleday, 1968 (1907).
Lang, Andrew. *The Blue Fairy Book,* illustrated by Reisie Lonette. New York: Random House, 1959 (1889).
Larrick, Nancy, ed. *I Heard a Scream in the Street: Poems by Young People in the City.* M. Evans, 1970.

Lear, Edward. *Edward Lear's Nonsense Books.* Grosset & Dunlap, 1967 (*More Nonsense,* 1872).

Le Guin, Ursula K. *The Farthest Shore,* illustrated by Gail Garraty. Atheneum, 1972.

——. *The Tombs of Atuan,* illustrated by Gail Garraty. Atheneum, 1971.

——. *A Wizard of Earthsea,* illustrated by Ruth Robbins. Parnassus, 1968.

Lewis, Richard, ed. *Miracles.* Simon & Schuster, 1964.

Lindgren, Astrid. *Pippi Longstocking,* illustrated by Louis Glanzman. Viking, 1950.

Lofting, Hugh. *The Story of Doctor Dolittle.* Lippincott, 1920.

London, Jack. *The Call of the Wild,* illustrated by Charles Pickard. Dutton, 1968 (1903).

McCloskey, Robert. *Homer Price.* Viking, 1943.

McDermott, Gerald. *Anansi the Spider.* Holt, Rinehart and Winston, 1972.

——. *Arrow to the Sun,* a Pueblo Indian tale. Viking, 1974.

MacDonald, George. *At the Back of the North Wind,* illustrated by E. H. Shepard. Dutton (1871).

Maxwell, Gavin. *Ring of Bright Water.* Dutton, 1961.

Merriam, Eve. *The Inner-city Mother Goose,* photos by Lawrence Ratzkin. Simon & Schuster, 1969.

Miles, Miska. *Mississippi Possum,* illustrated by John Schoenherr. Little, Brown, 1965.

Milne, A. A. *Winnie the Pooh,* illustrated by Ernest H. Shepard. Dutton, 1926.

Mitchell, Lucy Sprague. *Here and Now Story Book,* edited by Van Loon, *et al.* Dutton, 1948 (1921).

Mohr, Nicholasa. *Nilda.* Harper & Row, 1973.

Monjo, F. N. *Poor Richard in France,* illustrated by Brinton Turkle. Holt, Rinehart and Winston, 1973.

Moore, Clement C. *A Visit from St. Nicholas,* facsimile ed., illustrated by T. C. Boyd. Simon & Schuster, 1971 (1822).

Mure, Eleanor. *The Story of the Three Bears.* Walck, 1967 (1831).

Nesbit, Edith. *The Story of the Treasure Seekers.* Penguin.

Ness, Evaline. *Amelia Mixed the Mustard and Other Poems,* selected and illustrated by Evaline Ness. Scribner's, 1975.

Nicholson, William. *Clever Bill.* Farrar, Straus, 1972 (1926).

North, Sterling. *Rascal: A Memoir of a Better Era,* illustrated by John Schoenherr. Dutton, 1963.

Perkins, Lucy Fitch. *The Twins* Series. Walker, 1968, 1969 (1911).

Perrault, Charles. *Perrault's Classic French Fairy Tales,* illustrated by Janusz Grabianski. Hawthorn, 1967 (*Contes de ma Mere L'Oye,* 1697).

——. *Puss in Boots,* illustrated by Marcia Brown. Scribner, 1952.

Perry, John. *Our Polluted World: Can Man Survive?* F. Watts, 1972.

Potter, Beatrix. *The Tale of Benjamin Bunny.* Warne, 1904.

——. *The Tale of Jemima Puddleduck.* Warne, 1908.

——. *The Tale of Peter Rabbit.* Warne, 1902.

Pyle, Howard. *Pepper and Salt: Or, Seasoning for Young Folk.* Harper & Row, 1886.

——. *The Wonder Clock.* Harper & Row, 1888.

Rand, Ann, and Paul Rand. *I Know a Lot of Things,* illustrated by Paul Rand. Harcourt Brace Jovanovich, 1956.

Reed, W. Maxwell. *The Earth for Sam,* rev. ed. Harcourt Brace Jovanovich, 1960.

Richter, Hans Peter. *Friedrich,* translated by Edite Kroll. Holt, Rinehart and Winston, 1970.

Rossetti, Christina. *Sing-Song,* illustrated by Marguerite Davis. Macmillan, 1952 (1872).

Ruskin, John. *The King of the Golden River.* World Publishing, 1946 (1851).

Schaefer, Charles E., and Kathleen C. Mellor. *Young Voices.* Macmillan, 1971.

Sendak, Maurice. *In the Night Kitchen.* Harper & Row, 1970.

——. *The Nutshell Library.* Harper & Row, 1962.

——. *Where the Wild Things Are.* Harper & Row, 1963.

Seton, Ernest Thompson. *Wild Animals I Have Known.* Grosset & Dunlap, 1966 (1898).

Sewell, Anna. *Black Beauty.* World Publishing, 1972 (1877).

Shotwell, Louisa R. *Roosevelt Grady,* illustrated by Peter Burchard. World Publishing, 1963.

Sidney, Margaret, pseud. (Harriet Lathrop). *Five Little Peppers,* illustrated by Anna Magagna. Macmillan, 1962 (1880).

Slobodkina, Esphyr. *Caps for Sale.* W. R. Scott, 1947.

Smith, E. Brooks, and Robert Meredith. *The Coming of the Pilgrims,* illustrated by Leonard Everett Fisher. Little, Brown 1964.

———. *Pilgrim Courage,* illustrated by Leonard Everett Fisher. Little, Brown 1962.

Spyri, Johanna. *Heidi,* illustrated by Greta Elgaard. Macmillan, 1962 (1884).

Steptoe, John. *My Special Best Words.* Viking, 1974.

———. *Stevie.* Harper & Row, 1969.

Sterling, Dorothy. *Mary Jane,* illustrated by Ernest Crichlow. Doubleday, 1959.

Stevenson, Robert Louis. *A Child's Garden of Verses,* illustrated by Brian Wildsmith. F. Watts, 1966 (*Penny Whistles,* 1885).

———. *Treasure Island,* illustrated by N. C. Wyeth. Scribner, 1911 (1883).

Swift, Jonathan. *Gulliver's Travels,* illustrated by Arthur Rackham. Dutton, 1952 (1726).

Tappan, Eva M. *When Knights Were Bold.* Houghton Mifflin, 1911.

Terhune, Albert P. *Lad: A Dog,* illustrated by Sam Savitt. Dutton, 1959 (1919).

True Book of . . . Series. Children's Press.

Twain, Mark, pseud. (Samuel Clemens). *The Adventures of Huckleberry Finn.* Harper, 1884.

———. *The Adventures of Tom Sawyer.* Harper, 1876.

Udry, Janice May. *Let's Be Enemies,* illustrated by Maurice Sendak. Harper & Row, 1961.

Van Loon, Hendrik W. *The Story of Mankind,* rev. ed. Liveright, 1972 (1921).

Verne, Jules. *Around the World in Eighty Days,* illustrated by W. F. Phillips. Dutton, 1968 (1872).

———. *Twenty Thousand Leagues under the Sea,* illustrated by Charles Molina. Macmillan, 1962 (1870).

Ward, Lynd. *The Biggest Bear.* Houghton Mifflin, 1952.

Weik, Mary Hays. *The Jazz Man,* illustrated by Ann Grifalconi. Atheneum, 1966.

White, E. B. *Charlotte's Web,* illustrated by Garth Williams. Harper & Row, 1952.

———. *Stuart Little,* illustrated by Garth Williams. Harper & Row, 1945.

Wilder, Laura Ingalls. *Little House in the Big Woods,* illustrated by Garth Williams. Harper & Row, 1953 (1932).

Wildsmith, Brian. *Brian Wildsmith's Puzzles.* F. Watts, 1971.

Women in America Series. Crowell.

Wyss, Johann. *Swiss Family Robinson,* illustrated by Lynd Ward. Grosset & Dunlap, 1949 (1814).

Zei, Alki. *Petro's War,* translated from the Greek by Edward Fenton. Dutton, 1972.

———. *Wildcat under Glass,* translated from the Greek by Edward Fenton. Holt, Rinehart and Winston, 1968.

PART **2** Knowing Children's Literature

3 Picture Books

Annie, aged 2½, returned home from a morning visit with her 4-year-old play-mate. While waiting for her lunch, Ann looked thoughtfully at her mother and said, "Do you know, Robin can't read." There was a mixture of pity and amazement in her voice, for Annie could "read." True, she could not identify the printed words, but she could read pictures with understanding. In fact, her favorite entertainment was "reading" books or magazines by herself, with her mother, or any other willing interpreter of the printed page. Annie had already discovered the joys and pleasure that can be derived from reading. She was amazed and a little sad to learn that all children actually did not share her favorite pastime.

First Experiences with Books

Children cannot be introduced to books too soon. At age 2½, Annie had already entered the world of literature. To know exactly why she enjoyed books and her friend Robin did not, would require an intimate knowledge of their family backgrounds. We know that Annie came from a home in which books were a part of her natural environment. She saw her mother, father, and sister reading. She frequently went to the library with them. After they had selected their books, Annie was taken to the children's room for her books. The bedtime story was a ritual for her. But enjoyment of books was not limited to just this time; rainy days meant reading days; the quiet and lonely time right after her daddy had gone to work and her sister had gone to school, a few moments before her naptime, at dusk when the family was waiting dinner for father, these were all times when Annie could say, "Read to me, please."

Annie is learning to love books, as she has many opportunities to snuggle up close to her mother and father for a storytime. She is also increasing her vocabulary as she points to pictures and names them, or hears new words used in the context of a story. The language development of children of this age is phenomenal; preoccupation with words and the sounds of words is characteristic of the very young child. Books help to fulfill this insatiable desire to hear and learn new words. Hearing writing of good quality read aloud helps the child to develop his full language potential.

The young child who has the opportunity to hear and enjoy many stories is also getting ready to learn how to read. The process of learning to read should hold no terror for Annie—only the opportunity to become independent in a skill that she knows gives pleasure. Her experiential background has been widened as a result of exposure to many books. Research has shown that the nature and extent of children's past experiences influence their progress in learning to read. The meaning and comprehension of the printed page depends upon the meaning and understanding that the reader brings to that page. Annie's background of experience is rich and not limited to books alone. However, her enjoyment and appreciation of the world of literature will facilitate the transition from *hearing* stories to *reading* stories independently.

Children who have not had such a fortunate literary upbringing as Annie has, should have the opportunity to hear many stories read aloud during their pre-school and primary years. By listening to records and seeing filmstrips, they may have the chance to hear or see their favorite story over and over again; they may experience the same joy that Annie did when she was able to say "read it again."

LAP BOOKS

The young child's first experience with a book is usually associated with being held in the lap

A whole family enjoys a popular edition of Mother Goose. Photographed by Francis Haar, Honolulu, Hawaii.

The young child's first experience with a book is usually associated with being held in the lap of a loving adult.

Illustration by Maurice Sendak from *Little Bear* by Else Holmlund Minarik. Pictures Copyright © 1957 by Maurice Sendak. Reprinted by permission of Harper & Row, Publishers, Inc.

of a loving adult. These "lap books" might be the nonsense of Mother Goose, a simple baby's book, or even a family magazine in which toddlers find pictures of "mother," "daddy," "sister," or themselves. The child enjoys the love and attention that he receives at this time, and he delights in the game of pointing out familiar objects. Recognizing this need of the young child to identify and name objects, publishers have produced simple "first books." These are usually constructed with heavy, durable pages and portray such articles as favorite toys, clothing, and animals. "First books" may have an accompanying text, but there is little or no continuity of plot to these stories. The fun is in naming the pictures. The illustrations should be simple, uncluttered, and easily identifiable, with usually only one object, or a group of two or three on a page. *Baby's First Book*, illustrated by Garth Williams, is an excellent example of this type of book. Phoebe and Tris Dunn have used clear colored photographs to illustrate their book of *Things*— things to do, things to hold, things to taste, and things to wonder about. The simple text and pictures show young children blowing bubble gum, drinking orange juice, making a snowball, or holding a starfish for the first time.

Two books by Peter Spier invite the identification of many animals and their sounds. *Gobble Growl Grunt* presents accurate detailed pictures of hundreds of animals, while the text only includes their proper identification and a phonetic approximation of the sounds they make. The front endpaper shows a small horrified mouse facing a horde of bellowing animals; the last endpaper portrays the little mouse squeaking, while the rest of the animals listen in silence. The rrringgg of a classroom bell . . . the grunch-grunch of boots on new snow, the sounds made by everything from a tugboat to a tuba are presented in *Crash! Bang! Boom!* Both of these books by Spier invite the noisy participation of preschoolers, much to their delight.

Some books have a kind of "built-in participation" as part of their design. These books may serve well as the transition between toys and real books. One such book by Kunhardt, *Pat the Bunny,* has been a best seller for the very young child for many years. In this little book the child is invited to use senses other than sight and sound. A "pattable" bunny made of flannel is on one page; flowers that really smell on another; and daddy's unshaven face, represented by sandpaper roughness, is on still another. Young children literally wear out this "tactile" book. Sophisticated cutout books by Bruno Munari also have immediate appeal for young children. In *Who's There? Open the Door!* the first double-page spread shows Lucy, the giraffe, with a crate. Open the crate (which is a page) and there is Peggy, the zebra with a trunk (a smaller page), and so the story continues. One 3-year-old was first introduced to this book by knocking at the cover and repeating the title of *Who's There? Open the Door!*. It became a book that he requested again and again, along with the established ritual of knocking on the cover.

The Birthday Present, also by Munari, has a similar format. A truck driver is taking a birthday present home to his 3-year-old son. When the trucker is ten miles from home, his truck breaks down, and the various means of transportation by which he reaches home are presented on smaller and smaller-sized pages. Another uniquely designed book by Munari is *The Circus in the Mist,* which has graphic surprises on every page. All of Munari's books are well-designed and well-constructed. Sturdy construction is an essential requirement for books for the very young child. Simplicity of format and clear, recognizable pictures are equally important.

First experiences with books should be enjoyable ones. If participation is not built into the book, the reader can provide some by using imaginative questions. For example, when sharing Slobodkina's *Caps for Sale,* the child might be told: "Find the monkey—not the one in the red hat, not the one in the blue hat, but the one in the green hat!" Such participation will help children develop visual discrimination, and, more importantly, it will make storytime fun.

MOTHER GOOSE

For many children, Mother Goose is their first introduction to the world of literature. Even a 1-year-old child will respond with delight to the language games of "Pat-a-Cake! Pat-a-Cake!" or "This Little Pig Went to Market" or "Ride a Cock Horse." Many of the Mother Goose rhymes and jingles continue to be favorites among the 4s and 5s. What is the attraction of Mother Goose that makes her so appealing to these young children? What accounts for her survival through these many years? Much of the language in these rhymes is obscure; for example, no modern-day child has any understanding of curds and whey, yet he delights in Little Miss Muffet. Nothing in current literature has replaced the venerable Mother Goose for the nursery-school age.

Appeals of Mother Goose

LANGUAGE PATTERNS

Much of the appeal of Mother Goose lies in the musical quality of the varied language patterns, the rhythm and rhyme of the verses, the alliteration of such lines as: "Wee Willie Winkie runs through the town" or "Deedle, deedle, dumpling, my son John." Children love the sound of the words, for they are experimenting with language in this period of their lives. The greatest growth in language development is achieved between the ages of 2 and 6 years. The child learns new words every day; he likes to try them out, to chant them in his play. Mother

Goose rhymes help the young child satisfy his preoccupation with language patterns and stimulate further language development.

PARTICIPATION

Mother Goose rhymes offer young children many opportunities for active participation and response. Most of the verses are short and easily memorized; they can be chanted in unison, or children may join in the refrains. Some of the rhymes—such as "Pease Porridge Hot," "London Bridge," or "Ring a Ring o'Roses"—are games or involve direct action from the child. Other verses include counting rhymes—as in "1, 2, buckle my shoe/3, 4, shut the door." Slightly older children enjoy answering the riddles in some of the Mother Goose verses, or attempting to say their favorite tongue twisters. Every child likes to fool someone with the well-known riddle: "As I was going to St. Ives, I met a man with seven wives." And they never fail to delight in successful recitation of the entire verse of "Peter Piper picked a peck of pickled peppers."

NARRATIVE QUALITY

Another attraction of many of the Mother Goose rhymes is their narrative quality; they tell a good story. In just six lines "Little Miss Muffet" proves to be an exciting tale with action, a climax, and a satisfying conclusion. This is also true of "Simple Simon," "Sing a Song of Sixpence," "The Old Woman in the Shoe," and "Three Blind Mice." These stories in Mother Goose are characterized by their quick action. They are not moralistic, but justice does prevail, as in the ending of "The Queen of Hearts." Pre-school and kindergarten children enjoy pantomiming or dramatizing these well-known verse stories.

CHARACTERS

Many of the characters in Mother Goose have interesting, likeable personalities: Old King Cole *is* a merry old soul; Old Mother Hubbard not only tried to find her poor dog a bone but she ran all over town at his special bidding; and although Tommy Lynn put the pussy in the well, Johnny Stout pulled her out! "The Crooked Man" is a grotesque character, but he has a crooked smile; and one can't help liking poor old "Simple Simon." Unpleasant character traits are suggested by "Crosspatch," "Tom, Tom, the Piper's Son," and "Lazy Elsie Marley."

CONTENT

The content of the verses reflects the interests of young children. Many favorites are rhymes about animals—such as "The Three Little Kittens," "The Cat and the Fiddle," and "The Mouse Who Ran Up the Clock." While many of the animals are personified, others are not. For example, the kitten in "I Love Little Pussy" is very real.

Some of the verses are about simple everyday experiences, and include such incidents as "Lucy Locket" losing her purse, "The Three Little Kittens" losing their mittens, and "Little Bo Peep" who lost her sheep. Children's pranks are enacted in "Ding, Dong, Bell!" and "Georgie Porgie." Everyday misfortunes are included in "Jack and Jill" and "Humpty Dumpty." "Peter, Peter, Pumpkin-Eater" had a housing problem, as did the "Old Woman in the Shoe." There are many verses about seasons and the weather, a concern of both young and old. The pleading request of one boy for "Rain, Rain, Go Away" reflects the universal feelings of childhood.

HUMOR

A major appeal of Mother Goose is the varied humor. There is the jolly good fun of a ridiculous situation in:

One misty, moisty morning
When cloudy was the weather,
I chanced to meet an old man
Clothed all in leather;
He began to compliment
And I began to grin-
"How do you do" and "How do you do"
And "How do you do" again!

Two 7-year-olds interpreted this verse in action by pretending to pass each other; as one moved to the left, the other moved in the same direction. Their movements were perfect for this amusing and familiar situation.

The young child's rather primitive sense of humor, which delights in other persons' misfortune, is satisfied by the verses about "Jack and Jill" and "Dr. Foster":

Doctor Foster went to Gloucester
In a shower of rain;
He stepped in a puddle up to his middle
And never went there again.

When this kind of humor is exaggerated, it is apt to become sadistic. Children's humor can be cruel, however, and they are quite insensitive to the dire punishment of the "old man/Who would not say his prayers/I took him by the left leg/And threw him down the stairs." For children, such action is fun and thoroughly relished.

Finally, the pure nonsense in Mother Goose tickles children's funny bones. Chukovsky,[1] a Russian poet, reminds us that there is sense in nonsense; a child has to know reality to appreciate the juxtaposition of the strawberries and the herrings in this verse:

The man in the wilderness asked me
How many strawberries grew in the sea.
I answered him as I thought good,
As many as red herrings grew in the wood.

Different Editions of Mother Goose

Today's children are fortunate in being able to choose among many beautifully illustrated Mother Goose editions. There is no *one* best Mother Goose book, for this is a matter for individual preference. The children in every family deserve at least one of the better editions, however. Pre-school and primary teachers will also want to have one that can be shared with small groups of children who may not have been fortunate enough to have ever seen a really beautiful Mother Goose.

ENGLISH EDITIONS

Three English editions of Mother Goose have been treasured classics for many generations. While they are, perhaps, not the most appropriate selections for the modern American child, they still appeal to children. They are important for the student of children's literature, for they are the forerunners of many of our present editions. *Mother Goose, or The Old Nursery Rhymes,* illustrated by Kate Greenaway, is tiny in format, with quaint, precise, old-fashioned pictures. Greenaway's children have a quiet decorum that is in keeping with their nineteenth-century finery. However, there is action in these tiny pictures and a feeling for the English rural countryside and villages.

Quite different in effect is the edition by

Arthur Rackham entitled *Mother Goose, Old Nursery Rhymes.* Rackham uses three different types of illustrations for his verses—pen-and-ink sketches, silhouettes, and colored pictures. The latter are painted in the typical Rackham fashion, with eerie trees and weird little men peering from under their mushroom hats.

Leslie Brooke's *Ring O'Roses* presents a very different impression from that of the Rackham edition. Brooke's pictures are delightfully humorous and gay. The pigs in "This Little Pig Went to Market" are happy and complacent, except for the poor dejected fellow who had no roast beef.

Modern English editions of Mother Goose are equally outstanding. *Lavender's Blue* was compiled by Kathleen Lines and illustrated by Harold Jones. The colored pictures are in muted tones of blue, green, and brown and are unmistakably English in setting, costume, and mood. Raymond Briggs has produced a comprehensive *The Mother Goose Treasury* which includes over 400 rhymes and more than twice as many illustrations. Almost all of the verses are from the authentic Opie collection and include most of the well-loved rhymes, plus some that are less well known to Americans. The book appears crammed with many vivid little scenes, objects, and comic people. Each rhyme has its own illustrations, and in some instances, each verse or line has an accompanying picture. This gives a feeling of clutter, but it provides much for the child to look at and enjoy.

Probably the most striking and unusual Mother Goose edition is *Brian Wildsmith's Mother Goose.* Painted in brilliant watercolors, these pictures capture the gaiety of Mother Goose for twentieth-century children. The typical Wildsmith trademark is seen in the harlequin designs on the clothing of his characters. Another unusual characteristic of Wildsmith's style is the frequency with which he shows just the backs of people. By illustrating the back of "Tom, Tom, the Piper's Son" and that of the "Ten O'clock Scholar," Wildsmith includes the reader as a witness to the scene. The careful planning of this book is reflected in the combination of rhymes that are presented on facing pages. For example, "Little Boy Blue" is shown opposite "Diddle, Diddle, Dumpling"; both boys are sleeping, one in the haystack and the other in his bed. While

---

[1] Kornei Chukovsky, *From Two to Five,* translated by Miriam Morton (Berkeley, Calif.: University of California Press, 1963), p. 95.

Doctor Foster nonchalantly walks toward a puddle and the reader, the crooked man walks away with his back to the viewer. A contrast of rich and poor is seen in the placement on facing pages of the rhymes of "Ride a cock horse to Banbury Cross/To see a fine lady upon a white horse," and "Hark, hark, the dogs do bark/The beggars have come to town." Mindful of the medieval origin of some of the Mother Goose rhymes, Wildsmith has used this period as the setting for many of the verses.

AMERICAN EDITIONS

Counterparts of the English editions may be seen in some of the American ones. The good humor that is so characteristic of Brooke is equally characteristic of Rojankovsky's illustrations in *The Tall Book of Mother Goose.* His pictures are bright and happy; his children are natural looking, sometimes homely and disheveled. Rojankovsky is particularly skilled in capturing children's expressions; his "Little Miss Muffet" is terrified; "Lucy Locket" is thoughtful and pensive; "Jack Horner" is a picture of greedy innocence. Some of the pictures are moralistic; for example, little Johnny Green, who was responsible for pushing the pussy in the well, is shown smoking. A large "X" is drawn through his face in order to leave no doubt in the reader's mind as to the kind of boy who would do such a thing. Rojankovsky has portrayed his Humpty Dumpty as Hitler. Since one theory maintains that the first nursery rhymes were really political satire, this portrayal seems quite appropriate, particularly in 1942 when this edition was first published.

The Real Mother Goose by Blanche Fisher Wright has long been an established favorite in American nurseries. The large traditional pictures remind one of Brooke's work, but these lack his delightful humor. First published in 1916, the golden anniversary edition was printed in 1965. Although the flat pictures are old-fashioned in appearance, the book continues to be a favorite as it is passed down from one generation to another.

The *Mother Goose* by Tasha Tudor is reminiscent of the work of Kate Greenaway. Her soft pastel pictures are quaint and charming; her characters, loveable. The costumes of the characters represent many periods; American colonial, pioneer, Kate Greenaway, and Elizabethan. The settings of interiors are as authentic as the costumes. Rural scenes portray the changing seasons delightfully. Miniatures in flowered frames on the endpapers and title page add to the old-fashioned feeling of this book.

One of the most beautiful editions of Mother Goose is *The Book of Nursery and Mother Goose Rhymes* by Marguerite de Angeli. This is a large book containing nearly 250 pictures, some of which are full-page illustrations painted in soft watercolors. No one could ever forget the lovely picture that illustrates the fine lady on her beautiful horse. The rich detail of the English countryside is similar to *Lavender's Blue* and suggests that the illustrator was very aware of the origin of Mother Goose. De Angeli's children and babies are beautifully portrayed, and show her love and knowledge of her own children and grandchildren.

Carefully designed wood engravings in six colors illustrate Philip Reed's *Mother Goose and Nursery Rhymes.* His rustic human characters and spirited animals provide humor and charm. The total format of this book represents superb bookmaking. The fine paper and well-designed use of space give a feeling of quality and richness. This selection of Mother Goose rhymes includes several that are less well known than the usual verses—for example, the English "Guy Fawkes Day."

Two books of Mother Goose in other languages—*Mother Goose in French* and *Mother Goose in Spanish*—have been illustrated by Barbara Cooney. Both of these books reflect the research and authenticity of setting that is characteristic of Cooney's work. The Gallic flavor of a small French town is shown in every scene of her *Mother Goose in French,* while the setting of several locales in Spain serves beautifully for her *Mother Goose in Spanish.*

A variant of Mother Goose is *Chinese Mother Goose Rhymes* selected by Robert Wyndham. This book includes both Chinese and English texts for poems and riddles that have been traditionally told to Chinese children. The intricate illustrations by Young faithfully reproduce the ancient art of paper cutting. The book is designed to be read vertically like a scroll, and the Chinese letters flow lengthwise down the pages. The total format of this book is one of beautiful design—a Chinese feast for the eyes of all young children.

The Rooster Crows by the Petershams has sometimes been called an American Mother Goose, for it includes many such well-known American rhymes and jingles as "A bear went over the mountain" and "How much wood would a woodchuck chuck . . ." Another bit of Americana is found in the highly original *Father Fox's Pennyrhymes* written by Clyde Watson and illustrated by her sister, Wendy Watson. These nonsense rhymes and jingles have the lilt and rhythm of traditional rhymes of folklore. Some are as gay as "Knickerbocker Knockabout/Sausages & Sauerkraut"; while others are as sad as Mrs. Fox's lament, "The rain falls down/The wind blows up:/I've spent all the pennies/In my old tin cup."[2] The little watercolor-and-ink illustrations detail the antics of Father Fox and his friends and relatives in old-fashioned pictures. Some of these are done in sequences with balloon blurbs, as with comic strips. The pictures are surely as much fun as the highly amusing rhymes.

A delightful nursery rhyme book is N. M. Bodecker's *It's Raining Said John Twaining*. Recalling his childhood in Denmark, Bodecker, a poet and artist, translated and adapted the rhymes into English so he could share them with his three sons. His pictures are as droll and humorous as some of the rhymes, particularly the title verse.

SINGLE VERSE OR LIMITED VERSE EDITIONS

A recent publishing trend has been the production of picture books portraying only one Mother Goose rhyme or a limited number of rhymes around a single theme. Nonny Hogrogian's *One I Love, Two I Love and Other Loving Mother Goose Rhymes* is an example of the small (only 27 verses) theme collection. Droll illustrations portray such loving creatures as "Willy, Willy Wilkin who kissed the maids a-milking," Georgie Porgie, and Peter Pumpkin Eater. Each page has a pastel border, which helps to create the total effect of a somewhat shy valentine.

[2]From *Father Fox's Pennyrhymes*. Copyright © 1971 by Clyde Watson, with permission of Thomas Y. Crowell Company, Inc., publisher.

Mother Fox laments the rain and her penniless cup in this delightful book of nursery rhymes.

From *Father Fox's Pennyrhymes* by Clyde Watson. Illustrations Copyright © 1971 by Wendy Watson, with permission of Thomas Y. Crowell Company, Inc., publisher.

In a succession of carefully selected nursery rhymes, Spier tells the story of a farmer's day in New Castle, Delaware, during the early nineteenth century. Spier's detailed, colorful pictures begin before dawn as Mr. Marley (Lazy Elsie is asleep in the log farmhouse) prepares to go to market. A cohesive story is told with many nursery rhymes until the Marleys return to the farm on "silver Saturday" for "the morn's the resting day." The scenes of the Market Place show the Town Hall and colonial brick homes facing the Delaware River. Authentic interiors of the church, the blacksmith's, and the sheep barn help children visualize earlier times in U.S. history. *To Market, to Market* is far more than just another Mother Goose book; it is American history combined with old-fashioned fun!

The whole history of London Bridge is detailed in a similar fashion by Spier in his beautiful book, *London Bridge Is Falling Down*. Notes on the back pages provide a history of London Bridge and the music for the well-known song. In sharp contrast to the historical details of this book is Ed Emberley's rendition of the same verse and song. The stylized pictures of pen and ink and pastel colors are as formal and understated as the verse's quiet announcement to the "fair lady" of the impending collapse of the bridge!

Paul Galdone has illustrated several single-verse editions, including *The Old Woman and Her Pig, The House that Jack Built, Old Mother Hubbard and Her Dog, Tom, Tom, the Piper's Son,* and *The History of Simple Simon.* These narrative verses have action and humor and lend themselves well to individual presentations. Galdone's colorful pictures are large, clear, and especially good for sharing with young children. It is fun to compare Galdone's *Old Mother Hubbard* with the sophisticated humor of the *Old Mother Hubbard* done by Evaline Ness. In this very modern version the dog is a huge English sheep dog that has a harassed Mother Hubbard running all over town to buy him delicacies while he romps about the house, reads the funny papers, and smokes a pipe! In sharing this book, an adult might ask children to say what picture usually comes to their minds when they think of Old Mother Hubbard. Then they may compare their visual images with the full-page color painting that shows Mother Hubbard's pampered pet.

A modern interpretation of Mother Hubbard and her pampered dog.

From *Old Mother Hubbard and Her Dog* by Evaline Ness. Copyright © 1972 by Evaline Ness. Reproduced by permission of Holt, Rinehart and Winston, Inc.

Janina Domanska has used dramatically stylized pen, ink, and watercolor pictures to illustrate her single editions of *If All the Seas Were One Sea* and *I Saw a Ship A-Sailing.* Pattern on top of pattern gives a very modern, clean-looking character to the little ship that sails off with its duck captain and its four-and-twenty sailors, all of whom were white mice.

Susan Jeffers' *Three Jovial Huntsmen* was a Caldecott Honor Book. It is the story of the three men who decided to go hunting, but who couldn't find an animal. Throughout their search, watchful animals are seen hidden in the woods. Children always enjoy finding hidden figures in a picture, and this story abounds with them. The softly muted colors of the forest provide perfect hiding places. This is a beautiful book, which contrasts the stupidity of the hunters with the quiet harmony of nature.

A handsome edition of *The House that Jack Built* has been presented in two languages with bold woodcuts by Antonio Frasconi. While this verse does not regularly appear in Mother Goose books, it is a well-known traditional nursery rhyme. Frasconi's four-color woodcuts have a strength and a rusticity appropriate for this old rhyme.

Maurice Sendak chose to illustrate two less well-known rhymes in *Hector Protector and As I Went Over the Water.* His illustrations greatly expand the original text of four lines into a story of their own. Sendak has told the tale of Hector, a small rebellious boy who hates green *and* the queen, in twenty-four pictures! In the second rhyme a little boy conquers a boat-swallowing dragon with the greatest of aplomb.

Barbara Cooney has illustrated in minute detail *The Courtship, Merry Marriage, and Feast of Cock Robin and Jenny Wren, to which is added the Doleful Death of Cock Robin.* For her wedding, Jenny Wren wears a white dress with train, pearls, and a hat with a beautiful plume. Later, in a widow's veil, she stands quite apart from the other mourners at Cock Robin's grave. Cooney has captured both the gaiety of the wedding and the solemnity of the funeral in this distinguished little book.

EVALUATING MOTHER GOOSE BOOKS

With so many editions of Mother Goose, what factors should be considered when evaluating them? The following points may be useful in studying various editions.

Coverage: How many verses are included? Are they well-known rhymes or are there some fresh and unusual ones?

Illustrations: What medium has been used? What colors? Are the illustrations realistic, stylized, or varied? Are the illustrations consistent with the text? Do they elaborate the text? What is the mood of the illustrations (humorous, sedate, high-spirited)?

Period: Is the setting modern or in the past? What period do the costumes, houses, furnishings, and activities represent?

Setting: What background is presented—rural or urban? Does the book take place in any particular country?

Characters: Do the characters portray multiethnic types or only Caucasians? Do the characters have distinct personalities? Are adults and children portrayed? How are animals presented—as humans or realistically?

Arrangement: Is there a thematic arrangement of the verses? Is there a feeling of unity to the whole book, rather than just separate verses?

Format: What is the quality of the paper and the binding? Is the title page well designed? Is there an index or table of contents? Is there harmony between endpapers, cover, and jacket? Are pictures and verses well spaced or crowded?

No matter what edition is selected, children should be exposed to the rhythm and rhyme of Mother Goose. It is part of their literary heritage and may serve as their first introduction to the realm of literature.

ABC, COUNTING, AND CONCEPT BOOKS

ABC Books

In colonial days a child began his reading instruction by memorizing his "Great A's." Today we know that it is not necessary for the beginning reader to recite the entire alphabet before learning to read. He does not "call letters" in order to read, but reads whole words in a context that is highly meaningful to him. Nevertheless, children do need to know the names of the letters as they begin to read and write, and parents and teachers feel good about the child "who knows his ABC's."

ABC books are frequently used as a kind of organizing structure by which adults present an array of objects or animals for the young child to identify and talk about. If, in the process of identifying such alliterative phrases as the bumbling bear or the buzzing bee, the child becomes aware of the sound of the letter "B," well, fine and good! In the meantime, he has had lots of fun extending his vocabulary and looking at beautiful and interesting illustrations.

Certain factors need to be considered in selecting alphabet books, however. Only one or two objects should be presented on a page and these should be easily identifiable and meaningful for the age level of the child for whom the book was planned. It is best to avoid portraying those objects that might have several correct names. For example, if a rabbit is presented for "R," the very young child might refer to it as a "bunny." Similarly, the more common sounds of the letter should be represented, rather than blends or silent letters. To present a "gnu" for a "G" is most confusing. Since text is necessarily limited, the pictures usually "carry" the story. For this reason they should be both clear and consistent with the text, reflecting and creating the mood of the book.

One of the earliest ABC books, by Edward Lear, was filled with nonsense rhymes for each letter. A new edition of this book has been reproduced in Lear's own handwriting under the title *ABC*. Two almost classic alphabet books are C. B. Falls' *An ABC Book*, with its simple illustrations of animals from the zoo and farmyard, and Fritz Eichenberg's *Ape in a Cape*, a humorous alphabet book with rhyming captions such as "Goat in a Boat" and "Fox in a Box." Another, earlier but beautifully designed alphabet book, is Wanda Gág's *The ABC Bunny*. Here, a little rabbit provides the continuity and slight story line for each letter. The illustrations are woodcuts and the large capital letters stand out in scarlet color reminiscent of children's alphabet blocks.

Vivid, full-color photographs of single objects illustrate *ABC An Alphabet Book* by Matthiesen. Uncluttered, clear photographs of common objects make this a book for the youngest child. A touch of whimsy in the simple, direct text amuses children; for example, "It is not good to drop an egg unless you like to mop the floor."[3]

Many handsome alphabet books have come to us from artists abroad. The current trend of including the illustrator's name in the title can be noticed in these books: *Bruno Munari's ABC*, *Brian Wildsmith's ABC*, *Celestino Piatti's Animal ABC*, *John Burningham's ABC*, and *Helen Oxenbury's ABC of Things*. Munari, an Italian artist, has created a book that is notable for its simple but beautiful design. Objects are clearly presented, with a fly adding a touch of humor at intervals throughout the text. As usual, *Brian Wildsmith's ABC* book is a riot of attractive color. Most of the letters are represented by a painting of a single animal or bird, although a queen still stands for "Q" and a violin, windmill, and xylophone are given their allotted places. Background pages of solid colors provide stunning contrasts for each subject. Celestino Piatti is a Swiss artist and graphic designer. His ABC book shows unusual animals in striking, bold colors. Using a heavy black outline, his artwork resembles that of the French painter, Georges Rouault. However, the book lacks unity because the four-line verses fail to interpret the action in the pictures.

John Burningham has given youngsters a good solid straight-forward ABC book. The letter "T" is represented by a determined little man on his very fine tractor; "V" is an erupting volcano; and "Y" is a seaworthy yacht. Helen Oxenbury's *ABC of Things* is richly illustrated with a variety of objects that provide a small vignette for each letter. For example, the letter "H" is represented by a very funny picture of a hare and a hippopotamus lying in bed in the hospital. Oxenbury's illustrations frequently present an interesting perspective, such as in the bird's-eye picture of the tops of umbrellas with only feet sticking out below.

A well-known American artist, Leonard Baskin, has illustrated a most sophisticated alphabet book for his son and titled it simply *Hosie's Alphabet*. This was an Honor Book for the Caldecott Award in 1972; one of the few alphabet books to have received this distinction. Young children

will love the brilliant pictures and the sound of the words, even though they may have difficulty in comprehending some of them, such as a "quintessential quail" or a "quasi kiwi."

Some alphabet books incorporate riddles or hidden puzzles in their formats. In *The Alphabet Tale* by Jan Garten each letter is introduced on the preceding page by showing just the tail of an animal. Turning the page, you see the whole animal. Children have four clues by which they may determine what each animal is called—the content of the verse referring to the animal's characteristics, the sound of the rhyme, the picture of the tail, and the beginning letter. The letter "G" is introduced with this verse: "A neck so long it makes you laugh/This tail is the tail of the tall—(giraffe)."[4] Peter Parnall has hidden the letters in the grass of *Apricot ABC*, an ecological story of the adventures of an apricot seed. Detailed illustrations of a meadow complement the beauty of the text by Miska Miles. For the letter "Q" we read:

> Quietly from special places
> In the flickering shadow of Queen Anne's laces,
> Quickly ventured queer little things
> On fluttering, fragile gossamer wings.[5]

Butterflies flit lightly through the pages of Marcia Brown's unique alphabet book, *All Butterflies*. Superb, double-page woodcut spreads illustrate paired letters and words such as "Cats Dance," "Elephants Fly," and "Mice Nibble." Children enjoy discovering the organizing principle of this book; then they can tell or write their own alphabet books.

Several alphabet books present various aspects of city or country living. *A Big City* by Grossbart shows brightly colored silhouettes of such familiar city objects as a fire escape, garbage can, and hydrant. The simplicity and clarity of the graphic design makes this an excellent book for the pre-school child. A novel design is seen in *The City-Country ABC* by Marguerite Walters. The first half of the book describes an alphabet walk in the country; the reader turns the book over and begins again with an alphabet ride in the city. Phyllis McGinley's *All Around the Town*

[3]Thomas Matthiesen, *ABC An Alphabet Book* (New York: Platt & Munk, 1966), unpaged.

[4]Jan Garten, *The Alphabet Tale,* illustrated by Muriel Batherman (New York: Random House, 1964), unpaged.

[5]Miska Miles, *Apricot ABC*, illustrated by Peter Parnall (Boston, Mass.: Little, Brown, 1969), unpaged.

Mice Nibbling

Marcia Brown has designed a clever alphabet book using paired letters and imaginative woodcuts.

Illustration used by permission of Charles Scribner's Sons from *All Butterflies* by Marcia Brown. Copyright © 1974 Marcia Brown.

contains lively, happy verse about city sights and sounds. The illustrations by Helen Stone reflect busy city life. *Adam's ABC* by Dale Fife follows a small black boy through his daily experiences in the city. Letters are represented by those objects and activities that would appeal to the black city child; for example, "E" is a carved EBONY elephant from Africa. Today, both urban and suburban children face the all too frequent experience of moving. In *M Is for Moving*, Velma Illsley has created a rhyming text that presents

a child's-eye view of moving day: "L is for Left-overs./I made the Lunch-/Liverwurst sandwiches, Lemonade punch."[6] The letter "M" stands for mess and moving! And the use of "X" to mark the spot on the map where the family is going is an ingenious idea.

Many other topical themes have been used to tie the alphabet together. Tasha Tudor's *A Is for Annabelle* pictures an old-fashioned doll with her different belongings representing the various letters. In contrast to the delicate detailed watercolors of Tudor are the big, bold, circus-poster pictures painted by Brinton Turkle for *C Is for Circus* by Chardiet. A unique alphabet book for older children features photographs of the great pantomimist, Marcel Marceau, in the guise of a clown acting out such key words as "Awakening," "Love," "Old," and "Vanish." Children in the middle grades might enjoy developing their own lists of words to pantomime after reading *The Marcel Marceau Alphabet Book* by George Mendoza.

Jambo Means Hello is a beautiful Swahili alphabet book by Muriel and Tom Feelings. Selecting twenty-four words, one for each letter of the

[6]Velma Illsley, *M Is for Moving* (New York: Walck, 1966), unpaged.

Tom Feelings' rich and detailed illustrations introduce the Swahili alphabet, as well as extend an understanding of African culture.

From *Jambo Means Hello* by Muriel Feelings, illustrated by Tom Feelings. Illustrations, copyright © 1974 by Tom Feelings. Used with permission of The Dial Press.

Swahili alphabet, Muriel Feelings gives children a simple lesson in the Swahili language while introducing them to some important aspects of the geography and culture of East African life. Tom Feelings uses a unique art technique to obtain his soft gray, black, and white pictures. The art is prepared with water-soluble black ink, white tempera, and linseed oil. At one stage in his painting, he covers the paint board with wet tissue paper, which causes the ink and paint to bleed together. The effect is a soft, luminous picture. Older boys and girls will enjoy and learn from this unique book.

Children's interest in technological and scientific advances is met by Zacks' *Space Alphabet*, Shuttlesworth's *ABC of Buses*, and Alexander's *ABC of Cars and Trucks*. Older children will be encouraged to try some of the experiments in *ABC Science Experiments*, and will be alerted to what they can do for their environment in *ABC of Ecology*. Both these books have been prepared by Harry Milgrom, director of science in the New York City Public Schools.

Obviously there is no lack of ABC books, both general and specialized, for the pre-schooler and for the older child. Each ABC book should be evaluated on its own merits in concept and design, considering the purpose for which it will be used and the projected age level of its audience. The concept of an ABC book is one that can be utilized in every area of study. Children would thoroughly enjoy making their own, such as an "ABC of Pioneer Life" or an "ABC of Favorite Books," and then sharing them with their peers or younger children.

Counting Books

Ideally, boys and girls should learn to count by playing with real objects such as blocks, boxes, bottle caps, or model cars. They can manipulate and group these as they wish, actually seeing what happens when you add one more block to nine, or divide six blocks into two groups. Since time immemorial, however, we have been providing children with counting books, substituting pictures for real objects. The young child can make this transition from the concrete to its visual representation, provided he first has experienced the real and that the visual illustrations are clearly presented.

In evaluating counting books, then, we look to see if the objects to be counted stand out clearly on the page. Various groupings of objects should avoid a cluttered, confusing look. Illustrations and page design are most important in evaluating counting books. Accuracy is essential.

Clear, beautifully designed photographs are used to illustrate the book *Count and See*. Tana Hoban has photographed objects that are familiar and meaningful to the young child, such as three school buses, six candles on a birthday cake, nine firemen's hats, a dozen eggs in their carton, fifteen cookies, and, amazingly, 100 peas in ten pea shells! A pair of young boys—one black, the other white—represent the numeral 2. The cover pictures an integrated group of seven boys and girls with balloons. The photographs are reinforced on opposite pages with the number as word, as numeral, and as model set represented by white dots.

Another book of *Numbers* utilizes color photographs by Weissman. In the text of this book Robert Allen relates the concept of five cars to the number of fingers a child has on his hand; ten is related to both hands, and two to the number of things that come in twos such as gloves and shoes. The author also attempts to develop the notion of one-to-one relationship and conservation of number regardless of arrangement. These concepts seem especially difficult for children just beginning to understand numbers.

Many of the same author-illustrators who have published alphabet books have also written counting books. Eichenberg's *Dancing in the Moon* explains the numbers 1 through 20 in one-line rhymes. Tudor's book, *1 Is One*, is illustrated in her old-fashioned, dainty style. Oxenbury's *Numbers of Things* is as delightfully amusing as her alphabet book. Her picture of seven chairs shows a large shaggy dog occupying the largest, most comfortable overstuffed chair; granny is in her rocker; the baby in his high chair; and the cat, smaller dog, dolls, and girl in the other ones. Fifty is represented by the appropriate number of lady bugs, and the final page shows an astronaut on the moon with the caption, "How many stars?"

Brian Wildsmith's 1, 2, 3's is handsome but confusing. He utilizes basic geometric forms—

circle, triangle, and rectangle—in combination with a kind of patchwork design. The designs within the basic shapes are distracting and might well be miscounted. For example, the picture for number ten is an engine. The two black circles of smoke are difficult to discern against the dark navy background, yet they are essential for the development of the concept of ten. The smoke stack is a rectangle made of two squares of different colors. Most children will count these squares as two objects rather than see them as one. This is an exciting, brilliantly designed book that is too complex for most young children.

A circus train serves as a vehicle for Eric Carle's counting book, *1, 2, 3 to the Zoo*. Each colorful page has a car with an increasing number of animals in it, such as two hippos and nine snakes. The cumulative train at the bottom of each double-page spread gives the child added practice in knowing how many cars have passed. Carle's novel book, *The Very Hungry Caterpillar*, is really the story of the life cycle of a caterpillar from a small egg to a beautiful butterfly. However, it can be used both as a counting book and in helping children learn the days of the week. For the hungry caterpillar eats through one apple on Monday, two pears on Tuesday, three plums on Wednesday, and so on through the week; and he is so hungry that he literally eats his way through the pages of the book leaving small holes to prove it!

Ezra Jack Keats has illustrated his version of the old counting rhyme *Over in the Meadow* with colláge pictures in jewel-like colors. The fine recording by Marvin Hayes increases children's enjoyment of the lilt and rhythm of this favorite poem. Primary grade children can compare Keats' illustrations with those done by Rojankovsky for another version of this story of all the animals who lived in the sunny meadow by the cool pond.

Many counting books present a cumulative procession of objects with a thread of a story to hold them together. Some also reverse the sequence of the plot and include the concept of deletion or subtraction. Maurice Sendak's counting book, *One Was Johnny*, is a part of the very small Nutshell Library; however, it may be ordered for school use in an approximately 5 by 7 inch size. Typically Sendak in humor, it is the story of "Johnny who lived by himself" until he is disturbed by one noxious animal after another. Not knowing what to do, he starts counting backward with the threat "'and when/I am through-/If this house isn't empty/I'll eat/all of you!!!!'"[7] Needless to say, the house is emptied and Johnny is left to enjoy his solitude.

Krüss has utilized the mathematical concept of grouping in his brilliantly illustrated book, *3 × 3 Three by Three*. Three hunters, three foxes, three dogs, three cats, three mice, and three chickens chase each other in and out of a very busy house. The excitement of the chase is good fun, and children enjoy the simple three-line verses.

Krüss has utilized the mathematical concept a Swahili counting book written by Muriel Feelings. It contains superb soft brown paintings of East Africa by Tom Feelings. A map of Africa, showing the countries where Swahili is spoken, is included. Older children will find this a beautiful presentation of African life, but younger children will find it a confusing counting book. The number six is represented by six persons in different kinds of dress, but only five kinds of clothing are identified. Again, it would be difficult for the young children to differentiate the eight market stalls in the scene of the marketplace.

The folk tales, *Six Foolish Fishermen*, by Elkin, and *Nine in a Line*, by Kirn, are not really counting books, but their stories revolve around the ability to count. In the Elkin book six brothers go out to fish in various places. When it is time for them to go home, each counts the others, neglecting himself, and decides that one must have drowned. Then a small boy counts the brothers and assures them that they are all there. *Nine in a Line* is based upon an Arabic tale with the same theme. Each time Amin counts his camels he has only eight, until he is convinced that "the Evil One" has taken a camel. Both of these books give children an opportunity to participate in counting several times, plus the added fun of being "in" on the joke.

Concept Books

A concept book is one that describes the various dimensions of an abstract idea through the

[7]Maurice Sendak. *One Was Johnny* (New York: Harper & Row, 1962), unpaged.

use of many comparisons. In some respects, it is a young child's information book. Rather than presenting specific facts, a concept book explores many facets of an idea, object, or concept. Well-defined concepts are necessary for children's cognitive and language development.

Watch a very young child learn a new word and struggle to understand its meaning. The word "dog" may be applied to his dog and also to the cat or the squirrels in the yard, until he has abstracted the essential qualities of "dogginess." Later he will be able to make finer differentiations and discriminate between his dog and the dog next door; and later still, to name a St. Bernard and a Pekinese while grouping them in the central class of dogs. Concept books help children to identify these essential elements of an abstract idea, object, or class of objects.

ABC books and counting books are really concept books. So, too, are those books which help children to identify and discriminate colors. John Reiss has illustrated a book of *Colors* for very young children with clear bright graphics showing several pages of familiar objects for each color; for example, the color green is depicted by green leaves, grass, a snake, frogs, turtles, pickles, cucumbers, gooseberries, and peas in a pod. The Provensens have produced a large oversized volume titled *What Is a Color?* Boldly painted pictures portray everyday things in the child's surroundings in their appropriate colors.

Striking black-and-white photographs by Tana Hoban depict fifteen pairs of opposites in her book *Push Pull, Empty Full.* The same scene of a city is portrayed for night and day; a turtle pulls his head in for "in" and pokes it out for "out"; two eggs represent "whole," while the same two are seen smashed on the floor for "broken." The endpapers reflect the theme of this well-designed book by showing a tree with leaves and one that is quite bare. Twelve spatial concepts are explored in Tana Hoban's *Over, Under and Through.* Often, several concepts are pictured in one photograph, and children would enjoy testing each other and discussing these well-planned photographs. However, a child needs much real experience of what is "over," "between," and "across" before he can gain much benefit from the book.

Square shapes, round shapes, fat and thin shapes are part of the fun of the book *Are You Square?* by Ethel and Leonard Kessler. With provocative questions and illustrations, the Kesslers help children become aware of the various shapes around them. In *The Wing on a Flea*, Emberley presents the basic concepts of a triangle, rectangle, and circle, and suggests that children look to see how many examples of these shapes they can find. Miriam Schlein's books, *Heavy Is a Hippopotamus* and *Fast Is Not a Ladybug,* are both concept books that discuss the comparative values of weight and speed. They give more specifics than most concept books and are more appropriate for second- or third-graders.

All the different uses and delights to be had in, with, or under a tree are described in the award-winning book, *A Tree Is Nice*, by Udry. The joyous illustrations by Marc Simont picture children, adults, and animals enjoying trees in various ways. Margaret Wise Brown's *The Important Book,* illustrated by Leonard Weisgard, helps children to make generalizations concerning the most significant aspects of such different objects as a spoon or an apple. Children could be encouraged to abstract what they consider to be the essential characteristics of favorite objects and so develop their own "important books." Such an activity would stimulate critical thinking and interest.

Picture Books

Picture books are essential to the development of the young child's visual and verbal imagination. In fact they may be the only "real art" that the child sees. James Johnson Sweeny, formerly Director of the Museum of Modern Art, emphasizes the importance of picture books in this statement:

> A child's book is essentially a work of visual art . . . It should be aimed primarily to stimulate the imagination through the eye—to educate in the true sense, by drawing something out of the observer—to mature the observer through stimulation, to exercise the imagination and develop the power for creating images.[8]

[8]*Children's Book Show 1945–1950* (New York: American Institute of Graphic Arts, 1951), Introduction.

DEFINITIONS OF PICTURE BOOKS

Some authorities differentiate between the picture book and the picture storybook. The difference is contingent upon the development of plot and characters. A picture book may be an alphabet book, a counting book, a first book, or a concept book. In these the pictures must be accurate and synchronized with the text; however, it is not essential that they provide the continuity required by a story line. The illustrations for a concept book or an alphabet book may depict a different object or animal on each page, providing for much variety in the pictures. Examples would be *John Burningham's ABC* or Brown's *The Important Book.* In a picture storybook, however, the same characters and settings are frequently drawn, while variety is achieved through the action of the characters. The artist must consider plot and character development in the picture storybook, rather than just the unifying idea or concept of the picture book itself. Symeon Shimin has drawn lovely, sensitive illustrations for the picture storybook *Sam* by Ann Scott. In this story of a little boy's rejection by members of his family, the artist had to show Sam's increasing frustration at being told to stop what he was doing and go somewhere else to play. Finally, when Sam begins to cry at the simple rebuke of his father, the family come together and realize the cumulative effect they have all had on Sam. The illustrations show a happier Sam who chooses to make raspberry tarts with his mother! Both the artist and author must sustain children's interest, carry the story line, and portray subtle changes in expression and mood. For this reason, the picture storybook probably places a greater demand on the talent of both author and illustrator than does the picture book. It is important to recognize the different requirements of these two types of books. Yet in many instances, the two terms are used interchangeably to refer to that large group of books in which pictures and text are considered to be of equal importance. While the fusion of pictures and text is essential for the unity of presentation in a picture book, this fusion does not exist in the illustrated book. In the latter the pictures are mere extensions of the text. They

A rebuked Sam receives comfort from his mother. Symeon Shimin's realistic illustrations dramatize a universal childhood experience.

Illustration © 1967 by Symeon Shimin. From *Sam* by Ann Herbert Scott & Symeon Shimin. Used with permission of McGraw-Hill Book Co.

may enrich the interpretation of the story, but they are not necessary for its understanding. For example, Beth and Joe Krush have illustrated *The Borrowers* by Mary Norton. Their intricate line sketches greatly add to the fantasy of this delightful book, but they are not essential for its understanding. Illustrated books are usually written for those children who have already achieved considerable fluency in reading skills.

Sometimes it is difficult to differentiate between a profusely illustrated book and a picture storybook. *Annie and the Old One* by Miska Miles has such complete unity between text and illustrations that it is hard to imagine one without the other. The book received consideration for both the Newbery and Caldecott awards but finally became an honor book for the Newbery on the basis of the quality of its very sensitive story. A final criterion for differentiating a picture book from an illustrated book is simply to ask yourself the question: "Having heard the text and seen the pictures once, could a child accurately retell the story from just the pictures?"

Wordless Picture Books

Special definition must be given to the increasing number of books without words which have been published in the past few years. These books are particularly helpful in stimulating the language development of children. They have no text and encourage the child to tell the story from pictures only. *The Good Bird* by Wezel presents the story of a friendly pink bird who shares his worm with an unhappy goldfish. The crayoned pictures are simple and childlike, but clearly show the sequence of action. In *Do You Want to Be My Friend?*, Eric Carle has given the child more latitude to create his own story about a little mouse who in seeking a friend follows the lead of one tail after another, only to be very surprised at what is at the other end! The brilliant collage pictures will delight children as much as the opportunity to tell their own versions of this story.

A highly original wordless book is *Changes, Changes* by Pat Hutchins. Here, two wooden dolls arrange and rearrange wooden building blocks to tell a fast-paced story. When their block house catches fire, the resourceful couple dismantle it and build a fire engine, whose hose quickly douses the fire thereby creating a flood! Undaunted, the wooden dolls then build a boat, which becomes a truck, which is changed to a train, until eventually they reconstruct their original block house. Hutchins has written and illustrated an even funnier story with the use of only one sentence. In this book Rosie—a very determined, flat-footed hen—goes for a walk, unmindful of the fact that she is being stalked by a hungry fox. At every turn of *Rosie's Walk*, the hen unwittingly foils the fox in his plans to catch her. The brightly-colored comic illustrations help youngsters to tell Rosie's story. Even children in the middle grades enjoy creating sound effects on a tape for this story, or retelling the story from the point of view of the frustrated fox. Its appeal really has no age level limitations.

John Goodall has produced several old-fashioned books without words that remind one of Beatrix Potter's works. Lovely, detailed watercolors portray *The Midnight Adventures of Kelly, Dot, and Esmeralda*; a koala bear, a doll, and a tiny mouse, who climb through a picture on the wall and into a charming landscape of a river and boat. Their river outing meets with disaster, as does their trip to a village fair. The three just manage to make it back to the boat, the river, and through the picture, and onto the safety of their own toy shelf. The ingenious use of half pages adds to the excitement and movement of this book. *Shrewbettina's Birthday* is also in full color and uses the same imaginative format. Black-and-white pictures detail *The Adventures of Paddy Pork*, who runs away from his mother to follow the circus. These are long stories with several incidents in each plot, yet the pictures show the action clearly and make them easy and exciting to narrate.

A rather subtle picture story, *Apples* by Nonny Hogrogian, shows the magical growth of an apple orchard as men and animals carelessly toss their apple cores away. Passage of time is shown by the increasing size and number of trees; while the parade of animals and people always going from left to right across the large double-page spreads creates a remarkable feeling of movement. Even the first village on the left disappears as the larger one on the right comes into view. These subtleties of time and change might be wasted on the pre-schooler, but delight the more observant 6- or 7-year-old.

Another sophisticated and highly amusing story with few words is *Look What I Can Do* by Jose Aruego. In this book two brown-and-gray carabaos (a kind of Phillipine water buffalo) match each other's antics in a game of follow-the-leader. After some narrow escapes and complete exhaustion, they are both challenged by a third carabao, who is quite literally sat upon by his two friends. This is a very funny story that even older children enjoy interpreting.

Lynd Ward's *The Silver Pony* is unique in that it contains some eighty pictures and no words. This is the story of a lonely farm boy who imagines that he sees a winged horse. He fantasizes the many trips that he takes on the back of his beautiful Silver Pony, helping a young person caught in a flood, saving a lamb from a mountain lion, bringing flowers to a lonely girl in a lighthouse. Finally, in his dreams he and his pony are caught in the midst of a battle of rockets and shot down. His family do find him lying ill outside the house. In order to bring his two worlds together, the boy receives his own silver pony—without wings. This is a story that will fascinate young and old, but its appeal will be mostly to the middle-graders who can sustain attention throughout the story. The pictures have the power and realism that we have come to associate with Ward.

Other wordless books that are well-liked by children include *A Boy, a Dog, and a Frog* and its sequel, *Frog, Where Are You?*, by Mercer Mayer. Martha Alexander has two very funny ones called *Out! Out! Out!* and *Bobo's Dream. What Whiskers Did* by Carroll was one of the first books without words. The pictures in all these books must carry the entire narration. Therefore action and sequence need to be clearly portrayed so that the child has no difficulty in telling the story.

"Easy-to-Read" Books

Picture books should not be confused with ones written with a controlled vocabulary for the beginning reader. Most picture storybooks require a reading ability level of at least third-grade and are generally read *to* children. They are written for the young child's interest and appreciation level, not his reading ability level. A new genre of book was created when Dr. Seuss wrote *The Cat in the Hat* in 1957. This book was written with a controlled vocabulary (derived from the Dolch vocabulary list of 220 words) for the young child to read independently. In format, such books tend to look more like basic readers than picture storybooks, although they do have illustrations on every page. Some of these books, such as *Little Bear* by Minarik and the superb *Frog and Toad* series by Arnold Lobel, can take their rightful place in children's literature. In fact, while *Frog and Toad Are Friends* was a 1971 Caldecott Honor Book, *Frog and Toad Together* was a 1973 Newbery Honor Book, suggesting that quality writing can be achieved with a limited vocabulary. *Mouse Tales* also by Lobel consists of seven short bedtime stories which Papa Mouse tells, one for each of his seven mouse boys. The warmth, humor, and literary quality of these tales are complemented by Lobel's amusing illustrations of a tiny world of mouse people.

Unfortunately, most of these books do not achieve such literary excellence, and appear very contrived and restricted by the controlled vocabulary. They do serve the useful purpose of providing a transition from stilted basic readers to "library books," and help the young child begin to develop independence in reading. They also serve to help stimulate interest and confidence, even in reluctant readers.

Picture Books for Older Children

The number of picture books designed for older children is growing rapidly. This trend merely reflects the greater role of visual presentation in books and magazines for all ages. Many of these picture books for older boys and girls may be classified as informational books in the science or social studies areas, and are reviewed in Chapter 9. Occasionally, however, a picture storybook designed for somewhat older children is shelved with other picture books and, consequently, is lost to the age level for which it was intended. This may easily happen to such beautiful but oversized books as Valens' *Wingfin and Topple* or the d'Aulaires' *Abraham Lincoln.* The humor and subtle commentaries on human nature as presented in Thurber's *Many Moons* are completely wasted on very young children, as is the irony of *The Shrinking of Treehorn* by Heide. Keeping's rather sombre tale of what Jacob can see *Through the Window* that looks out on London's East End is also for somewhat older boys and girls. The highly symbolic pictures, with the cross from the church across the street reflected in almost every scene and the pattern of the lace curtains forming the frames for most of the pictures, tend to confuse young children. It is also well to remember that some picture books are ageless—appealing to a wide age range of children. A 13-year-old boy from Kentucky enjoyed Lynd Ward's wonderful story of *The Biggest Bear* as much as do second- and third-graders. Books by Leo Lionni—such as *Swimmy, The Biggest House in the World,* and *Tico and The Golden*

Wings—may be read to older boys and girls for their many layers of meaning.

Many schools are now encouraging the practice of having children in the middle grades read to boys and girls in the kindergarten or primary grades. Older boys and girls are always amazed at how much they enjoy such books as *Let's Be Enemies* by Udry or *Amos and Boris* by Steig. They are also impressed with the difficulty of the vocabulary. Increasingly, picture storybooks are for all ages.

THE CONTENT OF PICTURE BOOKS

In evaluating a picture book both the text and the pictures need to be appraised. Too frequently we may be impressed with the beauty of the illustrations and do not pay enough attention to the quality of the language or the appropriateness of the content for the age level of its intended audience. A particular danger in writing for young children is that the author will write *about* a child rather than *for* a child. Beware of the book that is too sweet or too coy. Children resent being chucked under the chin whether by an author or a great aunt! Joan Walsh Anglund's books, *Spring Is a New Beginning* or *Morning Is a Little Child*, are examples of books that are about childhood, not for children. These little books are filled with nostalgia, an emotion seldom felt by the young child.

Adult emotions are also the theme of the picture book *Joseph's Yard* by Charles Keeping. This is a story of a very lonely young boy who plants a flower in his backyard. When the rose begins to grow, Joseph picks the bud too soon and it withers and dies. The next year he waits patiently for his flower to grow, and then fearful of the birds and cats, he covers it with his coat and smothers it. The author makes Joseph's feelings very explicit in didactic adult terms, which seem inappropriate for today's child.

> Joseph was bitterly ashamed. First his love and now his jealousy had killed a beautiful thing in his yard.[9]

Sex stereotyping begins early and frequently can be seen in the content of picture books. This

[9]Charles Keeping. *Joseph's Yard* (London: Oxford University Press, 1969), unpaged.

may be as subtle and unconscious as the pictures for *A Tree Is Nice*, which portrays boys climbing trees while girls boost them up; or as blatant as the text for Darrow's book, *I'm Glad I'm a Boy! I'm Glad I'm a Girl!*, which contains such insidious statements as "Boys are doctors. Girls are nurses." Or "Boys fix things. Girls need things fixed." Or, again, "Boys build houses. Girls keep houses!"[10]

In the highly imaginative story *Can I Keep Him?* by Steven Kellogg, Albert asks his mother if he can keep one pet after another, ranging from real, imaginary, to human. His distraught mother is always pictured attending to such household chores as scrubbing, ironing, and cleaning the toilet bowl. She explains in very practical terms why Albert cannot keep his pets; for example, a snake's scales could clog the vacuum. While the contrast between Albert's highly original ideas and his mother's mundane preoccupation with household duties is funny, it is also devastating to the image of the liberated housewife.

Racial stereotypes in picture books are slowly disappearing with the raised consciousness level of publishing houses. Many more picture books

[10]Whitney Darrow, Jr. *I'm Glad I'm a Boy! I'm Glad I'm a Girl!* (New York: Simon and Schuster, 1970), unpaged.

A highly imaginative little boy is contrasted with his stereotyped mother who is always pictured in her frilly apron doing various household chores.

From *Can I Keep Him?* by Steven Kellogg. Copyright © 1971 by Steven Kellogg. Used with permission of The Dial Press.

have black characters than was true ten years ago. Most of these—such as the well-loved stories of Peter by Keats, the Benjie books by Lexau, and *Stevie* by John Steptoe—have universal appeal. Others, such as *Uptown* and *Train Ride* by Steptoe, are more related to the specific ethnic differences of the black experience. In at least one instance, objectionable black stereotypes have been eliminated from a previously published picture book. In the fourteenth printing of the Caldecott Award winning book *The Rooster Crows* by the Petershams, two rhymes written in black-face dialect and accompanying pictures of stereotyped Negroes were removed. This action received praise from the majority of persons who were offended by these rhymes and pictures in an award book that continued to be purchased by most schools and libraries; some, however, objected to the deletion in an award-winning book on the basis that history should not be altered, even from the more enlightened perspective of today.

Increased attention is being directed to the publication of picture books portraying modern American Indians and Hispanic-Americans. These groups have been maligned in print and television as bloodthirsty warriors and sleeping peons in sombreros. Picture books frequently give children their first impressions of various ethnic or racial groups. Only when our books portray characters of both sexes, all races, and all colors in a wide range of occupations and from a great variety of socioeconomic backgrounds and settings will we have moved away from stereotyping to a more honest portrayal of a world literature for children.

THE LANGUAGE OF PICTURE BOOKS

The words of picture books are as important as the illustrations, and may help children develop an early sensitivity to the imaginative use of language. Since most of these books will be read to children rather than by them, there is no reason to oversimplify or write down to today's knowledgeable and sophisticated child. Television does not talk down to children; neither should parents, teachers, or books. Beatrix Potter knew that given the context of the story and the picture of Peter caught in the gooseberry net, most children would comprehend the sentence

"... his sobs were overheard by some friendly sparrows, who flew to him in great excitement, and implored him to exert himself."[11]

Certainly one way to extend the child's experiences and vocabulary is by reading aloud to him. *Amos and Boris* is a comical story of the friendship between two mammals, a mouse and a whale. Hurricane Yetta blows the whale upon the beach where he is found by his friend, the mouse. "'Amos, help me,' said the mountain of a whale to the mote of a mouse."[12] By contrasting the words "mountain" and "mote," children will obtain the general idea of the word, if not the specific meaning. Following story hour in first grade, one child was heard chanting the word "humiliated, humiliated" after he had heard it used in Ward's *The Biggest Bear*.

Children delight in the repetition of words and will join in the refrains of such books as *Millions of Cats* by Wanda Gág or *Plum Pudding for Christmas*, which tells of the frantic search of the Duchess for plums to make the king's pudding, for he had said he would come:

"If you serve a pudding
      and that pudding is plum,
Plums that are purple,
      Plums in a clump
So that each bumpy lump
      is a plum that is plump."[13]

In *Long Ago Elf* the mood of an eerie moonlit night is created by luminous black-and-white pictures and the mysterious refrain:

Silently he creeped
By blue-white shimmer
Through thorn bush shiver
By firefly glimmer
Through tall grass quiver—[14]

This same quiet mood is sustained in the lovely story of *The Tomten*, the little troll who on silent, small feet walks about the lonely farmhouse on a winter night and talks to all the animals of the

[11] Beatrix Potter. *The Tale of Peter Rabbit* (London: Frederick Warne, n.d.), p. 45.
[12] William Steig. *Amos and Boris* (New York: Farrar, Straus, 1971), unpaged.
[13] Virginia Kahl. *Plum Pudding for Christmas* (New York: Scribner, 1955), unpaged.
[14] Mary Smith and R. A. Smith. *Long Ago Elf* (Chicago: Follett, 1968), p. 17.

promise of spring. Beautiful full-color winter-scapes illuminate the poetic text by Victor Rydberg.

Children can appreciate figurative language, provided the comparisons are within the realm of their experiences. The vivid word pictures in Tresselt's *White Snow, Bright Snow* are thoroughly enjoyed by 5-and-6-year-olds and reflect a child's point of view. Even older children respond to the similes and metaphors of this poetic prose.

In the morning a clear blue sky was overhead and blue shadows hid in all the corners. Automobiles looked like big fat raisins buried in snow drifts.

Houses crouched together, their windows peeking out from under great white eyebrows. Even the church steeple wore a pointed cap on its top.[15]

In his beautiful book, *Swimmy*, Lionni has described strange sights in the unknown depths of the ocean in terms children will understand and visualize: "a lobster who walked about like a water-moving machine," "a forest of seaweeds growing from sugar-candy rocks," and "an eel whose tail was too far away to remember."[16]

The dialogue of a story can be rich and believable or it can be dull and stilted. *Dazzle* by Diane Massie is the story of a very vain peacock who decides he must be Lord of the Jungle because he is so magnificent. Making lordly pronouncements, which are always shown in capital letters, Dazzle decrees that all the other birds must wait on him. When the lion hears all the commotion, he confronts the bird and asks him why he thinks he is Lord of the Jungle. Dazzle asserts that he is "exquisite from quill to tip"—then there is a SNAP! SHUNCH! and Dazzle's tail disappears into the lion's jaws.

"GOOD HEAVENS!"
screeched Dazzle. "WHERE IS MY TAIL?"
"It seems to have vanished," said the lion.
"It was here a minute ago," said Dazzle.
"You've taken it!"
"I?" said the lion, smiling.
"HOW CAN I BE LORD OF THE JUNGLE
WITHOUT MY TAIL?" shouted Dazzle.

"I guess you can't," said the lion.
"I shall have to be Lord of the Jungle myself."[17]

Light, bright pictures are as archly funny as the dialogue of this well-written book.

In evaluating picture storybooks it is well to remember that the attention span of the young child is limited, and so the story must be told rather quickly. Picture storybooks are short—usually thirty-two to sixty-four pages. Even within this limitation the criteria developed in Chapter 1 for all fiction apply equally well to picture storybooks. Both text and illustrations should be evaluated in a picture storybook. The beauty of the words should be equal to the beauty of the illustrations.

THE ART OF PICTURE BOOKS

The picture storybook is one that conveys its message through two media, the art of illustrating and the art of writing. Both media must bear the burden of narration in a well-designed book that reflects its whole character. It is difficult to think of Wanda Gág's *Millions of Cats* without hearing its frequent refrain about the millions and billions and trillions of cats. At the same time, the rhythmical picture of the gnomish little old man wandering over the rolling hills and down the winding roads followed by all those cats is inseparable from the repetitive text. The action in the text is reflected by the action in the illustrations. One can almost hear the howls of the terrific cat fight and the subsequent silence when only one little kitten remains. Although one of our earliest[18] picture books, it still serves as an outstanding example of a book in which text and illustrations seem to flow together.

Another well-loved picture storybook is *Blueberries for Sal* by Robert McCloskey. This is a story that children can tell by themselves just by looking at the clear blue-and-white pictures. The illustrations help the "reader" anticipate both the action and climax as Sal and her mother are seen going berry-picking up one side of Blueberry Hill, and Little Bear and his mother are seen coming up the other side. McCloskey uses a false climax, a good storytelling technique. Sal hears a noise and starts to peer behind an ominously

[15]Alvin Tresselt. *White Snow, Bright Snow*, illustrated by Roger Duvoisin (New York: Lothrop, 1947), p. 20.
[16]Leo Lionni. *Swimmy* (New York: Pantheon, 1963), unpaged.

[17]Diane Massie. *Dazzle* (New York: Parents', 1969), unpaged.
[18]First published in 1928 (New York: Coward-McCann).

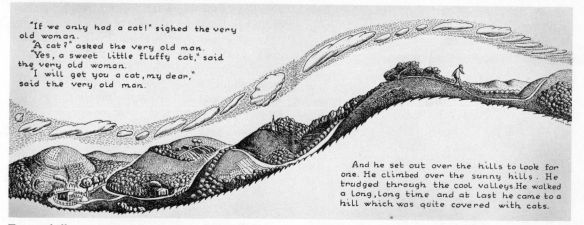

"If we only had a cat!" sighed the very
old woman.
"A cat?" asked the very old man.
"Yes, a sweet little fluffy cat," said
the very old woman.
"I will get you a cat, my dear,"
said the very old man.

And he set out over the hills to look for
one. He climbed over the sunny hills. He
trudged through the cool valleys. He walked
a long, long time and at last he came to a
hill which was quite covered with cats.

Text and illustrations move together to create the feeling of the little old man's journey over the rolling hills and down the winding roads. This is a most effective use of a double-page spread.

Reprinted by permission of Coward, McCann & Geoghegan, Inc., from *Millions of Cats* by Wanda Gág. Copyright 1928 by Coward-McCann, Inc.

dark rock; the reader expects her to meet the bears, but instead she sees a mother crow and her children. On the next page she calmly meets Mother Bear and tramps along behind her. A parallel plot gives Little Bear a similar experience, but Sal's mother is not so calm about meeting him! The human expressions of surprise, fear, and consternation on the faces of both mothers express emotion as well as action.

Ward has used another technique to show the climax in his well-loved story, *The Biggest Bear*. In order to dramatize the growth of Johnny's bear, he shows him first as a lovable but mischievous cub. The next four pictures illustrate the chaos the bear created in the kitchen during the summer, Mr. McCarroll's trampled cornfield in the fall, the half-eaten and ruined bacon and hams in the smokehouse during the winter, and the overturned sap buckets in the spring. The bear is not shown in any of these pictures; only the results of his destructive actions. The text suggests the passage of time, but in no way prepares the reader for the shock of the next picture of a gigantic bear, standing on his hind legs gorging himself on the McLeans' maple syrup! This adventure story has moments of real pathos, compassion, and humor. The illustrations help to create these feelings as well as the text does.

The size of the imaginary characters who come to see a little boy in *One Monday Morning* increases with each of their daily visits and with each level of stairs that they climb. Finally, when the king, the queen, the prince, and their entourage reach the sixth floor, the little boy invites them in and they fill his entire drab tenement room. Only the last page reveals their true size and the extent of the boy's (and Uri Shulevitz's) imagination!

Size of picture may increase with the mounting tension of the story. One of the best-known examples of this is seen in Sendak's well-loved story, *Where the Wild Things Are*. The pictures in this book become larger and larger as Max's dream becomes more and more fantastic. Following the climatic wild rumpus, which is portrayed on three full-sized spreads with no text whatsoever, Max returns home. The pictures decrease in size, although never down to their original size; just as symbolically, Max will never be quite the same again after his dream experience.

The creative introduction of color provides just the right climax for Arnold Lobel's black-and-white illustrations in *Hildilid's Night*. This delightful story by Cheli Ryan has a modern folk tale quality to it. It tells the story of a little old woman who hates the night above all things, so she tries to chase it away by sweeping it outside with a broom, by spanking it, stuffing it in a sack; she even digs a grave for it, but still it will not go away. After all her vain endeavors she is exhausted and returns home to sleep just as the sun comes up and drives away the detested night.

The royal visitors struggle up the stairs of a tenement building to make a visit. Their figures appear larger and larger on each successive visit until the surprise ending.

Illustration used by permission of Charles Scribner's Sons from *One Monday Morning* by Uri Shulevitz. Copyright © 1967 Uri Shulevitz.

The only use of color is on the last three pages, when Hildilid is too tired to see the faint yellow gold of dawn. On the final page her little hut is ablaze with sunlight and Hildilid is sound asleep.

Pictures should not only reflect the action and climax of the plot, they should help to create the basic mood of the story. In a perfection of words and watercolors, McCloskey has captured the changing mood of the Maine coast in his *Time of Wonder.* Using soft grays and yellow, he conveys the warmth and mystery of the early morning fog in the woods. His ocean storm scene, on the other hand, is slashed with streaks of dark blues and emerald greens, highlighted by churning whites. The text is no longer quiet and poetic, but races along with "the sharp choppy waves and slamming rain." The storm subsides; the summer ends; and it is time to leave the island.

The beauty of this book will not reach all children, but it will speak forever to young and old alike who have ever intensely loved a particular place on this earth. Words and pictures so complement each other that the reader is filled with quiet wonder when he sees the family's boat slip into the sunset and reads the poetic prose:

> Take a farewell look
> At the waves and sky.
> Take a farewell sniff
> Of the salty sea.
> A little bit sad
> about the place you are leaving,
> A little bit glad
> About the place you are going.
> It is a time of quiet wonder—
>   for wondering, for instance:
> Where do hummingbirds go in a hurricane?[19]

Besides creating the basic mood of a story, illustrations also help portray convincing character delineation and development. The characterization in the pictures must correspond to that of the story. There is no mistaking the devilish quality of the incorrigible *Madeline* as she balances herself on the ledge of the Pont des Arts in Paris, or says "pooh-pooh to the tiger in the zoo." Madeline is always her roguish self in the four other books that Bemelmans wrote about her. She shows little or no character development, but the delineation of her character is unmistakable. Madeline is a real personality.

One of the few picture storybooks that portrays character development is *Crow Boy* by Yashima. In the very first picture of this wonderfully sensitive story, "Chibi" is shown hidden away in the dark space underneath the schoolhouse, afraid of the schoolmaster, afraid of the children. In subsequent pictures he is always alone, while the other children come to school in two's and three's. With the arrival of the friendly schoolmaster and his discovery of Chibi's talent to imitate crows, Chibi grows in stature and courage. On graduation day he is pictured standing tall and erect, having been the only one honored for perfect attendance at school for six years. Chibi does not completely change with his new name of Crow Boy, for this story

[19]Robert McCloskey. *Time of Wonder* (New York: Viking, 1957), p. 62.

Randolph Caldecott was one of the first illustrators for children to show action in his pictures. The design for the Caldecott Medal is taken from the picture.

From "John Gilpin," *Picture Book Number 1*, illustrated by Randolph Caldecott. Reproduced by permission of the publisher, Frederick Warne & Co., Inc.

Early Illustrators

Quaint costumes and prim and proper decorum characterized the art work of Kate Greenaway.

From *A Apple Pie* by Kate Greenaway. Reproduced by permission of the publisher, Frederick Warne & Co., Inc.

A trusting Jemima Puddle-Duck listens to the "foxy-whiskered gentleman." Beatrix Potter created real personalities in both the text and pictures of her many books.

From *The Tale of Jemima Puddle-Duck* by Beatrix Potter. Reproduced by permission of the publisher, Frederick Warne & Co., Inc.

Detailed cardboard cuts by Blair Lent capture the delicacy and strength of this Japanese folktale.

Illustration by Blair Lent from *The Wave* by Margaret Hodges. Copyright © 1964 by Margaret Hodges; Copyright © 1964 by Blair Lent. Reprinted by permission of the publisher, Houghton Mifflin Company.

Media: printing and scratchboard

A menacing wolf is created with scratchboard illustrations for the story of Peter and the Wolf.

Illustration by Frans Haacken from *Peter and the Wolf* by Serge Prokofieff, originally published by Alfred Holz Verlag, Berlin. English edition first published by Bancroft & Company Limited, and used with their permission.

Well-designed woodcuts portray the transformation of a dog to a magnificent tiger. Notice the dog shadow of the tiger's former self.

Illustration used by permission of Charles Scribner's Sons from *Once a Mouse* by Marcia Brown. Copyright © 1961 Marcia Brown.

The crisp clear lines of wood engravings portray rustic characters that are reminiscent of the earliest Mother Goose books.

Copyright © 1963 by Philip Reed. Cover from *Mother Goose and Nursery Rhymes*. Used by permission of Atheneum Publishers.

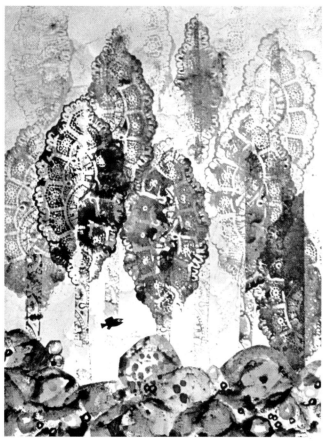

The little fish, *Swimmy*, is almost lost in a forest of seaweed made by printing with lace paper doilies. Leo Lionni has used colláge, paper stamping, and many muted watercolors to create this watery world of fantasy.

From *Swimmy* by Leo Lionni. © Copyright 1963 by Leo Lionni. Reprinted by permission of Pantheon Books, a Division of Random House, Inc.

No longer a tadpole, the frog leaves his friend the fish to discover the wonders of the world. A patchwork of textured crayon creates the lake and the bank.

From *Fish Is Fish* by Leo Lionni. Copyright © 1970 by Leo Lionni. Reprinted by permission of Pantheon Books, a division of Random House, Inc.

A Variety of Media

One winter morning Peter woke up and looked out the window. Snow had fallen during the night. It covered everything as far as he could see.

A colláge of red-patterned paper conveys the warmth of Peter's room in contrast to the snowy city roofs.

From *The Snowy Day* by Ezra Jack Keats. Copyright © 1962 by Ezra Jack Keats. Reprinted by permission of The Viking Press, Inc.

Soft gray and green watercolors portray a foggy morning in a forest so quiet that you can hear "the sound of growing ferns."

From *Time of Wonder* by Robert McCloskey. Copyright © 1957 by Robert McCloskey. Reprinted by permission of The Viking Press, Inc.

At that moment the sun climbed over the hills of Hexham. But Hildilid was too tired from fighting the night to enjoy the day.

Hildilid is too tired from trying to chase the night away to enjoy the day. Arnold Lobel's amusing black-and-white pictures end appropriately in a burst of yellow sunshine.

From *Hildilid's Night* by Cheli Duran Ryan. Illustrations by Arnold Lobel. Illustrations copyright © 1971 by Arnold Lobel. Used by permission of Macmillan Publishing Co., Inc.

Effective Use of Color

John Burningham has made extravagant use of color in this foldout poster scene of summer. Brilliant yellow and green acrylic paints give the feeling of a dazzling summer day.

From *Seasons*, written and illustrated by John Burningham, published in England by Jonathan Cape, Ltd., and in the United States by The Bobbs-Merrill Company, Inc.

Using only shades of blue chalk, Weisgard has created a wet misty world as seen through the gentle slanting rain.

Reprinted from *Where Does the Butterfly Go When It Rains*, text © 1961 by May Garelick, illustrations © 1961 by Leonard Weisgard, a Young Scott Book, by permission of Addison-Wesley Publishing Company.

Realistic wash drawings and watercolors reflect the drama of the moment a boy discovers a nest of baby rabbits. Fine draftsmanship is evident in Shimin's natural sketches of people and animals.

From *Listen Rabbit!* by Aileen Fisher. Illustrations copyright © 1964 by Symeon Shimin with permission of Thomas Y. Crowell Company, Inc., Publisher.

The Style of Art:
Realistic and Impressionistic

A sophisticated rabbit and serious-minded little girl wander through impressionistic landscapes while selecting appropriate presents for her mother. Sendak has extended the text by adding little details and creating definite characters in these luminous watercolors.

Illustration by Maurice Sendak from *Mr. Rabbit and the Lovely Present* by Charlotte Zolotow. Pictures copyright © 1962 by Maurice Sendak. Reprinted by permission of Harper & Row, Publishers, Inc.

A Variety of Styles

John Steptoe's powerful paintings with heavy dark contours and glowing colors are somewhat reminiscent of Rouault. Robert waits in the hall while a lady (nameless and so headless) delivers *Stevie* to his house to stay with his mother.

Illustration from *Stevie* by John Steptoe. Copyright © 1969 by John Steptoe. Reprinted by permission of Harper & Row, Publishers, Inc.

Jewel-like colors in abstract designs are characteristic of many of the pictures by Brian Wildsmith.

Illustration by Brian Wildsmith, from *Brian Wildsmith's Mother Goose*, copyright 1964 by Brian Wildsmith. Used by permission of the American publisher, Franklin Watts, Inc. Published in England by Oxford University Press and used with their permission.

Brilliant graphics illustrate the story of Anansi by McDermott. Based on the designs of the Ashanti people, this book was first adapted from an animated film.

From *Anansi the Spider* adapted and illustrated by Gerald McDermott. Copyright © 1972 by Landmark Production, Incorporated. Reproduced by permission of Holt, Rinehart and Winston, Inc.

across the yard

Pattern on pattern is characteristic of the stylized comical drawings of Pat Hutchins. Action and anticipation are in every line of the fox, while flat-footed Rosie goes on in her determined way.

From *Rosie's Walk* by Pat Hutchins. Copyright © 1968 by Patricia Hutchins. Used by permission of Macmillan Publishing Co., Inc.

Cartoonlike illustrations are used in the popular Walt Disney version of Snow White.

From *Walt Disney's Snow White and the Seven Dwarfs*. Illustrations by the Walt Disney Studio, adapted by Campbell Grant. Story adapted by Jane Werner. Published by Golden Press. © Walt Disney Productions.

© Walt Disney Productions

Compare and Contrast these Two Interpretations of Snow White

Nancy Burkert has shown careful attention to detail in her representational illustrations of Snow White.

Reprinted with the permission of Farrar, Straus & Giroux, Inc., from *Snow-White and the Seven Dwarfs*, a tale from the Brothers Grimm, translated by Randall Jarrell, illustrated by Nancy Ekholm Burkert, Pictures copyright © 1972 by Nancy Ekholm Burkert.

has the integrity of life itself. He remains aloof and independent as he assumes his increased adult responsibilities. He has lost the gnawing loneliness of Chibi, however, as the final pages of text and pictures combine to tell us of his character development:

> Crow Boy would nod and smile as if he liked the name. And when his work was done he would buy a few things for his family. Then he would set off for his home on the far side of the mountain, stretching his growing shoulders proudly like a grown-up man. And from around the turn of the mountain road would come a crow call—the happy one.[20]

Character change is also evident in Samantha (everyone calls her Sam), the heroine of the Caldecott Award book, *Sam, Bangs and Moonshine.* Sam's fantasies are responsible for the near loss of her devoted friend Thomas at high tide out on Blue Rock. Sensitive pictures by Evaline Ness clearly portray a miserable and remorseful Sam huddled in her chair sobbing uncontrollably. When Thomas is safely rescued, Sam decides to give him her pet gerbil, named "Moonshine." Symbolically, Sam gives away her "Moonshine" tendencies at the same time.

Another requirement of an excellent picture book is one of accuracy and consistency with the text. If the story states, as Bemelmans does in *Madeline,* that "In an old house in Paris that was covered with vines lived twelve little girls in two straight lines,"[21] children are going to look for the vines; they are going to count the little girls; and they are going to check to see that the lines are straight. Bemelmans was painstakingly careful to include just eleven little girls in his pictures after Madeline goes to the hospital. He failed in one small picture that shows twelve girls breaking their bread, even though Madeline was still hospitalized. A 7-year-old child noticed the error and called attention to it one day during a story hour.

Pictures and text should be synchronized, then, for as the adult reads the text, the child is reading the pictures. For this reason, children prefer that the picture be on the same page or facing the part of the story that it illustrates.

[20]Taro Yashima. *Crow Boy* (New York: Viking, 1955), p. 37.
[21]Ludwig Bemelmans. *Madeline* (New York: Viking, 1939, 1962), unpaged.

A miserable and remorseful Sam huddled in her chair sobs uncontrollably.

From *Sam, Bangs & Moonshine* written and illustrated by Evaline Ness. Copyright © 1966 by Evaline Ness. Reproduced by permission of Holt, Rinehart and Winston, Inc.

Many picture books today are quite authentic and show the result of hours of research. Barbara Cooney spent much time studying rare, illuminated manuscripts before she illustrated *Chanticleer and the Fox,* adapted from *The Canterbury Tales.* The results of her research are to be seen in every picture. The book begins in the style of an illuminated manuscript with a strawberry plant placed inside the capital letter of the first word. The thatched roof cottage, the wattle fence, and every flower and blade of grass shown in the book are indigenous to the England of Chaucer's time. True to the superstitions of the day, Cooney placed a magpie, thought to be an evil omen, on the second page of the story to foretell the disaster that was to befall the proud rooster.

Another beautiful picture book that reflects

this same painstaking care in research and authenticity is *Snow White and the Seven Dwarfs* (*see* Chapter 4), illustrated by Nancy Burkert. Set in medieval times, every detail of the illustrations reflect the period; the interiors of huts and palaces, fabric and tapestries, even the pieces of crockery were copied after those found in the Museum of Decorative Arts in Paris. The headdress that Snow White wears when serving the dwarves is copied from a portrait by the German engraver Albrecht Dürer; her apron is embroidered with meadow rue, an herb to ward off witches; while the white dog, cherries, and lilies in the bouquet on the table all signify virginity. The detail and authenticity of these exquisite illustrations should help children develop an appreciation for beautiful bookmaking.

Not only are settings in the past carefully documented, but settings of today are faithfully presented in children's picture storybooks. Every young American may visit the public gardens of Boston in McCloskey's almost classic story, *Make Way for Ducklings*. Don Freeman has illustrated the magnificent beauty of San Francisco in his *Fly High, Fly Low*, the story of two pigeons. Leo Politi has captured the excitement and beauty of a Mexican Christmas procession in Los Angeles in his book *Pedro, the Angel of Olvera Street*.

Foreign settings have been authentically represented in Bemelmans' books, *Madeline* and *Madeline's Rescue*. In these stories Bemelmans has used well-known landmarks of Paris—such as Notre Dame, the opera building, Sacre Coeur, the Tuileries, and the Pont Neuf—as background for his striking colored pictures of Madeline and her eleven friends. In brilliant blues, pinks, and lavender Marcia Brown has recreated the charm of Venice in her book *Felice*, the story of a young gondolier's cat. Her pictures recall the extravagant beauty of St. Mark's Square, the Grand Canal swarming with barcas and gondolas, and the intriguingly narrow back canals.

The authenticity of the setting is not as important to boys and girls as is the plot of the book. However, where a specific setting is suggested, it should be accurate and authentic. It is hoped that young children's horizons will be widened by these occasional glimpses of other worlds that serve as background for their favorite stories.

THE MEDIA AND STYLE OF THE ILLUSTRATIONS

Children accept and enjoy a variety of media in the illustrations of their picture books. Many artists today are using the picture book as a vehicle for experimentation with new and interesting media. Since the primary purpose of an illustration is to reflect, interpret, and extend the text of the book, only two questions need to be asked about the medium used: (1) How appropriate is this particular medium to the story? and (2) How effectively has the artist used it?

The question of evaluating media still remains one of harmony between text and illustrations. Was the choice of medium an appropriate one for that particular story? For medium does impose a certain form of its own; one can't imagine *The Tale of Peter Rabbit* done in woodcuts, for example, any more than one can imagine *Once a Mouse* painted in delicate watercolors! Occasionally, there will be a book whose illustrations are superb and whose story is a good one, but text and pictures do not go together. *The Happy Owls* is a rather sentimental story of two old owls who never quarrel. It is illustrated by Piatti with bold, beautifully colored pictures heavily outlined in black in a fashion similar to Rouault. The pictures alone are magnificent; the story alone is peaceful and quiet. The choice of opaque paints, rich heavy colors, and a bold style of illustration seems inappropriate for the theme of this story.

Woodcuts and Similar Techniques

In the beginning of printing the woodcut was the only means of reproducing art. It is still used effectively today. In making a woodcut, the nonprinting areas are cut away, leaving a raised surface which, when inked and pressed on paper, duplicates the original design. If colored overlays are to be used, the artist must prepare as many woodcuts as colors. Woodcut illustrations produce a bold simplicity and have a power that is not found in any other media.

Marcia Brown has used woodcuts superbly in her fable of India, *Once a Mouse*. Taking full advantage of her medium, she has allowed the texture or grain of the wood to show through, adding depth and interesting patterns to these dramatic illustrations. The woodcuts by Ness for

Josefina February are both bold and compassionate, as they portray the poverty and richness of native life in Haiti. Frasconi is well known for his well-designed woodcuts in such books as *See Again, Say Again* and *The House that Jack Built.* Although Emberley used only three colors for the woodcuts for *Drummer Hoff,* the book appears to explode with as much color as the powder of Drummer Hoff's cannon. This effect was created by careful overprinting of Emberley's very stylized designs. This artist owns and operates a small printing press on which he prints the woodcuts and most of the type for the books that he and his wife create.

Wood engravings are cut on the end-grain of very hard wood (usually boxwood) rather than with the grain on the plank side of a soft wood. This process of wood engraving gives a delicate, finer line to the illustrations than the more crude woodcut. Not many modern picture books have been illustrated with wood engravings. Artzybasheff's illustrations for *Aesop's Fables* are fine examples of this medium, as are Philip Reed's *Mother Goose and Nursery Rhymes.*

Linoleum block prints also give a finer line than woodcuts. The simple, direct story of *Dick Whittington and His Cat* was illustrated by Marcia Brown with linoleum block prints. Clement Hurd has placed linoleum block prints on a background of a print previously made from the grain of weathered wood. This intriguing technique of print on print produced an effect of water for *Wingfin and Topple* and a forest fire in *Wildfire.* Both of these books were written by Valens.

Cardboard cuts resemble wood or linoleum cuts, although a hard, medium-weight laminated cardboard is used. The artist draws with a lead pencil on the cardboard and then cuts away the area he does not want to reproduce. When the illustration is finished, it is shellacked in order to prevent the cardboard from deteriorating when the ink is applied. Block printing ink is rolled or brushed on to the raised surface of the cardboard and then the print is made. Blair Lent has produced some striking art using this medium in illustrating Dayrell's *Why the Sun and the Moon Live in the Sky,* Hodges' *The Wave,* Small's *Baba Yaga,* and his own *John Tabor's Ride.* Lent is able to adapt this particular medium to express

many moods. In *The Wave,* he created a delicate, almost fragile Japanese village that was completely engulfed by a mighty tidal wave. By contrast, action and tall-tale humor are captured in his illustrations of John Tabor riding on the back of a whale. Yet another mood is created by the fiendish Russian witch, Baba Yaga, who rides her mortar and pestle on great swooping air currents. In skilled hands this medium has infinite possibilities and much flexibility.

Scratchboard illustrations may be confused with wood engravings, since their appearance is similar. However, the process of making them is very different. In making scratchboard illustrations a very black ink is usually painted on the smooth white surface of a drawing board or scratchboard. When it is thoroughly dry, the picture is made by scratching through the black-inked surface with a sharp instrument. Color may be added with a transparent overlay, or it may be painted on the white scratchboard prior to applying the black ink. Scratchboard technique produces crisp black-and-white illustrations. Handsome pictures for Prokofieff's *Peter and the Wolf* were made with scratchboard by Frans Haacken of Germany. Cooney has achieved a dramatic effect with this technique combined with color overlays in *Chanticleer and the Fox.*

Stone Lithography[22]

Another very old method of illustrating is that of drawing directly on stone. Using a grease crayon or pencil, the artist transfers his designs to the surface of the stone. The stone is dampened with an ink repellent. When the ink is placed on the stone, it will adhere only to the greased area. In the U.S. all the Currier and Ives prints were made with stone lithography. McCloskey used this method in illustrating his well-known *Make Way for Ducklings* and the d'Aulaires have utilized it in their picture books, *Ola, Abraham Lincoln,* and *Pocahontas.* Felix Hoff-

---

[22] Today, "lithography" is a term that has come to be synonymous with photo offset, which is a printing process. The term "offset" merely means that the original plate does not touch the paper; it first makes an impression on another, or "blanket," roller which, in turn, prints the illustration. Stone lithography, however, refers to the old-fashioned method of printing from an image that has been drawn directly on stone.

man has illustrated many single fairy tales (*see* Chapter 4) with this medium. Stone lithography can be identified by the subtle grain of the stone, which is visible in each picture. However, a new printing process which uses acetates to imitate this grainy texture has been developed. Soon, then, the actual use of stone may be obsolete.

Collágé

The use of collágé for illustrating children's books has become very popular. The effect of this medium is simple and childlike, not unlike pictures children might make themselves. The word "collágé" is derived from the French verb *coller*, meaning "to paste," and refers to the kind of picture that is made by cutting out a variety of different kinds of materials—newspaper clippings, patterned wallpaper, fabric, and the like, and assembling them into a unified, harmonious illustration. Ezra Jack Keats has proven himself a master of this technique with his award-winning *The Snowy Day*. Using patterned and textured papers and pen and ink, Keats has captured young Peter's delight in a snowy day.

Lionni used collágé with patterned crayon shapes to create the grass, leaves, and birds in his highly original *Inch by Inch*. Circles of torn paper were used to convey the abstract families of *Little Blue and Little Yellow*. In his own version of the ant and grasshopper fable, Lionni has created a favorite character, *Frederick*, a mouse-poet torn from two shades of gray paper. In the story of *Alexander and the Wind-up Mouse*, Lionni arranges scraps of newspapers, tissue paper, marbleized paper, and wallpaper to tell the story of the friendship of a house-mouse with a wind-up toy mouse. Children enjoy looking closely at the visual images created by the medium of collágé. After seeing some of these books by Keats and Lionni, they will want to make their own collágé stories.

Paints and Pen and Ink

The vast majority of illustrations for children's books are done in paint, pen and ink, or combinations of these media. The creation of new materials, such as plastic paints, and new techniques frequently make it very difficult to determine the medium used.

Generally, paint may be divided into two

kinds, that which is translucent and has a somewhat transparent quality, such as watercolor, and that which is opaque and is impenetrable to light, such as tempera, gouache, and oils.

We usually think of old-fashioned delicate pictures when we think of watercolor, but this is not necessarily the case. Ardizzone, England's master of watercolor and pen-and-ink sketches, has produced full-color seascapes for his *Little Tim and the Brave Sea Captain* that have tremendous vitality and movement. The storm scenes in McCloskey's *Time of Wonder* have this same power, contrasted with the soft diffused light of the fog scene. Broad comic humor is hilariously interpreted in Margot Zemach's pastel watercolors for *The Judge*, a cumulative tale written by her husband. Slobodkin's watercolors seem most appropriate for Thurber's delightful fairy tale, *Many Moons*. Other artists who have successfully employed the use of watercolors are Burton in *The Little House*, Marcia Brown with *Felice*, Bemelmans in *Madeline*, and all of Marguerite de Angeli's and Tasha Tudor's work.

Acrylics or plastic paints produce vibrant, almost shocking colors. Jose Aruego and Ariane Aruego have used this medium to achieve brilliant pictures for "the follow-the-leader" story of *The Chick and the Duckling* by Ginsburg. Very young children reach out to touch these shiny pictures of the chick, who thought he could do everything that the duckling could. These artists have used even more colors to illustrate the amusing story of a panda by Robert Kraus, *Milton the Early Riser*. Wildsmith also uses some acrylics in many of the brilliant illustrations for his *Brian Wildsmith's ABC* and La Fontaine's fable, *The Lion and the Rat* (*see* Chapter 4).

Some of Keats' picture books are a combination of collágé and acrylic paintings. The brilliant sky scenes in *Dreams* are made from marbleized paper, first created by floating acrylic paints on water and then lightly placing a piece of paper over it. Contrasted against the dark tenement building, where Amy and Roberto live, these brilliant backdrops give the feeling of a hot city night.

Opaque paint may give a brilliant sparkling look, such as that Weisgard achieved in *The Little Island*, or it may produce the rather somber colors of Politi's *Song of the Swallows*. Sidjakov has created a stained-glass effect for Robbins' story of *Baboushka and the Three Kings* by using bright blue, red, and yellow tempera paints and a black felt pen to outline his wooden, doll-like figures. Sendak contrasted dark green and blue tempera with shades of purple to create Max's weird fantasy world in *Where the Wild Things Are.* Texture and shading are achieved with pen-and-ink cross-hatching strokes. The characters in Sendak's *In The Night Kitchen* are painted in bold flat colors that resemble a comic-book world, while details are reserved for the intricate labels and pictures that are on the cartons, bottles, and jars that make up the city of the night kitchen.

Gouache paint is the same as powder color or tempera, with the addition of white. Roger Duvoisin used this medium most effectively to create the fog-shrouded world of *Hide and Seek Fog* by Alvin Tresselt. The use of gouache is also characteristic of the many books illustrated by

In Mickey's dream he falls out of his clothes and into the world of the "night kitchen."

Illustration from *In the Night Kitchen* by Maurice Sendak. Copyright © 1970 by Maurice Sendak. Reprinted by permission of Harper & Row, Publishers, Inc.

the Provensens; for example, their large animated pictures for *Aesop's Fables* (*see* Chapter 4).

Kota Taniuchi used oil paints for his illustrations of *Up on a Hilltop,* the quiet story of a boy who rides to a hilltop to watch a train pass and that night dreams he is a train himself. This book has a tactile quality that makes young children want to touch its canvaslike pages and layered paint. It received a graphic award at the International Children's Book Fair in Bologna.

Crayon and Chalk

Crayon and soft pencil illustrations are frequently employed for children's books. The subtle texture of crayon is easily discernible. Rojankovsky used crayon, brush, and ink to make his delightful illustrations for *Frog Went A-Courtin'!* In *Fish Is Fish,* Lionni creates an underwater world with crayons, but he portrays the fish's conception of the frog's world with the brilliant colors of a felt pen. The difference in color and media helps to separate the imagined from the real. The textured quality of Yashima's colored-pencil trees is always recognizable. These can be seen in *The Village Tree, Plenty to Watch* and *Crow Boy.*

Leonard Weisgard created a rainy world in his lovely illustrations for *Where Does the Butterfly Go When It Rains?* by Garelick. In order to achieve the textured haziness of a light summer rain, soft blue chalk was sponged on paper that had been placed on a rough-grained board. Scratching with a needle added the slanting rain lines. The general conception of this book is one of complete harmony of words and pictures.

The soft furry look of the illustrations for *The Burning Rice Fields* was created with pastels (a kind of chalk stick) by Funai. The pictures have a childlike quality that is appropriate for Sara Cone Bryant's telling of this well-known folk tale (*see* Chapter 4). Hogrogian illustrated an old Scottish song entitled *Always Room for One More* in a book by Sorche Nic Leodhas, with intriguing pen-and-ink illustrations combined with heathery colored pastels. Using cross-hatching and parallel lines, the figures appear as misty as the Scottish moors themselves.

Photography

More and more children's books are being illustrated with photographs. A photograph, like a painting, can simply record an incident or, in the hands of a photo-artist, it can interpret, extend, contrast, and develop real insight. The most exciting photographic work for children's books is being done by Tana Hoban. Her book *Look Again!* does not present a narrative but helps the child develop his perception and sharpen his awareness of the world. A two-inch square peep hole allows the viewer to see only a portion of the black-and-white photograph, while he guesses what it is. Turning the pages, he then sees a detailed close-up of a snail, a fish, the face of a zebra, and so on. As the square frame falls back on the previous photograph, another pattern is seen, causing the reader to *Look Again!* The book provides an exercise in seeing, a way of expanding the child's consciousness. Its total graphic conception is simple, yet superbly complex.

Beautiful photographs of animals by Ylla have illustrated rather slight stories: *Two Little Bears* and *Animal Babies* by Gregor and *The Sleepy Little Lion* by Margaret Wise Brown. Ylla's photographs also illustrate the picture puzzle book *Whose Eye Am I?* by Bonsall. The pictures for these books are simple, large, and beguiling. The stories seem somewhat contrived, and obviously were created for the pictures rather than the other way around.

Laughing Camera for Children by Hanns Reich derives its humor from the juxtaposition of some superb photographs. A picture of a mother duck crossing the street with her baby ducklings behind her is placed opposite a photograph of a teacher crossing the street with each of her pupils holding on to a long rope. The braided tail of a horse is compared to the pigtail of a college graduate. Middle-grade children would find much to interest them in these humorous pictures. A more serious response would develop from the thought-provoking photographs of *Children of Many Lands*, also assembled by Reich. These photographs have some of the same qualities of that magnificent photo essay, *The Family of Man* by Edward Steichen.

The world that is Paris has been brilliantly photographed in both the film and book entitled *The Red Balloon* by Lamorisse. Pascal's magical balloon takes him down side streets and narrow alleys, follows him on the streetcar, flies up to his shuttered apartment windows, and hovers miserably outside his school. The balloon becomes so real that the reader feels empathy for Pascal at the "death" of his red balloon.

Gordon Parks took the illustrations for the book *J. T.* during its filming for the CBS Children's Hour. The story by Jane Wagner takes place in Harlem at Christmastime, and concerns a boy and his struggle to save an old one-eyed near-dead alley cat. The cat is killed, but J. T. survives and gains some surprising strength in the process.

Sensitive photographs illustrate the story *We Are Having a Baby* by Viki Holland. Told from the point of view of 4-year-old Dana, this picture story relates the adventure of the new baby's arrival. Hospital scenes are included, but not scenes of the actual birth. Dana is delighted with the baby at first; then she has some doubts about the whole idea of a baby brother. The story seems real and not contrived to suit the pictures—a fault of many stories illustrated with photographs.

The Use of Color

Children generally prefer brightly colored illustrations, although they readily accept pastels and black and white, provided the pictures and text tell a good story. Many perennial favorites do not use color in their illustrations—the sepia pictures of McCloskey's *Make Way for Ducklings* and Ward's *The Biggest Bear*, the black-and-white humorous illustrations by Lawson for both *The Story of Ferdinand* and *Wee Gillis* by Leaf, and the well-loved black-and-white illustrations of *Millions of Cats* by Wanda Gág. The use of color alone is no guarantee of success for a book. The appropriate use of color is significant.

The choice of color or colors depends on the theme of the book. Certainly, the choice of blue for both pictures and text in *Blueberries for Sal* by McCloskey was appropriate. Tawny yellow and black were the natural choices for Don Freeman's wonderfully funny story of the lion who suddenly decided to live up to the double meaning of his name, *Dandelion*. Quiet stories—such as *Play with Me* and *Gilberto and the Wind* by Marie Hall Ets—are illustrated with pastels of white, browns, and pale yellow against a soft gray background. Wildsmith has used vibrant jewel-like colors to illustrate the fable *The North Wind and the Sun* by La Fontaine. In cool greens and blues Wildsmith portrays the wind blowing violently to make a man remove his new cloak. With brilliant oranges, yellows, and reds the artist shows that the sun is able to achieve by warmth what the wind could not achieve by coldness!

Certain artists have made effective use of color to show a change in mood for the story. In order to convey the loneliness of *Swimmy* after the tuna fish had gulped down all of his friends, Lionni places the tiny black fish on a large double-page spread of watery gray. In *White Snow, Bright Snow,* Duvoisin has utilized a gray-blue to give the feeling of cold. The reader sees the day grow darker as the snow becomes thicker and heavier. The next morning the storm is over. With brilliant splashes of red, yellow, and dazzling white Duvoisin emphasizes the contrast of this dramatic weather change. The pictures in *Dawn* by Uri Shulevitz start with the deep blue of nighttime, when an old man and his grandson are curled up outdoors in their bedrolls. The moon casts a luminous light on the shimmering lakes, making the shadows on the mountains even darker. Gradually the sky lightens, the birds begin to call, and the old man and the boy break camp and push their boat into the waiting water. Then the dawn breaks and the quiet world of lake, mountain, and boat is suffused with golden, pink, and green light. Changing color and increasingly larger pictures create the beauty and drama of this everyday miracle.

In order to signify danger Marcia Brown has added red to her pictures for *Once a Mouse.* Starting with cool forest green, mustard yellow, and a trace of red, the red builds up in increasing amounts until the climax is reached and the tiger is changed back to a mouse. Only cool green and yellow is seen in the last picture as the hermit is once again "thinking about big—and little. . . ."

The Style of the Illustrations

Occasionally, the question is raised as to what style of illustration is best for children's books. There can be only one answer to that question: There is no *one* style that is most preferred by all children, any more than one medium is enjoyed more than another. A young child's taste in art is quite catholic, including realistic, impressionistic, stylized, abstract, and caricatured art. Again, the primary question concerning style is its harmony with the text; Is the art conveying the same message, the same feelings as the story itself?

Modern picture book styles will help the child to broaden and deepen his receptive powers. Since appreciation is learned, opportunity to view some of the best artistic talents in children's literature may have a lasting effect on children's taste in art in general.

The age of the child for whom the book is intended places a few restrictions on style. It is difficult for a child in the preoperational stage of mental development to grasp the idea of perspective. One young child of 3 looked at a picture that showed a man in the distance and remarked: "That's a funny tiny man down there." Some of Helen Oxenbury's pictures (such as the "U" for umbrellas in her *ABC of Things*) are painted from a bird's-eye point of view and may confuse 3- and 4-year-olds. Just as many young children have difficulty comprehending perspective, so, too, are they bothered by the incomplete picture of a hand, part of an animal, or other object. They want to know where the missing parts are. Imagine the concept of a flamingo that a very young child might derive from Lionni's picture of an inchworm (in *Inch by Inch*) measuring just the neck of a flamingo! If the child had seen a flamingo, or if a complete flamingo was pictured before showing only a partial illustration of it, his imagination could fill in the rest of the bird. With increased experience and visual maturity, children are ready for more complex and varied art styles.

Style is the arrangement of line, color, and mass into a visual image. The style of an illustrator will be influenced by his particular skill as an artist and his vision of the story that is being interpreted.

Some artists' styles have stabilized to the point that they are quite recognizable. They frequently persist in their preference for one style, one medium, and even in their choice of content. Thus, we have come to associate quaint and quiet pastel illustrations with Tasha Tudor's work. Lois Lenski's rounded adult personages in 5-year-old bodies are always distinctive. Whether Mr. Small is *Cowboy Small* or *Policeman Small,* he is easily identified as he gaily goes about the important details of his daily life. Slobodkin's work is almost always in watercolors, with figures that are sketchy and incomplete. With only a few lines he is able to suggest the throne of the king, or the huge bed of Princess Lenore in *Many Moons.* His illustrations seem almost to float on the page and complement the fairy-tale quality of this modern fantasy. Equally distinctive are Leo Politi's panoramic views of villages or missions in Mexico, California, and Italy. His people are usually painted in primitive fashion with large hands and feet. The peasant art style of Francoise for the *JeanneMarie* books is most appropriate for her stories and the nursery-school children who enjoy them. All her little doll-like people have pink, rosy circles on their cheeks, and the pages frequently contain decorative folk designs of hearts and flowers. This same kind of peasant art is used with more brilliant colors by Virginia Kahl for her amusing story of the Duke and Duchess and their thirteen daughters in *The Duchess Bakes a Cake.* Janina Domanska has employed humorous folk art for her book *The Turnip.* The illustrations for the nursery rhymes, *If All the Seas Were One Sea* and *I Saw A Ship A-Sailing,* are very stylized with pattern on pattern in pen and ink and bright-colored overlays. The amusing animals in the stories by Pat Hutchins are equally stylized with patterned fur and feathers. Her squirrels in *The Surprise Party* and *Good Night, Owl!* are easily recognizable, and the hen in *Rosie's Walk* is without doubt the most self-sufficient hen in the barnyard! Some illustrators are cartoon artists such as H. A. Rey, Jean de Brunhoff, and Dr. Seuss. The illustrations of *Curious George,* the monkey; Babar, the French elephant; and all the zany animals of Dr. Seuss are refreshing, amusing, and recognizable.

Several artists are experimenting with both style and media and seem to gather strength with each new book. Sendak's droll little whimsical characters are as recognizable as Jennie, the white sealyham terrier that appears in many of his books. However, his pictures for *The Moon Jumpers, Mr. Rabbit and the Lovely Present, Where the Wild Things Are,* and *In the Night Kitchen* vary, despite the fact that each has a moonlight setting. The luminous illustrations for *The Moon Jumpers* by

Udry give a dreamy effect for the children's dance in the night. The children have a look of almost arrested motion. The "Wild Rumpus" scenes in *Where the Wild Things Are* have an effect almost of caricature and are an extension of the dance in *The Moon Jumpers.* The impressionistic Monetlike pictures for *Mr. Rabbit and the Lovely Present* written by Zolotow are easily identifiable. The little girl looks like an old woman in the way she walks and with the worried look on her face. The rabbit, however, is a very sophisticated rabbit; at times, smug, puzzled, or pleased, but always in complete control of the situation. The trees and end papers of *Where the Wild Things Are* have been compared to Henri Rousseau's French primitive paintings. However, Max, with his roguish smile, and the big ludicrous beasts with their "terrible eyes and terrible teeth" are very much Sendak. While the illustrations for *In the Night Kitchen* reflect the influence that Disney and the comics had on Sendak in his youth, they are very definitely Sendak's own creation. Max has now become Mickey, who sheds the last of his inhibitions in a dream in which he falls out of his clothes and into the night kitchen. Comic-book characters have been refined to a work of art that captures the feelings and dream-wishes of childhood. Each new book of Sendak's represents a deeper involvement with the child that he was and a greater mastery of interpretation.

Marcia Brown's sensitivity to the varying requirements of different stories has led her to use different media and styles of illustrating. Look at the movement of her wonderful *The Three Billy Goats Gruff* as they come prancing over that bridge in the Norwegian fiord country. Her troll is a muddy, ugly one that you are glad to see crushed to bits! Compare these vigorous crayon and gouache drawings to the fluff and frills of *Cinderella* or to the bold, vigorous concentration of lines and design in the woodcuts for *Once a Mouse.* The exquisite beauty of her two-color illustrations in black and white and delicate peach are most appropriate for the symbolic story of *The Wild Swans* by Hans Christian Andersen. Leo Lionni is also experimenting with style and media. His colláge pictures for *Inch by Inch, Little Blue and Little Yellow, Frederick,* and *Alexander and the Wind-up Mouse* have been most successful. The ocean background of *Swimmy* is watercolor, but he has also used collàge and lino-leum block print in this book. Textured fish swim near seaweed that has been made by printing with lace doilies. Despite the many techniques that have been used to make this lovely book, it has unity of theme and is harmonious with the text. The rich use of crayon is seen in *Fish Is Fish*, while crayon and paint are combined to make the beautiful pictures of *The Biggest House in the World*. The influence of his trip to India is reflected in the decorative design of some of his symbolic paintings for *Tico and the Golden Wings*.

Style, then, is an elusive quality of the artist changing and varying over the years and with the particular demands of the work. There is, perhaps, more freedom to experiment in illustrating children's books than ever before. Many of our contemporary artists are taking advantage of this new freedom and producing fresh and original art.

The Format of the Book

The actual format of the book is important in creating its total impact. Today, picture books have many sizes and shapes. Children enjoy large and beautiful books, but the continuous popularity of Potter's *The Tale of Peter Rabbit* and her other well-loved books show children like small-sized books also. Sendak's *The Nutshell Library* consists of four tiny books, measuring $2\frac{1}{2} \times 3\frac{5}{8}$ inches, that fit in their own small case.

The shape of some books suggests their content; for example, *A Tree Is Nice* by Udry is tall and vertical in shape. The horizontal shape of McCloskey's *Blueberries for Sal* is quite appropriate for portraying Sal and her mother on one side of a long, sloping hill and the bear cub and his mother on the other. The cumulative old rhyme of *A Boy Went Out to Gather Pears* fits perfectly in a long, narrow format designed by Felix Hoffmann.

Both the cloth cover and dust jacket of a book should receive careful attention. The primary purpose of the jacket is to call attention to the book. It should not be just a duplicate of an illustration from the book but should be carefully designed to express the general character or mood. Too often the binding design or cloth cover of a book is just a repeat of the jacket; yet, the cloth material will not take the color of an illustration in the same way as the paper of the jacket. Good cloth designs are usually small and symbolic of the content. For example, a small, single white cricket is stamped on the gray cover of *A Pocketful of Cricket* by Caudill. The jacket design shows Jay standing with his hands in his overalls and a satisfied look on his face. He is framed by leaves and branches of the hickory nut tree and the cricket that he took to the first day at school is on the jacket. Most library bindings do incorporate the jacket design on the cloth since these covers are washable and will take color as well as paper will. This type of binding preserves the gay attractiveness of the jacket in a permanent form, but destroys the contrast in color and texture between a cloth cover and the jacket design.

The endpapers of a picture book may also add to its attractiveness. These are the first and last pages of the book, one of which is glued to the reverse of the cover, while the other is not pasted down. Endpapers are usually of stronger paper than printed pages. In picture books endpapers are usually of a color that harmonizes with the cover or other pictures in the book, and frequently these are illustrated. Again, their patterns usually give a hint of the general theme of the book. The striking endpapers of Marcia Brown's *Felice*, with their design of interlacing black-and-white gondolas against a dark blue background, suggest the setting of the story. The brilliant red-and-blue design on the endpapers of *Chanticleer and the Fox* by Cooney represents the eye of that proud rooster. The endpapers of *Crow Boy* by Yashima show a flower and butterfly alone against a dark background. They seem to symbolize the metamorphosis of Crow Boy's life from one of dark despair to brilliant hope.

Even the title page of a picture book can be beautiful and symbolic. The title-page spread for *Bear Circus* by William Pène du Bois shows curious kangaroos peering into the tent bearing the name of the book. The title page of *The Happy Lion* by Louise Fatio introduces the reader to the tame nature of this wise beast. On another double-page spread, Duvoisin has drawn a golden, serene lion peacefully sleeping, while a small bird eats a meal not more than a paw's length away from his mouth.

Attention should be given to the spacing of

A well-designed title page that invites the reader into the *Bear Circus*.

From *Bear Circus* by William Péne du Bois. Copyright © 1971 by William Péne du Bois. Reprinted by permission of The Viking Press, Inc.

pictures and text so that they do not appear monotonously in the same position on each page. Arnold Lobel has contained many of his pictures for *On the Day Peter Stuyvesant Sailed into Town* within a frame that resembles the Dutch tiles used as a design for the endpapers. However, every now and then a figure or a feather of a hat will break through the framing, or just the text will be framed. Three double-page spreads depicting Peter's arrival at the run-down town of New Amsterdam, its reformed appearance twelve years later, and Peter's prophetic dream of the future—all help to add variety to this well-planned book.

The spacing of the text on the page, the choice of margins, the white space within a book contribute to the making of a quality picture book.

In Burton's *The Little House* the text flows in the same rhythmical pattern as the road. Poetic text and well-placed illustrations describe one week in a little black boy's life in the book *Some of the Days of Everett Anderson* by Lucille Clifton. The picture for "Saturday Night Late" shows a police car parked outside of Apartment 14A, while a single plain white page faces the next poem for "Sunday Morning Lonely."

Daddy's back
is broad and black
and Everett Anderson loves to ride it.

Daddy's side
is black and wide
and Everett Anderson sits beside it.

Daddy's cheek
is black and sleek
and Everett Anderson kisses it.

Daddy's space
is a black empty place
and Everett Anderson misses it.[23]

In illustrating *Crow Boy*, Yashima has made skillful use of space to help intensify the feeling of Chibi's isolation and loneliness. In the picture of the schoolroom Chibi looms large in the foreground, with empty space separating him from the children across the room. The wide margins of clear white paper in *Time of Wonder* give a rich spacious feeling to this book. Only in the storm scene is the text placed over the illustration in order to have a full page of dark, violent storm.

The appropriate choice of type design is also a matter for consideration. Type is the name given to all printed letters, and type face refers to the over 6,000 different styles available today. These type faces vary in legibility and the feeling they create. Some seem bold; others delicate and

graceful; some crisp and businesslike. Sidjakov[24] describes the difficulty he and his editor had in finding a suitable type face for *Baboushka and the Three Kings*. When they did find one they liked, it was obsolete and not easily available. They finally located enough fonts to handset *Baboushka* a page at a time!

Other factors in a picture book must be considered from a utilitarian standpoint. The paper should be dull so that it does not easily reflect light, opaque to prevent print showing through, and strong to withstand heavy usage. Its color, texture, and receptivity to ink must be considered. Side-sewing in the binding of many picture books makes them more durable, but may distort double-page spreads, unless the art work is prepared with the gutter separation in mind. Tall narrow books with side-sewing will not lie flat when the book is open. Many librarians complain that the binding that is being done today is of poor quality and will not last for the life of the book. These, then, are some of the practical considerations which may affect the beauty

[23]From *Some of the Days of Everett Anderson* by Lucille Clifton. Copyright © 1970 by Lucille Clifton. Reprinted by permission of Holt, Rinehart and Winston, Inc.

[24]Nicolas Sidjakov. "Caldecott Award Acceptance" in *Newbery and Caldecott Medal Books: 1956–1965*, edited by Lee Kingman (Boston: Horn Book, 1965), pp. 223–225.

At first
the Little House
was frightened,
but after she got used to it
she rather liked it.
They rolled along the big road,
and they rolled along the little roads,
until they were way out in the country.
When the Little House saw the green grass
and heard the birds singing, she didn't feel sad any more.
They went along and along, but they couldn't seem to find
just the right place.
They tried the Little House here,
and they tried her there.
Finally they saw a little hill
in the middle of a field . . .
and apple trees growing around.
"There," said the great-great-granddaughter,
"that's just the place."
"Yes, it is," said the Little House to herself.
A cellar was dug on top of the hill
and slowly they moved the house
from the road to the hill.
37

Text and road follow the same rhythmical pattern of the picture.

Illustration from *The Little House* by Virginia Lee Burton. Copyright © renewed 1969 by George Demetrios. Reprinted by permission of the publisher, Houghton Mifflin Company.

Yashima's use of space intensifies Chibi's feelings of loneliness and isolation.

From *Crow Boy* by Taro Yashima. Copyright 1955 by Mitsu and Taro Yashima. Reprinted by permission of The Viking Press, Inc.

and the durability of a book. Librarians, teachers, and publishers must be aware of all these factors.

GUIDES FOR EVALUATING PICTURE BOOKS

Probably the best way to learn to judge a picture storybook is to look searchingly at the finest that have been produced. The following questions will summarize the factors that have been discussed in the last section:

The content of the book: What is the story or content of the book? In what genre of literature does it belong? Where does it take place? When does it take place? Are characters well delineated and developed? Are stereotypes of sex, race, and others avoided? What is the quality of the language? What theme is presented? For what age group does it seem most appropriate?

The illustrations: How are the pictures made an integral part of the text? How is action in the text reflected by action in the pictures? Do the pictures reflect the mood of the story? How do the pictures show character delineation? Are the pictures accurate and consistent with the text? Do they extend the text? Are the pictures authentic?

The media and style of illustrations: What medium or combinations of media have been used (watercolor, chalk, crayon, woodcut, colláge, ink)? Does the medium complement the tone of the story? How many colors have been used? Are the colors bright, soft, varied? How would you describe the style of illustrating (delicate, vigorous, realistic, stylized, decorative)? Is the style appropriate to the story? How has the illustrator varied style and technique? What techniques seem to create movement or rhythm? How has the artist created balance in composition?

The format of the book: What is the size of the book? Does the jacket design express the theme of the book? Does the cover design convey the spirit of the book? How do the endpapers reflect the theme of the book? Does the title page add to the book? In what way? Is the type design well chosen for the theme and purpose of the book? What is the quality of the paper? How durable is the binding?

Comparison with others: How is this work similar to or different from other works of the artist? How is this book similar to or different from other books with the same subject or theme? What comments have reviewers made about this book? What has the artist said about his work? What contribution will this book make to the growing body of literature for children? How lasting will it be?

TYPES AND THEMES OF PICTURE BOOKS

Young children have many and varied interests. They are filled with "insatiable curiosity" about their world. As boys and girls reach out for richer and wider experiences, they are ready for many different types of picture books.

Family Stories

The young child's world is egocentric and revolves around himself and his immediate family. *Zeek Silver Moon* by Amy Ehrlich is the quiet recital of all the wondrous events that have occurred in the five years of life of Zeek, child of a contemporary family. These include his father's song for him when he was a baby, dancing with his mother, picnicking with his father, and solving the mystery of how bread is made. Luminous watercolors by Parker celebrate the beauty of these significant moments in a family whose life style rejects the materialism of today in their search for more enduring values.

Sibling rivalry over the arrival of a new baby is the theme of Alexander's *Nobody Asked Me If I Wanted a Baby Sister.* Oliver is indignant about all the attention that his new baby sister, Bonnie, is receiving, so he puts her in his little red wagon and sets forth to give her away. However, Bonnie herself lets him know that he is very special to her when one one else can quell her howls. His vanity restored, Oliver changes his mind about giving Bonnie away. The humorous little pictures are just right for this childlike story about real feelings. Peter in *Peter's Chair* by Keats doesn't give his sister away, but he decides to run away himself before all of his possessions are painted pink for his new baby sister. Taking his dog, a picture of himself when he was small, his toy crocodile, and his favorite blue chair, he goes outside his house. However, when he discovers that he no longer fits in his chair, he decides that maybe it would be fun to paint it pink himself. The colláge pictures add greatly to this universal story.

The title of Joan Lexau's book, *Emily and the Klunky Baby and the Next-door Dog* describes how Emily feels about her task of taking care of her baby brother while their mother works on income taxes. Emily feels very put-upon and decides to run away and go live with her Daddy— only she doesn't know the way. She has promised her mother that she will not cross any streets, but she becomes disoriented while going around the block. She finally reaches home after a frustrating experience. Martha Alexander's pictures have captured the genuine emotions of a modern divorced mother who has had all the noise she can stand, and those of Emily who is equally vexed with her "klunky baby brother."

Lexau has also written a moving story of a black child's reaction to divorce, and his growing concern about whether he will hear from his father on his birthday. His mother sends him on a mysterious errand and Rafer has his *Me Day*, a whole day to spend gloriously with his father! Children from divorced homes will find real security in Rafer's discussion with his father:

> Daddy said slowly, "Look, your mother and me are divorced. Not you kids. No way! You and me are tight, buddy. Together like glue, O.K.?" "O.K., Daddy," Rafer said.[25]

In *A Father Like That* a little boy (whose father went away before he was born) wistfully tells his mother what kind of father he would have been. He would have played checkers with him each night, talked to him when he had nightmares, known all his friends by name, and always taken his side. The little boy's mother listens patiently and then says:

> "I like the kind of father you are talking about. And in case he never comes, just remember when you grow up you can be a father like that yourself!"[26]

Zolotow has utilized these same wish-fulfilling approaches to portray different sibling relationships in *Do You Know What I'll Do?* and *If It Weren't for You*. In *Do You Know What I'll Do?*, an older sister lovingly tells her little brother of all the thoughtful things that she wants to do for him. Some of her promises are beautiful and include: "I'll bring you a shell to hold the sound of the sea" and "I'll remember my dreams and tell them to you."[27] The softly shaded illustrations by Garth Williams reflect the dignity and deep feelings of the little girl's promises. In *If It Weren't for You*, Zolotow realistically presents an older brother's feelings of jealousy for his younger brother. *Titch*, on the other hand, is the youngest in his family and the smallest. He is too small to ride a two-wheel bicycle, or fly a kite, or use a hammer. But he is not too small to plant a tiny seed! Pat Hutchins understands the humiliation of always being the littlest. The ending of the story of *Titch* is a beautiful example of the poetic justice children so appreciate. The classic story by Ruth Krauss titled *The Carrot Seed* has a similar theme of a small boy triumphing over all the doubts of his family. Little children need to feel big, if only through their stories!

Helen Buckley has written several books about the joy of the extended family. *Grandfather and I* is a favorite with many children. Buckley describes the leisurely pace of a walk with grandfather in contrast to the way mothers and fathers and big sisters and brothers race along. Young children enjoy the rhythm and repetition of the lines: "But Grandfather and I never hurry. We walk along and walk along And stop . . . And look . . . just as long as we like."[28] Others in this series include *Grandmother and I* and *My Sister and I*, all illustrated with Galdone's refreshingly modern pictures.

A warm perceptive grandmother is the only one who can understand her grandson's longing for a doll in Zolotow's *William's Doll*. William has a basketball and a tiny train set that his father has given him, but he still wants a doll. His brother thinks he is a creep, and the boy next

---

[25]Joan Lexau. *Me Day*, illustrated by Robert Weaver (New York: Dial Press, 1971), unpaged.
[26]Charlotte Zolotow. *A Father Like That*, illustrated by Ben Shecter (New York: Harper & Row, 1971), unpaged.

[27]Charlotte Zolotow. *Do You Know What I'll Do?*, illustrated by Garth Williams (New York: Harper & Row, 1958), unpaged.
[28]Helen Buckley. *Grandfather and I*, illustrated by Paul Galdone (New York: Lothrop, 1959), unpaged.

door calls him a sissy. Only his grandmother understands how he feels and says "wonderful" and "nonsense" to the arguments of the males. She buys him a baby doll "to hug . . . so that when he's a father . . . he'll know how to care for his baby. . ."[29] In this gentle story Zolotow has successfully challenged the usual sex roles that society assigns to boys. The illustrations by William Pène du Bois reflect and extend the theme of this story from the first page, where William looks longingly at his sister and her doll, to the title page, where the sister skips off with it and William is left alone. William doesn't look like a sissy, but is very much a real boy—a real boy who just happens to want a doll.

Benjie is a very shy little black child who refuses to speak to people. When his granny loses a cherished earring Benjie goes out to search for it. Forced to ask others if they have seen it, Benjie begins to overcome his shyness. Lexau has written an excellent sequel to this story in *Benjie On His Own.* When Benjie's grandmother is not at school to meet him, he must find his way home alone. Worrying about his grandmother, Benjie reaches home to find she is sick and he must go for help. These two books have excitement and a well-developed narrative. Benjie's character growth is natural and believable, with his love for his grandmother serving as the motivating force for his changed behavior. *I Love Gram* by Ruth Sonneborn is another very believable story of a little black girl's love and concern for her grandmother, who has had to go to the hospital. Waiting for the grandmother's homecoming seems interminable, but an understanding teacher helps the child prepare for the big day when her beloved Gram comes home.

Familiar Everyday Experiences

Books can help children keep alive the wonder of first-time experiences. All too frequently the familiar grows commonplace and the excitement of daily living is lost. Myra Brown appears able to see the "big things" that happen in the lives of small children. In *First Night Away from Home,* Brown shows Stevie packing such essential things as his rock collection and his squirt gun, and walking to Davie's house five houses away

from his own home. Stevie gets ready for bed, but he finds he can't go to sleep in the unfamiliar surroundings until his mother sends over his teddy bear.

All children are concerned about their first day at school, and Jim is no exception. He worriedly asks his father, *Will I Have a Friend?.* Miriam Cohen has written a story answering that question. At first, it seems all the friends are taken. Jim makes a clay statue, but he has no friend to show it to; no one talks to him at juice-time; and when the others play silly games, Jim just watches. By the time school is over, however, Jim does have a friend, and he proudly tells his dad about him. Jim feels the same apprehension about *The New Teacher* as he did about the first day of school; and his fears are equally false. In another book, *Best Friends,* Paul and Jim cope with the near disaster of the light failing in the class incubator. They find that in working together to solve the problem, their friendship grows in the process. Lillian Hoban's illustrations are just right for these funny (for adults) and very serious (for 5- and 6-year-olds) stories.

Other picture books about friendship include *My Friend John* by Zolotow and *Steffie and Me* by Phyllis Hoffman. John's friend knows everything about him, and John knows everything about his friend. For example, only John knows that his friend sleeps with his light on, but then John is afraid of cats! Friends share secrets and stick together! *Steffie and Me* is also a very warm, funny story of two little girls who are fast friends. They ride the same school bus together and are in the same class at school. Perceptive teachers will recognize the sad truth which underlies some of the observations of their school room:

> Our room is on the first floor.
> It has lots and lots of windows
> With stupid tulips on them.
> We made everything that's hanging on the walls.
> Except some of the stuff is from last year.[30]

Mary Jo worries about what to share during "Show and Tell Time" at school, until she has the brilliant idea of sharing her father! Janice Udry has told this story in *What Mary Jo Shared.*

---

[29]Charlotte Zolotow. *William's Doll,* illustrated by William Pène du Bois (New York: Harper & Row, 1972), unpaged.

[30]Phyllis Hoffman. *Steffie and Me,* illustrated by Emily McCully (New York: Harper & Row, 1970), p. 13.

A sequel to the book is *What Mary Jo Wanted,* which turns out to be a puppy of her very own. Mary Jo lives up to her promise to care for and train her long-desired pet.

Other "firsts" may include the first time a child learns how to do something, such as sliding down a slide, learning to whistle, or writing his name. In *Michael Is Brave,* Buckley tells the story of Michael, who is too frightened to go down the slide until his teacher asks him to go up and stand behind a little girl who is more frightened than he. After she goes down the slide, Michael does too, and finds he likes it. Emily McCully's illustrations change perspective and let you see how very high the slide seems to Michael when he is at the top. In *Whistle for Willie,* Keats has captured a small boy's delight in learning how to whistle. With colorful colláge pictures Keats suggests a hot city afternoon, but not too hot or noisy for Willie, the dog, to hear Peter's first whistle and come running. Sue Felt has written of *Rosa-Too-Little,* who loved to go to the library but who was too little to write her name and thus be allowed the privilege of her own library card. There is a moment of pride and joy when Rosa learns to write her name and can borrow books from the library.

Books may help children extend their experiences or see their everyday world in a new perspective. A little girl sees her world quite differently when for her birthday present she goes out with her father *In the Middle of the Night.* In lovely poetic style, Aileen Fisher describes the wondrous discoveries that both of them make. A boy and his father get up early to explore the changing seashore in Kumin's book, *The Beach before Breakfast.* They dig clams and watch the seagulls fish for food. There is a kind of joy in recalling similar previous experiences and in doing the unusual at an early hour alone with your father. Weisgard's horizontal lines and luminous color convey a feeling of space and the peace of the beach at dawn.

The preceding books are quiet, almost mood, stories. In recent years authors have portrayed all facets of children's emotions, including their angry, quarreling moments. Udry's story, *Let's Be Enemies,* is a tongue-in-cheek parody on children's quarrels (*see* Chapter 2). *The Quarreling Book* by Zolotow recounts the cumulative effect of a rainy gray morning and the fact that Mr. James forgot to kiss Mrs. James goodbye. Mrs. James is then quite cross with Jonathan who, in turn, is nasty to his sister, who hurts her best friend's feelings, who then calls her brother, Eddie, a sissy, and so forth, until the chain is broken by Eddie's little dog who plays with him and licks his face until he laughs. Then the whole dismal process is reversed and the day is saved. Zolotow is also the author of *The Hating Book,* which begins with a rhythmical kind of chant of "I hate hate hated my friend,"[31] and pictures a frowning little girl. The little girl recounts all the mean things which her friend has done, and her mother simply tells her to ask why. Finally, the girl does, only to find out that each one of the girls had misunderstood what the other one had said or done, and their friendship is restored. In these two books Zolotow reveals her consistent understanding of the world of the young child.

Every day *Stevie* is brought to Robert's mother's house, much to Robert's disgust. Robert tells how Stevie plays with his toys and breaks them, climbs all over his bed with his dirty shoes, and gets him into trouble. But then Stevie's mother and father come to take him away for good and Robert realizes that he misses him:

> We used to have some good times together.
> I think he liked my momma better than
> his own, cause he used to call his mother
> "Mother" and he called my momma "Mommy."
> Aw, no! I let my cornflakes get soggy
> Thinkin' about him.
> He was a nice little guy.
> He was kinda like a little brother
> Little Stevie[32]

While Robert and Stevie are black, the theme of their story is universal; for man seldom learns to appreciate what he has until it is gone. A 9-year-old girl described Stevie as "a nice nuisance"—we have all experienced one!

In *I'll Fix Anthony* by Judith Viorst a younger brother dreams of revenge, planning all the different ways that he can think of to "fix Anthony," his older brother. The contrast between his plans and the ending provides much of the humor of this book. Everyone has a bad

[31]Charlotte Zolotow. *The Hating Book,* illustrated by Ben Shecter (New York: Harper & Row, 1969), p. 4.
[32]John Steptoe. *Stevie* (New York: Harper & Row, 1969), unpaged.

I went to sleep with gum in my mouth and now there's gum in my hair and when I got out of bed this morning I tripped on the skateboard and by mistake I dropped my sweater in the sink while the water was running and I could tell it was going to be a terrible, horrible, no good, very bad day.

Pictures and text combine to tell the hilarious story of *Alexander and the Terrible, Horrible, No Good, Very Bad Day.*
Pictures copyright © 1972 by Ray Cruz. From *Alexander and the Terrible, Horrible, No Good, Very Bad Day* by Judith Viorst. Used by permission of Atheneum Publishers.

day occasionally, but few of us have experienced the kind of day that Viorst has written about in *Alexander and the Terrible, Horrible, No Good, Very Bad Day.* Alexander knew it was going to be a miserable day from the moment he woke up with gum in his hair. And he was right. It was a bad, bad day at school; he had lima beans for supper; and there was kissing on TV. When Alexander went to bed his bath was too hot and he got soap in his eyes; but the worst affront was the fact that he had to wear the railroad-train pajamas that he hated. He thought of moving to Australia, but "Mom says some days are like that. Even in Australia."[33]

[33]Judith Viorst. *Alexander and the Terrible, Horrible, No Good, Very Bad Day*, illustrated by Ray Cruz (New York: Atheneum, 1972), unpaged.

Viorst has written a quieter, more serious story about the death of a young boy's cat, *The Tenth Good Thing about Barney.* After Barney died, the little boy's mother told him to think about ten good things to say about Barney, and that they would have a funeral for him the next day. The little boy could only think of nine things, but later, while he was helping his father plant seeds, he thought of the tenth: Barney was in the ground helping the flowers to grow. The little black-and-white ink sketches by Erik Blegvad help create the sincerity of this story of a boy's first experience with death. The children in the story of *The Dead Bird* by Margaret Wise Brown also conduct a funeral for the little bird they had found, make a stone marker, and carry flowers to the grave. But the children soon return to their play and forget the bird. In Viorst's story, however, the continuity of life is there, but the reader feels that somehow the little boy will always remember Barney, the cat that purred in his ear and "sometimes . . . slept on my belly and kept it warm."[34]

Stories of the Country and City

Young children should be ever extending their horizons, not confined within them. Books about the city may give the city child a new perspective on a familiar experience, or they will offer new experiences to the rural or suburban child. Likewise, books about the farm may be enjoyed for their familiarity by the country child, and appreciated for their newness by the urban child. In *A Thousand Lights and Fireflies*, Tresselt has contrasted city life with country life while emphasizing the universal qualities of both. He compares the settings of city and country in rich descriptive prose:

> In the city everything is squeezed together. The buildings are so close they have to stretch up into the sky to find room.
> The country is stretched out for miles and miles, rolling over hills and valley and broad flat farms.
> The houses sit apart so they can look at one another.[35]

Other differences are noted, such as city noises—"the shriek of the fire engines"—and country noises—"Brooks gossiping with the pebbles"[36]—but similarities include mothers and fathers and children playing and going to school. In *Wake Up, City!* Tresselt describes how morning comes to the city from the first chirping of the sparrow to the honking of the bus that picks the children up for school. A companion book is *Wake Up, Farm!* The book *Sun Up*, also by Tresselt and illustrated by Duvoisin, traces a hot midsummer day on the farm from the cock's early morning crow through a late afternoon's sudden storm, to the peacefully cool coming of the night.

Six-year-old Jay is a young farm boy who loved the sights and sounds of everything around him. One day on his way home with the cattle Jay finds a cricket and puts him in his pocket. In *A Pocketful of Cricket*, Rebecca Caudill describes what happens when Jay takes his pet cricket to school. A perceptive teacher helps Jay find a way to keep his noisy cricket in the classroom and share it with the other children. Caudill's sensory descriptions of the countryside make the reader vitally aware of the sounds and sights of Jay's world:

> Jay climbed the fence. He sat on the top rail.
> He heard the wind rustling in the ripening corn.
> He heard bugs and beetles ticking.
> He heard a cicada fiddling high notes in the August heat.
> He heard an owl hooting in the dusky woods.
> On the hill beyond the cornfield he heard a cow bawling.[37]

The quality of the pictures by Evaline Ness complements the quality of the language of this beautiful picture book.

A stifling hot day in the city is described by Bourne in *Emilio's Summer Day*. The writing is as realistic as the drab brown pictures of the slums. For example:

> He felt his damp shirt sticking to his damp back.
> He smelled orange peel in an open garbage can.
> Around the corner he heard a car start.
> Music floated out of the windows across the street.
> A baby cried. But nothing moved.[38]

Relief and fun do come in the form of the street washer that sprays the children with icy water. This book would be interesting to compare with *The Snowy Day* by Keats, which describes a city child's delight in the new-fallen snow.

Keats' stories about Peter begin with *The Snowy Day*, *Peter's Chair*, and *A Letter to Amy*. As Peter grows up he is joined by his friend Archie in *Goggles*, *Hi Cat!*, and *Pet Show!* All of these

[34]Judith Viorst. *The Tenth Good Thing about Barney*, illustrated by Erik Blegvad (New York: Atheneum, 1971), p. 8.
[35]Alvin Tresselt. *A Thousand Lights and Fireflies*, illustrated by John Moodie (New York: Parents' Magazine Press, 1965), unpaged.
[36]Tresselt.

[37]Rebecca Caudill. *A Pocketful of Cricket*, illustrated by Evaline Ness (New York: Holt, Rinehart and Winston, 1964), unpaged.
[38]Miriam Anne Bourne. *Emilio's Summer Day*, illustrated by Ben Shecter (New York: Harper & Row, 1966), p. 23.

stories take place in the inner city and have exciting story lines and convincing characterization. In *Goggles,* Peter, Archie, and Willie, Peter's dachshund, fool some big boys who want to take away the motorcycle goggles that the two friends have found. In *Hi Cat!,* Peter is adopted by a crazy cat. There is less excitement in this story than in perhaps any of the others. In *Pet Show!* the crazy cat disappears just when Archie needs him for his entry. Being highly creative, Archie substitutes an empty bottle which contains his pet, a germ! He receives an award for the quietest pet. Keats has used bright acrylic paints for these well-loved stories of Peter and his friends.

Uptown by Steptoe has little plot and seems to go nowhere in the same way as the dead-end people that two black boys, John and Dennis, pass while walking through Harlem. The boys see junkies, cops, brothers, karate experts, and hippies, and wonder what it would be like to be one of them. They decide they wouldn't want to be a cop because you wouldn't have any friends. They discuss the way the army changes a man. Finally they decide not to decide; they don't know what they want to be when they grow up. The book ends with John saying: "Guess we'll just hang out together for a while and just dig on everythin' that's goin' on."[39] *Train Ride,* also by Steptoe, is a good exciting story of Charles and his friends who decide to take the subway to Times Square. They sneak on the train, spend all their money at a penny arcade, have to persuade the man at the token booth to let them back on, and then return home for the beating that each of them knows he will get. The next morning they all decide that they had a "boss time," but they wouldn't go again for a while! Both of these books contain black speech rhythms and the powerful paintings which are characteristic of Steptoe's style.

Ruth Sonneborn has told the story of Pedro and his three sisters and brothers in *Friday Night Is Papa Night.* On this particular night a Puerto Rican family is waiting in vain for papa—he does not come. Finally they go to bed without seeing him. Pedro, who sleeps in the kitchen, awakens and turns on the light just in time to greet a very tired Papa, who had been delayed because he had taken a sick friend home. Papa gives all the children his usual Friday night gifts, but his safe arrival is the best gift of all. Many children cannot imagine a family that is too poor to have a telephone, just as many have never known the rich love and family loyalty that is such an inherent part of this story.

Today's concern about aging and the role of the elderly is reflected in a delightful story titled *Maxie* by Mildred Kantrowitz. Maxie is an old woman who lives alone, except for her canary bird and cat, in a tenement building. One morning, feeling unwanted and unnecessary, Maxie just decides not to bother getting up. By 9:45 A.M., Maxie finds out how many people depend upon her raising her shades at exactly 7:10, or uncovering her bird, getting her milk, or the sound of her whistling tea kettle. Maxie knows now that she is important and needed.

Weather and the Seasons

Weather and seasonal changes are important events in a young child's life, often more significant than they are for adults. One of the most handsome books on this subject is Burningham's *Seasons.* Full-color scenes follow the cycle of the seasons from Spring, with "birds nesting" and "ducks dabbling," to Summer, with "holidays" and "heat waves," to Autumn, with "leaves flying" and "geese soaring," to Winter, with "ice and snow" and "endless rain," until it is Spring again, with a nest of baby birds. Some of the scenes and captions have an English flavor, as one would expect from one of England's finest illustrators. The text is as terse as the pictures are breathtaking.

The team of Alvin Tresselt and Roger Duvoisin has produced the book, *It's Time Now,* which shows the seasonal cycle in an unspecified city in the U.S. This text is more detailed and descriptive:

Slowly the days grow longer.
Slowly the air turns warm once more.
A gentle softness spreads over the city
And at last it is time. . . .[40]

---

[39] John Steptoe. *Uptown* (New York: Harper & Row, 1970), unpaged.

[40] Alvin Tresselt. *It's Time Now,* illustrated by Roger Duvoisin (New York: Harper & Row, 1969), unpaged.

The page facing the title page pictures the same tree at four different seasons. This could serve as the impetus for children to observe a particular tree in their school yard or neighborhood.

Tresselt and Duvoisin have presented a contrast between adults' and children's reactions to weather in *White Snow, Bright Snow* and *Hide and Seek Fog*. In the first book adults' displeasure over the inconvenience of a snowstorm is contrasted with the children's joy over its arrival. Repeating this same pattern, Tresselt has described the children's ready response to a fog that came and stayed for three days in a little seaside village on Cape Cod, while their parents grumbled about spending their vacations in the middle of a cloud. Duvoisin's hazy pearl-gray illustrations effectively convey the mystery of a fog-shrouded day.

In *The Storm Book* by Zolotow, children may follow the progress of a storm from the oppressive dry stillness broken by the first faint rumble of thunder to the last graceful arch of the rainbow. Iwasaki has made lovely abstract paintings to capture the mood of a little girl who is *Staying Home Alone on a Rainy Day*. Allison's mother had to go to the store, so she told her daughter not to answer the door and that she would be right back. The little girl felt very grown up staying all alone in the house until it started to storm. The rain subsides and the sun comes out just as her mother returns with the groceries. In *Rain Rain Rivers*, Shulevitz has produced a beautiful book that expresses the mood of a rainy day in the city and the country. Indoors, a little girl watches, listens, and feels safe and cozy in her own small room. Outdoors it rains on the windowpanes, the roof tops; it rains on the fields, the hills, and the ponds. The streams, the brooks, the rivers, the seas, surge and swell, rage and roar. Tomorrow will bring puddles and mud. "I'll jump over pieces of sky in the gutter"[41] thinks the little girl. Watercolors in greens and blues are the appropriate media and colors used for these lovely illustrations.

In *Umbrella* by Yashima, Momo is impatient for rain so that she can wear her new red rubber boots and carry her new umbrella to nursery school. At last the rain comes, and Momo walks straight like a lady, listening to the rhythmic patter of the raindrops on her new umbrella. A little Mexican boy pretends that wind is his playmate in *Gilberto and the Wind* by Marie Hall Ets. Some days wind is good company for Gilberto; sometimes he whispers to him; at other times he roars and tears things from his hands; still other days he is all tired out and says nothing at all. The quiet pictures of Gilberto's expressive face, even his very stance, reflect his response to this changeable playmate.

Nature Stories

Increased concern for ecology and preserving the balance of nature has been reflected in recent picture books for children. Most of these books have a thread of a story and also give some accurate information. All of them are distinguished by beautiful pictures. Some of these books make their own statements about the danger to our world in a subtle, quiet fashion; others make it through a very funny story; and some are so overburdened with their messages that they sound like didactic tracts.

Tresselt has described the life and death of a huge oak tree in the forest in his book *The Dead Tree*. The tree provides shelter for the small creatures that nestle by its roots, but it also provides a home and food for the very insects which will destroy it. "Even as the tree grew, life gnawed at its heart."[42] Carpenter ants and termites ate passageways through the tree; woodpeckers enlarged the holes; and a hurricane crashed it to the forest floor. Gradually the tree is reclaimed by the earth to create new acorn trees. Robinson's pictures beautifully portray the patterns of light sifting through the forest.

In *The Beaver Pond*, Tresselt describes the life story of a pond—its birth, maturity, and its final transformation to a meadow. The pond creates and sustains the lives of many other living things—the fish, frogs, birds, insects, raccoons, and, of course, the beavers. Duvoisin has made striking full-color illustrations. Many of them reflect a childlike perspective of looking down at the whole pond. Duvoisin also illustrated the story of *The Old Bullfrog* by Berniece Freschet.

---

[41] Uri Shulevitz. *Rain Rain Rivers* (New York: Farrar, Straus and Giroux, 1969), unpaged.

[42] Alvin Tresselt. *The Dead Tree*, illustrated by Charles Robinson (New York: Parents' Magazine Press, 1972), unpaged.

Using a combination of collàge and paint, he shows the heron silently stalking the old bullfrog. The title page, showing just the wise bulging eyes of the frog, suggests the ending of this beautifully integrated book. Freschet has also written *The Turtle Pond,* which Carrick has illustrated with lovely, soft watercolors. The story is of a warm day in June when a mother turtle lays her eggs. Two months later eleven baby turtles hatch, and make their long, dangerous journey down the short distance to the pond. They all make it, but one little one will always have a crook in his tail where the kingfisher nearly got him!

One of the most beautiful books that Duvoisin has illustrated is *The Web in the Grass* by Freschet. This book, like *The Old Bullfrog,* is done in full-color collàge. The jeweled pictures of the spider and her web should increase a child's awareness of the beauty that might be as near as the bush outside his door. *All Upon a Stone* by Jean George describes the microcosm that exists upon a single stone. The poetic text details the life of a mole cricket who crawls out from under the stone, spends a summer day exploring, and crawls back in. Don Bolognese's pictures are enlargements from a single painting, which is reproduced at the end of the book. Each picture appears as it might look through a hand lens. Seven- and 8-year-olds need to hear and see this story before they take a walk in the woods. If they can take a hand lens with them, they might discover their own stories and pictures upon a stone, tree, or stump.

The Last Free Bird by Stone carries a clear eco-logical warning in its text, which tells how the land changed after people came—the bubbling brook was spoiled; the crisp clean air polluted; the dense forest paved. The front endpaper shows many birds flying freely against a blue sky, while the last one pictures only an empty sky. Beautiful clear watercolors become increasingly muddied to convey the book's visual message. The story does not preach, but its statement is profound.

Following the cumulative form of the "House that Jack Built," Peter Parnall has told the grim story of *The Mountain* that stood in the west. The ironic theme of this picture book is that humans always destroy that which they love best. For the destruction of the mountain occurs after it had been made a national park by the people who loved it so much that they wanted to preserve its beauty forever!

Realistic Animal Stories

There are more animal stories, including realistic and fanciful tales, than any other kind of story for young children. Scientific accounts of particular species are included in Chapter 9 ("Informational Books"). Picture stories of animals that are true to their animal nature are included here. Because young children tend to humanize animals, many of these stories do ascribe speech and human thoughts to their animal characters.

The story of *Make Way for Ducklings* by Robert McCloskey has become a classic for primary grade children. No child worries about the vintage of the cars in this story, for he is too concerned with the safety of Mrs. Mallard and her ducklings in the bustle of Boston traffic.

The lilting narrative poem *Listen, Rabbit* by Aileen Fisher portrays a realistic story of a wild rabbit and a boy who wants it for a pet. Patiently the boy watches for his rabbit all year, until finally in the spring he discovers a wonderful surprise, "a nest/like a furlined cup/and five baby rabbits/to watch grow up!"[43] This same author has described all the various little houses that insects and animals build in *Best Little House.* The parallel stories of a family and a possum caught in a flood are presented in *Mississippi Possum* by Miles. The stunning black-and-white pictures by John Schoenherr show how Rose Mary gradually tames the little possum while both wait in the tent city for the flood waters to recede. When the family returns to its shack at the bottom of the hill, the possum goes home with them. This same team produced *Wharf Rat,* the story of a victim of an oil slick. Injured birds were cleaned and sheltered, but the rescuers threw stones at the poor wharf rat. He saves himself by fleeing down a pier and scrambling aboard a tanker. Schoenherr has written and illustrated *The Barn,* a straightforward story of a skunk who hunts and is hunted one night by an owl. Realistic black-and-white pictures capture the silent drama of this encounter.

[43] Aileen Fisher. *Listen, Rabbit,* illustrated by Symeon Shimin (New York: Crowell, 1964), unpaged.

There are surprisingly few realistic stories of pets. Clare Newberry's many books about cats have slight story lines, but the beautiful pictures of soft, cuddly kittens and sleek, shiny cats appeal to children. In *April's Kittens,* Father finally agrees to move to a "two-cat" apartment rather than a "one-cat" one. *Joey's Cat* by Robert Burch is a very satisfying story of how Joey persuaded his mother, who didn't like cats too well, to allow him to bring a mother cat and her kittens into the house. His mother agrees to let them stay only until they grow up, but the mother cat gives Joey a wink and looks as if she could manage that situation very easily. Don Freeman's illustrations portray a convincing black family meeting a universal problem of cats, kittens, and children who want them all in the house!

Fanciful Animal Stories

Ever since the day Peter Rabbit disobeyed his mother and squeezed through Mr. MacGregor's garden fence children have enjoyed stories in which animals act like people, frequently like small children. Boys and girls can easily see their own behavior mirrored in *Bedtime for Frances* by Russell Hoban, the story of an engaging badger who finds as many excuses to avoid going to sleep as any 5-year-old child. In *A Baby Sister for Frances,* also by the Hobans, Frances decides that Gloria is receiving entirely too much attention, so she packs her knapsack, says goodbye to her parents, and runs away—under the dining-room table. Frances continues to want to be the center of attention, even on Gloria's birthday. *A Birthday for Frances* is uproariously funny as the egocentric badger eats most of her present for her little sister! Frances outmaneuvers Albert and the rest of the boys in *Best Friends for Frances;* but Thelma nearly gets the best of her in an easy-reading book titled *A Bargain for Frances.* Frances is a funny, opinionated badger character that all primary grade children should have the chance to meet.

Children easily recognize themselves, the situations, and their own reactions in *The Temper Tantrum Book* by Edna Preston. Eight different verses portray a particular animal having a temper tantrum; for example, the lion is "roaring and raging." The next page shows the cause of his rage; his mother is combing the tangles from his hair. An elephant hates it when he gets soap in his eyes; a turtle dislikes it when he is told to stay inside because it is raining! The last verse has a surprise ending that delights young children. *Squawk to the Moon, Little Goose,* also by Preston, tells the engaging story of Little Goose's disobedient moonlight swim, her clever escape from the fox, and her return to the inevitable spanking. Beautifully executed watercolors by Barbara Cooney make the most of this book's nighttime setting.

The warmth of a mother's love is portrayed in Margaret Wise Brown's book *The Runaway Bunny.* When the bunny warns his mother that he is going to run away, she says that she will follow him. The bunny imagines many things that he will become, and his mother tells him how she can find him regardless of what he is. The popularity of this book is seen in the fact that it has never been out of print since it was first published in 1942. Thirty years later Clement Hurd has redrawn some of his pictures for a fine new edition of this classic. This same feeling of love and warmth permeates the story and pictures of *Little Bear* by Minarik. Maurice Sendak's illustrations are in perfect harmony with the tone of this book. He portrays a large Mother Bear whose Victorian dress and apron provide a very ample lap for Little Bear. When Little Bear decides to go to the moon, his mother joins in the fun of pretending that she is on the moon too, until Little Bear tells her to stop fooling:

> "You are my Mother Bear and I am your Little Bear, and we are on Earth, and you know it. Now may I eat my lunch?"
> "Yes" said Mother Bear, "and then you will have your nap. For you are my little bear, and I know it."[44]

Other stories about Little Bear include *Father Bear Comes Home, Little Bear's Friend, Little Bear's Visit,* and *A Kiss for Little Bear.*

Many animal characters in children's literature have real personalities of their own. Almost all first-graders love the stories of a silly goose, *Petunia,* who thinks she has acquired wisdom

---

[44]Else Holmelund Minarik. *Little Bear,* illustrated by Maurice Sendak (New York: Harper & Row, 1957), p. 48.

when she finds a book. She does not know that it is important to learn to read what is in the book, and as a result gives all kinds of poor advice to her unfortunate friends in the barnyard. Duvoisin's gay pictures show Petunia holding her head higher and higher with pride until it stretches off the page. Duvoisin has also illustrated his wife's many stories about that sophisticated French lion, *The Happy Lion.* One day, this king of the beasts finds his cage door open and observes that anyone could walk in! It then occurs to him that he could take a stroll himself. He is completely mystified by the strange antics of his friends, the townspeople, when he walks into their village. Only the zookeeper's son, Francois, calls out "Bonjour, Happy Lion," and seems glad to see him as he calmly walks him back to the zoo. Another sophisticated French "animality" is Tomi Ungerer's *Crictor,* a most affectionate boa constrictor pet of Madame Bodot, who teaches school in a peaceful French village—peaceful until a burglar breaks into her apartment only to meet Crictor! *Anatole* by Eve Titus is a cheese-tasting mouse who is as French as his little beret and bicycle. He saves M'sieu Duval's cheese factory from financial ruin and becomes first Vice-president in charge of cheese-tasting! *Broderick,* by Ormondroyd, is a very sophisticated mouse who learns to read and is greatly influenced by all the famous mice in literature, including Anatole, Norman in Freeman's *Pet of the Met, Miss Bianca,* and others. Determined to make his mark in the world, Broderick takes up surfing and is very successful indeed. Children also might enjoy reading all the stories about mice that were so influential in Broderick's life.

Other favorite animal personalities include Jean de Brunhoff's *The Story of Babar,* a little elephant who runs away from the jungle and goes to live with an understanding lady in Paris. His cousins, Arthur and Celestine, come to visit and persuade him to return to Africa where his poise and elegant wardrobe are so impressive that he is made King of the Jungle. The Babar stories are now being continued by Jean de Brunhoff's son, Laurent. The *Curious George* stories by H. A. Rey, are also children's favorites. This comical monkey has one escapade after another, but the man in the yellow hat always manages to save him

from real danger. When the Primm family move into their apartment in *The House on East 88th Street,* they find Lyle, a performing crocodile, in the bathtub. They become fast friends and live happily together. Several other stories by Waber continue the adventures of Lyle. The preposterous animals of Dr. Seuss need little introduction to children. They love the story of *Horton Hatches the Egg* that tells of the good-natured elephant who helps the ungrateful lazy bird, Mazie, to hatch her egg. The incongruity of a great big elephant sitting on a nest in a tree tickles the funny bone in all of us. Another lovable Seuss animal is *Thidwick, the Big-hearted Moose,* whose generosity nearly costs him his life. These earlier books by Dr. Seuss have more spontaneity and originality than many of his recent ones which are written with a controlled vocabulary and appear to be following a formula of exaggeration.

First-graders faced with the formidable task (for some of them) of learning to read can sympathize with *Leo the Late Bloomer* by Robert Kraus. Leo, a baby tiger, can't do anything right; he can't read, write, or draw; he is a sloppy eater and never talks. His mother assures his father that Leo is a late bloomer. And she is right. Eventually, and in his own good time, Leo blooms! Beautiful, brilliant pictures by Jose Aruego add much to the humor of this story. The same team has written and illustrated *Milton the Early Riser,* a book which capitalizes upon the current interest in pandas. Milton, a baby panda, gets up early and does everything he can think of to awaken his sleeping friends. Finally they do wake up, but predictably, Milton is exhausted by his efforts and goes back to sleep. *Good Night, Owl!* by Pat Hutchins is a brilliant, beautifully designed book that has somewhat the reverse plot of *Milton the Early Riser.* In this story poor owl tries to sleep during the day, but the bees buzz; the crows croak; the starlings chitter; the woodpecker taps his hollow nest—and sleep is impossible. Then, when night falls and there isn't a sound, owl screeches and screeches until everyone is wide awake! Young children will be intrigued by the onomatopoetic text that imitates the sounds of the birds and by the surprise ending. *The Surprise Party* by the same author-illustrator is based upon the well-loved party game of "pass-it-on." Rabbit's whispered invitation to a surprise party becomes more and more distorted as each animal tells the next. Five- and 6-year-olds would enjoy playing "pass-it-on" either before hearing this story or as a follow-up activity.

Friends abound in many of the stories of fanciful animals. All ages appreciate the friendship of that loyal pair, *Frog and Toad Are Friends* and *Frog and Toad Together* written and illustrated by Lobel. Each book has five short chapters, which can be read as separate stories. In one of the stories Frog discovers Toad looking very sad indeed and he asks him what is wrong.

> "This is my sad time of day. It is the time when I wait for the mail to come. It always makes me very unhappy."
> "Why is that?" asked Frog.
> "Because I never get any mail," said Toad.[45]

[45] Arnold Lobel. *Frog and Toad Are Friends* (New York: Harper & Row, 1970), p. 54.

Frog and Toad Are Friends

by Arnold Lobel

An I CAN READ Book

Arnold Lobel's pictures and text for his Frog and Toad stories are proof that quality can be achieved in writing an easy-to-read book.

Illustration from *Frog and Toad Are Friends* by Arnold Lobel. Copyright © 1970 by Arnold Lobel. Reprinted by permission of Harper & Row, Publishers, Inc.

Frog leaves quickly, goes home and writes a letter to Toad, and gives it to a snail to deliver. He returns to Toad's house and together the two friends wait—four days later the letter arrives! These stories are droll, tender, and funny.

Friendship between a whale and a mouse seems highly unlikely. Yet in the tale of *Amos and Boris*, Steig has created a modern version of the fable of the "Lion and the Rat." Amos, a seafaring mouse, falls off his boat, "The Rodent," and is saved by Boris, a monstrous whale. Boris agrees to give Amos a ride home, and the two become fast friends. The quality of the language of this story is equalled only by the quality of the superb illustrations. Steig describes the growing friendship between Amos and Boris and their admiration for each other in this way:

> Boris admired the delicacy, the quivering daintiness, the light touch, the small voice, the gemlike radiance of the mouse.
> Amos admired the bulk, the grandeur, the power, the purpose, the rich voice, and the abounding friendliness of the whale.[46]

A universal theme in many fanciful animal stories is that of being true to one's own nature. *Dandelion* by Freeman is the story of a lion who becomes such a "dandy" in order to go to a party that his hostess, Jennifer Giraffe, does not recognize him and shuts the door in his face! The children do not recognize their own dog in the story of *Harry, The Dirty Dog* by Gene Zion. Harry, once a white dog with black spots, hides his scrub brush and so becomes a black dog with white spots! He digs up his scrub brush and when the children give him a bath, they finally recognize him. In *Pig Tale*, Oxenbury has told the very funny story of Briggs and Bertha, two bored pigs, until the day they dug up a treasure chest. Then the two go on a buying spree that includes a new house with a swimming pool, the latest model car, new clothes, TV, washing machines, power lawnmowers, and so on. Finally, their mechanical gadgets become too complicated for them and the pigs long for the good old days when they romped in the mud. They shed their materialistic world with their clothes and joyously

[46] William Steig. *Amos and Boris* (New York: Farrar, Straus and Giroux, 1971), unpaged.

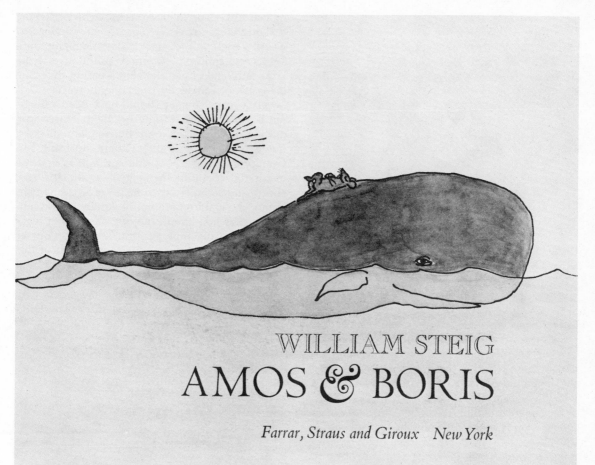

WILLIAM STEIG
AMOS & BORIS

Farrar, Straus and Giroux   New York

The title page of *Amos & Boris* suggests the incongruous friendship of a monstrous whale and a tiny mouse.
Reprinted with the permission of Farrar, Straus & Giroux, Inc., from *Amos & Boris* by William Steig, Copyright © 1971 by William Steig.

return to their rural paradise, where they once again can be their pig selves. The rollicking verse of this tale is as delightful as the happy pictures. Waber's book, *"You Look Ridiculous," Said the Rhinoceros to the Hippopotamus*, is as funny as its title. Each animal that the sensitive hippopotamus meets tells her that she looks ridiculous without the distinctive characteristic of his particular species. Steig won the Caldecott Award for his book *Sylvester and the Magic Pebble.* Sylvester is a young donkey who finds a magic red pebble that will grant his every wish. Hurrying home to show it to his family, he meets a lion and foolishly wishes himself a stone. The seasons pass but Sylvester remains a boulder. One day

in May his mother and father have a picnic, and by chance use Sylvester's stone as their table! In trying to forget Sylvester, they remember him. Having just found the red pebble, they place it on the stone and Sylvester wishes he were his real self again—and he is! In *Walter Was a Frog*, by Diane Massie, Walter is very happy to be a frog until his mother gives him lily-petal broth. Then Walter decides to be a bird, and he makes a nest. Nest-making becomes a bit of a bore, so Walter tries being a fish. Each of these various roles brings disastrous results, until Walter learns the importance of being himself. *Fish Is Fish* by Leo Lionni emphasizes this same theme of being true to one's own nature. In the story of *Alexander*

Briggs and Bertha shed their clothes and wealth to celebrate the joy of returning to their natural state.

Reprinted by permission of William Morrow & Co., Inc., from *Pig Tale*, written and illustrated by Helen Oxenbury. Copyright © 1973 by Helen Oxenbury. Also by permission of the British publishers, William Heinemann, Ltd.

and the Wind-up Mouse, also by Lionni, Alexander envies the wind-up mouse, Willie, and wants to become one himself. However, fortunes change, and in order to save his friend Alexander asks the magic lizard to make Willie a real mouse, just like Alexander.

In *Frederick* Lionni celebrates the story of a mouse who is different. The other mice bring in the harvest for the long winter, but Frederick does not work. He is gathering a harvest of sights and feelings. When the wind is cold and there is no food, Frederick shares his contribution of words and colors with his friends. He makes up poetry about the sun and the flowers and warms their souls. Lionni's statement is direct and clear; we each have a contribution to make that must be true to our individual natures. One of the best-loved tales of children's literature is Leaf's *The Story of Ferdinand,* the unique bull who prefers smelling flowers to bull-fighting. When he sits on a bee, his ferocious behavior causes him to be chosen for the bull fight. Once in the arena, he sits—smelling the flowers!

Humorous and Fanciful Picture Books

Young children's humor is simple and obvious. They laugh uproariously at the large comic pictures in *Animals Should Definitely Not Wear Clothing* by the Barretts. The broad humor of a

moose tangled up in his trousers, a chicken trying to lay an egg in stretch pants, and oppossums wearing their clothes upside down delights both adults and children. The more subtle joke of the large lady and larger elephant wearing the same dress is not caught by everyone, however.

Mr. Gumpy's Outing should have been a disaster, but it turned out to be a delight. This warm, humorous story by John Burningham is very English and very funny. Patient, tolerant Mr. Gumpy goes for a boat ride and allows first the children to join him, then a goat, a calf, chickens, sheep, and so on. To each he gives an admonishment: The children are not to squabble; the rabbit mustn't hop about; the dog should not tease the cat; the pig mustn't "muck about." But of course they all do these things; and the boat tips over. They dry out in the sun and all troop back to Mr. Gumpy's house for tea! Glorious watercolor pictures and sunny yellow endpapers help create the happy mood of this story. The long-suffering Mr. Gumpy takes the whole gang for another outing in the story of *Mr. Gumpy's Motor*

The humor of this picture proves that *Animals Should Definitely Not Wear Clothing.*

Illustrations copyright © 1970 by Ron Barrett. From *Animals Should Definitely Not Wear Clothing* by Judi Barrett. Used by permission of Atheneum Publishers.

Car. For a while it looks as if the rain is going to spoil this trip, since the car becomes stuck in the mud. However, with everyone's cooperation, they push the car out of the mud and arrive at Mr. Gumpy's just in time for a swim. Burningham suggests there may be further adventures with Mr. Gumpy, as this kind, patient man waves goodbye and invites them all to come again for another ride.

Slapstick and nonsense are the order of the day at another party in *May I Bring a Friend?* by Beatrice Schenk de Regniers. A little boy is invited to tea by the King and Queen and each time he goes he takes a friend: a giraffe, monkeys, lions, and hippos—not all of whom are very polite. The monkeys swing on the chandeliers; the hippopotamus puts his foot in the cake; the lions roar; and the seal plays "Long Live Apple Pie" on his bugle. Through it all their royal majesties retain their equanimity. The brilliant purple, pink, and yellow illustrations by Beni Montresor resemble stage settings for the passing parade of incongruities.

Nonsense can only be funny when it is contrasted with sense. The juxtaposition of Chester, a very bored boy who complains that *Nothing Ever Happens on My Block* with the amazing happenings that are actually occurring on his street makes for a very funny book. While Chester sits on the curb and stares at the reader, a house catches on fire behind him; a robber is chased by a policeman; a man finds buried treasure; a house fills up with witches; a car hits an armored Brinks' truck and money flies all over; and much, much more occurs. Chester sees none of it, but the reader sees it all. Children want to look at this book by Ellen Raskin over and over again, for they see something more to laugh at with each viewing.

Silly, ridiculous situations tickle children's funny bones. They laugh at the absurd antics of the boy in Ruth Krauss' book who decides to spend *The Backward Day* by putting his coat on first, then his suit and underwear, walking backward to breakfast, and saying "Goodnight" to his father and mother! In fact, after hearing this story, they like to plan their own "backward day." *Lazy Tommy Pumpkinhead* by William Pène Du Bois is pure mechanical slapstick! Tommy was so lazy that he had electrical gadgets that bathed

him, dressed him, and fed him. A violent storm causes a power failure and utter turmoil in the timing of these services when power is restored. Lazy Tommy falls head first into the dressing machine, the tooth-brushing machine scrubs his toes, and the feeding machine pours scrambled eggs and seven quarts of orange juice over his feet! Six- and 7-year-olds think this story is hysterical.

Three funny stories of urban Jewish family life make up the book *Tell Me a Mitzi* by Lore Segal. A "mitzi" is a story about a character named Mitzi, who might be any child. The first story details Mitzi's early morning efforts to visit her grandparents. She changes her baby brother's diaper, dresses him, dresses herself, takes the elevator downstairs, and catches a taxi—only to realize she doesn't have her grandparents' address! The second "Mitzi" describes the time when the whole family came down with sneezes and bad colds. Grandmother arrives and cares for them all, only to become sick herself on the next day. The third story is more fanciful, but just as funny. The writer is skillful in using sentence patterns that make you feel someone is telling this story. The pictures of the flat comic-book characters with lumpish faces add to the humor of the book.

Surprise endings frequently appeal to the young child's sense of humor. They love Karla Kuskin's repetitious story *Just Like Everyone Else*, which describes how Jonathan James gets up in the morning; how he gets dressed; what he has for breakfast; and how he says good-bye to his mother, father, dog, and little sister—just like everyone else. Then, "Jonathan James flew off to school." One kindergarten child, on hearing this story, said, "It sounded just like a broken record, but I knew it had to end funny." The surprise ending of *The Camel Who Took a Walk* by Tworkov intrigues children. Their excitement grows as the gentle young camel walks down the path toward the place where the tiger plans to pounce upon her; and then they feel a surge of relief as the camel stops, yawns, and says, "I think I'll return now."

Young children are past masters at exaggeration, so they appreciate the humor of the tall tale. Dr. Seuss' stories, *And to Think that I Saw It on Mulberry Street* and *McElligot's Pool*, are models of humorous tall tales. *Burt Dow, Deep-water Man* by McCloskey is a tall tale of an old fisherman who catches a whale by the tail and then binds the wound with a candy-striped bandaid. The grateful whale swallows him whole, boat and all, in order to protect him from a storm. With the help of some bilge water and the giggling gull, Burt Dow is burped back into the ocean and home to his sister Leela, but not before he has put candy-striped bandaids on a whole school of whales.

Many picture storybooks portray children's fantasies or dreams. Some of these are very humorous, such as *A Very Special House* by Ruth Krauss. The glory of this remarkable house is that you can do anything you want in it, such as swing on the doors or draw on the walls—in fact, all of the things that are not allowed in a regular house! The little boy admits that it is a pretend house on the last page:

> I know a house—
> and it's not up in a tree
> or underneath the bed—
> Oh it's right in the middle—
> Oh it's ret in the meddle—
> Oh it's root in the moodle of my head head head.[47]

Maurice Sendak has portrayed the droll little boy who is telling the story in blue, while everything else is drawn in pen and ink in order to contrast reality with the child's imagination. In *Conrad's Castle*, Ben Shecter has told a highly original fantasy of a little boy who literally builds castles in the air. One day Conrad throws a rock in the air and it stays there. Then he begins to build a castle. All the children try to dissuade him from his castle building with such childlike enticements as promising him he can be captain of the team or asking if he wants to see a dead mouse. But Conrad keeps building until a bird flies by and tells him that what he is doing is impossible. Then for the first time Conrad has some doubts and his castle collapses. Only momentarily defeated, however, the determined Conrad looks at the bird and speaks his only utterance: "I can too!"[48] This time even the bird believes him, and she starts to build a nest in Conrad's castle! On

the surface this is a highly fanciful story that is good fun; deeper meanings suggest the value of believing in yourself and your "impossible dreams." *Andy and the Lion* by Daugherty is a wonderful mixture of fantasy and reality. Andy is returning the story of "Androcles and the Lion" to the library when he meets his own lion. Andy extracts a thorn from the lion's paw and thereby becomes his friend for life. The vigorous black-and-white illustrations reflect the power and strength of this favorite story. Books that have been discussed elsewhere in this chapter also portray children's dreams. These include Sendak's *Where the Wild Things Are* and *In the Night Kitchen* and Shulevitz's *One Monday Morning.*

Another form of fantasy for young children is the personification of inanimate objects, such as toys and machines. Most all children know and love Watty Piper's story of *The Little Engine that Could,* . . . and did get the toys over the mountain. Most of the books written by Virginia Lee Burton contain personification: *Katie and the Big Snow, The Little House,* and *Mike Mulligan and His Steam Shovel.* The modern problem of obsolescence is solved easily in the story of Mike and his beloved steam shovel, Mary Ann. After proving that Mary Ann could dig a basement for the new town hall in a day, Mike was forced to convert her into a furnace, since he had neglected to plan a way for Mary Ann to get out of the excavation. Katie is a snowplow who saves the day by plowing out a whole village. The encroachment of the city on the country is portrayed in Burton's classic story of *The Little House* that stood on the hill and watched day and night and the seasons pass. Gradually, a road is built, cars come, and soon the city grows up around the little house. Elevated cars speed by her; subway trains speed under her; and people rush to and fro in front of her. One day the great-great-granddaughter of the original owner sees the little house, buys her, and has her moved back to the country where she can once again see the stars.

Hardie Gramatky has written several books that personify the inanimate. *Little Toot* is the story of a headstrong tugboat in New York harbor who refuses to accept his tugboat responsibilities until a time of crisis makes him a hero. *Loopy* by the same author-illustrator tells of a

[47] Ruth Krauss. *A Very Special House,* illustrated by Maurice Sendak (New York: Harper & Row, 1953), unpaged.
[48] Ben Shecter. *Conrad's Castle* (New York: Harper & Row, 1967), unpaged.

disobedient airplane. Gramatky's illustrations have action and the same engaging humor that characterizes his stories. However, they also reflect the years Gramatky worked for Walt Disney.

One of the earliest stories to personify toys was *The Velveteen Rabbit* by Margery Williams. Any child who has loved a stuffed animal of his own will understand the conversation between the old skin horse and the velveteen rabbit on the subject of becoming real. The skin horse tells the rabbit, " 'Real isn't how you are inside. . . . It's a thing that happens to you when a child loves you for a long long while.' " When the rabbit asks how it happens, he replies, " 'It doesn't happen all at once. . . . you become. It takes a long while.' "[49] It took a long time for a teddy bear named *Charles* to become. He was first given as a present to a little girl who didn't understand him. But a boy traded a kitten for him and then Charles "became"—for he was very loved by the little boy and understood. Liesel Skorpen also wrote the story of *Elizabeth*, a doll that belongs to a little girl. Don Freeman's *Corduroy* is a warm, delightful story of a wistful teddy bear who wears green corduroy overalls. Every day he waits patiently in a department store for someone to buy him. A little girl, Lisa, sees him and wants to buy him, but her mother discourages her by pointing out that he doesn't look very new, and besides one of the buttons on his shoulder strap is missing. That night Corduroy has many exciting adventures in the store as he goes in search of a new button. He doesn't find one, but the next morning he does find what he has wanted most—a home and a friend, for Lisa returns with the contents of her piggy bank and buys him. This book is a completely satisfying story containing pathos, excitement, and love. It was the favorite story of a group of 7-year-olds in an inner city.

Many picture storybooks are written in the traditional folk-tale style. These stories are original and modern, yet they have the rhythm, repetition, and refrains of the old tales. For very young children Holl's *The Rain Puddle* has the classic pattern of the animal folk tale. When the barnyard animals see their reflections in the rain

puddle they call for help for the poor creatures trapped in the water. When the sun dries out the puddle they assume the animals have climbed out safely. Only the wise old owl and the reader know the joke! Wanda Gág's stories of *Millions of Cats* and *Nothing at All* ring of the oral tradition with their rhythmical refrains. *Hildilid's Night* by Cheli Ryan has the glorious lilt of an oft-told tale. It begins:

> High in the hills near Hexham
> there lived an old woman named Hildilid.
> She hated bats and owls and moles and voles
> and moths and stars and shadows and sleep,
> and even the moonlight, all because she hated the
> night.[50]

The popular *Caps for Sale* by Slobodkina utilizes repetition and refrains. In this story a peddler who is selling caps tries vainly to recover his merchandise from some mischievous monkeys. Only after he becomes very angry and throws his own cap on the ground do the imitating monkeys return his caps. The story of *Finders Keepers* by Will and Nicholas has a touch of both folklore and fable in it. Two dogs quarrel over a bone and so they ask a farmer, a goat, an apprentice barber, and a big dog whose bone it is. When the big dog threatens to take it from them, they quickly resolve their quarrel and work together to save the bone. A very funny story told in cumulative verse is *The Judge*, written and illustrated by the Zemachs. Prisoner after prisoner appears before a judge and each is accused of telling a fearsome and fabricated tale. Each new witness adds one more descriptive detail of the horrible thing that is coming. The judge has them all dragged off to jail. In perfect poetic justice the ending shows the monster devouring the judge, while the prisoners are free to go on their way. In this delightful tongue-in-cheek book it is difficult to know who is fooling whom. One of the prisoners appears to have a wooden leg, but a closer look reveals that he is just pretending. The slightly Hogarthian caricatures suggest the whole tale is a lovely farce. *A Penny a Look* by the same husband and wife team has a similar folk-tale twist and ironic ending.

Fanciful tales with more complex plots include

[49]Margery Williams. *The Velveteen Rabbit*, illustrated by William Nicholson (New York: Doubleday, 1922), p. 17.

[50]Cheli Duran Ryan. *Hildilid's Night*, illustrated by Arnold Lobel (New York: Macmillan, 1971), unpaged.

several stories of dragons and monsters. These appeal to more sophisticated 7- and 8-year-olds. The Belsakis were a very ordinary family until Mrs. Belsaki called Mr. Belsaki a "fuddy-duddy." In order to prove that he was not anything so dull Mr. Belsaki buys their son, Gaylord, a pet dragon. This establishes Mr. Belsaki as some kind of local hero, until the dragon starts growing. The mayor then informs them that their dragon is much too large for a "built-up area," so the Belsakis ride off to the Isles of Magic on the back of their pet. The surprise ending of this tale of *The Dragon of an Ordinary Family* by Mahy would suggest some further adventures for the Belsakis. Oxenbury has illustrated this story with most amusing pictures that suggest a real change in the "fuddy-duddy" family.

Mr. Drackle and His Dragons by Elizabeth Froman is about an ogre who starts raising dragons, much to the consternation of the other ogres. It just isn't done; no other ogre has ever raised dragons! The anti-dragon movement grows and finally Mr. Drackle and his dragons settle the question in a positive but firm manner. The illustrator of this story, David McKee, has also written and illustrated several original fantasies of his own. *Mr. Benn—Red Knight* is invited to a fancy-dress ball, so he goes to a costume shop and tries on a splendid suit of red armor. The next thing he knows, he is in a magical land with a large unhappy dragon. Mr. Benn solves the dragon's problem and becomes a real hero. Just as he is about to join the feast to celebrate the return of the dragon, he steps into a small room and realizes he is back in the fitting room of the costume shop. A very funny sequel to this story is titled *123456789 Benn*, and tells of Mr. Benn's adventures as a prisoner after he has tried on a convict's costume. David McKee's illustrations have a childlike perspective, which details the action of the story in a circular fashion. Castle and prisons appear horizontally on the page; all four sides of a room or a courtyard are shown just as children might draw them. These stories have rich possibilities for creative writing. Boys and girls may want to select a "pretend costume" and create their own "Mr. Benn Adventure."

Zeralda's Ogre only eats little children until he meets 6-year-old Zeralda, who cooks such delicacies as watercress soup, snails, and suckling pigs for him. Under Zeralda's influence the ogre and his friends completely lose their taste for children! This book, with its oversized pictures and text by Tomi Ungerer, is obviously a glorious spoof on the usual fairy tale. An even funnier farce is *The Beast of Monsieur Racine* by the same author-artist. This highly imaginative tale tells of the friendship between Monsieur Racine, a retired tax collector, and a rare beast which appeared to be nothing more than a conglomerate of living lumps. After meticulous research on the origin of the beast, Monsieur Racine decides to present it before the Academy of Sciences. What happens there throws all Paris into an uproar. One of Ungerer's trademarks for his illustrations for adults are his "leaky faucet" pictures. This farce provides him with a showcase for his own personal indulgence, and he delights in showing bandaged frames, a tramp carrying a dripping foot, and men with umbrellas sticking out of their heads. While these illustrations are in keeping with the satire of the story, the violence appears to be overdone.

Picture Books of Other Times and Places

Many picture storybooks of today emphasize the universal qualities of childhood, while they provide familiarity with cultures of other parts of the world or other periods. Young children have little understanding of chronology, but they still enjoy some stories of "the olden days." It is also difficult for them to imagine how it would feel to live in another land, yet television has made the world smaller and more familiar to all.

Brinton Turkle has written and illustrated three books about the adventures of a little Quaker lad who lived in Nantucket. In the first story, *Obadiah the Bold*, Obadiah changes his mind about becoming a pirate. *Thy Friend, Obadiah* is a delightful story of a seagull who follows Obadiah around, much to the little boy's annoyance. But one bitter winter day, when Obadiah needs a friend, his seagull is not to be found. Then, Obadiah realizes how much he misses it. Later, when the seagull is in trouble, Obadiah is able to be a friend to him. The deeper meanings and responsibilities of friendship are explored in this warm story of a little red-haired Quaker boy. Glowing pictures with interesting perspectives capture the flavor of living in old

Brinton Turkle provides a bird's-eye perspective of old Nantucket.

From *Thy Friend, Obadiah* by Brinton Turkle. Copyright © 1969 by Brinton Turkle. Reprinted by permission of The Viking Press, Inc.

Nantucket. *The Adventures of Obadiah* are continued in a very happy tale about Obadiah's wild ride at the Sheep-shearing Squantum. *Yonie Wondernose* is a well-loved story of a Pennsylvania Amish boy whose insatiable curiosity earned him his name. Lovely watercolors by Marguerite de Angeli illustrate this classic story. In humorous verse and striking illustrations, Lobel has created a vivid picture of New Amsterdam in 1647 in his book, *On the Day Peter Stuyvesant Sailed into Town.* The ecological theme has a real basis in history and carries an important message for today. In drawing the picture of New York City today (as

seen in Peter Stuyvesant's dream), Lobel[51] said that he first made a very authentic representation of the New York skyline. But even as he was sketching it, new buildings were going up, so he decided to make a more stylized abstraction.

Certain picture books create only the flavor and feeling of a country, while others vividly portray recognizable scenes. Politi gives the feeling of the warmth and gaiety of the Italian hill towns in his autobiographical picture book *Little*

[51] At *The Children's Book Showcase* sponsored by the Children's Book Council at Bank Street College of Education, New York City, May 1972.

Leo. While this book portrays such unfamiliar scenes as hillside vineyards, olive trees, and oxen teams, it also shows the love of play in children throughout the world.

A Bell for Ursli and *The Snowstorm* by Chönz vividly portray village children's preparations for two Swiss festivals. *Florina and the Wild Bird* is the story of Ursli's sister, who rescues a wild ptarmigan and raises the bird over the summer in the mountain hut where the brother and sister have come to pasture the goats. These stories are told in verse form with brilliant watercolors of the Swiss mountains by Carigiet. Two books— *Anton the Goatherd* and *The Pear Tree, the Birch Tree, and the Barberry Bush*—were written and illustrated by Carigiet alone. While the plots are slight in these books, the glorious pictures more than compensate. Carigiet is the only Swiss artist to have won the Hans Christian Andersen Award, an international award for illustrating children's books. In Krasilovsky's story of *The Cow Who Fell in the Canal* children may see Peter Spier's lovely, detailed pictures of the Dutch countryside and market day in the town. While the story of *Ola* by the d'Aulaires is fantasy, the pictures of the interior scenes of Norwegian houses and the Norwegian stave churches provide an authentic background for the setting. Duvoisin, in his illustrations for *Red Bantam* by Fatio, has portrayed a beautiful French farm scene in this story of a brave little banty rooster who saves his favorite hen, Nanette, from the fox, and so proves his courage and superiority over the Big Rooster.

Don Freeman has portrayed a panorama of Paris from a pigeon's eye view in his sophisticated story, *Inspector Peckit.* Peckit is a "private eye" with a perch on the Eiffel Tower. In his attempts to solve the case of the missing knit bag, he covers the Luxembourg Gardens and the Paris sidewalk cafés. The solution to the mystery lies much closer to home than that, however; in fact, you could say it had come home to roost! No one has surpassed the distinctive watercolors of Paris by Bemelmans for *Madeline* and *Madeline's Rescue.* Not only did he paint authentic landmarks of the city but he captured something of the independence of that well-loved city in the character of Madeline. Just before his death Bemel-

mans wrote and illustrated *Madeline in London,* and so presented that lovely city to his many Madeline fans.

Ets and Labastida have carefully portrayed both the old Mexico in the market scene and the new, modern Mexico showing Dairy Queens, supermarkets, and TV aerials in *Nine Days to Christmas.* Using bright yellows, fuchsia pinks, and orange against a pearl gray background, Ets has created a modern child's delight in the Christmas Posada and piñata party. The flavor of Haiti has been accurately conveyed by Evaline Ness in her story, *Josefina February.* Like the little burro that she finds, Josefina seems to be all skinny arms and legs, with a thatch of unruly hair atop her head.

Yashima's stories—*Crow Boy, The Village Tree,* and *Plenty to Watch*—recall his childhood in rural Japan. The pictures of the lovely sweeping branches of the village willow tree and the patterned hills of the countryside give a distinctive picture of Japan. Matsuno tells the story of Mako, a little Japanese girl who cracks her brand new red clogs by playing the weather-telling game, in *A Pair of Red Clogs.* Mako tries to deceive her mother by walking in the mud, but, like all mothers, Mako's seems to know the whole story. The illustrations by Mizumura express the little girl's pride in her new shoes and her misery over trying to deceive her mother. In *Chie and the Sports Day,* Matsuno relates a modern story of how a Japanese girl finds an unusual way to help her brother run in the races.

There are, as yet, no picture stories of modern China. Children continue to love Flack's classic *The Story about Ping,* the little Chinese duck and his adventure on the Yangtze River. The handsome, black-and-white illustrations for *Mei Li* by Handforth tell the story of the Chinese girl who went all alone to the New Year's Fair in the city.

Picture storybooks of other times and places can enlarge children's lives and enhance their living. The phenomenal growth of beautiful picture books for young children is an outstanding accomplishment of the past fifty years of publishing. Children may not always recognize the beauty of these books, but early impressions do exert their influence on the development of permanent tastes for children growing up.

SUGGESTED LEARNING EXPERIENCES

1. Read a story to a 3-year-old. See how many different ways you can provide for the child's participation in the story.

2. Observe children during a story hour either at school or at the library. Record their reactions—verbal comments, facial expressions, or body movements.

3. Working in pairs and using the criteria established in this chapter, compare three different editions of Mother Goose, or three ABC or counting books.

4. Compare two very inexpensive picture books (other than paperbacks) with two or more picture books from a major publisher. Note the quality of paper, binding, and printing; compare illustrations in terms of media and technique; look for originality of plot and well-chosen language in the stories. Which of these books would you rather share with children, and why?

5. Look closely at three or more picture storybooks to discover how the illustrations carry the story's meaning beyond the words. Note the effect of the artist's choice of medium, style, and color; look for content details present in the pictures but not in the text.

6. Study the work of one Caldecott Award-winning illustrator. What media does this artist use? What terms would you use to describe his or her style? How do earlier books compare to the most recent ones? Read his or her acceptance speech for the Caldecott. How has the illustrator's style been influenced by his or her concepts of childhood?

7. Form a mock Caldecott Award Committee and review the Honor Books and Award-winning Book for one specific year. Would you have made the same decision as the ALA Committee? Why or why not?

8. Find three or four books which are examples of the use of one medium—such as cardboard cut, scratchboard, or colláge. Experiment with the materials used in this medium to make a picture of your own.

9. Find examples of picture books which you think might increase children's sensitivity to well-used language. Look for vivid descriptions, repetition of unusual words or phrases, figures of speech within the child's experience.

10. Interview primary grade teachers to see how often they read to the children, how long a time they read, and what their favorite books are.

RELATED READINGS

1. Alderson, Brian. *Looking at Picture Books 1973.*
   A catalogue for the 1973–74 exhibition prepared by Brian Alderson and arranged by The National Book League, London. Distributed in the U.S. by The Children's Book Council.
   This is far more than a catalogue listing information about an exhibition of books; it is in many instances a critical review of picture books in general. The exhibition was designed, according to Mr. Alderson, to do two things: (1) show the range of picture books available today; and (2) by juxtaposing selected books, suggest a critical standpoint for judgment. This is, indeed, a witty and discerning look at picture books.

2. Cianciolo, Patricia. *Illustrations in Children's Books.* Dubuque, Iowa: W. C. Brown Co., 1970.
   Part of a paperback series on literature for children, this book examines the style, the media, and techniques of illustrations in children's books. The last chapter suggests ways in which book illustrations may be used with children.

3. Cianciolo, Patricia, ed., *Picture Books for Children.* Chicago, Ill.: The American Library Association, 1973.
   A thorough discussion and annotated listing of all kinds of picture books for children, including biographies and informational books, picture book editions of single poems, and folk tales. Appropriate age levels for each book are suggested; these range from 3 to 18.

4. Colby, Jean Poindexter. *Writing, Illustrating and Editing Children's Books.* New York: Hastings, 1967.

All phases of juvenile publishing from techniques of writing, illustration, and production to the duties of the editor. Part Two includes a clear discussion of illustrating books, printing methods, typography, and book design.

5. Hurlimann, Bettina. *Picture-book World,* translated and edited by Brian W. Alderson. London: Oxford University Press, 1968.

A survey of modern picture books from all over the world. Twenty-two countries are represented in this book about the international aspect of modern-day picture books.

6. Kingman, Lee, Joanna Foster, and Ruth Lontoft. *Illustrators of Children's Books: 1957–1966.* Boston, Mass.: Horn Book, 1968.

The third book in a series on children's book illustrators. Contains an interesting article, "Color Separation," by Adrienne Adams. A source for many brief biographical sketches of illustrators.

7. Kingman, Lee, ed. *Newbery and Caldecott Medal Books: 1956–1965.* Boston, Mass.: Horn Book, 1965.

This volume contains the acceptance papers, biographies, and related materials concerning the Newbery and Caldecott awards for the ten years from 1956–1965. Norma R. Fryatt's excellent article, "Picture Books Today," is a critical review of the award winners.

8. Klemin, Diana. *The Art of Art for Children's Books.* New York: Potter, 1966.

A contemporary survey of those artists who have illustrated children's books for a decade or more. Sixty-four artists are represented through examples, eight of these in full color. Under the name of each artist is the title of the book illustrated, the technique used, and the size of the original illustration. This is a most useful reference.

9. ———. *The Illustrated Book: Its Art and Craft.* New York: Potter, 1970.

A sequel to number 8 above, this concentrates on the contributions of some forty-eight illustrators of both children's and adult books.

10. MacCann, Donnarae, and Olga Richards. *The Child's First Books: A Critical Study of Pictures and Texts.* New York. H. W. Wilson Company, 1973.

A thorough and critical review of both the literary and graphic elements of picture books. The brief chapters on "Stereotypes in Illustration" would help both teachers and librarians to distinguish between the cliché in art form and the truly imaginative.

11. Mahony, Bertha E. *Illustrators of Children's Books: 1744–1945.* Boston, Mass.: Horn Book, 1947.

The history and development of illustrated books. The article by Helen Gentry, "Graphic Processes in Children's Books," gives a detailed, clear description of the various methods and processes used in printing illustrations. Lynd Ward's article, "The Book Artist: Yesterday and Tomorrow," describes the importance of picture books for children, the contributions of artists from abroad, and the variety of styles in illustrating.

12. ———. *Illustrators of Children's Books: 1946–1956.* Boston, Mass.: Horn Book, 1958.

A supplement to number 11 above. It contains many short biographical sketches of illustrators and several excellent discussions of the art in children's books. Marcia Brown's article, "Distinction in Picture Books," and Lynd Ward's "The Book Artist: Ideas and Technique" are both highly recommended.

13. Miller, Bertha Mahony, and Elinor W. Field. *Caldecott Medal Books: 1938–1957.* Boston, Mass.: Horn Book, 1957.

Includes a biography and the acceptance speech of each artist who has won the Caldecott Award up to 1957. The acceptance papers frequently reveal artists' convictions about illustrating for children; these are fascinating reading. In a final article, "What Is a Picture Book," Esther Averill candidly evaluates the award-winning books.

14. Pitz, Henry C. *Illustrating Children's Books.* New York: Watson-Guptill, 1963.

Pitz describes the history of illustrating books, the techniques of the process, and the actual production. This book is profusely illustrated; unfortunately, many of the illustrations are from a single press. A useful index and bibliography are included.

RECOMMENDED REFERENCES[52]

MOTHER GOOSE AND NURSERY RHYMES

Bodecker, N. M. *It's Raining Said John Twaining.* Atheneum, 1973.

Briggs, Raymond. *The Mother Goose Treasury.* Coward-McCann, 1966.

Brooke, Leslie. *Ring O'Roses.* Warne, 1923.

Cooney, Barbara. *The Courtship, Merry Marriage, and Feast of Cock Robin and Jenny Wren, to which is added the Doleful Death of Cock Robin.* Scribner, 1965.

———. *Mother Goose in French,* translated by Hugh Latham. Crowell, 1964.

———. *Mother Goose in Spanish,* translated by Alastair Reid and Anthony Kerrigan. Crowell, 1968.

De Angeli, Marguerite. *The Book of Nursery and Mother Goose Rhymes.* Doubleday, 1954.

Domanska, Janina. *I Saw a Ship A-Sailing.* Macmillan, 1972.

———. *If All the Seas Were One Sea.* Macmillan, 1971.

Emberley, Ed. *London Bridge Is Falling Down.* Little, Brown, 1967.

Frasconi, Antonio. *The House that Jack Built.* Harcourt Brace Jovanovich, 1958.

Galdone, Paul. *The History of Simple Simon.* McGraw-Hill, 1966.

———. *The House that Jack Built.* McGraw-Hill, 1961.

———. *Old Mother Hubbard and Her Dog.* McGraw-Hill, 1960.

———. *The Old Woman and Her Pig.* McGraw-Hill, 1960.

———. *Tom, Tom, the Piper's Son.* McGraw-Hill, 1964.

Greenaway, Kate. *Mother Goose, or The Old Nursery Rhymes.* Warne, n.d.

Hogrogian, Nonny. *One I Love, Two I Love and Other Loving Mother Goose Rhymes.* Dutton, 1972.

Jeffers, Susan. *Three Jovial Huntsmen, A Mother Goose Rhyme,* Bradbury, 1973.

Lines, Kathleen. *Lavender's Blue,* illustrated by Harold Jones. F. Watts, 1964.

Ness, Evaline. *Old Mother Hubbard and Her Dog.* Holt, Rinehart and Winston, 1972.

Petersham, Maud, and Miska Petersham. *The Rooster Crows.* Macmillan, 1945.

Rackham, Arthur. *Mother Goose, Old Nursery Rhymes.* Appleton, 1913.

Reed, Philip. *Mother Goose and Nursery Rhymes.* Atheneum, 1963.

Rojankovsky, Feodor. *The Tall Book of Mother Goose.* Harper & Row, 1942.

Sendak, Maurice. *Hector Protector and As I Went Over the Water.* Harper & Row, 1965.

Spier, Peter. *London Bridge Is Falling Down.* Doubleday, 1967.

———. *To Market, to Market.* Doubleday, 1967.

Tudor, Tasha. *Mother Goose.* Walck, 1944.

Watson, Clyde. *Father Fox's Pennyrhymes,* illustrated by Wendy Watson. Crowell, 1971.

Wildsmith, Brian. *Brian Wildsmith's Mother Goose.* F. Watts, 1963.

Wright, Blanche Fisher. *The Real Mother Goose.* Rand McNally, 1965 (1916).

Wyndham, Robert, compiler. *Chinese Mother Goose Rhymes,* illustrated by Ed Young. World Publishing, 1968.

ABC BOOKS

Alexander, Anne. *ABC of Cars and Trucks,* illustrated by Ninon. Doubleday, 1956.

Baskin, Leonard, illustrator. *Hosie's Alphabet;* words by Hosea, Tobias, and Lisa Baskin. Viking, 1972.

Brown, Marcia. *All Butterflies.* Scribner, 1974.

Burningham, John. *John Burningham's ABC.* Bobbs-Merrill, 1967.

Chardiet, Bernice. *C Is for Circus,* illustrated by Brinton Turkle. Walker, 1971.

Eichenberg, Fritz. *Ape in a Cape.* Harcourt Brace Jovanovich, 1952.

Falls, Charles Buckles. *An ABC Book.* Doubleday, 1923.

Feelings, Muriel. *Jambo Means Hello, Swahili Alphabet Book,* illustrated by Tom Feelings. Dial, 1974.

---

[52] All books listed at the end of this chapter are recommended subject to the qualifications noted in the text. *See* Appendix D for publishers' complete addresses.

Fife, Dale. *Adam's ABC,* illustrated by Don Robertson. Coward-McCann, 1971.
Gág, Wanda. *The ABC Bunny.* Coward-McCann, 1933.
Garten, Jan. *The Alphabet Tale,* illustrated by Muriel Batherman. Random House, 1964.
Grossbart, Francine. *A Big City.* Harper & Row, 1966.
Illsley, Velma. *M Is for Moving.* Walck, 1966.
Lear, Edward. *ABC.* McGraw-Hill, 1965 (1871).
McGinley, Phyllis. *All Around the Town,* illustrated by Helen Stone. Lippincott, 1948.
Matthiesen, Thomas. *ABC An Alphabet Book.* Platt & Munk, 1966.
Mendoza, George. *The Marcel Marceau Alphabet Book,* photographs by Milton Greene. Doubleday, 1970.
Miles, Miska. *Apricot ABC,* illustrated by Peter Parnall. Little, Brown, 1969.
Milgrom, Harry. *ABC of Ecology,* photographs by Donald Crews. Macmillan, 1972.
———. *ABC Science Experiments,* photographs by Donald Crews. Macmillan, 1970.
Munari, Bruno. *Bruno Munari's ABC.* World Publishing, 1960.
Oxenbury, Helen. *Helen Oxenbury's ABC of Things.* F. Watts, 1972.
Piatti, Celestino. *Celestino Piatti's Animal ABC.* Atheneum, 1966.
Shuttlesworth, Dorothy. *ABC of Buses,* illustrated by Leonard Shortall. Doubleday, 1965.
Tudor, Tasha. *A Is for Annabelle.* Walck, 1954.
Walters, Marguerite. *The City-Country ABC,* illustrated by Ib Ohlsson. Doubleday, 1966.
Wildsmith, Brian. *Brian Wildsmith's ABC.* F. Watts, 1963.
Zacks, Irene. *Space Alphabet,* illustrated by Peter Plasencia. Prentice-Hall, 1964.

COUNTING BOOKS

Allen, Robert. *Numbers,* photographs by Mottke Weissman. Platt & Munk, 1968.
Carle, Eric. *1, 2, 3 to the Zoo.* World Publishing, 1968.
———. *The Very Hungry Caterpillar.* World Publishing, 1969.
Eichenberg, Fritz. *Dancing in the Moon.* Harcourt Brace Jovanovich, 1955.
Elkin, Benjamin. *Six Foolish Fishermen,* illustrated by Katherine Evans. Children's Press, 1957.
Feelings, Muriel. *Moja Means One: Swahili Counting Book,* illustrated by Tom Feelings. Dial, 1971.
Hoban, Tana. *Count and See.* Macmillan, 1972.
Keats, Ezra Jack. *Over in the Meadow.* Four Winds, 1972.
Kirn, Ann. *Nine in a Line.* Norton, 1966.
Krüss, James. *3 × 3 Three by Three,* translated by Geoffrey Strachan, illustrated by Johanna Rubin. Macmillan, 1965.
Langstaff, John. *Over in the Meadow,* illustrated by Feodor Rojankovsky. Harcourt Brace Jovanovich, 1957.
Oxenbury, Helen. *Numbers of Things.* F. Watts, 1968.
Sendak, Maurice. *One Was Johnny (Nutshell Library,* vol. 3). Harper & Row, 1962.
Tudor, Tasha. *1 Is One.* Walck, 1956.
Wildsmith, Brian. *Brian Wildsmith's 1, 2, 3's.* F. Watts, 1965.

CONCEPT BOOKS

Brown, Margaret Wise. *The Important Book,* illustrated by Leonard Weisgard. Harper & Row, 1949.
Emberley, Ed. *The Wing on a Flea.* Little, Brown, 1961.
Hoban, Tana. *Over, Under and Through.* Macmillan, 1973.
———. *Push Pull, Empty Full.* Macmillan, 1972.
Kessler, Ethel, and Leonard Kessler. *Are You Square?,* illustrated by Leonard Kessler. Doubleday, 1966.
Provensen, Alice, and Martin Provensen. *What Is a Color?* Golden Press, 1967.
Reiss, John J. *Colors.* Bradbury, 1969.
Schlein, Miriam. *Fast Is Not a Ladybug,* illustrated by Leonard Kessler. W. R. Scott, 1953.
———. *Heavy Is a Hippopotamus,* illustrated by Leonard Kessler. W. R. Scott, 1954.
Udry, Janice May. *A Tree Is Nice,* illustrated by Marc Simont. Harper & Row, 1956.

WORDLESS PICTURE BOOKS

Alexander, Martha. *Bobo's Dream.* Dial, 1970.
———. *Out! Out! Out!* Dial, 1968.
Aruego, Jose. *Look What I Can Do.* Scribner, 1971.
Carle, Eric. *Do You Want to Be My Friend?* Crowell, 1971.
Carroll, Ruth. *What Whiskers Did.* Walck, 1965.
Goodall, John S. *The Adventures of Paddy Pork.* Harcourt Brace Jovanovich, 1968.
———. *The Midnight Adventures of Kelly, Dot, and Esmeralda.* Atheneum, 1972.
———. *Shrewbettina's Birthday.* Harcourt Brace Jovanovich, 1971.
Hogrogian, Nonny. *Apples.* Macmillan, 1972.
Hutchins, Pat. *Changes, Changes.* Macmillan, 1971.
———. *Rosie's Walk.* Macmillan, 1968.
Mayer, Mercer. *A Boy, a Dog, and a Frog.* Dial, 1967.
———. *Frog, Where Are You?* Dial, 1969.
Ward, Lynd. *The Silver Pony.* Houghton Mifflin, 1973.
Wezel, Peter. *The Good Bird.* Harper & Row, 1964.

PICTURE BOOKS

Aesop's Fables, selected and adapted by Louis Untermeyer, illustrated by A. and M. Provensen. Golden Press, 1965.
Alexander, Martha. *Nobody Asked Me If I Wanted a Baby Sister.* Dial, 1971.
Andersen, Hans Christian. *The Wild Swans,* illustrated by Marcia Brown. Scribner, 1963.
Ardizzone, Edward. *Little Tim and the Brave Sea Captain.* Walck, 1955.
Artzybasheff, Boris. *Aesop's Fables.* Viking, 1933.
Asbjørnsen, P. C., and J. E. Moe. *The Three Billy Goats Gruff,* illustrated by Marcia Brown. Harcourt Brace Jovanovich, 1957.
d'Aulaire, Ingri, and Edgar d'Aulaire. *Abraham Lincoln.* Doubleday, 1957 (1939).
———. *Ola.* Doubleday, 1932.
———. *Pocahontas.* Doubleday, 1946.
Barrett, Judi. *Animals Should Definitely Not Wear Clothing,* illustrated by Ron Barrett. Atheneum, 1970.
Bemelmans, Ludwig. *Madeline.* Viking, 1962 (1939).
———. *Madeline in London.* Viking, 1961.
———. *Madeline's Rescue.* Viking, 1953.
Bonsall, Crosby. *Whose Eye Am I?,* photographs by Ylla. Harper & Row, 1969.
Bourne, Miriam Anne. *Emilio's Summer Day,* illustrated by Ben Shecter. Harper & Row, 1966.
Brown, Marcia. *Dick Whittington and His Cat.* Scribner, 1950.
———. *Felice.* Scribner, 1958.
———. *Henry-Fisherman.* Scribner, 1949.
———. *Once a Mouse.* Scribner, 1961.
Brown, Margaret Wise. *The Dead Bird,* illustrated by Remy Charlip. W. R. Scott, 1958.
———. *The Runaway Bunny,* illustrated by Clement Hurd. Harper & Row, 1972 (1942).
———. *The Sleepy Little Lion,* photographs by Ylla. Harper & Row, 1947.
Brown, Myra Berry. *The First Night Away from Home,* illustrated by Dorothy Marino. F. Watts, 1960.
Bryant, Sara Cone. *The Burning Rice Fields,* illustrated by Mamoru Funai. Holt, Rinehart and Winston, 1963.
Buckley, Helen E. *Grandfather and I,* illustrated by Paul Galdone. Lothrop, 1959.
———. *Grandmother and I,* illustrated by Paul Galdone. Lothrop, 1961.
———. *Michael Is Brave,* illustrated by Emily McCully. Lothrop, 1971.
———. *My Sister and I,* illustrated by Paul Galdone. Lothrop, 1963.
Burch, Robert. *Joey's Cat,* illustrated by Don Freeman. Viking, 1969.
Burningham, John. *Mr. Gumpy's Motor Car.* Jonathan Cape Ltd., 1973.
———. *Mr. Gumpy's Outing.* Holt, Rinehart and Winston, 1971.
———. *Seasons.* Bobbs-Merrill, 1970.

Burton, Virginia Lee. *Katie and the Big Snow*. Houghton Mifflin, 1943.

———. *The Little House*. Houghton Mifflin, 1942.

———. *Mike Mulligan and His Steam Shovel*. Houghton Mifflin, 1939.

Carigiet, Alois. *Anton the Goatherd*. Walck, 1966.

———. *The Pear Tree, the Birch Tree, and the Barberry Bush*. Walck, 1967.

Caudill, Rebecca. *A Pocketful of Cricket*, illustrated by Evaline Ness. Holt, Rinehart and Winston, 1964.

Chönz, Selina. *A Bell for Ursli*, illustrated by Alois Carigiet. Walck, 1953.

———. *Florina and the Wild Bird*, illustrated by Alois Carigiet. Walck, 1953.

———. *The Snowstorm*, illustrated by Alois Carigiet. Walck, 1958.

Clifton, Lucille. *Some of the Days of Everett Anderson*, illustrated by Evaline Ness. Holt, Rinehart and Winston, 1970.

Cohen, Miriam. *Best Friends*, illustrated by Lillian Hoban. Macmillan, 1971.

———. *The New Teacher*, illustrated by Lillian Hoban. Macmillan, 1972.

———. *Will I Have a Friend?*, illustrated by Lillian Hoban. Macmillan, 1967.

Cooney, Barbara. *Chanticleer and the Fox*. Crowell, 1958.

Daugherty, James. *Andy and the Lion*. Viking, 1938.

Dayrell, Elphinstone. *Why the Sun and the Moon Live in the Sky*, illustrated by Blair Lent. Houghton Mifflin, 1968.

De Angeli, Marguerite. *Yonie Wondernose*. Doubleday, 1944.

De Brunhoff, Jean. *The Story of Babar*. Random House, 1960.

De Regniers, Beatrice Schenk. *May I Bring a Friend?*, illustrated by Beni Montresor. Atheneum, 1964.

Domanska, Janina. *The Turnip*. Macmillan, 1969.

Du Bois, William Pène. *Bear Circus*. Viking, 1971.

———. *Lazy Tommy Pumpkinhead*. Harper & Row, 1966.

Dunn, Judy. *Things*. Photographs by Phoebe and Tris Dunn. Doubleday, 1968.

Duvoisin, Roger. *Petunia*. Knopf, 1950.

Ehrlich, Amy. *Zeek Silver Moon*, illustrated by Robert Andrew Parker. Dial, 1972.

Emberley, Barbara. *Drummer Hoff*, illustrated by Ed Emberley. Prentice-Hall, 1967.

Ets, Marie Hall. *Gilberto and the Wind*. Viking, 1963.

———. *Play with Me*. Viking, 1955.

Ets, Marie Hall, and Aurora Labastida. *Nine Days to Christmas*, illustrated by Marie Hall Ets. Viking, 1959.

Fatio, Louise. *The Happy Lion*, illustrated by Roger Duvoisin. McGraw-Hill, 1954.

———. *Red Bantam*, illustrated by Roger Duvoisin. McGraw-Hill, 1962.

Felt, Sue. *Rosa-Too-Little*. Doubleday, 1950.

Fisher, Aileen. *Best Little House*, illustrated by Arnold Spilka. Crowell, 1966.

———. *Listen, Rabbit*, illustrated by Symeon Shimin. Crowell, 1964.

———. *In the Middle of the Night*, illustrated by Adrienne Adams. Crowell, 1965.

Flack, Marjorie. *The Story about Ping*, illustrated by Kurt Wiese. Viking, 1933.

Francoise, pseud. (Francoise Seignobosc). *Jeanne-Marie Counts Her Sheep*. Scribner, 1957.

———. *Springtime for Jeanne-Marie*. Scribner, 1955.

———. *What Time Is It, Jeanne-Marie?* Scribner, 1963.

Frasconi, Antonio. *See Again, Say Again*. Harcourt Brace Jovanovich, 1964.

Freeman, Don. *Corduroy*. Viking, 1968.

———. *Fly High, Fly Low*. Viking, 1957.

———. *Inspector Peckit*. Viking, 1972.

Freeman, Don, and Lydia Freeman. *Pet of the Met*, illustrated by Don Freeman. Viking, 1953.

Freschet, Berniece. *The Old Bullfrog*, illustrated by Roger Duvoisin. Scribner, 1968.

———. *The Turtle Pond*, illustrated by Donald Carrick. Scribner, 1971.

———. *The Web in the Grass*, illustrated by Roger Duvoisin. Scribner, 1972.

Froman, Elizabeth. *Mr. Drackle and His Dragons*, illustrated by David McKee. F. Watts, 1971.

Gág, Wanda. *Millions of Cats*. Coward-McCann, 1928.

———. *Nothing at All*. Coward-McCann, 1941.

Garelick, May. *Where Does the Butterfly Go When It Rains?* illustrated by Leonard Weisgard. W. R. Scott, 1961.

George, Jean Craighead. *All Upon a Stone,* illustrated by Don Bolognese. Crowell, 1971.

Gill, Joan. *Hush, Jon!,* illustrated by Tracy Sugarman. Doubleday, 1968.

Ginsburg, Mirra. *The Chick and the Duckling,* illustrated by Jose Aruego and Ariane Aruego. Macmillan, 1972.

Goudey, Alice. *Houses from the Sea,* illustrated by Adrienne Adams. Scribner, 1959.

Gramatky, Hardie. *Little Toot.* Putnam, 1939.

———. *Loopy.* Putnam, 1941.

Grimm, The Brothers. *Snow-White and the Seven Dwarfs,* translated by Randall Jarrell, illustrated by Nancy Ekholm Burkert. Farrar, Straus, 1972.

Handforth, Thomas. *Mei Li.* Doubleday, 1938.

Heide, Florence P. *The Shrinking of Treehorn,* illustrated by Edward Gorey. Holiday, 1971.

Hoban, Russell. *A Baby Sister for Frances,* illustrated by Lillian Hoban. Harper & Row, 1964.

———. *A Bargain for Frances,* illustrated by Lillian Hoban. Harper & Row, 1970.

———. *Bedtime for Frances,* illustrated by Garth Williams. Harper & Row, 1960.

———. *Best Friends for Frances,* illustrated by Lillian Hoban. Harper & Row, 1969.

———. *A Birthday for Frances,* illustrated by Lillian Hoban. Harper & Row, 1968.

Hoban, Tana. *Look Again!* Macmillan, 1971.

Hodges, Margaret. *The Wave,* illustrated by Blair Lent. Houghton Mifflin, 1964.

Hoffman, Phyllis. *Steffie and Me,* illustrated by Emily McCully. Harper & Row, 1970.

Hoffmann, Felix. *A Boy Went Out to Gather Pears.* Harcourt Brace Jovanovich, 1963.

Holl, Adelaide. *The Rain Puddle,* illustrated by Roger Duvoisin. Lothrop, 1965.

Holland, Viki. *We Are Having a Baby.* Scribner, 1972.

Hutchins, Pat. *Good Night, Owl!* Macmillan, 1972.

———. *The Surprise Party.* Macmillan, 1969.

———. *Titch.* Macmillan, 1971.

Iwasaki, Chihiro. *Staying Home Alone on a Rainy Day.* McGraw-Hill, 1969.

Kahl, Virginia. *The Duchess Bakes a Cake.* Scribner, 1955.

———. *Plum Pudding for Christmas.* Scribner, 1956.

Kantrowitz, Mildred. *Maxie,* illustrated by Emily A. McCully. Parents', 1970.

Keats, Ezra Jack. *Dreams.* Macmillan, 1974.

———. *Goggles.* Macmillan, 1969.

———. *Hi, Cat!* Macmillan, 1970.

———. *A Letter to Amy.* Harper & Row, 1968.

———. *Pet Show!* Macmillan, 1972.

———. *Peter's Chair.* Harper & Row, 1967.

———. *The Snowy Day.* Viking, 1962.

———. *Whistle for Willie.* Viking, 1964.

Keeping, Charles. *Through the Window.* F. Watts, 1970.

Krasilovsky, Phyllis. *The Cow Who Fell in the Canal,* illustrated by Peter Spier. Doubleday, 1957.

Kraus, Robert. *Leo the Late Bloomer,* illustrated by Jose Aruego. Windmill, 1971.

———. *Milton the Early Riser,* illustrated by Jose Aruego and Ariane Aruego. Windmill, 1972.

Krauss, Ruth. *The Backward Day,* illustrated by Marc Simont. Harper & Row, 1950.

———. *The Carrot Seed,* illustrated by Crockett Johnson. Harper & Row, 1945.

———. *A Very Special House,* illustrated by Maurice Sendak. Harper & Row, 1953.

Kumin, Maxine W. *The Beach before Breakfast,* illustrated by Leonard Weisgard. Putnam, 1964.

Kunhardt, Dorothy. *Pat the Bunny.* Golden Press, 1962 (1940).

Kuskin, Karla. *Just Like Everyone Else.* Harper & Row, 1959.

La Fontaine, Jean de. *The Lion and the Rat,* illustrated by Brian Wildsmith. F. Watts, 1964.

———. *The North Wind and the Sun,* illustrated by Brian Wildsmith. F. Watts, 1964.

Lamorisse, Albert. *The Red Balloon.* Doubleday, 1956.

Langstaff, John. *Frog Went a-Courtin',* illustrated by Feodor Rojankovsky. Harcourt, 1955.

Leaf, Munro. *The Story of Ferdinand,* illustrated by Robert Lawson. Viking, 1936.

————. *Wee Gillis,* illustrated by Robert Lawson. Viking, 1938.

Lenski, Lois. *Cowboy Small.* Walck, 1949.

————. *Policeman Small.* Walck, 1962.

Lent, Blair. *John Tabor's Ride.* Little, Brown, 1966.

Lexau, Joan. *Benjie,* illustrated by Don Bolognese. Dial, 1964.

————. *Benjie on His Own,* illustrated by Don Bolognese. Dial, 1970.

————. *Emily and the Klunky Baby and the Next-door Dog,* illustrated by Martha Alexander. Dial, 1972.

————. *Me Day,* illustrated by Robert Weaver. Dial, 1971.

Lindgren, Astrid. *The Tomten,* adapted from a poem by Viktor Rydberg, illustrated by Harald Wiberg. Coward-McCann, 1961.

Lionni, Leo. *Alexander and the Wind-up Mouse.* Pantheon, 1969.

————. *The Biggest House in the World.* Pantheon, 1968.

————. *Fish Is Fish.* Pantheon, 1970.

————. *Frederick.* Pantheon, 1967.

————. *Inch by Inch.* Astor-Honor, 1960.

————. *Little Blue and Little Yellow.* Astor-Honor, 1959.

————. *Swimmy.* Pantheon, 1963.

————. *Tico and the Golden Wings.* Pantheon, 1964.

Lobel, Arnold. *Frog and Toad Are Friends.* Harper & Row, 1970.

————. *Frog and Toad Together.* Harper & Row, 1972.

————. *Mouse Tales.* Harper & Row, 1972.

————. *On the Day Peter Stuyvesant Sailed into Town.* Harper & Row, 1971.

McCloskey, Robert. *Blueberries for Sal.* Viking, 1948.

————. *Burt Dow, Deep-water Man.* Viking, 1963.

————. *Make Way for Ducklings.* Viking, 1941.

————. *Time of Wonder.* Viking, 1957.

MacDonald, Golden, pseud. (Margaret Wise Brown). *The Little Island,* illustrated by Leonard Weisgard. Doubleday, 1946.

McKee, David. *Mr. Benn—Red Knight.* McGraw-Hill, 1968.

————. *123456789 Benn.* McGraw-Hill, 1970.

Mahy, Margaret. *The Dragon of an Ordinary Family,* illustrated by Helen Oxenbury. F. Watts, 1969.

Massie, Diane Redfield. *Dazzle.* Parents', 1969.

————. *Walter Was a Frog.* Scribner, 1970.

Matsuno, Masako. *Chie and the Sports Day,* illustrated by Kazue Mizumura. World Publishing, 1965.

————. *A Pair of Red Clogs,* illustrated by Kazue Mizumura. World Publishing, 1960.

Miles, Miska. *Mississippi Possum,* illustrated by John Schoenherr. Little, Brown, 1965.

————. *Wharf Rat,* illustrated by John Schoenherr. Little, Brown, 1972.

Minarik, Else Holmelund. *Father Bear Comes Home,* illustrated by Maurice Sendak. Harper & Row, 1959.

————. *A Kiss for Little Bear,* illustrated by Maurice Sendak. Harper & Row, 1968.

————. *Little Bear,* illustrated by Maurice Sendak. Harper & Row, 1957.

————. *Little Bear's Friend,* illustrated by Maurice Sendak. Harper & Row, 1960.

————. *Little Bear's Visit,* illustrated by Maurice Sendak. Harper & Row, 1961.

Munari, Bruno. *The Birthday Present.* World Publishing, 1959.

————. *The Circus in the Mist.* World Publishing, 1969.

————. *Who's There? Open the Door!* World Publishing, 1957.

Ness, Evaline. *Josefina February.* Scribner, 1963.

————. *Sam, Bangs and Moonshine.* Holt, Rinehart and Winston, 1966.

Newberry, Clare Turlay. *April's Kittens.* Harper & Row, 1940.

Nic Leodhas, Sorche, pseud. (Leclaire Alger). *Always Room for One More,* illustrated by Nonny Hogrogian. Holt, Rinehart and Winston, 1965.

Ormondroyd, Edward. *Broderick,* illustrated by John M. Larrecq. Parnassus, 1969.

Oxenbury, Helen. *Pig Tale.* Morrow, 1973.

Parnall, Peter. *The Mountain.* Doubleday, 1971.

Piatti, Celestino. *The Happy Owls.* Atheneum, 1964.

Piper, Watty. *The Little Engine that Could,* illustrated by George Hauman and Doris Hauman. Platt & Munk, 1954 (1930).

Politi, Leo. *Little Leo.* Scribner, 1951.

————. *Pedro, the Angel of Olvera Street.* Scribner, 1946.

————. *Song of the Swallows.* Scribner, 1949.

Potter, Beatrix. *The Tale of Peter Rabbit.* Warne, 1902.

Preston, Edna Mitchell. *Squawk to the Moon, Little Goose,* illustrated by Barbara Cooney. Viking, 1974.

————. *The Temper Tantrum Book,* illustrated by Rainey Bennett. Viking, 1969.

Prokofieff, Serge. *Peter and the Wolf,* illustrated by Frans Haacken. F. Watts, 1961.

Raskin, Ellen. *Nothing Ever Happens on My Block.* Atheneum, 1966.

Reich, Hanns. *Children of Many Lands.* Hill & Wang, 1964.

————. *Laughing Camera for Children.* Hill & Wang, 1971.

Rey, Hans Augusto. *Curious George.* Houghton Mifflin, 1941.

Robbins, Ruth. *Baboushka and the Three Kings,* illustrated by Nicolas Sidjakov. Parnassus, 1960.

Ryan, Cheli Duran. *Hildilid's Night,* illustrated by Arnold Lobel. Macmillan, 1971.

Scheer, Julian. *Rain Makes Applesauce,* illustrated by Marvin Bileck. Holiday, 1964.

Schoenherr, John. *The Barn.* Little, Brown, 1968.

Scott, Ann Herbert. *Sam,* illustrated by Symeon Shimin. McGraw-Hill, 1967.

Segal, Lore. *Tell Me a Mitzi,* illustrated by Harriet Pincus. Farrar, Straus, 1970.

Sendak, Maurice. *In the Night Kitchen.* Harper & Row, 1970.

————. *The Nutshell Library.* Harper & Row, 1962.

      Alligators All Around

      Pierre

      One Was Johnny

      Chicken Soup with Rice

————. *Where the Wild Things Are.* Harper & Row, 1963.

Seuss, Dr., pseud. (Theodor S. Geisel). *And to Think that I Saw It on Mulberry Street.* Vanguard, 1937.

————. *The Cat in the Hat.* Random House, 1957.

————. *Horton Hatches the Egg.* Random House, 1940.

————. *McElligot's Pool.* Random House, 1947.

————. *Thidwick, the Big-hearted Moose.* Random House, 1948.

Shecter, Ben. *Conrad's Castle.* Harper & Row, 1967.

Shulevitz, Uri. *Dawn.* Farrar, Straus, 1974.

————. *One Monday Morning.* Scribner, 1967.

————. *Rain Rain Rivers.* Farrar, Straus, 1969.

Skorpen, Liesel. *Charles,* illustrated by Martha Alexander. Harper & Row, 1971.

————. *Elizabeth,* illustrated by Martha Alexander. Harper & Row, 1970.

Slobodkina, Esphyr. *Caps for Sale.* W. R. Scott, 1947.

Small, Ernest. *Baba Yaga,* illustrated by Blair Lent. Houghton Mifflin, 1966.

Smith, Mary, and R. A. Smith. *Long Ago Elf.* Follett, 1968.

Sonneborn, Ruth. *Friday Night Is Papa Night,* illustrated by Emily McCully. Viking, 1970.

————. *I Love Gram,* illustrated by Leo Carty. Viking, 1971.

Spier, Peter. *Crash! Bang! Boom!* Doubleday, 1972.

————. *Gobble Growl Grunt.* Doubleday, 1971.

Steig, William. *Amos and Boris.* Farrar, Straus, 1971.

————. *Sylvester and the Magic Pebble.* Windmill, 1969.

Steptoe, John. *Stevie.* Harper & Row, 1969.

————. *Train Ride.* Harper & Row, 1971.

————. *Uptown.* Harper & Row, 1970.

Stone, A. Harris. *The Last Free Bird,* illustrated by Sheila Heins. Prentice-Hall, 1967.

Taniuchi, Kota. *Up on a Hilltop.* F. Watts, 1971.

Thurber, James. *Many Moons*, illustrated by Louis Slobodkin. Harcourt Brace Jovanovich, 1943.

Titus, Eve. *Anatole*, illustrated by Paul Galdone. McGraw-Hill, 1956.

Tresselt, Alvin. *The Beaver Pond*, illustrated by Roger Duvoisin. Lothrop, 1970.

———. *The Dead Tree*, illustrated by Charles Robinson. Parents', 1972.

———. *Hide and Seek Fog*, illustrated by Roger Duvoisin. Lothrop, 1965.

———. *It's Time Now*, illustrated by Roger Duvoisin. Harper & Row, 1969.

———. *Sun Up*, illustrated by Roger Duvoisin. Lothrop, 1949.

———. *A Thousand Lights and Fireflies*, illustrated by John Moodie. Parents', 1965.

———. *Wake Up, City!*, illustrated by Roger Duvoisin. Lothrop, 1957.

———. *Wake Up, Farm!*, illustrated by Roger Duvoisin. Lothrop, 1955.

———. *White Snow, Bright Snow*, illustrated by Roger Duvoisin. Lothrop, 1947.

Turkle, Brinton. *The Adventures of Obadiah*. Viking, 1972.

———. *Obadiah the Bold*. Viking, 1965.

———. *Thy Friend, Obadiah*. Viking, 1969.

Tworkov, Jack. *The Camel Who Took a Walk*, illustrated by Roger Duvoisin. Dutton, 1951.

Udry, Janice May. *Let's Be Enemies*, illustrated by Maurice Sendak. Harper & Row, 1961.

———. *The Moon Jumpers*, illustrated by Maurice Sendak. Harper & Row, 1959.

———. *What Mary Jo Shared*, illustrated by Eleanor Mill. A. Whitman, 1966.

———. *What Mary Jo Wanted*, illustrated by Eleanor Mill. A. Whitman, 1968.

Ungerer, Tomi. *The Beast of Monsieur Racine*. Farrar, Straus, 1971.

———. *Crictor*. Harper & Row, 1958.

———. *Zeralda's Ogre*. Harper & Row, 1967.

Valens, Evans G. *Wildfire*, illustrated by Clement Hurd. World Publishing, 1963.

———. *Wingfin and Topple*, illustrated by Clement Hurd. World Publishing, 1962.

Viorst, Judith. *Alexander and the Terrible, Horrible, No Good, Very Bad Day*, illustrated by Ray Cruz. Atheneum, 1972.

———. *I'll Fix Anthony*, illustrated by Arnold Lobel. Harper & Row, 1969.

———. *The Tenth Good Thing about Barney*, illustrated by Erik Blegvad. Atheneum, 1971.

Waber, Bernard. *The House on East 88th Street*. Houghton Mifflin, 1962.

———. *"You Look Ridiculous," Said the Rhinoceros to the Hippopotamus*. Houghton Mifflin, 1966.

Wagner, Jane. *J. T.*, photographs by Gordon Parks. Van Nostrand, 1969.

Ward, Lynd. *The Biggest Bear*. Houghton Mifflin, 1952.

Will and Nicholas, pseud. (William Lipkind and Nicholas Mordvinoff). *Finders Keepers*. Harcourt Brace Jovanovich, 1951.

Williams, Garth. *Baby's First Book*. Golden Press, 1955.

Williams, Margery. *The Velveteen Rabbit*, illustrated by William Nicholson. Doubleday, 1958 (1922).

Yashima, Taro, pseud. (Jun Iwamatsu). *Crow Boy*. Viking, 1955.

———. *Umbrella*. Viking, 1958.

———. *The Village Tree*. Viking, 1953.

Yashima, Taro, and Mitsu Yashima. *Plenty to Watch*. Viking, 1954.

Ylla, pseud. (Camilla Koffler). *Animal Babies*, text by Arthur Gregor. Harper & Row, 1959.

———. *Two Little Bears*. Harper & Row, 1954.

Zemach, Harve. *The Judge*, illustrated by Margot Zemach. Farrar, Straus, 1969.

———. *A Penny a Look: An Old Story*, illustrated by Margot Zemach. Farrar, Straus, 1971.

Zion, Gene. *Harry, the Dirty Dog*, illustrated by Margaret Bloy Graham. Harper & Row, 1956.

Zolotow, Charlotte. *Do You Know What I'll Do?*, illustrated by Garth Williams. Harper & Row, 1958.

———. *A Father Like That*, illustrated by Ben Shecter. Harper & Row, 1971.

———. *The Hating Book*, illustrated by Ben Shecter. Harper & Row, 1969.

———. *If It Weren't for You*, illustrated by Ben Shecter. Harper & Row, 1966.

———. *Mr. Rabbit and the Lovely Present*, illustrated by Maurice Sendak. Harper & Row, 1962.

———. *My Friend John*, illustrated by Ben Shecter. Harper & Row, 1968.

———. *The Quarreling Book*, illustrated by Arnold Lobel. Harper & Row, 1963.

———. *The Storm Book*, illustrated by Margaret Bloy Graham. Harper & Row, 1952.

———. *William's Doll*, illustrated by William Pène du Bois. Harper & Row, 1972.

4 Traditional Literature

Ever since humans realized they were unique among animals in that they could think and talk, they have tried to explain themselves and their world. Who was the first human? How did he come to be? What made the sun and the moon and the stars? Why were the animals made the way they were? What caused night and day, the seasons, the cycle of life itself? Why were some people greedy and some unselfish, some ugly and some handsome, some dull and others clever? As people pondered these questions and many more, they created stories that helped explain the world to their primitive minds. The story tellers told these tales again and again around the fires of the early tribes, by the hearths of humble cottages, before the great fire in the king's hall; they told them as they sat in the grass huts of the jungle, the hogans of the Navajo, and the igloos of the Eskimo. Their children told them, and their children's children, until the stories were as smooth and polished as the roundest stones in the stream. And so people created their myths, and their folk tales, their legends and epics; the literature of the fireside, the poetry of the people, and the memory of mankind.

A Perspective on Traditional Literature

ORIGIN OF FOLK LITERATURE

We have no one word that encompasses all of the stories that are born of the oral tradition. They are most often grouped under the heading of folklore, folk literature, or mythology. Generally, we say that myths are about gods and the creation of things; legends are about heroes and their mighty deeds before the time of recorded history; and folk tales, fairy tales, and fables are simple stories about talking beasts, woodcutters, and princesses who reveal human behavior and beliefs while playing out their roles in a world of wonder and magic.

Children will sometimes identify these stories as "make-believe," as contrasted with "true" or "stories that could really happen." Unfortunately, the word *myth* has sometimes been defined as an "imagined event" or a "pagan falsehood," as opposed to "historical fact" or "Christian truth." In literary study, however, *myth* does not mean "untrue"; rather the term refers to a generalized meaning or a universal idea, a significant truth about man and his life. A single *myth* is a narrative that tells of origins,[1] explains natural or social phenomena, or suggests the destiny of humans through the interaction of people and supernatural beings. A *mythology* is a group of

[1]Sylvan Barnet, Morton Berman, and William Burto, *The Study of Literature* (Boston, Mass.: Little, Brown, 1960), pp. 315–316.

159

myths of a particular culture. Myth-making[2] is continuous and in process today. Usually myth is a product of a society rather than of a single author.

The origin of the myths has fascinated and puzzled mythologists, anthropologists, and psychologists. How, they wonder, can one account for the similarities found among these stories that grew out of ancient cultures widely separated from each other? The Greek myth of "Cupid and Psyche" (291) is very much like the Norwegian tale of "East of the Sun and West of the Moon."(8)[3] Again, the Norwegian story of "The Princess on the Glass Hill" (6) is similar to the French "Cinderella" (186), except that the main character is a boy instead of a girl. And the story of Cinderella is found throughout the world, with nearly 500 versions appearing in Europe alone.

In trying to explain this phenomenon one group of early mythologists proposed the notion of *monogenesis*, or inheritance from a single culture. The Grimm brothers, who were among the first of the nineteenth-century scholars of folklore, theorized that all folk tales originated from one prehistoric group called Aryans, later identified as Indo-Europeans by modern linguists. As this group migrated to other countries the scholars reasoned that they took their folklore with them, which led to the theory of *diffusion*.

Another group of mythologists explained myths in terms of movements of the sun or moon. They believed that all the myths and folk tales expressed the basic plot of the sun or sun hero battling against the powers of darkness. Little Red Riding Hood, for example, was viewed as the sun being devoured by the wolf (night), only to be disgorged and reappear. This solar-myth theory is no longer accepted by scholars.

Another approach to folklore involves the theory of *polygenesis*, or multiple origins. It is argued that each story could have been an independent invention growing out of universal desires and needs of humankind. Early anthropologists viewed myth as the religion of the people derived from rituals that were recounted in drama and narratives. They identified recurrent themes in myths of different cultures. Kluckhohn's study[4] of the myths of fifty cultures revealed such recurring themes as the flood, slaying of monsters, incest, sibling rivalry, and castration. He also found several patterns repeated in the myth of the hero. Sir James Frazer's twelve-volume analysis of ritual, taboos, and myths in *The Golden Bough*[5] was of major importance. This anthropological study, written in the form of a quest, gave sexual symbolic meaning to primitive myths and greatly influenced modern literature.

Freud's analysis[6] of myth as dream, or disguised wish fulfillment, was the beginning of psychological literary criticism. This interpretation is based on the idea that distressful stimulation leads an individual to dream of an object, situation, or an act. If the dream is felt to be sinful, it will include punishment and serve as a deterrent for the act. Freud held the view that all myths expressed the Oedipus theme with its incest motive, guilt, and punishment. Another psychological viewpoint was that of Carl Jung, a contemporary of Freud, who thought that a "collective unconscious" is "inherited in the structure of the brain."[7] These unconscious, recurring images created the primitive mythic heroes and still exist as individual fantasies for the civilized person as a kind of "race memory," according to Jung.

The folklorist, however, may disagree with such psychological interpretations. Dorson notes that "folk literature cannot all be prettily channeled into the universal mono-myth," and "the folklorist looks with jaundiced eye at the excessive straining of mythologists to extort symbols from folk tales."[8] Whether or not folk tales and

[2] Jerome Bruner, "Myth and Identity," in *The Making of Myth,* Richard M. Ohrmann, ed. (New York: Putnam, 1962), pp. 159–170.
[3] The numbers in parentheses following the title of a folk tale or myth indicate the number of the reference in the bibliography at the end of this chapter. These references list the book in which the tale may be found.

[4] Clyde Kluckhohn, "Recurrent Themes in Myth and Myth-making," in Ohrmann, pp. 52–65.
[5] Sir James Frazer, *The Golden Bough,* 3rd ed. (London: Macmillan, 1911–1915).
[6] Stanley E. Hyman, *The Armed Vision,* rev. ed. (New York: Vintage, 1955).
[7] Carl C. Jung, "On the Relation of Analytic Psychology to Poetic Art," in O. B. Hardison, Jr., ed., *Modern Continental Literary Criticism* (New York: Appleton, 1962), pp. 267–288.
[8] Richard Dorson, "Theories of Myth and the Folklorist," in Ohrmann, p. 45.

myths express symbolic images or unconscious dreams, they are literature derived from human imagination to explain the human condition. Literature today continues to express our concern about human strengths, weaknesses, and the individual's relationships to the world and to other people. Traditional literature forms the foundation of understandings of life as expressed in modern literature.

THE VALUE OF FOLK LITERATURE— FOR CHILDREN

When Jacob and Wilhelm Grimm published their first volume of "Household Stories" in 1812, they did not intend it for children. These early philologists were studying the language and grammar of such traditional tales. In recent years, as we have seen, anthropologists study folklore in order to understand the inherent values and beliefs of a culture. Psychologists look at folk tales and myths and discover something of the motivations and inner feelings of humans; while folklorists themselves collect and categorize various stories, types, and motifs from around the world. These are all adult scholars of folk literature, which was first created by adults and usually told to an adult community. How then did folk literature become associated with children's literature; and what value does this kind of literature have for children?

Originally, folklore was the literature of the people; stories were told to young and old alike. Families, or tribes, or the king's court would gather to hear a famous storyteller in much the same way that an entire family today will watch their favorite television program. With the age of scientific enlightenment, these stories were relegated to the nursery and kept alive, in many instances, by resourceful nursemaids or grandmothers, much to the delight of children.

Children today still enjoy such tales because they are first and foremost good stories. Born of the oral tradition, these stories are usually short and have fast-moving plots. They are frequently humorous and almost always end happily. Poetic justice prevails; the good and the just are eventually rewarded, while the evil are punished. This appeals to the child's sense of justice and his moral judgment. Wishes come true, but usually not without the fulfillment of a task or trial. The littlest child, the youngest son, or the smallest animal succeeds, while the oldest or the largest is frequently defeated. Youngsters who are the little people of their world thrive on such a turn of events.

Beyond the function of pure entertainment, folk tales can kindle the child's imagination. This spark of creativity, which educators say is a part of all of us, must be quickened before it is extinguished. Behind every great author, poet, architect, mathematician, or diplomat is a dream of what the person hopes to achieve. This dream or ideal has been created by the power of imagination. If we always give children stories of "what is," stories that only mirror the living of today, then we have not helped them to imagine what "might have been" or "what might be."

Chukovsky,[9] the Russian poet, tells of a time when it was proposed that all folk tales and fairy tales be eliminated from the education of the Soviet child in favor of simple realistic stories. Then, one of the major Russian educators began keeping a diary of her child's development. She found that her child, as if to compensate for the fairy tales which he had been denied, began to make up his own! He had never heard a folk tale, but his world was peopled with talking tigers, birds and bugs! Chukovsky concludes this story with the statement: "Fantasy is the most valuable attribute of the human mind and should be diligently nurtured from earliest childhood."[10]

Traditional literature is a rightful part of a child's literary heritage and lays the groundwork for understanding all literature. How can one enjoy a modern fable, for instance "The Little Girl and the Wolf" from the *Thurber Carnival*, without knowing the Red Riding Hood story and the fable form? Poetry and modern stories are replete with allusions to traditional literature, particularly the Greek myths, Aesop's fables, and Bible stories. Northrup Frye maintains that "all theme and characters and stories that you encounter in literature belong to one big interlocking family."[11] As you meet such recurring

[9]Kornei Chukovsky, *From Two to Five*, translated and edited by Miriam Morton (Berkeley, Calif: University of California Press, 1963), p. 119.
[10]Chukovsky, p. 119.
[11]Northrup Frye, *The Educated Imagination* (Bloomington, Ind.: Indiana University Press, 1964), p. 48.

patterns or symbols in myth as floods, savior heroes, cruel stepmothers, the seasonal cycle of the year, the cycle of a man's life, you begin to build a framework for literature. Poetry, prose, and drama become more emotionally significant as you respond to these recurring archetypes.

Our speech and vocabulary reflect many contributions from traditional literature. Think of the figures of speech that come from Aesop's fables: "sour grapes," "dog in the manger," "boy who cried wolf." Our language is replete with words and phrases from the myths—such as "narcissistic," "cereal," "labyrinth," "siren," and many more. Isaac Asimov has written a fascinating book, *Words from the Myths*, which tells the stories of how such words originated. Our vocabulary, then, is thoroughly embedded in references to traditional literature. The child who has the opportunity to hear or read traditional literature cannot help but extend the meaning of language.

A very practical value of these traditional tales is the enrichment they provide for the school social studies program. Every culture has produced a folklore. A study of the folk tales of Africa, Russia, or the American Indian will provide insights into the beliefs of these peoples, their values, their jokes, their life styles, their histories. A cross-cultural study of folk literature will help children discover the universal qualities of humankind.

Folk Tales

DEFINITION OF FOLK TALES

Folk tales have been defined as "all forms of narrative, written or oral, which have come to be handed down through the years."[12] This definition would include epics, ballads, legends, and folk songs, as well as myths and fables. In using folk literature in the elementary school we have tended to confine the rather simple folk tales—such as the popular "The Three Billy Goats Gruff," "Little Red Riding Hood," and "Rumpelstiltskin"—to the primary grades; while we recommend the so called "fairy tales"—such as "Snow White" and "Cinderella"—for slightly older children, since these tales are longer and

[12]Stith Thompson, *The Folktale* (New York: Holt, Rinehart and Winston, 1951), p. 4.

contain romantic elements. Such a division appears arbitrary and is based more on use than any real difference in the stories. To complicate matters even further, modern fanciful stories created by a known author are often also referred to as fairy tales. Hans Christian Andersen's fairy tales are becoming part of the heritage that might be described as folk tales, but they *originated in written* rather than *oral form*. Thus they are distinguished from the stories told by the common folk that were finally collected and recorded. This chapter will discuss the folk and so-called fairy tales that are a part of the oral tradition. It also includes a description of the epics, myths, and stories from the Bible, which are all a part of traditional literature. Modern fanciful stories written by known authors will be discussed in Chapter 5.

TYPES OF FOLK TALES

Cumulative Tales

Very young children are fascinated by such cumulative stories as "The Old Woman and Her Pig" (80) with its "Rat! rat! gnaw rope; rope won't hang butcher; butcher won't kill ox; ox won't drink water; water won't quench fire; fire won't burn stick; stick won't beat dog; dog won't bite pig; piggy won't get over the stile; and I shan't get home tonight." The story itself is not as important as the increasing repetition of the details building up to a quick climax. The story of the naughty Gingerbread Boy who ran away from the old woman defiantly crying "Catch me if you can" has been told in many different versions, including the Norwegian "The Pancake" (3), the Russian "The Bun" (24), the Scottish "The Wee Bannock" (221), and the English *Johnny-Cake*. William Stobbs has made a handsome picture book of *Johnny-Cake* (222). Ruth Sawyer's *Journey Cake, Ho!* (200) is an adaptation of this well-loved story. "Henny Penny" (78) thinks the sky is falling and shouts to all the other animals to run until one wise one shows the truth. The same pattern is found in "Plop" (247), a Tibetan story of six rabbits who heard a ripe fruit fall into the water and started to flee from "Plop." A deer, pig, buffalo, rhinoceros, elephant, and other animals run wildly until a lion traces the origin of the fear.

A Scottish counting rhyme, *All in the Morning Early* (180) is also a cumulative tale, and one loved by younger children. Sandy is joined by one huntsman, two ewes, three gypsies, four farmers, and, finally, ten bonny lasses. The children enjoy joining the chorus:

Over the burn and over the hill,
And down the road that leads to the mill,
Where the old mill wheel is never still—
Clicketty-clicketty-clicketty-clack!
All in the morning early.[13]

The Fat Cat (144) is a wonderful Danish folktale that Jack Kent has illustrated in a picture-book format. The fat cat eats the gruel he was watching for the little old lady; then he eats the pot and the little old lady herself! He continues his eating binge, growing larger and larger with each victim. Finally, the fat cat is stopped when he makes the mistake of trying to eat the woodcutter. All his victims are released, and the last picture shows the woodcutter carefully applying a bandaid to the fat cat's tummy. Certainly the best known of all cumulative tales is the popular "The House that Jack Built" (76). However, you will find these repetitive stories in practically all folklore.

Pourquoi Stories

Some of the folk tales are "why" or *pourquoi* stories that explain certain animal traits or characteristics, or customs of people. The Norwegians have a story about a fox tricking a bear into thinking that he could catch fish by holding his tail in a hole in the ice. His tail froze and came off when he tried to pull it out, which is "Why the Bear Is Stumpy-Tailed" (121). Many American Indian stories are "why" stories, explaining certain animal features. For example, a California Indian tale, "The Theft of Dawn" (300), tells how the animals were surprised by the sudden appearance of the sun. When Blue Jay and Ground Squirrel go to steal dawn, Ground Squirrel takes a large piece of black obsidian rock that can be used for a tool. His back is blistered from carrying it, and that is how he got the stripes on his back.

A very funny Burmese tale, "The Tiger's Minister of State" (47), explains why the rabbit

[13]Sorche Nic Leodhas, *All in the Morning Early*, illustrated by Evaline Ness (New York: Holt, Rinehart and Winston, 1963).

twitches his nose constantly. Tiger tests the applicants for the position of minister by asking each if his breath is sweet. The boar denies the truth and is rejected as a flatterer. The monkey agrees the tiger's breath is very offensive; he is rejected for being too frank. The rabbit diplomatically twitches his nose and says he has such a cold he can't smell anything. So he is chosen to be minister of state; and to this day he twitches his nose to show he cannot smell.

The old Chinese custom of binding women's feet is explained in the amusing story of "The Big Feet of the Empress Tu Chin" (35). The venerable lady had a very bad habit of walking in her sleep. In trying to find the cause of this, she decided it must be that her large feet did not do enough walking during the day. The Emperor suggested the cure for that was to make her feet one-third as long as they were, and then she would not need to do so much walking!

Beast Tales

Probably the favorite folk tales of young children are the beast tales in which animals act and talk like human beings. The best known of these are "The Three Billy Goats Gruff" (7), "The Three Little Pigs" (206), "Little Red Hen" (61), and "The Bremen Town Musicians" (93). "Puss in Boots" (188) is a favorite tale in which the clever puss helps his master obtain riches, a palace, and a beautiful bride.

Many West African stories are wise beast-foolish beast tales of how one animal, such as the rabbit or the spider, outwits hyena, leopard, and other friends. *The Extraordinary Tug-of-War* (201) is a Nigerian folk tale that has been retold by Letta Schatz and put in picture-book form by John Burningham. It is the delightful story of how a hare bet first a hippopotamus and then an elephant that he could win over each of them in a tug-of-war. The hare obtained a long rope and then proceeded to pit each of the huge beasts against the other, while he stayed halfway between the two laughing heartily! When the two great beasts realize that they have been tricked by a little hare:

They stormed through the woods, hunting for Hare. They stamped and trampled, and mashed and thrashed and thundered and blundered and raged and roared. But not one hair of Hare did they find.[14]

John Burningham has made superb illustrations that portray this great contest from every possible vantagepoint through day and night. The book suggests rich possibilities for making other single tales of these African beast stories.

Talking animals appear in folk tales of all cultures. Fish are often found in English, Scandinavian, German, and South Sea stories. Tales of bears, wolves, and the firebird are found in Russian folklore. Goats and blackbirds often appear in Italian tales. Spiders, rabbits, tortoises, crocodiles, monkeys, lions, and tigers are very much a part of African tales; while rabbits, badgers, monkeys, and even bees are represented in Japanese stories. A study of just the animals in folklore would be a fascinating search.

Noodlehead Stories

So called "noodlehead" or numbskull stories are a part of every folk culture. These tales frequently follow a set pattern. The story of the fool who literally follows the right advice at the wrong time is a well-known recurring theme. In the Swiss tale, "Silly Jean" (66), told by his mother to be friendly to people as he goes to the mill and to answer politely if someone asks the way, tries offering the advice but is rebuffed. His mother tells him he should have commented, "So you're leading your goat to the fair." When he makes this remark to the bride and groom he next meets, he is beaten. And so it goes, until his mother decides he cannot go out into the world. The Turkish tale *Just Say Hic!* (237) and the English "Lazy Jack" (221) story have similar motifs. In a very contemporary and funny collection of tales from Majorca, "Tony Di-Moany" (167) sits on hen's eggs to keep them warm, throws flour by the handful into the air so the wind can carry it home, and uses big cheeses for stepping stones when he floods the house with wine!

The confused identity story appears frequently. In a Persian tale, "Who Am I?" (247), a country man on going into the city for the first time is convinced that he won't be able to know himself amidst such crowds. So he ties a pumpkin to his right leg for the sake of identification.

That night a trickster removes the pumpkin from the farmer's leg and ties it to his own instead. In the morning when the poor man awakes and sees the pumpkin on his companion's leg, he calls to him:

> Hey! get up, for I am perplexed in my mind. Who am I, and who are you? If I am I, why is the pumpkin on your leg? And if you are you why is the pumpkin not on my leg?[15]

In a collection of noodlehead stories from Italy, the title tale, "The Disobedient Eels" (18) tells of a man who was carrying a heavy sack of eels that he had caught. When he came to a canal, he dumped them all in and told them to meet him on the other side!

In the Hodja stories from Turkey (64), the Hodja—a local scholar, teacher, preacher, and judge all rolled in one—could be very clever or very stupid. In one tale the Hodja was sawing the very branch of a tree that he was sitting on. A passer-by told him that he would fall if he continued to do that. He did fall, so he considered the man a prophet. If this man knew when the Hodja was going to fall, perhaps he could also tell when the Hodja would die. The stranger said the Hodja would probably die when his donkey brayed twice. So when his donkey brayed twice, the Hodja laid down on the road, shut his eyes, and announced he was dead. His friends got a coffin and started to carry him home. But when they came to a fork in the road they began to argue which way to go. Finally, the Hodja could endure it no longer. "'When I was alive,' he snapped, 'I took the left fork!'"[16]

A Russian noodlehead story, "How the Peasant Helped His Horse" (89), tells how, when the horse was having difficulty pulling a heavy load, the peasant got out, put one of the bags of wheat on his shoulder, then climbed back into the wagon saying; "Giddy-up, giddy-up! It's easier for you now! I'm carrying a whole bag on my shoulder!"[17]

Several collections of these stories have been compiled. *Noodles, Nitwits, and Numbskulls* by

[14]Letta Schatz, *The Extraordinary Tug-of-War*, illustrated by John Burningham (Chicago, Ill.: Follett, 1968), p. 47.

[15]Carl Withers, *A World of Nonsense*, illustrated by John E. Johnson (New York: Holt, Rinehart and Winston, 1968), p. 81.
[16]Charles Downing, *Tales of the Hodja*, illustrated by William Papas (New York: Walck, 1965), p. 42.
[17]Mirra Ginsburg, *Three Rolls and One Doughnut*, illustrated by Anita Lobel (New York: Dial Press, 1970), p. 6.

Maria Leach (152) is one source; another is *Noodle-head Stories from Around the World* by Jagendorf (138). *The Lazies* by Mirra Ginsburg (86) is a sparkling collection of stories from the Russian people—all based on the common theme of indolence. Most of the noodlehead stories are great for story-telling. The humor of these tales is their complete nonsense and absurdity. Children know they couldn't possibly happen.

Wonder Tales

Children call wonder tales of magic and supernatural "fairy tales." Very few of them have even a fairy godmother in them, but still the name persists. These are the stories that include giants such as "Jack and the Beanstalk" (221) or elves and goblins in "The Elves and the Shoemaker" (93). Wicked witches, called Baba Yagas in Russian folklore, demons such as the *oni* of Japanese tales, or monsters and dragons abound in these stories. Traditionally, we have thought of the fairy tale as involving romance and adventure. "Cinderella," "Snow White and the Seven Dwarfs," or "Beauty and the Beast" all have elements of both. *The Provensen Book of Fairy Tales* (191) is a fine collection of twelve classic and literary fairy tales, including "Beauty and the Beast," "The Three Wishes," "The Seven Simons," and "The Prince and the Goose Girl." This collection is beautifully illustrated with the Provensens' rich and colorful paintings. The long quest tales—such as the Russian *The Story of Prince Ivan, The Firebird and the Gray Wolf* (241); the Norwegian "East of the Sun and West of the Moon" (149); or the extended tale from Ceylon of *The Three Princes of Serendip* (125)—are complex wonder tales in which the hero, or heroine, triumphs against all odds to win the beautiful princess, or handsome prince, and makes a fortune. Children know that these tales will end with ". . . and they lived happily ever after." In fact, one of the appeals of the fairy tale is the secure knowledge that no matter what happens the virtues of love, kindness, and truth will prevail; while hate, wickedness and evil will be punished. Fairy tales have always represented the glorious fulfillment of human desires.

Realistic Stories

Surprisingly, there are a few realistic tales included in folklore. The story of *Dick Whittington* (156) could have happened; in fact, there is historical reason to suggest that a Richard Whittington did indeed live and was mayor of London. The Norse tale of the loving wife who thought her husband could do no wrong is realistically told in "Gudbrand on the Hillside" (8). A funny tale of marital conflict is presented in the Russian story of "Who Will Wash the Pot?" (86). It is based on the familiar folk-tale pattern of the married couple declaring that the first to speak will have to do some unwanted task—in this instance, wash the pot. The well-loved Japanese tale of *The Burning Rice Fields* (32), as told by Sara Cone Bryant, is a realistic story based on the self-sacrifice of the old man who set his fields ablaze in order to warn the villagers of a coming tidal wave. *Zlateh, The Goat* (217), the title story in a collection of Jewish tales by Singer, is a realistic survival story. Aaron, the young son of a poor peasant family, is sent off to the butcher to sell Zlateh, the family goat. On the way to town he and the goat are caught in a fierce snowstorm. They take refuge in a haystack where they must stay for three days. Zlateh eats the hay, while Aaron exists on Zlateh's milk and warmth. Finally the storm is over and Aaron and Zlateh return home to a grateful family. No one ever again mentions selling Zlateh, the goat. The Weston Woods film of this folktale catches the drama of the storm and the special relationship between the boy and his goat.

Generally, however, while a tale may have had its origin in a real person or experience, it has become so embroidered through various tellings that it takes its place among the folklore of its culture.

CHARACTERISTICS OF FOLK TALES

Since folk tales have been told and retold from generation to generation within a particular culture, we may ask how they reflect the country of their origin and their oral tradition. An authentic tale from Africa will include references to the flora and fauna of Africa, to the food that was eaten by the tribesmen, to their huts, their customs, their foibles, and their beliefs; and it will sound as if it is being *told*. While folk tales will have many elements in common, it should not be possible to confuse a folk tale from the Congo with a folk tale from the fiords of Norway.

What then are the characteristics common to all folk tales?

Plot Structures of Folk Tales

The plot structure of the longer folk-tale narrative is usually simple and direct. A series of episodes maintains a quick flow of action. If it is a wise beast-foolish beast story, the characters are quickly delineated; the action shows the inevitable conflict and resolution; and the ending is usually brief. If the tale is a romance, the hero sets forth on his journey, often helps the poor on his way, frequently receives magical power, overcomes obstacles, and returns to safety. The plot that involves a weak or innocent child going forth to meet the monsters of the world is another form of the "journey-novel." "Hansel and Gretel" (94) go out into a dark world and meet the witch, but goodness and purity triumph. Almost all folk-tale plots are success stories of one kind or another.

Repetition is a basic element in many folk-tale plots. Frequently, three is the magic number for building suspense. There are three little pigs (221) whose three houses face the puffing of the wolf. Then the wolf gives three challenges to the pig in the brick house—to get turnips, apples, and to go to the fair. *The Three Billy Goats Gruff* (7) face the troll under the bridge, and the repetition of the trip, trap, trap, the troll's demands and the goats' responses are essential elements in this well-loved tale. In the longer tales each of the three tasks becomes increasingly more difficult, and the intensity of the wonders becomes progressively more marvelous. For example, in the Norwegian tale of "The Princess on the Glass Hill" (6) Boots first rides his horse one-third of the way up the hill; the next day he goes two-thirds of the way up, and the last day he reaches the top. There is a satisfying sense of order that comes from this heightened expectation of recurring tasks.

Repetition of responses, chants, or poems is frequently a part of the structure of the tale.

"Now, I'm coming to gobble you up!" roared the troll.
"Well, come along! I've got two spears,
And I'll poke your eyeballs out at your ears.
I've got besides two great big stones,
And I'll crush you to bits, body and bones."

Marcia Brown's setting and use of the traditional text are faithful to the Norse origin of this familiar tale.

© 1957 by Marcia Brown. Reproduced from *The Three Billy Goats Gruff* by Asbjørnsen and Moe by permission of Harcourt Brace Jovanovich, Inc.

"Mirror, mirror on the wall, who is fairest of them all" and "Fee, fi, fo, fum" are repetitive verses that are familiar to all. The somber and beautiful Scottish tale, "The Black Bull of Norroway," (221) is filled with lovely verses. A young girl at last finds her lover after searching for him for many years. She bargains with the witch-woman, who is going to marry him, for just three nights alone with him. However, the witch-bride drugs him and so all night long the lovely girl sighs and sings:

> "Far have I sought for thee,
> Long have I wrought for thee,
> Near am I brought to thee,
> Dear Duke o' Norroway
> Wilt thou say naught to me?"[18]

Time and place are established quickly in the folk tale. Time is always past, and frequently described by such conventional terms as "Once upon a time," or "In the first old time," or "In olden times when wishing still helped one." Time passes quickly in the folk tale. The woods and brambles encircle Sleeping Beauty's palace (149) in a quarter of an hour, and "when a hundred years were gone and passed," the prince appears at the moment the enchantment ends. The setting of the folk tale is not specific, but in some far-away land, in a cottage in the woods, in a beautiful palace.

The introduction to the folk tale usually presents the conflict, characters, and setting in a few sentences. In "Anansi and Nothing Go Hunting for Wives"(49) the problem is established in the first two sentences:

It came to Anansi one time, as he sat in his little hut, that he needed a wife. For most men this would have been a simple affair, but Anansi's bad name had spread throughout the country and he knew that he wouldn't be likely to have much luck finding a wife in near-by villages.[19]

With little description, the storyteller goes to the heart of his story, capturing the interest of his audience.

The conclusion of the story follows the climax very quickly and includes few details. After Sleeping Beauty was awakened by the Prince there is a fine dinner. "After supper, without losing any time, the Prince and Princess were married in the chapel of the palace. In two years, the Prince's father died. The Prince and Princess became the new King and Queen, and were given a royal welcome at the capital."[20] Even this is a long ending compared with, "and so they were married and lived happily ever after."

The structure of the folk tale, with its quick introduction, economy of incident, and logical and brief conclusion maintains interest through suspense and repetition. Because the storyteller has to keep the attention of his audience, each episode must contribute to the theme of the story. Written versions, then, should follow the oral tradition, adding little description and avoiding lengthy asides or admonitions.

Characterization in Folk Tales

Characters in folk tales are shown in flat dimensions, being symbolic of the completely good or entirely evil. Character development is seldom depicted. The beautiful girl is usually virtuous, humble, patient, and loving. Stepmothers are ugly, cross, and mean. The hero, usually fair-haired, or curly-haired, is strong, virile, brave, kind, and sympathetic. The poor are often kind, generous, and long suffering; while the rich are imperious, hard-hearted, and often conniving, if not actually dishonest. Physical characteristics may be described briefly, but the reader forms his own picture as he reads: "Pretty children they all were, but the prettiest was the youngest daughter, who was so lovely there was no end to her loveliness."[21](6) In describing "The Daughter of the Dragon King" the Chinese grandmother says: "Now this young woman was poorly dressed, but her face was as fair as a plum blossom in spring, and her body was as slender as a willow branch."[22] (35)

[18]Flora Annie Steel, *English Fairy Tales,* illustrated by Arthur Rackham (New York: Macmillan, 1962), p. 116.

[19]Harold Courlander and George Herzog, *The Cow Tail Switch and Other West African Stories* (New York: Holt, Rinehart and Winston, 1947), p. 95.

[20]Virginia Haviland, *Favorite Fairy Tales Told in France,* illustrated by Roger Duvoisin (Boston, Mass.: Little Brown, 1959), p. 75.

[21]P. C. Asbjørnsen and Jorgen E. Moe, *East of the Sun and West of the Moon, and Other Tales,* illustrated by Tom Vroman (New York: Macmillan, 1963), p. 1.

[22]Frances Carpenter, *Tales of a Chinese Grandmother,* illustrated by Malthe Hasselriis (New York: Doubleday, 1949), p. 75.

Qualities of character or special strengths or weaknesses of the characters are revealed quickly, because this factor will be the cause of conflict or lead to resolution of the plot. The stepmother and stepsister of Marushka are contrasted with the pretty girl in the Czechoslovakian story, "The Twelve Months"(116). Marushka was made to do all the hard work, "But Marushka never complained. Patiently she bore the scoldings and bad tempers of the mother and daughter. Holena's ugliness increased, while Marushka became even lovelier to look at."[23] A rich merchant in Addis Ababa was characterized in one sentence: "Haptom Hasei was so rich that he owned everything that money could buy, and often he was very bored because he had tired of everything he knew, and there was nothing new for him to do."[24]

Seeing folk-tale characters as symbols of good, evil, power, wisdom, and other traits, children begin to understand the basis of literature that distills human experience.

Style of the Folk Tales

Folk tales offer children many opportunities to hear rich qualitative language and a wide variety of language patterns. Story introductions may range from the familiar "once upon a time" to the Persian tales that begin with "there was a time and there wasn't a time" or the African tale that starts: "We do not mean, we do not really mean that what we are going to say is true."

The introductions and language of the folk tale should maintain the "flavor" of the country, but still be understood by its present audience. Folk tales should not be "written down" to children, but they may need to be simplified. Wanda Gág states her method of simplification in adapting folk tales for children:

By simplification I mean:

(a) freeing hybrid stories of confusing passages

(b) using repetition for clarity where a mature style does not include it

(c) employing actual dialogue to sustain or revive interest in places where the narrative is too condensed for children

However, I do not mean writing in words of one or two syllables. True, the careless use of large words is confusing to children; but long, even unfamiliar words are relished and easily absorbed by them, provided they have enough color and sound value.[25]

American children have probably never heard the words "pawkiest piece" or "cosseted," yet they could easily grasp the meaning of them in the context of the Scottish folk tale, "The Laird's Lass and the Gobha's Son"(183).

An old laird had a young daughter once and she was the pawkiest piece in all the world. Her father petted her and her mother cosseted her till the wonder of it was that she wasn't so spoiled that she couldn't be borne.[26]

However, in introducing the story, the teacher would need to tell the children that the "gobha" in the title meant a blacksmith.

Language is rich and seems to invite modification and invention in the black-American stories of *The Knee-high Man and Other Tales* by Julius Lester (154). The description of Mr. Rabbit eating lettuce is an example: "He had never tasted such delicious, scrumptious, crispy, luscious, delectable, exquisite, ambrosial, nectareous, yummy lettuce in aaaaaaaall his life."[27]

Unusual phrases appear in many folk tales. In the *Russian Wonder Tales* (239) the narrative includes "whether the way was long or short," "across three times nine kingdoms," and "the morning is wiser than the evening." Some folk tales include proverbs of the country. For example, in the silly Turkish tale, *Hilili and Dilili* (236), Walker adds: "The poor have empty pockets but full hearts," "Trust in God, but first tie your

---

[23]Virginia Haviland, *Favorite Fairy Tales Told in Czechoslovakia*, illustrated by Trina Schart Hyman (Boston, Mass.: Little, Brown, 1966), p. 3.

[24]Harold Courlander and Wolf Leslau, *The Fire on the Mountain and Other Ethiopian Stories*, illustrated by Robert W. Kane (New York: Holt, Rinehart and Winston, 1950), p. 7.

[25]Wanda Gág, *Tales from Grimm* (New York: Coward-McCann, 1936), p. ix.

[26]Sorche Nic Leodhas, *Thistle and Thyme, Tales and Legends from Scotland*, illustrated by Evaline Ness (New York: Holt, Rinehart and Winston, 1962), p. 17.

[27]Julius Lester, *The Knee-high Man and Other Tales*, illustrated by Ralph Pinto (New York: Dial Press, 1972), p. 13.

camel," and "A good companion shortens the longest road."[28]

Although there is a minimum of description in the folk tale, figurative language and imagery are employed by effective narrators. Isaac Singer uses delightful prose to introduce the Jewish tale about the wager between the spirits of good luck and bad luck:

> In a faraway land, on a sunny spring day, the sky was as blue as the sea, and the sea was as blue as the sky, and the earth was green and in love with them both.[29](215)

In an African tale, when Zomo's trick frightens the cock he has "a feeling in his belly as if the hairy caterpillar that he had swallowed earlier that morning has come to life and is going on a tour of inspection."[30](224)

In the story of "The Tortoise and the Hyena" (68) the listener can share in the tortoise's delight at seeing real fresh mushrooms:

> "Mushrooms!" exclaimed Kamba, the Tortoise, joyfully. "Do I see mushrooms? *Real* mushrooms?" Yes, they were real mushrooms, little white satiny, buttony mushrooms, with lovely pink underneath; little white mushrooms that had pushed all night at the dark brown earth above them, and had struggled through its hard crust just in time to see the sun rise, just in time to make a fine breakfast for a hungry Tortoise.[31]

In selecting various editions of folk tales, teachers and librarians will want to consider the style of writing. A consideration of the rich prose of Walter de la Mare's telling of Cinderella (57) illustrates the importance of style in folk tales:

> Indeed, all was so hushed at last in the vacant kitchen that the ashes, like pygmy bells in a belfry, tinkled as they fell; a cricket began shrilly churring from a crevice in the hob, and she could hear the

tiny tic-a-tac-tac of the mice as they came tippeting and frisking 'round her stool. Then, suddenly, softly, and without warning, there sounded out of the deep hush a gentle knock-knocking at the door.[32]

Surely children in the primary grades would be cheated linguistically if they had to hear this version of "The Elves and the Shoemaker":

> Once upon a time there was a poor shoemaker. The poor shoemaker had a wife. The poor shoemaker had a shop. He made shoes. He made little shoes. He made big shoes. He made long shoes. He made short shoes.[33]

This kind of distortion is not justified even for ease of beginning reading. Folk tales were meant to be heard and enjoyed, not made the object of labored reading.

Since folk tales originally were told, the written version should suggest the flavor of an oral telling. Many of the African tales retain the cadence and rhythm of the original telling. Read this paragraph from "Kigbo and the Bush Spirits" (48) aloud and listen to the echoes of the oral tradition:

> In a certain village there was a young man named Kigbo. He had a character all his own. He was an obstinate person. If silence was pleasing to other people, he would play a drum. If someone said, "Tomorrow we should repair the storage houses," Kigbo said, "No, tomorrow we should sharpen our hoes."[34]

When the tales are written as though the storyteller is speaking directly to the reader, the oral tradition is more clearly communicated. Arkhurst uses this style effectively in *The Adventures of Spider* (4): "So spider threw his hat on his head, and, of course, you can guess what happened." Again the storyteller says, "My friends, can you imagine what happened? I don't think

[28] Barbara K. Walker, *Hilili and Dilili*, illustrated by William Barss (Chicago: Follett, 1965), pp. 5, 9, 14.

[29] Isaac Bashevis Singer, *Mazel and Shlimazel, or The Milk of a Lioness*, illustrated by Margot Zemach (New York: Farrar, Straus, Giroux, 1967), p. 1.

[30] Hugh Sturton, *Zomo the Rabbit*, illustrated by Peter Warner (New York: Atheneum, 1966), p. 22.

[31] Geraldine Elliot, *The Long Grass Whispers*, illustrated by Sheila Hawkins (New York: Schocken Books, 1968), p. 17.

[32] Walter de la Mare, *Tales Told Again*, illustrated by Alan Howard (New York: Knopf, 1927), p. 49.

[33] Frances Pavel, *The Elves and the Shoemaker*, illustrated by Joyce Hewitt (New York: Holt, Rinehart and Winston, 1961), p. 1.

[34] Harold Courlander and Ezekiel A. Eshugbayi, *Olode, the Hunter and Other Tales from Nigeria* (New York: Harcourt Brace Jovanovich, 1968), p. 45.

so, so I will tell you."[35] The vigorous style of *Tom Tit Tot* (178) reflects this old form of story-telling:

> Well, she was that frightened, she'd always been such a gatless girl, that she didn't so much as know how to spin, and what was she to do tomorrow with no one to come nigh her to help her? She sat down on the stool and LAW, HOW SHE DID CRY![36]

The use of dialogue makes a folk tale more readable and interesting, and few folk tales are written without conversation. The words of the characters convey the action and tone. Some writers omit "he said" or "she said" and merely write the words of the speakers. Most writers use little description in expressing the feelings of the characters, but let the dialogue convey emotion. In the well-loved tale of *The Goose Girl* (55), only Falada, the magical horse, knew that the goose girl was the real princess. But the wicked servant who had taken the princess's place had the horse's head cut off. Each day the goose girl stopped and spoke to the horse's head that hung on the gateway, and each day the horse revealed the sadness of her situation:

> . . . the princess said:
> "Alas! dear Falada, there thou hangest."
> Falada answered:
> "Alas! Queen's daughter, there thou gangest.
> If thy mother knew thy fate,
> Her heart would break with grief so great."[37]

Dialect enhances the story, but it is difficult for children to read. The teacher will need to practice reading or telling a story with dialect, but it is worth the effort if it is done well. Richard Chase recorded stories from the Appalachian mountain folk in *The Jack Tales* (37). He notes: "The dialect has been changed enough to avoid confusion to the reading eye; the idiom has been kept throughout." In this dialogue from "The Heifer Hide" the mountaineer vocabulary and dialect are clear:

> "Well, now," she says, "hit's just a little I was a-savin' for my kinfolks comin' tomorrow."
> "Me and Jack's your kinfolks. Bring it on out here for us."
> So Jack and him eat a lot of them good rations. Jack was awful hungry, and he knowed she hadn't brought out her best stuff yet, so he rammed his heifer hide again, says, "You blabber-mouthed thing! I done told you to hush. You keep on tellin' lies now and I'll put you out the door."[38]

In Courlander's collection of black-American folk tales, *Terrapin's Pot of Sense* (46), dialect has been modified, but speech rhythms and patterns have been preserved. The dialect of the Brer Rabbit stories in *The Complete Tales of Uncle Remus* by Harris is so heavy as to be most difficult to tell and equally hard to understand.

The major criteria for style in the written folk tale, then, are that it maintain the atmosphere of the country and culture from which it originated, and that it truly seems to be a tale *told* by a storyteller.

Themes in Folk Tales

The basic purpose of the folk tale was to tell an entertaining story, yet these stories do present important themes. Some tales may be merely humorous accounts of foolish people who are so ridiculous that the listeners see their own foolish ways exaggerated. Many of the stories provided an outlet for feelings against the kings and nobles who oppressed the poor. Values of the culture were expressed in folklore. The virtues of humility, kindness, patience, sympathy, hard work, and courage were invariably rewarded. These rewards reflected the goals of people—long life, a good husband or loving wife, beautiful homes and fine clothing, plenty of food, freedom from fear of the ogre or giant. The power of love, mercy, and kindness is one of the major themes of folk tales. "The Pumpkin Child" (168), a Persian tale, was a little girl born to a woman who expressed a deep wish for a daughter even if she looked like a pumpkin. When a prince agreed to marry the girl, love released her from the enchantment and she became "as beautiful as the moon on its fourteenth night." The thematic wis-

[35] Joyce Cooper Arkhurst, *The Adventures of Spider, West African Folk Tales*, illustrated by Jerry Pinkney (Boston: Little, Brown, 1964), pp. 26, 10.

[36] Evaline Ness, *Tom Tit Tot* (New York: Scribner, 1965), unpaged.

[37] Marguerite de Angeli, *The Goose Girl* (New York: Doubleday, 1964), p. 21.

[38] Richard Chase, *The Jack Tales*, illustrated by Berkeley Williams (Boston, Mass.: Houghton Mifflin, 1943), p. xi.

dom of *Beauty and the Beast* (56) is that one should not trust too much to appearances. The lesson that inner qualities of love and kindness are more important than the outer semblance is clearly presented.

A tale written in China in 350 B.C. is the basis of Jean Merrill's story, *The Superlative Horse* (172). When the Chief Groom and trusted adviser of the Duke Mu nears retirement age, the Duke tries to find someone to take his place. A peasant boy is suggested by the old man, Po Lo, as his successor. Accompanied by the Chief Minister, a rather gross character who was unaware of deeper values, the boy journeys forth to locate a superlative horse. Duke Mu speaks wisely: "There are two kinds of men," he said, "those who ask 'What is the value?' and those who ask 'What is the price?'"[39] The theme of the story is that external details have little to do with the heart or spirit.

Parents, teachers, and some psychologists have expressed concern about themes of cruelty and horror in folk tales. "Little Red Riding Hood" (137), for example, has been rewritten so that the wolf eats neither the grandmother nor the heroine. Cruel deeds occur very quickly with no sense of pain and no details of the action. No blood drips from the Ravens' sister's hand when she cuts off a finger; not an "ouch" escapes her lips (104). The wolf is cut open so the six kids can escape, and the mother goat sews the stones into his stomach without any suggestion that the wolf is being hurt (93). Children accept these stories as they are—symbolic interpretations of life in an imaginary land of another time. Long ago, young children heard the stories within the reassuring circle of family and friends. This is one reason why it is good to tell or read the stories so that the child can sense an adult's communication of security at this moment. Three- to 5-year-olds who have not distinguished the real world from the imaginary one are not ready for many folk tales. By the time children can read folk tales for themselves, they can enter the land of make-believe where the horror is seldom as grim or detailed as some children's programs on television.

Motifs in Folk Tales

Folklorists analyze folk tales according to motifs or patterns, numbering each tale and labeling its episodes.[40] *Motifs* have been defined as the smallest part of a tale that can exist independently. These motifs can be seen in the recurring parade of characters in folk tales—the younger brother motif, the wicked stepmother, the abused child, the clever trickster—or in such supernatural beings as the fairy godmother, the evil witch, or the terrifying giant. The use of magical objects—such as a slipper, a magic doll, a ring, or tablecloth—is another pattern found in many folk tales. Stories of enchantment, long sleeps, or marvelous transformations are typical motifs. Some of the motifs have been repeated so frequently that they have been identified as a type of folk story. Thus we have noodlehead stories about fools and simpletons, beast tales about talking animals, and the wonder tales of supernatural beings that children generally call fairy tales.

Even the plots of the stories have recurring patterns—such as three tasks to be performed, three wishes that are granted, or three trials to be endured. A simple tale will have several motifs; a complex one will have many. Recognizing some of the most common motifs in folklore will help a teacher to suggest points of comparison and contrast in a cross-cultural approach to folk literature.

THE LONG SLEEP OR ENCHANTMENT

The long sleep is a motif that appears time and again in folklore and may symbolically represent the coming of winter or death. Perhaps the best-known tales that include this motif are Grimm's "Snow White and the Seven Dwarfs" (206) and "The Sleeping Beauty in the Wood" (149) first recorded by Perrault. A Japanese story, "Urashima Taro and the Princess of the Sea" (233) tells of a boy who remains under the sea in a beautiful palace for three years, only to discover he was gone three hundred years. In the modern picture book, *Seashore Story*, Yashima has told this tale as a story within a story (252).

---

[39] Jean Merrill, *The Superlative Horse*, illustrated by Ronni Solbert (New York: W. R. Scott, 1961), p. 27.

[40] Stith Thompson, *Motif Index of Folk-literature* (Bloomington, Ind.: Indiana University Press, 1955–1958), 6 vols.

MAGICAL POWERS

Magical powers are frequently given to persons or animals in folk tales. A common pattern in folklore is seen in the story by the Grimms titled *Six Companions Find Their Fortunes,* illustrated as a handsome picture book by Lilo Fromm. A soldier is dissatisfied with his dismissal pay of only threepence and is determined to make the king give him all of his treasure. He is joined in his journey to the palace by Strong, Hunter, Blow, Speed, and Frost—five men each of whom had one remarkable talent that went with his unusual name. When the six of them are united, no trial the king could devise can defeat them. This same motif is used in a Bohemian fairy tale adapted and illustrated by Evaline Ness. *Long, Broad and Quickeye* (176) are three engaging characters who help the young prince rescue the princess from her imprisonment in a mysterious castle. In Turska's beautiful Polish story, *The Woodcutter's Duck* (232), Bartek, a woodcutter, is taught how to whistle a magic tune by a Frog King whose life he has saved. When the commander of the army demands Bartek's beloved duck for his dinner, Bartek whistles his magic tune and creates a terrific storm which saves the duck. Finally, the soldiers are so ashamed of a leader who will not keep his word that they make the poor woodcutter their commander; utilizing another common motif of the humble and most lowly overcoming the exalted. This book received the Kate Greenaway Award for the best-illustrated book in England for the year of its publication.

MAGICAL TRANSFORMATIONS

The transformation of an animal to a person, or vice-versa, is a part of many folk tales. "Beauty and the Beast" (149) is one of the most familiar of the tales using this motif. "The Frog Prince" (108) is one such popular story collected by the Grimm brothers. A frog retrieves the princess' ball in exchange for her promise that he can eat from her plate and sleep with her. He becomes a prince when allowed on her pillow. In a Shawnee Indian story, *The Ring in the Prairie* (205) Waupee, the Indian brave, transforms himself into a small mouse so that he might creep up and capture one of the twelve sisters who come down from the sky to dance. The horse in the Norwegian story of the "Widow's Son" (8) begs the young boy to cut off his head. The lad finally agrees, and there stands a handsome young prince! A Japanese duck hunter is changed into a duck himself and then trapped in the same way he had caught ninety-nine ducks. His tears dissolve the rope trap and he once again becomes a man; but a changed man, for Gombei resolves then and there never to trap another living thing. This Japanese folk tale, "Gombei and the Wild Ducks" (234) would be an interesting one to compare with Roald Dahl's modern fantasy, *The Magic Finger.* Both would be useful in an ecology study.

MAGIC OBJECTS

Magic objects are essential aspects of many tales that also reflect other themes. From Japan comes the story of *The Dancing Kettle* (233) that makes a fortune for a junkman. The magic tablecloth is a frequent device for providing food. In "Little One-Eye, Two-Eyes, and Three-Eyes" (51) the magic cloth appears when Two-Eyes says, "Little goat bleat, Little table appear!" In the Norwegian tale, "The Lad Who Went to the North Wind" (6), and also the Armenian variant, "The Enormous Genie" (227), a table provides food on the command of "Table, spread thyself." Both these stories include an animal that spits out gold coins, and a club that beats a person on command. *The Witch's Magic Cloth* (165) is a picture-book version of the story of the old Japanese woman who takes care of the witch of the mountain and in return is given a roll of magic cloth that always renews itself. Both a ring and a lamp play an essential part in the story of "Aladdin" from *The Arabian Nights.* Ruth Manning-Sanders has included a short, exciting version of this complex tale in her collection, *A Choice of Magic* (162). A prince who disguises himself as a shepherd in the delightful Czechoslovakian folk tale, "The Shepherd's Nosegay" (116), is granted four magic gifts for each of the four loaves of bread he gives to beggars. The Zemachs have combined their talents to produce an hilarious Italian folk tale called *Too Much Nose* (257). In this story each of three poor sons is given a magical object. In a real switch on folktale patterns, the second son outwits the scheming, cheating queen by discovering the magic secret of how to change the sizes of people's noses. In the end he recovers all of the magical objects and leaves the queen with too much nose! Other magic objects that figure in folk tales are dolls, purses, harps, the hen that lays the golden egg, and many more. In *A Book of Charms and Changelings* (161), Manning-Sanders has collected a group of tales from all over the world that involve the use of magic objects.

WISHES

Many stories are told of wishes that are granted and then used foolishly, or in anger or greed. *The Three Wishes* is the tale of the woodsman who was so hungry that he wished for a sausage; his wife was so angry at this wish that she wished the sausage would stick to his nose; then of course they have to use the third wish to get it off. Paul Galdone's amusing picture-book version of this tale delights primary grade children (84). A Japanese tale of the foolish use of wishes has been told in picture book form by Eve Titus under the title *The Two Stonecutters* (229). In return for their kindness the Goddess of the Forest granted two brothers seven wishes between them. The younger brother, who is quite content with his life, gives all his wishes except one to his elder brother, who longs to be rich and powerful. The elder brother promptly uses his six wishes to satisfy his desire for riches and to become a prince. Wanting more and more power, he wishes to become the wind, the sun, a storm cloud, and finally a stone. Luckily, the younger brother who remained a contented stonecutter, found the elder brother and was able to save him with the one remaining wish.

TRICKERY

Both animals and people trick their friends and neighbors in folk literature. The wolf tricked Little Red Riding Hood into believing he was her grandmother; and Hansel and Gretel tricked the mean old witch into crawling into the oven.

Almost every culture has an animal trickster in its folklore. In European folk tales it is usually a wolf or a fox; in Japan it is a badger or a hare; Indonesia has Kantjil, a tiny mouse deer; and Africa has three well-known tricksters, Anansi the spider, Zomo the rabbit, and Ijapa the tortoise; while Coyote and the raven play this role in American-Indian tales.

Anansi, from West Africa, is perhaps the best known of the animal tricksters. In "Anansi and the Old Hag" (209) there is an account of the way Anansi tricked people into giving him food by saying he dreamed the Old Hag was coming if people didn't stop talking about their neighbors. Frequently, however, Anansi is caught by his own tricks.

In *The Arabian Nights* (41) Scheherazade tricks the sultan by continuing her stories for one thousand and one nights. Harold Berson has illustrated a very amusing picture book about how a rich man foiled a robber in *The Thief Who Hugged a Moon Beam* (19). When the man hears a thief on the roof, he tells his wife in a very loud voice that the way he obtained his wealth was to speak a magic word and then ride a moonbeam into the open windows of houses. When the thief tries to do it, disaster follows. Berson has also adapted and illustrated a delightful French tale of trickery that explains *How the Devil Gets His Due* (18). *Balarin's Goat* (17), another story by Berson, is the amusing French tale of how a wife decides to trick her husband into giving her as much attention as he showers on his favorite goat, Fluerette. Surely this tale was first told by a woman! In a funny tale from Majorca, *Granny Shelock* (167) tricks the king into marrying her by just showing him her little finger, which she had sucked all of her life so it was white and tender. When the king takes off her veil following the ceremony, he can't believe his eyes. He throws her out the window into the royal garden, where some kind fairies find her and really do make her young and beautiful again.

A peasant tricks a king in the Russian story of "The Best Liar" (89). To amuse himself a king once said he would give a golden apple to a man that could tell him the biggest lie. Many persons try, but none of their stories pleases the king. One day a poor shepherd comes to the palace with a large pot. He tells the assembled court that the king owes him a potful of gold. The king says that is ridiculous, in fact it's the biggest lie he ever heard. Whereupon the peasant claims the golden apple!

In an Hawaiian story, *Punia and the King of the Sharks* (173), the king of the sharks refused to allow fishermen to get lobsters, but Punia tricks him by diving in one spot, although he announces his intention to dive at another place. At last, Punia tricks the shark into swimming into such shallow water that he dies.

Enchantments and long sleeps, magical powers, transformations, use of magic objects, wishes, and trickery are just a few of the motifs that run through the folklore of all countries as we have seen. Others may include the power of naming, as in "Rumpelstiltskin" (95); the ability to make yourself invisible, as the gardener did in "The Twelve Dancing Princesses" (53); becoming stuck to a person or object, as in the African tale, *Beeswax Catches a Thief* (145); causing royalty or a rich person to laugh, as in "Lazy Jack" (121); or the "Lazy Jack" pattern itself, of the simpleton who follows his mother's directions at the wrong time. You can make your own list of motifs or have the children in your classroom do so. It is one way to understand the common elements of all folklore.

Variants of Folk Tales

The number of variants of a single folk tale fascinates beginning students of folklore. A variant will have basically the same story or plot as the original, but it may have different characters, different setting, and use some different motifs. For example, a Japanese Rumpelstiltskin story (234) is about an ogre who built a bridge for a carpenter. If the carpenter couldn't discover the ogre's name, he had to forfeit one of his eyeballs. In an Armenian tale, "The Talking Fish" (226), a demon loans a poor peasant a cow for three years on the basis that at the end of the time the demon will return to ask a question. If the peasant cannot answer it, he and his wife must become the demon's slaves. In a twist to the usual ending a traveler who was visiting their house answered all the demon's questions correctly. The traveler turns out to have been a fish that the kind peasant had returned to the sea. Other better-known variants of Rumpelstiltskin are the English *Tom Tit Tot* (178); the Scottish "Whippety Stourie" (246); and a tale from Cornwall, *Duffy and the Devil* (254). These are all discussed under the section "British Folk Tales."

An English folk tale, retold in picture-book format, is called *Tops and Bottoms* (42) by Lesley Conger. In this Northamptonshire tale an indus-

trious farmer and a lazy goblin match wits. The farmer had been told by his father, who had been told by his father, never to plant anything in the west field, for nothing would grow there. One spring the farmer decided to challenge tradition and plant the field. As soon as his plow dug into the good dirt, a goblin stood in front of him saying that he would take the crop. The quick-thinking farmer suggested they go halves on it. He would do all the work and he would give the goblin his choice of whether he wanted the top half or the bottom half of the crops. The goblin chose the bottom. And so the farmer planted wheat. The next year the goblin reappeared, wanting the top half this time. And so the farmer planted carrots. The third year the goblin challenged him to a mowing contest, but again the crafty farmer tricked him. Harold Berson has made a picture book of a similar tale from Africa called *Why the Jackal Won't Speak to the Hedgehog* (20). In this story the two animals share the work and split the crops (wheat and onions) in the same way. The result is seen in the title of the book! A Russian tale, "The Peasant and the Bear" (89), has the same plot, but turnips and wheat are planted. In "The Devil's Partnership" (65), a Latvian story, God and the Devil share the crops. You can guess who wins that time!

In Marcia Brown's lively story, *Stone Soup* (28), French soldiers trick a whole village into providing them with the ingredients for a delicious soup which they claim they have made from three stones. In the Swedish version, *Nail Soup* by the Zemachs (255), an old man teaches a stingy old woman how to make soup from a nail in the same fashion. In the Russian variant a man makes "Hatchet Gruel" (89).

A comparison of the variants of Cinderella illustrates differences in theme and motif. Scholars have found versions of this story in ancient Egypt, in China in the ninth century, and in Iceland in the tenth century. Cinderella receives her magic gifts in many different ways; in the French and most familiar version, a fairy Godmother gives them to her (186); in Grimm's version (93) a dove appears on the tree that grew from the tears she had shed on her mother's grave; in the English "Tattercoats" (221) she receives her beautiful gowns from a herdboy. Cleaning peas, or retrieving peas thrown into the fire by the stepmother, are obstacles to her attendance at the ball. She attends three balls in some variants; for example, in the Italian version (119), Cenerentola throws coins as she leaves the ball the first night, pearls on the second escape, and loses her slipper on the third night. The treatment of the stepsisters varies from blinding them to inviting them to live with her at the palace. An Indian Cinderella (3) wins the Great Chief by giving an honest answer to his sister's questions, for he is truly invisible. Her own sisters leave the wedding feast in disgrace, weeping with shame.

Knowledge of the different variants of a tale, common motifs, and common types of folk tales will enable a teacher to help children see similar elements in folk tales across cultures. Knowledge of the folklore of a particular country or cultural group will aid in identifying the uniqueness and individuality of that group. Both approaches to a study of folklore seem essential. For this reason the two charts that follow, "A Cross-cultural Study of Folk Tales" and a "Cultural Study of Folk Tales," have been developed.

FOLK TALES OF THE WORLD

British Folk Tales

The first folk tales that most children in the United States hear are the English ones. This is because Joseph Jacobs, the folklorist who collected many of the English tales, deliberately adapted them for young children, writing them, he said, "as a good old nurse will speak when she tells Fairy Tales." His collection includes cumulative tales such as *The Old Woman and Her Pig* and *Henny Penny*, and the much-loved talking beast stories of *The Little Red Hen*, *The Three Bears*, and *The Three Little Pigs*. Paul Galdone has illustrated single editions of all of these nursery tales with large, colorful, and humorous pictures that appeal to the young child. Today, when children see such beautiful modern picture books, it is good to have these well-loved classic tales in handsome single picture-book editions.

English folk tales are known for their humor, particularly those stories that are about fools and simpletons. "Mr. and Mrs. Vinegar" (221) is a favorite among many children. It is a cheerful story of a couple who lived in a glass pickle jar until Mrs. Vinegar smashed it with her vigorous sweeping. They then set out to find their fortune and do when they frighten away some robbers and retrieve their stolen gold. Mrs. Vinegar sends her husband off to buy a cow which will keep them in comfort all of their lives. But Mr. Vinegar trades the cow for some bagpipes which he fancies. Then he trades the bagpipes for a warm pair of gloves, the gloves for a walking stick, and finally he throws the stick at a magpie. He returns home to receive a beating from his wife, but he remains unperturbed and says quite cheerfully: "You are too violent, lovey. You broke the pickle jar, and now you've nearly broken every bone in my body. I think we had better turn a new leaf and begin afresh."[41]

"Lazy Jack" (221) is the story of a simpleton who follows the right directions at the wrong time, a motif found in many folk tales. Jack earns a penny but loses it coming home. His mother scolds him for not putting it in his pocket and he promises to do so next time. The next day he gets a jar of milk and, remembering his mother's advice, he puts it in his pocket! Finally, the simpleton, again following the advice for the way to carry home a piece of meat, staggers home carrying a live donkey! He passes by the house of a rich man who has promised his daughter's hand in marriage to any man who can make her laugh. Needless to say Lazy Jack succeeds. Mollie Clarke has written and illustrated a simplified picture-book version of this story titled *Silly Simon* (39).

The tale of *The Three Sillies* (258) has comic illustrations by Margot Zemach. It is a droll story about people who borrow trouble before it comes. A young girl goes down in the cellar to draw beer for her suitor and parents. She sees an axe stuck in the cellar beam, and she imagines what might happen if, after her marriage, she has a son and he goes down in the celler and is struck by the axe. Her parents soon join her in weeping over this imagined tragedy.

There are many foolish tales of "The Wise Men of Gotham" (221), including one "Of Drowning Eels" (221). The funniest and the one

---

[41]Flora Annie Steel, *English Fairy Tales*, illustrated by Arthur Rackham (New York: Macmillan, 1918), p. 144.

CROSS-CULTURAL STUDY OF FOLK TALES

Types of Folk Tales	Tale	Culture	Sample Motifs	Tale	Culture	Sample Variants	Culture
Cumulative	*The Old Woman and Her Pig* (80) *All in the Morning Early* (180) "The Pancake" (3) "Plop!" (247)	England Scotland Norway Tibet	Magical Powers	*Six Companions Find Their Fortune* (106) *The Fool of the World and the Flying Ship* (192) *The Woodcutter's Duck* (232)	Germany Russia Poland	*Cinderella* (186) "Tattercoats" (221) "Aschenputtel" (95) "The Princess on the Glass Hill" (121) *Nomi and the Magic Fish* (166) "Little Burnt Face" (3)	France England Germany Norway Africa American-Indian
Pourquoi Tales	"Why the Bear is Stumpy-Tailed" (121) *Why the Sun and the Moon Live in the Sky* (54) "How the Duck Got His Bill" (286)	Norway Africa American-Indian		*The Five Chinese Brothers* (21) *Long, Broad and Quick-eye* (176)	China Bohemian	*Rumpelstiltskin* (103) *Tom Tit Tot* (178) *Duffy and the Devil* (254) "The Talking Fish" (226) "Whippety Stourie" (246) "Ogre Who Built a Bridge" (234) "Fareedah's Carpet" (151)	Germany England Cornwall Armenian Scotland Japan Arabia
Beast Tales	*The Three Billy Goats Gruff* (82) *The Three Little Pigs* (83) *The Traveling Musicians* (111) *Anansi the Spider* (157) "Kantjil and Monkey Business" (23)	Norway England Germany Africa Indonesia	Transformations	*Beauty and the Beast* (185) "The Frog Prince" (108) "The Crane Maiden" (163) "The Little Crow" (122) "The Theft of Fire" (153) "The Prince Who Was Taken Away by the Salmon" (113)	France Germany Japan Africa American-Indian American-Indian	"The Lad Who Went to the North Wind" (6) "The Table, the Donkey and the Cudgel" (93) "The Enormous Genie" (227)	Norway Germany Armenian
Noodlehead Stories	"Clever Elsie" (108) "Who Am I?" (248) *Three Rolls and One Doughnut* (89) "The First Shlemiel" (217) *The Disobedient Eels* (38)	Germany Persia Russia Jewish Italy	Magical Objects	*The Dancing Kettle* (233) *Vasilisa the Beautiful* (242) *Too Much Nose* (257) "The Shepherd's Nosegay" (116) "Aladdin" (162)	Russia Italy Czechoslovakia Arabia	"Jack and the North West Wind" (37) "Bottle Hill" (162)	American-Appalachian Ireland
Wonder Tales	*Little One-Inch* (199) "Jack and the Bean Stalk" (221) *Beauty and the Beast* (185) *The Ring in the Prairie* (205) *The Three Princes of Serendip* (125)	Japan England France American-Indian Ceylon	Trickery	*Nail Soup* (255) *Balarin's Goat* (17) "The Best Liar" (89) "Anansi and the Old Hag" (209) "Shrewd Todie and Lyzer, the Miser" (216)	Sweden France Russia Jamaica Jewish	"Lazy Jack" (222) *Just Say Hic!* (237) "Boy and the Cloth" (47) "A Time for Everything" (59)	England Turkey India Russia
Realistic	"Gudbrand on the Hill-side" (8) *Dick Whittington and His Cat* (25) "Who Will Wash the Pot?" (86) *The Wave* (127) *Zlateh, the Goat* (217)	Norway England Russia Japan Jewish				*Epaminondas* (171) "Tony Di Moany" (167)	American Majorca

CULTURAL STUDY OF FOLK TALES

Cultures	Collectors	Typical Tales	Characters	Characteristics
British Folk Tales	Joseph Jacobs (1854–1916)	*The Old Woman and Her Pig* (80) *The Three Little Pigs* (83) *The Little Red Hen* (79) *Tom Tit Tot* (178) "Jack and the Beanstalk" (221) "Whippety Stourie" (246)	Mr. Vinegar Lazy Jack Giants "Wee folk" Dick Whittington	Cumulative tales for the youngest Well-loved beast tales Droll humorous stories Giant killers Simpletons
German Folk Tales	The Grimm Brothers Jacob (1785–1863) Wilhelm (1786–1859)	*The Traveling Musicians* (111) *The Shoemaker and the Elves* (105) *Rumpelstiltskin* (103) *Hansel and Gretel* (94) "*Frog Prince*" (108) *The Seven Ravens* (102) *Rapunzel* (102) *Snow-White and the Seven Dwarfs* (107)	"Clever" Elsie Tom Thumb Rumpelstiltskin Hansel and Gretel Snow White Evil witches Dwarfs and elves Bears Wolves	More somber frightening tales Some children as characters Harsh punishment (Snow White) Romances—Rapunzel, Snow White, King Thrushbeard Transformations
Norse Tales	Peter Christian Asbjørnsen (1812–1885) Jorgen E. Moe (1813–1882) Translated into English by George Webbe Dasent (1817–1896)	*The Three Billy Goats Gruff* (7) "Why the Sea Is Salt" (121) "Why the Bear Is Stumpy-tailed" (121) "Gudbrand on the Hillside" (8) "The Lad Who Went to the North Wind" (6) "Princess on the Glass Hill" (121) *East O' the Sun and West O' the Moon* (5) "Lord Per" (8)	Trolls, Tomte Many-headed giants Youngest sons or "Boots" North wind White bears Salmon Cats Reindeer, elk	Tongue-in-cheek humor Some pourquoi stories Helpful animals Magic objects Magic enchantments Many trials and tasks Poor boy succeeds
French Folk Tales	Charles Perrault (1628–1703)	*The Little Red Riding Hood* (187) *Puss in Boots* (188) *Cinderella* (186) *The Sleeping Beauty* (190) *The Twelve Dancing Princesses* (150) *Beauty and the Beast* (185) "Chanticleer the Cock's Story" (30)	Fairy godmothers Jealous stepsisters Kings and queens Princes and princesses Courtiers Reynard the Fox	Traditional fairy tale Romance Wicked enchantments Long sleep Unselfish youngest daughter succeeds

Cultures	Collectors	Typical Tales	Characters	Characteristics
Russian Folk Tales	Alexander Afanasyev (1855–1864)	*The Great Big Enormous Turnip* (230) *The Fox and the Hare* (85) *Vasilisa the Beautiful* (242) *Salt* (256) *The Fool of the World and the Flying Ship* (192) *The Story of Prince Ivan, the Firebird and the Gray Wolf* (241) "*Marya Moryevna*" (240)	Fox is the trickster Vasilisa, the beautiful or the wise Ivan, the youngest brother Baba Yagas, witches Koshchei, the Deathless, an evil wizard The Firebird Wolves Falcons Bears	Ivan, the fool, triumphs over all Peasants and youngest brothers outwit generals and tsars Many sets of tasks and trials Quest of the firebird, frequent theme Helpful animals Dire punishments Frightening, bloody tales Wry humor
African Folk Tales	Harold Courlander and other present-day collectors	"*How Spider Got a Thin Waist*" (4) *Why the Sun and the Moon Live in the Sky* (54) "*Zomo Pays His Debts*" (224) "*The Man and the Mango Trees*" (131) "*Anansi and Nothing*" (11) *The Cow-Tail Switch* (49)	Anansi, the Spider Zomo, the Rabbit Ijapa, the Tortoise Mama Semamingi Crocodiles Leopards	"How and why" stories Many talking beast tales Animal tricksters Small defenseless animal or man outwits others Wry humor Play on words Dilemma tales
Japanese Folk Tales		*Little One-Inch* (199) *The Mud Snail Son* (155) *The Funny Little Woman* (174) *The Crane Maiden* (163) *The Golden Crane* (251) *The Burning Rice Fields* (32)	Inchling Monotaro, Little Peach Boy Ogres, *Oni* Goblins, *Tengu* Magic badgers, *Tanuki* Urashima	Poor farmers or fisherman Childless couples who have "different" children Transformation into bird Respect for the aged Kindness to animals rewarded Self-sacrifice
American Indian Folk Tales	Henry Rowe Schoolcraft (1820's–1850's)	*The Long-tailed Bear* (286) *The Fire Bringer* (126) "*Prince Who Was Taken Away by the Salmon*" (123) *The Ring in the Prairie* (205) "*Red Swan*" (204)	Glooscap Manabozho, "The Hare" Coyote Raven Badger	Many legends and nature myths Tricksters Transformation tales Romance Struggle for survival Use of pattern of four

that delights 6- and 7-year-olds the most, is the story of the men going fishing and then counting each other to see if they are all there. The person doing the counting always forgets to count himself and then decides one of them has drowned. The simplified version that children in the United States know best is Elkin's *Six Foolish Fishermen* (67). This same tale is told of camels in *Nine in a Line* (146) by Ann Kirn and *How Many Donkeys?* (143), a Turkish folk tale by Alice Geer Kelsey. All three of these stories are available in picture-book versions.

There is an element of realism that runs through some of the English folk tales. The story of Dick Whittington and his cat has its basis in history. There was once a real Richard Whittington who was three times mayor of London in 1396, 1406, and 1419. And what an exceptional mayor he must have been—enacting prison reforms, providing the first public lavatory and drinking fountain, and building a library and a wing on the hospital for unmarried mothers. It is no wonder that the common people made him the popular hero of one of their most cherished tales. The story of "Dick and His Cat" was found in some of the very earliest chapbooks of the day. Kathleen Lines, who has written a noteworthy edition of *Dick Whittington* (156), illustrated by Edward Ardizzone, maintains that this story "has no real parallel amongst the folk tales of other countries."[42] Children will also enjoy Marcia Brown's picture story book of *Dick Whittington and His Cat* (25), which is illustrated with handsome linoleum block prints appropriately printed in gold and black.

The British version of Cinderella is called "Tattercoats" (221) and is a more poignant romance than the better-known French story. For in this tale the prince falls in love with Tattercoats even when she is dirty and wearing an old torn petticoat. To prove his love he invites her to come as she is with her herdboy and his geese to the King's ball that evening. Only after the Prince greets them and presents her to the King as the girl he has chosen for his bride does the herdboy begin to play his magical pipe and Tattercoats' rags are changed to shining robes while

the geese become dainty pages. The herdboy is never seen again.

Rumer Godden retells a modern version of her favorite English tale in *The Old Woman Who Lived in a Vinegar Bottle* (91). Mairi Hedderwick's lovely watercolor illustrations show the changes in both the character and condition of the old woman who first lived in an old house the shape of a stone vinegar bottle. She is very happy and contented until she saves the life of a fish who then grants her every wish. These include a new cottage, new clothes, furniture, and a maid! Finally, when she demands a chauffeur and a big shining car like the Queen's, the fish has had enough, and returns her to her original house and condition. Unique to this version is the ending in which the old woman goes back to the lake and apologizes to the fish for being such a "greedy

Rumer Godden has written a modern version of her favorite fairy tale. Lovely watercolors picture the interior of the old woman's cozy vinegar-bottle house.

From *The Old Woman Who Lived in a Vinegar Bottle* by Rumer Godden, illustrated by Mairi Hedderwick. Illustrations copyright © 1972 by Macmillan London Ltd. Reprinted by permission of The Viking Press, Inc.

---

[42]Kathleen Lines, *Dick Whittington*, illustrated by Edward Ardizzone (New York: Walck, 1970), background notes: p. 48.

grabbing old woman." The fish offers to return her riches, but the old woman has enough sense to refuse them. She knows she is happiest in her old oast house rocking her cat, Malt. In the story which the Grimm brothers collected called "The Fisherman and His Wife" (108) the wife never finds contentment, even after she has been made Emperor and Pope!

Giant killers are also characteristic of some English stories. Everyone knows the story of "Jack and the Beanstalk" (206). Less well-known in the United States is the story of "Molly Whuppie and the Double-faced Giant" (221). Molly is a girl that would delight the heart of any ardent supporter of women's liberation, for she is clever enough to trick the double-faced giant four times, each time narrowly escaping over the One Hair Bridge. This is a somewhat bloody story in that Molly tricks the giant into choking his own children rather than her sisters, and beating his own wife to death after she had traded places with Molly.

Mr. Miacca (177) is not a giant but he delights in catching naughty little boys, putting them in his sack, and taking them home to eat at supper. Such was the fate of Tommy Grimes, but being as clever as Molly Whuppie, he escaped from Mr. Miacca's house two different times. Evaline Ness has used the setting of Victorian London for her illustrations of this rather scary but humorous English folk tale.

Using crude woodcuts, Ness has also illustrated a picture-book version of *Tom Tit Tot*, the English variant of "Rumpelstiltskin." It is not known which variant came first, but the English one is much funnier than the German. Both tales include boasting parents, who make great claims to the king of their daughters' ability to spin. However, in *Tom Tit Tot* the daughter is described as a "gatless" girl who was too dimwitted to learn how to spin. Therefore, on the last month of the year when her husband, the king, tells her she must spin five skeins of flax a day or lose her head, she just sits down on a stool and cries. Then she notices a creature, a black "impet" with a tail, who offers to do the spinning for her. Each night he will give her three chances to guess his name, and if at the end of the month she hasn't guessed it, then she will be his. On the last night of the bargain the king tells her that while out

hunting he saw this funny little creature spinning and twirling his tail and singing this song:

> Nimmy Nimmy not
> My name's Tom Tit Tot[43]

Lusty, broad humor also characterizes a Cornish version of this same tale titled *Duffy and the Devil* (254). The Zemachs have produced a single picture-book edition of this delightful story about Squire Lovel who hires a local girl, Duffy, to help old Jone, his housekeeper, with the spinning, sewing, and knitting. Duffy doesn't know the first thing about a spinning wheel and curses the thing, saying the devil can make the Squire's stockings for all she cares! At that moment a little creature with horns and a long tail appears and makes a pair of stockings! He agrees to help Duffy with all her knitting and spinning for three years, after which time she must tell him his name or he'll take her away. Squire Lovel is more pleased with Duffy all of the time, so he asks her to marry him and Duffy becomes Lady Duffy Lovel. When her three years are nearly up she confides in old Jone, who advises her to be sure to wait up until the Squire returns from hunting. The Squire tells her of following a hare into an underground cavern and interrupting a midnight meeting of witches and a "squinny-eyed creature" with a long tail who was singing this song:

> Tomorrow! Tomorrow! Tomorrow's the day!
> I'll take her! I'll take her! I'll take her away!
> Let her weep, let her cry, let her beg, let her pray—
> She'll never guess my name is Tarraway!"[44]

When Duffy guesses the devil's name he disappears in a flash of flame, but at the same time everything that he had knitted turns to ashes! Squire Lovel is on the moors when this happens and he has to come home with nothing on but his hat and shoes! Duffy swears she'll never knit again, and she doesn't. Both the language and the pen-and-wash illustrations retain the flavor and character of this folklore comedy.

"Whippety Stourie" (246) is the strange Scottish version of Rumpelstiltskin. In this tale a

[43] Evaline Ness, *Tom Tit Tot* (New York: Scribner, 1965), unpaged.
[44] Harve Zemach, *Duffy and the Devil*, illustrated by Margot Zemach (New York: Farrar, Straus, 1973), unpaged.

young wife outmaneuvers her husband when he announces that she must spin twelve hanks of fine thread a day. While weeping under a rowan tree she spies six wee ladies in gowns of green all sitting around a spinning wheel. They quickly agree to do her spinning for her, and their only request is to take supper with her and her husband. Now the strange thing about the wee ladies is that they all have lopsided mouths and laugh with a lopsided laugh. When the husband asks them why their mouths are this way, Whippety Stourie tells him it is because of their constant spinning. Since the husband does not care to have this happen to his fair wife, he orders that her spinning wheel be burned immediately.

While there are few fairies such as fairy godmothers in the British folk tales, the folklore of Scotland and Ireland is replete with the "little folk." All of them are not as helpful as the little lopsided ladies in the story of "Whippety Stourie." In fact, one motif that runs through the stories of these countries is that of the "changeling"—when the fairies exchanged their own crying ugly babies for a human one. Sorche Nic Leodhas has told such a story in her fine collection, *Thistle and Thyme* (183). This folklorist produced some five other collections before her death. Her *Gaelic Ghosts* (181), *Ghosts Go Haunting* (182), and *Twelve Great Black Cats and Other Eerie Scottish Tales* (184) contain supernatural stories that could give Alfred Hitchcock competition!

British folklore, then, is more robust and humorous than some other European tales. While British folklore includes giants and wee folk, it has developed relatively few complicated wonder tales as in French and Russian folklore. Its greatest contribution has been made to the youngest children in providing such nursery classics as "The Three Little Pigs," "Goldilocks and the Three Bears," and "The Little Red Hen."

German Folk Tales

Next in popularity to the English folk tales are those of German origin. Jacob and Wilhelm Grimm spent over twelve years collecting the tales which they published in 1812 as the first volume of *Kinder-und Hausmarchen* (Household Stories). They did not adapt their stories for children as Jacobs did, but were very careful to preserve the form and content of the tales as they were told (without benefit of a tape recorder!). These were then translated into English by Edgar Taylor between the years 1823–1826.

New and beautiful collections and single tales of Grimm's stories continue to be published today. Maurice Sendak[45] visited Kassel, Germany, prior to illustrating his two volumes of *The Juniper Tree and Other Tales from Grimm* (97). In the museum there he was fortunate enough to find a version illustrated by none other than the Grimms' younger brother, Ludwig. The size of this little-known version with only six engravings served as the inspiration for Sendak's small volumes. Mindful of the fact that these tales were first told to country folk, Sendak used adults as his subjects. His view of Rapunzel is from within her room looking out, rather than the cliché of Rapunzel hanging her hair out of the castle window. Sendak has pictured a pregnant Rapunzel, for the story states that she had her twin babies with her when she was at last united with her prince. This is an authentic and distinguished edition of Grimm; one that reflects the origin of the stories, yet makes us look at them with a new wonder and delight. Nonny Hogrogian has used simple but very expressive line etchings for the stories translated by Elizabeth Shub titled *About Wise Men and Simpletons: Twelve Tales from Grimm* (92). Fortunately there are an increasing number of well-illustrated single tales of Grimm, also.

German folk tales are not as funny as the English ones. They have a few drolls and simpletons, such as "Clever Elsie" whose story is similar to that of *The Three Sillies* (258) in which she cries because the baby she might have could someday be cut by the axe in the cellar. When Clever Elsie goes to the fields to reap the rye, she cuts her clothes instead of the rye and does not know herself. She decides to go home to see who she is. Upon arriving at the house, she asks her husband if Elsie is at home. Thinking that his wife is upstairs, her husband answers, "Yes."

> "Ach!" cried Clever Elsie. "Then I'm already at home, and this is not I, and I'm not Elsie but somebody else, and I don't live here."[46]

[45] Described in a lecture at Ohio State University, November 10, 1972.
[46] Wanda Gág, *Tales from Grimm* (New York: Coward-McCann, 1936), p. 132.

Sendak has given the Grimm stories back to adults with his symbolic, distinguished illustrations. Here, for example, he portrays a pregnant Rapunzel.

Reprinted with the permission of Farrar, Straus & Giroux, Inc., from *The Juniper Tree and Other Tales from Grimm*, selected by Lore Segal and Maurice Sendak, translated by Lore Segal, with four tales translated by Randall Jarrell, illustrated by Maurice Sendak. Pictures copyright © 1973 by Maurice Sendak.

Elsie runs away, "but is probably getting along all right because she is so clever." Elizabeth Shub has adapted a tale similar to *Gone Is Gone* (77) for beginning readers in her tale, *Clever Kate* (210). Kate, a bride of only one week, makes unbelievable mistakes, including giving her husband's gold away. All is recovered in the end and the well-meaning lovable Kate truly earns the title of *Clever Kate*. Anita Lobel's decorative peasant art adds to the fun of this tale. "Goose Hans" (108) is about the foolish boy who receives gifts from a prospective bride. He puts the needle in a haystack, the knife in his sleeve, a goat in his pocket—literally following his mother's directions. Left alone, he causes havoc in the house, but ends the day by rolling in honey and goose feathers to sit on the eggs, replacing the goose he kills. "The Golden Goose" (93) is the story of the third and youngest son, named Dunderhead, who finds a golden goose. The goose has magical properties such that anyone who touches her is stuck tight. Dunderhead has seven persons stuck to his goose when he hears that the king will give his daughter in marriage to anyone who can make her laugh. When she sees Dunderhead and the train of persons following his golden goose, she, of course, laughs.

The well-known tale of "The Bremen Town Musicians" (93) is the story of the cooperative efforts of the donkey, the hound, the cat, and the rooster in routing robbers out of their house. Hans Fischer has created lively pen-and-ink illustrations for a sophisticated picture-book version of this story, titled *The Traveling Musicians* (111). The wolf is usually the villain in the few beast stories that exist in German folklore. In the story of "The Wolf and the Seven Little Kids" (93) the wolf tricks the little goats into believing that he is their mother. Once they open the door he devours them all with the exception of the one little goat who hid in the clock. When the mother goat returns, her littlest one tells her what happened. They cut open the stomach of the sleeping wolf, let out the little goats, fill it with stones, and sew him up again. When he goes for a drink, he falls in the lake and is drowned. This is the same ending that is used in the Grimm brothers' *Little Red Riding Hood* (a longer version titled "Little Red Cap" appeared in later editions of Grimm). Harriet Pincus has illustrated a single edition of the Grimms' *Little Red Riding Hood* (100) with rather comic droll sketches. Edward Gorey's old-fashioned yet sophisticated pictures seem most appropriate for a *Red Riding Hood* (58) retold in humorous verse by Beatrice Schenk de Regniers:

> When the hunter saw the wolf,
> he said,
> > "So, there you are,
> > You mean old sinner!
> > Have you eaten Red Riding Hood's
> > Grandma for dinner?"
> > He took his knife
> > And he cut the wolf's belly.
> Out jumped Red Riding Hood.
> "Oh, it was smelly
> > in there," she said.[47]

[47] Text copyright © 1972 by Beatrice de Regniers. From *Red Riding Hood Retold in Verse* by Beatrice de Regniers. Used by permission of Atheneum Publishers.

Edward Gorey's sophisticated fox and naïve Red Riding Hood complement this humorous version written in verse form by Beatrice Schenk de Regniers.

Illustrations copyright © 1972 by Edward Gorey. From *Red Riding Hood* retold by Beatrice Schenk de Regniers. Used by permission of Atheneum Publishers.

Tom Thumb (110), the little lad not much bigger than his mother's thumb, also ends up in the wolf's belly, having first been in a mouse hole, a snail's shell, and down a cow's throat. However, quick-witted Tom tricks the wolf into taking him home, where Tom's parents kill the wolf and cut him open to find Tom safe and alive. Felix Hoffmann has illustrated a handsome single edition of this favorite tale.

Some of the Grimm tales are just that—grim, dark, and forbidding. Children can be frightened by the story of "Hansel and Gretel" (108), the somber tale of a young brother and sister who were abandoned in the woods by their parents and then nearly baked and eaten by a horrible witch. Joan Walsh Anglund's pictures for *Nibble Nibble Mousekin* (2), a single tale of Hansel and Gretel, are less sentimental than most of her artwork, and they do soften this rather frightening tale. Less well known but equally scary is the story of *Jorinda and Joringel* (96), which has been beautifully illustrated by Adrienne Adams. In this tale a wicked witch transforms a lovely girl into a nightingale. Joringel, a shepherd, finds a magic flower, and with it and his love to protect him, he goes to the castle in the dense forest and frees Jorinda and the seven thousand other girls who had all been transformed into birds. It is also a witch who keeps Rapunzel locked in her tower until a prince hears her lovely singing and persuades her to let down her hair as a ladder for him to climb. Felix Hoffmann, the well-known Swiss artist, has illustrated many single tales of Grimm. To illustrate *Rapunzel* (102), he has created large romantic pictures in muted colors that seem most appropriate for this classic fairy tale.

German folklore is livened by little elves. Children everywhere love the story of "The Elves and the Shoemaker" (93), the tale of the little men who helped the old shoemaker and his wife. Every night they made shoes for the old couple until one night the shoemaker and his wife made them a beautiful set of clothes. Then off the elves scampered never to be seen again. Using a picture-book form, Adrienne Adams (105) has been faithful to the origin of this tale by portraying German dress, the village, and a cobbler shop of the seventeenth century. The little man in *Rumpelstiltskin* was not as unselfish as the elves who helped the shoemaker. He had his price for spinning straw into gold; the queen's first-born child. William Stobbs (103) has illustrated a single edition of this tale with brightly colored illustrations that portray a rather jovial little elf-man. The text, which has been edited by Kathleen Lines, is short without much embellishment, particularly the undiluted ending when the Queen has guessed the name:

> "The devil told you that! The devil told you that!" shrieked the little man; and in his anger he stamped so hard with his right foot that it went into the floor above his knee; then he seized his left leg with both hands in such a fury that he split himself in two. And that was the end of him.[48]

Some of the German tales are laced together with a heavy thread of morality—kindness is always rewarded, while dire punishment faces the evil doer. The so-called "grandmother tale" of *Mother Holly* (10) is a popular story of two sisters, one kind and beautiful, the other lazy and ugly but nevertheless her mother's favorite. Yet the kind child's diligence earns a reward of gold from old Mother Holly at the bottom of the well,

[48]Grimm Brothers, *Rumpelstiltskin*, illustrated by William Stobbs (New York: Walck, 1970), unpaged.

while the lazy sister merits only a shower of pitch. Bernadette Watts has retold and illustrated a striking version of this story. Her pictures glow with color, many of them having the look of a child's crayoned drawing. This story has a theme similar to the favorite French tale of "Toads and Diamonds" (149). Another morality tale is the story of the humbling of a haughty princess by her husband, *King Thrushbeard* (99). Felix Hoffmann has illustrated this classic tale with his usual handsome pictures; while Sendak has made a merry comedy of the same tale with his picture-book version, *King Grisly-Beard* (98), in which two reluctant children play the prince and princess on a miniature stage. The importance of keeping a promise, even to a frog, is emphasized in the story of "The Frog Prince" (108). The princess did not relish sharing her little gold plate with the frog, or her bed, but her father made her honor her promise to do so when the frog retrieved her golden ball from the fountain. When the petulant princess threw the frog against the wall, she broke his enchantment and a handsome prince emerged. Of course they were married and lived happily everafter.

Wicked enchantments and magical transformations are characteristic of German folk tales. *The Seven Ravens* (104) is the story of seven boys who are changed into ravens by the curse of their father when the boys break a jug of water

Collected from the common folk, Grimm's fairy tales were realistic and honest. Hoffmann has captured these elements in his illustrations of *Tom Thumb*.

Copyright © 1972 by Sauerlander AG, Aarau, Switzerland. English translation copyright © 1973 by Oxford University Press and Atheneum Publishers. Illustrations by Felix Hoffmann—A Margaret K. McElderry Book. Used by permission of Atheneum Publishers. Schweizerische Bankgesellschaft CH-5001, *Aarau Schweiz*.

Mindful of the origin of the story of "The Shoemaker and the Elves," Adrienne Adams has used an authentic seventeenth-century German cobbler shop for the setting.

Illustration used by permission of Charles Scribner's Sons from the Brothers Grimm *The Shoemaker and the Elves*, illustrated by Adrienne Adams. Copyright © 1960 by Adrienne Adams.

with which he was going to christen their new baby sister. When the sister is older and very lonely, she sets off to find her brothers. Coming at last to the glass mountain where the ravens are kept, she must cut off her finger and use it as a key to the door and so release her brothers. Hoffmann has illustrated this well-known tale with rustic pictures of simple peasant folk. It is fun to notice the boots and hats of the boys as they turn into ravens. Hoffmann's pictures faithfully show the length of time the brothers were kept in the form of ravens, for when they are restored to boys again, they are noticeably older.

The story of the "Six Swans" (93) is one of treachery and true faithfulness. A king's sons are turned into swans by a wicked stepmother. The price for their transformation is difficult, indeed, for their sister must make them six shirts from star flowers and she may neither laugh nor speak

for six years. A king falls in love with her and marries her with the hope that she will speak. She is cruelly tricked by his mother and sentenced to burn at the stake. Just as the fire is about to be lit, the swan brothers appear. She throws the little shirts over them and they are transformed into men, except for one brother whose shirt was not quite finished; he has a swan wing for the rest of his life. Hans Christian Andersen took the inspiration for his very complex literary tale called *The Wild Swans* from this story of the Grimms.

While Walt Disney may be credited with making Snow White the best known of fairy tales today, he is also responsible for having bowdlerized it to such an extent that the Grimm Brothers would not recognize it. The Disney dwarfs are cute little men with names that came out of the Disney Studio rather than the Black Forest. Snow White is a sweet little sex symbol who dances with the dwarfs; at the same time she plays the role of little mother and makes them wash their hands before supper! For over thirty years no one challenged this Disney interpretation, until Nancy Burkert (107) created a beautifully illustrated edition translated by the late Randall Jarrell (*see* the first color section). Burkert used her own daughter as the model for Snow White, a beautiful 14-year-old girl, not a child, but not yet a woman. Weeks of medical library research revealed the characteristic proportions of dwarfs, and so Burkert drew not funny grotesque elves but real people, who look at Snow White with love and pride in their eyes. The medieval cottage of the dwarfs is as authentic as their proportions. Every architectural detail, the rich fabrics on the walls, the braided floor mat, the very plates and mugs on the table were copied from museum pieces. Appropriately, Snow White's mug is different from the seven that belonged to the dwarfs. Snow White herself wears a headdress borrowed from an Albrecht Dürer portrait. The white dog, basket of cherries, and the lilies on the table all signify virginity, while the meadow rue that is embroidered on Snow White's apron was believed to have been a protection against witches. No detail has been overlooked in creating this authentic beautiful scene. Disney used a "Sleeping Beauty" ending to his story, with Snow White being awakened by the kiss of the

Prince. Randall Jarrell was true to Grimm's story, in which the apple that had become lodged in the heroine's throat was shaken free when the Prince carried her off to Italy. For the climax Burkert has painted a triumphal judgment scene in which the white dog stands with his tail between his legs as he looks down the long flight of stairs where the jealous queen was taken after she had danced to her doom in red-hot slippers. Snow White and her Prince ascend the stairs that lead up to the King and their future paradise. The dwarfs are all there waiting to greet their lovely Snow White. Hopefully, such a book can restore the dignity, the beauty, and symbolic meaning to the story of *Snow White and the Seven Dwarfs*.

The German Cinderella story is called "Ash Maiden" (93), and is a somber, gruesome tale. There is no fairy godmother in this version; rather the little ash girl goes to her mother's grave beneath the hazel tree and a white dove grants her every wish. The stepsisters and stepmother tease the poor girl unmercifully as they throw peas and lentils into the ashes and then promise her she can go to the dance if she will pick them out. The eldest step-sister cuts her toe off in trying to fit her foot to the golden slipper, while the second stepsister mutilates her heel. At the wedding of Ash Maiden to the King's son, the two false sisters are blinded by birds who peck out their eyes.

While there is little mercy for the wicked in these German tales, there is much joy for the righteous. The plots are exciting, fast-moving, and a little frightening. Evil stepmothers, wicked witches, and an occasional mean dwarf hold princes and princesses in magical enchantments that can be broken only by kindness and love. Such were the dreams and wishes of the common folk of Germany when the Grimm Brothers recorded their tales.

Scandinavian Folk Tales

Most of the Scandinavian folk tales are from the single Norwegian collection titled *East of the Sun and West of the Moon*. These stories were gathered in the early 1840's by Peter Christian Asbjørnsen and Jorgen Moe. They rank in popularity with Grimm's fairy tales and for the same reason; they were written down in the vigorous language of the storyteller. Ten years after the

publication of these tales in Norway, they were ably translated by an Englishman, George Dasent, and made available to the English-speaking world.

Perhaps the best known of all of these stories is that of *The Three Billy Goats Gruff* (7) who "trip-trapped" across the troll's bridge to eat the green grass on the other side. It is the perfect example of folk-tale structure; the use of three billy goats, the increasing size of each one, and the anticipated downfall of the mean old troll. Fast action and an economy of words lead directly to the storyteller's conventional ending:

> Snip, snap, snout
> This tale's told out.

Marcia Brown's matchless picture-book version has been faithful to the Norwegian origin of this tale in both the setting for her lively illustrations and in the text. Paul Galdone's picture book (82), showing large close-up illustrations of the goats and the troll, will appeal particularly to the younger child.

Two very funny Norwegian folk tales deserve to be told together, for they complement each other. One, "Gudbrand on the Hillside" (8) tells of the contented wife who thinks everything her husband does is fine. One miserable day things go wrong for him—he sets out to buy a cow and trades it for one thing after another until he has nothing left, but still certain of his wife's infinite faith in his judgment, he bets his neighbor that she will not say a word against him. The good woman does not disappoint him and he wins his bet! William Wiesner has made a humorous picture-book version of this tale titled *Happy-Go-Lucky* (243). The incredulous facial expression of the neighbor hiding behind the door adds much fun to this tale of marital bliss. The English artist David McKee has created hilarious pictures for the companion tale to this story titled *The Man Who Was Going to Mind the House* (159). Wanda Gág illustrated a delightful little version of it under the title *Gone Is Gone* (77), while Wiesner titled his version *Turnabout* (244). In this story a bragging husband tells his wife how hard he works while she just "putters and potters about the house." His wife suggests that they trade places; he can take care of the house and she'll do his work in the field. The next day is an utter disaster for the husband and he never again says that his work is harder than his wife's!

The Norwegians tell of a Cinderlad, rather than Cinderella, in the story of "The Princess on the Glass Hill" (6). While the youngest son in this tale was not mistreated, he was not credited with much intelligence either, and given all the odd jobs to do. Dasent usually called him "Boots" in his English translations, since he did the same menial tasks as the boys who polished boots in England at that time. In this story only the youngest son, Boots, is brave enough to stand guard over the hayfields on St. John's Night. Three times he hears a noise as loud as an earthquake, followed by the sound of a horse cropping hay. Each time the horse, the saddle, and the armor near him was more beautiful than the last. Boots hid the horses and the armor and returned home. Now the king of the country had a daughter whom he would give in marriage to anyone who could ride up the glass hill and obtain the three golden apples in her lap. Boots, as in the Cinderella story, is laughed at by his brothers and denied the opportunity of entering the contest. However, as soon as his brothers are out of the house, Boots saddles his wonderful steed and rides one-third of the way up the hill. The next day he goes two-thirds of the way; and the final day, dressed in resplendent gold, he easily rides to the top of the hill where he takes the last golden apple from the Princess. This story is more exciting than Cinderella. And Boots, himself, seems quite nonchalant about his amazing accomplishments!

Equally as determined as Boots was "The Lad Who Went to the North Wind" (6) and complained to the Wind about blowing the grain out of his hand. The gruff North Wind then gives the boy a magic tablecloth that will spread itself and serve a full meal. Unfortunately, the boy is so proud of it that he shows it to the landlady of the inn, who promptly steals it and replaces it with a plain cloth. When the cloth won't work for his mother, the brave lad goes back to the North Wind and receives a ram that will make gold coins. Again the innkeeper robs him, so again the boy returns to the North Wind. This time the North Wind gives the boy a stick that will beat persons on command. When the innkeeper tries to steal the stick, he is so beaten that

he agrees to return the tablecloth, ram, and stick. And so the boy calmly returns home with all of his magical gifts from the North Wind.

The title story of *East O' the Sun and West O' the Moon* (5) is a complex tale that is similar to the French "Beauty and the Beast" (149) and the Scottish "Black Bull of Norroway" (206). In this tale a poor man gives his youngest daughter to a white bear, who promises to make the family rich. The girl is taken to a beautiful palace and given all that she wants. The white bear comes to her every night and throws off his beast shape, but he leaves before dawn so she never sees him. Her mother tells her to light a candle and look into his face, but to be careful not to drop any tallow on him. When her light shines on him, she sees a handsome prince, but three hot drops of tallow awaken him. Then he tells her of his wicked enchantment in which for one year he must be a bear by day. Now that she has seen him, he must return to the castle which lies east of the sun and west of the moon and marry the princess with a long nose. When the girl awakens in the morning, the bear and the castle have vanished and she is in a thick wood. She then seeks directions for the castle that lies east of the sun and west of the moon. She must make four long trips on each of the winds, finally arriving at the castle on the back of the North Wind. Before the prince will marry, he sets one condition, namely that he will only marry the one who can wash out the tallow spots on his shirt. Neither his long-nose bride-to-be nor an old hag can do it, but the girl who has posed as a beggar can wash it white as the snow. The wicked trolls burst and the prince and princess marry and leave the castle that lies east of the sun and west of the moon.

In many of the Norwegian tales the hero is aided in the accomplishment of seemingly impossible tasks by animals that he has been kind to. For example, in "The Giant Who Had No Heart in His Body" (6), a raven, a salmon, and a wolf all help to find the giant's heart. Then Boots squeezes it and forces the giant to restore to life his six brothers and their wives who had been turned to stone.

"Lord Per" (8) is the Norwegian tale of "Puss in Boots." The cat presents the king with the gifts of a reindeer, a stag, and an elk. After she gets the troll's castle for Lord Per, she asks him to cut off her head. He refuses and she says she'll claw out his eyes if he doesn't do it. When he does, she becomes a lovely princess and he makes her his queen.

In most instances, then, the animals in these tales are helpmates in overcoming giants or wicked trolls. Frequently, they are human beings who are held by an evil spell. While the Scandinavian tales are characterized by many trolls, magic objects, and enchantments, they are also frequently humorous, exciting, and fast-moving. The youngest son, or Boots, performs impossible tasks with ease and a kind of practical resourcefulness.

French Folk Tales

French folk tales were the earliest to be recorded, and they are also the most sophisticated and adult. This is probably because these tales were the rage among the court society of Louis XIV. In 1697 Charles Perrault, a distinguished member of the French Academy, published a little volume of eight fairy tales. The title page bore no name and there has been some debate as to whether they were the product of Charles Perrault or his son, Pierre. While the stories were probably very close to the ones told Pierre by his governess, they have the consciously elegant style of the "literary tale" rather than the "told tale" of the Grimms. It is thought these stories were translated into English about 1729; certainly "Cinderella," "Red Riding Hood," "Puss in Boots," and "Sleeping Beauty" are very much entrenched in English folklore.

The godmother in Cinderella is Perrault's invention, as are the pumpkin coach, the six horses of dappled mouse gray, and the glass slipper. In this French version Cinderella is kind and forgiving of her two stepsisters, inviting them to live at the palace with her. Marcia Brown was faithful to both the French setting and original text in her Caldecott Award-winning book *Cinderella* (186). Ethereal illustrations in delicate blues and pinks portray the splendid palace scenes. Cinderella's stepsisters are haughty and homely, but hardly cruel. Another beautiful picture book rendition of *Cinderella* has been created by Errol Le Cain. The rich, lavish illustrations are interesting to compare with Brown's delicate ones. (See Chapter 12 for an illustration and a lesson comparing several editions of *Cinderella.*)

The sister story to "Cinderella" is the well-known "Sleeping Beauty." The opening suggests that this is not a story told for peasants but one to be enjoyed by a wealthy and traveled society:

> Once upon a time there were a king and a queen who were very unhappy that they did not have any children, so unhappy that it can hardly be expressed. They went to all the watering places in the world, tried vows, pilgrimages, and acts of devotion but nothing would do. Finally, however, the queen did become pregnant and gave birth to a daughter.[49](53)

It is interesting to compare the wishes that the fairies gave to the newborn baby. In Grimm's tale they endow Briar Rose with virtue, beauty, riches, and "everything in the world she could wish for"; in Perrault's version they bestow her with beauty, angelic disposition, grace, and the ability to dance perfectly, sing like a nightingale, and play musical instruments! In both versions the jealous uninvited fairy predicts the child will prick her finger on a spindle and die. This wish is softened by the last fairy who changes it to the long sleep of one hundred years to be broken by the kiss of a prince. A long retelling of both *Cinderella* (71) and *The Sleeping Beauty* (72) was done by C. S. Evans in the 1920's and illustrated with silhouettes by the renowned English artist, Arthur Rackham. Both of these books were reissued by their publisher in 1972.

Certainly, "Little Red Riding Hood" (149) is as popular today as it was in the French courts. The French version never saves the little girl, but ends suddenly when the wolf gobbles her up. Actually, Perrault was telling his story on two levels: one as a straightforward entertaining tale and, then, as a warning to the ladies in the court to beware of soft-spoken strange gentlemen! Originally all of his stories had long stated morals, which were dropped when the tales were produced as chapbooks in England. Nonny Hogrogian has illustrated a little gem of a book titled *The Renowned History of Little Red Riding Hood* (130). Written in verse form, this old nine-

[49]Charles Perrault, "Sleeping Beauty" in *The Twelve Dancing Princesses and Other Fairy Tales* edited by Alfred David and Mary Elizabeth David (New York: New American Library, 1964), p. 125.

teenth-century version contains a cautionary moral for children:

> This story demonstrates that children discreet
> Should never confide in each stranger they meet;
> For often a Knave, in an artful disguise,
> Will mark out an innocent prey for his prize:
> Take warning, dear children, before 'tis too late,
> By Little Red Riding-hood's tragical fate.[50]

William Stobbs has used brightly colored illustrations for his picture-book version (187) which is quite faithful to the Perrault text.

Marcia Brown's *Puss in Boots* (188) is French from the tip of the feathered plume in his hat to the toe of his grand boots. She refers to him as "Puss," but also "Master Cat," "Sly Rogue," "Master Slyboots," and "Great Lord." And what a clever French cat he was! You recall that while

[50] *The Renowned History of Little Red Riding Hood,* illustrated by Nonny Hogrogian (New York: Crowell, 1967), unpaged.

he was the only inheritance of the youngest son of a poor miller, he proved to be a very rich inheritance indeed. Each day "Puss" sent fresh vegetables, a hare, or pheasant to the king, telling him that they were from an imaginary Marquis of Carabas, his master. Dashing ahead of the royal carriage, the cat tells the peasants to say the land belongs to the Marquis of Carabas or he will make mincemeat of them. Reaching a castle, he tricks the ogre into changing into a mouse which he promptly eats. The castle then becomes his master's, and Puss remains the dashing hero in boots and plumed hat. Children would enjoy comparing Marcia Brown's lavishly dressed French Puss with Hans Fischer's handsome virile cat (189).

Adrienne Adams has created two beautiful picture-book fairy tales of French origin, *The Twelve Dancing Princesses* (150) and *The White Rat's Tale* (203), retold by Schiller. The mystery of how the twelve lovely princesses who are locked in

Two artists' interpretations of *Puss in Boots*—Marcia Brown's (*left*) and Hans Fischer's (*right*).

Illustration used by permission of Charles Scribner's Sons from *Puss in Boots,* illustrated by Marcia Brown. Copyright 1952 by Marcia Brown.

Illustration by Hans Fischer reproduced from *Puss in Boots* by permission of Harcourt Brace Jovanovich, Inc.

their rooms each night wear out their dancing slippers is discovered by Michael, a gardener's helper. Although he is entitled to marry one of the princesses, he will not do so until Lina, the youngest, proclaims her love for him. Then the mysterious enchantment is broken and the princes who had been the dancing partners of the lovely ladies are freed to become their husbands. *The White Rat's Tale* is a delightful switch on the usual fairy tale. A childless king and queen own a wonderful white rat. However, she was not as satisfying to them as a daughter might be, so they ask a good fairy to turn her into a princess. This the fairy does. "A lovely pink and white princess. A little too pink of eye, a bit too white of hair, said the courtiers behind their hands. But still infinitely more adorable than a white lady rat."[51] When the time comes for the princess to marry she is very choosy and settles on only one suitor, a rat! So the good king and queen ask the fairy queen to change their princess back into a white lady rat, and the two are properly married.

The best-known French fairy tale, other than those by Perrault, is *Beauty and the Beast,* adapted from a longer story by a Madam de Beaumont in 1757. Philippa Pearce (185), the gifted English writer, has retold the story for today's children in beautiful prose, while Alan Barnett's gouache paintings provide a rich mysterious background. His beast is hideous. Only Beauty's true unselfish love for the beast, himself, could break his wicked enchantment and release the handsome young prince. This is an exquisite fairy tale of love and sacrifice and understanding.

The folk tales of France were not the tales of the poor but those of the rich. They have all the trappings of the traditional fairy tale including fairy godmothers, stepsisters, and handsome princes. Tales of romance and sophisticated intrigue, they must surely have been the "soap operas" of their day.

Russian Folk Tales

Russian folk tales reflect universal folklore patterns with many stories of tasks and trials, transformations, and tricksters. However, the Russian tales are longer and more complicated

[51]Barbara Schiller, *The White Rat's Tale,* illustrated by Adrienne Adams (New York: Holt, Rinehart and Winston, 1967), unpaged.

than those of other countries and frequently involve several sets of tasks, as in *The Story of Prince Ivan, the Firebird and the Gray Wolf* (241). This story begins with three sons being charged to find the thief who steals the golden apple from a certain tree. The youngest, Ivan, gets the feathers of the firebird and sets out to find it. He is kind to a wolf which later reciprocates this help. However, each time the boy has a task, he disregards the wolf's advice and has an even more difficult task assigned. Finally, on the completion of all the tasks, including obtaining the firebird, the beautiful princess Elena, and the horse with the golden mane, Ivan is murdered by his two brothers who wish to obtain Ivan's reward from their father. Thirty days later his friend the gray wolf finds Ivan and with the help of a crow restores him to life. Ivan arrives at the palace just in time to prevent the marriage of Princess Elena to his evil brother. Nonny Hogrogian has richly illustrated this firebird story that was translated by Whitney. In "The Fire-Bird and the Princess Vasilisa" (242) a horse, rather than a wolf, advises his young master and so saves his life. The Princess Vasilisa tricks the old Tzar into jumping into the boiling water that had made the warrior so young and handsome. The Tzar is burned to death and the Princess and the warrior marry. A picture book version of *The Fire Bird* (22) has glowing illustrations by Toma Bogdanovic. Rich in color and design these pictures beautifully complement this well-loved Russian tale. The firebird theme runs throughout Russian folklore and was the inspiration for Stravinsky's "Firebird" music. Middle-grade children would enjoy both the stories and the exciting music.

There is a grim, frightening aspect to many of the Russian tales. For example, *Vasilisa the Beautiful* (242) is the Russian counterpart to Cinderella. But in this tale Vasilisa is sent to the wicked witch, Baba Yaga, to obtain a light for her stepsister who hopes that the witch will eat Vasilisa up. Ever protected by the little doll Vasilisa's mother had given her before she died, Vasilisa carries the light home in a human skull. Upon her return, the intensity of the light's rays consumes her stepmother and stepsister.

Koshchei, the Deathless One, is another evil character in Russian folklore. In the complex tale of "Marya Moryevna" (240) Prince Ivan disobeys his wife Marya and opens a closet only to find

A Russian Cinderella, Vasilisa, is sent by her step-sisters to the wicked witch, Baba Yaga.

From *Vasilisa the Beautiful*, Thomas Whitney, Translator. Illustrations by Nonny Hogrogian. Illustrations copyright © 1968 by Nonny Hogrogian. Used by permission of Macmillan Publishing Co., Inc.

Koshchei, the Deathless, shackled by twelve chains. He takes pity on him and gives him water to drink, which restores Koshchei's strength and enables him to escape. After a long chase and a series of trials, Ivan and Koshchei have a grim fight, and the Deathless One is finally killed:

> [Koshchei] jumped to the ground and tried to slash him with a saber. But Prince Ivan's steed kicked Koshchei the Deathless, smashing his head, and the prince finished him off with a club. Then Prince Ivan placed a pile of firewood on top of him, lighted it and Koshchei the Deathless was burned up. Prince Ivan scattered his ashes in the wind.[52]

These fierce tales are matched only by the cold, vast harshness of the climate of Siberia. Mirra Ginsburg has edited several excellent collections of Russian tales; among them is *The Master of the Winds and Other Tales from Siberia*

(87). These tales blow with the cold of wind and snow. In one of them even the devil feels the isolation as he says: "Who can I ask? . . . There is no one around, no one less than a day's journey away from you and me!"[53]

Luckily, not all Russian folk tales have such grim settings or stories. There are many animal stories for younger children about bears and hares and the fox, who is the trickster of Russian folklore. Ginsburg has made a collection of nine such tales in the book, *One Trick Too Many: Fox Stories from Russia* (88). The cunning of the fox is evident in all these tales as he succeeds in outwitting peasants and animals. In *The Neighbors* (27), Marcia Brown tells of one time when the rooster was a true neighbor and helped the hare get the best of Mr. Fox! Brown's illustrations are filled with brilliant color and vigorous action in this folk-tale picture book. Victor Nolden has illustrated Ginsburg's version of the same tale in *The Fox and the Hare* (85).

Several cumulative Russian tales have delighted children all over the world. Tolstoy retold the old folk tale that emphasizes the theme of cooperation in pulling out *The Great Big Enormous Turnip*. The old man did not know that when he planted his turnip and told it to grow sweet and strong that it would do both! The story tells how it required the old man, the old woman, her granddaughter, the dog, the cat, and the mouse to pull the turnip out. Two delightful and quite different picture books have been made of this tale. One is illustrated by Helen Oxenbury, and shows a very English family pulling up the turnip (230). She portrays the struggle from several vantage points—from the side, the rear, even from a bird's-eye point of view of looking down on the family. The illustrations by Domanska for her book simply titled *The Turnip* (62) are more faithful to the origin of the story using patterned, stylized folk art. Both editions would be fun to share with primary grade children. The tale is superb for story-telling and dramatization.

A variant on the cumulative tale of the gingerbread boy is *The Bun: A Tale from Russia* illustrated by Marcia Brown. A more frightening cumulative story is about *The Clay Pot Boy* (139) that gobbles up the childless couple that created him

[52]Thomas P. Whitney, translator, *In a Certain Kingdom*, illustrated by Dieter Lange (New York: Macmillan, 1972), p. 120.

[53]Mirra Ginsburg, *The Master of the Winds and Other Tales from Siberia* (New York: Crown, 1970), p. 28.

and everything else in his way. Lobel portrays "the boy" as a rather rounded monster that grows larger and larger as he goes on his voracious path. Finally he is stopped by a little goat that butts him to pieces. This story, which suggests man may be destroyed by that which he creates, has many implications for the twentieth century.

Another well-loved Russian folk tale, *My Mother Is the Most Beautiful Woman in the World* by Reyher (196), contains the universal truth that beauty is in the eye of the beholder. When Varya falls asleep in the wheat fields, she is separated from her mother. Running through the fields she finally comes upon a group of villagers. Exhausted and crying, she will only say that her mother is the most beautiful woman in the world. After the townsfolk have called all the local beauties together for Varya's inspection, a large toothless woman pushes her way through the crowd to embrace her daughter. Varya had proved the old Russian proverb: "We do not love people because they are beautiful, but they seem beautiful to us because we love them."[54]

Russian peasants enjoyed telling their children stories in which the common people succeeded

[54]Becky Reyher, *My Mother Is the Most Beautiful Woman in the World*, illustrated by Ruth Gannett (New York: Lothrop, 1945), unpaged.

or got the best of their generals and Tsars. Uri Shulevitz has illustrated two handsome picture books that glorify the underdog. In *Soldier and Tsar in the Forest* (212), a simple soldier saves a helpless Tsar who has become lost in the woods on a hunting trip. *The Fool of the World and the Flying Ship* (192) follows the typical pattern of the youngest son who, with the help of his eight companions, each of whom has a magical power, outwits a treacherous Tsar and wins the princess for himself. Magnificent pictures capture the sweep of the Russian countryside and the richness of the Tsar's palace, in contrast to the humble huts and dress of the peasants. This book received the Caldecott Award.

Luckily, Russian folklore is also replete with stories of fools and noodleheads. Daniels translated the story of *Foma the Terrible* (52) from the large collection of the folklorist, Afanasyev. Foma, who has squinty eyes, a bulbous nose, and a thatch of hair like a haystack goes on a fly-killing binge and decides he is a great hero. After bragging of his exploits he is sent by the King of Prussia to battle against the Emperor of China. Foma so befuddles the enemy that he conquers them, thereby winning the hand of the lovely princess. Ivan was as clever a fool as Foma in the Russian tale *Salt* (256) by Harve Zemach. In

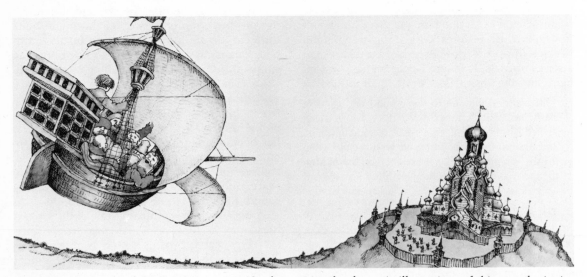

Sweeping panoramas of the Russian countryside characterize the dramatic illustrations of this award-winning folk tale.

Reprinted with the permission of Farrar, Straus & Giroux, Inc., from *The Fool of the World and the Flying Ship*, a Russian tale retold by Arthur Ransome, illustrated by Uri Shulevitz. Pictures Copyright © 1968 by Uri Shulevitz.

this well-illustrated single tale, a wealthy merchant gives each of his three sons a ship and cargo to trade in foreign lands. Only Ivan, "the fool," makes his fortune and wins the princess, much to his father's amazement!

Another successful "fool" was the youngest son in the story of "How the Sons Filled the Hut" (250). A father offered to give a small house to any of his three sons who could fill it completely. The eldest son bought a large horse, but it only filled one corner; the second son bought a load of hay, but it only filled one-half the hut; while the youngest son, the fool, bought a fat candle and the whole hut was filled with light!

The title story of *Three Rolls and One Doughnut* is a lovely noodlehead tale. A peasant walks a long way from his village to the city and is very hungry. He buys one roll, but he is still hungry. He buys another, and another; finally he buys a doughnut and he is no longer hungry.

> "Ah," he clapped himself on the forehead. "What a fool I was to have wasted all that good money on rolls. I should have bought a doughnut to begin with!"[55]

The same collection contains the story "Hatchet Gruel," which is similar to the Swedish *Nail Soup* (255) and the French *Stone Soup* (28). In the Russian version a soldier asks an old woman for a bite of food. "The old woman was rich and stingy. She was so stingy that she would not give you a piece of ice in winter."[56] The enterprising soldier teaches her to make a delicious gruel by boiling an old hatchet; though at his suggestion she adds salt, a handful of oats, and a spoonful of butter! And so the Russian tales celebrate the cleverness of the peasant and his gullibility. Their wry humor balances the dark grim tales of evil enchantments and horrendous punishments.

Jewish Folk Tales

Only in the past eight to ten years have Jewish folk tales been made available for children in written form. In *Zlateh the Goat* (217) and *When Shlemiel Went to Warsaw* (216), Isaac Singer has told warm, humorous stories based upon the Yiddish tradition and his own childhood memories. Here are tales of the amiable fools of Chelm (that fabled village where only fools live), lazy Shlemiels, and shrewd poor peasants who outwit rich misers. In Chelm the wise elders are the most foolish of all, and their "solutions" to people's problems make for some hilarious stories. One night they planned to gather the pearls and diamonds of the sparkling snow so the jewels could be sold for money. Worrying about how they might prevent the villagers from trampling the snow, they decided to send a messenger to each house to tell the people to stay inside. But then the "wise elders" realized the messenger's feet would spoil the snow, so their solution was to have him carried on a table supported by four men so that he would not make any footprints as he went from house to house! The story of Lemel, a silly bridegroom who follows advice in the wrong way, is similar to the English "Lazy Jack" (221) stories and the black *Epaminondas* (171) tales. When Lemel's child was born, an Elder asked if it were a boy. To Lemel's response of "no," the Elder inquired if it were a girl. "How did you guess?" Lemel asked in amazement. And the Elder of Chelm replied, "For the wise men of Chelm there are no secrets."[57]

Singer has also written a book just about *The Fools of Chelm and Their History* (214). Illustrated by Shulevitz, this collection provides more humorous stories about Gronam Ox and his fellow sages, Shmendrick Numskull, Berel Pinhead, Shmerel Thickwit, and the inevitable Shlemiel.

The story of "Shrewd Todie and Lyzer the Mizer" (216) is a delightful tale of chicanery in another book by Singer. Todie borrows a silver tablespoon from Lyzer on the pretext of needing it for a party for his daughter's rich suitor. He returns it with thanks along with the gift of a silver teaspoon, saying that the tablespoon had given birth to the teaspoon. The next time Lyzer is delighted to loan him a tablespoon, and again it is returned with the gift of its baby spoon. The third time Lyzer so believes Todie's tale that he asks, "'Does it ever happen that a spoon has twins?'"[58] When Todie then asks to borrow

---

[55] Mirra Ginsburg, *Three Rolls and One Doughnut: Fables from Russia*, illustrated by Anita Lobel (New York: Dial, 1970), p. 7.

[56] Ginsburg, *Three Rolls and One Doughnut*, pp. 25, 26.

[57] Isaac Bashevis Singer, *Zlateh the Goat, and Other Stories*, translated by the author and Elizabeth Shub, illustrated by Maurice Sendak (New York: Harper & Row, 1966), p. 50.

[58] Isaac Bashevis Singer, *When Shlemiel Went to Warsaw and Other Stories*, translated by the author and Elizabeth Shub, illustrated by Margot Zemach (New York: Farrar, Straus, 1968), p. 9.

some silver candlesticks, Lyzer, eager to increase his wealth, presses eight of them on Todie, who immediately sells them. When Todie does not return the candlesticks, he explains that the "candlesticks died." Lyzer swears that candlesticks cannot die and calls the rabbi for advice. The rabbi hears both sides and then tells Lyzer the miser that if he believes spoons can give birth, then he must accept "the fact" that candlesticks can die! This same tale is told in a slightly different version in the story called "The Borrower" (207) in *Let's Steal the Moon,* a collection of Jewish tales by Serwer. The title story of this book relates to the time the foolish people of Chelm decided to capture the moon in a barrel of water in order to save it for a dark night. "The Mechanical Man of Prague" in this same collection is the rather frightening story of the Golem, a mechanical man created to protect the Jews in Prague. The clay man begins to develop a will of his own by learning to love the children he had saved from the fire at the children's home. This story would be interesting to present prior to reading the modern fantasy *The Master of Miracle* by Ish-Kishor.

A terribly funny picture book is about Simon Boom, a boaster who only buys "The Best." Naturally, when *Simon Boom Gives a Wedding* (225) he wants the very best for his daughter. He decides to buy two hundred pounds of the very best fish for his daughter's reception and cautions the fish dealer to sell him only the best. The fish dealer replies that "his fish are as sweet as sugar." This convinces Simon that sugar is better to serve and so he goes to buy sugar. But the sugar merchant swears his sugar is as "sweet as honey." And so it goes until Simon ends up serving clear water that is the *very* best for it is:

sweeter than sugar
clearer than honey
purer than oil. . . .[59]

A matchless picture book, illustrated by Margot Zemach, is *Mazel and Shlimazel, or the Milk of a Lioness* (215) by Isaac Singer. Based on a folk tale that his mother had told him when he was

a boy, this is a long complicated story of a wager between Mazel, the spirit of Good Luck, and Shlimazel, the spirit of Bad Luck, and Tam, a poor peasant lad who is the subject of their bet. Shlimazel wagers that he can destroy in a second (not using death or illness) what it would take Mazel a year to build up. At first it seems that Shlimazel has won the bet. For just as Tam, who has found amazing favor in the court, takes the milk of the lioness to the ill king, his luck runs out. He's nearly hanged before Good Luck gets Bad Luck drunk on the wine of forgetfulness and comes to Tam's rescue. But Tam ". . . learned that good luck follows those who are diligent, honest, sincere and helpful to others. The man who has these qualities is indeed lucky forever."[60] The illustrations by Margot Zemach are some of the best she has done. Using thick black lines and muted royal colors in a variety of patterns, she has contrasted rich scenes of Byzantine Russian palaces with poor peasant huts crowded together in miserable little villages. In almost every picture one can find the joyful figure of Good Luck watching over his special charge. On the last page we see just his jaunty back as he goes on his merry way.

In pictures and text adapted from a Yiddish story by I. L. Peretz, *The Magician* (211), Uri Shulevitz has presented one of the legends of Elijah. This poignant story tells how Elijah in the guise of a magician appears in a village on the eve of Passover and conjures a feast for a desperately poor couple who had nothing in the house to eat. The poor peasants cannot believe their good fortune, so they go to the rabbi to ask if it is evil or good magic. When they return home, the magician is gone, but the feast and the wine are real. Another Hebrew legend about *Elijah the Slave* (213) has been retold by Issac Singer and magnificently illustrated by Antonio Frasconi. In this story Elijah, a messenger from God, sells himself as a slave in order to help a poor faithful scribe. To earn his freedom he then builds a beautiful palace with the assistance of angels who laugh for joy at their work. The pictures appear to have been made from woodcuts and then cut out and pasted on radiant back-

[59] Yuri Suhl, *Simon Boom Gives a Wedding,* illustrated by Margot Zemach (New York: Four Winds, 1972), unpaged.

[60] Isaac Bashevis Singer, *Mazel and Shlimazel, or the Milk of a Lioness,* illustrated by Margot Zemach (New York: Farrar, Straus, 1967), p. 42.

Zemach's rhythmical illustrations portray humankind's continuous route from good luck to bad luck to good luck.

Reprinted with the permission of Farrar, Straus & Giroux, Inc., from *Mazel and Shlimazel or The Milk of a Lioness* by Isaac Bashevis Singer, illustrated by Margot Zemach. Pictures © 1967 by Margot Zemach.

grounds. The effect is breathtaking and reminiscent of medieval art.

These Jewish tales have a poignancy, wit, and ironic humor that is not matched by any other folklore. Many of them have been preserved by the masterful writing of Isaac Singer, who has retained the flavor of both the oral tradition and the Yiddish origin.

The Folk Tales of the East

To describe the folk tales of the Near Eastern countries, India and Indonesia, and the Orient would take several books. For this area was the cradle of civilization and the birthplace of many of our folk tales. Unfortunately, these tales are not as well known in the United States as they deserve to be. Rather than confuse the reader with a description of many unfamiliar stories, only those tales or books which might serve as an introduction to the folklore of these countries will be discussed.

THE NEAR EAST

Armenian folk tales usually have the formal beginning of *Once There Was and Was Not*, and end with the traditional phrase *Three Apples Fell from Heaven:* one for the teller, one for the listener, and one for all the peoples of the world. Two fine collections of Armenian tales by Virginia Tashjian derive their titles from these traditional beginnings and endings (226, 227). Nonny Hogrogian has created superb humorous illustrations that reflect the folk wisdom of the stories. The tale of "The Enormous Genie" (227) reminds one of the Norwegian story, "The Lad Who Went to the North Wind" (6), while the story of "The Miller-King" (226) is a variant of "Puss in Boots" (206). In this Armenian version, however, the helpful animal who boasts of his master's wealth, and then proceeds to get it for him, is a fox that a miller let out of a trap. In the picture book *One Fine Day* (129) an old woman caught a fox licking up her pail of milk and she cut off his tail. She agreed to sew it back on only when he replaced the milk, which proved a difficult task. Nonny Hogrogian won the Caldecott Award for this fine picture book. The matchless simplicity of her drawings are perfect for the rustic humor found in most of these folk tales.

The Hodja stories are known throughout the Middle East, the Balkans, and Greece. Nasreddin Hodja was thought to have lived several hundred years ago in Turkey, where he served as a religious leader, teacher, or judge as the occasion demanded. He could be wise or he could be foolish, but he was always able to laugh at himself. The wisdom of Hodja is seen in the way he settled disputes between villagers. One day he watched a woodcutter chopping trees while his companion rested nearby (238). Everytime the ax fell, however, the companion groaned. When the woodcutter finished and sold his load of wood at the bazaar, his companion demanded half of the pay. The Hodja carefully listened to both sides of the case and then, taking each of the coins, he dropped them on the stone:

> As they rang out with a pleasant jingle he said to the companion, "Do you hear this?"
> "Yes," the companion answered.
> "Fine," said the Hoca [Hodja]. "The *sound* is yours, and the *coin* is the woodcutter's."[61]

The foolishness of the Hodja is seen in this typical Hodja story (64):

> One day a friend came up to the Hodja with an egg hidden in his hand.
> "Hodja," he said "if you guess what I've got in my hand, I'll treat you to an omelette. An *omelette.*"
> "Give me a clue," said the Hodja.
> "It's white on the outside, and yellow in the middle."
> "I know, I know!" cried the Hodja. "It's a turnip with a carrot inside!"[62]

Just Say Hic! (237) (pronounced "heech") is an amusing Turkish folk tale in picture-book form that follows the "Lazy Jack" (221) pattern. However, instead of carrying something the wrong way, this boy always says the wrong thing. Sent by his master to buy some salt, the servant boy, Hasan, repeats the word for salt, "Hic, hic, hic." In Turkey, "hic" also means "nothing." He repeats the word as he watches a fisherman who tells him to say, "May there be five or ten of them," instead of "nothing." He then repeats *this* phrase as he sees a funeral procession! And so it goes, as Hasan creates comic scenes with his right phrases in the wrong places.

Marcia Brown has richly illustrated *The Flying Carpet* (26), one of the tales from *The Arabian Nights.* Originally published in English in 1712, children find these tales very long and complicated, even in the adapted versions by Padriac Colum (41) and Andrew Lang (148). More stories retold in the picture-book format, such as with *The Flying Carpet,* might make them more popular.

An amusing variant of the Rumpelstiltskin story is found in the tale of "Fareedah's Carpet," one of seven tales from Arabia in the collection entitled *Palace in Bagdad* by Larson (151). In this version a camel offers to weave a carpet for a lazy girl whose mother won't let her back into the house until she finishes it. However, by the time the girl has waited on the camel, she is no longer lazy. The last story in this fine collection is titled "Caravan" and tells of the quests of two sons who were asked by their father, the Sultan, to find out what is the most powerful force in

[61] Barbara K. Walker, *Watermelons, Walnuts and the Wisdom of Allah and Other Tales of the Hoca,* illustrated by Harold Berson (New York: Parents', 1967), p. 36.

[62] Charles Downing, *Tales of the Hodja,* illustrated by William Papas (New York: Walck, 1965), p. 11.

the world. The startling discovery of the youngest son concerning the power of "an idea" would lead to an interesting discussion with middle-graders.

INDIA

Many of the tales from India are moralistic or religious in nature. The *Jataka* (Birth) tales are stories of the previous reincarnations of the Buddha. The Buddha appears as a lamb, a crane, a tiny deer, and many other animals in stories in which he always serves as a noble example. These beast tales were actually fables and always taught a moral lesson. They were known to have existed as early as the fifth century A.D. Later a guide for princes was composed as a series of moralistic animal stories known as the *Panchatantra*, literally meaning five books. These stories usually had a framing narrative leading into many other narratives that were loosely strung together. The *Panchatantra* was printed in Persia under the title of *The Fables of Bidpai*. When these stories are translated into English, the morals and teaching verses are usually eliminated. Without their morals or references to the Buddha, these Indian fables become more like folk tales.

The story of "The Banyan Deer" (118) is a Jataka tale of a self-sacrificing king deer who was willing to give his life for the sake of a mother deer and her baby. When the king who hunted in the forest saw the kindness and mercy of the Banyan deer, he saved his life and the mother deer's and promised never again to hunt in the park or forest.

Usha, the Mouse-Maiden (90) has been retold and illustrated in a picture book form by Mehlli Gobhai, a native of Bombay, India. This story, taken from the *Panchatantra*, is the tale of the tiny mouse who becomes a beautiful maiden through the magic of the holy man who then gives her to his wife to raise. When it is time for the girl to choose a husband, none will do until her eyes alight on a beautiful mouse. Reluctantly, the holy man transforms his daughter back into a mouse and the two mice run swiftly into the thick green forest. This story dates back several thousand years ago, and was certainly the antecedent for the French version of *The White Rat's Tale* (203).

A collection of tales from the *Panchatantra* simply titled *Tales from India* (235) includes "The Moneylender's Trick." In this story a merchant leaves his valuable iron scale with a moneylender in return for a loan. When he attempts to pay his debt and recover his scale, the moneylender claims he no longer has them, that mice had eaten them up. The merchant who knows he is being tricked, asks the moneylender if his son might go with him to carry his things down to the river. The moneylender agrees and the boy goes with the merchant, who promptly shuts him up in a cave. When he returns alone the moneylender asks for his son and is told that he was carried off by a tiny bird! The two men tell their stories to the village council, where it is suggested that the scale and the boy be restored to their rightful owners. Indian folk tales appear to be full of these stories of tricks and trades.

The animal trickster in Indian tales is the jackal. He is always tricking the crocodile, who is portrayed as fierce but stupid. Occasionally the jackal can be helpful, as he was in the very funny story of "The Tiger, the Brahman, and the Jackal" (118). In this tale a Brahman, or wise man, lets a tiger out of a cage. The tiger promptly decides to eat his benefactor, but gives him the opportunity to ask others if the tiger is being unjust. The Brahman meets the jackal and tells him of all that has occurred. The jackal pretends to be very confused and insists on going back to the scene of the incident, where he then attempts to reconstruct it in his mind:

> "Yes! I was in the cage—no I wasn't—dear! dear! Where are my wits? Let me see—the tiger was in the Brahman, and the cage came walking by—no, that's not it either! Well, don't mind me, but begin your dinner, for I shall never understand."
>
> "Yes, you shall!" returned the tiger, in a rage at the jackal's stupidity. "I'll *make* you understand."[63]

The tiger then proceeds to demonstrate what happened, including getting back into the cage, which is precisely what the jackal intended, as he quickly shuts the door on him.

"The Valiant Chattee-Maker" (118) is the funny story of a poor man who makes pots. He rides a tiger by mistake, and then is attributed

[63]Virginia Haviland, *Favorite Fairy Tales Told in India*, illustrated by Blair Lent (Boston, Mass.: Little, Brown, 1973), p. 88.

with more courage than he feels. The story has many of the same motifs as *Seven at One Blow* (245) or "The Brave Little Tailor" (149). Courlander includes an Indian "Lazy Jack" story in his collection, *The Tiger's Whisker* (47). It is titled "The Boy and the Cloth," and would amuse children no end. The poor boy refuses to take the seven rupees offered to him for his mother's cloth, because she had told him to sell it for four! Not only does this unfortunate do all the wrong things at the right times, but he says all the right things at the wrong times!

Since Indian tales were originally told to instruct the young, many of them contain a lesson as has been noted. "The Prince of the Six Weapons" (47) tells the story of a prince's struggle with a demon covered with long blue hair. The prince has tried to kill the demon with his five weapons—the bow, the spear, the shield, the war-ax, and his sword. He had failed, for nothing would penetrate that thick blue hide. However, the prince is not frightened, for he has told the demon that he has a sixth weapon within him and that if the demon ate him, the demon would be destroyed. The weapon is knowledge. "Whenever they come together knowledge destroys evil."[64]

One long book-length fairy tale from Ceylon is responsible for the introduction of a word to the English language—"serendipity," meaning "the gift of finding valuable or agreeable things not sought for." *The Three Princes of Serendip* (125) (the ancient name of Ceylon) were sent on a quest by their father to find the secret formula, "Death to Dragons," that would rid the seas around their island homeland of the great beasts that hindered travel. The three princes journeyed far seeking the formula, but happening always instead upon adventures and rare pleasures. One of the first written versions of this tale was published in Italian in 1557. Elizabeth Hodges drew on several different sources to write her version of the well-known tale. A companion volume contains seven mysterious tales that the Princes heard in the seven Persian palaces of their travels after the Dragon Secret. This volume is titled *Serendipity Tales* (124).

INDONESIA

Two foolish characters, Guno and Koyo, play a low-comedy role in many tales of Java and Ceylon. One is the well-known story of "The Well Diggers" (47) who keep digging new holes in which to put the dirt from the last hole. Another funny tale, "The Learned Men," (47) reminds one of *The Ransom of Red Chief* by O. Henry. The two foolish old men seize a buffalo boy and make him their servant—except the boy won't do anything for them. They have to carry him, and provide food and water for him. They even try to run away and leave him, but he stops them. Finally, in despair, they carry him back to where they found him!

The trickster in Indonesian folklore is the tiny mouse deer called Kantjil, and there are countless stories about him. Kantjil is clever, mischievous, with a high opinion of himself; always ready to outwit or out-trick any opponent of any size. Each of the stories in the book *How the Mouse Deer Became King* can be told separately, but collectively they deal with the increasing sphere of influence that this tiny deer exerts over all of the animals. In some cases he tricks other animals into accepting his kingship, such as the day he got the monkeys to dig in the beehive; and in other situations he works for their loyalty, as in the six days he spent in keeping the reapers from finding the owl's nest full of baby owlets. The owl is grateful to Kantjil and called him "most kind":

> For once Kantjil had no reply. No one had ever called him kind before, and it seemed to him a very great thing. He hung his head modestly, but from the corner of his eye he saw his doe was absolutely beaming. Kantjil was amazed. Now wasn't that just like the female, more proud of kindness than of canniness or courage.[65]

Of all of the animal characters in folklore, surely the little mouse deer, Kantjil, must be the most lovable.

THE ORIENT

Long a favorite with boys and girls in the United States, the story *Tikki Tikki Tembo* (175)

---

[64]Harold Courlander, *The Tiger's Whisker and Other Tales and Legends from Asia and the Pacific,* illustrated by Enrico Arno (New York: Harcourt Brace Jovanovich, 1959), p. 57.

[65]Marguerite Harmon Bro, *How the Mouse Deer Became King,* illustrated by Joseph Low (Garden City, N.Y.: Doubleday, 1966), p. 106.

tells why the Chinese use short names for their children. When Chang, the youngest son of a Chinese family, falls in the well, his brother quickly tells his mother and the Old Man with the Ladder. However, a few months later, when the "first and honored" son with the grand long name of Tikki-Tikki-Tembo-no-sa-rembo-chari-bari-ruchi-pip-peri-pembo also falls in the well, it takes so long for his brother Chang to tell both his mother and the Old Man with the Ladder that the elder son is nearly drowned! And that is why to this day all Chinese have short names. Young children love to repeat the rhythmical long name of the elder brother. Both the text and Blair Lent's stiff, stylized illustrations capture the tongue-in-cheek humor of the danger of too much respect!

Ed Young, a Chinese artist, has illustrated several beautiful picture books of Chinese folk tales. *The Emperor and the Kite* is a delightful story of the faithfulness of the tiny youngest daughter of the emperor. "She was so tiny, she was not thought very much of—when she was thought of at all."[66] But of all his eight children, only Djeow Seow attempted to help her father when he was captured and imprisoned in a high tower. Each day she sent him food in a basket attached to her kite. Finally, one day she sent up a long, strong rope which she had been patiently weaving of vines, grasses, and her own long black hair. The emperor tied it to the iron bar of his window and climbed down to kneel before his tiny daughter. Using the authentic Chinese art form of cut paper design, the intricate illustrations are as delicate as the sensitive story of love and faithfulness. In the folk tale, *8000 Stones* (249), a Chinese governor's clever son solves the problem of how to weigh the marvelous elephant given to his father by the Satrap of India. Embedded in this unusual tale of the ingenuity of Little Pei are principles of water displacement and methods of physics! Seven- and 8-year-olds could be challenged to think how they would weigh an elephant before they hear of Pei's solution. Ed Young has created an Oriental effect of cut paper design with glowing watercolors to illustrate this interesting tale told by Diane Wolkstein. Young has also created brilliant,

beautiful collàges for his illustrations of the hauntingly sad tale of *The Golden Swans* by Krueger (147). This is the strange and lovely legend from Thailand that explains why there is a statue of a swan in a place where swans have never been found, and why the water of the Lake of the Swans is always clear and pure. It is a tragic story, and one that could well be a part of a unit on ecology. For only when children deeply feel the reverence for life that is expressed in this legend can they apply such knowledge to their own lives.

The lovely *The Legend of the Willow Plate* (231) has been told by Alvin Tresselt and Nancy Cleaver. The illustrations by Joseph Low are faithful to the Oriental setting of this tale of fated romance. A poor poet and the daughter of a mandarin run off together, but their island hiding place is discovered by her former suitor. Chang is killed and Koong-se sets fire to her house and perishes in the flames. The two are turned into doves to fly together for eternity. The setting for the entire story is symbolically recreated in the traditional blue-willow pattern. This is a story that would delight middle-graders—it demands but a single prop, a blue-willow plate.

The Black Heart of Indri (128) adapted by Hoge is a kind of Chinese beauty and the beast tale. Not truly a variant, it is the story of Indri, an ugly fellow who had webbed feet and hands and the face of a toad. Since he controlled the stream of the water of life, he had much power over the people. Told that his ugliness would vanish if he would live in the presence of virtue for nine days and nights, he learns that it is only when he tries to make others happy that he is transformed both physically and spiritually into a handsome, kind prince.

A tender tale from ancient Vietnam titled *The Fisherman and the Goblet* (228) has been told by Mark Taylor and illustrated by Yashima. This is the story of a beautiful princess who falls in love with a poor young fisherman she has never seen, but who plays haunting songs on his flute under her window. When the princess finally sees him, she rejects him because he is so ugly. The fisherman dies of a broken heart, leaving an exquisite crystal that was said to have been made from his unanswered love. A beautiful goblet is made from the crystal and given to the mandarin's

[66]Jane Yolen, *The Emperor and the Kite,* illustrated by Ed Young (Cleveland, Ohio: World, 1967), unpaged.

daughter. When the girl holds the goblet in her hands she can see the fisherman and hear his song of love. Now, too late, the maiden realizes her love for the fisherman transcends his ugliness. A tear falls on the goblet, dissolving it, and her soul leaves her body. This tragic tale reminds one of the hauntingly beautiful stories of Hans Christian Andersen.

Oriental folk tales have a delicacy and quiet sedateness not found in other folklore. Even the humor is dignified and dry—and can be devastating, as seen in the story of "The Ambassador from Chi" (47). According to tradition there was bad feeling between the Prince of Chu and the Prince of Chi. However, the Prince of Chi wanted to have better relations with Chu, so he sent an ambassador who was a master of diplomacy and "saving face." The Prince of Chu was determined to ridicule him at a formal banquet given for all the foreign dignitaries. After subjecting him to one embarrassing situation after another, the Prince finally asked him why he was chosen as the ambassador and if a more worthy citizen couldn't have been found. The ambassador from Chi gave this withering explanation:

> "Oh, Prince of Chu, you see it is this way. In my country we have a guiding principle about sending ambassadors abroad. We send a good man to a state with a good ruler. To a state with a bad and vulgar ruler we send a bad and vulgar ambassador. So, as I am the most useless and worthless man in all of Chi, I was sent to the court of the Prince of Chu."[67]

Japanese folklore is filled with the wishes of childless couples for children. "Little One-Inch" (199) or *Issun Boshi, the Inchling* (135) (as he is called in a picture-book version) was the answer to an old couple's prayer for a child even if he was as small as a thumb. When Inchling had grown older, but no larger, he announced that he was going to the capital to seek his fortune. Inchling arrived at the house of a great lord who hired him to be a companion for his beautiful daughter. Here he became a favorite, eventually defending the princess from three demons, and won the red demon's mallet, which allowed him

[67]Harold Courlander, *The Tiger's Whisker and Other Tales and Legends from Asia and the Pacific*, illustrated by Enrico Arno (New York: Harcourt Brace Jovanovich, 1959), p. 45.

to wish to be as tall as other men. He grew into a full-sized man, married the princess, and invited his old parents to come and live with them. The watercolors of this picture story book by Fuku Akino remind one of Japanese scrolls. Akino has also illustrated the story of *The Mud Snail Son* (155) by Lifton. This again is the tale of a childless couple who give birth to a tiny son in the form of a mud snail. In "Monotaro" (120) the hoped-for child comes floating down the river inside a peach! He grows to be a fine young man and at 15 is determined to go off to an island and destroy the demons who live there. Following the typical folk-tale pattern, he shares his food with three animals who join him in his quest and aid him in conquering the demons and the treasure that they had stolen. He returns home and shares his good fortune with the old couple who had been so kind to him.

The Crane Maiden (163) has been beautifully illustrated with glowing watercolors that portray a Japanese village in the snow. An old man thoughtfully frees a beautiful white crane from a trap. That evening a lovely young girl taps at his door and stays to help him and his wife. The couple are delighted and say that at last in their old age they have a daughter. Seeing how desperately poor they are, the young girl offers to weave a bolt of cloth for them, providing they promise that they will not look at her while she weaves. Eventually, the old woman grows so curious that she can't help herself and looks in. There she sees a great white crane pulling feathers from her body and weaving them. Once seen, the beautiful girl identifies herself as the crane the old man had rescued. Kissing the old man and woman good-bye, she walks out of the house and instantly becomes a crane and flies away. In another version of this story, titled "The Cloth of a Thousand Feathers" (10), the crane marries the woodcutter only to be discovered.

Yamaguchi's Japanese story, *The Golden Crane* (251), tells of Toshi, a deaf-and-dumb child who is befriended by an old fisherman. Each day golden cranes fly over the shore, but one is wounded. Toshi is able to speak as he defends the crane. On the day the bird is to be caged, there is a flash of golden wings and the bird, boy, and old man are borne away.

How the Withered Trees Blossomed (164) is an

intriguing folk tale bound and printed in the Japanese tradition with the story beginning on the back page and moving forward. Japanese script reads down the side of the page below the printed text. The story follows the familiar folk-tale pattern of animals and objects rewarding a kind couple, and producing nothing but trouble for the evil couple who borrow them. Children studying Japan would be fascinated with both the format and the story.

Arlene Mosel has retold the story of *The Funny Little Woman* (174) who spent most of her time laughing at the wicked *Oni* or demons who capture her in their underground cavern and make her cook for them. They give her a magic paddle that makes a potful of rice from one grain. After nearly a year has passed, the funny little lady steals their magic paddle and a boat and starts to escape. The *Oni* suck all the water into their mouths, which causes the woman to get stuck in the mud. Her giggling must have been contagious, because the *Oni* laugh at her and all the water flows back into the river. The funny little woman gets back to her house and then becomes the richest woman in Japan by making rice cakes with her magic paddle. Blair Lent won the Caldecott Award for his imaginative pictures of the funny little woman, the wicked green *Oni* in their underground cavern, and the detailed insets showing the little woman's house during the passing seasons.

Lent also illustrated *The Wave* (127) as retold by Margaret Hodges. He used intricate cardboard cuts in shades of brown and black to portray this story of the old man who sacrificed his own rice fields in order to warn the villagers of a coming tidal wave. Another version, told by Sara Cone Bryant, is illustrated with simple childlike pictures in bright colors. *The Wave* has a richness of language and a quiet dignity in both the text and illustrations that the more simplified version, *The Burning Rice Fields* (32), does not have. Children enjoy comparing these two interpretations, however.

Many Japanese tales are similar to European folk tales. "The Ogre Who Built a Bridge" (234) is a Rumpelstiltskin variant with a different task and reward. A river ogre agrees to build a bridge for a well-known carpenter. If he fails to guess the ogre's name, the carpenter must give him one of his eyeballs! Luckily the carpenter comes upon a group of ogre children who are singing about "Mr. Ogre Roku," so he successfully thwarts the river ogre. When he is named, the ogre disappears into the depths of the river.

Three Strong Women (219) by Claus Stamm is a Japanese tall tale that has some of the same characteristics as U.S. tall tales. Wrestlers have always been especially esteemed in Japan, so Forever-Mountain was more than a little conceited about his strength and ability, until he meets Maru-Me, her mother, and her grandmother, who were strong women and also wrestlers! The three months' training they give to Forever-Mountain enables him to win the emperor's match easily. In fact, he is so good that he promises never to wrestle again, but to become a farmer with Maru-Me for his wife. She is so delighted to see him return that she carries him halfway up the mountain. Then she giggles and puts him down, and lets him carry her the rest of the way! Claus Stamm has also told the humorous story of the cheat-and-change contest of *The Very Special Badgers* (220). The *Tanuki*, or magic badgers, are the tricksters of Japanese folklore who can change themselves into almost any form. This story of the contest to see who can best the powerful Bald Badger makes a delightful picture folk tale.

The folklore of Japan is more easily characterized than that from other parts of the Orient, perhaps because it has been more readily accessible to Westerners. Here we have stories of poor farmers, many childless couples who have their dreams fulfilled. Gentleness and kindness to others and to animals is rewarded. Respect for older persons and aged parents is a constant pattern in this folklore. Wicked *Oni* are pictured as blue, green, or red ogres, while the *Tengu* are long-nosed little creatures who are frequently tricked by the magic badgers, the change-artists of Japanese folklore. Beautiful picture-book versions of these magical tales are making them more widely available to a world audience.

Folk Tales from Africa

Today our children are the fortunate recipients of a rich bounty of folk tales that have been collected in Africa by such well-known present-day folklorists as Harold Courlander. Some collections, such as Heady's *When the Stones Were Soft* (122), have been greatly enriched by the lovely, mild pencil-gray pictures of Tom Feelings. Other single tales have been recognized for their outstanding illustrations. *A Story a Story* (112) by Gail Haley won the Caldecott Award in 1971; while both Gerald McDermott's brilliant graphics for *Anansi, the Spider* (157) and Blair Lent's distinguished illustrations for *Why the Sun and the Moon Live in the Sky* (154) by Dayrell made them Honor Books for their respective years.

Story-telling in Africa is a highly developed art, particularly in West Africa. These tales have a rhythm and cadence found in no other stories of the world. They ring of the oral tradition, and sound as if they are really being told. They are frequently written from the point of view of the story-teller, as in this tale of "How Spider Got a Thin Waist" (4):

> Many dry seasons ago, before the oldest man in our village can remember, before the rain and the dry and the rain and the dry that any of us can talk about to his children, Spider was a very big person. He did not look as he looks today, with his fat head and his fat body and his thin waist in between. Of course, he had two eyes and eight legs and he lived in a web. But none of him was thin. He was big and round, and his waistline was very fat indeed. Today, he is very different, as all of you know, and this is how it came to pass.[68]

Short sentences, frequent use of parallel constructions, repetition, and much dialogue characterize the style of many of the African tales. All these elements are apparent in the story of "Ticky-Picky Boom-Boom" (209), an Anansi story that came to us by way of Jamaica. One can almost hear the story-teller increasing his tempo as he tells of the foolish tiger who is chased by the yams that he had tried to dig out of Anansi's garden:

> Tiger began to run. The yams ran, too. Tiger began to gallop. The yams galloped, too. Tiger jumped. The yams jumped. Tiger made for Brother Dog's house as fast as he could, and he called out at the top of his voice,

"Oh, Brother Dog, Brother Dog, hide me from the yams."

Dog said, "All right, Tiger, hide behind me and don't say a word."

So Tiger hid behind Dog.

Down the road came the yams stamping on their two legs, three legs, four legs:

> "Ticky-Picky Boom-Boom
> Ticky-Picky Boom-Boom, Boof!"[69]

Many of the African tales are about personified animals, including those tricksters Anansi the spider, Zomo the rabbit, and Ijapa the tortoise. In one collection (63), recorded by a chief of Lower Nimba County, Liberia, Anansi is characterized in one brief sentence: "You see, Old-man Spider is a friend to any living thing, but the only obstacle about him is that one cannot depend on him."[70] Both Anansi and Zomo the rabbit are lazy characters who are continually tricking other animals into doing their work for them. In the story "Zomo Pays His Debts" (224), the rabbit is introduced to the reader in this way:

> Zomo The Rabbit is never a great one for work. He will tell you that he likes using his head, not his hands, but the truth is that unless he has to, he will not use either.[71]

Zomo became Br'er Rabbit in the black folklore of the United States when the Hausa peoples of Africa were captured as slaves. Ijapa the tortoise has survived in the black literature of the United States as Brother Terrapin. "Like Anansi, Ijapa is shrewd (sometimes even wise), conniving, greedy, indolent, unreliable, ambitious, exhibitionistic, unpredictable, aggressive, generally preposterous, and sometimes stupid"[72](48).

While all three of these tricksters—the spider, the hare, and the tortoise—have bad characters, one has to admire their ingenuity and wit. They

---

[68]Joyce Cooper Arkhurst, *The Adventures of Spider, West African Folk Tales* (Boston, Mass.: Little, Brown, 1964), p. 5.

[69]Philip M. Sherlock, *Anansi the Spider Man, Jamaican Folk Tales*, illustrated by Marcia Brown (New York: Crowell, 1954), p. 79.

[70]Peter G. Dorliae, *Animals Mourn for Da Leopard and Other West African Tales*, illustrated by S. Irein Wangboje (Indianapolis, Ind.: Bobbs-Merrill, 1970), p. 4.

[71]Hugh Sturton, *Zomo the Rabbit*, illustrated by Peter Warner (New York: Atheneum, 1966), p. 14.

[72]In "Notes on the Stories" by Harold Courlander and Ezekiel A. Eshugbayi, *Olode the Hunter and Other Tales from Nigeria* (New York: Harcourt Brace Jovanovich, 1968), p. 127.

are not always successful, and occasionally the tricksters are tricked by someone else. In "Anansi the Spider in Search of a Fool" (31) Anansi looks for someone to do all of his work for him. Anene the Crow agrees to go fishing with him and even volunteers his help in such a way that Anansi ends up doing the work:

> "Now let me make the fish traps," said Crow. "Yes, let me. I'll show you how. You can take the fatigue of my labors."
>
> Spider replied, "Anene, never! Everyone knows that I'm a great weaver. Leave the trap making to me. You take the fatigue."[73]

Many other African animal tales may be described as, "Why Stories," such as "Why the Lion, the Vulture, and the Hyena Do Not Live Together" (48), "Why Dogs Live With Men" (122), "Why Cats Live with Women" (122). The last story gives an interesting perspective on the esteem of women in Eastern Africa. The story tells of Paka the Cat who was very lonely and wanted to live with the strongest animal in the jungle. Each animal that he stays with fears another one until he at last decides to live with man, since even the cheetah is fearful of him. However, when man arrives home late for his supper, his wife is angry and won't let him come in. Paka decides that "Man is not the strongest creature. Woman is stronger. I will stay with her."[74]

A beautifully written and illustrated picture-book edition of an African tale is *The Third Gift* (34) by Jan Carew. It tells the story of how the Jubas, after learning of the gifts of work and beauty, learn of the most important gift that can be given to humans—the gift of imagination, fantasy, and faith. Leo Dillon and Diane Dillon have created brilliantly colored illustrations for this thought-provoking tale.

African folk tales are marked by a sophisticated and wry humor that delights in exposing the foibles of human nature. In a Nigerian story Seidu always boasted that he was "The Brave Man of Golo" (43). Therefore when some of the women were going to attend a funeral in another village, it was decided that Seidu should accompany them through the forest. Seeing some enemy warriors, Seidu and the women raced for the nearest trees. The warriors ridiculed him, and when he returned to his own village everyone there laughed at the courage of the great boaster. At last Seidu could stand it no longer and he sent his wife to tell them this:

> "Seidu who was formerly the bravest of men was reduced to being the bravest in his village. But from now on he is not the bravest in the village. He agrees to be only as brave as other people."[75]

Indecision is the theme of the humorous story of "The Man and the Mango Trees," one of the *Bantu Tales* (131) told by Virginia Holladay. In this story a man is unable to decide which fruit of two mango trees he should eat first. He asks a stranger, who tells him that the fruit on the right tree looks best. The man then cannot decide whether to eat the best fruit first or save it until last. While he ponders this question the ripened fruit falls to the ground and rots!

A play-on-words is another favored form of humor in some African tales. Courlander tells the story of the very wealthy man named Time (49). Change of fortune reduced him to a beggar and persons remarked that "Behold, Time isn't what it used to be!"[76] The same collection has a story about the young hunters who tried to capture "The One You Don't See Coming," which was their name for sleep. In another Anansi story, there is a character named Nothing. Anansi kills him and all the villagers "cry for nothing!" (49).

Frequently, an African tale will present a dilemma and then the storyteller will invite the audience to participate in suggesting the conclusion. In the story of "Three Sons of a Chief" (43), a chief decides to test the strength of each of his sons in a contest. One son throws his spear at a baobab tree and rides his horse through the hole; the second son jumps his horse over the tree; while the third son pulls the tree up and moves it over his head. The audience is asked to decide which is the greatest among them. The

[73] Ashley Bryan, *The Ox of the Wonderful Horns and Other African Folktales* (New York: Atheneum, 1971), pp. 6, 7.
[74] Eleanor B. Heady, *When the Stones Were Soft, East African Fireside Tales*, illustrations by Tom Feelings (New York: Funk & Wagnalls, 1968), p. 89.

[75] Harold Courlander, *The King's Drum and Other African Tales*. (New York: Harcourt Brace Jovanovich, 1962), p. 55.
[76] Harold Courlander and George Herzog, *The Cow-tail Switch and Other West African Stories* (New York: Holt, Rinehart and Winston, 1947), p. 77.

problem of which son should receive the famous Cow-tail Switch as a reward for finding their long lost father is asked in the title story of the book by Courlander (49). Lost for many years, the search is undertaken only after the youngest child learns to speak and asks for his father. Each of the sons has a special talent, which he uses to help restore his father to life. Then it is that the storyteller asks who should receive the father's cow-tail switch. In this instance the father decides in favor of the little boy who had been born while he was lost in the forest:

> The people of the village remembered then that the child's first words had been, "Where is my father?" They knew that Ogaloussa was right.
>
> For it was a saying among them that a man is not really dead until he is forgotten.[77]

Magical transformations are found in African folk tales also. Mama Semamingi tells the story of "Little Crow" (122) who was raised by a good woman who had no children. When Akakona the Crow was grown up he saw a beautiful maiden of a nearby village whom he wished to marry. He went to her father's hut and asked if he could see his daughter alone. There he circled the hut three times and turned into a handsome boy! Kakumba gladly accepted him for her husband.

A frog turns into a handsome man in one of the stories in the collection of *Black Fairy Tales* (16) by Berger. These tales were adapted from fairy tales collected from South Africa in 1908. While the stories have African settings, many of their motifs are common to European fairy tales. "The Serpent's Bride" is very similar to "Beauty and the Beast," except that the beast is a huge serpent, king of the waters. This book is dedicated to black children who had never read black fairy tales. Certainly the descriptions of the kings and princesses belong to the traditional fairy tale:

> At the sight of the green Kraal, the hopes of the ambassador rose. They soared even higher when the Princess came to the door to greet him, for there she stood, her blackness glistening from head and foot in the bright sunlight. Round her neck were thick bars of red-gold copper.[78]

Verna Aardema has retold ten short tales in her book *Behind the Back of the Mountain: Black Folktales from Southern Africa* (1). Some of these tales have a fairy-tale feeling, such as the Zulu story of the king's faithful daughter and the beast. Many of them are animal tales of trickery. Leo Dillon and Diane Dillon have created beautiful well-designed illustrations for this fine collection.

Nomi and the Magic Fish (166) is an African Cinderella story that would make for interesting comparisons with European stories. Based on a Zulu folk tale, it was written in English by a 15-year-old African girl. It tells of a second wife

Akakona the Crow selects the most beautiful woman of an East African tribe to be his wife. Tom Feelings' soft, penciled illustrations enhance this transformational tale.

From *When the Stones Were Soft* by Eleanor B. Heady. Illustrations Copyright © 1968 Tom Feelings, with permission of Funk & Wagnalls Publishing Company, Inc., Publisher.

[77]Harold Courlander, *The Cow-tail Switch*, p. 12.
[78]Terry Berger, *Black Fairy Tales*, illustrated by David Omar White (New York: Atheneum, 1969), p. 70.

who is cruel to her husand's beautiful tall daughter, Nomi. The wife dotes on her own child who is short and ugly. A magic fish comes to the aid of Nomi and saves her, even though the wicked stepmother has him killed. The fish instructs Nomi to hide his bones in the chief's garden. When no one is able to pick up the bones, the chief announces that he will marry any girl in the village who is able to remove the fish skeleton. Of course, only Nomi can do it.

Obviously, there is no dearth of folk literature from Africa. This is where the oral tradition has been maintained. Children in the United States who hear these tales will be able to enter another culture, another country, and listen to the rhythmical chord of the ancient storytellers. They will learn of a land where baobab trees grow and people fear crocodiles, leopards, droughts, and famines. More importantly, they will learn something about the wishes, dreams, hopes, humor, and the despair of other peoples. They may begin to see literature as the universal story of humankind.

Folk Tales in the United States

When the early settlers, immigrants, and slaves came to North America they brought their folk tales with them from England, Scotland, and Ireland; from Germany, Russia, and Scandinavia; from West Africa; and China. Children in the United States are the fortunate inheritors of the folklore of the world. As these stories were told over and over again, some of them took on an unmistakable North American flavor. For example, the "Brave Little Tailor" (149) became "Jack and the Varmints" (37) in a mountaineer variant of that popular folk tale. Many of the tales of Brer Rabbit in black folklore have Zomo, the rabbit trickster from West Africa, as their antecedent as we have seen.

The only folk tales that are indigenous to the United States are those which were already here; namely, the folklore of the American-Indian, and those marvelous tall tales which developed from the pioneer spirit of a young country. In discussing folk tales of the United States it is impossible to describe any one body of folklore such as the Grimms discovered in Germany, for example. The folklore of the United States can be placed into three large categories:

1. That which was here originally: American-Indian, Eskimo, and Hawaiian.
2. That which came from other countries and was changed in the process: Black folklore and European variants.
3. That which developed: Tall tales and other Americana.

FOLK TALES OF THE AMERICAN INDIAN

To try to characterize all the folklore of the various American-Indian tribes as one cohesive whole is as unreasonable as to lump all of the folklore of Europe together. For there is as great a diversity between the folk tales of the Indians of the Northwest Coast, as compared to the Eastern Woodland Indians, as there is between the fierce totem poles of the one group and the delicate beadwork of the other. There are, however, some common characteristics among the various tribes and between the folklore of the Indians and some of the Northern European tales.

Many of the Indian tales are a combination of tribal lore and religious beliefs. Quite properly, some of them should be categorized as mythology, for they include creation myths and sacred legends. As with the Greek and Roman mythology, some of these tales were told as separate stories out of context of the original creation tale. Because history does not give us complete information about the religious beliefs of the individual tribes, we have put all the tales together to form an amorphous body of Indian folklore.

The very act of storytelling was considered of ceremonial importance among various tribal groups. Storytelling was done at night, and among certain tribes, such as the Iroquois, it was only permitted in the winter. Men, women, and children listened reverently to stories, which in some instances were "owned" by certain tellers and could not be told by any other person. The sacred number of four is found in all Indian tales, rather than the pattern of three that is common to other folk tales. Four hairs may be pulled and offered to the four winds; or the ceremonial pipe will be smoked four times; or four quests must be made before a mission will be accomplished. The stories, when originally told, were loosely plotted rather than following the highly structured form of certain European fairy tales.

Thomas Leekley, who retold some of the stories of the Chippewa and Ottawa tribes in his book *The World of Manabozho* (153), says:

> Indian folklore is a great collection of anecdotes, jokes, and fables, and storytellers constantly combined and recombined these elements in different ways. We seldom find a plotted story of the kind we know. Instead, the interest is usually in a single episode; if this is linked to another, the relationship is that of two beads on one string, seldom that of two bricks in one building.[79]

Many of the Indian tales are nature myths—"how and why" animals have certain characteristics or explanations for natural phenomena. Belting's collection, *The Long-tailed Bear* (286), is a good source for such stories as "How the Birds Came to Have Many Colors," "How the Duck Got His Bill," and "How Frogs Lost Their Tails." The title story is similar to the Norse story of how the bear was tricked into using his tail for fishing in the ice where it became frozen tight. The Raskins have also included many of these nature myths in their book, *Indian Tales* (193). An explanation for the stars we call the Pleiades is given in Anne Rockwell's easy to read picture book, *The Dancing Stars, An Iroquois Legend* (197). The story of the contest of prowess between winter and spring was first recorded by Henry Rowe Schoolcraft in the 1800's, and has been edited by John Bierhorst in *The Fire Plume* (204).

The Cherokees were noted for their many animal tales. Some of them have a gentle humor that reminds one of the Brer Rabbit tales. In the story of "Why the Terrapin's Shell Is Scarred," the terrapin has been caught by the wolves. The wolves think of all the ways they can punish him and finally decide to throw him into the deepest hole in the river and drown him. The terrapin begs them not to do that, so of course they do, which is what he really wanted! When he is thrown in the river, he strikes a rock which breaks his back in a dozen places. He sings a medicine song:

"I have sewed myself together
I have sewed myself together"[80]

The pieces come together, but forever after the scars remain on his shell.

Almost all the folklore of the various tribes contain tales of animal tricksters. Rabbit is the trickster in the Cherokee tales, while Coyote plays that role among the tribes of the West, and the raven is the clever rogue in the tales of the Indians of the Northwest Coast. Interestingly, while both the coyote and the raven are mischief-makers, they are credited with stealing fire and giving it to the peoples of their tribes. *The Fire Bringer* (126) by Margaret Hodges has been effectively illustrated by Peter Parnall with clear line drawings and an economy of color. These pictures reflect the taut race of the coyote and the boy to snatch fire from the slopes of Burning Mountain. To this day, the legend says, coyote's fur is singed and yellow along the sides where the flames blew backward as he ran down the mountain carrying the burning brand. Hettie Jones has retold four *Coyote Tales* (140) in a collection by that name. These detail the coyote's uncanny ability to trick others—animals and humans alike. Frequently, however, his wily schemes backfire, which creates the humor in these stories. Louis Mofsie, a native American, has made the handsome black-and-white illustrations for these tales.

In the Glooscap stories one Indian was so troublesome that he came to be known as Badger, the Mischief Maker. Badger had one redeeming characteristic, his concern for his little brother. One winter Little Brother became ill, so Badger decided to steal the summer for him. The story of "The Year Summer Was Stolen" (123) tells of this escapade.

Manabozho was a kind of half-god, half-super-Indian among the Algonquian family of Indian tribes. He was a boasting trickster who could be cruel at times and thoughtful at other times. He could turn himself into all kinds of animal shapes, although his favorite disguise was that of a hare—Manabozho means "Great Hare."

---

[79]Thomas B. Leekley, *The World of Manabozho: Tales of the Chippewa Indians,* illustrated by Yeffe Kimball (New York: Vanguard, 1965), pp. 7–8.

[80]George F. Scheer, *Cherokee Animal Tales,* illustrated by Robert Frankenberg (New York: Holiday, 1968), p. 68.

He used this shape in order to steal fire from the old man and his two daughters who guarded it. Some of the stories of Manabozho picture him as less than a super-hero; in fact, the story of "Sleepy Feet" (153) is a real noodlehead tale. Waiting for some rabbits to roast, Manabozho put his feet in charge of watching them, while he went to sleep! A canoeload of Indians came by and quickly stole his dinner. Manabozho promptly punishes his feet by burning them, because they had failed in their duty to guard his dinner!

Indians personified all living things, giving personalities to the mysterious elements of the sun, the moon, the stars, thunder, lightning, rivers, and lakes. They characterized their animals and thought their strengths could enter man's form. It is not surprising, then, to find many tales of transformation in Indian folklore. *Longhouse Winter* (141) by Hettie Jones contains four Iroquois transformation tales. These are memorable for the style of writing and for the unusual tightly controlled geometric watercolor designs by Nicholas Gaetano. In one story Sky Holder, attempting to restore peace to his peoples, suggested they hold a dance so friendships could be renewed. But the spirit of the Evil-Minded one entered the wild dancers and caused them to beat to death a score of braves. They are branded as outcasts by Sky Holder and turned into rattlesnakes:

> Trembling, their faces in the dust, they felt the power of the Sky Holder. The very fibers of their bodies ripped, and they twisted in agony as their clothing grew fast to their skin and became scaly. Legs merged with the rattles where their feet had been, arms melted into their sides. Their tongues divided, their teeth fell out, sharp fangs pierced the bleeding gums, and now they were rattlesnakes, the Evil-Minded's children, despised and hated crawlers of the ground![81]

During the long winter nights, when the wind howled in from the wild North Pacific, the Indians had their great feasts or potlatches and

heard the exciting stories told in those excellent collections by Harris, *Once Upon a Totem* (114) and *Once More Upon a Totem* (113). One of their favorite tales was the story of "The Prince Who Was Taken Away by the Salmon" (113). This is a story which explores the mystery of the Pacific salmon, their disappearance and their return to the rivers of the West; it also explores many of the customs of the Indian tribes—the inheritance into the maternal tribe, the high expectations for a prince, the duties of slaves. This story reads more like fiction than a folk tale, as we understand the conflict between Yaloa and his mother who longs to have him take his place as chief of the killer whale family. But Yaloa, the lazy boy, has no "sea-power," until the day he catches the chief of all the salmon. The transformation of Yaloa's character is as sure as his final transformation into a salmon.

In the romantic story of *The Ring in the Prairie* (204), edited by Bierhorst, Waupee transforms himself into a mouse in order to catch the youngest of the twelve princesses who come down from the sky to dance on the prairie. The youngest daughter of the stars marries Waupee and seems content in his lodge with the addition of their baby boy. However, she still yearns for her sisters in the sky and so she fashions a basket large enough for her son and herself to return to the sky. Years later, following the instructions of her father, she returns for Waupee who is to bring back a feather, a paw, or a tail of every kind of bird and animal he kills while hunting. When Waupee presents his gift, each of the stars is allowed to select one. They then become that animal or bird. Waupee, his wife, and son select the feathers from a white hawk and together they descend to the earth. This story, originally recorded by Schoolcraft in the early 1800's, is illustrated in glowing colors by Leo Dillon and Diane Dillon. "The Red Swan" (204) is a complex, mysterious tale of transformation also recorded by Schoolcraft. This story was mentioned by Longfellow in *The Song of Hiawatha*.

Another complex quest story is that of the Tlingit Indians, *The Angry Moon* (218), retold by William Sleator and illustrated in full-color designs by Blair Lent. An Indian girl, Lapowinsa, who dared to laugh at the moon is spirited away

---

[81]Hettie Jones, adaptor, *Longhouse Winter: Iroquois Transformation Tales*, illustrated by Nicholas Gaetano (New York: Holt, Rinehart and Winston, 1972), unpaged.

and made his prisoner. Her friend, Lupan, shoots his arrows into the sky all that night. The arrows link into a ladder, which Lupan climbs into the sky country. An old grandmother gives him four gifts which enable him to impede the moon's chase as it races after Lupan and Lapowinsa. Gerald McDermott has created stunning yellow, orange, and brown graphic designs for the Pueblo Indian tale, *Arrow to the Sun* (158). This is another hero quest story in which a boy goes in search of his father, Lord of the Sun. An arrow-maker constructs a special arrow that shoots the boy to the Sun, where he then must undergo four trials to prove his kinship. Upon the successful completion of the trials he is filled with the power of the Sun and sent back to earth to bring the Sun's spirit to the world of men. McDermott received the 1975 Caldecott Award for his vibrant illustrations of this Indian tale.

These recent, well-written, carefully researched, attractive books should increase children's interest in the folklore of native Americans.

FOLK TALES OF THE ESKIMO

The Eskimo believed that the Raven created the world out of a snowball. In *Raven, Creator of the World* (170), Melzack has retold ten legends about Raven, a super-human being who could take the shape of a man or a bird. These are well-told, sometimes poignant tales of a creator who was lonely and could not become a part of the world he had made. Melzack, a Canadian psychologist, also collected ten Eskimo tales for *The Day Tuk Became a Hunter* (169). These are exciting stories, short and fine for story-telling. "The Witch" reminds one of Hansel and Gretel, as the Eskimo children also find a way to escape. And there is something of the Cinderella tale in the story about how the lovely but rejected Leealura wins the heart of Maleyato, the best hunter in the village. "Magic in the Carved Chests" appears in a collection of tales called *The Rescue of the Sun* (179) by Newell. It is a curious twist on the story of Pandora, who opened the box filled with the evils of the world. In this story a man and his son must guard two chests that have been in their family for years. A stranger arrives and opens the chests, which contained the magic of water and fire.

The theme of survival is a constant one in all the Indian and Eskimo tales. A powerful yet simple Eskimo tale (40) tells of Ana, a widow who goes to beg food from her brother-in-law. Instead of food her cruel sister-in-law fills her bag with three stones. Two strangers hear her tale and give her a tiny sealskin poke which, when she awakens, is filled with seal meat and blubber. And the amazing poke is always full! Glo Coalson has illustrated this fine single tale, *Three Stone*

In this Indian transformation tale Waupee becomes a mouse in order to catch the youngest daughter of the stars. The link between humans and nature is a prevailing element in American Indian tales.

From *The Ring in the Prairie* by John Bierhorst. Illustration, copyright © 1970 by Leo and Diane Dillon. Used with permission of The Dial Press.

Woman, with bold black sumi brush drawings that reflect its Eskimo origin.

Tikta Liktak (133), a legendary Eskimo hunter, is isolated when an ice pan broke away. In desperate hunger, he becomes obsessed with the idea that the island he reaches is his grave. He builds a coffin and climbs into it to die. The dreams of the past bring refreshment of spirit, and he wakens saying, "I will not die." Still living in the dream, he kills a seal, and gains the strength to survive and to finally find his way home. This is a dramatic tale of courage and triumph over nature. James Houston has written two other superb Eskimo legends, *The White Archer* (134) and *Akavak* (132). The White Archer seeks only vengeance, but he finally succumbs to the kindness and wisdom of Ittock and his wife. Akavak helps his grandfather survive on their long and difficult journey only to see him die at the end of the trip. These tales reveal the hardships and the difficulties which are the daily pattern of the Eskimo's life.

BLACK FOLKLORE IN THE UNITED STATES

When the slaves were brought to this country from Africa, they continued to tell many African tales, particularly the talking-beast tales. Some of these stories took on new layers of meaning about the relations between the slave and his or her owner. Richard Dorson has collected over a thousand black folk tales in the United States and classified them under such headings as "Animal and Bird" stories in his book, *American Negro Folktales.* Julius Lester has retold several of these tales for children in his book, *The Knee-high Man and Other Tales* (154), amusingly illustrated by Ralph Pinto. Some of these stories are about those favorite characters, Mr. Rabbit and Mr. Bear. Mr. Rabbit always gets the best of Mr. Bear, as in the story in which Mr. Rabbit volunteers to provide Mr. Bear with the answer to "What Is Trouble?" The story of "The Farmer and the Snake" is a realistic one of a farmer who helps a poor frozen snake and is bitten in return. The moral is a sad commentary on the nature of beast or man.

Joel Chandler Harris became interested in collecting the tales he heard black people tell in Georgia. He published these tales in 1880 under the title of the *Uncle Remus Stories.* The stories are transcribed in Harris' written interpretation of the dialect of the Southern Negro. Unless the dialect is simplified, these tales are almost impossible to tell, and even more difficult to understand. Margaret Wise Brown prepared the simplest version in her edition titled, *Brer Rabbit* (29). Rees selected three of his favorite Brer Rabbit stories and recreated them in rhyming verse in *Brer Rabbit and His Tricks* (194). He included "Brer Rabbit and the Tar Baby" in this first book. His second collection, titled *More of Brer Rabbit's Tricks* (195), includes "Fishing for Suckers," "Brer Fox Bags a Lesson," and "Brer Rabbit's Visit to Aunt Mammy Bammy." In this last funny tale Brer Rabbit goes to visit Aunt Mammy Bammy to have his confidence restored. When he finishes catching a rattlesnake for her, he feels pretty good about himself indeed!

Courlander also includes some of "Buh Rabbit's" stories in his collection of black folklore in the book *Terrapin's Pot of Sense* (46). He has preacher stories of outsmarting the devil, and some variants of European and African tales. "Sharing the Crops" is the old tops and bottoms motif found in many tales. In this one, the sharecropper gets the best of the plantation owner three years in a row by first choosing the bottoms of the crops and planting potatoes; then the tops and planting oats; and finally he agrees to take just the middle of the crops and plants corn! "Old Boss, John, and the Mule" is similar to "Talk" in Courlander's *Cow-tail Switch* (49), but much funnier somehow. John is frightened by his mule, who starts talking and saying he's going to tell the Boss how lazy John is and how badly he treats the mule. John runs home and says he is going to quit; he won't work with a talking mule. The boss goes out to get the mule and can't make him say a thing. He comes back and scolds John:

> "I'm pretty put out with you," Boss say and start on up to the house. Halfway there he shake his head, sayin', "Don't know what I'm goin' to do with that boy. Sure don't know."
>
> Right then his yellow dog speak up, saying, "Fire him, Boss. You got no choice."[82]

---

[82] Harold Courlander, *Terrapin's Pot of Sense*, illustrated by Elton Fax (New York: Holt, Rinehart and Winston, 1957), p. 89.

EUROPEAN VARIANTS IN THE UNITED STATES

Richard Chase collected and published *The Jack Tales* (37) and *Grandfather Tales* (36), which are American variations of old stories brought to this country by English, Irish, and Scottish settlers in the seventeenth and eighteenth centuries. They are as much a part of Americana as the Brer Rabbit stories. In some respects Jack is an equivalent figure to Brer Rabbit. He is a trickster hero who overcomes his opponent through quick wit and cunning rather than strength, as in the tall tales of the United States. All of these stories come from the mountain folk of the southern Appalachians. Cut off from the main stream of immigration and changing customs, these people preserved their stories and songs in the same way that they continue to weave the Tudor rose into their fabrics.

The Jack Tales represent a cycle of stories in which Jack is always the central figure. You'd expect to find him playing this role in "Jack in the Giant's Newground" and "Jack and the Bean Tree." However, he shows up again in "Jack and the Robbers," which is a variant of "The Bremen Town Musicians" (93). The delightful aspect of these tales is Jack's nonchalance about his exploits and the incongruous mixing of the mountaineer dialect with unicorns, kings, and swords. In the story of "Jack and the Varmints," Jack kills seven little blue butterflies with his paddle. He has the blacksmith make a sign on his belt with some beads. Pretty soon the King comes by on his horse and says "Hello" to Jack:

> "Howdy do, King."
>
> "What's all that writin' you got around ye, Jack? Turn around so's I can read it."
>
> The old King read off:
>
> 'STRONG-MAN-JACK
>
> KILLED SEVEN AT A WHACK'
>
> "You mean you've done killed seven at one lick, Jack? You must be gettin' to be an awful stout feller. I reckon you could do pretty nigh anything, couldn't ye?"
>
> "Well," says Jack, "I don't know, I've pulled a few tricks."[83]

Students would enjoy comparing these stories with the original versions. They might enjoy writing their own variants of a particular tale using a modern setting.

TALL TALES AND OTHER AMERICANA

Ask any visitor to the United States what he has seen and he is apt to laugh and reply that whatever it was, it was the "biggest in the world"—the longest hotdog, the highest building, the largest store, the hottest spot. This is the land of superlatives, "the best." While many countries have tall tales in their folklore, only the United States has developed such a number of huge legendary heroes. Perhaps the vast frontier made man seem so puny that he felt compelled to invent stories about superheroes. Whatever the reasons, North American tall tales contain a glorious mixture of the humor, the bravado, the pioneer spirit that was needed to tame a wilderness.

Of all the heroes only Johnny Appleseed was of a gentle, tame nature who lived to serve others. Such a person as Johnny Appleseed did exist, and his real name was John Chapman. Davy Crockett and Daniel Boone actually lived also, but stories about them have been embroidered or invented. They swagger, exaggerate, and play tricks, yet solve problems with good humor. Paul Bunyan was a huge lumberjack who bossed a big gang of lumbermen in the Northwoods of Michigan, Minnesota, and Wisconsin. Children will enjoy stories about his school problems, for: "Just to write his name Paul had to put five copy books one on top of the other, and even then the teacher would only see part of each letter and he would mark him wrong."[84](74) Paul's light lunch one day was "three sides of barbecued beef, half a wagon load of potatoes, carrots and a few other odds and ends."[85](198) One of the favorite stories about Paul is the popcorn blizzard that he created to help his men cross the hot desert plains on their way to California. When the heat made the corn so hot, it started to pop. Then the men thought it was a blizzard and made snowshoes, while the horses almost froze to death

[83]Richard Chase, *The Jack Tales*, illustrated by Berkeley Williams, Jr. (New York: Houghton Mifflin, 1943), p. 59.

[84]Roberta Strauss Feuerlecht, *The Legends of Paul Bunyan*, illustrated by Kurt Werth (New York: Macmillan, 1966), p. 17.
[85]Glen Rounds, *Ol' Paul, the Mighty Logger* (New York: Holiday, 1949), p. 28.

until the men put blankets on them! Only Babe the Blue Ox and Paul really knew what caused the blizzard.

What Paul Bunyan meant to the North, Pecos Bill (223) meant to the West. Bill was one of eighteen children, so his parents didn't miss him when he bounced off the wagon when crossing the Pecos River. Raised by a coyote, Bill finally went back to the ranch and became an amazing cowboy. He invented the lasso and taught the cowhands how to rope cattle. Later, he is credited with the idea of branding cattle and developing the round-up, the cowboy song, and many other uniquely Western customs. Old Stormalong (73) was a sailor whose size made life on a ship, on a ranch, or on a farm quite uncomfortable; but his adventures are exciting. A famous keelboatman who lived on the Mississippi was Mike Fink. In his words:

> I'm thunder and lightnin' and hurrycane all rolled into one! With a mite o' earthquake throwed in for good measure. I'm a Mississippi whirlpool! I'm a river snag! I'm half hoss and half alligator! I'm all that and a long chalk more! I can outrun, outjump, knock down and mud waller any man as wants to try me! Whoopee! Make way for the king of the keelboatmen![86](9)

Industry has its heroes, too. "Joe Magarac" (223) is a man of steel who came to Hunkietown. Magarac means Jackass, and Joe works like a mule and eats like a mule. He can stir molten iron with his arm, but when there is no more work to be done, he melts himself and becomes part of a new steel mill. "John Henry" (223) is a powerful black who swings his hammer mightily to build the transcontinental railroad. His contest with a steam drill is a dramatic story. Ezra Jack Keats used a picture-book format (142) to create huge, bold figures to tell of this legendary hero. We need more such attractive single editions of these North American tall tales.

Some excellent collections of these tall tales have been made by Malcolmson in *Yankee Doodle's Cousins* (160), Shapiro in *Heroes in American Folklore* (208), and Stoutenburg in *American Tall Tales* (223).

The chart, "Some American Tall-Tale Heroes," details some of the characteristics of eight of these legendary heroes, including their occupations and their unique childhoods. Other legendary heroes that could be researched and added to the chart might include Casey Jones, Febold Feboldson, Tony Beaver, and more.

Other North American folklore has been collected in *The Hodgepodge Book* (69) by Duncan Emrich. This includes riddles and jokes, proverbs, cumulative stories and songs—such as the favorite, "The Little Old Lady Who Swallowed a Fly"—and many more wise and witty bits of American folklore. Emrich has also compiled *The Nonsense Book of Riddles, Rhymes, Tongue Twisters, Puzzles and Jokes from American Folklore* (70). Carl Withers' *A World of Nonsense: Strange and Humorous Tales from Many Lands* (248) is an entertaining anthology of nonsense stories garnered from the folklore of many lands.

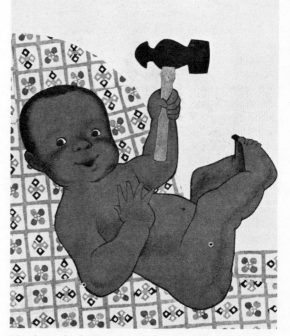

The legend of John Henry begins with his unusual strength as a baby. Large, bold colláges by Ezra Jack Keats depict the power of this hero.

From *John Henry*, by Ezra Jack Keats. Copyright © 1965 by Ezra Jack Keats. Reprinted by permission of Pantheon Books, a Division of Random House, Inc.

[86]Zachary Ball, *Young Mike Fink*, illustrated by Paul Lantz (New York: Holiday, 1958), p. 196.

Other Folk Tales

Obviously, it is impossible to discuss all the folk tales around the world in this chapter. Most of the Hawaiian folk tales more properly belong with Polynesian mythology, for they are tales of gods and demi-gods, such as the tall tale stories of Maui. *The Legs of the Moon* (136) by Jacobs is the warm appealing story of Paka, the smallest of the menehune (tiny red-bearded people) who volunteered to hold the legs of the moon so the light would last longer and enable all to escape a volcanic eruption. Woodcuts by Rocco Negri illustrate this fine picture-book version. *Kama Pua'a* (33) was an Hawaiian god who was born in the form of a boar. Known as a kupua, he could change his shape into a boy, a huge boar, a leaf, a fish. When he steals the king's prize rooster, it takes a whole tribe to subdue him. Kama Pua'a then becomes a huge eight-eyed, eight-legged monster and turns them all into stone. Bold, bright watercolors capture the beauty of the islands and the pride of the people in this book, which would be a fine story to use in the study of the state of Hawaii.

Not as many folk tales from Latin American countries have been published in the United States as from other cultures. Certainly, one should become acquainted with Courlander's *Ride with the Sun* (44) and Charles Finger's award-winning *Tales from Silver Lands* (75). The Puerto Rican tales collected by Pura Belpré in *The Tiger and the Rabbit* (15) are excellent for telling. And children thoroughly enjoy the picture-book version of two tales by Belpré illustrated by Galdone; *The Dance of the Animals* (12) and *Oté, A Puerto Rican Folk Tale* (13). Another favorite of Spanish-speaking children everywhere is the tale of the cockroach and the mouse, *Perez and Martina* (14), also by Belpré and illustrated by Carlos Sanchez.

No one can know every folk tale, but you can learn something about the values and characteristics of the folk tale form, you can begin to develop a list of *your* favorite tales, and you should realize that every country has its own special folklore. By immersing yourself in it, you can learn something of the values and beliefs of the culture. It is hoped that you'll discover what fun folk tales are and communicate this same enthusiasm to children.

Fables

ORIGIN OF FABLES

Fables are usually associated with the name Aesop, a Greek slave who is supposed to have been born in Asia Minor about 600 B.C. Some scholars doubt his actual existence and believe that his works were the product of several story-tellers. We know that some of the fables appeared in Greek literature two centuries before Aesop's birth, and in India and Egypt prior to that. The first written fables were in Greek, were translated into Latin, and again into English by William Caxton, and printed in 1484.

Another source for fables, as we have seen, was the *Jatakas,* animal stories that told of the previous births of the Buddha, and the *Panchatantra,* which was written for the purpose of instructing the young princes of India. These stories are far longer than Aesop's fables and had moralistic verses interspersed throughout. When these are removed, the tales are closer to folk tales, where they were discussed. One exception, however, is Marcia Brown's *Once a Mouse* (264), which is obviously a fable, with its implied moral on the pride of self. Beautifully illustrated with striking woodcuts, this fable from India received the Caldecott Award.

A third common source for fables is the work of La Fontaine, a French poet, who wrote his fables in verse form. However, he drew largely upon the collections of Aesop's fables that were available in the seventeenth century.

CHARACTERISTICS OF FABLES

Fables are brief, didactic tales in which animals, or occasionally the elements, speak as human beings. Examples of these might be the well-known race between "The Hare and the Tortoise" or the contest between "The Sun and the North Wind." Humans do appear in a few fables, such as "The Country Maid and the Milk Pail," or "The Boy Who Called Wolf." The characters are impersonal, with no name other than "fox," "rabbit," or "cow." They do not have the lively personalities of Anansi, the spider, or Kantjil, the mouse deer, of folk-tale fame. The animals are merely representative of different aspects of human nature—so that the lion stands for kingliness, the fox for cunning, the sheep for

SOME AMERICAN TALL-TALE HEROES

Name	Occupation	Locale	Characteristics	Childhood
Johnny Apple-seed (John Chapman) (1774–1845)	Wanderer, planter of apple trees	Pennsylvania, Ohio, Indiana	Selfless, gentle, a healer. Tame wolf as companion. Dressed in ragged clothes, with cooking pot for hat. Always carried apple seeds.	Loved apple trees and animals; could make things grow.
Pecos Bill	Cowboy	Texas, the Southwest	Normal size, great strength and daring (could hug a bear to death or ride a cyclone like a bronco). Clever—invented lasso, six-shooter, spurs, branding iron. Owned beautiful white mustang named Widow-Maker.	One of 18 children. As a baby drank mountain lion's milk; lost by his parents and raised by a pack of coyotes.
Paul Bunyan	Lumberman	North Woods	Of huge proportions, enormously strong, a good problem-solver. Pet—"Babe," a giant blue ox.	Dangerously strong, even as a baby—cradled in a boat at sea.
Davy Crockett (1786–1836)	Frontiersman	Tennessee	Tall, known for wide grin. Good hunter and soldier. Talked with animals, had many pets. Often battled nature, such as comets and cold weather. Tamed and rode a bear named "Death-Hug." Rifle named "Betsy."	Very tall. Good woodsman and hunter.
Mike Fink	Keelboatman	Ohio, Mississippi and Missouri Rivers	Loud and quick-tempered. Given to bragging. Expert marksman, good fighter. Rifle named "Bang-All."	Lived in the woods. Not big, but tough.
John Henry	Railroad man (hammerman)	The South	Huge black hero known for strength, great endurance, natural ability for steel-driving. Companion—Li'l Willie.	First thing he reached for as a baby was a hammer.
Joe Magarac (Jackass)	Steel worker	Pittsburgh ("Hunkietown")	Bigger than usual, made of steel. Works like a mule and eats like one. Could stir molten iron with his arm.	Born from an ore pit or a rolling mill.
Alfred Bulltop Stormalong	Sailor, whaler, ship's captain	Massachusetts, North East Coast	Huge in size and strength—5 fathoms tall. Prodigious appetite. Skillful and daring. Always needed a still-bigger ship. Made the White Cliffs of Dover with soap.	Born with oceanwater in his veins.

innocence and simplicity, and so on. Fables seldom have more than three characters, and the plots are usually based on a single incident. Primarily, fables were meant to instruct. Therefore, all of them contain either an implied or a stated moral.

Because of their brevity fables appear to be simple. However, they are conveying an abstract idea in relatively few words, and for that very reason are highly complex stories. In selecting fables, then, it is wise to look at both the quality of language and the illustrations. Compare the following two interpretations of the story of "The Ass in the Lion's Skin.":

> An Ass once found the skin of a dead lion. Putting it on, he frightened all the animals by strutting about without a sound. Only the clever fox was suspicious. In an attempt to frighten him, the Ass tried to roar. As soon as he heard the familiar bray, the fox laughed and said, "I, too, might have been alarmed if you had kept your mouth shut."
>
> *Clothes do not make the man*
> *Your talk gives you away.*[87](261)

James Reeves has added details and uses modern conversational style in telling his story of how a donkey used a lion's hide to frighten all the animals. Here is an example of Reeves' interpretation:

> So Reynard only laughed and ran right up to Donkey; he lifted the corner of Lion's skin and saw Donkey's dusty grey hair.
> "Good day, Your Majesty," said Reynard slyly. "I shouldn't be surprised to see a pair of long ears under that mane of yours. Why, what a donkey you are, to think you could frighten me! Whoever heard a lion bray like that?" And he ran off to tell all the other animals what a donkey Donkey was, and how silly they had been to be scared of him.
>
> *If you play a part you are not fitted for, you're sure*
> *to give yourself away.*[88](263)

Artzybasheff's collection is illustrated with superb woodcuts. While his stories are brief, the morals, or applications as he calls them, are pedantic and reminiscent of the earliest editions as seen in this one for "The Ass in the Lion's Skin":

> Application: They who assume a character that does not belong to them generally betray themselves by overacting it.[89](259)

VARIOUS EDITIONS OF FABLES

Unquestionably, the most popular collection of fables among children is the oversized book of *Aesop's Fables* edited by Untermeyer (261) and illustrated with large animal cartoon-figures who make comments about the stories. Thus, a talking dog usurps the manger and barks words of warning to a hungry cow, donkey, and ram. The animal bystanders who watch the tortoise win the race with the hare murmur such comments as "strange," or "I wouldn't have thought it possible." This is a witty, sophisticated edition of the fables which should delight 9- and 10-year-olds.

Older and more standard editions include the well-written Reeves one (263) and the beautifully illustrated Artzybasheff collection (259). Forty of the best-known fables have been retold by Anne Terry White and illustrated with handsome woodcuts by Helen Siegl (262). A reprint of a 1912 edition translated by Vernon Jones, illustrated by the well-known English artist, Arthur Rackham, has been recently made available (260). It is comprehensive, containing nearly 300 fables.

Richard Scarry has illustrated and adapted *The Fables of La Fontaine* (270) for younger children. The stories are very brief, while the pictures portray the large dressed-up animals in bright primary colors that we tend to associate with Scarry's work.

Paul Galdone's *Three Aesop Fox Fables* (268) include two stories in which the fox is outsmarted and one in which he triumphs. Galdone's bright-eyed fox provides the continuity for these three lively stories. Other single fables which Galdone has illustrated include *The Town*

---

[87]*Aesop's Fables,* selected and adapted by Louis Untermeyer, illustrated by Alice Provensen and Martin Provensen (New York: Golden Press, 1966), p. 32.

[88]*Fables from Aesop,* retold by James Reeves, illustrated by Maurice Wilson (New York: Walck, 1962), p. 24.

[89]*Aesop's Fables,* illustrated by Boris Artzybasheff (New York: Viking, 1933), p. 41.

Cartoon-figures and imaginative conversation extend the meanings of Aesop's fables. A dog in the manger prevents others from enjoying what he cannot eat.

Illustration from *Aesop's Fables*, illustrated by A. and M. Provensen. © 1965 by Western Publishing Company, Inc., reproduced by permission.

Mouse and the Country Mouse (269), *Androcles and the Lion* (266), and a Jataka tale, *The Monkey and the Crocodile* (267).

Brian Wildsmith's glowing colors and geometric patterns distinguish his illustrations for oversize books based on a single fable. *The Rich Man and the Shoemaker* (274), *The North Wind and the Sun* (273), and *The Lion and the Rat* (271) portray the characters in interesting designs. Squares, triangles, and trapezoids are repeated in the designs of clothing, towns, or houses. The rat in *The Lion and the Rat* fairly bristles. He is painted in grayed blues, greens, and browns with purple eyes and orange ears.

Various artists have interpreted the story of *The Miller, the Boy and the Donkey,* including a brilliant edition by Wildsmith (272). By way of contrast, Tomi Ungerer created humorous cartoonlike pictures for this fable adapted by Showalter and titled *The Donkey Ride* (278). Both pictures and text have extended this familiar tale

to make a very funny picture book. *Hee Haw* (277) by Ann McGovern also capitalizes on the comedy act of the miller and his son carrying their donkey in their attempt to please everyone.

Children in the middle grades might enjoy comparing different collections, as well as interpretations of single stories. In this way they could become more sensitive to the style and possible meanings of the stories, while appreciating various artistic interpretations. After reading such modern fables as Steig's *Amos and Boris* (279), Lionni's *Tico and the Golden Wings* (276) and *Frederick* (275), or John Ciardi's *John J. Plenty and Fiddler Dan* (265), they might want to try writing their own. By comparing Frederick and Fiddler Dan with the original fable of "The Ant and the Grasshopper," they could see that both Ciardi and Lionni were saying something significant about different kinds of work—namely, the place of the artist in our society. Such a discussion would help children understand the deeper layers of meaning that are inherent in the form of the fable.

Myths

THE NATURE OF MYTH

Mythology evolved as primitive man searched his imagination and related events to forces, as he sought explanation of the earth, sky, and human behavior. These explanations moved slowly through the stages of a concept of one power or force in human form, who controlled the phenomena of nature; to a complex system in which the god or goddess represented such virtues as wisdom, purity, or love; to a worshipping of the gods in organized fashion. Gods took the form of man and woman, but they were immortal and possessed supernatural powers.

Myths deal with human relationships with the gods, with the relationships of the gods among themselves, with the way people accept or fulfill their destiny, and with the struggle of people within and without themselves between good and evil forces. The myths are good stories, too, for they contain action, suspense, and basic conflicts. Usually, each story is short and can be enjoyed by itself, without deep knowledge of the general mythology.

TYPES OF MYTHS

Creation Myths

Every culture has a story about how the world began, how people were made, how the sun and the moon got in the sky. These are called creation myths, or origin myths; they give an explanation for the beginnings of things. Maria Leach has collected some sixty-two creation myths from around the world in her book, *The Beginning* (335). These range from the farmer's almanac that maintained the world began at nine o'clock on the morning of October 26, 4004 B.C. to the Haida Indian story that says Raven created man from a clam shell. Leach makes the point that it does not matter if the early explanations were not true.

"A wrong answer does not belittle the seeking for an answer."[90] Another book by Leach, which is more appropriate for children, is *How the People Sang the Mountains Up* (336). The title story of this book tells of the Apaches' belief in the power of song to make the mountains rise. Curry's book *Down from the Lonely Mountain* (300) relates a California Indian tale of Coyote's part in making the mountain ranges. Another good source for creation myths is the book by Fahs and Spoerl, *Beginnings: Earth Sky Life Death* (303). They include the stories of Adam and Eve; the Greek story of the creation of man by Prometheus; and the Norwegian tale of the giant cow who licked an ice block into the shape of a man called Buri, grandfather of Odin. In a creation story from *Hawaiian Myths of Earth, Sea, and Sky* (369) by Thompson, the God of Creation, Kane, tossed a calabash into the air to make sky. Pieces broke off to become sun, moon, and stars. Kane made man and later made woman from man's shadow. Betty Baker has retold the hauntingly beautiful creation myths of the Pima and Papago Indian tribes in a continuing narrative, *At the Center of the World* (283). Earth Magician was supposed to have created the world and man three different times while the Buzzard watched him. The first time no one died and soon there was nothing to eat. The second time the people were born old. The third time the people smoked, even the babies! Buzzard observed each creation and criticized it. Finally, Earth Magician tried once more, and Buzzard said: You're still making mistakes. . . . The lizards' legs are too short and the snakes have none at all."[91] But Earth Magician said he was tired and he stopped. This is an exciting well-written story that children in the middle grades would enjoy.

Nature Myths

The nature myths include stories that explain seasonal changes, animal characteristics, earth formation, constellations, and the movements of

---

[90]Maria Leach, *The Beginning: Creation Myths around the World,* illustrated by Jan Bell Fairservis (New York: Funk & Wagnalls, 1956), p. 21.

[91]Betty Baker, *At the Center of the World,* illustrated by Murray Tinkelman (New York: Macmillan, 1973), p. 5.

the sun and earth. Many Indian nature myths are appropriate for children in the primary grades. Belting's collections, *The Long-tailed Bear* (286) and *The Earth Is on a Fish's Back* (285), contain both nature and creation myths. The familiar story of Narcissus and Echo, as well as the less familiar one, "The Two Bears," appears in the book by Green titled *Tales the Muses Told* (319). The story of "The Two Bears" tells how the constellations of the Great Bear and the Little Bear were put in the sky. Dayrell's African story *Why the Sun and the Moon Live in the Sky* (54) is a fine example of a nature myth.

The Greek story of "Demeter and Persephone" explains the change of seasons. Hades, god of the underworld, carried Persephone off to his land to be his bride, and Demeter, her mother, who made plants grow, mourned for her daughter. When she learned of Persephone's fate, she asked Zeus to intercede, and it was granted that the girl might return if she had eaten nothing in Hades. Since she had eaten the seeds of a pomegranate, she was compelled to return for four months each year. Several beautiful picture-book interpretations of this story have been published. Ati Forberg has used mixed-media including finger-painting to create the artwork for *Persephone, Bringer of Spring* by Tomaino (370). Her dramatic pictures have the quality of an exquisite Greek vase—particularly the one that shows Persephone within the outline of a pomegranate tasting the four seeds that would bind her to Hades for four months of the year. Margaret Hodges has retold this story under the title *Persephone and the Springtime* (329). The illustrations by Stewart seem overly-romantic and old-fashioned in appearance. The text does not read as smoothly as the Tomaino one. Homer's "Hymn Number Two" celebrated the story of *Demeter and Persephone*. Translated into simple clear prose by Proddow (347), this book is distinguished by the fine illustrations of Barbara Cooney. Persephone is beautiful and desirable in her diaphanous dress. The size and grief of her mother, Demeter, is awesome. The settings are faithful in every detail to the Greek origin of this story. Children in the middle grades should have an opportunity to compare and contrast all three versions of this well-known nature myth.

Barbara Cooney's brilliant illustrations for the picture-book edition of *Demeter and Persephone* reflect the Greek style of art, architecture, and dress.

From *Demeter and Persephone,* translated and adapted by Penelope Proddow, illustrated by Barbara Cooney. Illustration copyright © 1972 by Barbara Cooney Porter.

Hero Myths

Another kind of myth does not attempt to explain anything at all. These are the hero myths that are found in many cultures. They differ from the epic in form and usually do not relate the entire life of the hero. Some hero tales come from the epic tradition, however. These hero myths have some of the same qualities as wonder stories, in that the hero will be given certain tasks or, in the case of Hercules, twelve labors, to accomplish. Frequently the gods intercede and help (or hinder) a particular favorite mortal. Monsters such as gorgons, hydreas, and chimaeras in the Greek stories are plentiful, but these provide the hero with his challenge. Characteristic of the hero role is that he accepts all dangerous assignments, accomplishing his quest or dying in one last glorious adventure.

One of the great Greek hero tales is the story of Perseus. The birth and life of Perseus follows the pattern of many heroes. Foretold that a grandson would kill him, Acrisius imprisoned his daughter so she would have no children. However, Zeus, the king of the gods, came to her in a shower of golden rain and a child was born from their union. Acrisius put mother and child in a wooden chest and pushed it into the sea. They were found by a fisherman who accepted the child as his son. When Perseus was but 15 he rashly promised the king of the island the head of the terrible gorgon, Medusa. Her hair was made of snakes, and anyone who looked upon her turned to stone. The goddess Athena gave Perseus her sword and shield, while Hermes lent him his winged sandals. After first going to the back of the North Wind to ask directions from the three hideous gray sisters, Perseus went to the island of the nymphs, and finally to the Gorgon's isle, where he succeeded in slaying her. He returned to the land of his birth, stopping on the way home to save the beautiful maiden, Andromeda, from a sea monster. He then became king, making Andromeda his queen. Margaret Hodges has retold this story in clear prose, while Charles Mikolaycak has provided dramatic pictures for the book, *The Gorgon's Head* (327). Ian Serrailler has given us a slightly longer but somehow more vivid retelling of this hero tale in his book of the same title (362).

In *The Other World* (328), Margaret Hodges has recounted some of the lesser-known tales of the Celts. She tells one of the stories about the epic hero, Cuchulain, in "The Champion of Ireland." Typical of the hero tale, Cuchulain exhibited great strength and skill at an early age, beating all others in games before he was 5, and wearing sword and armor at 7. In his early manhood he is described by a princess as the epitome of the hero. "His hair is black, his look draws love, his glance shoots fire, and the hero light gleams around him."[92] In this particular tale three chiefs

are vying for the title of champion of Ireland. They must fulfill tests set by the king and the great wizard. The final test is given by a stranger, who enters the camp looking for a man who will keep a certain promise. He asks to have his head cut off on the one provision that he can cut off the head of the man who did it the next day! All three chiefs agree, but are horrified when the headless body picks up his rolling head and walks away. Only Cuchulain has the courage to keep his promise and return. However, the ax cannot harm him, and he is acclaimed Champion of Ireland. This tale is similar to the well-loved story of "Gawaine and the Green Knight" (342) from the King Arthur legend.

Maui is a Polynesian hero who is a human with supernatural power. Because he was deformed when he was born, his mother cast him into Moana, the ocean. After he was cared for by the god of the sky, he returned to earth. Maui changes himself into a dove and seeks his parents in another world. To help the people get their work done, Maui snares the sun and exacts its promise to cross the sky more slowly. New Zealand was created from a giant fish caught by Maui, but it is mountainous because his brothers did not wait for him to give thanks to the gods. Stories of Maui are found in books by Hill (326), Colum (297), and Thompson (369).

GREEK MYTHOLOGY

The myths with which we are the most familiar are those of the Ancient Greeks which were collected by the poet Hesiod sometime during the eighth century B.C. The Roman versions of these myths were adapted by the poet, Ovid, during the first century B.C. in his well-known work, *Metamorphoses*. This has caused some confusion in that the Roman names for the gods are better known than the Greek, and yet the stories originated with the Greeks. However, the more recent versions of these myths are using Greek names. In working with children it is best to be consistent in your choice of names, or they will become confused. You might wish to reproduce the following chart for their reference.

Greek mythology is composed of many stories of gods and goddesses, heroes, and monsters.

---

[92] Margaret Hodges, *The Other World, Myths of the Celts*, illustrated by Eros Keith (New York: Farrar, Straus, 1973), pp. 21, 22.

SOME GODS AND GODDESSES OF GREEK AND ROMAN MYTHOLOGY

Greek	Roman	Title	Relationship
Zeus	Jupiter or Jove	Supreme Ruler, Lord of the Sky	
Poseidon	Neptune	God of the Sea	Brother of Zeus
Hades or Pluto	Dis	God of the Underworld	Brother of Zeus
Hestia	Vesta	Goddess of the Home and Hearth	Sister of Zeus
Hera	Juno	Goddess of Women and Marriage	Wife and sister of Zeus
Ares	Mars	God of War	Son of Zeus and Hera
Athena	Minerva	Goddess of Wisdom	Daughter of Zeus
Apollo	Apollo	God of Light and Truth, the Sun God	Son of Zeus and Leto
Aphrodite	Venus	Goddess of Love and Beauty	Daughter of Zeus, Wife of Hephaestus
Hermes	Mercury	Messenger of the Gods	Son of Zeus and Maia
Artemis	Diana	Goddess of the Moon and Hunt	Twin sister of Apollo
Hephaestus	Vulcan	God of Fire	Hera's son
Eros	Cupid	God of Love	Aphrodite's son (in some accounts)
Demeter	Ceres	Goddess of Corn	Daughter of Cronus and Rhea
Dionysus or Bacchus	Bacchus	God of Wine	Son of Zeus and Semele
Persephone	Proserpine	Maiden of Spring	Daughter of Demeter

The Greeks were the first to see their gods in their own image. As their culture became more sophisticated and complex, so, too, did their stories of the gods. These personified gods could do anything that humans could do, but on a much mightier scale. The gods, while immortal, freely entered into the lives of mortals, helping or hindering them depending upon their particular moods. Their strength was mighty and so was their wrath. Many of the myths are concerned with conflicts and the loves of the gods. Jealousy and the struggle for power among them often cause trouble for humans. Some of the stories of the loves and quarrels of the immortals, however, are inappropriate for children.

Greek mythology includes the creation story that Earth and Sky were the first gods. Their children were giant Cyclops and the Titans, one of whom was Cronus who drove his father away with a scythe (thus, the picture of Father Time). Cronus swallowed each of his children so they would not usurp his place, but his wife gave him a stone instead of her last child, Zeus. Of course, Zeus overthrew his father and made him disgorge his brothers and sisters, who were still alive. Zeus married Hera, a very jealous vindictive woman,

who caused all kinds of trouble. Prometheus was a Titan who defied the other gods in order to give man fire. Zeus then chained him to Mount Caucasus, where an eagle devoured his liver each day, but it was renewed each night. Zeus also sent Pandora, with her box of trouble, as a punishment for Prometheus and man. Told not to open the box, Pandora was so curious that she could not help herself. All the evils of the world came forth, and only hope remained in the box.

Children who have a good background in folk tales will find many of the same elements present in the myths. They will enjoy the story of King Midas, who foolishly wished that everything he touched would turn to gold. While Hawthorne's sentimental version (320) of this story emphasized the evilness of greed, earlier translations suggested that the sin of Midas was his continued defiance of the gods.

The gods could not tolerate human pride any better than defiance or arrogance, which the Greeks called *hubris,* a word we still use today. *Hubris* was always swiftly followed by Nemesis, the goddess of retribution. Arachne was transformed into a spider because of her *hubris.* She foolishly claimed to be a better weaver than the goddess Athena, who challenged her to a contest and won. Bellerophon tamed the mighty winged-horse, Pegasus, and together they slew the monster, Chimaera, defeated the Amazons in battle, and overcame many other dangers. As Bellerophon's fame spread, he grew proud and arrogant. One fatal day he decided to challenge the gods themselves. Springing on the back of Pegasus he shouted aloud that he would fly to Olympus, the home of the gods. This was too much for Zeus, who caused a gadfly to sting Pegasus and Bellerophon was thrown to his death far below. Krystyna Turska has given children a dramatic interpretation of this favorite story in picture-book format. Simply titled *Pegasus* (372), her glorious pictures of the winged horse capture the excitement of this tale.

Eight- and 9-year-olds delight in the story of *Daedalus and Icarus,* as told by Farmer and illustrated in a picture book by Connor (304). They are intrigued with the idea of the labyrinth designed by Daedalus to house the monstrous Minotaur. The ingenious escape from this maze, climaxed with the first flight of man, makes a fascinating tale. But as in the story of Bellerophon, Icarus became so enchanted with his own power that he flew too close to the sun and the wax of his wings melted and caused his downfall. Serraillier has written a slightly longer version of this story in *A Fall from the Sky* (361). Children would be interested in comparing the different methods of escape used in these two editions.

Another reckless boy was Phaëthon, son of the Sun-God, Hebris. Phaëthon's one consuming wish was permission to drive the sun chariot across the sky for a day. Reluctantly his father granted him this wish, and the results were disastrous. Pollack's poetic retelling of this story (346) describes the flight:

> The horses reared and pawed at the sky, fighting to get more slack. They snorted and neighed and whinnied and kicked, strong and wild and wanting their heads. . . . They climbed more sharply, resisting the driver. . . . Wider and wider the chariot swung, finally out of control.[93]

[93]Merrill Pollack, *Phaëthon,* illustrated by William Hofmann (Philadelphia, Pa.: Lippincott, 1966), pp. 46–47.

After children have been introduced to these exciting single myths, they will be ready for the longer hero tales of Perseus, the gorgon-slayer; Theseus, who killed the Minotaur; the many labors of Heracles; and the tale of the Argonauts' search for the golden fleece. Serraillier has provided us with fine well-written books about each of these heroes. *The Way of Danger* (364) chronicles the story of Theseus from the time that he was able to lift the rock at the foot of the olive tree, and discovered his own identity as the son of the King of Athens, to his dramatic rescue from Hades by his friend Heracles and the ultimate treachery of his murder. *Heracles the Strong* (363) is the amazing story of the persistence and accomplishments of the hero who is better known by his Roman name of Hercules. The story of Jason's quest for the golden fleece is told in the book *The Clashing Rocks* (360). All these retellings by Serraillier provide a continuous narrative of the hero. Written in short chapters, they would be excellent to read aloud to a group of middle-graders.

Benson's *Stories of the Gods and Heroes* (287) were derived from *The Age of Fable* (291) written by Thomas Bulfinch in 1855. Benson has kept the flavor of the older storytellers, but has presented the tales in very readable style. Conversation is used wisely to create interest. The indicated pronunciation of a word or name follows immediately in the text. Sellew's *Adventures with the Gods* (359) contains sixteen stories of gods and goddesses written in a simple and interesting style. The author includes a useful pronunciation guide. *Tales of the Greek Heroes* (318) by Roger Lancelyn Green is a somewhat more difficult but well-written retelling of these same myths.

Two books which are available in paperback employ modern vernacular in their retellings, *Heroes and Monsters of Greek Myth* (302) and *The Greek Gods* (301). The pace of the text and the language makes them appealing to today's child. For example, Procrustes was showing Perseus his remarkable six-foot bed into which he fitted everyone by the expedient method of either cutting off their feet or stretching them. He explains:

> "And I am a very neat, orderly person. I like things to fit. Now, if the guest is too short for the bed,

we attach those chains to his ankles and stretch him. Simple."

"And if he's too long?" said Theseus.

"Oh, well then we just lop off his legs to the proper length."

"I see."

"But don't worry about that part of it. You look like a stretch job to me. Go ahead, lie down."[94]

Robert Graves has utilized this same rather flippant approach to the myths in his book *Greek Gods and Heroes* (313). This style makes the stories seem very contemporary, but as the same time they lose part of their mystery and grandeur.

The Provensens' illustrations are outstanding features of two Golden Books, *The Golden Treasury of Myths and Legends* (375) by White and *The Iliad and the Odyssey* (373) by Watson. The design is excellent, and colors create the mood. A masklike quality of the faces painted in charcoal, gray, or brown is in keeping with the myths. There is no pronunciation guide, but the style is readable.

Another book which is memorable for the quality of the illustrations is the d'Aulaires' *Book of Greek Myths* (381). The beautiful, full-page colored lithographs convey the sense of power in the gods. The stories are very brief, and for the child or adult not well acquainted with the myths, this book can be overpowering, with too many names and episodes. It is best to share these handsome illustrations and short tales after reading a more completely plotted story, such as may be found in books by Benson, Sellew, or Serraillier.

Doris Gates has written a series of books featuring all of the stories related to one god or goddess. These provide a continuing theme and avoid the fragmentation of books that attempt to give a complete coverage of the myths. *Lord of the Sky, Zeus* (310) includes the lovely story of the poor couple, "Baucis and Philemon," who were willing to share all that they had with the stranger who stopped at their humble hut, never dreaming that he was Zeus. The longer stories of Theseus and Daedalus are well-written, as are the other books in the series: *The Warrior Goddess:*

[94]Bernard Evslin, Dorothy Evslin, and Ned Hoopes, *Heroes and Monsters of Greek Myth* (New York: Scholastic, 1970), p. 53.

Athena (312), *The Golden God: Apollo* (309), and *Two Queens of Heaven,* the story of Demeter and Aphrodite (311). These would be fine stories to read aloud to 10- to 12-year olds.

Finally, the most exciting books based upon the Greek myths are *The God Beneath the Sea* (307) and *The Golden Shadow* (308) by Leon Garfield and Edward Blishen. The first is a long continuous narrative that evokes an emotional response from the reader. We are captured on the first page with Hephaestus the "fiery shrieking baby . . . ," who falls from the sky into the sea and is cared for by the sea-goddesses Thetis and Eurynome. When they finally tell him about his origin, they in effect tell the reader too about the making of the gods. The characterizations are remarkably clear—Zeus the lusty patriarch of a huge, quarrelsome family; Hera his cruel and jealous wife; Hermes the lovable rogue. All of them assume a dimension not usually given in simple retellings. These are the gods the Greeks must have known, while we have had only the shells of their stories. Many of the episodes are beyond the maturity and experience of elementary-school children. The strange black-and-white illustrations are somewhat grotesque. *The Golden Shadow* is illustrated with startling black-and-white sketches by Charles Keeping. This is the recreation of the Greek legends around the sustained story of the mighty Heracles. It contains such traditional tales as the Calydonian Boar Hunt and the twelve labors of Heracles, including the frightening description of the killing of the many-headed hydra and the amusing account of the cleaning of the Augean Stables. Again, these are vital, sensuous, dramatic tellings that completely absorb the reader. These books would be appropriate at the junior high-school level and are strongly recommended for teachers to provide a new perspective on the Greek myths and legends.

NORSE MYTHOLOGY

A mythology derives its characteristics from the land and peoples of its origin. The land of the Norsemen was a cold, cruel land of frost, snow, and ice. Life was a continual struggle for survival against these elements. It seems only natural that Norse mythology was filled with

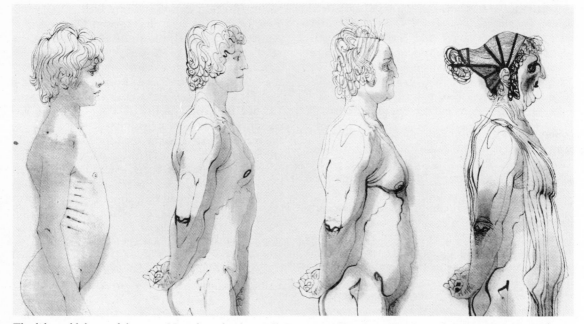

The life and labors of the great Heracles take their toll. Keepings' illustrations portray the sensuousness, violence, and despair of Greek mythology.

Copyright © 1973 by Charles Keeping. Reprinted from *The Golden Shadow*, by Leon Garfield and Edward Blishen, illustrated by Charles Keeping, by permission of Pantheon Books, a Division of Random House, Inc. © Leon Garfield and Edward Blishen, 1973. Illustrations © Charles Keeping, 1973. Reproduced by permission of Penguin Books Ltd.

gods who had to battle against huge frost giants also. These were heroic gods who, unlike the immortal Greek gods safe in their home on sunny Mount Olympus, knew that they and their home on Asgard would eventually be destroyed. And in a way their prophecy was fulfilled, for Christianity all but extinguished the talk of the old gods except in Iceland. There, in the thirteenth century, Snorri Sturluson—a poet, scholar and historian—collected many of the Norse myths and legends into a book called the *Prose Edda*. Much of his writing was based upon an earlier verse collection called the *Poetic Edda*. These two books are the primary sources for our knowledge of Norse mythology.

It is too bad that children do not know these myths as well as they know those of the Greeks. In some ways the Norse tales seem more suited to children than the highly sophisticated, gentle Greek tales. These stories appeal to the child's imagination, with their tales of giants and dwarfs,

eight-legged horses and vicious wolves, and magic hammers and rings. Primarily they are bold, powerful stories of the relationships among the gods and their battles against the evil frost giants. The Norse gods are heroic in nature. Odin is the serious protector of the men he created, willingly sacrificing one of his eyes to obtain wisdom that would allow him to see deep into the hearts of men. The largest and the strongest of the gods is Thor, owner of a magic hammer that will hit its mark and then return to his hands. And Balder, the tragic god of light, was the most loved by all the other gods.

Some of the stories are amusing. Seven- and 8-year-olds would enjoy the picture-book version of *The Hammer of Thunder* (348) retold by Ann Pyk. In this tale the enormous Thor is dressed as a bride and goes with Loki, who is his "bridesmaid," in order to trick the giant Thrym into returning Thor's magic hammer.

Another story tells of Thor's and Loki's contest with the giants, in which the gods were the losers. For the giants were able to out-drink them, out-run them, and out-wrestle them. Thor felt disgraced until the giant Utgard told him that they had been trying to drink the sea, to out-run "thought," and to wrestle with "old age," which no one can survive.

Loki is a puzzling character who seems a likeable mischief-maker in the beginning of the tales, but becomes increasingly evil. Finally, he is responsible for the death of Balder. He guides the hand of Hoder, Balder's blind brother, who shoots a fatal arrow made of mistletoe, the only object that could harm Balder. The gods enforce a cruel punishment on Loki that reminds one of the punishment of Prometheus.

The best collection of these myths remains *The Children of Odin* (295) by Colum. Hosford's *Thun-*

With his single eye flashing under his golden helmet, Odin, the all-father of Norse mythology, rides his great eight-legged horse into battle.

Illustration from *Norse Gods and Giants* by Ingri and Edgar Parin d'Aulaire. Copyright © 1967 by Ingri and Edgar Parin d'Aulaire. Reproduced by permission of Doubleday & Company, Inc.

der of the Gods (331) is easier to read and maintains a style in keeping with the serious themes of struggle. *Adventures with the Giants* (358) by Sellew is also a good source for simple yet dramatic retellings of fourteen of these tales.

The d'Aulaires have provided a continuous narrative of these stories, along with handsome lithographs, in their book, *Norse Gods and Giants* (282). Their retelling of these tales maintains the flavor of the original *Edda*. For example, the description of the making of a special bond to chain the fierce Fenris wolf reminds one of the Witches' Chant in Macbeth:

> [The gnomes] spell-caught the sound of cat paws, the breath of fish, the spittle of birds, the hairs of a woman's beard, the root of a mountain, and spun them around the sinews of a bear. That made a bond that looked as fine as a ribbon of silk, but since it was made of things not in this world, it was so strong nothing in the world could break it.[95]

Green has provided a more thorough treatment of these tales in his book *The Myths of the Norsemen* (316). For her long book, *In the Morning of Time* (333), Cynthia King has interwoven many of the myths with the central story of the Norse god, Balder. The theme of this well-written, long narrative runs throughout all the Norse myths, namely the tension between good and evil. Hoder identifies it as he considers the unknowing part he played in his brother's death:

> The blind god said, "Two brothers, two sides of a coin, good and evil, darkness and light, insight and innocence, that is all that any of us have been."[96]

OTHER MYTHOLOGIES

If children have time to become acquainted with only one mythology they should know the Greek stories (or their Roman adaptations). No other tales have so influenced the literature and art of the Western world. Norse mythology, too, has left its mark upon Western culture, as in the names for Wednesday (Odin's day) and Thurs-

[95]Ingri d'Aulaire and Edgar d'Aulaire, *Norse Gods and Giants* (Garden City, N.Y.: Doubleday, 1967), p. 52.
[96]Cynthia King, *In the Morning of Time*, illustrated by Charles Mikolaycak (New York: Four Winds, 1970), p. 136.

day (Thor's day). Also, these tales have a special appeal for children. However, there are many other important mythologies which may be sampled as a part of the study of a culture, or be simply enjoyed as literature.

Stories from other mythologies such as the Egyptian tale of "Isis and Osiris" or the Persian "Mithras" or the Mexican "Quetzalcoatl" might enrich the study of one of these countries. Roger Lancelyn Green has brought together some of these myths from earlier cultures in his *A Book of Myths* (315). The text and illustrations are distinguished in a later book by Green entitled, *Tales of Ancient Egypt* (317). Burland has made a fine collection of *North American Indian Mythology* (292). This is really an adult reference book, but the many excellent photographs of relics and paintings make it a good resource for children. *The Serpent and the Sun* (354) by Roy is a readable collection of myths from the Mexican world.

Epic Literature

QUALITIES OF EPICS

The epic is a long narrative or cycle of stories clustering around the actions of a single hero. It grew out of the myths or along with them, since the gods were still intervening in earlier epics such as the *Iliad* and the *Odyssey*. Gradually, the center of action shifted from the gods to a human hero, so that in such tales as Robin Hood the focus is completely upon the daring adventures of the man himself.

The epic hero is a cultural or national hero embodying all the ideal characteristics of greatness in his time. Thus, Odysseus and Penelope, his wife, represented the Greek ideals of intelligence, persistence, and resourcefulness. He was a man who survived by his wit rather than his great strength. Both King Arthur and Robin Hood appealed to the English love of justice and freedom; King Arthur and his knights represented the code of chivalry, while Robin Hood was the champion of the common man—the prototype of the "good outlaw." The epics, then, express the highest moral values of a society. A knowledge of the epics will give children an understanding of a particular culture; but, more importantly, it will provide them with models of greatness through the ages.

Many of the epics were originally written in poetic form, although a few, such as Malory's *Morte d'Arthur*, were in prose. Some, such as the story of Robin Hood, came from ballads. The translations used should keep the poetic rhythm, for the epics were sung in measured dignity with rich images and a suggestion of deep emotion. Such tales should not be rewritten in a "thin" style, nor should they omit the dangers, grim horrors, or weakness of humans. For even though the epic hero is a "larger than life" character, he is human and his humanity should show. Rewritten versions should communicate the excitement and the nobility that are characteristic of these great tales.

EPIC HEROES

Gilgamesh

The legend of Gilgamesh is believed to be the first story ever written. Even before the invention of writing, it is said to have been told or sung to the accompaniment of the harp. When cuneiform writing was first developed by the Sumerians, some three thousand years before the birth of Christ, the story of Gilgamesh was recorded on clay tablets. When the Sumerian civilization collapsed just before 2000 B.C., their writing and mythology was taken over by the Babylonians. Even though their cities disappeared, the story of Gilgamesh persisted.

This first known heroic epic tells of the mighty deeds of Gilgamesh, King of Uruk, his friendship with Enkidu, and his search to know the secret of life and death. Together Enkidu and Gilgamesh overcame the monster Humbaba and killed the Great Bull of Heaven. Incurring the wrath of the goddess Ishtar, Enkidu died. Then it was that the anguished Gilgamesh set out on his journeys that took him through the great caverns to the Eastern gardens, across the Bitter River to the underworld itself. He met at last with Enkidu, but he was not able to bring him back from the dead. In despair, Gilgamesh willed his own death so that he might rejoin his friend. Although Gilgamesh was mortal, his song and deeds lived for centuries, proclaiming him the true hero:

He who saw everything
He who knew everything,
He stood seven cubits high;
Two-thirds of him was god,
One-third of him was man.
He was the most glorious of heroes,
The most eminent of men,
And Enkidu was his companion.[97](290)

Bernarda Bryson's version of *Gilgamesh* is distinguished for its language and authentic watercolors suggested by the designs of the actual relics of the period. She has included a story of a great flood within the story of Gilgamesh that bears a striking resemblance to the Genesis story. Westwood has presented the flood story as a separate tale in her more difficult interpretation of *Gilgamesh and Other Babylonian Tales* (374). The easiest version of this epic is *He Who Saw Everything, The Epic of Gilgamesh* (305) by Anita Feagles. Handsome reproductions of plaster friezes and paper sculpture illustrate this text. Children studying ancient civilizations should know the legend of Gilgamesh. It is somehow gratifying to think that man's first story was based upon the theme of friendship.

The *Iliad* and the *Odyssey*

According to tradition, a blind minstrel named Homer composed the epic poems, the *Iliad* and the *Odyssey*, about 850 B.C.; but scholars generally believe that parts of the stories were sung by many persons and that they were woven into one long narrative before they were written. The *Iliad* is an account of the Trojan War fought by the Greeks over Helen, the most beautiful woman in the world. Paris, son of King Priam of Troy, had taken her away from the Greek king, Menelaus. After a siege of ten years, Agamemnon and Achilles, Greek leaders, quarrelled bitterly over the spoils of the war. The gods and goddesses had their favorites, and they, too, quarrelled among themselves as they witnessed the battles, almost as one would watch a football game! The complex story is long and difficult to understand, although specific incidents do intrigue some children. They particularly enjoy hearing about the final defeat of the Trojans by the cunning device

97Bernarda Bryson, *Gilgamesh: Man's First Story* (New York: Holt, Rinehart and Winston, 1967), p. 105.

Bernarda Bryson's illustrations for *Gilgamesh*, believed to be the first story ever written, were copied from decorations found on ancient relics.

From *Gilgamesh* written and illustrated by Bernarda Bryson. All rights reserved. Reproduced by permission of Holt, Rinehart and Winston, Inc.

of the Trojan Horse. Fortunately, James Reeves has retold this classic tale through the eyes of 10-year-old Illias (352). The first-person account gives vitality and excitement to the story, as do the dramatic pictures by Krystyna Turska. This picture-book version, simply titled *The Trojan Horse*, would acquaint children with the meanings of such expressions as "Beware of Greeks bringing gifts" and the Trojan Horse strategy of conquering an enemy from within. More importantly, however, this is a great story in a handsome new format, which children should have the opportunity to enjoy. *The Siege and Fall of Troy* (314) by Robert Graves gives the complete story of Troy, including one chapter on the return home of Odysseus. This account is written in modern contemporary language.

The *Odyssey* is the story of the hazardous ten-year journey of Odysseus, called Ulysses by the Romans, from Troy to his home in Ithaca, following the end of the war. Odysseus has one terrifying experience after another, which he manages to survive by his cunning. For example, he defeats the horrible one-eyed Cyclops by blinding him and then strapping his men to the undersides of sheep, which were allowed to leave the cave. No one has heard the song of the Sirens and lived, until Odysseus puts wax in his men's ears and has himself bound to the mast of his ship with strict orders to his men to ignore his pleas for release. His ship safely passes between the whirlpool of Charybdis and the monster, Scylla, but later is shipwrecked, and delayed for seven years. A loyal servant and his son aid the returned hero in assuming his rightful throne and saving his wife, Penelope. For Penelope herself has had a difficult time discouraging the many suitors who wish to become king. While children or teachers may be acquainted with episodes from the story, it is the total force of all his trials that presents the full dimensions of this hero.

The Iliad and the Odyssey (373) by Watson is enriched by the powerful illustrations of the Provensens. The modern text maintains the flow of action, but it does not recall the stately language of more traditional translations. A pronunciation guide is very helpful. Both of Barbara Picard's retellings, *The Odyssey of Homer Retold* (344) and *The Iliad of Homer* (343), are distinguished and give emphasis to development of characters. The two books written by Church in 1906 and 1907 have been combined and printed as *The Iliad and the Odyssey of Homer* (293). The style seems somewhat formal and includes such phrases as "You speak truly, fair lady." Padraic Colum's version, *The Children's Homer* (296), keeps the essence of the traditional poem and Pogany's illustrations distinguish this book.

King Arthur

Some historians believe there was a King Arthur who became famous around the sixth century. Defeated by the invading Saxons, his people fled to Wales and Brittany and told stories of his bravery and goodness. Other stories became attached to these, and the exploits of Tristram, Gawaine, and Lancelot were added to the Arthurian cycle. The religious element of the quest for the Holy Grail, the cup used by Christ at the Last Supper, was also added. Whether or not the chalice actually existed, it remains as a symbol of purity and love. In the fifteenth century Sir Thomas Malory's *Morte d'Arthur* was one of the first books printed in England and became a major source of later versions.

While many of the brave deeds of the knights were performed for the love of a fair lady, others, such as the intriguing tale of "Gawaine and the Green Knight," contain elements of mystery and wonder. These are noble tales and children delight in them. They are fascinated by the story

of "The Sword in the Stone," "How Arthur Gained Excalibur," and the puzzling "Passing of Arthur." Picard, in her book notes for *Hero Tales from the British Isles* (342), relates the old tradition that Arthur and his knights are not dead but sleeping in a cave, and that they will awaken and fight again when England has need of them. William Mayne utilized this legend in his eerie modern fantasy titled *Earthfasts* (see Chapter 5).

There are many fine collections and single tales of King Arthur. Two earlier editions are still popular: Sidney Lanier's *The Boy's King Arthur* (334) which first appeared in 1880, and Howard Pyle's *The Story of King Arthur and His Knights* (349). Picard's *Stories of King Arthur and His Knights* (345) includes the deceit of Guinivere. The style is stately and follows the old form. Told in simple, direct language, Jay Williams' *Sword of King Arthur* (376) is based on Malory, but is the easiest version to read of the legends of Arthur. MacLeod's distinguished retelling in *King Arthur and His Knights* (338) is also designed for easier reading. Several books relate single episodes of particular knights. The story of Gareth or Fairhands, one of King Arthur's court, is retold by Schiller in *The Kitchen Knight* (356). Placed in the kitchen, the boy volunteers to help a lady whose sister is besieged. She taunts the lad, but he overcomes the Indigo, Green, and Red Knights. Schiller has also retold the romantic tale of *Erec and Enid* (355). Constance Hieatt continues the story of Erec and Enid in her well-written *The Joy of the Court* (322). Following his marriage to Enid, Erec was quite content to stay at home with his lovely wife. Mocked by his fellow knights, however, Erec takes his wife on a hazardous journey that proves his courage and her loyalty. Hieatt has told a longer version of the story of the kitchen knight in her book *The Castle of Ladies* (321). The illustrations by Laliberté are drawn with white chalk on black paper in much the same fashion as children's art. *Sir Gawain and the Green Knight* (324), *The Knight of the Cart* (323), and *The Sword and the Grail* (325) are other single tales related by Constance Hieatt. *Sir Gawain and the Loathly Damsel* (371) by Troughton is a picture-book tale that has the same motif as the French fairy tale "Beauty and the Beast." In this instance, Sir Gawain must agree to marry a hideous woman in order to save the good King

Arthur. These short tales of single adventures will serve to introduce children to the tales of King Arthur.

The romantic *Tristan and Iseult* (368) which was added to the Arthurian cycle, has been beautifully retold by Rosemary Sutcliff. The language has a lyrical quality reminiscent of the old storytellers:

> It was young summer when they came to the hidden valley; and three times the hawthorn trees were rusted with berries and the hazelnuts fell into the stream. And three times winter came and they huddled about the fire in the smoky bothie and threw on logs from the wood-store outside. . . .[98]

Taliesin and King Arthur (353) by Ruth Robbins is extracted from Welsh legendry in the *Mabinogion* and tells of the experiences of a young Welsh poet, Taliesin, when he entered the contest of the bards on Christmas Eve day at King Arthur's court. Youngest of the poets, he wins the high honor of the day by singing the riddle of his birth. All of these books become a part of the magic mystique which surrounds the story of King Arthur. Children seldom discover these tales on their own, but once introduced to them, children delight in taking their place at that round table of adventure.

Robin Hood

Scholars have been unable to agree over whether there was indeed a medieval outlaw by the name of Robin Hood or whether he was really a mythical character derived from festival plays given in France at Whitsuntide. But by the fifteenth century Mayday celebrations in England were called "Robin Hood's Festivals," and the story of Robin Hood had become a legend for all time.

Children love this brave hero who lived in Sherwood Forest, outwitted the Sheriff of Nottingham, and shared his stolen goods with the poor. Others in the band were the huge Little John, Friar Tuck, the minstrel Alan-a-Dale, and Robin's sweetheart Maid Marian. According to one story, the king came in the disguise of a monk and shared their dinner and games. Con-

[98]Rosemary Sutcliff, *Tristan and Iseult* (New York: Dutton, 1971).

vinced of their loyalty to him, he granted them pardon. Some stories include Robin's death through the treachery of the false Prioress.

Howard Pyle's *Some Merry Adventures of Robin Hood* (350) is a shorter version of his classic, *The Merry Adventures of Robin Hood* (349). Ann McGovern has retold this familiar legend in clear, direct language. A few words, such as "perchance" and "thou," retain the spirit of the medieval language without making *Robin Hood of Sherwood Forest* (337) too difficult to read. McSpadden's *Robin Hood and His Merry Outlaws* (339) is also a simplified version. The lively illustrations of Slobodkin add appeal to this edition. Virginia Lee Burton spent three years making the scratchboard illustrations for *The Song of Robin Hood* (340) edited by Malcolmson and Castagnetta. Every verse of every song has its own small black-and-white etching similar to the illuminated manuscripts of medieval days. Large full-page illustrations with rhythmical design sweep the eye around a road to a castle, or around the cowled figures of men seated by an open fire, and then up with the swirls of the smoke. This is one of the most beautiful examples of bookmaking that we have. Surely it should be shared, along with every prose edition, for it somehow captures the spirit of that delightful adventurer, Robin Hood.

The Ramayana

The Ramayana is the great epic tale of India which tells how the noble Rama, his devoted brothers, and his beautiful virtuous wife Sita manage to defeat the evil demon, Ravana. Heir to the throne, Rama is banished from his home through the trickery of his stepmother. Prince Rama, his brother, and the devoted Sita spend fourteen years in wandering and adventure. One day Sita vanishes, kidnapped by Ravana. Rama searches for her unsuccessfully and then turns to a tribe of monkeys for their help. Finally Sita is found, and with the help of an entire army of monkeys, Rama rescues her. In order to be cleansed from her association with the demon, Sita must stand a trial by fire. Her faithfulness proved, she is united with her beloved Rama. Peace and plenty prevail during the reign of Rama.

Composed in India by the sage Valmiki during

Three years of care and dedication went into the superb scratchboard illustrations for *The Song of Robin Hood*. Virginia Lee Burton's distinctive art style is seen in these rhythmical illustrations, as well as in *The Little House* and her other picture books.

Illustration by Virginia Lee Burton from *The Song of Robin Hood* by Anne Malcolmson. Copyright 1947 by Anne Burnett Malcolmson and Virginia Lee Demetrios. Reprinted by permission of the publisher, Houghton Mifflin Company.

the fourth century B.C., the Ramayana represented some 24,000 couplets which were memorized and repeated. It constitutes part of the gospel of Hindu scripture, for Rama and his wife are held as the ideal man and woman. Rama is believed to be an incarnation of the god Vishnu come to earth in human form.

Elizabeth Seeger has created a prose version of *The Ramayana* (357) that reads smoothly as one long and exciting narrative. Joseph Gaer has told the story for children in *The Adventures of Rama* (306). Mukerji's version, *Rama, the Hero of India* (341), tells how the Hindus memorize these stories. Surely Western children should know something of this epic hero who is so important to a large part of the world.

Other Epics

Other epic heroes include the legend of the famed Irish warrior, Cuchulain. He earned the name of "Hound of Ulster" because he killed a ferocious guard dog with his bare hands when he was yet a boy. His strength increased when angered in battle, and a kind of insanity overcame him. Rosemary Sutcliff has woven the legends of this hero into a continuous narrative in a way that portrays the epic and tragic quality of *The Hound of Ulster* (367). Sutcliff has also written *The High Deeds of Finn MacCool* (366), another well-known Irish hero. In *Hero Tales from the British Isles* (342), Barbara Picard relates tales of these two heroes and others, such as the Welsh tale of "Bran, Son of Llyr."

On the European continent Roland was a French hero who served Charlemagne. "Chanson de Roland" dates from the eleventh century and includes the well-known tale of Roland blowing his enchanted horn so that Charlemagne, many miles distant, could come to his rescue. Baldwin has written *The Story of Roland* (284), while Sherwood (365) and Clark (294) have recorded this epic as *The Song of Roland*. Clark's version gives a fine description of medieval life.

Havelok the Dane (299) by Crossley-Holland is based upon a thirteenth-century Danish narrative. Havelok and his wife Goldborough both lose their kingdoms as children, but regain them through wit, courage, and strength. The story of Sigurd (Siegfried) was known both by the Norsemen and among Germanic groups. The Volsunga Saga tells of the many adventures of Sigurd, including the killing of the dragon, Fafnir. Padriac Colum includes the saga of Sigurd in *The Children of Odin* (295). It has been retold in both Hosford's *Sons of the Volsungs* (330) and in Coolidge's *Legends of the North* (298). The German epic, the *Nibelungenlied,* was taken from the Volsunga Saga, and it was upon this epic that Wagner based his four operas of the Ring cycle.

Backbone of the King, The Story of Pakaa and His Son Ku (289) is Marcia Brown's dramatic retelling of a legend of Hawaii about the faithfulness of a father and son who serve as chief guardians to the king. When the father is relieved of this responsibility, he carefully trains his son to avenge his enemies and take his place as the rightful "Backbone of the King." The many Hawaiian words and difficult chants suggest this is a book to read aloud. The inclusion of the chants has kept the story faithful to the original Polynesian legend.

An exciting addition to African literature for children is the legend of *Sundiata, The Epic of the Lion King* (288) retold by Roland Bertol. It is the magnificent tale of Sundiata, the twelfth son of a good king, who is scorned by most of the kingdom because he was born physically handicapped. But only Sundiata survives to defend his people, and indeed all Africa, from the evil Sumanguru, who has sold his soul to the devil (in this case, a dwarf). Sundiata grows to legendary strength and wisdom and in a climactic battle defeats Sumanguru. This is a brief, exciting tale that children would really enjoy. The language of the book is rich, and conveys the impression of being told aloud.

Gassire's Lute (332) is an epic poem from the Sudan of West Africa. A proud fighter, Gassire longs to carry his father's sword and shield into battle and become a hero who will be remembered forever. A wise man predicts he will bear a lute instead of arms and that his kingdom of Wagadu will fall. The prophecy is fulfilled as Gassire loses all but one of his sons in battle. He then becomes a bard, renouncing his noble birth. Through his vanity he has lost both his sons and his kingdom; only in song will he achieve greatness. The poetic form of this epic reminds one of chants. The language is cadenced and rhythmical. The final refrain for each of the verses could be recited in unison or played to the accompaniment of drums. *Gassire's Lute* has been illustrated with handsome woodcuts by the Dillons. Another version of this story has been told by Harold Courlander in *The Son of the Leopard* (45). In this tale the prophecy relates to one man alone, Wolde Nebri. Three times he attempts revenge upon his tribe for their abuse of him, and three times he fails. Through sorrow he at last finds his true identity as a singer of the joys of the world. No longer known as Wolde Negri, he is called Brother of the Harp. Both versions of this story could be shared, for each casts its light on the other and makes the legend more understandable.

The Bible as Literature

THE PLACE OF THE BIBLE IN LITERARY STUDY

The Bible has an important and rightful place in any comprehensive discussion of traditional literature. For the Bible is a written record of man's continuing search to understand himself and his relationships with others and his creator. It makes little sense to tell children the story of Jack the Giant Killer but to deny them the stories about David and Goliath or Samson. They read of the wanderings of Ulysses, but not those of Moses. They learn that Gilgamesh built an ark and survived a flood, but do not know the story of Noah. Our fear should not be that children will know the Bible; rather it should be that they will *not* know it. Whatever our religious persuasion or non-persuasion, children should not be denied their right to knowledge of the traditional literature of the Bible. For other literature cannot be fully understood unless children are familiar with the outstanding characters, incidents, poems, proverbs, and parables of this literature of the Western world of thought. It is time that we clarified the difference between the practice of religious customs and indoctrination of one viewpoint, and the study of the Bible as a great work of literature. In 1963 the Supreme Court asserted that "religious exercises" violated the First Amendment, but the Court also encouraged study of the Bible as literature:

In addition, it might well be said that one's education is not complete without a study of compara-

tive religion or the history of religion and its relationship to the advancement of Civilization. It certainly may be said that the Bible is worthy of study for its literary and historic qualities.[99]

The literary scholar, Northrop Frye, believes it essential to teach the Bible, for it presents humans in all their history. "It's the *myth* of the Bible that should be the basis of literary training, its imaginative survey of the human situation which is so broad and comprehensive that everything else finds its place inside it."[100] Some critics will be disturbed by the use of the term *myth* unless they understand its larger literary context as the human search for and expression of truth and meaning.

BOOKS FOR THE STUDY OF THE BIBLE

Collections of Bible Stories

When a school staff agrees that children should have an opportunity to hear or read some of the great stories from the Bible, it faces the task of selecting materials. Walter de la Mare's introduction to *Stories from the Bible* (389) provides an excellent background for understanding the problems of translation. He compares versions of the story of Ruth in the Geneva Bible (1560), the Douai Bible (1609), and the Authorized Version (1611). The old form of spelling is used in his quotations from Wycliffe of 1382, John Purvey of 1386, and Miles Coverdale of 1536. He clearly explains the differences between literal, allegorical, moral, and analogical meanings given words and phrases. This book presents the Creation; the flood; and stories of Moses, Joseph, Samson, Samuel, Saul, and David. The text combines modern style with imagery in description and a biblical form in conversation. For example: "As Joseph grew older, and in all that he was and did showed himself more and more unlike themselves, jealousy gnawed in their hearts like the fretting of a cankerworm."[101]

The text for *Brian Wildsmith's Illustrated Bible Stories* (401) was written by Philip Turner, a winner of the British Carnegie Medal for distin-

---

[99]Quoted by Betty D. Mayo, "The Bible in the Classroom," *The Christian Science Monitor* (September 30, 1966), p. 9.
[100]Northrop Frye, *The Educated Imagination* (Bloomington, Ind.: Indiana University Press, 1964), p. 111.
[101]Walter de la Mare, *Stories from the Bible*, illustrated by Edward Ardizzone (New York: Knopf, 1961), p. 62.

guished writing for children. The Bible story has been presented in chronological order as a consecutive narrative, including stories of both the Old and New Testaments. The writing has dignity and simplicity and Wildsmith's pictures illuminate every page. Alvin Tresselt (400) has retold twelve of the traditional stories from the Old Testament which Lynd Ward illustrated with handsome lithographs. The prose has retained the poetic quality of the Old Testament and at the same time has been artfully simplified. Marguerite de Angeli closely followed the text of the King James version in her edition of *The Old Testament* (388). Her soft, watercolor illustrations are superb, and the pencil character studies are especially fine.

Single Bible Stories

Many individual picture-book stories from the Bible are especially useful for sharing with children. Wynants has created fascinating textured collage illustrations for his *Noah's Ark* (405). Colored spreads alternate with black and white, while a brilliant rainbow forms the last endpaper. Helga Aichinger's full-color paintings for *Noah and the Rainbow* (385) have an exquisite simplicity of line that matches the fine retelling of this ancient story translated from the German by Clyde Bulla.

Bulla has also retold the story of *Jonah and the Great Fish* (386) and again Aichinger has created distinguished pictures of great simplicity. The all-blue great fish fills a double-page spread, while the sea seems to splash and swirl out of some of the pages. Margaret Gordon has interpreted this story with more stylized pictures, portraying her men similar to stiff figures on Assyrian bas-relief with textured beards and huge fat hands. Curling green waves encircle the poetic text by George MacBeth for this book titled *Jonah and the Lord* (397). A comparison of both the language of these texts and the art work would help children appreciate the various interpretations of the same tale.

Another attractive book is Galdone's *Shadrach, Meshach, and Abednego* (391). Nebuchadnezzar is pictured as a huge golden creature, and the figures of the other characters are powerful. Although the story is simplified, the author retains the rhythm of the chant and uses repetition effectively.

In *A Basket in the Reeds* (398) by Saporta, the illustrations are patterned after Egyptian wall paintings. The text includes a poetic description of the river as the basket floats in the reeds carrying the baby Moses. Children should be made aware of the way this author used his imagination to extend the brief account in the Bible. Clyde Bulla has provided a complete story of the life of *Joseph the Dreamer* (387), lavishly illustrated with watercolors by Gordon Laite. The *Story of Saul the King* (403) was first written by Helen Waddell in England and illustrated with colorful pictures by Doreen Roberts.

David and Goliath (390) by De Regniers is a very good retelling of the story of the youngest son going forth to meet the giant. The folk-tale pattern is used; for example, David passes certain tests before his father consents to his journey. The longer part of his life is concluded briefly, noting he fought battles, married the king's daughter, and took Saul's place as king. Brilliant oranges and pinks contrast with blue and green tones in the illustrations by Powers.

Lorenz Graham has retold five Bible stories in the idiomatic language of African-English, which he heard in Liberia. *David He No Fear* (392) is the well-loved story of David and Goliath, told in the following words and speech patterns:

> The Giant say
> "Ho! Small boy come to say how-do."
> David say
> "I come for fight."
> Giant say
> "Do you mommy know you out?"
> David say
> "Now I kill you!"
> Giant say
> "Go from my face less I eat you!"[102]

Ann Grifalconi's strong and powerful woodcuts are most appropriate for this story. The other books in the series are *God Wash the World and Start Again* (394), *A Road Down in the Sea* (396); and from the New Testament, *Every Man Heart Lay Down* (birth of Jesus) (393) and *Hongry Catch the Foolish Boy* (Prodigal Son) (395). These retellings provide an immediacy and simplicity to Bible stories for all children.

---

[102]Lorenz Graham, *David He No Fear*, illustrated by Ann Grifalconi (New York: Crowell, 1971), unpaged.

Then David see the giant.
He be high past ten men
He be strong same way
He got iron helmet on him head
And more iron on him front.
He walk about and laugh

Ann Grifalconi's bold woodcuts are most appropriate for this African retelling of the story of David and Goliath.

From *David He No Fear* by Lorenz Graham. Text Copyright 1946 by Lorenz Graham, illustrations Copyright © 1971 by Ann Grifalconi, with permission of Thomas Y. Crowell Company, Inc., publisher.

The story of *The Tower of Babel* (404) has been retold by William Wiesner in picture-book form. The richly designed illustrations are busy and full of details. The figures are flat and stiff as in Mesopotamian art, but they become very animated as their language is confused and they can no longer communicate with one another. This is very much a pourquoi story explaining the division of one people into many nations and languages. It is essentially a good story, but it would also be very useful in a unit on communication.

Isaac Bashevis Singer has vividly retold the Old Testament story of the destruction of Sodom in *The Wicked City* (399). The text is substantial, with a strong sense of story and the underlying layer of meaning for today's world. For example, when Abraham comes to visit Lot, neighbors talked:

"Why did Lot allow his crazy uncle to come here?" one of the bystanders asked. Others pelted Abraham and his two companions with the dung of asses.

"This is what happens when one admits stran-

gers," said another. "Sooner or later they bring foreigners with them."[103]

The scratchboard pictures by Fisher provide fine details of texture and facial expression.

The Christmas story has been retold in words and pictures many times. Everyone has his favorite telling, but certainly Piatti's *The Holy Night* (402) and Aichinger's *The Shepherd* (377) must be among the most beautiful. *The Christ Child* (380) illustrated by the Petershams has long been a favorite to share with children. *Baboushka and the Three Kings* (see Chapter 3), a Caldecott Award winner written by Robbins and illustrated by Sidjakov, tells the old story of the little Russian woman who was too busy cleaning her house to accompany the wise men and her subsequent search for the meaning of the star. The story of the three wise men has been portrayed in jewel-like colors in *They Followed the Star* (406) by Stepán Zavrel.

[103]Isaac Bashevis Singer, *The Wicked City*, translated by the author and Elizabeth Shub, illustrated by Leonard Everett Fisher (New York: Farrar, Straus, 1972), unpaged.

Three books illustrated by Tony Palazzo have presented poetry from the Bible in a way that would be meaningful for children. Animals and birds exhibiting natural behavior illustrate *The Lord Is My Shepherd* (381). A colt lies in a green pasture; as a happy rooster crows, his soul is restored; a squirrel finds a table prepared; a polar bear licks her cub, anointing it with love; and a dove promises hope. In *A Time for All Things* (382) a beaver at work illustrates "a time to break down, and a time to build up." A puppy at an empty swing experiences "a time to mourn." Animals are again used to illustrate verses from the Bible in *Wings of the Morning* (384). Some of Tasha Tudor's loveliest pictures illustrate a very

tiny book of *The Twenty Third Psalm* (383). This is a personal book for the child's own library.

In two related books about the Bible, *Words in Genesis* (379) and *Words from the Exodus* (378), Asimov shows how our modern language has been enriched by words derived from the Old Testament. As in his book, *Words from the Myths* (280), Asimov presents the story behind the words and our present-day use of them.

The Bible, the myths, the fables and folk tales represent the literature of the people down through the ages. Folk literature has deep roots in basic human feelings. Through this literature, children may form a link with the common bonds of humanity from the beginnings of time.

SUGGESTED LEARNING EXPERIENCES

1. Read as many folk tales and myths of one country as you can find. Assuming that these stories provided your only basis for understanding the country, what characteristics of the land and the people could you identify? Look for such things as food, climate, typical occupations, beliefs, and values.
2. Take one motif, such as transformations or a magical object, and see how many different tales you can find that utilize it.
3. Working with one type of folk tale, such as the trickster tales or simpleton stories, make an annotated bibliography of the stories that fall into that category.
4. Find as many different editions as you can of such well-known tales as "Cinderella," "Snow White," or "Puss in Boots." Compare both the language of the retellings and the illustrations.
5. Find as many variants as you can for a particular folk tale, such as "The Valiant Tailor" or "Puss in Boots." Bring them to class to share and compare.
6. Select one folk tale that you think you would like to learn to tell. Prepare it and tell it to four or five members of your class, or to a group of children. What suggestions do they have for improving your presentation?
7. Write a modern fable for such well-known morals as "Pride goeth before a fall" or "Don't count your chicks before they hatch." Use present-day objects, animals, or people.
8. Collect advertisements that show our use of words from the myths; for example, Atlas tires, Mercury cars, Ajax cleanser. Using the book *Words from the Myths* by Asimov determine the story behind the advertisement.
9. Make a list of titles or literary allusions of any literature that were derived from myth or scriptural writings.
10. On the basis of your knowledge of the characteristics of an epic, what do you think the hero of a North American epic might be like? Consider personal qualities, obstacles, achievements.
11. Develop a simple inventory of names from folk tales, fables, myths, and biblical characters. Give it to your class or ask to give it to a group of children. How well known is traditional literature today?

RELATED READINGS

1. Anderson, William, and Patrick Groff. *A New Look at Children's Literature.* Belmont, Calif.: Wadsworth Publishing Co., 1972.
   Chapter Two presents a scholarly analysis of mythology, folklore, and related forms.

2. Brean, Herbert, and the editors of *Life. The Life Treasury of American Folklore,* illustrated by James Lewicki. New York: Time, 1961.

   Picture maps would be of interest to children. Includes lesser-known American heroes and such unsavory characters as Jesse James.

3. Bulfinch, Thomas. *The Age of Fable or Beauties of Mythology.* New York: New American Library, 1962.

   This classical survey of mythology is presented in paperback. Notes and references are very helpful.

4. Carlson, Ruth Kearney, ed. *Folklore and Folktales around the World.* Newark, Del.: International Reading Association, 1972.

   This paperback contains all of the papers that were presented at a special conference on folklore held in conjunction with the International Reading Association Meeting. Teachers would find the article by Carlson on "World Understanding through the Folktale" and the article by Rosemary Weber on "The American Hero in American Children's Literature" particularly useful. This is a rich and easily obtainable resource.

5. Cook, Elizabeth. *The Ordinary and the Fabulous.* Cambridge, England: Cambridge University Press, 1969.

   A senior lecturer in English discusses myths, legends, and fairy tales for teachers and storytellers. A particularly helpful section is the author's critical analysis of the presentation of some scenes from myths and legends in various editions.

6. Frye, Northrop. *The Educated Imagination.* Bloomington, Ind.: Indiana University Press, 1964.

   A literary critic develops a theory of literature and presents a plan for literary study in the school that includes intensive study of the Bible and other traditional literature.

7. Garfield, Leon, and Edward Blishen. *The God Beneath the Sea,* illustrated by Zevi Blum. New York: Pantheon, 1971.

   These English authors have retold the Greek myths as one continuous narrative and in such a way as to make them live for today.

8. Hamilton, Edith. *Mythology,* illustrated by Steele Savage. Boston, Mass.: Little, Brown, 1944.

   The introduction summarizes the emergence of Greek ideas. Genealogical tables are helpful. A very readable source presenting Creation, Stories of Love and Adventure, and Heroes of the Trojan War.

9. Haviland, Virginia. *Children and Literature: Views and Reviews.* Glenview, Ill.: Scott, Foresman, 1973.

   Haviland, well-known for her many fine collections of fairy tales from around the world, has compiled an excellent book of readings on children's literature. Chapter 6 is devoted to folk literature and fantasy. The article by Chukovsky on "The Battle for the Fairy Tale" and the one by Buchan on "The Novel and the Fairy Tale" have particular relevance for this chapter.

10. McKendry, John J. *Aesop: Five Centuries of Illustrated Fables.* New York: Metropolitan Museum of Art, 1964.

    An excellent introduction that gives information about the origins of fables. A history of printing is illustrated with examples of work from Bewick to Calder.

11. McHargue, Georgess. *The Impossible People,* illustrated by Frank Bozzo. New York: Holt, Rinehart and Winston, 1972.

    Half in wit and half-serious, Georgess McHargue has made a compendium of all the impossible mythological beings. She also includes practical speculations as to their possible origin, noting that the activities of a Boggart sound precisely like the phenomenon of a poltergeist.

12. Ohrman, Richard, ed. *The Making of Myth.* New York: Putnam, 1962.

    Viewpoints of the anthropologist, psychologist, and folklorist are presented. Bruner's essay, "Myth and Identity," discusses myth-making today.

13. Thompson, Stith. *The Folktale.* New York: Holt, Rinehart and Winston, 1951.

    Various theories of the origins of folk tales and folk-tale themes are presented in a thorough manner in this book.

RECOMMENDED REFERENCES[104]

FOLK TALES

1. Aardema, Verna. *Behind the Back of the Mountain: Black Folktales from Southern Africa*, illustrated by Leo Dillon and Diane Dillon. Dial, 1973.
2. Anglund, Joan Walsh. *Nibble Nibble Mousekin: A Tale of Hansel and Gretel.* Harcourt Brace Jovanovich, 1962. (S—Germany)
3. Arbuthnot, May Hill, compiler. *The Arbuthnot Anthology of Children's Literature*, rev. ed. Scott, Foresman, 1961.
4. Arkhurst, Joyce Cooper. *The Adventures of Spider, West African Folk Tales*, illustrated by Jerry Pinkney. Little, Brown, 1964.
5. Asbjørnsen, Peter Christian, and Jorgen E. Moe. *East O' the Sun and West O' the Moon*, translated by George Webbe Dasent. Dover, 1970 (1888). (Norway)
6. ———. *East of the Sun and West of the Moon, and Other Tales*, illustrated by Tom Vroman. Macmillan, 1963. (Norway)
7. ———. *The Three Billy Goats Gruff*, illustrated by Marcia Brown. Harcourt Brace Jovanovich, 1957. (S—Norway)
8. d'Aulaire, Ingri, and Edgar d'Aulaire, editors and illustrators. *East of the Sun and West of the Moon.* Viking, 1969 (1938). (Norway)
9. Ball, Zachary. *Young Mike Fink*, illustrated by Paul Lantz. Holiday, 1958. (United States)
10. Bang, Garrett, translator and illustrator. *Men from the Village Deep in the Mountains and Other Japanese Folk Tales.* Macmillan, 1973.
11. Barker, W. H. and Cecelia Sinclair. *West African Folk-Tales*, illustrated by Cecelia Sinclair. Metro Books, 1972 (1917).
12. Belpré, Pura. *The Dance of the Animals: A Puerto Rican Folk Tale*, illustrated by Paul Galdone. Warne, 1972. (S)
13. ———. *Oté: A Puerto Rican Folk Tale*, illustrated by Paul Galdone. Pantheon, 1969. (S)
14. ———. *Perez and Martina*, rev. ed., illustrated by Carlos Sanchez. Warne, 1961. (S—Puerto Rico)
15. ———, ed. *The Tiger and the Rabbit and Other Tales*, illustrated by Tomie DePaola. Lippincott, 1965. (Puerto Rico)
16. Berger, Terry. *Black Fairy Tales*, illustrated by David Omar White. Atheneum, 1969. (Africa)
17. Berson, Harold. *Balarin's Goat.* Crown, 1972. (S—France)
18. ———. *How the Devil Gets His Due.* Crown, 1972. (S—France)
19. ———. *The Thief Who Hugged a Moonbeam.* Seabury, 1972. (S—France)
20. ———. *Why the Jackal Won't Speak to the Hedgehog.* Seabury, 1969. (S—Tunisia)
21. Bishop, Claire Huchet. *The Five Chinese Brothers*, illustrated by Kurt Wiese. Coward-McCann, 1938. (S)
22. Bogdanovic, Toma, illustrator. *The Fire Bird.* Scroll Press, 1972. (S—Russia)
23. Bro, Marguerite Harmon. *How the Mouse Deer Became King*, illustrated by Joseph Low. Doubleday, 1966. (Indonesia)
24. Brown, Marcia. *The Bun: A Tale from Russia.* Harcourt Brace Jovanovich, 1972. (S)
25. ———. *Dick Whittington and His Cat.* Scribner, 1950. (S—England)
26. ———. *The Flying Carpet.* Scribner, 1956. (S—Arabia)
27. ———. *The Neighbors.* Scribner, 1967. (S—Russia)
28. ———. *Stone Soup.* Scribner, 1947. (S—France)
29. Brown, Margaret Wise. *Brer Rabbit: Stories from Uncle Remus*, illustrated by A. B. Frost. Harper & Row, 1941. (Black American)
30. Brown, Roy. *Reynard the Fox*, illustrated by John Vernon Lord. Abelard-Schuman, 1969. (France)
31. Bryan, Ashley. *The Ox of the Wonderful Horns and Other African Folktales.* Atheneum, 1971.

[104]Single tales are identified with the code letter S. Where country of origin is not obviously indicated within the reference, it is supplied in parentheses at the end. All books listed at the end of this chapter are recommended, subject to the qualifications noted in the text. *See* Appendix D for publishers' complete addresses.

32. Bryant, Sara Cone. *The Burning Rice Fields,* illustrated by Mamoru Funai. Holt, Rinehart and Winston, 1963. (S—Japan)

33. Buffet, Guy, and Pam Buffet. *Kama Pua'a,* illustrated by Guy Buffet. Island Heritage, 1972. (S—Hawaii)

34. Carew, Jan. *The Third Gift,* illustrated by Leo Dillon and Diane Dillon. Little, Brown, 1974. (S—Africa)

35. Carpenter, Frances. *Tales of a Chinese Grandmother,* illustrated by Malthe Hasselriis. Doubleday, 1949.

36. Chase, Richard. *Grandfather Tales.* Houghton Mifflin, 1948. (United States)

37. ———. *The Jack Tales,* illustrated by Berkeley Williams, Jr. Houghton Mifflin, 1943. (United States)

38. Cimino, Maria. *The Disobedient Eels and Other Italian Tales,* illustrated by Claire Nivola. Pantheon, 1970.

39. Clarke, Mollie. *Silly Simon,* illustrated by Eccles. Follett, 1967. (S—England)

40. Coalson, Glo. *Three Stone Woman.* Atheneum, 1971. (S—Eskimo)

41. Colum, Padraic. *The Arabian Nights,* illustrated by Lynd Ward. Macmillan, 1953 (1923).

42. Conger, Lesley. *Tops and Bottoms,* illustrated by Imero Gobbato. Four Winds, 1970. (S—England)

43. Courlander, Harold. *The King's Drum and Other African Tales.* Harcourt Brace Jovanovich, 1962.

44. ———. *Ride with the Sun,* illustrated by Roger Duvoisin. McGraw-Hill, 1955. (International)

45. ———. *The Son of the Leopard,* illustrated by Rocco Negri. Crown, 1974. (S—Africa)

46. ———. *Terrapin's Pot of Sense,* illustrated by Elton Fax. Holt, Rinehart and Winston, 1957. (Black American)

47. ———. *The Tiger's Whisker and Other Tales and Legends from Asia and the Pacific,* illustrated by Enrico Arno. Harcourt Brace Jovanovich, 1959.

48. Courlander, Harold, and Ezekiel A. Eshugbayi. *Olode the Hunter and Other Tales from Nigeria.* Harcourt Brace Jovanovich, 1968.

49. Courlander, Harold, and George Herzog. *The Cow-tail Switch and Other West African Stories,* illustrated by Madye Lee Chastain. Holt, Rinehart and Winston, 1947.

50. Courlander, Harold, and Wolf Leslau. *The Fire on the Mountain and Other Ethiopian Stories,* illustrated by Robert W. Kane. Holt, Rinehart and Winston, 1950.

51. Curcija-Prodanovic, Nada. *Yugoslav Folk Tales,* illustrated by Joan Kiddell-Monroe. Oxford, 1957.

52. Daniels, Guy, translator. *Foma the Terrible,* illustrated by Imero Gobbato. Delacorte, 1970. (S—Russia)

53. David, Alfred, and Mary Elizabeth David, ed. *The Twelve Dancing Princesses and Other Fairy Tales.* New American Library, 1964.

54. Dayrell, Elphinstone. *Why the Sun and the Moon Live in the Sky,* illustrated by Blair Lent. Houghton Mifflin, 1968. (S—Africa)

55. De Angeli, Marguerite. *The Goose Girl.* Doubleday, 1964. (S—Germany)

56. De Beaumont, Marie Leprince. *Beauty and the Beast,* translated by Richard Howard, illustrated by Hilary Knight. Macmillan, 1963. (S—France)

57. De la Mare, Walter. *Tales Told Again,* illustrated by Alan Howard. Knopf, 1946 (1927).

58. De Regniers, Beatrice Schenk. *Red Riding Hood,* illustrated by Edward Gorey. Atheneum, 1972. (S—Germany)

59. Deutsch, Babette, and Avrahm Yarmolinsky. *More Tales of Faraway Folk.* Harper & Row, 1963.

60. Dobbs, Rose. *No Room, An Old Story Retold,* illustrated by Fritz Eichenberg. McKay, 1944. (S—Russia)

61. Domanska, Janina. *Little Red Hen.* Macmillan, 1973. (S—England)

62. ———. *The Turnip.* Macmillan, 1969. (S—Russia)

63. Dorliae, Peter G. *Animals Mourn for Da Leopard and Other West African Tales,* illustrated by S. Irein Wangboje. Bobbs-Merrill, 1970.

64. Downing, Charles. *Tales of the Hodja,* illustrated by William Papas. Walck, 1965. (Turkey)
65. Durham, Mae. *Tit for Tat and Other Latvian Folk Tales,* illustrated by Harriet Pincus. Harcourt Brace Jovanovich, 1967.
66. Duvoisin, Roger. *The Three Sneezes and Other Swiss Tales.* Knopf, 1941.
67. Elkin, Benjamin. *Six Foolish Fishermen,* illustrated by Katherine Evans. Children's Press, 1957. (S)
68. Elliot, Geraldine. *The Long Grass Whispers,* illustrated by Sheila Hawkins. Schocken Books, 1968. (Africa)
69. Emrich, Duncan. *The Hodgepodge Book: An Almanac of American Folklore,* illustrated by Ib Ohlsson. Four Winds, 1972.
70. ———. *The Nonsense Book of Riddles, Rhymes, Tongue Twisters, Puzzles and Jokes from American Folklore,* illustrated by Ib Ohlsson. Four Winds, 1970.
71. Evans, C. S. *Cinderella,* illustrated by Arthur Rackham. Viking, 1972 (1919). (S—France)
72. ———. *The Sleeping Beauty,* illustrated by Arthur Rackham. Viking, 1972 (1920). (S—France)
73. Felton, Harold W. *True Tall Tales of Stormalong: Sailor of the Seven Seas,* illustrated by Joan Sandin. Prentice-Hall, 1968. (United States)
74. Feuerlecht, Roberta Strauss. *The Legends of Paul Bunyan,* illustrated by Kurt Werth. Macmillan, 1966. (United States)
75. Finger, Charles, *Tales from Silver Lands,* illustrated by Paul Honoré. Doubleday, 1924. (Latin America)
76. Frasconi, Antonio. *The House that Jack Built.* Harcourt Brace Jovanovich, 1958 (S—England)
77. Gág, Wanda. *Gone Is Gone.* Coward McCann, 1935. (S—Norway)
78. Galdone, Paul. *Henny Penny.* Seabury, 1968. (S—England)
79. ———. *The Little Red Hen.* Seabury, 1973. (S—England)
80. ———. *The Old Woman and Her Pig.* McGraw-Hill, 1960. (S—England)
81. ———. *The Three Bears.* Seabury, 1972. (S—England)
82. ———. *The Three Billy Goats Gruff.* Seabury, 1973. (S—Norway)
83. ———. *The Three Little Pigs.* Seabury, 1970. (S—England)
84. ———. *The Three Wishes.* McGraw-Hill, 1961. (S—England)
85. Ginsburg, Mirra. *The Fox and the Hare,* illustrated by Victor Nolden. Crown, 1969. (S—Russia)
86. ———. *The Lazies: Tales of the Peoples of Russia.* Macmillan, 1973.
87. ———. *The Master of the Winds and Other Tales from Siberia.* Crown, 1970.
88. ———. *One Trick Too Many: Fox Stories from Russia,* illustrated by Helen Siegl. Dial, 1972.
89. ———. *Three Rolls and One Doughnut: Fables from Russia,* illustrated by Anita Lobel. Dial, 1970.
90. Gobhai, Mehlli. *Usha, the Mouse-Maiden.* Hawthorn, 1969. (S—India)
91. Godden, Rumer. *The Old Woman Who Lived in a Vinegar Bottle,* illustrated by Mairi Hedderwick. Viking, 1972. (S—England)
92. Grimm Brothers. *About Wise Men and Simpletons: Twelve Tales from Grimm,* translated by Elizabeth Shub, illustrated by Nonny Hogrogian. Macmillan, 1971.
93. ———. *Grimm's Fairy Tales,* introduction by Frances Clarke Sayers, illustrated by children of fifteen nations. Follett, 1968.
94. ———. *Hansel and Gretel,* illustrated by Arnold Lobel. Delacorte, 1971. (S)
95. ———. *Household Stories,* translated by Lucy Crane, illustrated by Walter Crane. McGraw-Hill, 1966 (1886).
96. ———. *Jorinda and Joringel,* translated by Elizabeth Shub, illustrated by Adrienne Adams. Scribner, 1968. (S)
97. ———. *The Juniper Tree and Other Tales from Grimm,* translated by Lore Segal and Maurice Sendak, illustrated by Maurice Sendak. Farrar, Straus, 1973.
98. ———. *King Grisly-Beard,* translated by Edgar Taylor, illustrated by Maurice Sendak. Farrar, Straus, 1973. (S)

99. ———. *King Thrushbeard*, illustrated by Felix Hoffmann. Harcourt Brace Jovanovich, 1970. (S)

100. ———. *Little Red Riding Hood*, illustrated by Harriet Pincus. Harcourt Brace Jovanovich, 1968. (S)

101. ———. *Mother Holly*, retold and illustrated by Bernadette Watts. Crowell, 1972. (S)

102. ———. *Rapunzel*, illustrated by Felix Hoffmann. Harcourt Brace Jovanovich, 1961. (S)

103. ———. *Rumpelstiltskin*, illustrated by William Stobbs. Walck, 1970. (S)

104. ———. *The Seven Ravens*, illustrated by Felix Hoffmann. Harcourt Brace Jovanovich, 1963. (S)

105. ———. *The Shoemaker and the Elves*, illustrated by Adrienne Adams. Scribner, 1960. (S)

106. ———. *Six Companions Find Their Fortune*, translated by Katya Sheppard, illustrated by Lilo Fromm. Doubleday, 1971. (S)

107. ———. *Snow-White and the Seven Dwarfs*, translated by Randall Jarrell, illustrated by Nancy Ekholm Burkert. Farrar, Straus, 1972. (S)

108. ———. *Tales from Grimm*, translated and illustrated by Wanda Gág. Coward-McCann, 1936.

109. ———. *Three Gay Tales from Grimm*, translated and illustrated by Wanda Gág. Coward-McCann, 1943.

110. ———. *Tom Thumb*, illustrated by Felix Hoffmann. Atheneum, 1973. (S)

111. ———. *The Traveling Musicians*, illustrated by Hans Fischer. Harcourt Brace Jovanovich, 1955. (S)

112. Haley, Gail E. *A Story a Story*. Atheneum, 1970. (S—Africa)

113. Harris, Christie. *Once More upon a Totem*, illustrated by Douglas Tait. Atheneum, 1973. (American-Indian)

114. ———. *Once Upon a Totem*, illustrated by John Frazer Mills. Atheneum, 1963. (American-Indian)

115. Harris, Joel Chandler. *The Complete Tales of Uncle Remus*, compiled by Richard Chase, illustrated by Arthur Frost and others. Houghton Mifflin, 1955. (Black American)

116. Haviland, Virginia. *Favorite Fairy Tales Told in Czechoslovakia*, illustrated by Trina Schart Hyman. Little, Brown, 1966.

117. ———. *Favorite Fairy Tales Told in France*, illustrated by Roger Duvoisin. Little, Brown, 1959.

118. ———. *Favorite Fairy Tales Told in India*, illustrated by Blair Lent. Little, Brown, 1973.

119. ———. *Favorite Fairy Tales Told in Italy*, illustrated by Evaline Ness. Little, Brown, 1965.

120. ———. *Favorite Fairy Tales Told in Japan*, illustrated by George Suyeoka. Little, Brown, 1967.

121. ———. *Favorite Fairy Tales Told in Norway*, illustrated by Leonard Weisgard. Little, Brown, 1961.

122. Heady, Eleanor B. *When the Stones Were Soft, East African Fireside Tales*, illustrated by Tom Feelings. Funk & Wagnalls, 1968.

123. Hill, Kay. *More Glooscap Stories: Legends of the Wabanaki Indians*, illustrated by John Hamberger. Dodd Mead, 1970.

124. Hodges, Elizabeth J. *Serendipity Tales*, illustrated by June A. Corwin. Atheneum, 1966. (Ceylon)

125. ———. *The Three Princes of Serendip*, illustrated by Joan Berg. Atheneum, 1964. (S—Ceylon)

126. Hodges, Margaret. *The Fire Bringer: A Paiute Indian Legend*, illustrated by Peter Parnall. Little, Brown, 1972. (S)

127. ———. *The Wave*, illustrated by Blair Lent. Houghton Mifflin, 1964. (S—Japan)

128. Hoge, Dorothy. *The Black Heart of Indri*, illustrated by Janina Domanska. Scribner, 1966. (S—China)

129. Hogrogian, Nonny. *One Fine Day*. Macmillan, 1971. (S—Armenian)

130. ———, illustrator. *The Renowned History of Little Red Riding Hood*. Crowell, 1967. (S—France)

131. Holladay, Virginia. *Bantu Tales,* edited by Louise Crane, illustrated by Rocco Negri. Viking, 1970. (Africa)

132. Houston, James. *Akavak: An Eskimo Journey.* Harcourt Brace Jovanovich, 1968. (S)

133. ———. *Tikta Liktak: An Eskimo Legend.* Harcourt Brace Jovanovich, 1965. (S)

134. ———. *The White Archer: An Eskimo Legend.* Harcourt Brace Jovanovich, 1967. (S)

135. Ishii, Momoko. *Issun Boshi, the Inchling: An Old Tale of Japan,* translated by Yone Mizuta, illustrated by Fuku Akino. Walker, 1967. (S)

136. Jacobs, Francine. *The Legs of the Moon,* illustrated by Rocco Negri. Coward-McCann, 1971. (S—Hawaii)

137. Jacobs, Joseph. *English Fairy Tales,* illustrated by John D. Batten, 3rd rev. ed. Putnam, n.d.

138. Jagendorf, Moritz A. *Noodlehead Stories from Around the World,* illustrated by Shane Miller. Vanguard, 1957.

139. Jameson, Cynthia. *The Clay Pot Boy,* illustrated by Arnold Lobel. Coward-McCann, 1973. (S—Russia)

140. Jones, Hettie. *Coyote Tales,* illustrated by Louis Mofsie. Holt, Rinehart and Winston, 1974. (American-Indian)

141. ———. *Longhouse Winter: Iroquois Transformation Tales,* illustrated by Nicholas Gaetano. Holt, Rinehart and Winston, 1972.

142. Keats, Ezra Jack. *John Henry, An American Legend.* Pantheon, 1965. (S)

143. Kelsey, Alice Geer. *How Many Donkeys?,* illustrated by Bob Binkley and Regina and Haig Shekerjian. Scott Foresman, 1971. (S—Turkey)

144. Kent, Jack. *The Fat Cat: A Danish Folktale.* Parents', 1971. (S)

145. Kirn, Ann. *Beeswax Catches a Thief.* Norton, 1968. (S—Africa)

146. ———. *Nine in a Line.* Norton, 1966. (S—Arabia)

147. Krueger, Kermit. *The Golden Swans: A Picture Story from Thailand,* illustrated by Ed Young. World, 1969. (S)

148. Lang, Andrew. *The Arabian Nights,* illustrated by Vera Bock. McKay, 1951.

149. ———. *The Blue Fairy Book,* illustrated by Reisie Lonette. Random House, 1959.

150. ———. *The Twelve Dancing Princesses,* illustrated by Adrienne Adams. Holt, Rinehart and Winston, 1966. (S—France)

151. Larson, Jean Russell. *Palace in Bagdad; Seven Tales from Arabia,* illustrated by Marianne Yamaguchi. Scribner, 1966.

152. Leach, Maria, *Noodles, Nitwits and Numbskulls,* illustrated by Kurt Werth. World, 1961.

153. Leekley, Thomas B. *The World of Manabozho: Tales of the Chippewa Indians,* illustrated by Yeffe Kimball. Vanguard, 1965.

154. Lester, Julius. *The Knee-high Man and Other Tales,* illustrated by Ralph Pinto. Dial, 1972. (Black American)

155. Lifton, Betty Jean. *The Mud Snail Son,* illustrated by Fuku Akino. Atheneum, 1971. (S—Japan)

156. Lines, Kathleen. *Dick Whittington,* illustrated by Edward Ardizzone. Walck, 1970. (S—England)

157. McDermott, Gerald. *Anansi the Spider.* Holt, Rinehart and Winston, 1972. (S—Africa)

158. ———. *Arrow to the Sun.* Viking, 1974. (S—American-Indian)

159. McKee, David. *The Man Who Was Going to Mind the House.* Abelard-Schuman, 1973. (S—Norway)

160. Malcolmson, Anne. *Yankee Doodle's Cousins,* illustrated by Robert McCloskey. Houghton Mifflin, 1941. (United States)

161. Manning-Sanders, Ruth. *A Book of Charms and Changelings,* illustrated by Robin Jacques. Dutton, 1972.

162. ———. *A Choice of Magic,* illustrated by Robin Jacques. Dutton, 1971.

163. Matsutani, Miyoko. *The Crane Maiden,* illustrated by Chihiro Iwasaki, English version by Alvin Tresselt. Parents', 1968. (S—Japan)

164. ———. *How the Withered Trees Blossomed,* illustrated by Yasuo Segawa. Lippincott, 1969. (S—Japan)

165. ———. *The Witch's Magic Cloth*, illustrated by Yasuo Segawa, English version by Alvin Tresselt. Parents', 1969. (S—Japan)

166. Mbane, Phumla. *Nomi and the Magic Fish*, illustrated by Carole Byard. Doubleday, 1972. (S—Africa)

167. Mehdevi, Alexander. *Bungling Pedro and Other Majorcan Tales*, illustrated by Isabel Bodor. Knopf, 1970.

168. Mehdevi, Anne Sinclair. *Persian Folk and Fairy Tales*, illustrated by Paul E. Kennedy. Knopf, 1965.

169. Melzack, Ronald. *The Day Tuk Became a Hunter and Other Eskimo Stories*, illustrated by Carol Jones. Dodd Mead, 1967.

170. ———. *Raven, Creator of the World*, illustrated by László Gál. Little, Brown, 1970. (Eskimo)

171. Merriam, Eve. *Epaminondas*, illustrated by Trina Schart Hyman. Follett, 1968. (S—United States)

172. Merrill, Jean. *The Superlative Horse*, illustrated by Ronni Solbert. W. R. Scott, 1961. (S—China)

173. Mohan, Beverly. *Punia and the King of the Sharks*, illustrated by Don Bolognese. Follett, 1964. (S—Hawaii)

174. Mosel, Arlene. *The Funny Little Woman*, illustrated by Blair Lent. Dutton, 1972. (S—Japan)

175. ———. *Tikki Tikki Tembo*, illustrated by Blair Lent. Holt, Rinehart and Winston, 1968. (S—China)

176. Ness, Evaline. *Long, Broad and Quickeye*, adapted from Andrew Lang. Scribner, 1969. (S—Bohemian)

177. ———. *Mr. Miacca: An English Folk Tale*. Holt, Rinehart and Winston, 1967. (S)

178. ———. *Tom Tit Tot*. Scribner, 1965. (S—England)

179. Newell, Edythe W. *The Rescue of the Sun, and Other Tales from the Far North*, illustrated by Franz Altschuler. A. Whitman, 1970.

180. Nic Leodhas, Sorche, pseud. (Leclaire Alger). *All in the Morning Early*, illustrated by Evaline Ness. Holt, Rinehart and Winston, 1963. (S—Scotland)

181. ———. *Gaelic Ghosts*, illustrated by Nonny Hogrogian. Holt, Rinehart and Winston, 1963.

182. ———. *Ghosts Go Haunting*, illustrated by Nonny Hogrogian. Holt, Rinehart and Winston, 1965.

183. ———. *Thistle and Thyme, Tales and Legends from Scotland*, illustrated by Evaline Ness. Holt, Rinehart and Winston, 1962.

184. ———. *Twelve Great Black Cats and Other Eerie Scottish Tales*, illustrated by Vera Bock. Dutton, 1971.

185. Pearce, Philippa. *Beauty and the Beast*, illustrated by Alan Barnett. Crowell, 1972. (S—France)

186. Perrault, Charles. *Cinderella*, illustrated by Marcia Brown. Scribner, 1954. (S—France)

187. ———. *The Little Red Riding Hood*, illustrated by William Stobbs. Walck, 1972. (S—France)

188. ———. *Puss in Boots*, illustrated by Marcia Brown. Scribner, 1952. (S—France)

189. ———. *Puss in Boots*, illustrated by Hans Fischer. Harcourt Brace Jovanovich, 1959. (S—France)

190. ———. *The Sleeping Beauty*, illustrated by Felix Hoffmann. Harcourt Brace Jovanovich, 1959. (S—France)

191. Provensen, Alice, and Martin Provensen. *The Provensen Book of Fairy Tales*. Random House, 1971.

192. Ransome, Arthur. *The Fool of the World and the Flying Ship*, illustrated by Uri Shulevitz. Farrar, Straus, 1968. (S—Russia)

193. Raskin, Joseph, and Edith Raskin. *Indian Tales*, illustrated by Helen Siegl. Random House, 1969. (American-Indian)

194. Rees, Ennis. *Brer Rabbit and His Tricks*, illustrated by Edward Gorey. Young Scott Books, 1967. (Black American)

195. ———. *More of Brer Rabbit's Tricks*, illustrated by Edward Gorey. Young Scott Books, 1968. (Black American)

196. Reyher, Becky. *My Mother Is the Most Beautiful Woman in the World*, illustrated by Ruth Gannett. Lothrop, 1945. (S—Russia)

197. Rockwell, Anne F. *The Dancing Stars, An Iroquois Legend.* Crowell, 1972. (S)

198. Rounds, Glen. *Ol' Paul, the Mighty Logger.* Holiday, 1949. (S—United States)

199. Sakade, Florence. *Little One-Inch and Other Japanese Children's Favorite Stories*, illustrated by Yoshisuke Kurosaki. Tuttle, 1958.

200. Sawyer, Ruth, *Journey Cake, Ho!,* illustrated by Robert McCloskey. Viking, 1953. (S)

201. Schatz, Letta. *The Extraordinary Tug-of-War*, illustrated by John Burningham. Follett, 1968. (S—Africa)

202. Scheer, George F. *Cherokee Animal Tales*, illustrated by Robert Frankenberg. Holiday, 1968.

203. Schiller, Barbara. *The White Rat's Tale*, illustrated by Adrienne Adams. Holt, Rinehart and Winston, 1967. (S—French)

204. Schoolcraft, Henry Rowe. *The Fire Plume: Legends of the American Indians*, edited by John Bierhorst, illustrated by Alan E. Cober. Dial, 1969.

205. ———. *The Ring in the Prairie: A Shawnee Legend*, edited by John Bierhorst, illustrated by Leo Dillon and Diane Dillon. Dial, 1970. (S)

206. Sekorová, Dagmar, compiler. *European Fairy Tales*, illustrated by Mirko Hanák. Lothrop, 1971.

207. Serwer, Blanche Luria. *Let's Steal the Moon*, illustrated by Trina Schart Hyman. Little, Brown, 1970. (Jewish)

208. Shapiro, Irwin. *Heroes in American Folklore*, illustrated by Donald McKay and James Daugherty. Messner, 1962.

209. Sherlock, Philip M. *Anansi the Spider Man, Jamaican Folk Tales*, illustrated by Marcia Brown. Crowell, 1954.

210. Shub, Elizabeth, adapter. *Clever Kate: Adapted from a Story by the Brothers Grimm*, illustrated by Anita Lobel. Macmillan, 1973. (S—Germany)

211. Shulevitz, Uri. *The Magician*, adapted from the Yiddish of I. L. Peretz. Macmillan, 1973. (S—Jewish)

212. ———, illustrator. *Soldier and Tsar in the Forest: A Russian Tale*, translated by Richard Lourie. Farrar, Straus, 1972. (S)

213. Singer, Isaac Bashevis. *Elijah the Slave*, translated by the author and Elizabeth Shub, illustrated by Antonio Frasconi. Farrar, Straus, 1970. (S—Jewish)

214. ———. *The Fools of Chelm and Their History*, illustrated by Uri Shulevitz. Farrar, Straus, 1973. (Jewish)

215. ———. *Mazel and Shlimazel, or the Milk of a Lioness*, illustrated by Margot Zemach. Farrar, Straus, 1967. (S—Jewish)

216. ———. *When Shlemiel Went to Warsaw and Other Stories*, translated by the author and Elizabeth Shub, illustrated by Margot Zemach. Farrar, Straus, 1968. (Jewish)

217. ———. *Zlateh, the Goat, and Other Stories*, translated by the author and Elizabeth Shub, illustrated by Maurice Sendak. Harper & Row, 1966. (Jewish)

218. Sleator, William. *The Angry Moon*, illustrated by Blair Lent. Little, Brown, 1970. (S—American-Indian)

219. Stamm, Claus. *Three Strong Women, A Tall Tale from Japan*, illustrated by Kazue Mizumura. Viking, 1962. (S)

220. ———. *The Very Special Badgers, A Tale of Magic from Japan*, illustrated by Kazue Mizumura. Viking, 1960. (S)

221. Steel, Flora Annie. *English Fairy Tales*, illustrated by Arthur Rackham. Macmillan, 1962 (1918).

222. Stobbs, William. *Johnny-Cake.* New York: Viking, 1973. (S)

223. Stoutenberg, Adrien. *American Tall Tales*, illustrated by Richard M. Powers. Viking, 1966.

224. Sturton, Hugh. *Zomo the Rabbit*, illustrated by Peter Warner. Atheneum, 1966. (Africa)

225. Suhl, Yuri. *Simon Boom Gives a Wedding,* illustrated by Margot Zemach. Four Winds, 1972. (S—Jewish)

226. Tashjian, Virginia. *Once There Was and Was Not, Armenian Tales Retold,* illustrated by Nonny Hogrogian. Little, Brown, 1966.

227. ———. *Three Apples Fell from Heaven, Armenian Tales Retold,* illustrated by Nonny Hogrogian. Little, Brown, 1971.

228. Taylor, Mark. *The Fisherman and the Goblet,* illustrated by Taro Yashima. Golden Gate, 1971. (S—Vietnam)

229. Titus, Eve. *The Two Stonecutters,* illustrated by Yoko Mitsuhasi. Doubleday, 1967. (S—Japan)

230. Tolstoy, Alexei. *The Great Big Enormous Turnip,* illustrated by Helen Oxenbury. F. Watts, 1969. (S—Russia)

231. Tresselt, Alvin, and Nancy Cleaver. *The Legend of the Willow Plate,* illustrated by Joseph Low. Parents', 1968. (S—China)

232. Turska, Krystyna. *The Woodcutter's Duck.* Macmillan, 1973. (S—Poland)

233. Uchida, Yoshiko. *The Dancing Kettle and Other Japanese Folk Tales,* illustrated by Richard C. Jones. Harcourt Brace Jovanovich, 1949.

234. ———. *The Sea of Gold and Other Tales from Japan,* illustrated by Marianne Yamaguchi. Scribner, 1965.

235. Upadhyay, Asha. *Tales from India,* illustrated by Nickzad Nodjoumi. Random House, 1971.

236. Walker, Barbara K. *Hilili and Dilili,* illustrated by William Barss. Follett, 1965. (S—Turkey)

237. ———. *Just Say Hic!,* illustrated by Don Bolognese. Follett, 1965. (S—Turkey)

238. ———. *Watermelons, Walnuts and the Wisdom of Allah and Other Tales of the Hoca,* illustrated by Harold Berson. Parents', 1967. (Turkey)

239. Wheeler, Post. *Russian Wonder Tales,* illustrated by Bilibin. A. S. Barnes, 1957.

240. Whitney, Thomas P., translator. *In a Certain Kingdom,* illustrated by Dieter Lange. Macmillan, 1972. (Russia)

241. ———. *The Story of Prince Ivan, the Firebird and the Gray Wolf,* illustrated by Nonny Hogrogian. Scribner, 1968. (S—Russia)

242. ———. *Vasilisa the Beautiful,* illustrated by Nonny Hogrogian. Macmillan, 1970. (S—Russia)

243. Wiesner, William. *Happy-Go-Lucky.* Seabury, 1970. (S—Norway)

244. ———. *Turnabout.* Seabury, 1972. (S—Norway)

245. Williams, Jay. *Seven at One Blow,* illustrated by Friso Henstra. Parents', 1972. (S)

246. Wilson, Barbara Ker. *Scottish Folk-tales and Legends,* illustrated by Joan Kiddell-Monroe. Walck, 1954.

247. Withers, Carl. *I Saw a Rocket Walk a Mile,* illustrated by John E. Johnson. Holt, Rinehart and Winston, 1965.

248. ———. *A World of Nonsense: Strange and Humorous Tales from Many Lands,* illustrated by John E. Johnson. Holt, Rinehart and Winston, 1968.

249. Wolkstein, Diane. *8,000 Stones: A Chinese Folktale,* illustrated by Ed Young. Doubleday, 1972. (S)

250. Wyndham, Lee. *Tales the People Tell in Russia,* illustrated by Andrew Antal. Messner, 1970.

251. Yamaguchi, Tohr. *The Golden Crane,* illustrated by Marianne Yamaguchi. Holt, Rinehart and Winston, 1963. (S—Japan)

252. Yashima, Taro, pseud. (Jun Iwamatsu). *Seashore Story.* Viking, 1967. (S—Japan)

253. Yolen, Jane. *The Emperor and the Kite,* illustrated by Ed Young. World, 1967. (S—China)

254. Zemach, Harve. *Duffy and the Devil,* illustrated by Margot Zemach. Farrar, Straus, 1973. (S—England)

255. ———. *Nail Soup,* adapted from the text by Nils Djurklo, illustrated by Margot Zemach. Follett, 1964. (S—Sweden)

256. ———. *Salt: A Russian Tale,* illustrated by Margot Zemach. Follett, 1965. (S—Russia)

257. ———. *Too Much Nose, An Italian Tale,* illustrated by Margot Zemach. Holt, Rinehart and Winston, 1967. (S)
258. Zemach, Margot. *The Three Sillies.* Holt, Rinehart and Winston, 1963. (S—England)

FABLES

259. Aesop. *Aesop's Fables,* illustrated by Boris Artzybasheff. Viking, 1933.
260. ———. *Aesop's Fables,* translated by Vernon Jones, illustrated by Arthur Rackham. F. Watts, 1967 (1912).
261. ———. *Aesop's Fables,* selected and adapted by Louis Untermeyer, illustrated by Alice Provensen and Martin Provensen. Golden Press, 1966.
262. ———. *Aesop's Fables,* edited by Anne Terry White, illustrated by Helen Siegl. Random House, 1964.
263. ———. *Fables from Aesop,* retold by James Reeves, illustrated by Maurice Wilson. Walck, 1962.
264. Brown, Marcia. *Once a Mouse.* Scribner, 1961.
265. Ciardi, John. *John J. Plenty and Fiddler Dan,* illustrated by Madeleine Gekiere. Lippincott, 1963.
266. Galdone, Paul. *Androcles and the Lion.* McGraw-Hill, 1970.
267. ———. *The Monkey and the Crocodile.* Seabury, 1969.
268. ———. *Three Aesop Fox Fables.* Seabury, 1971.
269. ———. *The Town Mouse and the Country Mouse.* McGraw-Hill, 1971.
270. La Fontaine. *The Fables of La Fontaine,* adapted and illustrated by Richard Scarry. Doubleday, 1963.
271. ———. *The Lion and the Rat,* illustrated by Brian Wildsmith. F. Watts, 1963.
272. ———. *The Miller, the Boy and the Donkey,* illustrated by Brian Wildsmith. F. Watts, 1969.
273. ———. *The North Wind and the Sun,* illustrated by Brian Wildsmith. F. Watts, 1963.
274. ———. *The Rich Man and the Shoemaker,* illustrated by Brian Wildsmith. F. Watts, 1965.
275. Lionni, Leo. *Frederick.* Pantheon, 1967.
276. ———. *Tico and the Golden Wings.* Pantheon, 1964.
277. McGovern, Ann. *Hee Haw,* illustrated by Eric von Schmidt. Houghton Mifflin, 1969.
278. Showalter, Jean B. *The Donkey Ride,* illustrated by Tomi Ungerer. Doubleday, 1967.
279. Steig, William. *Amos and Boris.* Farrar, Straus, 1971.

MYTHS AND EPICS

280. Asimov, Isaac. *Words from the Myths,* illustrated by William Barss. Houghton Mifflin, 1961.
281. d'Aulaire, Ingri, and Edgar Parin d'Aulaire. *Book of Greek Myths.* Doubleday, 1962.
282. ———. *Norse Gods and Giants.* Doubleday, 1967.
283. Baker, Betty. *At the Center of the World,* illustrated by Murray Tinkelman. Macmillan, 1973.
284. Baldwin, James. *The Story of Roland,* illustrated by Peter Hurd. Scribner, 1930.
285. Belting, Natalia. *The Earth Is on a Fish's Back: Tales of Beginnings,* illustrated by Esta Nesbitt. Holt, Rinehart and Winston, 1965.
286. ———. *The Long-tailed Bear and Other Indian Legends,* illustrated by Louis Cary. Bobbs-Merrill, 1961.
287. Benson, Sally. *Stories of the Gods and Heroes,* illustrated by Steele Savage. Dial, 1940.
288. Bertol, Roland. *Sundiata, The Epic of the Lion King,* illustrated by Gregorio Prestopino. Crowell, 1970.
289. Brown, Marcia. *Backbone of the King, The Story of Pakáa and His Son Ku.* Scribner, 1966.
290. Bryson, Bernarda. *Gilgamesh: Man's First Story.* Holt, Rinehart and Winston, 1967.
291. Bulfinch, Thomas. *The Age of Fable.* New American Library, 1962 (1855).
292. Burland, Cottie Arthur. *North American Indian Mythology.* Tudor Publishing, 1965.
293. Church, Alfred J., ed. *The Iliad and the Odyssey of Homer,* illustrated by Eugene Karlin. Macmillan, 1967 (1906, 1907).

294. Clark, Eleanor. *The Song of Roland,* illustrated by Leonard Everett Fisher. Random House, 1960.

295. Colum, Padraic. *The Children of Odin,* illustrated by Willy Pogany. Macmillan, 1920.

296. ———. *The Children's Homer: The Adventures of Odysseus and the Tale of Troy,* illustrated by Willy Pogany. Macmillan, 1962.

297. ———. *Legends of Hawaii,* illustrated by Don Forrer. Yale University Press, 1937.

298. Coolidge, Olivia. *Legends of the North,* illustrated by Edouard Sandoz. Houghton Mifflin, 1951.

299. Crossley-Holland, Kevin. *Havelok the Dane,* illustrated by Brian Wildsmith. Dutton, 1965.

300. Curry, Jane Louise. *Down from the Lonely Mountain,* illustrated by Enrico Arno. Harcourt Brace Jovanovich, 1965.

301. Evslin, Bernard, Dorothy Evslin, and Ned Hoopes. *The Greek Gods,* illustrated by William Hunter. Scholastic, 1966.

302. ———. *Heroes and Monsters of Greek Myth,* illustrated by William Hunter. Scholastic, 1970.

303. Fahs, Sophia, and Dorothy Spoerl. *Beginnings: Earth Sky Life Death.* Starr King Press, 1958.

304. Farmer, Penelope. *Daedalus and Icarus,* illustrated by Chris Connor. Harcourt Brace Jovanovich, 1971.

305. Feagles, Anita. *He Who Saw Everything, The Epic of Gilgamesh.* Young Scott, 1966.

306. Gaer, Joseph. *The Adventures of Rama,* illustrated by Randy Monk. Little, Brown, 1954.

307. Garfield, Leon, and Edward Blishen. *The God Beneath the Sea,* illustrated by Zevi Blum. Pantheon, 1971.

308. ———. *The Golden Shadow,* illustrated by Charles Keeping. Pantheon, 1973.

309. Gates, Doris. *The Golden God: Apollo,* illustrated by Constantinos CoConis. Viking, 1973.

310. ———. *Lord of the Sky: Zeus,* illustrated by Robert Handville. Viking, 1972.

311. ———. *Two Queens of Heaven, The Story of Demeter and Aphrodite,* illustrated by Trina Schart Hyman. Viking, 1974.

312. ———. *The Warrior Goddess: Athena,* illustrated by Don Bolognese. Viking, 1972.

313. Graves, Robert. *Greek Gods and Heroes.* Doubleday, 1960.

314. ———. *The Siege and Fall of Troy,* illustrated by C. Walter Hodges. Doubleday, 1962.

315. Green, Roger Lancelyn. *A Book of Myths,* illustrated by Joan Kiddell-Monroe. Dutton, 1965.

316. ———. *The Myths of the Norsemen,* illustrated by Brian Wildsmith. Dufour, 1964.

317. ———. *Tales of Ancient Egypt,* illustrated by Elaine Raphael. Walck, 1968.

318. ———. *Tales of the Greek Heroes.* Penguin Books, 1958.

319. ———. *Tales the Muses Told,* illustrated by Don Bolognese. Walck, 1965.

320. Hawthorne, Nathaniel. *The Golden Touch,* illustrated by Paul Galdone. McGraw-Hill, 1959.

321. Hieatt, Constance. *The Castle of Ladies,* illustrated by Norman Laliberté. Crowell, 1973.

322. ———. *The Joy of the Court,* illustrated by Pauline Baynes. Crowell, 1971.

323. ———. *The Knight of the Cart,* illustrated by John Gretzer. Crowell, 1969.

324. ———. *Sir Gawain and the Green Knight,* illustrated by Walter Lorraine. Crowell, 1967.

325. ———. *The Sword and the Grail,* illustrated by David Palladini. Crowell, 1972.

326. Hill, W. M. *Tales of Maui,* illustrated by Jacques Boullaire. Dodd, 1964.

327. Hodges, Margaret. *The Gorgon's Head,* illustrated by Charles Mikolaycak. Little, Brown, 1972.

328. ———. *The Other World, Myths of the Celts,* illustrated by Eros Keith. Farrar, Straus, 1973.

329. ———. *Persephone and the Springtime, A Greek Myth,* illustrated by Arvis Stewart. Little, Brown, 1973.

330. Hosford, Dorothy G. *Sons of the Volsungs,* illustrated by Frank Dobias. Holt, Rinehart and Winston, 1949.

331. ———. *Thunder of the Gods,* illustrated by Claire Louden and George Louden. Holt, Rinehart and Winston, 1952.

332. Jablow, Alta, translator. *Gassire's Lute,* illustrated by Leo Dillon and Diane Dillon. Dutton, 1971.

333. King, Cynthia. *In the Morning of Time: The Story of the Norse God Balder,* illustrated by Charles Mikolaycak. Four Winds, 1970.

334. Lanier, Sidney. *The Boy's King Arthur,* illustrated by N. C. Wyeth. Scribner, 1880.

335. Leach, Maria. *The Beginning: Creation Myths around the World,* illustrated by Jan Bell Fairservis. Funk & Wagnalls, 1956.

336. ———. *How the People Sang the Mountains Up: How and Why Stories,* illustrated by Glen Rounds. Viking, 1967.

337. McGovern, Ann. *Robin Hood of Sherwood Forest,* illustrated by Arnold Spilka. Crowell, 1968.

338. MacLeod, Mary. *King Arthur and His Knights,* illustrated by Alexander Dobkin. World, 1950.

339. McSpadden, J. Walker. *Robin Hood and His Merry Outlaws,* illustrated by Louis Slobodkin. World, 1946.

340. Malcolmson, Anne, ed. *The Song of Robin Hood,* music arranged by Grace Castagnetta, illustrated by Virginia Lee Burton. Houghton Mifflin, 1947.

341. Mukerji, Dhan Gopal. *Rama, the Hero of India,* illustrated by Edgar Parin d'Aulaire. Dutton, 1930.

342. Picard, Barbara Leonie. *Hero Tales from the British Isles,* illustrated by Gay Galsworthy. Penguin Books, 1969.

343. ———. *The Iliad of Homer,* illustrated by Joan Kiddell-Monroe. Walck, 1960.

344. ———. *The Odyssey of Homer Retold.* Walck, 1952.

345. ———. *Stories of King Arthur and His Knights,* illustrated by Roy Morgan. Walck, 1955.

346. Pollack, Merrill. *Phaëthon,* illustrated by William Hofmann. Lippincott, 1966.

347. Proddow, Penelope, translator. *Demeter and Persephone,* illustrated by Barbara Cooney. Doubleday, 1972.

348. Pyk, Ann. *The Hammer of Thunder,* illustrated by Jan Pyk. Putnam, 1972.

349. Pyle, Howard. *The Merry Adventures of Robin Hood.* Scribner, 1946 (1883).

350. ———. *Some Merry Adventures of Robin Hood.* Scribner, 1954.

351. ———. *The Story of King Arthur and His Knights.* Scribner, 1933 (1903).

352. Reeves, James. *The Trojan Horse,* illustrated by Krystyna Turska. F. Watts, 1969.

353. Robbins, Ruth. *Taliesin and King Arthur.* Parnassus, 1970.

354. Roy, Cal. *The Serpent and the Sun: Myths of the Mexican World.* Farrar, Straus, 1972.

355. Schiller, Barbara. *Erec and Enid,* illustrated by Ati Forberg. Dutton, 1970.

356. ———. *The Kitchen Knight,* illustrated by Nonny Hogrogian. Holt, Rinehart and Winston, 1965.

357. Seeger, Elizabeth. *The Ramayana,* illustrated by Gordon Laite. Young Scott, 1969.

358. Sellew, Catharine F. *Adventures with the Giants.* Little, Brown, 1950.

359. ———. *Adventures with the Gods,* illustrated by George Hauman and Doris Hauman. Little, Brown, 1945.

360. Serraillier, Ian. *The Clashing Rocks: The Story of Jason,* illustrated by William Stobbs. Walck, 1964.

361. ———. *A Fall from the Sky: The Story of Daedalus,* illustrated by William Stobbs. Walck, 1966.

362. ———. *The Gorgon's Head: The Story of Perseus,* illustrated by William Stobbs. Walck, 1962.

363. ———. *Heracles the Strong,* illustrated by Rocco Negri. Walck, 1970.

364. ———. *The Way of Danger: The Story of Theseus,* illustrated by William Stobbs. Walck, 1963.

365. Sherwood, Merriam, translator. *The Song of Roland,* illustrated by Edith Emerson. McKay, 1938.

366. Sutcliff, Rosemary. *The High Deeds of Finn MacCool,* illustrated by Michael Charlton. Dutton, 1967.

367. ———. *The Hound of Ulster,* illustrated by Victor Ambrus. Dutton, 1963.

368. ———. *Tristan and Iseult.* Dutton, 1971.
369. Thompson, Vivian. *Hawaiian Myths of Earth, Sea, and Sky,* illustrated by Leonard Weisgard. Holiday, 1966.
370. Tomaino, Sarah F. *Persephone, Bringer of Spring,* illustrated by Ati Forberg. Crowell, 1971.
371. Troughton, Joanna. *Sir Gawain and the Loathly Damsel.* Dutton, 1972.
372. Turska, Krystyna. *Pegasus.* F. Watts, 1970.
373. Watson, Jane Werner. *The Iliad and the Odyssey,* illustrated by Alice Provensen and Martin Provensen. Golden Press, 1956.
374. Westwood, Jennifer. *Gilgamesh and Other Babylonian Tales,* illustrated by Michael Charlton. Coward-McCann, 1970.
375. White, Anne Terry. *The Golden Treasury of Myths and Legends,* illustrated by Alice Provensen and Martin Provensen. Golden Press, 1959.
376. Williams, Jay. *Sword of King Arthur,* illustrated by Louis Glanzman. Crowell, 1968.

BIBLE

377. Aichinger, Helga. *The Shepherd.* Crowell, 1967.
378. Asimov, Isaac. *Words from the Exodus,* illustrated by William Barss. Houghton Mifflin, 1963.
379. ———. *Words in Genesis,* illustrated by William Barss. Houghton Mifflin, 1962.
380. Bible, N. T. *The Christ Child,* illustrated by Maud Petersham and Miska Petersham. Doubleday, 1931.
381. Bible O. T. *The Lord Is My Shepherd, The Twenty-Third Psalm,* illustrated by Tony Palazzo. Walck, 1965.
382. ———. *A Time for All Things,* illustrated by Tony Palazzo. Walck, 1966.
383. ———. *The Twenty Third Psalm,* illustrated by Tasha Tudor. Achille J. St. Onge, 1965.
384. ———. *Wings of the Morning, Verses from the Bible,* selected by Robin Palmer, illustrated by Tony Palazzo. Walck, 1968.
385. Bolliger, Max, reteller. *Noah and the Rainbow,* translated by Clyde Robert Bulla, illustrated by Helga Aichinger. Crowell, 1972.
386. Bulla, Clyde Robert. *Jonah and the Great Fish,* illustrated by Helga Aichinger. Crowell, 1970.
387. ———. *Joseph the Dreamer,* illustrated by Gordon Laite. Crowell, 1971.
388. De Angeli, Marguerite. *The Old Testament.* Doubleday, 1959.
389. De la Mare, Walter. *Stories from the Bible,* illustrated by Edward Ardizzone. Knopf, 1961.
390. De Regniers, Beatrice. *David and Goliath,* illustrated by Richard M. Powers. Viking, 1965.
391. Galdone, Paul. *Shadrach, Meshach, and Abednego.* McGraw-Hill, 1965.
392. Graham, Lorenz. *David He No Fear,* illustrated by Ann Grifalconi. Crowell, 1971.
393. ———. *Every Man Heart Lay Down,* illustrated by Colleen Browning. Crowell, 1970.
394. ———. *God Wash the World and Start Again,* illustrated by Clare R. Ross. Crowell, 1971.
395. ———. *Hongry Catch the Foolish Boy,* illustrated by James Brown, Jr. Crowell, 1973.
396. ———. *A Road Down in the Sea,* illustrated by Gregorio Prestopino. Crowell, 1970.
397. MacBeth, George. *Jonah and the Lord,* illustrated by Margaret Gordon. Holt, Rinehart and Winston, 1970.
398. Saporta, Raphael. *A Basket in the Reeds,* illustrated by H. Hechtkopf. Lerner, 1965.
399. Singer, Isaac Bashevis. *The Wicked City,* translated by the author and Elizabeth Shub, illustrated by Leonard Everett Fisher. Farrar, Straus, 1972.
400. Tresselt, Alvin. *Stories from the Bible,* illustrated by Lynd Ward. Coward-McCann, 1971.
401. Turner, Philip. *Brian Wildsmith's Illustrated Bible Stories,* illustrated by Brian Wildsmith. F. Watts, 1969.
402. von Jüchen, Aurel. *The Holy Night,* translated by Cornelia Schaeffer, illustrated by Celestino Piatti. Atheneum, 1968.
403. Waddell, Helen. *The Story of Saul the King,* abridged by Elaine Moss, illustrated by Doreen Roberts. D. White, 1966.
404. Wiesner, William. *The Tower of Babel.* Viking, 1968.
405. Wynants, Miche. *Noah's Ark.* Harcourt Brace Jovanovich, 1965.
406. Zavrel, Stepán. *They Followed the Star.* Scroll Press, 1969.

5

Modern
Fantasy

A wonderfully perceptive teacher maintained a diary in which she recorded significant events in her teaching day. These excerpts reveal her students' responses to a reading aloud of the well-known fantasy, *Charlotte's Web*, by E. B. White:

January 18

A wisp of a girl with dark dreaming eyes, Judy F. sits transfixed, listening to *Charlotte's Web*. When I read aloud, I'm aware of an irreplaceable group feeling. But beyond that, if children aren't read to, how will they see the purpose of such a difficult skill? . . .

February 6

Judy came in glowing.
"We've bought a baby pig. Mother took me to a nearby farm."
"How marvelous. What's his name?"
"Wilbur," she said, in a matter-of-fact voice—as if the name of the pig in *Charlotte's Web* was the only one possible. "He's quite cuddly for a pig. We bathe him every day."

February 20

When I'm alone with Judy, I ask about Wilbur.
"Oh, he's getting along just fine. We bought him a large pink ribbon and only take it off when he goes to bed."
"Where does he sleep?"
"In my bed," said Judy, as if I ought to know.

March 2

Everyone was silent at the end of *Charlotte's Web*. David wept when Charlotte died. Later he asked to borrow the book. It'll be interesting to see how he maneuvers such difficult reading. But there's the motivation they talk about.

April 3

Judy's mother hurried over to me at the P.T.A. meeting.
"What's all this about your pig?" she queried.
"My pig?" I answered incredulously. "You mean your pig; the one you and Judy bought at the farm."

"Come now," said Mrs. F. "This is ridiculous. Judy's been telling me for weeks about the class pig. The one you named for Wilbur in *Charlotte's Web*."

We looked at each other, puzzled, and suddenly the truth dawned upon us.

Wilbur, that immaculately clean pig in his dazzling pink ribbon, belonged to neither Mrs. F. nor me. He was born in dreams—a creature of Judy's wonderful imagination.[1]

A book of fantasy had seemed so real to these children that David had cried at its end, and Judy had continued the story in her imagination, convincing both her teacher and her mother that Wilbur did indeed exist.

Fantasy for Today's Child

Some educators and parents have questioned the value of fantasy for today's child. They argue that children want contemporary stories that are relevant and speak to the problems of daily living. Today's generation, they maintain, want "now" books about the real world, not fantasies about unreal worlds. They point to books by Judy Blume, the Cleavers, John Neufeld, and others (*see* Chapter 7) as examples of books which speak directly to today's child.

The tremendous increase in the publication of informational books also indicates that children are seeking "useful" books that provide real facts, such as the most recent NFL statistics on football players or a report on underwater archeology. Of what use, the realists ask, is a 400-page story about talking rabbits (*Watership Down* by Richard Adams) or one about a bizarre family that includes a hunter, a mermaid, a bear and a lynx (*The Animal Family* by Randall Jarrell)?

Children themselves have denied the truth of some of these statements by choosing many books of fantasy as their favorites. Certainly, *Charlotte's Web* is one of the most popular children's books, if not *the* most popular, to be published within the past twenty-five years. Selden's *The Cricket in Times Square*, Dahl's *Charlie and the Chocolate Factory*, and L'Engle's *A Wrinkle in Time* are all fantasies that rank high among children's favorite books. And many of the classics, books that have endured through several generations—such as *Winnie the Pooh*, *Wind in the Wil-*

lows and *Alice's Adventures in Wonderland*—are also fantasies.

Fantasy is as relevant for today's children as it was for the Victorians. The great fantasies frequently reveal new insights into the world of reality. Both *Charlotte's Web* and *Wind in the Willows* detail the responsibilities and loyalties required of true friendship. The fundamental truth underlying LeGuin's story, *A Wizard of Earthsea*, is that man is responsible for the evil he creates and is only free of it when he faces it directly. Such a theme might appear to be a thinly disguised Sunday School lesson in a book of realism; in fantasy it becomes an exciting quest for identity and self-knowledge. Fantasy consistently asks the universal questions concerning the struggle of good versus evil, the humanity of man, the meaning of life and death.

A modern contemporary novel may be out of date in five years, but well-written fantasy endures. Andersen's story, *The Emperor's New Clothes*, had as much relevance to Watergate as to the kings of his time. Another Andersen tale, *The Nightingale*, speaks directly to the twentieth century's adoration of mechanical gadgetry to the neglect of that which is real. Adams has portrayed the horrors of a Nazi-like warren of rabbits in *Watership Down*; while in *A Wrinkle in Time*, L'Engle details the loss of freedom on the planet Camazotz, where even the children must skip rope and bounce balls in time to the terrible rhythm of the heartbeat of "It." Fantasy frequently proclaims ancient truths in a way that makes children see their own reality in a new perspective.

Most importantly, however, fantasy helps the child to develop imagination. The ability to imagine, to conceive of alternative ways of life,

[1]Jean Katzenberg. "More Leaves from a Teacher's Diary: On Reading" in *Outlook*, Issue II (Spring 1974), pp. 28–29. Published by the Mountain View Center for Environmental Education, University of Colorado.

to entertain new ideas, to create strange new worlds, to dream dreams are all skills vital to the survival of humankind. Paul Fenimore Cooper wrote of the importance of nourishing the child's imagination:

> Fancy is to the imagination what the seed is to the tree. Let it lie in barren ground and it will not grow. But nourish it and care for it through the years and it will grow into imagination, (as dear a possession for the man as fancy is for the child). He who lacks imagination lives but half a life. He has his experiences, he has his facts, he has his learning. But do any of these really live unless touched by the magic of the imagination? So long as the road is straight he can see down it and follow it. But imagination looks around the turns and gazes far off into the distance on either side. And it is imagination that walks hand in hand with vision.[2]

Modern Fairy Tales

The traditional folk or fairy tale had no identifiable author, but was passed by word of mouth from one generation to the next. While the names of Grimm and Jacobs have become associated with some of these tales, they did not *write* the stories; they compiled the folk tales of Germany and England. The modern literary fairy tale utilizes the form of the old, but has an identifiable author.

THE BEGINNINGS OF THE MODERN FAIRY TALE

Hans Christian Andersen is generally credited with being the first *author* of modern fairy tales, although even some of his stories, such as *The Wild Swans*, are definite adaptations of the old folk tales. (Compare Andersen's *The Wild Swans* with Grimm's "The Six Swans," for example.) Every Andersen story bears his unmistakable stamp of gentleness, melancholy, and faith in God. Even his adaptations of old tales were embellished with deeper hidden meanings, making them very much his creations.

Two of Andersen's tales are said to be autobiographical, *The Ugly Duckling* and *The Steadfast Tin*

Soldier. The little ugly duckling was the jest of the poultry yard until he became the beautiful swan. Andersen himself suffered all kinds of indignities as a young boy and youth, but later he was honored by his king and countrymen— truly a duckling turned into a swan. The sad tale of the painfully shy but loyal tin soldier and his love for the cold and unbending toy ballerina is said by some authorities to represent Andersen's rejection by the woman he loved.

Many of Andersen's fairy tales are really commentaries on what he saw as the false standards of society. In "The Princess and the Pea," sometimes called "The Real Princess," Andersen laughs at the snobbish pride of the princess who claimed she could feel a pea through twenty mattresses and twenty eiderdown beds. The farce of *The Emperor's New Clothes* is disclosed by a young child who had no reason to assume the hollow pretense of his elders and so told the truth—that the Emperor was stark naked! Both of the stories, *The Nightingale* and *The Swineherd,* show the foolishness of preferring the mechanical and the spurious over that which is real.

Andersen was not afraid to show children cruelty, morbidity, sorrow, and even death. In the long tale, *The Snow Queen,* the glass splinter enters Kay's eye and stabs his heart, which becomes cold as ice. He then becomes spiteful and angry with Gerda, his former friend. Gerda is hurt by the changed behavior of her companion but, still loving him, searches for him in the Snow Queen's palace. At last she finds him, and her tears melt the splinter and his icy coldness. "The Little Mermaid" suffers terribly for her selfless love of a mortal prince. She dies on the night of his marriage to another, unwilling to kill him as her sisters had planned and unable to speak to him of her love. Her goodness brings a promise of immortality, however. The story of *The Little Match Girl* ends in the gentle death of a little girl who is freezing to death and who had seen a vision of her grandmother in the last flicker of her matches. A few stories, such as the tender *Thumbelina,* end happily, but most of Andersen's tales contain a thread of tragedy.

Many of Andersen's stories have been beautifully illustrated in single editions. Marcia Brown has captured the mystical beauty of *The Wild Swans* with her subdued pen-and-wash drawings in black and gray tones, with the shyest touch

---

[2]Paul Fenimore Cooper. "On Catching a Child's Fancy," in *Three Owls,* Third Book, Annie Carroll Moore, ed. (New York: Coward-McCann, 1931), pp. 56–57.

Marcia Brown's subdued pen-and-wash drawings convey the mystical quality of this Hans Christian Andersen tale.

Illustration used by permission of Charles Scribner's Sons from *The Wild Swans* by Hans Christian Andersen, illustrated by Marcia Brown. Copyright © 1963 Marcia Brown.

of coral for warmth. This illustrator used no color in the many fine-line drawings for *The Snow Queen*, a fact which served to emphasize the coldness of the Queen's icy halls. A proud red and blue seemed to be the appropriate colors for *The Steadfast Tin Soldier;* while gold was used for the little dancer's spangle (all that was left of her) and charcoal for the charred breast of the soldier. The symbolic use of color is one of the characteristics of Marcia Brown's art work. Another edition of *The Steadfast Tin Soldier* was first published in Switzerland. These illustrations by Monika Laimgruber emphasize the tiny toy qualities of the tin soldier and his fragile ballerina doll. The picture of the enormous green fish in the process of swallowing the poor soldier is a study in contrasts!

Adrienne Adams has portrayed *Thumbelina* and her enchantingly small world with delicate details and bright watercolors. Her drawings for *The Ugly Duckling* are, more properly, subdued and somber. Before making these illustrations, Adams paid a special visit to Denmark to become familiar with Andersen's native land. Erik Blegvad also revisited his native Denmark before he illustrated the small but amusing tale of *The Swineherd.* Nancy Burkert has richly portrayed the Chinese setting of *The Nightingale* in Oriental tradition. Many of her pictures resemble paintings on old Chinese silk screens. She has also illustrated Andersen's poignant Christmas tale, *The Fir Tree,* with delicate full-color paintings and black-and-white drawings. Blair Lent uses intricate detail, but muted colors, to portray the cold harsh city that allowed *The Little Match Girl* to freeze to death on New Year's Eve. The large towering buildings and blinding snow emphasize the helplessness of the freezing little girl.

The popular and amusing *The Emperor's New Clothes* is available in several editions. The Delanos' emperor is a fat, pompous, and quite naked monarch! In Virginia Lee Burton's version rhythmical illustrations seem to move with the farcical procession of the Emperor.

The Woman with the Eggs is a delightful adaption of one of Andersen's poems. Robust illustrations by Ray Cruz show a proud and greedy woman going to market with a basket of eggs on her head. As she walks along, she plans what she will do with all the riches she will derive from the sale of her eggs. An unfortunate toss of her head quickly destroys the eggs and her dreams.

Kaj Beckman is illustrating two of Andersen's stories each year until all forty-two of his tales are in picture-book format. Those that have been published so far—including *The Nightingale* and *Thumbelina*—utilize collágo techniques in an interesting fashion. All these many new picture-book editions of Andersen's single tales will serve the useful purpose of acquainting today's child with these classic stories.

Oscar Wilde wrote two fairy tales, *The Happy Prince* and *The Selfish Giant.* The first has been illustrated by Gilbert Riswold in a striking single edition. It is a somewhat sentimental story of the love of a swallow and the golden statue of a prince. In real life the prince had been happy, for he had known nothing of the misery of his people. Now, from his high pedestal he can look out over his city and see all the suffering that exists. Making the swallow his emissary of mercy, he sends the great ruby of his sword to a poor seamstress for her sick son. One by one, he asks the swallow to pluck out his sapphire eyes and give them to the poor. Now the happy prince is blind, so the swallow stays with him, flying over the city and relieving suffering by stripping the statue of its gold leaf and giving it away. No longer able to live in such a cold climate, the bird kisses his friend goodbye and falls dead at his feet. The town councilors, seeing the shabbiness of the statue, pull it down and melt its lead. All will burn except its heart, which is thrown on the same ash heap as the body of the dead bird. Together, the two are received in Heaven as the most precious things in the city. *The Selfish Giant* has even more religious symbolism and is less appropriate for children.

Many of George MacDonald's fairy tales were religious in nature, including *The Golden Key,* which has been sensitively illustrated by Maurice Sendak. Sendak also illustrated MacDonald's *The Light Princess,* which is the amusing story of the princess who had been deprived of her gravity by an aunt who was angry at not being invited to her christening. This story is pure fun, and somehow seems more appropriate for today's children who understand the principle of weightlessness than for the children of the nineteenth century for whom MacDonald wrote. It is interesting to compare Sendak's tender yet humorous illustrations for this story with the detailed, amusing, and colorful pictures by William Pène du Bois.

FAIRY TALES TODAY

In many instances modern writers have written farcical versions of the old fairy-tale form. The story may be set in the days of kings and queens and beautiful princesses; the language will reflect the manners of the period; and the usual "Once upon a time" beginning and "They lived happily ever after" ending will be present; but the conflict may have a modern twist. True to all fairy tales, virtue will be rewarded and evil overcome. An example of one of these modern literary fairy tales is the fresh and original story by Phyllis McGinley of *The Plain Princess,* who

owns the handsomest two-wheeled bicycle in the world. Yet this story of the transformation from a plain to a beautiful princess has a familiar ring. *A Birthday for the Princess* by Anita Lobel has a unique and unusual ending. It is the story of an over-directed, over-protected, unloved princess. No one ever asks the princess how *she* feels or what *she* wants—even on her birthday. In the midst of her very planned birthday party, the princess slips away and invites an organ-grinder and monkey to be her guests. The king and queen are horrified, and the poor organ-grinder is thrown in the dungeon. The lonely little princess lets him out and rides away with him forever. Anita Lobel's illustrations are humorous, yet elegantly rich in detail.

Jay Williams is the author of several modern fairy tales, including *The Practical Princess* and *Petronella.* Both these stories liberate women from the state of helplessness in which the traditional tale usually portrays them. Bedelia, the practical princess, proves that she is not only very practical but brave and wise. *She* slays the dragon and rescues the prince from his tower prison! *Petronella* is a delightful and amusing twist on the usual fairy tale as the princess rides off to seek her fortune and find her prince! Traditional roles are altered in *The Good-for-Nothing Prince* also by Williams, in which the princess has to demand that the lazy prince rescue her. Only after she throws his food out the window does Prince Palagon respond to her request.

Three books written by Jane Yolen and illustrated by Ed Young follow the pattern of traditional Oriental tales. In *The Emperor and the Kite,* his youngest daughter rescues the emperor from imprisonment in a high tower by weaving a strong rope from her own hair, and then attaching it to the tail of a kite which she flies to her father so that he can escape. Ed Young's illustrations for this lovely tale of loyalty are done in an intricate Oriental cut-paper style. A kite also plays a major role in the dramatic tale of *The Seventh Mandarin,* whose principal duty was to fly the king's dragon kite which was the carrier of the king's soul. Like the other mandarins and the king himself, the seventh mandarin never had been outside the palace walls. But one night the king's kite was blown outside the palace gates and the mandarin had to go in search of it. There

A young, liberated princess goes off to find her own prince in this modern version of a fairy tale.

Illustration by Friso Henstra from *Petronella*. Copyright © 1969 by Friso Henstra. By permission of Parents' Magazine Press.

he saw suffering and sadness, which he had never known existed. That same night the king dreamed of the suffering of his people and demanded to know if it were true. Only the seventh mandarin could give him an honest answer and take him outside the palace walls to see for himself. *The Girl Who Loved the Wind* has a similar theme; only in this instance the king had high walls built around the palace and the garden and tried to protect his daughter, Princess Danina, from ever seeing or hearing an unlovely thing. But for all his care, the king could not prevent the wind from singing a true song about the reality of the world. Finally, Danina listened

more to the wind's song than her father's, and using her cape for a sail she flew off with the wind. Ed Young studied Persian miniatures before he designed the richly textured pictures for this beautiful book.

Another handsome literary tale that reflects an Oriental setting is *The Blue Bird* by Fiona French. In this tale of evil enchantment, a beautiful young girl and Chiang Ti, a young scholar, set out to ask the Enchantress why the girl's blue bird has stopped singing. Along the way they are kind to a tortoise, a cat, and the rain dragon. In true folk-tale manner these three friends save the lives of the young couple and destroy the Enchantress. At the same time all the birds that were frozen in her power are released. The striking blue-and-white illustrations were inspired by old Chinese porcelain. After the destruction of the evil spell, the final pictures seem to burst into color, as all the birds fly free. This story is reminiscent of Grimm's tale of *Jorinda and Joringel* (*see* Chapter 4). Children might compare the two for their similarities and differences.

Other popular modern fairy tales are Thurber's *Many Moons* and Slobodkin's *The Amiable Giant*. *Many Moons* is the story of a petulant princess who desires the moon. The characterizations of the enraged king, the perplexed wise men, and the understanding jester are well drawn. Princess Lenore solves the problem of obtaining the moon in a completely satisfying and childlike manner. Louis Slobodkin received the Caldecott Medal for his illustrations of *Many Moons*. Slobodkin also wrote and illustrated *The Amiable Giant*, which is a disarming tale of a friendly, but misunderstood giant. As in *Many Moons*, a child solves the problem, for Gwendolyn is the only one who hears the giant's message. She convinces the villagers that they are being fooled by the wicked wizard's interpretations of the giant's conversations. The giant is so grateful that he gives Gwendolyn a birthday party, baking the cake himself. Both of these stories lend themselves to interpretation through creative dramatics.

The 13 Clocks and *The Wonderful O* by James Thurber are more sophisticated and mature fairy tales. A cold duke who was afraid of "now" had frozen time in Coffin Castle, where he kept the beautiful Princess Saralinda. A prince in the disguise of a ragged minstrel accomplishes the impossible tasks set by the Duke and wins her hand. However, it is only with the bungling and amusing help of the Golux that the Prince is able to obtain the one thousand jewels and start the thirteen clocks, so that the time is Now and he may marry his Princess. This is an imaginative spoof on fairy tales and one that middle-graders thoroughly enjoy. *The Wonderful O* is the story of what happens to an island when a black-hearted pirate in search of treasure banishes the use of the letter "o." He has had a hatred for "o" ever since his mother became wedged in a porthole. Terrorizing the islanders to produce a treasure they do not own, the pirate eliminates not only words beginning with "o" but the objects they represent. Finally, he is overcome when the people of the island find and use four words that contain "o"—hope, love, valor, and freedom. *The Wonderful O* is restored to its rightful place, and a monument is erected to recall the horrible time when it did not exist. The play on words in this book is clever, but requires considerable maturity.

The 500 Hats of Bartholomew Cubbins by Dr. Seuss is the hilarious tale of a small boy who is commanded to take off his hat for the king. Bartholomew complies, only to find that another hat appears in its place. The king is enraged and takes the boy to court. Sir Snipps, the royal hat maker, cannot remove Bartholomew's hat; his wise men have no practical suggestions, and the royal magicians cannot even charm it off his head. Finally, he is sent to the executioner, who is a very proper kind of person and refuses to execute anyone wearing a hat. The king's horrid nephew, The Grand Duke Wilfred, suggests that he be allowed to push poor Bartholomew off the highest parapet of the castle. As they climb the stairs, Bartholomew desperately tears off his hats which become more and more elaborate. The 500th hat is so "befeathered and bejeweled" that the king offers to spare Bartholomew's life in exchange for his gorgeous hat. Bartholomew gladly removes it. Much to his relief, his head remains bare. *Bartholomew and the Oobleck* is a sequel to the magical medieval tale of Bartholomew Cubbins.

In *The Truthful Harp*, one of Lloyd Alexander's

An evil enchantress has laid a spell on all the birds in the land. Notice the birds frozen in the pillars, the lattice work, and the railing, while the enchantress herself has claws and wings.

Illustration from *The Blue Bird* © Fiona French, 1972. Used by permission of Henry Z. Walck, Inc., publishers.

humorous fairy tales, the harp has magical powers. Every time its owner, Fflewddur Flam, exaggerates the truth to suit his story, the harp breaks a string. The pictures by Evaline Ness contrast the reality of Fflewddur's world with his vivid imaginings. When Flam goes forth to see his kingdom he calls for his wild and mettlesome charger; Ness portrays a plump swayed-back dappled gray pony! Again, the text suggests that all of Flam's subjects come down to wish him well on his venture, and the picture shows one small child! Despite Flam's tendency to stretch the truth, he has a kind and noble heart, as his deeds do show. Children may first be introduced to the characters in Alexander's Prydain Series by reading the exciting picture-book tale of *Coll and His White Pig*. When King Arawn, the Lord of the Land of Death, spirits away Hen Wen, the magical pig, Coll has no choice but to go after her. Using the traditional folk-tale motif of providing aid to three animals in distress, Coll, in turn, is helped to save his pig. Alexander's style of writing captures the sound of the traditional tale. Notice, for example, his ending:

> Such is the tale of Coll and the rescuing of Hen Wen, with the help of the owl, Ash-Wing, the stag, Oak-Horn, and the digging and delving of the moles.
>
> And such is the end of it.[3]

The Four Donkeys, also by Alexander, is a spirited modern version of the well-known fable, "The Miller, His Son and the Donkey." In this extended tale it is easy to determine the identity of the four donkeys. As always, one can delight in Alexander's apt and amusing descriptions in which the tailor, the baker, and the shoemaker perceive things in terms of their trades. For example the baker describes the tailor as being ". . . skinny as a breadstick, but he has twice the crust!"[4] The watercolor illustrations by Lester Abrams are as richly detailed as the text, and add much to the humor of this lively tale.

The King's Fountain by Alexander is a modern

parable with the somber theme of personal responsibility. It is the story of a poor man who wanted to stop the king from building a great palace that would cut off the flow of water to all the poor people in the city. The wisest scholar could not speak clearly and convincingly, the smooth-tongued merchants were afraid of the king's anger, and the bravest man would use uncontrolled brute strength. And so the poor man had to go to see the king himself. Ezra Jack Keats has been criticized for using overly bold and dramatic pictures for this quiet story of personal courage. Perhaps the critics have a point, and yet the message of assuming personal responsibility for righting wrongs needs to be proclaimed loudly and boldly in our times, as well as in the past.

Kenneth Grahame's *The Reluctant Dragon* is the droll tale of a peace-loving dragon who is forced to fight St. George. The dragon's friend, called simply the Boy, arranges a meeting between St. George and the dragon, and a mock fight is planned. St. George is the hero of the day, the dragon is highly entertained at a banquet, and the Boy is pleased to have saved both the dragon and St. George. The pictures by Ernest Shepard add to the subtle humor of this book.

A popular fairy tale of our time for adults and children is the haunting story of *The Little Prince* by Antoine de Saint-Exupéry. Written in the first person, the story tells of the author's encounter with the Little Prince on the Sahara Desert where he made a forced landing with his disabled plane. Bit by bit, the author learns the strange history of the Little Prince, who lived all alone on a tiny planet no larger than a house. He possessed three volcanoes, two active and one extinct, and one flower unlike any other flower in all the galaxy. However, when he saw a garden of roses, he doubted the uniqueness of his flower until a fox showed him that what we have loved is always unique to us. This gentle story means many things to different people, but its wisdom and beauty are for all.

Modern Fantasy

Fantasy, like poetry, means more than it says. Underlying most of the great books of fantasy is a metaphorical comment on society today.

---

[3]Lloyd Alexander. *Coll and His White Pig*, illustrated by Evaline Ness (New York: Holt, Rinehart and Winston, 1965), unpaged.
[4]Lloyd Alexander. *The Four Donkeys*, illustrated by Lester Abrams (New York: Holt, Rinehart and Winston, 1972, unpaged).

Some children will find the hidden meanings in a tale such as *The Little Prince;* others will simply read it as a good story; and still others will be put off reading it altogether because it isn't "real." Children vary in their capacity for imaginative thinking. The literal-minded child finds the suspension of reality a barrier to the enjoyment of fantasy; other children relish the opportunity to enter the world of enchantment. Children's reactions to books of modern fantasy are seldom predictable or mild; they appear to be either vehemently for or against them. Frequently, taste for fantasy may be developed by having the teacher or librarian read aloud such well-known books as Milne's *Winnie the Pooh,* Alexander's *The Cat Who Wished to Be a Man,* or Merrill's *The Pushcart War.*

GUIDES TO EVALUATING MODERN FANTASY

Books of modern fantasy are usually longer than fairy tales and may take a variety of forms. All contain some imaginary elements that are contrary to reality as we know it today; for example, they may personify animals or toys, create new worlds, change the size of human beings, give humans unusual powers, or manipulate time patterns. Some fantasies utilize several of these approaches. Characteristic of most fantasy, like the fairy tales of old, is the presentation of a universal truth or a hidden meaning—love overcomes hate, the fools may be wiser than the wise men, the granting of wishes may not bring happiness. Well-written fantasy, like other fiction, will have a well-constructed plot, convincing characterization, a worthwhile theme, and an appropriate style. However, additional considerations are needed to guide the evaluation of fantasy.

The primary concern is the way the author makes his fantasy believable. A variety of techniques may be used to create belief in the unbelievable. Many authors firmly ground a story in reality before gradually moving into fantasy. Not until Chapter 3 in *Charlotte's Web* does author E. B. White suggest that Fern can understand the farm animals as they talk. And even then, Fern never talks to the animals; she only listens to them. By the end of the story Fern is growing up and really is more interested in listening to Henry Fussy than to the animals.

Another method for creating belief is careful attention to the detail of the setting. Mary Norton's graphic description of the Borrowers' home beneath the clock enables the reader to visualize this domestic background, and to feel what it would be like to be as small as *The Borrowers.* The well-written fantasy includes details of sensory imagery helping the reader to experience the sounds, smells, and tastes of this new world.

Characters' acceptance of the fanciful nature of the book is another device for developing credibility. In *Earthfasts,* Mayne has portrayed David and Keith as two rather mature scientifically knowledgeable children. Therefore, their acceptance and horror of an eighteenth-century drummer rising out of the earth create the same kind of reaction from the reader. In another well-written fantasy Max could very easily have picked up the twelve toy soldiers and taken them to the Haworth Museum in *The Return of the Twelves* by Clarke. However, he respected the integrity of the little soldiers and helped them in their march to safety. The reader, too, comes to think of these soldiers as being alive.

The use of appropriate language adds a kind of documentation to fantasy. Underground for nearly two hundred years, the drummer uses such obsolete words as "arfish" for "afraid" in *Earthfasts,* and his lack of understanding of such modern words as "breakfast" seems very authentic indeed. Richard Adams created his own lapine language for the rabbits in *Watership Down.* "Tharn," for example, describes a state somewhere between panic and exhaustion, a sort of paralysis of fear. By the time you finish reading this remarkable book, you find yourself thinking with some of these words.

The proof of real objects gives an added dimension of truth in books. How can one explain the origin of Greta's kitten or her father's penknife, if not from Blue Cove in Julia Sauer's story, *Fog Magic?* When the elderly Mrs. Oldknow mends a quilt, she reminisces over pieces from Susan's dresses, as she tells Tolly about the little blind girl in Boston's *The Treasure of Green Knowe.* All these devices may increase the readers' belief in the fantasy.

Another point to be considered when evaluating fantasy is the consistency of the story. Each fantasy should have a logical framework and an internal consistency within the rules that the author has developed. Characters cannot become invisible whenever they face difficulty, unless invisibility is a well-established part of their natures. The laws of fantasy may be strange indeed, but they must be obeyed.

Lloyd Alexander, master of the craft of writing fantasy, explains the importance of internal consistency within the well-written fantasy:

> Once committed to his imaginary kingdom, the writer is not a monarch but a subject. Characters must appear plausible in their own setting, and the writer must go along with the inner logic. Happenings should have logical implications. Details should be tested for consistency. Shall animals speak? If so, do *all* animals speak? If not, then which—and how? Above all, why? Is it essential to the story, or lamely cute? Are there enchantments? How powerful? If an enchanter can perform such-and-such, can he not also do so-and-so?[5]

Finally, while all plots should be original, the plots of fantasy must be ingenious and creative. A contrived or trite plot seems more obvious in a fanciful tale than in a realistic story.

In summary, the following specific questions might guide the evaluation of modern fantasy:

What are the fantastic elements of the story?
How has the author made the story believable?
Is the story logical and consistent within the framework established by the author?
Is the plot original and ingenious?
Is there a universal truth underlying the metaphor of the fantasy?

STRANGE AND CURIOUS WORLDS

When Alice followed the White Rabbit down his rabbit hole and entered into a world that grew "curiouser and curiouser," she established a pattern for many modern books of fantasy. Starting in the world of reality they move quickly into the world of fantasy, where the everyday becomes extraordinary in a believable fashion. The plausible impossibilities of *Alice's Adventures in Wonderland* include potions to drink and edibles to eat that make poor Alice grow up and down

[5] Lloyd Alexander. "The Flat-Heeled Muse" in *Children and Literature* by Virginia Haviland (Glenview, Ill.: Scott Foresman and Co., 1973), p. 243.

like an elevator. At the famous "Mad Hatter's Tea Party" there is no room nor tea. The Mad Hatter, the Dormouse, and the Rabbit are just a few of the individuals whom Alice meets in her wanderings. Other characters include the Red Queen, who has to keep running in order to stay "in the same place"; the hurrying White Rabbit, who keeps murmuring that he'll be late—yet no one knows where he is going; the terrifying Queen of Hearts, who indiscriminately shouts, "Off with her head." Alice's matter-of-fact acceptance of these nonsensical statements makes them seem believable. Always the proper Victorian young lady, Alice maintains her own personality despite her bizarre surroundings. She becomes the one link with reality in this amazingly fantastic world.

Not all children enjoy *Alice's Adventures in Wonderland,* for many of them do not have the maturity or imagination required to appreciate this fantasy. Teachers and librarians might read certain popular selections from the story and then encourage those who enjoy them to read the entire book.

The cyclone that blew Dorothy into the Land of Oz continues to blow swirling controversies around this series of books by L. Frank Baum and others. Some maintain that *The Wizard of Oz* is a skillfully written fantasy, a classic in its own right. Others condemn the first book because of some of the poorly written volumes that followed. Altogether, there are some forty Oz books, of which Baum himself wrote nineteen. *The Wizard of Oz* was the first book and is the most popular. In this story Dorothy, her dog, Toto, the Scarecrow, the Tin Woodman, and the Cowardly Lion make the long, hazardous trip to the Emerald City to seek special gifts from the Wonderful Wizard. The Scarecrow wishes for brains; the Tin Woodman, a heart; and the Lion wants to be brave. Dorothy only wants to get back to Kansas to her Aunt Em and Uncle Henry. Eventually each of the characters achieves his or her particular wish, but the wizardry is in the way they think of themselves, rather than in anything that the Wizard does for them. For the most part this fantasy depends upon the strange situations and creatures that Dorothy and her companions meet, rather than anything they do or say. One never doubts that the four will overcome all odds and achieve their wishes. Even the Wizard holds no terror for practical, matter-of-fact Dorothy. This lack of wonder and awe—the basic ingredients of most fantasy—makes *The Wizard of Oz* seem somewhat pedestrian when compared with other books of its kind.

For many years the Moomintroll family has delighted the children of Sweden. Now children in the United States are taking to these strange but endearing creatures that look slightly like hippopotamuses. The Moomin live in a lonely valley with various peculiar friends—the Snork Maiden, restless Snufkin, the moody stamp-collector, Hemulen, who comes to visit and never leaves, and the horrid Hattifatteners. Each member of the Moomin family is an individual and remains faithful to his characterization throughout the series of books. *Tales from Moominvalley* is the first and, perhaps, best of this fantastic series. Each episode is stranger and more frightening than the last, but the inner life of the characters is what gives them depth. Tove Jansson won the Hans Christian Andersen International Award for this contribution to the literature of children. Not all children in the United States react favorably to these strange creatures, but those who do become enthusiastic "Moomin-fans."

One of the most popular fantasies for children is Roald Dahl's tongue-in-cheek morality tale, *Charlie and the Chocolate Factory.* Mr. Willie Wonka, owner of the mysterious, locked chocolate factory, suddenly announces that the five children who find the gold seal on their chocolate bars will be allowed to visit his fabulous factory. And what an assortment of children win—Augustus Gloop, a greedy fat pig of a boy; Veruca Salt, a spoiled little rich girl whose parents always buy her what she wants; Violet Beauregarde, the world's champion gum chewer; Mike Teevee, a fresh child who spends every waking moment in front of the television set; and Charlie Bucket, the Hero, who is honest, brave, trustworthy, obedient, poor, and starving. One by one the children are disobedient and meet with horrible accidents in the chocolate factory. Nothing, of course, happens to the virtuous Charlie. At the end of the story Charlie and Mr. Wonka fly an elevator back to Charlie's house to pick up his starving family and take them to live at the choc-olate factory, while Charlie learns all of Mr. Wonka's secrets in order to become the future owner of this marvelous place. The book has been the subject of some criticism[6] since the chocolate factory is worked by a tribe of pygmies called the Oompa-Loompas, who supposedly were imported from Africa by Mr. Wonka. While all the white characters (with the exception of Charlie) suffer dreadful fates, the black pygmies are exploited as workers and presented as a group rather than as individuals. True, the entire story is exaggerated satire and is a product of the early 1960s, but one would wish that Roald Dahl had been more sensitive to the portrayal of any minority group. In the film version of the story the pygmies were changed into little green people. Exploitation of others—whether in fantasy or fact; whether benevolent or deliberate; or whether the persons are large or small, or black, red, or green—is still exploitation, and should be an anathema to all thinking persons. The sequel to this book, *Charlie and the Great Glass Elevator*, lacks the humor and the imaginative sparkle of the first book.

Going through *The Phantom Tollbooth*, Milo discovers a strange and curious world indeed. Norton Juster, the author, creates "The Lands Beyond," which includes the Foothills of Confusion, the Mountains of Ignorance, the Lands of Null, the Doldrums, and the Sea of Knowledge. Here Milo meets King Azoz the Unabridged, the unhappy ruler of Dictionopolis, the Mathemagician who serves them subtraction stew and increases their hunger, and the watchdog, Tock, who keeps on ticking throughout all their adventures. Among the many funny episodes in the book is the Royal Banquet, where the guests must eat their words! But the substance of this fantasy is in its play on words rather than its characters or situations. Its appreciation is dependent upon the reader's knowledge of the various meanings of words. For this reason it is funny only for children with mature vocabularies.

Rather than create their own imaginary worlds many authors have successfully blended fantasy with reality to produce strange elements in the known world. A hauntingly beautiful fantasy is

[6]Lois Kalb Bouchard "A New Look at Old Favorites: 'Charlie and the Chocolate Factory'" in *Interracial Books for Children*, Vol. 3 (Winter, Spring 1971), pp. 3, 8.

a story of the Appalachian Mountains titled *You Better Come Home with Me* by John Lawson. No one saw the Boy come down the mountains; he just appeared on Main Street one Saturday night and joined the men as they sat around the stove at Nagles' store. As they got up to leave, the Scarecrow said, "You'd better come home with me," which, as everyone in the mountains knows, is a way of saying goodbye. But the Boy, who had no home and did not know who he was, accepted the statement for the welcome it offered. At the Scarecrow's house he met the clever Mr. Fox, the witch, and the wise Snowman, who thought he recognized the Boy but melted before he could tell him who he was. The Boy felt at home at the Scarecrow's house and he savored the beauty of the woods and the hay fields— somehow he belonged here. All the while the Boy was drawn to the Old Man, who had told him to get off his property. This mystical story of the Boy's quest for his identity blends reality with fantasy. Lawson's descriptions of the coming of the Appalachian spring are superb:

> Sometimes the thaw came suddenly. You smell it first, warm and sweet. Then the rain came. It was almost as if just then he felt a drop. Then he did hear it coming softly in the mountains—ten thousand million thousand drops falling on bare branches, onto the snow, each drop making a dent.[7]

> The cherry tree was reaching, and where its branches had been bare the night before because it had lost last year's leaves, now the branches were bare because this year's leaves had not yet come.[8]

The Sea Egg by L. M. Boston is the haunting story of two young boys and their magical summer on the Cornish coast of England. The boys buy an unusual egg-shaped rock from a lobsterman and place it in a sheltered pool of sea water that can be reached only at low tide through a tunnel. They hope that whatever it might be—sea serpent, sea horse, or genii—can hatch in secrecy and safety in this hidden spot. The egg hatches into a baby triton (a merman), with whom they swim and play most of the day. On the last night of the boys' holiday, their companion shares the most remarkable experience of all—a magical night swimming with the seals through the underwater tunnels of Seal Island. L. M. Boston evokes an eerie beauty in this strange, suspenseful sea adventure.

A mermaid is a part of the bizarre *The Animal Family* created by Randall Jarrell. A man and woman and their son are shipwrecked on an uninhabited coast, where they live an isolated life. The boy's mother and father grow old and die; and the boy, now a man and a hunter, is left completely alone. His loneliness is intensified by his desire to share beauty. The hunter's loneliness is assuaged as a mermaid, bear, lynx, and, finally, a shipwrecked baby become his family. This is a strange and haunting story of man's need to create a home and share love and companionship in the context of a family, even if the family consists of a mermaid and animals. Maurice Sendak has wisely illustrated the original home of every member of this family, thereby emphasizing the theme of the story.

For his fantasy, *A Grass Rope,* William Mayne has created belief in Mary's unicorn by acknowledging everyone else's disbelief. Nan, her older sister, did not believe in the legend at all. Adam, however, tried to find rational explanations behind the old story of a unicorn and a treasure. Mary was too young to bother about science; she simply believed and wove a grass rope to catch the unicorn. The old sign at the Unicorn Inn gave the children their first clues. The rest of the story is told almost entirely through conversation, until the very end when Mary's action frightens everyone. She doesn't find her unicorn at the bottom of the old mine shaft; but she does find the nine silver collars that had belonged to the dogs in the legend and a genuine unicorn's skull! The Yorkshire setting of this story is made more vivid by old Charlie's dialect. However, Mary's childlike expressions are characteristic of all children who still wonder—for example: "What colour is a thing you can't see?"

Andrew Peterson Smith did not believe in fantasy, or make-believe, or anything that was imaginary. Imagine Andrew's reaction when he comes upon an old "Book of Beasts" describing obviously impossible creatures, like the unicorn or the manticore, as though they were real.

---

[7] John Lawson. *You Better Come Home with Me,* illustrated by Arnold Spilka (New York: Crowell, 1966), p. 68.

[8] Lawson, p. 70.

Andrew decides he must report this unscientific book to the proper authorities in the library. Reading further to tabulate all the untruths he finally falls asleep. In his dreams he enters *The Land of Forgotten Beasts* and saves the beautiful, brave—and once believable—inhabitants from oblivion. This book by Barbara Wersba continues to be a favorite of 9- and 10-year-olds.

Both of Natalie Babbitt's fantasies, *The Search for Delicious* and *Kneeknock Rise,* comment on the truth of myth within the framework of their kind of quest story. Young Gaylen is sent out as the king's messenger to poll the kingdom as to which food should stand for the word "delicious" in the dictionary that the prime minister is compiling. Before he finishes, Gaylen uncovers Hemlock's plot to overthrow the king. With the help of all the creatures that the people no longer believe in, but that are the subject of the minstrel's songs and tales—such as woldwellers, the dwarfs, and Ardis, the mermaid—Gaylen is able to foil Hemlock and save his king. In the epilogue the minstrel returns and the prime minister tells him Gaylen's strange story, thinking that it would make a very pretty song indeed! And so myth-making continues. In *Kneeknock Rise,* Egan climbs the mountain and finds a perfectly rational explanation for the groaning noises of the mythical Megrimum. Egan eagerly relates his findings to the villagers, but they refuse to listen to him. Egan discovers that man does not relinquish his myths easily, and harmless monsters may be preferable to facts.

The private world of dreams can be a strange and curious blend of reality with the fanciful. Ben wished for a dog so intensely that he began to dream he had one in the story of *A Dog So Small* by Philippa Pearce. His grandfather had promised him a dog for his birthday, but his parents had said it was impossible to have a dog in London. Instead, his grandparents gave him a little wool-embroidered picture of a Chihuahua. Ben lost the picture on the train, but he didn't lose the one he carried in his mind—Chiquitito, the little dog that always appeared in his dreams and responded to his call. Ben drifted into his dream world more and more, closing his eyes to see his dog. But one day Ben closed his eyes and stepped into the street, following Chiquitito, and was struck by a car. After his recovery from the accident, Ben's parents allowed him to have a puppy. He is overwhelmingly disappointed because it is so big, not small like his dream dog. His grandmother wisely comments: "People get their heart's desire . . . and then they have to begin to learn to live with it."[9] Finally, Ben learns that it's best to be satisfied with possible things rather than to dream of the impossible.

In Mary Steele's book, *Journey Outside,* Dilar escapes from the subterranean river tunnels where his people have lived for generations. In his quest for "The Better Place" that his grandfather had told him about, Dilar learns much about four strange and curious worlds. The first one is inhabited by the People against the Tigers, warm fun-loving people who give no thought to tomorrow. Next, Dilar meets Wingo, who spends all of his time tenderly caring for small creatures who promptly became the prey of the hawks and tigers. Wingo refuses to recognize the cruelty of his love. Dilar, too, becomes a prisoner of his possessive care and escapes only because he is caught in a landslide. In the desert Dilar meets the complete opposite of Wingo's obsessive concern, the "Not People," who wanted and needed no one. Finally, on the cliffs behind the sea, Dilar finds a brusque old man named Vigan who knows something of the raft people. Dilar asks him if he is a wise man and he replies:

'If you mean am I an old man who has learned a lot and thought about it some, yes, I am. If you mean can I tell you what to do and how to do it, yes, I may be. If you mean can I tell you whether to do it and why you should or shouldn't, no, I'm not. Oh, I might know, but only a fool tries to answer such questions for another. Wisdom is like water: there comes a point where it runs into the ground and if you want it you must dig it out yourself.'[10]

There is no doubt that Dilar has become a wiser boy as the result of his journey outside. And one hopes that he will be able to rediscover the underground river and so show his raft people the light of day. Yet in this mysterious allegory, the reader is left with the impression that all the

[9]Phillippa Pearce. *A Dog So Small,* illustrated by Antony Maitland (Philadelphia, Penn.: Lippincott, 1962), p. 138.
[10]Mary Q. Steele. *Journey Outside* (New York: Viking, 1969), p. 123.

persons Dilar met were circling in the dark as much as his grandfather was. Only Vigan, the old goat man, really understood, but he had no answers. Children will read this story for its excitement, but they may be puzzled by its underlying message.

IMAGINARY KINGDOMS

Frequently, authors have created long fairy tales about mythical kingdoms. Carefully detailing the settings, even providing maps of these strange lands, the authors have made them seem very real. The laws of the kingdom and the customs of the people are described—they may be very different from ours, but once stated, they do not deviate.

Many children know the land of Narnia as well as their own backyards or city blocks. C. S. Lewis, a well-known English scholar and theologian, created seven fantasies about the country of Narnia. The best of the series is the first one published, *The Lion, the Witch, and the Wardrobe,* although it was the second in the sequence according to the history of Narnia. Beginning quite realistically in our time and world, four children find their way into the land of Narnia through the back of a huge wardrobe (or closet) in one of the large rooms of an old English house. They find Narnia wrapped in a blanket of snow and ice, under the wicked Snow Queen's spell that controls the weather so it is "always winter and never Christmas." The children and the Narnians pit themselves against the evil witch and her motley assortment of ghouls, boggles, minotaurs, and hags. With the coming of the great Aslan, the Lion, signs of spring are seen in the land. The children successfully aid the lion king in destroying the evil forces, and he crowns them Kings and Queens of Narnia. Narnia has its own history and time, and in *The Magician's Nephew* the reader is told of the beginnings of Narnia, born from the Lion's song of creation. Narnian time is brief, as measured against our time, so with each visit of the children several hundred Narnian years have passed. In the seventh and last of the books of Narnia, King Tirian remembers the stories of his ancestors about the Earth Children and calls on them to come to his aid in this, *The Last Battle.* Narnia is destroyed; yet the real Narnia, the inner Narnia, is not. The children learn that no good

thing is ever lost, and the real identity of the Great Lion, Aslan, is finally revealed to them. These stories are mysterious, intriguing, and beautifully written. If children do not always understand their religious allegory, they may appreciate them as wondrous adventures that somehow reveal more than they say.

Welsh legends and mythology are the inspiration for the intriguing chronicles of the imaginary land of Prydain as told by Lloyd Alexander. In *The Book of Three* the reader is introduced to Taran, an assistant pigkeeper who dreams of becoming a hero. With a strange assortment of companions he pursues Hen Wen, the oracular pig, and struggles to save Prydain from the forces of evil. Probably no one was less prepared for this role than Taran, but he grew as he erred, and matured under stress. The chronicles are continued in the most exciting of all of the books, *The Black Cauldron.* Once again the faithful companions fight evil as they seek to find and destroy the great cauldron in which the dread Cauldron-Born are created, "mute and deathless warriors" made from the stolen bodies of those slain in battle. Taran is proud to be chosen to fight for Lord Gwydion, for now he will have more opportunity to win honor than when washing pigs or weeding a garden. His wise and sensitive companion, Adaon, tells him:

> "I have marched in many a battle host . . . but I have also planted seeds and reaped the harvest with my own hands. And I have learned there is greater honor in a field well plowed than in a field steeped in blood."[11]

Gradually, Taran learns what it means to become a man among men—the sacrifice of his gentle Adaon, the final courage of the proud Ellidyr, and the faithfulness of his companions. He experiences treachery, tragedy, and triumph, yet a thread of humor runs throughout this sinister tale to lighten its tension. Good does prevail, and Taran has matured and is ready for his next adventure. In the third book of the series, *The Castle of Llyr,* Taran escorts Princess Eilonwy to the Isle of Mona, where Queen Teleria is expected to teach the temperamental Eilonwy to

[11]Lloyd Alexander. *The Black Cauldron* (New York: Holt, Rinehart and Winston, 1965), p. 43.

behave in the manner of a proper princess. This is not an easy task, and supporters of the women's liberation movement would be proud of Eilonwy. In the fourth book of the Prydain Cycle, *Taran Wanderer*, Taran goes questing in search of his identity. His search takes him through the awful marshes at Morva, the rugged wastelands, and at length to the Llawgardarn Mountains where, in a moving climax, he looks into the Mirror of Llunet. More important than the identity of his parents, however, is Taran's self-discovery of who he is and what he dares to become. *The High King* is the masterly conclusion to this cycle of stories about the kingdom of Prydain. This title received the Newbery Award. However, the recognition carried praise for all five of these chronicles which provide the story of the maturing of the Assistant Pig-keeper Taran from a proud hotheaded boy to a thoughtful unselfish human being. When given the choice of becoming immortal or staying to finish his task on earth, Taran chose to stay with these words:

'Long ago I yearned to be a hero without knowing, in truth, what a hero was. Now, perhaps, I understand it a little better. A grower of turnips or a

The five titles in the Prydain Cycle by Lloyd Alexander.

Illustrations by Evaline Ness for *The Black Cauldron, The Book of Three, The Castle of Llyr, The High King,* and *Taran Wanderer* by Lloyd Alexander. Reproduced by permission of Holt, Rinehart and Winston, Inc.

shaper of clay, a common farmer or a king—every man is a hero if he strives more for others than for himself alone. Once . . . you told me that the seeking counts more than the finding. So too must the striving count more than the gain.'[12]

Each of these titles may be read independently, but together they represent an exciting adventure in some of the best-written fantasy of our time.

One of the six short stories from *The Foundling* by Alexander could serve as a good introduction to the Prydain Cycle. These tales deal with happenings before the birth of Taran, the Assistant Pig-Keeper. The title story is about Dalben, not as the age-worn enchanter but as a baby floating in a wicker basket in the marshes of Morva. Each of these tales is complete in itself. Some of them, such as "The Stone," would be excellent for dramatic activities with children in the middle grades.

Two other books by Alexander that are lighter and more humorous than the Prydain Cycle are *The Cat Who Wished to Be a Man* and *The Marvelous Misadventures of Sebastian.* In the former story Lionel, the cat of Magister Stephanus, wishes to be a man, even though the grumbling wizard warns him what a sorry lot humans are. Lionel is finally transformed into a man and he goes exploring the world in the town of Brightford. There he meets Gillian, Mistress of the Crowned Swan (kissing is entirely new to him but he is willing to practice), and Dr. Tudbelly, an engaging quack who spouts Latin, knows little medicine, but has basic integrity. The villains are the scheming, greedy Swaggart and Mayor Pursewig, who contrive to hold the townspeople slaves to taxes and tolls and plan to take over the Crowned Swan for themselves. Gillian is a determined lass who is not going to let them succeed. Lionel, of course, could escape being involved by becoming a cat again, but the more he knows of Gillian, the less he feels like leaving her with her troubles. He uses his one magic wish not to return to the wizard but to get to Gillian's side. So Lionel chooses to be human in much the same way that Taran chooses to be human in *The High King.* This is a gem of a book—fast-moving, slapstick, but wise and witty also. As a fantasy it

[12]Lloyd Alexander *The High King* (New York: Holt, Rinehart and Winston, 1968), p. 274.

borrows all that is finest from folk tales and adds the best of literary style. Seven-, 8- and 9-year-olds will delight in its action, dialogue, and comic humor.

The Marvelous Misadventures of Sebastian is equally lighthearted and will delight middle-graders. The story is about an eighteenth-century court musician in the imaginary realm of Hamelin-Loring. The book has all the trappings of a fast-paced adventure story as Sebastian helps a runaway princess, meets a dancing bear, joins a theatrical troupe, is imprisoned, and saves the princess. Episode tumbles after episode, but soaring above them all is the haunting music of the strange enchanted violin that Sebastian has found among the costumes of the entertainers. The beauty of the violin is almost as enticing as the deadly voice of the Lorelei, and twice it nearly proves to be the death of Sebastian. It is difficult to tell whether Sebastian plays the violin or if the magical instrument plays him; he only knows that he has never played so well and that he cannot stop. This amusing fantasy does not have the usual "and they lived happily ever after" ending. For Sebastian hears the sound of what he could become in the magic of his own broken violin. He leaves the Princess to begin his apprenticeship by rediscovering that glory. This is a book that received and deserved the National Book Award.

ANIMAL FANTASY

Ever since Kipling first told his humorous *Just-So Stories* about the origins of certain animal characteristics, authors have been writing imaginative tales of amusing animals. The humor of the *Just-So Stories* is based on Kipling's wonderful use of words and his tongue-in-cheek asides to the reader. The favorite with children is the story of *The Elephant's Child,* whose nose originally was no bigger than a bulgy boot. His "'satiable curiosity" causes him all kinds of trouble and spankings. To find out what the crocodile has for dinner he departs for the "banks of the great grey-green, greasy Limpopo River, all set about with fever-trees. . . ." Here he meets the crocodile, who whispers in his ear that today he will start his meal with the Elephant's Child! The Elephant's Child is finally freed from the crocodile, but only after his nose has been badly pulled out of shape. As he waits for it to shrink, the Bi-Colored-Python-Rock-Snake points out all of the advantages of having an elongated nose. It is convenient for eating, for making a "cool-schloopy-sloshy mud-cap all trickly behind his ears," but most of all it would be wonderful for spanking! Some of these stories—such as *The Elephant's Child, How the Leopard Got His Spots,* and *How the Rhinoceros Got his Skin*—have been beautifully illustrated in single picture-book editions by Leonard Weisgard.

Seven- and 8-year-olds who are just discovering the pleasure of reading will enjoy Michael Bond's series of books about the very endearing *A Bear Called Paddington.* The Brown family finds him in Paddington Station in London, obviously looking for a home, and so they name him and bring him to their house. Paddington earnestly tries to help the Browns, but invariably ends up in difficulty. His well-meaning efforts produce a series of absurdities that make amusing reading. One of the funniest incidents is in the book, *More about Paddington,* and describes the day Paddington decided to wallpaper his room. He covers over the doors and windows and then can't find his way out! Other adventures of this lovable bear are included in *Paddington at Large, Paddington Helps Out, Paddington Takes the Air,* and many more—all amusingly illustrated by Peggy Fortnum.

Another easy introduction into animal fantasy are Beverly Cleary's books *The Mouse and the Motorcycle* and *Runaway Ralph.* Like the Paddington series, these two stories require little suspension of disbelief and are just pure fun. In the first story a young mouse named Ralph makes friends with Keith, a boy staying at the Mountain View Inn and the owner of a toy motorcycle. *Runaway Ralph* continues the adventures of this intrepid mouse. These books are Cleary's first excursions into the world of fantasy, and they have met with as much acceptance by children as her humorous stories about that all-American boy, Henry Huggins.

Macaroon by Julia Cunningham is the gentle story of a raccoon who thought he knew how to obtain all the comforts of life without any of the disadvantages. In the fall, when the leaves turned to scarlet and the air became crisp, the raccoon knew it was time for him to adopt a human child.

Each year he allowed himself to be hugged and loved in return for soft rugs in front of a fire and his meals delivered in a special saucer. It was a good arrangement, the raccoon felt, far better than a cold hole in a tree, except for the leaving. Each year it became increasingly difficult to abandon his adopted children on the first day of spring. This year, therefore, he decides to adopt the most impossible of all impossible children, so the spring departure will be a relief. The raccoon does find such a girl, named Erika, living at the big house. The relationship is perfect—she calls him a rotten old macaroon and throws food at him. Slowly and quite believably Macaroon reforms Erika and loses his heart to her in the process. Evaline Ness has portrayed the temperament and tenderness of this story with her fine illustrations.

Cricket Winter by Felice Holman is a charming story of an inventive 9-year-old boy and the friendship he develops with a tender-hearted cricket who lives below the floor boards in his room. Simms wants to build his own telegraph set, but his family is not interested. However, the cricket is intrigued with the sounds that this human can make; they are very much like his language. Soon the boy and the cricket have learned Morse Code and are communicating with each other. The cricket helps Simms catch the rat which had so bothered his family; and Simms, in turn, helps the cricket regain his lost love. This is a gentle, humorous fantasy that intrigues both boys and girls in the middle grades.

Unquestionably the most beloved animal fantasy of our time is E. B. White's delightful tale, *Charlotte's Web.* While much of our fantasy is of English origin, *Charlotte's Web* is as American as the Fourth of July, and just as much a part of our children's heritage. Eight-year-old Fern can understand all of the animals in the barnyard—the geese who always speak in triplicate ("certainly-ertainly-ertainly"); the wise old sheep; and Templeton, the crafty rat—yet she cannot communicate with them. The true heroine of the story is Charlotte A. Cavatica—a beautiful, large, gray spider who befriends Wilbur, an humble, little pig. The kindly old sheep inadvertently drops the news that as soon as Wilbur is nice and fat he will be butchered. When Wilbur becomes hysterical Charlotte promises to

A loyal Charlotte spins her opinion of her friend Wilbur in this best-loved fantasy of our time.

Illustration by Garth Williams from *Charlotte's Web* by E. B. White. Copyright, 1952, by E. B. White. Reprinted by permission of Harper & Row, Publishers, Inc.

save him. By miraculously spinning words into her web that describe the pig as "radiant," "terrific," and "humble," she makes Wilbur famous. The pig is saved, but Charlotte dies alone on the fairgrounds. Wilbur manages to bring Charlotte's egg sac back to the farm so that the continuity of life in the barnyard is maintained. Wilbur never forgets his friend Charlotte, though he loves her children and grandchildren dearly. Because of her, Wilbur may look forward to a secure and pleasant old age:

> Life in the barn was very good—night and day, winter and summer, spring and fall, dull days and bright days. It was the best place to be, thought Wilbur, this warm delicious cellar, with the garrulous geese, the changing seasons, the heat of the sun, the passage of swallows, the nearness of rats, the sameness of sheep, the love of spiders, the smell of manure, and the glory of everything.[13]

This story has humor, pathos, wisdom, and beauty. Its major themes speak of the web of true friendship and the cycle of life and death. All ages find meaning in this most popular fantasy. An earlier book by White tells the story of *Stuart Little,* the mouse son of the Frederick C. Littles. Children are intrigued by Stuart's many exciting adventures. While adults are somewhat disturbed by the calm acceptance of a mouse born to human parents, this in no way bothers children.

White's most recent book, *The Trumpet of the Swan,* is the story of a mute swan who had to learn to play an instrument in order to woo his mate, Serena. Like *Stuart Little,* this story is a curious blend of fantasy and reality. While not a great book, it still has much appeal for children. And as in all of his books for children White celebrates the joy of living so that he can say through Louis, a swan:

> All his thoughts were of how lucky he was to inhabit such a beautiful earth, how lucky he had been to solve his problems with music, and how pleasant it was to look forward to another night of sleep and another day tomorrow, and the fresh morning, and the light that returns with the day.[14]

The Mousewife by Rumer Godden is a tender story of the friendship between a small, industrious mousewife and a caged turtledove. At first the mouse is only interested in the dried peas in the bird's cage, but later she comes to know the dove as a friend. The dove tells her about dew, about night, and the glory of flying. It is with wonder and awe that the little mousewife learns of the outside world. At last she can no longer stand to think of her friend imprisoned in a cage and she jumps on the catch, releasing the dove. As she sees him fly away she cries tears the size of millet seeds. But she knows now what it means to fly, for she has seen the stars and some of the world beyond. There is a gentle sadness in this story that reminds the reader of some of Andersen's tales. William Pène du Bois has captured mouse expressions of wonder and compassion in his soft gray-and-white illustrations, so appropriate for this animal fantasy.

Robert Lawson has written a gay and gentle

---

[13] E. B. White. *Charlotte's Web,* illustrated by Garth Williams (New York: Harper & Row, 1952), p. 183.

[14] E. B. White. *The Trumpet of the Swan,* illustrated by Edward Frascino (New York: Harper & Row, 1970), p. 210.

story about all the little animals who live on *Rabbit Hill.* The story opens with excitement and wonder about the new folks who are moving into the big house on the hill. Will they be planting folks, who like small animals, or shiftless, mean people? Each animal character responds in his own unique way to this sudden bit of news. Mother Rabbit is a worrier and tends to be pessimistic; Father Rabbit, stately and always eloquent, feels that there are many auspicious signs (he is a Southern gentleman and always speaks in this fashion), and young Georgie delightedly leaps down the hill chanting, "New folks coming, new folks coming!" Uncle Analdas, who visits his sister on Rabbit Hill, is somewhat disinterested but debonair, as befits a worldly bachelor. Although on probation for several days after their arrival, the new folks win the approval of all the animals of Rabbit Hill by putting up a large sign that says: "Please Drive Carefully on Account of Small Animals." They plant a garden without a fence, provide much garbage for Phewie, the skunk, and do not permit the use of poison or traps. Little Willie, the fieldmouse, is rescued from drowning in the rain barrel and Georgie is saved from an automobile accident. Finally, on Midsummer's Eve, the animals on Rabbit Hill have an opportunity to return the kindness of the gentle folks who live in the house. *The Tough Winter* is a sequel to *Rabbit Hill,* and describes the plight of all the animals when the "Folks" go away for the winter and leave a neglectful caretaker and a mean dog in charge. Both these books are more thoroughly enjoyed by fourth- and fifth-graders if they can be savored together during story time. They would be most appropriate for enriching a unit on ecology.

These same qualities of wonder and tenderness are found in the story of a small brown bat who becomes a poet. *The Bat-Poet* written by the late well-known poet, Randall Jarrell, is both a delightful animal fantasy and a commentary on the writing of poetry itself. For some reason a bat once couldn't sleep during the days, so he opened his eyes and saw squirrels and chipmunks, the sun and the mockingbird. He tried to get the other little bats to open their eyes and see the world, but they refused. Admiring the mockingbird's many songs, the little bat makes up some of his own. He first tries his poems out on the bats, but they aren't interested. The

mockingbird deigns to listen, but comments only on the form not the content of his poem. At last, the bat finds the perfect listener, the chipmunk who is delighted with his poems and believes them. The fine pen-and-ink drawings by Maurice Sendak give the impression of steel engravings. They are as faithful to the world of nature as are the little animals in this story. For, while they talk and write poetry, their behavior is otherwise true to life.

The urban counterpart of *Charlotte's Web* and *Rabbit Hill* is *The Cricket in Times Square* by George Selden. A fast-talking Broadway mouse named Tucker and his pal, Harry the Cat, initiate a small country cricket called Chester into the vagaries of city living. Chester spends only one summer in New York City, having been transported in someone's picnic lunch basket. The climax of Chester's summer adventures comes when the cricket begins giving nightly concerts from the Bellinis' newsstand, saving his benefactors from bankruptcy. On his last night before his return to Connecticut, Chester brings traffic in New York City to a standstill as he chirps the sextet from *Lucia di Lammermoor.* After his friends, Tucker and Harry, find him a small corner out of the wind on the Late Local Express, they return to Tucker Mouse's home in the drainpipe and plan their vacation for next summer in the country in Connecticut! This vacation turns into a crusade to save the Connecticut countryside and is detailed in the book *Tucker's Countryside.* The incongruous friendship of these three friends with their varying backgrounds and sophisticated dialogue makes the stories both warm and witty. Garth Williams has created human expressions for each of the animals in such a way as to endow them with real personalities.

Garth Williams also illustrated the series of tongue-in-cheek melodramas by Margery Sharp about the pure and beautiful white mouse *Miss Bianca.* The first story is titled *The Rescuers,* and tells of the breathtaking adventure of three mice—Miss Bianca, Bernard, and Nils—as they rescue a Norwegian poet from the grim, windowless Black Castle. *Miss Bianca* is the exciting story of the rescue of a little girl, Patience, from the clutches of a hideous wicked duchess, who lives in the Diamond Palace. She has twelve mechanical ladies-in-waiting who regularly bow to her every hour and say, "as your Grace pleases." The fiendish duchess wants at least one human being who will react to her cruelty, however, so Patience is kidnapped for this purpose. The beautiful and gracious Miss Bianca and the humble and resolute Bernard effect Patience's rescue with the aid of the mouse members of the Ladies Guild. Williams' illustrations portray the hideousness of the duchess, as well as the gentle beauty of Miss Bianca. *The Turret, Miss Bianca in the Salt Mines* and *Miss Bianca and the Bridesmaid* continue the adventures of these intrepid mice.

Dominic, the expansive hound dog created by William Steig, leaves home one day to see the world. He has no particular plan; he is just moving along on his way to wherever he gets, to find whatever he finds. He's advised at the beginning to go up the road where adventure is, not the one where there is ". . . no adventure, no surprise, nothing to discover or wonder at."[15] Dominic is an adventuring hero in the mold of every picaresque character who sets out to see the world—he meets good fortune and bad (mostly in the form of the wicked Doomsday Gang), a little magic, and, in the end, following the best tradition of fairy tales, he finds a beautiful dog sleeping in an enchanted garden. The book is more than a delightful spoof on fairy tales, however, for it makes its own comment on the personal and social values of our world. Dominic's difficulty in carrying his treasure speaks of the encumbrance of wealth, for instance. The story makes you laugh out loud, but leaves you thinking. *The Real Thief* is even more serious, in that it tells of the unjust accusation of Gawain, the goose and Chief Guard of the King's Royal Treasury. Gawain escapes from his faithless friends and goes into a miserable, lonely self-exile. When the "real thief" is discovered, the king and the entire community are themselves in misery until the goose is found and his good name restored. Again Steig is discussing such important issues as guilt by association and the whole notion of assuming innocence until proven guilty. While these may appear to be heavy themes for children's books, they are always lightly incorporated in humorous nonsensical tales. In many respects they are funny cartoons made visible by superb prose.

[15]William Steig. *Dominic* (New York; Farrar, Straus, 1972), p. 7.

What E. B. White has done to popularize and humanize spiders, Robert O'Brien has accomplished for rats in his Newbery Award-winning book, *Mrs. Frisby and the Rats of NIMH*. Really two stories within one, the first is a warm and brave animal tale of Mrs. Frisby, a widowed mouse mother, and her concern for her family. The plot turns on Mrs. Frisby's determination to save the family's winter home in the garden from spring plowing so that her son Timothy has sufficient time to recuperate from pneumonia. Mrs. Frisby is sent to the rats for help in saving her house and gradually begins to piece together their story, a process speeded up by the device of a long first-person account by Nicodemus, their leader. The rats, as well as Mrs. Frisby's late husband, have escaped from a laboratory called NIMH (National Institute for Mental Health—although it is never so identified in the story), where they had been given DNA and steroid injections to develop their intelligence so they could read and write and also extend their life spans. When Mrs. Frisby meets them, the rats are just completing a plan to move into a wilderness preserve where they hope to establish a self-sufficient farming community and at last live without stealing. In the process of helping the rats prepare to move her house, Mrs. Frisby is able to discover and warn them about the government exterminators who are coming with cyanide gas. All of the rats but two escape to their hidden valley; but the reader never knows if the unlucky ones included Justin, Mrs. Frisby's friend. The epilogue suggests many possibilities for discussion questions or further adventures.

American children who have enjoyed *Mrs. Frisby and the Rats of NIMH* will welcome the much longer (429 pages) and very British story of a band of rabbits that live on *Watership Down*. Originally published in England as a children's book, where Richard Adams, its author, won the Carnegie Medal for the best juvenile, it has been promoted in the United States as adult fiction. While its theme of migration and animal survival is similar to that in *Mrs. Frisby*, its complexity, vocabulary, and sheer length will make it less accessible to many children.

Essentially, this is the story of a band of rabbits who cherish freedom enough to risk their lives to fight for it. The central character of *Watership Down* is Hazel, a young male rabbit who leads a little band of bucks away from the flourishing, well-established Sandleford Warren into new territory to establish a warren of their own. He does so reluctantly but at the urging of his younger and somewhat weaker brother, Fiver, who has a form of extrasensory perception and feels the old warren is in grave danger. The reader is privileged to know that the warren is threatened by a new housing tract (the rabbits had noticed the signboards announcing this, but unlike the rats of NIMH, they can't read). Hazel and Fiver are joined in their search for a new warren by nine others, including Bigwig, the strongest of them all; Blackberry, one of the most intelligent and creative thinkers; and Dandelion, an accomplished storyteller. One of the feats of the author's characterization is the slow, steady growth of Hazel as a leader. He is firm but gentle, wise enough to recognize the talents of others, and always considerate. His actions in saving a terrified mouse from a kestrel and nursing a crippled gull back to health pay handsome dividends, true to the folklore tradition.

The wanderers escape one danger after another and eventually are joined by Bluebell and Captain Holly from the original warren, who tell of its destruction with dogs, poison gas, and a bulldozer. Holly makes this sad commentary, which reflects the author's philosophy: "Men will never rest until they've spoiled the earth and destroyed the animals."[16] Eventually the rabbits do establish a new warren on Watership Down. The rest of the book centers on the necessity of obtaining some does if the new settlement is to continue. They organize a raid on the overcrowded warren at Efrafa, where the Chief Rabbit is General Woundwort, a real Fascist of a rabbit. A dangerous and daring rescue of nearly a dozen does is accomplished by Bigwig with the help of Kehaar, the seagull that Hazel had helped. However, General Woundwort orders pursuit and eventually attacks the warren at Watership Down. Largely because of Hazel's wit and daring and Bigwig's physical courage, the warren is saved.

This is a surprisingly unsentimental, even tough story. It is more realistic than most "realism" because the story is firmly rooted in a world we know. The details of rabbit life are accurately

presented and nothing is passed over or "prettied up." They mate, make droppings, and they talk and joke about both, very much as humans do. The rabbits get hurt and bleed and suffer; they grow ugly with age and they die. According to the rabbits: "We've all got to stop running one day, you know. They say Frith [the sun god] knows all the rabbits, every one."[17]

What is perhaps the most interesting of all, Adams has created a complete rabbit civilization including a religion, a mythology, and even a lapine language, with at least a partial set of linguistic rules to go with it. For example, a "hrududu" is lapine for any large machine and "hrair" designates any number over four, an uncountable number in the rabbits' world. During the story-telling sessions the reader learns of El-ahrairah, the great chief rabbit and trickster; he hears a remarkable creation legend and a deeply moving story of a rabbit redeemer who braves the palace of death to offer his own life for his people. And at the end of the book, when one of the does tells her little one a new story of El-ahrairah, we know that she is telling a garbled version of the story of the establishment of Watership Down and adding Hazel's accomplishments to those of the legendary rabbit—a comment on the entire process of mythmaking.

This remarkable story about rabbits is also very much about human beings, who live in communities, develop leaders, and must cope with their world. There is no way to read this book and not remember it. But the simple act of reading it will take some doing. One hopes teachers will read it aloud and discuss it with 11- and 12-year-olds, and that it might also serve to restore the family story hour.

Watership Down has been compared with *Wind in the Willows* by Kenneth Grahame. In fact, one English reviewer maintained that the "story is what one might expect had *Wind in the Willows* been written after two world wars, various marks of nuclear bomb, the Korean and Vietnam obscenities and half a dozen other hells created by the inexhaustibly evil powers of man."[18] Certainly, *Wind in the Willows* seems slower, much more idyllic, and sentimental by comparison with the Adams book. Yet it is not a story of harsh

---

[16]Richard Adams. *Watership Down* (New York: Macmillan, 1974), p. 136.

[17]Adams. p. 204.

[18]Aidan Chambers. "Letter from England: Great Leaping Lapins!" in *The Horn Book,* Vol. 49, No. 3 (June 1973), p. 255.

survival, as is *Watership Down,* but a peaceful, tender, sometimes humorous story of the friendship among four animals; Water Rat, Mole, Toad, and Badger. Kindly Badger is the oldest and wisest of the quartet, the one they all seek when they are in trouble. Rat is a practical soul, good-natured and intelligent. Mole is the appreciative, sometimes gullible one. The comic relief of the story is provided by Toad, who develops one fad after another. He is always showing off and becoming involved in situations from which Rat, Mole, and Badger are forced to rescue him. Despite his wild fantasies and changing crazes, Toad is a good-hearted, generous friend. As Rat says: "It's never the wrong time to call on Toad. Early or late he's always the same fellow. Always good-tempered, always glad to see you. Always sorry when you go!"[19] It is Toad's expansive, open-hearted personality that enables his loyal friends to put up with him at all. After a long hot journey in a gypsy caravan (one of Toad's fads) Toad, jubilant as ever says:

> "Well, good night, you fellows! This is the real life for a gentleman! Talk about your old river!"
>
> "I *don't* talk about my river," replied the patient rat. "You *know* I don't, Toad. But I *think* about it," he added pathetically, in a lower tone: "I think about it—all the time!"
>
> The Mole reached out from under his blanket, felt for the rat's paw in the darkness, and gave it a squeeze. "I'll do whatever you like, Ratty," he whispered. "Shall we run away tomorrow morning, quite early—*very* early—and go back to our dear old hole on the river?"[20]

Besides friendship, the sense of home and love of nature are the other two themes that pervade this fantasy. Each of the character's homes is described in detail, from the costly Toad Hall to Ratty's snug little dwelling place in the riverbank. And in one chapter, titled "Dulce Domum," Mole catches a whiff of his old home and can't continue his journey with Rat. Choking back his tears, he tries to describe his feelings:

> "I know its a shabby, dingy little place," he sobbed forth at last, brokenly: "not like—your

cozy quarters—or Toad's beautiful hall—or Badger's great house—but it was my own little house—and I was fond of it—and I went away and forgot all about it and then I smelt it suddenly—on the road . . . and I *wanted* it."[21]

Long, loving descriptions of the riverbank, the wild wood, and more abound in this animal pastoral. All children will not have the background of experience to appreciate its beauty, but those who do, love this book above all others. It is best read aloud a chapter at a time, just as Grahame wrote it for his son.

THE WORLD OF TOYS AND DOLLS

As authors have endowed animals with human characteristics, so, too, have they personified toys and dolls. Young children enjoy stories that personify the inanimate, such as a tugboat or a steamshovel.[22] Seven-, 8-, and 9-year-olds still like to imagine that their favorite playthings have a life of their own. Hans Christian Andersen utilized this approach in his stories of "The Steadfast Tin Soldier," "The Fir Tree," and many others. One of the most popular of all children's stories, *The Adventures of Pinocchio* by Collodi, is a personification type of story. The mischievous puppet that old Geppetto carves out of wood becomes alive and has all kinds of adventures. He plays hookey from school, wastes his money, and tells lies. Each time he lies to the Blue Fairy his nose grows longer, until it is so long that he has difficulty turning around in a room. When Pinocchio at last does something for someone else, he becomes a real boy. Written in Italy in 1880, this story has been translated into many different languages and is a universal favorite.

Probably no one has made toys seem quite so much like people as has A. A. Milne in his well-loved Pooh stories. Each chapter contains a separate adventure about the favorite stuffed toys of Milne's son, Christopher Robin. The good companions include *Winnie-the-Pooh,* a bear of little brain; doleful Eeyore, the donkey; Piglet, the happy follower and devoted friend of Pooh; and Rabbit; Owl; Kanga; and little Roo. A bouncy new friend, Tigger, joins the group in Milne's second book, *The House at Pooh Corner.* They all

---

[19]Kenneth Grahame. *The Wind in the Willows,* illustrated by E. H. Shepard (New York: Scribner, 1908, 1940), p. 34.
[20]Grahame, pp. 42–43.

[21]Grahame, pp. 102–103.
[22]*See* Chapter 3.

live in the "100 Aker Wood" and spend most of their time getting into—and out of—exciting and amusing situations. One time, Pooh becomes wedged in a very tight place and has to abstain from eating his "hunny" for a whole week until he grows thin again. Eight- and 9-year-olds thoroughly enjoy the humor of the Heffalump story, and appreciate the self-pity of gloomy Eeyore on his birthday. They like kindly but forgetful Pooh, who knocks at his own door and then wonders why no one answers. They are delighted when Piglet and Roo exchange places in Kanga's pocket, and even more pleased when Piglet gets a dose of Roo's medicine! The humor in these stories is not hilarious but quiet and subtle, with a gentle touch of whimsy. Such humor is usually lost on primary-grade children, but is greatly appreciated by children in the middle grades. However, younger children may enjoy the Pooh stories when they are read within a family circle. Parents' chuckles are contagious, and soon the whole family has become Pooh admirers.

Rumer Godden makes the world of dolls seem very much alive in several of her books—*The Dolls' House, Impunity Jane, The Fairy Doll, Candy Floss, The Story of Holly and Ivy,* and *Home Is the Sailor.* The idea expressed in all Godden's doll books is stated best by Toddie in *The Dolls' House.* She says: "It is an anxious, sometimes a dangerous thing to be a doll. Dolls cannot choose; they can only be chosen; they cannot 'do'; they can only be done by."[23] Another characteristic of Godden's stories is that many of them are stories about boy dolls, or even boys who enjoy playing with dolls. For example, *Impunity Jane,* so named because the salesclerk said she could be dropped "with impunity," belongs to a boy named Gideon. Jane pilots his airplane, rides his bicycle, and sails his boat. No doll could have more exciting or wonderful adventures. *Home Is the Sailor* is the story of a doll family's house that had for many years stood by a window in a house in Wales overlooking the sea. A touch of sadness had pervaded this household of dolls, for there was not a male doll left except for Curly, who was only a boy. Curly's chance meeting with Bertrand, a lonely French boy visiting Wales for

the summer, gives him an opportunity for a marvelous adventure. Part of this unusual doll's story is the way Curly helps Bertrand grow up.

A unique fantasy about toy soldiers is *The Return of the Twelves* by Pauline Clarke. Eight-year-old Max finds twelve wooden soldiers under an attic floor in a Yorkshire farmhouse not far from Haworth, the village where the Bronte family once lived. Warmed by his delight, the little soldiers come to life and talk to him of a time past when four "genii"—Branwell, Charlotte, Emily, and Anne—loved them and played with them. Max and his sister learn that an American has offered 5,000 pounds for Branwell Bronte's soldiers in order to give them to an American museum. The children reason that the toys belong in their ancestral house at Haworth, which is now the Bronte Museum. However, they respect the sturdy independence of the Twelves and help them make their hazardous march to Haworth rather than carry them there. Their flight makes for an exciting story, even without knowing the literary background of the soldiers.

Miss Hickory by Bailey is the story of a unique country doll whose body is an applewood twig and whose head is a hickory nut. Miss Hickory has all the common sense and forthright qualities that her name implies. She survives a severe New Hampshire winter in the company of her friends—Crow, Bull Frog, Ground Hog, and Squirrel. It was Squirrel who ended it all when he ate Miss Hickory's head; but then some might say that was just the beginning—and so it was.

The end of a pair of wind-up toys was their beginning in a strangely cruel yet tender story by Russell Hoban titled *The Mouse and His Child.* New and shiny in the toy shop the day before Christmas, the naïve little toys end up on the rubbish heap in the cruel clutches of Manny Rat. Their long and tedious journey fulfills the prophecy predicted by the frog:

> Low in the dark of summer, high in the winter light; a painful spring, a shattering fall, a scattering regathered. The evening you flee at the beginning awaits you in the end.[24]

The wind-up toys' adventures in the outside world began when a lonely tramp found them

[23] Rumer Godden, *The Dolls' House,* illustrated by Tasha Tudor (New York: Viking, 1962; first published in England in 1947), p. 13.

[24] Russell Hoban. *The Mouse and His Child* (New York: Harper & Row, 1967), p. 28.

in the trash can, wound them up, and told them to "Be Tramps." Searching for a home, a family, and "their territory," the wind-ups seem completely dependent upon blind fate. A combination of many coincidences return them to the dump, where they find "their doll house," establish their family, and defeat Manny Rat. In fact, Manny becomes "Uncle Manny" in his total conversion. In the end the same tramp sees them and advises them to "Be Happy." The story is not a gentle one. It is filled with images of death and decay, violence and vengeance, tears and laughter. The ideas are complex and are conveyed in symbolism and satire. Like *Alice's Adventures in Wonderland*, the story's appeal may be more adult than childlike. Yet it is a fantasy that is not easily forgotten.

LILLIPUTIAN WORLDS

Humans have always been intrigued with the possibility of little people. Swift explored the land of the Lilliputians in *Gulliver's Travels*, and Andersen left us the tale of the lovely *Thumbelina*. In the great tradition of English fantasy, Mary Norton has told a fascinating story about tiny people, *The Borrowers*, and their miniature world under the grandfather clock. There are not many borrowers left, for the rush of modern life does not suit them. They derive their names from their occupation, which is "borrowing" from human "beans," those "great slaves put there for them to use." "Borrowing" is a dangerous trade, for if one is seen by human beings, disastrous things may happen. Therefore, it is with real alarm that Pod and Homily Clock learn of their daughter Arrietty's desire to explore the world upstairs. Finally, Pod allows Arrietty to go on an expedition with him. While Pod is borrowing fibers from the hall doormat to make a new brush for Homily, Arrietty wanders outside, where she meets the boy. Arrietty's disbelief about the number of people in the world who are the boy's size, compared to those of her size, is most convincing:

> "Honestly—" began Arrietty helplessly and laughed again. "Do you really think—I mean, whatever sort of world would it be? Those great chairs . . . I've seen them. Fancy if you had to make chairs that size for everyone? And the stuff for their

Arrietty meets a "human bean." The artists have skillfully shown the comparative sizes of the tiny borrower and the boy.

Illustration by Beth and Joe Krush from *The Borrowers*, copyright, 1952, 1953, by Mary Norton. Reproduced by permission of Harcourt Brace Jovanovich, Inc.

clothes . . . miles and miles of it . . . tents of it . . . and the sewing! And their great houses, reaching up so you can hardly see the ceilings . . . their great beds . . . the food they eat . . . great smoking mountains of it, huge bags of stew and soup and stuff."[25]

In the end, the Borrowers are "discovered" and have to flee for their lives. This surprise ending leads directly to the sequel called *The Borrowers Afield*. The characterizations in these stories are particularly well drawn. Homily is a worrier and Pod is her solid, kindly husband. Prim and properly brought up, Arrietty still cannot control her natural curiosity. These are real people that Mary Norton has created. Her apt descriptions of setting, and the detailed illustration by Beth Krush and Joe Krush, make the small-scale world of the Borrowers come alive. Other titles in the series include *The Borrowers Afloat* and *The Borrowers Aloft*.

A very readable fantasy from the United States is *The Gammage Cup* by Carol Kendall. For 880 years the Minnipins had lived securely in their villages along the Watercress River in the Land Between the Mountains. Revering their relics, their traditions, and their first family, the Periods, most of the Minnipins were sober, sedate people who wore green cloaks and had green front doors to their homes—"the proper color for Minnipins." A few of the Minnipins rebel against this stuffy tradition and paint their doors red and wear orange sashes. Such actions can no longer be tolerated, for the village of Slipper-on-the-Water is preparing to enter a contest for the "best village" in The Land Between the Mountains. At a town meeting it is decided that in order to win the coveted Gammage Cup, all homes must be painted green and have scalloped roofs—and of course all Minnipins must wear green. Muggles, uncertain and embarrassed to speak before the whole village, has the courage to try to explain her reasons for nonconformity:

"Well, I don't think it's doors or cloaks or . . . orange sashes. It's us. What I mean is, it's no matter what color we paint our doors or what kind of clothes we wear, we're . . . well, we're those colors inside us. Instead of being green inside, you see, like other folk. So I don't think it would do any good if we just changed our outside color."[26]

Muggles' explanation is not accepted, however, and the five friends are outlawed to the mountains. Here, the little group of exiles establish a home for themselves and make the startling discovery that the Minnipins' ancient enemies, the Mushrooms, have found a way into the valley and are preparing to attack! Sounding the alarm, the five save the village and are welcomed back as heroes. The tart commentary on false values in a society and the timely theme of the individual versus the group give an added dimension to this well-written fantasy. *The Whisper of Glocken* continues the adventures of the Minnipins, but tells of another village and a new set of heroes.

Perhaps the best-known fantasy of little people in our time is *The Hobbit* by J. R. R. Tolkien, a retired professor at Oxford in England and a scholar of the folk tale and myths of northwest Europe. With his background it seems only natural that he should choose to create a world in which the little folk—dwarfs, elves, and hobbits—dwell. And what is a hobbit?

They are (or were) small people, smaller than dwarves (and they have no beards) but very much larger than lilliputians. There is little or no magic about them, except the ordinary everyday sort which helps them to disappear quickly when large stupid folk like you and me come blundering along making a noise like elephants which they can hear a mile off. They are inclined to be fat in the stomach; they dress in bright colors (chiefly green and yellow); wear no shoes, because their feet grow natural leather soles and thick warm brown hair like the stuff on their heads (which is curly); have long clever brown fingers, good-natured faces, and laugh deep fruity laughs (especially after dinner, which they have twice a day when they can get it).[27]

Generally the hobbits are very respectable creatures who never have any adventures or do any-

[25] Mary Norton. *The Borrowers*, illustrated by Beth Krush and Joe Krush (New York: Harcourt Brace Jovanovich, 1953), p. 78.

[26] Carol Kendall, *The Gammage Cup*, illustrated by Eric Blegvad (New York: Harcourt Brace Jovanovich, 1959), pp. 91–92.
[27] J. R. R. Tolkien. *The Hobbit* (Boston, Mass.: Houghton Mifflin, 1938), p. 12.

thing unexpected. The book is the story of one hobbit, Bilbo Baggins, who has an adventure and finds himself doing and saying altogether unexpected things. He is tricked by the dwarfs and the elves into going on a quest for treasure when he would much rather stay at home where he could be sure of six solid meals a day rather than be off fighting dragons. On the way, he is lost in a tunnel and nearly consumed by a ghoulish creature called Gollum, who is "dark as darkness except for his two big round pale eyes." Gradually the hobbit's inner courage emerges, as he struggles on through terrifying woods, encounters with huge hairy spiders, and battles with goblins to a somewhat enigmatic victory over the dragon (a more heroic figure is allowed to slay it). *The Hobbit* gives children an introduction to middle-earth and its creatures. As adults they may pursue this interest in Tolkien's vastly expanded view of middle-earth in *Lord of the Rings,* a 1,300-page trilogy.

"FABULOUS FLIGHTS"

Before the age of 7, Peter Peabody Pepperell III was a perfectly normal boy. But shortly after his seventh birthday he stopped growing; in fact he started shrinking! By the time Peter was 13, he had "grown down" to almost four inches. Both Peter and his family had adjusted to this reversal of growth; and Peter had a wonderful time training an army of small animals, riding a rabbit, and sailing in a model sailboat. One day Peter met Gus, an uneducated seagull with a great deal of common sense. Gus offered to give Peter a ride, the first of many wonderful flights. *The Fabulous Flight,* which is the name Robert Lawson gave his tongue-in-cheek story, was a dangerous mission across the Atlantic Ocean to steal a small capsule more deadly than any atom bomb. Peter was sure that he and Gus might fly into a heavily guarded castle completely unnoticed. His father thought the plan had possibilities. Finally, they convinced the Secretary of State, and Gus and Peter made their flight. Upon reaching Zargonia they discovered that the "professor" involved was really a crook from the United States who had taken over when the scientist had died. At a dramatic moment Peter obtained the capsule, and Gus dived to safety. Halfway over the ocean Peter decided that no country should own such an

explosive, and he and Gus agreed to unload the capsule. The terrific force of the explosion restored Peter's "sacropitulianphalangic gland" to its normal functioning and his growth once again became normal. Although written over twenty-five years ago, this story now appears to be more appropriate for today's world of international hijacking and hostages than when it was first written.

No one ever had a more fabulous flight than did James in the book, *James and the Giant Peach* by Roald Dahl. James is one of the saddest and loneliest boys in the world, living with two wicked aunts, Aunt Sponge and Aunt Spiker, in an old, ramshackle house on a high hill in the south of England. James meets a queer old man who thrusts a bag of green crystals into his hands and tells him to mix them with water and drink them and he'll never be miserable again. After cautioning him not to let the crystals escape, the old man disappears. James is so excited and so intent upon getting to the kitchen without being seen by his aunts that he slips and falls, and all of the magic crystals disappear into the ground right under the old peach tree. In no time at all an enormous peach grows on the tree, bigger than a house. One night James discovers a door in the side of the peach. Upon entering he finds six amazing creatures who say they had been waiting for him—a grasshopper the size of a large dog, a giant ladybug, an enormous spider, a centipede, an earthworm, and a silkworm. Early the next morning the centipede gnaws off the stem and the huge peach starts to roll down the hill, incidentally smashing Aunt Spiker and crushing Aunt Sponge on its mad dash to the sea. The marvelous adventure has begun! Threatened by sharks, James saves the peach by throwing strands of silk and spider webbing over 502 seagulls who gently lift the peach from the ocean and sail away across the sea. This is a wonderful spoof on Victorian morality tales. The characters are well drawn and their grumbling conversations are very believable. The plot is original and ingenious. The illustrations by Nancy Burkert are beautifully detailed and reflect the pathos and joy of James' "fabulous flight."

The Pott family had a very different kind of flight in their amazing car, *Chitty-Chitty-Bang-Bang.* This sophisticated parody on a detective story is the only children's book written by the late Ian Fleming, the creator of the well-known James Bond mysteries. Commander Caractacus Pott was a famous inventor, but he couldn't account for all the magical abilities of his mysterious green car. Chitty-Chitty could be an airplane or a boat whenever she wanted to. So the Potts took a sea voyage from their English home and accidentally found a gangsters' hidden cave across the Channel in France. The cave contained all the ammunition of a mob of gangsters—Joe the Monster, Man-Mountain Fink, Soapy Sam, and Blood-Money Banks. With the help of the great green car, Commander Pott and his family blew up the cave, but not before the gangsters had seen them. The children are kidnapped and held as hostages. However, by this time the reader is certain that Chitty-Chitty will use the marvelous radar scanner on her hood and find the twins. And she does! The gangsters are turned over to the police. At the very end of the book Chitty-Chitty soars up to the sky, and the Potts are off on an unknown adventure.

Still another fabulous flight is recorded in the story of *The Twenty-one Balloons* by William Pène du Bois. Professor Sherman left San Francisco on August 15, 1883, in a giant balloon, telling reporters that he hoped to be the first man to fly across the Pacific Ocean. He was picked up three weeks later in the Atlantic Ocean clinging to the wreckage of a platform which had been flown through the air by twenty-one balloons. The story is told as the Professor's speech at the Explorers' Club. On the seventh day of his voyage a seagull plummeted through the Professor's balloon, and he was forced to land on the island of Krakatoa. There, Professor Sherman discovered that he was to be a permanent visitor, since the twenty families who lived over the most fabulous diamond mine in the world wished to remain unknown. They were extremely gracious to the Professor and escorted him on a tour of their amazing island, which heaved like the ocean from its volcanic activity. However, each of the houses was built on a diamond foundation and so did not move. The houses were amazing; they included a replica of Mount Vernon, a British cottage with a thatched roof, the Petit Trianon, a Moroccan house, and so on. Mr. F. told the Professor the story of the discovery of the mines and the selection of the twenty families to come and live on the island:

> Each family was required to have two things in order to be chosen. They had to have: a) one boy and one girl between the ages of three and eight; and b) they had to have definite creative interests, such as interests in painting, writing, the sciences, music, architecture, medicine. These two requirements would not only assure future generations of Krakatoa citizens; but he assumed that people with creative interests are not liable to be bored on a small desolate island; and people with inventive interests can more easily cope with unusual situations and form a stronger foundation for a cultured heredity.[28]

The Professor describes the houses, the amazing inventions, and customs of Krakatoans and their escape when the volcano erupted in graphic detail. As usual, the minute description of Du Bois' text is matched only by the meticulous perfection of his pen-and-ink drawings.

ECCENTRIC CHARACTERS AND PREPOSTEROUS SITUATIONS

Many humorous books for children are based upon eccentric characters who are unreal and preposterous situations that could not happen. The forerunner of all nonsense stories in the United States was Lucretia Hale's *The Peterkin Papers*. One of these stories, "The Lady Who Put Salt in Her Coffee," first appeared in a juvenile magazine in 1868. Over one hundred years later children continue to be amused by the tales of the Peterkin family and their friend, the lady from Philadelphia, who offers simple, ridiculous solutions to whatever problem perplexes them.

Amelia Bedelia might well be a descendant of the lady from Philadelphia. As the literal-minded maid of the Rogers family, Amelia follows Mrs. Rogers' instructions to the letter. She can't understand why Mrs. Rogers wants her to dress the chicken or draw the drapes, but she cheerfully goes about making a pair of pants for the chicken and drawing a picture of the drapes. Her wonderful lemon-meringue pie saves the day—and Amelia's job. Peggy Parish has written several

[28] William Pène du Bois. *The Twenty-one Balloons* (New York: Viking, 1947), pp. 83–84.

other books in which Amelia Bedelia continues to do things in her own special way. These modern noodlehead stories include *Thank You, Amelia Bedelia; Play Ball, Amelia Bedelia;* and *Amelia Bedelia and the Surprise Shower.*

A riotously funny character in children's literature is *Pippi Longstocking,* created by a Swedish writer, Astrid Lindgren. Pippi is an orphan who lives alone with her monkey and her horse in a child's utopian world where she tells herself when to go to bed and when to get up! Pippi takes care of herself most efficiently and has a wonderful time doing it. When she washes her kitchen floor, she ties two scrubbing brushes on her bare feet and skates over the boards. She is a tidy housekeeper—in her fashion—as witnessed by the way she cleans the table at her own birthday party:

> When everybody had had enough and the horse had had his share, Pippi took hold of all four corners of the tablecloth and lifted it up so that the cups and plates tumbled over each other as if they were in a sack. Then she stuffed the whole bundle in the woodbox.[29]

Although she is only 9 years old, Pippi can hold her own with anyone, for she is so strong that she can pick up a horse or a man and throw him into the air. Her "logical thinking" delights children. For example, she decides to go to school because she feels it really isn't fair for her to miss Christmas and Easter vacation by not attending! However, one day at school is sufficient for both Pippi and her teacher. Children love this amazing character who always has the integrity to say what she thinks, even if she shocks adults; actually, children are quite envious of Pippi's carefree existence. Seven-, 8-, and 9-year-olds enjoy her madcap adventures in the two sequels to the original Pippi book, *Pippi Goes on Board* and *Pippi in the South Seas.*

Third- and fourth-graders thoroughly enjoy the fun of *Miss Osborne-the-Mop* by Wilson Gage. One very dull summer Jody discovers that she has the power to change people and objects into something else and back again. Complications arise when Jody turns a dust mop into a person

who strongly resembles her fourth-grade teacher, and then finds that she cannot turn the tireless, spindly-legged Miss Osborne back into an ordinary dust mop.

When the east wind blew *Mary Poppins* into the Banks' house in London to care for Michael and Jane, it blew her into the hearts of many thousands of readers. Wearing her shapeless hat and white gloves, carrying her parrot-handled umbrella and a large carpet bag, Mary Poppins is as British as tea, yet many children in the United States love this nursemaid with strange magical powers. Probably their favorite story is that of the laughing-gas party. Jane, Michael, and Mary Poppins visit Mary Poppins' uncle for tea, only to be overcome by fits of uncontrollable laughter. As a result, they all blow right up to the ceiling. Mary Poppins raises the table in some way, and they have birthday tea suspended in midair! Nothing seems impossible for this prim autocrat of the nursery to perform in her matter-of-fact, believable fashion. Not all children enjoy the British flavor of this book, but many adore Mary Poppins as much as did Michael and Jane. Mary Poppins goes serenely on her way through other excruciatingly funny adventures in *Mary Poppins Comes Back, Mary Poppins Opens the Door,* and *Mary Poppins in the Park.* Children hope that the west wind will never blow her away permanently, for she has become a classic character in many a family's reading. While the movie of Mary Poppins by Walt Disney introduced her to thousands of children, it also destroyed some of the acerbity of the character created by P. L. Travers. For Walt Disney's Mary Poppins is beautiful, gay, and fun; while the original is unpredictable, abrupt, and mysterious.

Not all of the strange and eccentric characters in children's literature are women. Robert Lawson has created the droll and inimitable character of Professor Ambrose Augustus McWhinney, inventor of Z-Gas. In fact, it is this same Z-Gas in his bicycle tires that takes him on *McWhinney's Jaunt,* a kind of gliding trip across the country. With Z-Gas, the professor's bicycle tires just won't stay on the ground. He soars westward from the George Washington Bridge, wins $500 in a professional bike race, and is given $1,000 for crossing the Grand Canyon on a kite string. *Mr. Twigg's Mistake* is another humorous story

---

[29] Astrid Lindgren. *Pippi Longstocking,* illustrated by Louis S. Glanzman (New York: Viking, 1950), p. 150.

by Robert Lawson. This is the preposterous tale of what happens to a mole when he eats pure vitamin X instead of Bita-Vita breakfast food. It is all Mr. Twigg's fault because, as a scientist for a breakfast-food company, he pulled the wrong lever and put all of the vitamins intended for thousands of packages into one. It was quite by accident that Squirt Appleton fed this box of "Bities" breakfast food to his pet mole, named General Charles de Gaulle. The results of the mixup are amazingly funny.

The story of *Mr. Popper's Penguins* by Richard Atwater and Florence Atwater has long been the favorite funny story of many primary-grade children. This is the tale of Mr. Popper, a mild little house painter whose major interest in life is the study of the Antarctic. An explorer presents Mr. Popper with a penguin which he promptly names Captain Cook. In order to keep Captain Cook from becoming lonely, Mr. Popper obtains Greta from the zoo. After the arrival of ten baby penguins, Mr. Popper has a freezing plant put in the basement of his house and his furnace moved upstairs to the living room. The Atwaters' serious accounting of a highly implausible situation adds to the humor of this truly funny story.

Keeping penguins in the basement doesn't seem nearly as preposterous as trying to raise a dinosaur in a small New Hampshire town. However, that is precisely what Nate Twitchell does when *The Enormous Egg* which he is taking care of hatches into a baby Triceratops. When government figures in Washington, D.C., are consulted about the problem, members of the Congress attempt to have "Uncle Beazley" (the dinosaur) destroyed, since he is extinct and probably un-American! Nate Twitchell tells the story of his efforts to save Uncle Beazley's life in a grave manner and with a sincere earnestness that makes this book seem even funnier. Oliver Butterworth's satire on politics in the United States is a delightful mixture of humor and truth. The anachronism of a dinosaur in today's world greatly appeals to a child's sense of the ridiculous. A more serious story with a somewhat similar plot is recorded in *Emma Tupper's Diary* by Peter Dickinson. This is an account of a plan concocted by a group of Scottish children to fool tourists into thinking that they had discovered a monster in the lake in their glen. The plan

backfires when they do find real monsters and decide they must be protected.

A satire that is both funny and pathetic is *The Shrinking of Treehorn* by Florence Parry Heide. One day a very strange thing happened to Treehorn, a boy of 7 or 8; he started shrinking. His mother and father ignored his predicament except to tell him to sit up at the table. His friend, Moshie, told him that it was a stupid thing to do, and his teacher said: "'We don't shrink in this class.'"[30] Poor Treehorn spends an unhappy day and night until he finds a magical game that restores his growth. The next night, however, as he is watching one of his fifty-six favorite TV programs, he notices that his hand has turned green. Looking in the mirror he sees that his face and hair are green also. He decides not to tell his parents and see if they notice anything different. They don't. While this book appears in a picture-book format with Edward Gorey's wonderful tongue-in-cheek pen-and-ink drawings, it is not a story for young children. Satire requires maturity. The situation is impossible, but the uncaring self-centered attitude of the parents is possible. Fortunately, most children see it as a very funny story and are very quick to say: "Well, my parents would certainly notice if I started shrinking!"

Freaky Friday by Mary Rodgers is well-named, indeed. The opening statement sets the stage for one of the funniest books published:

> You are not going to believe me, nobody in their right mind could *possibly* believe me, but it's true, really it is!
>
> *When I woke up this morning, I found I'd turned into my mother.*[31]

The plot hinges on this one impossible switch; Annabel looks like her mother, is treated as her mother, must meet her mother's appointments; but thinks and acts as Annabel! Despite the humor of the situation, Annabel does really see herself as others see her, and she comes to have a new appreciation of her mother's role in the family. Students in the middle grades love this

[30]Florence Parry Heide. *The Shrinking of Treehorn*, illustrated by Edward Gorey (New York: Holiday, 1971), unpaged.
[31]Mary Rodgers. *Freaky Friday* (New York: Harper & Row, 1972), p. 1.

mixed-up tale. It is a great book for reading aloud in a fifth- or sixth-grade class.

MAGICAL POWERS

Folk tales are replete with characters or objects that possess particular magical powers of enchantment. Modern authors, like Roald Dahl, have been quick to utilize this motif in many of their fanciful tales. Zak, an 8-year-old girl, had a terrible power and a highly developed sense of righteous indignation. When she became irate at her neighbors for hunting, she put *The Magic Finger* on them. The next morning when Mr. and Mrs. Gregg awaken, they find that they have shrunk to the size of the ducks they were shooting and have grown wings where their arms were. Imagine their consternation when they are out in the backyard trying out their wings, and see a family of enormous ducks with long arms instead of wings moving into their house! Sizing

Copied after the well-known picture of Uncle Sam, an 8-year-old girl puts *The Magic Finger* on her neighbors and stops their hunting forever!

Illustration by William Pène du Bois from *The Magic Finger* by Roald Dahl. Pictures copyright © 1966 by William Pène du Bois. Reprinted by permission of Harper & Row, Publishers, Inc.

up the situation, Mr. Gregg builds a nest for the night. They awaken after a damp, rainy night to find themselves peering down the ends of three double-barreled shotguns. The Greggs promise the ducks that they will never go hunting again, at which point they are suddenly standing in their own yard once more with arms instead of wings. Their reform is complete. At the end of the story Zak hears more guns, and once again her magic finger begins to grow very hot. The theme of this fast-paced fantasy is very much in keeping with today's increased concern for the preservation of wildlife. There is no mistaking the message in William Pène du Bois' pictures, one of which shows Zak pointing her finger at the reader in the same manner as the well-known picture of Uncle Sam by James Montgomery Flagg.

No one knew what made *The Bongleweed* grow so lushly and extravagantly, but it covered Becky's house, the church cemetery, and threatened to invade the formal garden of Pew. Soon it became the center of controversy, since Becky's father, the Harpers' gardener, refused to destroy the weed that had flowers the color and size of fox heads. Becky developed a new respect for her father who for the first time in his life stood up to his employers. The frost finally killed the Bongleweed, but not until it had made a tremendous difference in Becky's life. This well-written fantasy by Helen Cresswell also speaks of the need to preserve beauty in our world even if some see it as undesirable.

The children in the many books of fantasy by Edward Eager frequently possess a magic object, know a magic saying, or have magical powers themselves. In *Half Magic*, Jane finds what she believes to be a nickel, but it is a magic charm, or at least half of a magic charm, for it provides half of all the children's wishes. For example, Katherine wished that their cat would talk, but no one could understand its garbled language. Thereafter, the children learned to double their wishes, so that half of them would come true. Each child in the family has an exciting adventure, including a trip to the Sahara Desert and one through time to the days of King Arthur! Another of Eager's stories, *Seven-day Magic*, tells of a magic book that the children borrow from the library. When they open the book, they find it is about themselves; everything they had done that morning was in the book and the rest of the book was shut tight waiting for them to create it. The children all agree that the best kind of book is a magic one, where:

> . . . the people in the book would be walking home from somewhere and the magic would start suddenly before they knew it. . . . and then they'd have to tame the magic and learn its rules and thwart it.[32]

When their wonderful book is due to be returned to the library at the end of seven days, they take it back. Logic and humor are characteristic of the many books of fantasy that were Eager's legacy of modern magic for today's children.

The Genie of Sutton Place by George Selden was adapted from a TV play. It blends the reality of New York City today with an authentic Arabian Genie, the transformation of a dog into a man, and a turbaned antique dealer turned medium. The combination is light, breezy, and thoroughly entertaining. It has its serious moments, of course. Dooley (Abdullah, the genie that Tim Farr charmed out of the carpet) must decide whether to become forever human or give up his love for Rose, Aunt Lucy's very modern maid. Sam, Tim's half-basset hound, half-springer spaniel also finds out that being turned into a man involves complications:

> "When I woke up this morning, the biggest problem I had was to choose between Alpo and Chuck Wagon."[33]

And beneath all the irreverent carrying on at the National Museum, is a reverence for the secrets of the past. This book would make a fine introduction to fantasy for middle-graders.

The primitive magic of the Aborigines comes to life in the modern city of Sydney, Australia, in Patricia Wrightson's fine story, *An Older Kind of Magic*. This story is well-grounded in realism. A brother and sister, Rupert and Selina, and their friend, Benny, like to play in the Botanical Gardens and are shocked to discover that Sir Mortimer Wyvern plans to urge the Ministry to turn part of the Gardens into a parking lot. It looks as if the forces of commercialism will prevail, but no one had considered the influence of the older magic:

> The city trod heavily down on the land, crushing it under its concrete feet. Yet under the city, strong and silent, lay the living rock; and in caverns and crevices within the rock lived the Nyols, old things of the land.[34]

On the night of the appearance of a thousand-year-old comet, the three children are witness to many strange happenings. Store mannequins come to life and participate in a demonstration to save the park; a stone eagle moves its wing to protect a kitten; Benny practices a charm from an old magic book, "To Call a Toad to Your Hand," and gets a Potkoorok instead; and, finally, Sir Mortimer escapes from the underground Nyols only to be turned to stone when he hears a dog talk! It is a lot to believe, and the magic of this book is that the author has created a mood and setting where it all seems quite possible.

In *The Nargun and the Stars*, also by Wrightson, men disturb the ancient creatures once again; this time at Wongadilla, a sheep ranch in northern Australia. Simon Brent, a silent boy, shocked at the accidental death of both of his parents, comes to live with Charlie and Edie, second cousins whom he has never met. Slowly he comes to terms with the simple, direct ways of the middle-aged brother and sister and with the steep, lonely countryside itself. A city boy, he is awed by the size and beauty of the ranch and delighted by the swamp, where he discovers the Potkoorok, a green-and-golden froglike creature who likes apples and speaks! Simon learns too of the shadowy, elusive spirits who live in the trees, the Turongs. But on the night of the storm Simon is terrified by another, older presence, the ancient Nargun, the huge stonelike creature that "oozed from rose-red fire into darkness." Disturbed by the vibrations of the bulldozer and the road scraper, the Nargun was moving, searching for his primeval silence, and he was crushing everything in his path. Quite believably, Simon finds

[32]Edward Eager. *Seven-day Magic*, illustrated by N. M. Bodecker (New York: Harcourt Brace Jovanovich, 1962), p. 25.
[33]George Selden. *The Genie of Sutton Place* (New York: Farrar, Straus, 1973), p. 89.

[34]Patricia Wrightson. *An Older Kind of Magic*, illustrated by Noela Young (New York: Harcourt Brace Jovanovich, 1972), p. 124.

that Charlie and Edie had known the Potkoorok and the Turongs when they were children. Now Charlie sees the Nargun and realizes the danger to all their lives and the ranch. Calmly, courageously, he tries to discover all he can about the ancient creature, and then he and Simon develop an ingenious plan to drive the Nargun away. Trapped at last in a cavern:

> The Nargun never moved. In this place of nothing—no light, no wind, no heat, no cold, no sound—it waited. It felt the old, slow pulse, deep and enduring, and remembered the earth swinging on its moth-flight around the sun. Its dark, vacant eyes waited: for the mountain to crumble; for a river to break through; for time to wear away.[35]

This is a haunting and powerful fantasy which suggests man's unending struggle with primordial forces.

The setting for *The Summer Birds* by Penelope Farmer is a small village in England. Here, a strange boy meets Charlotte and Emma in the lane one morning. One by one, he teaches the village children how to fly like birds, and all enjoy a magical summer of enchantment. There are an eerie and exciting moonlight flight, daylong expeditions to a remote and lovely lake, and Charlotte's daring swoop like a gull from a cliff top. Yet, running throughout the children's excitement and pleasure is the brooding, ominous question as to the boy's identity. The climax occurs when the boy attempts to take the children with him to a special island, and the children learn who and what he is. He is a bird, the last of his race, who has been given the summer to come and restore his kind with any creatures he can find, for they would take his form once on the island. Charlotte, who is attracted to the boy more than any of the others, has the courage to demand that he tell them where they are going. In the end Maggot, an orphan with no ties, joins the bird and the two fly off, leaving the rest of the children desolate and without the power to fly. An intriguing part of the story is the closed child society that is formed, and the boy's struggle for leadership within it. The characterization is excellent, and the eerie mood of the story is

sustained throughout. *Emma in Winter* is a sequel to *The Summer Birds*. With her sister, Charlotte, away at boarding school, the lonely Emma begins to dream of the joyous summer when the strange boy had taught them to fly. When fat Bobby Fumpkins, even lonelier and more friendless than Emma, begins to appear in her dreams, Emma treats him with the same cruel mockery as she does when she is awake, until she learns that they actually are sharing the same dreams. Emma's growing companionship with Bobby in her dreams affects her relationship with him in real life. Conflict and friendship are also the theme of another of Farmer's books, *The Magic Stone*. Alice, the oldest daughter of a family recently moved to the country from the London slums, meets Caroline, who has lived all of her life in the country and is planning to go off to boarding school. The two girls are immediately antagonistic toward each other, until they find the magic stone. Because of the stone they become more sensitive to nature and to each other. Finally, they surrender their stone so that their two brothers, hostile to each other, may have the same experience they have had.

Farmer's *A Castle of Bone* utilizes the device of a magic cupboard made of apple wood (the wood of mythological immortality) to reduce objects or persons to their origins or infancy. A pigskin wallet when placed in the cupboard becomes a pig again—and Hugh's friend, Penn, is reverted to babyhood. Hugh himself, through the cupboard, lives in a dream world in which a castle and trees exert a strange power over him. He wonders if he can enter that castle, only to discover that he is already inside the magic castle of bone which is his own skeleton. This is a more difficult book for children than the others by Penelope Farmer, but it is for adolescent readers. The power of the characterization and the sheer terror of the magic make this a memorable story.

TRICKS WITH TIME

Probably every human being at one time or another has wondered what it would be like if he could visit the past. We have looked at old houses and wished they could tell us of the previous lives they contained; we have held antique jewelry in our hands and wondered about the former owners. Our curiosity has usually been

[35] Patricia Wrightson. *The Nargun and the Stars* (New York: Atheneum, 1974), p. 184.

more than just an historical interest; we have wished to communicate, to enter into the lives of the past without somehow losing our own particular place in time.

Recognizing this fascination with being transported to another age, authors of books for children have written many fantasies that are based upon tricks with time. Characters appear to step easily from their particular moment in the present to a long-lost point in someone else's. Usually these time leaps are linked to a certain tangible object or place that is common to both periods. In L. M. Boston's Green Knowe stories it is the memory of the house itself that provides the base for the mingling of the children who have lived there at one time or another. In *Tom's Midnight Garden* by Pearce, the old grandfather clock that strikes thirteen hours serves as the fixed point of entry for the fantasy. And in *Charlotte Sometimes* by Farmer, Charlotte becomes Clare only if she sleeps in the bed with wheels in the school dormitory. The rules of time fantasy are as binding as the relentless ticking of our own time period.

Julia Sauer's *Fog Magic* is the tender, moving story of Greta Addington, a young girl of Nova Scotia. One day, while walking in the fog, Greta discovers a secret world, the village of Blue Cove. This fishing village is only present in the fog; on sunny days there are just empty cellar holes of houses from the past. Midst the fog magic, Greta meets a girl her own age named Retha Morrill. Retha's mother senses that Greta is from "over the mountain" and quietly reminds her each time the fog is lifting that it is time for her to go home. Some occasional knowing looks and comments from Greta's father make her realize that he, too, has visited Blue Cove. Greta is particularly anxious that her twelfth birthday be a foggy day. It isn't; but that evening, when she is on the way home from a church picnic with her father, the fog comes in. She runs back to enter Blue Cove, where Retha's mother gives her a soft gray kitten as a birthday present and quietly wishes her a "Safe passage for all the years ahead." Greta senses that this will be the last time that she will be able to visit Blue Cove. She walks slowly down the hill to find her father waiting for her. As she shows him her kitten, he reaches into his pocket and pulls out an odd little knife that he had received on his twelfth birthday at Blue Cove. This hauntingly beautiful story appeals to perceptive children in the middle grades.

When Marnie Was There by Joan Robinson tells the story of an introspective, solitary child, Anna, who first sees Marnie at the window of the old empty Marsh House. Elusive young Marnie appears at odd times and places, but she provides Anna with the friendship she has never before had. When Marnie "leaves," a warm delightful family moves into Marsh House, and Anna finds she is no longer the shy child that she was before she knew Marnie. Gradually the pieces of the puzzle fit together, and Anna discovers that Marnie was her long dead grandmother and that she, too, had had a lonely childhood growing up in the Marsh House. Compelling and mysterious, this is a favorite fantasy of many 9-, 10-, and 11-year-old girls.

Nan Chauncy's memorable fantasy, *The Secret Friends*, won the award for the best Australian children's book for the year of its publication. It is the story of Lexie, a solitary fair-haired girl of Tasmania, who meets and plays with Merrina, an "abo" girl. But the aborigines had all been cruelly killed or had died years ago when Lexie's great-great-aunt Rita had known and played with one. Lexie was 9 when she first felt someone watching her. Her instinct was right, for one day Merrina stepped out of the cleft in a rock above a hidden valley. With growing curiosity, trust, and affection, the children meet almost daily, unknown to anyone. Merrina is fascinated with Lexie's clothes, her zipper, and the fact that she can "unpeel" her shoes and socks. Merrina wears no clothes. One day the "fathers" invite Lexie to a kangaroo feast—never before had she joined in the tribal festivals. The feast ends in terror, however, as two starving escaped convicts find the tribe and shoot them. Merrina gets Lexie safely away both from the convicts and her tribe, who think Lexie had betrayed them. While hurrying over the rocks, Lexie falls and is found unconscious and in deep shock by her father. Gradually, she recalls part of the story and only confides in Kent, her brother. The dream is gone, and Lexie will never again play with Merrina. But Merrina has told her that she would always know when Lexie wanted her. Years later, Merrina keeps that promise when she mysteriously appears and guides Lexie to her brother, who has fallen down the cleft of the same valley and hurt his knee. Lexie wants to thank her, and finds her as Kent said she would be, huddled over her "yearning fire," calling back all her loved ones—for Merrina is all alone. The unusual setting of this story, the convincing characterization, and the smooth stepping back and forth in time make this an outstanding fantasy.

No one is more skillful in fusing the past with the present than L. M. Boston in her stories of Green Knowe, that mysterious old English house in which the author still lives. In *The Children of Green Knowe*, the first in this series, Boston tells the story of a small boy called "Tolly" who is sent to live with his great-grandmother. Over the large fireplace in the drawing room hangs a picture of three children who grew up at Green Knowe in the seventeenth century. Tolly's great-grandmother tells him stories about them: of Toby and his pony Festi, of Linnet and her birds, of Alexander and his flute. The children seem so real that Tolly is convinced they often play hide and seek with him. His great-grandmother believes him, and soon the reader does too! In *The Treasure of Green Knowe*, Boston has included a mysterious search for lost jewels, but the real interest of the book is the story-within-a-story of blind Susan Oldknow's life at Green Knowe some two centuries ago. Children may appreciate the problems and joys of the blind after hearing Susan's story of misunderstanding and mistreatment. Even Tolly, in another generation, becomes concerned that Susan had never seen the stars. His great-grandmother reminds him that Susan could smell the spring night and maybe even the stars:

> "I nearly can myself tonight. She could certainly smell the kind of things that stars belong to and happen in. Sometimes you make things smaller by giving them a name to themselves, like 'star.' Imagine Susan taking a breath of it and just thinking all that!"
>
> Tolly took a lungful of star and cherry blossom and fresh-water river and yew and sleeping violets, and then leaped into bed.[36]

The old house at Green Knowe is also the setting for *The River at Green Knowe*. New characters are

introduced, but the reader misses Tolly and his great-grandmother, who just naturally seem to belong to Green Knowe.

One of the best time fantasies to be written is the mysterious and exciting *Tom's Midnight Garden* by Philippa Pearce. Forced to spend part of a summer with a rather boring aunt and uncle, Tom's visit is quite dull until he hears the grandfather clock in the hall strike thirteen. That is the time for him to slip into the most exciting garden in the world and play with Hatty, a child of the past. Hatty and the gardener, Abel, are the only ones who can see Tom in his pajamas; he is invisible to everyone else. Tom becomes so absorbed in his midnight visits when "there is time no longer," that he does not wish to return home. One fateful night Tom opens the back door and sees only the paving and the fences that stand there in daylight—Hatty and her garden have vanished. When Tom meets the real Hatty, a little old lady who has been dreaming about her past, he understands why the weather in the garden has always been perfect, why some nights it has been one season and the next night a different one, why Hatty was sometimes young and sometimes older; it all depended upon what old Mrs. Bartholomew had chosen to remember. Lonely and bored, Tom had joined her in her dreams. This is a fascinating story that should please both boys and girls in the middle grades. The book won the Carnegie Medal as the outstanding English children's book for the year of its publication.

Charlotte is *Charlotte Sometimes*, but at other times she is Clare Moby, a girl who had been at the same boarding school some forty years before. At first, the girls exchange places on alternate days, leaving each other notes in Clare's diary describing assignments and problems. But one day Charlotte is moved from her regular room and caught in Clare's time. Charlotte enlists the help of Emily, Clare's younger sister, in order to return to the present, but not before she has established a deep affection for Emily and Clare. Underneath the suspense and mystery of Penelope Farmer's well-written fantasy is Charlotte's search for her self-identity. Once back in her own time, Charlotte has developed a clear understanding of her self-worth.

Another English tale of persons trapped in a time period is Helen Cresswell's *Up the Pier*. The

[36]L. M. Boston, *The Treasure of Green Knowe,* illustrated by Peter Boston (New York: Harcourt Brace Jovanovich, 1958), p. 93.

seaside amusement area had been boarded up for the season when Carrie came to visit her aunt in October. Lonely and bored, Carrie is delighted when she meets a strange boy and his family who live on the pier. They are not always there, and when they do appear, it is very sudden. Gradually, Anna learns that the family are trapped by the memory of the gruff old pier-keeper and by her wishes for company. She willingly sacrifices her needs in order to help the Pontifexes to return to their time of 1921.

Fantasy in the United States seems much more lighthearted than that of the British. For example, Edward Ormondroyd's *Time at the Top* is a refreshingly different time fantasy. It starts out with a windy, wretched day when everything had gone wrong, until Susan met a funny little old lady who had lost her hat, had her umbrella blown inside out, and had her bag of groceries ripped. After Susan helped the old lady, the "Mary Poppins-ish" woman said she'd "give her three," and off she went. That had started it, for when Susan pushed the elevator button for the top floor where she and her father lived, the elevator had kept right on going to the eighth floor—except there was no eighth floor. Susan got off and found herself in a different time and at a different place. How she made friends with Victoria and her brother, Robert, solved their financial difficulties and their widowed mother's marital problems makes for a fast-paced, amusing story that middle-graders will particularly enjoy. *Castaways on Long Ago* also by Ormondroyd is almost more mystery than fantasy. Three children on their vacation spend most of their time trying to discover the identity of the mysterious redhaired boy who keeps waving to them from the island where their hosts have forbidden them to go. The children do visit and have a frightening, dreamlike adventure. In the process they

Frank, the Flower, shoots down another truck during the Pea Shooter Campaign of the Pushcart War of 1976.

Reprinted from *The Pushcart War*, text © 1964, by Jean Merrill, illustrations © 1964 by Ronni Solbert, a Young Scott Book, by permission of Addison-Wesley Publishing Company.

discover the identity of the boy on Long Ago Island.

One of the few satires really enjoyed by children is Jean Merrill's *The Pushcart War*. Written from the point of view of 1986, the story is presented as a "documented report" of the famous Pushcart War of 1976. Believing that we cannot have peace in the world unless people understand how wars start, the "author-historian" proceeds to describe the beginning of the war between the giant trucks of New York City and the Pushcarts. The Daffodil Massacre has been established as taking place on the afternoon of March 15, 1976, when Mack, driver of the Mighty Mammoth, rode down the cart of Morris the Florist. Like the Minutemen of the American Revolution, the 509 pushcart peddlers unite in their fight against the three largest trucking firms in the city, known simply as The Three. At first their fragile carts are crushed like matchboxes, but then the loyal band of defenders develops the old-fashioned peashooter into a highly effective weapon. The straight-faced account that provides details of the progress of the war and the eventual triumph of the pushcart peddlers is both a funny and pathetic commentary on life today. Children thoroughly enjoy this satire; in fact, one fifth-grade class returned for their report cards on the last day of school and stayed an extra hour while their teacher finished reading the book. Few books can claim such devotion!

Some authors have made history particularly vivid, as they shift modern characters to interesting historical periods. *A Traveler in Time* is based on the dream experiences of its author, Alison Uttley. Penelope, who is visiting her aunt and uncle at an old manor house, The Thackers, in Derbyshire in England, steps through a door and finds herself talking to her great-aunt, who is kneading dough in an Elizabethan kitchen. At first, Penelope's visits are brief, but then she finds herself caught up with the old tragedy of Anthony Babington and his plot to save Mary Queen of Scots. Knowing Mary's fate, Penelope tries to communicate the dangers involved, but no one will listen to her pathetic pleas. Penelope slips back and forth in time, but she sadly realizes that she will outgrow her visions.

Mystery and political intrigue are also a part of the complex fantasy by Eleanor Cameron titled *The Court of the Stone Children*. The story of modern-day Nina, who has a "Museum Feeling" and thinks she would like to be a curator, becomes intertwined with the story of Dominique, a young noblewoman of nineteenth-century France whose father was executed by Napoleon's regime and whose family possessions are now housed in the French Museum in San Francisco. Domi appears to Nina in the museum and becomes her friend. She enlists Nina's help in the task of clearing her father's name of the charge of murder. What then develops is a suspenseful mystery, with telling clues foreshadowed in one of Nina's "real-life" dreams, in which one of the statues in the Museum's Court of Stone Children points the way to a painting which serves as evidence of the Count's innocence. The fantasy of the fused time periods seems more believable than the characterization of Nina and her friend Gil, who appear to have only the best capacities of youth, including superintelligence and maturity. Both characters are very interested in the subject of "Time." Gil is doing personal research on it; and Nina has a real feeling for the antiquities in the museum. The Chagall painting, "Time Is a River without Banks," which hangs in the museum, is used throughout the story as a symbolic reference point. Nina understands:

> . . . the connection between her Museum Feeling and the painting. "Time is a river without banks"—yes, immeasurable and indefinable. And she understood, with no need for words, that it was the paradox and, somehow, the sadness of Time that drew her to the possessions of those long gone: objects, unthinking, unfeeling objects that yet have their own voices, and that outlast the loving flesh that created them.[37]

This book won the National Book Award in the children's category for 1974. Certainly the quality of the writing is accomplished, but its appeal will be limited to the most sensitive and mature children.

Earthfasts by William Mayne is a chilling story that combines many of the elements of fantasy, legend, and science fiction. David and Keith meet

[37] Eleanor Cameron. *The Court of the Stone Children* (New York: Dutton, 1973), p. 91.

at dusk at the place where Keith had seen a swelling in the earth the day before. Tonight it is larger, and the ground is vibrating with the sound of drumming. The boys speculate as to the cause. Could it be water, a giant mushroom, or badgers? As the noise increases, the boys are frozen in terror as a person emerges from the ground beating a drum and clutching a steady, cold white flame. David identifies this stranger as Nellie Jack John, who according to legend went underneath the castle more than 200 years ago to seek the treasure of King Arthur. The boys protect him and feed him, but Nellie Jack John only stays above the earth for two days, leaving his strangely cold candle behind him. Fascinated by the glow of the taper, David realizes that the many bizarre events occurring throughout the countryside are related to Nellie Jack John's disturbance of time. Ancient stones, called earthfasts, work up in a farmer's ploughed field; a family's boggart returns after an absence of many years; and one terror-filled night David vanishes in what looks like a flash of lightning. Trying to find a clue to David's disappearance, Keith stares at the brilliant cold flame of the candle. Suddenly he understands:

> On the skyline, where lightness filled the air, stood a row of huge stones, or giants. Keith was not sure which they were, but it did not matter, because standing stones were giants, and giants became standing stones whilst the King's time was standing still. And the King's time stood still when the candle Keith held was in its proper place under the ground, because King Arthur's time was not yet come. . . . When Nellie Jack John took up this candle and brought it out from its place he disturbed the time that slept and the King that slept with it, and he woke what was asleep before, and things that slept since, like giants that had become standing stones, and the boggart; and the things that whirled.[38]

This is an unforgettable book that creates belief in the inexplicable.

A more terrifying story that moves from the present to the past and into the future is Joan Phipson's first fantasy, *The Way Home.* Three

[38] William Mayne. *Earthfasts* (New York: Dutton, 1967), p. 140.

young people miraculously survive a flash flood in Australia which kills the mother of one of them and sweeps away their car. The three children find each other, and their subsequent search for rescue turns into a long quest story in which they journey backward in time, meeting variously with Aborigines, with dinosaurs, glaciers, and volcanoes. Toward the end, when they think they are home, they find themselves in a kind of Orwellian future with places they know scarcely recognizable and the people they meet farther and farther out of tune with earth and time, more and more mechanized and immersed in their schedules. Two of the children see an ever-changing "Protector," who brings them through danger in unexplainable ways and who gives them a sense of complete peace. The older boy sees only what he in terror calls "a hater," and dies before he finds his way home. Considering children's fascination with dinosaurs and volcanoes this would be an intriguing book to discuss with boys and girls of 10, 11, or 12.

OVERCOMING EVIL

The age-old conflict between good and evil, light versus darkness, life over death is a recurring theme in modern fantasy as well as in traditional literature. Frequently these tales employ wicked enchantments, transformations, or time magic as a means of subduing one side or the other. Boston has created a sinister mood for her story, *An Enemy at Green Knowe.* Granny Oldknow tells Tolly and his Chinese friend, Ping, about a mad alchemist who lived as a tutor at Green Knowe in the year 1630. In order to gain power and wealth, the alchemist practiced witchcraft. Soon after hearing this story a Miss Melanie Powers, an oddly unattractive woman who had rented a house nearby, comes to call on Granny in search of some of the alchemist's books that she believes might still be in the house. Drawn into the search, the boys find themselves fighting evil as mysterious and dark as it was in the 1600s. Plagues of maggots, birds, and snakes are as repulsive as Miss Powers herself. The boys' discovery of Melanie Powers' real name leads to her downfall. Suspense and imagination in this evil story quite captivates readers in the middle grades.

Better sometimes not to know the powers ranged against you, who is your enemy, and how heavy the odds.[39]

So begins the chilling story of Andrew Badger, a lonely orphan who lives with his unfeeling stepmother as the only boy in a girls' boarding school in England. Andrew makes one friend in the girls' school, Ronnie Peters, a self-sufficient, matter-of-fact girl. The two of them discover the Annerlie ring of power, although they do not guess its significance. However, the ring makes Andrew feel braver, somehow, and much more aware of the beauty around him. He is also sure that there is some relationship between the ring and his dreams of *The Cloud Forest*—that mystical place where he meets the other Andrew, his true self. And yet he doesn't understand the connection of the ring with Sir Edward Annerlie, the proud and contemptuous owner of Annerlie Hall. Ronnie overhears the headmistress and Sir Edward discussing the ring and Andrew. She suspects his true identity and also realizes the danger they are in. Enlisting the aid of a rather timid rector, Ronnie's overprotective mother, and an ineffective teacher, Andrew and Ronnie attempt to fight the forces of evil that include Sir Edward, a neuropsychologist who wants the ring for the power it will give him, the headmistress, and a social scientist with a strange program of self-development. The good do overcome the evil forces, but the latter are not completely eliminated, for evil is never completely vanquished. This is a strong story with a theme that gives warning of ruthless men of science who would try to control men's minds.

Both mystery and fantasy combine in Jane Langton's spellbinding tale, *The Diamond in the Window*. Edward and Eleanor live with their aunt and uncle in a strange old turreted house in Concord, Massachusetts. Their Uncle Freddy had been a world-renowned authority on Emerson and Thoreau until the mysterious disappearance of his younger brother and sister had left him slightly deranged. In the tower room the two beds were made up in a vain hope of the return of the two missing children. Edward and Eleanor move to the tower room and search in their dreams for the two missing members of the family. Their

[39]Joan North, *The Cloud Forest* (New York: Farrar, Straus, 1966), p. 1.

dreams include excitement, terror, and romance. Finally, the two children overcome their adversaries and free the lost children and their prince from a spell cast upon them by the prince's evil uncle. The magnificent star diamond of India is returned to its rightful owner and even Uncle Freddy regains his senses! *The Swing in the Summerhouse* is an exciting sequel to *The Diamond in the Window*, and once again the children must thwart the powers of darkness. In the third book of the series, *The Astonishing Stereoscope*, Eddy finds that they can do more than just look at his Temples of the World stereoscopic cards; they can enter those worlds! Here the children have many adventures and make further discoveries about the truths of good and evil.

Susan Cooper, an Englishwoman now living in Boston, has planned a series of five books about the cosmic struggle between light and dark. The first story is titled *Over Sea, Under Stone*. The three Drew children on a holiday in Cornwall had found an old map and were hunting for an ancient treasure linked with King Arthur. The treasure, which lay "over sea, under stone," if found by the right people, would keep at bay the ancient forces of evil. The children soon find themselves faced with deadly danger somehow connected with the local vicar and a curiously menacing man and his sister. The children turn for help to their Great-uncle Merry, a known scholar of ancient lore. They find the treasure in a cave along the coast only to be trapped by the rising tide and their enemies. They save what they call "The Grail," but lose the manuscript that was the key to the cup's inscriptions. Simon discovers the clue to Great-uncle Merry's real identity, and then he has no doubts as to the authenticity of the grail. The third book of this series, *The Greenwitch*, continues this quest for the grail and the key to its inscription. The forces of evil have stolen the grail from its honored place in the museum. Great-uncle Merry, Simon, Jane, and Barney search for it in Cornwall. Their visit coincides with a local ceremony in which the women of the small Cornish village create a Greenwitch from leaves and branches and cast her into the sea for good luck in fishing and harvest. Jane is present at the making of the Greenwitch and feels strangely drawn to the huge figure. Each woman may touch the witch and make a wish. For some inexplicable reason, Jane wishes the Greenwitch could be happy. Because Jane pitied the Greenwitch, she gave up "her secret," the leaden tube which contained the key to the inscriptions on the grail. In a series of dangerous and exciting episodes, the boys discover the whereabouts of the grail.

Greenwitch is less complex and easier to read than the remarkable second book, *The Dark Is Rising,* which was the only Newbery Honor book for 1974. On the Midwinter Day that is his eleventh birthday, Will Stanton, seventh son of a seventh son, discovers that he is the last of the Old Ones, immortals dedicated throughout the ages to keeping the world from domination by the forces of evil, the Dark. Will is the "Sign-Seeker" who must find the six Signs of Life—each in the shape of a quartered circle (a cross within a circle) in order to complete the "Circle of the Old Ones." The completing of this circle is the only thing which can defeat, even temporarily, the rising of the Dark. Will finds himself with strange powers, able to move in and out of Time. In one of his encounters from an earlier time he meets Merriman Lyon, the first of the Old Ones, who becomes his teacher and mentor. In Lyon's words:

> For the Dark, the Dark is rising. The Walker is abroad, the Rider is riding; they have woken, the Dark is rising. And the last of the Circle is come to claim his own, and the circles must now all be joined. The white horse must go to the Hunter and the river take the valley; there must be fire over the sea. Fire to burn away the Dark, for the Dark, the Dark is rising![40]

While the writing is rich in symbolism and allegory, the author keeps the story grounded in reality, so that Will's "real" life and quest in suspended time are distinct yet interwoven. The Old Ones and the forces of the Dark appear as quiet everyday people in his real life, their significance felt only by Will. The story is played out between Christmas and Twelfth Night, contrasting the family's celebration of love and joy against the cold fierce assault of the Dark. Finally, the six Signs of Life are joined in power and the Dark is at least temporarily defeated. This book is one that needs to be shared and discussed with children. The story is gripping, but complex. A perceptive teacher can help 11- and 12-year-olds find clarity in its complexity. Once interested, they can read the first and third books of the series on their own.

Another superb tale of high fantasy is *A Wizard of Earthsea* by Ursula LeGuin. This is the story of a young boy growing up in an imagined world of many islands, and learning to become a wizard or mage. While studying at the School for Wizards he is taunted by a jealous classmate to use his powers before he is ready. Pride and arrogance drive him to call up a dreadful malignant shadow that threatens his life and all of Earthsea. Thus begins the chase and the hunt between the young wizard and the shadow-beast across stone-peaked islands and the farthest reaches of the waters of Earthsea. This book is memorable for many reasons. LeGuin has created a believable world with its own geography, peoples, beasts, culture, and beliefs. One is almost persuaded that such a world exists, and the fine detailed map by Ruth Robbins gives substance to such credibility. The characterization of young Sparrowhawk, or Ged, which was his true name known only to his most trusted friends, is well developed; he grows from an intelligent, impatient adolescent to a wise and grateful mage. The loyalty and constancy of his friend, Vetch, is beautifully portrayed. One of the major themes running throughout the story is the responsibility that each choice carries with it. While attending the School of Wizardry Ged asks the Master Hand how transformation of objects can be made permanent. He is answered:

> . . . you will learn it, when you are ready to learn it. But you must not change one thing, one pebble, one grain of sand, until you know what good and evil will follow the act. The world is in Equilibrium. A wizard's power of Changing and of Summoning can change the balance of the world. It is dangerous, that power. It is most perilous. It must follow knowledge, and serve need. To light a candle is to cast a shadow.[41]

The word "shadow" is one of the recurring motifs of this story. Ged sets sail for the island of Roke in a boat named "The Shadow." And

---

[40] Susan Cooper. *The Dark Is Rising,* illustrated by Alan E. Cober (New York: Atheneum, 1973), p. 36.

[41] Ursula LeGuin. *A Wizard of Earthsea,* illustrated by Ruth Robbins (Berkeley, Calif.: Parnassus, 1968), p. 57.

Ursula LeGuin has created a geography and a culture for the land and peoples of Earthsea. Ruth Robbins' detailed map gives substance to this imaginary land.

Map of Earthsea, drawn by Ruth Robbins for the book *A Wizard of Earthsea* by Ursula K. LeGuin, illustrated by Ruth Robbins, published by Parnassus Press © 1968.

the evil that he has released into the world is called a shadow, since it has no name. It follows Ged like a shadow until, at the advice of his first mage, Ged begins to hunt the shadow. In the end it is recognized as a shadow of himself and the evil he did. It obtains substance only as Ged embraces it and names it with his own name. True to traditional literature the power of naming or knowing a person's true name is of central importance in this book. Ged's first test on the wizard's island of Roke is to find the password to enter, and five years later his last test is to name the same Master Doorkeeper. In both instances he has to be humble enough to admit his own ignorance. And finally Ged's recognition that the shadow bears his own name suggests

once again that he was responsible for the evil he had released. When Ged has recovered from the horrible struggle with the shadow, Vetch looks at him and understands what has happened:

> And he began to see the truth, that Ged had neither lost nor won, but, naming the shadow of his death with his own name, had made him whole: a man: who knowing his whole true self, cannot be used or possessed by any other power other than by himself, and whose life therefore is lived for life's sake and never in the service of ruin, or pain, or hatred, or the dark.[42]

[42] LeGuin, p. 203.

The next story in this trilogy of Earthsea is the sinister tale of a child priestess sacrificed at the age of 5 to a cult of darkness and evil. At 15 Arha discovers Ged trapped in *The Tombs of Atuan,* a place no man is allowed. Arha must decide between death or life for them both. She is terrified to leave the service of the Dark Ones for fear their evil spirits will overpower her; yet she knows if she stays, she must kill Ged. Arha chooses life and freedom, and together she and Ged escape from the underground labyrinth. This is a slower, more somber story than the first, but it provides important insights into human trust and the price of freedom. The last of the trilogy focuses once again upon the Wizard of Earthsea. Titled *The Farthest Shore,* it completes the mighty deeds of Ged. In this moving tale Ged uses all his wisdom and wizardry to defeat the evil forces of destruction which threatened to overcome the islands of Earthsea. Its metaphor for today's world is profound and clear. The National Book Award in the Children's Category was given to Ursula LeGuin in 1973 for *The Farthest Shore.*

Legend is a rich source upon which to build modern fantasy. While LeGuin has used the ancient archetype of legend to create her books, Ish-Kishor has written *The Master of Miracle* based on the Jewish legend of the creation of the Golem. This legend had its origin in sixteenth-century Prague, when the Jews were being severely persecuted. In order to save them from destruction, a huge living being was created from clay by a great rabbi who could invoke the power of God. The story is told through the eyes of an orphan boy, Gideon Ben Israyel. The High Rabbi asks Gideon to dig and carry the clay from which the giant man, the Golem, is made. With the Golem's help a plot is foiled, for a greedy Count had pretended that ghetto Jews had stolen his daughter to use her blood for the Passover. The Golem and Gideon find Maria Agnes where the Count himself has hidden her, and the ghetto is saved. Then Gideon makes one fateful mistake. He does not follow the rabbi's instructions to destroy the Golem once he had fulfilled his usefulness. The Golem goes on a rampage. As the High Rabbi intervenes, Gideon runs to protect the rabbi's granddaughter, Leah, and is severely injured by the collapse of the Golem. Brain-

damaged, Gideon (according to the legend) is doomed to live and guard the remains of the Golem until the return of the Jews to Palestine. In *A Wizard of Earthsea,* Ged had to assume responsibility for the evil he created by using a power for which he was not ready. Gideon, too, felt he knew more than the High Rabbi and decided to let the Golem live. In a reflection at the end of the story Gideon says: "I must learn that to put away death is to misunderstand the purpose of life."[43]

Alan Garner's book, *The Owl Service,* is based upon the Welsh legend in the *Mabinogion* about Leu Llaw Gyffes and his wife Blodeuwedd, who was made for him out of flowers and who then destroyed him when she turned into an owl. Garner uses a modern China set (service)—seen in one way it resembles flowers or by piecing the pattern together it becomes an owl—as a symbol and device for reliving the tragic Welsh legend in today's world. The cast of characters is complex, particularly when one is not acquainted with the legend. The modern story centers on a group of teenagers—Alison and Roger, a stepbrother and sister from an English upper-class family, and Gwyn, a Welsh lad whose mother, Nancy, rents part of her large house to summer visitors. Gwyn hopes to leave his Welsh village and become better educated. The next group of characters involve the older generation, particularly Huw, the gardener and handyman who, we later discover, is Gwyn's father. The third layer of characters include those who make up the ancient legend of Blodeuwedd. The story begins when Alison discovers a whole set of dishes in the attic over her room. She had heard noises up there when she was sick in bed. The pattern on the dishes look like owls, particularly when she traces the lines and then folds the paper to join them. The pattern then disappears on the plates, but the house becomes filled with a strange menace emanating from them. Poltergeist events occur and increase the many tensions which exist among the characters; the English superiority against the Welsh clannishness, upper social class against the servant class, educated against uneducated superstition, the

[43]Sulamith Ish-Kishor. *The Master of Miracle: A New Novel of the Golem,* illustrated by Arnold Lobel (New York: Harper & Row, 1971), p. 104.

younger generation against the older. A kind of nastiness in human relations pervades the house, along with owl feathers and droppings. The mounting tension is climaxed by an owl attack upon Alison, which is relieved only by Roger's apology to Gwyn and his insistence that Alison see flowers not owls on the plate. This strange playing out of the old Welsh legend appears to be more for adults than children. Yet *The Owl Service* won the Carnegie Medal for the outstanding children's book in England, and appears to be very popular with English children.

North American boys and girls prefer one of Garner's earlier books, *Elidor*, which has the same mounting terror as *The Owl Service* but is less complex. It is the adventure of four children who, while exploring a church that is being dismantled for slum clearance, enter the other world of Elidor which is threatened by the powers of darkness. It would seem that this would be the better book to introduce to children and then share *The Owl Service* with those who are ready

The endpapers for the English edition of *The Owl Service* show the pattern on the plates which, seen in one way, resembles flowers or can be folded to become owls.

From *The Owl Service* by Alan Garner. Used with permission of Collins Publishers.

to take its complexity and overlaid stories. The most recent book by Garner is *Red Shift*, a fascinating tale of three time periods—second-century England, seventeenth-century, and modern England. The genre is difficult to identify. It could be historical fiction or fantasy, depending upon your perspective. Certainly there can be no doubt that with this book, Garner has moved into the young adult or the adult category of literature.

SUSPENSE AND THE SUPERNATURAL

Interest in the occult and the supernatural, a recent adult preoccupation, has captured the imagination of children also. They enjoy spooky, scary stories, just as they like being frightened by terror on TV or horror films. Increasingly, publishers are printing finely-crafted suspense fantasies which are very superior to the usual ghost story or mystery tale. These well-written tales of suspense and the supernatural deserve attention.

Mollie Hunter mingles long-ago legend with present-day mystery in her tale *The Haunted Mountain*. In the lonely mountain passes of the Scottish Highlands the country folk still heed the ancient lore, which bids them give a parcel of their land to the "Good People," so called to disguise their evil nature. But MacAllister was a strong and stubborn crofter and so he ignored the Skeelie Woman's warning not to defy these shadowy creatures. He needed money if he was to marry his Peigi-Ann, and so he dared to plough the Goodman's Croft. Later, the Good People capture him and chain him to the haunted mountain for seven years. His young son Fergus, cast in the same rugged mold as his father, breaks the evil spell by enduring a time of terrible testing. Freed of his chains, the father with his son face a final confrontation with the blind great stone man who haunts the mountain. Their valiant old dog, Colm, gives his life to save them. They bury him in the Goodman's Croft, thus satisfying the demand of the sacrifice of blood before the land of the "Good People" can be rightfully theirs. *The Walking Stones* is a more gentle, loving story of an old Scotsman called Bodach and his friendship with young Donald. Together the two of them call up their co-walkers from the other world to hold back the flooding of their Highland Glen until after the time of the secret walking of the magic ring of stones. The old Bodach is ill and young Donald must go by himself at sunrise and see this event that takes place every hundred years. He is frightened, until he remembers the words of the Bodach: "Magic is just something that happens when everything is right for it to happen."[44] The old Bodach dies, and the dam floods the glen, but not until Donald has received the gift of Second Sight and holds the Bodach's staff in his hand. This mystical story blends the lore and language of old Scotland with the modernization in the new. Rings of standing stones are still found in secluded glens in Scotland. If you have ever listened to the silence that permeates the center of one, it would not be difficult to believe Hunter's superb story of *The Walking Stones. Thomas and the Warlock,* also by Hunter, is really a tall tale of witchcraft. It is the amusing story of a blacksmith who incurs the wrath of a warlock because he is hunting on his land. In the story titled *The Kelpie's Pearls* the townsfolk all thought that old Morag was a witch, for she had been seen talking to a kelpie, or water sprite. Two saw her ride away on the back of a beautiful black horse—one said she was old and crying and the other said she was young and smiling—and both had seen her with their own eyes.

In recent years there has been an increasing interest in witchcraft and books about witches. *Moon Eyes* by Josephine Poole is a chilling tale of a young girl's struggle to save her 5-year-old brother, Thomas, from a "familiar" in the form of a black dog and an evil "aunt" with designs on the boy and his inheritance. The children seem particularly vulnerable in this story, for the boy is mute, unable to speak since his mother's death, and Kate is caring for him alone while her father is away. At first Kate is relieved to have a relative stay at the manor house, and then she becomes suspicious of the evidence of witchcraft in Aunt Rhoda's room. The tension mounts until Kate finds Rhoda forcing Thomas to swear obedience to his master the "devil dog." At that point Thomas speaks his first words, which are, "Get out of this house, Moon Eyes." Rhoda has

lost her control over him and runs down the road into the path of a speeding car. Kate's concern and love for her little brother are very real and add to the reader's involvement in the story.

Jane-Emily by Patricia Clapp is the eerie tale of a spoiled, undisciplined child who still demands her own way even though she is dead. Eighteen-year-old Louisa expects to spend a dull summer when she takes her orphaned niece Jane to stay with her grandmother Canfield. However, she so enjoys the company of attractive Dr. Frost that Louisa tries not to be concerned about Jane's obsession to know everything about Mrs. Canfield's long-dead daughter, Emily. When Dr. Frost describes Emily's almost willful death and the strange sudden deaths of her father and brother, Louisa becomes concerned for Jane. One rainy night Jane thinks she hears Emily calling and she goes outside, only to have the door lock behind her. Cold and dripping wet, she becomes ill and develops pneumonia. The illness abates only when old Mrs. Canfield absolutely denies the self-indulgent spirit of Emily the right to have Jane. For the first time Emily receives the discipline she had never known. All the characters are well-drawn in this unusual story, but perhaps the reader knows Emily the best.

William Sleator's first novel, *Blackbriar*, creates a haunting sense of place. From the moment Danny and his guardian, Phillipa, move into the ancient house, Danny can feel its strange powers. His sleep is filled with sounds of chanting and laughter. Then he discovers the list of names carved on the cellar door. After each name is a date, either 1665 or 1666, except for the last name of Mary Peachy. It stands alone. Strange, weird events occur in rapid succession. One night a shadowy figure knocks at the door and asks for Mary Peachy. Another time, upon returning from the village, Danny and Phillipa see a fire burning in their fireplace and a robed figure seated in front of it. When they enter the house the man is gone, but the fire continues to burn. Islington, the Siamese cat, finds a strange little wooden doll that terrifies Phillipa, but somehow fascinates Danny. In fact, Danny consistently draws strength from meeting each of these challenges, while Phillipa becomes more pettish and quarrelsome. With the aid of the girl, Lark, Danny finds a tunnel leading from the cellar of Black-

[44]Mollie Hunter. *The Walking Stones* (New York: Harper & Row, 1970), p. 86.

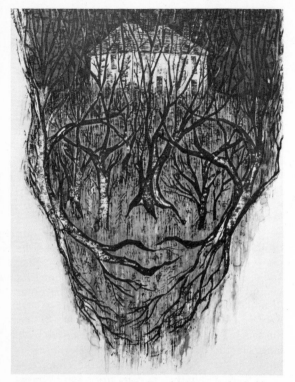

The trees that surround the old house of *Blackbriar* form the shape of a skull, suggesting the sense of mystery that permeates this eerie tale.

From *Blackbriar* by William Sleator, illustrated by Blair Lent. Illustration copyright © 1972 by Blair Lent. Reprinted by permission of the publishers, E. P. Dutton & Co., Inc.

briar and a room full of skeletons. In a dramatic climax the two children uncover the mystery of Blackbriar and Mary Peachy, and, with the help of the police, the mad Lord Harleigh is apprehended. The woods gradually reclaim Blackbriar for the ghost of Mary Peachy; while Danny claims his self-hood and growing independence. This remarkable book, which sustains interest and suspense throughout, is a great one to read aloud to 10- and 11-year-olds.

Another book which is memorable for setting and mood is *The Satanic Mill* by Otfried Preussler. Krabat, a 14-year-old beggar boy in seventeenth-century Germany, apprentices himself to a master of a mill in the dark fen of Kosel. He soon discovers that the mill is actually a school for black magic and that he and the mill's journeymen are virtual prisoners. During the week

Krabat pursues the normal work of the mill, but on Friday nights he is turned into a raven for instruction in the Black Art. The more Krabat learns of the mill, the more danger he realizes that he must face. Each New Year one of the miller's men must die in place of the miller himself according to his pact with the "Goodman." The only escape from the mill is to have his release requested by a girl who loves him and can identify him from all others despite the master's tricks. This book is clearly rooted in the folklore of Eastern Europe. Its very structure follows the pattern of three in describing Krabat's three years at the mill. The only comic relief from the sinister atmosphere comes from the magical transformations. These episodes seem very much like folktales, particularly in the chapter "Military Music," where the miller's men make fools of groups of soldiers. Another interesting aspect of this haunting tale is the accurate detail about the life and times of seventeenth-century Germany—what they ate, what sort of work was necessary to run a mill, village life and customs. It is easy to see why this book won the German Children's Book Prize for 1972.

For sheer nightmare quality no one can compete with the books of Leon Garfield. He establishes an eerie ominous mood from the very first paragraph of *Mister Corbett's Ghost:*

A windy night and the Old Year dying of an ague. Good riddance! A bad Old Year, with a mean spring, a poor summer, a bitter autumn—and now this cold, shivering ague. No one was sorry to see it go. Even the clouds, all in black, seemed hurrying to its burying—somewhere past Hampstead.[45]

Mister Corbett's Ghost is the story of Benjamin Partridge, apprentice to an unbelievably harsh taskmaster, an apothecary named Corbett. On New Year's Eve, when Benjamin was hurrying to join the celebration with his friends and family, Mr. Corbett demanded that he deliver a prescription to an old man three miles away. Benjamin knows that such a long walk will keep him from the New Year's party, and he can think only of revenge against Mr. Corbett. It seems he has come to the right place, for the strange old man,

[45]Leon Garfield. *Mister Corbett's Ghost*, illustrated by Alan E. Cober (New York: Pantheon, 1968), p. 1.

who seems to be either the devil himself or a close relative, offers to arrange Mr. Corbett's death for a reasonable fee. When Benjamin discovers Mr. Corbett's body on the road on the way home he thinks he might be suspected of murder. In a series of macabre incidents he tries to cart the body off to the cemetery for burial. At a point of desperation the old man appears and offers to change the dead weight of Corbett's body for a ghost, although he warns Benjamin that the ghost may prove too heavy for his soul. And so it does, as the boy begins to feel pity for the shivering ghost who begs to go back to the shop for one more peek at his children and Mrs. Corbett. When Ben learns that Mr. Corbett had regretted sending him on the thankless delivery and had set out to bring him back, he feels an agony of guilt. The strange old man suddenly appears and Ben offers him anything to have Mr. Corbett restored. The fee is relatively small (a quarter of the boy's next week's earnings) in contrast to the wisdom gained. Mr. Corbett's ghost does rejoin his body and the family is reunited. Ever afterward, Ben thinks differently about his master. And when he looks at him, he sees a soul as well as a body. This story is enough like *A Christmas Carol* so that children can see and enjoy making comparisons. In Dickens, the man develops compassion for the boy; in this story, the boy develops compassion for the man.

The Ghost Downstairs by Garfield is in many ways similar to *Mister Corbett's Ghost*. It is short, grim, and deals with a bargain made ostensibly with the devil, but which turns out to be a soul-saving bargain in the end. A lonely but very greedy solicitor's clerk makes a contract with a Mr. Fishbane to receive a million pounds for seven years off the end of his life. Mr. Fast, who lives up to his name, specializes in "clever contracts," and gives him the first seven years of his life. Then to Mr. Fast's horror, he finds Mr. Fishbane going around with a pale little ghost who is Dennis Fast, himself at age 7. With the sale of his childhood go all of his dreams and remembrances of the roots of love. While the suspense is here, the themes of lost childhood, lost dreams, and being jaded by desire and obsession for wealth appear to be more adult concerns than children's desires.

It is difficult to describe Joan Aiken's work as anything but fantastic Victorian melodrama. *The Wolves of Willoughby Chase* has all of the ingredients of a nineteenth-century chiller, including wicked wolves without and an outrageously wicked governess within. It takes place in a period of history that never existed—the Stuarts in the person of good King James III are on the throne in the nineteenth century! To adults this spoof on Victorian writing is riotously funny; to children it seems a believable mystery fantasy. *Black Hearts in Battersea* is the mad and exciting sequel to *The Wolves of Willoughby Chase*. It includes shipwrecks, stowaways, more wolves, and a desperate climax to save the king by means of a balloon. *Nightbirds on Nantucket* is the tale of the quest for a pink whale. Feminists will applaud the return of the resourceful 11-year-old Dido as much as they will dislike the quaking 9-year-old Dutiful Penitence and her sinister Aunt Tribulation. Even the chapter subtitles read like old-fashioned Victorian novels: "Chapter Ten: Ways and Means. Penitence eavesdrops. Aunt Tribulation is suspicious. The rocket. The gun's last ride."[46] Essentially, these books represent suspenseful melodrama at its best. While they contain no universal truths, they do provide exciting and lively entertainment.

Science Fiction

The line between science fiction and fantasy has always been difficult to draw, particularly in relation to children's literature. Younger children call anything that has to do with outer space "science fiction," while older children recognize that most science fiction deals with scientific possibilities and the potential changes these may bring about in society. Sylvia Louise Engdahl, writing in *The Horn Book Magazine*, states: ". . . science fiction differs from fantasy not in subject matter but in aim, and its unique aim is to suggest real hypotheses about mankind's future or about the nature of the universe."[47]

Science fiction is very relevant for today's rapidly changing world. Almost all technological and

[46]Joan Aiken. *Nightbirds on Nantucket* (Garden City, N.Y.: Doubleday, 1966), p. 187.
[47]Sylvia Louise Engdahl. "The Changing Role of Science Fiction in Children's Literature," *The Horn Book Magazine*, Vol. 47 (October, 1971), p. 450.

scientific advances have been predicted in science fiction many years before their invention. Over a century ago a Frenchman, Jules Verne, wrote of atomic submarines and rocket ships taking passengers to distant places. He not only forecast man's flight to the moon, he predicted that the United States would lead the way!

Science fiction does more than just speculate about future technological advances, however. Writers must imagine how these new discoveries will affect the daily lives and thoughts of people. In order to do this, the writer must construct a future world in which certain unknowns are accepted as proven fact. As in modern fantasy, detailed descriptions of these "scientific facts" and the characters' acceptance of them make the story believable. However, good writers of science fiction will do more than create fast-moving adventure stories with all the modern gadgetry of the twenty-first century, just as fine writers of historical fiction must refuse to rely only upon such trappings as coonskin caps, buckskin clothing, and encounters with Indians. The author who speaks to today's youth about the future must say what he believes about the interaction of science upon every aspect of society, from politics to warfare, from religion to sports, from education to entertainment. Only a few science-fiction writers for children have been able to rise above scientific novelty to see the human dimensions of this new knowledge.

One of the values of science fiction for children is its ability to develop imagination, speculation, and flexibility in the minds of its readers. Most literature offers a static picture of society; whereas, science fiction assumes a future that is vastly different from the one we know today. In his introduction of *Worlds to Come*, Damon Knight makes this statement:

> What science fiction has been doing for the last forty years is to shake up people's thinking, make them skeptical of dogma, get them used to the idea of change, let them dare to want new things. Nobody will ever know for sure how much effect these stories have had, but it is almost impossible to believe they have had none.[48]

Some of the easiest science fiction for young readers appears in such science-fiction series as Slobodkin's *The Space Ship under the Apple Tree* Series, the *Miss Pickerell* Series by Ellen MacGregor, and the *Mushroom Planet* Series by Eleanor Cameron. There are some five books about Marty, the Martian who visits Eddie Blow on earth. The first book, *The Space Ship under the Apple Tree*, is nearly a picture book, while each story thereafter has become slightly longer. Willie, a black friend of Eddie's, joins the series in *The Space Ship in the Park*. The books are divided into easy chapters, with such amusing titles as "Klunko . . . Junko!" and "Cyfarchiad Dieidhryn."[49] Children in second and third grades find these tales very funny.

Children in the middle grades continue to enjoy the many books by Ellen MacGregor about that intrepid traveler, Miss Pickerell. Returning from her vacation, the elderly Miss Pickerell is amazed to find a spaceship parked in her pasture. In a rage she endeavors to remove the trespassers, but instead finds herself involved in a flight to Mars, where she becomes a heroine in spite of her lack of knowledge about space. The story of her trip is told in *Miss Pickerell Goes to Mars*. There are at least eight titles in the series, including *Miss Pickerell and the Weather Satellite* and *Miss Pickerell Goes on a Dig* both co-authored with Dora Pantell. The mixture of humor and scientific facts delights children who are just discovering science fiction.

Eleanor Cameron's series about the people who visit Basidium, the Mushroom Planet, are exciting and convincingly written. The names of the characters are intriguing: Tyco Bass, a scientist who is actually one of the space people and is old enough to have known Galileo; Prewyt Brumblydge, who has invented the Bumblitron that can make sea water fresh; and King Ta, who comes to visit earth. In *The Wonderful Flight to the Mushroom Planet* two extraordinary California boys go by space rocket to Basidium where they save the people by restoring an essential food to their diet. *Stowaway to the Mushroom Planet*, *Mr. Bass's Planetoid*, and *A Mystery for Mr. Bass* con-

---

[48] Damon Knight, ed., in the introduction to *Worlds to Come* (New York: Harper & Row, 1967), p. xi.

[49] Louis Slobodkin. *The Space Ship in the Park* (New York: Macmillan, 1972).

tinue the fascinating story with moments of suspense and fast action. *Time and Mr. Bass* has more elements of fantasy than science fiction. Other popular space fantasies include the *Danny Dunn* Series by Jay Williams and Raymond Abrashkin and Jerome Beatty's *Mathew Looney* stories.

The Forgotten Door by Alexander Key is a science-fiction story with an unusual theme. Little Jon wakens in a mossy cave and finds himself cold and bruised; he cannot remember who he is or where he came from. He is found by the kindly Bean family, who gradually discover some amazing facts about the quiet, sensitive boy. He cannot speak English, but he understands what they are thinking and gradually translates it into words. He can communicate with animals, even their cross dog. He eats only vegetables and knows nothing of money, guns, robbery, murder, war, or other evils. It soon becomes apparent to the Beans that he is not from this world. The local folk call Jon a wild boy and are afraid of his extraordinary powers. Accused of a robbery, Jon demonstrates his innocence in an exciting scene in the closed session of the judge's chambers. Rumors continue to spread, however, and soon the federal government demands custody over Little Jon. Other political groups would like to use Jon's powers, and the Beans are desperate for help. Finally, Jon is able to hear his parents calling him and he communicates his concern for his friends, the Beans. He is told to bring them with him. As various forces close in on the tiny cabin, Jon and the Beans disappear through the Forgotten Door to the world Jon had described to them—a world so simple as to need no laws, no leaders, and no money, where intelligent people work together and are friends with the deer. The pace of the story is breathtaking. In addition, the characters have substance and the theme is thought-provoking. *Escape to Witch Mountain* also by Key has a similar theme. It is the story of two orphans, Tony and Tia, and their search for their own people, people who have more than ordinary powers and more than ordinary understanding.

Another well-written story of a visitor from outer space is *Down to Earth* by Patricia Wrightson. When Cathy and George discover the space boy living in an old abandoned house, they don't believe his story until they see him curled up asleep in an old stove glowing with a strange green color. They also find that he bounces when he falls. Dropping naturally into the role of his protectors, the children's greatest difficulty is to keep Marty, the Martian, as they called him, from announcing he is a space man to everyone they meet. He can't understand why, when he is just visiting the country until the next new moon, he can't make his presence known. Finally, Marty realizes some of the problems when he is put in custody in a child-welfare home. Hiding in the meter box until the children come to save him, Martin is most indignant at his treatment at the hands of adults. He is grateful for the friendship of the children, and as he awaits his space ship on the night of the new moon he comments:

> "A pity about all the trouble; the police, and the ships and rockets. A great pity. But I'll remember the people, and you and Cathyn . . . Strange, all the same . . . that the sum should be so much smaller than its parts."[50]

The Endless Pavement by Jackson and Perlmutter describes a strange bleak future, where everyone lives in a Home-a-rolla and has his own personal vehicle, a rollabout. Josette goes to school, goes shopping, and even sleeps in her rollabout. People's legs have become useless, because they never walk. The Great-Computer-Mobile's electronic dashboard controls everything, including people's thinking. But one evening, while the family is watching the great auto races on TV, their screen goes blank and they have time to talk to each other. This is when Josette's father tells her about a time where there was grass and green trees. Josette is filled with a curious longing that is fulfilled only when she sees something green sticking up through the endless pavement. This is a strange futuristic story with an obvious message for today's world. It contains satire that 8- and 9-year-olds can understand. They delight in the pledge of allegiance to the Great Computer-Mobile, for example. This is a book which will help children to consider the shape of a future that values mechanized life above all.

[50]Patricia Wrightson. *Down to Earth*, illustrated by Margaret Horder (New York: Harcourt Brace Jovanovich 1965), p. 201.

The many pictures by Richard Cuffari help to visualize this sterile world of concrete.

If there is a classic that emerges in the field of science fiction for children it may be Madeleine L'Engle's *A Wrinkle in Time,* a Newbery Award winner. This exciting story concerns Charles Wallace, a 5-year-old boy brilliant beyond his age and time; Meg, his 12-year-old sister, whose stubbornness becomes an asset in space encounters; and Calvin O'Keefe, a 14-year-old friend upon whose stability the others often rely. The three become involved in a frenzied search for Meg's and Charles' missing father, a scientist who has been working for the government. The children are helped in their search by three ladies who appear to have supernatural powers—Mrs. Whatsit, Mrs. Who, and Mrs. Which. To accomplish the rescue the children must travel in space by the fifth dimension, a tesseract, which reduces the distance between two points by creating a wrinkle in time. Their first tesser takes the children to a friendly planet where they learn that their father is being held prisoner on the distant planet, Camazotz. Camazotz had surrendered to the Power of Darkness, a giant black cloud that represents all evil in the universe. On their second tesseract the children go alone to Camazotz to rescue their father. Here, they find that the people have given up their identity and do everything in a mechanical, robot fashion. Charles Wallace attempts to overcome the Prime Coordinator of the Central Intelligence Building with his superior reasoning and is hypnotized instead into another dehumanized citizen of Camazotz. By using Mrs. Who's glasses, Meg is able to pass through a transparent wall and rescue her imprisoned father. In a frightening scene she is nearly brainwashed by the disembodied, pulsating brain named It. Her father saves her only by tessering her and Calvin to another planet, leaving Charles Wallace behind. Still under the influence of the Black Thing of hate, Meg is furious with her father and Calvin for leaving Charles. She slowly recovers from her ordeal, nursed back to love and peace by one of the planet's strange, faceless inhabitants whom she calls Aunt Beast. The three ladies return and tell Meg that she alone has the necessary power to save her brother. Meg is frightened but agrees to go. When she confronts Charles Wallace, she

suddenly realizes what she has that It does not. She saves Charles from the power of It by repeating her love for him. Together, they rejoin Mr. Murray and Calvin, and with one more tesser they are all back safe on Earth. This story has many layers of meaning. It may be read for its exciting science-fiction plot alone, or it may be read for its themes of love conquering evil and the need to respect individual differences. It is a strange and wonderful combination of science fiction, modern fantasy, and religious symbolism.

L'Engle has written a companion story to *Wrinkle in Time* entitled *A Wind in the Door,* which involves such familiar characters as Meg, Charles Wallace, and Calvin, plus a whole host of new and strange creatures. The story concerns the fight to save Charles Wallace from a baffling illness. Meg, Calvin, and Mr. Jenkins, the cold remote principal of the school, are led to a planet in galactic space where size does not exist. Here they are made small enough to enter Charles Wallace's body and help fight the attacking forces of evil, the Echthroi. Only when Meg names them (and with her own name) does she overcome them and save Charles. The theme of the story emphasizes the importance of every miniscule part of the universe in carrying out its purpose in living, to be all that it was meant to be. For the universe to thrive, the balance of life must be maintained. A recurring motif in this complex tale is the ancient magical power of naming. This is a theme that runs throughout · traditional literature, including the Old and New Testaments. *A Wind in the Door* is a deeper, more complex book than *A Wrinkle in Time.* But L'Engle is capable of "kything" her message to perceptive children of 10 and up to whatever the reader's own age is. One 10-year-old boy returned *A Wind in the Door* to his teacher with real tears in his eyes, saying: "You know this is just a beautiful book."

In writing futuristic stories most authors assume advances in technology or thought control or biochemical feedback. Peter Dickinson has written a trilogy of books in which following so-called "changes," the people of England regress to a feudal state. During the time of "The Changes" mankind learns to fear and dread all machines and so they destroy them. The first book to be published, *The Weathermonger* describes the events long after "The Changes" and tells how two children reverse these strange events. The second story about the changes, called *Heartsease*, is concerned with the narrow prejudice and oppression that exist in a small village. Most of the people still fear machines, hate strangers, and believe in witches. Margaret and her cousin, Jonathan, rescue a downed U.S. pilot who has been stoned by the hysterical villagers as a "witch." The children care for him in the forbidden tractor shed. When he is well, they find a way to get him on board an old tugboat, *Heartsease*, leaving the angry villagers behind. This is the most exciting of the three stories, including the "witch-hunt" and the mad chase down the canals. Dickinson's third book, *The Devil's Children*, takes the reader back to the beginning of the changes. Nicky, separated from her parents at the time, is left alone in London. She joins a group of Sikhs who are unaffected by the changes and becomes their "canary," someone who can warn them lest they offend the suspicious villagers. Gradually Nicky comes to love the "Devil's Children," the name the local group gives the Indians. Once the reader accepts the notion of the changes this book becomes completely believable. The characters are well drawn; the suspense is real; and the plot is original and intriguing. The theme of brotherly love as a necessity for survival is a recurring motif in many science-fiction stories.

The White Mountains trilogy by John Christopher also describes a future world that has been reduced to a primitive society. However, men in this twenty-first-century world are controlled by machine creatures who are called the Tripods. At 14 each human being must be "capped," a ceremony in which a steel plate is inserted into the skull to make the wearer a servant of the state. No one is allowed to discuss the capping ceremony, but Will finds out that his friend, Jack, has some real reservations about it. After Jack's capping he appears to be a different person—docile, too busy working to be a friend. Will talks to a seemingly crazy Vagrant, and finds out that there are a colony of free people living in *The White Mountains* to the south. In the rest of his story Will describes the terrifying journey that he and two other boys make to reach this

refuge. In the second book of the trilogy, *The City of Gold and Lead*, Will wins an athletic contest in order to have "the privilege" of serving the master Tripods. Actually, he goes as a spy to learn the secrets of this alien culture. He succeeds and is able to escape at the end of a suspenseful story. In the last book of the series, *The Pool of Fire*, the Tripods are defeated and mankind is free to set up its own government. The reader hopes that Will's plan for world unity will succeed; but Christopher is a realistic writer, so Will is forced to give up his plans for world peace by quarreling, dissident groups.

The question of free will is also central to another book by Christopher titled *The Guardians*. This Orwellian tale is set in England in the year 2052, when society is divided into two distinct groups—the masses who live in the huge megalopolis called The Conurb and the English aristocracy who live in a kind of controlled Victorian culture. Rob, who is an orphan, runs away from the Conurb and is befriended by Mike, who although he lives in the County, belongs to a secret group of young revolutionaries. Rob, who is passed off as Mike's distant cousin from India, learns to enjoy his role in the County, and the reader can see him begin to change, to conform, and settle down. The story then becomes Mike's and his part in an unsuccessful uprising. When Rob is questioned about Mike's whereabouts he learns that his true identity has been known all along. The authorities offer to make him one of the Guardians, the elite who rule, if he will help in the capture of Mike, whose punishment will be a minor brain operation that will "cure" him of his creative and independent thought. It is chilling to find that Mike's mother approves of the operation (rather like thinking a child's tonsils should be taken out) and that Mike's father had endured a similar "correction" as a young man. Rob balks at this and prepares to escape back to the Conurb, where he hopes to keep in touch with the revolutionaries. This is a sobering book that raises many questions. The very conception of a future society full of its own contrasts and ironies, as well as references to contemporary life, will make students consider their part in shaping our future world.

Christopher's second science-fiction trilogy (*The Prince in Waiting, Beyond the Burning Lands*, and *The Sword of the Spirits*) deals, like *The Guardians*, with England in the twenty-first century. But the imagined society is totally different. People measure time since "The Disaster," a period of volcanic activity, earthquakes, and extra strong radiation from the sun, which has destroyed all of man's technical accomplishments. Amid the ruins a kind of medieval society has sprung up, with independent city-states not far advanced from barbarian tribes. Religion takes the form of Spiritism in this society, and the use of machines or the pursuit of science is as strictly forbidden as in the stories by Peter Dickinson. The Seers, or priests of Spiritism, are comparable to the Guardians of Christopher's earlier book, and the reader soon learns that they have a plan to unite the civilized city-states and lure the people back to the acceptance of science. This does occur and in the last book civilization seems "safely" on the road to science once more, but with as little direction as ever. These books have much more violence in them than the White Mountain trilogy, which is in keeping with their imagined setting. It also may be justified on the basis that it raises the ethical questions of whether violence impersonalized by distance and machine is any different from hand-to-hand violence and whether it is possible to keep "rules" in war. All of John Christopher's books will help children consider the problems of the future of humankind, but the themes never overburden the suspense or action of the stories.

Andre Norton is another prolific writer of science fiction. In *Breed to Come* she uses one of her favorite themes, that of the intelligent animal mutant. For background, we learn that the polluted world has been deserted by people in space ships and is now dominated by "The People" (highly intelligent cats), the Barkers (dogs), the Tusked Ones (pigs) and their common enemy the Rattons (rats). As these animal people become more intelligent, physically refined (the feline People are developing fingers for paws), and acquire more of the knowledge that humans left behind, they also face problems of the human conditions—such as greed, hostility, fear, and doubt. Gammage, an old feline adventurer of the People, wants to rally all the groups together to take a stand against the Demons (humans), whose return is expected. The dreaded return

does occur when two young couples arrive in their scouting space ship. The conflicts that develop are fundamental: Who has real power? Who will gain and be able to use the old knowledge? To what use will the knowledge be put? The story is absorbing and the questions are worth discussion. There is a minimum of space jargon in this book, lots of action, and the characterization is very good. The animal people seem to have greater dimension than the humans, however. Most of Norton's stories are for teenagers, but some middle-grade science-fiction fans are capable of reading such books as *The Crystal Gryphon*, *The Night of Masks*, and *Zero Stone*.

Enchantress from the Stars by Sylvia Louise Engdahl is a most unusual story that almost goes beyond science fiction in its scope. The mission of Elana, her father, and Evrek, her betrothed, is to save the Andrecians from the Imperialists. Elana and her team belong to the Anthropological service of the Federation of Planets occupied by the most advanced human beings in the universe. The Andrecians by contrast are at a medieval stage of development, where people still believe in magic and the king has offered a reward to anyone who can kill the "terrible dragon" that is ravaging his land. The "dragon" is really an earth-moving machine brought by the invading Imperialists from their planet to aid their expedition in destroying the forests of Andrecia, as well as the people, in order to make room for their colonists.

The Federalists are dedicated to the service of saving one Youngling planet from another Youngling planet that may be advanced in scientific knowledge but not in humanity. The assignment is dangerous; in fact, one of the team is killed early in the mission. In working with different societies the Federalists allow the same freedom of choice, the freedom even to fail, as they themselves have. They do not work against the archaic beliefs of the various groups, but with them. For example, they allow Georyn, the fourth son of a woodcutter, to believe that Elana is an Enchantress. They will not kill the dragon for the Andrecians, but help them to find a way to destroy it that is acceptable to their beliefs. Elana asks her father if they couldn't speed up the process of evolution, and he replies: "No! you can't give evolution, anymore than you can give

This decoration is symbolic of the trinity of workers who came from a highly developed world to settle the problems of other "youngling" planets.

Copyright © 1970 by Sylvia Louise Engdahl. Illustrated by Rodney Shackell. From *Enchantress from the Stars*. Used by permission of Atheneum Publishers.

personal maturity. Could you take a small child and teach him to function as an adult?"[51] Eventually Georyn and Elana defeat the invaders by what he believes to be magic, but Elana recognizes as pure faith and love. The power of love triumphs in this story as it does in L'Engle's *A Wrinkle in Time* and *A Wind in the Door*. Despite the differences in the worlds of the Andrecians, the Imperialists, and the Federalists, the values of love, faith, and sacrifice transcend all levels of development. This story will make the reader see his own world in a different perspective, which is one of the functions of good science fiction. The sequel to this book is *The Far Side*

of Evil. Elana is given the assignment of observing a planet that is in the Critical Stage—its people have learned enough about nuclear power to destroy themselves but not enough about self-control to keep from doing so. This story seems more didactic than the *Enchantress*. Two other books, *This Star Shall Abide* and *Beyond the Tomorrow Mountains*, deal with Noreen and his society with its three distinct groups—the villagers, the technicians, and the scholars. The work of Sylvia Engdahl is a major contribution to the field of science fiction for young persons.

Fantasy for children needs no defense. Whether it is a modern fairy tale, such as *Many Moons* or *The Little Prince*, modern fantasy, such as *Charlotte's Web* or *The Dark Is Rising*, or the science fiction of *A Wrinkle in Time* or *Enchantress from the Stars*, these are lasting books that can speak for our time and the times to come. They may stretch a child's imagination and help him to view the world with a new perspective. In accepting the National Book Award for 1973, Ursula LeGuin had this to say about fantasy:

> The fantasist, whether he uses the ancient archetype of myth and legend or the younger ones of science and technology, may be talking as seriously as any sociologist—and a great deal more directly—about human life as it is lived, and as it might be lived, and as it ought to be lived.[52]

[51]Sylvia Louise Engdahl. *Enchantress from the Stars*, illustrated by Rodney Schackell (New York: Atheneum, 1970), p. 137.

[52]From the "Acceptance Remarks of Ursula LeGuin on Receiving the National Book Award in Children's Books for *The Farthest Shore*," reprinted in *The Horn Book Magazine*, Vol. 49 (June 1973), p. 239.

SUGGESTED LEARNING EXPERIENCES

1. Compare the chronicles of Narnia by C. S. Lewis with Lloyd Alexander's Prydain Series; or compare two animal fantasies, such as *The Wind in the Willows* with *Watership Down*. In what ways are they alike; how are they different?
2. The importance of naming or having a secret name is a motif that is central to such books as L'Engle's *A Wind in the Door* or LeGuin's *A Wizard of Earthsea* and *The Tombs of Atuan*. Find other such examples in traditional literature or in anthropological reports of primitive societies. Prepare a chart of your findings.
3. Make a display or a chart of the many symbols and their meaning found in the book, *The Dark Is Rising* by Susan Cooper.
4. Ask a group of middle-graders, or your friends, to list their ten favorite children's books. How many of these could be categorized as modern fantasy?
5. Working with children, or your peers, plan a mural showing favorite characters or animal personalities from fantasy writing.
6. Ask a group of children to tape one chapter from *Charlotte's Web* or *Winnie the Pooh* with different children reading the different animal roles. Play the tape for the class.

7. Write a modern fairy tale, fable, or tall tale using the old forms, but with twentieth-century content and reflecting today's changing values. For example, you might want to consider reversing the stereotyped sex roles of the prince and princess.

8. Ask yourself what might happen to the world of tomorrow if hunger were eliminated, or if robots became practical, or if hydrogen fusion were made a workable source of energy. Think through the impact of one such scientific advancement.

RELATED READINGS

1. Anderson, William, and Patrick Groff. *A New Look at Children's Literature.* Belmont, Calif.: Wadsworth Publishing Co., 1972.

     In Chapter Three these authors present an in-depth analysis of five fantasies. Over half of the chapter is devoted to *Alice's Adventures in Wonderland* and *Through the Looking Glass.*

2. Cameron, Eleanor. *The Green and Burning Tree.* Boston, Mass.: Little, Brown and Company, 1969.

     The title essay in this fine book of literary criticism is a study of time fantasy. As the author of many fantasies herself, Cameron is in a unique position to evaluate the fantasies in this category.

3. Egoff, Sheila, G. T. Stubbs, and L. F. Ashley. *Only Connect: Readings on Children Literature.* New York: Oxford University Press, 1969.

     All the selections under "Fairy Tales, Fantasy, Animals" would be appropriate reading for this chapter. However, don't miss reading the article by C. S. Lewis, "On Three Ways of Writing for Children," or P. L. Travers' (creator of Mary Poppins) fine article, "Only Connect."

4. Frye, Northrup. *The Educated Imagination.* Bloomington, Ind.: Indiana University Press, 1964.

     Frye stresses the social utility of developing the imagination and sees literature as one way in which humans reach out to the environment and find their place in it.

5. Haviland, Virginia. *Children and Literature: Views and Reviews.* Glenview, Ill.: Scott Foresman and Co., 1973.

     The well-known children's librarian of the Library of Congress has made an excellent selection of readings for this book. All of the entries for Chapter Six would be appropriate, but two seem to have great significance for this chapter: Lloyd Alexander's "The Flat-Heeled Muse" and Sylvia Engdahl's "The Changing Role of Science Fiction in Children's Literature."

6. Higgins, James E. *Beyond Words: Mystical Fancy in Children's Literature.* New York: Teachers College Press, Columbia University, 1970.

     A remarkable little paperback that suggests the value of fantasy for the development of the child's imagination, perceptions, and sensibilities.

7. Jago, Wendy. "'A Wizard of Earthsea' and the Charge of Escapism," *Children's Literature in Education,* Vol. 8 (July 1972), pp. 21–29.

     Jago presents the values of fantasy for children, and then gives a thoughtful explication of *The Wizard of Earthsea.* This periodical comes from England and certainly deserves the attention of every serious student of children's literature.

8. Tolkien, J. R. R. *Tree and Leaf.* Boston, Mass.: Houghton Mifflin, 1965.

     The author of *The Hobbit* has written a critical essay on the technique and purposes of writing "On Fairy Stories." This discusion is followed by a short story, "Leaf by Niggle," which is an illustration of the points Tolkien makes in his essay.

RECOMMENDED REFERENCES[53]

Adams, Richard. *Watership Down.* Macmillan, 1974.

Aiken, Joan. *Black Hearts in Battersea,* illustrated by Robin Jacques. Doubleday, 1964.

[53] All books listed at the end of this chapter are recommended subject to the qualifications noted in the text. *See* Appendix D for publishers' complete addresses.

————. *Nightbirds on Nantucket*, illustrated by Robin Jacques. Doubleday, 1966.

————.*The Wolves of Willoughby Chase*, illustrated by Pat Marriott. Doubleday, 1963.

Alexander, Lloyd. *The Black Cauldron*. Holt, Rinehart and Winston, 1965.

————. *The Book of Three*. Holt, Rinehart and Winston, 1964.

————. *The Castle of Llyr*. Holt, Rinehart and Winston, 1966.

————. *The Cat Who Wished to Be a Man*. Dutton, 1973.

————. *Coll and His White Pig*, illustrated by Evaline Ness. Holt, Rinehart and Winston, 1965.

————. *The Foundling*, illustrated by Margot Zemach. Holt, Rinehart and Winston, 1973.

————. *The Four Donkeys*, illustrated by Lester Abrams. Holt, Rinehart and Winston, 1972.

————. *The High King*. Holt, Rinehart and Winston, 1968.

————. *The King's Fountain*, illustrated by Ezra Jack Keats. Dutton, 1971.

————. *The Marvelous Misadventures of Sebastian*. Dutton, 1970.

————. *Taran Wanderer*. Holt, Rinehart and Winston, 1967.

————. *The Truthful Harp*, illustrated by Evaline Ness. Holt, Rinehart and Winston, 1971.

Andersen, Hans Christian. *The Emperor's New Clothes*, illustrated by Virginia Lee Burton. Houghton Mifflin, 1949.

————. *The Emperor's New Clothes*, illustrated by Jack and Irene Delano. Random House, 1971.

————. *The Fir Tree*, illustrated by Nancy Burkert. Harper & Row, 1970.

————. *The Little Match Girl*, illustrated by Blair Lent. Houghton Mifflin, 1968.

————. "The Little Mermaid" in *Hans Christian Andersen: The Complete Fairy Tales and Stories*, translated by Erik Christian Haugaard. Doubleday, 1974.

————. *The Nightingale*, translated by M. R. James, illustrated by Kaj Beckman. Van Nostrand, 1969.

————. *The Nightingale*, translated by Eva Le Gallienne, illustrated by Nancy Ekholm Burkert. Harper & Row, 1965.

————. "The Princess and the Pea" in *Seven Tales*, translated by Eva Le Gallienne, illustrated by Maurice Sendak. Harper & Row, 1959.

————. *The Snow Queen*, illustrated by Marcia Brown. Scribner, 1972.

————. *The Steadfast Tin Soldier*, translated by M. R. James, illustrated by Marcia Brown. Scribner, 1953.

————. *The Steadfast Tin Soldier*, illustrated by Monika Laimgruber. Atheneum, 1971.

————. *The Swineherd*, translated and illustrated by Erik Blegvad. Harcourt Brace Jovanovich, 1958.

————. *Thumbelina*, illustrated by Adrienne Adams. Scribner, 1961.

————. *Thumbelina*, translated by M. R. James, illustrated by Kaj Beckman. Van Nostrand, 1973.

————. *The Woman with the Eggs*, adapted by Jan Wahl, illustrated by Ray Cruz. Crown, 1975.

————. *The Ugly Duckling*, illustrated by Adrienne Adams. Scribner, 1965.

————. *The Wild Swans*, illustrated by Marcia Brown. Scribner, 1963.

Atwater, Richard, and Florence Atwater. *Mr. Popper's Penguins*, illustrated by Robert Lawson. Little, Brown, 1938.

Babbitt, Natalie. *Kneeknock Rise*. Farrar, Straus, 1970.

————. *The Search for Delicious*. Farrar, Straus, 1969.

Bailey, Carolyn Sherwin. *Miss Hickory*, illustrated by Ruth Gannett. Viking, 1962 (1946).

Baum, L. Frank. *The Wizard of Oz*. World, 1972 (1900).

Beatty, Jerome, Jr. *Matthew Looney and the Space Pirates*, illustrated by Gahan Wilson. Young Scott, 1972.

Bond, Michael. *A Bear Called Paddington*, illustrated by Peggy Fortnum. Houghton Mifflin, 1960.

————. *More about Paddington*, illustrated by Peggy Fortnum. Houghton Mifflin, 1962.

————. *Paddington at Large*, illustrated by Peggy Fortnum. Houghton Mifflin, 1963.

————. *Paddington Helps Out*, illustrated by Peggy Fortnum. Houghton Mifflin, 1961.

————. *Paddington Marches On*, illustrated by Peggy Fortnum. Houghton Mifflin, 1965.

————. *Paddington Takes the Air,* illustrated by Peggy Fortnum. Houghton Mifflin, 1971.

✓ Boston, L. M. *The Children of Green Knowe,* illustrated by Peter Boston. Harcourt Brace Jovanovich, 1955.

————. *An Enemy at Green Knowe,* illustrated by Peter Boston. Harcourt Brace Jovanovich, 1964.

————. *The River at Green Knowe,* illustrated by Peter Boston. Harcourt Brace Jovanovich, 1959.

————. *The Sea Egg,* illustrated by Peter Boston. Harcourt Brace Jovanovich, 1967.

————. *The Treasure of Green Knowe,* illustrated by Peter Boston. Harcourt Brace Jovanovich, 1958.

Butterworth, Oliver. *The Enormous Egg,* illustrated by Louis Darling. Little, Brown, 1956.

✓ Cameron, Eleanor. *The Court of the Stone Children.* Dutton, 1973.

————. *Mr. Bass's Planetoid,* illustrated by Louis Darling. Little, Brown, 1958.

————. *A Mystery for Mr. Bass,* illustrated by Leonard Shortall. Little, Brown, 1960.

————. *Stowaway to the Mushroom Planet,* illustrated by Robert Henneberger. Little, Brown, 1956.

————. *Time and Mr. Bass,* illustrated by Fred H. Meise. Little, Brown, 1967.

————. *The Wonderful Flight to the Mushroom Planet,* illustrated by Robert Henneberger. Little, Brown, 1954.

✓ Carroll, Lewis, pseud. (Charles L. Dodgson). *Alice's Adventures in Wonderland and Through the Looking Glass,* illustrated by John Tenniel. Macmillan, 1963 (1865, 1872).

Chauncy, Nan. *The Secret Friends,* illustrated by Brian Wildsmith. F. Watts, 1962.

Christopher, John. *Beyond the Burning Lands.* Macmillan, 1971.

————. *The City of Gold and Lead.* Macmillan, 1967.

————. *The Guardians.* Macmillan, 1970.

————. *The Pool of Fire.* Macmillan, 1968.

————. *The Prince in Waiting.* Macmillan, 1970.

————. *The Sword of the Spirits.* Macmillan, 1972.

————. *The White Mountains.* Macmillan, 1967.

Clapp, Patricia. *Jane-Emily.* Lothrop, 1969.

Clarke, Pauline. *The Return of the Twelves,* illustrated by Bernarda Bryson. Coward-McCann, 1963.

Cleary, Beverly. *The Mouse and the Motorcycle,* illustrated by Louis Darling. Morrow, 1965.

————. *Runaway Ralph,* illustrated by Louis Darling, Morrow, 1970.

✓ Collodi, C. *The Adventures of Pinocchio,* illustrated by Naiad Einsel. Macmillan, 1963 (1892).

✓ Cooper, Susan. *The Dark Is Rising,* illustrated by Alan E. Cober. Atheneum, 1973.

————. *The Greenwitch.* Atheneum, 1974.

————. *Over Sea, Under Stone,* illustrated by Marjorie Gill. Harcourt Brace Jovanovich, 1966.

Cresswell, Helen. *The Bongleweed.* Macmillan, 1973.

————. *Up the Pier,* illustrated by Gareth Floyd. Macmillan, 1972.

Cunningham, Julia. *Macaroon,* illustrated by Evaline Ness. Pantheon, 1962.

✓ Dahl, Roald. *Charlie and the Chocolate Factory,* illustrated by Joseph Schindelman. Knopf, 1964.

————. *Charlie and the Great Glass Elevator,* illustrated by Joseph Schindelman. Knopf, 1972.

————. *James and the Giant Peach,* illustrated by Nancy Burkert. Knopf, 1961.

————. *The Magic Finger,* illustrated by William Pène Du Bois. Harper & Row, 1966.

Dickinson, Peter. *The Devil's Children.* Little, Brown, 1970.

————. *Emma Tupper's Diary,* illustrated by David O. White. Little, Brown, 1971.

————. *Heartsease,* illustrated by Nathan Goldstein. Little, Brown, 1969.

————. *The Weathermonger.* Little, Brown, 1969.

✓ Du Bois, William Pène. *The Twenty-one Balloons.* Viking, 1947.

Eager, Edward. *Half Magic,* illustrated by N. M. Bodecker. Harcourt Brace Jovanovich, 1954.

————. *Seven-day Magic,* illustrated by N. M. Bodecker. Harcourt Brace Jovanovich, 1962.

Engdahl, Sylvia Louise. *Beyond the Tomorrow Mountains,* illustrated by Richard Cuffari. Atheneum, 1973.

————. *Enchantress from the Stars,* illustrated by Rodney Shackell. Atheneum, 1970.

————. *The Far Side of Evil*, illustrated by Richard Cuffari. Atheneum, 1971.

————. *This Star Shall Abide*, illustrated by Richard Cuffari. Atheneum, 1972.

✔ Farmer, Penelope. *A Castle of Bone*. Atheneum, 1972.

————. *Charlotte Sometimes*, illustrated by Chris Connor. Harcourt Brace Jovanovich, 1969.

————. *Emma in Winter*, illustrated by James Spanfeller. Harcourt Brace Jovanovich, 1966.

————. *The Magic Stone*, illustrated by John Kaufmann. Harcourt Brace Jovanovich, 1964.

————✔. *The Summer Birds*, illustrated by James Spanfeller. Harcourt Brace Jovanovich, 1962.

✔ Fleming, Ian. *Chitty-Chitty-Bang-Bang*, illustrated by John Burningham. Random House, 1964.

French, Fiona. *The Blue Bird*. Walck, 1972.

Gage, Wilson. *Miss Osborne-the-Mop*, illustrated by Paul Galdone. World, 1963.

Garfield, Leon. *The Ghost Downstairs*, illustrated by Antony Maitland. Pantheon, 1972.

————. *Mister Corbett's Ghost*, illustrated by Alan E. Cober. Pantheon, 1968.

Garner, Alan. *Elidor*. Walck, 1967.

————. *The Owl Service*. Walck, 1968.

————. *Red Shift*. Macmillan, 1973.

Godden, Rumer. *Candy Floss*, illustrated by Adrienne Adams. Viking, 1960.

————. *The Dolls' House*, illustrated by Tasha Tudor. Viking, 1962 (1947).

————. *The Fairy Doll*, illustrated by Adrienne Adams. Viking, 1956.

————. *Home Is the Sailor*, illustrated by Jean Primrose. Viking, 1964.

————. *Impunity Jane*, illustrated by Adrienne Adams. Viking, 1954.

————✔. *The Mousewife*, illustrated by William Pène du Bois. Viking, 1951.

————. *The Story of Holly and Ivy*, illustrated by Adrienne Adams. Viking, 1958.

Grahame, Kenneth. *The Reluctant Dragon*, illustrated by Ernest H. Shepard. Holiday, 1938.

————✔. *The Wind in the Willows*, illustrated by E. H. Shepard. Scribner, 1940 (1908).

Hale, Lucretia P. *The Complete Peterkin Papers*. Houghton Mifflin, 1960.

Heide, Florence Parry. *The Shrinking of Treehorn*, illustrated by Edward Gorey. Holiday, 1971.

Hoban, Russell. *The Mouse and His Child*, illustrated by Lillian Hoban. Harper & Row, 1967.

Holman, Felice. *Cricket Winter*. Grosset & Dunlap, 1967.

Hunter, Mollie, pseud. (Maureen McIlwraith). *The Haunted Mountain: A Story of Suspense*, illustrated by Laszlo Kubinyi. Harper & Row, 1972.

————. *The Kelpie's Pearls*, illustrated by Joseph Cellini. Funk & Wagnalls, 1966.

————. *Thomas and the Warlock*, illustrated by Joseph Cellini. Funk & Wagnalls, 1967.

————. *The Walking Stones: A Story of Suspense*, illustrated by Trina Schart Hyman. Harper & Row, 1970.

Ish-Kishor, Sulamith. *The Master of Miracle: A New Novel of the Golem*, illustrated by Arnold Lobel. Harper & Row, 1971.

Jackson, Jacqueline, and William Perlmutter. *The Endless Pavement*, illustrated by Richard Cuffari. Seabury, 1973.

✔ Jansson, Tove. *Tales from Moominvalley*, translated by Thomas Warburton. Walck, 1964.

Jarrell, Randall. *The Animal Family*, illustrated by Maurice Sendak. Pantheon, 1965.

————. *The Bat-Poet*, illustrated by Maurice Sendak. Macmillan, 1964.

✔ Juster, Norton. *The Phantom Tollbooth*. Random House, 1961.

Kendall, Carol. *The Gammage Cup*, illustrated by Erik Blegvad. Harcourt Brace Jovanovich, 1959.

————. *The Whisper of Glocken*, illustrated by Imero Gobbato. Harcourt Brace Jovanovich, 1965.

Key, Alexander. *Escape to Witch Mountain*, illustrated by Leon B. Wisdom, Jr. Westminster, 1968.

————. *The Forgotten Door*. Westminster, 1965.

Kipling, Rudyard. *The Elephant's Child*, illustrated by Leonard Weisgard. Walker, 1970.

————. *How the Leopard Got His Spots*, illustrated by Leonard Weisgard. Walker, 1972.

————. *How the Rhinoceros Got His Skin*, illustrated by Leonard Weisgard. Walker, 1974.

————. *Just-So Stories*, illustrated by Etienne Delessert. Doubleday, 1972.

Langton, Jane. *The Astonishing Stereoscope*, illustrated by Erik Blegvad. Harper & Row, 1971.

————. *The Diamond in the Window*, illustrated by Erik Blegvad. Harper & Row, 1962.

———. *The Swing in the Summerhouse*, illustrated by Erik Blegvad. Harper & Row, 1967.

Lawson, John. *You Better Come Home with Me*, illustrated by Arnold Spilka. Crowell, 1966.

Lawson, Robert. *The Fabulous Flight*. Little, Brown, 1949.

———. *McWhinney's Jaunt*. Little, Brown, 1951.

———. *Mr. Twigg's Mistake*. Little, Brown, 1947.

———. *Rabbit Hill*. Viking, 1944.

———. *The Tough Winter*. Viking, 1954.

LeGuin, Ursula K. *The Farthest Shore*, illustrated by Gail Garraty. Atheneum, 1972.

———. *The Tombs of Atuan*, illustrated by Gail Garraty, Atheneum, 1971.

———. *A Wizard of Earthsea*, illustrated by Ruth Robbins. Parnassus, 1968.

L'Engle, Madeleine. *A Wind in the Door*. Farrar, Straus, 1973.

———. *A Wrinkle in Time*. Farrar, Straus, 1962.

Lewis, C. S. *The Horse and His Boy*, illustrated by Pauline Baynes. Macmillan, 1962.

———. *The Last Battle*, illustrated by Pauline Baynes. Macmillan, 1964.

———. *The Lion, the Witch, and the Wardrobe*, illustrated by Pauline Baynes. Macmillan, 1961.

———. *The Magician's Nephew*, illustrated by Pauline Baynes. Macmillan, 1964.

———. *Prince Caspian, the Return to Narnia*, illustrated by Pauline Baynes. Macmillan, 1964.

———. *The Silver Chair*, illustrated by Pauline Baynes. Macmillan, 1962.

———. *The Voyage of the "Dawn Treader,"* illustrated by Pauline Baynes. Macmillan, 1962.

Lindgren, Astrid. *Pippi Goes on Board*, translated by Florence Lamborn, illustrated by Louis S. Glanzman. Viking, 1957.

———. *Pippi in the South Seas*, translated by Florence Lamborn, illustrated by Louis S. Glanzman. Viking, 1959.

———. *Pippi Longstocking*, illustrated by Louis S. Glanzman. Viking, 1950.

Lobel, Anita. *A Birthday for the Princess*. Harper & Row, 1973.

MacDonald, George. *The Golden Key*, illustrated by Maurice Sendak. Farrar, Straus, 1967.

———. *The Light Princess*, illustrated by William Pène du Bois. Crowell, 1962.

———. *The Light Princess*, illustrated by Maurice Sendak. Farrar, Straus, 1969.

McGinley, Phyllis. *The Plain Princess*, illustrated by Helen Stone. Lippincott, 1945.

MacGregor, Ellen. *Miss Pickerell Goes to Mars*, illustrated by Paul Galdone. McGraw-Hill, 1951.

MacGregor, Ellen, and Dora Pantell. *Miss Pickerell and the Weather Satellite*, illustrated by Charles Geer. McGraw-Hill, 1971.

———. *Miss Pickerell Goes on a Dig*, illustrated by Charles Geer. McGraw-Hill, 1966.

Mayne, William. *Earthfasts*. Dutton, 1967.

———. *A Grass Rope*, illustrated by Lynton Lamb. Dutton, 1957.

Merrill, Jean. *The Pushcart War*, illustrated by Ronni Solbert. W. R. Scott, 1964.

Milne, A. A. *The House at Pooh Corner*, illustrated by Ernest H. Shepard. Dutton, 1928.

———. *Winnie-the-Pooh*, illustrated by Ernest H. Shepard. Dutton, 1926.

North, Joan. *The Cloud Forest*. Farrar, Straus, 1966.

Norton, Andre. *Breed to Come*. Viking, 1972.

———. *The Crystal Gryphon*. Atheneum, 1972.

———. *The Night of Masks*. Harcourt Brace Jovanovich, 1964.

———. *Zero Stone*. Viking, 1968.

Norton, Mary. *The Borrowers*, illustrated by Beth Krush and Joe Krush. Harcourt Brace Jovanovich, 1953.

———. *The Borrowers Afield*, illustrated by Beth Krush and Joe Krush. Harcourt Brace Jovanovich, 1955.

———. *The Borrowers Afloat*, illustrated by Beth Krush and Joe Krush. Harcourt Brace Jovanovich, 1959.

———. *The Borrowers Aloft*, illustrated by Beth Krush and Joe Krush. Harcourt Brace Jovanovich, 1961.

O'Brien, Robert C. *Mrs. Frisby and the Rats of NIMH*, illustrated by Zena Bernstein. Atheneum, 1971.

Ormondroyd, Edward. *Castaways on Long Ago,* illustrated by Ruth Robbins. Parnassus, 1973.

————. *Time at the Top,* illustrated by Peggy Bach. Parnassus, 1963.

Parish, Peggy, *Amelia Bedelia,* illustrated by Fritz Siebel. Harper & Row, 1963.

————. *Amelia Bedelia and the Surprise Shower,* illustrated by Fritz Siebel. Harper & Row, 1966.

————. *Play Ball, Amelia Bedelia,* illustrated by Wallace Tripp. Harper & Row, 1972.

————. *Thank You, Amelia Bedelia,* illustrated by Fritz Siebel. Harper & Row, 1964.

Pearce, Philippa. *A Dog So Small,* illustrated by Antony Maitland. Lippincott, 1962.

————. *Tom's Midnight Garden,* illustrated by Susan Einzig. Lippincott, 1959.

Phipson, Joan. *The Way Home.* Atheneum, 1973.

Poole, Josephine. *Moon Eyes,* illustrated by Trina Schart Hyman. Little, Brown, 1967.

Preussler, Otfried. *The Satanic Mill,* translated by Anthea Bell. Macmillan, 1973.

Robinson, Joan G. *When Marnie Was There.* Coward-McCann, 1968.

Rodgers, Mary. *Freaky Friday.* Harper & Row, 1972.

Saint-Exupéry, Antoine de. *The Little Prince,* translated by Katherine Woods. Harcourt Brace Jovanovich, 1943.

Sauer, Julia. *Fog Magic,* illustrated by Lynd Ward. Viking, 1943.

Selden, George. *The Cricket in Times Square,* illustrated by Garth Williams. Farrar, 1960.

————. *The Genie of Sutton Place.* Farrar, Straus, 1973.

————. *Tucker's Countryside,* illustrated by Garth Williams. Farrar, Straus, 1969.

Seuss, Dr., pseud. (Theodor Seuss Geisel). *Bartholomew and the Oobleck.* Random House, 1950.

————. *The 500 Hats of Bartholomew Cubbins.* Vanguard, 1938.

Sharp, Margery. *Miss Bianca,* illustrated by Garth Williams. Little, Brown, 1962.

————. *Miss Bianca and the Bridesmaid,* illustrated by Erik Blegvad. Little, Brown, 1972.

————. *Miss Bianca in the Salt Mines,* illustrated by Garth Williams. Little, Brown, 1967.

————. *The Rescuers,* illustrated by Garth Williams. Little, Brown, 1959.

————. *The Turret,* illustrated by Garth Williams. Little, Brown, 1963.

Sleator, William. *Blackbriar.* Dutton, 1972.

Slobodkin, Louis. *The Amiable Giant.* Macmillan, 1955.

————. *The Space Ship in the Park.* Macmillan, 1972.

————. *The Space Ship under the Apple Tree.* Macmillan, 1952.

Steele, Mary Q. *Journey Outside,* illustrated by Rocco Negri. Viking, 1969.

Steig, William. *Dominic.* Farrar, Straus, 1972.

————. *The Real Thief.* Farrar, Straus, 1973.

Thurber, James. *Many Moons,* illustrated by Louis Slobodkin. Harcourt Brace Jovanovich, 1943.

————. *The 13 Clocks,* illustrated by Marc Simont. Simon & Schuster, 1950.

————. *The Wonderful O,* illustrated by Marc Simont. Simon & Schuster, 1957.

Tolkien, J. R. R. *The Hobbit.* Houghton Mifflin, 1938.

Travers, Pamela L. *Mary Poppins,* illustrated by Mary Shepard. Harcourt Brace Jovanovich, 1934.

————. *Mary Poppins Comes Back,* illustrated by Mary Shepard. Harcourt Brace Jovanovich, 1935.

————. *Mary Poppins in the Park,* illustrated by Mary Shepard. Harcourt Brace Jovanovich, 1952.

————. *Mary Poppins Opens the Door,* illustrated by Mary Shepard and Agnes Sims. Harcourt Brace Jovanovich, 1943.

Uttley, Alison. *A Traveler in Time,* illustrated by Christine Price. Viking, 1964 (1939).

Wersba, Barbara. *The Land of Forgotten Beasts,* illustrated by Margot Tomes. Atheneum, 1964.

White, E. B. *Charlotte's Web,* illustrated by Garth Williams. Harper & Row, 1952.

————. *Stuart Little,* illustrated by Garth Williams. Harper & Row, 1945.

————. *The Trumpet of the Swan,* illustrated by Edward Frascino. Harper & Row, 1970.

Wilde, Oscar. *The Happy Prince,* illustrated by Gilbert Riswold. Prentice-Hall, 1965.

————. *The Selfish Giant,* illustrated by Herbert Danska. Harlan Quist, 1967.

Williams, Jay. *The Good-for-Nothing Prince*, illustrated by Imero Gobbato. Norton, 1969.
———. *Petronella*, illustrated by Friso Henstra. Parents', 1973.
———. *The Practical Princess*, illustrated by Friso Henstra. Parents', 1969.
Williams, Jay, and Raymond Abrashkin. *Danny Dunn and the Homework Machine*, illustrated by Ezra Jack Keats. McGraw-Hill, 1958.
———. *Danny Dunn and the Smallifying Machine*, illustrated by Paul Sagsoorian. McGraw-Hill, 1969.
———. *Danny Dunn and the Swamp Monster*, illustrated by Paul Sagsoorian. McGraw-Hill, 1971.
Wrightson, Patricia. *Down to Earth*, illustrated by Margaret Horder. Harcourt Brace Jovanovich, 1965.
———. *The Nargun and the Stars*. Atheneum, 1974.
———. *An Older Kind of Magic*, illustrated by Noela Young. Harcourt Brace Jovanovich, 1972.
Yolen, Jane. *The Emperor and the Kite*, illustrated by Ed Young. World, 1967.
———. *The Girl Who Loved the Wind*, illustrated by Ed Young. Crowell, 1972.
———. *The Seventh Mandarin*, illustrated by Ed Young. Seabury, 1970.

6 Poetry

Sharing time was nearly over in Mrs. Hill's first-grade room when Jeannie shyly raised her hand and said: "I have a pair of new shoes."

"Of course you do, Jeannie," responded Mrs. Hill, "and they are very special shoes, too. Do you want to stand up and show them to us?"

Her new red sandals brought admiring comments from the rest of the children. Mrs. Hill encouraged Jeannie to tell the group about buying them by asking: "Did you look at other shoes? Did you have a hard time choosing these? How did you decide?" Then the teacher and the children talked about how new shoes made them feel. Mrs. Hill told them that new shoes had made one person feel this way:

NEW SHOES

I have new shoes in the Fall-time
And new ones in the Spring.
Whenever I wear my new shoes
I always have to sing!

    Alice Wilkins (14)[1]

This poem reminded the children of another favorite, "Choosing Shoes" (294) by Ffrida Wolfe. Mrs. Hill suggested that the children stand around the edge of the rug and say this poem together. Then one group on each side of the rug repeated a verse, while all of the children joined in the last verse, stamping to the rhythm of "Flat shoes, fat shoes, Stump-along-like-that shoes . . ."

Poetry was a natural part of these children's lives. Their creative, sensitive teacher enjoyed poetry herself and was alert to the various opportunities in the school day when poetry could extend and enrich children's experiences. She had memorized many poems so they could be introduced spontaneously at the right "teachable moment." In addition to those poems she knew, she had her own personal collection filed on four-by-six cards in categories that complemented her knowledge of 6-year-olds' interests. Hardly a day passed in her classroom when there were not a few moments in which to share a poem. Sometimes, the children joined Mrs. Hill in saying the poem, as they did in "Choosing Shoes." More frequently, they just listened and enjoyed the poem for its own sake.

---

[1] The numbers following poems in this chapter refer to the book number in the Recommended References where the poem may be found. Many of the poems are in several anthologies, however.

The Meaning of Poetry

WHAT IS POETRY?

There is an elusiveness about poetry that defies precise definition. It is not so much what it is that is important as how it makes us feel. Eleanor Farjeon tells us that "Poetry" (91) is "not a rose, but the scent of the rose . . . Not the sea, but the sound of the sea." Fine poetry is this distillation of experience that captures the essence of an object, feeling, or thought. Such intensification requires a more highly structured patterning of words than does prose. Each word must be chosen with care, both for its sound and meaning, for poetry is language in its most connotative and concentrated form. Laurence Perrine in his text, *Sound and Sense*, defines poetry as "a kind of language that says more and says it more intensely than ordinary language."[2]

Poetry may both broaden and intensify experience, or it may present a range of experiences beyond the realm of personal possibility for the individual listener. It may also illuminate, clarify, and deepen an everyday occurrence in a way the reader never considered, making him see more and feel more than he ever had before. For poetry does more than mirror life; it reveals life in new dimensions. Robert Frost stated that a poem goes from delight to wisdom. Poetry does delight children, but it also helps them develop new insights, new ways of sensing their world.

Poetry communicates experience by appealing to both the thoughts and feelings of its reader. It has the power to evoke in its hearers rich sensory images and deep emotional responses. Poetry demands total response from the individual—his intellect, senses, emotion, and imagination. It does not tell *about* an experience as much as it invites its hearers to *participate in* the experience. Poetry can only happen when the poem and the reader connect. Eve Merriam writes about the experience this way:

"I," says the poem matter-of-factly,
"I am a cloud,
I am a tree.

I am a city,
I am the sea,

I am a golden
Mystery."
But, adds the poem silently,
I cannot speak until you come.
Reader, come, come with me.

Eve Merriam (202)

Much of what poetry says is conveyed by suggestion, by indirection, by what is not said. Carl Sandburg made the statement that "What can be explained is not poetry. . . . The poems that are obvious are like the puzzles that are already solved. They deny us the joy of seeking and creating."[3] A certain amount of ambiguity is characteristic of poetry, for more is hidden in it than in prose. The poet does not tell the reader "all," but invites him to go beyond the literal level of the poem and discover its deeper meanings for himself.

Robert Frost playfully suggested that poetry is what gets lost in translation—and translation of poetry into prose is as difficult as translation of poetry into another language. To paraphrase a poem is to destroy it. Would it be possible to reduce Frost's "Mending Wall" to prose? The scene, the situation, the contrast of the two men's thoughts about the wall they are repairing may be described, but the experience of the poem cannot be conveyed except by its own words.

POETRY FOR CHILDREN

Poetry for children differs little from poetry for adults, except that it comments on life in dimensions that are meaningful for children. Its language should be poetic and its content should appeal directly to children. Myra Cohn Livingston has described "Winter and Summer" in a way that reflects how children might view these contrasting seasons:

WINTER AND SUMMER

The winter
    is an ice-cream treat,
    all frosty white and cold to eat.
But summer
    is a lemonade
    of yellow sun and straw-cool shade.

Myra Cohn Livingston (190)

---

[2]Laurence Perrine. *Sound and Sense: An Introduction to Poetry*, 3rd ed. (New York: Harcourt Brace Jovanovich, 1969), p. 3.

[3]Carl Sandburg. "Short Talk on Poetry," in *Early Moon* (New York: Harcourt Brace Jovanovich, 1930), p. 27.

Such poetry appeals to children's sensory experiences and helps them think about the differences between winter and summer in a creative, imaginative way. It speaks to the child, but in the language of poetry. Poetry for children appeals to their emotions as well as to their senses. Young persons may experience emotions that are similar to adults, but the circumstances that provoked them will generally differ. They get angry, but it may be because they have to go to bed too early. They are easily hurt, but it may be because no one will play with them, as in Marci Ridlon's poem "Sunday Morning" (252). The scope of poetry for children, then, encompasses all the feelings, all the experiences of childhood.

The limitations of poetry for children are surprisingly few. Poems of passion and nostalgia seem to have little place in childhood as these are not children's emotions (*see* Chapter 1). Literary allusions are necessarily limited, and metaphors should be related to children's experiences. Figurative language tends to obscure meaning, unless it is based upon familiar experiences or well-known objects. Young children readily respond to the figures of speech in this poem, however:

DECEMBER LEAVES

The fallen leaves are cornflakes
That fill the lawn's wide dish,
And night and noon
The wind's a spoon
That stirs them with a swish.

The sky's a silver sifter
A-sifting white and slow,
That gently shakes
On crisp brown flakes
The sugar known as snow.

Kaye Starbird (272)

The freshness of the comparison between brown leaves and breakfast food will have immediate appeal for today's young child. The poet has helped children see two common, disparate objects in a new relationship. Capitalizing upon children's interests, this poem helps the child to view the world of nature in a new way, through the language of poetry. Its metaphor is childlike, but not "childish."

Space-age children need fresh comparisons that are relevant to their background of experiences. The child's hero of today works in space and not under the spreading chestnut tree. Many children who would have little understanding of "The Village Blacksmith" (299) would comprehend the comparison that Eve Merriam makes in her poem:

SATELLITE, SATELLITE

Satellite, satellite
The earth goes around the sun.

Satellite, satellite,
The moon goes around the earth.

Satellite, satellite,
I have a little satellite:

My little brother orbits me
And pesters day and night.

Eve Merriam (210)

Children might be encouraged through discussion to think of other satellite situations in their lives—a little dog that faithfully follows its master, a bee buzzing around a clover blossom, even Mary's little lamb!

While children's taste in poetry has become more sophisticated, they frequently do not understand the use of complex symbolism until they have reached the formal stage of mental operations, usually around the age of 12. If a symbol is *obvious* and connects with their background of experience, it may be understood. The title provides the clue to the symbolic meaning of this poem:

HOPE'S FORECAST

As a water lily only blooms
When rooted deep in slime,
So peace shall flower, white, cool,
On a future hidden pool
From the murky residue
Of an atomic time.

Ethel Romig Fuller (264)

Understanding could be extended by reading Oliver Hereford's "I Heard a Bird Sing in the Dark of December" (13) or Emily Dickinson's "Hope is the thing with feathers" (13). Some symbolism, then, is appropriate in poetry for children, provided it is linked to what they know.

The emotional appeal of children's poetry should reflect the real emotions of childhood.

Poetry that is cute, coy, nostalgic, or sarcastic may be *about* children, but it is not *for* them. Whittier's "The Barefoot Boy" (92) looks back upon childhood in a nostalgic fashion characteristic of adults, not children. "The Children's Hour" (92) by Longfellow is an old man's reminiscences of his delight in his children. Some poems patronize childhood as a period in life when children are "cute" or "naughty." Joan W. Anglund's poetry is as cute and sentimental as her little pictures of "sweet little boys and girls." Even the best of children's poets occasionally have been guilty of this kind of portrayal of childhood. For example, "Vespers" (212) by A. A. Milne appeals more to adults who are amused and pleased by the sweet description of a child's desultory thoughts during prayer, while children find little humor in this poem which makes them the object of laughter. John Ciardi has written many poems that make children laugh; he has also written some poems that laugh at children. Frequently, he appears to be talking to parents when he refers to children as "monsters," "the little dears," or the "sillies." Exasperated parents or teachers may occasionally think of children in this way; but do children think of themselves like this? Eugene Field's "Little Boy Blue" (92) describes an adult's reaction to the loss of a child— it, too, is inappropriate fare for children. Many poems are didactic and preachy. Unfortunately, some teachers will accept moralizing in poetry that they would never accept in prose. Sentimentality is another adult emotion, seldom felt by children. The poem "Which Loved Best," frequently quoted before Mother's Day, drips with sentiment and morality. Poems that are *about* childhood or aim to instruct are usually disliked by children.

There are two schools of thought concerning what is appropriate poetry for children. Some would disallow any poetry written by the so-called children's poets, and present only poems of recognized poets who write for adults. They would search for the few poems of Tennyson, Shakespeare, and Dickinson, for example, that might be appropriate for children. Others have limited poetry in the classroom to such childhood poets as Stevenson, Farjeon, and Aldis. This seems an unnecessary dichotomy. In evaluating a poem for children it makes little difference who the author is, provided the poem speaks *to chil-*dren in the *language* of poetry. Children deserve excellence in poetry regardless of its source, but it must speak to them at their point of time.

THE ELEMENTS OF POETRY

A child responds to the total impact of a poem and should not be required to analyze it. However, teachers need to understand the language of poetry, if they are to select the best to share with children. How, for example, can you differentiate between real poetry and mere verse? *Mother Goose*, jump-rope rhymes, tongue twisters, and some of the lyrics to pop and rock music are not poetry; but they *can* serve as a springboard for diving into real poetry. Elizabeth Coatsworth, who has written much fine poetry and verse for children, refers to rhyme as "poetry in petticoats."(64)[4] Such rhymes may have the sound of poetry, but they do not contain the quality of imagination or the depth of emotion that characterizes real poetry.

It is a difficult task to identify elements of poetry for today's children, for contemporary poets are breaking traditional molds in both content and form. These poems speak directly to the reader about all subjects. Frequently the words are spattered across pages in a random fashion or they become poem-pictures, as in concrete poetry. As children become more sophisticated by their exposure to films and television, the dividing line between what is poetry for adults and what is poetry for children becomes fainter and fainter. It is, however, possible to identify those poems that contain the elements of fine poetry, yet still speak to children.

Rhythm

The young child is naturally rhythmical. He beats on the tray of his highchair, kicks his foot against the table, and chants his vocabulary of one or two words in a singsong fashion. He delights in the sound of "Pat-a-cake, pat-a-cake, baker's man," or "Ride a cock-horse to Banbury Cross" before he understands the meaning of the words. This response to a measured beat is as old as humans themselves. Primitive people had chants, hunting and working songs, dances, and crude musical instruments. Rhythm is a part of

[4]Elizabeth Coatsworth. *The Sparrow Bush,* illustrated by Stefan Martin (New York: Norton, 1966), p. 8.

the daily beat of our lives—the steady pulse rate, regular breathing, and pattern of growth. The inevitability of night and day, the revolving seasons, birth and death provide a pattern for everyone's life. The very ebb and flow of the ocean, the sound of the rain on the window, and the pattern of rows of corn in a field reflect the rhythm of the world around us.

Poetry satisfies the child's natural response to rhythm. Eve Merriam has described the importance of rhythm in the first verse of the title poem of her book, *It Doesn't Always Have to Rhyme:*

INSIDE A POEM

It doesn't always have to rhyme,
but there's the repeat of a beat, somewhere
an inner chime that makes you want to
tap your feet or swerve in a curve;
a lilt, a leap, a lightning-split:—

　　　　　　Eve Merriam (208)

It is this built-in rhythm or meter that helps to differentiate poetry from prose. A poem has a kind of music of its own, and the child responds to it.

The very young child enjoys the monotonous rocking-horse rhythm of Mother Goose and expects it in all other poems. Mary Ann Hoberman has explored other rhythms in the child's life as she links weather and seasonal patterns to the rhythm of a child's swinging:

Hello and good-by
Hello and good-by

When I'm in a swing
Swinging low and then high
Good-by to the ground
Hello to the sky.

Hello to the rain
Good-by to the sun,
Then hello again sun
When the rain is all done

In blows the winter,
Away the birds fly.
Good-by and hello
Hello and good-by

　Mary Ann Hoberman (128)

Stevenson's well-known poem "The Swing" (278) suggests a different meter for the physical sensation of swinging. Read both of these poems to children and let them pantomime swinging as they chant the lines. Then they can discuss which poem was the easier one to respond to.

The galloping rhythm of Stevenson's "Windy Nights" compares the sound of the wild wind to a mysterious horseman riding by. The refrain of the last four lines may be read loudly and then softly to give the effect of the wailing wind:

. . .

By, on the highway, low and loud,
By at the gallop goes he:
By at the gallop he goes, and then
By he comes back at the gallop again.

　　　Robert Louis Stevenson (278)

Stevenson has also captured the fast pace of a train with the clipped rhythm of his poem "From a Railway Carriage" (278). The sliding, gliding movement of "Skating" is well portrayed by the rhythm of Herbert Asquith's poem (13), while the slow steady beat of "Lullaby" by Hillyer (88) imitates the strong strokes of the paddle moving "The long canoe/toward the shadowy shore." The rhythm of a poem, then, should be appropriate to its subject matter, reinforcing and creating its meaning.

In some poems both the rhythm and pattern of the lines are suggestive of the movement or mood of the poem. The arrangement of these poems forces the reader to emphasize a particular rhythm. The words of Farjeon's "Mrs. Peck-Pigeon" and the repetition of the hard sounds of "b" and "p" help to create the bobbing rhythm of the pigeon herself:

MRS. PECK-PIGEON

Mrs. Peck-Pigeon
Is picking for bread,
Bob—bob—bob
Goes her little round head.
Tame as a pussy-cat
In the street,
Step—step—step
Go her little red feet.
With her little red feet
And her little round head,
Mrs. Peck-Pigeon
Goes picking for bread.

　　　Eleanor Farjeon (91)

In Dorothy Baruch's "Merry-go-Round" (13) the pattern of the line and the rhythm can be read to suggest the increasing and decreasing speed of a merry-go-round. The somewhat pensive mood of A. A. Milne's "Halfway Down" (212) is heightened by the arrangement of the words and lines. The reader has to interpret the slow descent of a little boy going down the stairs until he stops at his favorite step, halfway down.

A change of rhythm is indicative of a new element in the poem: a contrast in mood, a warning, or a different speaker, for example. Mary Austin has contrasted the ominous movement of "The Sandhill Crane" (13), as he goes "slowly solemnly stalking," with the fast scuttling movements of the frogs and minnows who fear for their lives. A similar warning is seen in the change of rhythm in this poem:

> The sea gull curves his wings,
> The sea gull turns his eyes.
> Get down into the water, fish!
> (If you are wise.)
>
> The sea gull slants his wings,
> The sea gull turns his head.
> Get down into the water, fish!
> (Or you'll be dead.)
>
> Elizabeth Coatsworth (13)

The first two lines of each verse soar with the flight of the gull, but the last two lines change the pace of the poem and issue a staccato warning.

Rhyme and Sound

In addition to the rhythm of a poem children respond to its rhyme. For rhyme helps to create the musical qualities of a poem, and children enjoy the "singingness of words." The Russian poet, Chukovsky[5] maintains that in the beginning of childhood we are all "versifiers," and that it is only later in life that we begin to speak in prose. He is referring to the young child's tendency to double all syllables so that "mother" becomes "mama" and water "wa-wa." This, plus the regular patterning of such words as daddy, mommie, granny, and so on, makes for a natural production of rhyme. Karla Kuskin capitalized on

[5] Kornei Chukovsky, *From Two to Five*, translated and edited by Miriam Morton (Berkeley, Calif.: University of California Press, 1963), p. 64.

this phenomenon among children with her amusing story of *Alexander Soames* (155) who could only "speak in poems!" The young child's enjoyment of Mother Goose is due almost entirely to the rhyme and rhythm of these verses.

Children need to be freed from the notion that all poetry must rhyme in order to be poetry. They should be introduced to some poetry that doesn't rhyme, such as free verse or haiku, so that they begin to listen to the meaning of a poem as well as the sound of it.

Rhyme is one aspect of sound; alliteration, or the repetition of initial consonant sounds, is another; while assonance, or the repetition of particular vowel sounds, is still another. The repetition of the hard "g" sounds in "Godfrey Gordon Gustavus Gore" (13) adds to the humor of this poem about the boy who would never shut the door. Younger children delight in the "splishes and sploshes and slooshes and sloshes" which Susie's galoshes make in Rhoda W. Bacmeister's poem "Galoshes" (294). The quiet "s" sound and the repetition of the double "o" in "moon" and "shoon" suggest the mysterious beauty of the moon in "Silver" (13). Onomatopoeia is a term that refers to the use of words that make a sound like the action represented by the word, such as "crack," "hiss," and "sputter." Occasionally, a poet will create an entire poem that resembles a particular sound. David McCord has successfully imitated the sound of hitting a picket fence with a stick in his popular chant:

> The pickety fence
> The pickety fence
> Give it a lick it's
> The pickety fence
> Give it a lick it's
> A clickety fence
> Give it a lick it's
> A lickety fence
> Give it a lick
> Give it a lick
> Give it a lick
> With a rickety stick
> Pickety
> Pickety
> Pickety
> Pick.
>
> David McCord (197)

"Railroad Reverie" (202) by E. R. Young captures the sound of a train far away in the distance and then coming closer and closer. Children love the first loud and then soft refrain of:

> . . .
> Catch-a-teacher, catch-a-teacher, patch-his-
> britches,
> Patch-his-britches, catch-a-teacher, patch-his-
> britches
> Catch-a-teacher Whoosh! . . .

Repetition, then, is another way that the poet creates the sound effects of his poem. He may repeat a particular word or phrase for emphasis, for a special sound, or to create a recurring theme as in a symphony. In this poem, Zilpha Snyder has repeated the word "tree" to emphasize how often we see a tree and think nothing of it—until one day we really see:

TREE

> Tree—
> Tree, tree, tree.
> It's a simple sound—a common word.
> Everyone uses, everyone's heard
> Over and over and over again,
> 'Til it's only a noise, like steady rain.
> Tree, tree, tree, tree.
> Everyone everywhere's certainly seen
> A tree. You know it's usually green,
> Or yellow or red. You know it's good
> For swings and shade or fruit or wood.
> But it's only a tree, a tree, a tree.
>
> But then, perhaps, on a certain day,
> Without any warning—a sudden ray
> Of light catches you—jars you free.
> Opens your eyes and then you see
> The secret magic meaning—
> TREE.

> Zilpha Keatley Snyder (269)

Robert Frost frequently used repetition of particular lines or phrases to emphasize meaning in his poems. The repetition of the last line "miles to go before I sleep" in his famous "Stopping by Woods on a Snowy Evening" (118) adds to the mysterious element in that poem.

Children are intrigued with the sound of language and enjoy unusual and ridiculous combinations of words. The gay nonsense of Laura

Richards' "Eletelephony" (13) is as much in the sound of the ridiculous words as in the plight of the poor elephant who tried to use the "telephant." Children love to trip off the name of "James James Morrison Morrison Weatherby George Dupree," who complained about his mother's "Disobedience" (212). Harry Behn's "Tea Party" is a delightful mumble of scolding:

> Mister Beedle Baddlebug,
> Don't bandle up in your boodlebag
> Or numble in your jumblejug,
> Now eat your nummy tiffletag
> Or I will never invite you
> To tea again with me. Shoo!

> Harry Behn (27)

Poets use rhyme, rhythm, and the various devices of alliteration, assonance, repetition, and coined words to create the melody and sound of poetry loved by children.

Imagery

Poetry draws on many kinds of language magic. To speak of the imagery of a poem refers to direct sensory images of sight, sound, touch, smell, or taste. This aspect of poetry has particular appeal for children, as it reflects one of the major ways they explore their world. The very young child grasps an object and immediately puts it in his mouth. Children love to squeeze warm, soft puppies or they squeal with delight as a baby pet mouse scampers up their arms. Taste and smell are also highly developed in the young child.

The sadness of our modern society is that children are increasingly deprived of natural sensory experiences. One of the first admonitions they hear is "Don't touch." In the endless pavement of our cities, how many children have an opportunity to roll in crunchy piles of leaves? Air-pollution laws assure that they will never enjoy the acrid autumn smell of burning bonfires (rightly so, but still a loss). Many also miss the warm yeasty odor of homemade bread or the sweet joy of licking the bowl of brownie batter. Some of our newest schools are windowless, so children are even deprived of seeing the brilliant blue sky on a crisp cold day, or the growing darkness of a storm, or the changing silhouette of an oak tree on the horizon.

Poetry can never be a substitute for actual sensory experience. A child can't develop a concept of texture by hearing a poem or seeing pictures of the rough bark of a tree; he must first touch the bark and compare the feel of a deeply furrowed oak with the smooth surfaced trunk of a beech tree. Then the poet can call up these experiences, extend them or make the child see them in a new way. John Moffitt describes how to really "see" with the eyes of the poet:

TO LOOK AT ANY THING

To look at any thing,
If you would know that thing,
You must look at it long:
To look at this green and say
'I have seen spring in these
Woods,' will not do—you must
Be the thing you see:
You must be the dark snakes of
Stems and ferny plumes of leaves,
You must enter in
To the small silences between
The leaves,
You must take your time
And touch the very peace
They issue from.

John Moffitt (88)

Since most children are visual-minded they respond readily to the picture-making quality of poetry. Louise Allen has looked with the eyes of a young child at a familiar world made strange with snow. Her poem, "First Snow," may well be the first snow of the season or the child's first experience with snow:

FIRST SNOW

Snow makes whiteness where it falls,
The bushes look like popcorn balls.
And places where I always play,
Look like somewhere else today.

Marie Louise Allen (12)

Robert Frost has made us see a "Patch of Old Snow" (88) in the city as if it were an old blown-away newspaper bespeckled with grimy print. How many different ways can snow be described?

Tennyson's description of "The Eagle" is rich in the use of visual imagery. In the first verse the reader can see the eagle perched on the crest of a steep mountain, poised ready for his swift descent whenever he sights his quarry. While in the second verse the poet has "entered into" the eagle's world and describes it from the bird's point of view. Looking down from his lofty height, the might of the waves is reduced to wrinkles and the sea seems to crawl:

THE EAGLE

He clasps the crag with crooked hands;
Close to the sun in lonely lands,
Ringed with the azure world, he stands.

The wrinkled sea beneath him crawls;
He watches from his mountain walls,
And like a thunderbolt he falls.

Alfred, Lord Tennyson (164)

The lonely, peaceful scene is shattered by the natural metaphor of the final line, "And like a thunderbolt he falls." In your mind's eye you can see, almost feel the wind on your wings, as you plunge down the face of the cliff. Some poets are so skilled in presenting a particularly vivid picture that they can direct "eye movements" and change the reader's focus on a certain scene. Harry Behn has done this in:

FAR AND NEAR

Farther away than a house is a lawn
    A field and a fence and a rocky hill
    With a tree on top, and farther still
    The sky with a cloud in it gold at dawn.
Closer than dawn in the sky is a tree
    On a hill, and a fence and a field and a
        green
    Lawn and a house and a window screen
    With a nose pressed against it—
        and then me.

Harry Behn (28)

Did you stand at the house and see a panoramic view of the lawn, the field, the hill, and the tree silhouetted against the sunrise; and then did you see the picture in reverse, as gradually you shifted your focus from the sky to the tree, to the field, to the lawn, the house, and yourself? The poet created these shifting images without the use of any figurative language, relying solely upon his picture-making ability.

Most poetry depends on visual and auditory imagery to evoke a mood or response, but imagery of touch, taste, and smell is also used. Children have always enjoyed the poem that begins, "Mud is very nice to feel/all squishy—squash between the toes! . . ." (13). Zilpha Snyder's "Poem to Mud" also wallows in this delightful feeling:

POEM TO MUD

Poem to mud—
Poem to ooze—
Patted in pies, or coating your shoes.
Poem to slooze—
Poem to crud—
Fed by a leak, or spread by a flood.
Wherever, whenever, wherever it goes,
Stirred by your finger, or strained by your toes,
There's nothing sloppier, slipperier, floppier,
There's nothing slickier, stickier, thickier,
There's nothing quickier to make grown-ups
    sickier,
Trulier coolier
Than wonderful mud.

Zilpha Keatley Snyder (269)

Aileen Fisher creates a vivid sensory impression by contrasting the various textures of the skins of fruits in her poem, "Skins." Before introducing this poem, put a variety of fruit in a paper bag and have children describe the first one they touch. Encourage them to use descriptive words and then see if their classmates can guess the name of the fruit from their description of how it feels. Compare their descriptions with those of Fisher's:

SKINS

Skins of lemons are waterproof slickers.
Pineapple skins are stuck full of stickers.
Skins of apples are skinny and shiny
and strawberry skins (if any) are tiny.

Grapes have skins that are juicy and squishy.
Gooseberry skins are vinegar-ishy.
Skins of peaches are fuzzy and hairy.
Oranges' skins are more peely than pare-y.

Skins of plums are squirty and squeezy.
Bananas have skins you can pull-off-easy.

A realistic photograph effectively captures the sensory imagery of "Poem to Mud" by Zilpha K. Snyder.

Photographs copyright © 1969 by John Arms. From *Today Is Saturday* by Zilpha Keatley Snyder. Used by permission of Atheneum Publishers.

. . .
I like skins that are thin as sheeting
so what-is-under is bigger for eating.

Aileen Fisher (110)

In the poem "Gravel Paths" (141), Patricia Hubbell describes the crinkled feel of gravel. It would be fun to compare this poem with Kim Worthington's "I Held a Lamb" (294), in which the poet responds to the warm soft feel of a baby lamb.

Most children have a very delicate sense of taste that responds to the texture and smell of a particular food. Yet there are few poems for children that appeal to a child's sense of taste. Patricia Hubbell has described all the various dimensions of lemons, contrasting lemons with other fruit, telling how lemons look and how lemons do not look. Then she identifies the unique aspect of lemons:

LEMONS

A lemon's a lemony kind of a thing,
It doesn't look sharp and it doesn't look sting,
It looks rather round and it looks rather square,
It looks almost oval, a yellow pear.

It looks like a waxy old, yellow old pear,
It looks like a pear without any stem,
It doesn't look sharp and it doesn't look sting,
A lemon's a lemony kind of a thing.
But cut it and taste it and touch it with tongue
You'll see where the sharp and the sting have
　　been hiding—
Under the yellow without any warning;
I touch it and touch it again with my tongue,
I like it! I like it! I like to be stung!

Patricia Hubbell (140)

In "A Matter of Taste," (210) Eve Merriam relates the way food tastes to the way it feels and sounds when it is being chewed! This poem is a favorite with all age levels.

Christopher Morley's poem "Smells (Junior)" (13) describes all the smells that delight a small boy, including the way his dog smells when he has been out in the rain! Zhenya Gay's poem which begins, "The world is full of wonderful smells" (120) tells of the luscious smell of hot bread and cake, of a haymow, and a warm dog lying in the sun. Much of children's poetry evokes this rich sensory response from its hearers and serves to sharpen children's perceptions.

Figurative Language: Comparison and Contrast

Since the language of poetry is so compressed, every word must be made to convey the message of the poem. Poets do this by comparing two objects or ideas with each other in such a way that the connotation of one word gives added meaning to another. Rowena Bennett in describing the look of "Motor Cars" from a high city window compares them to little black beetles:

MOTOR CARS

From a city window, 'way up high,
I like to watch the cars go by.
They look like burnished beetles, black,
That leave a little muddy track
Behind them as they slowly crawl.
Sometimes they do not move at all
But huddle close with hum and drone
As though they feared to be alone.
They grope their way through fog and night
With the golden feelers of their light.

Rowena Bennett (13)

Having established the "look-alikeness" of cars and burnished beetles in the first simile, the poet then extends the comparison in the metaphor of the last two lines, in which the cars have *become* beetles, their lights now assuming such beetle properties as "feelers." When a writer compares one thing with another, using such connecting words as *like* or *as*, he is using a simile. In a metaphor the poet speaks of an object or idea as if it *were* another object. In recent years in schools we have paid little attention to the difference between these two techniques, referring to both as examples of metaphorical or figurative language.

It is not important that children know the difference between a simile and a metaphor. It is important that they know what is being compared, and that the comparison is fresh and new and helps them view the idea or object in a different and unusual way. In Harry Behn's book, *Chrysalis*, he describes meeting with a group of gifted children and asking them to tell him what they thought poetry was. One child stood up and read this poem as his answer:

"THE MOUNTAIN"

Did you think
about the mountain?
Did you think?
Did you see it today
or some other day
in another way? (22)

In evaluating poetry, then, we look at the imaginative quality of the poem. Some figurative language is so commonplace that it has lost its ability to evoke new images. Language and verse are filled with such clichés as "it rained cats and dogs," "a blanket of snow," "quiet as a mouse," or "thin as a rail." Eve Merriam describes a "cliché" as ". . . what we all say/when we are too lazy/to find another way" (208). Her poem "Metaphor Man" (209) also pokes fun at such expressions as "drives a hard bargain," "stands four square," or "flies in a rage."

In a book titled *Small Poems,* Valerie Worth has written some twenty-four simple yet vivid poems which describe quite ordinary objects in fresh new terms. Her clear observations of a tractor would be understood by any child who had seen a grasshopper:

TRACTOR

The tractor rests
In the shed
Dead or asleep,

But with high
Hind wheels
Held so still

We know
It is only waiting
Ready to leap—

Like a heavy
Brown
Grasshopper.

    Valerie Worth (307)

Most children are intrigued with the subject
of dinosaurs and readily respond to Charles
Malam's poem that compares a steam shovel
with those enormous beasts. The image, which
the poem projects, reinforces the idea of the
poem throughout:

STEAM SHOVEL

The dinosaurs are not all dead.
I saw one raise its iron head
To watch me walking down the road
Beyond our house today.
Its jaws were dripping with a load
Of earth and grass that it had cropped.
It must have heard me where I stopped,
Snorted white steam my way,
And stretched its long neck out to see,
And chewed, and grinned quite amiably.

        Charles Malam (88)

James Reeves compares the sound of the sea
with the howls of a hungry dog in his poem "The
Sea." He also effectively contrasts a stormy sea
with a quiet one, while sustaining his original
metaphor:

THE SEA

The sea is a hungry dog,
Giant and gray.
He rolls on the beach all day.
With his clashing teeth and shaggy jaws
Hour upon hour he gnaws
The rumbling, tumbling stones,
And "Bones, bones, bones!"

The giant sea-dog moans,
Licking his greasy paws.

And when the night wind roars
And the moon rocks in the stormy cloud,
He bounds to his feet and snuffs and sniffs,
Shaking his wet sides over the cliffs,
And howls and hollos long and loud.

But on quiet days in May or June,
When even the grasses on the dune
Play no more their reedy tune,
With his head between his paws
He lies on the sandy shores,
So quiet, so quiet, he scarcely snores.

        James Reeves (76)

Carl Sandburg's well-known poem "Fog" (237)
likens the fog hovering over the city to a cat that
sits "on silent haunches." Langston Hughes sees
the city as a bird in the first stanza of this poem,
"City," and personifies it in the last:

CITY

In the morning the city
Spreads its wings
Making a song
In stone that sings.

In the evening the city
Goes to bed
Hanging lights
About its head.

  Langston Hughes (202)

Personification is a way of speaking about
inanimate objects as though they were persons.
Aileen Fisher uses personification to describe
"The Voice of the Sky" (105) as the oldest voice
that has ever been heard. The wind becomes a
person in Adrien Stoutenberg's free verse titled:

THE STORM

In a storm
the wind talks
with its mouth wide open.
It yells around corners
with its eyes shut.
It bumps itself
and falls over a roof
and whispers
Oh. . . . Oh. . . . oh. . . .
  Adrien Stoutenberg (279)

Rachel Field has personified "Skyscrapers" (93) when she wonders if they ever "grow tired of holding themselves up high" or if they ever "shiver on frosty nights." In one of Gwendolyn Brooks' poems, "Lyle" (47) sadly laments the fact that he is going to have to move, whereas the tree in his backyard won't have to pack his bag; "tree can stay and stay." Children frequently personify their toys and pets; poetry extends this process to a wider range of objects.

Another way of strengthening an image is through contrast. Elizabeth Coatsworth employs this device in much of her poetry. Her best-known "Poem of Praise" (63) contrasts the beauty of swift things with those that are slow and steady. Similarly, she compares the speeds at which "Morning and Afternoon" (63) pass, in the poem by that title. Marci Ridlon presents two points of view concerning life in the city. This poem could be read as two contrasting speakers or as the same speaker revealing different feelings. Read the poem first as two voices. Then read the poem straight across both parts, reading by four-line phrases rather than lines—and it becomes one voice.

CITY CITY

I	II
City, city	City, city
Wrong and bad,	Golden-clad,
Looms above me	Shines around me
When I'm sad,	When I'm glad,
Throws its shadow	Lifts me with its
On my care,	Strength and height,
Sheds its poison	Fills me with its
In my air,	Sound and sight,
Pounds me with its	Takes me to its
Noisy fist,	Crowded heart,
Sprays me with its	Holds me so I
Sooty mist.	Won't depart.
Till, with sadness	Till, with gladness
On my face	On my face,
I long to live	I wouldn't live
Another place.	Another place.

Marci Ridlon (252)

In the poem "Fueled," the poet contrasts the launching of a man-made rocket with the miraculous growth of a seedling pushing its way through the earth. The first feat receives much acclaim, while the second goes virtually unnoticed. There seems to be no doubt in the poet's mind which is the greater event, for she has even shaped her poem to resemble half of a tree:

FUELED

Fueled
by a million
man-made
wings of fire—
the rocket tore a tunnel
through the sky—
and everybody cheered.
Fueled
only by a thought from God—
the seedling
urged its way
through the thickness of black—
and as it pierced
the heavy ceiling of the soil—
and launched itself
up into outer space—
no
one
even clapped.

Marcie Hans (88)

Even though all children know about rockets and seeds, they may not be able to see the connection between the two images that the poet has created. Among one group of educationally and economically advantaged 8-year-olds, not one child saw both of these ideas; yet 11-year-olds in the same school easily recognized them. This suggests the importance of knowing the comprehension level of a group before selecting poetry for them.

The Shape of a Poem

The first thing children notice about reading a poem is that it looks different from prose. And usually it does. Most poems begin with capital letters for each line and have one or more stanzas.

Increasingly, however, poets are using the shape of their poems to reinforce the image of the idea. David McCord describes the plight of "The Grasshopper" that fell down a deep well. As luck would have it, he discovered "a rope/ that/dangled/some/hope." And up he climbed one word at a time! The reader must read up the page to follow the grasshopper's ascent.

THE GRASSHOPPER

Down
a
deep
well
a
grasshopper
fell.
By kicking about
He thought to get out.
   He might have known better,
   For that got him wetter.
To kick round and round
Is the way to get drowned,
   And drowning is what
   I should tell you he got.
      But
      the
      well
      had
      a
      rope
      that
      dangled
      some
      hope.
And pure as molasses
On one of his passes
   He found the rope handy
   And up he went, and he
      it
      up
      and
      it
      up
      and
      it
      up
      and
      it
      up
      went
and hopped away proper
as any grasshopper.

      David McCord (197)

The Emotional Force of Poetry

We have seen how sound, language, and the shape of a poem may all work together to create the total impact of the poem. Considered individually the rhyme scheme, imagery, figurative language, or the appearance of the poem are of little importance unless all of these interrelate to create an emotional response in the reader. The craft of the poem is not the poem.

In Randall Jarrell's remarkable fantasy *The Bat-Poet* (150), the little bat shares the poem he has written with the sophisticated mockingbird. When he has finished reading it, the mockingbird tells him it is quite good, although the last line is two feet short! The chipmunk, however, responds to the total impact of the poem, which describes the owl as a deadly shadow. ". . . when the poem was over the chipmunk gave a big shiver and said, 'It's terrible, just terrible! Is there really something like that at night?'"[6]

Good poetry has the power to make the reader catch his breath in fear, gasp in wonder, smile with delight, or sit back and think. For poetry heightens emotions and increases one's sensitivity to an idea or a mood. All elements of the poem should work together to create this response.

Children and most adults react to the total force of a poem. Only after they have had a chance to hear much poetry and developed a taste for it, should they give any consideration to the technical elements of a poem.

Teachers need to be able to identify the characteristics of good poetry in order to make wise selections to share with children. They need to know the various kinds of poetry and the range of content of poetry for children. Then they can provide children with a balance of form and subject. Hopefully, teachers will allow children the chipmunk's response of awe and wonder, rather than the mockingbird's concern with mechanical techniques.

FORMS OF POETRY FOR CHILDREN

Children are more interested in the "idea" of a poem than in knowing about the various forms of poetry. However, teachers will want to expose children to various forms of poetry and note their reactions. Do these children like only narrative poems? Do they think all poetry must rhyme, or

[6]Randall Jarrell, *The Bat-Poet*, illustrated by Maurice Sendak (New York: Macmillan, 1963), p. 17.

will they listen to some free verse? Are they ready for the seemingly simple, yet highly complex form of haiku? Understanding and appreciation for a wide variety of poetry grows gradually as children are exposed to different forms and types. Teachers will want to begin at the level of children's interests, which may be jump-rope rhymes or the newest rock lyrics, and then move to higher quality poetry when children seem ready for it.

Ballads

Ballads are narrative poems that have been adapted for singing or that give the effect of a song. Originally, they were not made or sung for children but were the literature of all the people. Characteristics of the ballad form are the frequent use of dialogue in telling the story, repetition, marked rhythm and rhyme, and refrains that go back to the days when ballads were sung. Popular ballads have no known authors, as they were handed down from one generation to the next; the literary ballad, however, does have a known author. Ballads usually deal with heroic deeds, and include stories of murder, unrequited love, feuds, and tragedies.

Children in the middle grades enjoy the amusing story of the stubborn man and his equally stubborn wife in "Get Up and Bar the Door" (37). As in many ballads, the ending is abrupt, and the reader never does find out what happened to the two sinister guests, other than that the good husband finally locked them all in the house together! "The Outlandish Knight" (299) and "Robin Hood and the Widow's Sons" (299) will appeal to youngsters' sense of poetic justice; while true love reigns in "The Bailiff's Daughter of Islington" (299), "Robin Hood and Allan-a-Dale" (299), and "Lochinvar" (238). There are many different versions of the story of the wealthy young bride who runs off with gypsies. Children might compare the variations found in the folk song, "The Raggle Taggle Gypsies" (299), and the traditionally tragic ballad, *The Gypsy Laddie* (124), richly illustrated in a picture-book edition by Dorothy Rice.

Ballads from the United States include the well-known story of the dying cowboy in "The Streets of Laredo" (238). Brinton Turkle has illustrated a picture-book edition of Stephen

Vincent Benét's literary ballad, *The Ballad of William Sycamore (1790–1871)*. Unlike the dying cowboy, William Sycamore was a frontiersman who was killed by an unbroken colt, but he died content:

. . .

> Now I lie in the heart of the fat, black soil,
> Like the seed of a prairie-thistle;
> It has washed my bones with honey and oil
> And picked them clean as a whistle.
>
> And my youth returns, like the rains of Spring,
> And my sons, like the wild-geese flying;
> And I lie and hear the meadow-lark sing
> And have much content in my dying.
>
> Go play with the town you have built of blocks,
> The towns where you would have bound me!
> I sleep in the earth like a tired fox,
> And my buffalo have found me.

Stephen Vincent Benét (30)

Other literary ballads that are appropriate for use with children include "A Legend of the Northland" (299) by Phoebe Cary and "Beth Gêlert" (299) by William Spencer. The first ballad tells of the origin of a redheaded woodpecker from a selfish old woman; while the latter ballad is the appealing story of a faithful dog. Older children will enjoy the poignant tale of "The Ballad of the Harp-Weaver" (13) by Edna St. Vincent Millay. The picture-book edition of *The Ballad of the Burglar of Babylon* by Elizabeth Bishop (32) is a modern tragedy of a man who preferred death to the living death of a ninety-nine-year sentence in jail. This book serves as an excellent introduction to the ballad form for older boys and girls.

Narrative Verse

The narrative poem relates a particular event or episode, or tells a long tale. It may be a lyric, a sonnet, or written in free verse; its one requirement is that it *must* tell a story. Many of children's favorite poems are these so-called story poems. One classic that has been enjoyed for years is Browning's "The Pied Piper of Hamelin" (299). This poem has been richly illustrated in a single tale by Lieselotte Schwarz (49), and presents a striking contrast to the traditional pictures of the Pied Piper. Another well-loved narrative

Lieselotte Schwarz portrays an angry Pied Piper of Hamelin Town in her unusual picture-book edition of this favorite poem.

Illustration by Lieselotte Schwarz from *The Pied Piper*. Used by permission of Scroll Press.

poem is "A Visit from St. Nicholas" (92) by Clement Moore, known to children as "Twas the Night Before Christmas." Moore created the prototype for the North American Santa Claus in this poem that was published in 1823. Other traditional favorites include Laura E. Richards' ironic tale of "The Monkeys and the Crocodile" (13), Eugene Field's "The Duel" (13), and that swashbuckling "Pirate Don Durk of Dowdee" (13).

One of the favorite narrative poems of young children is the simple story of the parents who lovingly pretend to look for their son in the poem "Hiding" (7) by Dorothy Aldis. The triumphant ending of "The Little Turtle" (13) who caught a mosquito, a flea, and a minnow, "But he didn't catch me," always delights younger children. A. A. Milne's poems of a lost mouse, "Missing" (212), and the disappearing beetle, "Forgiven" (211), are also favorites with this age group.

Six-, 7-, and 8-year-olds delight in "The King's Breakfast" (213) and "King John's Christmas" (213); and they are old enough to enjoy Christopher Robin's humorous deception of adults in "Sneezles" (213). The long narrative verses in the many books by Dr. Seuss have their greatest appeal for this age group, as does the humorous story of "Custard the Dragon" (299) by Ogden Nash.

A modern narrative poem that has become a favorite of many children is "Mummy Slept Late and Daddy Fixed Breakfast" (59) by John Ciardi. Another popular story poem is Karla Kuskin's hilarious tale of the boy who got stuck in the glue:

HUGHBERT AND THE GLUE

Hughbert had a jar of glue.
From Hugh the glue could not be parted,
At least could not be parted far,
For Hugh was glued to Hughbert's jar.
But that is where it all had started.
The glue upon the shoe of Hugh
Attached him to the floor.
The glue on Hughbert's gluey hand
Was fastened to the door,
While two of Hughbert's relatives
Were glued against each other.
His mother, I believe, was one.
The other was his brother.
The dog and cat stood quite nearby.

They could not move from there.
The bird was glued securely
Into Hughbert's mother's hair.

Hughbert's father hurried home
And loudly said to Hugh:
"From now on I would rather
That you did not play with glue."

Karla Kuskin (158)

While many narrative poems for children are humorous, some are not. Older children respond to the pathos of "Nancy Hanks" (29) and the irony of "Abraham Lincoln" (29), both by the Benéts. They are stirred by the galloping hoofbeats in *Paul Revere's Ride* (192) and the actions of that intrepid heroine of Fredericktown, *Barbara Frietchie* (306). One of their favorite romantic tales is the dramatic *The Highwayman* (226) by Alfred Noyes which has been illustrated with eerie ruby reds and shadowy purples by Gilbert Riswold in his picture-book version.

One of the best ways to capture children's interest in poetry is to present a variety of narrative poems. Teachers will want to build a file of story poems appropriate to the interests of children in their classes, and will want to read them often.

Lyrical

Most of the poetry written for children is lyrical. The term is derived from the word "lyric," and means poetry that sings its way into the minds and memories of its listeners. It is usually personal or descriptive poetry, with no prescribed length or structure other than its melody.

Much of William Blake's poetry is lyrical, beginning with the opening lines of his introductory poem to *Songs of Innocence:* "Piping down the valleys wild/Piping songs of pleasant glee" (36). Stevenson's poems have a singing quality that makes them unforgettable. Everyone knows the poem "The Swing" (278) and "The Wind" (278) and the mysterious "Windy Nights" (277). In Stevenson's poem "Where Go the Boats?" the tempo of the words reminds one of the increasing swiftness of the flow of the river toward the sea:

Dark brown is the river,
　Golden is the sand.
It flows along forever,
　With trees on either hand.

Green leaves a-floating,
   Castles of the foam,
Boats of mine a-boating—
   Where will all come home?

On goes the river
   And out past the mill,
Away down the valley,
   Away down the hill.

Away down the river,
   A hundred miles or more,
Other little children
   Shall bring my boats ashore.
              Robert Louis Stevenson (278)

The music-making quality of Christina Rossetti's poems is unmistakable. Most children will know her poem that begins: "Who has seen the wind?" (13). Her delight in a rainbow is captured in the poem "Boats sail on the rivers" (13). The singing, soaring flight of a "Kite" (27) is described by Harry Behn, as is its sudden fall into a tree. Older children enjoy the lyrical beat of Masefield's "Sea-Fever" (13) or Allan Cunningham's "A Wet Sheet and a Flowing Sea" (37). Both boys and girls respond to the strong beat and internal rhyme of "The Lone Dog" that will have no master but himself. The first verse provides an example of its rhythm:

THE LONE DOG

I'm a lean dog, a keen dog, a wild dog, and
   lone;
I'm a rough dog, a tough dog, hunting on my
   own;
I'm a bad dog, a mad dog, teasing silly sheep;
I love to sit and bay the moon, to keep fat souls
   from sleep.
. . .

              Irene Rutherford McLeod (13)

Lyrical poetry is characterized by this singingness of words that gives children an exhilarating sense of melody.

Limerick

A nonsense form of verse that is particularly enjoyed by children is the limerick. This is a five-line verse with the first and second line rhyming, the third and fourth agreeing, and the fifth line usually ending in a surprise or humorous statement. Freak spelling, oddities, and hu-

morous twists characterize this form of poetry. David McCord in his book, *Take Sky*, suggests that "a limerick, to be lively and successful, *must* have *perfect* riming and *flawless* rhythm." He gives several suggestions of how to write a limerick using the limerick form:

Write a limerick now. Say there was
An old man of some place, what he does,
   Or perhaps what he doesn't,
   Or isn't or wasn't.
Want help with it? Give me a buzz.
              David McCord (199)

Although Edward Lear did not originate the limerick, he did much to popularize it. Modern writers continue to produce limericks, particularly, William Jay Smith. In *Typewriter Town*, his unusual typewriter illustrations add to the enjoyment of the humorous limericks.

The limerick form lends itself to modern satire, as is seen in Paul Dehn's poem:

LITTLE MISS MUFFET

Little Miss Muffet
   Crouched on a tuffet,
Collecting her shell shocked wits.
   There dropped (from a glider)
   An H-bomb beside her
Which frightened Miss Muffet to bits.
              Paul Dehn (88)

Middle-grade children might want to write their own limericks, following McCord's instructions,

There was an old person of Nice,
Whose associates were usually Geese.
They walked out together, in all sorts of weather.
That affable person of Nice!

Edward Lear's laughable illustrations are as humorous as his well-known limericks.

Reprinted by permission of Dodd, Mead & Company, Inc., from *The Complete Nonsense Book* by Edward Lear. Edited by Holbrook Jackson. Published in England by Faber and Faber, Ltd., and used with their permission.

try their hand at making typewriter pictures, and consider the potential for social comment as seen in such modern limericks as "Little Miss Muffet." Certainly this is an easier form for children to write than the highly abstract form of haiku.

Free Verse

Free verse does not have to rhyme but depends upon rhythm or cadence for its poetic form. It may use some rhyme, alliteration, and pattern. It frequently looks different on a printed page, but it sounds very much like other poetry when read aloud. Children who have the opportunity to hear this form of poetry will be freed from thinking that all poetry must rhyme. The teacher may read them some of the descriptive and arresting poems written by Hilda Conkling when she was a child. Boys and girls enjoy listening to the way another child describes a "Mouse" (78) in his "gray velvet dress," or the "Hills" (78) that are "going somewhere." When Conkling was 6 years old, she wrote this poem:

The world turns softly
Not to spill its lakes and rivers.
The water is held in its arms
And the sky is held in the waters.
What is water,
That pours silver,
And can hold the sky?

Hilda Conkling (78)

Langston Hughes' melodic "April Rain Song" (237) is another example of the effective use of free verse. Probably one of the best-known poems of our day is "Fog" (237) by Carl Sandburg. This metaphorical description of the fog characterized as a cat is written in free verse.

Haiku

Haiku is an ancient Japanese verse form that can be traced back to the thirteenth century. There are only seventeen syllables in the haiku; the first and third lines contain five syllables, the second line seven. Almost every haiku may be divided into two parts; first, a simple picture-making description that usually includes some reference, direct or indirect, to the season; and second, a statement of mood or feeling. A relationship between these two parts is implied, either a similarity or a telling difference.

The greatest of haiku writers, and the one who crystallized the form, was Basho. In his lifetime Basho produced more than 800 haiku. He considered the following poem to be one of his best:

An old silent pond . . .
A frog jumps into the pond,
splash! Silence again.

Basho (23)

The silence reverberates against the sudden noise of the splash, intensified by the interruption. Another poet has contrasted destruction of material things with the everlasting beauty of nature in this haiku:

Ashes my burnt hut . . .
But wonderful the cherry
Blooming on my hill.

Hokushi (149)

The meaning of haiku is not expected to be immediately apparent. The reader is invited to add his own associations and meanings to the words, thus completing the poem in his mind. Each time the poem is read, new understandings will be developed. Harry Behn has written a haiku to explain the deeper meanings of this form of poetry:

A spark in the sun,
this tiny flower has roots
deep in the cool earth.

Harry Behn (23)

Haiku is deceiving in that the form appears simple, yet it requires much from its reader. Unless children have reached the level of formal operations in their thinking, haiku may be too abstract a form of poetry for them to fully understand.

Concrete Poetry

Many poets today are writing picture poems that make you see what they are saying. The message of the poem is presented not only in the words (sometimes just letters or punctuation marks) but in the arrangement of the words. Meaning is reinforced, or even carried, by the shape of the poem. Myra Cohn Livingston creates the shape of a building with the words for her poem:

BUILDINGS

Buildings are a great surprise,
Every one's a different size.

Offices
grow
long
and
high,
tall
enough
to
touch
the
sky.

Houses seem
more like a box,
made of glue
and building blocks.

Everytime you look, you see
Buildings shaped quite differently.

Myra Cohn Livingston (190)

Robert Froman has created picture poems about pollution, traffic, loneliness, skyscrapers, fire hydrants, and a garbage truck for his book *Street Poems.* One that will please children particularly pictures a candy bar in words (see bottom of this page).

Froman has continued his innovative way of *Seeing Things* in a book by that title. An excellent source of concrete poetry is A. Barbara Pilon's book, *Concrete Is Not Always Hard* (239). Younger children will enjoy "Lick Smack" and "Ice Cream," while middle-graders will be amused by "Apfel" by Dohl and "Showers, Clearing Later in the Day" by Merriam, which is made entirely with exclamation points and asterisks. Merriam's "Windshield Wiper" in her own book, *Out Loud* (209), is another concrete poem that intrigues children.

Once children have been exposed to concrete poetry, they invariably want to try writing some of their own, and that is fine. However, some children become so involved in the picture-making process that they forget that the meaning of the poem is carried by both words and arrangement. If emphasis is placed on the meaning first, then the shaping of the words will grow naturally from the idea of the poem. In the words of Pilon, "Concrete is not always hard"; frequently it is simply fun!

WELL, YES

Candy bar—

Too much.
Too much.
But I'll have one more.

Robert Froman (114)

Selecting Poetry for Children

CHILDREN'S POETRY PREFERENCES

Children's interest in poetry was the subject of many research studies in the 1920s and 1930s.[7] The interesting fact about all these studies is the similarity of their findings and the stability of children's poetry preferences over the years. Prior to conducting her own research on children's response to poetry, Ann Terry[8] summarized the findings of these earlier studies:

1. Children are the best judges of their preferences.
2. Reading texts and courses of study often do not include the children's favorite poems.
3. Children's poetry choices are influenced by the (1) poetry form, (2) certain poetic elements, and (3) the content, with humor and familiar experience being particularly popular.
4. A poem enjoyed at one grade level may be enjoyed across several grade levels.
5. Children do not enjoy poems they do not understand.
6. Thoughtful, meditative poems are disliked by children.
7. Some poems appeal to one sex more than another; girls enjoy poetry more than boys.
8. New poems are preferred over older, more traditional ones.
9. Literary merit is not necessarily an indication that a poem will be liked.

In her own report of this national survey of children's poetry preferences, Terry[9] found much consistency with the results of these earlier studies. Narrative poems, such as Ciardi's "Mummy Slept Late and Daddy Fixed Breakfast" (59), and limericks, including both modern and traditional, were the favorite forms of poetry for children. Haiku was consistently disliked by all grade levels. Elements of rhyme, rhythm, and sound increased children's enjoyment of the poems, as evidenced by their preference for David McCord's "The Pickety Fence" (196) and "Lone Dog" (13). Poems that contained much figurative language or imagery were disliked. Children's favorite poems at all grade levels contained humor or were about familiar experiences or animals. All children preferred contemporary poems containing modern content and today's language more than the older, more traditional poems.

This last finding is particularly important when compared with a study done by Chow Loy Tom,[10] which indicated that teachers were primarily reading such older poems as "Paul Revere's Ride," "The Daffodils," "Fog," and "Who Has Seen the Wind" to their middle-grade students. In fact, all but four of the forty-one poems most frequently read to children were written before 1928. "Paul Revere's Ride," a narrative poem published in 1861, was the most frequently read poem at all grade levels. By comparing these two studies, one can conclude that teachers are not selecting the poems that children would enjoy hearing the most.

How then can one most effectively select poetry for children? Certainly a teacher will want to consider children's needs and interests, their previous experience with poetry, and the types of poetry that appeal to them. A sound principle to follow is to begin where the children are. Using some of the findings from the research mentioned above, teachers can share poems that

[7]Helen K. Mackintosh. "A Study of Children's Choices in Poetry," *The Elementary English Review*, I (May 1924); Helen K. Mackintosh. "A Critical Study of Children's Choices of Poetry," University of Iowa Studies in Education, VII, No. 4 (September 1932); Miriam B. Huber, Herbert B. Bruner, and Charles McCurry. *Children's Interest in Poetry* (Chicago, Ill.: Rand McNally and Company, 1927); Blanche E. Weekes. *The Influence of Meaning on Children's Choices of Poetry*, Contributions to Education No. 354 (New York: Teachers College, Columbia University, 1929); Ruth E. Bradshaw. "Children's Choices in the First Grade," *Elementary English Review*, XIV (May 1937), pp. 168–176; 188; Lucy Kangley. *Poetry Preferences in the Junior High School*, Contributions to Education, No. 758 (New York: Teachers College, Columbia University, 1938), p. 138.
[8]Ann Terry. *Children's Poetry Preferences: A National Survey of the Upper Elementary Grades* (Urbana, Ill.: National Council of Teachers of English, 1974), p. 10.

[9]Ann Terry. "A National Survey of Children's Poetry Preferences in the Fourth, Fifth, and Sixth Grades" (Unpublished dissertation, The Ohio State University, Columbus, Ohio, 1972).
[10]Chow Loy Tom. "Paul Revere Rides Ahead: Poems Teachers Read to Pupils in the Middle Grades," *The Library Quarterly*, Vol. 43 (January 1973), pp. 27–38.

have elements of rhyme, rhythm, and sound, such as Susie's "Galoshes" (294) or "The Pickety Fence" (196). Teachers can read many narrative verses and limericks and look for humorous poems and poems about familiar experiences and animals.

The poetry selected should have relevance for today's child. "The Village Blacksmith" (92) was a favorite of our grandfathers, but it has little meaning for today's child, who has probably never even seen a blacksmith. It is best to avoid poems with forbidding or archaic vocabulary, those that "talk down" to children, nostalgic poems about childhood, and those that try to teach a lesson. Poetry should be appropriate to the background and the age level of the child, and to the age in which he lives.

A teacher's prime purpose should be to increase enjoyment of poetry in children. However, taste needs to be developed, too; and children should go beyond their delight in humorous and narrative poetry to develop an appreciation for various other types of poetry.

It may well be that the consistency in children's poetry preferences over the years simply reflects the poverty of their experience with poetry. We tend to like the familiar. If teachers only read traditional narrative poems to children, then these children will like narrative poems. Or having had little or no exposure to fine imaginative poetry, children may not have gone beyond their natural intuitive liking for jump-rope rhymes or humorous limericks. In brief, the results of the studies of children's interests in poetry may be more of an indictment of the quality of their literature program than on the quality of their preferences. We need to ascertain children's poetry preferences *after* they have experienced a rich, continuous exposure to poetry throughout the elementary school. It is hoped that as children have increased experience with a wide range of quality poetry, they will grow in appreciation and understanding of the finer poems.

THE CONTENT OF POEMS FOR CHILDREN

Children derive certain satisfactions from hearing and reading poetry, but their preference for particular poems is usually based upon the idea or content of the poems they like best. Form may influence choice, but it does not necessarily determine it. Teachers will want to become familiar with a wide range of poetry so they may select the appropriate poem for the appropriate moment. Acquaintance with the work of individual poets is important, but knowledge of the subject matter of poetry will prove most helpful. In making a choice, the teacher does not think: "What poem by Elizabeth Madox Roberts should I read to the group?" Instead, "The Woodpecker" (13) by Roberts is selected because the class has seen this bird eating the suet at their bird-feeding station.

Young children want their poems to be simple, vivid, and to the point, much the same pattern that they demand of stories they read. Each poem should present one clear thought or image, or a succession of such thoughts. Children will accept poems they do not completely understand, such as the mysterious poems of Walter de la Mare; but they are not as tolerant about poetry that is vague and deliberately confusing. They cannot "take" too many figures of speech, long descriptions, or much philosophizing.

Children's preferences for poetry are very similar to their preferences for prose. The young child enjoys poems of everyday occurrences. His interest in animals, both comical and real, is reflected in many poems. The changes in the weather and the seasons continue to be a source of wonder to him. All children enjoy humorous poetry, whether it is gay nonsense or an amusing story. Yet children today are well aware of the evils and inequities in modern society. Middle-grade children are deeply concerned about what is happening in the world and are writing and reading poems of social commentary. More sophisticated, more "aware" than children ten years ago, today's child wants his poetry to be straightforward and, above all, honest.

Me, Myself and I

The young child is egocentric and views the world as revolving about himself. He is fascinated with his uniqueness, his individuality. He is a very special person, and he wants the world to recognize this. When it does not, he is very provoked, as is shown in this long-time favorite poem by Dorothy Aldis:

EVERYBODY SAYS

Everybody says
I look just like my mother.

Everybody says
I'm the image of Aunt Bee.
Everybody says
My nose is like my father's
But I want to look like me.

Dorothy Aldis (7)

Primary-grade children can crawl outside of themselves just long enough to ponder on their uniqueness. In "Just Me" (127) by Margaret Hillert the child speaker reveals that "Nobody sees what I can see,/For back of my eyes there is only me." In the final line, she rightly maintains, "And there's nobody like me anywhere." Eve Merriam writes about the amazing stability of personality in the poem "Me Myself and I" (210), in which the child observes that no matter how much he grows and changes he still is the same interior person.

Older children still puzzle about the miracle of self. They wonder who they really are and what they will become. Gwendolyn Brooks has described this bewilderment of an older child who looks in a mirror and finds "Robert, Who Is Often a Stranger to Himself" (47). Similarly, Merriam has captured a child's confrontation with himself in:

CONVERSATION WITH MYSELF

This face in the mirror
stares at me
demanding *Who are you? What will you become?*
and taunting, *You don't even know.*
Chastened, I cringe and agree
and then
because I'm still young,
I stick out my tongue.

Eve Merriam (208)

In the poem "I Wonder" (252) Marci Ridlon explores the idea of how someone else might feel about her things. Would he like them as much, or maybe more? If she weren't here to own them, where would she be? Would she be? Slowly the poet questions her very existence. Older children

will be interested in Eve Merriam's poem "Thumbprint" (208) in which she describes the uniqueness of each individual as revealed by the whirls and lines of his thumb. In the poem "maggie and milly and molly and may" e. e. cummings suggests that our personalities determine the quality of experience that we have, even in such a simple experience as a trip down to the beach:

MAGGIE AND MILLY AND MOLLY AND MAY

maggie and milly and molly and may
went down to the beach (to play one day)

and maggie discovered a shell that sang
so sweetly she couldn't remember her troubles, and

milly befriended a stranded star
whose rays five languid fingers were;

and molly was chased by a horrible thing
which raced sideways while blowing bubbles: and

may come home with a smooth round stone
as small as a world and as large as alone.

For whatever we lose (like a you or a me)
it's always ourselves we find in the sea

e. e. cummings (126)

More mature students might want to consider the way in which one's traits and physical characteristics may live on through time and inheritance. In "Heredity" (241), Thomas Hardy considers the continuity of self: "The eternal thing in man,/That heeds no call to die."

Family, Friends, and Feelings

Family relationships have been described honestly and naturally in poetry for young children. Secure and loved, the child in Myra Cohn Livingston's poem asks his mother to "Be My Circle" (178). Dorothy Aldis tells of the child who views his mother at "The Dinner Party" (7) and sees her ". . . looking strange and new/as though she'd never done/The marketing. Or made a stew./Or scolded anyone." Deeper emotions are evoked by Coatsworth's poem "Asleep," which describes the reactions of a child who, unable to sleep, sought comfort in her mother's room. Peeking in the door, she sees her mother asleep, a stranger to her:

. . .
It seemed to me some enemy
Was lying in my mother's place
With eyes closed tight to shut
    me out,
    and a forgetting face.

    Elizabeth Coatsworth (64)

Theodor Roethke's remembrance of "My Papa's Waltz" (203) was not happy but somewhat terrifying, as he hung on to his father who had had too much to drink. A poignant poem by Gwendolyn Brooks reveals the pride of the poor and the quiet ache of a disappointed child:

OTTO

It's Christmas Day. I did not get
The presents that I hoped for. Yet
It is not nice to frown or fret.

To frown or fret would not be fair.
My Dad must never know I care
It's hard enough for him to bear.

    Gwendolyn Brooks (47)

In "Andre" (47) the same poet describes a dream in which a boy had an opportunity to select new parents and, much to his surprise, he found he chose the same ones.

Given a chance, it would seem that many children might not select their own brothers or sisters. "Little" (7) by Dorothy Aldis tells of a young child who shows her favorite toys to her baby brother, and each day he is too little to look. In "My Brother" (252) Marci Ridlon describes the feelings of a sister who thinks her baby brother is worth about two cents, while the child in the following poem is so disgusted with her brother, she tries to exchange him for another!

BROTHER

I had a little brother
And I brought him to my mother
And I said I want another
Little brother for a change.
But she said don't be a bother
So I took him to my father
And I said this little bother
Of a brother's very strange.

But he said one little brother
Is exactly like another

And every little brother
Misbehaves a bit he said.
So I took the little brother
From my mother and my father
And I put the little bother
Of a brother back to bed.

    Mary Ann Hoberman (85)

"Tag Along" (235) could be either a brother or a sister, but he or she is obviously a nuisance. This poem and "Satellite Satellite" (210), quoted earlier, would be good ones to read in conjunction with the picture book *Stevie* by John Steptoe.

Sisters come in for their share of mistreatment in a poem by Ted Hughes titled "My Sister Jane" (203), in which the speaker maintains that his sister Jane is a bird! "Oh it never would do to let folks know/My sister's nothing but a great big crow." It is easy to guess who the speaker of the following poem might be, and how many sisters he had to contend with:

TRIOLET AGAINST SISTERS

Sisters are always drying their hair.
    Locked into rooms, alone,
They pose at the mirror, shoulders bare,
Trying this way and that their hair,
Or fly importunate down the stair
    To answer a telephone.
Sisters are always drying their hair,
    Locked into rooms, alone.

    Phyllis McGinley (238)

Friends are as unpredictable as brothers and sisters according to the sad lament of one child in the poem "Nobody Loves Me" (133) by Charlotte Zolotow. This poem could be read along with Zolotow's picture story, *The Hating Book*, or Udry's *Let's Be Enemies*. Children's quarrels are just as momentary as these stories and poems suggest.

Children are as quick to adapt to new situations as they are to forget a quarrel. In "New Neighbors" (103) Aileen Fisher describes the apparent heartache of the child who cried all day because the next-door neighbors had moved away. Yet, by the end of the verse, the Browns had moved in with a cat, a dog with puppies, and a girl; and Judy, the life-long friend who had moved away, was nearly forgotten! In Rose Fyleman's poem with almost the same title, "The

New Neighbor" (13), a newcomer is faced with a barrage of questions, including the final one in which the welcomer invites himself in for tea! Harry Behn treats this same situation quite candidly in his poem "New Little Boy" (27). In this instance, the new neighbor won't answer any questions, and so the speaker concludes: "Well, all I know is his name is Tim/And I don't think very much of him."

Stephen Spender describes the agony of the overprotected child who wants desperately to make friends with the bullies who frighten him:

MY PARENTS KEPT ME FROM CHILDREN
WHO WERE ROUGH

My parents kept me from children who were
  rough
Who threw words like stones and who wore
  torn clothes.
Their thighs showed through rags. They ran in
  the street
And climbed cliffs and stripped by the country
  streams.

I feared more than tigers their muscles like iron
Their jerking hands and their knees tight on my
  arms.
I feared the salt-coarse pointing of those boys
Who copied my lisp behind me on the road.

They were lithe, they sprang out behind hedges
Like dogs to bark at my world. They threw mud
While I looked the other way, pretending to
  smile.
I longed to forgive them, but they never smiled.

                    Stephen Spender (236)

Poetry reflects the fears, joys, anger, the resentments of children caught in a world they did not make and cannot control. Primary-grade children quickly identify with the child in Karla Kuskin's poem, "I Woke Up this Morning," who had not been able to do anything all day that pleased her parents. The increasing size of the print reinforces a rising crescendo of resentment that ends with her final threat "That tomorrow/At quarter past seven,/They can/come in and get me/I'M STAYING IN BED" (158). The same tone is reflected in Marci Ridlon's "Questions," which was one of the best-liked poems in the Terry study (*see* footnote 8 of this chapter).

QUESTIONS

What did you do?
Where did you go?
Why weren't you back
An hour ago?

How come your shirt's
Ripped on the sleeve?
Why are you wet?
When did you leave?

What scratched your face?
When did you eat?
Where are your socks?
Look at your feet!

How did you get
Paint in your hair?
Where have you been?
Don't kick the chair!

Say something now.
I'll give you till ten.
. . .
"See if I ever
Come home again."
           Marci Ridlon (252)

Two open-ended poems that express anger without stating the cause are "Crosspatch" (235) by Nina Payne and Eve Merriam's "Mean Song" (210), which is a remarkable combination of nonsense syllables that sound very angry indeed! Children might enjoy writing stories or talking about times when they feel the same anger expressed in these poems.

When children are hurt and upset many of them want to be alone. Most children have private places, their own secret hideouts that are unknown to adults. A. A. Milne's poem "Solitude" represents some children's feelings about the need to have a special place of their own:

SOLITUDE

I have a house where I go
  When there's too many people,
I have a house where I go
  Where no one can be;
I have a house where I go
Where nobody ever says "No";
Where no one says anything—so
  There is no one but me.

            A. A. Milne (213)

Trina Schart Hyman has drawn a contemporary child's private place to illustrate A. A. Milne's timeless poem, "Solitude."

Illustration by Trina Hyman, copyright © 1972 by Harcourt Brace Jovanovich, Inc., and reproduced with their permission from *Listen, Children, Listen*, edited by Myra Cohn Livingston.

"Keziah," one of Gwendolyn Brooks' *Bronzeville Boys and Girls* (47), tells how he uses his secret place as a retreat from family quarrels, while "Charles" (47) has only himself to withdraw into. For children, like adults, frequently find themselves in moments of solitude.

Trees seem to be a favorite hiding place for children. Kathleen Fraser's poem "Tree Climbing" (133) describes a tree as a special place to be alone in. Dorothy Aldis has written about "The Secret Place" of a child, where two branches of a tree form a little chair. The child is delighted because no grown-up ever goes there, "and if he should, and climbed to it—/He would not fit, he would not fit!" (7). The child in Aileen Fisher's "Hideout" (105) seems to want to reveal her presence, for she throws acorns down from her hiding place in an old oak tree. A boy lovingly calls "The Maple" (64) his "whispering tree," for when his friends climb in to his "great green thimble," they sit quietly and whisper. This poem reflects some of the same quiet peace that can be found in McCord's favorite place:

THIS IS MY ROCK

This is my rock,
And here I run

To steal the secret of the sun;
This is my rock,
And here come I
Before the night has swept the sky;
This is my rock,
This is the place
I meet the evening face to face.

David McCord (197)

This contemplative poem might be introduced to children at the end of a cycle of poems about secret or special places. After children have discussed places where they go when they are angry or frightened, and after they have heard "Solitude" (213), "The Secret Place" (7), or "Keziah" (47), they would be ready to hear about a poet's special place where he goes to enjoy the beauty and wonder of the world. Children will like such poetry when they have been helped to develop a background for its appreciation.

Everyday Experiences

Poetry may help children see a familiar object or interpret an everyday experience in a fresh, meaningful way; for poetry has the capacity of making the commonplace seem distinctly uncommon. Dorothy Aldis has playfully described the fun of brushing your teeth in "See, I Can Do It" (7). In "Not That" (7), this same poet has identified the young child's wish to be independent in every respect except one—he hopes he won't have to tuck himself in bed! Children who plead for "five minutes more" before going to bed will see themselves in "Bedtime" (91) by Farjeon.

Many other common experiences of children have been portrayed in poetry. The difficulty of "Choosing Shoes" (14) was described in the introduction to this chapter. Children's concerns with clothes is a frequent topic of modern verse for children. In "Clothes" (233) by Elizabeth Jennings, an older girl suddenly realizes that someday her children may tease her about her clothes in the same way she laughs at what her mother used to wear. A little boy complains because he had to put on "Company Clothes" (103), but he is delighted when his mother's friends have a boy named John who wears jeans. He then makes a quick change to keep his "company, company." In the poem "Visitors" (103) Aileen Fisher portrays every child's wish to explore all the rooms of the house where he is visiting. Fisher also captures a child's amazement at the fact that when "Staying All Night" (103) at his friend's house, he likes oatmeal for breakfast! Another poet has shown that even such routine experiences as watering flowers and washing dishes can be new and exciting if done "At Josephine's House" (294). The joy of a picnic, coupled with the minor disaster of dropping a jelly sandwich in the sand, is ably described by Dorothy Aldis in "The Picnic" (7). Aileen Fisher emphasizes the fact that campfire "Picnics" (103) are the best, because you can capture the smell of them in your sweater! In "Beach Fire" (13), Frances Frost has pictured a moment of family togetherness, as they linger after a picnic on the beach to watch the sparks from their fire and the stars and moon lighten the evening darkness.

Just the pure joy of running, or climbing a tree, or messing about on Saturday has been captured in poetry for children. Marci Ridlon has written "The Running Song" (252), while David McCord tells of all the things that happen to a boy "Every Time I Climb a Tree" (196). In the title poem of her book, *Today Is Saturday* (269), Snyder describes the fun that four resourceful boys have on a Saturday.

Some experiences can be disappointing, as one child discovered on a "Sunday Morning" (252) when he couldn't find anyone who would play with him. Marci Ridlon describes another loser in her amusing verse titled "I Never Win at Parties!" (252). The thought of homework can also ruin the end of a glorious weekend as everyone knows:

HOMEWORK

Homework sits on top of Sunday, squashing
    Sunday flat.
Homework has the smell of Monday, homework's
    very fat. . . .

                Russell Hoban (136)

All children love to play games, but "Hiding" isn't any fun if no one finds you or if you can't find anyone else. The child in Mary Ann Hoberman's poem "Hiding" (128) solves this problem, however. In "Hide and Seek" (136) by Vernon

Scannell, the child waits and waits until he is sure he is the winner. Then he crawls out of his cold, dark hiding place in the shed to call "I've won," only to find the sun is gone and so are his playmates.

Many children must face the wrench of leaving their friends permanently when they move away. "Maurice" (47) is intrigued with the idea at first and "Peacocks up and down," but then he realizes that he can pack his balls and bats but not his friends. "Lyle" (47), on the other hand, sadly ponders the fact that he has had to move seven times while the tree in his backyard gets to stay in its favorite place.

Most children experience the death of a pet, friend, or loved one during their young lives, yet there are few children's poems about death. Gwendolyn Brooks has written a sensitive poem about a dying goldfish named "Skipper" (133); and Myra Cohn Livingston wrote a lament "For a Bird" (85) that she found lying dead near a tree. She wraps him carefully in a blue shirt and sings a song to him. Frances Cornford in "A Recollection" (73) has captured real childlike feelings about death, which may shock some adults. Having known her father's friend for just a short while before he died, this poet recalls that: "Deep in my heart I thought with pride,/'I know a person who has died.'" In "Italian Extravaganza" (162) by Gregory Corso, the child is impressed with the size of the dead baby's coffin and the ten black Cadillacs that were used in the funeral!

Time, Weather, and the Seasons

The child measures his time not so much by days as by events; the time until Christmas, summer vacation, or his birthday; time until the next baseball game, or spelling test; time for story hour or lunch. Time is not regular but variable, depending upon how engrossed the child may be in a particular activity. Phyllis McGinley notices this in her poem:

LENGTHS OF TIME

Time is peculiar
And hardly exact
Though minutes are minutes
You'll find for a fact
(as the older you get

and the bigger you grow)
That time can
Hurrylikethis
Or plod, plod, slow.

. . .

Phyllis McGinley (85)

Robert Francis has likened the passage of time to the slow nibbling away of a mouse in his poem "The Mouse Whose Name Is Time" (305); while the child, "Marie Lucille," maintains "The clock is ticking/Me away!" (47). In the poem "Time" (136), Patricia Hubbell writes of the child who took today to bed with her, but no matter how hard she held on to it, it became morning the next day! Eleanor Farjeon probably speaks for both adults and children in her well-known poem:

THERE ISN'T TIME!

There isn't time, there isn't time
To do the things I want to do,
With all the mountain-tops to climb,
And all the woods to wander through,
And all the seas to sail upon,
And everywhere there is to go,
And all the people, everyone
Who live upon the earth, to know.
There's only time, there's only time
To know a few, and do a few,
And then sit down and make a rhyme
About the rest I want to do.

Eleanor Farjeon (136)

Besides being aware of certain times, the child is alive to the wonder and beauty of night and day, the weather, and the seasons. Many nature poems for children evoke the loveliness of the revolving seasons, the changing weather, and the variable moods of the day. Beginning with Emily Dickinson's "I'll tell you how the sun rose,/a ribbon at a time" (86), there are poems for almost every hour of the day. Elizabeth Coatsworth uses personification to contrast the speeds at which "Morning and Afternoon" (63) pass. She also personifies night in a rather eerie poem:

SONG TO NIGHT

Night is something watching
something that is unseen,

something that moves a little,
patient and fierce and lean.
Night comes close to the window,
breathing against the pane,
and follows the lonely traveler
swiftly down the lane.

Elizabeth Coatsworth (200)

James Stephens has used a similar technique in his poem "Check" (13), which describes the night as creeping on the ground. Sara Teasdale's poem "Night" (289) contains the well-known line: "Look for a lovely thing and you will find it." Her poem, "The Falling Star" (289), is also a favorite of children.

Robert Louis Stevenson has given children two of their favorite poems about the "Wind" (278)—the one that begins, "I saw you toss the kites on high," and "Windy Nights" (278), with its galloping rhythm and mystery. Another much-loved favorite is Christina Rossetti's "Who has seen the wind?" (13). In a poem titled "Wind Song," Lilian Moore has provided a catalogue of the various kinds of wind sounds:

WIND SONG

When the wind blows
the quiet things speak.
Some whisper, some clang,
Some creak.

Grasses swish.
Treetops sigh.
Flags snap
and snap at the sky.
Wires on poles
whistle and hum.
Ashcans roll.
Windows drum.
When the wind goes—
suddenly
then,
the quiet things
are quiet again.

Lilian Moore (85)

"The Storm" (7) by Dorothy Aldis is described by a little child from the security of her safe, warm bed, while the child, or adult, in Patricia Hubbell's poem "Night Storm" stands at the window relishing "the night of the midnight rain" (142). Harry Behn portrays the golden summer day that follows "The Storm" (24); and he has also pictured a quiet and lovely "Spring Rain" (25). Rachel Field has described "City Rain" (93) with its "streets of shiny wetness" and "umbrellas bobbing to and fro." And children love the sound of Aileen Fisher's well-known poem:

I LIKE IT WHEN IT'S MIZZLY

I like it when it's mizzly
and just a little drizzly
so everything looks far away
and make-believe and frizzly.

I like it when it's foggy
and sounding very froggy.
I even like it when it rains
on streets and weepy windowpanes
and catkins in a poplar tree
and *me*.

Aileen Fisher (202)

In a poem called "Rain Sizes" (57), John Ciardi depicts rain as small mist that tickles, and as big as a nickel that "comes down too heavy to tickle." In "April Rain Song" (273), Langston Hughes conveys delight and joy in the rain that "plays a little sleep-song on our roof at night." James Tippett has captured the staccato sound of rain turned to ice in his "Sleet Storm" (40). The next morning the cold sun shines on a glittering world, still at last. Lew Sarett paints a similar picture for older children in his "Brittle World" (293).

Snow intrigues children both for its beauty and its fun. Children who have just made a snowman will enjoy hearing Aileen Fisher's "The Snowman's Resolution" (121). "Snow" (13) by Alice Wilkins, "The First Snow" (121) by Marie Louise Allen, and "Snow" (7) by Dorothy Aldis all present different childlike pictures of new-fallen snow that are interesting to compare. Lilian Moore describes the silence of a city that is hushed by snow in her poem "Snowy Morning" (217). Gwendolyn Brooks also emphasizes sound in her poem "Cynthia in the Snow," which begins "IT SUSHES./It hushes/The loudness in the road" (47). "Snow Color" (110) by Aileen Fisher suggests the variety of colors that snow may

reflect. Harry Behn's description of "Morning in Winter" (27) begins: "Shadows blue, sun bright/And everything else in the world white." His "Winter Night" (24) falls with the cadence of softly drifting snow. "The Snowstorm" (273) by Kaye Starbird describes a world that is changed by a big snow. Some children in the middle grades will appreciate the silent world of new-fallen snow in Wylie's "Velvet Shoes" (237). If children have developed an appreciation for such quiet poems, they may be introduced to Robert Frost's contemplative "Stopping by Woods on a Snowy Evening" (118). However, too early an introduction to this poem may destroy children's appreciation of it forever.

Changing seasons are a never-ceasing wonder to children. Many poems describe the arrival of spring and summer particularly. One of children's favorites suggests a race between spring and winter:

MARCH

A blue day,
a blue jay
and a good beginning.
One crow
melting snow—
spring's winning!

Elizabeth Coatsworth (136)

The harsh nature of March is revealed in Lew Sarett's touching tragedy of the "Four Little Foxes" (92), which are left shivering in the March rain. Late March has its beautiful harbingers of spring, also. Lilian Moore describes a "Forsythia Bush" (136) that "explodes into yellow," while Charlotte Zolotow writes of the "Little crocus/ like a cup,/holding all that sunlight up!" (308). Marcia Lee Masters welcomes April as a special time:

APRIL

It's lemonade, it's lemonade, it's daisy.
It's a roller-skating, scissor-grinding day;
It's gingham-waisted, chocolate flavored, lazy,
With the children flower-scattered at their play.

It's the sun like watermelon,
And the sidewalks overlaid
With a glaze of yellow yellow
Like a jar of marmalade.

. . .

It's lemonade, it's lemonade, it's April!
A water sprinkler, puddle winking time,
When a boy who peddles slowly, with a smile
    remote and holy,
Sells you April chocolate flavored for a dime.

Marcia Lee Masters (88)

Children who have enjoyed "Stopping by Woods on a Snowy Evening" (118) might want to compare it to this twelfth-century Oriental poem that contemplates the fragile beauty of spring:

Whose are this pond and house?
I lean on the red door, yet dare not knock.
But a fragment of sweet spring cannot be
    hidden,
As over the colored wall there peeps the tip of
    an apricot branch.

Chang Liang-Ch'en (173)

Rachel Field has personified summer in her well-known "A Summer Morning" (13), while Kaye Starbird's poem about "Summer" (272) is refreshing and childlike in its point of view.

The birds proclaim the approach of fall even sooner than does the brilliant coloring of the leaves. In "The Last Word of a Bluebird" (118) by Robert Frost, a young crow relays a bluebird's message to his daughter, Lesley, that "He just had to fly/But he sent his 'Good-by'" and a promise to return in the spring. Perhaps the best-known fall poem is the rather ominous warning contained in Rachel Field's "Something Told the Wild Geese" (13). The first two stanzas of "The Mist and All" (237) by Dixie Willson provoke a response similar to "Something Told the Wild Geese," but the last verse provides a decided contrast.

Animal Poems

Poems about animals are proven favorites with children. The behavior of wild animals is so closely linked to seasonal changes that it is sometimes difficult to distinguish between animal and seasonal poetry. Lew Sarett's poem, "Four Little Foxes" (92), is as much about animals as it is about spring. Coatsworth's poem, "The Song of Rabbits Outside the Tavern" (63), contrasts the plight of the rabbits out in the bitter cold with the warmth of the interior of the inn. The poet tells us that those who seek the warmth of the fire have never known the rabbits' delight in their wild and hungry dance by the light of the moon. In "Cold Winter Now Is in the Wood" (13), this same poet compares the condition of the favored cat and dog with the horses and cows in the dark barn and the hungry fox and lean hawk. Frances Frost notes the effect of season on the changing pelt of the rabbit in this picture:

WHITE SEASON

In the winter the rabbits match their pelts to the
    earth.
With ears laid back, they go,
Blown through the silver hollow, the silver
    thicket,
Like puffs of snow.

Frances Frost (117)

In "Green Hill Neighbors" (115), this poet tells about the little creatures who have their homes on one small hill. "The House of the Mouse" (121) has been described by Lucy Sprague Mitchell in words young children love to hear, particularly the ending that goes: "This sweet little, neat little, wee little green little cuddle-down hide-away house in the grass." Aileen Fisher contrasts the huge darkness of the night with the size of a mouse "In the Dark of Night" (98). "Night of Wind" (13) by Frances Frost pictures a little lost fox "caught by the blowing cold of the mountain darkness." In "Little Things" (13), James Stephens asks for forgiveness for mankind from the little creatures that have been trapped and must die in silence and despair. In "The Snare," he makes the reader *feel* the pain and cruelty inflicted by humans as he describes the cries of the little rabbit caught in a trap. Note the mounting intensity of the poem as the poet becomes more frustrated in his search for the wounded rabbit:

THE SNARE

I hear a sudden cry of pain!
There is a rabbit in a snare;
Now I hear the cry again,
But I cannot tell from where.

But I cannot tell from where
He is calling out for aid!
Crying on the frightened air,
Making everything afraid!

Making everything afraid!
Wrinkling up his little face!
As he cries again for aid;
—And I cannot find the place!

And I cannot find the place
Where his paw is in the snare!
Little one! Oh, Little One!
I am searching everywhere!

James Stephens (13)

W. H. Davies has also deplored human cruelty to little animals in his poem "The Rabbit" (68), while "The Ballad of Red Fox" (68) is a scathing commentary on the "sport" of fox hunting.

Mary Austin's lovely poem about "The Deer" (303) has the chanting refrain of "Follow, follow/By hill and hollow." Lilian Moore describes her "Encounter" (218) with a deer when they ". . . both stood/heart-stopping/still." Children enjoy the mysterious mood created by Thomas Hardy in his picture of "The Fallow Deer at the Lonely House" (37). Older children will appreciate Millay's delicate description of her unexpected meeting with a "Fawn" (67); while they will be saddened by the poignant picture of the dying "Buck in the Snow" (68). William Stafford's thoughtful poem "Traveling through the Dark" (238) reminds us that people kill with cars as well as guns. His decision to roll the dead doe with her live unborn fawn into the canyon was not an easy one to make. He hesitates a moment and "Hears the wilderness listen."

Some recent poems suggest the wilderness is listening for the human decision to save or destroy it. In the poem "Ecology" (218), Lilian Moore describes the disappearance of the muskrat due to the trapping of a farmer and a hunter; and now "The pond is/choking/on/its own wild/grass." A family vacationing in Wisconsin's Great North Woods drives to a "garbage grove" to view a native bear who regularly feeds there on the refuse of humankind. Disturbed by the spectators, the booing children, and the sad picture of a wild bear reduced to eating garbage, the bereaved poet goes home feeling a "Part of the Darkness" (68).

Compassion for caged animals is the subject of both D. H. Lawrence's poem, "Elephants in the Circus" (68), and Hockman's "The Elephant" (68). In *The Dreaming Zoo* (304), John Unternecker presents fourteen dreams of zoo animals who reveal their desires to be free in their natural habitats. For example, the hippopotamus dreams of "a steaming river" where he can soak himself in the mud and become "a brown island with eyes." *Prayers from the Ark* is a collection of twenty-seven poems, each one representing a prayer from a particular animal. The prayers reveal the distinctive characteristic of each animal and speak profoundly of their places in the world:

THE PRAYER OF THE COCK

Do not forget, Lord,
it is I who make the sun rise.
I am Your servant
but, with the dignity of my calling,
I need some glitter and ostentation
Noblesse oblige. . . .
All the same,
I am Your servant,
only . . . do not forget, Lord,
I make the sun rise.
    Amen

Carmen Bernos De Gasztold (119)

Frances Frost has described the proud rooster in a similar fashion in "Rise, Sun!" (115). The "Prayer of the Foal" (119) might be read to middle-grade children and compared with Robert Frost's "The Runaway" (118), the little Morgan colt, who is skittish at the sight of his first snow. Young children readily accept Robert Frost's invitation in his poem "The Pasture" (118) to go out and clean the spring and fetch the little calf. Children continue to enjoy Stevenson's friendly "The Cow" (278), "all red and white." James Reeves has caught the lazy rhythm of cows chewing their cuds in the refrain of his poem:

COWS

Half the time they munched the grass,
    and all the time they lay
Down in the water-meadows, the lazy month
        of May,
    A-chewing,
    A-mooing,
To pass the hours away.
  . . .

James Reeves (276)

Valerie Worth paints a slow-motion picture of a "Cow" (307) that moves like a mountain. "Her hoofs/Thump like dropped/Rocks:/Almost/Too late/She stops." If you have ever been out in a pasture with a cow, you will appreciate this accurate description of a cow's movements. Anyone who has heard the muffled clucking in a hen house at twilight will recognize Elizabeth Madox Roberts' description of "The Hens" (254). Young children who have visited a farm will respond to the sensory imagery of Kim Worthington's poem, "I Held a Lamb" (294) and Zhenya Gay's "Did You Ever Pet a Baby Goat?" (294). Dorothy Aldis has captured children's universal delight in newborn baby animals in her poem, "In Spring in Warm Weather" (294).

Cats are well represented in poetry for children. Eleanor Farjeon describes "A Kitten" (13) who "has a giant purr and a midget mew." Mary Britton Miller depicts the movements of a "Cat" (13) in her poem by that title. "The Mysterious Cat" (13) by Vachel Lindsay is written in his characteristically rhythmical style. Roselle Moore's "Catalog" (299) proclaims that "cats sleep fat and walk thin"; while Valerie Worth describes the delicate manner in which cats settle down for a nap—"arranged, shaped for sleep" (307). T. S. Eliot has written two amusing story poems about cats that older boys and girls generally like. One is called "The Rum Tum Tugger"

Natalie Babbitt's precise black-and-white illustrations complement the simplicity of Valerie Worth's *Small Poems*. Here, the artist depicts a cat "shaped for sleep."

Reprinted with the permission of Farrar, Straus & Giroux, Inc., from *Small Poems* by Valerie Worth, illustrated by Natalie Babbitt, Pictures copyright © 1972 by Natalie Babbitt.

(92), and the other is about "Macavity" (200), "A fiend in feline shape, a monster of depravity." John Ciardi has written an amusing poem about "My Cat, Mrs. Lick-A-Chin" (59), who can't ever make up her mind whether she wants to go out or come in!

It does not seem that there are as many good poems about dogs as there are about cats. Milne's "Puppy and I" (213) is a favorite. "The Hairy Dog" (202) by Herbert Asquith presents an amusing picture. In "Sunning" (136), James Tippett tells of an old dog happily lying in the sun, "Much too lazy to rise and run." James Reeves sings a song to "Mick" (67), his "mongrel-O." The ending is no surprise to anyone who has ever owned a dog! The origin of "The Dog's Cold Nose" (67) is explained in a poem with this title by Arthur Guiterman. "The Prayer of the Dog" (119) in *Prayers from the Ark* reflects the dog's sense of responsibility "to keep watch."

These represent only a few of the poems that have been written about wild animals, barnyard animals, and pets. Children might be encouraged to bring their favorite animal poems to school and begin a class collection of them.

Humorous Poetry

Many so-called animal poems are really humorous poems about all kinds of preposterous animals or humorous situations involving animals. One of children's favorites is Ogden Nash's "The Adventures of Isabel." This is the well-known narrative verse of the unflappable young girl who meets a bear that threatens to eat her:

. . .

Isabel, Isabel didn't worry.
Isabel didn't scream or scurry.
She washed her hands and straightened her hair up,
Then Isabel quietly ate the bear up.

. . .

Ogden Nash (85)

Arnold Spilka provides excellent advice for any time you should meet "The Talking Tiger" (271). The child in Spilka's amusing poem is more apprehensive than Isabel, but he handles the situation very cleverly. Mary Austin also explains what one should do upon meeting a "Grizzly Bear" (13). The child who met the "Boa Constrictor" (265) in Shel Silverstein's poem by that name needed help; but it never came! Sophisticated children delight in the humor of Ogden Nash's "The Octopus" (223) and "The Porcupine" (223). They also appreciate the sage advice given in the poem, "The Panther" (223), which suggests that when called upon by a panther, "Don't Anther." Children particularly like the following nonsense poem on when and how to tickle a lizard:

THE LIZARD

The Time to Tickle a Lizard
Is Before, or Right After, a Blizzard.
Now the place to begin
Is just under his Chin—
And here's more Advice!
Don't Poke more than Twice
At an Intimate Place like his Gizzard.

　　　　　　　　　Theodor Roethke (72)

In the poem "Beware, My Child" (72), Shel Silverstein warns of meeting the snaggle-toothed beast who sleeps till noon and eats Hershey bars. James Reeves has written a whole book of poems titled *Prefabulous Animiles* (249). These include everything from the "Hippacrump" to the "Snitterjipe." Children would enjoy creating their own animals using box construction, papier maché, or painting. Many of the poems by John Ciardi are descriptive of weird imaginary animals; for example, "The Saginsack" (57) or the "Bugle-Billed Bazoo" (57). One of his best poems for children is about the "grin-cat":

THE CAT HEARD THE CAT-BIRD

One day, a fine day, a high-flying-sky day,
A cat-bird, a fat bird, a fine fat cat-bird
Was sitting and singing on a stump by the high-
　　way.
Just sitting. And singing. Just that. But a cat
　　heard.

A thin cat, a grin-cat, a long thin grin-cat
Came creeping the sly way by the highway to
　　the stump.
"O cat-bird, the cat heard! O cat-bird, scat!
The grin-cat is creeping! He's going to jump!"

—One day, a fine day, a high-flying-sky day.
A fat cat, yes, that cat we met as a thin cat
Was napping, cat-napping on a stump by the
　　highway.
And even in his sleep you could see he was a
　　grin-cat.

Why was he grinning?—He must have had a
　　dream.
What made him fat?—A pan full of cream.
What about the cat-bird?—What bird, dear?
I don't see any cat-bird here.

　　　　　　　　　John Ciardi (54)

Children could contrast this poem with Theodor Roethke's "The Kitty-Cat Bird" (256) who met with a similar fate. In "The Lady and the Bear" (256), Roethke describes the peculiar fishing habits of the "Biddly Bears." This narrative verse will delight children's somewhat sadistic humor, as will the clues given by Carolyn Wells for "How to Tell the Wild Animals" (13). Charles Carryl's "The Plaint of the Camel" (237), who is most unhappy with his "bumpy humpy lumpy shape," is another favorite with children in the middle grades. Palmer Brown informs the reader that "The Spangled Pandemonium" (13) is missing from the zoo, but reveals little else about him. For this reason, the poem would be excellent for creative interpretations.

Much of the humor in children's poetry revolves around the description of funny, eccentric characters with delightful-sounding names. Laura E. Richards immortalized "Mrs. Snipkin and Mrs. Wobblechin" (13), "Little John Bottlejohn" (251), and Antonio (223), who was tired of living "alonio." James Reeves introduces children to such funny people as "Mrs. Golightly," "Little Minnie Mystery," and "Mrs. Gilfillan" (248), who "when troubled with troubles" goes to the kitchen and blows bubbles! "Jonathan Bing" (13) by Beatrice Brown is another favorite with 8- and 9-year-olds. They enjoy the inconsistencies of this strange character who in "A New Song to Sing about Jonathan Bing" (48) has "a curious way/Of trying to walk into yesterday." E. V. Rieu has written the comical tale of "Sir Smasham Uppe" (253), whose visit was a disaster for the china, the chair, and his host!

Many humorous poems are based upon ludicrous situations and funny stories. A. A. Milne writes of "King John's Christmas" (213) and "The King's Breakfast" (213). Both are delightful tales of petulant kings, one of whom wants only a "little bit of butter" for his bread, while the other desires only a big red India-rubber ball! "Bad Sir Brian Botany" (213) relates the metamorphosis of bold Sir Brian to plain Mr. Botany B. in a story that is the epitome of poetic justice. In "The Monkeys and the Crocodile" (251), Laura Richards has also portrayed poetic justice in a tale of a monkey's "comeuppance." Eve Merriam's poem, "Teevee" (204), is a satire of Mr. and Mrs. Spouse, who never spoke to each other until the day their television set was broken. They were just in the process of introducing themselves when the TV came back on! Third- and fourth-graders love the story of the "Alligator on the Escalator" (204) in the same book. Other funny tales in poetry include "A Tragic Story" (69), "The Twins" (92), and "After the Party" (92). A longer story that has become quite a favorite is Ogden Nash's "The Tale of Custard the Dragon" (299).

Much of what children consider funny is really sadistic and even ghoulish. They love the tale that begins: "As I was going out one day/My head fell off and rolled away./But when I saw that it was gone,/I picked it up and put it on" (72). John Ciardi's recommendation for "The Happy Family" (72) is to be sure to screw the children's heads on each night (Doubtful cases must be glued!). In the poem "Bones" (62), by Walter de la Mare, a man complained of a pain in his bones and so the doctor took them all out and gave them to him in a parcel! Newman Levy has recounted the horrible tale of Paul Mac-Gregor James D. Cuthbert Hall who got caught in "The Revolving Door" (62) and might still be there for all we know. Modern macabre nursery rhymes include "Little Miss Muffet" (88), who was blown to bits by an H-bomb, and the tale of "The Hydrogen Dog and the Cobalt Cat" (44) by Frederick Winson.

Much of what we would call pure nonsense delights children. They love to hear Hoberman's story of "The Folk Who Live in Backward Town" (72), who live upside down and take their walks across the ceiling! Gelett Burgess's well-known limerick that begins: "I wish that my room had a floor" (62) has always provoked laughter. The contradictory statements in this traditional North American chant intrigue children:

ONE BRIGHT MORNING

One bright morning in the middle of the night,
Two dumb boys got up to fight.
Back to back they faced each other,
Drew their swords and shot each other.

A deaf policeman heard the noise,
Came and arrested those two dumb boys.

(281)

Myra Cohn Livingston's title for her fine anthology of humorous verse is from the nonsense verse "What a wonderful bird the frog are" (189). Dozens of such nonsense rhymes and humorous narrative verses are available for school-age children. Frequently, these are the poems that will open the door to poetry which may otherwise become rusty with neglect.

Fanciful and Mysterious Poems

Lee Bennett Hopkins, in his fine book for teachers, *Pass the Poetry Please*, suggests the time has come "To Bury the Fairies."[11] Certainly, we inherited a surfeit of "fairy poems for little ones" from the poets of the past. Children in the United States who have watched newscasts of war, assassinations, race riots, and space flights understandably do not believe in the "Good Fairy," and reject most of the fairy poems.

Children still like to experience the feelings of mystery and wonder that are evoked by the best of certain fanciful poems, however. They enjoy Elizabeth MacKinstry's "The Man Who Hid His Own Front Door" (13). The neighbors, the Banker, and the Mayor went to call upon this elvish man and could not find his door; but a little girl in fading calico found the wandering door easily and entered the strange and mossy hall. A similar story is told by Winifred Welles in her mysterious poem, "Behind the Waterfall" (13). Here, a little old woman beckoned a child to come through a waterfall and into the crystal city that lay behind the misty spray. "Musetta of the Mountains" (250) by James Reeves is the hauntingly beautiful tale of a golden-haired girl who lives in the snowy mountains and rides a white doe. Though her thin voice cries, "follow me," none will ride with Musetta to her mountainside.

Walter de la Mare was a master at writing mysterious, eerie poetry. One of children's favorite poems is the story of "Someone" (82) who came knocking at the door. The poet never reveals the identity of the mysterious visitor, however. In the poem "The Old Stone House" (82)

[11] Lee Bennett Hopkins. *Pass the Poetry Please*. New York: Citation, 1972, p. 137.

the child is outside the house, but can feel a "friendless face" peering at him from within. In "Nothing" (79) and "Which?" (281) the reader never knows what is there! While the poem "The Old House" carries the connotation of death, most children enjoy its eerie quality and haunting language:

THE OLD HOUSE

A very, very old house I know—
And ever so many people go,
Past the small lodge, forlorn and still,
Under the heavy branches, till
Comes the blank wall, and there's the door.
Go in they do; come out no more.
No voice says ought: no spark of light
Across that threshold cheers the sight;
Only the evening star on high
Less lonely makes a lonely sky,
As, one by one, the people go
Into that very old house I know.

Walter de la Mare (81)

Elizabeth Madox Roberts' poem about the "Strange Tree" (92) which looked at her has the same spooky feeling as have the poems by Walter de la Mare. "Footprints in the Night" (219) by Coatsworth is equally disquieting.

All these poems that suggest the mysterious, the mystical, the things we don't quite understand will help to stretch children's imaginations. Siddie Joe Johnson's poem "I Did Not See a Mermaid?" (183) ends with a question mark and makes children wonder if perhaps she really did see one. Children should be encouraged to wonder, to dream dreams, and to share their fantasies.

Poems of Adventure and Accomplishment

Many narrative poems are historical in nature—they tell of the accomplishments of great men and small. Included in this group are the well-known poems of "Paul Revere's Ride" (192) by Longfellow, Whittier's "Barbara Frietchie" (306), and "Columbus" (13) by Miller. This latter poem could be compared with Squire's "The Discovery" (200), which is told from an Indian's point of view as he watches the arrival of the "huge canoes with bellying cloths." In "Indian," the Benéts have ironically described the white

man's treatment of the Indian. One stanza provides an example:

. . .

He knows his streams are full of fish,
His forests full of deer,
And his tribe is the mighty tribe
That all the others fear.
—And, when the French or English land,
The Spanish or the Dutch,
They'll tell him they're the mighty tribe
And no one else is much.

Rosemary Benét and Stephen Vincent Benét (29)

Both Annette Wynne's "Indian Children" (13) and Elizabeth Coatsworth's lovely "The Wilderness Is Tamed" (65) speak of the changes that have been wrought in our country. Stephen Vincent Benét helps children appreciate the origin and excitement of "American Names" (200). He and his wife, Rosemary Benét, have written the stirring, rhythmical "Western Wagons" (29). Older children respond to the exhilaration and challenge expressed in "The Coming American" by Foss (200). John T. Alexander has presented an ironical twist in his "The Winning of the TV West" (200), a poem that could stimulate much discussion about new frontiers.

Children in the middle grades enjoy biographical poetry as much as they appreciate biographies. Rosemary Benét and Stephen Vincent Benét have written verses about great Americans which give capsule biographies and summarize the events in which men and women played a part. *A Book of Americans* includes "Miles Standish," "Aaron Burr," "Andrew Jackson," and "Thomas Jefferson," as well as poems of "Clipper Ships and Captains" and "Pilgrims and Puritans." The latter poem portrays the self-righteousness of our forefathers, as well as their resolute character in the face of difficulties. The authors suggest that as "punishment for sinners/They invented New England dinners!" Although some of their poems are humorous, most present a serious theme. One about Abraham Lincoln quietly comments on the inability of Lincoln's neighbors to recognize greatness when it was a part of their daily lives.

. . .

"Need a man for troubled times?
Well, I guess we do.

Wonder who we'll ever find?
Yes—I wonder who."

That is how they met and talked,
Knowing and unknowing.
Lincoln was the green pine.
Lincoln kept on growing.

Rosemary Benét and Stephen Vincent Benét (29)

Eve Merriam has also celebrated the great—
such as Benjamin Franklin and Frederick
Douglass—and the unsung great—such as
Elizabeth Blackwell and Lucretia Mott—in her
book of long biographical poems titled *Independent
Voices.* Her poem of Elizabeth Blackwell, the first
woman doctor, provides a social commentary on
the prejudice of that day and today:

. . .
"Is this some kind of joke?"
asked the proper menfolk.
"A woman be a doctor?
Not in our respectable day!
A doctor? An M.D.! Did you hear what she said?
She's clearly and indubitably out of her head!"

"Indeed, indeed, we all thoroughly agreed,"
hissed the ladies of society all laced in and
    prim,
"its a scientific fact a doctor has to be a him."
"Yes, sir"
" 'twould be against nature
if a doctor were a her."

. . .

Eve Merriam (207)

For too long U.S. history books and television
programs have glorified war. Poetry brings to the
preadolescent and adolescent another view of
war—its pain, loneliness, and horror. In "Epitaph
for a Concord Boy" (200) the poet describes the
death of a young, sleepy lad, routed from his bed
by his father, who died at Concord without
knowing why he had fought. Southey's poem,
"The Battle of Blenheim" (299), tells of an old
man's memory of a battle in the early eighteenth
century. When the children find a skull and
question him about it, he recalls how the English
won a "famous victory." But he cannot tell "what
good came of it at last." When children study
the Civil War in the United States, they learn of
the conflicting loyalties of many individuals.

Girls enjoy Woolson's narrative poem, "Kentucky Belle" (299), which tells how a Southern
woman living in Ohio helped a rebel soldier by
giving him her horse, Kentucky Belle. Robert
Nathan's long poem, "Dunkirk," is a moving
story of two British children who sailed their
patched sailboat, *The Sarah P,* across the English
Channel to rescue fourteen soldiers; 600 small
boats sailed that night and reached Dunkirk:

. . .
They raised Dunkirk with its harbor torn
By the blasted stern and the sunken prow;
They had raced for fun on an English tide,
They were English children bred and born,
And whether they lived, or whether they died,
They raced for England now.
. . .
For Nelson was there in the Victory,
With his one good eye, and his sullen twist,
And guns were out on the Golden Hind,
Their shot flashed over the Sarah P.
He could hear them cheer as he came about.

By burning wharves, by battered ships,
Galleon, frigate, and brigantine,
The old dead Captains fought their ships.
And the great dead Admirals led the line.
It was England's night, it was England's sea.

Robert Nathan (300)

Modern accomplishments of both the mean
and the great have been recorded in poetic form.
Children may be brought to understand the dignity of their own worth when they hear Mary
Austin's "A Song of Greatness" (13). In this
poem an Indian boy hears of the heroic feats of
his forefathers and knows that when his time
comes, he, too, "Shall do mightily." In Langston
Hughes' well-known poem, "Mother to Son"
(143), a black mother tells her son that "Life for
me ain't been no crystal stair." But despite her
difficulties she kept on climbing and she admon-
ishes her son to do the same. Mature students
will appreciate the moving poem, "The Gift to
Be Simple" (241), which was written at the time
of Einstein's death. In his beautiful and reverent
poem, "High Flight" (200), the poet-pilot, John
Gillespie Magee, has captured the sense of accomplishment and exhilaration that flying can

produce. Poetry can help children realize that there are still frontiers and achievements to be won—these may be of the mind or the spirit.

Social Commentary and Protest

Children of today are more sophisticated and more cynical than they were even ten years ago. Television has made children aware of the bigotry and sham, the waste and corruption that are a part of modern society. The statistics of crime are repeated on every newscast—the killings and rapes of the day. The Vietnam War, Watergate, and the energy crisis are a part of the history of their lives. The voices of the new poets are protesting this human-made-mess of a world in poems about pollution, poverty, prejudice, politics, and war. And young persons themselves are writing their own protests in poetic form.

The impersonalization of our lives and the seeming inability to communicate with others is a common theme of contemporary poetry. In this poem Gerald Raftery comments on the crowded, anonymous life of the apartment dweller:

APARTMENT HOUSE

A filing-cabinet of human lives
Where people swarm like bees in tunneled
    hives,
Each to his own cell in the towered comb
Identical and cramped—we call it home.

Gerald Raftery (88)

In the poem titled "Why Do They?" (161) a student asks the question why does everyone walk by without looking or speaking, afraid to become involved; and then she wonders why she does the same thing. In "Husbands and Wives" (88) Miriam Hershenson tells of families who ride the train from station to station without ever speaking to each other. The sharply cynical "Forecast" (88) by Dan Jaffe suggests that when the end of the world does come, humankind will probably hear about it on the weather report on television.

Concern about visual pollution is not new. Many years ago Ogden Nash wrote the amusing verse, "Song of the Open Road," which parodies the well-known Joyce Kilmer poem, "Trees":

SONG OF THE OPEN ROAD

I think that I shall never see
A billboard lovely as a tree.
Indeed, unless the billboards fall
I'll never see a tree at all.

Ogden Nash (62)

The poem, "Landscape" (205), by Eve Merriam asks what we expect to find at the rim of the earth—"eternal sunrise," "immortal sleep," or "cars piled up in a rusty heap?" "Parking Lot" (252) by Marci Ridlon is a favorite counting poem about all the old cars in a junkyard. A sharply satirical poem by Myra Cohn Livingston is titled "Only a Little Litter" (184). In this poem the poet asks the moon if he likes the footprints and flags that have been left on his face. Two students collaborated on a poem about the litter in the city and titled it "Nobody Collects the Papers" (161); while another student wrote about the graffiti "Scribbled on a Once-clean Wall" (161).

The dirt, the grime, the poverty of the ghetto are a frequent subject of protest poems written by young people and incorporated by Nancy Larrick in an anthology titled *I Heard a Scream in the Street.* In "Odyssey of a Slum" (161) Vanessa Howard recalls a bare table with no tablecloth, brothers and sisters sleeping six in a bed, the smell of urine in the hallway, and cold outdoor showers. This same 16-year-old poet suggests that despite "trips" on alcohol and drugs, there is no way to "Escape the Ghettos of New York" (161).

Beginning in the 1920s Langston Hughes was the first to write poems of black protest and pride. It was his voice that asked: "What Happens to a Dream Deferred?" (145), and reminded the world that: "I, too, sing America" (143). Some of his poems are bitter, proud, and militant; others are as soft and sensitive as his lovely tribute "My People" (143). The voices of Gwendolyn Brooks, Le Roi Jones, Mari Evans, Nikki Giovanni, and others have joined with Hughes to produce a fine body of black poetry. Many of these have been collected in the anthology edited by Arnold Adoff titled *Black Out Loud* (2). One poem by Nikki Giovanni may be read in several ways—as a black militant poem or as a protest against the status quo; as an invitation to destroy, or as an opportunity to build:

WORD POEM

(Perhaps Worth Considering)

as things be/come
let's destroy
then we can destroy
what we be/come
let's build
what we become
when we dream

Nikki Giovanni (2)

Young writers have added their voices to the chorus of protest, as is seen in the poem "A Black Man's World" (161) by Lorenza Loflin, "Mine" (161) by Alice Jackson, and "This Is a Black Room" (161) by Joshua Beasley. All these poems appear in the anthology *I Heard a Scream in the Street.*

The harsh realities and futility of war have been the subject of many poems of protest. Randall Jarrell's grim poem, "The Death of the Ball Turret Gunner" (236), details the abortion of a life that had never really had a chance to live. Inner struggles of the fighting man are revealed by William Butler Yeats, who writes: "Those I fight I do not hate/Those that I guard I do not love," in his poem, "An Irish Airman Foresees His Death" (38). Young people all over the world are protesting war. A boy from Pennsylvania writes of "A War Game" (161) and "the menagerie that newspapers call war." A student from California maintains that he would rather go to "Jail" (161) than to kill without his will. A 15-year-old in Russia writes of "The Last Soldier" (221), and wonders who will be the last soldier to perish—a Russian, a Greek, Zulu, or German? The well-known rock lyric by Pete Seeger titled "Where Have All the Flowers Gone?" (236) ends with the refrain: "Oh, when will they ever learn?" In a poem titled "Fantasia" (205), Eve Merriam tells of a woman who dreams of giving birth to a son who will someday ask her, "What was war?" And in a poem simply titled "Peace" (145), Langston Hughes bitterly speaks for the dead who care not who won or lost the war. Sara Teasdale's poem, "There Will Come Soft Rains" (288),

maintains that it would make little difference to the coming of the Spring if mankind were to perish from the face of the earth. Many of these are angry poems; some are bitter and cynical; while others are sad and despairing. All of them have the power to evoke thoughtful, serious responses from young people today.

Beauty, Wisdom, and Hope

Each succeeding generation finds solace in Dickens' words: "It was the worst of times, it was the best of times." While there is much in modern life in America to provoke protest and cynicism; there is also much that is good, beautiful, and worthy of praise.

Children's eyes need to be opened to the natural beauty around them. Even in the squalor of a tenement there is joy in laughter, the delight of a smile, the warmth of love, and the beauty of neon signs against a summer's black night. An energy crisis may temporarily darken the lights of the streets, but the lights in young people's eyes should not be darkened. Poems of protest and despair need to be balanced by poems of hope and beauty. Poetry can be an invitation, a summons to see more clearly, to live more fully:

SUMMONS

Keep me from going to sleep too soon
Or if I go to sleep too soon
Come wake me up. Come any hour
Of night. Come whistling up the road.
Stomp on the porch. Bang on the door.
Make me get out of bed and come
And let you in and light a light.
Tell me the northern lights are on
And make me look. Or tell me clouds
Are doing something to the moon
They never did before, and show me.
See that I see. Talk to me till
I'm half as wide awake as you
And start to dress wondering why
I ever went to bed at all.
Tell me the walking is superb.
Not only tell me but persuade me.
You know I'm not too hard persuaded.

Robert Francis (88)

Sara Teasdale gives similar advice in her well-known poem, "Night" (289); namely, "Look for a lovely thing and you will find it." In "The Coin" (289) this same poet suggests that each beautiful scene be tucked away into the heart's treasury, for far better than money "Is the safe-kept memory/Of a lovely thing." Elizabeth Coatsworth's best-known poem contrasts the beauty of swift things with those that are slow and steady. Her message is much the same as in Teasdale's "Night": seek beauty in all living things:

POEM OF PRAISE

Swift things are beautiful:
Swallows and deer,
And lightning that falls
Bright-veined and clear,
Rivers and meteors,
Wind in the wheat,
The strong-withered horse,
The runner's sure feet.

And slow things are beautiful:
The closing of day,
The pause of the wave
That curves downward to spray.
The ember that crumbles,
The opening flower,
And the ox that moves on
In the quiet of power.

Elizabeth Coatsworth (63)

Poems may be about the concept of beauty or quicken children's responses to that which is beautiful.

One characteristic of childhood is its ability to dream dreams and sustain hope. Emily Dickinson's poem "Hope is the thing with feathers" (13) appeals to older boys and girls, as does Victor Hugo's "Be Like the Bird" (13). In the first, hope is metaphorically represented as a bird; while in the second, the confident action of the bird implies hope and faith. Langston Hughes' well-known poem warns of the dire consequences of losing one's "Dreams":

DREAMS

Hold fast to dreams
For if dreams die
Life is a broken-winged bird
That cannot fly.

A young child "holds fast to dreams" in this handsome woodcut by Ann Grifalconi.

Copyright © 1969 by Ann Grifalconi. Reprinted from *Don't You Turn Back*, by Langston Hughes, illustrated by Ann Grifalconi, edited by Lee Bennett Hopkins, by permission of Alfred A. Knopf, Inc.

Hold fast to dreams
For when dreams go
Life is a barren field
Frozen with snow.

Langston Hughes (143)

Robert Frost[12] is quoted as saying that all poetry should begin in delight but end in wisdom. Certainly, this is characteristic of the poetry of Robert Frost, who subtly examines the meaning of walls and the definitions of home in his well-known poems "Mending Wall" (118) and "The Death of the Hired Man" (118). These are poems that teach, not preach. While children

[12]Hyde Cox in the "Foreword" of *You Come Too* by Robert Frost (New York: Holt, Rinehart and Winston, 1959), p. 7.

reject the didactic, they do appreciate poems that make them think. Flashes of Carl Sandburg's keen wisdom penetrate all his poems, as in:

CIRCLES

The white man drew a small circle in the sand and
  told the red man,
"This is what the Indian knows,"
And drawing a big circle around the small one,
"This is what the white man knows."
The Indian took the stick
And swept an immense ring around both circles:
"This is where the white man and the red man
  know nothing."

Carl Sandburg (261)

Sandburg frequently gives advice in his poetry. His "Primer Lesson" speaks directly to boys and girls in terms they can understand:

Look out how you use proud words.
When you let proud words go, it is not easy to
  call them back.
They wear long boots, hard boots; they walk off
  proud; they can't hear you calling—
Look out how you use proud words.

Carl Sandburg (202)

Emily Dickinson's poem "A Word" might be compared with Sandburg's "Primer Lesson." As always, the Dickinson poem is stripped of any embellishment; like a beautifully-designed Shaker table, its grace and beauty speak for themselves:

A WORD

A word is dead
When it is said,
  Some say.

I say it just
Begins to live
  That day.

Emily Dickinson (13)

The wisdom of the Bible and beauty of many of the Psalms should be a part of children's poetic heritage (*see* Chapter 4). "Proverbs" and certain portions from both the Old and New Testaments are truly poetic. For example, listen to the poetic quality of these verses from "Isaiah":

But they that wait upon the Lord shall renew
  their strength;
They shall mount up with wings as eagles;
They shall run, and not be weary;
And they shall walk, and not faint.

Isaiah 40:31

Paul's advice to the Philippians in Chapter 4:8 sings with poetry in the well-known admonition: "Whatsoever things are true/whatsoever things are honest/whatsoever things are just/whatsoever things are pure/whatsoever things are lovely . . . think on these." The Bible may be considered both a source of wisdom and a source of great literature.

POETS AND THEIR BOOKS

Recent years have seen an increase in the number of writers of verse for children and the number of poetry books published for the juvenile market. Poetry itself has changed, becoming less formal, more spontaneous and imitative of the child's own language patterns. The range of subject matter has expanded with the tremendous variation in children's interests. It is difficult to categorize the work of a poet on the basis of the content of his poems, for many poets interpret various areas of children's experience. However, an understanding of the general subject matter of the works of each poet will help the teacher select poems and make recommendations to children.

Interpreters of the World of Childhood

William Blake was the first poet to discover the world of childhood, which he celebrated in his *Songs of Innocence,* published in 1789. Many of these poems are symbolic and religious in tone, and have little meaning for today's child. Some, however, sing with joy; for example, "The Laughing Song," "Infant Joy," and "Piping Down the Valleys Wild." Ellen Raskin (36) has illustrated a new edition of *Songs of Innocence* with strikingly modern woodcuts.

Robert Louis Stevenson was the first poet to write of childhood from the child's point of view. *A Child's Garden of Verses,* published in 1885, continues in popularity today. Stevenson was himself a frail child and spent much of his early life in bed or confined indoors. His poetry reflects a solitary childhood, but a happy one. In "Land of Counterpane" and "Block City," he portrays a resourceful, inventive child who can create his own amusement. He found playmates in his shadow, in his dreams, and in his storybooks. Occasionally, Stevenson lapsed into the moralistic tone of his time with such poems as "System," "A Good Boy," and "Whole Duty of Children." "Foreign Children" presents a narrow, parochial point of view that is contrary to the beliefs of modern society. However, the rhythm of Stevenson's "The Swing," "Where Go the Boats," and "Windy Nights" appeals to children today as much as to the children of nearly a century ago. Currently, some fifteen illustrated editions of *A Child's Garden of Verses* are in print. They range in interpretation from Tasha Tudor's (277) quaint pastel pictures that portray Stevenson as a young child, to Brian Wildsmith's (278) edition that is a brilliant kaleidoscope of color.

Perhaps the best-loved of children's poets is A. A. Milne. Some of his poems show perceptive insight into the child's mind, such as "Halfway Down" and "Solitude." "Happiness" captures a child's joy in such delights as new waterproof boots, a raincoat, and hat. Told in the first person, "Hoppity" reveals a young child's enjoyment of the state of perpetual motion! The majority of Milne's poems are delightfully funny. His Christopher Robin is an only child, whose playmates are toys or adults. Perhaps this is why he has to resort to entertaining his adult friends with "Sneezles." In the poem "Missing," the reader never does hear Aunt Rose's reply to the query concerning a mouse with a "woffelly nose"—we hope the lady liked mice, however. Milne's solitary child is so engrossed in his play and himself that he never seems lonely—only creatively busy. His activities include the well-known trip to "Buckingham Palace" for the changing of the guards, or walking on just the "Squares" of the sidewalks. The poetry from both of Milne's poetry books has now been collected into one volume titled *The World of Christopher Robin* (213). Illustrations by Ernest Shepard seem as much a part of Milne's poetry as Pooh belongs with Christopher Robin; it is hard to imagine one without the other.

Another well-loved British poet for children is Eleanor Farjeon. Her knowledge and understanding of children's thoughts and behavior are reflected in her books, *Eleanor Farjeon's Poems for Children* (91) and *The Children's Bells* (90). The simple poem, "New Clothes and Old," tells of a child's preference for his old things. "Over the Garden Wall" is a hauntingly beautiful poem that makes the reader feel as lonely as the child who is left out of the ball game on the other side of the wall. This poet also wrote the lovely nature poem "The Night Will Never Stay" and the graphic description of "Mrs. Peck-Pigeon."

Before her death in 1965 Eleanor Farjeon had received notable recognition for her poetry and prose. She was the first recipient of the international Hans Christian Andersen Medal in 1956; and in 1959 she received the Regina Medal for her life's work. No other poet who has written exclusively for children has received such recognition.

The poetry of Dorothy Aldis is attuned to the everyday experiences of young children. She catches the child's delight in the simple routines of home life as expressed in "Ironing Day," "After My Bath," "The Windy Wash Day," and "Going to Sleep." This poet shows sensitivity to the child's emotions in "Bad," "The Secret Place," and "Alone." Family relationships are lovingly portrayed in "Little," "My Brother," and "Hiding." Poems from the first four books by Dorothy Aldis have been collected in a single volume entitled *All Together* (7). Two other books are *Hello Day* (9) and *Quick as a Wink* (10). A picture-book paperback edition containing thirty poems is available under the title *The Secret Place and Other Poems* (11). After the poet's death her publishers put together a book of *Favorite Poems of Dorothy Aldis* (8).

Primary-grade children also enjoy Rachel Field's poems. The book simply titled *Poems* (93) includes her first book of poetry, *The Pointed People* (1924) (94), and also *Taxis and Toadstools* (1926) (95). Many of these poems are written from the city child's point of view, including "Skyscrapers," "Taxis," "City Rain," and "Snow in the City." However, Rachel Field spent four months of every year on an island off the coast of Maine, hence the "toadstools" in one book's title. Field has immortalized the experience of sleeping on an island in the lines of her poem: "If once you have slept on an island/You'll never be quite the same." Other favorite country poems are "Roads," with its surprise ending, and "General Store," with its "tinkly bell" and "drawers all spilly." The warning conveyed in "Something Told the Wild Geese" may have provided the signal for Field to return to the city and her "Taxis."

James Tippett has written poems about the city and traveling in his books *I Go A-Traveling* (296), *I Spend the Summer* (298), and *I Live in the City* (297). His images are clear and childlike, whether he is describing a "cricket" or the "underground rumbling" of the subway. His poem "Sh" deals with one of the problems of a boisterous child who lives in an apartment. "Ferry-Boats" evokes the constant shuffling to and fro of the boats, while the increasing speed of engines is reflected in the tempo of "The Trains." A new collection of his best-loved poems is titled *Crickety Cricket!* (295). Mary Chalmers' little detailed pencil sketches seem just right for these poems for the young child.

Beatrice Schenk de Regniers has presented ten childlike poems in a small volume called *Something Special*, which Irene Haas has illustrated gaily. These poems have a bouncing rhythm and wonderful nonsense. The title poem includes the chant: "What did you put in your pocket/in your pockety pocket . . . ?" A quiet poem with charming imagery includes the line, "a feather is a letter from a bird." Children of all ages might well heed De Regniers' advice in this poem:

Keep a poem in your pocket
and a picture in your head
and you'll never feel lonely
at night when you're in bed.

Beatrice Schenk de Regniers (84)

Myra Cohn Livingston brings a charm and freshness to poetry for children that is gay and refreshing. Her book, *Whispers and Other Poems*, is filled with laughter, curiosity, and tenderness. Some of the imagery is as delicate as her title poem:

WHISPERS

Whispers
tickle through your ear
telling things you like to hear.

Whispers
are as soft as skin
letting little words curl in.
Whispers
come so they can blow
secrets others never know.

Myra Cohn Livingston (190)

Other books of poems by Livingston include *Wide Awake* (191) and *The Moon and a Star* (185). *I'm Hiding* (180), *See What I Found* (186), *I'm Not Me* (181), *Happy Birthday* (179), and *I'm Waiting* (182) are written in simple rhythmic prose that approaches poetic form. Erik Blegvad's detailed black-and-white illustrations for these books are completely harmonious with the mood of the texts. Two other collections of Livingston's poems are *A Crazy Flight and Other Poems* (178) and *The Malibu and Other Poems* (184). These reflect a wide variety of subject matters that would appeal to slightly older children, including the author's increasing interest in ecological concerns: "Hey moonface,/man-in-the moonface,/do you like the way we left your place? . . ." Children could compare the following poem with "Whispers":

IT HAPPENED

Well, it happened
(Just like I knew it would).

I told her once,
I told her twice
I told her never to tell
a secret to Michelle

(Who can't keep a thing to herself)
and she told her.
And now *everybody* knows!

Myra Cohn Livingston (184)

The childlike verses of Karla Kuskin's *In the Middle of the Trees* (157) and *The Rose on My Cake* (158) are a welcome addition to poetry for younger children. These contain such favorites as "Lewis Had a Trumpet" and "I Woke Up This Morning," which tells of a young child who does nothing right all day. (This would make a wonderful poem to compare with the picture book, *Alexander and the Terrible Horrible No-Good Very Bad Day* by Viorst; *see* Chapter 3). Gay nonsense characterizes Kuskin's verse in *Alexander Soames, His Poems* (155), while *Sand and Snow* (159) contrasts two children's responses to summer and winter. Her book, *Any Me I Want to Be* (156), is written from the point of view of the subject. Instead of writing how a cat, or the moon, or a pair of shoes appear to her, the poet tries to get inside the object and be its voice. Children then enjoy guessing what the verse is about. Kuskin illustrates all her own books with amusing stylized pictures.

Another modern poet who is attuned to the world of childhood is Patricia Hubbell. Her first book, *The Apple Vendor's Fair* (140), includes some forty-one poems dealing with everything from clouds to dinosaurs. "When Dinosaurs Ruled the Earth" is a favorite with children. From *8 A.M. Shadows* (142), the title poem of her second book, to "Bedtime," the last poem, lies a full day of a young child's thoughts, games, and encounters with nature. The imagery is fresh and childlike in these poems. For example, "Squirrels" are described as having tails "like dandelion down"; and in "The Shepherd," "The wind is a shepherd/That herds the clouds/across the summer sky." The verses in *Catch Me a Wind* (141) find joy in a remembered day at the beach, the thrill of riding a carousel, the freedom that can be found in a tree house. This book speaks to all ages, even fathers "At Little League." The chant of "The Awakening Bulldozers" is frightening, as it evokes a picture of a child's Orwellian World of 1984.

Kaye Starbird's first book of poems for children was *Speaking of Cows* (275). Others include *Don't Ever Cross a Crocodile* (272), *A Snail's a Failure Socially* (274), and *The Pheasant on Route Seven* (273). Most of these poems include amusing observations of animals and people told from a child's point of view (*see* "December Leaves" p. 311). The problem of visiting a friend who is interested only in reading is the subject of a poem titled "Massie." "Minnie Morse" is a typical fourth-grade girl who is so engrossed with the subject of horses she might as well be one! The most outstanding camper by far was "Eat-It-All Elaine," who swallowed birch bark, prune pits, and stink bugs with quiet aplomb. Evaline Ness has included this poem in her amusing collection of poems about girls titled *Amelia Mixed the Mustard* (224).

Not all childhood experiences are happy ones, however. Pulitzer Prize-winner Gwendolyn Brooks has written some poignant poetry about black children who live in the inner city. *Bronzeville Boys and Girls* (47) contains some thirty-four poems, each bearing the name, thoughts, and feelings of an individual child. There is "John, Who Is Poor"; "Michael," who is afraid of the storm; and "Otto," who did not get the Christmas presents he had hoped for. But there is some joy—the happiness that "Eunice" feels when her whole family is in the dining room; "Beulah's" quiet thoughts at church; and "Luther and Breck," who have a make-believe dragon fight. Unfortunately, this poet has only written one volume of poetry for children.

Nikki Giovanni is well known for her adult poetry, but she has also written one book for children. Titled *Spin a Soft Black Song* (122), this book contains some poems that are both for and about black children. Others are about the things that happen to all children and their parents. "Poem for Rodney" expresses both a child's point of view and an adult's. Rodney is tired of everyone asking him what he is going to do when he grows up; his reply is simply that he'd like to grow up. Rodney's answer is typical of childhood; but projected against adults' knowledge of life in the ghetto, it carries a more pathetic plea.

Ronni Solbert has written prose poems to accompany her superb photographs of children in the city. These reflect the universal joys and sorrows of childhood. Children would enjoy interpreting just the photographs in the book entitled *I Wrote My Name on the Wall* (270); they could then compare their stories with the published poems. In *Who Look at Me*, June Jordan has written a long, sustained poem interpreting twenty-seven portraits of black life in the United States. Sometimes grim, always forceful, this is a book that would appeal to older children.

Lee Bennett Hopkins has compiled an anthology of the poems of Langston Hughes that speak directly to young people of today. The title of this book, *Don't You Turn Back*, is from a line of Hughes' most poignant poem, "Mother to Son":

. . .

So, boy, don't you turn back.
Don't you set down on the steps
'Cause you find it kinder hard.
Don't you fall now—

For I'se still goin', honey,
I'se still climbin'
And life for me ain't been no crystal stair.

Langston Hughes (143)

This collection contains such well-known poems as "The Negro Speaks of Rivers," "April Rain Song," "Dreams," and "I, Too, Sing America." Some of Ann Grifalconi's finest woodcuts illustrate this outstanding book.

Poets of Nature

Children, like poets, are fascinated with the constant changes in nature and enjoy poems that communicate a sense of wonder and appreciation for the world about them.

Christina Rossetti was a contemporary of Stevenson's, and some of her poetry has the distinctive lyrical quality that characterizes his poems as well. In her only book, *Sing-Song* (259), she writes of the wind, the rain, the rainbow, and small creatures. Her best-known poems are "Boats Sail on the Rivers," "Who Has Seen the Wind?," and the lovely color poem, "What Is Pink?"

Elizabeth Madox Roberts also wrote only one book of poetry for children, *Under the Tree* (254). Her poems show keen insight into the child's mind as she writes about digging for worms, the fun of wading, and listening to "Water Noises." Children enjoy the staccato rhythm of "The Woodpecker" and the description of "The Hens" going to roost and speaking their little "asking words."

Frances Frost has described nature as seen through the eyes of a child in her two books, *The Little Whistler* (116) and *The Little Naturalist* (115). Fox cubs, otters, a chubby woodchuck, and a wren that made its nest in a mailbox are a few of the small creatures that parade through these books. The poet uses such vivid phrases as "my heart is a grasshopper wild in my chest" in the tale of the "Little Fox Lost." Frances Frost's poems are based on accurate observations, and are filled with warmth and tenderness for the creatures of the natural world.

Aileen Fisher is equally adept at observing nature and children. Always she sees the natural world through the eyes of a child. In "Butterfly Tongues," for example, she accurately describes how the butterfly uncoils his tongue to sip the nectar from the flowers, but then observes, as a child would, that if humans only had tongues like that we'd never need straws! Her poems are filled with sensory imagery, as in this verse:

PUSSY WILLOWS

Close your eyes
and do not peek
and I'll rub Spring
across your cheek—
smooth as satin,
soft and sleek—
close your eyes
and do not peek.

Aileen Fisher (105)

Fisher's comparisons are simple and fresh, very much within the experience of a child. In the poem "Sky Net," she describes a spider as a "fisherman of the sky," while the constant maneuvering of bees from clover to hive, is referred to as an "Airlift." Most of her nature poems are in *Cricket in a Thicket* (98); *In the Woods, in the Meadow, in the Sky* (105); and *Feathered Ones and Furry* (99). Poems about children's activities are found in the delightful anthology, *In One Door and Out the Other* (103), illustrated by Lillian Hoban, and *Runny Days, Sunny Days* (108). Her longer narrative poems are told in lilting verse and include *Listen, Rabbit* (107); *Going Barefoot* (101); *Where Does Everyone Go?* (111); *Like Nothing at All* (106); *I Like Weather* (102); and *In the Middle of the Night* (104). Beautifully illustrated by such well-known artists as Adrienne Adams, Symeon Shimin, and Leonard Weisgard, these books are usually presented to children as picture storybooks (*see* Chapter 3).

Lilian Moore has captured the changing moods of both the city and the country in her books *I Thought I Heard the City* (217) and *Sam's Place* (218). Her earlier book *I Feel the Same Way* (216) identifies some of the thoughts and feelings of the young child. Moore's poems are simple and frequently appealing to the senses, as in this poem from her book about the city:

FOGHORNS

The foghorns moaned
in the bay last night

so sad
so deep
I thought I heard the city
    crying in its sleep.

        Lilian Moore (217)

Her images of country scenes are clear and evocative, as can be seen in the description of the "Winter Cardinal" or an "Encounter" with a deer.

Harry Behn's books—*The Little Hill* (25), *Windy Morning* (27), and *The Golden Hive* (24)—contain many poems about nature and the seasons. A favorite with children and teachers is:

DISCOVERY

In a puddle left from last week's rain,
    A friend of mine whose name is Joe
    Caught a tadpole, and showed me where
    Its froggy legs were beginning to grow.

Then we turned over a musty log,
    With lichens on it in a row,
    And found some fiddleheads of ferns
    Uncoiling out of the moss below.

We hunted around, and saw the first
    Jack-in-the-pulpits beginning to show,
    And even discovered under a rock
    Where spotted salamanders go.

I learned all this one morning from Joe,
But how much more there is to know!

        Harry Behn (24)

Undoubtedly, Harry Behn's sensitivity to nature led him to appreciate haiku. In *Cricket Songs* (23) and *More Cricket Songs* (26), he has translated many haiku from the Japanese masters of this form. *All Kinds of Time* (21) has some unusual poems about clocks, time, and the seasons.

The poetry of Elizabeth Coatsworth reflects the moods and perceptions of an astute observer of nature. Her delicate and beautiful verse reveals a deep love of nature and animals. She frequently employs a pattern of comparison in her poems. For example, she contrasts the beauty of swift things with that of slow things in "Poem of Praise"; and makes another comparison in "January," when snow is described as coming as quietly as a cat or with "windy uproar and com-

motion." Coatsworth's poems are included in: *Poems* (63), *Summer Green* (65), and *The Sparrow Bush* (64). The third volume is illustrated with delicate wood engravings by Stefan Martin.

Mary Austin has described the beauties of the Southwest in *The Children Sing in the Far West* (17). Her most popular poems include the amusing "Grizzly Bear" and "A Feller I Know." Children also enjoy "Prairie-dog Town" and "The Sandhill Crane." Her Indian poems reflect the quiet dignity of that ancient race, particularly "A Song of Greatness."

Some of the strong, quizzical poetry of Carl Sandburg is appropriately used with children in the middle grades. They enjoy the humor of "Phizzog," the advice of "Primer Lesson," and the wisdom of "Circles." Sandburg made two collections of his poems which were particularly appropriate for young people, *Early Moon* (260) and *Wind Song* (261). In the latter, available in paperback, the vivid imagery of "Haystacks," "Night," and "River Moons" will help children see with the eyes of a poet.

Many poems of Robert Frost are simple enough for a child to understand and complex enough for graduate study. Before his death, he selected some of his poems to be read to, or by, young people. Interestingly, the title of this collection, *You Come Too*, was taken from a line of "The Pasture," the first poem in this book and the introductory poem of the very first book of Frost's ever to be published. Upon initial reading this poem seems no more than a literal invitation to join someone as he cleans the pasture spring. However, the poem takes on more meaning when viewed in the context of its placement; the trip to the pasture to clean the spring may well be an invitation to the enjoyment of poetry itself— "you come too!" Robert Frost seemed to have had a preoccupation with clearing muddied waters, and it is significant that his last book was titled *In the Clearing*. Children can enjoy "The Runaway," "Dust of Snow," "The Last Word of a Bluebird," and "The Pasture" on their level of understanding. Older children will begin to comprehend the deeper meanings in "Mending Wall," "The Road Not Taken," and "The Death of the Hired Man." The poetry of Robert Frost is for all ages.

A small black-and-white wood engraving by Thomas Nason presents a literal interpretation of Frost's well-known poem, "The Road Not Taken."

From *You Come Too* by Robert Frost. Copyright © 1959 by Holt, Rinehart and Winston, Inc. Reproduced by permission of Holt, Rinehart and Winston, Inc.

Weavers of Magic and Fantasy

Children love eerie, "spooky" poetry. The master craftsman in creating mysterious moods is Walter de la Mare. Children enjoy the hushed mystery of "Someone," which ends with the enigmatic lines: "So I know not who came knocking, at all, at all, at all." The same kind of eeriness is felt in the poem "Nothing." The "Ride-by-Nights" is a vividly descriptive poem about witches who "surge pell-mell down the Milky Way." Two of Walter de la Mare's best-known poems are "Silver" and "The Listeners." Both create a mood of sustained stillness and mystery. De la Mare's most popular poems are found in *Peacock Pie* (81), first published in 1913. A recent edition has been illustrated by Barbara Cooney. A collection of all his poems has been published in one book—*Rhymes and Verses, Collected Poems for Young People* (82). And a selected group of poems have been delicately illustrated by Dorothy Lathrop in *Bells and Grass* (79).

James Reeves' books, *The Blackbird in the Lilac* (248) and *The Wandering Moon* (250), contain a wide variety of poems. Many of them are funny verses about strange people; some are thoughtful and quiet; some are fantasies of myth and legend, such as "Little Fan," "Pat's Fiddle," and "Queer

Things." Children will enjoy "The Old Wife and the Ghost," which is the amusing tale of a deaf woman who refuses to be frightened by a ghost. "A Garden at Night" and "The Toadstool Wood" also paint ghostly scenes. Imaginative and pleasantly scary for younger children are the poems in *Prefabulous Animiles* (249), which has been illustrated by Edward Ardizzone. Reeves has invented such creatures as the fearsome Hippocrump with a hundred teeth and the forty-legged Snyke. These verses must have been fun to illustrate.

Writers of Humorous Verse

Almost all poets have written some humorous verse, but only a few have become noted primarily for this form. In the nineteenth century the names of Edward Lear and Lewis Carroll became almost synonymous with humorous nonsense poems. Although Lear did not create the limerick, he was certainly master of the form as we have seen. His narrative verse includes the well-known "The Owl and the Pussycat," "The Jumblies," "The Quangle-Wangle's Hat" (166), and "The Duck and the Kangaroo." His limericks, alphabet rhymes, and narrative poems have been compiled into one book, *The Complete Nonsense Book* (165). Each absurd verse is illustrated by the poet's grotesque drawings, which add greatly to Lear's humor.

Most of Carroll's nonsense verse is included in *Alice's Adventures in Wonderland* and *Through the Looking-Glass* (50). Many of Carroll's poems were parodies of the popular poems of his time. "The Lobster Quadrille" mimics Mary Howitt's "The Spider and the Fly," "Father William" copies Southey's "The Old Man's Comforts," while "How Doth the Little Crocodile" parodies Watt's "How Doth the Busy Bee." Interest in the original poems has all but disappeared, but the parodies continue to delight. "Jabberwocky" is a "made language" of portmanteau words—namely, combining the meaning and parts of two words to create a new one. "Brunch," for example, carries the combined meaning and sound of both breakfast and lunch. The sound and play of words must have fascinated Carroll, for his poems and books abound with puns, double meanings, coined words, and wonderful nonsense.

Laura E. Richards' rhythmical nonsense poems are presented in her book, *Tirra Lirra* (251). Much of the humor of Richards' poems is based upon the manufacture of delightful-sounding words; her children go fishing for "pollothy-woogs" and get stuck in "bogothybogs"; and a "Wiggledywasticus" is in the museum along with the "Ploodlecumlumpsydyl." Many of Richards' poems are humorous narratives, such as "The Seven Little Tigers and the Aged Cook" and "The Monkeys and the Crocodile." Funny characters and situations pervade the poetry of this prolific writer.

Several of our modern poets are following in the tradition of Lear. William Jay Smith has included limericks, imaginary dialogues, and verse about various nonsense birds in his collection, *Mister Smith and Other Nonsense* (267A). Here are the verses about "Poor little pigeon-toed Dimity Drew/The more she ate, the smaller she grew" and "Big Gumbo"—"Great big gawky Gumbo Cole/Couldn't stop growing to save his soul." Smith's other books include *Laughing Time* (267); *Boy Blue's Book of Beasts* (266); and the unique limericks for *Typewriter Town* (268), which he illustrated with pictures made on the typewriter.

The sophisticated light verse and limericks of Ogden Nash appeal to both adults and children. They delight in "The Panther," "The Centipede," and "The Eel." Young children enjoy his longer narrative poems, including "The Adventures of Isabel," who eats a bear, and the sad demise of "The Boy Who Laughed at Santa Claus." These poems appear in *The Moon Is Shining Bright as Day* (223).

E. V. Rieu, an English classicist, finds relaxation in writing nonsense verse for children. Such verse has been collected in *The Flattered Flying Fish and Other Poems* (253). Several of these, such as "A Dirge for a Bad Boy" and "Two People," are about children's misbehavior and consequent punishment, a subject that never fails to amuse children.

The originator of poems about mischievous children and their grim punishments was Heinrich Hoffman in "Slovenly Peter." Harry Graham continued the tradition with his *Ruthless Rhymes for Heartless Homes*, first published in 1899, with such gems as:

THE STERN PARENT

Father heard his Children Scream
So he threw them in the stream
Saying, as he drowned the third,
"Children should be seen, not heard!"

Harry Graham (123)

John Ciardi appears to be following the Hoffman-Graham tradition in some of his poems. The first verse of "Children When They're Very Sweet" is an example:

Children when they're very sweet,
    Only bite and scratch and kick
A very little. Just enough
To show their parents they're not sick.
. . .

John Ciardi (55)

Ciardi's book, *You Know Who* (58), is filled with sly descriptions of different "someones" and their behaviors. *The Monster Den* (56) is the title of the book about his own children, and has more appeal for parents than children. Many of Ciardi's poems are enjoyed by boys and girls with enough sophistication to appreciate their tongue-in-cheek humor. His poems about imaginary animals, such as the "Shiverous Shreek" or the "Saginsack," are well liked. One fourth grade's favorite was about the disastrous custard made by "Some Cook," while all children enjoy "Mummy Slept Late and Daddy Fixed Breakfast." In *The Reason for the Pelican* (57), there are some fine lyrical poems, including "There Once Was an Owl," "The River Is a Piece of Sky," and "Rain Sizes." Humorous poetry characterizes his other books, which include *I Met a Man* (54); *The Man Who Sang the Sillies* (55); and *You Read to Me, I'll Read to You* (59). Sophisticated Victorian illustrations by Edward Gorey complement Ciardi's spoof on today's parent-child relations.

While most of Theodor Roethke's poems are written for adults, two collections of his poems have been put together for older children. The first one, *I Am! Says the Lamb* (257), is divided into two parts, nature poems and humorous poetry. *Dirty Dinky and Other Creatures* (256) contains poems selected for younger children by Beatrice Roethke and Stephen Lushington after Roethke's death. "Dinky" is a favorite with all children who

Art and poetry combine to make this one of children's favorite poetry books.

Illustrations Copyright © 1967 by Marc Simont. From *Every Time I Climb a Tree* by David McCord, by permission of Little, Brown and Co.

like to put the blame on someone else. One stanza serves as an example:

. . .
Suppose you walk out in a storm,
With nothing on to keep you warm,
And then step barefoot on a worm
—Of course, it's Dirty Dinky. . . .

        Theodor Roethke (256)

One of the funniest recent collections of poems is Silverstein's *Where the Sidewalk Ends* (265). Here you meet a boy who turns into a TV set, a king who eats only a "Peanut-Butter Sandwich," and "Sarah Cynthia Sylvia Stout" who will not take the garbage out!

"Of Cabbages and Kings"

It is difficult to characterize the wide variety of poems produced by certain poets. David

McCord's poetry, for example, ranges in subject from nature poems to verse about verse. Certainly one of the best-loved poetry collections published is his picture-book anthology, *Every Time I Climb a Tree* (196) illustrated by the Caldecott Award-winner, Marc Simont. This includes the favorite "The Pickety Fence," "Pad and Pencil," and "This Is My Rock." Much of the poetry in McCord's first book, *Far and Few, Rhymes of Never Was and Always Is*, concerns simple country sights or walking in the woods with his father. The unusual verse arrangement in "The Grasshopper," already quoted, reinforces the image of the grasshopper going down the well and then climbing back up. The poem "At the Garden Gate" portrays an exasperated parent questioning the tardiness of his children for dinner; while a pleading child begs her parents to let her stay up late in "Conversation." Both poems reveal McCord's knowledge of children and his ability to capture the intonations of an argument.

All Day Long (195) includes songs of nature, a trip to the laundromat, and other humorous verse. Some verse reflects McCord's persistent interest in language, such as "Figures of Speech," "Ptarmigan," and "Says Tom to Me." This special delight in words was the subject of most of the poems in his book *Take Sky* (199). The long "Write Me a Verse" contains Professor Swigly Brown's talk on "four kinds of Rime." In McCord's most recent book, *For Me to Say* (198), he gives riotous instructions on "How to Draw a Monkey" and how to use chopsticks while "Eating at the Restaurant of How Chow Now." He also includes some seven poems on the subject of "Write Me Another Verse."

Eve Merriam has written a trilogy of books for children about the nature of poetry, including *There Is No Rhyme for Silver* (210), *It Doesn't Always Have to Rhyme* (208), and *Catch a Little Rhyme* (204). Her poetry has a lilt and bounce that will capture the most disinterested child's attention, beginning with "How to Eat a Poem." Such poems as "Metaphor," "Cliché," "Simile," and "Onomatopoeia" are excellent for the language class. The poems in *Catch a Little Rhyme* are for children in the primary grades. City boys and girls who are accustomed to slum clearance will appreciate "Bam Bam Bam." They will also enjoy the ironic twist to "The Stray Cat." Humor is found in "Teevee," and "Alligator on the Escalator." In her books *Finding a Poem* (205) and *Out Loud* (209) Merriam continues her interest in playing with language, and at the same time shows her increasing interest in social and political satire. Thus, "The Wholly Family" is really a wholly plastic family, while "Basic for Irresponsibility" suggests that everything can be blamed on "It." Some of the poetry in this book is concrete; while other poems, such as "A Charm for Our Time," are chants of newly created words and products such as "freeze-dry, high-fi." *Independent Voices* (207) includes seven long poems on persons whom Merriam admires: Benjamin Franklin, Elizabeth Blackwell, Frederic Douglass, Henry Thoreau, Lucretia Mott, Ida B. Wells, and Fiorello La Guardia. Merriam has also written *I Am a Man: An Ode to Martin Luther King, Jr.* (206),

which appears in a picture-book format. Her political satire, written primarily for adults, has received much acclaim. These books include *The Inner City Mother Goose* and *The Nixon Poems*. Obviously, Eve Merriam writes on many subjects and for all ages.

Children from 7 up respond with enthusiasm to Mary O'Neill's poems about color in *Hailstones and Halibut Bones, Adventures in Color* (228). Using fresh imagery, the poet has explored the various sensory and emotional dimensions of each color; for example, "Green is an olive and a pickle. The sound of green is a water-trickle"; and "Brown is cinnamon and morning toast and the good smell of the Sunday roast." This same poet has used a similar approach in her books *Words, Words, Words* (232) and *What Is that Sound!* (231) and *Fingers Are Always Bringing Me News* (227). The first book contains poems about the history of the language, parts of speech, punctuation, and reflections upon particular meanings of words; for example, "Imagination is a new idea beginning to grow/In the warm, soft earth of all we know." The book of sounds imitates the hiss, crackle, and sputter of fire and the murmur, gurgle, splash of water. These are poems that help children understand the concept of onomatopoeia. The work of various kinds of fingers is described in *Fingers Are Always Bringing Me News*— city and country fingers, greedy fingers, fingers of the newborn and of old age. *People I'd Like to Keep* (229) are cameo poems of persons such as "Miss Hortense Rogers, the Grade School Principal" or "The Circus People," or "Darling Doctor de Plunkett." Even number concepts challenged O'Neill when she wrote *Take a Number* (230). All of O'Neill's poetry encourages children to see, hear, feel, and think in a new way. Frequently, her poems inspire children to create their own images and begin to write poetry too.

Anthologies of Poems for Children

COMPREHENSIVE POETRY COLLECTIONS

Every family will want to own at least one excellent anthology of poetry for children; while teachers will want to have several, including some for their personal use and some for the children. In selecting a general anthology of poetry, the following questions need to be considered:

What is the age level appeal of this book?

How many poems are included?

What types of poems are included?

How many poets are represented?

What is the quality of the poetry?

Are recent contemporary poems included, as well as old favorites?

What is the subject matter of the poems?

How are the poems arranged and organized?

How adequate are the indices in helping the reader find a poem?

How helpful are the introduction and commentaries?

Has the compiler achieved his stated or implied purpose in making the collection?

Are the illustrations and format appropriate for the poems and age appeal of the collection?

Teachers find *Time for Poetry* (13) by May Hill Arbuthnot and Shelton L. Root, Jr., almost indispensable. First published in 1952, the third edition retains many of the well-loved favorites of Stevenson, Rossetti, De la Mare, Lear, Farjeon, and Milne; while including some of the poetry of such contemporaries as Merriam, Kuskin, Behn, Ciardi, O'Neill, and others. A new section entitled "Keeping Children and Poetry Together" provides helpful suggestions for ways of using poetry in the classroom.

Primary-grade teachers will want to own a copy of the paperback, *Poems Children Will Sit Still For* (85) compiled by Beatrice Schenk de Regniers and others. Each of the 106 poems in this book was chosen with the title in mind: Would this be a poem that would really interest young children? The compilers have been successful in finding poems that speak to children yet maintain the language of poetry. Such poets as Robert Frost, John Ciardi, and e. e. cummings are represented along with Eve Merriam, Mary Ann Hoberman, Karla Kuskin, and Robert Louis Stevenson, A. A. Milne, and Walter de la Mare. The authors provide many fine suggestions of ways to involve children in the poems through discussion and participation.

Another distinctive collection for young children appears in Thompson's *Poems to Grow On*

(294). The format of this book and the selection of poems achieve a remarkable unity. It is unfortunate that the poets' names are only included in the table of contents and not directly under each poem. Even primary-grade children should begin to associate poets with particular poems. Kindergarten and primary-grade teachers continue to find the Geismer and Suter book, *Very Young Verses* (121), quite useful. Prepared by two teachers, it supplies many poems that have proven appeal. *Away We Go!* (201) contains 100 poems selected by Catherine McEwen to meet the needs of the young child. While the anthology presents some fresh contemporary poems, few are appropriate for city children. The crisp black-and-white scratchboard illustrations by Barbara Cooney add much to this collection.

Two anthologies which originated in England are now available here. *Fives Sixes and Sevens* (276) was compiled by Marjorie Stephenson and *Round about Eight* (233) by Geoffrey Palmer and Noel Lloyd. Both these collections will appeal to children. Humorous two-color illustrations appear on every page, and the print is large enough to encourage the child reading on his own. While some traditional poems are included, many are refreshingly modern and appropriate for today's child.

Listen, Children, Listen (183), edited by the poet Myra Cohn Livingston, is a remarkably fine collection for both teachers and children. The poems range from the nonsense of Hilaire Belloc and Edward Lear to the sensitive poems of Emily Dickinson, Langston Hughes, and Amy Lowell, with the fun of David McCord and Dorothy Aldis in between. The black-and-white drawings by Trina Schart Hyman portray modern children in jeans or shorts, city children and country children, black children and white, children wearing glasses, and spooky ugly trolls and goblins. Subtitled "An Anthology of Poems for the Very Young," the book seems most appropriate for children ages 7 through 11.

Some modern and indispensable paperback books for children of this age range are the *Arrow Book of Poetry* (202) selected by Ann McGovern, *Time to Shout* (136) and *Faces and Places* (135) both compiled by Lee Bennett Hopkins and Misha Arenstein. The *Arrow Book of Poetry* is a distinctive collection with more contemporary poets repre-

Invitation to a feast of paperback poetry books! All these books may be purchased for less than the cost of one general anthology.

sented than traditional ones. Included are such favorites as "The Pickety Fence," "Nancy Hanks," "The Snail," "The Cat Heard the Cat Bird," and some seventy-five other child-tested poems. *Time to Shout* is characterized by many humorous and contemporary poems. Children love "Sister Lettie's Ready" since she has hair made of spaghetti; they thoroughly enjoy "When Dinosaurs Ruled the Earth"; and easily identify with the feelings created by "Homework." *Faces and Places* includes poems about favorite times, favorite things, and favorite sports. Children will enjoy such contemporary poems as "The Winning of the TV West" and "Adventure House,"

a poem in praise of a movie theater. It is hoped that every teacher and every boy and girl in the middle grades would own copies of these excellent paperback collections.

Nancy Larrick has compiled a group of favorites for boys and girls in her anthology *Piper, Pipe that Song Again!* (163). Before she included any poem, Larrick tested it in a school classroom to determine children's responses. It includes such favorites as "Isabel" by Ogden Nash, Austin's "Grizzly Bear," and "Daddy Fell into the Pond" by Alfred Noyes, as well as selections by De la Mare, Fisher, Field, Sandburg, Frost, and others. Humorous black-and-white sketches by Kelly

Oechsli add to the delight of this book for children. Larrick also compiled *Piping Down the Valleys Wild* (164) for slightly older children. This again is a distinctive collection enriched by Ellen Raskin's stylized pictures for each section. Larrick was one of the first compilers to include a section of city poems in her anthologies.

Another book that contains tested children's favorites is *The First Book of Poetry* (237) compiled by Peterson, a teacher in the Laboratory School of the University of Chicago.

Favorite Poems, Old and New (92) by Helen Ferris continues to be a very popular anthology with both teachers and children in the middle grades. True to its title, it contains both traditional and contemporary poems. Children particularly enjoy the many narrative poems that can be found in this collection. Louis Untermeyer's anthology of poems, *The Golden Treasury of Poetry* (299), is profusely illustrated by Joan Walsh Anglund. Untermeyer has written a commentary on each poem, as he did in his other, older collections—*Stars to Steer By* (303), *This Singing World* (302), and *Rainbow in the Sky* (301). Untermeyer's collections rely heavily upon ballads and narrative poems such as "The Pied Piper of Hamelin," "Annabel Lee," and other traditional poems. Few contemporary poets are included. This same criticism may be directed at the *Oxford Book of Poetry for Children* (37) compiled by Edward Blishen and brilliantly illustrated by Brian Wildsmith. Here one may find classic poetry for children: poems by Lear, Carroll, De la Mare, Masefield, Stevenson, even Shakespeare, Thackeray, and Shelley. Walter de la Mare also looked to the past to select poetry "that wears well" for his two anthologies, *Tom Tiddler's Ground* (83) and *Come Hither* (80). The first ranges from a few Mother Goose rhymes to Tennyson, Keats, and Poe; while the second contains imaginative poems for young people and adults.

A discerning and unusual anthology of poems is McDonald's book, *A Way of Knowing* (200). These poems were originally selected for boys, but they appeal equally well to girls. The collection is varied, including light and serious, old, and some very modern poetry.

One of the most exciting modern anthologies is *Reflections on a Gift of Watermelon Pickle and Other Modern Verses* (88) by Dunning, Lueders, and Smith. Illustrated with superb photographs, many of the poems would appeal to the middle-grade child—for example, "Sonic Boom" by John Updike, "Ancient History" by Arthur Guiterman, "Dreams" by Langston Hughes, and "How to Eat a Poem" by Eve Merriam, to mention just a few. Fortunately, this volume is available in paperback along with a fine record of many of the poems. A series of four paperback books titled *First Voices* (280–283) has been edited by Geoffrey Summerfield. These anthologies contain fine colored photographs, etchings, or paintings that do not necessarily represent the poems but stand alone and make their own statements. In fact, the subtitle of the series reads: "An Anthology of Poetry and Pictures." Summerfield has mixed adult poems with poems by children, counting-out rhymes with serious poems, mostly contemporary poems with a few traditional poems—and yet the individual books have an amazing wholeness and integrity. Five other books simply titled *Voices* (284–288) are equally interesting, but appear to be geared for junior-high students or older.

An excellent collection, *This Way, Delight* (246), compiled by Herbert Read, will interest young people and adults. It is for those discerning few who have developed a keen appreciation for poetry. Another anthology for this group is *Lean Out of the Window* (126) by Hannum and Reed. It includes well-known selections from such twentieth-century poets as James Joyce, Robert Frost, Gwendolyn Brooks, and others. Sara Hannum and her husband, John Chase, have also edited an anthology of modern poems about the human condition under the title *To Play Man Number One* (125). Again, these are mostly poems for adults, but some of them will speak clearly to the sophisticated youth of today.

Richard Peck has edited a fine anthology for modern youth titled *Sounds and Silences* (236). It includes mostly contemporary adult poets writing on such subjects as dissent, identity, communication, war, love, and pain. Some popular lyrics, such as "Little Boxes" and "Where Have All the Flowers Gone?", are also included.

The Golden Journey is a distinguished anthology compiled by two poets, Louise Bogan and William Jay Smith (38). The title is derived from a modern poem entitled the "Golden Journey to

Samarkan." In the introduction the authors liken "the poet to a traveler whose itinerary covers every area of human experience from birth to death."[13] While many of these poems are well selected, some—such as Wordsworth's "Daffodils" or Herrick's "To Daffadills"—seem out of place in a modern collection. Stevenson's "Foreign Children" certainly reflects a superior attitude toward Eskimos and Indians that no sensitive teacher or librarian would want to present today.

A Flock of Words (203) is the title of an anthology compiled by David Mackay, a former teacher in England who felt strongly that children should have a chance to hear adult poetry. He collected poems from all over the world and tested them in his classroom. Some of the older, traditional English poems seem quite difficult, but others, such as the "Telephone Poles" by John Updike or "My Sister Jane" by Ted Hughes, would delight middle-grade children. Myra Cohn Livingston has provided older children with an unusual collection of poems from all over the world in *A Tune Beyond Us* (188). Some of the poems appear in the original Russian, Spanish, or German along with their translations. Some are very humorous, such as "King Tiet" and "Dirty Dinky." Many of these poems are not well known and provide a refreshing new source for teachers and children. *Beach Glass* (214) edited by Paul Molloy is an anthology of some 150 poems that will appeal to both adults and older children. These are modern poems from the United States, some of which are as realistic as Karl Shapiro's "Auto Wreck."

Specialized Collections

North American genius for organization is apparent in the number of specialized anthologies that have been published. Most of these are organized around a certain subject, such as humorous poems or animal poems. Some, however, are related to the origin of the poems or an ethnic background; while others are categorized by a form of poetry, such as haiku or limericks.

Since children enjoy humorous poetry more than any other kind, we have a great number of

Evaline Ness has selected and illustrated a lively collection of poems about girls of all shapes, sizes, and dispositions.

Reprinted by permission of Charles Scribner's Sons from *Amelia Mixed the Mustard and Other Poems* by Evaline Ness. Jacket illustration copyright © 1975 Evaline Ness.

anthologies of humorous verse. William Cole has produced four very funny collections which Tomi Ungerer has illustrated with comic line drawings. The titles of these books suggest their content: *Oh, What Nonsense!* (72); *Oh, How Silly!* (70); *Oh, That's Ridiculous!* (71); and *Beastly Boys and Ghastly Girls* (66). Cole deliberately left out the nonsense poems of Lear and Carroll, since their poems are so readily available in other collections. Instead, he included some of the amusing poems of Shel Silverstein, Spike Mulligan, and Theodor Roethke. These are books that will rescue any middle-grader who may have become disenchanted with poetry. A fifth book by Cole, *Humorous Poetry for Children* (69), contains many amusing narrative poems. Cole has also edited *Story Poems, New and Old* (77); *Poems of Magic and Spells* (75); *Poems for Seasons and Celebrations* (74); *The Birds and the Beasts Were There* (67); and *A*

---

[13]Louise Bogan and William Jay Smith, compilers. *The Golden Journey: Poems for Young People,* illustrated by Fritz Kredel (Chicago, Ill.: Reilley & Lee, 1965), p. xvii.

Book of Animal Poems (68). These are attractively illustrated and focus on themes that have much appeal for children in the middle grades.

A light-hearted anthology that will delight middle-graders is *What a Wonderful Bird the Frog Are* (189). Edited by Myra Cohn Livingston, this collection includes such zany verse as the title poem, limericks, amusing epitaphs, and the marvelous wit of such poets as Ogden Nash, David McCord, John Ciardi, and others. In another anthology, *Speak Roughly to Your Little Boy* (187), Livingston presents many well-known parodies and burlesques, along with the poems that inspired them. For example, "Pentagonia" by G. E. Bates is a clever parody about the building of the Pentagon following the form of "The House that Jack Built." Notes at the end of the book provide background on the original poems and parodies. Here we learn that there are countless parodies of Longfellow's poems, but the editor included only those she thought best. Children will certainly agree with her when they read:

THE MODERN HIAWATHA

When he killed the Mudjokivis
Of the skin he made him mittens,
Made them with the fur side inside,
Made them with the skin side outside,
He, to get the warm side inside,
Put the inside skin side outside;
He, to get the cold side outside,
Put the warm side fur side inside.
That's why he put the fur side inside,
Why he put the skin side outside,
Why he turned them inside outside.

George A. Strong (187)

The Brewtons have produced many excellent anthologies based upon such diverse subjects as animals, people, joy and beauty, holidays, seasons, and humor. The titles of their books are *Under the Tent of the Sky* (46), *Gaily We Parade* (42), *Bridled with Rainbows* (40), *Christmas Bells Are Ringing* (41), *Sing a Song of Seasons* (45), *Birthday Candles Burning Bright* (39), and *Laughable Limericks* (43). Another of their popular collections is titled *Shrieks at Midnight: Macabre Poems, Eerie and Humorous* (44). The foreword of this book suggests its content:

The poems in this book are about death and doom, ghosts and ghouls, bare bones and shiverous beasts. Ghoulish and grim, eerie and shivery—with a whiff of murder, death, and doom—these macabre verses also have a touch of humorous *grave* humor.[14]

Children from 7 and up will delight in the collection of "shivery poems" in *Catch Your Breath* (219). Selected by Lilian Moore and Lawrence Webster, and illustrated with purple-and-white line drawings by G. Wilson, this very readable book of some fifty poems would be great for Halloween and any other time children want "spooky poems." Fine poets are represented in this unusual anthology for children, including Dorothy Aldis, Harry Behn, John Ciardi, Aileen Fisher, Langston Hughes, and Eve Merriam.

Ogden Nash has collected a sparkling group of humorous poems for his two anthologies for older children: *The Moon Is Shining Bright as Day* (223) and *Everybody Ought to Know* (222). These include both contemporary poems and old favorites.

In *Sprints and Distances, Sports in Poetry and Poetry in Sport* (220), Lillian Morrison hopes to capture children's interest in poetry through building on their known interest in sports. Almost every sport is represented—from baseball to falconry. Arranged by the sport, the collection includes poems culled from such ancient and modern writers as Virgil, Shakespeare, Stevenson, Ogden Nash, David McCord, and Robert Francis. Some of the poems are humorous, as in "The Umpire"; some adulatory, as "To Lou Gehrig"; and some serious, as "To an Athlete Dying Young" by A. E. Housman. Another fine collection of poems about sports is *Hosannah the Home Run!* (112) by Alice Fleming. This anthology includes some thirty-four poems on every kind of sport, illustrated with striking black-and-white photographs. Middle-grade children who have been introduced to parodies would enjoy "Winter Trees," which begins, "I think that I shall never ski/Against against so stout a tree." Both humorous and serious poems are represented in this collection.

[14]Sara Brewton and John E. Brewton, compilers. *Shrieks at Midnight: Macabre Poems, Eerie and Humorous*, illustrated by Ellen Raskin (New York: Crowell, 1969), Foreword.

Here She Is

Mary Britton Miller

Jungle necklaces are hung
Around her tiger throat
And on her tiger arms are slung
Bracelets black and brown;
She shows off when she lies down
All her tiger strength and grace,
You can see the tiger blaze
In her tiger eyes, her tiger face.

Zebra

Isak Dinesen

The eagle's shadow runs across the plain,
Towards the distant, nameless, air-blue mountains.
But the shadows of the round young Zebra
Sit close between their delicate hoofs all day,
    where they stand immovable,
And wait for the evening, wait to stretch out, blue,
Upon a plain, painted brick-red by the sunset,
And to wander to the water-hole.

Poetry of Earth is a handsome anthology which reflects artistic design on each page. Note the complementary placement of these two poems and pictures.

Illustration used by permission of Charles Scribner's Sons from *Poetry of Earth* by Adrienne Adams. Copyright © 1972 Adrienne Adams. "Here She Is" from *Give a Guess,* by Mary Britton Miller. Copyright © 1957 by Pantheon Books, Inc. Reprinted by permission of Pantheon Books, a Division of Random House, Inc. "Zebra" from *Out of Africa,* by Isak Dinesen. Copyright 1937 by Random House, Inc., and renewed 1963 by Rungstedlundfonden. Reprinted by permission of the publisher. Also by permission of the British publisher, from *Out of Africa* by Karen Blixen published by Putnam & Co., London.

Four distinctive and unusual poetry collections for older readers have been made by Helen Plotz. In *Imagination's Other Place* (241), she has presented poems written about science and mathematics. The subject matter includes poems on dinosaurs, astronomy, physics, chemistry, biology, and medicine. The emphasis is on modern poetry, but well-known poets of other eras are represented. In *Untune the Sky* (243), Plotz has presented lovely poems of music and dance. The third book, *The Earth Is the Lord's: Poems of the Spirit* (240), is drawn from the inspirational literature of many ages and places; while the fourth book, *The Marvelous Light* (242), celebrates the theme of poetry itself. The first three titles are enriched with handsome wood engravings by Clare Leighton, who also provided the illustrations for a distinguished collection of world poetry titled *The Singing and the Gold; Poems Translated from World Literature* (234). Compiled by Elinor Parker, this distinctive anthology contains poetry from some thirty different countries and many different periods of history. All of these anthologies are for the discerning student of poetry and the mature child.

Poetry about animals is a popular subject for anthologies. *Poetry of Earth* (1) is a handsome collection of some thirty-three poems selected and illustrated by Adrienne Adams. Sharp, clear illustrations of birds, butterflies, and animals are printed on colored or white backgrounds of fine quality paper. The choice and arrangement of the poems have been carefully considered so that "Crows" by David McCord appears opposite "Dust of Snow" by Robert Frost; both poems share a picture of flying crows. Mary Britton Miller's poem "Here She Is," which describes the stripes of a tiger as her necklace and bracelets is juxtaposed with Isak Dinesen's poem about the shadow stripes of the "Zebra." Other selections include Edna St. Vincent Millay's "The Buck in the Snow," "The Sandhill Crane" by Mary Austin, "The Eagle" by Tennyson, and other familiar nature poems. This is a book that is pleasing to the images of both mind and eye.

A very different feeling is created in *Paper Zoo* (305), a collection of animal poems by modern poets of the United States compiled by Renee Weiss. Ellen Raskin has illustrated these poems with brilliant orange-and-green stylized creatures. Hidden within her patterned designs of the illustration for "The Magical Mouse" by Kenneth Patchen are the little birds and maidens that this mouse claims he eats. This is a sophisticated book in both illustrations and selection of poems.

Another unusual selection of poems about animals is Gwendolyn Reed's *Out of the Ark; An Anthology of Animal Poems* (247). Many of these are translated from the Chinese, Greek, French, or German. An equally fine collection that seems more appropriate for children's needs is William Cole's *The Birds and the Beasts Were There* (67), which has been mentioned earlier. Helen Siegl's distinguished woodcuts complement the selection of nearly three hundred animal poems. Robert Andrew Parker's subtle line drawings illustrate another collection of animal poems by Cole titled *A Book of Animal Poems* (68). Mostly contemporary, these poems have been gathered from all over the world.

Recent years have witnessed a trend away from poetry of nature to poetry of the city. No longer a rural nation, the United States has been slow to recognize that poetry may be found in the city too. Lee Bennett Hopkins has compiled several picture-book collections of city poems including *I Think I Saw a Snail* (132), *The City Spreads Its Wings* (130), and *Zoo! A Book of Poems* (134). Most of the poems are about the city and all of them are portrayed with a city setting. Poets such as Langston Hughes, Eve Merriam, Gwendolyn Brooks, and Patricia Hubbell are represented. These are small collections of some twenty poems each. Every poem is illustrated with a full-page picture and sometimes with a double-page spread. City children enjoy looking at and reading these books about themselves.

Three useful books for primary-grade teachers of urban children were edited by Donald Bissett. These include *Poems and Verses to Begin On* (35),

Verses about Animals (33), and *Poems and Verses about the City* (34). The point of view of the city child is the focus for all the poems. For example, the animal verses feature poems of zoo animals or animals of the park or pets. Each of these paperback books contains some seventy-five to one hundred poems. Even though they are not illustrated, they make a fine source for teachers.

The first and most exciting anthology of city poems was collected by Nancy Larrick under the title *On City Streets* (162). These poems were selected with the help of one hundred young readers in the inner city. These are not "pretty poems"; some tell of the bitter tragedies of city life, such as "The Sad Story about Greenwich Village" by Frances Park or "Mother to Son" by Langston Hughes. Clear black-and-white photographs extend the poems and frequently comment upon them. For example, Phyllis McGinley's verse "Q is for the Quietness" is accompanied by a picture of a man on his motorcycle in front of an apartment building! Available in both hardcovers and paperback, this is a collection that teachers and children in the middle grades will want to own. *City in All Directions* (3) edited by Arnold Adoff contains some eighty poems that will appeal to the more mature reader. The city setting for these poems has been richly illustrated by Donald Carrick.

Adoff has also edited several black poetry anthologies. The first one, *I Am the Darker Brother: An Anthology of Modern Poems by Black Americans* (4) was published in 1970 and contains some of the best-known poetry of Langston Hughes, Gwendolyn Brooks, and Countee Cullen, as well as some promising contemporary poets. *Black Out Loud: An Anthology of Modern Poems by Black Americans* (2) appeared in 1970 and contains many outspoken poems of love, hatred, protest, and pride. The bitterness in some of the poems makes the book more appropriate for older students, yet a teacher could find much to share with middle-graders. *My Black Me* (5), subtitled "a beginning book of black poetry," mixes black pride with power and protest. Children in the middle grades will enjoy many of these contemporary poems. The brief biographical notes on each of the poets add interest and would help children realize that poets are alive, well, and writing today.

Recent interest in the North American Indian has resulted in a handsome picture book of Indian poems titled *The Trees Stand Shining* (152), which was collected by Hettie Jones and illustrated with beautiful full-color paintings by Robert Andrew Parker. Many of these poems are really chants or songs which celebrate the changing seasons and the glory of the world as the Indian knew it. Weyman Jones' fine book of historical fiction *Edge of Two Worlds* (*see* Chapter 8) might be introduced with this chant from the Papago tribe:

> At the edge of the world
> It is growing light
> The trees stand shining
> I like it.
> It is growing light.
>
> (152)

In the Trail of the Wind: American Indian Poems and Ritual Orations (31) is a very scholarly collection of poems, chants, and prayers that have been translated from over forty languages representing the best-known Indian cultures of both South and North America. Edited by John Bierhorst, this interesting anthology is illustrated with old engravings of the American Indian.

Songs of the Dream People (138) by James Houston contains chants and images of both the Indians and Eskimos of North America. Grouped regionally by tribes of the Eastern Woodland, the Central Plains, the Northwest Coast, and the Eskimo—these poems are illustrated with striking drawings of artifacts, art objects, and weapons by Houston. They would be a rich resource for a study of the Indians or Eskimo.

Knud Rasmussen was the first to record the virile poetry of the Eskimo in his *Beyond the High Hills: A Book of Eskimo Poems* (245). Many of these poems were originally songs chanted to celebrate a hunt or the return of the caribou in the spring. Some were simply songs of praise, the joy of greeting a new day, or meeting new friends. The Eskimo's traditional struggle against the elements is the theme of many of these poems, for example:

> There is joy in
> Feeling the warmth
> Come to the great world
> And seeing the sun

> Follow its old footprints
> In the summer night.

> There is fear in
> Feeling the cold
> Come to the great world
> And seeing the moon
> —Now new moon, now full moon—
> Follow its old footprints
> In the winter night.
>
> (245)

Superb full-color photographs add greatly to the appeal of this book. Richard Lewis has edited a fine anthology titled *I Breathe a New Song: Poems of the Eskimo* (170). Edmund Carpenter, an anthropologist, has written a fascinating introduction to this collection in which he explains the beliefs of the Eskimo and their ways of forming poetry. Bold graphic illustrations by Oonark add strength to this collection of nearly one hundred poems. Lewis has also compiled the collection *Out of the Earth I Sing; Poetry and Songs of Primitive Peoples of the World*. While some of these poems and songs have come from Hawaii or the Bushman, many are Eskimo or North American Indian. Illustrated with photographs of primitive art, this is a book which would have much appeal for children.

Songs and chants of primitive African tribes have been compiled by Leonard Doob under the title *A Crocodile Has Me by the Leg: African Poems* (87). These are lively verses that were sung or spoken aloud when a person felt satisfied or frightened. The title comes from "Song of an Unlucky Man":

> Chaff is in my eye,
> A crocodile has me by the leg,
> A goat is in the garden,
> A porcupine is cooking in the pot,
> Meal is drying on the pounding rock,
> The King has summoned me to court,
> And I must go to the funeral of
>   My mother-in-law:
> In short, I am busy.
>
> (87)

Recent years have witnessed a revival of interest in Oriental poetry, particularly haiku. While this form is short, it is usually profound and requires the reader to make connections between two images or thoughts. For this reason it is more

How lovely,
Through the torn paper window
The Milky Way.
—Issa

The nightingales sing
In the echo of the bell
Tolled at evening.
—Ukō

Ezra Jack Keats creates dramatic effects with marblized paper colláge. This was one of the first books of haiku to break with traditional Oriental design.

From *In a Spring Garden*, edited by Richard Lewis, illustrated by Ezra Jack Keats, Illustration, copyright © 1965 by Ezra Jack Keats. Used with permission of The Dial Press. "The nightingales sing" from *The Pepper Pod* by Kenneth Yasuda, published by Alfred A. Knopf, Inc. Used by permission of the author. Haiku by Issa used by permission of the Hokuseido Press, from *Haiku in four volumes*, edited and translated by R.H. Blyth, The Hokuseido Press, Tokyo, Japan.

appropriate for older students. Richard Lewis has produced several exciting collections of haiku. *In a Spring Garden* (171), strikingly illustrated in full color by Ezra Jack Keats, makes an especially fine introduction to this poetry form. *The Moment of Wonder* (173), illustrated with authentic Oriental pictures in black and white, contains poems by both Japanese and Chinese writers. Two other books by Lewis, *The Way of Silence* (20) and *Of This World* (174) are in-depth studies of the poetry and lives of Basho and Issa respectively. Beautiful black-and-white photographs by Helen Buttfield complement and extend the haiku of these famous Japanese poets. Some of the best-loved of Issa's and Basho's haiku have been included in a collection for children titled *Don't Tell the Scarecrow* (148). The softly colored illustrations by Stubis relate these poems to the child's world

today, and at the same time reflect the origin of the poems. Basho and Issa are also represented among the haiku selected and translated by Cassedy and Suetake for their collection, *Birds, Frogs and Moonlight* (52). The Japanese calligraphy and brush and line drawings by Vo-Dinh add to the interest of this book. Jean Merrill and Ronni Solbert have selected haiku by Issa for their collection titled *A Few Flies and I* (147). Issa's reverence for life is reflected in many of these poems. The title is derived from this haiku:

A few flies
And I
Keep house together
In this humble home.
(147)

The delicate gray-wash illustrations are most

appropriate for this perceptive collection. *Cricket Songs* (23) and *More Cricket Songs* (26) are two fine collections of haiku sensitively translated by the poet Harry Behn. The accompanying pictures are chosen from the works of Japanese masters and add much to the Oriental flavor of these books.

In *Seasons of Time* (19) Virginia Baron has edited a book of tanka poetry. Tanka is similar to haiku but slightly longer. *The First Book of Short Verse* (139) by Coralie Howard contains haiku, tanka, cinquain (which is similar to tanka), and many other short arresting poems by such poets as Frost, Sandburg, and others. The introduction on "Why People Write Poetry" and the discussion of various forms of poetry in the postscript would make this an extremely useful book for helping children in the middle grades to write their own poetry.

Children will see that haiku is not just an ancient form of poetry if they can read some of the recent haiku created by modern poets. Such books as *Come Along* (53) by Rebecca Caudill or *Hello, Small Sparrow* (151) by Hannah Johnson are both beautifully illustrated; the first by Ellen Raskin and the second by Tony Chen. Such attractive books will help children see the potential in haiku for today. *The City . . . in Haiku* (255) by Roche uses the traditional form of verse with black-and-white photographs of the city. These poems and photographs point up the rhythm and contrasts that are found in the daily experience of urban life. Ann Atwood has created two modern books of haiku illustrated with exquisite full-color nature photographs that reflect the image of the haiku. Titled *Haiku: The Mood of Earth* (15), and *My Own Rhythm* (16), these books help us to see into the heart of haiku through the eyes of a poet-photographer.

Collections of Poems Written by Children

Creative teachers have always appreciated the writing and art of their own students. They have recognized that age alone does not make a poet, and that some of the creative talents of boys and girls deserve recognition.

Richard Lewis, an elementary-school teacher in New York City, decided to go around the world and make an international collection of children's poems. He collected over 3,000 poems from which he selected some 200 for his book *Miracles* (172). The poems do seem almost mirac-

Children's art work is appropriately used to illustrate a collection of children's poems from all over the world.

From *Miracles.* Copyright © 1966 by Richard Lewis. Reprinted by permission of Simon and Schuster.

ulous in their insight, imagination, and depth of feeling. The children wrote of fear, of "hurting," of death. One 10-year-old from Australia perceptively identified the function of doors in his house:

THE DOORS

The doors in my house
Are used every day
For closing rooms
And locking children away.
      Brian Andrews (172)

Other children described poetry itself. One 11-year-old suggested that a poem "must haunt the heart," while another one said, "Poems are friends," and then added, "Some last." Illustrated with black-and-white drawings by children, this book might well inspire a class or school to produce their own "miracles." Using a different format, Lewis published some twenty children's poems about *The Wind and the Rain* (177). Helen Buttfield's black-and-white photographs add an unusual dimension to this book. *There are Two Lives* (176) is an anthology of poems written by Japanese children and edited by Lewis. These are frank, honest poems from children who have been encouraged to be close observers. Sharing them with other children might encourage this same kind of personal writing.

Another collection which is highly personal and reflective is *The Moon Is Like a Silver Sickle*

(221) edited and translated by Miriam Morton. These poems were written by Russian children between the ages of 5 and 15. The subject matter ranges from a child's delight in a refrigerator to a thoughtful poem on who will be the last soldier to perish for humankind. This poem reminds one of the heartbreaking poetry of the children of the Theresienstadt Concentration Camp. Published under the title . . . *I Never Saw Another Butterfly* (146), these poems and drawings are all that remain of the more than 15,000 children who passed through this concentration camp on their way to death from 1942 to 1944. The poems and pictures are filled with the horror of dirt, disease, and death, yet courage and optimism shine through some of them as in the poem "Homesick":

> . . .
> People walk along the street,
> You see at once on each you meet
> That there's a ghetto here,
> A place of evil and of fear.
> There's little to eat and much to want,
> Where bit by bit, it's horror to live.
> But no one must give up!
> The world turns and times change.
> Yet we all hope the time will come
> When we'll go home again.
> Now I know how dear it is
> And often I remember it.
>
> Anonymous (146)

Here I Am! (18) edited by Virginia Olsen Baron is an anthology of poems written by young people of some U.S. minority groups. These are poems that affirm the pride and dignity, joys and despairs, dreams and sorrows of black, Eskimo, Puerto Rican, Navajo, and Aleut children. Haunting black-and-white drawings echo the message of these poems.

From the ghettos of our cities come outpourings of despair and outrage over the misery of mankind. Nancy Larrick has included many of these poems written by children and young people in her anthology *I Heard a Scream in the Street* (161). "Boys Don't Cry" is one of the poems found in this fine collection:

> And I've lived here all my lousy life
> but I don't cry about it.

> And I've had to fight for dear life
> but I don't cry about it.
> And I haven't seen all there is to see
> Haven't learned all there is to learn
> Haven't been loved like everyone
> should be,
> But,
> but I don't cry about it.
> Only sometimes painfully
> dry, dry tears.
>
> Lydia Martinez (161)
> New York, New York

Young Voices (262) is an excellent collection of some 122 poems that reflect children's concerns with contemporary problems. Collected by Charles Schaefer and Kathleen Mellor, these poems speak of fear, war, loneliness, school, boredom, and city life. All these writings bear witness to the fact that poetry is as frequently born of horror as of happiness.

Younger children's voices are heard in *City Talk* (131), a book of cinquain verse compiled by Lee Bennett Hopkins. Poems and black-and-white photographs celebrate the joys of childhood and the seasons of the city. *Green Is Like a Meadow of Grass* (160) is subtitled "An Anthology of Children's Pleasure in Poetry." Nancy Larrick selected these poems, written by children in response to *Hailstones and Halibut Bones* (228) by O'Neill and *Prayers from the Ark* by Carmen Bernos de Gasztold (119). Children might like to listen to the original sources that served as inspiration for these poems, and then hear what children their own age wrote in response. These can then serve as a springboard for their own writing. The major use of all of the published writing of children is to inspire further compositions by these authors and to encourage others to write.

Picture-book Editions of Single Poems

Traditionally, poetry books have had few illustrations in order to enable the reader to create vivid images on the screen of his imagination. This concept has changed, and today we have such books as the *Oxford Book of Poetry for Children* (37), profusely illustrated with Wildsmith's brilliant pictures. It was inevitable that poetry should also follow the trend to establish single-poem editions by the publishing of many beautifully illustrated single fairy tales or folk songs.

Paul Galdone lead the way by illustrating many books of a single narrative poem. Beginning with Lear's amusing tale of *The Two Old Bachelors* (167), Galdone then illustrated three patriotic poems: *Paul Revere's Ride* (192) by Longfellow, *Barbara Frietchie* (306) by Whittier, and *The Battle of the Kegs* (137) by Hopkinson. The stirring tale of how the colonists were warned by Paul Revere's midnight message is appropriately illustrated by Galdone's vigorous drawings in moonlit blues and blacks. During preparations for the illustrations of this book, Galdone made a special trip to New England in the spring, the time of the ride, and traced Paul Revere's route through the villages. In *The Battle of the Kegs,* he has captured the rollicking good humor of the old Revolutionary ballad that told of the colonists' plan to float kegs of gunpowder down the Delaware River in order to damage the English ships. His illustrations for *Barbara Frietchie* portray the courage of that intrepid old lady who waved the Union flag in defiance of Stonewall Jackson's orders. Oliver Wendell Holmes wrote *The Deacon's Masterpiece or the Wonderful One-Hoss Shay* (129) over a hundred years ago; but unlike the remarkable shay that was built to last a hundred years to a day, and then went to pieces all at once, the original humor of this poem endures. Galdone's amusing illustrations add to children's enjoyment of the poem. By way of contrast, his illustrations for *Three Poems of Edgar Allen Poe* (244) seem quite melodramatic. Perhaps the haunting love ballad of "Annabel Lee," terrifying rhythms of "The Raven," and singing repetition of "The Bells" demand such interpretation. Emotion is more difficult to portray than action, however.

The haunting tale of *The Highwayman* (226) by Alfred Noyes has been interpreted in ghostly lavenders and blood reds by Gilbert Riswold. The terror of this poem is captured in rather frightening pictures.

In *The Charge of the Light Brigade* (290), Tennyson paid tribute to the courageous, but hopeless, charge of the British troops in the Crimean War in 1854. Alice Provensen and Martin Provensen have caught the rigidity, nobility, and futility of this bloody massacre with their handsome, stylized illustrations. The cover of the book is cleverly fashioned after a newspaper report of the tragic event.

The Ballad of the Burglar of Babylon (32) by Elizabeth Bishop is also a modern tragic ballad. It relates the true story of a burglar in Rio de Janeiro who preferred ninety hours of freedom on the hill of Babylon to a ninety-year sentence in jail. Pursued by police and soldiers, the young criminal is shot down in the early morning light. The striking woodcuts of Ann Grifalconi add to the drama of this tragic ballad.

Both boys and girls in the middle grades will like Longfellow's haunting poem, *The Skeleton in Armor* (193), with eerie illustrations by Paul Kennedy. This would be an excellent poem to follow the reading of Polland's *Beorn the Proud* or *Hakon of Rogen's Saga* (see Chapter 7).

There are two illustrated editions of the popular *Casey at the Bat* by Ernest Thayer. Paul Frame (291) interpreted this poem with broad humor in comical, orange-and-black illustrations portraying baseball players of the 1880s. *The First Book Edition of Casey at the Bat* (292) has been illustrated in bold, black-and-white drawings by Leonard Everett Fisher. Sports enthusiasts of all ages thoroughly enjoy both books.

Janina Domanska has cleverly combined five of Lear's limericks into a kind of comic moving picture in the book titled, *Whizz!* (168). As each person of the limerick is described, he starts across a long bridge until the "young lady in blue" knocks down the bridge! Young children will delight in this cumulative nonsense.

One of Edward Lear's longer nonsense poems, *The Scroobious Pip* (169) has been beautifully illustrated with Nancy Burkert's delicate line drawings and full-color paintings. This poem was discovered in a nearly completed state at the time of Lear's death. Ogden Nash supplied the missing lines and phrases for this edition.

Helen Oxenbury received the Kate Greenaway Medal for her illustrations for *The Quangle Wangle's Hat* (166) by Lear. The color and humor of her illustrations, which depict the strange creatures who want to build their home in the Quangle Wangle's hat, complement this very funny poem. Oxenbury has also added to the nonsense of Lewis Carroll with her illustrations for *The Hunting of the Snark* (51). Again, she seems to be at her best when creating such imaginative and

Strong woodcuts by Ann Grifalconi illustrate the modern *The Ballad of the Burglar of Babylon,* the man who preferred death to imprisonment.

Reprinted with the permission of Farrar, Straus & Giroux, Inc., from *The Ballad of the Burglar of Babylon* by Elizabeth Bishop, illustrated by Ann Grifalconi. Pictures Copyright © 1968 by Ann Grifalconi.

weird creatures as the Jubjub bird and the Bandersnatch.

Ellen Raskin used brilliant stylized watercolors to present Christina Rossetti's classic poem *The Goblin Market* (258). This is a long narrative poem of two sisters who have to overcome the temptations of the goblins who offer them luscious but deadly fruits and potions.

Many of Aileen Fisher's long sustained poems have appeared in picture-book format and were discussed in Chapter 3. Lucille Clifton's stories about Everett Anderson (60–61) also belong in this category; as does Byrd B. Schweitzer's *One Small Blue Bead* (263). Doris Lund's *Attic of the Wind* (194) is a long poem that answers a little girl's question about what happens to all the things the wind blows away. Ati Forberg's illustrations vividly portray the treasures that may be found in the attic of the wind. Many children have been inspired by this book to write poems about other "lost" objects that might be found in the wind's attic.

Sharing Poetry with Children

DEVELOPING ENJOYMENT OF POETRY

The Misuse of Poetry in the Classroom

Very young children respond spontaneously to the sensory-motor action of "Ride a Cock Horse" or "Peas porridge hot/Peas porridge cold." They enjoy the damp adventures of poor old Dr. Foster, and they delight in the misfortune of "The Three Blind Mice." Children in the primary grades love to pantomime "Hiding" (7) by Dorothy Aldis or join in the chant of "The Pickety Fence" (197) by David McCord. The young child naturally delights in the sound, the rhythm, the language of poetry.

However, at some time toward the end of the primary grades, children begin to lose interest in poetry. The modern poet, William Jay Smith, comments: "How natural and harmonious it all is at the beginning; and yet what happens along the way later to make poetry to many children the dullest and least enjoyable of literary expressions?"[15] Norvell, in his extensive study of children's reading interests, indicated that boys and girls begin to show a dislike for both juvenile and adult poems between grades three and five.[16] Terry[17] also reported a decreasing interest in poetry as children progressed through the middle grades, with fourth-graders evidencing more interest in poetry than sixth-graders. These findings suggest that rather than develop enjoyment of poetry, many schools may actually destroy children's natural liking for this form of literature. Teachers have probably done more to mitigate against a love of poetry than they have ever done to promote it.

There are several ways in which teachers have alienated children from poetry. Poor selection of poetry is one of the most common mistakes made by both teachers and textbook publishers. The Tom study[18] found that teachers in the middle grades read many more traditional poems than contemporary ones which would be more suited to the modern child's maturity, experiences, and interests. Sentimental poems or poems that are about childhood rather than for children will turn today's young people from poetry very quickly. Poems that are too difficult, too abstract for children to understand will also be rejected.

Several studies have indicated teachers' neglect of poetry. Terry[19] found, for example, that over 75 percent of the teachers in the middle grades admitted reading poetry to their children only once a month or less! Children can hardly be expected to develop a love of poetry when they hear it less than nine times a year! It is also possible to hear too much poetry, particularly at one time. Teachers who read poetry for one hour, or have every child read one poem on a Friday afternoon are contributing to children's dislike of poetry as much as those who simply neglect it.

Another way to create distaste for poetry is by requiring memorization of certain poems, usually selected by the teacher. When everyone has to learn the same poem, it is especially dull. By the time a child has heard a poem thirty times "around the room," he has little desire to hear it again. One teacher was known to keep a record of the number of lines of poetry each child learned. When the class had an "extra" three minutes, a child would be called upon to recite. The recitation would end with the bell, not the end of the poem; the lines were tabulated; the class went to recess. No meaning, no comment, no selection of poem—what an effective way to kill poetry! Some teachers have even assigned a poem for memorization as punishment; the worse the misdeed, the longer the poem! Actually, many children enjoy memorizing favorite poems, provided it is done voluntarily and that they may select the poem. But choosing to commit a certain poem to memory is quite different from being required to do so.

Too detailed analysis of every poem is also detrimental to children's enjoyment of poetry.

[15] Virginia Haviland and William Jay Smith. *Children and Poetry* (Washington, D.C.: Library of Congress, 1969), p. iv.
[16] George W. Norvell. *What Boys and Girls Like to Read* (New York: Silver Burdett Company, 1958), p. 26.
[17] Ann Terry. *Children's Poetry Preferences: A National Survey of the Upper Elementary Grades* (Urbana, Ill.: National Council of Teachers of English, 1974), p. 29.
[18] Chow Loy Tom. "Paul Revere Rides Ahead: Poems Teachers Read to Pupils in the Middle Grades," *The Library Quarterly*, Vol. 43 (January 1973), pp. 27–38.
[19] Terry, p. 53.

An appropriate question or comment to increase meaning is fine; but critical analysis of every word in a poem, every figure of speech, and every iambic verse is lethal to appreciation! Everyone knows that if the point of a joke has to be explained, it is no longer funny. If one has to explain a poem, its beauty and resultant mood will vanish.

Poetry also suffers by being "used" to teach other subjects. One teacher decided to teach children their phonic blends from the delightfully funny poem "My Stomach Growls" (280) by Richard Margolis! A common assignment for practicing handwriting is to copy a poem from the chalkboard. Frequently, children must copy and illustrate a poem as part of their "seatwork." Some children are expected to memorize verses containing safety mottos, health rules, or admonitions on good manners. And while there is nothing wrong with enriching social studies with poetry, it is too bad to limit children's experience to only those poems which record historical events or have a patriotic theme such as "Paul Revere's Ride" or "Oh Captain My Captain!" Yet for many children, these are the only poems which they have heard in the classroom. Seldom, it seems, do teachers in the middle grades simply share poetry with their classes for pure enjoyment.

Promoting a Climate for Enjoyment

Fortunately, not all children have had such unpleasant classroom experiences with poetry. There have always been teachers who love poetry and who share their enthusiasm for poetry with students. These are teachers who make poetry a natural part of the daily program of living and learning. They realize that poetry should not be presented under the pressure of a tight time schedule, but should be enjoyed every day. Children should be able to relax and relish the humor and beauty that the sharing of poetry affords.

Such teachers will provide an abundance of many poetry books and not rely upon a single anthology which may overpower children with its sheer quantity of poems. Students will be encouraged to buy their own copies of some of the fine paperback collections such as the *Arrow Book of Poetry* (202) by Ann McGovern, *Faces and Places* (135) and *Time to Shout* (136) both by Hopkins and Arenstein, or *Reflections on a Gift of Watermelon Pickle* (88) by Dunning and others. Beautiful poetry books such as Ann Atwood's *Haiku: The Mood of Earth* (15) may be displayed in the science center; or Conrad Aiken's book *Cats and Bats and Things with Wings* (6) may be opened to his poem about "The Grasshopper" and placed near a glass bottle containing a live grasshopper. Marci Ridlon's poem about "Hamsters" (252) may be copied by a child and taped to the hamster's cage. Evidence of children's enjoyment of poetry is not limited to one time or one place.

The book center should contain many poetry books, plus a listening area where children may hear poets reading from their own works on tapes or recordings (*see* the section "Poetry and Media"). A bulletin board could be used to display children's favorite poems or some of their own poetry. Many teachers and children have enjoyed setting up displays of real objects and pictures of one predominant color to highlight their favorite poems from *Hailstones and Halibut Bones* (227) by Mary O'Neill.

A brief visit to a classroom, library, or school will reveal whether poetry is "alive and well" in that place, or sadly neglected and dying. A faculty might evaluate their own school by determining where they would place themselves on the continuum presented in the chart for "Developing Enjoyment of Poetry" (*see* p. 372). Teachers might also evaluate their own practices against those described as producing dislike or delight.

Finding Time for Poetry

Teachers who would develop children's delight in poetry will find time to share it with them during some time each day. They know that any time is a good time to read a poem to children, but they will especially want to capitalize on such exciting experiences as the first day of snow, a birthday party, or the arrival of a classmate's new baby brother. Perhaps there has been a fight in the playground and someone is still grumbling and complaining—that might be a good time to share poetry about feelings. The teacher could read Eve Merriam's "Mean Song" (210) or Marci

DEVELOPING ENJOYMENT OF POETRY

From *Dislike* of Poetry	Toward *Delight* in Poetry
Away from selecting only traditional poems	Toward selecting modern contemporary poems
Away from adult selection of "appropriate poems"	Toward beginning with students' interests—nonsense verse, narrative verse, jump-rope rhymes, rock lyrics
Away from teacher neglect and fear of poetry	Toward teachers and children discovering and enjoying poetry together
Away from reading poetry only once a month or less	Toward daily sharing of poetry
Away from study about a poem	Toward experiencing the poem
Away from dissection and analysis	Toward questions that contribute to the meaning and enjoyment of the poem
Away from teacher presentation of poetry from a single anthology	Toward use of many poetry books, records, and cassette tapes of poets reading their own works; student-recorded tapes with appropriate backgrounds of music or sound; slides, filmstrips, and pictures
Away from poetry presented in isolation	Toward poetry related to children's experiences, classroom activities, favorite books, art, music, drama, and so on
Away from required memorization of assigned poems	Toward voluntary memorization of self-selected poems
Away from required writing of poetry	Toward student's selection of the form of poetry as the most appropriate one for his thoughts

Ridlon's poems "Bad Day" (252) or "When Something Happy Happens" (252).

Such teachers will also plan ways to share specific poems. One way to be sure to share a poem with children each day is to relate poetry to prose. One teacher slipped cards of appropriate poems into the book that was going to be read during story hour. After finishing *Evan's Corner* by Elizabeth Hill, for example, the children heard poems about other "special places" as described in "Halfway Down" (213) by A. A. Milne, "Tree House" (265) by Shel Silverstein, and "This Is My Rock" (196) by David McCord. Taped in the back of the teacher's personal copy of *Where Does the Butterfly Go When It Rains* by May Garelick was Langston Hughes' quiet poem "April Rain Song" (202). This is a poem that middle-grade children rejected in the Terry study.[20] However, if presented in the right context and with prose that captures the same mood, children might begin to develop an appreciation for the more descriptive Hughes' poem. Teachers in the middle grades could read Spender's "My Parents Kept Me from Children Who Were Rough" (236) in conjunction with Betsy Byars'

book *The 18th Emergency* or *The Bully of Barkham Street* by Stolz (*see* Chapter 7).

Other subjects in the curriculum can be enriched with poetry. A "science discovery walk" could be preceded or followed by Moffitt's poem "To Look at Anything" (88). Aileen Fisher has written poetic texts for a series of beautifully illustrated books published by Bowmar. Accurate in every scientific detail, these nature books carry such titles as *Animal Houses* (97), *Animal Disguises* (96), *Tail Twisters* (109), *Filling the Bill* (100), and others. A math lesson might be introduced with Carl Sandburg's "Arithmetic" (88). Many poems may enhance the social studies, including those found in the Benéts' *A Book of Americans* (29) and Eve Merriam's *Independent Voices* (207) and *I Am a Man: Ode to Martin Luther King, Jr.* (206). Myth, art, and poetry are nicely linked together in the poem by William Carlos Williams, "Landscape with the Fall of Icarus" (282), in which the poet comments on the Brueghel painting that depicts the story of Icarus. Janet Gaylord Moore relates art and poetry in her magnificent book for older students titled *The Many Ways of Seeing* (215). Physical education is well served by two excellent poetry books, *Sprints and Distances* (220) by Lillian Morrison and *Hosannah the Home Run* (112) by

[20]Terry, p. 35.

Alice Fleming. Older children will enjoy the superb tension captured by Hoey's basketball poem, "Foul Shot" (88). Every taut move of the player is felt as he prepares to make the free throw that can win the game. "Base Stealer" (88) by Robert Francis is another poem that combines sports with poetry. Almost any poetry book will have poems that will enrich the language arts or music. However, teachers in the middle grades will find Mary O'Neill's book *Words, Words, Words* (232) particularly meaningful.

Finding the right poem for the right moment requires preparation and planning. Many teachers make their own collection of poems either on cards or in a notebook. These can be categorized in ways that teachers find the most appropriate for their own styles of teaching. A particularly useful reference that should be in every elementary-school library is the Brewtons' *Index to Children's Poetry*. The book lists poems by subject, author, first line, and title. It currently has three supplements, the most recent one titled *Index to Poetry for Children and Young People*, and indexes some 117 collections of poetry including many discussed in this chapter. Assuming a group were studying the ocean and its future exploration, this reference lists some forty-five titles of poems under the entry "sea," while four titles about dinosaurs are in the latest supplement. *The Subject Index to Poetry for Children and Young People*, edited by Sell and others and published by the American Library Association, is not as comprehensive or as up-to-date as the Brewton volumes, but it is still useful.

Children may want to make their own personal collections of poetry. Some classes set up their own collections, filing and categorizing their favorite poems in a card file or notebook. Children may enjoy making "Poetry Cycles"— collecting poems on particular subjects such

Children's interest in poetry may be aroused by the use of real objects in a simple table display.

as "Secret Places," "Dinosaurs," or "Cats." Children in the middle grades can be taught how to use a poetry index to facilitate making such collections. Other children may prefer to collect the poems of a favorite poet. Time needs to be provided for those children who want to make a collection. After they are completed, children should have the opportunity to share them with the class.

Presenting Poetry to Children

Poetry was meant to be read aloud. Some children do not have the skill in reading or the background of experience to read poetry effectively; and so teachers will want to read to them. Some poems need little or no introduction; others are more appreciated if children have some clue about what is to follow. Occasionally, they like to know the circumstances that surrounded the writing of a poem; knowing another poem by the same author may help build background.

Poetry should be read in a natural voice with emphasis placed upon the meaning of the poem rather than the rhyme. In this way the singsong effect that is characteristic of most children's reading of poetry is avoided. Generally, the appropriate pace for reading poetry is slower than for reading prose. It is usually recommended that a poem be read aloud a second time, perhaps to refresh children's memories, to clarify a point, or to savor a particular image. Most poetry, especially good poetry, is so concentrated and compact that few people can grasp its meaning in one exposure. Following the reading of a poem, discussion should be allowed to flow. In certain instances discussion is unnecessary or superfluous. Spontaneous chuckles may follow the reading of Mary Austin's "Grizzly Bear" (92)—nothing more is needed. Sometimes a moment of silence is the greatest applause. It is valuable for the teacher to record children's responses to poetry in order to guide future selections.

Poetry and Media

There are a growing number of records and tapes of poetry readings for children. Some of them provide children with the opportunity to hear live poets reading their own works. One particularly fine record, *Poetry Parade,* edited by Nancy Larrick, features readings by Aileen Fisher, Harry Behn, David McCord, and Karla Kuskin. In the teacher's guide that comes with the album, Larrick gives suggestions for "Using Poetry with Children." She wisely warns against playing an entire side of a record at one time, and gives hints for ways to use particular poems. John Ciardi reads his poetry for young people on two records produced by Spoken Arts. These include *You Read to Me, I'll Read to You,* in which the poet reads to his own children and they read back to him, and *You Know Who: John J. Plenty and Fiddler Dan and Other Poems.* These records are as popular with children as Ciardi's well-liked poetry. Eve Merriam may be heard reading several of her poems for children on a record titled *To Catch a Little Rhyme.* Richard Lewis selected the poems for a two-volume record set titled *A Gathering of Great Poetry for Children.* Some of these poems are read by the poets themselves—Carl Sandburg, Robert Frost, and T. S. Eliot; while others are read by actors Julie Harris, Cyril Ritchard, and David Wayne.

Book and record combinations have been made available by Scholastic Book Services. These include *Favorite Rhymes from a Rocket in My Pocket* by Carl Withers, which features nursery rhymes, riddles, and tongue twisters that delight children. A rhythmical jazz score accompanies the traditional counting rhyme, *Over in the Meadow.* Ezra Jack Keats has illustrated this favorite rhyme with sparkling collage designs. Excerpts from the *Arrow Book of Poetry* by Ann McGovern and *Faces and Places* by Lee Bennett Hopkins and Misha Arenstein have been packaged with paperback editions of these anthologies, and are available for older boys and girls. Male and female voices lend variety to these records, but, again, they should not be played in their entirety. Selections from the very popular *Reflections on a Gift of Watermelon Pickle* by Dunning and others have also been recorded.

Records and tapes allow children to hear live poets; they also provide an opportunity for them to hear different interpretations of poems; and they give children a chance to replay a poem as often as they wish. Recordings may supplement the teacher's presentation, but they should never substitute for it. There is no substitute for a teacher reading and enthusiastically sharing poetry with a class.

Some teachers and children have enjoyed selecting appropriate background music for their own readings of poetry. This is not an easy task, for it requires knowledge of music, poetry, and proper timing in the presentation. However, it does add a rich dimension to the reading, and requires the student to think about the meaning and rhythm of a poem. Some particularly happy combinations are "Silver" (13) read to Debussy's "Clair De Lune"; "Little Brand New Baby" (236) accompanied by the music of "Countdown at 6" from the Vanguard Record *In Sounds from Way Out;* and Eve Merriam's "Ping Pong" (205) to the Shostekovich "Polka" in *Listen, Move and Dance,* Vol. II, produced by Capitol Records. The challenge, of course, is to find your own combinations; tape them (it requires practice!); and then present them to the class. Children will listen with enthusiasm, but the person who has prepared the tape has had the richest experience.

Some packaged kits including slides, filmstrips, or flat pictures are now available along with records or tapes. Some of these provide lesson plans for teaching the poetry along with tapes of sounds, scent-impregnated cards, recommendations for a "tasting experience," or Braille cards for touch and other sensory-awareness materials. For the cost of these kits teachers would do better to develop their own materials, which would be more appropriate for the children in their classes. Then they can spend the extra money on more poetry books and records.

There is some argument as to the value of visual materials in the presentation of poetry. While slides, filmstrips, or lovely large flat pictures may capture children's interests, they may also prevent the child from responding to the image-making quality of the poem. Too frequently filmstrips of poetry simply provide a literal picture showing the objects or actions of the poem, but not conveying its mood or images. This criticism may be directed at the six sound filmstrips *Pick a Peck o' Poems* produced by the Miller-Brody Company. Lee Bennett Hopkins carefully selected the poems in this series, but the illustrations do not begin to capture the imaginative quality of the poems. Caedmon's program, *What Is Poetry?,* features imaginative pictures which only suggest and complement the content of the poems. These filmstrips are packaged with ten records of poetry read with distinction by Claire Bloom. They are for more mature students than the ones using *Pick a Peck o' Poems.* Lyceum Productions have published *Haiku: The Hidden Glimmering* based on Ann Atwood's book, *My Own Rhythm* (16). Stunning photography and lyrical narration are combined in a portrayal of visual haiku.

Weston Woods Studio has produced a film of cinematic haiku titled *The Day Is Two Feet Long.* One visual image flows into another in this very brief film which attempts to create the mood of haiku. Using only natural sounds and subtle color photography, the eight-minute film does capture the feeling of this poetry form. The film is in sharp contrast to the psychedelic presentation of six color poems in a film made from *Hailstones and Halibut Bones* (228) by Mary O'Neill. While some have found this film to be very stimulating, others were disappointed that the parts of the poems related to the feelings created by different colors had been deleted, while still others maintained that the film destroyed the visual images of nature that the poems had created in their minds. If the film is used *after* the poems have been read, children will have the opportunity to imagine their own "thought-pictures." These can then be compared with those created by the film artist.

Music and original art work form the background for the dramatic readings of seven films in the *Living Poetry* series by McGraw-Hill. While some of the films—such as those that feature the work of Whitman, Tennyson, and Browning—are for young people, children in the middle grades enjoy those depicting *The Deacon's Masterpiece, Paul Revere's Ride, Casey at the Bat, Hiawatha's Childhood,* and the poems of Lewis Carroll.

Some of these visual materials may inspire teachers or children to make their own slides, films, or taped recordings of sound effects for particular poems. This would appear to have far greater educational value for today's children than a more passive viewing of others' visual interpretations of their favorite poetry.

INVOLVING CHILDREN IN POETRY

Children Interpret Poetry

Children respond more readily to poetry when they can find a unique way to interpret it or to create their own. Finding sound effects for a poem, interpreting a poem in an art activity, creating body movements for poetry, or dramatizing it are all ways to make a poem a memorable experience.

Two 8-year-olds decided to present their favorite poems in a new and different way. They tape-recorded Patricia Hubbell's poem about "Lemons" (140) and invited a small group of children to listen to it while they gave each of them a slice of lemon to suck! Their teacher shared Eve Merriam's "A Matter of Taste" (210) with the class, and then they discussed what they thought was the sweetest taste, the bitterest, the most soothing. This led to some children writing their own poems about taste.

A student-teacher took two 12-year-old boys out to a freeway near their school. Standing on one of the roads that bridged the freeway, they taped the rush and roar of the traffic below. Then they played their tapes to the rest of the class and asked them to identify the sound. This was easily done, of course. However, the boys then asked the class to pretend that they were living in the fifteenth century and to imagine what kinds of noises might be heard. Since a group of boys had been studying about knights and armour, some of their guesses were quite appropriate. The student-teacher then read the group the poem "Central Park Tourney" (88) by Mildred Weston, and they saw how a metaphor in one century could be superimposed upon another one. One of the boys who did the taping also illustrated this poem with two pictures. The top one showed a medieval tourney with two knights on their horses jousting with their long spears; while the bottom picture depicted long sleek cars with their headlights piercing the darkness. Certainly, these activities greatly enriched these children's interpretations of "Central Park Tourney."

Another group of youngsters in a second grade enjoyed the poems in *Bronzeville Boys and Girls* (47). They constructed a large tenement building out of a cardboard box and put the names of the children in the poems under the windows where they imagined the children lived. Then, using a flashlight, a boy lit each window as one of his classmates read the poem about the child who might have lived there. This activity personalized these poems for the group and made them feel that they really knew "Charles," "Vern," and "Gertrude."

Increasingly, primary-grade teachers are seeing the importance of providing movement activities to increase children's total body management. While much movement is of the functional type, where children explore what their bodies can do, some movement is expressive, where children act out an idea or feeling. Poetry lends itself to this type of movement. A favorite poem for this kind of activity is "Jump or Jiggle" (13) by Evelyn Beyer, which describes how various creatures walk. "Tiptoe" by Karla Kuskin (13), "Sliding" (13) by Myra Cohn Livingston, and "Follow the Leader" (28) by Harry Behn are excellent to use in promoting appropriate movements; and children thoroughly enjoy doing them.

Some poems lend themselves well to dramatization, particularly ballads or those poems containing dialogue. Primary-grade teachers might want to try "Hiding" (7) by Dorothy Aldis, or "Puppy and I" (213), or "The King's Breakfast" (213) by A. A. Milne. Older children would enjoy doing "Questions" (252) by Marci Ridlon, "Overheard on a Saltmarsh" (88), or the hearty and amusing ballad "Get Up and Bar the Door" (37).

There is no reason to believe that a child must *do* something with every poem he reads. Surely that could destroy any interest in poetry. However, the occasional dramatization or pantomiming of a poem; the casual suggestion that this would be a good poem to illustrate or find sound effects for might stimulate a child's creativity and further his interest in poetry. The creative teacher will be able to see the potential in a poem and in the children being taught.

Writing Poetry

Children respond more enthusiastically to poetry once they have had an opportunity to create some of their own. Ideally, one would hope that if children had rich and meaningful experiences with poetry, they would choose to use this form as the best way of expressing certain kinds of thoughts and feelings. However, we know that many children do not have a rich background of experience with poetry and therefore must be given some encouragement to write it.

One way of stimulating children's writing of poetry is to read many of the published poetic works of other children, such as the poems in *Miracles* (172) edited by Lewis or *The Voice of the Children* (154) collected by June Jordan and Terri Bush. Each poem may be introduced or ended by giving the name of the poet, the age, and, in the case of *Miracles,* the nationality. Eventually children will realize that if a 9-year-old in Australia can write poetry or if 13- and 14-year-olds from the ghetto can do so, then, perhaps, they can too.

Some children feel more secure with this new medium if they can follow a model. After hearing Mary O'Neill's poems about color in *Hailstones and Halibut Bones* (228), children are frequently inspired to write their own feelings or thoughts about a particular color. O'Neill's thirteen poems give new dimensions of meaning to various colors by describing them in terms of objects, feelings, taste, and sound. Children quickly discover the pattern to the poems, and then eagerly write their own responses to color. One blind child described "Blue" in this way:

BLUE

Blue is the sky high over your head.
Blue is the blanket that's on a bed.
It's blueberry pie and juicy sweet plums.
It's the ink with which you write your sums.
It's water lapping the distant shore.
It's fresh new paint on the front door.
The air in spring is the smell of blue.
What scent brings forth this color to you?
Anchors Aweigh is a blue song to me,
I think of a sailor's uniform you see.
It's the loyalty I owe a friend,
Steadfast and true to the very end.[21]

After hearing Rumer Godden's translation of De Gasztold's *Prayers from the Ark* (119), a group of 8-, 9-, and 10-year-olds composed prayers for other animals:

PRAYER OF THE RAT

Dear God,
Why am I so ugly?
How come people must
scream when I'm around?
Why do I have to live in
a dirty leftover spot?
What reason did you have
To make me so hated?
I'm just a little different than the pretty white
mouse
Who lives in luxury,
Why then, should he be
Cared for and not I?
I do not understand
Do I have to be the one
To carry germs and make
Children dislike picking me up?
Grease and grime and hate.
Undernourishment. That's what
My life adds up to.
Dear Lord, Why???
Amen

Barbara Hammer, age 10

God, I am but a wiggling worm.
Who sees beauty in me?
I am brown and squishy,
and they feed me to the fish.
Is it because of *that;* they say I have no beauty?
They laugh and scream and run away.
I ask nothing of you
but that you consider my humble plea.
Dress me in riches!
Feed me apples!
So that people will not say "worm holes" in disgust
or fear that I might still be there.
I am just a worm,
your creation to plow the earth
So why do I bother?

Lisa Schiltz, age 10
Martin Luther King, Jr., Lab School,
Evanston, Ill.,
Barbara Friedberg, Teacher

[21]Mary Joyce Pritchard. *Elementary English,* Vol. 40 (May 1963), p. 543.

Nancy Larrick published children's poems that were inspired by *Hailstones and Halibut Bones* and

Prayers from the Ark in a small anthology titled *Green Is Like a Meadow of Grass* (160). Other poems in this book grew out of children's experimentation with seashells, singing nursery rhymes, and folk songs. In an afterword Larrick talks about the process of getting children to create their own poems, warning against emphasizing rhyme:

> At no time did we suggest use of rhyme. In fact, we discouraged attempts at rhyming lines because at this stage rhyme seems to force a child into goosestep thinking.[22]

Another book that suggests a theme and a kind of prose-poetry structure to children is *The Tiniest Sound* (89) by Mel Evans. Children enjoy recording their thoughts about the tiniest sound they ever heard. One 9-year-old in the same class that wrote their "Prayers from the Ark," chose to write her own book about "The Tiniest Sounds." These included such creative ideas as the tiniest sound is a slow wink, reading to yourself, or an ant sneeze!

One child's poem reflected her response to prose. Delighted by the book that her teacher was reading to the class. *Hurry Home Candy* by Meindert de Jong, this 9-year-old chose to put her thoughts into poetic form:

THE LOST DOG

On a cold chilly night
A little dog wandering
    with a wounded leg.
A soft gentle voice
Rang out of the night
Hurry Home Candy
Candy Come Home
A platter of meat
    at the doorstep
A big house all of his own
The lonely lost dog was home!

Kelly Wood
Upper Arlington Public Schools, Ohio,
                    Susan Lee, Teacher

Different forms of poetry may offer poetic structures to children and serve as models for creative poetry writing. Haiku frequently releases children from the problem of rhyme and focuses on the idea of the poem. However, this form of poetry has been overused with students too immature to understand the beauty of its concise thought and high level of abstraction. Frequently, the writer must imply a relationship between two disparate ideas, events, or scenes. These events must have some relationship to nature and take place at the present moment. To make matters even more complex, all these rules must be followed within a pattern of seventeen syllables, although an occasional deviation is allowed in English haiku. Obviously, haiku is not simple to write. Only when children are ready for the formal discipline imposed by haiku should they try it. Some middle-graders are challenged by it; others are only confused. Certainly, primary-grade children who are still at the cognitive level of concrete operations should not be asked to try anything so abstract and foreign to their way of thinking. The examples below illustrate two 12-year-olds' success in writing haiku:

> The cabin is small
> in the vast whiteness. Only
> the smoke reveals it.
>
>   Carol Bartlett

> The leaves on a tree
> Rustle, impatient, restless,
> Waiting to fall off.
>
>   Patti Krog
>   Boulder Public Schools, Colorado,
>   Allaire Stuart, Teacher

Some teachers have also had success in teaching children to write cinquain, which follows the formula of a five-line unrhymed stanza containing twenty-two syllables in a two, four, six, eight, two pattern. A variant of the form of cinquain emphasizes words, not syllables, and is easier for children to write. Cinquain consists of five lines in which a one-word title forms the first line. Two words describe the title in the second line, while the third line of three words expresses an action. The fourth line contains four words expressing a feeling. The last line is again one word, a synonym for the title. In the following cinquains one child expresses feelings for his small village, while another shows his consuming interest in racing cars:

[22]Nancy Larrick, ed. *Green Is Like a Meadow of Grass* (Champaign, Ill.: Garrard Publishing House, 1968), p. 63.

Harrisburg
Sleepy village
Busy and growing
Nice place to be—
Home.

Jerry Harris, age 12
Harrisburg Public Schools, Ohio,
        Joann Mason, Teacher

Tires
Black devils
Fast take-off
Clouds of blue smoke
Slicks.

John Calladine, age 13
Columbus Public Schools, Ohio,
        Art Prowant, Teacher

Other forms of poetry that have served as models are senryu—similar to haiku but not necessarily related to nature—tanka, and sijo. Lee Bennett Hopkins gives a description of each of these Oriental forms in his book *Pass the Poetry Please.* Kenneth Koch's *Wishes, Lies, and Dreams* also suggests subjects and forms that may inspire children to write poetry.

The danger in using any highly structured form of poetry with children is that we may just be substituting syllable-counting for versifying. Children can become too concerned with the mechanics of poetry, manipulating words not thoughts. Wallace Stevens always referred to a poem as the poem of the idea within the poem of the words. As teachers begin to help children in their writing of poetry, they will want to focus first upon the meaning of the poem, then the form. If following a model frees children from overemphasis upon rhyme and allows them to concentrate on meaning, then it will have served its purpose. Primarily, we want children to experience success in writing poetry that honestly reflects their thoughts and feelings. Our goal is not to create poets but young people who enjoy and appreciate poetry. Writing poetry is one way to promote this appreciation.

Choral Reading

The reading and sharing of poetry through choral speaking is another way to foster interest in poetry. Choral speaking or reading is the interpretation of poetry by several voices speaking as one. At first, young children *speak* it as they join in the refrains. Middle-grade children may prefer to *read* their poems. They are not always read in unison; in fact, this is one of the most difficult ways to present a poem. Four types of choral speaking are particularly suited for use in the elementary school. In the first, the "refrain" type, one person (teacher or child) reads the narrative and the rest of the class joins in the refrain. Another way, called antiphonal, is to divide the class into two groups. For example, when reading Rose Fyleman's poem, "Shop Windows" (13), boys may read the lines that tell what men like, and girls may read of women's preferences. The whole group can then join in on the last part that tells of a child's interest in a pet-shop window displaying puppy dogs. An effective approach with young children is the "line-a-child" arrangement, where different children say, or read, individual lines, with the class joining in unison at the beginning or end of the poem. "One, Two, Buckle My Shoe" is a good rhyme to introduce this type of choral reading. The dialogue of David McCord's "At the Garden Gate" (197) lends itself to this approach for children in the middle grades. A more difficult and formal version of this method is part speaking. Groups are divided according to the sound of their voices into high, middle, and low parts. The poem is then interpreted much as a song might be sung in parts. This is usually done with mature groups and is the method utilized by verse-speaking choirs. Another difficult method is to have children say the whole poem in unison, giving just one interpretation.

Many variations to these approaches will be used by creative teachers and children. A certain sound that complements both rhythm and the meaning of the poem may be an accompaniment; for example, "clickety clack" from the sound of Tippett's "Trains" (121). One group may repeat this phrase as another group says the words of the poem. Another poem that provides an interesting sound is "What the Gray Cat Sings" (223) by Guiterman. Alternate groups or solo voices could say the verses with the entire class joining in the cat's weaving song—"Pr-rrum, pr-rrum, thr-ree, thr-reads, in the thr-rum, Pr-rrum!"

The values of choral reading are many. Children derive enjoyment from learning to respond as a group to the rhythm and melody of the poem. They learn much about the interpretation of poetry as they help plan various ways to read the poem. Shy children forget their fears when participating with the group, and all children learn to develop cooperation as they work together with a leader to present a poem. It is important to remember that the process of choral reading is much more important than the final product. Teachers must work for the enjoyment of poetry, not perfection of performance. Too frequently choral reading becomes a "stunt" or a quick way to entertain a P.T.A. group. If teach-

ers and children are pressured for a "production," interpretation of poetry will be exploited for unnatural ends.

Boys and girls should have many opportunities to share poetry in interesting and meaningful situations, if they are to develop appreciation for the deep satisfactions that poetry brings. Appreciation for poetry develops slowly. It is the result of long and loving experience with poetry over a period of years. Children who are fortunate enough to have developed a love of poetry will always be the richer for it.

SUGGESTED LEARNING EXPERIENCES

1. Begin a poetry collection for future use with children. Make your own filing system. What categories will you include? Indicate possible uses for some poems, possible connections with prose, ways to interpret poems.
2. Make a study of one poet. How would you characterize his work both as to style and usual content? What can you find out about his background? How are these experiences reflected in his poetry?
3. Make a cycle of poems about one particular subject—for example, houses, secret places, the city, loneliness. Share these with the class.
4. Bring your favorite children's poem to present to the class or to tape record. Invite class members to evaluate both your selection and presentation.
5. Select three different kinds of poems and read them to a group of children. Record their responses. What poems had the greatest appeal? Why?
6. Select one or two poems that contain figurative language. Share them with children at different developmental stages. When do children appear to understand the metaphors being used?
7. Help children to interpret a poem in several media—for example, tape record an appropriate sound background for their presentation, find or make appropriate slides, set the poem to music, and so on.
8. Compare two general anthologies of poetry, using criteria suggested in the text.
9. Select several poems that you think would lend themselves to choral reading. Work with a group of children or classmates in planning ways to present one of these poems. If possible, tape record these interpretations.
10. Make a survey of the teachers in an elementary school to see how often they read poetry to their students, what their favorite poems are, what their favorite sources for poetry are. Make a visual presentation of your results.
11. Listen to some recordings of poetry read by authors and by interpreters. Contrast the presentations and appropriateness of the records for classroom use. Share these with children. Which ones do they prefer?
12. Try writing some poetry yourself. You may want to use some experimental verse forms, such as concrete poetry, found poetry, or some Oriental forms.

RELATED READINGS

1. Arnstein, Flora J. *Poetry and the Child.* New York: Dover Publications, 1970.
    Originally published under the title *Poetry in the Elementary Classroom,* this is an account of one teacher's techniques in encouraging children to create poetry. Many of the children's original poems are included and might inspire other children to try writing poetry. Arnstein's discussion of poetry will help an adult to recognize many of the qualities of fine poetry.

2. Boyd, Gertrude A. *Teaching in the Elementary School.* Columbus, Ohio: Charles E. Merrill Co., 1973.

This paperback presents many practical ways for the teacher to incorporate poetry into the elementary curriculum. It includes a good listing of films, filmstrips, tapes, and recordings, plus a selected bibliography of poetry books.

3. Chukovsky, Kornei, translated and edited by Miriam Morton. *From Two to Five.* Berkeley, Calif.: University of California Press, 1963.

A well-known Russian poet, Chukovsky, maintains that poetry is the natural language of little children. He emphasizes their delight in the sound of poetry and in nonsense verse.

4. Hopkins, Lee Bennett. *Pass the Poetry, Please.* New York: Citation Press, 1972.

This paperback book provides a wealth of ideas for making poetry come alive in a classroom. It includes suggestions for sparking children to write poetry, plus discussions of contemporary poetry for children. Many excellent references are cited.

5. Koch, Kenneth. *Wishes, Lies, and Dreams: Teaching Children to Write Poetry.* New York: Chelsea House, 1970.

Koch describes the success that he had in teaching children from grades one through six to write poetry in P. S. 61 on New York's Lower East Side. The author also discusses many of the poetry ideas, forms, and subjects that inspired children to try writing poetry.

6. Larrick, Nancy, ed. *Somebody Turned on a Tap in These Kids: Poetry and Young People Today.* New York: Delacorte, 1971.

Directed to teachers and parents, this book includes essays by such poets as Myra Cohn Livingston, June Jordan, Karla Kuskin, and Eve Merriam. The general theme of the talks, first presented at the Poetry Festival sponsored by Lehigh University in 1969, is that young people hunger for and respond positively to poetry that is meaningful to them.

7. Livingston, Myra Cohn. *When You Are Alone/It Keeps You Capone: An Approach to Creative Writing.* New York: Atheneum, 1973.

A well-known children's poet describes her joy and successes, despair and failures in teaching children to write poetry. Delightfully written, this book would help teachers develop a poetry-writing program that produces honest feelings and quality writing.

8. Painter, Helen W. *Poetry and Children.* Newark, Del.: International Reading Association, 1970.

A useful paperbound book, this is a general guide to the use of poetry in the classroom. The author provides many poems and gives suggestions and examples of how they can be incorporated into the curriculum.

9. Perrine, Laurence. *Sound and Sense, An Introduction to Poetry,* 3rd ed. New York: Harcourt Brace Jovanovich, 1969.

A college text for the serious student of poetry, the separate chapters introduce the student to elements of poetry, putting the emphasis on *how* and *why.* It is available in paperback.

10. Witucke, Virginia. *Poetry in the Elementary School.* Dubuque, Iowa: William C. Brown Co., 1970.

Part of the literature series written under the editorship of Pose Lamb, this paperback presents a balanced overview of a poetry program in the elementary school.

RECOMMENDED REFERENCES

1. Adams, Adrienne, compiler and illustrator. *Poetry of Earth.* Scribner, 1972.
2. Adoff, Arnold, ed. *Black Out Loud: An Anthology of Modern Poems by Black Americans,* illustrated by Alvin Hollingsworth. Macmillan, 1970.
3. ———, ed. *City in All Directions,* illustrated by Donald Carrick. Macmillan, 1969.
4. ———, ed. *I Am the Darker Brother: An Anthology of Modern Poems by Black Americans.* Macmillan, 1970.
5. ———, ed. *My Black Me.* Dutton, 1974.

6. Aiken, Conrad. *Cats and Bats and Things with Wings*, illustrated by Milton Glaser. Atheneum, 1965.

7. Aldis, Dorothy. *All Together*, illustrated by Marjorie Flack, Margaret Frieman, and Helen D. Jameson. Putnam, 1925.

8. ———. *Favorite Poems of Dorothy Aldis*. Putnam, 1970.

9. ———. *Hello Day*, illustrated by Susan Elson. Putnam, 1959.

10. ———. *Quick as a Wink*, illustrated by Peggy Westphal. Putnam, 1960.

11. ———. *The Secret Place and Other Poems*, illustrated by Olivia H. H. Cole. Scholastic, 1968.

12. Allen, Marie Louise. *A Pocketful of Poems*, illustrated by Sheila Greenwald. Harper & Row, 1957.

13. Arbuthnot, May Hill, and Shelton L. Root, Jr., eds. *Time for Poetry*, 3rd general ed., illustrated by Arthur Paul. Scott, Foresman, 1968.

14. Association for Childhood Education, Literature Committee. *Sung under the Silver Umbrella*, illustrated by Dorothy Lathrop. Macmillan, 1936.

15. Atwood, Ann. *Haiku: The Mood of Earth*. Scribner, 1971.

16. ———. *My Own Rhythm*. Scribner, 1973.

17. Austin, Mary. *The Children Sing in the Far West*. Houghton Mifflin, 1928.

18. Baron, Virginia Olsen, ed. *Here I Am! An Anthology of Poems Written by Young People in Some of America's Minority Groups*, illustrated by Emily McCully. Dutton, 1969.

19. ———. ed. *The Seasons of Time*, illustrated by Yashuhide Kobashi. Dial, 1968.

20. Basho. *The Way of Silence: The Prose and Poetry of Basho*, edited by Richard Lewis, illustrated by H. Buttfield. Dial, 1970.

21. Behn, Harry. *All Kinds of Time*. Harcourt Brace Jovanovich, 1950.

22. ———. *Chrysalis: Concerning Children and Poetry*. Harcourt Brace Jovanovich, 1968.

23. ———, translator. *Cricket Songs*. Harcourt Brace Jovanovich, 1964.

24. ———. *The Golden Hive*. Harcourt Brace Jovanovich, 1966.

25. ———. *The Little Hill*. Harcourt Brace Jovanovich, 1949.

26. ———, translator. *More Cricket Songs: Japanese Haiku*. Harcourt Brace Jovanovich, 1971.

27. ———. *Windy Morning*. Harcourt Brace Jovanovich, 1953.

28. ———. *The Wizard in the Well*. Harcourt Brace Jovanovich, 1956.

29. Benét, Rosemary, and Stephen Vincent Benét. *A Book of Americans*, illustrated by Charles Child. Holt, Rinehart and Winston, 1933.

30. Benét, Stephen Vincent. *The Ballad of William Sycamore (1790–1871)*, illustrated by Brinton Turkle. Little, Brown, 1972.

31. Bierhorst, John, ed. *In the Trail of the Wind: American Indian Poems and Ritual Orations*. Farrar, Straus, 1971.

32. Bishop, Elizabeth. *The Ballad of the Burglar of Babylon*, illustrated by Ann Grifalconi. Farrar, Straus, 1968.

33. Bissett, Donald J., ed. *Poems and Verses about Animals*. Chandler, 1967.

34. ———, ed. *Poems and Verses about the City*. Chandler, 1968.

35. ———, ed. *Poems and Verses to Begin On*. Chandler, 1967.

36. Blake, William. *Songs of Innocence*, music and illustrations by Ellen Raskin. Doubleday, 1966 (1789).

37. Blishen, Edward, compiler. *Oxford Book of Poetry for Children*, illustrated by Brian Wildsmith. F. Watts, 1963.

38. Bogan, Louise, and William Jay Smith, compilers. *The Golden Journey: Poems for Young People*, illustrated by Fritz Kredel. Reilly & Lee, 1965.

39. Brewton, Sara, and John E. Brewton, compilers. *Birthday Candles Burning Bright*, illustrated by Vera Bock. Macmillan, 1960.

40. ———, compilers. *Bridled with Rainbows*, illustrated by Vera Bock. Macmillan, 1949.

41. ———, compilers. *Christmas Bells Are Ringing*, illustrated by Decie Merwin. Macmillan, 1951.

42. ———, compilers. *Gaily We Parade*, illustrated by Robert Lawson. Macmillan, 1940.

43. ———, compilers. *Laughable Limericks*, illustrated by Ingrid Fetz. Crowell, 1965.

44. ———, compilers. *Shrieks at Midnight: Macabre Poems, Eerie and Humorous,* illustrated by Ellen Raskin. Crowell, 1969.

45. ———, compilers. *Sing a Song of Seasons,* illustrated by Vera Bock. Macmillan, 1955.

46. ———, compilers. *Under the Tent of the Sky,* illustrated by Robert Lawson. Macmillan, 1937.

47. Brooks, Gwendolyn. *Bronzeville Boys and Girls,* illustrated by Ronni Solbert. Harper & Row, 1965.

48. Brown, Beatrice. *Jonathan Bing and Other Verses.* Oxford, 1936.

49. Browning, Robert. *The Pied Piper of Hamelin,* illustrated by Lieselotte Schwarz. Scroll Press, 1970.

50. Carroll, Lewis. *Alice's Adventures in Wonderland and Through the Looking-Glass,* illustrated by John Tenniel. Macmillan, 1956 (1865).

51. ———. *The Hunting of the Snark,* illustrated by Helen Oxenbury. F. Watts, 1971.

52. Cassedy, Sylvia, and Kunihiro Suetake. *Birds, Frogs and Moonlight,* illustrated by Vo-Dinh. Doubleday, 1967.

53. Caudill, Rebecca. *Come Along,* illustrated by Ellen Raskin. Holt, Rinehart and Winston, 1969.

54. Ciardi, John. *I Met a Man,* illustrated by Robert Osborn. Houghton Mifflin, 1961.

55. ———. *The Man Who Sang the Sillies,* illustrated by Edward Gorey. Lippincott, 1961.

56. ———. *The Monster Den,* illustrated by Edward Gorey. Lippincott, 1966.

57. ———. *The Reason for the Pelican,* illustrated by Madeleine Gekiere. Lippincott, 1959.

58. ———. *You Know Who,* illustrated by Edward Gorey. Lippincott, 1964.

59. ———. *You Read to Me, I'll Read to You,* illustrated by Edward Gorey. Lippincott, 1962.

60. Clifton, Lucille. *Everett Anderson's Christmas Coming,* illustrated by Evaline Ness. Holt, Rinehart and Winston, 1972.

61. ———. *Some of the Days of Everett Anderson,* illustrated by Evaline Ness. Holt, Rinehart and Winston, 1970.

62. Clymer, Eleanor, compiler. *Arrow Book of Funny Poems,* illustrated by Doug Anderson. Scholastic, 1961.

63. Coatsworth, Elizabeth. *Poems,* illustrated by Vee Guthrie. Macmillan, 1958.

64. ———. *The Sparrow Bush,* illustrated by Stefan Martin. Norton, 1966.

65. ———. *Summer Green,* illustrated by Nora Unwin. Macmillan, 1948.

66. Cole, William, compiler. *Beastly Boys and Ghastly Girls,* illustrated by Tomi Ungerer. World, 1964.

67. ———, compiler. *The Birds and the Beasts Were There,* illustrated by Helen Siegl. World, 1963.

68. ———, compiler. *A Book of Animal Poems,* illustrated by Robert Andrew Parker. Viking, 1973.

69. ———, compiler. *Humorous Poetry for Children,* illustrated by Ervine Metzl. World, 1955.

70. ———, compiler. *Oh, How Silly!,* illustrated by Tomi Ungerer. Viking, 1970.

71. ———, compiler. *Oh, That's Ridiculous!,* illustrated by Tomi Ungerer. Viking, 1972.

72. ———, compiler. *Oh, What Nonsense!,* illustrated by Tomi Ungerer. Viking, 1966.

73. ———, compiler. *Pick Me Up: A Book of Short, Short Poems.* Macmillan, 1972.

74. ———, compiler. *Poems for Seasons and Celebrations,* illustrated by Johannes Troyer. World, 1961.

75. ———, compiler. *Poems of Magic and Spells,* illustrated by Peggy Bacon. World, 1960.

76. ———, compiler. *The Sea, Ships, and Sailors,* illustrated by Robin Jacques. Viking, 1967.

77. ———, compiler. *Story Poems, New and Old,* illustrated by Walter Buehr. World, 1957.

78. Conkling, Hilda. *Poems by a Little Girl.* Stokes, 1920.

79. De la Mare, Walter. *Bells and Grass,* illustrated by Dorothy Lathrop. Viking, 1963.

80. ———, compiler. *Come Hither,* illustrated by Warren Chappell. Knopf, 1957.

81. ———. *Peacock Pie,* illustrated by Barbara Cooney. Knopf, 1961 (1913).

82. ———. *Rhymes and Verses, Collected Poems for Young People,* illustrated by Elinore Blaisdell. Holt, Rinehart and Winston, 1947.

83. ———, compiler. *Tom Tiddler's Ground,* illustrated by Margery Gill. Knopf, 1961.

84. De Regniers, Beatrice Schenk. *Something Special,* illustrated by Irene Haas. Harcourt Brace Jovanovich, 1958.

85. De Regniers, Beatrice Schenk, Eva Moore, and Mary Michaels White, compilers. *Poems Children Will Sit Still For: A Selection for the Primary Grades.* Citation, 1969.

86. Dickinson, Emily. *Poems of Emily Dickinson,* edited by Helen Plotz, illustrated by Robert Kipness. Crowell, 1964.

87. Doob, Leonard W. *A Crocodile Has Me by the Leg: African Poems,* illustrated by Solomon I. Wangboje. Walker, 1967.

88. Dunning, Stephen, Edward Lueders, and Hugh Smith. *Reflections on a Gift of Watermelon Pickle and Other Modern Verses.* Scott, Foresman, 1966.

89. Evans, Mel. *The Tiniest Sound,* illustrated by Ed Young. Doubleday, 1969.

90. Farjeon, Eleanor. *The Children's Bells.* Walck, 1960.

91. ———. *Eleanor Farjeon's Poems for Children.* Lippincott, 1951.

92. Ferris, Helen, compiler. *Favorite Poems Old and New,* illustrated by Leonard Weisgard. Doubleday, 1957.

93. Field, Rachel. *Poems.* Macmillan, 1957.

94. ———. *The Pointed People.* Macmillan, 1924.

95. ———. *Taxis and Toadstools.* Macmillan, 1926.

96. Fisher, Aileen. *Animal Disguises,* illustrated by Tim Hildebrandt and Greg Hildebrandt. Bowmar, 1973.

97. ———. *Animal Houses,* illustrated by Jan Wills. Bowmar, 1973.

98. ———. *Cricket in a Thicket,* illustrated by Feodor Rojankovsky. Scribner, 1963.

99. ———. *Feathered Ones and Furry,* illustrated by Eric Carle. Crowell, 1971.

100. ———. *Filling the Bill,* illustrated by Betty Fraser. Bowmar, 1973.

101. ———. *Going Barefoot,* illustrated by Adrienne Adams. Crowell, 1960.

102. ———. *I Like Weather,* illustrated by Janina Domanska. Crowell, 1963.

103. ———. *In One Door and Out the Other: A Book of Poems,* illustrated by Lillian Hoban. Crowell, 1969.

104. ———. *In the Middle of the Night,* illustrated by Adrienne Adams. Crowell, 1965.

105. ———. *In the Woods, in the Meadow, in the Sky,* illustrated by Margot Tomes. Scribner, 1965.

106. ———. *Like Nothing at All,* illustrated by Leonard Weisgard. Crowell, 1962.

107. ———. *Listen, Rabbit,* illustrated by Symeon Shimin. Crowell, 1964.

108. ———. *Runny Days, Sunny Days.* Abelard-Schuman, 1933.

109. ———. *Tail Twisters,* illustrated by Albert John Pucci. Bowmar, 1973.

110. ———. *That's Why.* Nelson, 1946.

111. ———. *Where Does Everyone Go?,* illustrated by Adrienne Adams. Crowell, 1961.

112. Fleming, Alice. *Hosannah the Home Run: Poems about Sports.* Little, Brown, 1972.

113. Froman, Robert. *Seeing Things.* Crowell, 1974.

114. ———. *Street Poems.* McCall, 1971.

115. Frost, Frances. *The Little Naturalist,* illustrated by Kurt Werth. Whittlesey, 1959.

116. ———. *The Little Whistler,* illustrated by Roger Duvoisin. Whittlesey, 1949.

117. ———. *Pool in the Meadow.* Houghton Mifflin, n.d.

118. Frost, Robert. *You Come Too,* illustrated by Thomas W. Nason. Holt, Rinehart and Winston, 1959.

119. Gasztold, Carmen Bernos de. *Prayers from the Ark,* translated by Rumer Godden, illustrated by Jean Primrose. Viking, 1962.

120. Gay, Zhenya. *Jingle Jangle,* Viking, 1953.

121. Geismer, Barbara Peck, and Antoinette Brown Suter. *Very Young Verses,* illustrated by Mildred Bronson. Houghton Mifflin, 1945.

122. Giovanni, Nikki. *Spin a Soft Black Song: Poems for Children,* illustrated by Charles Bible. Hill & Wang, 1971.

123. Graham, Harry. *Ruthless Rhymes for Heartless Homes and More Ruthless Rhymes for Heartless Homes.* Dover, 1961 (1899).

124. *The Gypsy Laddie,* illustrated by Dorothy Rice. Atheneum, 1972.

125. Hannum, Sara, and John T. Chase, eds. *To Play Man Number One*, illustrated by Erwin Schachner. Atheneum, 1969.

126. Hannum, Sara, and Gwendolyn E. Reed, compilers. *Lean Out of the Window*, illustrated by Ragna Tischler. Atheneum, 1965.

127. Hillert, Margaret. *Farther than Far*, illustrated by Betty Fraser. Follett, 1969.

128. Hoberman, Mary Ann. *Hello and Good-by*, illustrated by Norman Hoberman. Little, Brown, 1959.

129. Holmes, Oliver Wendell. *The Deacon's Masterpiece or the Wonderful One-Hoss Shay*, illustrated by Paul Galdone. McGraw-Hill, 1965.

130. Hopkins, Lee Bennett, ed. *The City Spreads Its Wings*, illustrated by Moneta Barnett. F. Watts, 1970.

131. ———, ed. *City Talk*, illustrated by Roy Arenella. Knopf, 1970.

132. ———, ed. *I Think I Saw a Snail: Young Poems for City Seasons*, illustrated by Harold James. Crown, 1969.

133. ———, ed. *Me: A Book of Poems*, illustrated by Talivaldis Stubis. Seabury, 1970.

134. ———, ed. *Zoo: A Book of Poems*, illustrated by Robert Frankenberg. Crown, 1971.

135. Hopkins, Lee Bennett, and Misha Arenstein, compilers. *Faces and Places: Poems for You*. Scholastic, 1971.

136. ———, compilers. *Time to Shout: Poems for You*, illustrated by Lisl Weil. Scholastic, 1973.

137. Hopkinson, Francis. *The Battle of the Kegs*, illustrated by Paul Galdone, Crowell, 1964.

138. Houston, James, ed., illustrator. *Songs of the Dream People: Chants and Images from the Indians and Eskimos of North America*. Atheneum, 1972.

139. Howard, Coralie, compiler. *The First Book of Short Verse*, illustrated by Mamoru Funai. F. Watts, 1964.

140. Hubbell, Patricia. *The Apple Vendor's Fair*, illustrated by Julie Maas. Atheneum, 1963.

141. ———. *Catch Me a Wind*, illustrated by Susan Trommler. Atheneum, 1968.

142. ———. *8 A.M. Shadows*, illustrated by Julie Maas. Atheneum, 1965.

143. Hughes, Langston. *Don't You Turn Back*, edited by Lee Bennett Hopkins, illustrated by Ann Grifalconi. Knopf, 1969.

144. ———. *The Dream Keeper and Other Poems*. Knopf, 1945.

145. ———. *The Panther and the Lash: Poems of Our Times*. Knopf, 1967.

146. *. . . I Never Saw Another Butterfly*. Children's Drawings and Poems from Theresienstadt Concentration Camp 1942–1944. McGraw-Hill, 1964.

147. Issa. *A Few Flies and I: Haiku by Issa*, edited by Jean Merrill and Ronni Solbert, illustrated by Ronni Solbert. Pantheon, 1969.

148. Issa, *et al. Don't Tell the Scarecrow and Other Japanese Poems*, illustrated by Talivaldis Stubis. Four Winds, 1970.

149. *Japanese Haiku*, translated by Peter Beilenson. Peter Pauper, 1955–1956.

150. Jarrell, Randall. *The Bat-Poet*, illustrated by Maurice Sendak, Macmillan, 1963.

151. Johnson, Hannah. *Hello, Small Sparrow*, illustrated by Tony Chen. Lothrop, 1971.

152. Jones, Hettie, ed. *The Trees Stand Shining*, illustrated by Robert Andrew Parker. Dial, 1971.

153. Jordan, June. *Who Look at Me*. Crowell, 1969.

154. Jordan, June, and Terri Bush, eds. *The Voice of the Children*. Holt, Rinehart and Winston, 1970.

155. Kuskin, Karla. *Alexander Soames, His Poems*. Harper & Row, 1962.

156. ———. *Any Me I Want to Be*. Harper & Row, 1972.

157. ———. *In the Middle of the Trees*. Harper & Row, 1958.

158. ———. *The Rose on My Cake*. Harper & Row, 1964.

159. ———. *Sand and Snow*. Harper & Row, 1965.

160. Larrick, Nancy, ed. *Green Is Like a Meadow of Grass*, illustrated by Kelly Oechsli. Garrard, 1968.

161. ———, ed. *I Heard a Scream in the Street: Poetry by Young People in the City*. M. Evans, 1970.

162. ———, ed. *On City Streets*, photographs by David Sagarin. M. Evans, 1968.

163. ———, ed. *Piper, Pipe that Song Again!,* illustrated by Kelly Oechsli. Random House, 1965.

164. ———, ed. *Piping Down the Valleys Wild,* illustrated by Ellen Raskin. Delacorte, 1968.

165. Lear, Edward. *The Complete Nonsense Book.* Dodd, Mead, 1946.

166. ———. *The Quangle-Wangle's Hat,* illustrated by Helen Oxenbury. F. Watts, 1969.

167. ———. *The Two Old Bachelors,* illustrated by Paul Galdone. Whittlesey, 1962.

168. ———. *Whizz!,* illustrated by Janina Domanska. Macmillan, 1973.

169. Lear, Edward, and Ogden Nash. *The Scroobious Pip,* illustrated by Nancy Ekholm Burkert. Harper & Row, 1968.

170. Lewis, Richard, ed. *I Breathe a New Song: Poems of the Eskimo,* illustrated by Oonark. Simon & Schuster, 1971.

171. ———, ed. *In a Spring Garden,* illustrated by Ezra Jack Keats. Dial, 1965.

172. ———, ed. *Miracles, Poems by Children of the English-speaking World.* Simon & Schuster, 1966.

173. ———, ed. *The Moment of Wonder.* Dial, 1964.

174. ———, ed. *Of This World: A Poet's Life in Poetry,* photographs by H. Buttfield. Dial, 1968.

175. ———, ed. *Out of the Earth I Sing; Poetry and Songs of Primitive People of the World.* Norton, 1968.

176. ———, ed. *There Are Two Lives: Poems by Children of Japan,* translated by Haruna Kimura. Simon & Schuster, 1970.

177. ———, ed. *The Wind and the Rain,* illustrated by Helen Buttfield. Simon & Schuster, 1968.

178. Livingston, Myra Cohn. *A Crazy Flight and Other Poems,* illustrated by James J. Spanfeller. Harcourt Brace Jovanovich, 1969.

179. ———. *Happy Birthday,* illustrated by Erik Blegvad. Harcourt Brace Jovanovich, 1964.

180. ———. *I'm Hiding,* illustrated by Erik Blegvad. Harcourt Brace Jovanovich, 1961.

181. ———. *I'm Not Me,* illustrated by Erik Blegvad. Harcourt Brace Jovanovich, 1963.

182. ———. *I'm Waiting,* illustrated by Erik Blegvad. Harcourt Brace Jovanovich, 1966.

183. ———, ed. *Listen, Children, Listen: An Anthology of Poems for the Very Young,* illustrated by Trina Schart Hyman. Harcourt Brace Jovanovich, 1972.

184. ———. *The Malibu and Other Poems,* illustrated by James Spanfeller. Atheneum, 1972.

185. ———. *The Moon and a Star,* illustrated by Judith Shahn. Harcourt Brace Jovanovich, 1965.

186. ———. *See What I Found,* illustrated by Erik Blegvad. Harcourt Brace Jovanovich, 1962.

187. ———, ed. *Speak Roughly to Your Little Boy: A Collection of Parodies and Burlesques,* illustrated by Joseph Low. Harcourt Brace Jovanovich, 1971.

188. ———, ed. *A Tune Beyond Us: A Collection of Poetry,* illustrated by James Spanfeller. Harcourt Brace Jovanovich, 1968.

189. ———, ed. *What a Wonderful Bird the Frog Are.* Harcourt Brace Jovanovich, 1973.

190. ———. *Whispers and Other Poems,* illustrated by Jacqueline Chwast. Harcourt Brace Jovanovich, 1958.

191. ———. *Wide Awake,* illustrated by Jacqueline Chwast. Harcourt Brace Jovanovich, 1959.

192. Longfellow, Henry Wadsworth. *Paul Revere's Ride,* illustrated by Paul Galdone. Crowell, 1963.

193. ———. *The Skeleton in Armor,* illustrated by Paul Kennedy. Prentice-Hall, 1963.

194. Lund, Doris H. *Attic of the Wind,* illustrated by Ati Forberg. Parents', 1966.

195. McCord, David. *All Day Long,* illustrated by Henry B. Kane. Little, Brown, 1965.

196. ———. *Every Time I Climb a Tree,* illustrated by Marc Simont. Little, Brown, 1967.

197. ———. *Far and Few, Rhymes of Never Was and Always Is,* illustrated by Henry B. Kane. Little, Brown, 1952.

198. ———. *For Me to Say,* illustrated by Henry B. Kane. Little, Brown, 1970.

199. ———. *Take Sky,* illustrated by Henry B. Kane. Little, Brown, 1961.

200. McDonald, Gerald D., compiler. *A Way of Knowing,* illustrated by Clare Ross and John Ross. Crowell, 1959.

201. McEwen, Catherine Schaefer, compiler. *Away We Go!*, illustrated by Barbara Cooney. Crowell, 1956.
202. McGovern, Ann. *Arrow Book of Poetry*, illustrated by Grisha Dotzenko. Scholastic, 1965.
203. Mackay, David. *A Flock of Words: An Anthology of Poetry for Children and Others*, illustrated by Margery Gill. Harcourt Brace Jovanovich, 1970.
204. Merriam, Eve. *Catch a Little Rhyme*, illustrated by Imero Gobbato. Atheneum, 1966.
205. ———. *Finding a Poem*, illustrated by Seymour Chwast. Atheneum, 1970.
206. ———. *I Am a Man: An Ode to Martin Luther King, Jr.*, illustrated by Suzanne Verrier. Doubleday, 1971.
207. ———. *Independent Voices*, illustrated by Arvis Stewart. Atheneum, 1968.
208. ———. *It Doesn't Always Have to Rhyme*, illustrated by Malcolm Spooner. Atheneum, 1964.
209. ———. *Out Loud*, illustrated by Harriet Sherman. Atheneum, 1973.
210. ———. *There Is No Rhyme for Silver*, illustrated by Joseph Schindelman. Atheneum, 1962.
211. Milne, A. A. *Now We Are Six*, illustrated by E. H. Shepard. Dutton, 1927.
212. ———. *When We Were Very Young*, illustrated by E. H. Shepard. Dutton, 1924.
213. ———. *The World of Christopher Robin*, illustrated by E. H. Shepard. Dutton, 1958.
214. Molloy, Paul, compiler. *Beach Glass and Other Poems*. Four Winds, 1970.
215. Moore, Janet Gaylord. *The Many Ways of Seeing: An Introduction to the Pleasures of Art*. World, 1970.
216. Moore, Lilian. *I Feel the Same Way*, illustrated by Robert Quackenbush. Atheneum, 1967.
217. ———. *I Thought I Heard the City*, illustrated by Mary J. Dunton. Atheneum, 1969.
218. ———. *Sam's Place: Poems from the Country*, illustrated by Talivaldis Stubis. Atheneum, 1973.
219. Moore, Lilian, and Lawrence Webster, compilers. *Catch Your Breath: A Book of Shivery Poems*, illustrated by Gahan Wilson, Garrard, 1973.
220. Morrison, Lillian, compiler. *Sprints and Distances, Sports in Poetry and Poetry in Sports*, illustrated by Clare Ross and John Ross. Crowell, 1965.
221. Morton, Miriam, compiler and translator. *The Moon Is Like a Silver Sickle: A Celebration of Poetry by Russian Children*, illustrated by Eros Keith. Simon & Schuster, 1972.
222. Nash, Ogden, compiler. *Everybody Ought to Know*, illustrated by Rose Shirvanian. Lippincott, 1961.
223. ———, compiler. *The Moon Is Shining Bright as Day*. Lippincott, 1953.
224. Ness, Evaline, Compiler and illustrator *Amelia Mixed the Mustard and Other Poems*, Scribner, 1975.
225. *Now Poetry*. Charles L. Cutler, *et al.*, eds. English Unit Books. American Education Publications, 1970.
226. Noyes, Alfred. *The Highwayman*, illustrated by Gilbert Riswold. Prentice-Hall, 1968.
227. O'Neill, Mary. *Fingers Are Always Bringing Me News*, illustrated by Don Bolognese. Doubleday, 1969.
228. ———. *Hailstones and Halibut Bones, Adventures in Color*, illustrated by Leonard Weisgard. Doubleday, 1961.
229. ———. *People I'd Like to Keep*, illustrated by Paul Galdone. Doubleday, 1964.
230. ———. *Take a Number*, illustrated by Al Nagy. Doubleday, 1968.
231. ———. *What Is That Sound!*, illustrated by Lois Ehbert. Atheneum, 1966.
232. ———. *Words, Words, Words*, illustrated by Judy Piussi-Campbell. Doubleday, 1966.
233. Palmer, Geoffrey, and Noel Lloyd, compilers. *Round about Eight, Poems for Today*, illustrated by Denis Wrigley. Warne, 1972.
234. Parker, Elinor. *The Singing and the Gold: Poems Translated from World Literature*, illustrated by Clare Leighton. Crowell, 1962.
235. Payne, Nina. *All the Day Long*, illustrated by Laurel Schindelman. Atheneum, 1973.
236. Peck, Richard, ed. *Sounds and Silences: Poetry for Now*. Delacorte, 1970.
237. Peterson, Isabel J., compiler. *The First Book of Poetry*, illustrated by Kathleen Elgin. F. Watts, 1954.
238. Petitt, Dorothy. *Poems to Remember*. Macmillan, 1967.

239. Pilon, A. Barbara. *Concrete Is Not Always Hard.* Xerox Education Publications, 1972.
240. Plotz, Helen, compiler. *The Earth Is the Lord's: Poems of the Spirit,* illustrated by Clare Leighton. Crowell, 1965.
241. ———, compiler. *Imagination's Other Place,* illustrated by Clare Leighton. Crowell, 1955.
242. ———, compiler. *The Marvelous Light: Poets and Poetry.* Crowell, 1970.
243. ———, compiler. *Untune the Sky,* illustrated by Clare Leighton. Crowell, 1957.
244. Poe, Edgar Allen. *Three Poems of Edgar Allen Poe,* illustrated by Paul Galdone. McGraw-Hill, 1966.
245. Rasmussen, Knud. *Beyond the High Hills: A Book of Eskimo Poems,* photographs by Guy Mary-Rousseilère. World, 1961.
246. Read, Herbert Edward, compiler. *This Way, Delight,* illustrated by Juliet Kepes. Pantheon, 1956.
247. Reed, Gwendolyn, ed. *Out of the Ark: An Anthology of Animal Poems,* illustrated by Gabriele Margules. Atheneum, 1968.
248. Reeves, James. *The Blackbird in the Lilac,* illustrated by Edward Ardizzone. Dutton, 1959.
249. ———. *Prefabulous Animiles,* illustrated by Edward Ardizzone. Dutton, 1960.
250. ———. *The Wandering Moon.* Dutton, 1960.
251. Richards, Laura E. *Tirra Lirra,* illustrated by Marguerite Davis. Little, Brown, 1955.
252. Ridlon, Marci. *That Was Summer,* illustrated by Mia Carpenter. Follett, 1969.
253. Rieu, E. V. *The Flattered Flying Fish and Other Poems,* illustrated by E. H. Shepard. Dutton, 1962.
254. Roberts, Elizabeth Madox. *Under the Tree,* illustrated by F. D. Bedford. Viking, 1930.
255. Roche, A. K., ed., designer. *The City . . . in Haiku.* Prentice-Hall, 1970.
256. Roethke, Theodor. *Dirty Dinky and Other Creatures: Poems for Children,* selected by Beatrice Roethke and Stephen Lushington, illustrated by Julie Brinckloe. Doubleday, 1973.
257. ———. *I Am! Says the Lamb,* illustrated by Robert Leydenfrost. Doubleday, 1961.
258. Rossetti, Christina. *The Goblin Market,* adapted and illustrated by Ellen Raskin. Dutton, 1970.
259. ———. *Sing-Song,* illustrated by Marguerite Davis. Macmillan, 1924.
260. Sandburg, Carl. *Early Moon,* illustrated by James Daugherty. Harcourt Brace Jovanovich, 1930.
261. ———. *Wind Song,* illustrated by William A. Smith. Harcourt Brace Jovanovich, 1960.
262. Schaefer, Charles E., and Kathleen C. Mellor, compilers. *Young Voices.* Macmillan, 1971.
263. Schweitzer, Byrd Baylor. *One Small Blue Bead,* illustrated by Symeon Shimin. Macmillan, 1965.
264. Sheldon, William, Nellie Lyons, and Polly Rouault, compilers. *The Reading of Poetry.* Allyn and Bacon, 1963.
265. Silverstein, Shel. *Where the Sidewalk Ends,* Harper & Row, 1974.
266. Smith, William Jay. *Boy Blue's Book of Beasts,* illustrated by Juliet Kepes. Little, Brown, 1956.
267. ———. *Laughing Time,* illustrated by Juliet Kepes. Little, Brown, 1953.
267A. ———. *Mister Smith and Other Nonsense,* illustrated by Don Bolognese. Delacorte, 1968.
268. ———. *Typewriter Town.* Dutton, 1960.
269. Snyder, Zilpha. *Today Is Saturday,* illustrated by John Arms. Atheneum, 1969.
270. Solbert, Ronni. *I Wrote My Name on the Wall.* Little, Brown, 1971.
271. Spilka, Arnold. *A Lion I Can Do Without.* Walck, 1964.
272. Starbird, Kaye. *Don't Ever Cross a Crocodile,* illustrated by Kit Dalton. Lippincott, 1963.
273. ———. *The Pheasant on Route Seven,* illustrated by Victoria DeLarrea. Lippincott, 1968.
274. ———. *A Snail's a Failure Socially,* illustrated by Kit Dalton. Lippincott, 1966.
275. ———. *Speaking of Cows,* illustrated by Rita Fava. Lippincott, 1960.
276. Stephenson, Marjorie, ed. *Fives Sixes and Sevens,* illustrated by Denis Wrigley. Warne, 1968.
277. Stevenson, Robert Louis. *A Child's Garden of Verses,* illustrated by Tasha Tudor. Oxford, 1947 (1885).

278. ———. *A Child's Garden of Verses,* illustrated by Brian Wildsmith. F. Watts, 1966 (1885).
279. Stoutenberg, Adrien. *The Things that Are.* Reilly & Lee, 1964.
280. Summerfield, Geoffrey, ed. *First Voices: The First Book.* Random House (Singer School Division), 1970.
281. ———, ed. *First Voices: The Second Book.* Random House (Singer School Division), 1970.
282. ———, ed. *First Voices: The Third Book.* Random House (Singer School Division), 1970.
283. ———, ed. *First Voices: The Fourth Book.* Random House (Singer School Division), 1970.
284. ———, ed. *Voices: An Anthology of Poems and Pictures, The First Book.* Rand McNally, 1969.
285. ———, ed. *Voices: An Anthology of Poems and Pictures, The Second Book.* Rand McNally, 1969.
286. ———, ed. *Voices: An Anthology of Poems and Pictures, The Third Book.* Rand McNally, 1969.
287. ———, ed. *Voices: An Anthology of Poems and Pictures, The Fourth Book.* Rand McNally, 1969.
288. ———, ed. *Voices: An Anthology of Poems and Pictures, The Fifth Book.* Rand McNally, 1969.
289. Teasdale, Sara. *Stars Tonight,* illustrated by Dorothy Lathrop. Macmillan, 1954.
290. Tennyson, Alfred, Lord. *The Charge of the Light Brigade,* illustrated by Alice Provensen and Martin Provensen. Golden Press, 1964.
291. Thayer, Ernest L. *Casey at the Bat,* illustrated by Paul Frame. Prentice-Hall, 1964.
292. ———. *The First Book Edition of Casey at the Bat,* introduction by Casey Stengel, illustrated by Leonard Everett Fisher. F. Watts, 1964.
293. Thompson, Blanche Jennings, compiler. *All the Silver Pennies.* Macmillan, 1967.
294. Thompson, Jean McKee, compiler. *Poems to Grow On,* illustrated by Gobin Stair. Beacon, 1957.
295. Tippett, James S. *Crickety Cricket! The Best-Loved Poems of James S. Tippett,* illustrated by Mary Chalmers. Harper & Row, 1973.
296. ———. *I Go A-Traveling,* illustrated by Elizabeth T. Wolcott. Harper & Row, 1929.
297. ———. *I Live in the City.* Harper & Row. 1927.
298. ———. *I Spend the Summer.* Harper & Row. 1930.
299. Untermeyer, Louis, ed. *The Golden Treasury of Poetry,* illustrated by Joan Walsh Anglund. Golden Press, 1959.
300. ———, ed. *The Magic Circle: Stories and People in Poetry,* illustrated by Beth Krush and Joe Krush. Harcourt Brace Jovanovich, 1952.
301. ———, ed. *Rainbow in the Sky,* illustrated by Reginald Birch. Harcourt Brace Jovanovich, 1935.
302. ———, ed. *This Singing World.* Harcourt Brace Jovanovich, 1923.
303. ———, ed. *Stars to Steer By,* illustrated by Dorothy Bayley. Harcourt Brace Jovanovich, 1941.
304. Unternecker, John. *The Dreaming Zoo,* illustrated by George Weinheimer. Walck, 1965.
305. Weiss, Renee K., compiler. *Paper Zoo,* illustrated by Ellen Raskin. Macmillan, 1968.
306. Whittier, John Greenleaf. *Barbara Frietchie,* illustrated by Paul Galdone. Crowell, 1965.
307. Worth, Valerie. *Small Poems,* illustrated by Natalie Babbitt. Farrar, Straus, 1972.
308. Zolotow, Charlotte. *All that Sunlight,* illustrated by Walter Stein. Harper & Row, 1967.

POETRY INDEXES

Brewton, John E., and Sara W. Brewton. *Index to Children's Poetry.* H. W. Wilson, 1942.
———. *Index to Children's Poetry: First Supplement.* H. W. Wilson, 1954.
———. *Index to Children's Poetry: Second Supplement.* H. W. Wilson, 1965.
Brewton, John E., Sara W. Brewton, and G. Meredith Blackburn III. *Index to Poetry for Children and Young People 1964–1969.* H. W. Wilson, 1972.
Sell, Violet, *et al. The Subject Index to Poetry for Children and Young People.* American Library Association, 1957.

POETRY AND MEDIA[23]

Films

The Day Is Two Feet Long. Weston Woods.
Hailstones and Halibut Bones. Sterling Educational Films.
The Living Poetry Series. McGraw-Hill.

Filmstrips

Haiku: The Hidden Glimmering. Lyceum Productions.
Pick a Peck o' Poems. Miller-Brody Company.
What Is Poetry? Caedmon.

Records

A Gathering of Great Poetry for Children. Caedmon Records (distributed by D. C. Heath).
In Sounds from Way Out. Vanguard Records.
Listen, Move and Dance, Vol II. Capitol Records.
Poetry Parade. Weston Woods.
To Catch a Little Rhyme. Caedmon Records (distributed by D. C. Heath).
You Read to Me, I'll Read to You. Spoken Arts.
You Know Who: John J. Plenty and Fiddler Dan and Other Poems. Spoken Arts.

Book-Record Sets

Favorite Rhymes from A Rocket in My Pocket. Scholastic Book Services.
Over in the Meadow. Scholastic Book Services.
Reflections on a Gift of Watermelon Pickle. Scholastic Book services.
Selections from the Arrow Book of Poetry. Scholastic Book Services.
Selections from Faces and Places: Poems for You. Scholastic Book Services.

[23] *See* Appendix D for addresses of film and record companies.

7 Contemporary Realistic Fiction

In Wersba's *The Dream Watcher*, Albert Scully is portrayed as a young adolescent misfit in today's society. A lover of Shakespeare and Thoreau, Albert complains about the books he has to read in his English class:

> No matter what book we read in English it is always a story about youth going through experience and improving itself. Southern youth, Northern youth, European youth. To judge from these books you would think that youth did nothing but go through experience and come out great at the end. If Mr. Findley ever gave us a book in which youth went to pieces at the end, I would be more interested.[1]

If Albert Scully had been able to read his own story, *The Dream Watcher*, he might have been more interested in books. For on the day that Albert met aging Mrs. Woodfin he was contemplating suicide. His family did not understand him; he had no friends; and he was not doing well in school. The eccentric Mrs. Woodfin was the first person with whom he had had a real conversation in five years. Through his frequent visits to her house, Albert begins to find out who he is and to accept his difference. The old lady becomes a guardian of his dreams, someone who respects him, who doesn't think that he is odd because he likes gardening or Shakespeare. And so Scully is no longer embarrassed by his interests. ". . . it occurred to me that if Thoreau could have a different drummer, maybe I could too. I know this doesn't make much sense, but I kept wondering if there wasn't a drummer for me somewhere. A kind of beautiful person who was beating a drum with my name on it."[2] Albert gains enough strength from his relationship with Mrs. Woodfin to be able to accept her death and the destruction of her fantasy world. Her case worker reveals that Mrs. Woodfin was not the famous retired actress that she had claimed to be but a destitute alcoholic with a vivid imagination. Albert had needed someone who would listen to him, and Mrs. Woodfin had needed someone for whom she could give one last believable performance. Each had helped the other "to become." The book ends not with the youth going to pieces as Scully had said he wanted to do, but with a youth picking up the many pieces of his fragmented life and getting them all together.

The Dream Watcher is one of the best of the books representing the so-called

[1] Barbara Wersba. *The Dream Watcher* (New York: Atheneum, 1968), p. 78.
[2] Wersba, p. 112.

new realism for children. It contains many of the elements found in contemporary juvenile literature—alienated youth; uncaring, ineffectual parents; rejection of materialism; and an eccentric character who is willing to listen. Told in the first person, it reveals the thoughts of a lonely, alienated boy who desperately needs someone to understand him.

Realism in Contemporary Children's Literature

Realistic fiction may be defined as that imaginative writing which accurately reflects life as it was lived in the past or could be lived today. Everything in such a story can conceivably have happened to real people living in our natural, physical world, in contrast to fantasy where impossible happenings are made to appear quite plausible, even though they are not possible. Historical fiction (*see* Chapter 8) portrays life as it may have been lived in the past, while contemporary realism focuses upon the problems of living today.

When children ask if a story is true, they usually do not mean did it really happen but rather, could it possibly happen. Many children only want to read books about life today. In fact, one librarian maintains that the most common request of middle-grade girls is for a "book about a girl like me."

The books discussed in this chapter may be categorized as contemporary realistic fiction for children. Many of these are stories about youth growing up today, finding a place in the family, among their peers, and in modern society. All aspects of coping with the problems of the human condition may be found in contemporary literature for children. In addition to this content, books which reflect the special interests of some children—such as animal stories, sports stories, and mysteries—are also classified as realistic literature and so are included in this chapter.

The content of contemporary realism for children has changed dramatically in the past ten years. A discussion of some of these changes was included in Chapter 1, while Chapter 2 identified the recent trends in publishing books for children, including the increased publication of titles about minority groups; the growing number of translations of books from other countries; and the new freedom to present such formerly taboo subjects as profanity, alcoholism, premarital sex,

homosexuality, divorce, and death. All these changes have provoked controversy among writers, critics, librarians, teachers, and parents. For this reason attention will be given to some of the values of contemporary realism for children and some of these issues.

VALUES OF CONTEMPORARY FICTION

Realistic fiction serves children in the process of understanding and coming to terms with themselves as they acquire "human-ness." Books which honestly portray the realities of life may help children toward a fuller understanding of human problems and human relationships and, thus, toward a fuller understanding of themselves and their own potential. In describing her purpose in writing for children Emily Neville states:

> If I have any mission as an author, it is to show the reader, not how great a hero he could become, because I don't think most people are going to become heroes, but simply how hard it is to be a plain decent human being. . . . The values I write about will not lead to greater heroics; only, I hope, to fuller humanity.[3]

This is not a function unique to contemporary realism. Other types of books can give children a sense of their humanity. Some fantasy may be nearer to the truth than social realism, while biography and autobiography frequently provide readers with models of human beings who have lived compassionate lives. The ability to maintain one's humanity in the midst of degradation becomes clear in Hautzig's autobiography of her exile in Siberia, *The Endless Steppe*. The psychological importance of facing one's fears, even going to meet them, is as much the theme of the high fantasy, *The Wizard of Earthsea* by LeGuin, as it is the message of the modern story of *The 18th Emergency* by Byars. Stephen de Beauville in

---

[3] Emily Neville. "Social Values in Children's Literature," in *A Critical Approach to Children's Literature,* Sara Innis Fenwick, ed. (Chicago, Ill.: The University of Chicago Press, 1967), p. 52.

One Is One (Picard) was as much a misfit in his medieval society as Albert Scully is in today's world (*The Dream Watcher* by Wersba). However, most children appear to identify more readily with characters in books of modern realism than with those of historical fiction or fantasy. The horror of man's inhumanity to man overpowers the reader of *Sounder* (Armstrong) or *Boy of Old Prague* (Ish-Kishor), but *Berries Goodman* (Emily Neville) reveals the immediacy of the insidious sickness of prejudice in suburbia. Thus, modern realism may help the child to enlarge and deepen compassion and to see the world from a new perspective.

Realistic fiction may reassure young people that they are not the first in the world to have to face problems. They may read of other children whose parents have gotten a divorce in Blume's *It's Not the End of the World* or in Mann's *My Dad Lives in a Downtown Hotel*. Knowledge that you are not alone brings a kind of comfort. James Baldwin recognized the power of books to alleviate pain when he said:

> You think your pain and your heartbreak are unprecedented in the history of the world, but then you read. It was books that taught me that the things that tormented me the most were the very things that connected me with all the people who were alive, or who had ever been alive.[4]

While realistic fiction can cast a light upon personal problems, it can also illuminate those experiences which children have not had. It is probably far more important for the child who has loving parents, who has never known hunger, and whose only household chore consists of making a bed to read Fran Ellen's story in *The Bears' House* (Sachs), than for a child of poverty to read this book. Realistic fiction, then, becomes a way of experiencing worlds we do not know.

Some books also serve as a kind of warning or preparation for living. Far better to have read *Too Bad about the Haines Girl* (Sherburne) than to have to experience an unwanted pregnancy. Death is a part of everyone's life. Yet for many years this was a taboo subject in children's literature. As children face the honest realities of life

in books, they are developing a kind of courage for facing problems in their own lives. Madeleine L'Engle, who was one of the first authors to include the subject of death in a book for children (*Meet the Austins*), maintains:

> . . . to pretend there is no darkness is another way of extinguishing light. In literature, children and adults can find the heroes, the uncommon men who face these same dark clouds but show what a man can do. They do not always show the way, but serve as a point of reference.[5]

Realistic fiction for children does provide many possible models, both good and bad, for coping with the problems of the human condition. As the child experiences these stories, he may begin to filter out some meaning for his own life. Bruner emphasizes the important role that literature may bring to this shaping and organizing of life:

> Man must cope with a relatively limited number of plights—birth, growth, loneliness, the passions, death, and not very many more. They are plights that are neither solved nor bypassed by being "adjusted." An adjusted man must face his passions just as surely as he faces death. I would urge that a grasp of the basic plights through the basic myths of art and literature provides the organizing principles by which knowledge of the human condition is rendered into a form that makes thinking possible, by which we go beyond learning to the use of knowledge.[6]

ISSUES RELATING TO REALISTIC FICTION

There is more controversy surrounding the writing of contemporary realistic fiction for children than perhaps any other kind of literature. Everyone is a critic of realism, for everyone feels he is an expert on what is real in today's world. But realities clash, and the issue of "what is real for one may not be real for another" is a true and lively concern. Another question relates to how real, how graphic can writers of children's books be? What is appropriate for children? Are there limits to good taste, for example? A third

---

[4] James Baldwin. "Talk to Teachers," *Saturday Review* (December 21, 1963), pp. 42–44, 60.

[5] Madeleine L'Engle, in a speech before the Florida Library Association, Miami, May 1965.
[6] Jerome Bruner. "Learning and Thinking," *Harvard Educational Review*, Vol. 29 (Summer 1959), p. 186.

question centers on the negative aspects of how certain groups are presented, particularly sex-role stereotyping. Another issue relates to how realism is presented to children. Many authors become didactic when writing of the social problems of today. Their stories are overpowered by social themes of alienation, drugs, or ecology. Finally, much controversy centers on the authorship of these books. Must a story be derived from personal experience; can only blacks write about blacks, Chicanos about Chicanos, women about the girls they were, men about boys, and so on? What is the role of imagination in the writing of realistic fiction? These are some of the questions that seem uniquely related to contemporary realism in writing for children. They need to be examined.

What Is Real?

The question of what is "real" or "true to life" is a significant one. C. S. Lewis, the British author of the well-known Narnia stories (*see* Chapter 5 "Modern Fantasy)", described three types of realistic content:

> But when we say, "The sort of thing that happens," do we mean the sort of thing that usually or often happens, the sort of thing that is typical of the human lot? Or do we mean "The sort of thing that might conceivably happen or that, by a thousandth chance, may have happened once?"[7]

Middle-graders reading the Narnia series know they are fantasy and couldn't happen. You don't go into a closet and find yourself welcomed to the snow-covered land of Narnia by a faun! Things like that just don't happen, even if the faun is amazed to see you and has a book in his library titled *Is Man a Myth?* However, middle-graders may read *Sidewalk Story* by Mathis and believe that 9-year-old Lilly Etta could prevent the landlord from evicting her friend Tanya and her six brothers and sisters from their New York apartment. While such action is possible, it is highly improbable in today's world. *Sidewalk Story* is a warm, loving book which portrays the real friendship of two black girls. It is only the contrived resolution of the story that prompts one to ask: "What is real?" *Why Me?* by John Bran-

field is a popular, well-written story of a diabetic girl. Her bitterness about her illness is believable and reflected in the title of the book. But the fact that her dog suddenly develops diabetes, too, stretches the reader's credulity to the point of asking: "What is real?" The danger of such unlikely stories is that children will believe them and expect similar miraculous solutions to their problems. These are well-written books, cast in realistic settings with believable characters facing real problems. Only the solutions seem more fantastic than some fantasy.

How Real May a Children's Book Be?

Controversy also centers on how much graphic detail may be included in a book for children. How much violence is too much; how explicit may an author be in describing bodily functions or sexual relations? These are questions that no one would have asked ten years ago. But there are new freedoms today. Childhood is not the innocent time we like to think it is (and it probably never was). Children today are watching the same television shows as their parents, reading their magazines with centerfolds, and attending many adult films. Youth no longer needs protection, but it does need the perspective that literature can give. A well-written book makes the reader aware of the resulting human suffering of people's inhumane acts, whereas television or films are more apt to concentrate on the act itself. The National Commission on the Causes and Prevention of Violence[8] stated that 6.7 acts of violence occur every hour on the average on television. One authority has estimated that the average child in the United States will witness 1,300 video murders per year between the ages of 5 and 15. That equals nearly four killings a night. It is probable that today's youth witnesses more killings on television in an evening than his grandparents ever saw in a lifetime. Such mayhem and tasteless brutality blunts one's sensibility and makes violence seem commonplace.

By way of contrast to the plastic television world, a well-written story will provide perspective on the pain and suffering of humankind. In

[7] C. S. Lewis. *An Experiment in Criticism* (Cambridge, England: University Press, 1961), p. 57.

[8] U.S. Government Report. *To Establish Justice and Insure Domestic Tranquility: Final Report on the Causes and Prevention of Violence* (Washington, D.C.: U.S. Government, 1969), p. 194.

a literary story the author has time to develop his characters into full human beings. The reader knows the motives and pressures of each individual and can understand and empathize with the characters. If the tone of the author is one of compassion for his characters, if others in the story show concern or horror for a brutal act, the reader gains perspective.

Whichaway by the Swarthouts is a grim survival story of a 15-year-old boy in Arizona. Only son of the owner of the Box O Ranch, Whichaway is assigned an important job that no one else wants. He must grease and care for all thirty-seven windmills on the ranch. It is an endless job, one that brings no thanks from his father. A gust of wind catches him one day as he is fixing a windmill and the force of it spins him around twice, breaking both of his legs at the ankle. Caught on top of the platform, the boy tries to plan a way to get off. Two rustlers come by and refuse even to give him a drink of water. His last hope appears in the form of a crazed prospector who tries to shoot him so that he won't report his gold strike. Finally, after two days and nights of enduring unrelenting pain, he manages to get off the platform and on to his horse. Just at the moment he thinks he is dying, his father and two cowhands arrive. No one offers to help him; he has to ask them for water. His father's only cryptic comment is "You mean . . . it took you two whole days and nights just to figure out how to get down off a mill?"[9] And with that the boy attempts to ride the fifteen miles back to the ranch to prove that he is now a man! No one shows any pity or any sign of compassion for the boy. The description of his injured legs is graphic and detailed:

> These weren't legs or feet. They were fat sausages, horrible to look at, so swollen that the skin was a mottled blue and seemed to glisten from stretching. . . . He recalled the rustler's warning that if he thrashed around much, the jagged bones would slice into the veins. They'd bleed and rot the tissues, and then he'd have gangrene. And what did they do with rotten legs? They chopped 'em off.[10]

Forced to witness suffering and pain, the reader can only ask why. Nothing is put into any kind

of perspective. The boy's father is just as cold and indifferent to his son as he was before the accident. Since the authors show no sympathy for the boy and none of the characters do, the result is a dehumanizing experience for the reader.

By way of contrast there is a brutal scene in *Grover* by Vera Cleaver and Bill Cleaver, where the children sneak over to the house of a woman who had mistreated Grover and kill her prize turkey. Yet the reader knows it is not a wanton act of revenge. Grover's mother had cancer, and she had killed herself. His father was a changed man, wallowing in his own grief and showing no compassion for his son's feeling. Grover seeks the companionship of his friends, Ellen Grae and Farrell. Unsuspectingly, the three of them are talked into cleaning up the yard of the town's meanest and stingiest person. She puts them to work mowing her lawn and pulling the weeds and then finds ways to criticize them. She recognizes Grover as "the kid whose mother blew her brains out."[11] Then, when the children inadvertently frighten her tom turkey, she starts in again on Grover, telling him this time that: "Suicide is a coward's way."[12] The children leave without being paid for their work and the next morning at dawn they return and Grover cuts the head off the turkey. Ellen Grae tries to talk him out of it and Farrell is horrified as he avoids watching, but keeps asking if the bird is dead yet. Finally, Grover hits the bird again with his hatchet and severs its head:

> His head, the eyes horribly bulging, fell to the ground and his body jerked out of the hands that held it and flew up into the air and came down again and started dancing around. But after a minute or two it gave a big convulsive shudder, which sent some more blood spraying, collapsed, and was finally dead.
>
> They left it for Betty Repkin to find.
>
> On the way back down the hill Ellen Grae didn't speak to Grover nor did Farrell.[13]

Against the background of Grover's silent suffering and the mean words of the woman, the

[9] Glendon Swarthout and Kathryn Swarthout. *Whichaway* (New York: Random House, 1966), p. 100.

[10] Swarthout and Swarthout, p. 44.

[11] Vera Cleaver and Bill Cleaver. *Grover*, illustrated by Frederick Marvin (Philadelphia, Penna: Lippincott, 1970), p. 88.

[12] Cleaver and Cleaver, p. 89.

[13] Cleaver and Cleaver, p. 95.

reader sees the killing of the turkey as a kind of catharsis for Grover. Somehow he can't take anymore. It is almost as if he had to fight death with death. Later he says he is sorry he killed the turkey. The explicit details are necessary in this scene, and they do serve a purpose. Slowly Grover is putting the pieces of his mother's death into a framework that he can understand. He even tries to tell his father that he is sure she killed herself so they wouldn't have to see her change. But the father cannot hear his son, he is so consumed by his own grief. *Grover* is a story about death and how it affects the strong and the weak. It is not a sentimental story but a strong one that suggests we all have to wrestle with the grim reality of our lives in the ways that we know best.

In an article on violence in children's books James Giblin, a children's book editor, identifies six criteria by which he evaluates violence in the manuscripts he receives. These criteria are worthy of careful consideration:

1. *Appropriateness.* Very few subjects are inappropriate in and of themselves; it is all in how the author treats them.
2. *Realism.* Does the author portray the necessary facts of the situation, ugly as they may be?
3. *Honesty.* Does the author portray fully and fairly both sides of a conflict, the many dimensions of a personality?
4. *Depth.* Does the author present a textured many leveled experience?
5. *Emotion.* Does the author write with feeling and emotion?
6. *Thoughtfulness.* Does the author evince a spirit or breadth that extends beyond the particular subject. Does he help the child develop a perspective?[14]

These same criteria are appropriate for evaluating explicitness in sex and bodily functions in books for children. The theme of John Donovan's book *Remove Protective Coating a Little at a Time* is the physical and emotional maturing of a lonely, constrained 14-year-old. Harry is the only child in a success-oriented family with his still-young father in advertising and his mother going into and slowly coming out of a nervous breakdown. Preoccupied with his developing sexuality, Harry can't communicate with his parents. His understanding of sex must come from others. His first lesson is from his best friend in fifth grade, who asks him if he ever got "hard-ons."[15] Later on Harry attempts to have intercourse with Marilyn, the "sure score" at summer camp:

> Harry tried. He thought of every wonderful thought he had ever had about sex, but nothing happened. . . . Harry sat, silent, his shorts still tangled around his ankles.[16]

Harry's touch with reality is an eccentric old woman he meets in the park. She has great shock value in his life because, unlike his parents, she is so obviously sure of herself and so willing to talk with him forthrightly. Harry can't have conversations with his parents, but he can talk to Amelia; he can't touch his father in a satisfactory way, but he can lie comfortably with Amelia on her old beat-up mattress in her shabby room in a condemned building. The writing is vivid with the impact of modern poetry. The explicit references to sex are straightforward, not inserted for shock value but as a necessary part of understanding growing up in today's artificial world.

Sex-role Stereotyping

Since children's books have always reflected the general social and human values of a society, it is not surprising that they are now being scrutinized closely for sexist attitudes. The raised general consciousness level of the children's book world is reflected in the increasing number of books which present positive images of girls and women.

However, teachers, librarians, authors, and editors are more aware of racial stereotyping than of sex prejudice. (Racism in books will be discussed in the section "Appreciating Racial and Ethnic Diversity," later in this chapter.) All stereotyping is dehumanizing, for it treats individuals as a group, without regard to individual

[14] James C. Giblin. "Violence: Factors Considered by a Children's Book Editor," *Elementary English*, Vol. 1 (January 1972), pp. 64–67.

[15] John Donovan. *Remove Protective Coating a Little At a Time* (New York: Harper & Row, 1973), p. 8.
[16] Donovan, pp. 12–14.

differences, personalities, or capabilities. A book may be considered sexist if women and girls are exclusively assigned traditional female roles, or if men and boys are expected to behave in certain prescribed ways always assuming leadership roles and the exclusive rights to certain professions.

The difficulty in decrying a book as sexist is the fact that stereotypes develop from what was once considered the norm. One hundred years ago in this country most women were housewives; the agrarian society depended upon them. We should not reject such a fine book as *Witch of Blackbird Pond* (Speare) because the heroine's greatest problem appears to be whom she will marry. In 1688 Kit had little other choice. We can, however, delight in her rebellion against the strict Puritan way of life in Wethersfield, Connecticut; in her courageous friendship with the Quaker "Witch," Hannah; and in her compassion for the child, Prudence. Again there is no point in denouncing fairytales for their sexist portrayal of beautiful young girls waiting for the arrival of their princes, for evil stepmothers or nagging wives. Such stories reflected the longings and beliefs of a society long past. To change the folk tales would be to destroy our traditional heritage. A book should not be criticized, then, for being historically authentic or true to its traditional genre. However, we have every right to be critical when such stereotyped thinking is perpetuated and appears in contemporary literature. Today's books must reflect a more liberated point of view and allow for a wide range of occupation, education, speech patterns, and futures for all persons, regardless of race, sex, creed, or age.

Sex discrimination permeates our modern society to the point where it is seldom questioned. It is not surprising, then, to find examples of sex prejudice in books for children. But well-written contemporary literature must do more than mirror society, it must make its own comment about it and help the reader view society in a new perspective. In *Up a Road Slowly*, Irene Hunt has helped the reader to see many dimensions to the character, Uncle Haskell. Despite the fact that he was an alcoholic and a pathological liar, he could be kind and helpful to his niece, Julie. Because he is a sympathetic character, his advice to Julie carries more importance for her and, unfortunately, the reader. As Julie talks about her future, notice Haskell's answer:

> "If I [Julie] ever have a boy, I'm going to see that he gets the blame for the things he does just as much as the girls do," I said.
>
> "You're never going to get the chance to have a boy if you don't do something about that truculent little chin of yours." He got to his feet, hoisted the golf bag to his shoulder, and stooped to tweak my nose. "Accept the fact that this is a man's world and learn to play the game gracefully, my sweet."[17]

This is the kind of advice you might expect from the Uncle Haskells of this world, but both Julie and the author appear to accept it, for they make no rejoinder.

In the story of *Henry 3*, Joseph Krumgold was attempting to explore the hypocrisy of suburban living—the importance of having the "right" friends and living in the biggest house. Henry is hurt that his father evidently cares more about being vice-president of his firm than in being honest with his son. His mother obviously *likes* Crestview. Only his friend Fletcher and Fletcher's eccentric grandfather understand him. When there is a chance that Henry and his family will have to leave Crestview, Fletcher's grandfather tells him not to worry, that Crestview is no place for a boy to grow up in and be a man because it is a *woman's world*:

> ". . . you're living in a woman's world here. Crestview is her idea. . . . It is simply that these women have to be safe. They have their children to protect. Their first big idea is to get enough security to bring up a family. And the second, they have to be in fashion. Because in a place like this a woman can't grow old. Every year she has to look new again, as if she's just starting out. . . . I don't say there's anything wrong with those two ideas, style and security. But so help me, they're not big enough, that's all.[18]

Despite such deprecating passages some children's books do provide a positive image of women. In the story of *Queenie Peavy* (Burch), Queenie throws rocks and spits tobacco, but she

[17]Irene Hunt. *Up a Road Slowly* (Chicago, Ill: Follett, 1966), p. 31.
[18]Joseph Krumgold. *Henry 3* (New York: Atheneum, 1969), p. 134.

shows compassion for a classmate who faints from hunger. Gradually, Queenie learns that she doesn't have to fight the world because her father is in prison. She loses some of her antagonism, but she never loses the integrity of her own person.

Many books of children's literature present the "Tomboy Turned Beautiful Young Woman" theme. *Kick a Stone Home* by Smith does not follow this typical pattern. Fifteen-year-old Sara is a good football player and the boys *want* her on their team. However, she does not date the team members; she has few friends; and is still recovering from her parents' divorce of three years ago. She is unsure of everything except her vocation, having decided to be a veterinarian. How Sara gradually comes to terms with herself and her emotions makes for a well-written story of the difficulties of early adolescence. It may be, however, that the author has worked too hard to prove that her heroine is different from other girls, thereby making Sara too unique. This is a real danger when writing in a somewhat self-conscious area.

The two survival stories, *Island of the Blue Dolphins* (O'Dell) and *Julie of the Wolves* (Jean George) certainly portray strong female characters. Other positive images of independent girls are also found in such fantasies (*see* Chap. 5) as *Pippi Longstocking* (Lindgren), *The Summer Birds* (Farmer), and *A Wrinkle in Time* (L'Engle). In the latter book the friendship between Meg and Calvin is an honest friendship based upon mutual respect, rather than a romantic relationship. Meg's mother and father are both scientists, providing a model of a marriage in which both parents achieve career fulfillment. Historical fiction (Chapter 8) and, of course, biography (Chapter 9) provide many other positive models of independent females.

In preparing a revised list of non-sexist books about girls titled *Little Miss Muffet Fights Back*, the editors indicate the criteria they used in searching for appropriate books:

1. Looked for girls and women in fiction who were shown as active, interested and interesting people involved in exciting work and adventures.
2. Looked for stories of girls and women with positive personality characteristics—intelligence, independence, warmth, bravery, strength and competence.
3. Also concerned with the fictional portrayal of positive adult female roles other than that of mother. They searched for books in which girl characters *were* ambitious, in which girls did take pride in their own achievements.
4. Also looked for authors' explicit comments on sex discrimination where required by the plot.
5. Searched for books which dealt thoughtfully with the problems of friendship and of loving other people—books in which romantic love is not portrayed as a girl's only satisfaction.
6. Finally, looked for writing of quality and merit, books in which literary merit and valid themes combine to delight, and inspire, readers.[19]

Boys, too, have been victimized by sex-role stereotyping in children's literature. They have been consistently reminded that boys don't cry, for example, so that it is a relief to find in a story such as Eleanor Clymer's *Luke Was There* that tough Julius cries openly when he voluntarily returns to the children's home and finds his favorite social worker is there:

> I looked and there was Luke. He stood there looking at me over the kids' heads and then he grabbed me and I put my arms around him, and put my head against him and cried. I couldn't help it. I tried to stop but I couldn't. Luke didn't mind. He just kept patting me on the back and saying, Its okay, its okay, take it easy.[20]

In an article titled "The Cult of Kill in Adolescent Literature,"[21] Kelty points out that another form of sex-role stereotyping for boys is frequently found in animal stories. In books such as *Old Yeller* by Fred Gipson and *The Yearling* by Rawlings the main characters must kill the very animal that they have loved the most as their initiation into manhood. In *The Yearling*, Jody is ordered to shoot his pet deer because it is de-

[19] *Feminists on Children's Media. Little Miss Muffet Fights Back*, rev. ed. [Whitestone, N.Y. 11357: Feminist Book Mart (162-11 Ninth Avenue) 1974], pp. 18, 19, 20.
[20] Eleanor Clymer. *Luke Was There*, illustrated by Diane de Groat (New York: Holt, Rinehart and Winston, 1973), p. 64.
[21] Jean McClure Kelty, "The Cult of Kill in Adolescent Literature," in *English Journal* (February 1975), pp. 56–61.

Honest emotion is expressed in this picture as Luke welcomes home a runaway boy.
From *Luke Was There* by Eleanor Clymer. Illustrated by Diane de Groat. Copyright © 1973 by Eleanor Clymer. Copyright © 1973 by Holt, Rinehart and Winston, Inc. Reproduced by permission of Holt, Rinehart and Winston, Publishers.

stroying the family's crops. At the book's end he recalls his love for his pet:

> He did not believe he should ever again love anything, man or woman or his own child, as he loved the Yearling. He would be lonely all his life. But a man took it for his share and went on.[22]

In *Old Yeller*, the boy must shoot his beloved dog that just saved two of his family from an attack by a wolf because the wolf *might have been rabid.* After he has shot the dog, his father tells him: "Now the thing to do is to try and forget it and go on being a man."[23] The pattern is repeated in Peck's *A Day No Pigs Would Die;* the boy becomes a man the day he helps his father kill, Pinky, the boy's pet pig. As the boy kisses his father's bloody hands, his father tells him: "That's what being a man is all about, boy. It's just doing what's got to be done."[24] Girls are conditioned early to be dependent little girls; Kelty questions the way in which some of our "best" literature conditions boys to be hard and strong.

The "New" Didacticism

In writing a book on social or personal problems there is a very real danger that the author

[22] Marjorie Kinnan Rawlings. *The Yearling,* illustrated by Edward Shenton (New York: Scribners, 1938), p. 400.
[23] Fred Gipson. *Old Yeller,* illustrated by Carl Burger (New York: Harper & Row, 1956), p. 156.

[24] Robert Newton Peck. *A Day No Pigs Would Die* (New York: Dell, 1972), p. 129.

will attempt to preach or teach. The book written solely to promote an ideological position—such as a non-sexist book, or a story showing the evils of prejudice, or the narrow-mindedness of suburbia—may be overpowered by its theme, didactic in its approach.

A slight story for middle-grade children entitled *Meaning Well* by Shelia Cole is one of a number of books on the theme of child's inhumanity to child. A group of sixth-grade girls talk about one of their classmates whose father is an alcoholic. They decide to be nice to Peggy and the girl is delighted with her new-found friends, asking them all to her birthday party. At the last moment one of the girl's fathers offers to take some friends to Disneyland on the night of the party. Lisa's mother won't let her go, saying that she must go to the party no matter what the other two girls do.

> Susan was selfish, or as Lisa's mother said self-centered. The only person she thought of was herself. She shouldn't have taken everyone to Disneyland on the day of Peggy's party. But Susan was one of those people who did whatever she wanted to do, no matter what the consequences would be. Yes, she could be very nice when it suited her. She could also be very mean.[25]

Such commentary by the author seems very moralistic, leaving little opportunity for the reader to draw conclusions about Susan.

The problem in writing a book with a message is that the theme will dominate and the book will lack the quality of imagination that distinguishes literary merit. This seems particularly true of the "ad hoc book," the one written intentionally to expose a particular problem. The writing in such made-to-order books is usually sharply contrasted with those books that have grown from the author's own experiences and feelings.

The Background of the Author

A related controversy swirls about the racial background of the author. Must an author be black to write about blacks, Chinese to write about Chinese, American Indian to write about American Indians, and so on? One point of

view[26] urges that non-white minority authors should be the writers of so-called ethnic books. Certainly it is generally accepted that an author can write best about what he or she has experienced. Yet the hallmark of fine writing is the quality of the imagination with which that writing is involved. Imagination is not the exclusive property of any race or sex but the universal quality of all fine writers. There are more blacks writing and illustrating today than ever before. Some of these authors and artists are not going to want to be limited to writing only about the black experience, nor should they be limited in this way. We need to focus on two aspects of every book: (1.) What is its literary merit? and (2.) Will children enjoy it?

In preparing her bibliography of *The Black Experience in Children's Books*, Augusta Baker used another criterion for selecting books, namely their contribution to the Black Experience:

> Blacks and whites have each, from their own vantage point, made a contribution to the "Black Experience" in the past and in the present and they will both contribute in the future. Work of an author or artist, black or white, has been included and recognized wherever it has demonstrated a sensitivity to the black man's striving to fulfill the American dream or attempting to maintain his identity, with dignity, in the total human community.[27]

On "Becoming" One's Own Person

The story of every man, every woman is the story of growing up, of becoming a person, of struggling to become one's own person. The kind of person you become has its roots in the experiences of childhood—how much you were loved, how little you were loved; the people who were significant to you, the ones who were not; the places you've been, and those you did not go to; the things you wanted, and the things you did

---

[25]Shelia Cole. *Meaning Well,* illustrated by Paul Raynor (New York: F. Watts, 1974), p. 29.

[26]*Interracial Books for Children.* Vol. 3 (Autumn 1971). Particularly the editorial, "Criteria and Racism," and Ray Anthony Shepard, "Adventures in Blackland with Keats and Steptoe," pp. 2–3.

[27]Augusta Baker. *The Black Experience in Children's Books* (New York Public Library, 1971), p. iii.

not get. Yet a person is always more than the totality of his experiences; the way he organizes, understands, and relates to those experiences makes his individuality.

Childhood is not a waiting room for adulthood but the place where adulthood is shaped by one's family, peers, society, and, most importantly, the person one is becoming. The passage from childhood to adulthood is a significant journey for each person. It is no wonder that children's literature is filled with stories of growing up in our society today.

LIVING IN A FAMILY

Within the family the human personality is nurtured; here the growing organism learns of love and hate, of fear and courage, joy and sorrow. The first "family-life" stories tended to portray life without moments of anger and hurt, emphasizing only the happy or adventurous moments. Today the balance scale has tilted in the other direction, and it is difficult indeed to find a family story with well-adjusted children and happily-married parents.

In earlier stories the parents recede into the background as cardboard figures, and the emphasis is on the children. More recent books have included adults with both strengths and weaknesses, and show children interacting with them. In some almost "formula stories" parents are depicted as completely inept and unable to understand or cope with their children. It would seem a balance is needed if children are to see life wholly and gain some perspective from their reading.

Earlier Happy Family Stories

Eleanor Estes created believable children of the pre-television era in her books, *The Moffats, The Middle Moffat,* and *Rufus M.* Despite their economic hardships, these very independent children have fun and share each other's problems. The Halloween stunt they devise is especially amusing. There is adventure as Rufus Moffat rides the freight train to get little Hughie Pudge back to school; there is laughter and drama as Joe is unwillingly catapulted into a dance recital. These stories tend to be episodic, with little character development; however, they

do provide an opportunity for the vicarious experience of warm family relationships.

Another book in which a somewhat aloof father and unusually patient housekeeper seem relatively unimportant is *The Saturdays* by Enright. New York in the early 1940s was quite different from today, and the Melendy children seem amazingly close knit despite their age range. Their plan to pool their allowances so that each child, in turn, may enjoy a special Saturday excursion brings humor and pathos. Randy goes to an art museum, Rush to the opera, and Oliver goes alone to the circus. When Mona returns with haircut and curls from the beauty salon she feels guilty; yet, she feels secure in this process of emerging into an adolescent:

> She was safe in her bed, the house enclosed her in a shell of warm security and all about, on every side, were the members of her own family who loved and understood her so well. She felt calm and happy.[28]

Family life in a Lower East Side Jewish home is portrayed in Taylor's *All-of-a-Kind Family* books. The books recreate life in the 1930s, a life much slower than the modern tempo. Titled "All-of-a-Kind" because all are girls until a baby boy is born, the children also understood that all-of-a-kind means they are Jewish and "we're all close and loving and loyal—and our family will always be that." Children will better understand their parents' points of view after reading the incident in which Sarah refuses to eat her soup before the meat and vegetables. Mama holds to the rule, and the soup appears at Sarah's plate for two meals. This incident, as many others, is as modern as the newest cereal, and could well be used for role-playing and a discussion of parental roles. The descriptions of Jewish feasts and holy days contribute much to an understanding of religious faith. *More All-of-a-Kind Family* and *All-of-a-Kind Family Uptown* continue the family chronicle, and show the girls growing up.

Families in other countries have close relationships, too. Meindert DeJong sensitively interprets childhood in *Far Out the Long Canal* and *Shadrach.* Moonta of *Far Out the Long Canal* is the

---

[28] Elizabeth Enright. *The Saturdays* (New York: Holt, Rinehart and Winston, 1941), p. 102.

only son of two champion ice skaters, but he has not learned to skate although he is 9 years old. DeJong has captured Moonta's desperate anxiety to achieve skill in skating after his understanding mother gives up her skating tour in order to teach him. Although he disobeys and goes off alone to the far place where his father had promised to take him, Moonta heroically warns his father and grandfather of melting ice, and all return to the warmth of the home where the inner warmth of understanding glows as brightly as the fire.

In *Shadrach*, DeJong demonstrates his fine literary skill in the interpretation of a small boy's deep emotional attachment to a pet rabbit. This story also portrays Davie's secure place in a family that loves him all the more because he had been desperately ill. His grandpa and dad try to make the boy physically and emotionally well by giving him work, providing a pet to care for, and urging him to grow up. Davie's mother is overprotective, yet very understanding. To his father, Davie says: "You want to make me big all of a sudden, but Mother wants to keep me sort of sick, and sort of a baby."[29]

Joan Phipson has written several stories of the Barker family who live on a sheep station in Australia. In *The Family Conspiracy*, the children work to earn money for an operation for their mother. Their successes and failures unite this family in which each member has his place. In *Threat to the Barkers*, there is a mystery; and *The Boundary Riders* shows the development of courage in a crisis. Each story makes the Australian countryside and work on the station very real. These books present more than the facts about another land; the characters are well worth knowing.

One of the outstanding family stories of recent years is *Meet the Austins* by Madeleine L'Engle. No one character stands above the others, although the narrative is told in first person from the point of view of 12-year-old Vicki. Many difficult problems are faced by the Austins during one year. The quiet way in which the parents and children show their sympathy for Aunt Elena when her husband dies demonstrates the faith and security of the family. When Maggy, an orphan, comes to live with the Austins, her be-

havior corrodes the fine family unity. Vicki's accident creates another problem. When Mother takes the older children to a hilltop to look at the stars after they learn of Uncle Hal's death, the children express their curiosity about growing up and having things change. Their mother responds:

> "We can't stop on the road of Time. We have to keep on going. And growing up is all part of it, the exciting and wonderful business of being alive. We can't understand it, any of us, any more than we can understand why Uncle Hal and Maggy's father had to die. But being alive is a gift, the most wonderful and exciting gift in the world. And there'll undoubtedly be many other moments when you'll feel this same way, John, when you're grown up and have children of your own."[30]

Children in this family are included in serious discussions; grown-ups respect their difficult questions and share knowledge with the younger generation. When John, the eldest with the scientific bent, says Einstein didn't believe in God, his grandfather reads Einstein's own words to him. The author reflects this same kind of respect for children who read the book. Some will say that Dr. and Mrs. Austin are just too good to be true. However, there are adults whose inner convictions are sure, whose sights are set on the future to encourage children's values instead of their own temporary convenience. At a time when some are questioning the continued existence of family life as we have known it, it is indeed good to "Meet the Austins."

Relationships within a Family

Norma Klein has written two very contemporary stories about a child's reactions to the arrival of a new sibling. *Naomi in the Middle* is written from the point of view of Naomi, who is 7. Both Naomi and her mother are very frank and matter of fact about the conception of a baby. The story is slight, merely waiting for the baby's arrival. However, it is easy reading and the family is a warm and caring one. *Confessions of an Only Child* has more structure than *Naomi in the Middle* and reveals more change in the narrator-charac-

[29] Meindert DeJong. *Shadrach*, illustrated by Maurice Sendak (New York: Harper & Row, 1953), p. 104.

[30] Madeleine L'Engle. *Meet the Austins* (New York: Vanguard, 1960), p. 40.

A sleepy father and an older sister assume responsibility for the baby's night feeding.

Copyright © 1974 by Pantheon Books, a Division of Random House, Inc. Reprinted from *Confessions of an Only Child*, by Norma Klein and illustrated by Richard Cuffari, by permission of Pantheon Books, a Division of Random House, Inc.

ter. Antonia (Toe) is 9 years old and an only child. Her mother is pregnant and Toe's best friend, Libby, has a toddler sister who is the criterion against which Toe measures the idea of having another child in the family. Toe and Libby discuss the terrible things that this Baby Matilda does. But then the two friends decide that a boy baby would be much worse.

"Because they do this really awful thing," Libby said. "I saw it at my cousin's house. When you're changing their diaper they pee right up in the air, in your eye even, if you don't look out."

I made a face, "Ugh."

"It's pretty bad," Libby said. "Girls at least pee straight down."[31]

Toe's mother has a miscarriage, and during her hospital stay Toe is sent to stay with her Aunt Marjorie, her mother's sister. Toe feels a sense of loss so that when her mother becomes pregnant again very soon, Toe shares her parents' anticipation and their delight when a baby boy is born. This story reflects a feminist point of view. Toe's mother is in law school, and her father shares household chores as a matter of course; he fixes dinner at least one night of the week and he and Toe do the laundry together. Toe's Aunt Marjorie is young and attractive and shown living a single, enviable life. There is a contemporary frankness about the discussion of pregnancy ("See, Toe . . . my belly button's gone away!") and the language in general ("'God damn it,' Dad said as he tried to wall paper the back room").[32] Toe reflects the family's values of materialism as she wonders what presents she will get when the new baby arrives. Yet sophisticated as it is, the story does reveal considerable tenderness, acceptance, and a warm, if not traditional, family feeling. It is, however, a "slice of life" story picturing a modern liberal family. Unfortunately, it lacks the quality of imagination that one looks for in fine writing.

A very different family life and middle child are portrayed by Paula Fox in *The Stone-faced Boy*. Gus is the middle child of five in the Oliver family. They live in the country and their father commutes to New York City. Gus has learned to keep an expressionless face as a defense against his shyness and the teasing of his brothers and sisters, who call him "stone-face." On the day of the great snowstorm the family have a surprise visit from Great-Aunt Hattie who senses that there is something behind the mask that Gus wears. She gives him a geode, a symbol of his inner personality. That night his younger sister, Serena, talks him into going to rescue a stray dog that she has found just that day and which has now gotten caught in a foxtrap. Gus does go, but he is terrified during the whole ordeal and even considers coming back. He returns to find that his family has hardly missed him. Only Aunt Hattie realizes the significance of the journey out into the dark night. Gus has changed, and when the 4-year-old in the family hits him with a broom, Gus for the first time

[31] Norma Klein. *Confessions of an Only Child*, illustrated by Richard Cuffari (New York: Pantheon, 1974), p. 7.

[32] Klein, *Confessions of an Only Child*, p. 17.

picks him up by his ankles and holds him upside down until he promises not to do it again. He asserts himself again when he refuses to break open the geode when his brother asks him to:

> He knew how the stone would look inside, but he didn't choose to break it open yet. When he felt like it, he would take the hammer and tap the geode in such a way that it would break perfectly, in such a way that not one of the crystals inside would be broken.[33]

The reader knows that behind Gus's stone face lies a personality intact and as perfect as the crystals of the geode. This is more a story of a boy's finding himself than a family story. Yet it is the internal relationships of the family that have caused Gus to be the person he is and will become. *Portrait of Ivan,* also by Paula Fox, is another quiet, sensitive story of a boy's search for himself.

A pair of twins begin to assert their separate identities in a similar search for their dog in Barbara Corcoran's story, *A Trick of Light.* Always very close, Paige and Cassandra are the youngest of a warm, contemporary rural New Hampshire family. Paige is beginning to develop his current interests—ham radio and new close friendships with other boys—and his twin sister feels left out. At winter's end their dog Bingo is struck by a car and drags himself wounded across the snow. The twins follow him, but darkness catches them too far away from home to return. They spend the night in a camp closed for the winter and continue their search in the morning. They separate in order to cover more territory. Hearing barking, Cassandra runs across black ice and falls into a pond. She struggles out and Paige takes her back to the lodge to get her dry and warm. As he pulls her home on a sled, they see the dog lying in the snow. The doctor orders Cassandra to bed for a day or so, and the dog is taken to the vet, but can't be saved. Paige sticks close to his sister ("twin first" is an old family expression), and Cassandra has a long conversation with her mother that helps her understand Paige better. At last she urges him without resentment to visit his ham radio friend:

> She had to struggle to keep her new, calm, grown-up tone. "We're growing-up, that's all. We can't hang onto each other like little babies. You'll have your friends. I'll have mine."
>
> She looked at his face in the mirror, at her own face beside it. They didn't look as much alike as they used to, she thought. His face was getting longer or something.[34]

Few stories have been written about twins finding their own identities. Barbara Corcoran's writing is tight and understated. She faces reality without sentimentality. The dog does die. The twins must go their separate ways if they are to become individuals in their own right.

There are not many stories that depict a girl's relationship with her mother (*Freaky Friday* by Mary Rodgers is an exception and it is a fantasy!—*see* Chapter 5). Several books, however, portray father-son relations.

In the book, *The Grizzly,* David has been reared by his mother after she separated from his father. When he is 11, the boy, who has less than average physical skill and endurance, is taken on a camping trip by Mark, his rugged, outdoorsman father. David fears that his father will leave him alone to test him. He recalls the way Mark was always trying to make him strong when he was small, and so he is still afraid. The authors build a sense of threat in a rising crescendo. Even the description of the setting heightens the anxiety. For example, dawn is painted in taut prose:

> The fire made a small pinch of warmth in the vastness of the fog. . . . Around him out there in the haze the valley seemed to crouch, waiting. Even the mutter of the river was hushed in the ghostly white of dawn. David felt threatened.[35]

As the day wears on, Mark and David meet the unexpected—a grizzly that chases David and attacks Mark. David proves he does have skill, endurance, and courage in a crisis. His father experiences for the first time fear for himself and his boy. Each learns from the other, as respect and understanding grow between father and son.

In his second Newbery Award book Krumgold writes of Andrew Rusch, who wants to be like

---

[33] Paula Fox. *The Stone-faced Boy,* illustrated by Donald A. Mackay (Englewood Cliffs, N.J.: Bradbury, 1968), p. 106.

[34] Barbara Corcoran. *A Trick of Light,* illustrated by Lydia Dabcovich (New York: Atheneum, 1973), p. 115.

[35] Annabel Johnson and Edgar Johnson. *The Grizzly,* illustrated by Gilbert Riswold (New York: Harper & Row, 1964), p. 3.

his father, a hardware merchant in the small town of Serenity. However, Mr. Rusch hopes to realize his own dreams of becoming a scientist through his son. When Andy discovers he has an ability to communicate with an immigrant town bum, *Onion John*, he transfers his loyalty, and resents his father's interference with the superstitions and rituals of this character. Andy is hurt by the way his father and the townspeople try to change Onion John into a "proper citizen" by building an acceptable home for him. Finally, Andy is freed from his father's dominance and the superstition of Onion John. Each of these men contributes to Andy's growing independence.

Another Newbery Award book, *It's Like This, Cat* by Emily Neville, describes a boy's relationship with his father. Dave's insistence upon having a pet cat despite his father's disapproval symbolizes his growing independence. The opening scene in which Dave's father roars at him about a record he is playing is repeated in countless homes. Dave has some understanding of the reasons for his father's raving and realizes their arguments cause his mother's asthma. Dave's encounters with Nick, with girls, with Mary, whose intellectual parents seem to care little about her, Aunt Kate, the eccentric who liked cats, and the school are depicted in realistic first-person style. Dave sees his father in a new light when he helps Tom, an older boy who gets into trouble. Dave and his father do not settle all their quarrels. There is the beginning of tolerance, but the author leaves the family still struggling to attain some degree of harmony.

The title *Gull 737* is derived from the number given a seagull chick being studied by a biologist, Dr. Rivers. Author Jean George includes fascinating information about gulls and research procedures in this narrative that portrays a boy growing up and a father realizing he has a responsibility to his family as well as to science. When there is a plane crash caused by gulls on a runway, Dr. Rivers is called in to help solve the problem. His son Luke's suggestions are accepted by another scientist, and Luke becomes excited about his own investigation—not for money or for fame but *to find out for himself.* Luke realizes his father is self-centered and close-minded, so he defies his father by leaving to begin his own study. "He had just stepped out

of his father's image of him . . . a nice little boy . . . and he was finding the new suit of manhood a loose garb to wear."[36]

A father-daughter relationship is explored in *Sam* by Barbara Corcoran. Sam has spent the first fifteen years of her life on an island away from the civilized world that her father abhors. At the beginning of the book Sam is attending school with other children for the first time in her life. Unlike her brother Mark, Sam wanted to be with her peers. However, at first it seems as if her father is right—the girls are snobbish to her; the boys are tough. The aunt and uncle with whom Sam stays are also ineffectual human beings; the aunt is a helpless kind of woman, and the uncle a weak man who gambles. Yet, despite all these difficulties, Sam feels a part of the human race and realizes that her father's choice of life is a form of running away. A sub-plot of this story involves Sam's entry in a dog show, and would appeal to those readers who enjoy dog stories.

The extended family of grandparents and aunts and uncles also appears in children's books. In Eleanor Clymer's book the responsibility for *My Brother Stevie* was given to 12-year-old Annie Jenner. In fact, the last thing her mother had told Annie before she left, was: "Take care of your brother." Stevie is 8 years old and "full of the devil." Grandmother, who had reluctantly taken the children to live with her in a big city project apartment, can't cope with Stevie either. He breaks into candy machines and throws rocks at trains; and Annie is frightened. Then Stevie gets a new teacher, Miss Stover, and Annie has someone who can help her with him. Stevie does behave better in school until suddenly Miss Stover is called home, and Stevie reverts to his old ways. Annie devises a desperate scheme resulting in a train ride to Miss Stover's house in the country. Stevie changes, but so, too, does his grandmother, as Annie's notes show:

> So now everything is pretty much the same as before, but not quite the same, because as I said, we did this thing [the train ride] and it made us all a little different.
>
> Stevie is still a pain in the neck, but not as bad as before. . . .

[36] Jean George. *Gull 737* (New York: Crowell, 1964), p. 169.

Grandma doesn't yell at him so much and she doesn't hit him. I don't know if it's because he acts better—or does he act better because she's more patient.[37]

This is an honest, realistic story that shows the influence of each character upon the other. Clymer does not gloss over poverty, but neither does she wallow in it.

In *The House of Wings*, Sammy's parents leave him behind with his aged grandfather, a recluse in an old run-down house, while they go ahead to find a place to stay in Detroit. Sammy refuses to believe his grandfather and tries to follow them. The old man runs after the furious boy, but in the midst of the chase he calls him to come and look at a wounded crane. Together the two of them catch the crane and care for it. Suddenly the boy desperately wants his grandfather to know him the way he knows birds:

> He wanted his grandfather to be able to pick him out of a thousand birds the way he could pick out the blackbird, the owls, the wild ducks. . . . He said, "My name's Sammy."[38]

His grandfather looks at Sammy and then, instead of calling him "Boy," he calls him "Sammy," and the relationship is sealed. This is one of Betsy Byars' best books. Her two characters are well drawn; the eccentric old man, who is more interested in his geese and owl than his grandson; the boy, Sammy, furious at being left with the old man, uncertain of himself, and desperately wanting to love and be loved:

> Sammy kept looking at his grandfather in a funny way. He didn't know how it was possible to hate a person in the middle of one morning, and then to find in the middle of the next morning that you loved this same person.[39]

Keith Robertson's book *In Search of a Sandhill Crane* is a slower-moving story than *The House of Wings*, but it has some of the same characteristics. Link Keller decides to spend the summer in northern Michigan with an aunt whom he barely knows. Link's father had died when he was a young boy and now his mother has a chance to take a ten-week course in computer operation in Ohio. All her sisters, whom Link knows very well, have offered to have him come and stay with them, but in a perverse moment he announces he is going to Michigan. Once there, he discovers that Aunt Harriet is nothing like his mother's family. She is a poor cook, a timid driver, and rather quiet and reserved. Gradually Link discovers that she is a fine naturalist and an expert photographer. His Uncle Albert had lent him a set of expensive cameras on the condition that Link bring him back a slide of a sandhill crane. When Link sees the weather-beaten old cabin where they are going to stay—no electricity, no plumbing, no television, not even a refrigerator—he determines to get his picture quickly and return to his home in New Jersey. His uncle had said that he would need patience, and patience is just one of the qualities he develops that summer. He comes to appreciate his aunt for the intelligent capable woman she is. He becomes friends with Charlie Horse, an Indian who had gone to the University of Michigan; but most of all he comes to know the frightening power and fragile beauty of nature. In thinking about the chance remark that had brought him to the wilderness, Link comments to Charlie:

> "Funny how little accidents can change your whole life" . . .
> "Sometimes," agreed Charley. "But most of the time they just give you the chance to change it yourself."[40]

It is difficult to decide whether Irene Hunt has told the story of Julie Trelling or her Aunt Cordelia in the Newbery Award-winning book, *Up a Road Slowly*. Julia's mother dies when she is only 7 and Julia is sent to live in the country with her rather stern Aunt Cordelia, an English teacher. Julie is not an easy child to rear. She can be cruel at times, as she was to the dirty, smelly Aggie, a retarded child in her class; she is jealous of her sister's happy marriage, and scorns her alcoholic liar of an uncle. Yet it is Uncle Haskell

---

[37] Eleanor Clymer. *My Brother Stevie* (New York: Holt, Rinehart and Winston, 1967), p. 75.

[38] Betsy Byars. *The House of Wings*, illustrated by Daniel Schwartz (New York: Viking, 1972), p. 141.

[39] Byars, p. 141.

[40] Keith Robertson. *In Search of a Sandhill Crane*, illustrated by Richard Cuffari (New York: Viking, 1973), p. 99.

who saves her from becoming involved with a questionable boy who is exploiting her in many ways. When her father remarries a wise and charming woman, and they ask Julie to return to her own home, Julie finally realizes that she loves Aunt Cordelia dearly and wants to stay in her big old house. The book ends with Julie's graduation from school. Julie has grown up and become a lovely young woman appreciative of friends and family, particularly of Aunt Cordelia. She has plans to marry Danny, a special friend since childhood. This is a romantic tale with memorable characters.

Children of Divorce

With nearly one out of every two marriages now ending in divorce, it is only natural that we should have books describing children's pain and suffering in living through their parents' separation. Three stories, written for children 8 years old and up, depict a child's adjustment to seeing their fathers only occasionally. In *Me Day* by Joan Lexau, Rafer, a black boy, wakes up feeling the excitement that all children feel on their birthdays. He gets out of doing the chores, looks forward to a cake for supper and the treat of choosing the television shows. But even with all these special privileges Rafer has a growing feeling of disappointment. He hasn't heard from his father, and he had hoped he would. Then his mother sends him on a mysterious errand and he finds his father waiting to spend the whole long day with him—his day. This story is really a picture book with an extended text. Lexau writes with a special sensitivity to the problems of special days, such as birthdays, in broken homes. In *A Month of Sundays* by Rose Blue, Jeffrey at least knows that he will see his father every week. At the same time "it was hard having a dad who loved you on Sundays when he used to love you everyday."[41] This is only part of Jeffrey's adjustment since he and his mother moved to New York and Jeff has to go to a new school and make new friends. At first he is desperately lonely and has recurrent daydreams about having his mother home every day again. Then he begins to enjoy life and his multi-ethnic

friends. When one of his former classmates calls him to invite him to a party, Jeff has other plans with his newfound friends and he realizes he doesn't even want to go. Peggy Mann, in her story *My Dad Lives in a Downtown Hotel,* is the most realistic of all of these books in letting the reader *feel* the pain of the situation. Joey is awkward and self-conscious in talking to his dad in the rather sterile surroundings of a hotel room. His mother does have difficulty in telling Joey about the divorce:

> Mom took a dish towel from the back of the kitchen chair. She wiped the tears off her face. Then she started telling me.
>
> It was like a speech she'd been rehearsing over and over. She said the words pretty fast. And it didn't sound like Mom talking at all. "Joey—" she said, "there are some people who just don't seem to get on together. Each one may be perfectly fine as a person. But when the two are married—well, it—doesn't work, that's all. So the sensible thing for those people to do is to—well, break it up. Not live together any more."[42]

There is detail in this book which reveals the characters of Joey, his father, and his mother. Gradually Joey begins to accept his situation. He realizes he is not alone when Pepe Gonzalez (whose father is still in Puerto Rico), tells him there are fifty-three kids in his block living in a house with no father, and so the two of them decide to form a club!

Karen Newman thinks it is the end of the world when her father decided to go to Las Vegas to get a divorce. Suddenly she decides that if she could only get her parents together, they would change their minds. Her plan of showing them her Viking diorama isn't very successful, but then Jeff, her brother, runs away and they have to get together. And it is dreadful. Karen then learns that some very nice people are just impossible when they are together. She finds out that much as she thought divorce was the awful end, *It's Not the End of the World.* This is one of Judy Blume's best books. The characters are well realized, and she has created the tension of the situation. In typical Blume fashion, real humor re-

---

[41] Rose Blue. *A Month of Sundays,* illustrated by Ted Lewin (New York: F. Watts, 1972), p. 28.

[42] Peggy Mann. *My Dad Lives in a Downtown Hotel,* illustrated by Richard Cuffari (New York: Doubleday, 1973), p. 12.

lieves the seriousness of the problem. *I Trissy* by Norma Fox Mazer is also a girl's first-person account of the problems of being caught somewhere between divorced parents. Simultaneously funny and heartbreaking, this is another popular "divorce story" for middle-graders.

Blowfish Live in the Sea by Paula Fox has more depth than the books already mentioned. It is told in the first person from 13-year-old Carrie's point of view. Her half-brother Ben, 19, is a college dropout whose main preoccupation is to scribble "blowfish live in the sea" on old envelopes, oak tables, or dusty windows. This piece of information is important to Ben because it represents his final disillusionment with his own father. Near the end of the story the reader finds out that his father had sent him a blowfish when Carrie was born, saying that it had come from the upper reaches of the Amazon; so Ben's knowledge of the real source of blowfish indicates his resentment of a father who is less than honest. Carrie, who loves Ben, agrees to go with him to meet his father for the first time. They find him in a rundown Boston boarding house. He is fairly unreliable, drinks too much, and is a pathetic character. Ben no longer resents him and decides to stay and help him with his motel, his latest business venture. Carrie realizes that Ben has known what kind of a person his father was for a long time; this makes Ben's decision to try to help his father all the more poignant.

The Alternative Family

Alternative life styles have been explored in some contemporary books for children. One of the most sophisticated and amusing is Norma Klein's *Mom, the Wolf Man and Me.* Twelve-year-old Brett tells the story of her life with her never-been-married mother, who is a freelance photographer. Brett prefers their casual unscheduled life style to the restrictions that she imagines having a father and being part of a conventional family would bring. And so, though she likes Theo, the man with the wolfhound, she tries unsuccessfully to prevent a marriage. Klein describes Brett's reaction to the idea of her mother's marriage:

A week or two later a horrible thing happened. I was sound asleep, when all of a sudden Mom woke me up. She didn't even click on the light,

so I could at least see who it was. She said she and Theo were getting married.

I really felt horribly sick. I can't even describe it. At first, I thought she said they had gotten married, without even telling me. But to hear that they were going to do it anyway was more than I could believe. I couldn't believe Theo would do that after I had that long talk with him and told him how bad it would be.

"You'll have a father!" Mom said. She looked really excited and happy.

"I don't want one," I said.[43]

This is a frank and honest book that may shock some, but it does portray life as it is for some contemporary families. Despite the unconventional family life, this is a warm story that shows much love and caring for each other among its unorthodox characters.

An unusual story that was translated from the Swedish is titled *The Night Daddy* by Maria Gripe, a recent winner of the Hans Christian Andersen award. The story is really about the relationship between the "Night Daddy," a young writer who takes a job as a nighttime babysitter, and his charge, Julia, while her mother works as a nurse. Julia, who is about 9, is very secretive and at first resentful of the night sitter, feeling she is old enough to stay alone. Gradually, she comes to like the "Night Daddy," who is a sensitive young man, unpredictable and good fun. They have many good times together over the antics of Smuggler, his pet owl, and they share a moment of wonder when his night-blooming plant slowly opens. Julia insists that they must write a book together to prove that he does exist, since her friends tease her and tell her that she invented him in place of a real father. (No mention is ever made of her father; Julia's mother is not married, and the reader presumes she never was.) The book itself is supposed to be the result of their decision to write together. The structure of the book alternates between Julia and then the Night Daddy as the narrators. There is little plot and the story has a dreamlike quality appropriate for its nighttime setting.

Vera Cleaver and Bill Cleaver have looked at the harsher aspects of reality—suicide, death,

[43]Norma Klein. *Mom, the Wolf Man and Me* (New York: Pantheon, 1972), p. 119.

retardation, and theft. In the story *I Would Rather Be a Turnip*, they spotlight the problem of an illegitimate child in a small town. Annie is upset when she learns that her sister's illegitimate son, 8-year-old Calvin, is coming to live with them. She is determined to hate him. Only as she sees the senseless prejudice of others to the loving, amiable Calvin does Annie admit to herself how much she really likes him. Her change of heart is also influenced by a fair-minded black housekeeper who is sensitive to both children and the situation. The authors show compassion and humor in the tone of this story.

Children's Rights

Several recent books have focused upon alienated children in a family and their right to attention. M. E. Kerr is the author of a book with the deliberately shocking title of *Dinky Hocker Shoots Smack*. Actually, Dinky, the very fat daughter of a social "dogooder," does not shoot smack; but she does spend a great deal of her time eating and watching her tropical fish! Mrs. Hocker hardly notices her daughter until the night that Mrs. Hocker is to receive the Good Samaritan Award. Then the words "Dinky Hocker Shoots Smack" mysteriously appear on sidewalks, curbstones, and buildings all over Brooklyn Heights. Dinky had painted them there while the banquet was in progress. Horrified, Mrs. Hocker turns her attention from trying to cure drug addicts in the community to the needs of her own daughter. Caustic and witty, Kerr has written a sad social commentary on our times. Dinky's rebellion reflects the desperate need of all children to have their parents see them as individuals. Tucker, a friend of Dinky's, is talking with her cousin one day, and says:

> "I have trouble with relationships in general . . . I don't think I have any relationships . . . I have parents and I have a few friends, but I don't have relationships. I mean, my parents tell me what to do and I do it. And I tell my friends what I've done and they tell me what they've done. Are those relationships? No one even asks me my opinion on anything."[44]

Emma Sheridan, like Dinky, is a real person with a mind of her own. Emma is fat, black, 11 years old, and determined to become a lawyer like her father. However, the last thing in the world that the successful Mr. Sheridan can imagine is his daughter, a female, addressing a courtroom. Emma's little brother, Willie, is also the despair of his father, because Willie wants to be a famous tap dancer like his Uncle Dipsey. In this book, *Nobody's Family Is Going to Change*, written by Louise Fitzhugh just before her death, the author juxtaposes two kinds of stereotyping within one family, sexist and racist. Mr. Sheridan wants Willie to be the lawyer, and he doesn't really care what his daughter becomes. He can't bear the thought of his son filling the old stereotyped role of the black dancer, even though the uncle gets Willie a fine job in a musical. On the one hand Mr. Sheridan is faced with supporting a sexist point of view in not wanting Emma to be a lawyer, and on the other he is doing all he can to break a racial stereotype by refusing to allow Willie to dance. In both instances he is denying the rights of his children to determine the direction of their own lives. In a humorous and bizarre scene Emma falls in with an underground group called the Children's Army. They are organized to fight child-molesters and child-beaters. Emma soon realizes that they are powerless to help her with her father, and in the end she determines that nobody's family is going to change; it is up to the individual to change. So she drops her bombshell at the dinner table one evening by calmly announcing she is going to be a lawyer:

> "Stop saying things just to upset your father!" said Mrs. Sheridan.
>
> "Women lawyers are idiots! They're the laughing stock of any group of lawyers. I think any woman who tries to be a lawyer is a damned fool!" Mr. Sheridan glared at Emma.
>
> "That," said Emma, "is your problem, not mine." To herself she added, And frankly Daddy, I don't give a damn.[45]

All of the characters in this humorous yet serious story are larger-than-life in much the same way

[44]M. E. Kerr. *Dinky Hocker Shoots Smack* (New York: Harper & Row, 1972), p. 152.

[45]Louise Fitzhugh. *Nobody's Family Is Going to Change* (New York: Farrar, Straus, 1974), p. 221.

as were the characters in *Harriet the Spy,* Fitzhugh's earlier breakthrough book. Emma is a strong and likeable person. Her message—that the ultimate responsibility for what we become in life is ours—is an important one. The emphasis upon child rights is certainly timely and significant.

LIVING WITH OTHERS

Three- and four-year-olds have momentary concern for their sandbox companions, but it is not until children go to school that the peer group becomes important. By age 8, what other children think is often more significant than what parents or teachers think, and by 12, the place in the peer group is *all*-important. A few authors are especially sensitive to these patterns of childhood society.

Finding Acceptance by Peers

The classic example of children's cruelty to others who are "different" is the well-known story of *The Hundred Dresses* by Eleanor Estes. Wanda Petronski, a Polish girl from a poor, motherless family, attempts to win a place in the group by telling of the hundred dresses she owns. Of course, she wears the same faded dress to school day after day and is taunted by the other girls because she has a "funny" name and appears to be very stupid. After she moves away, her hundred dresses are presented in an art contest—one hundred fine drawings. The girls understand, too late, but it is Maddie who worries the most. Maddie is also poor, and as she recalls the way the taunting game started, she realizes her own cowardice:

> She had stood by silently, and that was just as bad as what Peggy had done. Worse, she was a coward. At least Peggy hadn't considered they were being mean, but she, Maddie, had thought they were doing wrong.[46]

Peggy and Maddie's letter to Wanda does not really contain an apology, but Wanda does reply with a friendly note. This is not a happy ending, for Maddie will always be burdened by the memory of her cruelty. Written over twenty years ago, this story seems didactic when compared to more contemporary fiction. However, children still respond to its forceful message.

If one can believe the story of *Blubber* by Judy Blume, modern children can be much more vicious to each other than Peggy and Maddie were to Wanda. When fat, 10-year-old Linda Fischer was giving her class report on "Whales," Caroline wrote a note saying: "Blubber is a good name for her." In no time everyone in the class had read the note and Linda was christened "Blubber." The cruelty is unrelenting and overdone. Wendy develops "a how to have fun with Blubber list," including forcing Linda to say: "I am Blubber the Smelly Whale of Class 206"[47] before she can use the toilet. The three girls make Linda show her underpants and force her to kiss one of the boys. They feed her candy, telling her they are chocolate-covered ants until she is sick. No one shows any compassion for the fat girl; even the teachers appear to be totally unaware of the cruelty of the group. In fact, the teachers are stereotyped, cardboard figures who never see a child as an individual and who use such outmoded discipline techniques as keeping the whole class after school or sending a child to stand in the corner. At the end of the book the narrator of the story becomes the next victim of Wendy's cruelty. While few of the characters have any redeeming qualities, this story does show how individuals may be manipulated by a strong leader. It would be an excellent book to discuss in order to help children clarify their values. Who could have stopped Caroline's cruelty to Linda? How could this be done? What could Linda have done, herself?

The characters in Constance Greene's story, *The Unmaking of Rabbit* have more depth than the two-dimensional characters in *Blubber.* Paul's father disappeared when he was 2; his mother was divorced and had no time for him; so he lived with Gran. Gran couldn't understand why the children at school were mean to Paul, putting pencil shavings in his lunch box and calling him "rabbit." And then, suddenly, Freddy Gibson and his gang became friendly with Paul, inviting him

---

[46]Eleanor Estes. *The Hundred Dresses,* illustrated by Louis Slobodkin (New York: Harcourt Brace Jovanovich, 1944), p. 49.

[47]Judy Blume. *Blubber* (Scarsdale, N.Y.: Bradbury, 1974), p. 72.

to their sleepout provided he will join them in their little "plan":

> Paul said nothing. He felt a sudden panic, an urge to run, to escape, combined with another sensation, which sent pleasurable shivers of anticipation down his spine, that he might be on the verge of becoming a member of a group. He had never come even close to being a member of anything, and the prospects were pleasing.[48]

Their "plan" consisted of using Paul to climb in a window of a house they intended to rob. Paul remembers the words of advice of an older boy on how to get out of a tight situation—pretend you are going to be sick. The trick works, and Paul runs home. He has the courage to write the whole story for his English assignment and then is asked to read it aloud. He tells Freddy off and finds a new integrity in himself. No longer "Rabbit," Paul does find a good friend in Gordon, the grandson of one of Gran's best friends. In this story the reader knows the background and motives of the characters. It is easy to empathize with lonely Paul, who loves his Gran but still keeps his suitcase packed under his bed in case his mother should ask him to come and live with her. The characters of Gran and her friends are well developed. Only Freddy and his gang seem one-dimensional. There is a wonderful discussion between Paul and Gordon in which they realize that they haven't told anyone that they love them since they were "little kids." At the end of the story, after Paul's unsuccessful visit with his mother, he tells Gran that he loves her. This, too, is part of the "unmaking of Rabbit."

Twelve-year-old *Amelia Quackenbush* (Sharlya Gold) has a funny name; she wears funny, hand-me-down clothes; she has no friends, and she has just enrolled in a new junior high school. Her family tries to be helpful, but they have their own concerns. Her mother escapes from cooking and the cares of a dingy house by constantly reading; her father loves his three daughters, but can't really support them; one of her sisters, Dorcas, is an ardent feminist; and the other sister, Courtney, is pregnant and unmarried. Then, Amelia meets Donna Rucker, who is nice to her.

[48]Constance C. Greene. *The Unmaking of Rabbit* (New York: Viking, 1972), p. 57.

Amelia is delighted; she has found a friend. Her delight changes to doubt and sickening regret when she is drawn into shoplifting by Donna. Threatening to tell on her, Donna and her boyfriend, Buzz, make Amelia hide a stolen bike in her garage. By this time Amelia is thoroughly frightened and wants to get out of the situation, but doesn't know how. By talking with her sympathetic older sister about "this friend" (really herself), Amelia derives the courage to return a stolen dress to the manager of the store. He is firm but fair, and makes Amelia pay for the necessary mark down of the dress. Free at last of the power of Donna, Amelia can join in the fun of her loving and unique family. The author does not preach, but she shows believable, warm human beings in a family trying to cope with many problems. Rather than just mirror reality, this story provides a window through which the reader may see some of the problems of growing up in a new light.

Harriet the Spy by Fitzhugh is the popular story of a precocious child who finds difficulty in relating to her parents and her peers. The author presents the story in first-person narrative and through the device of Harriet's diary. Harriet keeps careful notes about her parents, her peers, and the eccentric people she observes on her after-school "spy route" in her New York neighborhood. Her nurse, Ole Golly, has been Harriet's sole source of security; when she leaves, Harriet is very lonely. Her sophisticated parents are too busy with their social activities to give more than superficial attention to their daughter until she gets into trouble. When her classmates find Harriet's journal, they form an exclusive "Spy Catchers Club" to retaliate against Harriet. While Harriet is hurt by their treatment, she is never overcome. She does follow Ole Golly's advice—that sometimes you have to lie a little—when she prints a retraction of her statements in the school news. Basically, Harriet remains uncompromising and determined, despite her traumatic experience, but she has gained some understanding and wisdom. Underlying the humor of this story (and Harriet is really very funny) is a serious study of the way children respond to teachers, to their cliques, and to their cruelty to each other.

Two books by Mary Stolz should be read

together, but the sequence of reading *A Dog on Barkham Street* and *The Bully of Barkham Street* seems unimportant. The same characters and events are treated in each book, but from different points of view. Edward is frightened of the bully next door because he is two years younger and smaller. He teases Martin by calling him "Fatso" and "Plump Pudding" and then running to safety. Envious of the parental love Edward receives, and angry because his parents seem uninterested in him and partial to his sister, Martin becomes aggressive and sullen. In *A Dog on Barkham Street*, Edward and his friend recall that Martin had owned a dog briefly but had not taken care of it, and it had mysteriously disappeared. In the other book, *The Bully of Barkham Street*, the reader learns the details of the incident and the intensity of Martin's loss when the dog is peremptorily removed by his parents. There are moments of understanding between his teacher, his sister, his mother, and his neighbors. Martin does go on a diet and tries to reform, only to find that no one notices! The story of Martin and his struggle to find acceptance in his family and with his peers is humorous and heartwarming. Children can develop fresh insights into human behavior by reading both these stories of the same episodes told from two different points of view.

Developing Friendships

Almost all children long for a "special friend," someone to fool around with, to call on the phone, or to "sleep over" at each other's house. *A Girl Called Al* turned out to be this kind of friend for the narrator of her story:

> Al is a little on the fat side, which is why I didn't like her right at first . . . She is the only girl in the whole entire school, practically, with pigtails . . . She has gone to a lot of different schools. She has a very high I.Q., she says, but she doesn't work to capacity. She says things like this all the time but I don't like to let on I don't always know what she is talking about.[49]

The two girls become fast friends; their third best friend is Mr. Richards, the assistant superintend-

ent of their building. He lets them strap rags to their shoes and skate on his kitchen floor to polish it. And when the school won't let Al take shop, he helps both girls build a bookshelf. The girls find him after he has had a heart attack and get their mother to call the super and the doctor. They visit him once in the hospital before he dies in his sleep one night. Their friendship with each other and Mr. Richards has been a part of their growing-up process. Al loses weight and gets her pigtails cut off, much to the disappointment of her friend who misses them. The first-person telling of this book adds humor and verisimilitude to a story of a real friendship. *A Girl Called Al* is worth knowing as a person and as a book.

Only when the Almont was in danger of being torn down, did the tenants unite and try to do something about its condition—and then it was too late. In *We Lived in the Almont*, Eleanor Clymer has told the story of 12-year-old Linda Martin, whose father was the super of the old building. Carol Lopez, Linda's best friend, lived in apartment 5A, but Sharon Ross lived around the corner in a new luxury apartment house. Intertwined with the fate of the building is the friendship of the girls. Sharon is the first to move when her parents are divorced; then Linda and Carol must find new places to live. Clymer has portrayed well the transitory nature of friendship in a mobile urban environment.

Emily Blair was an only child until that amazing summer when she and her mother and father moved into an eighteen-room house and her four cousins came to stay with them. Not only did Emily have an instant family but she discovered Kate, a very special person who wrote poetry as she did. In *Look through My Window*, Jean Little has created the life that every only child might hope for. This is an affectionate story with real characters who come alive. An added serendipity for book lovers are Emily and Kate's rapt discussions about the books they love. Kate's search for her identity through her father's Jewish background is continued in a sequel simply titled *Kate*. In this story Kate makes a friend of young Susan, who becomes important in the untangling of the strands of her life; but Kate's friendship with Emily becomes strained. In the end Kate and Emily are better friends, even though they admit being a trial to each other. Kate comes to terms

---

[49] Constance Greene. *A Girl Called Al*, illustrated by Byron Barton (New York: Viking, 1969), pp. 10–11.

with her Jewishness and starts out for the synagogue alone, but is joined by her father. The story closes as the two of them enter hesitantly but together. The multiple themes of this book are deftly interwoven into a warmly satisfying story.

The long-term friendship between *Peter and Veronica* is tested when Veronica fails to come to Peter's bar mitzvah after Peter had spent days trying to convince his mother to invite his non-Jewish friend. The breach widens during the summer, when Veronica is away on a vacation. When she returns, Peter intends to give her a speech he has planned, only to find that she has one ready for him. In the end it is Peter who has to apologize. This is the sequel to Marilyn Sachs' first book about *Veronica Ganz*. In this story Veronica had been the class bully until little Peter Wedemeyer charmed her out of it. The story of *Peter and Veronica* is a better story with more substance than the earlier one.

Another fine girl-boy relationship is the friendship between Ellen Grae and Grover as portrayed in the book *Ellen Grae* by Vera Cleaver and Bill Cleaver. Ellen Grae has always entertained Grover and Mrs. McGruder (the woman with whom she stays since her parents are divorced) with her wild tales. For example, she told them both about a man who was asphyxiated because he kept his car windows shut in the summer so people would think he had an air-conditioned car! It is no wonder, then, that no one will believe her when she forces herself to reveal the dreadful secret of her friend Ira, a mentally retarded man who lives in an old tin shack by the river. Luckily for Ira, neither Ellen Grae's parents nor the sheriff will believe the weird tale of Ira's parents being killed by the very rattlesnake with which they had intended to eliminate Ira. Ellen's conscience is relieved of the burden of the story and, at the same time, she is freed of the guilt of telling Ira's secret. Unfortunately, in the sequel to this story titled *Lady Ellen Grae*, the authors decide they must tame Ellen Grae. Sent to Seattle to visit her Aunt Eleanor, Ellen Grae manages to pass a few of her tomboy ways along to Cousin Laura. Although Ellen is a strong heroine, who is not easily tamed, the reader has every right to ask if girls must be "tamed" in today's world.

Barbara Rinkoff has told of an unlikely but very believable friendship in *The Watchers*. Chris was a loner, a people-watcher who enjoyed observing people as long as he didn't have to get involved. He had his own problems—his parents were always fighting about his father's gambling; he'd gotten into trouble with the coach when he'd planted a laughing box in Jeff's locker; and now he had to find money for the paperweight that he'd taken from Mr. Schmid's candy store. What he didn't need was a friend like Sanford, the new kid downstairs who looked like a real loser. His hands twitched and his head jerked and the older kids teased him. One day when Jeff was trying to force Sanford to write "Jeff's the Greatest" on the sidewalk, Chris came to his rescue and became Sanford's idol. Chris takes him to the park and to his special "people watching rock"; he starts teaching him to throw a ball and to run. Sandy is sensitive to Chris' moods and finds out about the paperweight. Without being asked, he gives Chris the money and goes with him when he repays Mr. Schmid. The boys play hookey one day and Chris takes Sanford on the subway to the museum and to Brooklyn—all the places Sandy had never been allowed to go on his own. When they return, the boys have to face Sandy's mother and father. Sandy's mother is horrified, since she has always overprotected her brain-damaged son, but Sandy's father looks at him with new respect and plans to take both boys to a baseball game. As the story ends, the marriage of Chris' parents is not resolved, but his emotional problems are, and he has a newfound friend. Sandy's physical handicap remains, but he is beginning to free himself from his overprotective mother and become a person in his own right. Both children needed their friendship and grew stronger because of it.

Three books about friendships revolve around the secret play activities of very intelligent children. In *Jennifer, Hecate, MacBeth, William McKinley and Me, Elizabeth* by E. L. Konigsburg, two girls play at becoming a witch. The girls meet at a school Halloween party. Elizabeth, the narrator of the story, wears a hand-me-down Pilgrim costume, but Jennifer says she is a real Pilgrim witch in an authentic Pilgrim outfit with huge Pilgrim shoes made of buckles and cracked old leather. She agrees to take lonely Elizabeth on as an apprentice until Elizabeth learns to become a proper witch. The process is a long and tedious one, but Elizabeth does learn how to eat raw eggs, cast short spells, and get along with Jennifer. She endures well until the time comes to drop Hilary Ezra, her pet toad, into boiling water. Then Elizabeth refuses, the toad escapes, and Jennifer announces that Elizabeth will never make a proper witch because she is too sentimental! Fortunately the girls' friendship continues:

> Neither of us pretends to be a witch anymore. Now we mostly enjoy being what we really are . . . just Jennifer and just me . . . just good friends.[50]

In the story of *The Changeling* by Zilpha Snyder, Ivy Carson, member of the disreputable Carson family, insists she didn't really belong, that she was a changeling. Mousy Martha Abbott believed her and it became the basis for a long and exciting friendship. Ivy's vivid imagination creates a whole new world for Martha, peopled with fanciful animals and human trees. A beautiful natural dancer, Ivy gets the lead in the junior high-school play, and Kelly Peters begins to plot her revenge. When vandals break into the school, Kelly sees to it that Ivy and Martha are accused. Ivy and her family leave town before Martha's brother and two others of Rosewood's elite confess to the destruction. Only years later, when Martha is a popular and talented high-school sophomore, does she hear that Ivy is in New York as a dancer. She then realizes how much she owes to Ivy for helping her become the poised and talented person she is, instead of the mousy shy person she had been.

April and Melanie invented *The Egypt Game* (also by Snyder) that eventually includes six of the neighborhood children playing in an abandoned storage yard. The game is just good fun, until a child is murdered in the neighborhood and outdoor play is forbidden. Later, parents became more lax and April is attacked one night when she goes out into the yard for a book she had left. Four-year-old Marshall screams and the professor, who had been secretly watching their Egypt game for weeks, calls for help. The murderer is apprehended. Then the children find out

how important their game had been in restoring the professor's interest in living. The children come from a variety of ethnic backgrounds, but the author accepts that as naturally as the reader. Each of the characters has a distinct personality. At the end of the story the group is thinking about playing "Gypsies" next.

Good fun and friendship are also a part of the Joshua Cobb stories by Margaret Hodges. *The Hatching of Joshua Cobb* occurs during his first experience away from home at camp; *The Making of Joshua Cobb* tells of his adjustment to going to a preparatory school; while *The Freewheeling of Joshua Cobb* details the impact on Joshua of a summer bike trip with one of his former counselors, several classmates, and Cassandra, sister of his friend Helen Crane. Each of them changes for the better, and the trip suggests more open roads for Josh.

GROWING TOWARD MATURITY

In building his concept of self, each person comes to answer such questions as: "What kind of person am I?" "What are my roles in society to be?" "What do others think of me?" The self is built through mirrored reactions and interactions with people, places, and things. The child creates the concept of what he is: that he is a worthy person; a person who can succeed; a person who is loved; who can, in turn, respect and love others, as he receives these impressions from others.

As children grow toward adulthood, they may experience brief moments of awareness of this growth process. A conversation, an experience, or a book may bring the sudden realization that a step has been taken to a new level of maturity, and there is no turning back. This step may be toward adult responsibility or acceptance of one's developing sexuality or vocational choice. This process of "becoming," of finding the unique core of self is not easy. In literature, there are models of ordinary boys and girls who find the courage "to be," to stand firm despite pressures.

Developing Sexuality

Recent research (*see* Chapter 1) indicates that boys and girls are growing up physically and psychologically faster than ever before. Girls, particularly, are reaching puberty during the ele-

[50] E. L. Konigsburg. *Jennifer, Hecate, MacBeth, William McKinley and Me, Elizabeth*, illustrated by the author (New York: Atheneum, 1967), p. 117.

mentary-school years rather than during junior high school or high school, as their mothers did. Yet the first story to discuss menstruation was *The Long Secret* by Louise Fitzhugh first published in 1965. In this story Janie, Harriet's scientific friend, very matter-of-factly explains menstruation to Harriet and Beth Ellen. Beth Ellen's grandmother had given her false information, so Janie corrects it. The conversation is childlike and funny. None of the girls are pleased with the prospect, but take some satisfaction in the fact that when they have their periods they'll get to skip gym. By way of contrast, Margaret, in the story *Are You There God? It's Me Margaret* by Judy Blume prays for her period because she doesn't want to be the last of her secret club to start menstruating. She regularly does exercises which she hopes will increase her size 28 bust and she practices wearing a sanitary napkin! Mixed with her desire for physical maturation is a search for a meaningful relation with God. Adults find this book very funny indeed, but it is extremely serious for 11- and 12-year-old girls who share Margaret's concern for their own physical maturation.

Judy Blume has also written a book about the physical and emotional maturing of a boy, *Then Again, Maybe I Won't*. One strand of the story concerns the sexual awakening of Tony, a 13-year-old boy who is embarrassed and full of sexual fears about erection and nocturnal emissions. The other story line concerns the conflicts that Tony feels about his family's new life style. As a result of his father's success in selling an electrical invention, the Miglione family have moved from a cramped two-family house in Jersey City to a big white house on an acre of land on Long Island. Tony is painfully aware of the effects money has on his family, especially his mother, who is determined to keep up with the Joneses. Tony's mother even finds it more important to hire a maid like everyone else than to allow her own mother to continue to play a useful role by cooking for her family. Tony's brother "sells out" according to Tony, when he gives up his teaching career to join his father's business. Joel, Tony's new neighbor, makes crank telephone calls and shoplifts just to see if he can get away with it. Even though he feels it is wrong, Tony can't decide what to do about it. All these psychological pressures and conflicts combine to give Tony such severe stomach pains that he has to go to a hospital and afterward have regular visits with a psychiatrist. At the end of the book Tony is making a better adjustment and becoming interested in a girl in his own class, rather than worshipping 16-year-old Lisa. Joel is caught shoplifting but instead of going to a detention home, he is sent to a military school. At the same time the reader wonders if perhaps Tony has sold out to suburbia, as he looks forward to the new swimming pool that his dad has ordered. The title, *Then Again, Maybe I Won't*, conveys the same ambiguity as the direction of Tony's life. There is no doubt that Tony has achieved physical maturation, but will he be able to sustain his personal values in the difficult task of growing toward psychological and emotional maturity?

Freddy's Book by John Neufeld has only one thin story line—Freddy wants to know the meaning of the four-letter word that he sees in the boy's washroom, on the brick walls, and even on subway windows. The story is really Freddy's search for enlightenment about this hush-hush subject. He asks his mother, his friend, his dad, and his teenage football coach. His mother's explanation is amusing and confusing; his friend's is erroneous; his dad's is somewhat incomplete but loving; while the young coach's is clear yet still retains a fine, feeling tone. This story serves more of a psychological-informative purpose than a literary one. Yet there is no questioning Neufeld's ability as a writer. The writing is clever and some of the dialogue is perfect. However, the story is slight, and this is very much a single-track book. It succeeds best at giving information, and yet it provides a warm and loving background for that information that would be lacking in a nonfiction book. The most difficult task would be to match the book with the child who is ready for it. Most boys 8 and over know part of the sex information covered here, but not very many who haven't reached puberty would know it all or, like Freddy, have it straight. Perhaps the greatest value of the book is to recommend it for parents and teachers. Certainly it would help them see the kinds of questions children want to ask and the well-phrased answers to match. Some of the sexist critics are going to say that the book makes the sex act a male act.

But boys who need to know the answers to Freddy's questions need to accustom themselves to the physical facts before they can deal with the idea that the girl's role might be as important as theirs. Not all communities will be ready to accept *Freddy's Book,* which is too bad, because Freddy is a likeable wholesome boy asking the kinds of questions all boys want answered.

In *I'll Get There It Better Be Worth the Trip,* John Donovan has sensitively told the story of a 13-year-old boy's brief sexual encounter with a friend of his own age and sex. The reader is given enough background about Davy Ross to understand his loneliness and search for love. Following the death of his sympathetic grandmother, Davy is sent to live with his divorced mother in New York City. His mother is an alcoholic who smothers him with love one day and tells him he is ruining her life the next. Davy's father and second wife provide some love and stability, but he can only see them once a week. His only secure affection appears to be from his dachshund, Fred. And then he meets Altschuler, a boy in his class at school, and they have a good time fooling around together. One day, when the two of them are playing with Fred in Davy's apartment, Davy, impelled by an "unusual" feeling, kisses Altschuler and Altschuler kisses him. But as they part they pretend to box, "like tough guys." Davy reassures himself: "I mean a couple of guys like Altschuler and me don't have to worry about being queer or anything like that. Hell, no."[51] Their friendship grows although Davy's mother does not know that there is anything unusual about it until she comes home some days later and find the two boys asleep on the living room floor after they have been sampling her liquor. She becomes hysterical that something "unnatural" has been going on and calls Davy's father to come and talk to him. Davy's father has a sympathetic and understanding talk with him, saying that boys "play around in a lot of ways when they are growing up."[52] Davy feels better, but not for long. For during their talk, his mother has taken Fred out for a walk and the dog gets away from her and

is run over. Davy immediately blames himself for Fred's death. If he hadn't been fooling around with Altschuler, his dad wouldn't have had to talk with him and his mother wouldn't have taken the dog for a walk. Davy is inconsolable and refuses to talk with anyone. He has a fight with Altschuler in the showers after gym. Later he does resume his friendship with Altschuler, yet with the understanding that there will be no "queer business." The boys agree to respect each other, but Davy has lost Fred and his childhood in the encounter. Davy's concern over the rest of his journey into adulthood is captured in the second part of the title of the novel: "It Better Be Worth the Trip."

Charles Norstadt, like Davy, is searching for love and his self-identity when he meets *The Man without a Face.* At 14, Charles is trying to find a way to escape from living at home with his four-times-married mother and his nasty older sister, Gloria. The only solution seems to be to get into boarding school, so he arranges to take tutoring lessons with a local writer, known as "The Grouch," "The Man without a Face," or simply Justin McLeod. Charles slowly grows to respect this man with the badly scarred face. His respect deepens into love as the summer progresses:

> Except for Joey I'd never had a friend, and he was my friend; I'd never really, except for a shadowy memory, had a father, and he was my father: I'd never known an adult I could communicate with or trust, and I communicated with him all the time, whether I was actually talking to him or not. And I trusted him.[53]

The pressures of his family and the summer reach a climax one night when Charles arrives home to find Gloria's boyfriend has kicked his cat so hard that it is dying, and Gloria gives him newspaper clippings telling of the death by alcoholism of his long-lost father. Furious and sobbing, the boy runs to Justin's house for security. As Justin comforts him, Charles expresses his love for him physically and emotionally. The homosexual experience is treated with sensitivity, and the reader understands the situation in the

---

[51]John Donovan. *I'll Get There It Better Be Worth the Trip* (New York: Harper & Row, 1969), p. 143.
[52]Donovan, p. 166.

[53]Isabelle Holland. *The Man without a Face* (Philadelphia and New York: Lippincott, 1972), p. 129.

Through her art, Maria learns to see beauty in her own run-down neighborhood.

Illustrations copyright © 1974 by Frances Gruse Scott. From *Maria's House* by Jean Merrill. Used by permission of Atheneum Publishers.

context of the story. In no way is Justin to blame; he is simply portrayed as a thoughtful, sensitive person who is remarkably good at "salvaging flawed and fallen creatures."[54] Charles passes his exams and goes to school. Later he realizes the truth of what Justin has taught him about freedom and accepting the consequences of your actions and the importance of forgiving yourself. By the end of the story Charles is beginning to accept himself and his selfhood.

Sticks and Stones by Lynn Hall is also a junior novel which deals with the subject of homosexuality. Primarily, it is the story of a 17-year-old who is accused of being a homosexual when he

[54] Holland, p. 158.

is not. In reality, then, its theme speaks to injustice and the horrible power of gossip and rumor to destroy life. The age of its characters would make it more appropriate for older students in junior high school or high school.

Finding One's Self

Most of the stories of physical maturing also suggest a kind of emotional maturing or coming to terms with one's self. The process of becoming a mature person is a life-long task that begins in the latter stages of childhood and continues for as long as a person lives. Many stories of children's literature chronicle the steps along the way to maturity.

A growing point in Maria's life was achieved

when she learned that to be an artist one had to paint what was true. When her art teacher at the museum asked each of the children to paint their own houses Maria was ashamed—she couldn't paint the shabby tenement that was *Maria's House*. At first she decided to paint a storybook house, one she wished she lived in. But then Maria remembered what her proud mother, who worked hard to pay for her art lessons, had told her—that art has to be honest; you have to paint what is true. Jean Merrill has written an honest simple story about one child's decision.

In *After the Goat Man*, Betsy Byars describes one very important day in the life of a large, fat boy by the name of Harold V. Coleman. Harold's summer had been a miserable one of dieting and doing nothing except play Monopoly with his friend, Ada. And then Figgy, grandson of the old eccentric that everyone called "The Goat Man," had joined their Monopoly games. Figgy was very alone in the world except for his grandfather, who had turned strangely quiet when the government had forced him to give up his old cabin in order to make room for a new superhighway. Figgy was worried about his grandfather:

> His grandfather was the only person in the world to whom Figgy was tied. Figgy sometimes thought of other people as being all wound together as if they were caught in one huge spider web. He had only one tie, like a rowboat, and that was his grandfather.[55]

The old man takes his gun and leaves the row of houses built for persons displaced by the highway. Figgy knows his grandfather is going to return to the cabin to protect it. He blurts out the story to Harold and Ada and Ada promptly says they will ride their bikes to the site of the cabin and help Figgy get his grandfather. Harold, who is not the bravest of the three, has some doubts about going after an old man with a gun, but he does join them. Figgy rides behind Harold on his bike down the newly constructed, deserted highway. Going down the hill Harold loses control of the bike and has an accident. He is knocked out momentarily, but Figgy breaks his leg and cries for his grandfather. Harold hears himself offering to go and get the old man and then is frightened when Ada agrees that that is what must be done. Harold worries all the way there that the old Goat Man will shoot him. Once at the cabin he has a sudden awareness of what the place means to the old man, and his responsibility for the accident:

> "It was not at all the way Harold had thought it would be. There was nothing to be afraid of. Instead he felt run through with sadness. He who had avoided looking at hurt people all his life was now looking into the eyes of a man who had been mortally wounded.
>
> With great kindness in his voice Harold said, 'I've come to take you to Figgy.'"[56]

A moment of awareness, of empathy for an old man he never knew proves to be a beginning step toward maturity for Harold. As always, Byars helps the reader feel as the child must feel in a given situation. This is a simple straightforward account of a particular growing point in a child's life.

In *The 18th Emergency* Besty Byars has written another very funny book with the serious theme of facing up to one's responsibility. Benjie (better known as Mouse) and his best friend, Ezzie, have defined seventeen emergencies based upon old adventure movies—impossible situations with miraculous escapes. But neither of them can think of an escape for the eighteenth emergency— what to do about Marv Hammerman, the biggest and, Mouse thinks, the stupidest boy in school. Mouse writes Marv Hammerman's name under the "Neanderthal Man" on the evolution chart in the school hallway; his pleasure is short-lived, however, when he turns to find Marv glaring at him. Instead of facing the danger calmly, as Ezzie has taught him for the seventeen other emergencies, Mouse flees for his life, avoiding Hammerman for two days. Finally Mouse seeks Hammerman out and asks to get it over with. Afterward . . .

> Mouse turned and looked at Ezzie, squinting in the sunlight. He wet his swollen lip with his tongue

[55]Betsy Byars. *After the Goat Man*, illustrated by Ronald Himler (New York: Viking, 1974), p. 56.

[56]Byars, p. 106.

and said, "It was just sort of an honorable thing, Ezzie."

"A what?"

"An honorable thing."

"Hammerman? Honorable?"

Mouse nodded. He knew that he was not going to be able to explain it to Ezzie. He wasn't even sure he understood it himself now. But at the moment when he and Marv Hammerman had met in front of the Rialto, it had been clearly and simply a matter of honor.[57]

Being willing to face problems and certain pain rather than running away represents one aspect of growing up.

Robert Burch has told the poignant story of *Queenie Peavy*, a 13-year-old nonconformist living in a small Southern town during the Depression. Queenie carries a large chip on her shoulder, defying her teachers and being deliberately mean to her classmates because they torment her about her father, who is in jail. But the reader sees another side of Queenie as she helps her overworked mother; plays delightful games with the neighboring children; and talks with Dominick, her old rooster. Queenie lives for the day when her father will get out of jail and return home. He finally does get his parole, but once home, he ignores Queenie. One of the most dramatic scenes occurs when he drives off in a truck so quickly that she is knocked down. When Queenie sees that he has broken his parole by carrying a gun she asks him to give it to her, but he tells her it isn't any of her business. Queenie finally sees the man as he is: irresponsible, not put upon by others, and making his own choices—the wrong ones. Queenie herself is responsible for setting a trap so that Cravey Mason falls and breaks his leg. Fearful of being sent to the reformatory, Queenie determines to prove she can behave properly for an entire day. Both the school principal and a wise judge recognize Queenie's good qualities and see that she is not sent to reform school. When her friend, "Little Mother," faints from hunger Queenie goes along to the doctor's office and is very helpful. He offers to take Queenie on in a

parttime job. When the principal tells her about the offer he adds: "Who knows, you may grow up to be a nurse." Queenie smiles back at him saying, "I may grow up to be a doctor!" Queenie is a gutsy character, hard and defiant one moment and vulnerable and thoughtful the next. But with the help of sympathetic adults, Queenie is on her way to becoming a responsible, mature person.

The Loner by Ester Wier is the story of a migrant boy with no family, not even a name. His code of living is that he has to look after himself and not blame others when they think only of themselves, even though he is left sick and alone in a deserted camp. The grimness of life of the migrant is shown in the scene in which a service-station owner refuses to allow the migrants to drink at the water tap. The first person to show concern for the boy is a girl, Raidy, who plans to give him a name. Just as she is ready to say it, her long hair is caught in the potato-digging machine. With stark realism, yet avoiding details of the horror, Wier describes the accident: "Leaping forward he saw that her yellow hair was caught in the whirring moving parts of the machine. Powerless to help, he stood and watched in cold horror while the machine ripped and tore."[58]

The boy's first reaction is one of anger: "Why wasn't she taking care of herself?" He finishes the day's work in the fields and wanders until he is exhausted. The boy is found by Boss, a huge, stern woman, who manages a Montana sheep ranch. She is a loner, too, brooding over her son who has been killed by a grizzly bear. Tex, the herder, explains that he, too, had been a loner:

One of those who didn't believe anyone cared about them or wanted to help. I figured it was up to me to take care of myself and I didn't need help from anyone. . . . Somebody will care if you just give 'em a chance. . . . There's always people who need you as much as you need them. . . . All you got to do is find 'em, and when you do, you find you're happier carin' about someone else than just about yourself all the time.[59]

[57]Betsy Byars. *The 18th Emergency,* illustrated by Robert Grossman (New York: Viking, 1973), p. 120.

[58]Ester Wier. *The Loner,* illustrated by Christine Price (New York: McKay, 1963), p. 13.
[59]Wier, pp. 34–35.

The boy receives his name, David, from the Bible, and he tries to live up to the biblical example by working and learning. He makes mistakes, but gradually he learns what Boss is trying to teach him—a shepherd's responsibility for his sheep. Extending the ancient symbolism from sheep to helping others, David begins "to throw in his lot with others and work for everyone, not just himself."[60] He helps rescue Tex from a trap, nurses Boss when she is ill, and in a final dramatic scene kills the grizzly that had taken the life of Boss' son. A very real part of David's maturing involves learning how to accept as well as give love.

Gilly Ground is a loner also, a youth torn between his desire for freedom and his longing for peace and security. Kobalt's house seems a haven of peace after the noise of the bells and the clamor of children in the orphanage where Gilly had first lived following his grandmother's death. But gradually Gilly realizes that he is a "royal prisoner" in this house, just as much as he was an inmate of the orphanage. Instead of being channeled by loud bells, fifteen clocks softly determine his actions. Kobalt, the strange man with whom he lives, does provide warm clothing, good food, and fine shelter for Gilly; but there is still no love for him. Like Mash, Kobalt's dog, Gilly is taken care of, but eventually he acquires the same dull look in his eyes that he had first noticed in the eyes of the unresponsive dog. Gilly's attempt to make friends with the dog is his first reaching out to anything outside of himself. His one other outlet is the mysterious tall hunter whom he first met at the stone tower.

Gilly recognizes the terror of his situation when Kobalt beats the dog saying: "Mash must learn to die."[61] Then Gilly discovers a cage in Kobalt's room—just the size for a boy. When Kobalt knows he has turned his ankle, the sadist seems pleased. Gilly says: "My insides leap alive. I shovel my grief for Mash under as many layers of consciousness as I can. I recognize the danger now and it is as keen edged as the blade that kills."[62] Gilly escapes by using one of the ladders to crawl up the chimney. Kobalt finds him at the

tower and tries to kill him. Gilly is saved by Mash, who has survived, and is able to show his response to the love Gilly had given him. Free at last, Gilly goes down the hill presumably to find the hunter and begin a new life. He makes one brief stop at Kobalt's house and scribbles a last defiant message on Kobalt's door: "Dorp Dead." Only years later does he realize that one of the words is misspelled.

Dorp Dead is an intense and complicated novel for children. It is allegorical in nature. Gilly Ground represents all youth caught between its need for security and freedom; Kobalt, the ladder-maker, *is* evil, the eipitome of all evil that wants to control and damage basic personalities. The hunter whose gun has no bullets may represent love or the meaning of life. In an article for *The Horn Book*, Cunningham explains him in this way:

> I think the Hunter is no more or less than that person or, if one is lucky, persons who pass through every life for a moment, or sometimes longer, and give it strength and meaning. Why didn't he have a name? I guess I did not give him a name because he has so many.[63]

The plot of this story is sinister, but evil is overcome and the integrity of Gilly Ground's personality is preserved. Youth does find itself in the end of this very remarkable book.

Manolo was a Spanish boy who had to decide whether to follow his own conscience or to conform to the expectations of the community. *Shadow of a Bull* by Wojciechowska describes the darkening shadow of Manolo's fear of failure to be like his father, a famous bullfighter. Everything and everybody in Arcangel reminds Manolo of his destiny to face his first bull at the age of 12. On the night before his test, Manolo's mother tells him how tired his father had been after the bullfights, but she also tells him his father did what he wanted to do. "That was the great thing about your father: his own will to do what he was doing. What he did was for himself, most of all for himself."[64] Manolo's prayer is for

[60] Wier, p. 152.

[61] Julia Cunningham. *Dorp Dead*, illustrated by James Spanfeller (New York: Pantheon, 1965), p. 56.

[62] Cunningham, p. 71.

[63] Julia Cunningham. "Dear Characters," *The Horn Book Magazine*, Vol. 43 (April 1967), p. 234.

[64] Maia Wojciechowska. *Shadow of a Bull*, illustrated by Alvin Smith (New York: Atheneum, 1964), p. 128.

bravery to stand his ground, not to be saved from wounds or death. When he meets a famous critic before the bullfight, Manolo hears the words he should have heard earlier:

> "A man's life is many things. Before he becomes a man, he has many choices: to do the right thing, or to do the wrong thing; to please himself, or to please others; to be true to his own self, or untrue to it. . . . Real courage, true bravery is doing things in spite of fear, knowing fear. . . . Be what you are, and if you don't yet know what you are, wait until you do. Don't let anyone make that decision for you."[65]

Manolo proves both his physical and spiritual courage on the day of the test. He fights the bull long enough to prove his skill and bravery, and then he makes his choice; he turns the rest of the fight over to his friend, Juan, while he goes and sits with the doctor. His future will be healing not killing. For Manolo it took far greater courage to say no, to be what *he* wanted to be, than to follow in his father's footsteps.

More than anything else Rudi Matt *wanted* to follow in his father's footsteps. His burning desire is to climb the mountain, the Citadel, that claimed his father's life, the peak that no other guide has dared to climb. Rudi often runs away, although his mother and uncle have forbidden him to climb. On one excursion he saves an English climber. When Rudi learns the Englishman plans to climb the Citadel, he leaves work and goes to join the climber only to find that his uncle had agreed to climb with the Englishman and Saxo, the guide from another village. Rivalries and prejudice shadow the four, however, as they set out to reach the summit. Captain Winters, the Englishman, becomes ill, and according to the code of the mountains, the guide must remain with his "Master" if he becomes ill or is injured. Saxo cannot resist his own ambition and sets out alone to reach the top. Realizing what Saxo has done, Rudi leaves his uncle and Winters to pursue the guide. Saxo insists Rudi must return, for he alone will be the first to the top. In anger, the man turns, falls, and is injured. At that moment Rudi faces a terrible decision—to go on

to the top and leave an injured man, even an enemy, or to help Saxo. There is a way out, but it is down, not up. Titled *Banner in the Sky*, the book ends:

> That is the story they tell of the old days in the valley of Kurtal; of the conquest of the great mountain called the Citadel; and of how Rudi Matt, who was later to become the most famous of all Alpine guides, grew from a boy into a man.[66]

[66] James Ramsey Ullman. *Banner in the Sky* (Philadelphia, Penna.: Lippincott, 1954), p. 252.

In the intense story, *Dorp Dead*, Gilly Ground ponders the meaning of security and freedom.

From *Dorp Dead*, by Julia Cunningham, illustrated by James Spanfeller. Copyright © 1965 by Julia Cunningham. Reprinted by permission of Pantheon Books, a Division of Random House, Inc.

[65] Wojciechowska, pp. 145–146.

Most young people will not climb mountains but they will all face difficult decisions. When their time comes, let us hope that they, like Rudi, can make the choice between service to mankind and personal victory.

Stories of Survival

One test of achieving manhood in certain primitive tribes is a boy's ability to survive alone. The Australian aborigine has to go on his "Walkabout," living off the land and alone for a certain period of time. Surviving a particularly hazardous experience has frequently served as a kind of rite of passage from childhood to manhood in various cultures. Today, we have very modified forms of this ancient custom; going off to college alone, achieving a first job, living through boot training in the army. Certain camps and juvenile homes have even incorporated the idea of a "survival week" in their programs. And for many poor children throughout this country, problems of survival do not have to be simulated. Whatever the situation, children avidly read survival stories, wondering, if their time came, would they be up to the test?

One of the most popular survival stories is the tale of Karana, an Indian girl who lived alone on an island off the coast of California for some eighteen years. This Newbery Award book, *Island of the Blue Dolphins,* is based upon fact—the early missionaries did report finding such a person. Following an attack by the Aleuts who had come to kill otters, all of Karana's people leave their island home by boat. When Karana realizes her young brother is left on the island, she jumps overboard and returns to him. Within a few hours the island becomes a land of sadness—the boy is killed by wild dogs, and memories of the tribe are all Karana has left. The author does express Karana's feelings of despair when she realizes the boat will not return. Despite these feelings, she creates a life for herself. The island provides its resources, and the 12-year-old draws upon her memories to build a house, to make utensils, and to make weapons, although in so doing she violates a taboo. When she has weapons, she is able to hunt the wild dogs that killed her brother. For some deep reason she cannot bring herself to kill the leader of the pack, although she has wounded him. It is this act of mercy that saves Karana both physically and emotionally; as she gives love, she receives protection and companionship. Naming the dog Rontu, she talks to him. "Because of this I was not lonely. I did not know how lonely I had been until I had Rontu to talk to."[67]

Karana's days are filled with work, and the authentic details of her "Crusoe" efforts are interesting. There is excitement in her encounters with animals and her continuing battle against the elements. There is poignance—sharpest in her brief contact with an Aleut girl and in the death of the dog Rontu. Spanish priests at last find Karana, and her final parting from the island is sad with memories of her family, her pets, "and of all the happy days." The reader may ponder whether she found as much happiness at the mission with human companionship as she had known alone on her island.

Two survival stories that are interesting to compare with *Island of the Blue Dolphins* are *Call It Courage* by Armstrong Sperry (*see* lesson plan for Chapter 12) and *Tikta Liktak: An Eskimo Legend* by Houston (*see* Chapter 4).

Another exciting story of a girl's survival is Jean George's Newbery Award-winning story, *Julie of the Wolves.* Miyax, the Eskimo heroine of this beautiful story, finds herself alone on the Alaskan tundra. She realizes that her salvation or her destruction depends upon a nearby pack of wolves. Her father had once told her: " 'Wolves are brotherly . . . They love each other, and if

[67] Scott O'Dell. *Island of the Blue Dolphins* (Boston, Mass.: Houghton Mifflin, 1960), p. 101.

Miyax mourns the wanton killing of Amarog, leader of the wolves.

Illustration by John Schoenherr from *Julie of the Wolves* by Jean Craighead George. Pictures copyright © 1972 by John Schoenherr. Reprinted by permission of Harper & Row, Publishers, Inc.

you learn to speak to them, they will love you too.'"[68] Julie (Miyax is her Eskimo name) watches the wolves carefully, and gradually learns to communicate with them by glance, movement, and caress until Amarog, their leader, acknowledges her as a friend. Because of the wolves Julie survives and finds her way back to civilization. But it is that civilization that kills Amarog, as white hunters wantonly shoot him down from a plane for the "sport" of killing. Much of the story is based upon research on wolves that is being conducted at the Arctic Research Laboratory.[69] Only a naturalist, ecologist, and author like Jean George could turn the facts into such a poignant story of the Eskimo's love of the earth in conflict with the encroachment of modern civilization.

My Side of the Mountain, also by Jean George, is a book about a city boy who chooses to spend a winter alone on land in the Catskills once farmed by his ancestors. The crowded apartment, the pressures all around him impel Sam to prove he can live off the land. Armed with knowledge from reading about how to survive on the land, he makes a home in a hollow tree, sews buckskin clothing, and lays up stores for winter. The meals are described in mouth-watering fashion—even though acorn flour, bulbs, and strange herbs are the ingredients. A professor discovers the boy while on a mountain hike and respects his wish to be alone. At Christmas, "Bando" returns, and also Sam's father finds him. His pet falcon and a weasel provide Sam with entertainment, and work keeps his days busy. He writes in his journal, observes the birds, and keeps occupied with the chores of living. In the early spring a young news reporter discovers him, and Sam realizes he is now ready to be found. The professor tells Sam what he has already learned: "You can't live in America today and be quietly different. If you are going to be different, you are going to stand out, and people are going to hear about you. . . ."[70] In this modern "Robinson Crusoe"

story the details are so vividly related that the reader feels he is on the mountain with Sam. As a naturalist, Jean George has drawn upon her background to provide authentic facts of nature. This boy tests himself in an unusual way; children may consider other ways in which they can prove their ability to survive.

Wild Boy by Joan Tate is also a story of a modern city boy living in the wild on his own. Will, a Yorkshire boy of a very settled, secure couple, loves the moors above his town and goes there whenever he can to roam free. One day, by accident, he meets Mart, a "wild boy" of about his age who actually lives on the moors in a hut he has built for himself. He's an orphan, a runaway from the city; and he makes Will promise not to tell his secret. Will visits him often until school starts and it gets colder. On one of his fall visits he finds Mart ill and delirious, and he drags him down the long distance to his home. There Will's parents do all the right things, take care of Mart, nurse him back to health, and see that he gets a proper job—all without asking too many questions or calling in the authorities. They see him as another son, and Will certainly treats him as a brother. But Mart longs for the city and finally admits it:

> "It's something to do with belonging," said Mart . . ." You belong somewhere, don't you? You know who you are. Everybody does. And I know now that I belong in the city. Not really here. Perhaps I had to come here to find that out. Perhaps I had to meet you to find that out. That you can't run away. So I've got to go back. To find out all those things. To find out who I am. To start from where I belong."[71]

Felice Holman has written a grim story of survival in New York City titled *Slake's Limbo.* Slake is a 13-year-old nearsighted orphan who lives with his aunt and thinks of himself as a worthless lump. Slake has no friends; his vision makes him a poor risk for any gang, and a severe reaction to smoke and drugs makes him useless in other ways. Slake is a loner, and when he isn't shunned entirely, he is hunted and hounded for sport. It is just such an occasion that drives him

[68] Jean Craighead George. *Julie of the Wolves* (New York: Harper & Row, 1972), p. 78
[69] *See* the "Newbery Award Acceptance" speech by Jean Craighead George in *The Horn Book,* Vol. 49 (August 1973), pp. 337–347.
[70] Jean George. *My Side of the Mountain* (New York: Dutton, 1959), p. 170.

[71] Joan Tate. *Wild Boy,* illustrated by Susan Jeschke (New York: Harper & Row, 1973), pp. 91–92.

to take his fear and misfortune and hide them underground. Desperate, almost to the breaking point, Slake takes refuge in the subway. He stays 121 days. This is the story of his survival, the way he makes a little money reselling papers he picks up on the trains or in the trash until he gets a job sweeping up at one of the lunch counters. It tells of his home, a little hidden cave in the subway wall where he spreads newspapers to sleep. Only when the subway repair crew comes through does Slake realize that his "home" will be destroyed. Then he becomes ill and is taken to the hospital, and is given nourishment and proper eyeglasses. When he feels he is well enough he slips out of the hospital, not waiting for the social worker to find a proper "juvenile facility" for him. His first reaction is to return to the subway, but then he hears a bird sing and he looks up deciding he could perhaps exist on the roofs of some of the buildings:

> He turned and started up the stairs and out of the subway. Slake did not know exactly where he was going but the general direction was up.[72]

This story stands in sharp contrast to the two children who decide to run away from home and live in comfort in the Metropolitan Museum of Art! Claudia's reasons for running away are based upon what she considers injustice—she has had to both set the table and empty the dishwasher on the same night while her brothers did nothing. But Claudia is also bored with the sameness of her straight-A life; she wants to do something that is different and exciting. She chooses her brother Jamie to go along with her because he has money—$24.43. Claudia is a good organizer, and the two of them take up residence in the museum, even to taking baths in the museum's fountain, where Jamie finds another source of income—pennies thrown in the pool. They take their meals at the automat and the museum's cafeteria and join the tour groups for their education. It really isn't exciting until Claudia becomes involved in the mystery surrounding the statue of a little angel. The children's research finally takes them to the home of Mrs. Basil E. Frankweiler who arranges for Claudia to return home the way she had hoped

she would—different in some aspect. Now she is different because she knows the secret of the angel. In return for this knowledge the two children tell Mrs. Frankweiler the details of their survival. She carefully records it and then writes their story in *From the Mixed-up Files of Mrs. Basil E. Frankweiler.* This is a sophisticated, funny story by E. L. Konigsburg of the survival of two very modern and resourceful children.

Coping with Problems of the Human Condition

Men in all times and places must cope with problems of the human condition—birth, pain, loneliness, poverty, illness, and death. Children do not escape these human problems; but literature can give them windows for looking at different aspects of life, show them how some characters have faced personal crises, and help them ask and answer questions about the meaning of life.

In discussing the psychological significance of children's literature, Jacquelyn Sanders points out:

> Areas of life that are difficult . . . if avoided will not be understood; if simply presented will only be badly handled; but a valuable service can be rendered if these areas are presented together with help in learning how to cope with them.[73]

PHYSICAL HANDICAPS

Good stories of physically handicapped persons serve two purposes: They provide positive images with which handicapped youngsters may identify, and they may help physically normal children to develop an intelligent understanding of some of the problems which handicapped persons face. It is particularly important that stories of the handicapped be well written; not sentimental or maudlin. They should not evoke pity for what the child cannot do, but respect for what he *can* do. As in all well-written stories, characters should be multi-dimensional persons with real feelings and frustrations. The author

---

[72] Felice Holman. *Slake's Limbo* (New York: Scribner, 1974).

[73] Jacquelyn Sanders. "Psychological Significance of Children's Literature" in *A Critical Approach to Children's Literature,* Sara Innis Fenwick, ed. (Chicago, Ill.: The University of Chicago Press, 1967), p. 17.

should be honest in portraying the condition and future possibilities for the character.

Understanding of the difficulties faced by a family in helping a baby who is handicapped by cerebral palsy is sensitively portrayed by Killilea in her book *Wren.* When the parents learn that Karen may never walk, they help an older sibling understand and accept her sister. When Karen gets braces and struggles to walk, Marie is told that it is no kindness to do things for her or Karen will not learn to do them for herself. The faith expressed by the family and Karen herself is culminated in a beautiful moment at Christmas when she balances on one foot to lean toward the creche.

In another story of a child who has cerebral palsy a family has to learn to give love, but not to help too much. Jean Little's characterizations in *Mine for Keeps* are believable portraits. When Sally returns from a school for the handicapped to live at home, she attends regular school and meets many problems. A dog that may be hers "for keeps" helps her gain physical skill and emotional courage. Sally grows in maturity when she forgets about her problems and helps a Dutch boy who has been ill to find happiness and confidence.

Ivan Southall has vividly portrayed some of the desires and frustrations of a boy with a mild spastic condition in *Let the Balloon Go.* John Sumner attended a regular school in Australia and, except for occasional and unpredictable spasms and stuttering, he was like any other 12-year-old boy. And yet he had no friends. The children avoided him and his overanxious mother kept telling him what he couldn't do. John longed to be free, to do what he wanted. And one day, when he was home alone for the very first time, he did; he climbed a very tall tree all by himself. He had once heard a man say that a balloon wasn't a balloon until someone cut the string. John had cut the string that had bound him to his house and mother; at last he was truly free to grow in his own way.

Sarah, in the story *Why Me?* by John Branfield, has a physical handicap that doesn't show; she is a diabetic. Her moods fluctuate violently; she is frequently bitter and resentful. It just isn't fair, Sarah feels. Why should she have to give herself an injection every morning? Why can't she eat

sweets when she wants them? Why can't she live an ordinary life like her sister, Jane? Sarah's adolescent preoccupation with herself and her disease slowly changes as she becomes concerned about a dog which she rescues from a deserted mineshaft. From her actions, Sarah is convinced that the dog has diabetes, also. When tests confirm her suspicions, Sarah starts giving the dog injections of her own insulin. The dog appears to be much better but does die some six months later in a diabetic coma. By this time Sarah has learned to cope with her feelings about her illness and her family. Her savage rows with her sister and her mother decrease and she looks forward to training a new puppy. Branfield has a remarkable way of creating natural dialogue and real people. Toward the end of the story he does have a doctor give a brief, unnecessary lecture about the many things diabetics can do. By that time Sarah has shown us what she can do and what she intends to do with her life. The doctor's lecture seems a bit of an intrusion into a well-written story. Once the reader accepts the coincidence of both the dog and Sarah having diabetes, this is an intriguing tale of an adolescent girl coming to terms with her handicap.

A popular story of a boy who is blind is *Follow My Leader* by James Garfield. Jimmy tries to duck an exploding firecracker, but it is too late. "The world exploded in a white flash. Deafening thunder smashed against his ears. Then the light was gone, and the sound was gone. Everything became very dark, very quiet."[74] Eleven-year-old Jimmy's world was to remain dark forever, but it is far from quiet as he learns to eat, to walk, to read, and to use the dog, Leader, as his constant guide and companion. At the guide school Jimmy receives a warning about the sharp corner on a mantelpiece. When he suggests they put a piece of sponge on it the director asks: "Do you expect the world to pad its corners for you, just because you're blind?" The details of learning braille and of the training received at the guide-dog school are fascinating. Overcoming his hatred toward Mike, the boy who threw the firecracker, is very difficult for Jimmy. However, Jimmy visits Mike and they agree: "You can't be

[74]James B. Garfield. *Follow My Leader* (New York: Viking, 1957), p. 14.

happy until you quit hating." Here is a good story, one that communicates the feelings of those who must learn to live without sight.

All too frequently the handicap of deafness is forgotten. Robinson's *David in Silence* is a good story that tells of a boy who learns to live with this problem. Set in modern England, there is plenty of action as the children make overtures to a new boy who can only make grunting noises. David is delighted when Michael learns sign language so he can communicate through his wall of silence. The world of deafness, with its absolute absence of sound, is made quite clear to the reader in David's story. When David's actions in playing football are misinterpreted and he doesn't read lips clearly, the other boys become confused and angry:

> He can't hear. He can't hear. He makes noises like an animal. The creepiness was frightening. Fear, mistrust, and ignorance combined to arouse the mob instinct in them, and they drew close together. . . .[75]

When the boys give chase, David runs away and hides. Tension mounts as he moves into a dark tunnel of a canal and is overcome by a mirage of ugly faces. When he emerges he is lost, becomes hopelessly confused, and cannot tell anyone his problem:

> Suddenly he was swept by a wave of terror and desolation. People everywhere who could help him so easily if they were able to; ordinary homely people who looked kind until the moment they realized he was deaf, and then they would become frightened by their own ignorance of how to talk to him.[76]

The other boys come to accept David and to have a new awareness of the joy of hearing, but David remains in his silent world.

Julia Cunningham tells the moving story of a poor French boy caught in the silence of muteness until he enters Monsieur Hilaire's world of pantomime. This mystical story titled *Burnish Me Bright* has a fairytale quality, but the prejudice and violence of the French villagers seem very

real indeed. Auguste lived, or rather existed, on Madame Fer's farm, where he slept in the barn and received very little food for his labors. His only friends are Monsieur Hilaire and two children, Avril and Gustave, who are the only ones who take time to find out what Auguste is like and to accept him on those terms. After Monsieur's death Auguste continues to slip away to the woods, where he entertains his two friends with his mime. He calms a maddened dog in the village one day, and rumors of witchcraft begin to circulate. When the animals sicken and Gustave, too, becomes ill, a grim mob chase Auguste to Hilaire's old house and set fire to it. Auguste escapes, but he can never return to the prejudiced little village. He recalls Hilaire's words that to "the people of the village [their] enemy is anyone who is different."[77] Auguste remains handicapped, but he can communicate now through the magical gift of pantomime.

Other examples of children's courage in facing physical handicaps may be found in books of historical fiction, such as De Angeli's *The Door in the Wall,* Sutcliff's *The Witch's Brat,* and Forbes' *Johnny Tremain.* Biographies of Helen Keller, Annie Sullivan, and other handicapped persons portray strength in overcoming obstacles (*see* Chapters 8 and 9).

MENTAL DISABILITIES

Learning Problems

Sue Ellen (Edith Hunter) is a child of rural poverty with five brothers and sisters, a chronically ill mother, and a father whose hard work as a tenant farmer is inadequate to support the family. Sue Ellen herself is a learning-disability case, a non-reader at age 8 and identified for a special education class. After she enters Miss Kelly's room the book becomes a description, in some detail, of the effective teaching of children with educational handicaps. Sue Ellen has many interesting experiences, including a shopping trip that the class takes to get ready for a party and a money-raising auction. The children make baked goods and Sue Ellen's cake recipe is in-

[75] Veronica Robinson. *David in Silence,* illustrated by Victor Ambrus (Philadelphia, Penna.: Lippincott, 1966), p. 66.
[76] Robinson, p. 86.

[77] Julia Cunningham. *Burnish Me Bright,* illustrated by Don Freeman (New York: Pantheon, 1970), p. 19.

cluded. The story shows some scornful people (including Sue Ellen's regular classroom teacher) with a poor understanding of Sue Ellen's problems, but also many caring, helpful persons. One of Sue Ellen's favorite contacts is a high-school girl who is a frequent aide in Miss Kelly's room. The story also presents authentic attitudes of the rural poor. The Stokleys are not always eager to be helped, and the author conveys respect for their pride.

Jean Little's story *From Anna* is partially autobiographical. Anna was called awkward Anna by her four brothers and sisters and scolded by Frau Schmidt for not knowing her letters. But then the Solden family moved to Canada and Anna was put in a special class with nice Miss Williams. Most importantly, the doctor discovered that Anna had very poor vision. With her new glasses, her new school and country, Anna herself became a new person. While her teacher called her quick, her family continued to see her as slow, until that first Christmas when Anna had made them all special gifts and written "From Anna" on them. This is a warmly satisfying story of a little girl making many new adjustments.

Mental Retardation

The opening line of *Take Wing*, also by Jean Little, reads "James had wet the bed again."[78] As usual, 7-year-old James called on his sister, Laurel, to help him, rather than his mother. For Laurel had a special way and a special love for this younger brother who was "different." Laurel had always tried to hide her fear that he wasn't quite normal. Her mother wouldn't talk about him and her father was too busy to notice how slow and unsure his son was. When Laurel's mother breaks her hip, her Aunt Jessica and Cousin Alspeth come to stay at their house. Aunt Jessica recognizes that Laurel is carrying too much responsibility in having to care for James. At first, Laurel resents her aunt's interference, but finally she talks with her father and Aunt Jessica, and an appointment is made for James to have an examination at the medical clinic. Their findings confirmed Laurel's fears that her brother is retarded but educable. This is as much Laurel's

story as James. By refusing to face the facts of James' retardation, the family had overburdened his older sister. The symbolic title, *Take Wing*, refers to Laurel's freedom to begin to have a childhood of her own, to make friends and "to become."

Betsy Byars won the Newbery Award for her story about an adolescent girl and her retarded brother in *Summer of the Swans*. Sara felt very much like the ugly duckling during that difficult fourteenth summer. She had wept over her big feet and her skinny legs and her nose. She had even cried over her gross orange sneakers. But then, when her retarded brother got lost in the woods, her tears vanished in the terror she felt for Charlie. In her anguish Sara turned to Joe Melby—whom she had despised the day before——and together they found Charlie. It was the longest day of the summer and Sara knew that she would never be the same again. Like the awkward flight of the swans with their "great beating of wings and ruffling of feathers," Sara was going to land with a long perfect glide. Sara's love and fright for her brother's safety had helped her break through her moody adolescent shell.

One of the best stories of retarded children is Wrightson's *A Racecourse for Andy*. Andy is presented as a likable child with friends—not a pathetic loner. The author has managed to convey the foggy, somewhat removed mind of the child by using a window image:

> Andy lived behind a closed window. When he smiled his warm smile and spoke a little too loudly, it was as if he was speaking through the glass. When he listened carefully to what people said and paused for a second before he answered, it was as though their words came to him through a glass. . . . Even his face looked a little distorted, as things sometimes look through glass. Still, because he was Andy, always warm and admiring, always glad to see them and careful not to be a nuisance, the others were still his friends.[79]

Andy's four friends, who are not only tolerant but really interact with him, have a game in

---

[78] Jean Little. *Take Wing* (Boston, Mass.: Little, Brown, 1968), p. 3.

[79] Patricia Wrightson. *A Racecourse for Andy,* illustrated by Margaret Horder (New York: Harcourt Brace Jovanovich, 1968), p. 15.

which they pretend to own the public buildings in Sydney, Australia. Andy has difficulty in separating the real from the make-believe in this game. So when an old tramp jokingly offers to sell him the local racetrack for three dollars, Andy is excited and works a week to get the money to purchase Beecham Park. Events and people now conspire to make it seem that Andy really is the owner. Workmen who have heard of his "purchase" begin to call him "the owner" and make him a sort of mascot in a kindly fashion. Owners of the stalls at the racetrack pay him bags of chips for "rent." While the adults play along with the game, his friends are deeply concerned and attempt to persuade Andy that he is not the owner. Finally, the park committee, to whom the whole thing appears to have gotten out of hand, solves the problem by quietly "buying back" Beecham Park for ten dollars. Andy, very proud of his profit, is not disillusioned, and his friends are relieved. On one level the story is amusing; but the boys' concern for Andy, their discussions of what is real and whether the deception about ownership helps or hinders Andy raise the theme to a higher plane. Patricia Wrightson has told a story which could have been grim with much warmth and humor.

A Norwegian story by Friis-Baastad, *Don't Take Teddy* is a grim tale of the flight of a young boy and his older retarded brother. Mikkel runs away with Teddy because he fears that the police will take him away when they hear that a boy was hurt by a stone that Teddy threw. The two of them take a nightmarish journey across the countryside, arriving at their mountain cabin in a state of exhaustion. Both boys are ill by the time their father and uncle find them. The trip convinces the parents that they must find a special school for Teddy, one where he can learn something and be happy. Mikkel doesn't want him to go, but they take them both to the school, and he sees that the people are kind and that Teddy really likes it. Since it is near home, Teddy can commute by bus. The author has been very realistic in presenting the problems of trying to take care of a 15-year-old boy with the mentality of a 2- or 3-year-old. People in the bus and train stare and make cruel remarks. Teddy can't always wait to get to the bathroom. Certainly, he is far too great a responsibility for the younger

boy who tries to protect him. This story would help children feel what it was like to have a mentally defective brother.

Me Too by Vera Cleaver and Bill Cleaver is the story of twin girls, Lydia and Lorna. Lydia is bright, but Lorna is severely retarded. Twelve-year-old Lydia is determined to change Lorna; she hopes that one day Lornie will be so like her that no one can tell them apart. She has two motives for trying to "cure" Lorna; one is her love for her twin, and the other is her hope that her father would return to the family when he finds out that Lorna can learn. Lydia's mission leads her into trying a variety of methods to reach Lornie. She tries teaching her; she tries to put herself in Lornie's place; she even gives up her friends in order to devote more time to Lornie. She tries so hard that she stops seeing Lornie as a person, and she can't accept her for what she is. Only when Lydia realizes that her twin does have friends who like her just as she is does she understand the unreasonable demands that she had been placing on her sister. She had to learn that even love cannot change a permanent handicap. This is much more Lydia's story than it is Lornie's. In most instances the stories of mentally retarded children are stories of their impact upon others.

Mental Illness

Few stories about mental illness or drugs have been written for the elementary-school child. (*George*) by E. L. Konigsburg combines both in one of her less successful books. George, the reader finally realizes, is Ben's alter ego, a real and constant companion. Ben had managed to keep his schizophrenic symptoms to himself until he entered sixth grade. Then, because of the fear that he might be sent away to live with his father and stepmother and the pressure of knowing that his lab partners are stealing equipment from chemistry class to make LSD, George begins to speak out loud. Part of this story is very witty, as is typical of Konigsburg's stories, but part is very serious. George and Ben finally become one again and the book ends on a cheerful note of recovery.

Kin Platt has written an unusual and disturbing novel, *The Boy Who Could Make Himself Disappear*, about a boy who develops the withdrawal patterns of schizophrenia because he is so neglected by his rich father and so abused by his harsh, perfectionist mother. Roger Baxter used to pretend he was deaf so he wouldn't have to answer anyone; in fact, he could disappear. He was new to New York City, having just arrived with his divorced mother. An artist, she paid no attention to him, unless it was to hit him. Roger was lonely, and with his speech impediment he had a tough time making friends. Unfortunately, the teacher in the private school he attended was a sadist, and delighted in embarrassing Roger in front of the class. Although Roger knew more than his share of mean persons he also knew Roberta Clemm, his speech therapist; Miss Bentley, the beautiful model who lived in the penthouse in his apartment building; and, most importantly, Roger Tunnell, the kind Frenchman who loved Miss Bentley and Roger. Only because of these people did Roger survive the unbelievable neglect and cruelty of his parents. Platt has told Roger's poignant story through some of Roger's disjointed thoughts, which convey his gradual loss of reality. While Roger does recover at the end of the story, his future is still uncertain. Platt's story *Hey Dummy!* is the chilling tale of a sensitive boy who befriends a brain-damaged boy. Neil Comstock is the first to call stumbling Alan Harper "dummy." When he realizes Alan really is retarded, Neil tries to befriend him by giving him a toy drum. A girl is hurt, and Neil hides Alan in an effort to protect him. Then Alan is accidentally killed by a store guard as he and Neil search for food in the refuse bins. In deep shock, Neil's behavior and speech become similar to the "dummy's." While parts of this story are melodramatic, the author's efforts to enter the mind of a retarded child and copy his speech patterns seem very real. The reader is never told whether Neil recovers from his state of mental shock.

Friends were also the first to be concerned about a girl with mental illness in Neufeld's story of a teenager titled *Lisa, Bright and Dark.* This somewhat frightening but well-written story is more appropriate for older students.

DRUGS AND ALCOHOLISM

Few stories about drugs are satisfactory for younger children. Robert Coles' *Grass Pipe* might

better have been an informational book with its long discussions about the dangers of drugs given by one of the boy's fathers who is a doctor. A very simply written book of less than fifty pages is titled *Nikki 108* by Rose Blue. It is the story of a 12-year-old girl in a huge urban junior high school who is obviously intelligent and trying to overcome her surroundings. Her immediate problem is deciding whether or not to join the science honors class for which she has qualified. She receives no encouragement from her mother, who tells her that she'll only have her heart broken, that very few of her family or friends ever even finished high school. Nikki's mother works because her father has deserted them; and her older brother, Don, on whom she has depended for years, is hooked on heroin. He dies of an overdose. Nikki finds him, "his back against a lamppost, a needle inside an eyedropper still in his arm, dead on the fresh white ground."[80] After the funeral Nikki seeks out some of Don's old friends; one, who has taken a job in a bank and seems responsible, and others, who have dropped out and are having a tough time. Nikki realizes that it is time for her to decide what she is going to do with her life. She joins the science honors class, and the reader is led to believe she develops a better opinion of herself. Less didactic than Coles' book, this is still a moralistic story with rather cardboard, predictable characters. However, it does what the author set out to do; namely, tell a story with high interest for students in junior high school or high school who might not be very good readers.

Wojciechowska's book *Tuned Out* simply tells the story of a 16-year-old's love and concern for his brilliant older brother who is on drugs. Jim tries to dissuade Kevin from taking marijuana and LSD, particularly after he stays with him through a trip that is so bad that Kevin has to be hospitalized. The author does not moralize in the story, but lets the facts speak for themselves. *Go Ask Alice* is another grim tale of a girl's degradation through drugs. Alice's language becomes more vile and her morals more lax as she sinks deeper and deeper into the despair of drugs. The

[80] Rose Blue. *Nikki 108,* illustrated by Ted Lewin (New York: F. Watts, 1973), p. 20.

reader sees her try to kick the habit—in fact, thinks she is succeeding when the story ends with a notation that she died three weeks later from an overdose of drugs. Written anonymously in diary form, this has been one of the most criticized and censored books for young people. Certainly it is not appropriate reading for children, and yet some 11- and 12-year-olds *are* reading it. Grim as it may be, the total impact of this book is a believable testament *against* the use of drugs. Never does it preach or tell, rather it shows a young life destroyed by drugs.

The story of *Sara T* by Robin S. Wagner first appeared on television. It is the sad tale of a teenage alcoholic, detailing her gradual dependency upon liquor until it threatens to destroy her life. Sara's future appears somewhat promising as she joins an Alcoholics Anonymous group following her hospitalization.

AGING AND DEATH

In the early part of this century the aging and death of loved ones were accepted as a natural part of a child's first-hand knowledge. In most instances the modern child is removed from any such knowledge of senility and death. Few grandparents stay with their families anymore, living instead in retirement homes or whole "cities of leisure worlds." When older relatives become ill they are shunted off to hospitals and rest homes. Few persons die at home today, and many children have never attended a funeral. Seldom is death discussed with children. There is enough genuine mystery about death, without hiding it under this false cloak of secrecy.

Gradually, realistic fiction for children is beginning to reflect society's new concern for honesty about aging and dying. We have begun to move from a time when the subject of death was one of the taboos of children's literature to a time when it is being discussed openly and frankly.

Aging

A few stories tell of a child's relationship with a loved older person and the problems that occur as that person becomes ill or senile. This is the theme of Rose Blue's book *Grandma Didn't Wave Back*. Ten-year-old Debbie used to hurry home from school and wave at her grandma, who would be waiting at the window of their third-floor terrace apartment. But then one day Grandma doesn't wave back because she is feeling sick and becoming very forgetful. Some of Debbie's friends now say that her grandma is crazy, which hurts Debbie's feelings. After Grandma is found wandering the street at night, Debbie's parents do find a nursing home for her. Debbie thinks that it is a dreadful thing to have done, but she goes to visit her grandma and finds that the Shore Nursing Home is very elegant, with a lake view. As Debbie leaves, Grandma waves to her from her window. This is a very idealized treatment of the subject of aging, but it might lessen the concerns of some children.

In *A Figure of Speech* by Norma Fox Mazer the problems of an older person in the home are presented realistically. The theme that an older person is a person—not a senior citizen, a cliché, or figure of speech—is made very clear. This is a touching and poignant story of Jenny's love for her grandfather, who is tolerated by his family and then pushed aside when the older son and his wife come home to live. The book ends tragically with the death of the old man. It is certainly a fine story to promote discussion of the way in which we treat older persons, and lends itself nicely to a session on values clarification (*see* Chapter 12).

Death and Dying

A child's first experience with death is frequently the loss of a pet. *The Growing Time* by Warburg was one of the first books about death for younger children, and it is still among the best. In this story King, an old Collie dog, dies, and Jamie, his young owner, is desolate. His family console him; his mother tells him: "It hurts very badly to lose King, and it will not stop hurting right away. Death is not easy to bear."[81] Eventually, the family buys Jamie another puppy, and he doesn't even want to look at it. But in the middle of the night the new pup cries and needs someone to love it. Jamie comes downstairs to comfort and claim him.

More recent stories have depicted the death of a grandparent. One beautifully illustrated book, *Annie and the Old One* tells of a young

[81]Sandol Stoddard Warburg. *The Growing Time*, illustrated by Leonard Weisgard (New York: Harper & Row, 1969), p. 5.

Parnall's sensitive picture depicts Annie's love for her grandmother.

Illustrations Copyright © 1971 by Peter Parnall. From *Annia and the Old One* by Miska Miles, by permission of Little, Brown and Co. in association with The Atlantic Monthly Press.

Navajo girl's love for her dying grandmother. The old woman calmly accepts her coming death and even sets a date for it, saying that when the new rug is taken from the loom she will go to "Mother Earth." Annie does everything she can think of to forestall the completion of the rug until her grandmother guesses what she is doing and talks to her granddaughter:

> You have tried to hold back time. This cannot be done. . . . The sun comes up from the edge of the earth in the morning. It returns to the edge of the earth in the evening. Earth, from which good things come for the living creatures on it. Earth, to which all creatures finally go.[82]

Understanding at last, Annie picks up the Old One's weaving stick and begins to help with the weaving.

Sarah Somebody by Florence Slobodkin is the heartwarming story of a poor 9-year-old girl who lived in Poland at the turn of the century. The story has a dual theme: Sarah's desire to go to school, "to be a somebody," and the death of her beloved Jewish grandmother. Her grandmother is instrumental in persuading Sarah's parents to let her go to school. Proud of her granddaughter, the old lady asks Sarah to write her name for her. Sarah hesitates, because she only knows her grandmother as "Grandmother", not her given name of Ruth. When their cousin comes the next morning to tell them of the old lady's death, he says that she had a piece of paper in her hand with the name "Ruth" written on it in beautiful handwriting.

> "Ruth was Grandma's name. I never knew that. Did you, Sarah?"
> "Yes," said Sarah. "I knew."[83]

The modern story of *The Mulberry Music* (Orgel) seems rather bland by way of contrast to these thoughtful books. Grandma Liza, or just Liza, as she preferred to be called, was very much her own person; she jogged, swam, and played the piano, and Libby, her granddaughter, loved her dearly. Then Liza became very ill and had to go to the hospital. Libby runs away to the hospital to see her, and by calling for one of the family's friends who is a doctor, does manage to visit her grandmother. However, the energetic Liza is in a coma, and Libby, horrified, runs away again, this time to her grandmother's home. Her patient family endure her outbreaks calmly, and even let Libby determine where the funeral for Grandma Liza will be held. At the funeral Libby arranges to have her mother play the "Mulberry Music," Liza's favorite selection from Mozart. The story is so centered on Libby and her stormy reactions to her grief that the rest of the characters seem one-dimensional. And what family would allow a 12-year-old to plan her grandmother's funeral?

A Taste of Blackberries by Doris Smith is a much more believable story of the sudden death of a young boy. Jamie and his friends were catching Japanese beetles for Mrs. Houser when Jamie shoved a slim willow limb down a bee hole. The bees swarmed out and Jamie was stung. Allergic to bee stings, Jamie screamed and gasped and fell to the ground. His best friend thought he was just showing off, until the ambulance arrived. Jamie was dead by the time they got to the hospital. His friend goes to the funeral and the au-

[82] Miska Miles. *Annie and the Old One,* illustrated by Peter Parnall (New York: Little, Brown, 1971), unpaged.

[83] Florence Slobodkin. *Sarah Somebody,* illustrated by Louis Slobodkin (New York: Vanguard, 1969), p. 71.

thor graphically describes his reaction to seeing Jamie:

> There was Jamie. He was out straight with one hand crossed over his chest. He didn't look like he was asleep to me. Jamie slept all bunched up. Jamie looked dead.[84]

After the funeral Jamie's friend picks blackberries because the two of them had planned to do so together. He shares his berries with Jamie's mother, who is very loving to him. Told in the first person, the reader views death through a child's eyes. Simple, yet direct, this story seems very real.

Virginia Lee's story *The Magic Moth* is about the death of 10-year-old Maryanne from a congenital heart defect. One of five children, Maryanne had been sick for a long while. She is loved by all of her family, but to Mark-o, her 6-year-old brother, she is very special. He shares with Maryanne his toys, his rocks, and even a caterpillar which made a cocoon in a jar. Gradually, Maryanne becomes weaker and weaker and their father tells the family that the doctors say they can do nothing else for her; Maryanne will die. At the time of her death the moth from the cocoon symbolically flies out the window.

Hang Tough, Paul Mather by Alfred Slote is the very genuine story of a Little Leaguer who develops leukemia. The family moves from California to Michigan to be close to the university hospital where Paul will have special treatments. He is not supposed to play baseball, but some children in the neighborhood come over and Paul's kid brother can't help bragging about Paul's pitching abilities. The team needs a pitcher for their big game, so Paul slips out without his parents' knowledge, having forged the permission slip, and pitches a great game. However, he is out of condition, is hit in a head-on collision, and nearly passes out. His father has found out where he is and takes him out of the game and to the hospital for a long stay. Once there, he has a young doctor who becomes his friend. Their discussion of death is one of the most honest in children's literature. Paul has just asked the doctor if he is afraid of dying:

He thought about it. "I guess I would be, sport." And then he looked at me. "How about you?"

Suddenly we weren't doctor and patient, but two friends, even though he was thirty-something and I was twelve. And I knew then that I knew things he didn't know. I knew them because I had death inside me, I could feel it sometimes hard as a rock and sometimes soft and running crazy through my veins. I knew it first-hand; he only knew it from books . . . from me.

"Yes," I said, "I'm scared. Even when I'm so nauseous I wish I were dead, I'm still scared of dying."

"That's interesting," Tom said, as if I'd told him something.[85]

Paul gets out of the hospital in his wheel chair, at least long enough to watch and help win another game. While Paul sounds hopeful at the end of the story, he is back in the hospital and his condition has worsened.

Grover by the Cleavers has already been discussed (pp. 397–398); it details the anger and frustration felt by a young boy following his mother's suicide. The story of *Home from Far* by Jean Little also tells of a child's anger and resentment following the accidental death of her twin brother. Jenny completely misunderstands her mother's determination not to wallow in grief but to begin to build a new life. She puts all of Michael's things away in the attic and the family decide that they will take in two foster children. It is all too fast for Jenny, who thinks that her mother is deliberately trying to forget Michael. This is a fine story with an exciting plot involving the adjustment of the two foster children to their new home. Finally, after a talk with her mother, Jenny does begin to develop some perspective on her actions and on her mother's. Both this book and *Grover* point up the need of children to have someone with whom they can talk about their feelings.

John Gridley in Donovan's story *Wild in the World* had no one that he could talk to except "Son," his wolf-like dog. John is the last of the Gridleys to survive on the mountain after twelve other members of his family have died from

---

[84] Doris Buchanan Smith. *A Taste of Blackberries*, illustrated by Charles Robinson (New York: Crowell, 1973), p. 34.

[85] Alfred Slote. *Hang Tough, Paul Mather* (Philadelphia, Penna.: Lippincott, 1973), p. 123.

various causes. John doesn't bother to tell anyone of the death of his two remaining brothers, one from an infection from a fish hook caught in his hand and the other from being kicked by a cow. John buries them both near Rattlesnake Mountain and then lives in solitude taking on the chores of all the other members of the family. He frequently visits the graves of his brothers, finding it easier to speak to them now that they are dead than when they were alive. John nurses Son back to life after he was bitten by a rattlesnake while trying to protect John. However, the boy catches a chill after swimming and begins to decline while nursing the dog. John reminisces feverishly and finally dies sitting outside his home. This is a strange death-ridden story that seems to speak to the hopelessness of living and the senselessness of dying.

Pearl Buck's classic story *The Big Wave* offers more hope, even though the villagers live under constant fear of death from the earth's volcanic eruptions or the tidal waves of the sea. Kino asks his father:

> "Must we always be afraid of something?" and his father replies, "'We must say, someday I shall die, and does it matter whether it is by ocean or volcano, or whether I grow old and weak?'"[86]

When a big wave does come, it engulfs the homes and the people who live on the beach. Kino's friend, Jiya, loses his entire family, and comes to stay with them. Kino's father describes death as a great gateway and reminds Kino that he did not want to be born. He explains that a baby does not know about the happy life that awaits it:

> "You are afraid only because you don't know anything about death," his father replied. "But someday you will wonder why you were afraid, even as today you wonder why you feared to be born."[87]

Again, Kino's father tries to help him understand how to console his friend Jiya:

> "Ah, no one knows who makes evil storms," his father replied. "We only know that they come.

When they come we must live through them as bravely as we can, and after they are gone, we must feel again how wonderful is life. Every day of life is more valuable now than it was before the storm."[88]

Jiya chooses to remain with the poor farmer instead of accepting the wealthy Old Gentleman's offer to make him his son. He does "live" again, returns to work, and laughs, because he does not want others to feel sad because he is sad. Eventually, he decides to return to the sea as a fisherman, and builds a house down on the beach. Life goes on.

Living in a Pluralistic Society

In a true democracy it is essential that we learn to respect and appreciate the diversity of all cultures within our pluralistic society. Books can never substitute for first-hand contact with other people, but they can raise the consciousness level of children and deepen their understanding for cultures that are different from theirs. Rather than falsely pretend that differences do not exist, children need to discover that which is unique to each group of persons and universal to the experience of being human.

APPRECIATING RACIAL AND ETHNIC DIVERSITY

The Civil Rights Movement of the 1950s led to the publication of many books about integration (*see* Chapter 2). These books tended to emphasize similarity of groups, rather than racial or ethnic identity. The Black Movement of the sixties and, more recently, the protestations of native Americans and Chicanos have created the need for books which authentically capture the unique experience and contributions of all minority groups.

Recognizing that books for children can be powerful socialization tools, various minorities have become more critical and demanding of how their culture should be represented in literature for children. At this time in our history it is necessary to evaluate minority literature not only with regard to its general literary value but in a special light according to the image presented by the group.

[86]Pearl Buck, *The Big Wave* (New York: John Day, 1947), p. 30.
[87]Buck, p. 37.

[88]Buck, p. 30.

Guidelines for Evaluating Minority Literature

While the emphasis should be placed upon the selection of quality literature, the following guidelines[89] may be useful in evaluating minority literature:

1. *Diversity and range of representation.* In the portrayal of any minority group we need to look for a wide range of representation among the books about that particular race or ethnic group. Currently, many of the books of the black experience have slum settings or rural backgrounds. As more and more blacks enter the middle and upper economic status, we need to have stories that reflect the reality of upward mobility. Many migratory workers are Chicanos, but many Chicanos hold positions of authority that have nothing to do with following crops. Only when a collection of books about a particular group offers a wide spectrum of occupations, educational backgrounds, living conditions, and life styles will we honestly be moving away from stereotyping in books, and offer positive images of minority groups.

2. *Avoidance of stereotyping.* The other side of the coin to offering a wide range of futures to young people is the obvious limiting of opportunities, which is a form of stereotyping. If the only books about Puerto Ricans picture isolated families living in the basements of all-white apartment buildings because the father is the "building superintendent," this suggests a kind of stereotyping. We also need more stories that include black fathers to counteract the number of books which feature the "absent father." Are sexist stereotypes avoided, particularly in the portrayal of women of minority groups? Does the native American woman play a significant role in the story, or only the men? Is the black mother always pictured as the large loving center of the family? Are the illustrations in the book stereotyped? Are the distinctive qualities of

[89] More detailed guidelines may be found in Augusta Baker. *The Black Experience in Children's Books,* New York Public Library, 1971; Bettye I. Latimer, ed. *Starting Out Right. Choosing Books about Black People for Young Children.* Madison, Wis.: Wisconsin Department of Public Instruction, 1972; and "Checklist for Evaluating Chicano Material," in *Bulletin: Interracial Books for Children,* Vol. 5, 1975.

various racial characteristics portrayed so that the reader knows he's looking at a native American, a Chicano, or black? Does the illustrator avoid picturing such stereotyped articles of clothing as the sombrero and poncho or feather headbands and moccasins or "pickaninny pigtails" or bandanas? A more subtle kind of stereotyping can be seen in street scenes or parks or stores that picture only white people. Further discussion of stereotyping through pictures is given in Chapter 3, "Picture Books," and Chapter 9, "Informational Books and Biographies."

3. *The factor of language.* Derogatory terms for particular racial groups should not be used in stories about minorities unless these are essential to a conflict in the story or used in a historical setting. Even then, it should be made clear that these are unacceptable terms and cast more aspersion on the speaker than the character to whom he is speaking. Another language consideration is the use of dialect or "broken English." Some recent books about blacks have made a conscious effort to reproduce the cadence and syntax of certain black language patterns without resorting to stereotyped dialect or phonetically written spellings, such as the old "I'se a comin" put-downs. If Spanish words are used in the context of the dialogue, they do not need English translations if the book truly represents Latinos. Children today need to develop an understanding of the linguistic principle that no language is any better or worse than any other, and that regional speech or a dialect is a perfectly proper mode of communication.

4. *The perspective of the book.* In evaluating a book about minority groups we need to ask if it truly represents the black experience or the Chicano perspective and so on. This is a difficult guideline to define because we don't want to fall into stereotyped thinking that would suggest only one kind of black experience, for example. At the same time we must ask from whose perspective the book is told. If the major theme of the story is a Latino's desire to master the English language so he can then become "one of us," we may be certain that that story is being told from a white perspective. We need to look to see who solves the

problems in stories. Do characters from the represented minority groups take the initiative in problem-solving, or is the solution provided by paternalistic whites? Does the story provide a positive image of the minority group, or a negative one? Is racial pride apparent in the story? How authentic are the details of the story to the experience of the represented minority?

These are some of the questions and guidelines that may be used in evaluating the books in this section. No one is free from his or her own particular bias or background, however. Teachers or librarians in various school settings may want to apply other or additional criteria for the books they select. The essential point is to provide books about minorities for *all* children. Books can be a moving force in developing children's appreciation for our pluralistic society.

The Black Experience in Books for Children

Today we have many fine picture books that portray the black experience for younger children (*see* Chapter 3). We also have several picture books with extended text for older children. For example, *The Song of the Empty Bottles* by Molarsky has excellent illustrations by Tom Feelings. This is the story of Thaddeus, who went to the Neighborhood House every Thursday to hear Mr. Andrews sing and play the guitar. More than anything Thaddeus wanted a guitar of his own. He started collecting old bottles and newspapers to earn enough money to buy one, but it was slow work. Finally, Mr. Andrews suggested Thaddeus make up a complete song and he'd pay him. Thaddeus creates the "Empty Bottle Song" while he is collecting bottles, and so makes his extra money to buy the guitar. Music for the song is included in this story of a young boy's successful achievement. It is obvious from the title, *I Wish I Had an Afro* (John Shearer) what little John wants. Illustrated with attractive photographs, Little John expresses his wish; then his mother shows what she thinks, while his father considers the request. Like *The Song of the Empty Bottles,* this story in picture-book format is for children age 8 through 10 or 11. *Gabrielle and Selena* (Desbarats) are two young girls—one black, the other white—who decide they are tired of being themselves and want to exchange places. They do trade places with each other in their respective homes. Their parents go along with them and then play a joke on the girls. This story is just honest good fun. The author describes skin color and facial features in the text, which is seldom done in books for children. The description is necessary for reading the book aloud and is a natural part of the joke. *Striped Ice Cream* by Joan Lexau tells of a family's preparation for a special present for Becky's eighth birthday. Last year Becky had asked for chicken-spaghetti and striped ice cream. This year she feared they were too poor to afford even that. However, Becky is doubly rewarded, for she receives a brand-new striped dress to match her special striped ice cream. Her sisters and mother had made the dress, which explains why they had hurt her feelings by coaxing her out of the house. This is a warm family story in which only the pictures indicate that it is about blacks.

Nellie Cameron is the story of a 9-year-old girl, one of six children in a black family living in Washington, D.C. Nellie is in third grade and can scarcely read. This makes her feel "dumb," particularly when her older brother is considered brilliant. The school gives her little help:

> They kept promoting her at school, always telling her she was dumb and keeping her with the dumb kids. Nellie didn't think she was dumb. . . . She did her numbers pretty well. But reading was like a mountain she would never cross. She could see the top and it was beautiful, but she had no idea how to get up there.[90]

Then Miss Lacey's reading clinic opens and Nellie has a second chance with a teacher she loves. Miss Lacey tape records her speech and gives Nellie confidence. The teacher types her stories out as her reading "book" and, gradually, Nellie learns to read. At the end of the story, when no one seems really interested that she can read or that she's going to be promoted, Nellie proves to herself that she is still important in the family by running away to a friend's house. The family's relief at discovering she is all right, even Mama's spanking, assures Nellie of who she is.

[90] Michelle Murray. *Nellie Cameron* (New York: Seabury, 1971), p. 31.

Older children can experience the good times that 12-year-old Beth Lambert has with her first "crush" on a boy in rural Arkansas. Titled *Philip Hall Likes Me. I Reckon Maybe*, Bette Greene has written an episodic novel about a spunky, energetic young girl and her friend, Philip. They set up "The Elizabeth Lorraine Lambert & Friend Vegetable Stand" together, capture chicken thieves, picket a local merchant for selling them bad merchandise, and compete in a calf-judging contest that Beth wins. Beth apologizes to Philip and says she should have let him win, which makes him angry. After he calms down he says:

> "Truth is . . . all you been doing lately is winning, and that ain't hard to live with. Hard thing is losing."[91]

Beth suggests they go try out for the square-dance contest so they can win together or lose together. Beth Lambert has the spunk of a Queenie Peavy without Queenie's chip on her shoulder. This lively story was an Honor Book for the 1975 Newbery Award.

Virginia Hamilton is the first black author to receive the Newbery Award. One of her early books, *Zeely*, is still one of the best loved by children. Spending the summer at her uncle's farm, 11-year-old Geeder Perry meets the proud and beautiful Zeely Taber. Zeely is more than six and a half feet tall and is very thin and dark. Geeder finds a picture of a Watusi Queen and imagines that Zeely is also a queen. Only Zeely herself can bring Geeder back to reality by discovering the real beauty of being what you are. This is a story that is full of dignity, beauty, and mystery.

Using the device of a secret diary about her "special days," Eloise Greenfield has presented an intimate picture of the peak experiences of Doretha, called *Sister* by her family. The diary begins when Doretha is age 10 and details the sudden death of her father while they are all attending a picnic. At age 11 Doretha learns the family's story of her freedom-fighting ex-slave ancestor. When she is 12 she records her tears and her mother's disappointment when her mother's man friend jilts her. Throughout the

Even though Zeely lived on the next farm, Geeder always saw her as a Watusi queen.

From *Zeely* by Virginia Hamilton. Illustrations by Symeon Shimin. Illustrations copyright © 1967 by Macmillan Publishing Co., Inc. Used by permission of the publisher.

book Doretha worries about her alienated sister who seems not to care how much she hurts their mother. It is while Doretha is waiting up for her sister that she rereads her diary and adds the ending comment.

> In a way, her Doretha Book was a book of hard times. And she never wanted to forget them. . . .
>
> But what she would remember most were the good times, the family and friend times, the love times that rainbowed their way through the hard times. She would remember them over and over, and look for more.[92]

[91] Bette Greene. *Philip Hall Likes Me. I Reckon Maybe*, illustrated by Charles Lilly (New York: Dial, 1974), p. 95.

[92] Eloise Greenfield. *Sister* (New York: Crowell, 1974), p. 82.

Gradually, Doretha emerges from the pages of her book and from her role of sister, to become a very real person in her own right.

The realities of ghetto culture are also depicted in some books about blacks. The impact of gangs upon individuals is the theme of Paula Fox's *How Many Miles to Babylon* and Barbara Rinkoff's *Member of the Gang*. In the first story 10-year-old James is sent on a school errand, and instead runs off to a deserted house where he is found by a gang of boys who steal dogs. They force James to go to Coney Island where they keep him a prisoner. He finally manages to escape, sets the dogs free, and returns home to find his mother is back from the hospital. In *Member of the Gang*, Woodie wants to join Leroy's gang against the wishes of his father who says that it would only bring trouble. But Woodie agrees to be the front man in a store robbery, and when one of the gang members is injured, Woodie stays with him and gets picked up by the police and is put on probation. A black probation officer convinces Woodie that his parents were right about getting an education and staying out of a gang. The story is convincing without being didactic. The reader feels that Woodie will make it, but that several of the gang members are only stalling until their probation period is over. Frank Bonham's social documentary, *Durango Street*, centers upon a black teenage gang in California. In this story a teenager returns to the same environment that had caused him to be sent to the reformatory in the first place. Poverty, no father, a mother who doesn't understand him, and gangs continue to plague the youth. To be safe from one gang, he must join another. A young social worker joins the gang, but is merely tolerated. The book ends on a note of slight hope, but the reader realizes there will be more fights, more trouble ahead.

The story of a *Teacup Full of Roses* by Sharon Bell Mathis is also for teenagers, and shows the devastating effect that drugs had on the circumstances of one black family. One brilliant son is killed, and the oldest boy is so thoroughly hooked on drugs that he might as well be dead. It is more appropriate reading for high schoolers.

A bold and honest story about a 13-year-old boy is Alice Childress' *A Hero Ain't Nothin' But a Sandwich*. How to salvage Benjie who is well on his way to being hooked on heroin is the theme of this Harlem tale. The story is told from many different points of view—from that of Butler Craig, Benjie's "stepfather"; Jimmy Lee Powell's, Benjie's friend; Benjie's mother, Rose; Walter, the pusher; and Benjie himself. Each of these persons have something important to say about Benjie and their relationship with him. They also reveal differing viewpoints on life in Harlem. Jimmy Lee tells how hard it is to be a friend to someone on drugs:

> Friendship begins to split when one is caught in a habit and the other not. I've seen it time and time, needles divide guys, because the user rather be round another junkie.[93]

Butler saves Benjie's life one night and Benjie looks to him as to a father, someone who would believe in him. At the end of the story Butler is waiting for Benjie to come from the rehabilitation center—Benjie is late, and both Butler and the reader hope that he makes it. This is a tough yet very tender story. It may shock some readers and save others.

The Planet of Junior Brown by Virginia Hamilton is a far more complex and symbolic story than the same author's *Zeely*. The main theme in *Planet* is man's need for others. Although the book is titled *The Planet of Junior Brown* there are really three planets in the book—all complementing each other until they physically and ideally come together at the end of the story at Tomorrow Billy's. The first Planet is a huge beige-and-black mass added to the plastic solar system that Mr. Poole and Buddy have set up in the school basement. Like the 300 pound-Junior, the planet is larger than anything else in the solar system. By creating this planet for Junior, Buddy is trying to tell him that Junior, too, can belong. The second set of planets are the sanctuaries for homeless boys throughout the city. Here, leaders like the Tomorrow Billies, teach their charges to survive from day to day, even though they have no family nor home. All the planets and people ultimately come together in the final planet of Junior Brown, and it is here in this new planet that the reader sees what the

---

[93] Alice Childress. *A Hero Ain't Nothin' But a Sandwich* (New York: Coward, 1973), p. 87.

future or new world can be—a place where everyone belongs, where people have learned to live for each other not for themselves. It is unfortunate and ironic to find an anti-Jewish passage in a book with such a strong message of the brotherhood of man.

M. C. Higgins, the Great, which won the 1975 Newbery Award and the National Book Award, is the story of 13-year-old Cornelius Higgins and his family, who live just below a strip mine in the Appalachian hills of Ohio. M. C. helps take care of the younger children while his parents work. He dreams of getting his family away from the danger of the slow-moving spoil heap that is left from the strip mines and threatens to engulf their mountain home. M. C.'s place of refuge, where he can go and survey his domain and at the same time rise above his problems, is a forty-foot steel pole. It is from this forty-foot height that he discovers two strangers who are entering the valley. One is a "dude" who M. C. imagines will make his mother a singing star and help them all escape the menacing spoil heap. The other is Lurhetta, a young wanderer who awakens M. C.'s initiative and helps him learn that both choice and action lie within his power. M. C. realizes that his dream of running away from the mountain, or swaying above it on a pole, will never solve his problems. At the end of the story his father helps him to begin to build a wall to hold back the slag by giving him the tombstone of the slave who had run away to the mountain and started the family. Again Virginia Hamilton has created a strange, symbolic book that speaks to the uniqueness of the black experience and the universal concerns of all human beings.

Books about Other Minorities

There is far better quality and greater range in books about blacks than there is for other minorities. Many of the books about Latinos, for example, have "forced" stories that are thin in content and characterization; frequently they perpetuate stereotypes rather than dispel them. A favorite theme for stories about Puerto Ricans is that of overcoming language problems. Children are pictured as being miserable and having no friends until they learn to speak English properly. In *Candita's Choice* by Lewiton, a Puerto

Rican refuses to speak at all until she can speak well enough to make the teacher proud of her. This same theme is apparent in the title of Bouchard's book, *The Boy Who Wouldn't Talk.* Carlos' family has moved from Puerto Rico to New York City and he is so confused and frustrated with his language problem that he, too, decides to give up talking—in English *and* Spanish. Finally, he meets Ricky Hermandez, a blind boy who asks for directions in order to get home. Ricky cannot read the signs or pictures that Carlos makes for him, thereby forcing Carlos to talk.

How Juan Got Home by Peggy Mann has more depth of characterization and a more interesting plot than the other two stories, but the language problem is still central. Juan receives money for an airline ticket to come and live with his godfather, Uncle Esteban, in New York City. There is much preparation for Juan's trip, including a farewell feast. His mother has coveted this chance for him, yet she hates to see him go. Juan asks why everyone is hurrying him off almost as if they were glad for him to go. His mother tells him that it is because they are glad to see him have such a chance:

> "Well, why are you rushing me off so soon? . . ."
> "Because," his mother said in a matter of fact voice, "if I don't do it quickly I might not find the strength inside me to let you go at all."[94]

When he arrives, Juan hates New York. He doesn't understand the language, doesn't make friends, and misses the familiar foods of home. It is his trip to a Spanish grocery in the Barrio that finally brings him a friend, and the friendship is cemented by the fact that Juan shows skill at playing stickball. Juan makes a home run for the team, which provides the double image for the title. This accomplishment is marred by the pat ending where Juan cheers for his team in English: "Loud and proud he yelled the words— the words of the English language."[95] Peggy Mann has written three other books about Puerto Ricans, including *The Street of the Flower Boxes, When Carlos Closed the Street,* and *The Clubhouse.* All three of these stories show a 9-year-old boy

[94] Peggy Mann. *How Juan Got Home,* illustrated by Richard Lebenson (New York: Coward-McCann, 1972), p. 20.
[95] Mann, p. 94.

taking the initiative in bringing about changes in his community. Children like these stories, but Carlos' accomplishments seem unrealistic in terms of what one child can do. Even though former New York Mayor Lindsay recommends the book, the problems of the Puerto Ricans living in the city are not going to be solved with flowerboxes!

Chicano stories suffer from the same shallowness as some of the slight stories of the Puerto Ricans. *Go Up the Road* by Lampman tells of the dream of Yolanda Ruiz to finish grade school. But every year the family goes north up the road to harvest the crops and Yolanda would have to leave school early. She was doing fourth-grade work for the third time because of this and prayed to pass into the fifth. Then her Uncle Luis, a logger in a small Oregon town dies, and so they all go to help his widow and children. Much to their surprise Uncle Luis' family are far better off than the Ruiz'. Yolanda has a good school experience and is tutored so she can pass into fifth grade. Her papa decides to "stabilize," to find a job and remain in Oregon. This story seems somewhat patronizing of the Chicanos. Yolanda has none of the spunk of Janey Larkin, the heroine in the classic migrant story of *Blue Willow* by Doris Gates. Janey's only friend in that story is a Mexican-American girl. A comparison of the two stories would be interesting.

One of the most widely read stories about persons of Spanish descent in this country is the award-winning . . . *And Now Miguel* by Joseph Krumgold. Miguel is the middle brother of an Hispanic family living on a New Mexico sheep ranch. Pedro, the younger brother, seems satisfied with what he has, but Miguel thinks his 19-year-old brother, Gabriel, can do everything and has everything he wants. Miguel expresses the problem of all who feel "in between":

> Both of them, they are happy. But to be in between, not so little any more and not yet nineteen years, to be me, Miguel, and to have a great wish—that is hard.[96]

Miguel has one all-consuming desire, and that is to be able to go with the men when they take the sheep to the Sangre de Cristo Mountains. His prayers are answered, but not as Miguel wished. Gabriel is drafted into the army, and Miguel is allowed to take his place. While this is a beautifully written story, it is representative of only a small, isolated segment of the Chicano population.

Chicano Girl by Hila Colman is more appropriate for teenagers. Sixteen-year-old Donna Martinez is tired of the isolation of a rural Mexican community and yearns to go to Tucson to attend beauty school and earn money. Donna is warmly welcomed by her relatives, but does not believe their comments regarding her acceptance in the Anglo community. After many days of job hunting and a date with an Anglo boy who thought she'd be a pushover, she has to admit her relatives are right. This story was selected as an American Library Association Notable book, but the pace is uneven and some incidents seem contrived.

David Gast in his article on the treatment of minority groups in literature outlines several typical approaches, including "The Invisible Man" (or no treatment approach), "The Noble-Savage Approach," and "The White Man's Burden Approach."[97] Certainly, books about the native American have fallen into all of these categories. In most of historical fiction the American Indian is portrayed as the "Ignoble Savage." A frequent theme in contemporary literature centers on the Indian child's conflict in choosing between the dominant culture and the traditional Indian one. In *Quiet Boy* by the Waltrips a 12-year-old boy lives on an Indian reservation in Arizona where the old and new ways conflict. Before his father was killed in war, he had written his son urging him to obtain as much education as possible. Carlson also wrote of the conflict between those who wanted to learn modern ways and those who wished to retain the Indian traditions in *The Tomahawk Family*.

In Clymer's *The Spider, the Cave and the Pottery Bowl*, two Indian children spend their summer with an ailing grandmother in her pueblo on the Painted Desert. Although they break their grandmother's ancient pottery bowl, they dis-

[96] Joseph Krumgold. . . . *And Now Miguel,* illustrated by Jean Charlot (New York: Crowell, 1953), p. 9.

[97] David Gast. "The Dawning of the Age of Aquarius for Multiethnic Children's Literature," *Elementary English,* Vol. 47 (May 1970), pp. 661–665.

cover a new source for her clay, and take pride in learning the traditions of making pottery themselves. *Annie and the Old One* (Miles) is a beautiful story in both text and pictures of a Navajo girl who does not want to weave a rug since her grandmother says she will die when it is finished (*see* page 433). At the end of this moving story, Annie does begin to work on the rug. The continuity of life goes on.

Two older stories, *Indian Hill* by Bulla and *Wigwam in the City* by Smucker, describe the Indian's adjustment to living in the city. In the latter story a Chippewa Indian and his daughter are traveling to Chicago. They have an unfortunate encounter with a food vendor:

> "Speaka English?" he asked and then waited.
> Father said nothing and looked straight ahead. Susan's face flushed. She did not want the man to think that they could not speak English. She wondered why he had asked . . . He stopped at the next row of seats where people laughed. . . .
> "The Indians back there don't speak English. I don't know what they'll do when they get to Chicago."
> "Maybe they'll hunt bears at Lincoln Park Zoo," a woman with a high voice giggled.
> Father spoke quietly in the language of the Chippewa. "They must think we do not live in America."[98]

When Thunders Spoke by Virginia Driving Hawk Sneve is representative of the newer "identity" books. Young Norman Two Bull is the third generation of his family to live on the Dakota (Sioux) reservation. His mother wears hose and heels to entertain the ladies' society and disapproves of Norman's grandfather, Matt Two Bull, who clings to the old customs. He urges Norman to go to Thunder Butte, where Sioux boys once went seeking visions to guide their future life. Norman does go and finds agates which he trades to a thoroughly unlikable white trader. He also finds a relic, an old *coup* stick which he gives his grandfather. The trader proposes a quarry on Thunder Butte as a way to benefit the Indians since Norman found the agates there, but he wants mostly to advance his own interests. However,

the Butte is sacred ground and Norman's grandfather does not approve. Together Norman and his father return the *coup* stick, and the reader is left with the impression that the traditional beliefs are still revered. There is some veiled hostility in this book, which is written from the Indian point of view. For example:

> The man smiled and Norman almost liked him . . . [But then] when he turned back to Norman the white man's pale blue eyes looked shifty and greedy.
> Norman's mouth tightened in anger. This white man felt free to take from the Indians just the way all white people did.[99]

While Asian-Americans have been portrayed in picture books for younger children, there are very few stories about them for middle-graders. Several well-written accounts of life in the Japanese relocation camps have been written (*see* Means' *The Moved-Outers* and Uchida's *Journey to Topaz* in Chapter 8). *Willy Wong: American* was written by Vanya Oakes over twenty years ago. In this story of a Chinese-American, Willy Wong wants to be considered totally American by his friends yet still retain his Chinese identity. He learns about his Chinese ancestors and the role that his great-grandfather played in helping to build the first American railroad. Willy does develop pride in his heritage, yet the theme is so heavy-handed as to be distracting. *Moon Guitar* by Marie Niemeyer is a much more interesting story of a 12-year-old Chinese-American girl. Su-Lin does not want to be sent to Taiwan to become a "proper Chinese girl," but her grandfather thinks she should be brought up in the traditional ways as befits a family that once owned the long-lost and beautiful moon guitar. How Su-Lin and her friend search San Francisco's Chinatown for the family treasure makes for an exciting story and changes both Grandfather and Su-Lin.

RESPECTING RELIGIOUS BACKGROUNDS

Although the United States was founded upon a belief in freedom of religion, misunderstanding

---

[98] Barbara Smucker. *Wigwam in the City,* illustrated by Gil Miret (New York: Dutton, 1966).

[99] Virginia Driving Hawk Sneve. *When Thunders Spoke,* illustrated by Oren Lyons (New York: Holiday, 1974), p. 79.

and religious prejudice have persisted in our society. *Hannah Elizabeth* by Rich is the quiet story of a year in the life of a 10-year-old Indiana Mennonite. She has to learn to accept the taunts of schoolmates because her father refused to fight in the war. Many quotations from the Bible and parts of sermons are included, as well as accounts of fun in family life. Hannah Elizabeth attends a movie and party with her music teacher, but realizes she is not being a good Mennonite. Faced with conflicting values, she has no difficulty in choosing.

Three stories detail the lives of girls who belong to the "plain people." Adjustment to the conflicting values of her Amish home and the school "outside" is also difficult for Esther, the central character in *Plain Girl.* Sorenson writes sensitively of a father's disappointment when his son leaves the religious community, and his fear when his daughter goes to the public school. As Esther grows up, she discovers that people who wear pink, blue, and red may be as kind and good as those who wear plain clothing. When her brother finally returns, the young people recognize they may need to change outward symbols, such as haircuts and use of machinery, but they can keep the inner values of their religion.

Shoo-Fly Girl by Lenski portrays life in an Amish family in Pennsylvania. This book paints a detailed picture of a different culture—the homes, language, work of the children, church, and values. Shoo-Fly's encounters with the outside world bring confusion, and she prefers home. She accepts the answer of her Great-Grossomommy, who explained why women used pins instead of buttons:

> To keep humble, to avoid false pride. We are plain people. We eat plain, we live plain, we dress plain, to show that our hearts are not set on the things of this world, but above. We are Amish. These things we have always done. So we will always do.[100]

In *Proud to Be Amish* (Jordan), Katie Zook wrestles with the temptations of the modern world and her religious upbringing. She is envious of Gloria's red dress, and she feels guilty about listening to the little radio that belonged

Stiff figures are typical of Lenski's drawings which present realistic details of Amish life.

From *Shoo-Fly Girl* by Lois Lenski. Copyright © 1963 by Lois Lenski. Reproduced by permission of J. B. Lippincott Company.

to her older brother. But then Katie finds out that even her mother and father do not always resist wordly temptations. This story gives a vivid glimpse of Amish life in Pennsylvania farming country. A glossary is provided for some of the Amish terms.

In *A Promise Is a Promise*, Cone helps children understand the Jewish faith. Essentially, this is the story of Ruth Morgen's growing understanding of the meaning and history of her religion. Ruthy's preparation for her Bas Mitzvah is interwoven with the decisions she must make about daily relationships with people. Ruth is concerned about an eccentric, lonely neighbor whose cats bother another neighbor. Ruthy promises Mr. Hainey she will care for his cats when he goes to the hospital, and when he re-

---

[100]Lois Lenski. *Shoo-Fly Girl* (Philadelphia, Penna: Lippincott, 1963), pp. 117–118.

turns briefly to close his house forever, she promises to find a home for them. Ruth's problems in finding a home for the cats becomes intertwined with her questions about the meaning of Judaism. The customs of the Jewish holidays and religious service are described in this sensitive story of a girl growing up.

Kate by Jean Little is the story of a young girl from a mixed marriage who becomes interested in searching out the roots of her Jewish background. The reader learns nothing about the Jewish religion, however, for the story ends just as Kate and her father are entering the synagogue (*see* page 414).

The effect of anti-Semitism is realistically presented in *Berries Goodman* by Emily Neville. The book begins with a meeting of two high-school boys, one of whom is defying his mother by going away from home on a holiday. The other, Berries, thinks about causes of behavior and begins a reminiscence of his relationship with Sidney, his Jewish friend. The rest of the book is a flashback to a New York suburb and the development of the friendship. Berries' parents provide love and interest in him, although his mother has little desire to cook or keep house. Sandra, next door, has to prove herself to others because her parents really give her little time. It is Sandra and her family who are prejudiced against Jews. Berries learns that parents can be weak when his mother acquiesces to "agreements" made by the real-estate agency for which she works. When Sidney is hurt because Sandra taunts him into skating in a dangerous area, his mother refuses to let Berries see him. In a discussion of the accident, Sidney says: "The trouble was, Mom couldn't see that your family were any different from Sandra's. If your Mother had called up or anything. . . ."[101] Berries' father makes no protest when Sidney's father insists that the boys must stop their clandestine meetings. In both instances it is the parents who are weak, not the children. In discussing realistic writing Neville has expressed the view that an author should show that parents can be "nice cowards" and there should be a puzzlement; ". . . and this may make a child look a little more

closely, a little more acutely at the people around him."[102] In this story Neville has shown the effects of anti-Semitism. She has not probed beneath the surface to get at the causes of such attitudes. This book could lead to some excellent value-clarification sessions that might help children examine some of the root causes of prejudice.

APPRECIATING REGIONAL DIFFERENCES

The name of Lois Lenski is closely associated with the term "regional fiction," for she was one of the first authors to write of children who lived in particular regions of our country. Lenski would go to live in a community, observe as an anthropologist might observe, listening to the people, asking them to tell what had happened in their lives. Then she would weave the facts into an interesting plot centering around one family. She wrote of the purposes of her books:

> I am trying to introduce the children of one region to another, thus widening their horizons. I want to tell how they live and why, to point out details in backgrounds, occupations and customs peculiar to each region. But along with these differences, I show also the inward likenesses.[103]

In *Strawberry Girl*, a Newbery Award book, Lenski describes life in the central Florida backwoods early in the twentieth century. In *Coal Camp Girl* the West Virginia family experiences hunger during a winter when there is no food; they know the agony of waiting for the rescue of men trapped in a mine and the hard economic lesson of being paid "scrip" in advance of a salary and buying at the high-cost company store.

Texas Tomboy is about a young girl who wants to become a ranchwoman. Riding over the plains with her father, "Charlie Boy" learns the lore of ranching. The child who reads this book learns about the problems of ranch life; he also gains insight into the conflicting demands of society and the individual, as a girl rebels against her expected sex role. In *Prairie School*, Lenski has written a modern story of the trials of life on a

---

[101] Emily Neville. *Berries Goodman* (New York: Harper & Row, 1965), p. 177.

[102] Emily Neville. "Social Values in Children's Literature," *Library Quarterly* (January 1967), p. 46.
[103] Lois Lenski. "My Purpose," *Lois Lenski: An Appreciation*, Charles Adams, ed. (Durham, N.C.: Christian Printing Company, 1963), pp. 40–41.

snowbound prairie of South Dakota. Lenski realistically portrays the snowbound days in the school, the dramatic episode when the teacher takes Dolores through the storm for an appendectomy, and the hay drop by helicopter to save the cattle.

Judy's Journey was one of the first stories about migrants. Conditions were so bad for Judy's family, who were sharecroppers, that they had to sell their possessions and begin following the crops. As the family works in Florida and up the coast, they learn there are few opportunities for the migrant. Too proud to accept help from the Salvation Army or the women's welfare society, they struggle on. "We're not destitute, and we don't take *charity* off nobody. We still got our pride."[104] Lenski seldom used metaphor in her writing; she builds detail upon detail until the reader receives the total impression of the scene. She describes Judy's work in the fields:

> Potatoes—potatoes—nothing but potatoes. . . . The sun got hotter and hotter. Her ragged overalls stuck to her, and she was red with sunburn and prickly heat. Her back ached badly—she must rest for a minute. She stretched out full length in the dirt.[105]

At school Judy fought the town kids, learned to read and to care for the cuts and bruises of others. She learned from her parents: "'People are what you think they are,' said Papa. 'If you think they're good and treat 'em right, they'll *be* good and treat *you* right. But first, you got to be plumb good your own self.'"[106] Although Judy herself does not show much character change, she does effect change in the family's condition. This is characteristic of many of Lenski's regional stories.

In *Hoagie's Rifle Gun* Miska Miles relates the story of two Appalachian boys who have an unsuccessful hunting trip. Hoagie is only 11, but he never misses a shot—until the day when he shoots at Old Bob, a bobcat who had caught the rabbit he'd wanted. The boys, too, needed the rabbit for their family's dinner. Hoagie had shot at the cat more out of frustration than need, for

he knew bobcat meat wasn't worth bringing home. Ira, Hoagie's brother, was glad he'd missed. When he tells his father, Hoagie says he aimed for the big cat but really didn't want to kill him. His brother says, "You can't kill a thing when you know it by its name."[107] That night the family only had potatoes for their dinner. This is a spare, understated story of an impoverished Appalachian family who were rich in character and self-respect. Crisp black-and-white illustrations by John Schoenherr portray the poverty and pride of these people.

The Fiddler of High Lonesome is a hauntingly beautiful story written and illustrated in deep blues by Brinton Turkle. The Fogles didn't think much of their new kinfolk, Bochamp, when he said he didn't believe in shooting creatures. In

[107] Miska Miles. *Hoagie's Rifle Gun,* illustrated by John Schoenherr (New York: Little, Brown, 1970), p. 37.

The day Charley tried to stop the running water, he didn't get to carry the flag either.

From *Did You Carry the Flag Today, Charley?* by Rebecca Caudill. Illustrated by Nancy Grossman. Copyright © 1966 by Rebecca Caudill. Copyright © 1966 by Nancy Grossman. Reproduced by permission of Holt, Rinehart and Winston, Inc.

[104] Lois Lenski. *Judy's Journey* (Philadelphia, Penna.: Lippincott, 1947), p. 58.
[105] Lenski, p. 147.
[106] Lenski, p. 186.

fact, they weren't going to let him stay until they found out he could play the fiddle for their Saturday night dances. Then, one moonlit night, they left him to walk home alone and they could hardly believe what he told them. This story has the quality of folklore in that it captures all that was the worst of the mountaineers in the Fogles and all that was the best in Bochamp. Children from 8-years-old and up love this story.

Rebecca Caudill has told the story of curious young Charles Cornett's first days in a one-room schoolhouse in Appalachia. Each day when he comes home his brothers and sisters ask him *Did You Carry the Flag Today, Charley?* for this was the signal honor for good behavior. Each day Charley has to answer no, for a curious boy can find lots of ways to get into trouble. A former schoolteacher herself, Rebecca Caudill knows children and Appalachia as is shown in this warm story of an Appalachian family.

The Cleavers' story of *Where the Lilies Bloom* is the best-known tale of Appalachia for children. The tortuous death of Roy Luther from "worms in the chest" puts the full responsibility of the family on Mary Call, his 14-year-old daughter. She and Romey, her younger brother, carry Luther up the mountain in a wagon and bury him so the "county people" will not find out that they are orphaned and separate them. Then Mary Call strives to keep her "Cloudy-headed" older sister, Devola, and her two younger sisters alive through the winter. Mary Call's fierce pride gives her fortitude to overcome such things as a wild gray fox who waits to kill their last chicken, a severe winter, a caved-in roof, and the constant pretense that Roy Luther still lives. At 14, Mary Call's strength and responsibility have made her old before her time, but she pulls the family through the crisis:

> My name is Mary Call Luther, I thought, and someday I'm going to be a big shot. I've got the guts to be one. I'm not going to let this beat me. If it does, everything else will for the rest of my life.[108]

Mary Call does survive, through wildcrafting on the mountains, through scheming, and just

[108] Vera Cleaver and Bill Cleaver. *Where the Lilies Bloom* (New York: Lippincott, 1969), p. 144.

pure grit. The authors have captured the beauty and the hurt of the Smokies and of this memorable family who live in what an old hymn calls the land "Where the Lilies Bloom So Fair."

The same authors have written *The Whys and Wherefores of Littabelle Lee,* which is the story of a young girl who lives in the Ozarks with her Aunt Sorrow and her grandparents, Maw Maw and Paw Paw. When Aunt Sorrow decides it is wrong to have to give up your life for your parents, she leaves the responsibility to Littabelle Lee. Littabelle, who was teaching school with very little education herself, solves the problem by going to court and demanding that the rest of the family help her. Littabelle is a strong character, but this story does not have the force of *Where the Lilies Bloom*.

The grimness and poverty of life near a swamp is presented in George Harmon Smith's story of life in Louisiana in *Bayou Boy*. In sharing this story and all other regional fiction teachers need to help children realize that each book presents only one small aspect of life in a particular region; *Bayou Boy* does not represent the kind of a life that a child growing up in New Orleans in the same state would have. Teachers will want to help children to appreciate the differences among the regions in the United States, but they also should be made aware of the dangers of generalizing about all people of one region, class, or occupation.

UNDERSTANDING VARIOUS WORLD CULTURES

Increasingly, we have fine informational books about life in other countries (*see* Chapter 9). However, as children are studying units on Australia or countries of Africa or Europe, they should be made aware of the stories that provide the feelings of people, as well as the nonfiction that provides the facts. It is impossible to describe all the books about various countries in this section, but outstanding ones will be mentioned. Again, it is good to remind children that a single book cannot convey a complete picture of a country. In order to make this point clear, children might consider what books, if any, they would like to have sent to other countries as *representative* of life in the United States.

To understand the changes that are coming to the Zulus in Africa children might read Mirsky's

Thirty-one Brothers and Sisters. Life in the kraal is authentically presented in this story of Nomusa and her chieftain father's family of six wives and thirty-one children. Cultural expectations, the roles each person plays, customs, and taboos show the old patterns of living. In *Nomusa and the New Magic* the girl, now 14, goes to school to learn to be a nurse. Zitu, her father, accepts new ways; but Damasi, a boy who likes her, is afraid she will not want him and will cost him too many cows to marry. When Buselapi, the nurse, and Nomusa go to treat a wounded man, it is clear to Nomusa that the witch doctor treated the fears of the wives while the nurse's penicillin made the man well. Damasi leaves his work in the mines to go to the agricultural school. Thus, Damasi and Nomusa, who recognize their love, prepare to bring a change to their people.

The Leopard by Cecil Bodker is an exciting story about a young Ethiopian boy who knew too much—he knew that it was the blacksmith who was stealing the cattle under the guise of being a leopard. When Tibeso reveals this knowledge, the smith binds and gags Tibeso and takes him to a deserted village where he will be at the mercy of the wild animals and spirits of the night. In the end the smith is killed by a leopard, which has a kind of just retribution to it. Written by a Danish author who had lived in Ethiopia, this story portrays some modern aspects of East African life overlaid with the traditional superstitions of the mountain villagers.

A girl is the heroic figure of a novel set in Kenya, *The Bushbabies* by Stevenson. The "bushbabies" were Jacqueline, daughter of a game warden whose job has been taken over by a native; Kamau, her pet tarsier; and Tembo, a native who had been her father's assistant. Thinking she has time to return to the ship, Jackie decides she must leave her pet so Tembo can take it back to its bush home. The ship sails, leaving her alone. She finds Tembo and persuades him to help her travel nearly 300 miles. The descriptions of the African landscape and the animals encountered are intriguing and provide some exciting moments. They survive a forest fire, a storm, and a perilous flood, and Jackie faces a wounded leopard in her attempt to help Tembo. This well-written book has the elements of a good adventure—a strange land, danger from nature and men, a theme of assuming responsibility and understanding needs of native peoples.

Two books by the Norwegian writer, Aimée Sommerfelt, describe the sharp edges of poverty in India. *The Road to Agra* won the Norwegian State Prize for Children's Literature, the Jane Addams Book Award, and several other awards. It is the story of a village boy, Lalu, who walks nearly three hundred miles with his 7-year-old sister to take her to a hospital where her blindness may be cured. On the way the children face hunger, danger from a cobra and jackals, and evil men. Lalu and his pretty sister, Maya, do meet a few kind people, but their exhaustion often leads to despair. When they learn that their grand-uncle has moved, and when the guard at the hospital gate turns them away, all hope disappears. They decide they must return home. Fortunately, they join a group of lepers and poor children at a jeep health station, where the World Health Organization doctors examine Maya and agree to operate on her eyes. Lalu's fortitude and courage are to be admired, and the change in his purpose for the journey gives a fine example of character development. Lalu's story is continued in *The White Bungalow*, in which his dream of becoming a doctor is washed away in the storms.

A boy in India is the first in his village to learn to read. *What Then, Raman?* is the title of the book that tells how the boy worked to achieve his dream and how he found an answer to the difficult question posed by the lady who befriended him. It becomes necessary for his father to go to the city to get work and for Raman to leave school to work for the family. He is isolated from the other boys, for school has made him different. One day, he says that he will be a great scholar and read shelves of books:

> "Good," the . . . lady nodded. "And then what?"
>
> Again Raman stopped short, puzzled. He shifted his feet a trifle uncomfortably.
>
> "What will you do then, after you have learned so many things? . . ."
>
> "Why—why then I shall know them, that's all," he answered, stammering a little.[109]

[109] Shirley L. Arora. *"What Then, Raman?"*, illustrated by Hans Guggenheim (Chicago, Ill.: Follett, 1960), p. 115.

Raman discovers the joy of teaching when he begins to teach his sister to read. He also discovers he has courage when he faces the "tiger" in the jungle. It requires even greater fortitude to buy things for his family instead of the beautiful book he had dreamed of owning. When Raman agrees to teach the boys of the village, he knows he is at last answering the puzzling question: "What Then, Raman?" This book was published in paperback under the title of *Tiger on the Mountain*.

It would be interesting for children to compare the slow-moving, mystical story *Secret of the Andes* by Clark with the modern, frightening tale *Pulga* by S. R. Van Iterson. *Secret of the Andes* appears to be realistic fiction, yet elements of legend and fantasy are included in this story of an Indian boy who is chosen to be the one who shall know of the secret gold and llama herd of the Incas. When Cusi is 8 he discovers other people; until this time he has known only old Chuto who has taught him his language, care of the llamas, and to be satisfied with little. The fantasy develops as Cusi's llama leads him down a hidden trail to an ancient temple. There he discovers golden sandals that are his, says his "heart." Now, Chuto says, he has received the sign; he must go to Cuzco to seek his heart's desire. Encounters there with strangers who seem to recognize him only leave him with more questions. He returns to the mountains, for only in the hidden valley can he feel secure. Chuto shows him the cave where the gold is hidden, and Cusi swears he will never reveal the secret and that he will train another to take his place. The pace of this award-winning book is as slow as the climb up the mountain trails, but the author's descriptions provide moments of real beauty. The mystery of Cusi's identity supplies the suspense of the story.

Pulga means "flea" in Spanish, and it is the name by which an undernourished urchin who roams the streets of Bogota is called. It is also the title of the book by Van Iterson, who tells his story. In all his 13 years Pulga has known only the slums around him. Then one night he creeps under a truck to escape the rain and his destiny is changed. Pulga is hired as a trucker's helper and makes the "run" from Bogota to the coast and back again. The trip is dangerous, for in places the countryside is controlled by bandits, but for Pulga it is a wonderful opportunity, and he develops some hope for the future and a measure of self-respect. He begins to make plans for his handicapped brother to go on the next trip and stay with his godmother. This story creates a vivid if unflattering picture of life in Colombia. While the author is Dutch, she does live in Bogota with her family.

Several Australian writers are producing excellent books of contemporary realism. Ivan Southall is known for his survival stories, such as *Hill's End* and *Ash Road*. *Josh* is the story of the psychological and physical survival of a 14-year-old city boy who goes to visit the country town that was settled by his great-grandfather Plowman. The people he meets there—including Aunt Clara; the two O'Connor boys and their beautiful sister, Betsy; Laura and Harry Jones—all baffle him and seem uncivilized. Josh is a dreamer and a poet, a boy who seems to do everything wrong. During the three days of his visit encounters with the young people of Ryan Creek move from veiled hostility to open violence. Told from the point of view of Josh, this is a fascinating tale of a boy's struggle to survive in a world he doesn't understand. Aunt Clara says Josh has been just what the small town needed—a catharsis. But for Josh it has been more than he can bear. He cuts his stay short and starts walking back to Melbourne town. This story won the English Carnegie Medal in 1971. It paints a vivid picture of contrasting values and backgrounds in Australia.

Boy Alone by Ottley takes place on an isolated Australian cattle station. The protagonist is given no name, nor do we know why he is there, a boy alone without family or friends. The very size of the ranch influences the boy's feelings. "It's the bigness that makes you lonely."[110] The boy cares for a dog and her pup, although he knows the hard-bitten master of the dog pack, Kanga, will take them away. The dog, Brolga, does die when Kanga makes her go back with the pack, although the dog wants to stay with the boy. In despair, the boy goes out to the desert to save the pup, Rags. When he is lost in the sand, he realizes he "needed someone human—

---

[110] Reginald Ottley. *Boy Alone,* illustrated by Clyde Pearson (New York: Harcourt Brace Jovanovich, 1965), p. 55.

someone to help and guide."[111] All the men search, but it is Kanga who finds the boy. Kanga gives him the pup, although the boy now realizes that Kanga needs the dog to lead the pack. The author's descriptions of the heat and scorched earth make the reader's throat feel parched. Without being sentimental, he conveys the love of boy and man for the dogs. The harshness of survival in the outback country of Australia is made clear in this story.

John Rowe Townsend is writing stories of rugged realism in England. His *Good-Bye to the Jungle* is the story of four young persons from the slums of a city in northern England. The Thompson family leaves the "jungle," a tumbledown district of dilapidated houses which are being razed for slum clearance. They are moving to Westwood Estate, a development project that holds the promise of a new life for them all. However, there is little reason to believe that Walter Thompson will change. Head of the family, he is lazy, a spendthrift, and spends most of his time at the pub. Doris is Walter's "friend," or common-law wife, and is just about as worthless. Walter is the uncle and guardian of the narrator, who is Kevin, age 15, and his sister, Sandra, age 14. They came to live with the Thompsons when their parents were killed in a car accident. Walter also has two children, Harold and Jean, by a wife who has left him. The focus of the plot is on Walter's setting fire to the furniture warehouse where he works. Kevin and his friend rescue Walter and receive much publicity. Then the police find evidence that Walter set the fire, and he is convicted of arson. Kevin and Sandra have to hold the family together. It is they who assure that the 11-year-old genius of the family, Harold, gets his chance at a scholarship at Cobchester College. In brief, this is a modern-day survival story; and the children cope amazingly well. This particular story was a sequel to *Trouble in the Jungle*, in which Walter deserts the children who then are left to fend for themselves in an old empty warehouse. These stories face the realities of living in a slum in a frank and honest fashion.

Janet McNeill has written of a similar topic in her books *The Battle of St. George Without* and *Goodbye, Dove Square*. Both of these books also involve some mystery and intrigue. Matt McGinley and his friends live in the overcrowded buildings surrounding Dove Square. In the center of the square is an untended park, and in the park, nearly hidden by a tangle of bushes and trees, stands the church of St. George Without. It had been damaged during World War II and closed ever since. Matt finds a tunnel through the undergrowth and it became a perfect meeting place for his five adventurous friends—until they find that it is also the hangout for a sinister gang. In *Goodbye, Dove Square* the houses are all demolished and the families moved to The Flats, except one of the old friends who never left. He lives in a supposedly deserted house. Both these stories give a flavor of living in the slums of London; both of them have elements of mystery.

Realistic stories from Sweden reveal much of the new freedom that is found in realism in the United States. Maria Gripe received the Hans Christian Andersen Award for her writing. The book *The Night Daddy* has been reviewed in this chapter in the section on alternative families. Her book *Hugo and Josephine* is a delightfully humorous story about two children who are just beginning school. Josephine, the minister's daughter, is shy and conforming. Then she meets Hugo, who has a mind of his own. His teacher tells Hugo that he must be still and quiet:

> The teacher does the talking, and the children just answer when the teacher asks them a question.
>
> Hugo listens attentively to this, but looks frankly astonished.
>
> "Now that's odd," he says.
>
> "What's so odd about it?" the teacher asks.
>
> "There's no sense in our answering, when we don't know anything. We're the ones who ought to ask the questions."[112]

Another very humorous story about a young girl is titled *Grandpa's Maria* (Hellberg). Seven-year-old Maria lives with her grandpa since her divorced mother has had a nervous breakdown. Maria learns to ride a bicycle much to her delight. She meets her father and his new family, which is puzzling but leaves her feeling that she is better off with Grandpa. There is a very amus-

[111] Ottley, p. 178.

[112] Maria Gripe. *Hugo and Josephine*, translated from the Swedish by Paul Britten Austin, illustrated by Harold Gripe (New York: Delacorte, 1969), pp. 60, 61.

ing scene at the railroad station when Maria has to go to the bathroom and finds the ladies room locked. Finally, in desperation, she relieves herself on the station floor when no one is looking! This is a funny warm story which tells more about the attitude of the Swedish toward children than about Sweden itself.

Reading the literature of another country or reading about another place will broaden children's outlook and deepen their appreciation for all peoples of the world. Realistic fiction makes it possible to use the imagination to enter other lives in other places, to know more of the world in which we live. As C. S. Lewis has noted, this process enables the individual to extend his life space ". . . [For] in reading great literature I become a thousand men and yet remain myself."[113]

Popular Types of Realistic Fiction

Certain subjects of realistic fiction are so popular with children that they ask for them by name; they want to read a good animal story (usually dog or horse story); they want a sports book (or baseball or football story); or they'll ask for a "funny" book (meaning humorous fiction); or a good mystery. Many of these stories are not the quality of literature that we would hope children will read; yet many of them serve the useful function of getting children "hooked" on books so that they then move on to reading better literature. Teachers and librarians need to identify the appeals of these popular kinds of books so as to be able to recommend other titles when children are ready for them. They also need to know some of the outstanding books among these popular types, since some of them are very well written indeed.

ANIMAL STORIES

Stories about animals provide children with the vicarious experience of giving love and receiving devotion and loyalty from an animal. Frequently, these animal tales are really stories of the maturing of their major characters. For example, the well-loved story of *Goodbye, My Lady* by James Street is as much the story of the

boy, Skeeter, and his Uncle Jesse as it is the story of the rare dog that Skeeter found in the swamp. *The Yearling* by Rawlings is really Jody's story, even though his young fawn was very instrumental in his maturation.

Challenge, risk, and suspense are elements of the adventures children seek in books. Animal stories provide these ingredients in overcoming the obstacles and conflicts presented in the plot. Animals need love, respond to affection given by humans, and give back responses akin to human love. This bond of love between an animal and a man is the theme of Walt Morey's book, *Gentle Ben.* Ben is a brown bear, an unpredictable and possibly dangerous creature to have as a pet. Mark's father agrees to buy the bear after he has observed Mark and Ben playing together. A fish cannery manager helps Mark treat Ben when he is tormented by his former owner. As he reads this story of a boy's love for an animal that finally has to be taken away, the child will learn much about life in an Alaskan fishing village. The story of storms, fish pirates, and drunken men is not gentle; but the theme of the responsibility of love is woven into each exciting incident.

The Bears and I by Robert Leslie is the story of three orphaned bear cubs—Rusty, Scratch, and Dusty. Even though their owner is determined to prepare them for self-sufficiency, his love for the three playful bears grows every day:

> Like elephants and boa constrictors, bears are among the hardest animals to ignore, especially when hungry for affection.[114]

The trio and Leslie share many happy, as well as frightening experiences. The pain and sorrow of losing pets is depicted when Rusty is killed by a hunter's bullet and Dusty dies after a hideous struggle with a snow grizzly. Finally, when Leslie finds out that there will no longer be a closed hunting season on bears, he knows he has to send Scratch away to a safer place.

> Tears streaming down my cheeks I was forced to leave the thought of betrayal in the mind of the third bear. With a switch, I struck him again and again across the bulge of his nose—the nose that

[113] C. S. Lewis. *An Experiment in Criticism* (Cambridge, England: Cambridge University Press, 1961), p. 141.

[114] Robert Franklin Leslie. *The Bears and I* (New York: Ballatine, 1968), p. 11.

had so often nudged me with affection and admiration. At last he turned, disbelieving and slowly swam to Mark who helped him aboard the launch.[115]

Sterling North's book about his pet raccoon recalls life in a small town early in the twentieth century. The boy and his father are lonely, worry about the older boy serving in World War I, and share the joy of building a canoe. *Rascal, A Memoir of a Better Era* has been rewritten for younger readers under the title, *Little Rascal*.

Incident at Hawk's Hill by Allan Eckert is based upon an extraordinary incident which took place in Canada in 1870. It is the story of 6-year-old Ben, who was adopted and protected by a female badger. A shy and lonely child, Ben wanders away from Hawk's Hill, the family farm, and is given up for lost after two days and nights of searching. But Ben is found alive weeks later by his older brother, who has to fight off the badger to get to the boy. At first Ben is as wild and silent as the badger, but they take him home only to have the badger come to their house the next day. The badger stays, and finally Ben began to talk, to tell his family all about his experiences. This is a hauntingly beautiful story of a family's love for their shy child and his strange protector.

Hanno, a gorilla that escaped from the London Zoo, was a "pet" of Ping, a Chinese refugee, for only two days, but a strange bond exists between the two. *A Stranger at Green Knowe* is one of L. M. Boston's few realistic stories about the old English mansion which is the mysterious setting of many of her fantasies (*see* Chapter 5). The story begins in Africa with the early life and capture of the gorilla. Ping admires the gorilla in the zoo; and he learns a great deal about the animal as he talks with the keeper. The concrete walls and steel bars of Hanno's cage recall Ping's life in refugee camps. When Ping hears that the huge animal has escaped from the zoo, he plans a place for him on a hidden island in the river. Hanno finds the place and the food that Ping has left there. Ping plays with the huge beast and tries to keep the police from discovering the "refugee." The boy is foolhardy, yet this mystical understanding between the two refugees protects him. An exciting climax brings death to the go-

Six-year-old Ben's ability to communicate with animals was later responsible for saving his life.

Illustration by John Schoenherr. Copyright © 1971 by Allan W. Eckert. From *Incident at Hawk's Hill* by Allan W. Eckert, by permission of Little, Brown and Co.

rilla and hope that Ping has found a happy refuge. *Gorilla Gorilla*, an informational book by Carol Fenner, could be shared along with this story (*see* Chapter 9).

More mature readers can appreciate the classic by Marjorie Kinnan Rawlings, *The Yearling*. This story of a boy, his pet fawn, and his growth in the "big scrub" of Florida reveals the suffering that can come to all who give love. Rawlings writes with vigor, humor, and quiet beauty in words that capture the essence of the moment.

Horse and dog stories comprise the greatest number of animal stories, and are favorites of both boys and girls at the intermediate levels. A picture storybook series about Blaze is written and illustrated by C. W. Anderson. Easy to read, there is enough action in the stories of Billy and his horse to maintain interest. In *Billy and Blaze,* the little boy gets his pony. Blaze is stolen in *Blaze and the Gypsies;* and in *Blaze and Thunderbolt* a wild horse becomes a friend of Blaze and his owner. Care of horses, kindness, and good feelings toward others are expressed. Some 7- and 8-year-olds read the Blaze series easily.

Walter Farley has written a favorite series about one horse, *The Black Stallion,* and his descendants. Alec Ramsey and a wild, black stallion are the only survivors of a shipwreck. When they are finally rescued, the boy is determined to train the horse. After patient, secret training and night trials at the track, the Black is ready to run in the Derby. This famous race is recalled in *Son of the Black Stallion,* when Alec receives Satan, the first foal of the Black. Training a horse that has the instinct to kill seems nearly impossible. The reader learns about the preliminary races that must be won before the attempt is made for the "Triple Crown" in *The Black Stallion's Filly.* Bonfire, sired by Black, becomes known for his harness racing in *The Blood Bay Colt.* In this story there is better characterization than in the others. Emphasis in all these books is on horse training and races. The people are merely shadows. Paced as fast as the races, the stories maintain high interest for readers who are absorbed in horse lore.

Marguerite Henry is one of the more skillful writers of horse stories. Careful research provides an authentic background for her accounts of horses and the people who train them. *Misty of Chincoteague* was the colt of Phantom, a descendant of the Spanish horses that struggled to Assateague Island when a ship was wrecked in a storm. Once each year the wild horses are herded across the channel to Chincoteague Island, where they are sold on Pony Penning Day. Paul and Maureen have their hearts set on buying Phantom and are delighted to learn they can also purchase her colt, Misty. Through Misty, they are able to gentle Phantom and win an exciting race. Phantom escapes to the island, but Misty remains with her human friends. *Stormy, Misty's Foal* continues the story.

The dramatic, sad, yet noble story of an Arabian horse shipped from Morocco to France is told in Henry's *King of the Wind,* winner of the Newbery Award. Sham is not accepted by the French king, and is put out to work. A series of owners leaves him bruised and worn, but the Earl of Godolphin finally recognizes his value and gives the small horse his true place. Sham becomes the sire of a new breed of fine horses. More than a horse story, this is the tale of the devotion of a deaf-mute Arabian boy, Agba, who stays with the horse until Sham dies. Agba's courage, patience, and unswerving loyalty are unequaled.

In *Mustang, Wild Spirit of the West,* Henry writes in a different style, as though Annie Bronn Johnston is telling her own story of the fight to protect the wild horses of the Western ranges. Based on a true story, this narrative describes in realistic detail the hunting of the mustangs by plane and truck, and the torture before the animals are slaughtered for dog food. The warm love of her parents helps Annie overcome the effects of polio; her own love of her mustang, Hobo, inspires her to fight against the mustang round-up by writing letters, taking pictures of the cruelty, and by speaking to a Congressional committee. Horse lovers of all ages will share the feelings of Wild Horse Annie, as she struggles to protect this endangered species.

The Wild Heart by Griffiths is a well-written novel of a wild horse on the Argentine pampas and of the men who tried to subdue her. La Bruja was an ugly mare, but she could run with the speed of the wind, so she was desired by men. Captured and cruelly treated, she escapes only to be hunted again and again. One day La Bruja runs into the open door of a church and the priest gives her the right of sanctuary. A handicapped orphan boy at the mission, Angel, cares for the horse, and must finally decide whether to give her the freedom she seeks or keep her in a small lot. An alternative—to cripple La Bruja so she could never run and thus never be hunted by men—is suggested when a folk singer says: "To let her free you must take away that which makes her coveted by other men."[116] The book closes

[116]Helen Griffiths. *The Wild Heart,* illustrated by Victor G. Ambrus (New York: Doubleday, 1963), p. 187.

on the note that to be kind one must sometimes be cruel. Was Angel's decision the wise one? Each reader will answer for himself. This is a horse story with substance and an unpredictable ending. It should appeal to many middle-graders.

Heroic dogs who overcome obstacles are the subject of two popular animal stories for children. Sheila Burnford's book of three runaway pets is an odyssey of courage and endurance, as a young Labrador retriever, an old bull terrier, and a Siamese cat make *The Incredible Journey.* Left with a friend of their owner, the animals try to reach their home more than 250 miles away. Hunger, storms, dangerous river crossings, and fights are the nearly insurmountable problems of these three animals. Their survival and care for each other make a remarkable story.

Where the Red Fern Grows by Wilson Rawls is a heartwarming but sentimental tale of the love between two hound dogs and their master. Young Billy trained his two dogs, Old Dan and Little Ann, to be the finest hunting team in the Cherokee county of the Ozarks. Twenty-five sets of hounds were entered in the big coon hunt. After five nights of hunting, catching the coons, skinning them, and turning in the hides, Billy's hounds won $300 and the first-place cup. During the hunt Old Dan and Little Ann had nearly frozen to death after getting lost during an unexpected blizzard. They stayed with their coon, running around and around the tree until they were covered with ice. This story has been made into a major motion picture.

Another dog story that is well-known through its film is Gipson's story of *Old Yeller.* Travis thinks the yellow dog that appears at the ranch one day is truly indispensable. Then Old Yeller saves Travis' brother from a mad animal. As a result, the dog must be shot. The author suggests that Travis takes one step toward maturity when he accepts this decision.

Meindert DeJong's moving story *Hurry Home, Candy* tells of a small dog's search for love and security. Candy had first been owned by two children and punished by their impatient mother. When he pulled things and played with them, the mother put a broom across the corner. Finally, he would sleep: "A troubled broom-haunted sleep in which his paws twitched nervously because in his sleep he was fleeing from the fretful broom."[117] In a storm Candy is separated from the family, and fear of a broom across the ditch prevents him from crossing to them. Alone, hungry, lost, and sorrowful, he at last finds shelter with a man, a retired captain turned artist. One night, the artist interrupts some thieves, and Candy is caught in the police crossfire while the man breaks a leg. The news story brings the original owners, but the children want only the reward, not the dog. Candy hides again, but is drawn to the house by hunger. Once more, a broom stands between the dog and love and security. The captain discovers the source of the dog's fear; at the same time he gains understanding of his own fears: "Let me explain it to you—there are brooms in my life, too. I think that's the real explanation."[118] The big man tosses the broom aside, and the dog edges his way to food, to love, and home.

Jack London's *The Call of the Wild* was written for adults, but is enjoyed by older boys and girls. The men in this book are ruthless; and the dog, Buck, returns to the wildness of nature just as the men revert to force and cruelty to survive.

Jim Kjelgaard communicates his knowledge of the wilderness and his love of animals through exciting dog stories. *Big Red* is the story of an Irish setter being groomed for championship dog shows. Danny, his 17-year-old trainer, shows patience and courage in holding back the dog when facing Old Majesty, the huge bear. *Snow Dog* is a wild puppy of the northern wilderness who finally finds a life with men.

In *Bristle Face,* Ball shows how a hound dog plays an important part in the lives of an orphan boy, a lonely man who gives the boy a home, and an aggressive widow who agrees to marry the man. The author adds humorous touches to his realistic picture of mountain life. The boy, Jase, courageously faces the knowledge that the dog must be returned to its owner, and accepts the necessity for putting Bristle Face to death after he is blinded.

The Greyhound by Griffiths is a dramatic story of a boy's love for a dog. Conflicts with family and society encountered after he purchases the

---

[117] Meindert DeJong. *Hurry Home, Candy,* illustrated by Maurice Sendak (New York: Harper & Row, 1953), p. 39.
[118] DeJong, p. 187.

dog and hides him in a bombed-out London basement make this a compellingly realistic story. When Jamie cannot return the money that he borrowed to buy Silver, he is forced into a gang and made to help them steal. Finally he refuses to rob an old lady and confesses the whole sordid predicament to his mother. The authorities accept his story, but do not apprehend the gang. When Jamie goes to get Silver, there is an ugly, brutal scene as the gang enters the basement and attacks the dog to take revenge on Jamie. Worry, lack of food, and exposure lead to a severe illness, but Jamie recovers. There is a happy ending for the reader who can withstand the shock of the dog's beating. The poverty of Jamie's environment looms larger than one boy's inner resources. This book is a dog story, but it is also a commentary on life in the slums. It raises important questions. Do the means justify the end? What is the limit of endurance, or loyalty, or honesty when one you love is alone, cold, and hungry? A dog story may be a vehicle for telling more about an owner than his dog.

HUMOROUS STORIES

Children today need the opportunity to laugh and have fun. Luckily, there are some very funny juveniles published in the United States that will provide them with wholesome humor about characters who become involved in all kinds of amusing, amazing, and exaggerated predicaments. The story line is built around the solution to such problems. Many of these humorous books are episodic, each chapter representing a complete story.

Humorous series are also very popular. Beginning as early as 7 or 8 years old, children can read the Carolyn Haywood books about Little Eddie or the Betsy series. Eddie Wilson is portrayed as a typical American boy with a passion for collecting all kinds of "valuable property" (junk in the eyes of his parents). In almost all of the many Little Eddie books, Eddie turns his collecting instinct into profit. These stories serve to stimulate interest in personal reading and to promote the request for more books that are "funny."

Children love to relate the amusing things that happened to them when they were younger.

Ramona in *Ramona the Pest* by Beverly Cleary finds herself in hilarious situations in her new kindergarten experience. Ramona can hardly wait for "Show and Tell Time" so she can share her doll with the green hair. She then proudly tells the class that her doll's name is "Chevolet," named after her aunt's car, and that the green hair is the result of a shampoo with soap, detergent, and Dutch cleanser. In *Ramona the Brave* a grown-up first-grade Ramona is not very happy about some of the things that happen to her, such as the time Susan copies her owl and gets the credit, or having to use workbooks. Unfortunately, Ramona has drawn the same teacher that her sister Beezus had several years ago. Time has not mellowed Mrs. Griggs, only made her more tired. After her father tells Ramona that she has "spunk," and the school secretary tells her she is brave to face a big dog, Ramona begins to feel better about herself and her school.

Beverly Cleary has also written a genuinely funny series of books about a very natural, normal boy named *Henry Huggins*. In the first book Henry's problems center on a stray dog named Ribsy, and Henry's efforts to keep him. In *Henry and Beezus,* Henry's major interest is in obtaining a new bicycle. At the opening of the Colossal Market he is delighted when he wins one of the door prizes, and then horrified to find out it is $50 worth of Beauty Shoppe permanent waves, facials, and false eyelashes! Cleary's intimate knowledge of boys and girls in the middle grades is very evident as she describes their problems, adventures, and hilarious activities. Her contribution to the literature of childhood was recognized when she received the Laura Ingalls Wilder Award in 1975.

Edie on the Warpath by E. C. Spykman is one of a series of books about the Carls family. Edie's inventive mind and rebellious nature lead her into amusing situations. Edie clicks her jaw at people when she chews; she chops some of her hair off with a carving knife; and gets put in jail at age 11 along with marching suffragettes. Although the Edie books are set in the early 1900s, the events are reflective of the humor in childhood during any period.

Peter Hatcher's endless problems with his 2-year-old brother, Farley Drexel Hatcher, better known as Fudge, are humorously told in Judy Blume's book *Tales of a Fourth Grade Nothing*. One of the funniest episodes in the book concerns Peter's pet turtle, Dribble. Fudge insists that he didn't chew the turtle when Peter questions him:

> Fudge babbled "No chew, no chew, Gulp . . . gulp . . . all gone turtle. Down Fudge's tummy.[119]

After a hurried trip to the hospital and dosages of castor oil, milk of magnesia, and prune juice, the turtle is out. Since Peter is such a good sport about losing his pet turtle, Peter's parents give him a dog. The dog is much too big for his brother to swallow! In order to remind himself of Dribble, the dog is named Turtle!

How to Eat Fried Worms by Thomas Rockwell is a very funny and vividly told escapade. After an argument climaxed by a dare and a $50 bet, Billy plans to eat fifteen worms in fifteen days. They are fried, boiled, and smothered with catsup, horseradish, and other toppings. The ingestion of each worm becomes more and more bizarre the closer Billy comes to winning his bet. The brief chapters, extensive and amusing dialogue, and the plot make this a favorite story among middle-grade readers.

"I'm a loser, a born loser" says 12-year-old George, who still has a childhood attachment for a Teddy bear. His story is told by James Collier in the *Teddy Bear Habit, or How I Became a Winner*. When George tries out for a part in a Broadway musical, he hides Teddy in a paper bag. The bag is inadvertently tossed behind the curtain and the audition is a flop. Usually the Teddy bear is hidden in the owner's guitar case when walking through Greenwich Village to his lessons. A mysterious element is added to this story when Teddy ends up with stolen gems in his stuffings.

Probably the classic of modern humorous stories is McCloskey's *Homer Price*. The six chapters of this book present extravagant yarns about life in Centerburg, as aided and abetted by Homer and his friends. One story tells how Homer captured four robbers singlehanded with the help of Aroma, his pet skunk. Probably the favorite Homer Price story is that of the dough-

nuts. Homer helpfully offers to make some doughnuts in his uncle's new doughnut machine. A rich customer volunteers to make the batter and Homer is doing beautifully, until he realizes he can't stop the machine! The shop becomes full of doughnuts and then, after his uncle finally stops their manufacture, there is the problem of how to dispose of them. The missing bracelet of the woman who had helped to make the doughnuts supplies the answer. *Centerburg Tales* continues the adventures of Homer Price.

McCloskey has also illustrated the story of *Henry Reed, Inc.*, written by Keith Robertson. This book is recorded as the journal of Henry Reed, who has come to spend the summer with his aunt and uncle at Grovers Corner, Princeton, New Jersey. Henry is planning to use the journal as part of a report, for his teacher had asked that students do something that can be used to illustrate free enterprise. Henry establishes a business firm named "Reed and Glass, Inc., Pure and Applied Research." A girl, Margaret Glass, is his partner. He gravely records the amusing details of his undertakings in the great tradition of free enterprise in the United States. More adventures of Henry are recorded in the stories of *Henry Reed's Journey*, which includes his observations and adventures on a cross-country trip, and *Henry Reed's Baby-Sitting Service*, where Henry and Margaret collaborate on a money-making scheme.

Books of humor need no justification other than pure enjoyment for the reader. They provide a healthy balance for a reading diet that may be overburdened with too many books dealing with the social problems of our day, and they form an important part of the child's literary heritage.

SPORTS STORIES

Children today are energetic participants in and spectators of a variety of individual and team sports activities. Both boys and girls devote large blocks of time to viewing sports events on television; or attending professional games; playing with organized team leagues, on school programs, at playground and recreation centers, or at neighborhood informal gatherings. Sports are "in," and books about sports are in demand.

---

[119]Judy Blume. *Tales of a Fourth Grade Nothing,* illustrated by Roy Doty (New York: Dutton, 1972), p. 111.

Fiction, biography, and informational books about sports extend and enrich the personal experiences of engaging in or viewing a sports event. The child who enjoys watching a professional hockey game or the child who plays on a midget hockey team might want to read a book about Bobby Orr, the Stanley Cup Playoffs, the technical terms used in the games, or a fictional account of a baseball game as described in *Jake* by Slote.

It is difficult to find well-written sports stories. Most of the characters are flat, one-dimensional figures. The dialogue tends to be stilted, and the plots predictable. Children do continue to select these stories because they are so personally involved and interested in the activities.

Sports stories by Marion Renick meet the interests of second- and third-graders who are eager to play team sports. Basic information about the game that is the focus of each book is included. The reader of *Take a Long Jump* learns something about the techniques of running in track contests through the coach's directions to Jay:

> "You are forgetting the L that gave elbows their name," Skilly was telling the boys. Remember to make L's with your arms and let them swing that way, forward and backward, loose and relaxed. Let your hand swing forward almost as high as your shoulder. Let it swing back past your hip.[120]

Other popular stories by Renick include *Five Points for Hockey* and *Pete's Home Run*. Slight plot and little character development characterize these books, which do provide excitement in the accounts of games and some practical tips for the participant.

Matt Christopher's books depend upon accounts of games for their interests, but this writer usually develops a problem theme. For example, a mentally handicapped boy is given help and independence by his family, and he finally wins acceptance on the team in *Long Shot for Paul*. In this story Christopher does not minimize the hardships the boy faces. Sandy, in the story of *Hard Drive to Short*, had superb athletic ability but it went to his head and made him lose his friends.

In *Face-Off*, Scott Harrison has to overcome his fear of being hit by the hockey puck. The descriptions of fast-paced actions in ice hockey create the excitement of writing about this sport. Christopher deals with racial prejudice and overcoming a weakness in playing style in *No Arm in Left Field*; while Curtis Bishop's *Little League Amigo* presents the problems of Cuban refugees.

Caary Jackson's stories also carry a theme of adjustment. In *Buzzy Plays Midget League Football*, a boy must learn to admit his mistakes. A junior high boy, who "carried a chip on his shoulder" because of his size, is the central figure in *Shorty at Shortstop*. Tips for baseball players are included in a special section of this book, and also in *Pee Wee Cook of the Midget League*.

In *The Last Series* by Hal Higdon two rookie players, who are trying to prove themselves at the baseball season's end, tie in with a vocal protest group opposing the construction of a new city ballpark. The combination of sports and comedy is achieved in this story through an assortment of entertaining characters. Humor also enlivens many of the easy-to-read books by Lord, including *Bats and Balls, Guard for Matt*, and *Shrimp's Soccer Goal*.

A more serious story that portrays characters of real depth and understanding is *Thank You, Jackie Robinson* by Barbara Cohen. While the story takes place in 1947–1948, it is written in the first person and told as a reminiscence to a contemporary child. Sam Green is the only son of a Jewish widow who runs an inn in New Jersey. For company he has a radio, a sports record book, and the Brooklyn Dodgers. He doesn't care much about sandlot ball, but he can recite the batting order and play-by-play for every Dodgers game since the time he became a fan. Sam's best friend is the inn's black cook, Davy. It was Davy who took Sam to his first Dodgers game. There are several descriptions of other games that the two of them see together, and the hero of all the games for both of them is Jackie Robinson. In the midseason of 1948 Davy has a heart attack. Sam gathers his courage, buys a baseball, and goes alone to a Dodgers game where he asks Jackie Robinson to autograph a ball for Davy. Then Davy's son-in-law, Elliott, helps Sam sneak into the hospital in a laundry cart so he can personally present the ball to Davy:

---

[120] Marion Renick. *Take a Long Jump*, illustrated by Charles Robinson (New York: Scribner, 1971), p. 22.

There was no magic in the ball. He loved it, but there was no magic in it. It was not going to cure him, the way deep down in my heart I had somehow thought it would. I knew that, my whole self knew that now.[121]

This book succeeds at many levels; first as a warm and understanding consideration of friendship, second as a realistic presentation of death, and third as a backward look at Jackie Robinson and the Brooklyn Dodgers during the height of their baseball fame.

Alfred Slote's fine book, *Hang Tough, Paul Mather*, is about the Little Leaguer who had leukemia. It was discussed among the books that dealt with death on page 434. *Jake*, also by Slote, is a sensitively told baseball story. Another strong strand in this book is the relationship between Jake and his Uncle Lenny, who is 24. Jake, who never knew his father and was deserted by his mother, lives with Lenny. Lenny reluctantly agrees to coach the last two ball games of Jake's team rather than have the boys forfeit them for lack of a regular coach. The final game of the season is vividly described, and keeps the reader very involved.

Another excellent baseball story by Slote is titled *My Father, the Coach*. The story is a familiar one—the rookie team beats the league champions. However, the team they most want to beat is the one sponsored by the bank and coached by its vice-president, who patronizingly makes it clear each day that Willie Corkins is only a parking lot attendant and hardly a suitable coach. Out of loyalty to their coach the team proves the vice-president wrong.

A baseball book that shows a realistic level of success is *Johnny Lee* by Donald Honig. The story is written in the first person and gives the reader more than a sequence of game descriptions to think about. Johnny Lee is black, and when he moves from Harlem to a small mountain town in Virginia, he has to confront prejudice. There is some discrimination on the field and in the town, but eventually Johnny finds friends on the ball club.

Kerstin Thorvall has written a book that will appeal to a growing number of soccer fans. *Gunnar Scores a Goal* is the story of the youngest of three boys. Gunnar turns out to have an aptitude for soccer. He discovers when he hurts his ankles that his brothers can be very kind, and, even better, that they are proud of his athletic ability. This is a story of a child finding his place in his family through sports.

Some 10- and 11-year-olds will enjoy the well-known sports stories by John Tunis. The idea that the team is more important than the individual is stressed in *Keystone Kids. Yea! Wildcats* focuses upon a young coach whose principles create enemies in an Indiana town where basketball is described as a "disease." The plot of *Go, Team, Go!*, published some ten years later, is very similar. Tunis includes details of games only when the score is tied or a player's decision will make a difference. Other plays are summarized. While some of the Tunis characters appear overdrawn, he was one of the first sports writers to include themes of substance in his books. His sports/war story, *His Enemy, His Friend*, details the futility of revenge. (It is discussed in Chapter 8.)

MYSTERIES

Almost all children enjoy mystery stories during some period in their lives. Even the very youngest readers are demanding them, and so we have a whole series of *I Can Read* mysteries that include such amusing titles as Bonsall's *The Case of the Cat's Meow* or *The Secret Three* by Myrick. The latter is about a boys' secret club and the coded messages they send to each other. *The Case of the Stolen Code Book* by Rinkoff is also about a group of children who play at being detectives and write each other notes in secret codes. These easy-reading books are appropriate for 6- and 7-year-olds.

Slightly older children usually become the mystery buffs who delight in reading one Nancy Drew book after another. These have predictable plots, cardboard characters, stilted dialogue, and cliché-ridden prose. Most librarians and teachers will not order these books, yet they have sold over forty million copies![122] Obviously, they

---

[121] Barbara Cohen. *Thank You, Jackie Robinson*, illustrated by Richard Cuffari (New York: Lothrop, 1974), p. 11.

[122] Joyce Bermel. "The Secret of the Old Saw," in *Bookletter*, Vol. 1 (February 3, 1975), p. 2.

must be doing something right! Rather than discount all mysteries, teachers and librarians should look for better-written mysteries and other books that contain elements of mystery, in order to capitalize on children's interests.

Both boys and girls enjoy the Encyclopedia Brown stories by Donald Sobol. In *Encyclopedia Brown Takes a Case* Mr. Brown, chief of police of Idaville, brings home all the cases his men cannot solve. When he comes home for dinner he describes them to his son, Encyclopedia Brown, who usually solves them before it is time for dessert. In *Encyclopedia Brown Lends a Hand* ten more cases are presented. The reader matches wits with Encyclopedia because the solutions to the mysteries are always included at the back of the book. Children like to participate in trying to solve these mysteries.

Scott Corbett writes mysteries as well as sports stories. *The Case of the Gone Goose* is concerned with discovering the person who killed two prize geese; while *Run for the Money* is a more complicated and exciting story involving a search for thieves and stolen coins from Mr. Jonas' coin shop. In *Take a Number* a girl and a college freshman who had taken karate save their friend who is kidnapped. These are all single-strand, straightforward plots.

Phyllis Whitney's mysteries involve subplots and character development related to a larger theme. Overcoming a physical handicap in *The Mystery of the Haunted Pool* and developing respect for a blind girl in *Secret of the Emerald Star* are subplots in two Whitney books both of which won the Mystery Writers "Edgar" for excellence in the juvenile category. The idea that the blind do not want pity is made very clear in *Secret of the Emerald Star*, for example:

> A real friend isn't someone who is sorry for you. I hate people who drool because I'm a poor little blind girl. Or the others who act as if I were a genius because I can walk across a room by myself. They're the ones who think about blindness all the time. And that's silly because I don't. Or anyway, I wouldn't if they didn't push it at me so much.[123]

Using the pen name Wilson Gage, Mary Steele has written two interesting mysteries for

[123] Phyllis A. Whitney. *Secret of the Emerald Star*, illustrated by Alex Stein (Philadelphia, Penna.: Westminster, 1964), p. 99.

children. *The Secret of Crossbone Hill,* is a chilling tale of two children who find a crude map hidden in a bird nest in a South Carolina swamp. Then they are warned by a mysterious stranger to stay out of the swamp. David and Kathy think they are on the track of real treasure when they discover the whole adventure is related to the birds—rare cattle egrets from Africa! In *The Secret of Indian Mound,* Alec and Jimmy keep losing their tools and their artifacts when they are digging in an ancient burial mound. They are quick to make superficial judgments about who is disturbing their dig. In the end they have learned much about Indian artifacts and more about themselves. The characterization in both of these books by Mary Steele is excellent.

Elisabeth and the Marsh Mystery by Holman is an ecological mystery for young readers. Elisabeth, her father, and Stewart Peebles enlist the aid of a museum director in solving the mystery of the strange call emanating from the marsh. Stewart gives the Latin names for the birds they see, and patiently explains to Elisabeth the meaning of the terms he uses. Elisabeth admires his erudition, as well as the braces on his teeth, and the tone is humorous so the facts do not seem dull. When the mysterious "exotic" is found to be a sandhill crane, both children learn about bird migration.

Another ecological mystery is Jean George's excellent and humorous story, *Who Really Killed Cock Robin?.* Saddleboro was proud of its green lawns and clean air. As an ecology-conscious community the people pointed with pride to the Cock Robin whose mate built a nest on Mayor Joe's porch in his Stetson hat. Cock Robin was a symbol for the city, and then he died. Tony Isidoro often watched the nest with a scientific interest, keeping meticulous notes. After the death of the bird, he and his friend Mary Alice pursue the investigation relentlessly. Their findings prove that DDT, PCB, Mercury, and a sparrow with parasitic flies had all contributed to the death of the bird. Mary Alice has nothing but admiration for Tony's research and she tells him so:

> "Aw, come on," he said. "I'm not great. A team of people killed Cock Robin and a team of people solved the crime. And that's how its going to be

from now until the day we live in balance with all beasts and plants, and air and water."[124]

This story is far more than a mystery, but it has many of the elements that children enjoy in mysteries—suspense, intrigue, danger, and problem-solving.

The Museum of Natural History is the setting for a double mystery told by Georgess McHargue in the book *Funny Bananas*. Ben Pollock spends almost all of his after-school hours in the Museum because his scientist parents both work there. One day he learns of some mysterious goings on—the feathers of the red jungle fowl have been destroyed, and the information desk was ransacked, the wastebasket dumped, and some "funny bananas" found. At first Ben suspects Carmen, a girl who has been acting strangely. But when Ben convinces her that he is trying to help her, the two become allies, as they look for her coatimundi, a little South American animal that she has let loose in the Museum. While they are chasing him, they run right into a thief! The atmosphere of the Museum and the characterizations of the children are very believable. Fast-paced, this is an exciting mystery that involves real characters, an animal, and an actual thief.

In *Mystery of the Fat Cat* by Bonham four Oak Street Boys' Club members set out to prove foul play in the death of a cat, so the slum neighborhood club can have the half-million-dollar legacy that an old eccentric originally left to the pet. The sequel to this popular mystery is *The Nitty Gritty*. Both of these stories are fast-paced mysteries.

Manhattan Is Missing by E. W. Hildick is the very amusing tale of a missing Siamese cat entrusted to an English family when they sublet the owner's New York City apartment. "Operation Catnet" is initiated by Peter Clarke, his brother Benjie, and friend Hugh in an effort to recover the prized cat. The dialogue and characterization in this story are distinctive.

The House of Dies Drear by Virginia Hamilton is a compelling story of the weird and terrifying happenings that threaten a black professor and his family, who are living in a house that was

a former Underground Railway station. The brooding old house holds many secrets for Thomas Small and his family, who find they are being threatened by dangers from within and without their home. This is a finely crafted novel with enough suspense to hold every reader.

Another haunting story that has many elements of mystery is *The Witch's Daughter* by Nina Bawden. Perdita, the so-called "daughter of a witch," is a lonely orphan who is shunned by the village children because of her odd clothes, strange green eyes, shy manner, and sensitivity to nature. She has never been to school, but has deep knowledge of the outdoors and expresses a special awareness of the needs of the blind girl, Janey, who comes with her family to the Scottish island for a holiday. Perdita is treated kindly by the mysterious Mr. Smith, who has rented a cottage and fishes for lobsters although he does not like lobster. Tim, Janey's brother, puts the pieces of the puzzle together, but the adults will not accept his theory of the stolen jewels. A strange visitor deliberately leaves the children in a cave, but blind Janey leads them to safety. Perdita's shyness is finally overcome in a moment of sharing with Janey. This is a beautiful, almost mystical tale of danger to innocents.

Another story by Bawden, titled *Squib*, has a mysterious plot. In the park Kate and Robin find an extremely shy little boy who has odd eyes and a bit of a bruise on one leg. He doesn't talk to them, but he does play with them. Kate is determined to find out more about the odd little frightened boy that they nickname Squib. Her curiosity draws her into a terrifying situation, but eventually she does save Squib. All Nina Bawden's books have well-drawn characters with believable, yet exciting plots.

Peter Dickinson's story *The Gift* can be read as a thriller, but it also contains real depth of character interaction and superb writing. The "gift" is the gift of seeing into other peoples' minds, and Davy has inherited it. His Gran discovers this when she takes the children in as their shiftless father loses his job again. She warns Davy to take care, that the gift has always brought tragedy. Certainly it brings Davy terror, for he is a key witness to a robbery and then is hunted down by a sick man whose mind Davy can read. More than a mystery, this story por-

---

[124]Jean Craighead George. *Who Really Killed Cock Robin?* (New York: Dutton, 1971), p. 149.

trays much about common people, their growing up, and their impact upon each other.

The criteria for evaluating all fiction should be used in considering mystery stories, with the recognition that the major appeal of a mystery is fast action and suspense. Children do develop skills in rapid reading, building vocabulary, and noting details as they read mysteries. Interest in reading as a pleasurable activity may begin with these books, and be extended to other types of literature if children's choices are not criticized. Children should have a wide variety of books of this type from which to select, and teachers should share those quality books which they know have elements of the mysterious.

SUGGESTED LEARNING EXPERIENCES

1. Select several books dealing with a particular minority group. What stereotypes do you find in the books? What are the prevalent themes in the books? Compare and evaluate books using the criteria in this chapter.
2. Select books about a minority group. Find poetry, biographical material, historical fiction, and informational books that would extend the use of these books.
3. Select a current theme in realistic fiction—such as drugs, death, or migrant workers. Find some nonfiction that can be used with the fictional books.
4. Make a chart of some current books dealing with social and personal problems. What are the major topics? Are problems resolved? What cause/effect situations occur?
5. Read some of the books in which characters have to make major decisions. Identify the forces that affect the way the decisions are made.
6. Find articles on censorship. Make a list of controversial books that are currently being censored. Compare your ideas with the evaluations used for censorship.
7. Select a topic—such as loneliness, death, physical handicap, or friendship. Talk to a group of children to explore with them the personal experiences they may have had in the selected area. What misconceptions are expressed? What books have they read dealing with the topic? How else have they received information about the subject?
8. Compare the treatment of a topic such as death in a picture book, a book for intermediate-grade children, poetry, and an informational book.
9. Make a list of ideas you hold about a specific region, such as Appalachia. Read several books—for example, *Did You Carry the Flag Today Charley?*, *Fiddler of High Lonesome*, and *Where the Lilies Bloom*. Were your concepts reinforced, changed? What else did you find out about the region?
10. Compare the relationships of parents and children in the following books:

    Meet the Austins by Madeline L'Engle
    The Moffats by Eleanor Estes
    Berries Goodman by Emily Neville
    A Hero Ain't Nothin' But a Sandwich by Alice Childress
    Nobody's Family Is Going to Change by Louise Fitzhugh

11. Examine the sex roles of a hero and heroine found in realistic fiction.

RELATED READINGS

1. Baker, Augusta. "The Changing Image of the Black in Children's Literature," *Horn Book* (February 1975), pp. 79–88.
    The author gives an historical perspective on the image of blacks in children's books during the last fifty years of publishing.
2. Broderick, Dorothy. *Image of the Black in Children's Fiction.* New York and London: Bowker (A Xerox Education Company), 1973.
    An historical, literary, and critical analysis of the portrait of the black that emerges

from children's books published between 1827 and 1967.

3. Fisher, Laura. "All Chiefs, No Indians: What Children's Books Say about American Indians," *Elementary English* (February 1974), pp. 185–189.

   The author discusses books about American Indians and the stereotypes that are reinforced, as well as books that pay attention to ethnic consciousness and are of literary quality.

4. Haynes, John. "No Child Is an Island: Three Books that Focus on Handicapped Children," *Children's Literature in Education.* APS Publications, No. 15 (1974), pp. 3–18.

   The author analyzes three books in terms of what they say about the problems of handicapped children, the ability to hold reader's interest, and the values underlying the books.

5. *Interracial Books for Children.* New York: Council on Interracial Books for Children, Vol. 4, Nos. 1 and 2 (Spring 1972).

   This special issue focuses on Puerto Rican materials. One hundred children's books published by U.S. firms between 1932 and 1972 were collected for evaluation. Most of them were not recommended.

6. *Interracial Books for Children.* New York Council on Interracial Books for Children, Vol. 5, Nos. 7 and 8 (1975).

   This special issue focuses on a Council survey of 200 children's books on Chicano themes. The survey revealed an overall pattern of cultural misrepresentation.

7. Kimmel, Eric A. "Jewish Identity in Juvenile Fiction, A Look at Three Recommended Books," *Horn Book* (April 1973), pp. 171–179.

   The author discusses three books which he feels, though highly recommended, are inadequate in dealing with the real problems of contemporary Jewish life.

8. Kingston, Carolyn T. *The Tragic Mode in Children's Literature.* New York and London: Teachers College Press (1974).

   The author identifies the elements of literary tragedy found in children's books. She discusses notable examples of the tragic mode found in realistic fiction for 8–12-year-olds.

9. Latimer, L. Bettye, ed. *Starting Out Right. Choosing Books about People for Young Children,* Pre-school through Third Grade (Madison, Wis.: Children's Literature Review Board, Wisconsin Department of Public Instruction. Bulletin No. 2374, 1972).

   This bulletin establishes criteria for judging books involving black people. There is an annotated bibliography, including a critique which shows whether the book is recommended or not recommended.

10. *Little Miss Muffet Fights Back.* New York: Feminists on Children's Media (1974).

   A bibliography of recommended non-sexist books about girls for young readers. The appendix suggests ways to encourage the production, purchase, and use of good books that portray girls and women positively.

11. MacCann, Donnarae, and Gloria Woodard. *The Black American in Books for Children, Readings in Racism* (Metuchen, N.J.: The Scarecrow Press, 1972).

   A series of articles about the black perspective in books, and examples of racism in books and in publishing.

12. Reid, Virginia. *Reading Ladders for Human Relations,* 5th. ed. (Washington, D.C.: American Council of Education, 1972).

   This is a unique and invaluable bulletin on the use of trade books in the classroom to promote better human relations. Annotated lists are provided for different age levels on four subjects: "Creating a Positive Self Image," "Living with Others," "Appreciating Different Cultures," and "Coping with Change."

13. Rollock, Barbara, selector. *The Black Experience in Children's Books.* (New York: N.Y. Public Library, 1975).

   This list is a revision of the former publication by the same title edited by Augusta Baker. While the number of books has been expanded, the original criteria were used for this selection.

14. Stensland, Anna Lee. *Literature by and about the American Indian* (Urbana, Ill.: National Council of Teachers of English, 1973).

   An annotated bibliography for junior and senior high students. Each annotation gives a brief summary of the book, mentioning in general its good points and its drawbacks.

RECOMMENDED REFERENCES[125]

Anderson, C. W. *Billy and Blaze.* Macmillan, 1936.
———. *Blaze and the Gypsies.* Macmillan, 1937.
———. *Blaze and Thunderbolt.* Macmillan, 1955.
Arora, Shirley. "*What Then, Raman?*", illustrated by Hans Guggenheim. Follett, 1960.
Ball, Zachary. *Bristle Face.* Holiday, 1962.
Bawden, Nina. *Squib.* Lippincott, 1971.
———. *The Witch's Daughter.* Lippincott, 1966.
Bishop, Curtis. *Little League Amigo.* Lippincott, 1964.
Blue, Rose. *Grandma Didn't Wave Back,* illustrated by Ted Lewin. F. Watts, 1972.
———. *A Month of Sundays,* illustrated by Ted Lewin. F. Watts, 1972.
———. *Nikki 108,* illustrated by Ted Lewin. F. Watts, 1973.
Blume, Judy. *Are You There, God? It's Me, Margaret.* Bradbury, 1970.
———. *Blubber.* Bradbury, 1974.
———. *It's Not the End of the World.* Bradbury, 1972.
———. *Tales of a Fourth Grade Nothing,* illustrated by Roy Doty. Dutton, 1972.
———. *Then Again, Maybe I Won't.* Bradbury, 1971.
Bodker, Cecil. *The Leopard,* translated by Gunnar Poulsen. Atheneum, 1975.
Bonham, Frank. *Durango Street.* Dutton, 1965.
———. *Mystery of the Fat Cat,* illustrated by Alvin Smith. Dutton, 1968.
———. *The Nitty Gritty,* illustrated by Alvin Smith. Dutton, 1968.
Bonsall, Crosby. *The Case of the Cat's Meow.* Harper & Row, 1965.
Boston, L. M. *A Stranger at Green Knowe,* illustrated by Peter Boston. Harcourt Brace Jovanovich, 1961.
Bouchard, Lois. *The Boy Who Wouldn't Talk,* illustrated by Ann Grifalconi. Doubleday, 1969.
Branfield, John. *Why Me?* Harper & Row, 1973.
Buck, Pearl. *The Big Wave.* John Day, 1947.
Bulla, Clyde. *Indian Hill,* illustrated by James Spanfeller. Crowell, 1963.
Burch, Robert. *Queenie Peavy,* illustrated by Jerry Lazare. Viking, 1966.
Burnford, Sheila. *The Incredible Journey,* illustrated by Carl Burger. Little, Brown, 1961.
Byars, Betsy. *After the Goat Man,* illustrated by Ronald Himler. Viking, 1974.
———. *The 18th Emergency,* illustrated by Robert Grossman. Viking, 1973.
———. *The House of Wings,* illustrated by Daniel Schwartz. Viking, 1972.
———. *Summer of the Swans,* illustrated by Ted Coconis. Viking, 1970.
Carlson, Natalie Savage. *The Tomahawk Family,* illustrated by Stephen Cook. Harper & Row, 1960.
Caudill, Rebecca. *Did You Carry the Flag Today, Charley?,* illustrated by Nancy Grossman. Holt, Rinehart and Winston, 1966.
Childress, Alice. *A Hero Ain't Nothin' But a Sandwich.* Coward, 1973.
Christopher, Matt. *Face-Off,* illustrated by Harvey Kidder. Little, Brown, 1972.
———. *Hard Drive to Short,* illustrated by George Guzzi. Little, Brown, 1969.

---

[125]All books listed at the end of this chapter are recommended subject to the qualifications noted in the text. *See* Appendix D for publishers' complete addresses.

————. *Long Shot for Paul,* illustrated by Foster Caddell. Little, Brown, 1966.

————. *No Arm in Left Field,* illustrated by Byron Groto. Little, Brown, 1974.

Clark, Ann Nolan. *Secret of the Andes,* illustrated by Jean Charlot. Viking, 1952.

Cleary, Beverly. *Henry and Beezus,* illustrated by Louis Darling. Morrow, 1952.

————. *Henry Huggins,* illustrated by Louis Darling. Morrow, 1950.

————. *Ramona the Brave,* illustrated by Alan Tiegreen. Morrow, 1975.

————. *Ramona the Pest,* illustrated by Louis Darling. Morrow, 1968.

Cleaver, Vera, and Bill Cleaver. *Ellen Grae,* illustrated by Ellen Raskin. Lippincott, 1967.

————. *Grover,* illustrated by Frederic Marvin. Lippincott, 1970.

————. *I Would Rather Be a Turnip.* Lippincott, 1971.

————. *Lady Ellen Grae,* illustrated by Ellen Raskin. Lippincott, 1968.

————. *Me Too.* Lippincott, 1973.

————. *Where the Lilies Bloom,* illustrated by James Spanfeller. Lippincott, 1969.

————. *The Whys and Wherefores of Littabelle Lee.* Atheneum, 1973.

Clymer, Eleanor. *Luke Was There,* illustrated by Diane de Groat. Holt, Rinehart and Winston, 1973.

————. *My Brother Stevie.* Holt, Rinehart and Winston, 1967.

————. *The Spider, the Cave and the Pottery Bowl,* illustrated by Ingrid Fetz. Atheneum, 1971.

————. *We Lived in the Almont,* illustrated by David K. Stone. Dutton, 1970.

Cohen, Barbara. *Thank You, Jackie Robinson,* illustrated by Richard Cuffari. Lothrop, 1974.

Collier, James L. *The Teddy Bear Habit, or How I Became a Winner.* Norton, 1967.

Colman, Hila. *Chicano Girl.* Morrow, 1973.

Cone, Molly. *A Promise Is a Promise,* illustrated by John Gretzer. Houghton Mifflin, 1964.

Corbett, Scott. *The Case of the Gone Goose,* illustrated by Paul Frame. Little, Brown, 1961.

————. *Run for the Money,* illustrated by Bert Dodson. Little, Brown, 1973.

————. *Take a Number.* Dutton, 1974.

Corcoran, Barbara. *Sam,* illustrated by Barbara McGee. Atheneum, 1967.

————. *A Trick of Light,* illustrated by Lydia Dabcovich. Atheneum, 1973.

Cunningham, Julia. *Burnish Me Bright,* illustrated by Don Freeman. Pantheon, 1970.

————. *Dorp Dead,* illustrated by James Spanfeller. Pantheon, 1965.

DeJong, Meindert. *Far Out the Long Canal,* illustrated by Nancy Grossman. Harper & Row, 1964.

————. *Hurry Home, Candy,* illustrated by Maurice Sendak. Harper & Row, 1953.

————. *Shadrach,* illustrated by Maurice Sendak. Harper & Row, 1963.

Desbarats, Peter. *Gabrielle and Selena,* illustrated by Nancy Grossman. Harcourt Brace Jovanovich, 1968.

Dickinson, Peter. *The Gift.* Little, Brown, 1974.

Dobrin, Arnold. *Scat!,* illustrated by the author. Four Winds, 1971.

Donovan, John. *I'll Get There, It Better Be Worth the Trip.* Harper & Row, 1969.

————. *Remove Protective Coating a Little at a Time.* Harper & Row, 1973.

————. *Wild in the World.* Harper & Row, 1971.

Eckert, Allan. *Incident at Hawk's Hill,* illustrated by John Schoenherr. Little, Brown, 1971.

Enright, Elizabeth. *The Saturdays.* Holt, Rinehart and Winston, 1941.

Estes, Eleanor. *The Hundred Dresses,* illustrated by Louis Slobodkin. Harcourt Brace Jovanovich, 1944.

————. *The Middle Moffat,* illustrated by Louis Slobodkin. Harcourt Brace Jovanovich, 1942.

————. *The Moffats,* illustrated by Louis Slobodkin. Harcourt Brace Jovanovich, 1941.

————. *Rufus M.,* illustrated by Louis Slobodkin. Harcourt Brace Jovanovich, 1943.

Farley, Walter. *The Black Stallion,* illustrated by Keith Ward. Random House, 1944.

————. *The Black Stallion's Filly,* illustrated by Milton Menasco. Random House, 1952.

————. *The Blood Bay Colt,* illustrated by Milton Menasco. Random House, 1950.

————. *Son of the Black Stallion,* illustrated by Milton Menasco. Random House, 1947.

Fitzhugh, Louise. *Harriet the Spy.* Harper & Row, 1964.

————. *The Long Secret.* Harper & Row, 1965.

————. *Nobody's Family Is Going to Change.* Farrar, Straus, 1974.

Fox, Paula. *Blowfish Live in the Sea.* Bradbury, 1970.

————. *How Many Miles to Babylon?,* illustrated by Paul Giovanopoulos. D. White, 1967.

————. *Portrait of Ivan.* Bradbury, 1969.

————. *The Stone-faced Boy,* illustrated by Donald A. Mackay. Bradbury, 1968.

Friis-Baastad, Babbis. *Don't Take Teddy,* translated by Lise McKinnon. Scribner, 1967.

Gage, Wilson, pseud. (Mary Q. Steele). *The Secret of Crossbone Hill.* Washington Square Press, 1969.

————. *The Secret of Indian Mound.* Washington Square Press, 1969.

Garfield, James B. *Follow My Leader.* Viking, 1957.

Gates, Doris. *Blue Willow,* illustrated by Paul Lantz. Viking, 1940.

Gault, William. *Gasoline Cowboy.* Dutton, 1974.

George, Jean. *Gull 737.* Crowell, 1964.

————. *Julie of the Wolves,* illustrated by John Schoenherr. Harper & Row, 1972.

————. *My Side of the Mountain.* Dutton, 1959.

————. *Who Really Killed Cock Robin?.* Dutton, 1971.

Gipson, Fred. *Old Yeller,* illustrated by Carl Burger. Harper & Row, 1956.

Gold, Sharlya. *Amelia Quackenbush.* Seabury, 1973.

Greene, Bette. *Philip Hall Likes Me. I Reckon Maybe,* illustrated by Charles Lilly. Dial, 1974.

Greene, Constance C. *A Girl Called Al,* illustrated by Byron Barton. Viking, 1969.

————. *The Unmaking of Rabbit.* Viking, 1972.

Greenfield, Eloise. *Sister.* Crowell, 1974.

Griffiths, Helen. *The Greyhound,* illustrated by Victor G. Ambrus. Doubleday, 1964.

————. *The Wild Heart,* illustrated by Victor G. Ambrus. Doubleday, 1963.

Gripe, Maria. *Hugo and Josephine,* translated by Paul Britten Austin, illustrated by Harold Gripe. Delacorte, 1969.

————. *The Night Daddy,* translated by Gerry Bothmer, illustrated by Harold Gripe. Delacorte, 1971.

Hall, Lynn. *Sticks and Stones.* Follett, 1972.

Hamilton, Virginia. *The House of Dies Drear,* illustrated by Eros Keith. Macmillan, 1968.

————. *M. C. Higgins, the Great.* Macmillan, 1974.

————. *The Planet of Junior Brown.* Macmillan, 1971.

————. *Zeely,* illustrated by Symeon Shimin. Macmillan, 1967.

Haywood, Carolyn. *Annie Pat and Eddie.* Morrow, 1960.

————. *"B" Is for Betsy.* Harcourt Brace Jovanovich, 1968 (1939).

————. *Betsy's Busy Summer.* Harcourt Brace Jovanovich, 1956.

————. *Eddie and His Big Deals.* Morrow, 1955.

————. *Little Eddie.* Morrow, 1947.

————. *Snowbound with Betsy.* Morrow, 1962.

Hellberg, Hans-Eric. *Grandpa's Maria,* translated by Patricia Crampton, illustrated by Joan Sandin. Morrow, 1974.

Henry, Marguerite. *King of the Wind,* illustrated by Wesley Dennis. Rand McNally, 1948.

————. *Misty of Chincoteague,* illustrated by Wesley Dennis. Rand McNally, 1947.

————. *Mustang, Wild Spirit of the West,* illustrated by Robert Lougheed. Rand McNally, 1971.

————. *Stormy, Misty's Foal,* illustrated by Wesley Dennis. Rand McNally, 1963.

Higdon, Hal. *The Last Series.* Dutton, 1974.

Hildick, E. W. *Manhattan Is Missing,* illustrated by Jan Palmer. Doubleday, 1969.

Hodges, Margaret. *The Freewheeling of Joshua Cobb,* illustrated by Richard Cuffari. Farrar, Straus, 1974.

————. *The Hatching of Joshua Cobb,* illustrated by W. T. Mars. Farrar, Straus, 1967.

————. *The Making of Joshua Cobb,* illustrated by W. T. Mars. Farrar, Straus, 1971.

Holland, Isabelle. *The Man without a Face.* Lippincott, 1972.

Holman, Felice. *Elisabeth and the Marsh Mystery,* illustrated by Erik Blegvad. Macmillan, 1966.

————. *Slake's Limbo.* Scribner, 1974.

Honig, Donald. *Johnny Lee.* Saturday Review Press (Dutton), 1971.

Hunt, Irene. *Up a Road Slowly*. Follett, 1966.

Hunter, Edith Fisher. *Sue Ellen*, illustrated by Bea Holmes. Houghton Mifflin, 1969.

Jackson, Caary Paul. *Buzzy Plays Midget League Football*, illustrated by Kevin Royt. Follett, 1956.

———. *Pee Wee Cook of the Midget League*, illustrated by Frank Kramer. Hastings, 1965.

———. *Shorty at Shortstop*, illustrated by Kevin Royt. Follett, 1951.

Johnson, Annabel, and Edgar Johnson. *The Grizzly*, illustrated by Gilbert Riswold. Harper & Row, 1964.

Jordan, Mildred. *Proud to Be Amish*, illustrated by W. T. Mars. Crown, 1968.

Kerr, M. E. *Dinky Hocker Shoots Smack*. Harper & Row, 1972.

Killilea, Marie. *Wren*, illustrated by Bob Riger. Dodd, 1954.

Kjelgaard, Jim. *Big Red*, illustrated by Bob Kuhn. Holiday, 1956.

———. *Snow Dog*, illustrated by Jacob Landau. Holiday, 1948.

Klein, Norma. *Confessions of an Only Child*, illustrated by Richard Cuffari. Pantheon, 1974.

———. *Mom, the Wolf Man and Me*. Pantheon, 1972.

———. *Naomi in the Middle*, illustrated by Leigh Grant. Dial, 1974.

Knight, Eric. *Lassie Come Home*, illustrated by Marguerite Kerinse. Holt, Rinehart and Winston, 1940.

Konigsburg, E. L. *From the Mixed-Up Files of Mrs. Basil E. Frankweiler*. Atheneum, 1967.

———. *(George)*. Atheneum, 1970.

———. *Jennifer, Hecate, MacBeth, William McKinley and Me, Elizabeth*, illustrated by the author. Atheneum, 1967.

Krumgold, Joseph. *. . . And Now Miguel*, illustrated by Jean Charlot. Crowell, 1953.

———. *Henry 3*. Atheneum, 1969.

———. *Onion John*, illustrated by Symeon Shimin. Crowell, 1959.

Lampman, Evelyn Sibley. *Go Up the Road*. Atheneum, 1973.

Lee, Virginia. *The Magic Moth*, illustrated by Richard Cuffari. Seabury, 1972.

L'Engle, Madeleine. *Meet the Austins*. Vanguard, 1960.

Lenski, Lois. *Coal Camp Girl*. Lippincott, 1959.

———. *Judy's Journey*. Lippincott, 1947.

———. *Prairie School*. Lippincott, 1951.

———. *Shoo-Fly Girl*. Lippincott, 1963.

———. *Strawberry Girl*. Lippincott, 1945.

———. *Texas Tomboy*. Lippincott, 1950.

Leslie, Robert Franklin. *The Bears and I*. Ballantine, 1968.

Lewiton, Mina. *Candita's Choice*, illustrated by Howard Simon. Harper & Row, 1959.

Lexau, Joan. *Me Day*, illustrated by Robert Weaver. Dial, 1971.

———. *Striped Ice Cream*, illustrated by John Wilson. Lippincott, 1968.

Little, Jean. *From Anna*, illustrated by Joan Sandin. Harper & Row, 1972.

———. *Home from Far*, illustrated by Jerry Lazare. Little, Brown, 1965.

———. *Kate*. Harper & Row, 1971.

———. *Look through My Window*, illustrated by Joan Sandin. Harper & Row, 1970.

———. *Mine for Keeps*, illustrated by Lewis Parker. Little, Brown, 1962.

———. *Take Wing*. Little, Brown, 1968.

London, Jack. *The Call of the Wild*, illustrated by Charles Pickard. Dutton, 1968 (1903).

Lord, Beman. *Bats and Balls*, illustrated by Arnold Spilka. Walck, 1962.

———. *Guard for Matt*, illustrated by Arnold Spilka. Walck, 1961.

———. *Shrimp's Soccer Goal*, illustrated by Harold Berson. Walck, 1970.

McCloskey, Robert. *Centerburg Tales*. Viking, 1951.

———. *Homer Price*. Viking, 1943.

McHargue, Georgess. *Funny Bananas: The Mystery at the Museum*, illustrated by Heidi Palmer. Holt, Rinehart and Winston, 1975.

McNeill, Janet, *The Battle of St. George Without*, illustrated by Mary Russon. Little, Brown, 1968.

———. *Goodbye, Dove Square*, illustrated by Mary Russon. Little, Brown, 1969.

Mann, Peggy. *The Clubhouse,* illustrated by Peter Burchard. Coward-McCann, 1969.

——. *How Juan Got Home,* illustrated by Richard Lebenson. Coward-McCann, 1972.

——. *My Dad Lives in a Downtown Hotel,* illustrated by Richard Cuffari. Doubleday, 1973.

——. *The Street of the Flower Boxes,* illustrated by Peter Burchard. Coward-McCann, 1966.

——. *When Carlos Closed the Street,* illustrated by Peter Burchard. Coward-McCann, 1969.

Mathis, Sharon Bell. *Sidewalk Story,* illustrated by Leo Carty. Viking, 1971.

——. *Teacup Full of Roses.* Viking, 1972.

Mazer, Norma Fox. *A Figure of Speech.* Delacorte, 1973.

——. *I, Trissy.* Delacorte, 1971.

Merrill, Jean. *Maria's House,* illustrated by Frances Gruse Scott. Atheneum, 1974.

Miles, Miska. *Annie and the Old One,* illustrated by Peter Parnall. Little, Brown, 1971.

——. *Hoagie's Rifle Gun,* illustrated by John Schoenherr. Little, Brown, 1970.

Mirsky, Reba. *Nomusa and the New Magic.* Follett, 1962.

——. *Thirty-one Brothers and Sisters,* illustrated by W. T. Mars. Follett, 1952.

Molarsky, Osmond. *The Song of the Empty Bottles,* illustrated by Tom Feelings. Walck, 1968.

Morey, Walt. *Gentle Ben,* illustrated by John Schoenherr. Dutton, 1965.

Murray, Michelle. *Nellie Cameron.* Seabury, 1971.

Myrick, Mildred. *The Secret Three,* illustrated by Arnold Lobel. Harper & Row, 1963.

Neufeld, John. *Freddy's Book.* Random House, 1973.

Neville, Emily C. *Berries Goodman.* Harper & Row, 1965.

——. *It's Like This, Cat,* illustrated by Emil Weiss. Harper & Row, 1963.

Niemeyer, Marie. *Moon Guitar,* illustrated by Gustave Nebel. F. Watts, 1969.

North, Sterling. *Little Rascal,* illustrated by Carl Burger. Dutton, 1965.

——. *Rascal, A Memoir of a Better Era,* illustrated by John Schoenherr. Dutton, 1963.

Oakes, Vanya. *Willy Wong: American,* illustrated by Weda Yap. Messner, 1951.

O'Dell, Scott. *Island of the Blue Dolphins.* Houghton Mifflin, 1960.

Orgel, Doris. *The Mulberry Music,* illustrated by Dale Payson. Harper & Row, 1971.

Ottley, Reginald. *Boy Alone,* illustrated by Clyde Pearson. Harcourt Brace Jovanovich, 1965.

Phipson, Joan. *The Boundary Riders,* illustrated by Margaret Horder. Harcourt Brace Jovanovich, 1963.

——. *The Family Conspiracy,* illustrated by Margaret Horder. Harcourt Brace Jovanovich, 1962.

——. *Threat to the Barkers,* illustrated by Margaret Horder. Harcourt Brace Jovanovich, 1965.

Platt, Kin. *The Boy Who Could Make Himself Disappear.* Chilton, 1968.

——. *Hey Dummy!* Chilton, 1971.

Rawlings, Marjorie Kinnan. *The Yearling,* illustrated by Edward Shenton. Scribner, 1938.

Rawls, Wilson. *Where the Red Fern Grows.* Doubleday, 1961.

Renick, Marion. *Five Points for Hockey,* illustrated by Charles Robinson. Scribner, 1973.

——. *Pete's Home Run,* illustrated by Pru Herric. Scribner, 1952.

——. *Take a Long Jump,* illustrated by Charles Robinson. Scribner, 1971.

Rich, Elaine Sommers. *Hannah Elizabeth,* illustrated by Paul Kennedy. Harper & Row, 1964.

Rinkoff, Barbara. *The Case of the Stolen Code Book,* illustrated by Leonard Shortall. Crown, 1971.

——. *Member of the Gang,* illustrated by Harold James. Crown, 1968.

——. *The Watchers.* Knopf, 1972.

Robertson, Keith. *Henry Reed, Inc.,* illustrated by Robert McCloskey. Viking, 1958.

——. *Henry Reed's Baby-Sitting Service,* illustrated by Robert McCloskey. Viking, 1966.

——. *Henry Reed's Journey,* illustrated by Robert McCloskey. Viking, 1963.

——. *In Search of a Sandhill Crane,* illustrated by Richard Cuffari. Viking, 1973.

Robinson, Veronica. *David in Silence,* illustrated by Victor Ambrus. Lippincott, 1966.

Rockwell, Thomas. *How To Eat Fried Worms.* F. Watts, 1973.

Sachs, Marilyn. *The Bears' House,* illustrated by Louis Glanzman. Doubleday, 1971.

——. *Peter and Veronica,* illustrated by Louis Glanzman. Doubleday, 1969.

——. *Veronica Ganz,* illustrated by Louis Glanzman. Doubleday, 1968.

Shearer, John. *I Wish I Had an Afro.* Cowles, 1970.

Sherburne, Zoa. *Too Bad about the Haines Girl*. Morrow, 1967.

Slobodkin, Florence. *Sarah Somebody*, illustrated by Louis Slobodkin. Vanguard, 1969.

Slote, Alfred. *Hang Tough, Paul Mather*. Lippincott, 1973.

————. *Jake*. Lippincott, 1971.

————. *My Father, the Coach*. Lippincott, 1972.

Smith, Doris Buchanan. *Kick a Stone Home*. Crowell, 1974.

————. *A Taste of Blackberries*, illustrated by Charles Robinson. Crowell, 1973.

Smith, George Harmon. *Bayou Boy*. Follett, 1965.

Smucker, Barbara. *Wigwam in the City*, illustrated by Gil Miret. Dutton, 1966.

Sneve, Virginia Driving Hawk. *When Thunders Spoke*, illustrated by Oren Lyons. Holiday, 1974.

Snyder, Zilpha K. *The Changeling*, illustrated by Alton Raible. Atheneum, 1970.

————. *The Egypt Game*, illustrated by Alton Raible. Atheneum, 1967.

Sobol, Donald. *Encyclopedia Brown Lends a Hand*, illustrated by Leonard Shortall. Nelson, 1974.

————. *Encyclopedia Brown Takes a Case*, illustrated by Leonard Shortall. Nelson, 1973.

Sommerfelt, Aimée. *The Road to Agra*, illustrated by Ulf Aas. Criterion, 1961.

————. *The White Bungalow*, illustrated by Ulf Aas. Criterion, 1964.

Sorenson, Virginia. *Plain Girl*, illustrated by Charles Geer. Harcourt Brace Jovanovich, 1955.

Southall, Ivan. *Ash Road*, illustrated by Clem Seale. St. Martin, 1965.

————. *Hill's End*, illustrated by Clem Seale. St. Martin, 1963.

————. *Josh*. Macmillan, 1972.

————. *Let the Balloon Go*, illustrated by Ian Ribbons. St. Martin, 1968.

Spykman, E. C. *Edie on the Warpath*. Harcourt Brace Jovanovich, 1966.

Stevenson, William. *The Bushbabies*, illustrated by Victor Ambrus. Houghton Mifflin, 1965.

Stolz, Mary. *The Bully of Barkham Street*, illustrated by Leonard Shortall. Harper & Row, 1963.

————. *A Dog on Barkham Street*, illustrated by Leonard Shortall. Harper & Row, 1960.

Street, James. *Goodbye, My Lady*. Lippincott, 1954.

Tate, Joan. *Wild Boy*, illustrated by Susan Jeschke. Harper & Row, 1973.

Taylor, Sidney. *All-of-a-Kind Family*, illustrated by Helen John. Follett, 1951.

————. *All-of-a-Kind Family Uptown*, illustrated by Mary Stevens. Follett, 1958.

————. *More All-of-a-Kind Family*, illustrated by Mary Stevens. Follett, 1954.

Thorvall, Kerstin. *Gunnar Scores a Goal*, translated by Anne Parker, illustrated by Serge Hollerbach. Harcourt Brace Jovanovich, 1968.

Townsend, John Rowe. *Good-bye to the Jungle*. Lippincott, 1967.

————. *Trouble in the Jungle*, illustrated by W. T. Mars. Lippincott, 1969.

Tunis, John R. *Go, Team, Go!* Morrow, 1954.

————. *Keystone Kids*. Harcourt Brace Jovanovich, 1943.

————. *Yea! Wildcats*. Harcourt Brace Jovanovich, 1944.

Turkle, Brinton. *The Fiddler of High Lonesome*. Viking, 1968.

Ullman, James Ramsey. *Banner in the Sky*. Lippincott, 1954.

Van Iterson, S. R. *Pulga*. Morrow, 1971.

Wagner, Robin S. *Sara T*. Ballantine Books, 1975.

Waltrip, Lela, and Rufus Waltrip. *Quiet Boy*, illustrated by Theresa Kalab Smith. McKay, 1961.

Warburg, Sandol Stoddard. *The Growing Time*, illustrated by Leonard Weisgard. Harper & Row, 1969.

Wersba, Barbara. *The Dream Watcher*. Atheneum, 1968.

Whitney, Phyllis A. *The Mystery of the Haunted Pool*, illustrated by H. Tom Hall. Westminster, 1960.

————. *Secret of the Emerald Star*, illustrated by Alex Stein. Westminster, 1964.

Wier, Ester. *The Loner*, illustrated by Christine Price. McKay, 1963.

Wojciechowska, Maia. *Shadow of a Bull*, illustrated by Alvin Smith, Atheneum, 1964.

Wrightson, Patricia. *A Racecourse for Andy*, illustrated by Margaret Horder. Harcourt Brace Jovanovich, 1968.

8 Historical Fiction

One 10-year-old boy was most indignant when he found a single sentence in his history text mentioning that there was dissension among the colonists in Jamestown. He compared this statement with Jean Lee Latham's emotion-packed story about the founding of that settlement, *This Dear Bought Land.* He could not believe the difference. "All that happened," he said, as he pointed to the novel, "and they reduced it to one single sentence!" Latham's story had shown that time after time Captain John Smith had held his men together when they would have fought each other. This first permanent English settlement in America *was* "dear bought" in every sense of the word. During the first year of its existence it lost nine-tenths of its population. But to Captain John Smith the effort was worth it, as he later wrote in a letter from England:

> Men like you will keep England alive in America. Wherever fate casts my lot, I shall work for it, and fight for it. It is my life. It has been my hawk, my hounds, my wife, my child, the whole of my content—this dear bought land![1]

A story had clothed the bare bones of history and made it live again in the mind of this 10-year-old boy. For the first time, perhaps, he was struck with how the struggles of a lifetime could be buried in a single sentence in a text, or recreated in such a vital way as to make the reader feel as if he were participating in the past.

Historical Fiction for Today's Child

VALUES OF HISTORICAL FICTION

Historical novels for children do more than just transmit facts; they help a child to experience the past; to enter into the conflicts, the suffering, the joys, and the despair of those who lived before us. There is no way that children can feel the jolt of a covered wagon, the tediousness of the daily trek in the broiling sun, or the constant threat of danger, unless they take an imaginative journey in such books as *Carolina's Courage* by Yates or *Oregon at Last!* by Van der Loeff. Well-written historical fiction offers young people the vicarious experience of participating in the life of the past.

Stories about the past may also develop a feeling for the continuity of life; they will help children to see themselves and their present place in time as a part of the *living past*. In *The Namesake*, King Alfred is speaking to his men at Stonehenge:

> I like to come here, because among these stones I know that I am standing where other men like

[1]Jean Lee Latham. *This Dear Bought Land*, illustrated by Jacob Landau (New York: Harper & Row, 1957), p. 246.

469

me have stood and thought the same thoughts as I, a thousand years before I was born, and where others like me will stand likewise after I am dead. . . . Everyman is a part of the bridge between the past and the future, and must feel how it stretches out both ways before and behind him. Whatever helps him to feel this more strongly is good.[2]

The reading of historical fiction is one way to help children develop this sense of history and to begin to understand their place in the sweep of human destiny.

An historical perspective also helps children to see and judge the mistakes of the past. They can read such books as Paula Fox's *The Slave Dancer*, or *Friedrich* by Richter or *Journey to Topaz* by Uchida and realize the cruelty that man is capable of inflicting on other men, whether by slavery, persecution, or the assignment of American-Japanese to "relocation centers." Such books will quicken the child's sensibilities and bring him to a fuller understanding of human problems and human relationships. Hopefully, he will learn not to repeat the injustices of the past. Many years ago George Santayana cautioned: "Those who cannot remember the past are condemned to repeat it." An awareness of the past should influence the events of the future, for an understanding of history can be the vantage point for observing and evaluating all that has happened to humankind.

A sense of history also enables children to see change as natural and essential. They should realize that there was a time in history when the burning of witches was considered the righteous thing to do. As they read Petry's *Tituba of Salem Village* they will learn how at one time in our history a person's life could hang on the testimony of three hysterical girls. Stories such as *The Faraway Lurs* by Behn, *Dawn Wind* by Sutcliff, or *Sing Down the Moon* by O'Dell can help children trace the rise and fall of nations in terms of what this meant to the individual. No nation has ever been assured permanent leadership in the world, yet every nation at the pinnacle of its power has thought it was indestructible.

Times change; nations do rise and fall; but the universal needs of humankind have remained relatively unchanged. Every individual needs and

wants respect, belonging, love, freedom, security, regardless of whether he lived during the period of the Vikings, the pioneers, or is alive today. It matters not how many different "Little Houses" the Ingalls family lived in as long as Pa's fiddle sang a song of love and security in each one. Children today living in tenements, trailers, or suburban homes seek the same feelings of warmth and family solidarity that Laura Ingalls Wilder portrayed so effectively in her Little House series. Stories of the past will help children see that situations may be vastly different, but such fundamental qualities as human needs and relationships remain the same.

Historical fiction also enables children to see the interdependence of humankind. In the well-known words of John Donne: "no man *is* an island." We are all interconnected and inter-related. We need each other as much as Calvin Harper needed the strange old Indian, Sequoyah, in *Edge of Two Worlds* by Jones, or Annie deLeeuw needed the Dutch Oosterveld family when she and her sister had to hide in *The Upstairs Room* by Reiss. Such books also dramatize the courage and integrity of the thousands of "common folk" who willingly take a stand for what they believe. History does not record their names, but their stories are frequently the source of inspiration for books of historical fiction.

An appreciation for one's historical heritage is developed slowly throughout life. Children are creatures of the here and now, and their time concepts are inadequate and inaccurate; "the olden days" are likely to be back "before television!" For young children, the understanding of the time between the arrival of Columbus and the Pilgrims in the New World is apt to be in direct relation to the calendar time between Columbus Day and Thanksgiving! But the purpose of historical fiction is not to give an exact chronological understanding of history, rather it is to develop an awareness of people living in the past. Such books will free children from the cocoon of their self-centered little worlds and enlarge their life spaces to include a feeling for the past.

TYPES OF HISTORICAL FICTION

Adults define historical fiction differently than children do. Generally, we think of the historical novel as an imaginative story in which the author

[2]C. Walter Hodges. *The Namesake: A Story of King Alfred* (New York: Coward-McCann, 1964), pp. 166–167.

has deliberately reconstructed the life and times of a period in the past. Children, however, think of historical fiction as any story that takes place in the "olden days" (that is, before they were born). This includes "true" historical fiction, plus books written from an author's memory of an earlier period, or books that may have taken on an aura of the past simply by virtue of having been around for a long time. All these types will be considered in this chapter, but the student of literature will want to distinguish the differing task required of an author who writes an historical novel in contrast to the writing demands of a memoir or a contemporary story.

Johnny Tremain is an example of an authentic historical novel. When Esther Forbes was doing the research for her definitive adult biography of Paul Revere, she was intrigued by the many stories that she read about the apprentices of that time. When she finished the biography, she wrote the story of Johnny Tremain, an apprentice to Paul Revere. Her historical novel is as accurate as to the details of life in Boston just prior to the Revolutionary War as her adult biography is. The story is not just an excuse to present the causes of the Revolutionary War in a palatable form for young people. Her character is inextricably a part of the times. Within three years Johnny Tremain grew from a cocky young silversmith's apprentice to an embittered boy with a maimed hand and finally to a man of ideals, fortitude, and courage. His development had been hammered and shaped on the anvil of his times as surely as his master's creations of silver. In order to write this story Forbes had to do thorough research on the period; she had to know all the Revolutionary activities of the Committee for Public Safety, the duties and responsibilities of the apprentices, the details of the first skirmish in the Revolution, and much much more. Such a story requires days and months of research. It also requires the masterful touch of a gifted writer who never allows research to overpower the imaginative story.

Reconstruction of a period in which the author did not live is a far different task from the imaginative retelling of a personal experience that happened in the past. The Little House books, for example, are all based upon actual childhood experiences in the life of their author, Laura Ingalls Wilder (or the boyhood of her husband,

as in the case of *Farmer Boy*). *The Upstairs Room* by Johanna Reiss is a moving account of the author's own experiences as a young Jewish girl living in Holland during World War II. Written after she became an adult, this book required a searching of her memory for details and then the imaginative retelling and sorting of significant events. Little or no research is required in the writing of a book from memory.

Occasionally a contemporary story about a significant event will endure until it, too, acquires historical significance. An example of such a book is *Snow Treasure* by Marie McSwigan. Written in 1942, this is the exciting story of how some Norwegian children strapped gold bullion under their sleds and slid down the hill to the port past the watchful eyes of the Nazi Commandant. The self-discipline and courage of these children win the admiration of today's readers as much as they did when the book was first published. Children read this story as historical fiction, since no child alive today has any recollection of the Nazi occupation of Norway. What may be vivid memory for some adults is history to children. All of these books—historical fiction, personal memoirs, or books written at the actual time of an historical event—are quite capable of conveying the life and spirit of a period in the past to children.

Not all books are classifiable, and it would be strange, indeed, if the twentieth century had not produced some new types of books for children as well as adults. One such book is E. L. Konigsburg's story of Eleanor of Aquitaine, *A Proud Taste for Scarlet and Miniver*. Eleanor is waiting in heaven to see if her second husband, Henry II of England, will be able to join her. With Eleanor is Henry's mother, Matilda-Empress; William the Marshal; and an old friend of Eleanor's from the time of her first marriage, Abbot Suger. Each person in turn tells of a part of Eleanor's lively life, capturing the excitement of living in twelfth-century England and France. Wife of two kings, mother of Richard the Lion-Heart and wicked King John, Eleanor is credited with setting the tone of court life in her times, including the sponsoring of poets and musicians and romanticizing the legend of King Arthur. She helped her husband to establish the concept of trial by jury and the English Common Laws, to unify the monetary system, and to rule a kingdom that spanned from Scotland to the Pyrenees. Eleanor knew what she wanted and how to get it; she appeared to be a feminist before her time. Her husband reciprocated by keeping her a prisoner in her castles. The author provides just retribution, however, by having Eleanor reach heaven before her husband, even though he died first. When he finally arrives, he is escorted by Winston Churchill on one side and Abraham Lincoln on the other. Henry's first comments are priceless, as he puzzles over how a common man such as Churchill could have governed England, and then pointing to his other escort he says:

> "And this one . . . says that he is Mr. Abraham Lincoln and that he is an American lawyer and president. What is a president? And what in Heaven's name is an American?"[3]

Fantasy, historical fiction, or biography? It is hard to say. Actually the book is a combination of all three, for everything about Eleanor and her family is authentic in the true sense of historical fiction and biography. The scenes in heaven, however, come out of Konigsburg's remarkable imagination. As a book this is unclassifiable, except to say that children will thoroughly enjoy it, and when they have finished it they will have a better understanding of the complex life and times of King Louis VII and King Henry II of England and the woman who kept them together and apart.

CRITERIA FOR HISTORICAL FICTION

Books of historical fiction are not exempt from the requirement of telling a good story. They should not just sugar coat history, but tell a story that is interesting in its own right. The unique problem of historical fiction is how to balance fact with fiction. Margery Fisher maintains that fact must always be subordinated to the story:

> For the more fact [the author] has to deal with, the more imagination he will need to carry it off. It is not enough to be a scholar, essential though this is. Without imagination and enthusiasm, the most learned and well-documented story will leave the young reader cold, where it should set him on fire.[4]

Historical fiction does have to be accurate and authentic in every detail. However, the research should be thoroughly digested. It should appear as an essential part of the story, not tacked on as interesting detail. Mollie Hunter, a well-known Scottish writer of fine historical fiction for children, maintained that an author should be so steeped in the historical period of the book that "you could walk undetected in the past. You'd wake up in the morning and know the kind of bed you'd be sleeping in, the kind of covers you'd have over you, the amenities of getting dressed, even to the change you'd have in your pocket!"[5]

In writing an account of the Great Fire of London in 1666 in the story of *Master Cornhill*, it pleased the author, Eloise McGraw, to be accurate in every detail, even to the weather. Checking Samuel Pepys' famous diary, she knew of the unnatural heat and dryness of the summer, the day it rained during the fire, and the malicious Belgian gale that fanned the flames.[6]

A plot may be created and characters developed, but historical fiction must give an accurate and authentic presentation of the fundamental record of the times. There can be no distortion of values any more than of facts. Stories must accurately reflect the spirit of the times, as well as the events. Historical fiction can't be made to conform to today's more enlightened point of view concerning women or blacks or knowledge of medicine. You can't save George Washington with a shot of penicillin any more than you can have Brink's *Caddie Woodlawn* join the women's liberation movement or the black mother in Armstrong's story of *Sounder* become a black militant. Characters have to act in accordance with the values and beliefs of the time. Caddie's father allowed her to be a tomboy while she was growing up in the Wisconsin backwoods, but she had to become a "proper lady" during the Victorian era; there was no other choice. In order to have the mother in the film production of *Sounder* show more resentment toward whites, the period of the story had to be changed to the 1930s. Such an attitude would not have been

[3] E. L. Konigsburg. *A Proud Taste for Scarlet and Miniver* (New York: Atheneum, 1973), p. 200.
[4] Margery Fisher. *Intent upon Reading: A Critical Appraisal of Modern Fiction for Children* (New York: F. Watts, 1962), p. 225.

[5] In a lecture given in Columbus, Ohio, November 1968.
[6] Eloise Jarvis McGraw. *Master Cornhill* (New York: Atheneum, 1973), p. 205.

tolerated in the South in the 1890s. We deplore the number of books in historical fiction that show the Indians only as bloodthirsty slaves and we welcome such books as *Bread and Butter Indian* by Colver, which depicts a kind Indian, or *The Valley of the Shadow* by Hickman or *Sing Down the Moon* by O'Dell, which depict the cruel treatment the Indians received from whites. Such books help to balance the record. However, Edmonds could not have written *The Matchlock Gun* with kind Indians and still have been faithful to the historical truth of his story. Fiction is seldom impartial. Any well-written story must take a consistent point of view. In the middle of a massacre scene it is impossible to say: ". . . but on the other hand the Indians were only fighting for what was theirs!" Increasingly, books for children represent many different points of view. Teachers and librarians will want to provide a balance of viewpoints for an objective presentation of history.

Careful attention should be given to the authenticity of the language used in historical fiction. The spoken word in a book with an historical background should give the flavor of the period. However, too many "prithees" and "thous" will seem artificial, and may discourage children's further reading. Some archaic words can be used if they are explained in the content. For example, the book, *The Cabin Faced West*, notes that George Washington "bated" at the Hamiltons. The author, Jean Fritz, makes it very clear by the action in the story that "bated" meant "stop by for dinner." The Beattys[7] write amusingly of the research they conducted while writing their first-person historical narrative, *At the Seven Stars*. At one point in the story they spoke of a door knob to a secret passage. On checking both *The Shorter Oxford English Dictionary on Historical Principles* and a concordance of the King James version of the Bible, they found that door knobs were very new-fangled contrivances and that "button" would have been the term that their heroine would have used in the seventeenth century. Well-written historical fiction will also make use of figurative language that is appro-

priate for the times and characters in the story. For example, in Haugaard's superb Viking story, young Hakon comments on the plan of attack with an appropriate metaphor: "A plan should be whole and tight like a cooking pot, and ours seemed to me to resemble a fishing net."[8] An inappropriate use of language will jar the reader and make the story less believable. John Christopher writes many exciting science-fiction stories where authenticity of language is perhaps not so important. In his first book of historical fiction, *Dom and Va*, Dom, a young man of prehistoric times, thinks to himself: "It was no good. The die had been cast when he took her away."[9] One wonders how much a prehistoric man could have known about dies or casting molds!

A book of historical fiction should do more than relate a good story of the past authentically and imaginatively. It should illuminate the problems of today by examining those of yesteryear. The themes of many historical books are such basic ones as the meaning of freedom, loyalty and treachery, love and hate, acceptance of new ways, closed minds versus questing ones, and, always, the age-old struggle between good and evil. Many tales of the past echo contemporary experience. *The Ghosts of Glencoe* by Mollie Hunter is the gripping account of the Massacre of Glencoe in Scotland in 1662; yet it recalls the horror and treachery of the Mai Lai "incident" in our own time. Unfortunately, the twentieth-century episode had no soldier such as Ensign Robert Stewart who risked his life and career to protect the innocent from bloodshed. The parallels between the departure of the Roman Legions from England, as depicted by Sutcliff in her book *The Lantern Bearers*, and the departure of the United States Armed Forces from Vietnam are striking. Many of the social problems which Hester Burton portrays in her novels still provoke thought today.

In Burton's book, *Beyond the Weir Bridge*, Richard finally realizes that his Quaker friends' constancy to their faith and conscience counted more than serving their country. In another story

[7]John Beatty and Patricia Beatty. "Watch Your Language— You're Writing for Young People," *The Horn Book Magazine*, Vol. 41 (February 1965), pp. 34–40.

[8]Erik Christian Haugaard. *Hakon of Rogen's Saga*, illustrated by Leo Dillon and Diane Dillon (New York: Houghton Mifflin, 1963), p. 96.
[9]John Christopher. *Dom and Va* (New York: Macmillan, 1973), p. 95.

by the same author, *Time of Trial,* a London bookstore owner tries to speak out for the poor and is imprisoned for his concern. All these books are capable of shedding light and understanding on the problems of today.

To summarize, historical fiction must first meet the requirements of good writing, but it demands special criteria beyond that. In evaluating historical fiction the reader will want to consider whether the story meets these specialized needs:

1. Does the book tell a good story, blending fact with fiction in such a way that the background is subordinate to the story?
2. Is the story accurate and authentic in every detail, including the setting and the known events of history?
3. Does the story adequately reflect the values and spirit of the times, or is it written from the point of view of today?
4. Is the authenticity of the language preserved in both the spoken word and in the description and comparisons of the written word?
5. Does its theme provide insight and understanding for today's living as well as in the past?

Historical fiction can dramatize and humanize the sterile facts of history. It can give children a sense of participation in the past and an appreciation for their historical heritage. It should enable the child to see that today's way of life is a result of what people did in the past, and that the present will influence the way people live in the future.

Stories of Prehistoric Times

Little is known about prehistoric man other than from records he left in cave paintings, artifacts found in his graves, and the very shape of those grave mounds themselves. While no one can be certain of the exact ways that early people lived, anthropologists and geologists are slowly uncovering scientific data that make it possible to imagine how life in prehistoric times might have been. Authors and their readers have been fascinated with trying to reconstruct the mind and feelings of primitive people. How did they discover that there were others living in the world? Were all the tribes at the same level of development, or did different groups mature ahead of others? What happened when two groups met? Who were the first farmers? Who, the first artists? How was progress achieved? These and other questions have provided the stimulus for some remarkably fine stories.

One Small Blue Bead by Schweitzer is a poetic picture book that describes prehistoric times among a tribe that is convinced it is the only people in the world. One man thinks differently and yearns for others of his kind. His chores are willingly assumed by a boy to enable the old man to roam free in quest of knowledge. As the boy goes about his daily chores, he wonders, too:

> I wonder . . . I wonder
> If on some far hillside
> There is a boy
> who sits alone.
> And thinks the same thoughts
> As my own.
> I wonder if he wonders if
> There's a boy with thoughts like his.
> I'd like to tell him that there is
> And I'm that boy.[10]

The boy's faithfulness is rewarded as the man returns with a boy from another tribe, who gives him one small blue bead. This is a moving story of unselfishness and man's quest for the unknown. It will be understood and appreciated by children as young as 7. A similar tale is told for older children in *Beyond the Gorge of Shadows* by Harvey. This is the story of Gahyaz, a 16-year-old boy who lived in the American Southwest some 10,000 years ago. Finding strange spear-points in a cave, he dared defy the Hunt Chief's lifelong belief that the only men on earth are those in their tribe. Gahyaz is killed in a fight with a lion, but his friends, Seska and Maitsoh, continue the search for others of their own kind. At last they do find other men, but ironically they meet with the same disbelief from them as they had faced in their own tribe; they could not have come from the east, they are told, for no men live there. Slowly, the boys prove that they did come from this direction, and they return to their

[10] Byrd Baylor Schweitzer. *One Small Blue Bead,* illustrated by Symeon Shimin (New York: Macmillan, 1965), p. 18.

Meeting for the first time, a boy from a primitive tribe learns that there are others of his kind outside his own clan.

From *One Small Blue Bead* by Byrd Baylor Schweitzer. Illustrations by Symeon Shimin. Illustrations copyright © Symeon Shimin 1965. Used by permission of Macmillan Publishing Co., Inc.

their preparations, and only Andor's family are saved. Andor is not vindicated, however, for he had wanted to lead his whole tribe to safety. Even as the flood comes, it is called "Andor's Flood" and he is blamed for it. Only the reader knows the vision of the man and senses his frustration at being unable to convince his people of their impending doom.

The misty dawn of humankind is as fascinating to speculate about as is the future. Perhaps that is why John Christopher, author of many popular science-fiction books, decided to write *Dom and Va,* a story of a boy and girl who come from two different primitive tribes. Dom is from the fierce hunter tribes of the north, driven southward by a drying climate. Va is from a village of weaker, gentler people who have some agricultural skills and can make tools. The inevitable clash between the two cultures is symbolically told through the story of Va and Dom. She finds Dom wounded and nurses him, only later realizing that he is as savage as the rest of the hunters. When his tribe destroys Va's village, he helps her escape, not out of compassion but because he wishes to have her for a mate rather than give her to his father, the tribal chief. And having defied his father, he too must run away or be killed. Va hates Dom for his part in the destruction of her village. She stays with him for the sheer physical need of his protection and hunting skill. He, in turn, finds her useful and a comfort, although he cannot understand why she will not sing and smile as she did in their first encounter. Still loathing him, she bears his son. When other hunters come and nearly kill her, she realizes her need for Dom and accepts her role as mate and mother. The story is exciting and convincing. However, since Christopher presents Dom and Va as the prototype of the first family unit, it's impossible not to wonder about the assumptions underlying his portrayal of the two sex roles. In the Epilogue, Christopher states:

> From Dom the boys learned to use clubs, to defend their home from attackers. From Va the children learned to love beauty and all beautiful things—to sing, and tell stories, and paint in bright colors.[11]

own tribe with living proof of other men. This book has a tightly knit plot, excellent characterization, and a theme as meaningful today as 10,000 years ago: the age-old conflict between the questing mind and the closed one.

This same theme runs through a remarkable story of primitive people entitled *And the Waters Prevailed* by Barringer. When Andor, the Little, journeyed to the ocean, he saw that at what is now the Straits of Gibraltar the water would some day break through the fragile natural dam and flood the valley that was his people's home. No one shares his vision, and Andor spends his life trying to convince the tribe of impending danger. When the flood does come, Andor is an old man, too old to make the long journey to the caves in the Pyrenees that he had long ago found as a suitable refuge. The tribe delays in

[11]John Christopher. *Dom and Va* (New York: Macmillan, 1973), p. 153.

The contrasts here seem too easy, too oversimplified. Do we know for sure that no men ever painted, that no woman ever wielded a club? Sex-stereotyping begins early; did it really begin in the dawn of history, or is Christopher writing out of his modern-day assumptions?

In *The Dream Time*, Henry Treece has portrayed a gentle boy who would rather make beautiful things than kill people. Punished for drawing the shape of a wolf in the sand, Crooklegs (later named Twilight) is told that as a part of his initiation into manhood he must forfeit his right forefinger. The sacrifice is delayed by the tribe's attack on the Fox Folk during which his father is killed. Dreading the initiation, and having now lost both parents, Twilight leaves the battle and wanders from one tribe to another. Some welcome him, and some fear him for his art; but none understand his dreams—his dream of a time when everyone would speak the same language and understand each other, a time for making rather than breaking, a time of peace instead of war. This was the last book Henry Treece wrote before his death. In simple, almost poetic words he has created a boy from prehistoric times who dreamed dreams that moderns still dream today.

Another fascinating tale about the dawning of creativity in primitive people is told in *The Sorcerer* by Crompton. Lefthand, like Twilight, had artistic ability and so was considered different from the rest of the tribe. In a hunting accident he is nearly killed by the crushing blow of a huge bear. His mother takes him on a painful journey to live with her father, the sorcerer. The old man, who has a withered arm and leg, forces Lefthand to help the women scrape and cure animal skins. When the tribe departs for the winter, Lefthand stays with the sorcerer and his daughter. With the coming of the storms, they go to the sacred cave of many paintings. Lefthand is awed when he sees the shadowy pictures of galloping ponies, a bellowing bison bull, and wild pigs with tusks. He longs to paint the orphaned reindeer fawn that he had followed all year. He makes a sketch for the sorcerer who nods and says:

> "You do not live in your stomach like my grandson, Onedeer, and he will kill more animals than you will paint. His children will eat. But he will never look at a fawn and see what you have seen. For Onedeer, a fawn will never be anything more than meat and hide and bone. But you, Lefthand, will live in your eyes and your heart. And sometimes you will stretch out your heart like a hand and reach beyond yourself."[12]

Lefthand does go "beyond himself" in his painting, his recovery, and his courage. The author does not gloss over the real cruelty of this primitive tribe but she does reveal the beginnings of humanity and creativity. Her style of writing is compelling and beautiful. Near the end of the story she describes the birth of a baby reindeer in vivid yet reverent detail. The passage symbolizes the struggle and pain of Lefthand's life and his new beginning as "The Painter."

Drawing his inspiration from the Neolithic stone carvings which line the rocky shores of the White Sea, A. Linevski has written an authentic story titled *An Old Tale Carved Out of Stone*. The author, a highly respected Soviet archeologist, did research in the journals of seventeenth- and eighteenth-century travelers to Siberia "who were amazed to discover tribes living virtually in the Stone Age." Using this background, Linevski has created a very believable story of a reluctant young shaman.

Madeleine Polland tells the story of Lumma, a semi-savage Celtic girl who is captured by a Roman scouting party and taken to Rome as a slave. There, she faces an unbelievable cultural shock as she sees streets paved wide enough for seven chariots and huge buildings with great pillars of carved marble:

> It was all as large as [Cassilus] had said and just as wonderful, but it was something else. Something that made her catch her breath and struggle with the tears pricking at her eyes as she saw this Roman city, and then remember that her people lived as she had lived, in their mud huts of chilly damp, along the lake shore. She did not know what it was that so upset her; she had not yet learned the name for beauty.[13]

Lumma had only one wish and plan, and that was to return to Britain *To Tell My People*. She

[12] Anne Eliot Crompton. *The Sorcerer*, illustrated by Leslie Morrill (Boston, Mass.: Little, Brown, 1971), p. 153.
[13] Madeleine Polland. *To Tell My People*, illustrated by Richard M. Powers (New York: Holt, Rinehart and Winston, 1968), p. 158.

achieved her goal and brought disaster to the Romans she had grown to love and to her family who refused to believe what they thought were her foolish tales of a more powerful tribe. Caught between two warring cultures, and knowing something of each, Lumma had naïvely hoped that understanding would prevent bloodshed. But no one would listen. Readers hope that the Romans will accept her back as she makes a wild dash down to the sea, but we are never told.

Rosemary Sutcliff's moving story, *Warrior Scarlet,* tells of Drem, a Bronze Age boy, who must kill a wolf singlehanded in order to win his right to wear the scarlet of manhood. Drem is determined to become a warrior rather than be forced to live with the Earth people and be a shepherd. His task would be a difficult one for most boys; it seemed almost impossible for a 15-year-old boy who had the use of only one arm. This story not only accurately presents the life of these primitive peoples; it also shows the hurt, loneliness, and defiance of the handicapped.

In *The Faraway Lurs,* Harry Behn has created a hauntingly beautiful story of the love between a young Stone Age girl, Heather, and Wolf Stone, son of the chieftain of the Sun People. One morning Heather hears the great bronze trumpets (called lurs) of the Sun People, who have camped beside a lake near her village. Later, she meets Wolf Stone in the forest, as he searches for the mighty tree that her Forest People worship. Heather's people are peaceful forest dwellers, while the Sun People are fierce warriors. The two fall in love, but there is no solution for them other than death in this Romeo and Juliet story of the Bronze Age. The author was inspired to tell Heather's tale after a journey to Denmark to visit the birthplace of his mother. An important archeological find had been made on a farm when they discovered the "wet grave" of an 18-year-old girl perfectly preserved for some 3,000 years. Behn listened to the details of her burial and then wrote his own interpretation of what might have happened. In his foreword Behn points out the relative brevity of human history and the slow progress in human relations since Heather's time.

Stories of the Old World

Children in the United States are more interested in stories of the American frontier, the Civil War, or World War II than they are in the fiction of ancient or medieval days. Increasingly, however, as we have access to books published in England and Europe, plus those written in the United States, there is a growing body of fine historical fiction of the Old World. Some of the most distinguished will be described in the following pages.

ANCIENT TIMES

The ancient world of Egypt with all of its political intrigue provides a rich background for Eloise McGraw's story of a slave girl, *Mara, Daughter of the Nile.* Mara, the mistreated slave of a wealthy jewel trader, is bought by a mysterious man who offers her luxury in turn for her services as a spy for the queen. On a Nile riverboat Mara meets Lord Sheftu, who employs her as a spy for the king! In this exciting and sinister story of espionage and counterespionage, Mara endures torture for her love of Lord Sheftu and her loyalty to Egypt and its rightful king. The transformation of Mara from a selfish, deceitful slave to a loyal and courageous young woman is made slowly and believably. Plot and characterization are just as skillfully developed in McGraw's second book about Egypt, *The Golden Goblet.*

Eventually, Rome became the major influence and power in the world, dominating even mighty Egypt. But Rome was seldom welcomed elsewhere and seemed constantly at war. Perhaps the best known of all the attempts to defeat the Romans was Hannibal's fifteen-day march over the Alps. In Baumann's *I Marched with Hannibal* an old man relives his experiences as a 12-year-old elephant driver with Hannibal on his march across the Alps to Rome with 45,000 men, 6,000 horses, and 39 elephants. In this first-person narrative the reader learns much about the intrepid young general, the tortuous journey, and the ways of war. Primarily, however, this is the story of Suru, Hannibal's favorite elephant, and the last to survive. Upon Suru's death the boy deserts the army and returns to the ruins of Sanguntum where Suru had first found him, the only living person in those smoldering ruins. This is a grim but powerful story of the ruthlessness of war.

Daniel Bar Jamin had but one all-consuming purpose in his life, to avenge the cruel death of his father and mother by driving the Romans out of his land of Israel. First with an outlaw band, and then with a group of boy guerrillas, Daniel nurses his hatred and waits for the hour to strike. He takes comfort in the verse from II Samuel 22:35—"He trains my hands for war, so that my arms can bend a bow of bronze." Seen as a symbol for what *no man* can do, *The Bronze Bow* is the title for Daniel's tormented journey from blind hatred to his acceptance and understanding of love. Only after he has nearly sacrificed his friends and driven his sister, Leah, deeper into mental darkness, does he seek the help of Simon's friend, Jesus. After he pours out his troubles and hatred, Jesus tells him:

> It is hate that is the enemy, not men. Hate does not die with killing. It only springs up a hundred-fold. The only thing stronger than hate is love.[14]

The healing strength of Jesus cures Leah and, at that moment, Daniel can forgive the Romans. He understands at last that only love can bend the bow of bronze. Each character stands out in this startling story of the conflict of good and evil, of love overcoming hate.

A bear, a boy, and a holy man are strange traveling companions in Peter Dickinson's historical novel set in sixth-century Byzantium, *The Dancing Bear*. This story provides a rich tapestry of characters, high adventure, and much humor. Silvester, a young Greek slave, is very happy at his master's large house, where he plays with Lady Adriane, the master's daughter, learns Latin and medicine, and has the sole responsibility of training Bubba, the bear, to dance. Silvester's world is destroyed on the night of Lady Adriane's betrothal feast, when a group of Huns enter the house and slaughter most of the guests. Silvester and Adriane spend the night in Bubba's cage and so are saved. However, just as the Huns are leaving, one of them discovers the girl and carries her off. Silvester, as the model of the faithful slave, takes Bubba to go in search of Adriane. They are joined by Holy John, the household saint who has lived on top of a twelve-foot pillar in the center of the household for years. He decides that it is his mission to try to convert the Huns to Christianity. The three have many ad-

ventures, including finding a wounded leader of the Huns and nursing him back to health. Their trip is frequently punctuated by the humorous antics of Bubba, who is a most lovable and amusing bear, yet as dangerous as a wild beast at times. Holy John's missionary work is very unorthodox, but effective. The three are successful in finding and freeing the Lady Adriane. However, the real accomplishment of the quest is the freeing of Silvester from his literal and psychological bondage to slavery. Gradually, as he learns to act and think like a free man, he loses "the look of a slave." This is a heady tale, rich in humor, imagination, and historical detail.

VIKING ADVENTURES

While ancient civilizations flourished and decayed in Egypt, Greece, and Rome, the beginnings of European history were just stirring in England, Scotland, and the Scandinavian countries. The stories of the Vikings are a part of the eerie half-light of the predawn of history, when facts were recorded only in legend and song. Historians and archeologists gradually have added to our knowledge of these people, but it remained for the creative writer to breathe life into each fact and clothe these rugged adventurers with purpose and being. In *Viking Adventure*, Clyde Bulla has made the Vikings live for 8- and 9-year olds. This is the story of young Sigurd, who joins the crew of a ship that sails to verify Leif Ericson's discovery of Wineland a century earlier. After enduring the hardships of the voyage, and witnessing the treacherous murder of his captain, Sigurd escapes from the ill-fated ship and is the only survivor of the trip to the New World. Returning home at last, he asks the old bard to instruct him in writing and reading so that he may record for others what he has seen. In *Beorn the Proud* by Madeleine Polland the Vikings go on an expedition to plunder rather than to explore. While an Irish village is being sacked, 12-year-old Ness is taken captive by Beorn, the willful son of Anlaf, the Sea King. The dramatic story recounts Ness' experiences as Beorn's slave on the doomed ship on which Beorn's father dies. When they finally return to Denmark, Beorn's pride and fiery temper lead him close to disaster time and time again, but the wisdom and gentle Christian ways of Ness

---

[14] Elizabeth George Speare. *The Bronze Bow* (Boston, Mass.: Houghton Mifflin, 1961), p. 224.

help him to overcome his worst enemy—himself. Banished from Denmark with his small band of faithful followers, Beorn swallows his pride and returns to the island off the Irish coast, to Ness' former home. Her family forgives him in the joy of her return, and Beorn finds a new life and a new God. The characterization is excellent in this stirring story of individual and tribal conflict placed against the larger conflict of paganism and Christianity.

Erik Haugaard has written two superb stories of the Vikings that sing with the cadences of traditional sagas—*Hakon of Rogen's Saga* and *A Slave's Tale*. In the first story Hakon is sure that his island home, Rogen, is indestructible—had it not been in his family for nine generations? But his widowed father has rashly kidnapped a chieftain's daughter for his new bride. With the spring thaws come vengeance, and Hakon is an orphan at the mercy of his evil uncle. Treated as one of his uncle's slaves, Hakon hides in the mountains while Rark and others loyal to his father come to his aid. At last, Hakon, grown wise beyond his years, achieves his birthright along with his manhood. Having tasted the bitter gall of enslavement, if only briefly, his first act is to free Helga, the slave girl with whom he had been reared, saying:

> That is everyone's birthright, his freedom, and the gods have only one message for us, that we must live.[15]

A Slave's Tale continues the story of Hakon and Helga. Anxious to keep his word to Rark, to return the former slave to his homeland, Hakon embarks for Brittany. Helga, determined not to be left alone, stows away on board the ship. All goes well on the trip until they reach their destination and find that Rark's wife has remarried and Rark's friends, the priests, have been killed in a Norse raid. The new priests do not trust the Vikings and unknowingly aid in a tragic plot to kill Rark and the others. Only Hakon, Helga, and two others make their escape to the ship and the handful of men left to guard it. The basic theme of *A Slave's Tale* is still freedom. Haugaard explores the various dimensions of enslavement;

[15]Erik Christian Haugaard. *Hakon of Rogen's Saga,* illustrated by Leo Dillon and Diane Dillon (Boston, Mass.: Houghton Mifflin, 1963), p. 132.

Powerful woodcuts portray both evil and heroic Norsemen. Here Eirik, the Fox, hunts for Hakon—a 13-year-old boy, owner of Rogen—as long as he lives.

Illustration by Leo and Diane Dillon from *Hakon of Rogen's Saga* by Erik Christian Haugaard. Copyright © 1963 by Erik Christian Haugaard. Reprinted by permission of the publisher, Houghton Mifflin Company.

the slavery of the mind that will not let Helga forget that she was once a slave, or the slavery of power, the desire to possess all. These books speak to all ages, as profound in the depth of their darkness as in the extent of their light.

Viking's Dawn, The Road to Miklagaard, and *Viking's Sunset* form a trilogy of the life of Harald Sigurdson as told by a well-known English writer, Henry Treece. The last tale is a splendid one that would probably intrigue children in the United States the most. Harald seeks revenge on a blood enemy for the burning of the village. Harald chases his enemy to Greenland and then to Vinland, where they meet red men. The jealousy of the red chief's maimed son is the cause of Harald's death. His men give him a Viking burial as they put his body on his ship, *Long Snake,* and send it burning on its last voyage. (A longship prow was found in one of the lakes in Newfoundland, so there is historical justification for the dramatic end of this triology.) Henry Treece, like Haugaard, wrote these stories with a poetic terseness that captures the saga tone of the old Norse tales. *The Last Viking,* also by Treece, tells the tale of the last great viking who met his death in 1066 at Stamford Bridge while fighting King Harold Godwinson of England.

TALES OF EARLY BRITAIN

The Vikings' control over Great Britain was not to last long. In *Escape to King Alfred,* Geoffrey Trease—another excellent English writer—has told the exciting story of three English hostages held by the Danes in Gloucester. After a hazardous escape, the hostages survive a long winter and the battles that restore English control. Some of the Danes are baptized and remain in England. With the marriage of Judith and Olaf, the author shows that the English became part of each group they conquered and were conquered by. Two other fine, yet complex, books about the defeat of the Danes are *The Namesake* and its sequel, *The Marsh King,* by C. Walter Hodges.

No one has surpassed Rosemary Sutcliff in her ability to recreate the life and times of early Britain. *The Eagle of the Ninth, The Silver Branch,* and *The Lantern Bearers* form a trilogy that describes the period when Britain was ruled by Romans. In the third book the last of the Roman auxiliaries set sail in their galleys and abandon Britain to the internal strife and menace of invasion by Saxons. At the final moment, one Roman officer decides that his loyalties lie with Britain rather than the Legions. Aquila returns to his family villa only to have all that he loves destroyed by the Saxons. His father is killed; his sister captured; and he is tied to a tree to be killed by the wolves. In the morning, however, another band of invaders capture and enslave him. Three years later he escapes his thralldom, but it is many years before he can rid himself of the black bitterness of his sister's marriage to a Saxon. At last, Aquila finds a measure of contentment—a contentment partly learned from the kind and

gentle Brother Ninnias, partly from the loving loyalty of his British wife, Ness, lastly for his part in saving his sister's son, an enemy Saxon. His life has come full circle; free of bitterness and revenge, Aquila can look to the future. His old friend reflects his thoughts and the theme of this fine book:

> I sometimes think that we stand at sunset. . . . It may be that the night will close over us in the end, but I believe that morning will come again. Morning always grows again out of the darkness, though maybe not for the people who saw the sun go down. We are the Lantern Bearers, my friend; for us to keep something burning, to carry what light we can forward into the darkness and the wind.[16]

Both light and the stirring of the wind symbolize the beginning of a new era in Sutcliff's *Dawn Wind.* These fine books of historical fiction may cast a light into the shadows of the past and illuminate the path ahead. For always there is hope in Rosemary Sutcliff's books—hope for the future and the eventual triumph of courage, compassion, and love.

MEDIEVAL TIMES AND TALES

The Dark Ages had two windows to the light: the learning of the monks and the chivalrous deeds of the knights. Young children of 7 and 8 are intrigued with stories of the days of knighthood. Some of them will be able to read Bulla's *Sword in the Tree,* which is the story of a boy who saved his father and Weldon Castle by bravely going to King Arthur. Through treachery, Shan's uncle makes his own brother a captive and takes control of the castle. Remembering where he hid his father's sword in a tree, Shan establishes his identity as the rightful owner of Weldon Castle. This is an easy-reading book with excitement on every page. It has more than just a lively plot, however, for it presents an interesting picture of the justice of the time.

In *Candle at Dusk,* E. M. Almedingen has told the story of Idrun, a Frankish boy whose one consuming desire was to learn to read. In the eighth century book learning was left only to the clergy and monks, while boys of wealthy fami-

---

[16]Rosemary Sutcliff. *The Lantern Bearers,* illustrated by Charles Keeping (New York: Walck, 1959), pp. 250–251.

lies, such as Idrun's, spent their days hunting and fishing and training for battle. However, Idrun has killed a wild boar to save a serving woman and as a reward has received his father's permission to go to the Abbey at Ligugé and be tutored. There, the kind monk-librarian Dom Defensor teaches him to read and write, while at home his mother struggles to teach the girl to whom Idrun is betrothed to sew and be a lady. Throughout the book the threat of a Saracen invasion gathers momentum. When the danger is iminent, Idrun is taken home from the Abbey and so escapes its total destruction by the Arabs. He does return to save Dom Defensor's book of quotations from the ruins and presumably he will be the first to copy it. This story illuminates the times, particularly the role of the church and the daily life of the people.

Marguerite de Angeli has written many books, but her finest is *The Door in the Wall,* a Newbery Award winner. Set against a background of fourteenth-century England, De Angeli has painted in words and pictures the dramatic story of Robin, crippled son of Sir John de Bureford. Robin's father has gone off to the Scottish wars; his mother is in service to the Queen; and Robin is to go to the castle in the north to serve as a page to Sir Peter de Lindsay. Robin becomes ill with a strange malady, however, and is taken to the monastery by Brother Luke. There, Robin learns many things: to whittle, to swim, to read, to write, and above all to have patience—all "doors in the wall," according to Brother Luke. For:

> Whether thou'lt walk soon I know not. This I know. We must teach thy hands to be skilled in many ways, and we must teach thy mind to go about whether thy legs will carry thee or no. For reading is another door in the wall, dost understand, my son?[17]

Robin does learn to walk, but only with the aid of the crutches that he makes with his own hands. When he is well enough to travel, Brother Luke takes him to Sir Peter's castle. Robin is fearful of the reception a page on crutches might

[17]Marguerite de Angeli. *The Door in the Wall* (New York: Doubleday, 1949), p. 28.

The Door in the Wall

BY MARGUERITE DE ANGELI

A handicapped Robin symbolically stands outside the many doors in his life. This well-designed title page suggests the illuminated manuscripts of the book's medieval setting.

From *The Door in the Wall* by Marguerite de Angeli. Copyright 1949 by Marguerite de Angeli. Reproduced by permission of Doubleday & Company, Inc.

receive, but Sir Peter, like Brother Luke, assures him that everyone has his place in the world and that there are many ways to serve. It is during a siege of the castle that Robin finds a way to aid the king. Finally, Robin, or Sir Robin as he becomes for his exploits, is reunited with his father and mother. This is a beautiful book in format and text. De Angeli visited England and saw many of the churches, castles, and inns that she has portrayed in the background of her pictures. The pageantry of medieval days, the hardships of living during that period—but particularly living as a handicapped person—are all well conveyed. Robin's rebellion, final acceptance, and then challenge to live a rich life *with* his handicap should provide inspiration for all children today.

Rosemary Sutcliff has written of two healings in her story of Norman England titled *The Witch's Brat*. One is the healing of mind and spirit of Lovel, crooked and misshapen from birth, as he comes to terms with his own deformity while caring for the sick and poor at St. Bartholomew Hospital and Priory. The other is Brother Lovel's healing of Nick Redpoll's stiff knee, so that he can once again dream of becoming a free mason and build cathedrals. Driven out of his village as the "Witch's Brat," Lovel has at last fulfilled his grandmother's prophecy that he would become ". . . one of the menders of this world; not the makers, nor yet the breakers; just one of the menders."[18] This is a shorter, less complex story than most of Sutcliff's books. The characters are well developed as in all this author's work. The action is somewhat slower, as it describes life in a monastery, the work of the builders and craftsmen, and the harsh laws of feudal life.

Norah Lofts is well known for her adult historical fiction; recently she has written some fine stories for boys and girls of 10 and up. *The Maude Reed Tale* is the lively story of a young girl of the fifteenth century who wanted to be a wool merchant like her grandfather. According to the customs of the times she is sent away to Beauclaire Castle to learn needlwork, to play the flute, and to develop good manners. This she does, but not willingly, and she regularly slips away to ride her horse and practice jousting with the young pages. Torn between the passive feminine world and the active masculine one, Maude discovers that her favorite lady-in-waiting can read. Asking for instruction, she discovers a new world: "And then I realized that there was yet another world, neither male nor female—the world of reading and writing."[19] Maude uses this newly learned skill when she returns home to find an unscrupulous manager of the manor taking advantage of her sick grandfather. She competently and believably restores order to the mismanaged household and gradually takes over the wool business. This uncommon story of a woman merchant in the fifteenth century is set against a flawless background of medieval society.

The haunting story of *One is One* by Picard derives its name from the lines of an English folk song: "One is one and all alone and evermore shall be so." When Barbara Picard was asked what happened to the misfits in medieval society, she promptly replied that they were sent to the monastery, for there was nowhere else for them to go. This was the destiny of Stephen de Beauville, a gentle, sensitive boy who had been branded a coward by his many half-brothers and sisters and who was considered unfit for the life of a knight. Sent to the monastery at 13, Stephen finds some comfort in learning to paint, a skill in which he has remarkable talent, but the gruff Brother Ernulf refuses to praise him. Still dreaming of knighthood, Stephen runs away from the monastery. Quite by chance, he is found half-starved by a wise and valiant knight, Sir Pagan Latourelle, who instructs Stephen in the arts of knighthood, jousting, riding, and archery. Stephen comes to love his friend, the first who ever accepted him just as he is. In an unsuccessful attempt to free the king, Sir Pagan is captured. Just before his grim execution, Stephen contrives to visit him and Pagan gives him advice that he follows for the remainder of his life:

> "Above all, always be yourself. Do not be afraid to do what you want to do, as long as it hurts no one else. We are each of us as God made us, and if God has seen fit to make you in an uncommon mould, be brave enough to be different. Promise me that, Stephen."[20]

When Stephen sees Sir Pagan's severed head raised above the crowd, he no longer wants to live. But time heals wounds of anguish as well as pain. Stephen wins his knighthood and the devotion of an incorrigible young squire. When young Thomas dies of the plague, Stephen remembers Pagan's words and returns to the solace of his painting at the monastery. He has found sorrow that he could have avoided if he had never run away, but he has also found happiness, two friends to love, and himself. Stephen's story is tragic but in the best sense of tragedy; it is uplifting and fulfilling. Children who read *One*

[18]Rosemary Sutcliff. *The Witch's Brat*, illustrated by Richard Lebenson (New York: Walck, 1970), p. 145.
[19]Norah Lofts. *The Maude Reed Tale* (Nashville, Tenn.: Thomas Nelson, 1972), p. 44.

[20]Barbara Leonie Picard. *One Is One* (New York: Holt, Rinehart and Winston, 1966), p. 169.

Is One will have lived most intensively with Stephen de Beauville—they will have experienced literature.

Again, Rosemary Sutcliff has recreated the period and people of feudal England in her book, *Knight's Fee*. Randall is an orphaned dog-boy who was won at a chess game by a minstrel who, in turn, gave him to Sir Everard as valet for his son, Bevis. Bevis and Randall grow up together on the Dean land, the grassy downs that reach back into the very roots of time. Randall is as faithful to Bevis as the dogs that first knew his care. When Bevis keeps his lonely all-night vigil in the church before the day of his knighting, Randall kneels quietly outside in the shadows. Such devotion is rewarded, but in a way that Randall would never have chosen—Bevis makes him a knight just before he dies of a wound received at the Battle of Tenchebrai. Randall, the mistreated dog-boy becomes Sir Randall, to hold the Dean land by knight's fee. Life was cheap and of little value in the Middle Ages. A boy could be won in a game of chess, for example, but given a chance, that same boy could develop qualities of loyalty and courage that were unsurpassed. In her characteristic fashion Sutcliff has dramatized the potential for goodness in mankind in this story of knighthood and friendship.

Thirteenth-century England is the setting for the Newbery Award winner, *Adam of the Road*, by Elizabeth Janet Gray. It is the story of Adam; his minstrel father, Roger; and Adam's devoted dog, Nick. Nick is stolen on their way to the great Fair of St. Giles. In the frantic chase that follows, Adam is separated from his father. It takes a whole long winter to find both Nick and Roger again. Adam has many adventures and some disasters, but he learns that the road is home to the minstrel and that people, generally, are kind. In *I Will Adventure*, Elizabeth Gray tells the story of Master Talbot against the authentic background of Shakespeare's England. The title of the book comes from the page's speech in *Romeo and Juliet:* "I am almost afraid to stand alone/Here in the churchyard; yet I will adventure." This was the first play Andrew Talbot had ever seen, and the words struck a particularly responsive note for him. He resolved that he, too, would "adventure." How Master Shakespeare helps him achieve that goal makes for an interesting tale.

Another fine book that pictures the colorful life and times of Shakespeare's England is *The Wonderful Winter* by Marchette Chute.

THE EMERGENCE OF MODERN EUROPE

Peasant life under the feudal system of Europe in the sixteenth century was a far cry from Shakespeare's England. In *Boy of Old Prague*, Ish-Kishor has told the grim story of a sensitive, intelligent, but quite uneducated peasant boy, Tomas, who grows up accepting without question the harshness of the feudal system. In this system the lord of the manor owns both the land and its wealth and his people as well. Tomas is equally accepting of all that he hears about the Jews in the Ghetto, believing them to be the foredoomed property of the Devil. Imagine his horror, then, when he is caught stealing a roast chicken from the kitchen for his ill and starving mother and is sentenced to act as a bond servant to an old Jew in the Ghetto. He would rather have faced public execution. However, Reb Pesach and his beautiful granddaughter, Rachel, are kind to Tomas. The sensitive boy is confused. How could he admire the young lord of the manor who starved his own family and nearly killed him for the theft of a chicken, yet fear and despise these kind and gentle people? Gradually, Tomas allows himself to think and feel as his heart tells him. While home on a visit Tomas escapes the cruel pogrom of the Jews instigated by the young lord whose affections Rachel had rejected. Tomas searches for "his family" amidst the bodies on the streets and those left charred by the human bonfire in the marketplace. He clings to the hope that some of the Jews escaped and ends his story with a moving plea for understanding that speaks as forcefully to our times as it does to sixteenth-century Prague:

> Perhaps some day I shall find them again, little Joseph, and my gentle maiden, Mademoiselle Rachel, and the old man who taught me from his Hebrew soul the loving-kindness which I had never known. I shall find them, and I shall help them and work for them with my two strong hands, and among us we shall learn that the God of mercy is the same God, no matter where we find him.[21]

[21]Sulamith Ish-Kishor. *A Boy of Old Prague*, illustrated by Ben Shahn (New York: Pantheon, 1963), p. 90.

Poland is also the setting for Eric Kelly's Newbery Award winner, *The Trumpeter of Krakow.* This is a complex tale of the quest for the shimmering Great Tarnov Crystal, coveted by a Tartar chieftain for possessing magical powers and zealously guarded by the ancestral oath of a Ukrainian family. Joseph and Elzbietka save the crystal through their knowledge of history. Ever since the Tartars had sacked the city of Krakow in 1241, the Trumpeter had ended the Heynal on a broken note to commemorate the steadfast soldier of that time who defiantly played the hourly hymn and was killed in the midst of his playing. The year is now 1461 and once again the Tartars are in the city. This time it is only a small band of them who are seeking the Tarnov Crystal, but they have captured Joseph's father. When it is the time of the second hour, Joseph is allowed to play the Heynal so no one will suspect any thing is wrong. Joseph, however, signals for help by playing the hymn through to its completion, something that had not been done for two hundred years. While this story received the Newbery Award many years ago, the tale of intrigue, loyalty, and the quest for the mysterious gem will appeal to children today. The background of fifteenth-century Eastern Europe is vividly portrayed.

In a book titled *The Untold Tale*, Eric Haugaard has related the harsh story of a 7-year-old boy whose parents both die at the end of a winter of famine in Sweden. Naïvely setting out to find the king to help him in his distress, Dag is helped and hindered by the many people he meets along the way—Black Lars, a poacher; Bodil, a woman of ill-repute; Kirsten, her 6-year-old daughter; and Peter Gram, a 19-year-old traveling minstrel. Many years after Dag has been killed while protecting Kirsten in a battle between Sweden and Denmark, Peter tells his tragic tale. The universal message of this story—namely, the pain and suffering inflicted on helpless victims of war and poverty—is the same theme used in Haugaard's book, *The Little Fishes*, set in Italy during World War II. Always it is the little people, the children, the peasants, who are destroyed by war, whether in seventeenth-century Sweden or twentieth-century Italy or Vietnam.

A dog story serves to illuminate the crumbling world of the Madingly Estate during the English Civil War. In *Blood Royal*, Rosemary Weir tells the story of the love and respect that Gil Colepepper and his father feel for the royal line of greyhounds that are entrusted to their care while Sir Hugh Burnett is away. The Roundheads come and take one of the best hounds as a raider's prize. Gil and a friend daringly rescue him from the Roundhead camp. In the climaxing adventure Gil hides with the hounds in a tunnel leading from the summer house, while Simon, a hunchback servant boy that Gil had thought was his enemy, distracts the soldiers from the tunnel's other doorway in the manor house, but sacrifices his life in the process. This is a fine book for children who love dogs. They will learn much about the care and breeding of them as well as develop a feeling for the slow disintegration of a way of life.

Eloise McGraw tells the story of an 11-year-old orphan who lived in London during two of its most severe crises, the Great Plague of 1665 and the Great Fire of London. *Master Cornhill*, a foundling, is sent away from the city when his foster mother succumbs to the dread plague. When Michael returns some eight months later, all of his family and friends have perished. His whole life seems as closed as the door to their house which still retains traces of the red-ochre-painted plague cross. Homeless and penniless, Michael finds two new friends that direct the future of his life: Tom, a ballad singer, and Susanna, an independent young girl who keeps house for an old Dutch map-maker. When the fire sweeps through London, Michael and Tom struggle through it attempting to find Susanna. As in any disaster, there are those who think only of themselves and those who think of others and how they can help. Tom is one of the latter, and so it takes them several days to make their way slowly through the smoking ruins and find Susannah. Finally, the three are reunited, and Michael gets his chance to stay and learn mapmaking from the old Dutch craftsman. Gradually, Michael and London begin to renew their lives:

> It was true, they were going to rebuild London. Master Haas was right. He was right about most things, and Michael was beginning to understand some of them.
>
> Even change. Always there was change, there

was no preventing it and no undoing it, either—
and all arrangements were temporary. Everything
changed except one's courage. But as long as that
remained, a person—or even a city—could look
ahead.[22]

This is an absorbing, authentic story of London
during disaster. The narrative fairly tumbles
along from one event to another. It is long, but
the story bears the burden of its research easily
and lightly.

Leon Garfield writes with similar excitement
about life in England during the eighteenth century. While he captures the flavor of the times
and vividly describes the grim social conditions
of the poor, he does not include any known
historical events. Rather, his books have a
Dickensian flavor compounded of violence, suspense, and intrigue. *Smith* is the story of a 12-
year-old pickpocket in the grimy, shadow-filled
underworld of eighteenth-century London. He is
witness to the murder of the man whom he has
just robbed of his possessions, which consisted
of only one document—and Smith cannot read.
The rest of the plot deals with a whole cast of
unscrupulous characters who seek the document
and its promise of buried treasure. *Devil-in-the-Fog*
also contains a rich mixture of adventure and
mystery. It is the story of 14-year-old George
Treet, eldest son of a family of strolling players.
The family appears very happy except when the
Stranger in Black visits them twice a year and
fixes a cold uncanny stare on George. Finally,
George is told that he is not the Treets' son but
is the son of a rich nobleman. George goes to
his new home inhabited by unfriendly servants,
a cold ironical mother, a dying father, a monstrous uncle, and a feeling of something sinister
waiting for him in the fog. *Jack Holborn* is also
a story of a young orphan seeking his identity.
He stows away on the *Charming Molly*, but the
ship is attacked by pirates. Jack endures bloody
battles, a terrible shipwreck, marches through the
sodden jungles of Africa, and witnesses the horrors of a slave market and a murder trial at Old
Bailey in London. Sam, too, is seeking to discover
his origins in the story, *The Sound of Coaches*. The
opening paragraph is typical of Garfield's ability

to create an eerie scene and set the mood for his
story:

Once upon a winter's night when the wind blew
its guts out and a fishy piece of the moon scuttled
among the clouds, a coach came thundering down
the long hill outside of Dorking. Its progress was
wild, and the coachman and his guard rocked from
side to side as if the maddened vehicle was struggling to rid itself of them before going on to hell
without benefit of advice.[23]

There is no doubt that these are exaggerated,
swashbuckling tales, yet Garfield is a masterful
storyteller. The larger-than-life drama reminds
one of the Gothic novels of Joan Aiken. In contrast to Aiken's books, however, Garfield provides a real eighteenth-century setting. Certainly,
readers would get a feel for the times; its cruelty
to children, the poor, and prisoners; its lawless-
ness; and its daily life.

Rupert Hatton's Story by Norah Lofts also provides a feeling for an historical period over and
above specific historical events. Her attention to
the details of daily life in England in the seventeenth century also reminds one of Dickens. The
book is the story of Rupert Hatton's obsession
to play the violin against his father's wishes, and
the disaster that follows.

Another story of a boy who was determined
to become a musician is *Young Mark: The Story
of a Venture* by E. M. Almedingen. Based on notes
of the journey undertaken by the author's great-
great grandfather, this is one of the few stories
of early Russia for English-speaking children.
Young Mark had a magnificent voice and was
dissatisfied with life on his father's horse farm
in the Ukraine. He did not want to become a
monk, where training could be easily obtained,
because he felt he would be owned by the
church. He therefore sets out on a long adventurous journey to the great city of St. Petersburg
to try to win the favor of the Hetman, the
Tsarina's "unofficial" husband. This Count is also
from the Ukraine and Mark hopes to obtain his
favor and the Tsarina's support. Mark finally
does get to St. Petersburg, and after considerable
disappointment, meets the Count by chance and

[22]Eloise Jarvis McGraw. *Master Cornhill* (New York: Atheneum, 1973), p. 204.

[23]Leon Garfield. *The Sound of Coaches,* illustrated by John
Lawrence (New York: Viking, 1974).

earns favor as a singer. He later achieves an almost legendary career. *Katia* is the story of the author's great-aunt nearly one hundred years later, between 1834 and 1842. It presents a splendid look at the privileged class in Czarist Russia. The contrast between Uncle Nicholas' gay and winning treatment of the children in the family and his harsh discipline of the peasants provides an interesting insight into the causes of future revolution. These are well-written books with strong stories in their own right.

The French Revolution provides the setting for a book for older children titled *The Rebel* by Hester Burton. Stephen is the young rebel—fiery, hot-tempered, and idealistic. He and his friends publish a radical student newspaper while he is at Oxford in England. This infuriates his professors and the uncle who has been his guardian since his parents died. Stephen's sympathy for the exploited poor both in England and France takes him to France just as the Revolution erupts in its full and shocking violence. Stephen is in perfect sympathy with the Revolutionaries, although he feels some revulsion when he sees the naked and beheaded bodies of the Palace's Swiss guards. Then Stephen observes a "royalist" peasant being tortured and taunted on the rack, and his sense of justice leads him to interfere. As a result of this, Stephen is thrown in prison. He is rescued only because a Frenchman at his trial thinks he might make a useful spy in England. Once home in England Stephen is filled with shame and disgrace, and nearly goes mad. He is taken in by his former schoolmaster, who directs his idealism into teaching the urban poor. The prime irony of the story is made clear—those who set about to correct injustices may create more injustices of their own. While Hester Burton's historical novels are usually related to the social problems of the day, they are well-written imaginative stories that are never overpowered by their messages. Stephen's history is continued in *Riders of the Storm,* where once again he is in the eye of turbulence as he starts a new kind of school—a free school for the children of the poor. Another fine novel by Burton is *Beyond the Weir Bridge,* which tells the story of three firm friends growing up in an England torn by civil war and religious strife. It is no ordinary friendship, for one of the boys is the son of a Roundhead; while

another comes from a Royalist family; and Richenda, who is loved by both, has espoused the treasonable faith of the Quakers. Burton's novels make demands on the reader, but they are well worth the effort.

Stories of the New World

THE EXPLORERS

Most children's books about the early explorers are biographical. However, Betty Baker has told the dramatic story of the epic journey through the American South, West Florida, and Mexico by Cabeza de Vaca and three other Spaniards in her book titled *Walk the World's Rim.* The story is primarily that of Esteban, a black slave of one of the Spaniards, and Chakoh, an Avavare Indian boy who accompanies the men on their long trek. Chakoh is faced with conflicting values when he discovers that Esteban, his friend, is a slave. For among the Indians a slave is a man without honor, a man who has allowed himself to be captured. And yet this slave is the only one of the four Spaniards who *has* honor. Only when Chakoh sees his friend forfeit his life for others does he understand the true meaning of courage and honor and realize that slavery, rather than the slave, is to be despised. This fictional account of de Vaca's long journey is based upon the same source materials as the biography by Maia Wojciechowska titled *Odyssey of Courage;* yet the interpretation is different indeed. A comparison of the two books would be most worthwhile.

In *A Stranger and Afraid,* Baker has told the story of the Indians' first contacts with the Spanish explorers. From the terraces of Cicuye Pueblo, the Indians watched with excitement and fear as the "strangers riding monsters" approached. However, for young Sopete, the visit of the Spaniards is a source of hope as well as fear. Taken prisoner when their Wichita village was raided, he and his little brother Zabe have lived at the pueblo for three years. His brother has adjusted to the way of life of the pueblo-dwellers, but Sopete still yearns to return to his family lodge on the plains. The arrival of the Spaniards does provide the way, for he is given to Coronado to serve as his guide. Based on the actual records of Coronado's expeditions of

1540–1542, this story is told with sensitivity and understanding from the point of view of Sopete, the Indian guide.

In *The King's Fifth*, Scott O'Dell has related the story of the Conquistadores' search for gold in the New World. Six men and Zia, an Indian girl, their guide and interpreter, have left Coronado's summer camp to search for the golden cities of Cibola. Only Esteban de Sandoval returns to tell their story in a series of flashbacks as he stands trial for having defrauded the King of Spain of his rightful share of one-fifth of the treasure. His story is the age-old tale of the greed of men and what they will sacrifice to the lust for gold— blood, honor, sanity, and life itself. Only when he realizes that he is responsible for the death of his friend, Father Francisco, does Esteban come to his senses and dispose of the gold in such a way that he prevents anyone from having it. In prison, he is at last free from the evil that had nearly cost him his sanity and the love of Zia. Honor and greed are contrasted in this complex but powerful story.

COLONIAL AMERICA

All children in the United States know the story of the Pilgrims and the first Thanksgiving. Many informational books tell us what these people did, but there are few records that tell how the Pilgrims felt about what they did. *The Thanksgiving Story* by Alice Dalgliesh details the life of one family on the *Mayflower*, including their hardships on the voyage and during their first winter. It tells, too, of joy in the arrival of their new baby, of spring in their new home, of planting, harvest, and giving thanks. The large stylized pictures by Helen Sewell capture the spirit of American primitive paintings. Meadowcroft's books, *The First Year*, describes the hardships of the Pilgrims in a way that makes them real people to 7- and 8-year-olds. Two books by Hays, *Christmas on the Mayflower* and *Pilgrim Thanksgiving*, are enjoyed by this same age group. Simple and attractive illustrations enrich both these texts. Only in *John Billington, Friend of Squanto* by Clyde Bulla does any one Pilgrim assume much individuality, however. Young John Billington is always in trouble and is considered the bad boy of the colony, but he is instrumental in effecting a friendship between the settlers and the Cape Cod Indians. Younger readers enjoy this simple, straightforward account of mischief in Plymouth.

According to Love Brewster, John Brewster's young son, all of the Billingtons were a trial to the Piligrims. *I Sailed on the Mayflower* by Pilkington is the young boy's quite candid account of the *Mayflower* voyage and the first year in a new land. Love describes their seemingly endless weeks at sea. He tells about their cramped quarters, and how they had to take turns sleeping because there were only half as many bunks as people. When they finally landed at Plymouth on a cold and dreary day in December, Love went along with the exploration party to find a suitable place to settle. He describes many hardships in their first months on land. Sickness strikes the settlement and the time of the "Great Dying" comes. Many of Love's close friends die, but work goes on just the same. The day-to-day activities of the settlers, as seen through the eyes of a young boy, make fascinating reading.

One of the liveliest stories about the Pilgrims is *Constance: A Story of Early Plymouth* by Patricia Clapp. Written in the form of a diary, the story of Constance Hopkins, daughter of Stephen Hopkins, begins in November of 1620 on the deck of the *Mayflower* and ends seven years later with her marriage in Plymouth to Nicholas Snow. Constance describes the grim first winter at Plymouth with its fear of the Indians, the deaths of many of the colonists, and the difficulties with the English backers of the settlement. The device of a diary allows the author to use first-person narrative, which creates an immediate identification of the reader with Constance. An excellent romance, this story reminds one of *The Witch of Blackbird Pond* by Speare, but is all the more fascinating for being the story of real people. It could be read in conjunction with Margaret Hodges' authentic biography, *Stephen Hopkins, Portrait of a Dissenter*; the latter part of this story of Constance's father covers the same time period as does *Constance*.

The Puritans soon forgot their struggle for religious freedom as they persecuted others who did not follow their beliefs or ways. Older girls will thoroughly enjoy the superb story of *The Witch of Blackbird Pond* written by Elizabeth Speare. Flamboyant, high-spirited Kit Tyler was a misfit in the Puritan household of her aunt and stern-faced uncle. For Kit was as different from her colorless cousins as the bleak barren shore of Wethersfield, Connecticut, differed from the shimmering turquoise bay of Barbados that had been her home for sixteen years. Before Kit ever landed on shore, she had cast suspicion on herself by diving overboard to rescue a small child's doll. Only witches were supposed to know how to swim in New England in the 1680s! The only place in which Kit feels any peace or freedom is in the meadows near Blackbird Pond. And it is here that she meets the lonely bent figure of Quaker Hannah, regarded as a witch by the colonists. Here, too, Kit meets Nathaniel Eaton, the sea captain's son, with his mocking smile and clear blue eyes. Little Prudence, whose doll Kit has rescued, also comes to the sanctuary in the meadows. One by one, outraged townspeople put the wrong things together and the result is a terrifying witch hunt and trial. The story is fast-paced and the characters are drawn in sharp relief against a bleak New England background that shows a greening of promise for spring and for Kit at the close of this magnificent story.

Although the subject is the same, the tone of *Tituba of Salem Village* by Petry is as forbidding as the rotten eggs found on the steps of the bleak parsonage the day that the Reverend Samuel Parris, his family and slaves, John and Tituba, arrived in Salem Village in 1692. Tituba, too, had come from sunny Barbados and then been sold as a slave to a self-seeking, pious minister. The fact that Tituba was both a slave and a Negro made her particularly vulnerable to suspicion and attack from the obsessed witch hunters in Salem. A sense of foreboding, mounting terror, and hysteria fill this story of great evil done in the name of God. A comparison of *The Witch of Blackbird Pond* and *Tituba of Salem Village* would provoke much critical thinking by mature readers.

Sophia Scrooby Preserved by Martha Bacon is another story of a slave during the Colonial Period. This is the intriguing chronicle of a small daughter of "the lesser chieftain of an African tribe," who is taken into slavery and then sold to a well-to-do-family of New Haven, Connecticut, as a companion to their intractable daughter, Prudence. Sophia (or Pansy as she has been nicknamed on board ship) is a gifted singer and marvelously intelligent, having taught herself to read. The Scroobys are Tories, and lose all their money following the Revolution. Sophia is taken away along with the foreclosure of their house and lands. Resold once again, she falls into the hands of pirates and is stowed away in the voodoo swamps of Louisiana with another slave girl and an English sea captain. This group eventually escape and make their way to the captain's family in London, where Sophia becomes the darling of their social circle because of her wit and talent. On a visit to Drury Lane she discovers her singing master from New Haven, who takes her back to New England where they are reunited with the Scroobys. With some complicated legal maneuverings dependent on the fact that the pirate who last bought her was Spanish and had been hanged, Sophia finds she is no longer a slave. Written in an exaggerated dramatic style, the book is imitative of the romantic novels of the eighteenth century.

After the Colonial Period, the westward drive began. One settler in particular has been immortalized for children of 7 and 8 by Alice Dalgliesh in her popular book, *The Courage of Sarah Noble.* This is the true and inspiring story of 8-year-old Sarah, who accompanies her father into the wilderness to cook for him while he builds a cabin for their family. Many times Sarah has to remind herself of her mother's final words to her when she left home: "Keep up your courage, Sarah Noble!" Sarah has reason to remember when she hears the wolves howl outside the campfire, or when alone one day she is suddenly surrounded by Indian children. The real test of her courage is faced when her father tells her that he must leave her with Tall John, a friendly Indian, while he returns to Massachusetts for the rest of the family. Symbolic of Sarah's courage is the cloak that Sarah's mother had fastened around her just before she left home. When her family are finally reunited in their new home in the wilderness, Sarah is secure in the knowledge that she has "kept up her courage."

This book might be compared with Jean Fritz's poignant story of lonely 10-year-old Ann Hamilton, who was the only girl in the wilderness of early western Pennsylvania. Ann kept a diary filled with her longing for her Cousin Margaret and the girl-fun she had enjoyed on the other side of the Allegheny Mountains in Gettysburg. The title of this book, *The Cabin Faced West*, characterizes Ann's father's attitude toward the family's new adventure. They were not to look back to the past, but forward; and so he built the cabin facing west. Ann grows to hate the word "someday," as she hears it again and again. Someday she would have books to read; someday they would have windows in the cabin; and someday there would be a special occasion to use the linen tablecloth and the lavender flowered plates that her mother kept in her chest. All the "somedays" seemed so very far away to Ann. At last, however, a special occasion does happen. George Washington stops at the Hamilton cabin for dinner. Ann wears ribbons in her hair and sets the table in the way she has longed to do. This final episode is based upon fact and really happened to Ann Hamilton, who was the author's great-great-grandmother.

Marguerite de Angeli is known for her many books about religious or regional minorities. Some of these have an historical background. *Elin's Amerika* describes the life of children in the settlement of New Sweden on the Delaware in 1648. The unique contributions of Swedish pioneers are emphasized throughout the story. *Skippack School* is the story of Eli Shrawder, who came from across the sea to make a home in the Mennonite Settlement on the Skippack River in Pennsylvania. Eli was a mischievous lad who preferred to go fishing, chase squirrels, and carve wood rather than go to school. However, with a schoolmaster such as Christopher Dock, who is remembered in the history of Germantown as one of the most beloved and farseeing schoolmasters in America, Eli soon mended his ways and found himself anxious to go to school.

Indian raids instigated by the French were of grim concern to the Dutch settlers living in the Hudson Valley in 1756. In *The Matchlock Gun*, Walter D. Edmonds tells the true story of the Van Alstyne family. Hearing that the Indians are raiding Dutch homes, Teunis, the sturdy Dutch father, is summoned to watch for marauding Indians. Before leaving, he takes the great matchlock gun down from the wall and shows young Edward how to fire it. When the Indians do come, Edward's mother gives the command to fire the matchlock gun. The shot kills the

Indians, but does not save the mother from a flying tomahawk that pierces her shoulder. Edward drags his unconscious mother from the step of the burning cabin and waits with Trudy for their father to return with the militia. When Teunis rides in with his friends, he finds his wife still unconscious, the baby asleep, and Edward with the matchlock gun in his lap aimed at three dead Indians.

This is much more than an exciting adventure story. The characters are very real and true to life. Readers sense the fear and anxiety of the parents when they hear of the Indian raid. After their father had gone, the children go to bed in the loft. Their mother is alone downstairs and fear seems to fill the silence in the tiny cabin:

> There was only the note of the wind in the chimney and the feeling of it on the roof, like a hand pressed down out of darkness. It was easy to think of it passing through the wet woods, rocking the bare branches where only the beech trees had leaves to shake.[24]

This story, which won the Newbery Award in 1941, has since been criticized for presenting the Indians as bloodthirsty savages and for having a child shoot them. Obviously, this true story is told from the colonists' point of view. Other stories representing the Indian point of view will be discussed in the section on American Indians.

Longfellow immortalized "Paul Revere's Ride" in his famous long poem, but most Americans do not know of another dramatic ride that was made to warn the leaders of the revolution of the approach of Tarleton's Raiders. Gail Haley has told the tale of *Jack Jouett's Ride* in a stunning picture book illustrated with bold linoleum cuts. The year is 1781 and Thomas Jefferson, Patrick Henry, Benjamin Harrison, and Thomas Nelson—all signers of the Declaration of Independence and members of the Virginia Legislature—were gathered at Charlottesville. Jack Jouett was sitting in the moonlight outside the Cuckoo Tavern when he saw Tarleton's Raiders and guessed their mission. Mounting his fine horse, Sallie, he rode forty miles by moonlight through brush and brambles to spread the alarm.

[24] Walter D. Edmonds. *The Matchlock Gun*, illustrated by Paul Lantz (New York: Dodd, 1941), p. 14.

Jack Jouett, a Southern Paul Revere, warns Jefferson of the approach of Tarleton's Raiders. Bold linoleum cuts establish the authentic background of Monticello.

From *Jack Jouett's Ride* by Gail E. Haley. Copyright © 1973 by Gail E. Haley. Reprinted by permission of The Viking Press, Inc.

When he reached his father's inn, The Swan, where the men were staying, he found that General Stevens had been wounded and was too weak to ride far. Jack put on a fresh uniform and borrowed his father's swiftest horse to lead the Tarleton men astray, while General Stevens slipped away in an old dark cloak. It would be interesting to share this story with one of the many fine illustrated versions of *Paul Revere's Ride* (*see* Chapter 6) and have children speculate as to why Paul's ride is so much better known than Jack Jouett's. They might discover something of the lasting power of poetry in their discussion. Another little-known story of the American Revolution is that of a spunky young girl named Tempe Wick. When 10,000 Revolutionary soldiers spent the winters of 1780 and 1781 in New Jersey, Temperance Wick and her family helped to feed and clothe them. But then the soldiers mutinied and turned against their captains, even stealing from the very farmers who had helped them. When they tried to take Tempe's horse, Bon, Tempe hid her in the bedroom for three days. Finally, when a soldier demanded to search the house, the feisty Tempe threw him out in the snow. This humorous legend of the Revolutionary War is told by Patricia Lee Gauch in *This Time, Tempe Wick?*

As boys and girls in the middle grades read *The Scarlet Badge* by Wilma Pitchford Hays, they may learn that there was justification for different points of view concerning the American Revolu-

A spunky young girl prevents mutinous Revolutionary soldiers from taking her horse by hiding it in her bedroom!

Reprinted by permission of Coward, McCann & Geoghegan, Inc., from *This Time, Tempe Wick?* by Patricia Lee Gauch. Illustrations copyright © 1974 by Margot Tomes.

tion. Rob Roberts was a Virginian, and fiercely proud of the colony in which his forebears had lived for more than 150 years. Now the flames of the revolution blazed, and the Roberts family could no longer hope for a peaceful settlement of the wrongs imposed on the Colonies by King George III; they had to choose between the Rebels and the Loyalists. They made their choice, and Rob soon learned the price to be paid—the courage needed to stand fast in an unpopular cause. In a world turned upside down he saw revolution and rebellion become patriotism, loyalty to the king called treason, and friends and neighbors become strangers and enemies. Well-documented, this book from the Colonial Williamsburg Press will help children see the Revolution in a different perspective and value the importance of standing up for what one believes to be right.

My Brother Sam Is Dead by the Colliers tells of conflicting loyalties within a family and the injustices that are always inflicted upon the innocent in time of war. Sam is the only member of his Connecticut family who is fighting for the rebel cause. Ironically, it is Sam who is falsely accused of stealing his own cattle and is executed as an example of General Putnam's discipline. No one will believe the real facts of the case, for despite Sam's excellent war record, his family were Tories. This story, which was an Honor Book for the Newbery Award, takes an honest look at the injustices of all war—even the American Revolution.

In her story *Early Thunder*, Jean Fritz describes the events of the year 1775 as the first rumblings of the coming storm of the Revolutionary War. Fourteen-year-old Daniel adopts his father's loyalty to the king. Daniel hates the growing violence in Salem and the activities of the rowdy Liberty Boys who creep up on Tory porches and distribute their "Liberty Gifts" of garbage or manure. Yet, as the year passes, he becomes equally disillusioned by the British attitude. Finally, Daniel knows where his loyalties lie when a confrontation occurs between the British troops and the people of his town. This is an authentic story based upon facts. Daniel's conflict is made believable by showing justified reasons for supporting both causes and for hating each side. The characters are well realized and the

theme of conflicting loyalties will help children see that issues in war are seldom clearcut.

Rebecca's War by Ann Finlayson is a fast-paced story about the occupation of Philadelphia under General Howe. Told from the point of view of Rebecca, who is just 14, the reader receives a clear picture of what it must have been like to have the British troops not only in charge of your city but billeted in your house. *Redcoat in Boston* by the same author shows pre-Revolutionary Boston through the eyes of a British soldier. Thrust into the tensions of the times, Harry grows increasingly confused about the lines between his duty as a soldier and his obligations as a human being. The characters are well developed and the problems of defining black and white in a gray world are thoughtfully presented.

Leonard Wibberly has written a series of four books about the Revolutionary War—*John Treegate's Musket, Peter Treegate's War, Sea Captain from Salem,* and *Treegate's Raiders*. John Treegate was a solid citizen of Boston who had fought for his king and country in the Battle of Quebec on the Plains of Abraham. He was loyal to his British king, and had taught his son Peter to be loyal, too. However, he could not tolerate a country that marched armed troops of 700 men through a peaceful countryside to seize two men. John and Peter Treegate, father and son, arm themselves for the battle against the British that will go down in history as the Battle of Bunker Hill. The first year of the Revolution as seen through Peter's eyes is recorded in *Peter Treegate's War.* In *The Sea Captain from Salem*, Captain Manly is sent on a mission by Benjamin Franklin in order to convince the French that the Americans are capable of winning battles at sea. Manly cruises around the British Isles attacking British ships, sinking them or taking them as prizes. The final book of the series, *Treegate's Raiders,* describes the Revolution in the South in the highlands of the Carolinas. This story ends with the surrender of Cornwallis at Yorktown.

Probably no story of the American Revolution for children is better known than the fine juvenile novel, *Johnny Tremain* by Esther Forbes. Johnny Tremain is a silversmith's apprentice, a conceited, cocky young lad who is good at his trade and knows it. The other apprentices are resentful of his overbearing manner and determined to get even with him. Their practical joke has disastrous results, and Johnny's hand is maimed for life. Out of a job and embittered, Johnny joins his friend, Rab, and becomes involved in pre-Revolutionary activities. As a dispatch rider for the Committee of Public Safety he meets such men as Paul Revere, John Hancock, and Samuel Adams. Slowly, gradually, Johnny regains his self-confidence and overcomes his bitterness. Rab is killed in the first skirmish of the Revolution, and Johnny is crushed, but not completely. Somehow, this greatest of blows toughens his fiber and he becomes a man—a man of fortitude and courage, a new man of a new nation.

Tree of Freedom by Rebecca Caudill describes the Revolution from the backwoods settlers' point of view. In the year 1780, 13-year-old Stephanie Venable made the long trek from North Carolina to Kentucky where her family had a tract of rich new land waiting for them. Each child of the family is allowed to take one prized possession. Stephanie takes an apple seed because that is what her grandmother had brought from France. She plants the little tree by the side of their cabin door and calls it her "Tree of Freedom," a symbol of the new way of life the pioneering families mean to have in this fresh green land. Kentucky is full of promise and hardship. After their cabin is built and their crops are planted, a Britisher arrives with rival claims to their land. Now the Revolution becomes more important than ever, for the legality of their claim depends upon belonging to a new nation. One by one their father, Noel, and Jonathan go to serve their country, leaving the back-breaking care of the crops to resourceful Stephanie, her mother, and young Rob. Always, Stephanie has time to prune and care for her little tree. When her family returns from war and the quarrel between Noel and her father is resolved, Stephanie tells herself:

> Everything was all right then. . . . A body couldn't kill freedom any more than he could kill a tree if it had good, strong roots growing, she reckoned. No matter what passed over the land and possessed the people, you couldn't kill freedom if somebody gave it uncommon good care.[25]

[25]Rebecca Caudill. *Tree of Freedom,* illustrated by Dorothy Morse (New York: Viking, 1949), p. 263.

AMERICAN INDIANS

The point of view of historical fiction that portrays American Indians is gradually changing. In earlier stories the Indians are seen as cruel, bloodthirsty savages attacking small groups of helpless settlers. The provocation for the attacks is seldom given. Thus, in Edmonds' story, *The Matchlock Gun,* the reader can only guess the Indians' reasons for wounding Edward's mother and burning their cabin. In Field's *Calico Bush,* the Indians seem equally cruel as they burn the settler's house. Other stories, however—such as *Moccasin Trail* by McGraw or *The Year of the Three-legged Dear* by Clifford—portray Indians in more three-dimensional terms, showing their amazing generosity in some situations, their integrity, and the provocation for many of their actions. Finally, in such fine books as Baker's *Killer-of-Death, Sing Down the Moon* by O'Dell, and Hickman's *The Valley of the Shadow,* the shocking story of the white man's destruction of the Indians' way of life is told.

Many stories that present fully-developed Indian characters are of white captives who observe and gradually come to appreciate the Indian way of life. Seven- and 8-year-old boys and girls thoroughly enjoy Anne Colver's *Bread and Butter Indian.* Too young to understand her parents' fear of Indians, Barbara befriends a hungry Indian, offering him the bread and butter with which she was having a tea party for her imaginary friends. Although they cannot speak, they look for each other every day, and always Barbara shares her sandwich with him. While following her pet crow one evening at dusk, Barbara is kidnapped by a strange Indian. How the "bread and butter" Indian comes to her rescue is the climax of a warm, exciting story. Garth Williams' illustrations portray the simple joys of a pioneer child as she listens to her mother tell a story, makes new friends at a picnic, and plays dress-up in her aunt's fine clothes. Williams' illustrations of Barbara's "bread and butter Indian" are as warm and reassuring as this story of an incident that really happened. Another popular tale of captivity is *Indian Captive, The Story of Mary Jemison* by Lois Lenski. This is the highly fictionalized account of a real 12-year-old girl who was captured by the Senecas and taken to live with them. The theme of the story is the basic conflict between Indian and white culture. Mary is treated kindly by the Indians as they adopt her into their tribe, but she is determined to remember her white ways. Almost without realizing it, she begins to understand the Indians and to love them. When the time comes for her to decide whether she will remain with them or go with the English, she chooses to stay.

A story of Indian capture for more mature readers is *Calico Captive* by Elizabeth Speare. Based upon real people and events, this is a fictionalized account of the experiences of young Miriam Willard, who had just been to her first dance when she was captured by the Indians. Her sister, brother-in-law, three children, and a neighbor are captured with her, taken to Montreal, and sold as slaves. Their hardships and ordeals are taken from a diary kept by a real "captive" in 1754. Speare tells this story with her usual fine characterizations and attention to authentic detail.

Two stories of whites brought up as Indians lend themselves well to purposes of comparison: *Moccasin Trail* by Eloise McGraw and *The Light in the Forest* by Conrad Richter. In the first book Jim Heath is rescued from a grizzly bear by the Crow Indians and brought up to think and feel like an Indian. When the braves return with a blond scalp, just the color of his mother's hair, Jim has a sudden longing to be with his own kind, and leaves the Indians to search for some whites. He joins forces with a trapper and learns some of the white man's ways, before his long-lost family contacts him. His mother and father have both died, but the three younger children have come West to claim land and to find him. Jim pitches in to help the family make a home, but at the same time he clings to his Indian ways. His long braids, fancy feathers, and trapping smell are offensive to his sister, Sally; puzzling to his brother, Jonnie; and acceptable only to his little brother, Daniel, who worships and admires everything he does. Jim longs for the sensible Indian ways; but more than that, he wants to be accepted by all his family. Everything that he does seems to be wrong. He steals a horse for Jonnie—the grandest present a Crow Indian can give—and is rebuffed in front of the other settlers and made to return the horse. A loner, Jim de-

cides to leave. Daniel is heartbroken and runs away only to be captured by the Umpqua Indians, who keep slaves. Jim rescues him but knows that for his sake and his brother's he must forsake the moccasin trail forever. He symbollically cuts his braids and is at peace with himself and his family at last.

Richter's book was written for adults but has been enjoyed by older children. In this story True Son, a white boy reared by an Indian chief, is forced to return to his original home. His love and loyalty for his Indian parents and his rejection of the white man's civilization arouse inevitable conflicts. At last, he runs away and rejoins the Indians. But he betrays the tribe when at the last moment he will not take part in tricking a boatload of whites into an Indian ambush. Instead of calling for help as planned, he sees a small boy who reminds him of his brother, and he shouts a warning. Condemned to die by the Indians, he is rescued by his Indian father who imposes the most severe punishment of all—banishment from the tribe and the forest forever. Forced back to the white man's trail, the boy, who truly felt he was Indian, faces unbearable loneliness:

> Ahead of him ran the rutted road of the whites. It led, he knew, to where men of their own volition constrained themselves with heavy clothing like harness, where men chose to be slaves to their own or another's property and followed empty and desolate lives far from the wild beloved freedom of the Indian.[26]

In her book *The Valley of the Shadow*, Janet Hickman has portrayed the grim story of a group of peace-loving Moravian missionaries and their Indian converts, who in 1781 were caught in the midst of the conflict between the Colonists and the British. The story is told from the point of view of Tobias, whose father is the stern Indian helper to Brother Heckewelder. Lonely, skinny, and feeling that he can never live up to his father's expectations, Tobias would have been miserable except for his friendship with Thomas and his family. The Delaware Chief comes to warn them that if they stay in their villages the Long

[26]Conrad Richter. *The Light in the Forest* (New York: Knopf, 1953), p. 179.

Richard Cuffari has painted a dramatic cover for this authentic story of two survivors of a grim massacre of Christianized Indians by the frontier militia.

From *The Valley of the Shadow* by Janet Hickman. Jacket design by Richard Cuffari. Copyright © 1974 by Janet Hickman. Used by permission of Macmillan Publishing Co., Inc.

Knives will come. But among the basic tenets of the Moravian faith are non-violence and helpfulness, so the congregation decides to stay and remain neutral. The Long Knives do come and trick the Indians into giving up their knives and guns. Then the Indians are herded together, put into two buildings, and systematically massacred. Because Tobias is small, he is able to crawl through a cellar window and escape. In the woods he meets Thomas, who had been scalped and left for dead.

This is a true story based upon the records of the Moravian missionaries. Two boys did escape from the massacre in the manner told in the story. Bitter and horrendous as the facts are, the narration fills them with meaning and feeling.

The characters are fully realized; the conflict between Tobias and his father is believable; and the language richly reflects the life and natural surroundings of the Indians. Grim as this story is, it is not one of despair. For just as Old Tobias had good hopes for his son, the reader is left with good hopes for the pitiful band of remaining Indians, who had, indeed, passed through their valley of the shadow.

The Year of the Three-legged Deer by Eth Clifford is the year 1819 along the Indiana frontier. The Revolution is over; Tecumseh is dead; and the Indian wars in that area have ceased. Life seems good to trader Jesse Benton, his Indian wife, a Lenni Lenape, and their two children—14-year-old Takawsu and Chilili, the beautiful and sensitive young daughter. The spring of the year is notable for two events: Takawsu brings home a wounded fawn for his sister to raise with the help of a pet wolf, and Takawsu's father purchases the freedom of Sakkaape, an educated black slave who had saved the boy's life. Then the bitter racial hatred of a few white men shatters the family's happiness and separates them forever. Sakkaape is kidnapped during an outdoor pioneer wedding by three men who want to resell him for two hundred dollars. While escaping through the woods, they come upon a small band of peaceful Indians and massacre them, mutilating their bodies to make it appear that other Indians are responsible. But they are apprehended and brought to trial. The men assume they will be freed, for no one would be convicted of murdering Indians, particularly on the basis of a black man's testimony. They had not counted on the growing sense of decency and honor among the settlers, however, and they become the first whites sentenced to hang for the killing of Indians. Unfortunately, they escape from jail and, having sworn vengeance on Jesse Benton, return to kill his only daughter. The men are caught and hanged, but Jesse's wife and son decide to go with the Indian tribes that are being moved to new lands in the West. Sakkaape, too, makes the choice to go where he will no longer be thought of as a slave, or even a freed slave, but as a man. Benton, who had been a friend to the Indians, the slave, and the settlers has now lost everything, except his land which he loved with such a passion that he could not leave it. This is far more than an Indian story, for it explores the very roots and depths of prejudice. Based upon many factual events, the story would be almost unbearable except for the Prologue which shows that Benton did rebuild his life, his house, and finally became a state senator in Indiana.

A moving story of Apache rivalry with the white man is paralleled by an inner story of conflict between two young boys in *Killer-of-Death* by Betty Baker. The long feud between the medicine man's son and Killer-of-Death quickly disappears when they see most of their people killed like rabbits at the feast the white trader has planned so carefully. Broken and disheartened, the remnants of the tribe are moved to a reservation. The missionary asks Killer-of-Death to send his son to the white man's school. For two days the father fasts and then goes to a hill on which stands a single pine tree split by lightning. He waits for the spirits to speak his name and to provide an answer. Finally, the sign comes in the brilliant dawn of the new day. Might there be a renewal of the people in the same way? Killer-of-Death makes his decision: He will send his son to school.

The creation stories of the Southwest Indians tell of "singing up the mountains," or creating them. Knowledge of these Indian legends makes the title of O'Dell's book, *Sing Down the Moon*, take on tragic significance. For this is the story of the Long Walk of the Navahos when they were chased out of their homes in the canyons and forced to walk some 300 miles to Fort Sumner, where they were held prisoners for nearly two years from 1863 to 1865. Over 1,500 Navahos died at Fort Sumner. Those who did not die lost the will to live, particularly the men of the tribe. This moving story is told from the point of view of Bright Morning, who lived up to her name and somehow maintained her hope for a better future. She tells her story beginning with the beautiful spring in Canyon de Chelly in 1864, when life seemed as full of promise as the blossoming fruit trees and new young lambs in the canyon. But her dreams are shattered, first by Spanish slaves who wound Tall Boy, the proud and handsome youth who was to be her husband. Then the United States sends Colonel Kit Carson and his forces to round up the Navahos and bring them to Fort Sumner. By burning their crops and

destroying their fruit trees they force the Navahos to surrender. Imprisonment maims Tall Boy's spirit as much as the Spaniard's bullet had mutilated his arm. Urged on by Bright Morning, however, the two do escape and return to a cave in their canyon. There, Bright Morning finds a ewe and her newborn lamb. Her young son reaches out to touch the lamb; at the same time Bright Morning symbolically steps on the spear which the son's father had made for him and breaks it. This is a haunting and beautiful story of the strength of the human spirit. Told in spare prose, it reflects the dignity of a people who have lived through tragic degradation.

In *Only Earth and Sky Last Forever* by Benchley, Dark Elk, a fictional character, moves through real events. Written for older children, this is the first-person account of a youth who wants only to live free and unshackled on the remaining Indian land and marry Lashuka. He has nothing to give for her, however, since his Cheyenne parents were killed by the "Blue Coats" and the Sioux parents who adopted him have become drunken "agency Indians." Dark Elk has no other choice than to join Crazy Horse's troops in order to prove himself a warrior worthy of Lashuka. He participates in Rosebud, Little Bighorn, and Custer's Last Battle. Jubilant with the knowledge that Long Hair and his men are "rubbed out," Dark Elk helps to pursue some of Major Reno's men who are hiding across the river. He discovers the damage done to one of the Indian camps, and finds that Lashuka is among the dead:

> . . . finally I turned away and went to the Oglala camp. The Cheyennes had nothing more for me, and with the Oglalas there was at least Crazy Horse, and freedom.
>
> If you could count that for anything; in little more than a year he was bayoneted to death by a reservation Bluecoat, while Little Big Man held his arms. After that I stopped trying for freedom, because it didn't seem to mean much. It means whatever the winner wants it to mean, and nothing more."[27]

It would be interesting to read this story with *Red Hawk's Account of Custer's Last Battle* by Paul

[27] Nathaniel Benchley. *Only Earth and Sky Last Forever* (New York: Harper & Row, 1972), p. 189.

Goble and Dorothy Goble, which juxtaposes a documentary description with a longer, fictionalized first-person account of a young participant in the battle. Both these books would help to bring the Indian point of view to young people today.

Mature readers will also enjoy the highly fictionalized biography of *Ishi, Last of His Tribe* by Theodora Kroeber. Most of the Yaha Indians of California had been killed or driven from their homes by the invading gold-seekers and settlers during the early 1900s. A small band of the tribe called Yahi resisted their fate by living in concealment. They covered every footprint, jumped from rock to rock, and cut tunnels in the underbrush; but everywhere it seemed the Saldu (white people) had come. One by one Ishi's family dies, and at last, he is the lone survivor of his tribe. Hungry and ill, he allows himself to be found in a corral outside Oroville. Haltingly, he tells his story to an anthropologist who takes him to live at the University of California's museum. Here he dwells happily for five years helping to record the language and ways of the Yahi world.

In 150 years the once proud and powerful Haidas, lords of the western waters of Canada, disappear. The people themselves are reduced to a mere handful. *Raven's Cry* by Christie Harris tells the dramatic story of these doomed people and their great heritage to the world—the art of the Haida:

"Critics don't quite believe Haida art," its modern disciple says. "It's so refined and highly evolved that they can't believe it emerged from an Indian culture."

After all, as the old fur traders told their shipmates, these were only savages; they hadn't fine feelings like civilized human beings.

Maybe a more enlightened generation will know better.[28]

It is hoped that such well-documented human stories about the American Indian may help to produce a more enlightened generation.

THE AMERICAN FRONTIER

No other period in United States history has been more dramatized by films and television than that of the westward movement of the American pioneer. For this reason even 7-year-olds ask for books about "the pioneers." One favorite for younger children is *Caroline and Her Kettle Named Maud* by Miriam E. Mason. Caroline is a pioneer tomboy who longs for a real gun for her birthday—like her seventeen uncles. Instead, she receives a copper kettle that proves just as effective as a gun in capturing the wolf that threatens the family cows.

Bread and Butter Journey by Anne Colver continues the narrative of the family first introduced in *Bread and Butter Indian*. In this story the family leaves the relative safety of their pioneer village and journeys by foot over the Alleghenies to find a new homestead in western Pennsylvania. The father has gone ahead and Barbara, her mother, and another family set off alone with Barbara's 15-year-old brother, Jonas, and Philip, a 22-year-old veteran of the Revolutionary War. Philip breaks his leg in an accident at Bedford, and the two women and three girls must continue their journey with only Jonas for their guide. Barbara hadn't wanted to go in the first place; she hates the long tedious journey, and mostly she resents her unsmiling brother, who goads them on and who has abandoned her favorite pony with the Indians because the animal had gone lame. The trip is beset with accidents and danger, including Philip's broken leg, Tess' infected ear, and the night an Indian boy tried to steal their horses. However, there are many good memories, too, of helpful folk along the way and peaceful Indians who protect their route beside the creek. Gradually, Barbara changes her viewpoint about her brother and the trip itself:

The whole journey had been the change, Barbara thought slowly. But where could she find the words to tell Papa about so many things? How could she say that home wasn't an old place or a new place but part of the journey?[29]

This is a very popular story with middle-graders. The fine black-and-white pictures by Garth Williams add to its appeal. Barbara's feelings about the journey could be compared to the way Ann Hamilton felt in *The Cabin Faced West* by Jean Fritz (*see* page 489).

[28]Christie Harris. *Raven's Cry*, illustrated by Bill Reid (New York: Atheneum, 1966), p. 193.

[29]Anne Colver. *Bread and Butter Journey* (New York: Holt, Rinehart and Winston, 1970), p. 100.

Carolina's Courage by Elizabeth Yates tells of another journey at a later time in the development of the West. Carolina, her brother, Mark, and her father and mother leave their farm in New Hampshire to homestead in Nebraska. Each member of the family can take only one personal possession in the crowded covered wagon. Carolina chooses her beloved doll, Lydia-Lou, with her painted china face, black buttoned shoes, and layers of petticoats and party dresses. All across that endless prairie Lyddy is good company for Carolina. As they near their claim, rumors of unfriendly Indians stir their hearts with fear, and Carolina's father sits all night by the fire, his gun across his knees. But the night passes without incident and morning comes:

> It was good to be alive on such a morning. They had been walking into the future for four months. Now it seemed that the future was at last coming to meet them. Fears felt during the night had shrunk to daylight size, and the family talked together easily and naturally.[30]

However, the trip is not finished, for the family comes to an encampment of wagons waiting for an interpreter before going any further into Indian territory. Carolina finds a green, mossy place in the woods, quite perfect for a tea party with Lyddy. Startled by a noise, she looks up to see that an Indian girl carrying a doll made of rawhide has joined her. After they exchange dolls, the Indian girl makes many strange motions with her hands and darts away still holding Carolina's doll, Lyddy. Heartbroken about losing her one chosen possession, Carolina remembers that her father had said that pioneers must learn to share. She goes to bed without telling her family what has happened. That evening her parents find her asleep clutching the greasy Indian doll as closely as she had slept with Lyddy. When she pours out her story to her father, he slowly interprets the Indian girl's signs as promising a safe passage through the mountains. So with "Safe Conduct," as they named the Indian doll, sitting on Carolina's knees, the Putnams lead the wagon train. At different times during the day Indians ride down, circle the wagon, and point the way for the friend of the

---

[30]Elizabeth Yates. *Carolina's Courage*, illustrated by Nora S. Unwin (New York: Dutton, 1964), p. 64.

Indian chief's daughter who has a new china doll with many petticoats. Another story of pioneer life by Elizabeth Yates is *Sarah Whitcher's Story*. This is an amazing tale based upon recorded fact—a little girl is lost in the woods for over four days and is cared for by a large bear. A man in a town some thirty miles away hears of the lost child, goes to bed, and dreams that he sees her in a cave. He walks back to the settlement and leads the searchers to the cave, where they find Sarah, slightly dirty and berry-stained, but alive. This story is for far younger children, but it has many of the same elements of the miraculous that can be found in Eckert's *Incident at Hawk's Hill*, another true story of an animal caring for a lost child (*see* page 451).

White Bird by Clyde Bulla is the poignant tale of a little boy who was found floating down the river in a cradle that had fallen out of an overturned wagon. The baby is rescued by Luke Vail, a young man who had helped his harsh father to farm the poor land that was Half-Moon Valley. The baby was the only human being that the lonely Luke had ever loved. After his parents died and his neighbors left, Luke was alone in the valley. In his love and need for another, Luke became possessive and forbad John Thomas to have any outside contacts with the world. Then John Thomas found a wounded albino crow, and against Luke's wishes, helped it and nursed it back to health. How the white bird enlarged the whole of the boy's life makes for a fine story of pioneer life in the Tennessee country in the early 1800s. Bulla's writing style is as clean and as sparse in its descriptions as the solitude of Half-Moon Valley.

In *The Lone Hunt*, William Steele writes vividly of a boy's yearning to take a man's part in the last buffalo hunt held in Tennessee in 1810. Ever since his father died, Yance Caywood had had to help his mother with fetching, carrying, and hoeing, while his older brother did the plowing and hunting. At last, Yance is allowed to go on the buffalo hunt, taking along his well-loved hound dog, Blue. It is a long trail, and one by one the men drop out. When the snow begins, the last one turns back, but not Yance. His lone hunt through the wilderness takes courage, ingenuity, and fortitude. Yance kills his buffalo, but loses his dog to the frozen river. Pride in his accomplishment is overshadowed by his grief for his dog. Yance is grown up when he returns from the hunt.

Frontier living had its terror and horror, and Steele recreates it with authentic detail. In *The Year of the Bloody Sevens* 11-year-old Kelsey Bond decides to go west to Kentucky to join his father at Logan's Fort. He joins two "woodsies" for safety and companionship, but one day they are ambushed by Indians. Kel knows he should go to their aid but he can't make his legs move. When he does return to the campsite, he finds both "woodsies" dead. Kel runs away, but he brands himself as a coward. Even after he reaches the Fort and finds his father, the knowledge of his cowardice festers inside of him. At last, he tells his father, who reassures Kel that it took much courage for him to come to Kentucky. Kel had not thought he was brave, but decides: "Maybe the bravest things were the things you did without knowing you were being brave, without expecting other people to know you were brave."[31] Realism, excitement, and much backwoods wisdom characterize Steele's writing. His other pioneer stories include *Winter Danger, The Buffalo Knife, Tomahawks and Trouble, Flaming Arrows, Trail through Danger,* and *The Far Frontier.*

No books of historical fiction are more loved than the nine "Little House" books by Laura Ingalls Wilder. These stories describe the growing up of the Ingalls girls and the Wilder boys. In the first book of the series, *Little House in the Big Woods,* Laura is only 6-years old; the last three books—*Little Town on the Prairie, These Happy Golden Years,* and *The First Four Years*—tell of Laura's teaching career and her marriage. Based upon the author's own life, these books portray the hardships and difficulties of pioneer life in the 1870s and 1880s, and describe the fun and excitement that was also a part of daily living in those days. Throughout the stories the warmth and security of family love runs like a golden thread that binds the books to the hearts of their readers. There are floods, blizzards, grasshopper plagues, bears and Indians, droughts and the fear of starvation; but there is the wonderful Christmas when Laura receives her rag doll, the

A tender Christmas scene exemplifies the warmth and simple joy of pioneer living.

Illustration by Garth Williams from *Little House in the Big Woods* by Laura Ingalls Wilder. Pictures copyright © 1953 by Garth Williams. Reprinted by permission of Harper & Row, Publishers, Inc.

new house with real windows, trips to town, and dances. Best of all, there are the long winter evenings of firelight and the clear singing of Pa's fiddle. These mean love and security whether the home is in Wisconsin, the wild Kansas country, as described in *Little House on the Prairie,* in the Minnesota of *On the Banks of Plum Creek,* or *By the Shores of Silver Lake* in Dakota Territory. Children who read these books sense the same feelings of love and family solidarity experienced by Laura in the closing pages of *Little House in the Big Woods:*

> But Laura lay awake a little while, listening to Pa's fiddle softly playing and to the lovely sound of the wind in the Big Woods. She looked at Pa sitting on the bench by the hearth, the firelight gleaming on his brown hair and beard and glistening over

---

[31] William O. Steele. *The Year of the Bloody Sevens,* illustrated by Charles Beck (New York: Harcourt Brace Jovanovich, 1963), p. 184.

the honey-brown fiddle. She looked at Ma, gently rocking and knitting.

She thought to herself, "This is now."

She was glad that the cosy house, and Pa and Ma and the firelight and the music, were now. They could not be forgotten, she thought, because now is now. It can never be a long time ago.[32]

The last book of the series describes *The First Four Years* following Laura's and Manley's marriage in 1885. The manuscript for this story was found among Laura's papers after her death in 1957. Garth Williams has illustrated a uniform edition of all the books in the series. His black-and-white pictures capture the excitement and terror of many of the episodes in the books, but they also convey the tenderness, love, amusement, and courage that were necessary requisites to the life of the early settlers.

Another favorite book of pioneer days is *Caddie Woodlawn* by Carol Ryrie Brink. While this story takes place in the Wisconsin wilderness of the 1860s, it is primarily the story of the growing up of tomboy Caddie. She had been a frail baby, and so Caddie's father had persuaded her mother to allow her to be reared more freely than her older sister, Clara, who was restricted by the rules of decorum for young ladies. Caddie was free to run about the half-wild Wisconsin frontier with her two brothers. Their escapades and adventures read like a feminine *Tom Sawyer*. Caddie is a self-willed, independent spirit who is assured a memorable place in children's literature. A new edition of this classic pioneer story was published in 1973. The illustrations by Trina Schart Hyman picture Caddie as a spirited young girl.

In *Trouble River*, Betsy Byars has written a suspenseful story of pioneer life on the prairie. Dewey Martin is left alone with his dog and his grandmother when it is time for his mother to have a baby. His father thought it was quite safe to leave them, but he was not aware of the fact that a small band of Indians were raiding the countryside. Dewey and his dog frighten one Indian away from their cabin, but Dewey knows that the Indian will return with his friends in no time. In desperation, Dewey persuades his grandmother to escape by means of his homemade log raft. The old lady will only agree to go provided he puts her rocking chair on it! The rest of the story details their hazardous forty-mile journey down the shallow muddy river. They escape an attack by wolves, find their neighbor's cabin burned out, and somehow stay on the raft as they dash madly over the rapids to safety. Throughout it all, the old lady keeps telling Dewey dire tales of former Indian raids or issues directives to him on how to steer the raft. Despite the imminent danger, her constant monologue is very funny indeed.

Calvin Harper was the only survivor of a Comanche massacre in Weyman Jones' fine frontier story, *Edge of Two Worlds*. Calvin had been wandering for days on the Texas prairie with only the heat and the grasshoppers which somehow became confused in his dazed mind with the faces of the Indians that had attacked the wagon train. He stumbled upon the cave of the old and ill Cherokee, Sequoyah, who had as many reasons to distrust Calvin as the boy had to fear the Indian. But the two were drawn together by their mutual need of each other. As they continued their journey, their respect for each other grew. Calvin was at the edge of two worlds, the old Indian tells him, "a boy's world and a man's world." Whereas, Sequoyah had always lived in two worlds—white and Indian. "On the edge of two worlds. And where two worlds meet, they make a lonely place."[33] When Calvin once again set out to continue his trip to Boston to enter law school, he has left the world of his boyhood behind. *The Talking Leaf* by the same author is the fictionalized account of how Sequoyah achieved the first written language for the Cherokee. Both these books are carefully researched and beautifully written.

Richard Wormser has told the tale of the two worlds of Will Mesteno—half-black, half-Apache—in the book *The Black Mustanger*. The story takes place in Texas after the Civil War. The Rikers from Tennessee come out to Texas with hopes of making a living by branding wild cattle. Building a herd is hard work, but the Rikers are progressing until Mr. Riker breaks his

---

[32] Laura Ingalls Wilder. *The Little House in the Big Woods*, illustrated by Garth Williams (New York: Harper & Row, 1932), p. 238.

[33] Weyman Jones. *Edge of Two Worlds* (New York: Dial, 1968), p. 107.

leg. Then 13-year-old Dan Riker finds no one wants to help a former Yankee family. If it hadn't been for Will, the family would never have survived. He doctors Mr. Riker's leg and gives Dan a paying job. Later Dan becomes Will's partner. This unusual story of pioneer days in Texas reveals the prejudice that was rampant toward blacks and Union soldiers alike. It also pictures warm characters who are able to overcome such attitudes. Wormser has also written the story of a 13-year-old cattle driver in the 1870s titled *Ride a Northbound Horse.* This tells of the agonizing dry drive of Little Cav, who literally rode alone across the desert to drop water barrels at intervals for the drovers who would follow. These are fast-paced novels of a little-known era in the West.

The great westward trek continued as the frontier was pushed back further and further each year. The moving story of the Sager children is told by A. Rutgers van der Loeff in *Oregon at Last!* When both their parents die on the westward trail, the rest of the settlers want to divide the family of seven children among them, but they have not counted on the determination of 13-year-old John. When the men decide to go to California rather than tackle the difficult trail over the mountains to Oregon, John plans secretly with the rest of the children and they quietly steal away from camp. How they survive bears, fire, quicksand, and a walk of over one thousand miles of mountainous trails to reach Oregon is an incredible story.

THE CIVIL WAR ERA

Slavery

Many stories of the pre-Civil War period relate to slavery and the activities of the Underground Railroad, when people faced the moral issue of breaking laws out of their compassion for humankind. F. N. Monjo titled his easy-reading book *The Drinking Gourd*, after the "code song" that the slaves sang. The song was used to point the direction for escape by following the North Star, using the Big Dipper as a guide. The words to the song are included in this short story of how a young mischievous boy helps a family on their way to freedom. In Marguerite de Angeli's book, *Thee, Hannah!*, a young Quaker girl

helps a black mother and her child to safety. While Hannah was a Quaker, she did not willingly wear the clothes that were necessary to fulfill her family's religious expectations. She particularly despised her stiff, drab bonnet that did not have flowers and a brightly colored lining like that of her friend, Cecily. Yet, it was her bonnet that identified her as a Quaker and one who could be trusted to give aid to a runaway slave. Later, when the blacks are safe and tell Hannah this, Hannah's feelings toward her hated bonnet change. In *A Lantern in the Window*, Peter is not a Quaker but he learns all about Quaker activities in the Underground Railroad at his Uncle Eb's farm in Ohio. This is an exciting story written by the poet, Aileen Fisher. *Voices in the Night* by Rhoda W. Bacmeister details the part that a young girl plays in helping fugitive slaves make their escape.

In *Brady,* Jean Fritz tells the story of a very believable boy who discovers his father is an agent for the Underground Railway. His parents had not told Brady of their forbidden activities, for Brady just could not keep a secret. However, Brady, always curious, discovers the secret for himself. On the very night that had been set to transfer a slave to the next station, Brady's father's barn is burned, and his father suffers a broken leg during the fire. On his own, Brady carries out the plan for moving the slave and earns his father's respect. When his father hears of his son's resourcefulness, he asks for the family Bible and painstakingly writes the following inscription on the page reserved for significant events in family history:

> On this day the barn burned down and Brady Minton did a man's work.[34]

Meadowcroft's *By Secret Railway* is another popular story about the workings of the Underground Railway. David Morgan brings a young black boy home with him one day after he had gone down to the wharf to find a job. David's family welcome Jim, but he is with them only a short while. After Jim's freedom papers are destroyed, he is kidnapped and sold again as a slave. From runaway slaves, the Morgans learn

[34]Jean Fritz. *Brady*, illustrated by Lynd Ward (New York: Coward-McCann, 1960), p. 219.

that Jim is in Missouri. David is determined to rescue him and eventually finds him. The suspense is high when the boys are captured on their way home. They work their way out of their difficulties and finally reach Chicago, where Jim decides to stay with the Morgans.

In most of these stories of the Underground Railway the action is initiated by whites, while the character of the slaves is not developed. This is not true of Peter Burchard's story of one crucial day in the life of a young slave by the name of *Bimby*. It was to have been a happy day, for Bimby was going to help his friend Jesse take supplies to the white folks' picnic. Instead, Bimby learns from Jesse that their master is bankrupt and that all the slaves will have to be sold. And then Jesse is killed while racing his wagon with the younger slaves. Bimby decides to escape, even if he dies in the attempt, as his father had. Although Bimby's mother knows that she will never see him again, she gives Bimby information that may aid his flight to freedom. The story ends as Bimby sets out alone in Jesse's little boat to follow the Georgia coast south to Jacksonville in the hope of finding a larger ship from Boston, New York, or Philadelphia.

Thomas Fall has told the moving story of the friendship of a young Scottish indentured boy and a former slave in his book *Canalboat to Freedom*. Benja did not know that indenture was illegal when he became a "hoggee" for Captain Roach in return for his passage to America. It was Benja's exhausting and lonely job to walk miles along the towpaths each day leading the horses that pulled the canalboat. His only friend was the deckhand Lundius, a former slave, who patiently taught him the ways of nature and protected him from the bullying captain. Benja joins Lundius in helping two fugitive slaves to escape. One frightening morning Lundius loses his life, and Benja must carry out the escape of another slave with only the help of Kate and Mrs. Robbins. Heartsick at the loss of their loyal friend, Kate and Benja climb to the crest of the mountain and recall his goodness:

> They sat in silence—a strangely satisfying silence that was filled with Lundius and a sense of what they had learned from him. He had been a slave, treated as an animal, brutally disfigured by the

hands of men—and he had come into their lives and by his strength and gentleness had taught them to love.[35]

Jessie Bollier was a 13-year-old white boy who was shanghaied in New Orleans and made to join the crew of *The Moonlight,* a slave ship. In this grim story by Paula Fox, Jessie was forced to play his fife and "dance the slaves" so their muscles would remain strong and bring a higher price on the slave market. Jessie, *The Slave Dancer*, is young, innocent, and still capable of feeling shock. Everyone else on board the ship is so hardened as to be indifferent to human suffering. And this is the real message of the story, the utter degradation that eventually engulfs everyone connected with slavery—from the captain to the black Portuguese broker, to the depraved Ben Stout, and even to Jessie himself. For at one point Jessie is surprised to find himself hating the blacks; he is so sick of the sight, smell, and sound of their suffering that he wishes they did not exist. In one of the most compelling and symbolic scenes in the book Jessie is forced into the hold of the ship to look for his fife. Here he must touch, literally step on, the black bodies who were so crowded together that there was no room to walk. Jessie's descent into that hold somehow represents the descent of the whole of humankind.

In her Newbery Medal acceptance speech, Paula Fox writes about the theme of *The Slave Dancer:*

> Slavery engulfed whole peoples, swallowed up their lives, committed such offenses against their persons that in considering them, the heart falters, the mind recoils. . . .
>
> There are others who feel that black people can be only humiliated by being reminded that once they were brought to this country as slaves. But it is not the victim who is shamed. It is the persecutor who has refused the shame of what he has done and, as the last turn of the screw, would burden the victims with the ultimate responsibility of the crime itself.
>
> When I read the records of the past, . . . I perceived that the people who had spoken so long

---

[35] Thomas Fall. *Canalboat to Freedom,* illustrated by Joseph Cellini (New York: Dial, 1966), p. 160.

ago of every conceivable human loss were not only survivors, but pioneers of the human conditions in inhuman circumstances.[36]

The Civil War

There are many fine stories for children about the Civil War itself. Most of these describe the war in terms of human issues and suffering, rather than political issues. One of the best is *Jed* by Peter Burchard. By a simple act of human kindness Jed, a 16-year-old Yankee soldier, shows that it is possible to maintain one's humanity even in war. Jed is distressed by the looting and foraging that his fellow soldiers accept as their right. He understands the fear and hatred with which local residents view the army. Therefore, when he finds a small boy who has been hurt, he quietly takes him home to his Confederate family. The writing style is as quiet and restrained as the beauty and simplicity of Jed's act.

The battle and siege of Vicksburg has been described in *The Vicksburg Veteran* by F. N. Monjo. Written in the form of a diary by Fred Grant, the 12-year-old son of Ulysses S. Grant, this story details the siege that lasted for some forty-seven days. The pictures by Douglas Gorsline resemble some of the early Brady photographs of the war and lend authenticity to an easy-reading book for 7- or 8-year-old children.

Steele's *The Perilous Road* is a thought-provoking story of a boy caught between the divided loyalties of the Civil War. Chris Brabson, not quite 12, lived in Tennessee and was certain he hated the Union troops. When Yankee raiders steal his family's newly harvested crops, the Brabsons' only horse, and his new deerskin shirt, Chris is determined to have revenge, and sets out singlehandedly to achieve it. He reveals the position of a Union wagon train to a person he believes is a spy. Too late, he realizes his brother, who is with the Union troops, could be with the group. Chris tries to find his brother to warn him, and finally spends the night with the Union troops who have befriended him. He is caught in a bitter battle at dawn when the Confederates make a surprise attack. Chris realizes that even

The Vicksburg Veteran

F. N. MONJO

PICTURES BY DOUGLAS GORSLINE

Gorsline's pictures recall some of the early Brady photographs of the Civil War.

From *The Vicksburg Veteran*. Illustration COPYRIGHT © 1971, by Douglas Gorsline. Reprinted by permission of Simon and Schuster, Children's Book Division.

a Union soldier may "be a good and decent man." He understands the full meaning of his father's words: "Like I told you before, war is the worst thing that can happen to folks and the reason is it makes most everybody do things they shouldn't."[37]

Joanne Williamson portrays the Civil War as seen through the eyes of a young immigrant boy recently arrived in New York from Germany. At first, the struggle between the states does not seem as important to Martin Hester as the internal strife among various national and political groups within New York City. But then he meets Aaron, a fugitive slave, and the battle for an individual's right to be free becomes Martin's consuming interest. As a young news reporter for the *Tribune*, he has ample opportunity to debate

---

[36]Paula Fox. "Newbery Award Acceptance," *The Hornbook Magazine*, Vol. 50 (August 1974), pp. 348, 349.

[37]William O. Steele. *The Perilous Road*, illustrated by Paul Galdone (New York: Harcourt Brace Jovanovich, 1958), pp. 188–189.

the issues of the day and even covers the Battle of Gettysburg. Few history or trade books for children present the intense feelings against the Civil War, President Lincoln, and the Abolitionists that were felt by many political groups in Northern cities. This dimension of the many-faceted struggle of the Civil War is effectively recreated in *And Forever Free*. . . .

In *Orphans of the Wind*, Erik Haugaard has told the story of the Civil War from various points of view expressed by an English crew when they discover that the ship they are sailing is a blockade runner. The men are divided in their hatred of slavery. Finally, a crazed carpenter sets fire to the old brig, and the men rush for the lifeboats. Four of the young sailors who land on the Southern coast are determined to walk north until they can join the Union. They decide it will be easier to hide *in* the Southern army than to hide *from* it, so they enlist and move rapidly to the North. They are caught in the Battle of Bull Run, and one of them is killed. The other two do join the Union Army, while Jim, the 12-year-old boy in the story, sails once again; but this time on an American ship. There is much strength and sensitivity in this story by Erik Haugaard.

The effect of the war on a frontier family in Illinois has been told by Irene Hunt in the fine historical novel, *Across Five Aprils*. Jethro Creighton is only 9 years old at the outbreak of the war that first seemed so exciting and wonderful. But one by one Jethro's brothers, cousins, and his beloved schoolteacher enlist in the Northern army. His favorite brother, Bill, after a long struggle with his conscience, joins the South. As the war continues, Jethro learns that the war is not glorious and exciting, but heartbreaking and disruptive to all kinds of relationships. Although the many letters used to carry the action of the story to different places and provide historical detail make difficult reading, this is a beautifully written, thought-provoking book.

Rifles for Watie by Harold Keith tells of the life of a Union soldier and spy engaged in the fighting of the Western campaign of the Civil War. Jefferson Davis Bussey, a young farm boy from Kansas, joins the Union forces, becomes a scout, and quite accidentally a member of Stand Watie's Cherokee Rebels. Jeff is probably one of the few soldiers in the West to see the Civil War from both sides. This vibrant novel is rich in detail, with fine characterizations.

U.S. THROUGH 1900

Stories of the Civil War and Westward Expansion constitute the settings for the bulk of children's historical fiction of the nineteenth century. The few stories of the late nineteenth and early twentieth centuries are frequently the stories of private lives rather than public ones. They create a feeling for the period and take a look at a different kind of frontier—the long process of developing a young country.

Patricia Beatty has written many authentic, interesting stories of both the Northwest and Southwest in the 1890s. In *A Long Way to Whiskey Creek*, she has somehow made humorous a tale of the grim journey of a 13-year-old boy who went four hundred miles from Cottonwood to Whiskey Creek, Texas, to bring back the body of an older brother for proper burial in the family graveyard. There was no one else to go, so Parker Quiney persuaded Nate Graber, an orphan, to go along with him. The two boys are easy prey for the violence of the old West, but they also receive help from an unlikely source, The Tonkawa Kid, an aging outlaw. Both boys mature on the trip—in their own relationships and with others. In *Red Rock over the River*, Patricia Beatty has chosen Fort Yuma, Arizona, in 1881 as the setting. Thirteen-year old Dorcas is the narrator of this exciting tale, but Hattie Lou Mercer, the tall half-Indian housekeeper of the Fox household, is the real heroine. She encourages Dorcas to visit the infamous Arizona Territorial Prison where the two of them write letters for illiterate prisoners. She also includes Dorcas in a daring rescue of her half-brother from the prison and their escape via a gas circus balloon!

Patricia Beatty turned to reminiscences of members of her family for *O the Red Rose Tree*. Amanda Barnett and her three 13-year-old friends join forces to help an 80-year-old widow make a quilt of her own design. Called "O the Red Rose Tree," the quilt will require three shades of green cloth and seven shades of red. The last request proves to be a real challenge, since only one kind of red cotton that won't fade was made in the United States in the 1890s. The girls have many adventures while obtaining the red material from some surprising sources. This story gives a fine feeling for the activities of the time, and gains added depth from its underlying theme of the young who enjoy helping the old.

Good fun and tongue-in-cheek humor enliven the story of *Mr. Mysterious and Company* by Fleischman. In this book a delightful family of traveling magicians journey to California in the 1880s in their gaily painted wagon, making one-night stands in many frontier towns. All the children share in the magic show: Jane as a floating princess; Paul as a Sphinx who knows all the answers, including the identity of the Badlands Kid; and Anne as the little girl who is transformed from a big rag doll. Pa trades his cherished chiming watch for a maltreated dog for the children, and the children, in turn, decide to spend their reward money to buy their father another watch. This is a fine family story that carries the flavor of life in frontier towns of the West.

The Face of Abraham Candle by Bruce Clements is representative of the new realism in historical stories that simply dramatize daily living—in this instance near the turn of the century in Colorado. Abraham Candle, just into his teens, lives with the Widow Stent and her three young children. His mother is long dead; his father has recently died. He was particularly close to his father and delights in retelling and just rethinking some of the stories his father had told him. At the beginning of the book Abraham is anxious to go away, to find some excitement, something that will be a change for the better. Maybe, he thinks, his face will begin to look more like his father's. He is invited to go on a trip with Mr. Malone, the Widow Stent's friend, to explore the Indian Caves at Mesa Verde. The "adventure" may disappoint some readers because not a great deal happens. However, Abraham does make one memorable discovery on his own—a cave with an Indian mummy and corn still in the storage jars. He doesn't tell Mr. Malone about his find, which would be most lucrative, because somehow it would destroy the old Indian's dignity to move him. When Abraham returns home, he doesn't think the treasure hunt has changed him much. However, he looks in the mirror and decides that his face is at least worth telling a story about:

. . . his father's kind of story. No big heroes, no big battles, no great victories. Just a lot of work and a somewhat better face.

Good enough. He was satisfied.[38]

Bruce Clements is also the author of *I Tell a Lie Every so Often,* a hilarious account of a 14-year-old boy's trip up the Missouri River. It takes place during an earlier time period than *The Face of Abraham Candle,* but it lives up to Abraham's father's kind of story—"no big heroes, no big battles, no great victories," but plenty of excitement and much good fun.

When Libby Fletcher moved to Vermont she was told that you have to get used to *The Taste of Spruce Gum,* which she thought resembled turpentine. But Libby also had to get used to a whole new way of life—a new Papa; a lumpy, straw mattress in a new house; and living up on a mountain in a lumber mill filled with rough characters. Formerly sheltered, Libby is spared little in this strange new environment. The lumberjacks get drunk and beat their wives; she helps as her mother is called upon to be midwife for the birth of a baby girl; she watches their home burn down on Christmas night; and she overhears her mother quarreling with her new husband about the dishonesty of his oldest brother. It is almost too much for an 11-year-old to bear, but Libby has as much gumption as her mother, and, like the taste of spruce gum, she gets used to her new Vermont home and comes to love it and her new papa. Jacqueline Jackson has told a realistic story of life in a lumber camp in 1903. The plot is fast-paced, occasionally melodramatic, but with characters that live and speak of their time.

Certainly the most moving story of this time period is the Newbery Award-winner *Sounder* by William Armstrong. This is the stark and bitter tale of a black sharecropper and his family who endure cruel injustice with dignity and courage. When the father is thrown into jail for stealing a ham for his starving family, his big hunting dog, Sounder, is cruelly wounded by the sheriff. The dog never bays again until years later, when his master returns. As in the story of Odysseus,

---

[38]Bruce Clements. *The Face of Abraham Candle* (New York: Farrar, Straus, 1969).

The sun casts a long shadow as the father comes home—at the end of the day, the end of a long imprisonment, and the end of his life.

Illustration by James Barkley from *Sounder* by William H. Armstrong. Pictures copyright © 1969 by James Barkley. Reprinted by permission of Harper & Row, Publishers, Inc.

the dog is the first to recognize the man. Crippled from a dynamite blast in the prison quarry, the father has come home to die. He and Sounder take their last hunt together, for only Sounder returns to get the son, who finds his father just "tired out" under a tree. Sounder, too, soon dies as the boy had expected. The story would be one of deep despair except for the fact that during the long searches that the boy made to try to find where his father was imprisoned, he met a kind schoolmaster who enlarged his world by educating him and offered some hope for the future. This is a magnificent story of a family who had the courage and faith to endure within such an

inhuman culture that they appeared nameless in contrast to their dog. They did not fight back because they could not fight back—not in the rural South near the turn of the nineteenth century.

Come by Here by Olivia Coolidge depicts a black family living in Baltimore in the early 1900s. Grandma Minty's story goes all the way back to the days when she was born a slave, while her daughter, Big Lou, holds the position of Supervisor in a hospital kitchen. Her husband has a steady job in a steel factory. And so Minty Lou Payson, their one daughter, knows far more luxuries in life than her parents or their parents ever did. The family's standard of living surpasses their neighbors and is resented by Minty Lou's cousins. Once the background is established, Minty's parents are both killed in a bizarre accident. Life is radically changed for Minty Lou as she is shuffled from one relative to another, none of whom really want her. Throughout most of the book Minty is a hateful child, fighting back at people and circumstances too powerful for her to overcome. Finally, she is sent unannounced to her Grandma Minty in the country town of Cambridge. She is not really wanted here, but there is enough compassion to make room for her and her Grandma hopes that, like her mother, she may make something of herself. This is a book that illuminates the history of blacks between the times of slavery and advancing civil rights. It depicts a grim picture of survival in a city that is every bit as cruel as the rural setting is in *Sounder*.

THE DEPRESSION YEARS

While some children today have known deprivation, few have experienced the depth of poverty that characterized the Great Depression. Not many stories have been written for children about this period, and those that have are for mature readers.

In *Pistol*, Adrienne Richard relates the life of a boy growing up in a Montana cowtown during the Depression. The book is divided into two sections—Sunup describes a young teenager's life as a horse wrangler; and Sundown depicts the terrible years following the bank failures. Billy's father, who was never a strong man, runs away during the worst of the Depression; his older brother, Conrad, grows cold and bitter; but for the first time Billy sees his mother as a strong, warm human being. When the father returns, they all move to a noisy open boom town, where the men can find work on the construction of a dam. The characters are well drawn in this story of the impact of the Depression on the West.

Irene Hunt describes the effect of the Depression on the world of 15-year-old Josh Grondowski and his little brother, Joey, in her book, *No Promises in the Wind.* The year is 1932 and haggard, beaten men wait outside a factory gate for work that is not there. Women and men stand for long hours in breadlines, their eyes downcast with shame. Josh's father was one of these. His defeat made him bitter and thoughtlessly cruel to his older son. Josh decides to run away, but hasn't counted on his younger brother following him. Taking to the road, the two boys experience the suffering and wretchedness of the times. They find jobs at a carnival in Baton Rouge, but later it is destroyed by fire. An unscrupulous shopkeeper keeps the bill they give him for Joey's shoes, maintaining it must be counterfeit. While some take advantage of their misfortunes, others do help them, particularly when Joey becomes ill. This is an honest picture of a time in our history that many young people of today cannot comprehend.

Duffy's Rocks by Edward Fenton was the name of a small town outside of Pittsburgh. It was here that Timothy Brennan grew up under the physical pall of black mill smoke and the spiritual pall of the Great Depression. Timothy lives with his strong-willed Irish grandmother, for his mother had died when he was young and his father had deserted the family. The father had been home once when Timothy was about 7, and had promised to take Timothy to the circus in the morning; but he disappeared before Timothy had awakened. While the Depression provides the background, the story primarily revolves around Timothy's search for his father and his own identity. He does go to New York and finds his father's second wife, but not the father. His father's former employer provides Timothy with another clue, but again a visit with Frieda Blaufeld reveals that his father has left for Mexico, or maybe Guatemala. Timothy at last faces the truth about his father: "It was as though he was forever running away, and the world was full of people who had loved him and whom he had left behind."[39] Suddenly, Timothy longs to be with Gran at home in Duffy's Rocks. He returns to find that his Irish Grandmother had suffered a second heart attack and was literally hanging on to life until he came back. She dies and Tim goes to live with his Uncle Matt, stronger for the love that his Grandmother had always given him and for finally letting go of the dream of finding his father. This is a deeply moving story that speaks to the condition of many of today's alienated youth as well as the youth of yesterday.

The World at War

Recent years have witnessed almost a deluge of stories about World War II. Oddly enough, very few books for children about World War I were ever published. It may be that the new freedom in writing realistic stories has allowed authors to write truthfully about the horror and grimness of war. For in these stories there are few heroes but many victims, and the common enemy is war itself. While most of them depict man's inhumanity to man, they also show many individual acts of humanity and extreme courage.

ESCAPE FROM GERMANY

Some of the most popular war stories are about families that escaped to freedom or endured long years of hiding from the Nazis. Two well-written stories of German-Jewish families who became refugees when Hitler came to power are *Journey to America* by Sonia Levitin and *When Hitler Stole Pink Rabbit* by Judith Kerr. Both books are fictionalized memoirs. In *Journey to America,* the mother and three daughters leave Berlin and go to Switzerland while waiting to rejoin the father who had gone ahead of them to the United States. The first part of the book establishes the mood of Nazi Germany—the many soldiers, the chanting in the streets, strange disappearances, uncertainty, and the constant worry of what it all means. The bulk of the book describes the lives of these women as refugees in Switzerland. Because she is an alien, the mother cannot take a job, so the two older girls live for a while in a refugee camp recommended by a rabbi. The

---

[39]Edward Fenton. *Duffy's Rocks* (New York: Dutton, 1974), p. 182.

girls try not to tell their mother how bad it really is—Lisa must sleep in a crib; there isn't enough food; and the manager is dishonest. However, their mother senses the situation and takes them away. But later she is hospitalized with pneumonia and the girls are farmed out to different Swiss families. The Werfels have a daughter Lisa's age and they are very kind to the whole family, particularly when they have news that the girls' aunt and uncle have been killed. At last their passports are in order and they say goodbye to their fine Swiss friends and leave for the United States. At the end of the trip, Papa is there waiting. At first little Annie isn't sure if she really knows Papa. But Lisa has no doubts, for home is where Papa is, wherever the family can be together:

> Home, I thought, home was a feeling more than a place. I gave Papa's hand a squeeze and he smiled down at me.
>
> Yes, we were home.[40]

The story is told simply in an understated manner which somehow makes it more moving. Its feeling of family solidarity reminds one of the Laura Ingalls Wilder books. For despite the desperation of the times, the reader feels that nothing can destroy this family's mutual love.

Along with its intriguing title, *When Hitler Stole Pink Rabbit* also has the validity of solid detail that comes from personal experience. This is the thinly disguised story of Judith Kerr's family, their narrow escape to Switzerland, and the family's trials in trying to earn a living in Switzerland, then France, and finally England. Again, this is a pre-war story taking place in the 1930s. It is a happier account than *Journey to America;* Anna never felt like a refugee, in fact, she liked the many moves as long as the family stayed together. As they leave France for England, she wonders if they will ever really belong anywhere. And her father says: "Not the way people belong who have lived in one place all their lives. But we'll belong a little in lots of places and I think that may be just as good."[41]

Others made their escape by hiding for the duration of the war. *Anne Frank: The Diary of a Young Girl* is the classic story of hiding from the

Nazis. Autobiographical, this is a candid and open account of the changes wrought upon eight people while hiding for two years in a secret annex of an office building in Amsterdam. Living in constant fear and degradation, these people never gave up, even though ultimately they were found and imprisoned by the Nazis. Anne's diary reveals the thoughts of a sensitive adolescent growing up under extraordinary conditions. No one who lived in the annex survived the war except Anne's father. He returned to their hiding place and found Anne's diary. When it was published, it became an immediate bestseller and was translated into many languages. Its popularity continues today, and is an appropriate tribute to Anne Frank's amazing spirit.

The Upstairs Room by Johanna Reiss is a moving account of the author's own experiences when she and her sister were hidden by a farm family, the Oostervelds—Johann, his wife Dientje, and his mother known as Opoe, which means Granny. The girls spent most of their time in an upstairs room so that they wouldn't be seen, but Johann built a false back in a closet to give them a sure hiding place in case of search. The greatest excitement occurs when German soldiers make the Oosterveld house their temporary headquarters. Mostly, however, this is a story of the reactions of all the characters in close confinement and secrecy, the getting on each others' nerves, the tension and fear. The real delight of the book is the Oosterveld family with their plain folks values, salty language, and generosity. The most touching part of the book is the last chapter when the town is liberated and Annie can go outside at last. Johann's pride in what his family has done is so obvious and so obviously real-life, as he brags to neighboring farmers:

> "We had 'em for over two years. They're good girls. We didn't tell anybody about 'em. Don't be mad. It would've been too dangerous if we had told everybody in Usselo. I know you're special, but don't forget I was responsible for them. No, I was never afraid. Not once. Hey, Groothius, take a look at my girls."[42]

At the time this book was recognized as an Honor Book for the Newbery Award, it was also

[40]Sonia Levitin. *Journey to America* (New York: Atheneum, 1970), p. 150.

[41]Judith Kerr. *When Hitler Stole Pink Rabbit* (New York: Coward-McCann, 1972), p. 186.

[42]Johanna Reiss. *The Upstairs Room* (New York: Crowell, 1972), p. 188.

criticized for the number of swear words that peppered the Oostervelds' conversations. Certainly, their common language was as much a part of them as their uncommon bravery in helping two Jewish children survive the war. The Newbery-Caldecott Committee deserves credit for their broad-minded position in recognizing a fine book.

Marilyn Sachs wrote the story *A Pocket Full of Seeds* based on a friend's experience in France. Nicole Nieman lived with her sister and parents in the picturesque old town of Aix-les-Bain. The Niemans, who were Jewish, felt quite secure under the dictatorship of Marshall Petain. But then Nazi soldiers began to institute a reign of terror in France, rounding up Jews for prison camps and arresting those who had befriended them. "We had always been sure of being French but not at all sure of being Jewish. Now, suddenly, we are sure of being Jewish, and not at all sure of being French."[43] Nicole is visiting a friend for the night; when she returns home she finds the apartment ransacked and her parents and sister gone. No one will take her in but the schoolmistress. There she hides and tells her story in flashbacks, ending on a note of hope but before the war is over. We watch Nicole growing into her teens and never learn the fate of her family.

One of the best survival stories is *The Endless Steppe* by Esther Hautzig. This is the author's own account of growing up in a slave labor camp in Siberia. The Rudomins, a wealthy Jewish family, lived in Vilna, a city in Poland. The Russians had occupied Vilna and confiscated the family business; and then one day they arrested the whole family as "capitalists and therefore enemies of the people." They were shipped in filthy, stiflingly hot cattle cars across the barren flat land that was to be their home for five endless years—Siberia. These were grim years when everything was a struggle, and yet the family had happy moments. Some Sundays Esther and her Grandmother walked three hours to the village to trade such useless items as a fancy slip and an umbrella in return for extra food for the family. During a summer of drought and typhus

Esther paid sixteen rubles to see Deanna Durbin four times at the village movie! She knitted two sweaters in exchange for an old chiffonier that the family didn't need, but she thought looked beautiful in their hut. Despite the poverty and privation, Esther found ways to satisfy her adolescent needs and to find hope in a hopeless situation. When they are finally allowed to go back to Poland, she finds she is sad to leave the place she had once hated:

> I said good-by to the steppe—to the wind and the snow and the heat and the monotony. And to its space that had at first filled me with so much terror and later had quieted and soothed me. I said good-by to the unique beauty of the steppe.[44]

Ironically, their five years of exile had saved their lives. For during the time they were in Siberia, the Nazis had entered Poland and killed all their Jewish relatives and friends. In retrospect they considered themselves supremely lucky to have been deported to "The Endless Steppe." The ending of this story is less grim than that of *The Diary of Anne Frank*, but both stories are a tribute to the courage of the human spirit.

RESISTANCE

Frequently refugees were helped to flee or hide from authorities by common folk who did what they could to resist the invaders. Many stories relate the roles that children played in helping these resisters. In the story *Twenty and Ten* by Bishop, twenty children in a Catholic French orphanage manage to hide ten Jewish children during a Nazi investigation. Their dramatization of "The Flight into Egypt" finally saves them and is symbolic of their whole situation. This is a story that children as young as 7 or 8 enjoy. Also popular with this age level is McSwigan's story *Snow Treasure*, which tells how a brave group of Norwegian children helped to smuggle gold out of the country.

An exciting story of the underground activities of a family living in the occupied Netherlands is realistically presented by Van Stockum in *The Winged Watchman*. The Dutch Verhagen family

---

[43] Marilyn Sachs. *A Pocket Full of Seeds* (New York: Doubleday, 1973), p. 72.

[44] Esther Hautzig. *The Endless Steppe* (New York: Crowell, 1968), p. 239.

help a downed English flyer to escape. One of the sons, Dirk Jan, proves his endurance and wit by delivering an important message to the underground, who send it on by setting the arms of the old windmills along the coast. This "Morse Code of windmills" was used throughout the Dutch resistance period. While this story is filled with suspense, its strength lies in the character of the Verhagens, who were as determined in their effort to resist as in their efforts not to hate.

Eva-Lis Wuorio has written two fine novels of the Resistance movements in Denmark and Poland. *To Fight in Silence* tells the little-known tale of Denmark's heroic effort to save their Jewish people from deportation to concentration camps. A large family of Danish and Norwegian cousins, aunts, and a grandfather help in this operation that saved nearly eight thousand Danish Jews. Teenager Thor Erickson is the pivotal character in this story. Strong-willed, he must learn the hard way that self-discipline is essential if one wants to work in the Resistance. While the characters of this story are fictionalized, the background is authentic and provides a record of almost unknown heroic acts. For example, when the Germans forbade the Danes their traditional Midsummer Night festive bonfires, the Swedes across the water lit beach fires to give their neighbors hope. And when the Danish Jews finally returned to their homes, they found them just as they had left them. Their neighbors had looked after them, cleaned and dusted them, and even put fresh flowers in the vases for their return. *Code: Polonaise* records the activities of a small band of children who secretly work for their country's freedom. They publish a children's underground newspaper at much risk to themselves, and are finally caught. The network of organized resistance workers free them and help them in their flight across Europe. Once in England, Jan and Wanda play Chopin's "Polonaise," the symbol of nationalism, on a broadcast beamed to occupied Poland. These are both strong stories, particularly for young people today who take their freedoms for granted.

Both books by Alki Zei, *Petros' War* and *Wildcat under Glass,* have won the Mildred L. Batchelder Award for outstanding books translated from a foreign language. Petros lives in Athens during the Italian and then the German occupations, as did the author of this story. During that period Petros grows from a boy of 10 to a man of 14. Many of his experiences mature him quickly. He is caught in a "blocko," for example, when people are rounded up and then chosen at random for imprisonment or death. His resistance friend, Drossoula, is shot during a demonstration. He helps another friend dump his dead grandmother by the cemetery wall to eliminate the necessity for a funeral, because a funeral would mean the end of the grandmother's food allotment. And, finally, his brave devilish friend, Sotiris, taunts the German soldier once too often and is killed. But despite the grimness of the story the author never loses the child's point of view. The book begins with Petros mourning for a dead cricket; and one of the few things that reduces him to tears is the Germans' appropriation of his pet tortoise for turtle soup. The story carries the ring of truth. Petros' only daring missions consist of liberating a dog from a German soldier and joining in the sign-painting activities of the youth resistance. Yet he and his family endure and they fight in the small ways open to them. The setting and characters in this story are marvelously drawn, from Petros to his old actor grandfather. In *Wildcat under Glass* the same author writes of the military takeover of the government of Greece in the 1930s. Again she gives a particularly vivid picture of the impact of war upon an extended family, children's private society, and social class structures.

IN THE MIDST OF CONFLICT

Germany

Hans Peter Richter has written two compelling books about his life inside Hitler's Germany. Of all the Nazi versus Jewish books, *Friedrich* perhaps has the most impact because it is written from the viewpoint of an "average" German family who were slowly seduced by the propaganda of the Hitler regime. The narrator and his family are never identified by proper name, which creates the effect of universality; they represent all of the German people. Friedrich Schneider and his Jewish family are given names however. Friedrich and the narrator are the same age, live in the same apartment building in an unnamed German city, and grow up as fast friends.

A reader with sufficient information about the growth of Nazism in Germany before World War II will see the terrible ironies in this story: the very casual attitude of both families to the beginning of persecution, job restrictions, and youth organizations. In fact, Friedrich wants to join the *Jungvolk* with his friend, and goes to a meeting with him proudly wearing a swastika. Friedrich's friend can spout all the anti-Jewish slogans and songs when he is expected to, and he finds it somehow exciting. Yet he goes to Friedrich's Bar Mitzvah and finds that exciting too. Friedrich's friend somehow never seems to make the association between the slogans and Friedrich, which shows the insidiousness of effective propaganda. There is one memorable scene which creates reaction to the power of a mob. The narrator (now in his early teens) rather idly watches a group of Nazis smashing Jewish shops and property and soon finds himself taking part. He is finally sickened by it and runs home. But the mob follows to destroy the Schneiders' apartment. Frau Schneider dies amid the ruins of their possessions. When her husband has fully paid for the property damage, he and Freidrich are allowed to hole up there. The secret police arrest the father, however, because he hides a rabbi. Friedrich escapes the same fate only because he is not home that night; and he is not seen for another year. When he comes back to the building very dirty and tired, he asks for a photo of his parents; he cannot remember what they look like. There is an air raid, and everyone must go to the shelter, but Friedrich is not allowed in. To their credit, most of the people want to let him in, including an army sergeant, but the air-raid warden, who had been the Schneiders' landlord, threatens to report them all and locks the boy out. When the raid is over they find Friedrich sitting in the shadow of the stoop of their apartment building, dead. This book is filled with the dilemmas, contradictions, and the shame of a people caught in a larger horror than they could ever imagine. The writing is distinguished for the power of its understatement.

Richter's story, *I Was There*, takes the narrator and his two closest associates, Heinz and Gunther, into the German army and into battle.

Throughout the book the boys have seen this as a kind of glorified goal, but the last of the book makes clear there is no glory in war. The story does let you crawl inside the skin of a German youth and get the narrower perspective of a boy who wishes to succeed with other boys, with his parents, and as a "good German." In the beginning note the author identifies his point of view:

> I am reporting how I lived through that time and what I saw—no more. I was there. I was not merely an eyewitness. I believed—and I will never believe again.[45]

This is an unusual story, for Richter has the courage to tell the truth when right was *not* on his side.

Two novels by Forman, *Ceremony of Innocence* and *Horses of Anger*, are powerful indictments of Nazism and war. Both stories are for mature teenagers, however. The first describes the lives of a German brother and sister who are executed by the Nazis for printing and distributing anti-Nazi leaflets. *Horses of Anger* is similar to Richter's book *I Was There*, for it tells the story of a 15-year-old German soldier who idolized Hitler and only slowly began to question anything he did.

Elsewhere in Europe

Forman also wrote about the Nazi invasion of Greece in *The Skies of Crete*. In this grim tale the author contrasts the attitude toward the war of a youth who has endured some of its horrors, as he made his way south, and his grandfather who lives on memories of the heroism and glory of the Turkish wars of the past. To Penelope, the granddaughter, war was: ". . . the private possession of her grandfather who brought it out on wintry nights with its curved swords and flapping flags like pictures carefully etched in a history book."[46] When their home is bombed and they are unable to reach the refugee boat, she realizes her cousin, Alexis, was right, for war is fear, weariness, "and a hopelessness mute beyond communication."[47] Alexis is haunted by his guilt

[45]Hans Peter Richter. *I Was There,* translated by Edite Kroll (New York: Holt, Rinehart and Winston, 1972). Beginning note, unpaged.
[46]James Forman. *The Skies of Crete* (New York: Farrar, Straus, 1963), p. 20.
[47]Forman, p. 25.

at killing a soldier, and says this guilt is worse than being bombed. Penelope and Alexis follow their old warrior grandfather over a tortuous mountain, accompanied by El Greco, a shepherd who symbolizes truth. After recounting the history of Crete, El Greco comments: "It's hard to be angry or sure of anything when you look back over thousands of years."[48] They eventually reach a port where Penelope and her mother escape to Alexandria. Alexis remains behind to help the partisans protect refugees. True to his word that he will never shoot another man, he gives Penelope the cartridges from his gun.

The moving story of a 12-year-old boy named *Boris* who lived through the siege of Leningrad during 1942 has been told by Dutch author Jaap ter Haar. Essentially, this is a survival story of the horrors of the 500-day German siege. People starve, die quietly, and the death wagons make daily rounds. Spilling your day's ration of soup may make a difference between life and death. Boris and his brave friend, Nadia, go foraging for potatoes in the No-Man's-Land between the lines of the Russian and German armies. Nadia collapses and the two children are returned to a Russian camp by a compassionate German soldier. Boris had expected to be killed, not treated with kindness. Now he is forced to see the Germans as individuals, not simply as the enemy. At the end of the story, when captured Germans are marched into the city through crowds filled with hate, Boris gives one of the prisoners a bit of his own precious food—a gesture of recognition that the enemy is human. Boris feels the reproachful eyes and hears the disapproving voices until one old woman puts her hand on his shoulder and says:

"You did right. . . . What use is our freedom to us if we still live in hate?"

There was a pause, then most people nodded. Because those who have suffered much, can forgive much.[49]

This same theme is reflected in the powerful story *The Little Fishes* by Erik Haugaard. The "Little Fishes" are the pathetic children of Naples who had no homes, no families, no friends. Three of them wander about Italy, begging food, hoping to find a home, and get caught in the midst of war. Guido, the oldest boy, somehow stays alive and develops a mature wisdom for one so young. When Anna asks him why after all their suffering he cannot hate, he replies:

"Anna, one should not waste oneself with hate. . . . The war . . . the suffering, it must have a point and if I hate that man who only saw that we were dirty . . . then I would be like him. And all we had gone through would be as meaningless as the seasons are to the sheep. It is understanding . . . that makes the difference between us and the animals. And when you understand you can feel a kind of happiness even in the worst misery."[50]

ENGLAND

In *Silence over Dunkerque*, John Tunis writes of the average people who helped in the heroic evacuation of the British from the beaches of Dunkirk in France in 1940. Sergeant Williams stays with his men instead of accepting a boat ride back to his home at Dover. Because of the courage of a 14-year-old French Girl Scout and her grandfather, the Sergeant and his buddy, Fingers, eventually make their escape to England. Tunis maintains a breathless suspense until the men and the faithful dog that has attached himself to them are safe in Dover. The deeper meaning of the story—that "courage wears many uniforms, or none"—is applicable to life in peace as well as war. The author himself had the courage to show that some English were less than brave in this battle. The book might be a springboard for discussion of the momentary weakness or courage of human beings.

The Dolphin Crossing by Jill Paton Walsh is also a tale of the evacuation of the British forces from the beaches of Dunkirk. Two adolescent boys from vastly different backgrounds are thrown together for this dangerous operation. John's large home along the coast has been taken over by the government, but he still lives with his mother in the coastal village and has access to his father's boat, *The Dolphin*. Pat is from London,

[48]Forman, p. 70.
[49]Jaap ter Haar. *Boris,* translated by Martha Mearns, illustrated by Rien Poortvliet (New York: Delacorte, 1970), p. 149.

[50]Erik Christian Haugaard. *The Little Fishes,* illustrated by Milton Johnson (Boston, Mass.: Houghton Mifflin, 1967), p. 213.

living with his stepmother in an old abandoned railroad car. He has never been on the water before, but he makes a courageous and resourceful crew for *The Dolphin*. These two adolescents were symbolic of the many ordinary people who quietly played their part in the drama of Dunkirk. Another war story by Walsh, *Fireweed*, tells of an adolescent boy and girl who seek each other's protection and friendship when caught in London during the World War II Blitz, or bombings. While emphasizing the difference in their backgrounds, the author also shows us their growing dependency upon each other. One day the building where they are both living is bombed, and Bill thinks Julie has been killed. He later finds that she has been wounded, so he goes to the hospital to see her. There he meets her wealthy family and feels rejected by them and by Julie. Years later, he looks at the rubble and the many wild plants that have started to cover the scars of the war. Fireweed, in particular, is growing in abundance, and Bill thinks about its significance in terms of his experience:

> It is a strange plant; it has its own rugged sort of loveliness, and it grows only on the scars of ruin and flame.
>
> I suppose they will build on this again, some day; but I like it best like this: grown over, healed.[51]

Hester Burton's story *In Spite of All Terror* shows wartime London through the eyes of a young girl. Liz is sent to live in the country on the Brereton's estate when the raids begin. At first she feels very uncomfortable with the aristocratic family, but gradually she comes to love them very much. She goes to London on the eve of Dunkirk to see if she can help in some way, and is horrified by the devastation caused by the Battle of Britain. She does aid in the evacuation. Primarily, however, this is a story of sharp contrasts—the contrast between life as Liz knew it and life as the Brereton's knew it. It also contrasts life in the country and in London during the Blitz. And all lives are vastly changed by the war.

Susan Cooper's first book was a war story titled *Dawn of Fear*. She tells the tale of a small group of boys who were hardly touched by the war, until one day one of them is killed in an air raid. Now, suddenly, their games of war take on terrible meaning. This is a very real story of children's attitudes toward danger.

One of the best "war stories" is Nina Bawden's *Carrie's War*. The only sense in which it may be called a war story is that it is about three children who are evacuees living in a Welsh mining town. Nick and Carrie, brother and sister, are sent to live with stern Mr. Evans and his sister, Auntie Lou. Another evacuee, Albert Sandwich, lives at the bottom of Druid's Grove with Mr. Evans' older sister, the invalid Dilys. Brother and sister haven't spoken since Dilys married the mine owner's son, shortly after their father's death in the mine. Carrie and Nick love their visits to Druid's Bottom where the housekeeper, Hepzibah Green, is warm and kind, and a distant family relation, Mr. Johnny Gotobed, presents perhaps the best portrayal of a mentally retarded adult yet found in children's books. The story moves ahead on two levels—the family's feud and the children's involvement in it. The characters are seen from a child's eye view, with a child's perception of adults. Relationships are revealed naturally through conversation and minor scenes, such as Nick being comforted on Hepzibah's lap, Carrie and Nick washing the chapel floor so Auntie Lou can have a moment alone with her Major Cass, or the remarkable scene of the birth of the calf:

> February came, and the calf was born at Druid's Bottom. It was born on a Sunday afternoon and Carrie and Albert and Nick saw it happen. The cow lowing and lowing and Mister Johnny talking to her in his soft, bubbly voice, and pulling on the little hooves when they slowly appeared. And the astonishingly big calf coming out with a slippery rush and then, a few minutes later, standing up in the straw on its thin, wobbly legs, its thickly lashed eyes mild and brown like its mother's.
>
> "I've never seen anything so exciting in my whole life," Nick said afterwards. "It's my *best thing!*"[52]

This is a remarkable story that tells much more of the personal wars of living both as children and adults than of the war of bombs and blitzes.

[51] Jill Paton Walsh. *Fireweed* (New York: Farrar, Straus, 1970), p. 133.

[52] Nina Bawden. *Carrie's War*, illustrated by Colleen Browning (New York: Lippincott, 1973), pp. 75–76.

THE IMPACT OF THE WAR IN THE U.S.

While thousands of families lost sons, fathers, and husbands in World War II, the United States never endured the physical horror of war on our land. For this reason, perhaps, we have fewer stories about the impact of the war in the United States.

Michele Murray in her book, *The Crystal Nights,* describes the impact on her family of the arrival of their Jewish refugee relatives. When Uncle Michael is imprisoned, spoiled Aunt Anna and Cousin Margot come to live with Elly's family on their farm in Connecticut. Margot is not the instant bosom companion that Elly had anticipated, and there is a good deal of friction and tension all around. It is difficult to talk about the action in this story because, like real life, it has many strands to it. Elly's father has a heart attack, so the family decides to sell the farm and trade their small-town grocery store for a Brooklyn bakery. There is much about family relationships, peer relationships, political values, beliefs, and prejudices. Well-written, this book presents a very complete picture of what it was like to live in that particular place at that particular time.

The Summer of My German Soldier by Bette Greene is the story of 12-year-old Patty Bergen, who is Jewish and is the elder, awkward daughter of a small-town Arkansas department-store owner. This is not a happy family story; the mother and father fight and they are cruel to Patty primarily in non-physical ways, but there are two or three scenes in which she is beaten with her father's belt. Except for the real love of Ruth, the Bergens' black cook, Patty lives in a loveless situation. Perhaps this explains her compassion for and interest in a handsome, well-educated German prisoner of war named Anton who lives in a prison camp near town and comes to her father's store. Patty begins to think of him as her friend and later, when she sees him running down the railroad tracks, she offers him the safety of her special hideout room over the garage. Anton is almost discovered, but only after he has gotten away and is captured elsewhere is Patty's role in his escape uncovered. She is arrested and sent to a Reform School, a completely joyless place where only Ruth comes to visit her. The book ends giving only the barest notion that

Patty will be able to go back to her family and wait out the time until she can leave them and become a "person of value," a term Anton had used. The author's choice of detail and dialogue is exceptional. Unfortunately, the ease with which Patty and Anton accept each other and her secrecy in hiding him from her family do not seem completely believable. This is a story for rather mature readers.

The Cay by Theodore Taylor is both a war survival story and one of overcoming prejudice. After the Germans torpedoed the freighter on which Phillip and his brother were traveling from wartime Curaçao to the U.S., Phillip finds himself cast up on a barren little Caribbean Island with an old black man named Timothy. A blow on the head during the wreck had left Phillip blind and completely dependent upon Timothy. Born in Virginia of Southern parents, Phillip was prejudiced toward blacks. Timothy, who has been criticized for being an "Uncle Tom," probably really was one. He had never been outside the West Indies, had no formal education, and had been taught to call white men "bahss." Both Phillip and Timothy are products and prisoners of their backgrounds. Gradually, Phillip begins to understand and trust the wisdom and selflessness of Timothy. His way of overcoming his prejudice is to make Timothy white in his mind. At one point in the story, he even asks the old man if he is still black. Timothy deliberately sets out to make Phillip independent of him, forcing him to make fishnets, to find his way around the camp, to survive without him. And following the hurricane in which Timothy bears the brunt of the storm while protecting him, Phillip has to live without him, for Timothy dies. Phillip is finally rescued and his sight restored after three operations. This story of a color-conscious white boy and a self-sacrificing black was not meant to provide a model for today's living; what it does do is present a realistic account of a survival story in the Caribbean in 1942. Similar to *Edge of Two Worlds* by Jones and *Cross-Fire* by Graham, this book suggests human interdependence in time of crisis. It is one of the few stories that details the gradual loss of prejudice. Theodore Taylor also has written *The Children's War,* the little-known story of the Japanese capture of a small island off the coast of Alaska. It does not sustain the suspense of the survival story, *The Cay.*

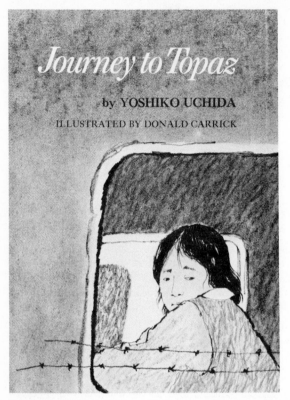

Journey to Topaz

by YOSHIKO UCHIDA

ILLUSTRATED BY DONALD CARRICK

The little-known history of the internment of the Japanese in the United States during World War II is sensitively told in *Journey to Topaz*.

Illustration by Donald Carrick, used by permission of Charles Scribner's Sons from *Journey to Topaz* by Yoshiko Uchida. Copyright © 1971 Yoshiko Uchida.

Citizens of the United States can take no pride in our treatment of Japanese-Americans at the beginning of the war against Japan. In *Journey to Topaz*, Yoshiko Uchida has given a fictionalized account of her family's evacuation and internment following the attack on Pearl Harbor. Yuki's father, a businessman, is taken away from his family on the very day of Pearl Harbor. It is almost a year before he is paroled. Yuki and her mother and older brother are taken first to a temporary center, a converted racetrack where their "apartment" is a hastily partitioned stall area in one of the stables. The walls have been so sloppily whitewashed that the bodies of cockroaches still cling to the boards. The latrines have no doors; the hot water never lasts; and the mealtime lines are interminable. At the "permanent" camp in

Topaz, Utah, the wind blows across the desert and through their scarcely-finished barracks. Here, Yuki's friend Emi's grandfather is shot by a guard, who sees him looking for arrowheads and thinks he is trying to escape. Also, Yuki's brother leaves camp to join a special Nisei Army Volunteer Unit. The author writes the story in a restrained way, with no bitterness. The quiet courage, dignity, and loyalty with which this Japanese family endures their unjust internment makes its own statement to the reader.

The Moved Outers by Florence Means is another record of this unpleasant chapter of our history. In this story one son is killed in war and the spirit of another is nearly broken by the humiliating treatment the family receives. Although the characters are in their teens, sixth-graders can understand their disillusionment and hopes for a future place. Discussion of the irrationality of human behavior during a war might follow the reading of these books.

THE WARS IN ASIA

The House of Sixty Fathers by DeJong is an example of a book that does not glorify war; it clearly, vividly tells of the horror of bullets coming in your direction and of the pains of hunger. DeJong's description of Tien Pao's fear, loneliness, and hunger are starkly realistic. The Chinese boy and his family flee before the Japanese invasion, but they are separated. Clutching his pet pig, Tien Pao struggles on, not knowing where to go. He finds a U.S. flier, and helps him survive. The boy is taken to the barracks and becomes a mascot of the soldiers, his sixty fathers. Although it seems impossible, he continues to believe his parents will be found. In a rather contrived ending he does identify his mother from a plane; she is working on the construction of an airfield. They land, the lieutenant finds a jeep and drives Tien Pao near the site, and the boy and his mother are reunited.

There is no such happy ending in the grim story of *The Man in the Box: A Story from Viet Nam* by Mary Lois Dunn. Chau Li is a Montagnard boy. His father had been the village chief until the Viet Cong had come and put him in a small wooden box and left him there to die. Now there is another man in the box, a U.S. soldier, and Chau Li is determined to save him. He does rescue the soldier and after an agonizing trip downstream, they reach a United States camp. Here, Dah Vid, as Chau Li called the soldier is put in a helicopter and flown to a hospital. Chau Li is supposed to go with him, but it is a Vietnamese crew and they push the Montagnard boy out, refusing to take him along. Chau Li stays near the compound with an old woman, who had helped him even though her son was a Viet Cong. There is an attack in the early dawn and the Americans are killed. Chau Li's friend, Ky, comes for him and, thinking he is a Cong, Chau throws a grenade at him. Everyone whom he knew is now dead. At the story's end he sets out in a sampan, floating down the river, dazed and without hope. Mary Dunn has given a realistic picture of the cruelty and the horror of the Vietnam War.

Even more devastating is *Cross-Fire* by Gail Graham. This is the story of the struggle for survival of four Vietnamese children and Harry, a lost U.S. soldier, who has been cut off from his platoon. Harry has reason to distrust the children, for he knows that Viet children are often employed by the Viet Cong. Everything about them is incomprehensible to him—their language, behavior, and attitudes. The point of view then switches to the oldest girl, Mi, and the reader comes to know why the children are alone in the jungle. Their village has just been destroyed by napalm from U.S. bombers, and they know that Harry is an American. Mi is inclined to trust Harry to a degree (a faltering mutual respect grows between them), but Ton, her 9-year-old brother, is bent on vengeance. It gradually becomes clear to Mi that her brother has had more contact with the Viet Cong than she had supposed.

Together the group sets out on a hopeless journey to a jungle town which, ironically, each of them sees as a haven. Harry remembers it as the seat of U.S. patrols; Ton thinks he can turn Harry over to the Viet Cong there; and Mi hopes to find a doctor for the sick baby at the Catholic Mission Hospital. But the baby dies long before they reach the town. Then Ton, seeing planes in the distance, shows himself as a target in order to draw fire to Harry. Harry runs to get the child to cover and is struck down. The soldier dies, never regaining consciousness. Then come the paratroopers, who have been ordered to shoot at anything that moves in the jungle; and they shoot all three of the children. The final dramatic irony is that it was the bare beginnings of trust and regard for human dignity in others that brings death to all of them. Harry dies because he tried to save Ton; the three children die at least partly because Mi's trust in Harry leads her to misjudge the paratroopers wearing the same uniforms. There is no glory in this devastating story, only the horrible evil that is war. The author worked in Vietnam; was once captured by and escaped from the Viet Cong. Her depth of understanding of the people and the country makes the book seem all the more grim.

THE AFTERMATH OF WAR

Peace does not always bring surcease of pain and trouble. Many children's and adults' lives remained twisted because of unhappy war experiences. A popular story that won the prize for the Best Scandinavian Children's Book is *North to Freedom* by Anne Holm. It concerns David, a boy who is given a chance to escape from a prison camp somewhere in eastern Europe where he has lived for most of his twelve years. David has no knowledge of his own background or of the world at large, and no feeling about people except that no one can be trusted. Luckily, he has learned seven languages from the prisoners and has been taught to read by Johannes, his one friend in the prison camp who had died. So much of David's learning is without the essential experience that brings meaning that it is difficult for him to relate to the world. Fearing recapture, David at first avoids people, preferring to observe and learn from a distance. Gradually, he makes tentative gestures toward human relationships, and some of these encounters are with people who are kindly and helpful. Slowly, his trust in human beings grows, and with it the desire to live and be a part of the world of sunshine, beauty, and color that is in such contrast to the drabness of the prison camp. David's change from an imprisoned creature completely shut off from normal human feelings to a responsive and responsible boy makes for a remarkable story. His eventual discovery of his own identity and his mother in Denmark seem almost anticlimatic in contrast to the self-understanding and the individual freedom that he has already achieved.

A quiet story of the strength required to rebuild one's life following a war is told by Margot Benary-Isbert in *The Ark*. Housing problems, labor office edicts, food rationing, and cold rooms are challenges faced by a German mother and her family of four children. Two of the children go to work on a farm, where they are allowed to make a home from an old railroad car—truly an ark, a refuge for the family that is finally united with their father who arrives home from a prison camp in Russia. Two sequels, *Rowan Farm* and *Castle on the Border*, continue the story of the Lechow family.

Perhaps the best-known story of World War II and its aftermath is the one by John Tunis titled *His Enemy, His Friend*. Written in two parts, the first tells of the German occupation of the small town of Nogent-Plage on the Normandy beach. Life is comparatively good in that small village during the war for one reason only—Sergeant Hans von Kleinschrodt is in charge of the town. Unlike other German soldiers, this one was a friend of the people, and particularly the children, whom he taught to play soccer. Then an explosive underground incident occurs and Hans is ordered to kill six hostages in reprisal; one is to be the school teacher, the father of his favorite soccer pupil, Jean-Paul Varin. The Sergeant does all he can to prevent the execution, and at the end it is his commanding officer who gives the order to fire. Hans cannot do it. Nevertheless, he becomes known as the Butcher of Nogent-Plage and is sentenced to ten years in prison by the War Trials Court at Rouen at the end of the war. Twenty years later to the day Hans and five of his soccer team members are stranded in the little town of Nogent-Plage when their mini-bus breaks down. He is recognized by the townspeople, who place the six Germans in the same cellar where the French hostages had been held. Crazy Pierre, the village madman, is already setting fire to the place when Jean-Paul Varin, who has played in the soccer game against the Germans, returns to the village. He calms the maddened crowd and pleads with them not to repeat the same crime that had been done twenty years before. "Somehow, somewhere, we must break this evil chain and look on each other as human beings."[53] Jean-Paul then rescues the men from the burning building. Once outside, his arm around the baron, a shot rings out and the German has been killed by Crazy Pierre. Jean-Paul falls weeping by the body of "his enemy, his friend."

Grim as these stories are, they do proclaim the futility and the tragedy of war. Only if young people can develop a clear understanding of what really happened in this period can they ever resolve that it must not happen again. In today's world there is no glory in war, only the threat of genocide.

Such well-written historical fiction as has been reviewed in this chapter may enable children to see the continuity of life and their own places in this vast sweep of history. The power of good historical fiction can give children a feeling for a living past. History can become an extension of their own personal experiences, rather than a sterile subject assigned to be studied in school. Such books can offer children a new perspective by which they come to realize that people make and shape their destinies through the decisions and actions of each individual. The events that are happening today do become the history of tomorrow.

[53]John R. Tunis. *His Enemy, His Friend* (New York: Morrow, 1967), pp. 194–195.

SUGGESTED LEARNING EXPERIENCES

1. Choose a recurring theme in history, such as the human search for freedom. Select a representative book from various periods in history that accurately explores the theme.
2. Choose a particular event in history, such as the American Revolution or Westward Expansion. Find books which express opposing points of view and compare the representations of these historical events.
3. Prepare a chart showing particular eras in history, and select books that would illuminate the periods.

4. If you have an opportunity, you may want to work with your classmates or children in the middle grades in making a videotape of famous trials found in historical fiction. Examples that could be used are the witch trial of Kit Tyler in *The Witch of Blackbird Pond* by Elizabeth Speare or the war trial of Sergeant Hans von Kleinschrodt from the book *His Enemy, His Friend* by John Tunis.

5. Prepare a decorated portfolio or box of materials of a particular event or period of time. You may want to include copies of newspaper clippings; artifacts; an annotated bibliography; copies of appropriate paperback books; and examples of art, music, and handcrafts. Plan activity cards for children's use and extension of these materials.

6. The class may want to make their own book of quotations from historical fiction that has relevance for today. One example might be the many statements about the meaning of freedom that are found in Haugaard's book, *Hakon of Rogen's Saga.*

7. Read four or five books about one particular period or place, and chart the references to kinds of food, clothing, houses, transportation, language, and so on. Evaluate which books give the most authentic picture.

8. Ask a group of middle-graders to each list their ten favorite books. What percentage of these can be classified as historical fiction?

9. What insights and understandings of child development may be derived from reading the Wilder books?

RELATED READINGS

1. Burton, Hester. "The Writing of Historical Novels" in *Children and Literature*, edited by Virginia Haviland. Glenview, Ill.: Scott Foresman, 1973, pp. 299–304.

    A well-known author of historical fiction describes the special requirements of writing stories of this genre for children.

2. Cianciolo, Patricia J., and Jean M. LePere. *The Literary Time Line in American History.* Garden City, N.Y.: Doubleday, 1969.

    A particularly useful paperback that is designed to provide teachers of children in the middle schools with references to enough resource materials to enable them to teach social studies entirely through the use of trade books. Suggestions for setting up such a program are provided, as well as an extensive annotated bibliography related to significant events in history.

3. Coughlan, Margaret N. *Creating Independence, 1763–1789.* Washington, D.C.: Library of Congress, 1972.

    A selected, annotated bibliography of books for young people that will be useful in connection with the Bicentennial of the American Revolution. Many of the books suggested show evidence of using primary sources. The list includes a limited number of historical novels and fictionalized biographies for children. It is well-illustrated with many prints, photocopies of which may be ordered from the Library of Congress.

4. Egoff, Sheila, G. T. Stubbs, and L. F. Ashley. *Only Connect: Readings on Children's Literature.* New York: Oxford University Press, 1969.

    The reader will enjoy three fine articles about the writing of historical fiction that appear in this book of readings. One, titled "Combined Ops," is by Rosemary Sutcliff and a second is titled "The Search for Selfhood: The Historical Novels of Rosemary Sutcliff." The third article is a tribute to the fine works of historical fiction by Henry Treece.

5. Fox, Paula. "Newbery Award Acceptance," *The Horn Book Magazine,* Vol. 50 (August 1974), pp. 345–350.

    In her Acceptance Speech for the Newbery Award for 1974, Paula Fox describes how she came to write *The Slave Dancer* and the research she did for this fine book.

6. Meek, Margaret. *Rosemary Sutcliff.* New York: Henry Z. Walck, Inc., 1962.

    This monograph gives a brief overview of the life of the historical novelist, Rosemary Sutcliff, and then presents an in-depth analysis of her works.

RECOMMENDED REFERENCES[54]

Almedingen, E. M. *A Candle at Dusk.* Farrar, Straus, 1969.
———. *Katia,* illustrated by Victor Ambrus. Farrar, Straus, 1967.
———. *Young Mark: The Story of a Venture,* illustrated by Victor Ambrus. Farrar, Straus, 1968.
Armstrong, William H. *Sounder,* illustrated by James Barkley. Harper & Row, 1969.
Bacmeister, Rhoda W. *Voices in the Night,* illustrated by Ann Grifalconi. Bobbs Merrill, 1965.
Bacon, Martha. *Sophia Scrooby Preserved,* illustrated by David Omar White. Little, Brown, 1968.
Baker, Betty. *Killer-of-Death,* illustrated by John Kaufmann. Harper & Row, 1963.
———. *A Stranger and Afraid.* Macmillan, 1972.
———. *Walk the World's Rim.* Harper & Row, 1965.
Barringer, D. Moreau. *And the Waters Prevailed,* illustrated by P. A. Hutchinson. Dutton, 1956.
Baumann, Hans. *I Marched with Hannibal,* illustrated by Ulrik Schramm. Walck, 1962.
Bawden, Nina. *Carrie's War,* illustrated by Colleen Browning. Lippincott, 1973.
Beatty, John, and Patricia Beatty. *At the Seven Stars,* illustrated by Douglas Gorsline. Macmillan, 1962.
Beatty, Patricia. *A Long Way to Whiskey Creek.* Morrow, 1971.
———. *O the Red Rose Tree,* illustrated by Liz Dauber. Morrow, 1972.
———. *Red Rock over the River.* Morrow, 1973.
Behn, Harry. *The Faraway Lurs.* World, 1963.
Benary-Isbert, Margot. *The Ark,* translated by Clara Winston and Richard Winston. Harcourt Brace Jovanovich, 1953.
———. *Castle on the Border.* Harcourt Brace Jovanovich, 1956.
———. *Rowan Farm.* Harcourt Brace Jovanovich, 1954.
Benchley, Nathaniel. *Only Earth and Sky Last Forever.* Harper & Row, 1972.
Bishop, Claire Huchet. *Twenty and Ten,* as told by Janet Joly, illustrated by William Pène du Bois. Viking, 1964.
Brink, Carol Ryrie. *Caddie Woodlawn,* illustrated by Kate Seredy. Macmillan, 1936.
———. *Caddie Woodlawn,* illustrated by Trina Schart Hyman. Macmillan, 1973.
Bulla, Clyde Robert. *John Billington, Friend of Squanto,* illustrated by Peter Burchard. Crowell, 1956.
———. *The Sword in the Tree,* Illustrated by Paul Galdone. Crowell, 1956.
———. *Viking Adventure,* illustrated by Douglas Gorsline. Crowell, 1963.
———. *White Bird,* illustrated by Leonard Weisgard. Crowell, 1966.
Burchard, Peter. *Bimby.* Coward-McCann, 1968.
———. *Jed: The Story of a Yankee Soldier & a Southern Boy.* Coward-McCann, 1960.
Burton, Hester. *Beyond the Weir Bridge,* illustrated by Victor Ambrus. Crowell, 1970.
———. *In Spite of All Terror,* illustrated by Victor Ambrus. World, 1969.
———. *The Rebel,* illustrated by Victor Ambrus. Crowell, 1972.
———. *Riders of the Storm,* illustrated by Victor Ambrus. Crowell, 1973.
———. *Time of Trial,* illustrated by Victor Ambrus. World, 1964.
Byars, Betsy. *Trouble River,* illustrated by Rocco Negri. Viking, 1969.
Caudill, Rebecca. *Tree of Freedom,* illustrated by Dorothy Morse. Viking, 1949.
Christopher, John. *Dom and Va.* Macmillan, 1973.
Chute, Marchette. *The Wonderful Winter,* illustrated by Grace Golden. Dutton, 1954.
Clapp, Patricia. *Constance: A Story of Early Plymouth.* Lothrop, 1968.
Clements, Bruce. *The Face of Abraham Candle.* Farrar, Straus, 1969.
———. *I Tell a Lie Every so Often.* Farrar, Straus, 1974.
Clifford, Eth. *The Year of the Three-legged Deer,* illustrated by Richard Cuffari. Houghton, Mifflin, 1971.
Collier, James Lincoln, and Christopher Collier. *My Brother Sam Is Dead.* Four Winds Press, 1974.
Colver, Anne. *Bread and Butter Indian,* illustrated by Garth Williams. Holt, Rinehart and Winston, 1964.

[54]All books listed at the end of this chapter are recommended, subject to the qualifications noted in the text. *See* Appendix D for publishers' complete addresses.

————. *Bread and Butter Journey,* illustrated by Garth Williams. Holt, Rinehart and Winston, 1970.

Coolidge, Olivia. *Come by Here,* illustrated by Milton Johnson. Houghton Mifflin, 1970.

Cooper, Susan. *Dawn of Fear,* illustrated by Margery Gill. Harcourt Brace Jovanovich, 1970.

Crompton, Anne Eliot. *The Sorcerer,* illustrated by Leslie Morrill. Little, Brown, 1971.

Dalgliesh, Alice. *The Courage of Sarah Noble,* illustrated by Leonard Weisgard. Scribner, 1954.

————. *The Thanksgiving Story,* illustrated by Helen Sewell. Scribner, 1954.

De Angeli, Marguerite. *The Door in the Wall.* Doubleday, 1949.

————. *Elin's Amerika.* Doubleday, 1941.

————. *Skippack School.* Doubleday, 1961.

————. *Thee, Hannah!* Doubleday, 1949.

DeJong, Meindert. *The House of Sixty Fathers,* illustrated by Maurice Sendak. Harper & Row, 1956.

Dickinson, Peter. *The Dancing Bear,* illustrated by John Smee. Little, Brown, 1972.

Dunn, Mary Lois. *The Man in the Box: A Story from Viet Nam.* McGraw-Hill, 1968.

Eckert, Allan. *Incident at Hawk's Hill,* illustrated by John Schoenherr. Little, Brown, 1971.

Edmonds, Walter D. *The Matchlock Gun,* illustrated by Paul Lantz. Dodd, 1941.

Fall, Thomas. *Canalboat to Freedom,* illustrated by Joseph Cellini. Dial, 1966.

Fenton, Edward. *Duffy's Rocks.* Dutton, 1974.

Field, Rachel. *Calico Bush,* illustrated by Allen Lewis. Macmillan, 1931.

Finlayson, Ann. *Rebecca's War.* Warne, 1972.

————. *Redcoat in Boston.* Warne, 1971.

Fisher, Aileen. *A Lantern in the Window.* Hale, 1957.

Fleischman, Sid. *Mr. Mysterious and Company,* illustrated by Eric von Schmidt. Little, Brown, 1962.

Forbes, Esther. *Johnny Tremain,* illustrated by Lynd Ward. Houghton Mifflin, 1946.

Forman, James. *Ceremony of Innocence.* Hawthorn, 1970.

————. *Horses of Anger.* Farrar, Straus, 1967.

————. *Ring the Judas Bell.* Farrar, Straus, 1965.

————. *The Skies of Crete.* Farrar, Straus, 1963.

Fox, Paula. *The Slave Dancer,* illustrated by Eros Keith. Bradbury, 1973.

Frank, Anne. *Anne Frank: The Diary of a Young Girl,* rev. ed., translated by B. M. Mooyart, introduction by Eleanor Roosevelt. Doubleday, 1967.

Fritz, Jean. *Brady,* illustrated by Lynd Ward. Coward-McCann, 1960.

————. *The Cabin Faced West,* illustrated by Feodor Rojankovsky. Coward-McCann, 1958.

————. *Early Thunder,* illustrated by Lynd Ward. Coward-McCann, 1967.

Garfield, Leon. *Devil-in-the-Fog,* illustrated by Antony Maitland. Pantheon, 1966.

————. *Jack Holborn,* illustrated by Antony Maitland. Pantheon, 1965.

————. *Smith,* illustrated by Antony Maitland. Pantheon, 1967.

————. *The Sound of Coaches,* illustrated by John Lawrence. Viking, 1974.

Goble, Paul, and Dorothy Goble. *Red Hawk's Account of Custer's Last Battle.* Pantheon, 1970.

Graham, Gail. *Cross-Fire: A Vietnam Novel,* illustrated by David S. Martin. Pantheon, 1972.

Gray, Elizabeth Janet. *Adam of the Road,* illustrated by Robert Lawson. Viking, 1944.

————. *I Will Adventure,* illustrated by Corydon Bell. Viking, 1962.

Greene, Bette. *The Summer of My German Soldier.* Dial, 1973.

Haar, Jaap ter. *Boris,* translated from the Dutch by Martha Mearns, illustrated by Rien Poortvliet. Delacorte, 1970.

Haley, Gail. *Jack Jouett's Ride.* Viking, 1973.

Harris, Christie. *Raven's Cry,* illustrated by Bill Reid. Atheneum, 1966.

Harvey, James O. *Beyond the Gorge of Shadows.* Lothrop, 1965.

Haugaard, Erik Christian. *Hakon of Rogen's Saga,* illustrated by Leo Dillon and Diane Dillon. Mifflin, 1963.

————. *The Little Fishes,* illustrated by Milton Johnson. Houghton Mifflin, 1967.

————. *Orphans of the Wind,* illustrated by Milton Johnson. Houghton Mifflin, 1966.

————. *A Slave's Tale,* illustrated by Leo Dillon and Diane Dillon. Houghton Mifflin, 1965.

————. *The Untold Tale,* illustrated by Leo Dillon and Diane Dillon. Houghton Mifflin, 1971.

Hautzig, Esther. *The Endless Steppe: Growing up in Siberia.* Crowell, 1968.

Hays, Wilma Pitchford. *Christmas on the Mayflower,* illustrated by Roger Duvoisin. Coward-McCann, 1956.

————. *Pilgrim Thanksgiving,* illustrated by Leonard Weisgard. Coward-McCann, 1965.

————. *The Scarlet Badge,* Illustrated by Peter Burchard. Holt, Rinehart and Winston, 1963.

Hickman, Janet. *The Valley of the Shadow.* Macmillan, 1974.

Hodges, C. Walter. *The Marsh King.* Coward-McCann, 1967.

————. *The Namesake: A Story of King Alfred.* Coward-McCann, 1964.

Holm, Anne. *North to Freedom,* translated by L. W. Kingsland. Harcourt Brace Jovanovich, 1965.

Hunt, Irene. *Across Five Aprils.* Follett, 1964.

————. *No Promises in the Wind.* Follett, 1970.

Hunter, Mollie. *The Ghosts of Glencoe.* Funk & Wagnalls, 1969.

Ish-Kishor, Sulamith. *A Boy of Old Prague,* illustrated by Ben Shahn. Pantheon, 1963.

Jackson, Jacqueline. *The Taste of Spruce Gum,* illustrated by Lilian Obligado. Little, Brown, 1966.

Jones, Weyman. *Edge of Two Worlds,* illustrated by J. C. Kocsis. Dial, 1968.

————. *The Talking Leaf.* Dial, 1965.

Keith, Harold. *Rifles for Watie.* Crowell, 1957.

Kelly, Eric P. *The Trumpeter of Krakow,* rev. ed., illustrated by Janina Domanska. Macmillan, 1966 (1928).

Kerr, Judith. *When Hitler Stole Pink Rabbit.* Coward-McCann, 1972.

Konigsburg, E. L. *A Proud Taste for Scarlet and Miniver.* Atheneum, 1973.

Kroeber, Theodora. *Ishi, Last of His Tribe,* illustrated by Ruth Robbins. Parnassus, 1964.

Latham, Jean Lee. *This Dear Bought Land,* illustrated by Jacob Landau. Harper & Row, 1957.

Lenski, Lois. *Indian Captive, The Story of Mary Jemison.* Lippincott, 1941.

Levitin, Sonia. *Journey to America,* illustrated by Charles Robinson. Atheneum, 1970.

Linevski, A. *An Old Tale Carved Out of Stone,* translated by Maria Polushkin. Crown, 1973.

Lofts, Norah. *The Maude Reed Tale,* illustrated by Anne Johnstone and Janet Johnstone. Thomas Nelson, 1972.

————. *Rupert Hatton's Story,* illustrated by Anne Johnstone and Janet Grahame Johnstone. Thomas Nelson, 1973.

McGraw, Eloise Jarvis. *The Golden Goblet.* Coward-McCann, 1961.

————. *Mara, Daughter of the Nile.* Coward-McCann, 1953.

————. *Master Cornhill.* Atheneum, 1973.

————. *Moccasin Trail.* Coward-McCann, 1952.

McSwigan, Marie. *Snow Treasure,* illustrated by Mary Reardon. Dutton, 1942.

Mason, Miriam E. *Caroline and Her Kettle Named Maud,* illustrated by Kathleen Voute. Macmillan, 1951.

Meadowcroft, Enid. *By Secret Railway,* illustrated by Henry C. Pitz. Crowell, 1948.

————. *The First Year,* illustrated by Grace Paull. Crowell, 1946.

Means, Florence. *The Moved-Outers,* illustrated by Helen Blair. Houghton Mifflin, 1945.

Monjo, F. N. *The Drinking Gourd,* illustrated by Fred Brenner. Harper & Row, 1970.

————. *The Vicksburg Veteran,* illustrated by Douglas Gorsline. Simon & Schuster, 1971.

Murray, Michele. *The Crystal Nights.* Seabury, 1973.

O'Dell, Scott. *The King's Fifth,* illustrated by Samuel Bryant. Houghton Mifflin, 1966.

————. *Sing Down the Moon.* Houghton Mifflin, 1970.

Petry, Ann. *Tituba of Salem Village.* Crowell, 1964.

Picard, Barbara Leonie. *One Is One,* Holt, Rinehart and Winston, 1966.

Pilkington, Roger. *I Sailed on the Mayflower,* illustrated by Douglas Bisset. St. Martins, 1966.

Polland, Madeleine. *Beorn the Proud,* illustrated by William Stobbs. Holt, Rinehart and Winston, 1961.

————. *To Tell My People,* illustrated by Richard M. Powers. Holt, Rinehart and Winston, 1968.

Reiss, Johanna. *The Upstairs Room.* Crowell, 1972.

Richard, Adrienne. *Pistol.* Little, Brown, 1969.

Richter, Conrad. *The Light in the Forest.* Knopf, 1953.

Richter, Hans Peter. *Friedrich,* translated by Edite Kroll. Holt, Rinehart and Winston, 1970.

———. *I Was There,* translated by Edite Kroll. Holt, Rinehart and Winston, 1972.

Sachs, Marilyn. *A Pocket Full of Seeds.* Doubleday, 1973.

Schweitzer, Byrd Baylor. *One Small Blue Bead,* illustrated by Symeon Shimin. Macmillan, 1965.

Speare, Elizabeth George. *The Bronze Bow.* Houghton Mifflin, 1961.

———. *Calico Captive,* illustrated by W. T. Mars. Houghton Mifflin, 1957.

———. *The Witch of Blackbird Pond.* Houghton Mifflin, 1958.

Steele, William O. *The Buffalo Knife,* illustrated by Paul Galdone. Harcourt Brace Jovanovich, 1952.

———. *The Far Frontier,* illustrated by Paul Galdone. Harcourt Brace Jovanovich, 1959.

———. *Flaming Arrows,* illustrated by Paul Galdone. Harcourt Brace Jovanovich, 1957.

———. *The Lone Hunt,* illustrated by Paul Galdone. Harcourt Brace Jovanovich, 1956.

———. *The Perilous Road,* illustrated by Paul Galdone. Harcourt Brace Jovanovich, 1958.

———. *Tomahawks and Trouble,* illustrated by Paul Galdone. Harcourt Brace Jovanovich, 1955.

———. *Trail through Danger,* illustrated by Charles Beck. Harcourt Brace Jovanovich 1965.

———. *Winter Danger,* illustrated by Paul Galdone. Harcourt Brace Jovanovich, 1954.

———. *The Year of the Bloody Sevens,* illustrated by Charles Beck. Harcourt Brace Jovanovich, 1963.

Sutcliff, Rosemary. *Dawn Wind,* illustrated by Charles Keeping. Walck, 1962.

———. *The Eagle of the Ninth,* illustrated by C. W. Hodges. Walck, 1954.

———. *Knight's Fee,* illustrated by Charles Keeping. Walck, 1960.

———. *The Lantern Bearers,* illustrated by Charles Keeping. Walck, 1959.

———. *The Silver Branch,* illustrated by Charles Keeping. Walck, 1959.

———. *Warrior Scarlet,* illustrated by Charles Keeping. Walck, 1958.

———. *The Witch's Brat,* illustrated by Richard Lebenson. Walck, 1970.

Taylor, Theodore. *The Cay.* Doubleday, 1969.

———. *The Children's War.* Doubleday, 1971.

Trease, Geoffrey. *Escape to King Alfred.* Vanguard, 1959.

Treece, Henry. *The Dream Time,* illustrated by Charles Keeping. Hawthorn, 1968.

———. *The Last Viking,* illustrated by Charles Keeping. Pantheon, 1966.

———. *The Road to Miklagaard.* S. G. Phillips, 1957.

———. *Viking's Dawn.* S. G. Phillips, 1956.

———. *Viking's Sunset.* Criterion, 1960.

Tunis, John R. *His Enemy, His Friend.* Morrow, 1967.

———. *Silence over Dunkerque.* Morrow, 1962.

Uchida, Yoshiko. *Journey to Topaz,* illustrated by Donald Carrick. Scribner, 1971.

Van der Loeff, Anna Rutgers. *Oregon at Last!,* illustrated by Charles Geer. Morrow, 1962.

Van Stockum, Hilda. *The Winged Watchman.* Farrar, Straus, 1963.

Walsh, Jill Paton. *The Dolphin Crossing.* St. Martin, 1967.

———. *Fireweed.* Farrar, Straus, 1970.

Weir, Rosemary. *Blood Royal,* illustrated by Richard Cuffari. Farrar, Straus, 1973.

Wibberley, Leonard. *John Treegate's Musket.* Farrar, Straus, 1959.

———. *Peter Treegate's War.* Farrar, Straus, 1960.

———. *Sea Captain from Salem.* Farrar, Straus, 1961.

———. *Treegate's Raiders.* Farrar, Straus, 1962.

Wilder, Laura Ingalls. *The First Four Years,* illustrated by Garth Williams. Harper & Row, 1971.

———. The Little House Series, illustrated by Garth Williams. Harper & Row, 1953.

By the Shores of Silver Lake (1939).

Little House in the Big Woods (1932).

Farmer Boy (1933).

Little House on the Prairie (1935).

Little Town on the Prairie (1941).

The Long Winter (1940).

On the Banks of Plum Creek (1937).

These Happy Golden Years (1943).

Williamson, Joanne S. *And Forever Free . . .*, illustrated by Jom McMullan. Knopf, 1966.

Wojciechowska, Maia. *Odyssey of Courage: The Story of Alvar Núñez Cabeza de Vaca*, illustrated by Alvin Smith. Atheneum, 1965.

Wormser, Richard. *The Black Mustanger*, illustrated by Don Bolognese. Morrow, 1971.

———. *Ride a Northbound Horse*, illustrated by Charles Geer. Morrow, 1964.

Wuorio, Eva-Lis. *Code: Polonaise*. Holt, Rinehart and Winston, 1971.

———. *To Fight in Silence*. Holt, Rinehart and Winston, 1973.

Yates, Elizabeth. *Carolina's Courage*, illustrated by Nora S. Unwin. Dutton, 1964.

———. *Sarah Whitcher's Story*, illustrated by Nora S. Unwin. Dutton, 1971.

Zei, Alki. *Petros' War*, translated from the Greek by Edward Fenton. Dutton, 1972.

———. *Wildcat under Glass*, translated from the Greek by Edward Fenton. Holt, Rinehart and Winston, 1968.

9 Informational Books and Biography

On the book jacket is a minutely detailed, black-and-white photograph that stops the eye. The fine texture suggests fur, but the pattern belies it—a butterfly wing perhaps? The book is the Wolbergs' *Zooming In, Photographic Discoveries under the Microscope;* and the picture shows the structure of arginine, an essential amino acid, magnified 320 times. Inside are a mosaic of human blood cells, the screen-wire pattern of an insect's eye, a patchwork of crystals in a piece of brass, the organs of a water flea seen through its transparent outer skeleton. There is a strong impulse to say: "Look at this!"—even if no one else is about. Equally exciting is Scheffer's *The Seeing Eye,* where brilliant color photographs illuminate the common roots of art and science: form in a bold shadow on sunlit rocks, texture in a crust of frost on fallen leaves, color in a bright sulfur fungus.

Here, in *City: A Story of Roman Planning and Construction* are Macaulay's detailed drawings of aqueducts, floor plans of Roman houses, cutaway sections of baths and an amphitheater, a birdseye view of a public toilet. Stepping stones in the Roman streets were placed there, the author tells us, not only to keep citizens' feet dry but to help enforce the speed limit, since animals and carts could straddle them only when traveling very slowly. Again, in *The Apprenticeship of Abraham Lincoln,* is something of note—a newly balanced perspective on the man who was "Lincoln" to his friends, "Paw" to his boys, the "Aboriginal Ape" to Secretary Stanton.

These are books with an uncommon vision of their subjects, intriguing books that beg to be shared. Most notably, these are books of nonfiction. Those who think that fiction alone has power to move and delight the reader are not familiar with the best of today's informational books and biographies. Some of the most original, most vital books that children's literature can offer are nonfiction.

Informational Books

Certainly there are more informational books for children, on a wider diversity of topics, than there have ever been before. They are an inviting lot, more attractive than ever, with some as well suited to leisure as to study. But such wealth creates its own problem—how to choose, or how to help children choose, the best books at the right time. It is not humanly possible for any one teacher or librarian to know all the informational books in print and keep abreast of the new ones; and despite the helpfulness of reference aids and reviewing sources, these cannot be carried about in one's pocket. There is no substitute for becoming aware of the criteria by which factual books should be judged, or for learning about the types of books in which information is presented.

CRITERIA FOR EVALUATING INFORMATIONAL BOOKS

A consideration of the following criteria should help teachers and librarians in the evaluation of informational books. No hierarchy of values is implied in the order of discussion, although accuracy ought always to be of primary importance. The reviewer will need to judge the various elements; there is no definite "scoring," for a book's major strengths may far outweigh a few minor weaknesses.

Accuracy and Authenticity

QUALIFICATIONS OF THE AUTHOR

Informational books are written by people who are authorities in their fields; or they are written by writers who study a subject, interview specialists, and compile the data. A few, like naturalist Jean Craighead George, are both specialists and writers. It is always a good idea to check the book's jacket copy, title page, introduction, or "About the Author" page at the back for information about the author's special qualifications, often expressed in terms of professional title or affiliation. Expertise in one field does not necessarily indicate competency in another, however, so one expects a high degree of authenticity only if the author has limited his book to what appears to be his specialty. This is the case with *Warriors and Worthies: Arms and Armor through the Ages* by Helmut Nickel. The author is Curator of Arms and Armor for New York City's Metropolitan Museum of Art; his text for this picture-history is combined with photographs of many items from the Museum's collection, which we can assume he is eminently qualified to describe. Young football buffs will appreciate the qualifications of the authors of *Defensive Football*—Dick Anderson and Nick Buoniconti—who play for the Miami Dolphins and here demonstrate, with the aid of photographs, such skills as are necessary for pass coverage, tackling, and reading keys. Another pair of authors who work in the field about which they write are Dr. Charles W. Gorodetzky and Dr. Samuel T. Christian, who are on the staff of the National Institute of Mental Health's Addiction Research Center. Their book, *What You Should Know about* DRUGS, is an objective, comprehensible account of the characteristics of various drugs, their effects, and the dangers of abuse. It should be recognized, however, that authorities do hold different views, especially on theoretical positions. Some writers of equal competence might disagree with statements in this book about marijuana, for instance.

If an informational book is written not by an expert in the field but by a "writer," facts can be checked by authorities and the authority cited. For example, the book *Peanut* by Millicent Selsam, with its striking magnified photographs by Jerome Wexler, acknowledges that both text and pictures were checked by the head curator of the New York Botanical Gardens. Add to this the knowledge—available in a note at the end of the book—that the author herself is not only a specialist, trained in botany, but also a writer who has produced many children's science books, and one can select this book with considerable assurance that the content is accurate. Selsam is only one of a number of authors who have earned the reputation of writing dependably good informational books. When in doubt, teachers and librarians are likely to turn first to writers who have proved their integrity with facts—Isaac Asimov, Herbert Zim, Dorothy Shuttlesworth, Jeanne Bendick, Edwin Tunis, Gerald White Johnson, and Genevieve Foster, among others. But authorship, while it may be a valuable rule of thumb, is a dangerous final criterion. The best of cooks sometimes makes a lumpy sauce; each book must be evaluated on its own merits.

ACCURACY OF FACTS

Fortunately, many of the errors of fact in children's informational books are minor ones. Johnson's book, *The Presidency*, mentions that the President's home is called the White House, ". . . although its official name is the Executive Mansion. . ."[1] Miller's *Story of the White House* plainly states that "White House" was made the official title by an Act of Congress in 1902, a fact easy to corroborate in various reference sources.

[1] Gerald W. Johnson. *The Presidency* (New York: Morrow, 1962), p. 11.

Children who have access to a variety of books on one topic should be encouraged to notice discrepancies and pursue the correct answer, a valuable exercise in critical reading. A more serious occasion which calls for reader alertness concerns the inclusion of questionable information, for example the suggestion in James P. Kenealy's *Better Camping for Boys* that survival campers should test plants for poison by tasting them.[2]

In many ways, however, the errors which teachers and children may recognize are less distressing than those which pass for fact because the topic is unfamiliar or highly specialized. Then the reader must depend on a competent reviewer to identify inaccuracies. Science books are regularly reviewed by Harry Stubbs in *The Horn Book Magazine;* Stubbs frequently points out minor errors and occasionally more serious ones. *School Library Journal* often provides helpful criticisms; for example, one review called attention to the errors in Frank Martin's *How Do You Say It? In English, Spanish, and French,* including improper grammatical constructions, misspellings, missing accents, and other slips.[3] Some of the other publications which review informational books are *Social Education, Science and Children,* and *Appraisal: Children's Science Books.*

BEING UP-TO-DATE

Some books that are free of error at the time of writing become inaccurate with the passage of time, as new discoveries are made in the sciences or as changes occur in world politics. Books which focus on the past are less likely to be soon outdated. A book like Baumann's *The Caves of the Great Hunters,* which describes the discovery of the caves at Lascaux and summarizes previous discoveries, will remain up-to-date unless some new theory should develop regarding the reason for primitive people's cave paintings. On the other hand, books which focus on areas of vigorous research and experimentation, such as viruses and disease or space technology, are quickly outdated. Ben Bova's 1974 book, *Workshops in Space,* could only anticipate events which are now history. It is worth noting, however, that the latest trade books are almost always more up-to-date than the latest textbooks or encyclopedias.

It is also difficult, but important, to provide children with current information about other countries where national governments are emerging or where future political developments are uncertain. Poole's *Thailand,* published in 1973, was welcomed as an update to earlier books about that country, although the situation in Southeast Asia changes so rapidly that often it is only the daily news that can provide completely up-to-date information.

Books about minority cultures need to include material on contemporary experience, as well as heritage. Too many studies of American Indians, for example, have dealt only with Indian life when the country was being explored and settled. It is refreshing now to have stories like Wolf's *Tinker and the Medicine Man,* which shows a modern Navajo family interested in preserving traditional ways, but willing to live in a trailer during the school year so that the children need not be separated from their parents.

Checking the copyright is the simplest way to get some idea of whether or not a book is up-to-date, but it is by no means a foolproof test. Even a recent edition, like the 1973 version of a 1952 book, *It's Fun to Know Why* by Schwartz, may be only superficially revised, with minimal new material tacked on to the end of each chapter and failure to eliminate old material which has little meaning for today's children—such as the discussion of coal furnaces (although the energy crisis could revive interest in even this subject).

INCLUDING ALL THE SIGNIFICANT FACTS

Though the material presented in a book may be current and technically correct, the book cannot be totally accurate if significant facts are omitted. Science books which deal with animal reproduction have frequently glossed over the specifics of birth or of mating, as happens in McClung's *Possum,* where the process is explained as: "All night long the two of them wandered through the woods together. But at dawn each went his own way again. Possum's babies were born just twelve days later."[4] Fortunately, changing social mores which have struck

---

[2] James P. Kenealy. *Better Camping for Boys* (New York: Dodd, Mead, 1971).

[3] Frank Martin. *How Do You Say It? In English, Spanish, and French,* illustrated by D. K. Stone (Platt & Munk, 1973).

[4] Robert McClung. *Possum* (New York: Morrow, 1963), p. 41.

It is born inside a sac.

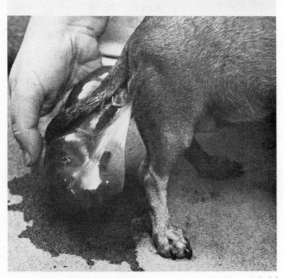

Clear photographs and forthright text help a child understand the birth of a puppy.

Reprinted by permission of William Morrow & Co., Inc., from *My Puppy Is Born* by Joanna Cole. Photographs by Jerome Wexler. Copyright © 1973 by Jerome Wexler.

down taboos in children's fiction have also encouraged a new frankness in books of information. Clear, close-up photographs in *My Puppy Is Born* by Cole, along with a brief but forthright text, serve to show birth through the delivery and early development of a dachshund's litter. Human reproduction and sexuality have so often been distorted by omissions that the many newer books, with accurate terminology and explicit information, are particularly welcome. *Love and Sex and Growing Up* by Eric Johnson and Corinne Johnson, for example, is meant for pre-adolescents. It includes not only the basic physiological facts but also material of less obvious but equally real concern to children, such as heredity, marriage and divorce, and adults who are sexually attracted to children. An attractive book designed for parents to share with young children is Stein's *Making Babies*, which deals head-on with questions that adults often find difficult to answer. After suggesting an uncomplicated way to explain the mechanics of inter-

course the author says: "It is sensible and honest to add that, because it feels nice, people make love together even when they are not starting a baby."[5] This book is part of the *Open Family* series, which also includes *About Handicaps* and *About Dying*, a topic often totally ignored or camouflaged by euphemisms. *Life and Death* by Zim and Bleeker briefly describes reproduction, life expectancies, and the burial customs of various societies, including our own. Most importantly, it does not pass over one of the central issues: "After burial a body, which is composed of nearly three-quarters water, soon changes. The soft tissues break down and disappear first. Within a year only bones are left."[6]

In many books the honest presentation of all the facts contributes to an effect of realism, as well as to total accuracy. This is certainly true in life-cycle animal books. *Possum* by McClung, mentioned earlier, avoids the word "mating," but nevertheless explains clearly that while thirteen young reached the mother's pouch, she had only eleven nipples and the "last two babies had no place to go. They eventually starved to death."[7] This sort of realism may also be achieved in historical or cultural accounts. There is no mincing of words in Rich's vivid telling of the hardships at Jamestown in *The First Book of the Early Settlers*:

> As the days grew shorter and colder, food became more and more scarce. They ate acorns, nuts, fruits, whatever they could find. Then they ate the dogs. . . .[8]

Bealer's chronicle of the Cherokee removal in *Only the Names Remain: The Cherokees and the Trail of Tears* is made to seem dramatic and immediate by the richness of detail. We learn that Andrew Jackson himself crossed out a treaty provision allowing Cherokee families to own Georgia farms, that soldiers sent to the Indian cabins forced even the sick out of their beds to march

[5] Sara Bonnett Stein, *Making Babies*, photographs by Doris Pinney (New York: Walker, 1974), p. 38.
[6] Herbert S. Zim and Sonia Bleeker. *Life and Death*, illustrated by René Martin (New York: Morrow, 1970), p. 46.
[7] McClung, p. 45.
[8] Louise Dickinson Rich. *The First Book of the Early Settlers*, illustrated by Douglas Gorsline (New York: F. Watts, 1959), p. 17.

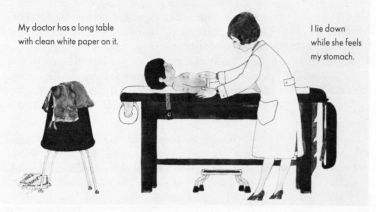

My doctor has a long table with clean white paper on it.

I lie down while she feels my stomach.

Informational books for children have been among the first to suggest a wide variety of career choices for women.

From *My Doctor* by Harlow Rockwell. Copyright © 1973 by Harlow Rockwell. Used by permission of Macmillan Publishing Co., Inc.

to the stockades, that government contractors supplied the journeying Cherokees with rotten meat and weevily corn. It is interesting to compare this authentic tale with Scott O'Dell's fictionalized account of the similar plight of the Navajos in *Sing Down the Moon* (*see* Chapter 8).

AVOIDING STEREOTYPES

A book that omits significant facts tells only part of the truth; a book that presents stereotypes pretends, wrongly, to have told the whole truth. One subtle but very common sort of stereotyping is by omission. The illustrations in science books, for instance, often create the impression that scientists must be male Caucasians, since so few women or minorities are pictured. A new level of awareness, however, has brought about the publication of books that, without fanfare, show women in a greater variety of roles. One such is the doctor in Rockwell's picture book, *My Doctor,* or the laboratory scientist in Lauber's *Of Man and Mouse.* Some books are directed toward breaking stereotypes. The series titled *What Can She Be?* features a woman as an architect, a newscaster, a veterinarian, and in other equally significant occupations. The subject in the Goldreichs' *What Can She Be? A Newscaster* is a black woman, and pictures of her family show that her husband is white—a notable breaking of stereotypes on three counts. Liebers' *Jobs in Construction* points out areas in that field now open to women,

and the photos show workers of both sexes. The cover of *Careers in a Medical Center* by Davis shows a black doctor and a white child; the fact that this picture is so uncommon as to be worthy of note indicates how far we have to go in dealing with stereotype by omission.

Perhaps the most blatant form of stereotyping occurs in books about other lands. Children can be taught to be alert to sweeping general statements such as this one in *Looking at Italy:* "Those who live in the north are tough, and make good businessmen. Those of the south are easy going and less efficient."[9] It is difficult to portray a country or region accurately in all its diversity of terrain, people, industry, housing, and such. One solution to the problem is exemplified by the Bernheims' *In Africa,* which has a very brief text accompanying nearly one hundred photographs. The pictures—which show differing life styles on the Savanna and in the forest, on the desert and in the city—speak largely for themselves. Another way to deal with diversity without presenting stereotypes is to limit the scope of the book as Sasek has done in *This Is Historic Britain.* The title indicates that the author's paintings of monuments, castles, and cathedrals are not intended to be a complete picture of the country.

[9] Rupert Martin. *Looking at Italy* (Philadelphia, Penna.: Lippincott, 1966), p. 12.

USING FACTS TO SUPPORT GENERALIZATIONS

A proper generalization, to be distinguishable from stereotype or simple opinion, needs facts for support. In *What You Should Know About* DRUGS, Gorodetzky and Christian use case studies to authenticate a generalization presented in carefully qualified terms:

> Marijuana can lead to the use of stronger drugs, although it does not always do so. Most narcotic addicts begin by smoking marijuana, but this is not the same as saying that all people who smoke marijuana go on to heroin. However, this experience with marijuana often increases the user's curiosity about the effects of other drugs. Smoking marijuana gets him accustomed to using drugs to run away from his problems. Probably those who have used marijuana are more likely to go on to other drugs than those who have never used any drugs at all.[10]

Pringle says in *The Only Earth We Have* that meat-eating birds at the end of food chains have been seriously affected by biocides. Three pieces of evidence are offered: the large amounts of DDT found in the bodies of dead eagles and in eggs that did not hatch, the lowered population of eagles and ospreys in areas where DDT is heavily used, and the thriving bird population in areas relatively free of biocides. Some generalizations, however, are difficult to support. The statement in Selsam's popular *Questions and Answers about Horses* that today's most popular riding horse is the American Saddle Horse would be arguable even if statistics were shown; preference is always subject to qualification. Critical readers need to be aware of generalizations and judge for themselves if adequate facts are offered for support.

MAKING THE DISTINCTION BETWEEN FACT AND THEORY

Careful writers make careful distinctions between fact and theory; but, even so, children need guidance in learning to recognize the difference. Often the distinction depends on key words or phrases—such as "scientists believe," "so far as

we know," or "perhaps." Consider the effect of a single "probably" in this sentence describing a prehistoric bird. "Gallornis had hollow bones and probably flew long distances with the flapping flight of flamingoes."[11] Shuttlesworth's discussion of fossil distribution in *To Find a Dinosaur* clearly labels as theory two different explanations of continent forms, then cites the evidence for one of them:

> For the most part, the "Gondwana land theory" was not taken very seriously. But during the past decade, a great amount of data gathered by scientists seemed to prove that Gondwana land really existed. And fossils, discovered very recently in Antarctica, gave final, convincing proof of the long-vanished continent.[12]

While it is important to distinguish between fact and theory in all of the sciences, and the social sciences as well, the matter receives most attention in books dealing with evolution and human origins. In some communities this remains a sensitive topic, but it would seem that children everywhere have a right to information about scientists' discoveries and theories regarding our origins. *Why Things Change: The Story of Evolution* by Bendick has a particularly good explanation of time relationships, as well as appropriate examples which demonstrate the meaning of such terms as "evolve," "adapt," and "extinct."

AVOIDING ANTHROPOMORPHISM

In poetry and fiction the assignment of human feelings and behavior to animals, plants, or objects is called personification—an accepted literary device that may be used with great effect. In science, however, the same device becomes unacceptable and is known as *anthropomorphism*. In a book that purports to be an informational book, this seems to say to the child: "You really do not have the intelligence or interest to understand or accept straightforward information." A comparison of Portal's *The Life of a Queen* and Shuttlesworth's *The Story of Ants* will show how otherwise accurate facts are distorted by anthropomorphism.

---

[10] Dr. Charles W. Gorodetzky and Dr. Samuel T. Christian. *What You Should Know About* DRUGS (New York: Harcourt Brace Jovanovich, 1970), p. 41.

[11] Elizabeth S. Austin. *Birds that Stopped Flying* (New York: Random House, 1969), p. 7.

[12] Dorothy E. Shuttlesworth. *To Find a Dinosaur* (New York: Doubleday, 1973), p. 86.

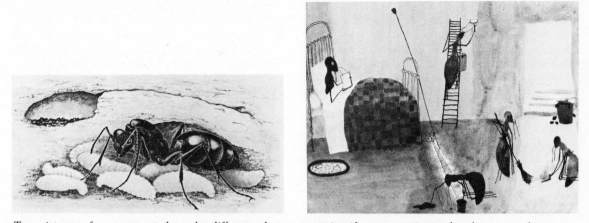

Two pictures of a queen ant show the difference between a scientific presentation and anthropomorphism. *(Left)* From *The Story of Ants* by Dorothy Shuttlesworth and Su Zan Noguchi Swain. Copyright © 1964 by Doubleday & Company, Inc. Reproduced by permission of the publisher. *(Right)* From *The Life of a Queen* by Colette Portal, published in German by Sellier GmbH Freising Verlag, and used with permission.

In Portal's book the activities of the queen ant and other members of the ant "realm" are described in an account that is basically accurate, but with a tone that suggests fantasy rather than fact: "High above the earth the young queen picks her mate. With him she disappears into the blazing sunset, leaving the others behind. This is the shining moment of her life."[13] The illustrations go even further toward personification, showing the ant queen variously in her brass bed, her ladderback chair, and her bentwood rocker. In contrast, *The Story of Ants* presents facts about ants in a straightforward manner, and the clearly detailed illustrations extend information rather than create the impression that ants are tiny humans with extra legs.

Selsam talks to her young readers about the problem of interpreting what animals do in the book, *Animals as Parents:*

> It is hard to keep remembering that animals live in a different kind of world from our own. They see, hear, smell, and taste things differently. And they do not have human intelligence or emotions, so we must avoid interpreting their behavior in terms of our own feelings and thoughts. For example, it looks to us as though parent birds are devoted to their young in the same way that human

parents are devoted to theirs. But only experimental work can show whether this interpretation is true.[14]

Knowing that young children perceive new things in terms of their own experiences and feelings, however, writers of books directed to this audience often give names to their animal characters and express behavior in a child's terms. In *Biography of a Polar Bear* by Steiner there comes a point during young Nanook's first experience with seal fishing when, like a child, he "could not sit still any longer" and a time when, finding Mother Bear asleep and himself awake, "he decided to look around." Very rarely are animal books at this level completely free of anthropomorphic touches. Fenner's excellent book *Gorilla Gorilla* does report only the observable behavior of an animal born wild, captured, and kept in a zoo; yet an undercurrent of emotion in the text allows the reader to suppose how such a creature feels. Although the animals in longer life-cycle stories are deliberately characterized, some come through with a minimum of anthropomorphic detail, as does Frosty, the partial albino, in Bancroft's intriguing account of *The White Cardinal*.

Closely related to anthropomorphism is an-

[13] Colette Portal. *The Life of a Queen,* translated by Marcia Nardi (New York: Braziller, 1964), unpaged.

[14] Millicent Selsam. *Animals as Parents,* illustrated by John Kaufmann (New York: Morrow, 1965), p. 16.

other error called *teleological explanation of phenomena*. A prime example is the personification of nature where Nature (capitalized) is given a supernatural or divine purpose. Such an explanation occurs in *Marvels of the Sea and Shore*, even though the manuscript was checked by scientists at the Scripps Institute of Oceanography:

> Whenever you come to the beach you enter the most important scientific laboratory in the world. Here in the sand and sea Nature herself is conducting the experiments. She is constantly mixing chemicals and testing forces. She works on microscopic bits and on objects huge in size. . . .[15]

While such a description has a certain poetic effect, it also conveys a basically unscientific attitude which has no place in a book of information.

Content and Perspective

PURPOSE

It is futile to try to pass judgment on the content of an informational book without first determining the purpose for which the book was designed. Identifying the scope of the book lets us know what we can reasonably expect. A quick look at Asimov's *ABC's of the Ocean* shows that this is a fascinating collection of facts for browsing, whereas both the title and appearance of the *Atlas of World Wildlife* indicate a comprehensive treatment of the topic. Titles can be misleading, particularly those which promise to tell "all about" a subject, but offer limited coverage instead. At best, titles both indicate the scope of the book's content and pique the reader's curiosity, as do Alderman's *The War We Could Have Lost: The American Revolution* and Hendrickson's *Who Really Invented the Rocket?*

INTENDED AUDIENCE

Before evaluating content we have to know not just for what the book was intended, but for whom. Book jackets or book reviews often indicate an age range according to reading level or interest. It is difficult to know whether one or both of these factors are reflected in the age recommended. Generally, the readability level of

a book is not as important as its content in relation to the reader's actual interest in a subject. In using informational books, children will read "beyond their abilities" when reading for particular facts. Children will frequently turn to difficult books if they contain many pictures or useful diagrams. At the same time, vocabulary, sentence length, size of type, and the organization of the book are factors to be considered. When children see crowded pages, relatively small type, and few pictures they may reject a book which contains useful information.

The choice of topic then is an important factor in determining whether a book will be suitable for its intended audience. Books for young children most often reflect their basic egocentric concerns, and their curiosity about themselves and other living things. It is a mistake to assume that these are the only appropriate topics, however. Radlauer's *Fast, Faster, Fastest*—designed for remedial reading at the upper elementary level—finds a great deal of interest at the primary level due to its color photographs of various vehicles, presented in triple sets to illustrate the title and other such concepts. Although the book by Kerr called *Shakespeare's Flowers* is handsomely illustrated in delicate, glowing colors, and has basically a picture-book appearance, it is not at all suited to the picture storybook age. The text combines quotes from Shakespeare with lore about the flowers he so frequently mentioned, and the paintings of these flowers are almost photographically accurate—a delightful book, but for a mature and rather specialized audience.

Examples chosen by an author to illustrate concepts have a great deal to do with the level of development needed for comprehension of the book. In *Less than Nothing Is Really Something*, with a picture-book format, Froman has considered the child's need to think in terms of the concrete and to manipulate objects. His explanation of negative integers asks children to recall their experience with thermometers, with steps descending below ground level, with the astronauts' countdown to blast-off. He also includes number lines to make and games to play. At the opposite end of the scale is Struble's good but difficult book, *The Web of Space-Time*. This explanation of Einsteinian relativity for older children (or per-

---

[15] Oren Arnold. *Marvels of the Sea and Shore*, illustrated by J. Yunge Bateman (New York: Abelard-Schuman, 1963), p. 17.

haps for their teachers) does avoid mathematical language, but understanding the text and diagrams requires a high level of abstract thinking.

ADEQUATE COVERAGE

Recognizing the purpose of a book and its intended level, the reader has a basis for deciding if the author has said too much about his topic or too little. *The Bread Book: All about Bread and How to Make It* by Meyer is an example of a book that looks at its topic from every conceivable angle. Nearly one hundred pages of legends, traditions, history, recipes, bakery techniques, and international types might become tedious if not for the author's lively narrative style and humorous drawings. In an equal number of pages De Garza's *Chicanos: The Story of Mexican Americans* attempts an overview of the four-hundred-year history and the contemporary affairs of this culture group. Some significant material, notably the Pueblo uprising against Spanish rule, is not given due attention; as a result the book, despite its good points, lacks balance. This matter of coverage in a book of history is extremely important. Johnson's introduction to *America Is Born* expresses the need for careful writing:

> Part of the story is very fine, and other parts are very bad; but they all belong to it, and if you leave out the bad parts you never understand it all. Yet you must understand it if you are to make your part one of the fine parts.[16]

The author who fails to acknowledge more than one viewpoint or theory fails to help children learn to examine issues. Even young children should know that authorities do not always agree, though the context may be very simple. In *A Book about Pandas*, Gross reports:

> The zoo keepers in China say that female pandas are friendlier than male pandas. Other zoo keepers do not agree. They say that pandas are like people—every one is different.[17]

Various theories about the origin of Stonehenge are presented in *The Mystery of Stonehenge* by Branley. Without bias, the author discusses the studies and conclusions of scientists from several fields and sums up: "But Stonehenge remains a challenge. Its mysteries may be locked forever within the silent stones."[18]

DEMONSTRATION OF SCIENTIFIC METHOD

Since we are concerned about *how* as well as *what* children learn, it is important to note what kind of thinking a book encourages, as well as the body of fact it presents. Informational books should illustrate the process of inquiry, the excitement of discovery. Children in the upper elementary grades are fascinated by the dramatic account of *Thor Heyerdahl and the Reed Boat Ra* by Murphy and Baker, a story which embodies the spirit of scientific investigation. Asimov describes the scientific processes used in bacteriological research in *How Did We Find Out about Germs?* The adventures of several nineteenth- and twentieth-century archaeologists come to life in Baumann's *In the Land of Ur: The Discovery of Ancient Mesopotamia*.

While these are fine accounts of the scientific method at work, the reader's involvement is still a vicarious one. Some books are designed to give children more direct experience with the skills of inquiry. The series, *A First Look at . . .* by Selsam and Hunt is particularly good for helping the primary-grade child develop his ability to observe and classify. In *A First Look at Leaves*, instead of pointing out that a ginkgo leaf resembles a fan, the authors direct the reader to find the leaf that looks like a fan, a mitten, a needle; clear line drawings of ginkgo, sassafras, and pine appear on the same page. Other characteristics with appropriate matching puzzles encourage independent thinking, and the possibilities are extended even further by the simple directions for making leaf prints. Other books in this series are about fish, mammals, insects, and birds. Another series, the *Science on Your Street* Books by Simon, encourages young children to explore and observe in a city environment. Here again the author uses questions and hints to encourage the child to do his own discovering:

---

[16]Gerald Johnson (in an introductory letter to Peter). *America Is Born*, illustrated by Leonard Everett Fisher (New York: Morrow, 1959), pp. viii–ix.

[17]Ruth Belov Gross. *A Book about Pandas* (New York: Dial, 1972), unpaged.

[18]Franklyn M. Branley. *The Mystery of Stonehenge*, illustrated by Victor Ambrus (New York: Crowell, 1969), p. 47.

Is a pigeon as large as your hand?
As large as your foot?
How large?
Use a ruler to measure an object that you think
is as large as a pigeon.[19]

A Building on Your Street calls attention to construction materials, sizes and shapes, and signs of age. An appealing book for slightly older children is Brenner's *A Snake-lover's Diary*, the record of a boy's experiences in collecting and taking care of a number of snake specimens. The emphasis is on the importance of keeping a careful account of observations and procedures; the text itself is in journal form.

Experiment books for all ages should avoid the "cookbook" approach that simply tells, step-by-step, what to do. Instead, children should be guided in problem-solving through the strategies of open-ended questions, guides to observation, and suggestions for further study. All these are employed by Rahn in *Seeing What Plants Do* and *More about What Plants Do*, both for middle readers. The questions to guide observation are particularly good—clear and direct, but allowing children to report their results as they see them. Expected outcomes and the reasons behind them are discussed in a separate section at the end of the book. Somewhat older children will reach their own conclusions through the open-ended activities in a timely book by Sootin, *Easy Experiments with Water Pollution*. Teachers will find a valuable discussion of the experimental method for their own reading in Moorman's book for high-school students, *How to Make Your Science Project Scientific*.

The scientific method applies to the social sciences too, but there are fewer books in this area designed to help children learn and use the inquiry approach. Strivastava's *Statistics*, for primary-grade children, is much livelier than its title indicates. It helps the reader learn to take samples, to gather data, and report it through simple charts and graphs. This is a most useful tool for children learning to explore their environment. Jean Fritz has illustrated techniques of historical research in a fictionalized account that children

like very much; it is called *George Washington's Breakfast*. The story illustrates the role of perseverance and good luck in problem-solving. After young George, who is trying to find out what George Washington customarily ate for breakfast, has asked questions, exhausted library resources, and gone on a futile fact-finding trip to Mt. Vernon, he happens to find the answer in an old book about to be discarded from his own attic. Practice in weighing evidence and making decisions is offered in Sidney Carroll's *You Be the Judge*, which describes actual court cases. The outcomes are reported on a different page, making each case a puzzle suitable for role-playing or discussion by children.

Mature readers can find a notable example of the use of interviews in examining an issue in Switzer's *How Democracy Failed*, in which the author has collected the opinions of German people who were growing up during the years that Hitler came to power. While a variety of attitudes are expressed, the author's commentary does give a strong point of view to the book as a whole. Older students who have read fictional accounts of life under the Nazi regime, such as Richter's *Friedrich* or *I Was There* (see Chapter 8), may want to read part of this book and compare the two.

INTERRELATIONSHIPS AND IMPLICATIONS

A list of facts is fine for an almanac, but most informational books are not almanacs and so should be expected to put facts into some sort of perspective. Basic information about geology is related to common urban sights in *City Rocks, City Blocks and the Moon* by Gallob. Intriguing black-and-white photographs compare an ancient fossil to a dog's footprints in wet cement; show weathered gravestones and brownstone houses, as well as more conventional rock specimens; and, finally, contrast the type of rocks found on the moon with those found on the earth. In a book about ecology, *The Living Community*, Hirsch states: "A poet once said that one could not pluck a flower without troubling a star. This is another way of saying that the living and the nonliving are linked together."[20] Perhaps the

---

[19] Seymour Simon. *Birds on Your Street*, illustrated by Jean Zallinger (New York: Holiday, 1974), unpaged.

[20] S. Carl Hirsch. *The Living Community, A Venture into Ecology*, illustrated by William Steinel (New York: Viking, 1966), p. 17.

chief strength of Billington's *Understanding Ecology* is this outlook, which shows that man is part of a total picture but not at its center. Interrelationships of a different sort are pointed out in Foster's *Year of the Pilgrims, 1620,* a horizontal history that helps children see the cultural context of a major event. Her brief account of the Pilgrims' journey and its background is given perspective by the descriptions of Shakespeare, Galileo, and other great artists and scientists of the day; even more significant is the inclusion of material that shows powerful contemporary kingdoms in Africa, India, China, and Japan. Other books by Foster provide similar treatment for *Year of Columbus, 1492; Year of Independence, 1776;* and *Year of Lincoln, 1861.*

The relationship of science and technology to society is a crucial one, and many recent information books have taken part of this problem as a focus. The Silversteins write about food additives, weighing advantages and disadvantages, in *The Chemicals We Eat and Drink;* Navarra stresses the need to be conscious of our environment in *The World You Inherit: A Study of Pollution;* Shuttlesworth and Williams present quite comprehensive information in *Disappearing Energy: Can We End the Crisis?.* Other books provide children with a strong impetus to social action, such as *The Organic Living Book* by Kohn, *Save the Earth: An Ecological Handbook for Kids* by Miles, and *Litter—The Ugly Enemy* by Shuttlesworth and Cervasio. This last describes how two children join in the activities intended to clean up their city.

But even those books which are not specifically designed to call attention to the related social problems of science and technology ought to acknowledge that such problems do exist. For instance, *The New Water Book* by Berger focuses on the characteristics of water and its uses, but also includes a list of organizations interested in pollution problems. De Rossi's *Computers: Tools for Today* explains much about how computers work, and includes a chapter on the history of their development. Despite the author's disclaimer that the book is not meant to tell everything about computers, it seems unfortunate to praise the advantages of computer technology without also mentioning the related problems of automation and cybernetics. Where the uses of science have serious implications for society, it would seem that the relationships should be made clear.

Style

CLARITY AND DIRECTNESS

Books that present information through the veil of fiction generally do not succeed in either category, although some of them are widely circulated. *Peter Gets the Chickenpox,* first published in 1959, went into its eighth printing in 1970. Its didacticism recalls the informational books of the last century, however:

> If new spots come, that's nothing to fear.
> It's customary for repeated crops to appear.
> For three to five days you may keep getting pox.
> While new blisters form, the old ones get crusts on their tops.[21]

While the information is not inaccurate, the awkward verse is a distraction. Children will certainly not care much about Peter as a character; the facts about chickenpox would have been better presented in a straightforward manner. Authentic stories, however—as opposed to such a contrived one—are welcomed by children. Life-cycle animal stories, for instance, and photographic essays featuring real people, such as Englebert's *Camera on Ghana: The World of a Young Fisherman,* can be very effective as vehicles for presenting information.

Precise use of language is another important factor in clarity. In his description of a new volcanic island, author William Stephens might have indicated, somewhat vaguely, that after the lava stopped flowing, flowers and birds and insects soon appeared. But his words are more specific, and therefore clearer:

> The lava flowed, off and on, until June 1967. Surtsey was now one and a half miles long and 567 feet high. That same month the first flower bloomed—a white sea rocket. Since then more than 25 species of birds have been recorded at Surtsey, as well as one spider and several dozen kinds of insects.[22]

[21] Marguerite Rush Lerner. *Peter Gets the Chickenpox,* illustrated by George Overlie (Minneapolis, Minn.: Lerner, 1959), unpaged.
[22] William M. Stephens. *Islands,* illustrated by Lydia Rosier (New York: Holiday, 1974), p. 39.

LEVEL OF DIFFICULTY

Although vocabulary does have to be within the child's range, books for primary-grade children need not be restricted to a narrow list of words. New terms can be explained in context as in one of the *I Can Read* series by Selsam. In her book, *Benny's Animals and How He Put Them in Order*, the museum professor says: "Another pile will be Amphibians—animals that live in the water when they are young and on land when they are grown up. Those are your frogs and toads."[23] Context does not serve to explain everything, however; a writer aware of the background of his audience will take pains to make new words clear. In *The Making of Man*, Collier warns his reader:

> One of the biggest nuisances you are going to face in this book is terminology—the naming of things. Unfortunately scientists have a tendency to put jawcracking names on their discoveries. The names usually stem from Latin or sometimes Greek. . . . When you see the word *anthropo*, you will know it has something to do with "man" or "mankind."[24]

Unfortunately some writers assume that children will have a wider understanding of words than is actually the case. Consider the background that a child would need to visualize this description of New Zealand:

> Gorse and broom cover the weathered hills in the south but toward the west coast sounds, or Findland, alternating hills and mountains rise beyond canyons, carved by rapidly flowing rivers, until heavy forest is reached.[25]

In the unlikely event that a child would know about "gorse," "broom," "sounds," and "weathering," he would still be put off by the length and complexity of the sentence.

Words that look unpronounceable are another stumbling block for most children. A glossary is helpful, but youngsters who are intent upon a book's content may not take time to look in the back. In *City Rocks, City Blocks and the Moon*, Gallob shows one way to solve the problem in a heading that reads: "Gneiss (say 'nice')."

READER INVOLVEMENT

Sometimes, when someone has done something very nasty to you, something mean and rotten and unfair, you might say:
"YOU'RE A REAL SKUNK!"
Why do you say that?
What's so bad about skunks?[26]

There are three good ways to get reader involvement, and Schlein has used all three in these opening lines for *What's Wrong with Being a Skunk?*: writing in a conversational tone; using the second person, "you"; and asking questions. The book continues as a superb example of lively language, as well as a clear and accurate presentation of facts about skunks.

Children are quickly drawn into an information book if it appears to be a "true story." In the preface to *The Travels of Monarch X*, Hutchins begins: "This is the true story of a Monarch butterfly. It was one of thousands of Monarchs tagged by Dr. Fred Urquhart of the University of Toronto, Canada, in his interesting studies of butterfly migration."[27] History can be made to seem more a "true story" if the writing is cast in the present tense. Phelan captures this sense of immediacy in *The Story of the Boston Tea Party*, an authentic account which makes the reader a contemporary of Sam Adams and Paul Revere. The present tense can be used to bridge space as well as time. Coombs gives the reader a here-and-now setting as he describes the astronauts' approach to *Skylab*:

> With small bursts of power they close the gap, coasting slightly behind the spacecraft. Continuing to trigger their small attitude thrusters, they nudge toward the cluster. . . . Then, with a comforting click, the nose of the command module slides into the port and locks itself solidly.[28]

[23] Millicent Selsam. *Benny's Animals and How He Put Them in Order*, illustrated by Arnold Lobel (New York: Harper & Row, 1966), p. 47.
[24] James Lincoln Collier. *The Making of Man: The Story of Our Ancient Ancestors* (New York: Four Winds, 1974), p. 42.
[25] Edna Kaula. *The Land and People of New Zealand* (Philadelphia, Penna.: Lippincott, 1964), p. 15.
[26] Miriam Schlein. *What's Wrong with Being a Skunk?*, illustrated by Ray Cruz (New York: Four Winds, 1974), unpaged.
[27] Ross E. Hutchins. *The Travels of Monarch X*, illustrated by Jerome P. Connolly (Skokie, Ill.: Rand McNally, 1966), p. 2.
[28] Charles Coombs. *Skylab* (New York: Morrow, 1972), p. 73.

One good reason for avoiding the past tense in this book, however, is that it appeared before the maneuver had actually taken place.

VIVID LANGUAGE

The writer of informational books uses the same techniques as the writer of fiction to bring a book to life, although the words must be accurate as well as attractive. Imagery is used to appeal to the senses, frequently to sight, as in Moore's distinguished book for mature readers, *The Many Ways of Seeing, An Introduction to the Pleasures of Art*:

> Suppose you are standing at the window on a rainy evening. Your attention might be caught by raindrops sliding against the outside of the pane, forming and reforming in vertical and diagonal patterns. But if you begin looking through the glass, you might see the wet, dark streets beyond, the pools of color; crimson, yellow, and blue reflections of neon lights; cars and people moving in dark silhouette against the lighted shops.[29]

Effective imagery does not have to be lyrical, as Aliki proves in this passage from *Green Grass and White Milk*:

> Last summer I visited a farm high up in the mountains.
> I went into the warm dark barn.
> It smelled of straw and cows.
> It smelled so much I had to hold my nose at first.
> Then I got used to the smell, and I liked it.[30]

Metaphorical language, since it is based on comparison, can be used to contribute to clarity in nonfiction. In his appealing and detailed book, *Chipmunks on the Doorstep*, Tunis aptly compares the little animal's seemingly insecure posture to "an egg balanced on its small end." Atwood uses metaphor to a somewhat different effect in her stunning photographic essay, *The Wild Young Desert*:

> . . . mountains that stole the moisture from the clouds may sink, or distant icecaps melt so that water pours back into the land. Then the rising

forests will send their green armies clambering over the sandstone castles to conquer the arid kingdom. And so the desert vanishes.[31]

The total effect of style is cadence. In scenes of action, suspense and excitement are created by the pace of the writing and the precise use of verbs. In *Bear Mouse*, Freschet makes the reader hold his breath:

> At the edge of the meadow, a bobcat slunk low.
> He crept forward, toward the mouse.
> Slowly, nearer and nearer crept the bobcat.
> Now he was close enough—
> He pounced![32]

And in *Man's Mark on the Land*, Gregor influences our thinking about the environment with the near poetry of his prose:

> In those far-off days the water was fit to drink and the air was fit to breathe. The constellations blazed in the clear night sky and the land was unspoiled. Man's mark on the earth was gentle.[33]

While children will probably not be able to describe an author's style, they will certainly respond to it. They will know that a well-written informational book somehow does not sound the same as an encyclopedia essay, and from the best they will take delight as well as information.

Organization

STRUCTURE

Even though a book is vividly written, accurate, and in command of its topic, children will not find it very useful unless it also furnishes a clear arrangement of information. McGovern effectively uses the relatively loose structure of questions and answers in her book . . . *If You Lived with the Sioux Indians*. Recognizing what kinds of things children will want to know, the author provides answers for: "Where would you sleep?" "Were grownups strict?" "Was there time for fun?" Also included are more conventional questions about hunting and ceremonies

---

[29] Janet Gaylord Moore. *The Many Ways of Seeing; An Introduction to the Pleasures of Art* (Cleveland, Ohio: World, 1968), p. 13.

[30] Aliki, pseud. (Aliki Brandenberg). *Green Grass and White Milk* (New York: Crowell, 1974), p. 11.

[31] Ann Atwood. *The Wild Young Desert* (New York: Scribner, 1970), unpaged.

[32] Berniece Freschet. *Bear Mouse*, illustrated by Donald Carrick (New York: Scribner, 1973), unpaged.

[33] Arthur S. Gregor. *Man's Mark on the Land: The Changing Environment* (New York: Scribner, 1974), p. 46.

and war. Several other books by McGovern make use of the same arrangement, including *If You Sailed on the Mayflower. Questions and Answers about Seashore Life* by List, a much longer book, groups the questions according to types of seashore life; under "Joint-Legged Animals," for instance, are questions about crabs, barnacles, and lobsters. This book has received recognition for its outstanding design—a striking combination of woodcuts, line drawings, and text carefully placed for optimum clarity.

A common and sensible arrangement for many books, especially about history or biological processes, is based on chronology. Marchette Chute has presented the growth of the right to vote in this way in *The Green Tree of Democracy*, which traces the franchise in the United States from the Jamestown colony to the Voting Rights Act of 1970. A very precise chronology of the development of a chick within the egg is made wondrously clear through descriptions and unique photographs in Flanagan's *Window into an Egg: Seeing Life Begin.*

Regardless of the topic, the general survey type of book should have a system of headings that will help the reader get an overview of the content. *Grocery Store Botany* by Rahn, a brief book that investigates the botanical characteristics of common produce items, has large boldface headings for "Roots," "Stems," "Leaves," and so on. Within each category, activities are set apart under the subheading "Something to Do." The longer the book and the more complex its topic, the greater its need for manageable division. In the Loeschers' comprehensive *The Chinese Way: Life in the People's Republic of China,* the chapter titles ("Government and Politics," for example, and "Women and the Family") are appropriately clear. A few of the chapters are so long, however, that the reader wishes for subheadings to break the flow of text.

REFERENCE AIDS

With the exception of certain simple and special types, factual books should offer help at both front and back for the reader who needs to locate information quickly. Since it is important for children to develop reference skills early, a table of contents and an index should not be omitted from books for primary-grade readers. *Secrets in Stones* by Wyler and Ames has a simple and readable text in spite of the difficult vocabulary that is necessary in a book about geology. The table of contents clearly lists major and minor headings; the two-page index is fortunately set in a typeface almost as large as the text, with plenty of leading between the lines. In short, the information in this book is accessible to its intended audience.

An index will be truly useful only if it is complete and has necessary cross references. It is difficult to think of the possible words children might use to look up a topic or to answer a question, yet writers should consider as many possibilities as would seem reasonable. If one wanted to find out about "language," "talk," "sound," or "speech" of dolphins, he would probably look under l, t, or s. In Lauber's *The Friendly Dolphins,* the topic is finally found under "d" as "dolphin talk." In this same book the words "size," "eyes," and "baby" are omitted, although there is information on these aspects of dolphin life.

Other helpful additions to a book are glossaries, bibliographies, suggestions for further reading, and informational appendixes. If children are to understand the method of inquiry, they need to learn that a writer uses many sources of information. Yolen's bibliography for *Ring Out! A Book of Bells* lists twenty-seven entries dated from 1848 to 1971. Suggestions for further reading by children are most helpful if separated from the adult's more technical resources; it is a bonus to find these entries annotated, as is the case in the Schwartzes' *Life in a Log.* Appendixes are used to extend information in lists or charts or tabulations of data. *And Then There Were None: America's Vanishing Wildlife* by Davis is weakened by its lack of an index, but it is correspondingly strengthened by the addition of three appendixes which list threatened species, extinct wildlife, and the names and addresses of environmentalist and conservation groups.

Perhaps the best way to learn the importance of clear organization in an informational book is to look carefully at a fine example, such as *A Natural History of Giraffes* by Dorcas MacClintock. This award-winning book is notable for its clar-

Striking silhouettes capture the sequence of movements as a giraffe gets up.

Illustration by Ugo Mochi is reprinted by permission of Charles Scribner's Sons from *A Natural History of Giraffes* by Dorcas MacClintock. Illustration copyright © 1973 by Ugo Mochi.

ity. After a preface which explains the technique of the pictures and gives a note on the author's sources, there are fifteen short chapters, clearly titled. These are further divided into subtopics, and the lesser headings are identified in large, bold type so that selected information can be easily located. Reference features include a table of contents, an adequate index, a glossary of technical terms, and a list of suggestions for further reading. This handsome book's arrangement makes it just as appropriate for quick reference as for deeper study. What is most striking, however, is the way it looks—the crisp black-and-white appearance of Ugo Mochi's silhouettes and the effective use of available space on each page. The organization of a book is closely related to format and illustration.

Illustration and Format

CLARIFICATION AND EXTENSION OF TEXT

While illustrations should serve to make a book more interesting and attractive, that is not their main purpose. The basic function of illustrations in informational books is to clarify and extend the text. *The Simple Facts of Simple Machines* by James and Barkin would not be so simple without diagrams and photographs. The use of jointed marionette figures in the photographs to demonstrate familiar actions, such as opening a bottle or swinging a tennis racket, seems a particularly good choice. The diagrams are well captioned and clear; unfortunately, they are awkwardly placed, often crowding the margins, so that the book is less attractive than useful. More abstract topics require pictures to help children "see" explanations. A good example is Baker's *The Vital Process: Photosynthesis,* where the drawings suggest what radiation-excited molecules might look like if they could be seen.

Illustrations are especially important in clarifying size relationships. Photographs and drawings often show magnified parts or wholes, in which case some information should be given about actual size. A photograph of air pollution particles in *The Only Earth We Have* by Pringle is clearly identified as having been magnified several thousand times. In Shuttlesworth's *The Story of Ants,* an ant figure in actual size is placed next to a large, detailed drawing of the same subject.

A pictured comparison of the subject with an object familiar to children is also effective. A huge museum skeleton of Tyrannosaurus is put into perspective in a photograph which shows a boy gazing up at it in *To Find a Dinosaur* by Shuttlesworth. Lasius flavus, the ant on the bottlecap in Jean George's *All upon a Sidewalk,* is greatly magnified, but there is no need to say so because the reference point is well known to children. The pictures in this book, by Don Bolognese, are in themselves an adventure in relative size. Each of the close-up scenes used throughout the story is contained in one of three paintings that appear at the end of the book.

While in many books the illustrations extend the information of the text, adding detail, in

Size relationship is shown by drawing an ant on an object well-known to children.

Illustration by Don Bolognese, from *All Upon a Sidewalk* by Jean George. Copyright © 1974 by Jean George. Reprinted by permission of the publishers, E. P. Dutton & Co., Inc.

others the illustrations themselves provide the bulk of the information, making the text subordinate. Glubok's series about the art of various cultures and countries, for instance, is centered on photographs which show examples of many different forms of art. *The Art of the Spanish in the United States and Puerto Rico*, like Glubok's other volumes, includes only a brief commentary; children will learn primarily by studying the pictures of paintings, furniture, textiles, tinware, homes, churches, and so on.

SUITABILITY OF MEDIA

Illustrations in any medium can be clear and accurate, but one medium may be more suitable than another for a given purpose. Photographs are necessary for the verité essay by Wolf, *Don't Feel Sorry for Paul*, which tells the story of a congenital amputee, born with incomplete hands and feet. Drawings or paintings could not as effec-tively show the nuances of posture and expression that make this book an accurate, moving account of a handicapped child. Von Frisch's *Animal Camouflage* is a different sort of book, but it is equally dependent on photography. The use of color is another asset here, where the pictures show the animals' success in concealment; with photographs there is no chance that an artist's perception will intrude upon the reader's. Contrasting photographs and photograms (or shadow photographs) are used by Gallob in *City Leaves, City Trees*, a handsome identification book. The photograms—showing leaves, buds, fruit, seeds, and flowers—have the advantage of emphasizing silhouette and structure in the manner of a drawn diagram, yet with greater visual impact.

Diagrams and drawings have an impact of their own, and also have many uses especially appropriate to science books. It's helpful to have X-ray eyes for seeing the skeletons in living things, a gift from the artist in Zim's book, *Bones*. The picture diagram of milk-processing in Aliki's *Green Grass and White Milk* well serves a purpose for young children: It reduces a complex procedure to its essentials, and at the same time helps the child see individual steps in relation to the whole. Diagrams are the only sort of illustration possible to show some of the relationships vital to Branley's discussion of *The Nine Planets*, although a few special photographs (notably from the Mariner space probe) are included. Diagrams are also fine for giving directions, and they can be charming as well as clear. This is true in Simon's popular *The Paper Airplane Book*, where scenes are interspersed with the how-to drawings to enliven the text.

Sometimes an artist's perception is vital to the purpose of a book. *Cathedral: The Story of Its Construction* is a venture in architecture, engineering, and esthetics that relies upon the author's fine pen-and-ink drawings for its effect. Macauley pictures his creation at various stages during the building; his choice of views puts the reader into the action and gives stunning contrasts of massive proportions and minute detail. Woodcut is the medium for the Hurds' *The Mother Beaver*. The three-color pictures are rich in texture, simple in form, and appealing—a good match for this nature story with its basic information for

The artist's point of view makes the reader feel that he is a builder on the uppermost scaffold of a cathedral.

From *Cathedral* by David Macaulay. Copyright © 1973 by David Macaulay. Reprinted by permission of the publisher, Houghton Mifflin Company.

very young children. The astonishingly precise watercolors in Dowden's *Wild Green Things in the City: A Book of Weeds* bear part of the author's message—weeds are beautiful—in a way that lesser illustrations could not have done. The delicacy and sensitivity of these pictures may help urban children find the same qualities in their own environments. Frequently, one book will employ more than one kind of illustration, meeting different needs where appropriate. Kaufmann uses mixed media for dramatic effect, along with representational studies, in *Bats in the*

Dark, which provides simple, clear information for young children. A teacher might want to call attention to this book when sharing Jarrell's *The Bat-Poet* (*see* Chapter 5).

CAPTIONS

Children need to be able to look at an illustration and know what they are seeing, and that requires wise use of captions and labels. Some writers use the text itself, if it is brief, to explain the pictures, thereby omitting captions. The photographs by Hess in *The Praying Mantis, Insect Cannibal* are sharp and magnified, and fascinating to see. But in order to grasp the significance of each one, the reader must deal with a considerable amount of text, and then perhaps remain confused. On the page opposite two photographs of one mantis making a meal of another, part of the text reads: "The mandibles are a pair of jaw-like appendages, placed at the side of the mouth."[34] In the flurry of antennae, legs, and body parts belonging to both eater and eaten, children may be uncertain which are the "jawlike appendages." A label would be useful. Selsam also uses text as caption in *The Tomato and Other Fruit Vegetables,* and even though the text is briefer, some of the photographs include labels printed directly on their surfaces. The cutaway photo of an eggplant flower is especially clear—a bracket indicates that the pistil contains the ovary, the style, and the stigma, and labels plainly identify these distinct parts. Since children learn much by reading captions and studying illustrations, it seems fair to demand that both be clear.

FORMAT

The total look of a book is its format, involving type size, leading, margins, placement of text and pictures, and arrangement of front and back matter—these include title and copyright pages in the front and indexes and bibliographies at the back. *A Great Bicycle Book* by Sarnoff and Ruffins has something of the design of a comic magazine. A more formal presentation might have made the book less "busy," but would also have lessened its appeal. The bonus space of a book's end-

papers is sometimes blank, but can be used to convey the general theme of the book or to add in some way to the information. In Cohen's *The Color of Man* children's faces at the front, representing different races, are contrasted with the faces of the elderly at the back. The endpapers of Fisher's *Two If by Sea,* which includes the story of Paul Revere's ride, show a map of Boston in 1775. In *Colonial Virginia* by Gill and Finlayson, one of the Colonial Histories series, the endpapers look like old parchment; numerous early prints, maps, and documents used for illustration give a feeling for the period under discussion. Even a book which is sparingly illustrated may be notable for its overall design, as is the complex *Great Civilizations of Ancient Africa* by Brooks. Spacious margins and tastefully ornamented headings make the length of the text seem less forbidding. The format of an informational book is an asset if it contributes to clarity or if it makes the book more appealing to its audience.

Summary of Criteria for Informational Books

The criteria for evaluating informational books are summarized here in question form, with the caution that every question will not necessarily apply to every book.

Accuracy and Authenticity

What are the qualifications of the author?
Are facts accurate?
Is the book up-to-date?
Are all the significant facts included? Is there an effect of realism?
Do text and illustrations reveal diversity and avoid stereotypes?
Are generalizations supported by facts?
Is there a clear distinction between fact and theory?
Do text and illustrations omit anthropomorphism?

Content and Perspective

For what purpose was the book designed?
Is the book within the comprehension and interest range of its intended audience?
Is the subject adequately covered? Are different viewpoints presented?

---

[34] Lilo Hess. *The Praying Mantis, Insect Cannibal* (New York: Scribner, 1971), p. 34.

Does the book lead to an understanding of the scientific method? Does it foster the spirit of inquiry?

Does the book show interrelationships? Do science books indicate related social problems?

Style

Is information presented clearly and directly?

Is the text appropriate for the intended audience?

Does the style create the feeling of reader involvement?

Is the language vivid and interesting?

Organization

Is the information arranged clearly, with appropriate subheadings?

Does the book have reference aids that are clear and easy to use, such as table of contents, index, bibliography, appendixes?

Illustrations and Format

Do illustrations clarify and extend the text?

Are size relationships made clear?

Are media suitable to the purposes for which they are used?

Are illustrations explained by captions or labels?

Does the total format contribute to the clarity and attractiveness of the book?

TYPES OF INFORMATIONAL BOOKS

Knowing the types of informational books now available will help the teacher and librarian provide balanced and rich resources for learning. Moreover, being able to recognize the significant characteristics of each type will facilitate the choice of particular books to serve particular purposes.

Concept Books

Too frequently we substitute the book for the experience, rather than enrich the experience with a book. Children who are given the opportunity to observe an ant hill over a period of time, for example, will develop an understanding of these insect colonies which will enable them to read Shuttlesworth's *The Story of Ants* with great

appreciation. Careful observation will also raise questions which will then send children to books for additional information. Concepts need to grow from firsthand experience as children gradually perceive common characteristics and relationships such as size, weight, space, order, sequence, self, community, justice. Books may reinforce this development in the same way that they contribute to language growth in very young children (*see* the discussion of "Concept Books" in Chapter 3 of this book). They may make explicit knowledge and concepts that children already know implicitly.

Concept books begin with what is already familiar and move toward the unfamiliar, some by showing new ways to consider well-known materials, others by furnishing new and different examples. Such books are often useful as idea sources for classroom experiences. Tana Hoban's *Shapes and Things*, although it is completely wordless, suggests that young children might use form and shape as well as function to identify and classify familiar objects. The white-on-black photograms are so striking in their arrangement that the book might also be used to sharpen older children's perceptions of form as an element of art. The title of Rinkoff's *A Map Is a Picture* is a concept statement. This book begins with the simplest of picture-maps, showing where a pirate buried his treasure; it goes on to show a neighborhood map that might have been made by a child; and eventually such complex maps as one of ocean depth and a star chart. Experiences are suggested directly, as part of the simple text: measure distance on the pictured map, make a map of your neighborhood, use a map of your own city to find the street where you live. *Measurements and How We Use Them* by Pine and Levine is an easy-to-read book which suggests such experiences as pacing out distances, measuring friends, and weighing pets. Reflection rather than action is called for in Tresselt's intriguing book, *How Far Is Far?* The collage illustrations are not only beautiful but essential in developing the concept through metaphors related to the child's experiences.

A growing number of books for children deal with concepts related to self. The idea that all people have physical forms that are both similar and unique is explored in *Bodies*. Brenner's text is written in caption form for Ancona's frank photographs. LeShan's *What Makes Me Feel This Way?* will help children in the upper elementary grades sort out their own experiences and feelings. *What Is Fear? An Introduction to Feelings* by Rosenbaum and McAuliffe goes into greater detail than the LeShan book, using brief case studies to demonstrate the relationship of such feelings as anger and forbidden desires to such fears as fear of the dark or of strangers or of school. None of these concept books can be substituted for experience, but they can be used to help children learn to discriminate and generalize; and this is the kind of thinking crucial to concept development.

Informational Picture Books

One of the first modern picture storybooks, *Pelle's New Suit*, came to this country from Sweden nearly fifty years ago. That story shows a little boy getting wool from his pet lamb, then having it carded, spun, dyed, woven, and finally taken to the tailor for a new suit. Interesting parallels may be drawn between this classic and the recent *"Charlie Needs a Cloak"* by De Paola, which also presents, as a story, basic information about making wool into cloth. Happily, this is an exception to the rule that says information is distorted by a veil of fiction. The story of Charlie's cloak is enhanced by humor, and the illustrations serve to emphasize the steps in the cloth-making process. Bright colors and an attractive format make this a satisfying picture storybook, as well as a resource. Another effective informational picture book that tells a story is *Elizabeth Gets Well* by Weber. This is a positive look at general hospital procedures through the eyes of a little girl with appendicitis; the full-color illustrations add feeling and gentle humor to the necessary details about discomfort and separation.

The more common form of informational picture book does not tell a story, but the text does depend in large part upon the illustrations. *When Clay Sings* by Baylor calls attention to the Indian heritage of the Southwest United States through its rhythmic, dramatically arranged text. But the substance of the book rests with Bahti's illustrations of the motifs found on shards of ancient pottery: turtles, butterflies, monsters, hunters,

abstract designs. Rockwell's *Games (And How to Play Them)* tells just that, with simple directions for more than forty children's games that call for no more elaborate equipment than a pebble or a few sticks. The watercolor illustrations show fancifully garbed animals in unlikely but appropriate settings—goats in togas, for instance, play "Statue Tag" before the Roman Coliseum.

Sasek's beautifully designed picture books of cities and countries, which are almost in a class by themselves, reflect the interests of a traveler looking at the region through the eyes of a child. The series titles begin *This Is . . .* and include Paris; London; New York; San Francisco; Washington D.C.; Australia; Greece; the United Nations; and several others. In *This Is Paris*, the well-known Czech painter has used the techniques of the artists Monet and Seurat to express the reflections of the "City of Light," as tiny dots of color shimmer below the Eiffel Tower. People's faces are reminiscent of the paintings of Modigliani in this notable interaction of art and subject matter.

Many informational picture books, despite oversize format and lavish illustration, are not directed to primary-grade children. Macaulay's *City* and *Cathedral* are books of this type, and so is the book by Tunis called *Shaw's Fortune: The Picture Story of a Colonial Plantation*. This last has a fairly detailed text, but the impact rests with the drawings, which are authentic in representation and creative in point of view. Exterior views and picture maps show the growing plantation in relation to its surroundings—interiors and cutaways show the grander and grander house; composite pictures show tools and costumes and children's games. The pictures in Kurelek's *Lumberjack* are paintings, not so strict in representation but nevertheless accurate in portraying the operations of a lumberjack before the advent of the mechanical tree harvester. The variety of scenes, rich in color and feeling, makes this book perhaps more memorable for its art than its information.

Photographic Essays

Many informational picture books display photographs in a significant way, but only some of these can be called photographic essays. Although the books by Selsam about plant growth

Authentic pictures by Tunis detail a plantation schoolroom.

From *Shaw's Fortune.* Reprinted by permission of Curtis Brown, Ltd. Illustration Copyright © 1966 by Edwin Tunis.

(*Bulbs, Corms and Such,* for example) depend on Wexler's photographs for clarification and support of the text on every page, they are not photographic essays. The essay relies upon the camera in different ways: to particularize general information, to document emotion, to assure the reader of truth in an essentially journalistic fashion. In Selsam's book, *How Kittens Grow,* the photographs by Bubley transform the facts. It is not just *any* kittens who "usually sleep on top of one another," it is these *particular* kittens. We see them crawling and nursing and playing and stepping in their food dish, and we gain a sense of personal involvement. It is this feeling of involve-

ment which makes Wolf's *Don't Feel Sorry for Paul* such an outstanding example of the form; and it is the same sensitivity and vitality in Ancona's photographs that make *Handtalk: An ABC of Finger Spelling and Sign Language* by Charlip and Miller more than a specialized ABC book. Inspired by the language of the deaf, this is a unique volume about communication, made memorable by the expressive photo demonstrations of the language in action. Teachers and librarians will want to call attention to *Handtalk* when children read stories such as *David in Silence* (*see* Chapter 7) or biographies of Helen Keller.

Numerous photographic essays present to

A photographic essay clearly shows all the many things that a handicapped child can do.

From *Don't Feel Sorry for Paul.* Written and photographed by Bernard Wolf. Copyright © 1974 by Bernard Wolf. Reproduced by permission of J. B. Lippincott Company.

children the way of life in other lands—some very simply, others in depth. *Zaire: A Week in Joseph's World* by Elisofon is brief, with large and cheerful pictures. The focus is on life style and the point of view is limited; it is well within the range of young children beginning to compare their own ways of life with others. The Jennesses' *Dwellers of the Tundra,* a study of a small Eskimo community, is more complex; the text and eloquent pictures portray the interaction of a traditional pattern of culture with encroaching technology.

A single incident may also be reported in this same journalistic fashion. The beaching of a whale at Provincetown on Cape Cod is the basis for *When the Whale Came to My Town* by Young. The photographs by Bernstein reflect one boy's observations and responses, and lead the reader, too, to consider the interrelationship of living things.

Identification Books

In its simplest form an identification book is a naming book, and this may well be the first

sort of book that a very young child sees. But just as children grow in their ability to discriminate and classify, so do naming books become more detailed, precise, and complex. The range is very wide. *The Toolbox* by the Rockwells features simple watercolor pictures of tools and a phrase or two to describe their functions; a plane, for example, "smooths wood and makes curly shavings." This is information for the youngest child. Older children will find more information and precisely detailed pictures in Jan Adkins' *Toolchest.* The plane in this handsome book has all its parts labeled, and five variations of the basic tool are shown. Young children enjoy the beautiful watercolors and rhythmic text of *Houses from the Sea* by Goudey. The delicately colored illustrations by Adrienne Adams relate familiar objects, one by one, to the names of shells. At the end of the book a double-page picture of all the shells serves for quick comparison and identification. *How to Be a Nature Detective* by Selsam teaches observation skills as it helps beginning readers identify some common animal tracks. Webster's *Track Watching* for older children covers many more examples and, like the Selsam book, contains some track-puzzle illustrations for practice.

When a child brings a stone, a leaf, or a wriggling snake to school and asks, "What is it?", the teacher or librarian needs to have some fairly comprehensive references. The *Golden Nature Guides* series by Zim and others are very useful small pocketbooks crammed with information. Another helpful series is *The First Book of . . .* published by Watts. Among these, Williamson's *The First Book of Birds* has basic material, though the identification clues in Blough's *Bird Watchers and Bird Feeders* may be clearer. Peterson's *Birds* is an authoritative reference; older children can use his *How to Know the Birds.*

Gallob's *City Leaves, City Trees* functions beautifully as an identification book, but is oversize for a field guide. For that purpose one might choose *The Doubleday First Guide to Trees* by Watts, a small but useful book. The trees are grouped according to areas where they would grow—sunny places, wet places, a shady forest. Leaf, flower, fruit, and shape of tree are conveniently shown on one page. A book that could help to make botanical excursions a year-round affair is Bette J. Davis' *Winter Buds,* which shows how to recognize dormant trees, vines, and shrubs by the characteristics of their buds. One recent specialized book which includes identification guides may well have value disproportionate to its scope—Limburg's *Watch Out, It's Poison Ivy!* The Polgreens' *The Stars Tonight* is designed to be used outdoors as well as in. Diagrams of constellations are clearly marked with month, time of night, and direction in which an observer should face. A commentary with each chart provides bits of history relating to astronomy, as well as information about recent discoveries. The topics covered by identification books are wide-ranging—from insects to sea life, from dinosaurs to stars. Regardless of subject, the books serve children in much the same way, by allowing for the discovery of specific facts.

Life-cycle Animal Books

A fascination with animals is one of the most general and durable of children's interests, beginning very early and often continuing through adolescence into adulthood. There is an eager audience for factual books that describe how animals live, with an emphasis on the inherent story element. These books cover all or some part of the cycle of life, from the birth of one animal to the birth of its progeny, or the events of one year in the animal's life, or the development of one animal throughout its lifetime. While the animal subject can sometimes be given a name, it may not be given powers of speech or human emotions. Even so, an accounting of authentic behavior often produces the effect of characterization; thus children frequently read these books as "stories" rather than as references.

Life-cycle books for young children are usually picture books as well, and the best are notable for both illustration and text. Soft blues and browns color the woodcuts in *The Mother Owl* by the Hurds, which traces a year in the mother screech owl's life, measured from one nestful of eggs to the next. The same author and illustrator have written *The Mother Beaver, The Mother Whale,* and *The Mother Deer.* All these books emphasize the continuity of the life pattern:

Just as she had done the autumn before and the autumn before that, the doe mated with a big buck. . . . The spring sun warmed her, and she gave birth to her two new little fawns, just as she

had done the spring before and the spring before that.[35]

Spring to spring also circumscribes the simple account of *Toad* by the Rockwells in an attractive picture book illustrated in crisp, flat colors. Skillfully, the text enlivens without anthropomorphism:

A mosquito! Still is Toad, still as a pebble or a lumpy chunk of earth. And then his sticky tongue flashes out, and the mosquito is eaten.[36]

Other one-year cycles are described for young children in Goudey's *Here Come the Squirrels, Here Come the Cottontails,* and other books in this series.

Longer life-cycle stories are often stories of survival against the elements and enemies in the environment. The books by John George and Jean George, such as *Vison the Mink* and *Vulpes the Red Fox,* remain outstanding examples of this type. Holling's beautifully illustrated *Minn of the Mississippi* and *Pagoo,* which trace the life histories of a turtle and a crawfish, are unique survival stories. The struggle for existence is central to Aileen Fisher's *Valley of the Smallest: The Life Story of a Shrew,* a suspenseful and beautifully written account that clarifies the "full circle" and interdependence of animal life.

Contemporary concerns about the environment and endangered species of wildlife are reflected in a number of life-cycle stories. McClung, author of many books of this type, has written *Screamer, Last of the Eastern Panthers* and *Thor, Last of the Sperm Whales.* The Annixters write of another threatened species in *Trumpeter: The Story of a Swan.* A new attitude toward wolves is dramatically evident in *The Wolf,* which reveals a strong social structure in the life of a family of wolves in Alaska's Arctic wilderness. Though the animals are named, they are portrayed without anthropomorphism. The author, Dr. Michael Fox, is an animal behaviorist, and the authenticity of the writing reflects this background. This book is a natural choice for comparison with or as an extension of *Julie of the Wolves* by George (*see* Chapter 7). Children who have enjoyed Fox's lively

---

[35] Edith Thatcher Hurd. *The Mother Deer,* illustrated by Clement Hurd (Boston, Mass: Little, Brown, 1972), pp. 29, 32.
[36] Anne Rockwell. *Toad,* illustrated by Harlow Rockwell (New York: Doubleday, 1972), p. 2

Clear black-and-white pictures show the life cycle of a long-tail shrew.

From *Valley of the Smallest* by Aileen Fisher, illustrated by Jean Zallinger. Copyright © 1966 by Aileen Fisher, with permission of Thomas Y. Crowell Company, Inc., publisher.

6. Full Circle

narrative style may also want to read his *Sundance Coyote,* which has equally precise information but includes one encounter with an Indian boy that must be classed as fiction.

Experiment Books

To some children the word "science" is synonymous with "experiment," and certainly experience is basic to scientific understandings. Many basic informational books suggest a few activities to clarify concepts; in contrast, experiment books take the activities themselves as content.

Many of these books focus on experiments keyed to one subject or one material. Milgrom's *Egg-ventures: First Science Experiments* invites the very young child to be an "egg explorer." Simple and safe activities are suggested by question and description; comments help explain the result. For instance, after the child has set two eggs

spinning—one raw, one boiled—and found that the cooked one spins longer and faster, he is told that the liquid in the raw egg acts like a brake. Selsam suggests many demonstrations to help young children understand plant growth in *Play with Seeds.* An interesting approach to chemistry is found in Cobb's *Science Experiments You Can Eat,* a book that is fun for children old enough to handle various cooking procedures safely.

Biology Project Puzzlers by Stone and Stein has several aspects of special appeal—the experiments have intriguing titles such as "What's This Fly Doing in My Soup?" and "A True Frogman Adventure." The cartoonlike illustrations add humor; and the various suggestions are clearly numbered within each experiment. Since results are not given, children must carry through the experiment to find out what will happen. Bendick's *Solids, Liquids and Gases,* a relatively easy book for upper-grade elementary children, is organized to help the experimenter develop skills in classifying the things found in his environment. Gould and Martin's *Think about It: Experiments in Psychology* represents an interesting but uncommon focus for this type of book. The suggested experiences are related to memory, attention, illusion, problem-solving, and the like.

A few experiment books are centered on the use of a special instrument. This is the case with Headstrom's *Adventures with a Hand Lens* and Schwartz's *Magnify and Find Out Why*. Franklyn Branley, an astronomer who writes fine books for children, shows how to make homemade instruments in *Experiments in Sky Watching*.

General experiment books, which include several experiments on varied topics, are also available. The Adlers, a team of outstanding science writers, cover a wide variety of topics in their books, *Why? A Book of Reasons* and *Why and How? A Second Book of Reasons*. The questions range from: "Why does a dog's tongue hang out. . . ?" to "Why can you skate on ice?". *Table Top Science* by S. H. Fisher has a variety of basic experiments which young children might carry out successfully, using only common and inexpensive materials. Rosenfeld's *Science Experiments for the Space Age* covers a wide range of fundamental subjects related to the physical sciences. An excellent book to encourage independent activity is *Science Teasers* by Wyler and Baird. Experiments are grouped under such titles as "Space Age Puzzles," "Magic—or So It Seems," "Weighty Problems," and "Trick or Tease." The style is interesting and leads the reader to think of an answer before he reads about it.

Documents and Journals

An important contribution to literature for children in recent years has been the publication of books based upon original documents and journals. *The Bayeux Tapestry* is a unique documentary record in English history as interpreted by artists of the eleventh century. Color photographs of the 230-foot tapestry which tells the story of the conflict between Harold of England and William of Normandy are explained by Denny and Filmer-Sankey. The text describes the embroidered figures, and the commentary explains historical data. This book provides an opportunity for comparing our way of life with that of nine centuries ago.

The journal of a Venetian nobleman who accompanied Magellan is a primary source edited by Sanderlin in *First around the World*. The introduction and commentaries for each selection provide continuity and further information. *Riding with Coronado* is based upon an eyewitness account of the Coronado exploration, and *The Quest of Columbus* is based upon a history written by the son of Columbus. These two documentaries by Meredith and Smith are enhanced by the illustrations of Leonard Everett Fisher. Further excellent historical material is presented by the same team in *Pilgrim Courage*, which uses Governor Bradford's journal as its source. An adaptation for primary-grade children titled *The Coming of the Pilgrims* is somewhat less satisfactory since it is not clear which words are exactly quoted and which are paraphrased.

Reproductions of twenty-six documents of American history are included in *Freedom* by Hays. Explanatory information helps the reader understand the setting and the author of each document. A rough draft of the Declaration of Independence, Theodore Roosevelt's letter about Cuba, the German surrender statement of 1945, and part of the log of *Old Ironsides* are included. An unusual approach is found in Brand's *Songs of '76: A Folksinger's History of the Revolution;* old newspapers, books, and magazines in the United States and in England have furnished more than sixty songs of Colonial America, reflecting both Tory and Rebel points of view. Colby's account of *Lexington and Concord, 1775: What Really Happened* is based on primary sources and is profusely illustrated with maps, engravings, and documents, as well as photographs.

A few notable books provide reproduction of primary sources as a background for the study of black history. Meltzer has compiled three volumes under the title *In Their Own Words, A History of the American Negro*, divided by time periods, 1619–1865, 1865–1916, 1916–1966. The sources include letters, speeches, excerpts from books, court testimony, and the like. Lester's extraordinary *To Be a Slave*, a Newbery Honor Book in 1969, combines the verbatim testimony of former slaves with the author's own commentary:

To be a slave. To be owned by another person, as a car, house or table is owned. To live as a piece of property that could be sold—a child sold from its mother, a wife from her husband. . . .

To be a slave was to be a human being under conditions in which that humanity was denied. They were not slaves. They were people. Their condition was slavery.[37]

Sterling's *Speak Out in Thunder Tones: Letters and Other Writings by Black Northerners, 1787–1865* brings to light many unfamiliar private documents that help students gain new perspectives on black history. Since the basic material of all these books was not written with children in mind, they do require mature reading skills.

A series by Hoff which also requires maturity is subtitled *Adventures in Eyewitness History.* The three volumes on *Africa, Russia,* and *America's Immigrants* provide excellent editorial comments, in addition to the original diaries, letters, and essays. One crucial point made by this author is that while eyewitness history has warmth and immediacy, it may lack accuracy and balance; an eyewitness, as part of the picture, cannot always see the picture in perspective.

Laura Ingalls Wilder fans will be interested in a book called *West from Home: Letters of Laura Ingalls Wilder, San Francisco 1915.* The letters were written to the author's husband while she was visiting her daughter, Rose, and attending the 1915 Panama Pacific International Exposition. The first-hand detail provides personal insights, as well as a measure of the country during that year. There is similar documentary value in Wilder's *The First Four Years,* a journal-like account discovered as a handwritten manuscript among the author's posthumous papers. In this book, which tells of the first years of the Wilders' married life on a claim that had to be made into a farm, the reader can see for himself the problems, attitudes, and some of the philosophies of another time. It is this information without benefit of an intermediary that is the unique contribution of documentary literature.

Children can learn a great deal from putting together their own collections of documentary materials based on a contemporary or historical event. These might include articles from newspapers and magazines, advertisements, photos, letters, rubbings, transcribed interviews, and so on. Several published collections, called "Jackdaws," are available; while some of these have contemporary material, most are made up of reproductions of early documents. *The Mayflower and the Pilgrim Fathers* by Tames, for instance, includes the first map of New England to be printed in the New World and the Plymouth Patent which was granted by King James I to the settlers. Tragle's *Nat Turner's Slave Revolt* furnishes a list of whites who were killed, the record of Turner's trial, and the draft of a bill intended to place blacks under stricter control. Ronan's *The Discovery of the Galaxies* reproduces early evidence to support theories of astronomy: maps of the heavens from a 1790 encyclopedia, photographs of the Milky Way, letters of the men who first identified the galaxies. Unlike a documentary book, these materials are not bound, making their use very flexible.

Survey Books

The purpose of a survey book is to give an overall view of a substantial topic and to furnish a representative sampling of facts, principles, or issues. Such a book emphasizes balance and breadth of coverage, rather than depth. *The Doubleday Nature Encyclopedia,* edited by Sheehan, is a sourcebook of general information about a wide variety of common plants and animals. Children will enjoy browsing through this book with its color illustrations, but for answers to many specific questions they will turn to separate topic books with more detail. The topic is narrowed considerably in Huntington's *Let's Look at Reptiles,* which focuses on various kinds of lizards, snakes, turtles, crocodiles, and alligators found in the United States. The information includes anatomical drawings and descriptions of the development and habitat of each reptile. The topic is still narrower in Simon's *Snakes: The Facts and the Folklore,* but the range of information marks this too as a survey. Various chapters cover folklore, evolution and anatomy, four broad categories of species, tips on keeping pet snakes, and the geographical range of common snakes in the United States. Detailed drawings in full color provide guides to identification and add greatly to the

---

[37] Julius Lester. *To Be a Slave,* illustrated by Tom Feelings (New York: Dial, 1968), p. 28.

appeal of this comprehensive book. Quite a different sort of survey is made by McKern in *The Many Faces of Man,* a book that explains theories and techniques of anthropology through a focus on the problem of defining race. The book is extensive but not formidable; the type is uncommonly readable and there are many interesting photographs.

A few books attempt to give children a survey of the important people, places, and events in the history of the world. Van Loon's *The Story of Mankind* was the first book to interpret world history to children in an interesting and informational fashion. This book, a pioneer in the field and the winner of the first Newbery Award in 1922, is now available in a revised edition. Genevieve Foster has made notable and unique contributions to children's literature with her horizontal treatments of history in several books that present a time slice of the world as it was. In *George Washington's World, Abraham Lincoln's World, Augustus Caesar's World, The World of Captain John Smith, The World of Columbus and Sons,* and *The World of William Penn,* this author writes of political affairs, economics, culture, and religion in relation to the span of one man's life. Each story or event is well written and could be read separately from the others, but continuity is given to all episodes by frequent mention of the life of the one man who serves as the pivotal point of the book. Foster's *Birthdays of Freedom,* now available in a single well-indexed volume, describes important people, places, and events in the development of individual liberty from the time of the earliest people to July 4, 1776. An objective overview of United States history is given in three volumes of beautifully clear prose by Johnson: *America Is Born, America Grows Up,* and *America Moves Forward.* Some historical surveys have a more limited focus. For instance, Prago's *Strangers in Their Own Land, A History of Mexican-Americans,* written for older children, begins with the first Europeans in the New World and moves toward an emphasis on the nineteenth and twentieth centuries. Despite this range there is a great deal of the sort of detail which raises questions and makes the reader want to pursue the topic further.

There are some definitive reference books which may be thought of as survey books. *The Modern Encyclopedia of Basketball,* edited by Hollander, is a volume to which sports fans of all ages turn again and again. Some 450 pages of information include history, brief biographies, statistics, records, official rules, photographs, and an all-important index. Survey books of this type have depth as well as breadth.

Specialized Books

Specialized books are designed to give specific information about a relatively limited topic. These are books that satisfy particular interests; they are more likely to be used intensively than extensively, on a one-time basis rather than as a frequent reference. For example, *What Did the Dinosaurs Eat?* by Ross is a book that briefly describes the prehistoric vegetation—ferns, mosses, and conifers (but not grasses, which had not yet developed)—upon which the dinosaurs fed. This will be useful information for children when they are working with projects or reports on prehistoric animals, a limited topic but a very popular one.

Many specialized books do provide extensions of content areas which are frequently part of the elementary-school curriculum. The *Colonial Craftsmen* series by Leonard Everett Fisher gives concise, detailed information, along with the author's distinguished scratchboard pictures, in *The Doctors, The Printers, The Weavers, The Shipbuilders,* and several other volumes. Schaeffer provides facts and pictures that would help youngsters in a reconstruction of pioneer life in *Dandelion, Pokeweed, and Goosefoot: How the Early Settlers Used Plants for Food, Medicine, and in the Home.* Phelan's paintings and diagrams in *The Whale Hunters* give children a clear look at this very specialized kind of life more than 150 years ago.

A study of Africa would be enhanced by Price's *Made in West Africa,* with its clear photographs of sculpture and carvings, pottery and beads, and decorated calabashes. The chapter on the textile arts—with its pictures of tie-dyed and appliqué cloth, strips of *kente* cloth and stamp-printed *adinkra* cloth—is a rich source of material that children might try to reproduce. Many groups will also find use for *Echoes of Africa* by Landeck, a music book of African songs and New World songs that reflect African origins. The commentary provides background information;

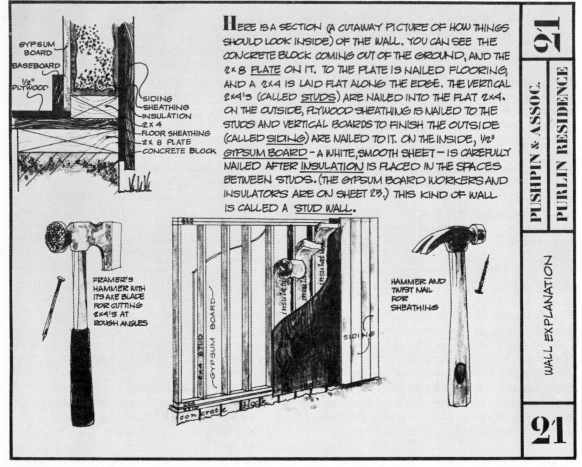

Clear text and drawings detail the steps that go into building a house. Each page resembles the layout of a blueprint.

From the book *How a House Happens* by Jan Adkins, published by Walker & Company, Inc., New York, N.Y., © 1971 by Jan Adkins.

and instrumental arrangements call for hand claps, claves, cowbells, thumb piano, and other authentic accompaniment.

Sometimes the use of one specialized book leads naturally to another. Macaulay's *City* may call for Pearlman's *The Zealots of Masada: Story of a Dig,* which has photographs of the excavated fortress in which the entire Jewish population chose to sacrifice themselves rather than to surrender to the Romans. Likewise, *Cathedral* may prompt a look at Hiller's impressive book of photographs called *Caves to Cathedrals: Architecture of the World's Great Religions.* Downer's *Roofs over*

America is a collection of photographs of representative structures in the United States that furnishes an overview of the history of American architecture. The step-by-step construction of a private residence is shown in Adkins' *How a House Happens,* a book in which the format itself contributes information: The endpapers show blueprints and the hand lettering is the same as that of an architect's drawing. The architect's rendering of plans, sections, and elevations is further explained in pictures that are at once accurate and good-natured. Still another construction book is Harman's *A Skyscraper Goes Up,* which uses both photographs and diagrams to show the entire process from excavation to the topping-off ceremony.

Many specialized books are geared to the personal interests of children. Dobrin's *Gerbils*—with its information about care, handling, and breeding—will prove helpful to the child who has or wants a gerbil for a pet. *Twins* by Cole and Edmondson is a book of basic information about multiple births that proves especially fascinating to a child who is a twin or who has one for a friend. An older child with a weight problem can find straightforward, sensible information in Gilbert's *Fat Free*. Part of the value of this book for young people is that it sets up some acceptable guidelines for determining whether or not the worrier really does have too much padding. *The Russian Ballet School*, a photographic essay by Harris, will intrigue young dancers with its pictures of a rigorously disciplined life. The same audience will respond to Marcia Brown's sensitive drawings in Verdy's telling of the story of the ballet *Giselle*. Among model-car enthusiasts a book that enjoys great popularity is *Famous Custom and Show Cars* by Barris and Scagnetti, with photographs and descriptions of nearly one hundred unusual vehicles from the Ala-Kart to the Zinger. Whatever the child's interest, it is likely that a specialized book can be found to extend it.

Activity and Craft Books

From chocolate-pudding fingerpaint to chess, a fascinating array of crafts and activities is featured in books that give directions for making and doing. Pride of accomplishment is emphasized in Harlow Rockwell's *I Did It*, a just-right combination of easy words and simple directions for primary-grade children. There are six activities, carefully chosen, each with an enjoyable result. The boy who has made a grocery-bag mask confounds his friends; the girl who has made a seed mosaic sees it every day in the place of honor where her mother has put it; and in the last and most complex activity a child shares bread that he has baked himself. *Beginning Crafts for Beginning Readers* by Gilbreath includes fourteen activities. In this book some of the needed materials are pictured within the text, rebus fashion.

Cookbooks for children ought to have sparkling clear directions and adequate warnings about the safe use of tools and equipment. *Cool Cooking: 16 Recipes without a Stove* by Hautzig has one safety precaution built in and others listed as general instructions at the beginning. Mothers are likely to appreciate the choice of recipes, which includes appetizers and salads, as well as desserts and drinks. Children will like the comic illustrations. Moore's *The Cookie Book* offers twelve basic recipes, one for celebrating a special day every month. The directions for *Let's Bake Bread* by Hannah Johnson are clarified at every step with a photograph; and there are suggestions for variation once the basic process is mastered.

Three books by Virginia Ellison have a special audience among lovers of Winnie the Pooh. *The Pooh Cook Book* delights all ages, although older children can manage the recipes better. *The Pooh Party Book*, while it does have some recipes, focuses on five celebrations with such enticing names as "A Honey-tasting Party" and "Woozle-Wizzle Snow Party," complete with instructions for invitations, decorations, and games. *The Pooh Get-Well Book: Recipes and Activities to Help You Recover from Wheezles and Sneezles* features simple crafts and games, but most of the recipes for "Strengthening Things to Eat and Drink" seem likely to require adult preparation.

Just as children's fiction reflects adult concerns, craft books tend to reflect popular adult interests. Sommer's *The Bread Dough Craft Book* marks a new awareness of folk-art forms. The recipe for this clay substitute calls for a dough of bread and glue, and requires no baking. Project directions in this book are so specific, however, that a child would need outside encouragement to make imaginative use of an essentially flexible medium. Meyer's *Yarn: The Things It Makes and How to Make Them* introduces beginners to crocheting, knitting, weaving, and macramé. Simple steps and clear illustrations make this a particularly functional book. In a time when celebrities, from football players to first families, have praised the satisfactions of needlepoint, it is not surprising to find children also mastering the craft. Lightbody's *Introducing Needlepoint* gives the necessary clear instructions, with a bonus of photographs that show children's original designs and finished work.

The Chess Book by Sarnoff introduces a venerable game which enjoyed a surge of popularity in the early seventies. For beginners, basic rules and simple strategy are presented with admirable clarity. Historic cartoon tidbits—a twelfth-century Danish king escaped death by using his chessboard as a shield—add humor to this book. Many children's books reflect a renewed interest in gardening, both indoors and out. *How to Make Things Grow* by Wickens and Tuey includes some experiments with plants, as well as tips and ideas for gardening. Soucie's *Plant Fun: 10 Easy Plants to Grow Indoors* is distinguished both in format and in the quality of its information; it is a particularly valuable addition to a classroom library.

Many activity and craft books seem to recommend themselves for classroom use. *Right Angles: Paper-folding Geometry* by Phillips is useful for working out mathematical concepts with younger children. Elsie Ellison's *Fun with Lines and Curves* shows upper elementary-school children how to draw beautiful geometric designs with lines, angles, and arcs. Directions are also given for work-

Informational books can encourage interesting classroom activities and displays.

Reprinted by permission of Four Winds Press, a division of Scholastic Magazines, Inc., from *Plant Fun, 10 Easy Plants to Grow Indoors* by Anita Holmes Soucie, illustrated by Grambs Miller.

ing designs in colored yarn or thread. In another area *Jug Bands and Handmade Music: A Creative Approach to Music Theory and the Instruments* by Collier gives fascinating material to older children. Chernoff's *Pebbles and Pods: A Book of Nature Crafts* for primary-grade children is an attractive book with concise explanations of rubbings, mosaics, spatter prints, sand paintings, and the like—all of which suggest interesting possibilities for combining science and art.

It is difficult to look at Newsome's *Egg Craft*, with its many techniques for egg decorating—including some from Poland, Czechoslovakia, and Mexico—without seeing that the book might also be used to extend experiences based on *The Egg Tree* by Milhous (see Chapter 3). Rockwell's book *Printmaking*, with well-illustrated directions for making twelve different kinds of prints, will be helpful for children who are experimenting with the media found in picture books. Three books by Weiss will help children who are involved in projects of book-making and photography. *Lens and Shutter: An Introduction to Photography* not only explains the workings of the camera and suggests techniques but provides demonstration pictures from the work of great photographers. Opportunities for using *How to Make Your Own Books* and *How to Make Your Own Movies* are discussed in Chapters 11 and 12. Photographer Viki Holland has produced a lively book called *How to Photograph Your World.* Her emphasis is on seeing and selecting; the last section, "Tell a Story," will help children make their own simple photo-documentaries.

The relationship of art to the social studies is emphasized by the structure of two books by the Kinneys, *21 Kinds of American Folk Art and How to Make Each One* and *How to Make 19 Kinds of American Folk Art from Masks to TV Commercials.* Directions for pinprick pictures, wax fruit molds, Indian beading, candle-dipping, toy carving, cartoon animation, and the like are combined with photographs of early products and comments about the times that produced them. A closely related book is Gladstone's *A Carrot for a Nose, The Form of Folk Sculpture on America's City Streets and Country Roads,* which encourages children to look closely at such common sights as pavement lids, trade signs, and snowmen.

Some craft books deal so specifically with

approaches and techniques common to the activity-centered classroom that it is likely they will be used as much by teachers as by individual children. The Parents' Nursery School book, *Kids Are Natural Cooks: Child-tested Recipes for Home and School Using Natural Foods,* is an example. With recipes planned for variation and experimentation, young children are encouraged to work with adults in growing sprouts, grinding peanuts, making vegetable soup, and other basic experiences. Sattler's *Recipes for Art and Craft Materials* will prove indispensable to teachers. Included are a variety of basic substances that children can make for their own use—such as paste, modeling and casting compounds, papier mâché, inks, and dried-flower preservatives. Skinner's attractively illustrated *How to Make Rubbings* is an excellent combination of directions for the use of materials, tips on procedure, and ideas for making flexible use of subject matter. In Wiseman's informal but comprehensive *Making Things: The Hand Book of Creative Discovery,* the commentary is directed to adults who work with children. Although the hand lettering is sometimes difficult to read, the drawings and ideas are clear and most notable for the emphasis on discovery and innovation. There are suggestions for fingerpainting with chocolate pudding, for cutting the basic shapes of African dashikis and Mexican rebozos, for weaving proof of the binomial theorem in red and black yarn, and for making improvised tools. In accord with the possibilities suggested, the last page bears the epigram "Never End."

Biography

While contemporary children enjoy reading about facts as facts, they also want to read stories about the lives of real people. The biographical narrative fulfills this need for a story "that really happened." Biography for children has reached a new, high level of popularity; children in first and second grades are clamoring for true stories about "people who really lived," while middle-graders continue to find satisfaction in reading of the lives and accomplishments of people in all walks of life. Biographies extend the child's opportunity for identification, not only with those who are great today but with those who have lived greatly in the past.

Biography fulfills children's needs for identification with someone "bigger" than they are. In this day of mass conformity, it may give them new models of greatness to emulate or suggest new horizons of endeavor. Children may look to the past and read of common persons who lived such uncommonly great lives as those of Sojourner Truth, Nathaniel Bowditch, or Elizabeth Cady Stanton; or they may take inspiration from the accomplishments of such contemporary figures as Shirley Chisholm, Maria Tallchief, or Cesar Chavez.

Publishers have been quick to capitalize upon children's interest in biography. They have also recognized the need to publish biographies to fulfill particular requirements in the changing social-studies curriculum. The recent emphasis on biographies about leaders in the American Revolution for use in connection with the Bicentennial is an example. Another identifiable trend is the increase of titles that relate to the study of blacks and, to a lesser degree, other minorities—such as native Americans and Mexican-Americans. More stories of famous American women are also being written. Publishers have recognized children's tremendous interest in sports and entertainment figures by producing biographies of Billie Jean King, Wilt Chamberlain, Bill Cosby, and many others.

Series after series have been developed until the proliferation of titles overwhelms librarians, teachers, and children. We begin to lose sight of a single biography of outstanding quality amidst the shelves of mass-produced ones. Children, and even teachers, ask for books by the publisher's trade name or the color of the cover, rather than by author or title. There are some fine biographies that have been written for children; there are many mediocre ones. The task of the teacher and librarian is to begin to distinguish among them.

CRITERIA FOR EVALUATING JUVENILE BIOGRAPHY

The criteria for evaluating biographies for boys and girls differ somewhat from those established for juvenile fiction. They also diverge from generally accepted patterns for adult biography.

Children read biography as they read fiction—for the story or *plot*. Children demand a fast-moving narrative. In biography, events and action become even more exciting because "they really happened." Thus, children want biography to be written as a story with continuity; they do not want a collection of facts and dates. An encyclopedia gives them facts in a well-organized fashion. Biography, to do more than this, must help them to *know* the person as a living human being.

Choice of Subject

Most of the biographies for children are about the more familiar figures of the past in the United States, particularly those whose lives offered the readiest action material, such as Daniel Boone or Abraham Lincoln. For the past few years, however, there has been an increase in biographies of poets, authors, artists, musicians, and humanitarians. Perhaps children are beginning to appreciate the challenges of the mind and spirit, as well as heroic physical accomplishments. World figures are also receiving more emphasis than previously; for example, two fine biographies, *Juárez, Man of Law* by De Treviño and *Juárez, The Founder of Modern Mexico* by Syme suggest other roots in our pluralistic society. The many biographies of contemporary world figures and persons in the sports or entertainment world reflect the influence of the mass media.

For many years biography for children was limited to those subjects whose lives were considered worthy of emulation. This is no longer true, as is seen by the increasing number of books about such unsavory persons as Jesse James or Billy the Kid in *Western Outlaws* by Frank Surge, *Benedict Arnold* by Ronald Syme, or Benjamin Appel's *Hitler, From Power to Ruin*. Such controversial persons as Fidel Castro, Ho Chi Minh, and Lenin have all been subjects of recent juvenile biographies. Children do know of these persons through the news media. As long as the biographies are objective and recognize the various points of view concerning the subjects, these books can serve a useful purpose in presenting a world view to boys and girls.

Formerly, authors of biographies for children avoided writing about certain aspects in the lives of their subjects. For example, in writing a biography of Alexander Hamilton, published in 1958,

authors Anna Crouse and Russel Crouse did not say that he was an illegitimate child. They did not alter any of the facts of his life, but simply never referred to his parents as husband and wife. In a recent biography, *Odd Destiny, A Life of Alexander Hamilton* by Milton Lomask, the fact of Hamilton's illegitimacy is mentioned on the very first page.

Serious criticism has been leveled at those biographies of Washington and Jefferson that did not include the fact that they owned many slaves. More recent biographies, even those for younger children, do include this information. In the note appended to the end of the biography of Jefferson titled *Grand Papa and Ellen Aroon,* Monjo points out that Jefferson's will did provide for freeing his personal slaves, but since all of his property (including slaves) was mortgaged and he was in debt, it was not possible to free the majority of them. The book also credits Jefferson with prohibiting slavery in the Northwest Territory, and indicates his distress at the fact that his condemnation of slavery was struck from the original draft of the Declaration of Independence at the insistence of South Carolina and Georgia.

Certain biographers when writing for younger children may present only a portion of a person's life. In planning their picture book of *Abraham Lincoln*, the D'Aulaires deliberately omitted his assassination and closed the book with the end of the Civil War. The authors' purpose was to present the greatness of the man as he *lived*, for too frequently, they believed, children remember only the manner of Lincoln's death. There is a danger, however, that omissions may oversimplify and thereby distort the truth of a person's life.

For many years it was thought that children were only interested in reading about the childhoods of great men and women, and that the complexities of adult activities would hold no interest for them. For this reason many earlier biographies focused primarily on childhood pranks and legends that suggested future accomplishments, but neglected, or oversimplified, real achievement. Today the trend is toward a more complete presentation of the subject's entire life. Increasingly, authors have respected children's right to read honest, objective, and complete biographies about a wide range of subjects—

famous persons, great human beings who were not famous, and even anti-heroes.

Style

Three kinds of biography are presented in children's literature:

1. Authentic biography.
2. Fictionalized biography.
3. Biographical fiction.

Authentic biography corresponds to that written for adults. It is a well-documented and re-searched account of a person's life. Only those statements that are actually known to have been made by the subject are included in the con-versation. Today there is an increase in the num-ber of authentic biographies available for chil-dren. *John and Sebastian Cabot* by Kurtz is one of a series of authentic biographies of explorers. The text is based on contemporary documents, with verbatim phrases or expressions carefully indicated by quotation marks. The illustrations are authentic also, with most of the maps and prints dating from the time of the Cabots. *America's Abraham Lincoln* by May McNeer is another excellent example of a biography based only upon known facts.

Fictionalized biography is grounded in thor-ough research, but allows the author more free-dom to dramatize certain events and personalize the subject than does the straight reporting of authentic biography. Fictionalized biography makes use of the narrative rather than the ana-lytical approach. Children do not want detailed interpretations and explanations. They come to know the character of the subject as it is pre-sented through his actions, deeds, and conversa-tions. In fictionalized biography the author may invent dialogue and even include the unspoken thoughts of the subject. These conversations are usually based upon actual facts taken from dia-ries and journals of the period. Clara Ingram Judson, a well-known biographer in the juvenile field, emphasized the importance of authentic conversation in the foreword of her book, *Abra-ham Lincoln, Friend of the People:*

> As I began writing, I saw that life is not a mere tale to be told: it includes talk as well as action. Talk is a kind of alchemy that brings reality. So

parts of my story are told through conversations. When actual words are a matter of authentic record, those words are used. When such record is lacking, but the incident is true, talk is recon-structed—much as the cabins are—from records and letters and the well-known manner of talk of each time and place.[38]

When dialogue is invented, it should make the scenes more effective and move the narrative forward. Some dialogue is unbelievably stilted and creates an impression of wooden characters. Read the following unnatural conversation be-tween George Washington and Martha Custis:

> One night George went to a party
> And he danced with a young woman.
> Her name was Martha.
> "How pretty you are!" said George.
> He went to see her many times.
> "Will you marry me?" he said.
> "Will you be my wife?"
> "Yes," said Martha, "I will be your wife."[39]

Believable dialogue characterizes the fictional-ized biography of Louis Braille, *Touch of Light* by Anne E. Neimark. When Louis was only 3 years old he received an injury in his father's harness shop that resulted in his total blindness. Cared for by a loving family, Louis complains to his sister that the village children don't want to play with him.

> "I know they don't want to play with me. They can still see things, can't they, Catherine?"
> ". . . you'll be like the bean seeds that grow, Louis. They can't see things under the ground, where it is dark, but nature helps them to grow very strong and tall . . ."
> "I don't want to be like the beans," he said.[40]

When the biography consists entirely of imagined conversation and reconstructed action, it becomes biographical fiction. An example of one of the most popular books of biographical

[38] Clara Ingram Judson. *Abraham Lincoln, Friend of the People,* "Author's Note." (Chicago, Ill.: Follett, 1950), p. ii.
[39] Gertrude Norman. *A Man Named Washington,* illustrated by James Caraway (New York: Putnam, 1960), unpaged.
[40] Anne E. Neimark. *Touch of Light, The Story of Louis Braille,* illustrated by Robert Parker (New York: Harcourt Brace Jovanovich, 1970), p. 24.

fiction is Lawson's funny *Ben and Me,* the story of Benjamin Franklin as told by his good friend Amos, the mouse who lived in Franklin's old fur cap. The facts of Franklin's life are truly presented, but Amos takes the credit for most of his accomplishments! Lawson used the same tongue-in-cheek pattern for his readable *Mr. Revere and I,* the story of Paul Revere as told by his horse, Scheherazade.

The choice of narrator, or point of view, is an important consideration in the style of a biography. Rather than write about the childhood of a famous person, a recent trend has been to tell his story from the point of view of a child who was close to the adult character. Monjo has been particularly successful in using this approach when writing about Franklin's visit to France with his grandson in *Poor Richard in France* and in seeing Jefferson through the eyes of his granddaughter in *Grand Papa and Ellen Aroon.* Such a point of view allows the reader to see greatness through the loving eyes of a grandchild. Ellen Aroon recounts such interesting times as the day Madison was imitating Patrick Henry and fell over backward in his chair. She also describes her delight in her Grand Papa's special whirligig desk chair and the day the French cook let her have a special new dessert called ice cream! These are joyful, childlike biographies that present authentic facts in a way that will capture the imaginations of 7- and 8-year-olds.

Aileen Fisher and Olive Rabe have used this same technique in writing about Louisa May Alcott and Emily Dickinson for boys and girls in the middle grades. In *We Dickinsons* the story is told by Austin Dickinson, the brother of Emily. This point of view provides intimacy in presenting the life of a famous person which could not be obtained in any other way.

A more dispassionate, third-person point of view is generally used for authentic biography. Yet even here, the narrator's tone pervades the presentation. Whatever the form or viewpoint, the biographical and background materials should be integrated into the narrative with smoothness and proportion. The judicious use of quotes from letters or journals may add to the authenticity of the biography, but it should not detract from the absorbing account of the life of the subject. Children enjoy a style that is clear and vigorous with a fast-moving narrative that reads like fiction. The research must be there; but it should be a natural part of the presentation.

Authenticity

Authenticity is the hallmark of good biographical writing, whether it is for adults or children. More and more writers of juvenile biography are acknowledging primary sources for their materials either in an introductory note or an appended bibliography. Conscientious authors of well-written children's biographies frequently travel to the locale of the setting in order to get a "feeling" for a place. They will visit museums in order to study actual objects that were used by their subjects; they will spend hours poring over original letters and documents. Much of this research may not be used in the actual biography, but its effect will be evidenced by the author's true insight into the character of the subject, by the accuracy of the historical detail, and by respect for verifiable reporting. Parson Weems was successful in perpetuating the myth of George Washington and his cherry tree upon generations. Modern biographers have more respect for fact and do not have to resort to the invention of moralistic stories to emphasize the worthy attributes of their subjects. They are much more concerned with presenting a true and accurate picture of a human being who once lived in a certain period and place, but who can live again in a child's imagination and appreciation.

The same kind of careful research should be reflected in the accuracy of the illustrations that convey the time, place, and setting. The costumes of the period, the interiors of the houses, the very utensils that are used must be authentic representations. Even the placement of illustrations may affect their accuracy, since children presume that text and pictures which occur together belong together. In Kaufman's biography of *Jesse Owens,* illustrated by Johnson, the description of Owens' Olympic triumph is unfortunately accompanied by a picture of the stadium at his home university.

But most difficult of all, perhaps, is the actual portrayal of the subject. There are many paintings and even photographs of some of our national heroes, yet some are more appropriate for use than others. In Fleming's biography of

George Washington, *First in Their Hearts,* only photographs of portraits that were made by artists who were *contemporaries* of Washington were used. Fleming also indicates which of the paintings were considered good likenesses of Washington by members of the family. Interestingly, the family never liked the Stuart portrait, which serves as the well-known image on the dollar bill. They maintained it was a poor choice, since Washington was suffering from an ill-fitting set of false teeth at the time the portrait was made. The teeth fit so poorly that they had to be held in place with bands of cotton, which caused a distortion of his mouth. Many photographs provide the authenticity for biographies of more recent presidents, such as *The Life and Words of John F. Kennedy* by James Wood, published soon after Kennedy's death. An interesting combination of modern photographs and drawings from rare books showing the same terrain is used to illustrate the authentic biography of *The Discoveries of Esteban the Black* by Elizabeth Shepherd. Maps of the routes taken by the Spanish explorers are also included.

Characterization

The characterization of the subject of a biography must be true to life, neither adulatory nor debasing in tone. The reader should have the opportunity to know the person as a real human being with both shortcomings and virtues.

Jean Fritz has presented Paul Revere as a busy and sometimes forgetful human being in her humorous yet authentic picture-book biography *And Then What Happened, Paul Revere?.* She tells about the time Revere built a barn and put part of it on a neighbor's property, which really happened. He didn't always meet his deadlines either, producing a hymn book some eighteen months after he had promised it! A dreamer, he even left one page in his "Day Book" simply for doodling. The author does not debunk her character; she simply makes him come alive by admitting his foibles, as well as describing his accomplishments.

Thomas J. Fleming has made George Washington seem like a very real person in his biography *First in Their Hearts,* written for older boys and girls. The author describes an incident in the wilderness in which Washington and his com-

And then what happened?

An unconcerned Paul Revere and John Lowell carry out a trunk of papers in the face of the enemy.

Reprinted by permission of Coward, McCann & Geoghegan, Inc., from *And Then What Happened, Paul Revere?* by Jean Fritz. Copyright © 1973 by Margot Tomes (illustrations), © 1973 by Jean Fritz (text).

panion were suddenly shot at by their Indian guide. Before the Indian had time to reload his gun, Washington wrestled the musket away from him and then prevented his companion from shooting the attacker in retaliation. In the very next paragraph, however, the author describes another side of Washington:

> If there were marks of maturity, there was much else in Washington's character during these years that was painfully raw. He was, for instance, hypersensitive to criticism. He returned from his defeat at Fort Necessity in a black mood, lashing out at anyone and everyone who dared to censure his tactics.[41]

Fleming not only shows the many sides of Washington's character but he portrays a growing, maturing man who had to overcome his own

[41] Thomas J. Fleming. *First in Their Hearts: A Biography of George Washington* (New York: Norton, 1968), p. 19.

personality problems at the same time that he struggled to save his country. This is a full and honest treatment of Washington that makes him seem a vibrant, living person.

There is danger in overdramatizing greatness. The result will be a two-dimensional person who can never emerge from the weight of his accomplishments. Martin suggests that many of the characters in biographical series are cut from the same pattern:

> There is a convention that great men and women invariably started out as normal and likeable youngsters, good mixers, and good sports. There is no inkling of the fact that loneliness and oddity often bear a dark fruit of their own. By pushing these books, we muff our best chance to show children that the awkward child, the poor athlete, the boy who comes to school in funny clothes may be the Lincoln or the Thomas Edison of the future.[42]

Biography must not degenerate into mere eulogy; neither should it include "debunking." Subjects should be presented so that they come alive for the reader. The background of their lives, their conversations, their thoughts, and their actions should be presented as faithfully with the facts as possible. The subject should also be seen in relationship to his times, for no person can be "read" in isolation.

Theme

Underlying the characterization in all biography—whether it be authentic, fictionalized, or biographical fiction—is the author's interpretation of the subject. No matter how impartial an author may be, a life story cannot be written without some interpretation. The very selection of facts that a biographer chooses may limit the dimensions of the portraiture or highlight certain features. In this context every author walks a thin line between theme and bias. Time usually lends perspective and objectivity, but contemporary biography may tend more toward bias.

John Gerassi—a former Latin-American editor for *Time* and *Newsweek*, a frequent visitor to Cuba with a personal acquaintance of Fidel Castro—would seem very well qualified to write an authentic biography of the Cuban leader. Examination of his book, however, shows many biases and omissions—no mention is made, for example, of the thousands of Cuban refugees who fled to Florida or the reason for their flight. In describing Castro's dictatorship Gerassi appears to have confused the political *form* with personal *style* of leadership:

> In fact, however, it is Fidel who rules Cuba. But in no way does that mean he is the kind of dictator which the American press pretends he is. Or else his form of dictatorship is one of the most democratic ever devised. It is a constant dialogue between him and the people.[43]

While this is an interesting biography of Castro, the interpretation is not objective; it is out of balance. Teachers and librarians need to help children realize that all biographies have a point of view which is determined by their authors. A comparison of several biographies of the same person will help children discover this fact.

The quality of a person's character (particularly one who is no longer living) must be deduced from known deeds, letters, diaries, pictures, canceled checks, and others' memories of him or her. Yet these primary sources should be interpreted by what is known about the person and the times in which the subject lived. These interpretations are usually made in terms of the way the author sees the life style of the subject. This emphasis becomes the theme of the biography. Frequently in juvenile biography, the theme will be identified in the title as in *Martin Luther King: The Peaceful Warrior* by Ed Clayton or *I'm Nobody! Who Are You? The Story of Emily Dickinson* by Edna Barth. Both these titles contain double meanings and point up the theme of the books. The title of the biography of Dickinson reflects the retiring attitude of the New England poet who in later life became a recluse. It is also, however, the title of one of Dickinson's well-known poems.

The remarkable story of Annie Sullivan, Helen Keller's teacher, is told in a biography

---

[42]Fran Martin. "Stop Watering Down Biographies," *Junior Libraries*, Vol. 6 (December 1959), p. 9.

[43]John Gerassi. *Fidel Castro, A Biography* (Garden City, N.Y.: Doubleday, 1973), p. 117.

appropriately titled *The Silent Storm*. Annie's early
life had left permanent scars on her spirit:

> On the surface, at least, she became more sure of
> herself, more poised, but underneath there was still
> the silent storm. Her own beginnings, the alms-
> house, the nightmare of losing Jimmie, the alone-
> ness, her utter lack of the simplest opportunities,
> the great gaps in her education—all these, in her
> own mind, set her apart and made her inade-
> quate.[44]

Yet these adversities prepared her to face and
understand the wild tornado that was young
Helen Keller. Annie's whole life seemed one of
continual turmoil until Helen graduated from
Radcliffe, and Annie met John Macy. "The silent
storm" was finally stilled.

There is a danger in oversimplifying and forcing all facts to fit a single mold. An author must
not recreate and interpret a life history in terms
of one fixed picture. The most common people
have several facets to their personalities; the great
are likely to be multi-dimensional. The perceptive biographer concentrates on those items from
a full life that helped to mold and form that
personality. It is this selection and focus that
creates the theme of the biography.

TYPES OF BIOGRAPHIES

Writers of adult biography are bound by definition to an attempt at recreating the subject's
life as fully as possible, with complete detail and
careful documentation. Writers of children's biography, however, may use one of several approaches. The resulting types of biography need
individual consideration, for each offers to children a different perspective and a different appeal.

Picture-book Biographies

A biography cast in picture-book form may
span the subject's lifetime, or a part of it; it may
be directed to a very young audience or to a
somewhat older one; it may be authentic or
highly fictionalized. Whatever the case, it remains for the pictures to carry a substantial part
of the interpretation. Jacob Lawrence's picture

Jacob Lawrence, a well-known black painter, has used
distortion and exaggeration in his pictures to symbolize the hardships and trials of Harriet Tubman.

From *Harriet and the Promised Land* by Jacob Lawrence. Reprinted by permission
of Windmill Productions, Inc.

book based on the life of Harriet Tubman, *Harriet
and the Promised Land*, gives only a skeletal outline
of fact, told in simple verse. The impact of the
book is made by Lawrence's paintings, which
convey feeling through a powerful exaggeration
of shape and color. This sometimes disturbing
intensity of emotion suggests that the best audience might be children of 7 and up, rather than
pre-schoolers.

In contrast, the charming, sometimes idealized
pictures of Ingri d'Aulaire and Edgar Parin
d'Aulaire serve to make their books appealing to
an audience not yet able to read the text. This
husband-and-wife team has written and illustrated beautiful picture-book biographies, including *George Washington; Abraham Lincoln*, for
which they received the Caldecott Award in 1940;
Buffalo Bill; Pocahontas; Columbus; Benjamin Franklin;
and *Leif, the Lucky*. Full-page, colored lithographs
printed by the old stone process appear on every
other page. Large black-and-white pictures are on
alternate pages, and many small pictures are interspersed throughout these books.

[44] Marion Brown and Ruth Crone. *The Silent Storm*, illustrated
by Fritz Kredel (Nashville, Tenn.: Abingdon, 1963), p. 189.

Their story of *Columbus* is one of the few for younger children that includes his discouraging last voyages. They picture his bitterness with sympathetic understanding, but do not gloss over the facts. It is interesting to compare this book with Dalgliesh's outstanding biography, *The Columbus Story.* This is a straightforward account of Columbus' boyhood, his difficulties obtaining support for his venture, and his successful first voyage. The pictures by Leo Politi are striking in their simplicity and clarity, and seem perfectly suited to the dignified narrative.

In the brief, easy-vocabulary picture biographies by Aliki, the childlike illustrations create a feeling of true Colonial primitives. In *The Story of Johnny Appleseed*, this author-illustrator has captured the humor and simplicity of the legendary pioneer. Delicately illustrated period pictures reflect the warmth and gentleness of the Quakers in *The Story of William Penn.* Their belief in the simple life is shown in the sharp contrast between William's plain dress and the King of England's frills and curls. Similar dignity and simplicity is communicated in *A Weed Is a Flower, The Life of George Washington Carver.* Again, Aliki has made meaningful for the youngest reader the inspiring story of a man who was born a slave but lived to become one of the greatest research scientists in the United States.

The mood or tone of a biography can be quickly established by its pictures. A glance at Morton's illustrations for *The Freedom Ship of Robert Smalls* by Meriwether lets us know that this account of a slave who commandeered a Confederate gunboat is a serious tale, despite its triumphant ending. The prevailing gray tones of the scenes near Fort Sumter, as Smalls pilots his family and friends north toward freedom, emphasize the menace of the situation; the fortress itself looms over its own reflection like a huge prison. A similar glance at Monjo's *Poor Richard in France* shows at once the high good humor of Brinton Turkle's illustrations, which match the lively tone of the text. Among the scenes are ones that show Franklin taking off his clothes in the ship's cabin for his daily "air bath," giving a French lady a polite kiss on the neck with rather obvious satisfaction, playing chess with Madame Brillon while she soaks in her bathtub, and dancing wildly to celebrate the news of the American

victory at Saratoga. This book relates the story of Franklin's mission to France through the eyes of his 7-year-old grandson, Benny, who accompanied him; the pictures reveal a warm relationship between boy and grandfather. Trina Schart Hyman's illustration of Samuel Adams thumbing his nose at the British flag helps set the tone for Jean Fritz's biography, *Why Don't You Get a Horse, Sam Adams?.* This book also humanizes a Revolutionary War hero by citing his failings as well as his accomplishments—Adams had difficulty escaping the battle of Lexington simply because he could not ride a horse.

A few picture books for older children focus on a subject's work and philosophy rather than his life. Raboff's series, "Art for Children," presents commentary and full-color reproductions of the work of great artists, along with brief biographical sketches. *Paul Klee, Marc Chagall,* and *Pablo Picasso* are among the subjects. Ann Atwood and Erica Anderson have used breathtaking color photographs to call attention to the words and work of Albert Schweitzer in *For All that Lives.*

Simplified Biographies

Not all children who have an interest in biographical information are in full command of the skills of reading. Some of these children are beginning readers; some read independently but are not ready for a long or complex text; some are older children with specialized interests but low skill levels. Various kinds of simplified biographies, usually short and with many illustrations, have been published in response to the needs of these children.

For beginning readers there are a number of biographies with limited vocabularies, such as those in Putnam's "See and Read" series, which includes books about Indian heroes, great women, and influential blacks, as well as famous men of U.S. history. One of the disadvantages of this kind of writing, however, is that it does frequently sound stilted. Often the sentences are set up line by line for ease of reading, rather than in paragraph form. Unfortunately, this creates a choppy effect. This type of jerky sentence pattern is avoided in Sullivan's *Willie Mays,* which also has a limited vocabulary. It seems condescending, however, to describe the accident in which

13-year-old Willie broke his leg with the words, "Down, down he fell."[45] Judson's beginning-to-read books about *Abraham Lincoln, George Washington,* and *Christopher Columbus* are simply written, complete biographies, describing the boyhood and accomplishments of these famous men. The vocabulary and length of the sentences is controlled for independent reading in first and second grade. However, the narratives read smoothly and do give the child a feeling for the subject.

Few writers can produce a book that is both easy to read and admirable for its style. Monjo has done it in his "I Can Read History Book," *The One Bad Thing about Father.* "Father" is Theodore Roosevelt, and the one bad thing about him, in his son Quentin's eyes, is that he is President of the United States and thus the whole family—including irrepressible sister Alice—must live in the White House.

> Some man once asked Father why
> he didn't do something about Alice.
> Father said, "I can do one of two things.
> I can be President of the United States.
> Or I can control Alice.
> I cannot possibly do both."[46]

Although easy-to-read biographies must be simplified, they should not be oversimplified. It is important to give children a basis for understanding cause-and-effect relationships, and for getting the meaning of unfamiliar terms. In *Abraham Lincoln: For the People* by Colver, little explanation of the Civil War is given, and war is introduced with the very brief sentence: "When the Civil War began the President was even busier."[47] Credence is given to the now-disproved story that Lincoln composed the famous Gettysburg Address while riding on a train. When the Lincolns go to the theater the text states: "The President and Mrs. Lincoln sat in a box."[48] No picture shows the Lincolns in their box seats, so one wonders what images young

readers who are not familiar with the legitimate theater will derive from this statement!

Many simple biographies, as in this last example, are not just for beginning readers but are directed toward an 8- or 9-year-old audience. Clyde Bulla has written two very popular biographies for new readers, *Squanto, Friend of the White Man* and *John Billington, Friend of Squanto.* The true story of Squanto is one that has always appealed to children, for it is filled with adventure, anxiety, and pathos. They identify readily with this Indian who was kidnapped by English explorers and spent some eight years in England. At last Squanto has the opportunity to return home, but once again he is captured and sent back across the Atlantic to be sold as a slave in Spain. Bulla tells this moving tale with simplicity and dignity. The pictures by Peter Burchard are as forceful as the text.

The "Crowell Biography" series, with an emphasis on contemporary figures and those from minority populations, is also directed to this age level. Though the books are produced by a variety of authors and illustrators, the formats are uniformly brief and are enhanced by many pictures. Eloise Greenfield has written the story of *Rosa Parks,* the black woman whose refusal to move to the back of a bus in Montgomery, Alabama, triggered events that grew into the Civil Rights Movement. The author has skillfully chosen a few anecdotes from Mrs. Parks' childhood which help to establish her character and the day-to-day effects of segregation: drinking from special water fountains, not being served at lunch counters, staying awake nights in fear of the Ku Klux Klan. Most of the story deals with Mrs. Parks' defiance of the law, the resulting boycott, and the progress of the protest until the Supreme Court ruled that the bus company must change its policies. This is a simple book but not a vague one, and it tells a moving story. The account by Sharon Bell Mathis of *Ray Charles,* the noted black musician, emphasizes his will and pride and sense of survival. In the opening anecdote 7-year-old Ray, newly arrived at St. Augustine School for the Blind, is tricked by the other children into running full speed against an iron post. In contrast, the examples of his self-sufficiency as an adult have great impact. He plays chess with a set that has the black pieces larger than the white, tells time with a Braille watch, picks out his own clothes,

---

[45] George Sullivan. *Willie Mays,* illustrated by David Brown (New York: Putnam, 1973), p. 7.

[46] F. N. Monjo. *The One Bad Thing about Father,* illustrated by Rocco Negri (New York: Harper & Row, 1970), p. 38.

[47] Anne Colver. *Abraham Lincoln: For the People,* illustrated by William Moyers (Champaign, Ill.: Garrard, 1960), p. 60.

[48] Colver, p. 72.

and can even ride a motor scooter. Such precise use of detail gives this simplified biography more depth than its thirty-three pages would indicate. There are many other books in this fine series, including *Leonard Bernstein* by Molly Cone, *The Mayo Brothers* by Jane Goodsell, *Jim Thorpe* by Thomas Fall, *Marian Anderson* by Tobi Tobias, *Cesar Chavez* by Ruth Franchere, and *Malcolm X* by Arnold Adoff.

The "Childhood of Famous Americans" series, begun by Bobbs-Merrill in 1932, was one of the first to popularize biography for young readers. More fiction than biography, each book attempts to recreate the childhood of a famous person, saving all of his or her adult accomplishments for one chapter at the end. Despite the obvious limitations of the approach, these simplified books do continue to appeal to middle-grade children.

Some simplified biographies fall into the high interest-low reading level category, where the most popular subjects seem to be from the sports and entertainment worlds. The text in these books may be very brief and illustrations or photographs may be used very liberally. In short, the books are designed to catch and keep the eye of the reluctant reader. An example is Creative's "Superstars" series from Children's Press. Olsen's book, *Billie Jean King, The Lady of the Court*, has a bright cover, a picture on every other page, and a short text which, for all its readability, is uneven in quality. For instance, the repetition of: "She believed in herself. Her teachers believed in her. Her friends believed in her. Her husband believed in her. Her parents believed in her,"[49] is out of tune with other, more interesting sentences on the same page. *Arnold Palmer*, another title in this series, is illustrated with garish poster-art pictures, and the text rambles within a loose chronological context. This series does command attention and favorable responses from older children because of their interest in sports heroes, but it is unfortunate that such a useful concept has not been executed with more care to produce really fine books.

Original paperback biographies are often available to provide information about popular figures. Cohen's book, *Cool Cos, The Story of Bill Cosby*, does not have a simplified text, but the many captioned photographs prove satisfying for children who cannot read the narrative. In Brondfield's *Hank Aaron . . . 714 and Beyond*, the text is very short, and again there are plenty of photographs. An addition, which gives bulk to this book, is a list of Aaron's home runs compared with a list of those by Babe Ruth. Other material, such as important dates in Aaron's life and quotes from fan letters he has received, is also furnished in list form. While this is not a conventional format, it admirably suits the purposes of those sports-minded readers who may not sustain attention long enough to read a fully detailed biography. A hardcover adaptation of United Press International's *Roberto Clemente* has been prepared for young readers by Alice Thorne under the title *Clemente*. The text is set in large type and the illustrations are reproduced from newspaper photos. One dramatic picture shows a Navy diver searching the wreckage of Clemente's plane for his body, which was never found.

Partial Biographies

One of the liberties allowed juvenile biographers is the freedom to write only part of the story of a subject's life, perhaps even to deal with as little as one episode. Just one day in the life of Joan of Arc has been reconstructed in *The Feast Day* by Edwin Fadiman, Jr., a beautifully written book of biographical fiction. The medieval background is detailed and authentic, the characterizations believable. When Joan confesses her first vision to the village priest, his skepticism and fear are ably demonstrated:

. . . some things are best left unsaid, some experiences best forgotten. Saint Michael was probably an undigested spoonful of soup or piece of meat.[50]

An Afterword puts the episode in perspective by giving the outline of later events; a bibliographic note suggests that children might find a transcript of Joan of Arc's trial in their public libraries. The gray-toned illustrations by Charles Mikolaycak are distinguished in their own right.

Some partial biographies do furnish information about the subject's entire life, but focus on

[49] James T. Olsen. *Billie Jean King, The Lady of the Court,* illustrated by John Nelson (Mankato, Minn.: Creative Education, 1974), p. 20.

[50] Edwin Fadiman, Jr. *The Feast Day,* illustrated by Charles Mikolaycak (Boston, Mass.: Little, Brown, 1973), p. 60.

a few incidents that are particularly memorable. *Mumbet, The Story of Elizabeth Freeman* by Harold Felton has two central incidents. The first and most striking tells how Bet, a slave in a well-to-do Massachusetts household in 1781 convinced a lawyer to appeal to the courts in her behalf. Her case for freedom rested on the grounds that the new state constitution guaranteed freedom and equality to all. After the court ruled in her favor, Bet worked as a paid nurse in her lawyer's household, and during Shays' Rebellion helped to protect his family, his silver, and his favorite horse from marauding ruffians—with the aid of a shovel and a hatpin! An introduction provides historical background and documentation which would otherwise have hindered the flow of this lively fictionalized account.

Other biographies are incomplete for the simple reason that a full treatment of the subject's complex life would make a book too long and unwieldy for young readers. There are several such biographies of Abraham Lincoln, for instance. Armstrong's book, *The Education of Abraham Lincoln*, furnishes details of the school life of the time and photographs of texts then in use. Scenes and dialogue are fictionalized, but authentically represent the times.

Carl Sandburg wrote a partial biography for children titled *Abe Lincoln Grows Up*. It was made from the first twenty-seven chapters of the longest and most definitive of biographies on Lincoln for adults, Sandburg's *Abraham Lincoln: The Prairie Years*. For his juvenile biography Sandburg included Lincoln's birth and boyhood, until he was 19 and "grown up." In singing prose that begs to be read aloud, the author describes the monotony of daily life on the frontier and Lincoln's desire for knowledge:

> He wanted to learn, to live, to reach out; he wanted to satisfy hungers and thirsts he couldn't tell about, this big big boy of the backwoods. And some of what he wanted so much, so deep down, seemed to be in books. Maybe in books he would find the answers to dark questions pushing around in the pools of his thoughts, and the drifts of his mind.[51]

[51]Carl Sandburg. *Abe Lincoln Grows Up*, reprinted from *Abraham Lincoln: The Prairie Years*, illustrated by James Daugherty (New York: Harcourt Brace Jovanovich, 1928), p. 135.

Frances Cavanah's book, *Abe Lincoln Gets His Chance*, covers a somewhat longer period than the Sandburg book, ending with Lincoln's departure for the White House. Cavanah makes good use of dialogue, and children will enjoy the conversation, the humor, and the inclusion of many interesting anecdotes. This is a book that middle-graders can easily read for themselves. Lincoln's departure for the White House also marks the end of a fine book by Olivia Coolidge called *The Apprenticeship of Abraham Lincoln*. Exacting scholarship went into the preparation of this authentic biography. The author encourages readers to weigh for themselves the evidence about Lincoln's absence from the bedside of his dying father; to consider carefully Herndon's comments on Mary Todd Lincoln, since there was long-standing animosity between them; to look through the eyes of an urbane New Yorker while the gawky Lincoln spoke at the Cooper Union. Lincoln himself, for all the detail that describes him, remains something of an enigma, a man who ". . . could put on dignity like a coat, yet shirtsleeves remained his natural costume."[52] This book is written for young adults and not for children, though upper elementary-school students might be interested in comparing the first chapter with other accounts of Lincoln's childhood. Certainly this is valuable background reading for teachers, and a good index makes it helpful for reference as well.

Many Lincoln biographies for children either omit the war years or pass over them very quickly. Not so Monjo's *Me and Willie and Pa*, which covers only the years 1860–1865. The first-person point of view is Tad Lincoln's, and through his eyes the reader sees the problems of a wartime president. There are also family anecdotes and descriptions of interesting visitors to the White House. Gorsline's illustrations, drawn from early photographs, support the documentary effect.

Complete Biographies

Complete biography spans its subject's lifetime. It may be relatively simple or difficult, authentic or fictionalized. Whatever the case may be, the reader should expect a view that has some

[52]Olivia Coolidge. *The Apprenticeship of Abraham Lincoln* (New York: Scribner, 1974), p. viii.

Willie and me, with Mama

Gorsline's pictures simulate the old daguerreotypes of Lincoln's family.

From *Me and Willie and Pa* by F. N. Monjo. Illustration Copyright © 1973, by Douglas Gorsline. Reprinted by permission of Simon and Schuster, Children's Book Division.

depth, some balance, some sense of perspective. Among types of biographies, this category is by far the largest. The following examples can do no more than suggest the range of books available.

ADVENTURERS AND PIONEERS

Since many young readers are more entranced by a life of action than a life of ideas, biographies of explorers are usually popular. A long list of concise and clearly written books about explorers can be credited to Ronald Syme. Some of his books are suited to 8- and 9-year-old readers; some are a bit harder to read. In *John Smith of Virginia*, Syme has drawn a picture of Smith that shows the leadership qualities which made men his willing followers, and also portrays those qualities which made men hate and envy him. Despite the magnificent seamanship of *Vasco da Gama*, Syme points out in his biography that this explorer was unable to make friends with native

people. The author has shown the dark side of Da Gama's character, his violent temper and revengeful nature. In his book *Verrazano*, the author describes how this explorer, the first to sail into New York Harbor, fell into disrepute more than 300 years after his death. An old document with careless spelling was misinterpreted by historians who concluded that Verrazano had been hanged as a pirate, a story not disproved until the turn of the last century when some of the Florentine's original papers came to light in a private Roman collection. Syme has also written two fine biographies of adventurous women: *African Traveler, The Story of Mary Kingsley* and *Nigerian Pioneer, The Story of Mary Slessor*. Mary Kingsley was the first woman to explore Africa, armed with nothing but curiosity, a sense of humor, and a British parasol. Syme has included some delightfully funny incidents in his account of this intrepid traveler.

Two fascinating accounts of exploration in the early sixteenth century will appeal to older children. Helen Parish's *Estebanico* is a first-person narrative of the slave who accompanied a Spanish expedition across the southern part of the American continent. Fictionalized and very readable, this book is based on the author's careful study of primary sources.

William O. Steele begins *The Wilderness Tattoo: A Narrative of Juan Ortiz* when the young Spaniard was 18. It was then, in 1528, that he was captured by Timucuan Indians on Tampa Bay, having been lured ashore from the ship of the explorer Narváez. What follows is a story of near death and slavery; then escape to a neighboring village, where Juan was treated as a friend and came himself to live as an Indian. Some eleven years later he joined the passing expedition of Hernando de Soto in the hope of one day returning to his homeland. But De Soto was determined to search for gold, and Juan Ortiz died, in some unrecorded way, while accompanying De Soto as his interpreter. This haunting story is presented in two ways—in numbered chapters which read like fiction and in separate interludes which provide the background. These interludes are based on careful research, particularly with respect to contemporary chronicles of the De Soto expedition.

Constance Fecher's *The Last Elizabethan, A Portrait of Sir Walter Ralegh*, tells the story of the courageous adventurer who was beheaded as a traitor by a hostile king. Ralegh showed uncommon courage in death, as he had in life:

He took the ax from the reluctant executioner.
  "Let me see it. Do you think I am afraid of it?" He smiled as he tried the edge against his thumb. "This is a sharp medicine, but it is a physician for all diseases."[53]

With a wealth of authentic detail, and dialogue reconstructed from early documents and letters, the author brings this complex, brilliant character to life. Margaret Hodges delineates a discontented English adventurer in *Hopkins of the Mayflower: Portrait of a Dissenter*. This book gives a fascinating glimpse of the first Massachusetts colonists against their Elizabethan background, and illustrates the diversity of beliefs among them. There is valuable material here for comparison with other accounts of Plymouth Plantation, but in its entirety the book would be very difficult for even advanced readers in elementary school.

For many years the name of James Daugherty seemed almost synonymous with that of biographer and illustrator of the North American scene. With singing, swinging pictures and rhythmical prose he portrayed Abraham Lincoln and Benjamin Franklin, as well as the great pioneers—Daniel Boone, Lewis and Clark, Marcus and Narcissa Whitman. His book *Daniel Boone* was a winner of the Newbery Award, and it portrays in almost epic prose the rigor and humor of pioneer life. During the grim nine-day siege of Boonesborough, the Indians offered friendship in exchange for a peaceful surrender. Daugherty describes the settlers' answer in these words:

They would not have been where they were if they had not been stubborn survivors of a rough, tough, restless race who lived and died in their own independent way by the rifle, the ax, the Bible and the plow. So they sent back the eagle's answer: "No surrender," the answer of the sassy two-year-old democracy, the answer of Man the Unconquerable to the hosts of darkness—"No surrender."[54]

[53] Constance Fecher. *The Last Elizabethan. A Portrait of Sir Walter Ralegh* (New York: Farrar, Straus, 1972), p. 231.
[54] James Daugherty. *Daniel Boone* (New York: Viking, 1939), p. 59.

There are joy and horror, courage and action in Daugherty's swirling, turbulent pictures, a perfect complement for the text. It must be pointed out, however, that Daugherty did not write objective biography. He rendered events as he interpreted them, in a poem of praise to the pioneers.

PRESIDENTS AND EARLY STATESMEN

One of children's most persistent requests is for books about United States presidents and early statesmen. Several complete biographies by Clara Ingram Judson, the products of scholarly research, have long helped to answer this need. Frequently, the theme of Judson's books can be seen in their titles; for example, *George Washington, Leader of the People*; *Andrew Jackson, Frontier Statesman*; *Thomas Jefferson, Champion of the People*; *Abraham Lincoln, Friend of the People*; and *Theodore Roosevelt, Fighting Patriot*. Many biographies have been written about these famous men, and it seemed to Judson that the only justification for writing more would be the presentation of a different interpretation of their lives. Her intensive research frequently revealed sidelights that had not previously been included in the more stereotyped biographies for children. For example, while reading the diary of a private soldier who served with Washington at Valley Forge, Judson came upon the comment that the General had joined in a game and that he was a good pitcher. Few biographies of Washington ever pictured him as a good ballplayer! And yet this side of his character would be much more appealing to children than the priggish presentation of the cherry-tree story. George Washington emerges as a real person, the Commander-in-Chief, the first President, but also as a farmer, father, and the man who loved his family as dearly as he loved his country. *Mr. Justice Holmes* is a somewhat more difficult book, but it tells the fascinating story of one of our greatest jurists, one whose famous father continued to call him "my little boy" even when the little boy had grown to be six feet four inches tall.

Biographies by Thomas J. Fleming are also difficult, though some children in upper elementary-school classes will read them easily. *Benjamin Franklin* is authentic biography, and a frank and balanced presentation of the life of a remarkable man. Though little space is devoted to Franklin's earliest childhood, there is ample coverage of his accomplishments, and occasional indiscretions, from his adolescent years to his death at 84. This is a lively book, with bits of dialogue quoted from Franklin's letters and publications. Older children, who will have previously read Monjo's *Poor Richard in France*, may be intrigued by the comparison of that book to the corresponding chapters in this one. While there is no contradiction of basic fact, the Fleming account shows that Franklin's humor and wit were only a part of the Paris experience, which also included discomfort and disappointment. Another notable but difficult book about an early political figure is Olivia Coolidge's *Tom Paine, Revolutionary*, which provides an objective look at Paine's impassioned and controversial beliefs.

REFORMERS AND CHAMPIONS OF FREEDOM

Many recent biographies tell exciting stories of black pioneers of freedom. A forerunner of these was *Amos Fortune, Free Man* by Elizabeth Yates, a moving account of a common man who lived simply and greatly. Born free in Africa, he was sold as a slave in North America. In time he purchased his own freedom and that of several others. Not until he was 80 years old did Amos Fortune spend money on himself; then he purchased twenty-five acres of land in the shadow of his beloved mountain, Monadnock—Indian for "the mountain that stands alone." Like Monadnock, Fortune stood alone, a rock of strength and security for all those he loved.

Shirley Graham tells *The Story of Phillis Wheatley, Poetess of the American Revolution*, who came to Boston at the age of 5 on a slave ship and was bought and educated by a gentle, prosperous family. As a young woman Phillis wrote poetry that was much admired and praised by such notables as Tom Paine and General Washington. But in the hard times that followed the war, the Wheatley family was separated by death and debts; Phillis' own husband, a free black man, was thrown into debtors' prison, and the young poet died, tragically alone.

She who sang so nobly of freedom was herself a victim of the war that freed thirteen separate colo-

nies and founded a nation on the proposition that "All men are created equal."[55]

Freedom Train, The Story of Harriet Tubman by Dorothy Sterling is a fast-moving biography of the amazing slave who brought freedom to more than 300 of her race. In this account of her life Harriet Tubman emerges as a strong, fearless woman with only one thought in mind, to lead her people out of slavery. No wonder the slaves called her "Moses." For *Captain of the Planter*, Sterling has told the story of Robert Smalls, the slave who claimed freedom by delivering a Confederate boat to the United States army. Later, he fought for freedom, and as a Congressman he worked for it through the hopes and bitter disillusionment of the Reconstruction. His name was Robert Smalls, but he was a big man in all that he did.

Journey toward Freedom, The Story of Sojourner Truth is a well-researched book, as gripping as a novel, by Jacqueline Bernard. Born a slave in Ulster County, New York, Sojourner Truth set out in her middle years, free, with her self-chosen name.

> She had been a slave. And she had been freed, in part through her own efforts. Now she would help free others. The Lord had pointed out her new task. It would be to testify against slavery.[56]

For the rest of her long life this remarkable woman spoke throughout the North on behalf of various social reforms: abolition, women's rights, fair treatment for freedmen. This long dramatic story would be a fine one for an adult to share, at least in part, with older children.

Another biography that will hold children's interest is that of *Forten, the Sailmaker* by Esther Douty. This well-documented story of a free and prosperous black man in the early nineteenth century invents some dialogue, but also includes direct quotes from letters and various papers. Forten's involvement with great questions of his time—abolition, American colonization of Africa, education and civil rights for blacks—and the

[55] Shirley Graham. *The Story of Phillis Wheatley, Poetess of the American Revolution* (New York: Washington Square Press, 1969), p. x.

[56] Jacqueline Bernard. *Journey toward Freedom, The Story of Sojourner Truth* (New York: Norton, 1967), p. 146.

character of the man himself make the book well worth reading. A more recent and somewhat simpler version of Forten's life is *Between the Devil and the Sea.* This book by Brenda Johnston places more emphasis on Forten's early life. Also of interest is *I, Charlotte Forten, Black and Free* by Polly Longsworth, a fictionalized account of James Forten's granddaughter. Based on her own journal, the story tells of young Charlotte's experiences as a teenager studying in Massachusetts, and as a teacher of newly freed slaves at Port Royal, South Carolina, during the Civil War.

Children who read these biographies will incidentally meet other nineteenth-century reformers whose stories they may want to know more about. The Fortens and Sojourner Truth, for instance, were all acquainted with William Lloyd Garrison, whose story is told by Doris Faber in *I Will Be Heard.* This biography is not fictionalized to a great extent, but the writing is lively and provides some interpretation of facts for young readers. The author admits Garrison's weaknesses, as she assesses the antislavery contributions of the publisher of *The Liberator:*

> He offered no specific plan for setting slaves free, he refused to accept advice from anybody, he was stubborn and far too fond of the sound of his own voice. *But he made people think about slavery.*[57]

Faber has also written a lively account of the life of Elizabeth Cady Stanton in *Oh, Lizzie!.* The daughter of a judge, young Lizzie learned Greek and secretly studied her father's law books in order to be as much pleasure to him as her dead brother might have been. When she found that married women in the early 1800s had no more rights than slaves, she determined to stay single. Her eventual marriage to journalist and abolitionist Henry Stanton, however, was an uncommon partnership that helped to involve her in the cause of women's rights. The historical background is precise, but the emphasis of the story is personal—on Lizzie's feelings, her sometimes unpredictable behavior, her amazing energy on long lecture tours, her fondness for thick cream and apple pie that made her size a matter for

caricature. Young readers will find many contemporary overtones in this story of a strong-minded, imaginative woman.

Mary Virginia Fox's biography of Belva Lockwood, *Lady for the Defense,* tells of an equal-rights advocate who deserves to be remembered for her accomplishments: first woman lawyer, first woman to run for president (in 1884), delegate to the first world peace conference, champion of the Cherokee Indians in their claims against the government for land payments. Young readers will welcome the amount of conversation in this book, although occasionally it seems that dialogue bears too much of the weight of the narrative. A different sort of reformer is described in Rachel Baker's story of *America's First Trained Nurse: Linda Richards.* Those who are fascinated by stories of Florence Nightingale will find their horizons widened by learning of this woman's efforts to win recognition for her profession and more humane conditions in treating the sick.

UNIQUE ACHIEVEMENTS

Frequently, biographers choose subjects who are credited with unique achievements, whatever the field. Most authors would be dubious about writing an interesting biography for children about a mathematician, but Jean Lee Latham was challenged. She studied mathematics, astronomy, oceanography, and seamanship. Then she went to Boston and Salem to talk with descendants of Nathaniel Bowditch and to do research on the geographical and maritime backgrounds of her story. The result of all this painstaking preparation was the Newbery Award-winner, *Carry On, Mr. Bowditch,* the amazing story of Nat Bowditch, who had little chance for schooling but mastered the secrets of navigation for himself. Before he was 30 he had written *The American Practical Navigator,* which was still used some 150 years later as a standard text in the United States Naval Academy! Latham has also written detailed biographies of inventors Eli Whitney and Cyrus Field; explorers James Cook and many others; as well as simpler books about such figures as Samuel F. B. Morse, George W. Goethals, and Rachel Carson. Latham is a gifted storyteller who also respects accuracy and authenticity.

Many other scientists, inventors, and re-

[57] Doris Faber. *I Will Be Heard, The Life of William Lloyd Garrison* (New York: Lothrop, 1970), p. 92.

searchers have served as subjects for biography. The Epsteins' book, *Michael Faraday, Apprentice to Science,* is suited to children just beginning to experiment with the principles of electric current, which he discovered. In *Joseph Henry, Father of American Electronics,* "A Hall of Fame" book by Jahns, the background of Washington D.C. during the Civil War and Henry's relationship with Lincoln is particularly interesting. The story of *Charles Richard Drew, Pioneer in Blood Research,* as told by Richard Hardwick, is an account of the singular accomplishments of a black physician.

Two fascinating biographies of naturalists are Hildegarde Hoyt Swift's story of John Muir, *From the Eagle's Wing,* and *The Edge of April, A Biography of John Burroughs.* The book about Muir, father of our national parks, is perhaps the more exciting of the two. A geologist with intense curiosity, Muir was determined to prove his glacial theory, and made frequent trips of exploration throughout the West. Swift has included the moving story of the rescue of his little dog Stickeen from near death on a glacier. Still exploring at 74, Muir's life was completely dedicated to the preservation of the natural beauty of our West. Lynd Ward's black-and-white pictures add strength and artistry to these fine biographies.

Stories of accomplishments earned in the face of great handicaps have special appeal for children; one teacher counted no less than thirteen biographies of Franklin D. Roosevelt on a public-library shelf. Helen Keller is another popular subject. Catherine Owens Peare has told *The Helen Keller Story* with much warmth and insight in an authentic biography which makes the reader feel and "see" as Helen Keller did. A related biography, and a somewhat easier one to read, is Edith Fisher Hunter's book about deaf and blind Laura Bridgman, *Child of the Silent Night.* Records of Laura's early education were used by Annie Sullivan in her preparation for teaching Helen Keller. The life of Annie Sullivan herself has been delineated by Mickie Davidson in a popular fictionalized biography, *Helen Keller's Teacher,* as well as in *The Silent Storm* by Brown and Crone.

ARTISTS AND AUTHORS

Children who have a special interest in the arts will also find numerous biographies to intrigue them. Anne Rockwell offers a brief reconstruction of the life of Giotto, an Italian painter of the fourteenth century, in *The Boy Who Drew Sheep.* The illustrations are reproductions of some of Giotto's paintings, showing his revolutionary use of authentic background and figures in realistic action. Since so little is known about the life of Velasquez and his celebrated black assistant, Elizabeth Borten de Treviño has had to invent a great deal of material for her Newbery Award-winning story, *I, Juan de Pareja.* The fascination of Juan's life lies in his beginnings as a slave, his secret and remarkable talent for his master's business of painting, and the growth of their relationship from master and slave to equals and friends.

In *Paintbrush & Peacepipe: The Story of George Catlin,* Rockwell tells the exciting and tragic story of a nineteenth-century North American whose paintings and writings are one of the chief sources of knowledge about the Plains Indians of that time. A more detailed account of Catlin's life and work is found in Haverstock's handsome book, *Indian Gallery.* An authentic biography which is not too difficult for older elementary-school children, it is liberally illustrated with photographs of Catlin's work and quotes from his letters and journals, including a recipe for "mosquito soup."

One way to encourage interest in fine books is to introduce biographies of children's authors. Those who have enjoyed some of Beatrix Potter's nursery tales will savor *Nothing Is Impossible, The Story of Beatrix Potter* by Dorothy Aldis. This well-written, fictionalized account gives contemporary children a glimpse of Victorian England and of parents whose strict dictates kept their talented daughter virtually isolated from the larger world until her middle age. Stories of the pets which were Potter's closest companions and of her education by governesses will intrigue children; perhaps the complete list of her books at the end will encourage middle-graders to look with keener eyes at their old favorites, or to read for the first time some of the Potter tales they had missed. Interest in this book could also be developed through love of Dorothy Aldis' poetry. Aileen Fisher and Olive Rabe have given children a special perspective on the author of *Little Women* in their book, *We Alcotts,* told from the first-person point of view of Louisa's mother. Because the Alcott family was so much a part of the vital intellectual climate of New England in the mid-nineteenth century, the book also includes biographical sidelights on such figures as Thoreau and Emerson, who were family friends. *America's Mark Twain* is one of the most handsome biographies available for young people. Thorough research is reflected in both May McNeer's perceptive text and Lynd Ward's magnificent pictures. Ward visited Samuel Clemens' hometown of Hannibal, Missouri, while preparing the many illustrations for this book. The author's life story is interspersed with reviews and pictures of some of the books he wrote.

The complex lives of very different poets, Edward Lear and Langston Hughes, have been frankly presented in two biographies for older children. Emery Kelen's *Mr. Nonsense, A Life of Edward Lear* probes the psychology of a man who was a literary clown bedeviled by personal troubles. Despite chronic asthma, epilepsy, and failing sight, Lear was an intrepid traveler, and Kelen points out how all these influences are reflected in his poems and pictures. Meltzer's biography of *Langston Hughes* will provide valuable insights for mature students who can consider the relationship of life and work for the first poet who gave voice to the condition of black Americans.

CONTEMPORARY FIGURES

Most biographies of living subjects fall into the simplified category, or are partial accounts based on a single achievement. Certainly a biographer's access to private material may be less complicated in the case of an historical subject—and his point of view more objective. Often biographies appear soon after a subject's death—*Young Man in the White House, John Fitzgerald Kennedy* by Levine and Jesse Jackson's biography of gospel singer Mahalia Jackson, *Make a Joyful Noise Unto the Lord!* are two examples. There are, however, a number of full-length, detailed biographies of contemporary figures.

The first black woman to be elected to Congress is the subject of two biographies which children might compare. *Shirley Chisholm* by Brownmiller is the easier of the two, with many reconstructed conversations. *The Honorable Shirley Chisholm, Congresswoman from Brooklyn* was written by Nancy Hicks, a young black journalist. This account has more detail and analysis, and raises more questions about the future. The story of another notable woman in government has been told in *A Life for Israel, The Story of Golda Meir* by Arnold Dobrin. Clearly written, with a length and vocabulary that put it within the reach of most 8- to 11-year-olds, this book shows the life of Golda Meir intertwined with the story of modern Israel. Photographs from both private and public sources support this dual image, and a separate chronology at the end of the book is helpful for reference.

Rosen's biography *Wizard of the Dome: R. Buckminster Fuller, Designer for the Future*, emphasizes the imagination and the world-consciousness of the man who has made spectacular use of the geodesic dome. Relatively little space is devoted to Fuller's childhood and quite a lot to the principles of "nature's own geometry," a combination that marks the book as one for advanced readers. The story of a man who was both an artist and a political figure is told in *Paul Robeson, The Life and Times of a Free Black Man.* This comprehensive book will be too difficult for all but the very best elementary-school readers, yet it has special appeal because it is written by a favorite author, Virginia Hamilton.

Perhaps the majority of biographies about contemporary figures are those of stars in sports and in the theater arts. *Kareem! Basketball Great* by Hano, from the "Putnam Sports Shelf," is the chronicle of Lew Alcindor, whose athletic prowess took him from Harlem through the University of California at Los Angeles to the world of professional basketball, where he became known by his Islamic name, Kareem Abdul-Jabbar. This book includes details of real games, scores, records—the same details that endear sports fiction to its readers. It also includes some striking use of language:

> Players dribble and pass like magicians, like carnival wizards hiding the pea beneath the walnut shell. Men leap softly into the air, unflex their wrists, and from any angle, any distances, drill the cords.[58]

Garrard has published a series of "Biographies about Creative People in the Arts and Sciences,"

[58] Arnold Hano. *Kareem! Basketball Great* (New York: Putnam, 1975), p. 20.

of which De Leeuw's *Maria Tallchief, American Ballerina* is one. The text is easy enough for 8- and 9-year-olds to read for themselves, and it emphasizes the determination of this fine dancer and her pride in her Indian heritage. Glowing quotes from reviews of successful performances are more memorable than the descriptions of hard work and practice, however. It might be interesting to read this book in conjunction with *The Russian Ballet School* by Harris (*see* page 553), which emphasizes the pain of striving for perfection.

Collective Biographies

Many children looking for biographical information want brief material about specific people or about specific endeavors. Literally hundreds of collective biographies have been published to meet this need. In scope and difficulty they run the gamut—some have one-paragraph sketches of many subjects, others have long essays on just a few. One particularly attractive book is Leonard Everett Fisher's *Picture Book of Revolutionary War Heroes*, with its distinctive scratchboard illustrations. The fifty patriots are widely representative: black Deborah Gannett, who dressed as a man to fight with the Massachusetts Regulars; wealthy Haym Solomon, whose origin was a Jewish ghetto in Poland; Baron Friedrich von Steuben of Prussia; Dr. Benjamin Rush of Philadelphia. The information about each is brief but tantalizing—Paul Revere once was court-martialed, financier Robert Morris died penniless. There are fewer subjects but more detail in Colonel Red Reeder's book, *Bold Leaders of the American Revolution*, which devotes a full chapter to each of a dozen people and is illustrated with handsome maps.

Like other books, collective biographies must be judged on more than title and appearance. *America's First Ladies 1789 to 1865* by Chaffin and Butwin promises to tell about the presidents' wives, but in reality tells more about the presidents themselves. However, the book is useful in a general way, and does include reproductions of paintings of each first lady and her husband. Hettie Jones uses a bit of song lyric for her title, *Big Star Fallin' Mama: Five Women in Black Music*. The book is in one sense a vehicle for information about the development of Afro-American

music; in the process the author tells the sometimes tragic stories of five singers: Ma Rainey, Bessie Smith, Mahalia Jackson, Billie Holiday, and Aretha Franklin. All told, there are so many collective biographies that teachers and librarians may find it helpful to use a reference such as Silverman's *An Index to Young Readers' Collective Biographies*,[59] which includes thousands of people in hundreds of books.

Autobiographies and Memoirs

Life stories are often recalled and written down by the subjects themselves, as autobiographies or memoirs. Some children's books based on autobiographical material have been discussed as historical fiction (*see* Chapter 8). Autobiography carries much the same advantages and disadvantages as informational books of eyewitness history—the warmth and immediacy of personal detail, but a necessarily limited perspective. The criterion of objectivity is reversed here; it is the very subjectivity of this sort of biography which

[59]Judith Silverman. *An Index to Young Readers' Collective Biographies*, 2nd ed. (New York: Bowker, 1975).

MARY LUDWIG HAYS 1754-1832

Crisp scratchboard illustrations portray the Revolutionary War heroine, "Molly Pitcher."

Picture Book of Revolutionary War Heroes, by Leonard Everett Fisher, published by Stackpole Books.

has value. But children do need to be aware of the inherent bias, and they may be encouraged to look to other sources for balance.

A series of black autobiographies published by Dutton offers modern adaptations of first-person accounts written in the eighteenth and nineteenth centuries. Knight's *In Chains to Louisiana, Solomon Northup's Story* was first published in 1853 as *Twelve Years a Slave, Narrative of Solomon Northup, a Citizen of New York, Kidnapped in Washington City in 1841, and Rescued in 1853, from a Cotton Plantation near the Red River, in Louisiana.* The updated language makes the book accessible to elementary-school children, although the raw violence of the detail presumes a certain maturity in the reader. Northup's master in Louisiana beat his slaves brutally and in drunken rages forced them to dance for his entertainment until dawn, then go to work in the fields without sleep, only to earn more punishment for working too slowly. The joyous scene of Northup's rescue is dimmed by the fact that he never won justice in the courts.

Another book in this series is *The Slave Who Bought His Freedom, Equiano's Story,* adapted by Karen Kennerly. Equiano's memories stretch back to his West African childhood, and his description of a slave ship crossing (published in 1789) is one of the earliest known. During the cruel trip Equiano wonders about his white captors:

> Why did they make us live in such filthy places below the deck and yet want us to stay alive—so much so that they would hold our mouths open by iron clamps and force food into our throats if we refused to eat?[60]

This account bears such striking similarity to the voyage described in Paula Fox's *The Slave Dancer* (*see* Chapter 8) that it seems Equiano's autobi-

ography might have been used as at least one source for that book.

Another type of autobiography which children may find interesting is that written by authors whose work they know. *Journey into Childhood, The Autobiography of Lois Lenski* includes a great deal about her adult work and will perhaps be of more interest to teachers and librarians than to young readers. A generous section of family-album photographs, as well as quotes from the author's own letters, have been included in this book.

Maia Wojciechowska, whom children know best as the author of *Shadow of a Bull* (*see* Chapter 7), has written a partial memoir, *Till the Break of Day, Memories: 1939–1942,* that includes her fascination upon seeing her first bullfight:

> I did not know the rules or why they had to do what they did to the animals. I did not understand why, at the end, the bull had to die. All I knew was that I was witnessing something terribly special when the man with the long, tired, sad face, the man they called Manolete, was down there on the sand.[61]

Older Winnie the Pooh fans may be drawn to the memoir written by the son of A. A. Milne, the "real" Christopher Robin. In *The Enchanted Places,* he offers an adult perspective on the surroundings of his childhood. Most interesting, perhaps, are his comments on the trials of separating his own identity from the image that became familiar to readers all over the world.

Biographies of all types give children a glimpse of other lives, other places, other times. The best of them combine accurate information and fine writing in a context that children enjoy—the story that really happened. Such books deserve to be part of every child's experiences with literature.

---

[60]Karen Kennerly, adapter. *The Slave Who Bought His Freedom: Equiano's Story* (New York: Dutton, 1971), p. 34.

[61]Maia Wojciechowska. *Till the Break of Day, Memories: 1939–1942* (New York: Harcourt Brace Jovanovich, 1972), p. 136.

SUGGESTED LEARNING EXPERIENCES

1. Talk to a group of children to find what special interests or hobbies they have. Make a survey of nonfiction to see what informational books or biographies might enrich these interests. Plan a display of some of these books for a classroom or library interest center.
2. Select several books on one topic—such as ecology, the solar system, or China. Evaluate

them, using the criteria in this chapter. Plan activity cards or questions which would interest children in the books and help them to use the books more effectively.

3. Compare different points of view in several books about one general topic—such as Alderman's *The War We Could Have Lost;* Colby's *Lexington and Concord, 1775;* Foster's *Year of Independence, 1776;* Fleming's *First in Their Hearts;* Reeder's *Bold Leaders of the American Revolution.* If possible, obtain a British account of the Revolutionary War. How are each of these books different? Can you identify a theme and point of view in each book?

4. Think of a specific activity—such as raising a hamster, building a terrarium, or using a microscope. Find informational books that would enrich the experience.

5. Collect specimens of leaves and plants; then choose several related identification books— such as Gallob's *City Leaves, City Trees;* Dowden's *Wild Green Things in the City;* or Selsam and Hunt's *A First Look at Leaves.* Which is easiest to use? What ideas do you get for new experiences built on the original activity?

6. Plan an environmental study. Assuming you might begin with a walking trip in the immediate neighborhood, what books would you take with you to use as immediate resources? What books might you have available for follow-up activities? Consider such possibilities as George's *All upon a Sidewalk,* Simon's *Birds on Your Street,* Gladstone's *A Carrot for a Nose,* or Downer's *Roofs over America.*

7. Working with one or a small group of children, select a craft or activity book which seems suited to their age level. Watch carefully as children follow the directions given. What difficulties do they have? What questions do they ask? Could you make the directions clearer, safer, or more imaginative?

8. Select a country such as Ghana in West Africa. Look at social-studies texts and encyclopedias. Compare the information in these books to recent informational books. Read some of the Anansi folk tales to see what additional insights can be gleaned from them about the Ashanti society.

9. Work with a group of children in writing an informational book modeled after one of the documentary accounts (*America's 200th Birthday: An Adventure in Eyewitness History*). Or, collect material for a Jackdaw on the same topic. What criteria should guide this activity?

10. Look at the selection of biographies in a school library. Make a checklist of how many biographies are about men. About women. What people have been the subject of many biographies? Few? One? What contemporary figures are presented in these biographies?

11. Select several biographies of one subject, such as Helen Keller. Make a chart to compare information, omissions, point of view of author, documentation. Read related biographies, such as *The Silent Storm* by Brown and Crone, to find out about Helen Keller through her teacher, Annie Sullivan. Make a list of books that might extend this focus—such as biographies of Louis Braille (*Touch of Light* by Neimark), informational books about seeing-eye dogs, and fictional accounts of blindness such as *Follow My Leader* by Garfield.

RELATED READINGS

1. "Aspects of Children's Informational Books," John Donovan, Guest Ed. *Wilson Library Bulletin,* Vol. 49:2 (October 1974), pp. 145–177.

   Almost the entire issue of this well-known periodical is devoted to an analysis of children's informational books. Zena Sutherland's excellent article, "Information Pleases— Sometimes," gives criteria for evaluating informational books and takes issue with some of Margery Fisher's criteria in *Matters of Fact.* Olivia Coolidge describes the process of writing authentic biography in her article, "My Struggle with Facts." In an essay, "To Each Generation Its Own Rabbits," Dennis Flanagan, editor of *Scientific American,* shows how *Watership Down* by Richard Adams embraces the two worlds of science and literature. Other articles relevant to this chapter are included in this fine special issue.

2. Eakin, Mary K. "The Changing World of Science and the Social Studies" in *Children and Literature, Views and Reviews,* Virginia Haviland, ed. Glenview, Ill.: Scott, Foresman, 1973.

Based upon a paper presented at the Congress of the International Board on Books for Young People, this is a plea for more honest informational books, science books which present the possible social implications of a discovery or new technique, social-studies books which face up to the errors and failures of the past. Some informational books, particularly those on ecology, are beginning to move in the direction suggested in this paper.

3. Fisher, Margery. *Matters of Fact: Aspects of Non-fiction for Children.* New York: Crowell, 1972.

   This authoritative book by an English author provides criteria for judging and selecting nonfiction books for children. The first chapter describes the various types of informational books, while the following chapters take an in-depth look at books about particular themes—such as bread, cowboys, honeybees, and atoms. Three chapters are devoted to an analysis of biographies about Bach, Helen Keller, and Abraham Lincoln. While many of the books discussed are British, publishers in the United States are given where appropriate.

4. Jurich, Marilyn. "What's Left Out of Biography for Children," *Children's Literature,* Vol. 1 (1972), p. 145.

   This author advocates a fuller treatment of subjects in biographies for children, and also more variety in the choice of subject. She believes we need more biographies on persons who are not famous, including some anti-heroes.

5. "Science Materials for Children and Young People," George S. Bonn, Issue Ed. *Library Trends,* Vol. 22:4 (April 1974).

   This entire issue of the University of Illinois Graduate School of Library Science publication is devoted to an analysis of science-information books. It contains excellent articles by two authors of science books, Glenn O. Blough and Illa Podendorf. Two librarians establish criteria for selection, and Zena Sutherland discusses "Science as Literature."

6. Selsam, Millicent. "Writing about Science for Children," in *A Critical Approach to Children's Literature,* Sara Innis Fenwick, ed. (Chicago, Ill.: The University of Chicago Press, 1967), pp. 96–99.

   One of the best-known authors of excellent informational books for children describes the qualities of a good science book for children. Her criteria are still very much up-to-date. Only her criticism of the non-scientific attitude toward evolution and sex is not quite applicable, as an increasing number of books on animal behavior do include the formerly taboo subject of mating. The reluctance to discuss evolution is also slowly changing.

RECOMMENDED REFERENCES[62]

INFORMATIONAL BOOKS

Adkins, Jan. *How a House Happens.* Walker, 1972.

———. *Toolchest.* Walker, 1973.

Adler, Irving, and Ruth Adler. *Why? A Book of Reasons.* John Day, 1961.

———. *Why and How? A Second Book of Reasons.* John Day, 1963.

Alderman, Clifford Lindsey. *The War We Could Have Lost: The American Revolution.* Four Winds, 1974.

Aliki, pseud. (Aliki Brandenberg). *Green Grass and White Milk.* Crowell, 1974.

Anderson, Dick, and Nick Buoniconti. *Defensive Football,* Bill Bondurant, ed. Atheneum, 1973.

Annixter, Jane, and Paul Annixter. *Trumpeter: The Story of a Swan.* Holiday, 1973.

Asimov, Isaac. *ABC's of the Ocean.* Walker, 1970.

———. *How Did We Find Out about Germs?* Walker, 1974.

Atlas of World Wildlife. Rand-McNally, 1973.

Atwood, Ann. *The Wild Young Desert.* Scribner, 1970.

[62] All books listed at the end of this chapter are recommended, subject to the qualifications noted in the text. (*See* Appendix D for publishers' complete addresses.)

Austin, Elizabeth S. *Birds that Stopped Flying.* Random House, 1969.

Baker, Jeffrey J. W. *The Vital Process: Photosynthesis,* illustrated by Patricia Collins. Doubleday, 1970.

Bancroft, Griffing. *The White Cardinal,* illustrated by Charles Fracé, Coward-McCann, 1973.

Barris, George, and Jack Scagnetti. *Famous Custom and Show Cars.* Dutton, 1973.

Baumann, Hans. *The Caves of the Great Hunters,* rev. ed. Pantheon, 1962 (1954).

———. *In the Land of Ur: The Discovery of Ancient Mesopotamia,* translated by Stella Humphries. Pantheon, 1969.

Baylor, Byrd. *When Clay Sings,* illustrated by Tom Bahti. Scribner, 1972.

Bealer, Alex W. *Only the Names Remain: The Cherokees and the Trail of Tears,* illustrated by William Sauts Bock. Little, Brown, 1972.

Bendick, Jeanne. *Solids, Liquids and Gases.* F. Watts, 1974.

———. *Why Things Change: The Story of Evolution,* illustrated by Karen Bendick Watson. Parents', 1973.

Berger, Melvin. *The New Water Book.* Crowell, 1973.

Bernheim, Marc, and Evelyne Bernheim. *African Success Story: The Ivory Coast.* Harcourt, 1970.

———. *In Africa.* Atheneum, 1973.

Billington, Elizabeth T. *Understanding Ecology,* rev. ed., illustrated by Robert Galster. Warne, 1971.

Blough, Glenn O. *Bird Watchers and Bird Feeders,* illustrated by Jeanne Bendick. McGraw-Hill, 1963.

Brand, Oscar. *Songs of '76: A Folksinger's History of the Revolution.* M. Evans, 1973.

Branley, Franklyn M. *Experiments in Sky Watching,* rev. ed., illustrated by Helmut K. Wimmer. Crowell, 1967.

———. *The Mystery of Stonehenge,* illustrated by Victor Ambrus. Crowell, 1969.

———. *The Nine Planets,* rev. ed., illustrated by Helmut K. Wimmer. Crowell, 1971.

Brenner, Barbara. *Bodies,* photographs by George Ancona. Dutton, 1973.

———. *A Snake-lover's Diary.* Young Scott, 1970.

Brooks, Lester J. *Great Civilizations of Ancient Africa.* Four Winds, 1971.

Carroll, Sidney. *You Be the Judge.* Lothrop, 1971.

Charlip, Remy, and Mary Beth Miller. *Handtalk: An ABC of Finger Spelling and Sign Language,* photographs by George Ancona. Parents', 1974.

Chernoff, Goldie Taub. *Pebbles and Pods: A Book of Nature Crafts,* illustrated by Margaret Hartelius. Walker, 1973.

Chute, Marchette. *The Green Tree of Democracy.* Dutton, 1971.

Cobb, Vicki. *Science Experiments You Can Eat,* illustrated by Peter Lippman. Lippincott, 1972.

Cohen, Robert. *The Color of Man,* photographs by Ken Heyman. Random House, 1968.

Colby, Jean Poindexter. *Lexington and Concord, 1775: What Really Happened,* photographs by Barbara Cooney. Hastings, 1975.

Cole, Joanna. *My Puppy Is Born,* photographs by Jerome Wexler. Morrow, 1973.

Cole, Joanna, and Madeleine Edmondson. *Twins,* illustrated by Salvatore Raciti. Morrow, 1972.

Collier, James Lincoln. *Jug Bands and Handmade Music: A Creative Approach to Music Theory and the Instruments.* Grosset & Dunlap, 1973.

———. *The Making of Man: The Story of Our Ancient Ancestors.* Four Winds, 1974.

Coombs, Charles. *Skylab.* Morrow, 1972.

Davis, Bette J. *Winter Buds.* Lothrop, 1973.

Davis, Joseph A. *And then There Were None: America's Vanishing Wildlife,* photographs by Nina Leen. Holt, Rinehart and Winston, 1973.

Davis, Mary. *Careers in a Medical Center,* photographs by Milton J. Blumenfeld. Lerner, 1973.

DeGarza, Patricia. *Chicanos: The Story of Mexican Americans.* Messner, 1973.

Denny, Norman, and Josephine Filmer-Sankey. *The Bayeux Tapestry, The Story of the Norman Conquest: 1066.* Atheneum, 1966.

DePaola, Tomie. *"Charlie Needs a Cloak."* Prentice-Hall, 1974.

DeRossi, Claude J. *Computers: Tools for Today,* illustrated by Margrit Fiddle. Children's, 1972.

Dobrin, Arnold. *Gerbils.* Lothrop, 1970.

Dowden, Anne Ophelia. *Wild Green Things in the City, A Book of Weeds.* Crowell, 1972.

Downer, Marion. *Roofs over America.* Lothrop, 1967.

Elisofon, Eliot. *Zaire: A Week in Joseph's World.* Crowell-Collier, 1973.

Ellison, Elsie. *Fun with Lines and Curves,* illustrated by Susan Stan. Lothrop, 1972.

Ellison, Virginia. *The Pooh Cook Book,* illustrated by Ernest H. Shepard. Dutton, 1969.

————. *The Pooh Get-Well Book: Recipes and Activities to Help You Recover from Wheezles and Sneezles.* Dutton, 1973.

————. *The Pooh Party Book.* Dutton, 1971.

Englebert, Victor. *Camera on Ghana: The World of a Young Fisherman.* Harcourt Brace Jovanovich, 1971.

Fenner, Carol. *Gorilla Gorilla,* illustrated by Symeon Shimin. Random House, 1973.

Fisher, Aileen. *Valley of the Smallest: The Life Story of a Shrew,* illustrated by Jean Zallinger. Crowell, 1966.

Fisher, Leonard Everett. *The Doctors.* F. Watts, 1968.

————. *The Printers.* F. Watts, 1965.

————. *The Shipbuilders.* F. Watts, 1971.

————. *Two If by Sea.* Random House, 1970.

————. *The Weavers.* F. Watts, 1966.

Fisher, S. H. *Table Top Science: Physics Experiments for Everyone,* illustrated by Al Nagy. Natural History Press, 1972.

Flanagan, Geraldine Lux. *Window into an Egg: Seeing Life Begin.* Young Scott, 1969.

Foster, Genevieve. *Abraham Lincoln's World.* Scribner, 1944.

————. *Augustus Caesar's World.* Scribner, 1947.

————. *Birthdays of Freedom: From Early Man to July 4, 1776.* Scribner, 1973.

————. *George Washington's World.* Scribner, 1941.

————. *The World of Captain John Smith 1580–1631.* Scribner, 1959.

————. *The World of Columbus and Sons.* Scribner, 1965.

————. *The World of William Penn.* Scribner, 1973.

————. *Year of Columbus, 1492.* Scribner, 1969.

————. *Year of Independence, 1776.* Scribner, 1970.

————. *Year of Lincoln, 1861.* Scribner, 1970.

————. *Year of the Pilgrims, 1620.* Scribner, 1969.

Fox, Michael. *Sundance Coyote,* illustrated by Dee Gates. Coward-McCann, 1974.

————. *The Wolf,* illustrated by Charles Fracé. Coward-McCann, 1973.

Freschet, Berniece. *Bear Mouse,* illustrated by Donald Carrick. Scribner, 1973.

Fritz, Jean. *George Washington's Breakfast,* illustrated by Paul Galdone. Coward-McCann, 1969.

Froman, Robert. *Less than Nothing Is Really Something,* illustrated by Don Madden. Crowell, 1973.

Gallob, Edward. *City Leaves, City Trees.* Scribner, 1972.

————. *City Rocks, City Blocks and the Moon.* Scribner, 1973.

George, Jean Craighead. *All upon a Sidewalk,* illustrated by Don Bolognese. Dutton, 1974.

George, John, and Jean George. *Vison the Mink.* Dutton, 1949.

————. *Vulpes the Red Fox.* Dutton, 1948.

Gilbert, Sara. *Fat Free: Common Sense for Young Weight Worriers.* Macmillan, 1975.

Gilbreath, Alice. *Beginning Crafts for Beginning Readers,* illustrated by Joe Rogers. Follett, 1972.

Gill, Harold B., Jr., and Ann Finlayson. *Colonial Virginia.* Nelson, 1973.

Gladstone, M. J. *A Carrot for a Nose: The Form of Folk Sculpture on America's City Streets and Country Roads.* Scribner, 1974.

Glubok, Shirley. *The Art of the Spanish in the United States and Puerto Rico,* designed by Gerard Nook, photographs by Alfred Tamarin. Macmillan, 1972.

Goldreich, Gloria, and Esther Goldreich. *What Can She Be? A Newscaster,* photographs by Robert Ipcar. Lothrop, 1973.

Gorodetzky, Dr. Charles W., and Dr. Samuel T. Christian. *What You Should Know about* DRUGS. Harcourt Brace Jovanovich, 1970.

Goudey, Alice E. *Here Come the Cottontails,* illustrated by Garry Mackenzie. Scribner, 1965.
———. *Here Come the Squirrels,* illustrated by Garry Mackenzie. Scribner, 1962.
———. *Houses from the Sea,* illustrated by Adrienne Adams. Scribner, 1959.
Gould, Laurence J., and William G. Martin. *Think about It: Experiments in Psychology,* illustrated by Gustave E. Nebel. Prentice-Hall, 1970.
Gregor, Arthur S. *Man's Mark on the Land: The Changing Environment.* Scribner, 1974.
Gross, Ruth Belov. *A Book about Pandas.* Dial, 1972.
Harman, Carter. *A Skyscraper Goes Up.* Random House, 1973.
Harris, Leon. *The Russian Ballet School.* Atheneum, 1970.
Hautzig, Esther. *Cool Cooking: 16 Recipes without a Stove,* illustrated by Jan Pyk. Lothrop, 1973.
Hays, Wilma P., ed. *Freedom.* Coward-McCann, 1958.
Headstrom, Richard. *Adventures with a Hand Lens.* Lippincott, 1962.
Hendrickson, Walter B., Jr. *Who Really Invented the Rocket?* Putnam, 1974.
Hess, Lilo. *The Praying Mantis, Insect Cannibal.* Scribner, 1971.
Hiller, Carl E. *Caves to Cathedrals: Architecture of the World's Great Religions.* Little, Brown, 1974.
Hirsch, S. Carl. *The Living Community, A Venture into Ecology,* illustrated by William Steinel. Viking, 1966.
Hoban, Tana. *Shapes and Things.* Macmillan, 1970.
Hoff, Rhoda. *Africa: Adventures in Eyewitness History.* Walck, 1963.
———. *America's Immigrants: Adventures in Eyewitness History.* Walck, 1967.
———. *Russia: Adventures in Eyewitness History.* Walck, 1964.
Holland, Viki. *How to Photograph Your World.* Scribner, 1974.
Hollander, Zander. *The Modern Encyclopedia of Basketball.* Four Winds, 1969.
Holling, Holling C. *Minn of the Mississippi.* Houghton Mifflin, 1951.
———. *Pagoo.* Houghton Mifflin, 1957.
Huntington, Harriet E. *Let's Look at Reptiles,* illustrated by J. Noël. Doubleday, 1973.
Hurd, Edith Thatcher. *The Mother Beaver,* illustrated by Clement Hurd. Little, Brown, 1971.
———. *The Mother Deer,* illustrated by Clement Hurd. Little, Brown, 1972.
———. *The Mother Owl,* illustrated by Clement Hurd. Little, Brown, 1974.
———. *The Mother Whale,* illustrated by Clement Hurd. Little, Brown, 1973.
Hutchins, Ross E. *The Travels of Monarch X,* illustrated by Jerome P. Connolly. Rand McNally, 1966.
James, Elizabeth, and Carol Barkin. *The Simple Facts of Simple Machines,* photographs by Daniel Dorn, Jr., diagrams by Susan Stan. Lothrop, 1975.
Jenness, Aylette. *Dwellers of the Tundra,* photographs by Jonathan Jenness. Crowell-Collier, 1970.
Johnson, Eric W., and Corinne B. Johnson. *Love and Sex and Growing Up,* illustrated by Visa-Direction Studio, Inc. Lippincott, 1970.
Johnson, Gerald W. *America Grows Up,* illustrated by Leonard Everett Fisher. Morrow, 1960.
———. *America Is Born,* illustrated by Leonard Everett Fisher. Morrow, 1959.
———. *America Moves Forward,* illustrated by Leonard Everett Fisher. Morrow, 1960.
Johnson, Hannah Lyons. *Let's Bake Bread,* photographs by Daniel Dorn. Lothrop, 1973.
Kaufmann, John. *Bats in the Dark.* Crowell, 1972.
Kerr, Jessica. *Shakespeare's Flowers,* illustrated by Anne Ophelia Dowden. Crowell, 1969.
Kinney, Jean, and Cle Kinney. *How To Make 19 Kinds of American Folk Art from Masks to TV Commercials.* Atheneum, 1974.
———. *21 Kinds of American Folk Art and How to Make Each One.* Atheneum, 1972.
Kohn, Bernice. *The Organic Living Book,* illustrated by Betty Fraser. Viking, 1972.
Kurelek, William. *Lumberjack.* Houghton Mifflin, 1974.
Landeck, Beatrice. *Echoes of Africa in Folk Songs of the Americas,* 2nd rev. ed., illustrated by Alexander Dobkin. McKay, 1969.
Lauber, Patricia. *The Friendly Dolphins,* illustrated by Jean Simpson and Charles Gottlieb. Random House, 1963.
———. *Of Man and Mouse: How House Mice Became Laboratory Mice,* illustrated by Hal Siegel. Viking, 1971.

LeShan, Eda. *What Makes Me Feel This Way?* Macmillan, 1972.

Lester, Julius. *To Be a Slave,* illustrated by Tom Feelings. Dial, 1968.

Liebers, Arthur. *Jobs in Construction.* Lothrop, 1973.

Lightbody, Donna M. *Introducing Needlepoint.* Lothrop, 1973.

Limburg, Peter R. *Watch Out, It's Poison Ivy!,* illustrated by Haris Petie. Messner, 1973.

List, Ilka Katherine. *Questions and Answers about Seashore Life,* woodcuts by the author, drawings by Arabelle Wheatley. Four Winds, 1970.

Loescher, Gil, with Ann Dull Loescher. *The Chinese Way: Life in the People's Republic of China.* Harcourt Brace Jovanovich, 1974.

Macaulay, David. *Cathedral, The Story of Its Construction.* Houghton Mifflin, 1973.

———. *City, A Story of Roman Planning and Construction.* Houghton Mifflin, 1974.

MacClintock, Dorcas. *A Natural History of Giraffes,* illustrated by Ugo Mochi. Scribner, 1973.

McClung, Robert. *Screamer, Last of the Eastern Panthers,* illustrated by Lloyd Sandford. Morrow, 1964.

———. *Thor, Last of the Sperm Whales,* illustrated by Bob Hines. Morrow, 1971.

McGovern, Ann. *. . . If You Lived with the Sioux Indians,* illustrated by Bob Levering. Four Winds, 1974.

———. *If You Sailed on the Mayflower,* illustrated by J. B. Handelsman. Four Winds, 1970.

McKern, Sharon S. *The Many Faces of Man.* Lothrop, 1972.

Meltzer, Milton. *In Their Own Words: A History of the American Negro 1619–1865.* Crowell, 1964.

———. *In Their Own Words: A History of the American Negro 1865–1916.* Crowell, 1965.

———. *In Their Own Words: A History of the American Negro 1916–1966.* Crowell, 1967.

Meredith, Robert and E. Brooks Smith. *The Quest of Columbus,* illustrated by Leonard Everett Fisher. Little, Brown, 1966.

———. *Riding with Coronado,* illustrated by Leonard Everett Fisher. Little, Brown, 1964.

Meyer, Carolyn. *The Bread Book: All about Bread and How to Make It,* illustrated by Trina Schart Hyman. Harcourt Brace Jovanovich, 1971.

———. *Yarn: The Things It Makes and How to Make Them,* illustrated by Jennifer Perrott. Harcourt Brace Jovanovich, 1972.

Miles, Betty. *Save the Earth: An Ecological Handbook for Kids.* Knopf, 1974.

Milgrom, Harry. *Egg-ventures: First Science Experiments,* illustrated by Giulio Maestro. Dutton, 1974.

Miller, Natalie. *Story of the White House,* illustrated by John Hawkinson. Children's, 1966.

Moore, Eva. *The Cookie Book,* illustrated by Talivaldis Stubis. Seabury, 1973.

Moore, Janet Gaylord. *The Many Ways of Seeing: An Introduction to the Pleasures of Art.* World, 1968.

Moorman, Thomas. *How to Make Your Science Project Scientific.* Atheneum, 1974.

Murphy, Barbara Beasley, and Norman Baker. *Thor Heyerdahl and the Reed Boat Ra.* Lippincott, 1974.

Navarra, John Gabriel. *The World You Inherit: A Study of Pollution.* Natural History Press, 1970.

Newsome, Arden J. *Egg Craft.* Lothrop, 1973.

Nickel, Helmut. *Warriors and Worthies: Arms and Armor through the Ages.* Atheneum, 1969.

Parents Nursery School. *Kids Are Natural Cooks: Child-tested Recipes for Home and School Using Natural Foods,* illustrated by Lady McCrady. Houghton Mifflin, 1974.

Pearlman, Moshe. *The Zealots of Masada: Story of a Dig.* Scribner, 1967.

Peterson, Roger T. *Birds.* Time-Life, 1969.

———. *How to Know the Birds.* Houghton Mifflin, 1962.

Phelan, Joseph, illustrator. *The Whale Hunters.* Time-Life, 1969.

Phelan, Mary Kay. *The Story of the Boston Tea Party,* illustrated by Frank Aloise. Crowell, 1973.

Phillips, Jo. *Right Angles: Paper-folding Geometry,* illustrated by Giulio Maestro. Crowell, 1972.

Pine, Tillie S., and Joseph Levine. *Measurements and How We Use Them,* illustrated by Harriet Sherman. McGraw-Hill, 1974.

Polgreen, John, and Cathleen Polgreen. *The Stars Tonight.* Harper & Row, 1967.

Poole, Frederick King. *Thailand*. F. Watts, 1973.

Prago, Albert. *Strangers in Their Own Land, A History of Mexican-Americans*. Four Winds, 1973.

Price, Christine. *Made in West Africa*. Dutton, 1975.

Pringle, Lawrence. *The Only Earth We Have*. Macmillan, 1969.

Radlauer, Edward. *Fast, Faster, Fastest*. Children's, 1973.

Rahn, Joan Elma. *Grocery Store Botany*, illustrated by Ginny Linville Winter. Atheneum, 1974.

———. *More about What Plants Do*, illustrated by Ginny Linville Winter. Atheneum, 1975.

———. *Seeing What Plants Do*, illustrated by Ginny Linville Winter. Atheneum, 1972.

Rich, Louise Dickinson. *The First Book of the Early Settlers*, illustrated by Douglas Gorsline. F. Watts, 1959.

Rinkoff, Barbara. *A Map Is a Picture*, illustrated by Robert Galster. Crowell, 1965.

Rockwell, Anne. *Games (And How to Play Them)*. Crowell, 1973.

———. *Toad*, illustrated by Harlow Rockwell. Doubleday, 1972.

———. *The Toolbox*, illustrated by Harlow Rockwell. Macmillan, 1971.

Rockwell, Harlow. *I Did It*. Macmillan, 1974.

———. *My Doctor*. Macmillan, 1973.

———. *Printmaking*. Doubleday, 1974.

Ronan, Colin. *The Discovery of the Galaxies*, Jackdaw #52. Grossman, n.d.

Rosenbaum, Jean, and Lutie McAuliffe. *What Is Fear? An Introduction to Feelings*, illustrated by Tomie de Paola. Prentice-Hall, 1973.

Rosenfeld, Sam. *Science Experiments for the Space Age*. Harvey House, 1972.

Ross, Wilda S. *What Did the Dinosaurs Eat?*, illustrated by Elizabeth Schmidt. Coward-McCann, 1972.

Sanderlin, George. *First around the World*, illustrated by Alan E. Cober. Harper & Row, 1964.

Sarnoff, Jane. *The Chess Book*, illustrated by Reynold Ruffins. Scribner, 1973.

Sarnoff, Jane, and Reynold Ruffins. *A Great Bicycle Book*. Scribner, 1973.

Sasek, Miroslav. *This Is Australia*. Macmillan, 1971.

———. *This Is Greece*. Macmillan, 1966.

———. *This is Historic Britain*. Macmillan, 1974.

———. *This Is London*. Macmillan, 1959.

———. *This Is New York*. Macmillan, 1960.

———. *This Is Paris*. Macmillan, 1959.

———. *This Is San Francisco*. Macmillan, 1962.

———. *This Is the United Nations*. Macmillan, 1968.

———. *This Is Washington, D.C.* Macmillan, 1969.

Sattler, Helen Roney. *Recipes for Art and Craft Materials*. Lothrop, 1973.

Schaeffer, Elizabeth. *Dandelion, Pokeweed, and Goosefoot: How the Early Settlers Used Plants for Food, Medicine, and in the Home*. Young Scott, 1972.

Scheffer, Victor B. *The Seeing Eye*. Scribner, 1971.

Schlein, Miriam. *What's Wrong with Being a Skunk?*, illustrated by Ray Cruz. Four Winds, 1974.

Schwartz, George I., and Bernice S. Schwartz. *Life in a Log*. Natural History Press, 1972.

Schwartz, Julius. *Magnify and Find Out Why*. McGraw-Hill, 1972.

Selsam, Millicent. *Animals as Parents*, illustrated by John Kaufmann. Morrow, 1965.

———. *Benny's Animals and How He Put Them in Order*, illustrated by Arnold Lobel. Harper & Row, 1966.

———. *Bulbs, Corms and Such*, photographs by Jerome Wexler. Morrow, 1974.

———. *How Kittens Grow*, photographs by Esther Bubley. Four Winds, 1973.

———. *Peanut*, photographs by Jerome Wexler. Morrow, 1969.

———. *Play with Seeds*, illustrated by Helen Ludwig. Morrow, 1957.

———. *Questions and Answers about Horses*, illustrated by Robert J. Lee. Four Winds, 1974.

———. *The Tomato and Other Fruit Vegetables*, photographs by Jerome Wexler. Morrow, 1970.

Selsam, Millicent, and Joyce Hunt. *A First Look at Birds*, illustrated by Harriet Springer. Walker, 1974.

———. *A First Look at Fish*, illustrated by Harriet Springer. Walker, 1972.

————. *A First Look at Insects,* illustrated by Harriet Springer. Walker, 1974.

————. *A First Look at Leaves,* illustrated by Harriet Springer. Walker, 1972.

————. *A First Look at Mammals,* illustrated by Harriet Springer. Walker, 1973.

Sheehan, Angela, ed. *The Doubleday Nature Encyclopedia.* Doubleday, 1974.

Shuttlesworth, Dorothy E., *The Story of Ants,* illustrated by SuZan N. Swain. Doubleday, 1964.

————. *To Find a Dinosaur.* Doubleday, 1973.

Shuttlesworth, Dorothy E., and Thomas Cervasio. *Litter—The Ugly Enemy: An Ecology Story.* Doubleday, 1973.

Shuttlesworth, Dorothy E., and Lee Ann Williams. *Disappearing Energy: Can We End the Crisis?* Doubleday, 1974.

Silverstein, Dr. Alvin, and Virginia Silverstein. *The Chemicals We Eat and Drink,* illustrated by Eva Cellini. Follett, 1973.

Simon, Hilda. *Snakes: The Facts and the Folklore.* Viking, 1973.

Simon, Seymour. *Birds on Your Street,* illustrated by Jean Zallinger. Holiday, 1974.

————. *A Building on Your Street,* illustrated by Leonard Shortall. Holiday, 1973.

————. *The Paper Airplane Book,* illustrated by Byron Barton. Viking, 1971.

Skinner, Michael Kingsley. *How to Make Rubbings.* Van Nostrand, 1972.

Smith, E. Brooks and Robert Meredith. *The Coming of the Pilgrims Told from Governor Bradford's Firsthand Account,* illustrated by Leonard Everett Fisher. Little, 1964.

————. *Pilgrim Courage,* illustrated by Leonard Everett Fisher. Little, 1962.

Sommer, Elyse. *The Bread Dough Craft Book,* illustrated by Giulio Maestro. Lothrop, 1972.

Sootin, Harry. *Easy Experiments with Water Pollution,* illustrated by Lucy Bitzer. Four Winds, 1974.

Soucie, Anita Holmes. *Plant Fun: 10 Easy Plants to Grow Indoors,* illustrated by Grambs Miller. Four Winds, 1974.

Stein, Sara Bonnett. *About Dying,* photographs by Dick Frank. Walker, 1974.

————. *About Handicaps,* photographs by Dick Frank. Walker, 1974.

————. *Making Babies,* photographs by Doris Pinney. Walker, 1974.

Steiner, Barbara A. *Biography of a Polar Bear,* illustrated by St. Tamara. Putnam, 1972.

Stephens, William M. *Islands,* illustrated by Lydia Rosier. Holiday, 1974.

Sterling, Dorothy, ed. *Speak Out in Thunder Tones: Letters and Other Writings by Black Northerners, 1787–1865.* Doubleday, 1973.

Stone, A. Harris, and Robert J. Stein. *Biology Project Puzzlers,* illustrated by David Lindroth. Prentice-Hall, 1973.

Strivastava, Jane J. *Statistics,* illustrated by John J. Reiss. Crowell, 1973.

Struble, Mitch. *The Web of Space-Time: A Step-by-Step Exploration of Relativity.* Westminster, 1973.

Switzer, Ellen. *How Democracy Failed.* Atheneum, 1975.

Tames, Richard. *The Mayflower and the Pilgrim Fathers,* Jackdaw #8. Grossman, n.d.

Tragle, Henry Irving. *Nat Turner's Slave Revolt,* Jackdaw #A1. Grossman, n.d.

Tresselt, Alvin. *How Far Is Far?,* illustrated by Ward Brackett. Parents', 1964.

Tunis, Edwin. *Chipmunks on the Doorstep.* Crowell, 1971.

————. *Shaw's Fortune: The Picture Story of a Colonial Plantation.* World, 1966.

Van Loon, Hendrik W. *The Story of Mankind,* rev. ed. Liveright, 1972.

Verdy, Violette. *Giselle,* illustrated by Marcia Brown. McGraw-Hill, 1970.

Von Frisch, Otto. *Animal Camouflage.* F. Watts, 1973.

Watts, May. *The Doubleday First Guide to Trees,* illustrated by Michael Bevans. Doubleday, 1964.

Weber, Alfons. *Elizabeth Gets Well,* illustrated by Jacqueline Blass. Crowell, 1970.

Webster, David. *Track Watching.* F. Watts, 1972.

Weiss, Harvey. *How to Make Your Own Books.* Crowell, 1974.

————. *How to Make Your Own Movies.* Young Scott, 1973.

————. *Lens and Shutter: An Introduction to Photography.* Young Scott, 1971.

Wickens, David, and John Tuey. *How to Make Things Grow.* Van Nostrand, 1972.

Wilder, Laura Ingalls. *The First Four Years,* illustrated by Garth Williams. Harper & Row, 1971.

———. *West from Home: Letters of Laura Ingalls Wilder, San Francisco 1915*, Roger MacBride, ed. Harper & Row, 1974.

Williamson, Margaret. *The First Book of Birds.* F. Watts, 1951.

Wiseman, Ann. *Making Things: The Hand Book of Creative Discovery.* Little, Brown, 1973.

Wolberg, Barbara J. *Zooming In, Photographic Discoveries under the Microscope*, photographs by Dr. Lewis R. Wolberg. Harcourt Brace Jovanovich, 1974.

Wolf, Bernard. *Don't Feel Sorry for Paul.* Lippincott, 1974.

———. *Tinker and the Medicine Man.* Random House, 1973.

Wyler, Rose, and Gerald Ames. *Secrets in Stones*, photographs by Gerald Ames. Four Winds, 1970.

Wyler, Rose, and Eva-Lee Baird. *Science Teasers*, illustrated by Jerry Robinson. Harper & Row, 1966.

Yolen, Jane. *Ring Out! A Book of Bells*, illustrated by Richard Cuffari. Seabury, 1974.

Young, Jim. *When the Whale Came to My Town*, photographs by Dan Bernstein. Knopf, 1974.

Zim, Herbert S. *Bones*, illustrated by René Martin. Morrow, 1969.

Zim, Herbert S., and Dorothea Barlowe. *Trees, A Golden Nature Guide.* Western, 1952.

Zim, Herbert S., and Sonia Bleeker. *Life and Death*, illustrated by René Martin. Morrow, 1970.

Zim, Herbert S., and Paul R. Shaffer. *Rocks and Minerals, A Golden Nature Guide.* Illustrated by Raymond Perlman. Western, 1957.

Zim, Herbert S., and Hobart M. Smith. *Reptiles and Amphibians, A Golden Nature Guide.* Illustrated by James G. Irving. Western, 1953.

BIOGRAPHY

Adoff, Arnold. *Malcolm X*, illustrated by John Wilson. Crowell, 1970.

Aldis, Dorothy. *Nothing Is Impossible, The Story of Beatrix Potter*, illustrated by Richard Cuffari. Atheneum, 1969.

Aliki, pseud. (Aliki Brandenberg). *The Story of Johnny Appleseed.* Prentice-Hall, 1963.

———. *The Story of William Penn.* Prentice-Hall, 1964.

———. *A Weed Is a Flower, The Life of George Washington Carver.* Prentice-Hall, 1965.

Appel, Benjamin. *Hitler, From Power to Ruin.* Grosset & Dunlap, 1964.

Armstrong, William H. *The Education of Abraham Lincoln.* Coward-McCann, 1974.

Atwood, Ann, and Erica Anderson. *For All that Lives*, with the words of Albert Schweitzer. Scribner, 1975.

d'Aulaire, Ingri, and Edgar Parin d'Aulaire. *Abraham Lincoln*, rev. ed. Doubleday, 1957.

———. *Benjamin Franklin.* Doubleday, 1950.

———. *Buffalo Bill.* Doubleday, 1952.

———. *Columbus.* Doubleday, 1955.

———. *George Washington.* Doubleday, 1936.

———. *Leif, the Lucky.* Doubleday, 1951.

———. *Pocahontas.* Doubleday, 1949.

Baker, Rachel. *America's First Trained Nurse: Linda Richards.* Washington Square Press, 1970 (1959).

Barth, Edna. *I'm Nobody! Who Are You? The Story of Emily Dickinson*, illustrated by Richard Cuffari. Seabury, 1971.

Bernard, Jacqueline. *Journey toward Freedom, The Story of Sojourner Truth.* Norton, 1967.

Brondfield, Jerry. *Hank Aaron . . . 714 and Beyond.* Scholastic, 1974.

Brown, Marion, and Ruth Crone. *The Silent Storm*, illustrated by Fritz Kredel. Abingdon, 1963.

Brownmiller, Susan. *Shirley Chisholm, A Biography.* Doubleday, 1970.

Bulla, Clyde Robert. *John Billington, Friend of Squanto*, illustrated by Peter Burchard. Crowell, 1956.

———. *Squanto, Friend of the White Man*, illustrated by Peter Burchard. Crowell, 1954.

Cavanah, Frances. *Abe Lincoln Gets His Chance*, illustrated by Paula Hutchison. Rand-McNally, 1959.

Chaffin, Lillie, and Miriam Butwin. *America's First Ladies 1789 to 1965.* Lerner, 1969.

Clayton, Ed. *Martin Luther King: The Peaceful Warrior,* 3rd ed., illustrated by David Hodges. Prentice-Hall, 1968.

Cohen, Joel H. *Cool Cos, The Story of Bill Cosby.* Scholastic, 1969.

Cone, Molly. *Leonard Bernstein,* illustrated by Robert Galster. Crowell, 1970.

Coolidge, Olivia. *The Apprenticeship of Abraham Lincoln.* Scribner, 1974.

———. *Tom Paine, Revolutionary.* Scribner, 1969.

Dalgliesh, Alice. *The Columbus Story,* illustrated by Leo Politi. Scribner, 1955.

Daugherty, James. *Daniel Boone.* Viking, 1939.

Davidson, Mickie. *Helen Keller's Teacher,* illustrated by Wayne Blickenstaff. Four Winds, 1965.

De Leeuw, Adele. *Maria Tallchief, American Ballerina,* illustrated by Russell Hoover. Garrard, 1971.

De Treviño, Elizabeth Borten. *I, Juan de Pareja.* Farrar, Straus, 1965.

———. *Juárez, Man of Law.* Farrar, Straus, 1974.

Dobrin, Arnold, *A Life for Israel, The Story of Golda Meir.* Dial, 1974.

Douty, Esther (Morris). *Forten, the Sailmaker: Pioneer Champion of Negro Rights.* Rand-McNally, 1968.

Epstein, Sam, and Beryl Epstein. *Michael Faraday, Apprentice to Science,* illustrated by Raymond Burne. Garrard, 1971.

Faber, Doris. *I Will Be Heard, The Life of William Lloyd Garrison.* Lothrop, 1970.

———. *Oh, Lizzie! The Life of Elizabeth Cady Stanton.* Lothrop, 1972.

Fadiman, Edwin, Jr. *The Feast Day,* illustrated by Charles Mikolaycak. Little, Brown, 1973.

Fall, Thomas. *Jim Thorpe,* illustrated by John Gretzer. Crowell, 1970.

Fecher, Constance. *The Last Elizabethan, A Portrait of Sir Walter Ralegh.* Farrar, Straus, 1972.

Felton, Harold W. *Mumbet, The Story of Elizabeth Freeman,* illustrated by Donn Albright. Dodd, 1970.

Fisher, Aileen, and Olive Rabe. *We Alcotts,* illustrated by Ellen Raskin. Atheneum, 1968.

———. *We Dickinsons,* illustrated by Ellen Raskin. Atheneum, 1965.

Fisher, Leonard Everett. *Picture Book of Revolutionary War Heroes.* Stackpole Books, 1970.

Fleming, Thomas J. *Benjamin Franklin.* Four Winds, 1973.

———. *First in Their Hearts, A Biography of George Washington.* Norton, 1968.

Fox, Mary Virginia. *Lady for the Defense, A Biography of Belva Lockwood.* Harcourt Brace Jovanovich, 1975.

Franchere, Ruth. *Cesar Chavez,* illustrated by Earl Thollander. Crowell, 1970.

Fritz, Jean. *And Then What Happened, Paul Revere?,* illustrated by Margot Tomes. Coward-McCann, 1973.

———. *Why Don't You Get a Horse, Sam Adams?,* illustrated by Trina Schart Hyman. Coward-McCann, 1974.

Goodsell, Jane. *The Mayo Brothers,* illustrated by Louis S. Glanzman. Crowell, 1972.

Graham, Shirley. *The Story of Phillis Wheatley, Poetess of the American Revolution.* Washington Square Press, 1969.

Greenfield, Eloise. *Rosa Parks,* illustrated by Eric Marlow. Crowell, 1973.

Hamilton, Virginia. *Paul Robeson, The Life and Times of a Free Black Man.* Harper & Row, 1974.

Hano, Arnold. *Kareem! Basketball Great.* Putnam, 1975.

Hardwick, Richard. *Charles Richard Drew, Pioneer in Blood Research.* Scribner, 1967.

Haverstock, Mary Sayre. *Indian Gallery, The Story of George Catlin.* Four Winds, 1973.

Hicks, Nancy. *The Honorable Shirley Chisholm, Congresswoman from Brooklyn.* Lion, 1971.

Hodges, Margaret. *Hopkins of the Mayflower: Portrait of a Dissenter.* Farrar, Straus, 1972.

Hunter, Edith F. *Child of the Silent Night,* illustrated by Bea Holmes. Houghton Mifflin, 1963.

Jackson, Jesse. *Make a Joyful Noise Unto the Lord! The Life of Mahalia Jackson, Queen of Gospel Singers.* Crowell, 1974.

Jahns, Patricia. *Joseph Henry, Father of American Electronics,* illustrated by Dave Hodges. Prentice-Hall, 1970.

Johnston, Brenda A. *Between the Devil and the Sea, The Life of James Forten,* illustrated by Don Miller. Harcourt Brace Jovanovich, 1974.

Jones, Hettie. *Big Star Fallin' Mama: Five Women in Black Music.* Viking, 1974.

Judson, Clara Ingram. *Abraham Lincoln*, illustrated by Polly Jackson. Follett, 1961.

------. *Abraham Lincoln, Friend of the People*, illustrated by Robert Frankenberg. Follett, 1950.

------. *Andrew Jackson, Frontier Statesman*, illustrated by Lorence F. Bjorklund. Follett, 1954.

------. *Christopher Columbus*, illustrated by Polly Jackson. Follett, 1960.

------. *George Washington*, illustrated by Polly Jackson. Follett, 1961.

------. *George Washington, Leader of the People*, illustrated by Robert Frankenberg. Follett, 1951.

------. *Mr. Justice Holmes*, illustrated by Robert Todd. Follett, 1956.

------. *Theodore Roosevelt, Fighting Patriot*, illustrated by Lorence F. Bjorklund. Follett, 1953.

------. *Thomas Jefferson, Champion of the People*, illustrated by Robert Frankenberg. Follett, 1952.

Kaufman, Mervyn. *Jessie Owens*, illustrated by Larry Johnson. Crowell, 1973.

Kelen, Emery. *Mr. Nonsense, A Life of Edward Lear*. Norton, 1973.

Kennerly, Karen, adapter. *The Slave Who Bought His Freedom, Equiano's Story*. Dutton, 1971.

Knight, Michael, adapter. *In Chains to Louisiana, Solomon Northup's Story*. Dutton, 1971.

Kurtz, Henry. *John and Sebastian Cabot*. F. Watts, 1973.

Latham, Jean Lee. *Carry On, Mr. Bowditch*, illustrated by John O'Hara Cosgrave II. Houghton Mifflin, 1955.

------. *Far Voyager, The Story of James Cook*. Harper & Row, 1970.

------. *George W. Goethals, Panama Canal Engineer*, illustrated by H. Greene. Garrard, 1965.

------. *Rachel Carson: Who Loved the Sea*, illustrated by Victor Mays. Garrard, 1973.

------. *Samuel F. B. Morse, Artist and Inventor*. Garrard, 1963.

------. *The Story of Eli Whitney*, illustrated by Fritz Kredel. Harper & Row, 1953.

------. *Young Man in a Hurry, The Story of Cyrus W. Field*, illustrated by Victor Mays. Harper & Row, 1958.

Lawrence, Jacob. *Harriet and the Promised Land*. Windmill, 1968.

Lawson, Robert. *Ben and Me*. Little, Brown, 1951 (1939).

------. *Mr. Revere and I*. Little, Brown, 1953.

Lenski, Lois. *Journey into Childhood, The Autobiography of Lois Lenski*. Lippincott, 1972.

Levine, I. E. *Young Man in the White House, John Fitzgerald Kennedy*. Washington Square Press, 1969 (1964).

Lomask, Milton. *Odd Destiny, A Life of Alexander Hamilton*. Farrar, Straus, 1969.

Longsworth, Polly. *I, Charlotte Forten, Black and Free*. Crowell, 1970.

McNeer, May. *America's Abraham Lincoln*, illustrated by Lynd Ward. Houghton Mifflin, 1957.

------. *America's Mark Twain*, illustrated by Lynd Ward. Houghton Mifflin, 1962.

Mathis, Sharon Bell. *Ray Charles*, illustrated by George Ford. Crowell, 1973.

Meltzer, Milton. *Langston Hughes, A Biography*. Crowell, 1968.

Meriwether, Louise. *The Freedom Ship of Robert Smalls*, illustrated by Lee Jack Morton. Prentice-Hall, 1971.

Milne, Christopher. *The Enchanted Places*. Dutton, 1975.

Monjo, F. N. *Grand Papa and Ellen Aroon, Being an account of some of the happy times spent together by Thomas Jefferson and his favorite granddaughter*, illustrated by Richard Cuffari. Holt, Rinehart and Winston, 1974.

------. *Me and Willie and Pa, The Story of Abraham Lincoln and His Son Tad*, illustrated by Douglas Gorsline. Simon & Schuster, 1973.

------. *The One Bad Thing about Father*, illustrated by Rocco Negri. Harper & Row, 1970.

------. *Poor Richard in France*, illustrated by Brinton Turkle. Holt, Rinehart and Winston, 1973.

Neimark, Anne E. *Touch of Light, The Story of Louis Braille*, illustrated by Robert Parker. Harcourt Brace Jovanovich, 1970.

Olsen, James T. *Billie Jean King, The Lady of the Court*, illustrated by John Nelson. Creative Education (Children's Press), 1974.

Parish, Helen Rand. *Estebanico*. Viking, 1974.

Peare, Catherine Owens. *The Helen Keller Story*. Crowell, 1959.

Raboff, Ernest. *Marc Chagall*. Doubleday, 1968.

------. *Pablo Picasso*. Doubleday, 1968.

————. *Paul Klee.* Doubleday, 1968.

Reeder, Colonel Red. *Bold Leaders of the American Revolution,* maps by Samuel H. Bryant. Little, Brown, 1973.

Rockwell, Anne. *The Boy Who Drew Sheep.* Atheneum, 1973.

————. *Paintbrush & Peacepipe: The Story of George Catlin.* Atheneum, 1971.

Rosen, Sidney. *Wizard of the Dome: R. Buckminster Fuller, Designer for the Future.* Little, Brown, 1969.

Sandburg, Carl. *Abe Lincoln Grows Up,* reprinted from *Abraham Lincoln: The Prairie Years,* illustrated by James Daugherty. Harcourt Brace Jovanovich, 1928.

Shepherd, Elizabeth. *The Discoveries of Esteban the Black,* maps by William Steinel. Dodd, 1970.

Steele, William O. *The Wilderness Tattoo: A Narrative of Juan Ortiz.* Harcourt Brace Jovanovich, 1972.

Sterling, Dorothy. *Captain of the Planter,* illustrated by Ernest Crichlow. Doubleday, 1958.

————. *Freedom Train, The Story of Harriet Tubman,* illustrated by Ernest Crichlow. Doubleday, 1954.

Sullivan, George. *Willie Mays,* illustrated by David Brown. Putnam, 1973.

Surge, Frank. *Western Outlaws.* Lerner, 1969.

Swift, Hildegarde Hoyt. *The Edge of April, A Biography of John Burroughs,* illustrated by Lynd Ward. Morrow, 1957.

————. *From the Eagle's Wing,* illustrated by Lynd Ward. Morrow, 1962.

Syme, Ronald. *African Traveler, The Story of Mary Kingsley,* illustrated by Jacqueline Tomes. Morrow, 1962.

————. *Benedict Arnold, Traitor of the Revolution,* illustrated by William Stobbs. Morrow, 1970.

————. *John Smith of Virginia,* illustrated by William Stobbs. Morrow, 1951.

————. *Juárez, The Founder of Modern Mexico,* illustrated by Richard Cuffari. Morrow, 1972.

————. *Nigerian Pioneer, The Story of Mary Slessor,* illustrated by Jacqueline Tomes. Morrow, 1964.

————. *Vasco da Gama, Sailor toward the Sunrise,* illustrated by William Stobbs. Morrow, 1959.

————. *Verrazano, Explorer of the Atlantic Coast,* illustrated by William Stobbs. Morrow, 1973.

Tobias, Tobi. *Marian Anderson,* illustrated by Symeon Shimin. Crowell, 1972.

United Press International. *Clemente,* text adapted by Alice Thorne. Grosset & Dunlap, 1973.

Wojciechowska, Maia. *Till the Break of Day, Memories: 1939–1942.* Harcourt Brace Jovanovich, 1972.

Wood, James Playstead. *The Life and Words of John F. Kennedy.* Scholastic, 1966.

Yates, Elizabeth. *Amos Fortune, Free Man,* illustrated by Nora S. Unwin. Dutton, 1950.

PART **3** Developing a Literature Program

10
Creating the Learning Environment

"What is honored in a country will be cultivated there."

Plato

A shrewd observer may walk through any school and tell you what is honored in that particular building. The physical environment may provide the most obvious clue. Is this a warm, friendly looking school? Are children's paintings and other art work proudly displayed in the halls, the cafeteria, the principal's office? Are there comfortable places to sit in the classrooms, a reading center with cozy nooks that provide for individual privacy? Is there a school library media center that has many books, easily and readily accessible to all children; and also nonprint materials such as slides, film strips, records, and films? Has nature been incorporated into the school so that doors can open onto patios and on nice days the outside can become an extension of the inside working space? On bad days can children look out their windows and see gathering storms and darkening skies, or are they closed within a cave of a windowless school? Are pets a natural part of this environment—a large bunny hopping on the floor, a canary outside the principal's office, a fascinating lighted aquarium in the library? Is there respect for beauty in this school? Are art prints of well-known painters, a lovely flower arrangement, artifacts from a nearby museum displayed?

What about the intellectual environment of this school? What can you learn from looking at the children's writing or art work? Is creativity fostered, or are children laboriously working in workbooks or with programmed materials? Do science and social studies activities show evidence of first-hand discoveries through experiments and trips, or is most of the work textbook centered? How much time is devoted to voluntary reading in contrast to reading instruction with basic readers? Do teachers in all grades read to children every day? Is child talk valued as much as teacher talk? What do children ask questions about—the content of the curriculum or the page number of their assignments? How do teachers encourage or discourage the child's natural curiosity?

And how would an observer determine the emotional climate of this school? What are the pressures on the teachers? Is the quietest room considered the best room? Is teacher performance determined by the children's test results? What are the relationships among the staff, and with the principal? What do teachers discuss in the faculty lounge? Do teachers treat children with respect? Do they trust the children? Are children free to come into the building, the library, the classrooms whenever they arrive, or must they all wait for a particular time? Do piercing bells punctuate the days into recess, lunch-time, recess, and dismissal; or may teachers and students make their own time schedules? Are students, parents, and teachers happy and proud of their school? Is it a place you would want to teach, or have your children attend? What is honored in this school; what is cultivated there?

The School Environment

Children learn what they live. Increasingly, educators are concerned that the quality of living in a school be equal to the quality of learning in that school. The physical environment of the school provides the context for that learning, but it is only one aspect of it. What teachers really believe in and want for their students will usually be taught.

COMMITMENT TO LITERATURE

Every primary-grade teacher sees himself or herself as a reading teacher who is truly committed to teaching each child to read. In fact, in many of our primary grades over one-half of the school day is devoted to the teaching of reading. Ironically, once children reach the middle grades, teachers provide little time for children *to read,* maintaining that the curriculum is too crowded with other important subjects. Yet this is the very time when children build power in reading; when they discover the real joy of reading; in brief, when they *learn to love reading.* This is also the time when children can begin to develop taste in reading and become discriminating readers of fine literature. Teachers must commit themselves not only to teaching children to read but to helping children become readers—children who can read, will read, and will want to read. Such a commitment requires the creation of an environment that will encourage, enrich, and extend the readers' experiences with good books. Only then will children begin to develop a lifetime habit of reading.

A faculty which is committed to the long-term goal of producing children who are readers will begin by providing many rich opportunities for language development. For reading is the product of much talk, of recording words and writing stories that are meaningful to the child, of hearing stories many times during the day, and of looking at and reading a vast multitude of books.

Such a faculty will plan a literature program that rests on the foundation of knowledge of literature, learning, and child development. Teachers will not rely upon an incidental literature program as a mere adjunct to reading instruction; but the study of literature will receive planned time in this program. Children's knowledge and understanding of literature will be assessed, as well as programs in other areas.

The school will provide libraries to make fine books and quality multi-media readily accessible to children and faculty. Library media programs will be closely identified with the total instructional program. No longer will teachers rely upon a single textbook to provide all the information that is needed in science or social studies. Children will use many books in all the content fields. The integration of print and non-print materials will be used to extend learning. Individualized, small group, and large group instruction will rely on a wide range of materials and a variety of books.

Finally, the greatest commitment to literature must be on the part of individual teachers and librarians. A few children discover books by themselves; in most instances, a parent, teacher, or librarian has served as the catalyst for bringing books and children together. As children grow up seeing significant adults as readers, they become readers. Find a teacher who is enthusiastic about children's books and you will find a class of children who enjoy reading. Invariably, the teacher who reads, who knows books, and who shares this enthusiasm with students will inspire a love of reading.

PROVISION OF SPACE AND TIME AND RESOURCES

Space

Children need private space where they can read comfortably. Such areas for individual reading should invite children with the feeling of

School library media centers can provide homelike environments for reading.
Martin Luther King, Jr., Laboratory School, Evanston, Illinois.

quiet, warm, cozy space. One primary-grade room achieved this by making "book cubbies" out of the regular bookcases. The shelves were taken out and pieces of carpet were put in. Children decorated them with their own special pictures. Paperback books were then placed on nearby racks and in movable bookcases. Another group of children extended a board from the top of a bookshelf to the window sill, carpeted and made their own private "upstairs" reading nook. One library media center provides small-sized rocking chairs for the primary-grade children to enjoy. Large, fireproofed pillows have been used in some school media centers to provide color and comfort in reading nooks. The media center and most reading areas in classrooms are carpeted to make for a quieter place for reading.

Books need to be housed in a space that cre-

ates interest and exploration. In primary-grade classrooms favorite stuffed animals of Eeyore and Piglet might be placed on the shelf with *Winnie the Pooh* by A. A. Milne. A collection of shells could call attention to a book on shell identification. Books related to the classroom pet might be displayed near the animal's cage. Dowden's lovely book on weeds, *Wild Green Things in the City,* could be placed on the science table with a bouquet of dried weeds. Children need to be surrounded by books; they need to have special books called to their attention. The natural curiosity of children should be encouraged by the invitation to browse and select from a wealth of material.

Children need free space—space for movement to avoid interfering with the work of others, space to provide a feeling of comfort and free-

A comfortable reading pit becomes the center of the school library.

Vista View School, Ocean View School District, Huntington Beach, California. Photographed by Susan Lee, teacher.

dom. When activity areas are separated by space, involvement in each activity is enhanced.

Time

A commitment to literature must involve a commitment of time every day for all children. Time to listen to the teacher or librarian tell stories or read them should be planned for every day. Wise choice of materials and challenging follow-up discussions are essential if the story hour is to go beyond mere entertainment to enlightenment. There should be time each day for the children and the teacher to select their own books and read quietly without disturbance. Time for conferences with the teacher and for in-depth discussion of books with small groups must be arranged. Finally, children need time to share their books through a variety of ways

which might include discussion; writing about their books; or interpreting them through drama, art, film, or music. Not every book needs to be shared this way, but certain books will be made more memorable if children do choose to use these various modes to interpret them.

The library media center should be open all day every day to serve students in its unique way. Story hours or lessons on library skills can take place in a special area of the room and still leave the rest of the resources free for others to use. Children can learn without the immediate presence of a teacher or librarian. A trained aide can help children find relevant books, films, tapes, and records. Parents have served most effectively as volunteers in the school media center. Children increase in their ability to do independent study by using a variety of sources. An abundance of materials should be readily and freely available. With a strong commitment to the value of literature, the school staff will plan time for a balanced program. (*See* Chapters 11 and 12 for further discussion of the requirements of a literature program.)

Resources

Obviously a commitment to a literature program also implies an allotment of resources, both of money and people. Children must be surrounded with books of all kinds, and books cost money. We know that wide reading is directly related to accessibility; the more books available and the more time for reading, the more reading children will do. Teachers should not have to scrounge for books or buy them with their own money, as many of them do. They should not have to go to public libraries and deplete their collections. Books must be readily available when children and teachers need them. Every elementary school must have a school library media center with a trained librarian; every classroom must have a reading center with many paperback books available and a changing collection of books. Books, films, records—all provide food for the mind; a school library is just as essential as a cafeteria or a gymnasium.

The most recent standards for *Media Programs: District and School* were published by the American Library Association in 1975. They were the result of the cooperative effort of The American Association of School Librarians and The Association for Educational Communications and Technology. These two groups recommend that in order to maintain an up-to-date collection of media and equipment that fulfills the instructional program, the annual expenditure of a school district per student should be at least 10 percent of the national per pupil operational cost as computed by the U.S. Office of Education.

Budgets must also include adequate monies for resource persons. Librarians need professional aides and clerks to free them from the menial tasks of book-shelving, carding, and the increasing care of audiovisual aids. One innovation which has brought rewards but costs money is the notion of having an author or poet-in-residence at a public school. Myra Cohn Livingston is poet-in-residence in the Beverly Hills School District. Here she works with children in creative writing of poetry, and she regularly shares poetry with groups. Knowing and working with a living poet gives children a new dimension in poetry appreciation.

When teachers and librarians are committed to the value of a literature program for their students they must have adequate support from the administration to put their plans into action.

The Classroom Reading Environment

The classroom in most elementary schools continues to be the center for children's living and learning. Teachers will want to provide children with many opportunities for stimulating experiences and rich resources for learning. This planned environment will allow for individual differences. Teachers today realize that each child is unique and learns in his or her own way. School must not cut across children's natural curiosity and desire to learn, but channel and extend each child's interests and abilities. In the ideal school ". . . teachers are open to the possibilities inherent in children; children open to the possibilities inherent in other children, in materials and in themselves."[1]

Books are an important part of the classroom environment, but they are only a part. We should be cautious about moving children into books too quickly at the expense of real experiencing. Books can inform, supplement, or extend real experience; but they seldom substitute for it, particularly with the young child. It would be too bad to show a child a pictorial representation of the life cycle of a tadpole *before* he himself had the opportunity to discover the gradual change from tadpole to frog over a period of time. The child should record or draw the various stages that he sees if he is to become a careful observer of the wonders of nature. Finally, he may turn to books to confirm, verify, and enlarge his experience. An older child can find and identify a

[1]Roland Barth. *Open Education and the American School* (New York: Agathon Press, 1972), p. 56.

Books are taken on a field trip to verify experiences.

From *Yesterday I Found . . .* by Dorothy and John Paull, Mountain View Center for Environmental Education, University of Colorado, 1972. Reprinted by permission.

flower. He can write about it or draw a detailed picture of it. Then, he is ready to hear Moffitt's poem "To Look at Anything" (*see* page 316). He now brings his experience to the poem, and this experience is enriched by the poem. He knows what it means to "Be the thing you see," and he learns that others have felt the same way he has. Perhaps the poem makes him see his flower in a whole new light, with new reverence and awe for its beauty. Books in the classroom are essential; the proper use of those books is just as important.

BOOKS IN THE CLASSROOM

Books should be a natural part of the classroom environment. There should be no argument as to whether to have a classroom collection of books or a library media center; both are necessary. Children should have immediate access to books whenever, wherever they need them. The importance of the accessibility of books in the classroom was investigated by Bissett. He reported that regardless of access to books in the home, the public library, and the school library, children in classrooms containing attractive col-

lections read 50 percent more books than children in the same school without such collections.[2]

The books in the classroom collection will vary from those in the library media center. Many classrooms have extensive paperback collections (200 to 300 titles). Frequently, there are five or six copies of the same title, so several children can read the same book and have an in-depth discussion of it.

The classroom teacher will also want to provide for a changing collection of books. These books will be related to the ongoing social studies or science programs. The librarian may provide a rolling cart of materials that will enhance children's study of a particular interest in social studies, science, or math. If the library media center does not have particular books that the children or the teacher need, they may be obtained from local public libraries or from a bookmobile. Some state libraries will send boxes of books to teachers in communities that are not serviced by public libraries.

CREATING THE READING INTEREST CENTER

Most teachers plan for some kind of a reading center in their classrooms. If possible this area should be somewhat secluded and away from the general traffic pattern. Teachers and children need to experiment with different arrangements to provide for a library corner. Shelves or bulletin boards may be used as dividers to create a separate area for quiet independent reading. One teacher of 8- and 9-year-olds clipped paperback books to clothespins and hung these by strings suspended from light fixtures to mark off the reading area. A rug provided comfort and quiet. A primary-grade teacher did the same thing, only the children clipped the books they had made to the clothespins. Comfortable and colorful chairs may make this a more inviting center. Informal classrooms will frequently have a comfortable couch for reading. Children also enjoy sitting or lying on the floor while they read. Squares of carpet samples make good mats or can be taped together to form a gay patchwork

[2] Reported by M. Ann Heibreder in "Research Needed in the Fields of Reading and Communications," Vol. 22, *Library Trends* (October 1973), p. 24.

rug. Inexpensive bookshelves may be constructed from salvaged materials, such as boards and bricks or apple crates.

Children will develop more interest in books when they share in the planning of a reading center. One group of 8-year-olds utilized an unused cloak room for their reading center. With the aid of the custodian they built and painted bookshelves. Others designed unbleached muslin curtains that were decorated with crayon drawings of their favorite characters from books. A mother provided a hooked rug and a rocking chair to complete the homey aspect of this reading center. Another school changed a storage closet that was between three rooms into a small primary-grade book center. Good lighting, carpeting, and some bookcases made this a quiet, comfortable place for children from several classrooms to meet and share books together.

Whenever possible, teachers should try to involve children in the process of selecting, obtaining, and arranging books for the reading center. Children may review new books and share in their selection. Excitement mounts as they unpack boxes of books, whether they come from the library or directly from the publisher. They may help with book arrangement and display. Sometimes, children's classifications of books will not be in agreement with the Dewey Decimal System, but the arrangement they develop will be meaningful to them.

Children also like private places in which to read their books. One teacher shared *Evan's Corner* by Hill with a group of 7- and 8-year-olds, and children paired off to make their own "reading corners." The room looked slightly like a rabbit warren, but the activity stimulated interest in construction and reading. Other children have made "book cubbies" out of bookshelves (*see* the second color section), or decorated their own folding cardboard screens which they can then · use to make a kind of floor carrel for their private reading. One library media center had a sturdy "reading tree" constructed with seats among the branches.

Creative teachers and children will enjoy setting up comfortable, attractive reading centers. Obviously, these centers should be filled with many quality paperback books and hardback books that children want to read. There is no

point in having an attractive center without the books; that would be like having a swimming pool without the water!

MOTIVATING CHILDREN TO READ

An Enthusiastic Teacher

The one most important element in children's development of a love of reading is the enthusiasm of the teacher. If the teacher loves books, shares them with children, provides time for children to read and a place for them to read, children will become enthusiastic readers. The teacher who reads to the children every day, talks about books and characters in books as if they were good friends, knows poems and stories to tell is serving the class as an adult model of a person who enjoys books. One teacher used to regularly read a new children's book while her class was reading. She would keep the book in an old beat-up briefcase that she delighted in carrying. A kind of game she played with her 7- and 8-year-old students was to keep the book hidden from them. Their delight was to find out what book she was reading, so they could read the same one. Of course, they always found out, which was what she had in mind in the first place. Walk into any classroom and you can tell if the teacher really respects the reading of books. You can look at the teacher's desk or ask the children what book their teacher is reading to them. You can see what provisions have been made to have books in the classroom; you can look at the quality of the books and talk to children about which ones they have read. Enthusiasm for books is contagious; if the teacher has it, so will the children. It is also very easy for an outsider to detect.

Displaying Books

The enthusiastic teacher who wants to bring books and children together will surround children with books. Trade books will be an integral part of all of the children's studies. A new book on growing house plants will be placed in the science center with a Piggy-Back plant and a Spider plant. The children might be studying ecology and investigating the effect of the laying of the Canadian Pipeline on the Eskimo way of life. To supplement their study and give them a

Books should be a natural part of the science center.

Diane Connett, teacher, Upper Arlington Public Schools, Columbus, Ohio. Photographed by Roy Wilson.

literature experience the teacher might share *Julie of the Wolves* by Jean George with the class. A soapstone sculpture might be displayed along with Shirley Glubok's superb book *The Art of the Eskimo* and some of the exciting legends by James Houston such as *Tiktá Liktak*.

Children should also be encouraged to use books and magazines in their displays. One child who studied bones included an identification book, the magazine *Wildlife*, and other books, along with his own collection of "bones." A group of 8-year-olds and their teacher arranged

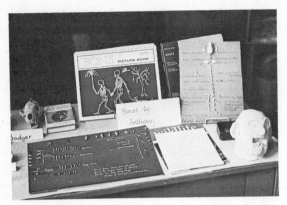

A child's project on "Bones" is displayed with books, magazines, and artifacts.

From *Yesterday I Found . . .* by Dorothy and John Paull, Mountain View Center for Environmental Education, University of Colorado, 1972. Reprinted by permission.

a "blue display" to accompany Mary O'Neill's poem about "Blue" from *Hailstones and Halibut Bones.* The display included a blue vase with a lovely bouquet of blue bachelor buttons and a piece of rich blue velvet draped behind the bookcase with a small reproduction of Reynolds' "Blue Boy" pinned to it. A book on *Pablo Picasso* by Raboff was opened to the picture of a "Young Girl on a Ball," painted during his so called "blue period." A bright blue ribbon cascaded down the center of the book and circled around a lovely, clay model of a blue cat made and painted by one of the children. When the children first heard "Blue," several of them wanted to make special displays for their favorite colors. Rather than do them all at once, they chose the top of the file cabinet as a safe place and really planned in advance for their display. As the teacher talked with them about various shades of color, various textures, and principles of arrangement, their displays became increasingly interesting, and they found examples of different colors in nature, art objects, and their own artistic creations.

Imaginative teachers and librarians will collect objects, models, and figurines related to social studies, science, and literature which may call special attention to a particular book. One teacher found an old Raggedy Ann doll and a very ancient velveteen rabbit in a trunk in the attic. Immediately recalling her love of Margery Williams' story, *The Velveteen Rabbit,* she realized that these old dolls would make an interesting display and be a wonderful introduction to that classic story. A display of a blue willow plate and a caption about the book, *Blue Willow,* by Gates would capture the attention of middle-grade children. Younger children might be introduced to the characters of Peter Rabbit, Jemima Puddleduck, and many others through the delightful Beatrix Potter figurines. The setting of a story can be suggested by arranging objects in a display. Rocks, sand, and a seashell might develop interest in reading McCloskey's *Time of Wonder,* or other books about islands and the sea. A shadow box could be constructed to provide an attractive display setting. The wooden box in the picture on page 598 is 28 by 18 by 15 inches and is lighted from the top by a bulb hidden behind the 3-inch frame. Teachers and children can plan for interesting displays in the shadow box.

An old Raggedy Ann doll and a long-ago cloth rabbit will create an interest in the book, *The Velveteen Rabbit.*

Making Bulletin Boards

Teachers and librarians may want to make small portable bulletin boards that might create an interest in a particular book. A picture of an author and brief biographical data could be shown along with his or her new book. One teacher who had a long waiting list for the popular book *Are You There God? It's Me, Margaret* asked the girls to list other books that they liked as well as this one. Then she prepared a mini-display of some of these books with the amusing caption: "Other Books May Bloom While You Are Waiting for Blume!"

Large bulletin boards should feature *children's* interpretations of literature (*see* Chapter 11). The teacher or librarian's time should not be spent in creating bulletin-board displays but rather in helping to arrange displays of children's work, which can be combined with other displays. An example is the "We Wrote to Authors" bulletin board on which children's letters were displayed along with photographs of their favorite authors.

The teacher might help children to prepare a "participation bulletin board" that would actively involve the class. A riddle bulletin board titled "Do You Know These People?" could be developed. Children can draw pictures and make up riddles about such favorite characters as Paddington, Charlotte, Wilbur, Pippi Longstocking, and others. Examples might be: "I wallpapered myself in my room, who am I?," "I am a very good speller.," "I look radiant.," "I've had only one day of school in my life.," and so on. Then

yarn could be linked between the riddle and the picture of the character. Children might see if they could connect all the riddles and pictures. Another type of participation bulletin board can be made by placing a large map of the United States under a sheet of acetate. Using a wax pencil, similar to grocers' marking pencils, children mark on the map the setting of books that have been listed on a sheet of paper. *Cotton in My Sack* by Lenski, *Little House on the Prairie* by Wilder, *My Side of the Mountain* by George, *From the Mixed-up Files of Mrs. Basil E. Frankweiler* by Konigsburg, and *Island of the Blue Dolphins* by O'Dell are some of the titles that could be included. The pencil marks are easily removed from the acetate by rubbing with a soft cloth, so many children can have a chance to locate the settings of these books.

The children may also use maps to trace routes followed by the characters in such books as *Carolina's Courage* by Yates, *The Loner* by Ester Wier, *North to Freedom* by Holm, or *Harriet Tubman* by Petry.

A bulletin board may be arranged to show the theme of one book, the books of one author, or books on one topic. New books can be introduced and titles may be suggested for summer or holiday reading through the use of interesting bulletin boards. The more children are involved in making such bulletin boards, the more interested they will become in reading the books.

Knowing Authors and Illustrators

To develop a concept of books as living literature, children need to learn about authors and illustrators. Even young children should be told the names of the author and illustrator of the book the teacher is reading. Increased interest in the story may be aroused if the teacher can supply some additional information about the author or illustrator.

After reading the description of McCloskey's detailed research on Mallard ducks, the teacher can tell the children of the painstaking hours he spent drawing hundreds of sketches. They would be much more excited about the illustrations in *Make Way for Ducklings*[3] if they knew the artist

[3] *See* the report of McCloskey's work in creating *Make Way for Ducklings* in Nancy Larrick. *A Teacher's Guide to Children's Books* (Columbus, Ohio: Merrill, 1960), pp. 188–191.

Teachers, librarians, and children can use a shadow box to display favorite books and objects. Here, a small doll and an old sampler replicate a picture in *Hitty, Her First Hundred Years* by Rachel Field.

once kept six ducklings in the bathtub of his New York apartment!

Recognizing the need for young children's reading materials about authors and artists, one teacher wrote brief biographical sketches of her first graders' favorite authors and illustrators. These were printed in large type for the children to read, and placed in a notebook with the author's or artist's picture obtained from their publishers.

The teacher and librarian can develop a file of biographical information, pictures, and anecdotes about authors and illustrators. Many sources can be used to build such a file. Publishers have pictures and brief biographies on many of their authors and artists. Lee Bennett Hopkins has written two books about his in-

terviews with authors and illustrators in such an informal chatty style that children would enjoy hearing the brief sketches or reading these themselves. The first, *Books Are by People*, is primarily about the people who create picture books for children; while his second, *More Books by More People*, is about persons who write books for children in the middle grades and up. Both books are in paperback and would be a valuable resource for libraries to own. The reference set published by Gale Research and titled *Something about the Author* presents facts and pictures about contemporary authors and illustrators of books for young people. A brief biography including education, current address, and list of writings are a part of each entry. Frequently, quotes about how the author or illustrator works are included.

Fourth-graders display their letters to authors with the answers and pictures received from the publishers.

Washington School, Evanston, Illinois, Public Schools, Barbara Friedberg, teacher.

References for obtaining more information are also listed. This is a useful and attractive series that every school should own. *The Junior Book of Authors* edited by Kunitz and Haycraft, *More Junior Authors* edited by Fuller, and *The Third Book of Junior Authors* are all comprehensive resources. These books contain much biographical data, but fewer anecdotes. *Newbery Medal Books, 1922–1955* (*see* Related Readings, Chapter 1) edited by Miller and Field provides background material about the winners of the awards; while *Caldecott Medal Books 1938–1957* (*see* Related Readings, Chapter 3) gives similar information on the artists. *Newbery and Caldecott Medal Books, 1956–1965* (*see* Related Readings, Chapter 1) edited by Kingman adds to the series. *The Pied Pipers* by Wintle and Fisher presents in-depth interviews with twenty-four authors and illustrators. These provide insights into the work of such persons. The Walck monographs also give biographical sketches of such English authors as Potter, De la Mare, Grahame, and Sutcliff.

Several magazines provide current information about authors and illustrators. Frequently, *Language Arts* features an article about the work of an author or illustrator. *The Horn Book Magazine* regularly publishes essays about the writers and artists of children's literature. A periodical from England, *Children's Literature in Education,* will frequently have a critical review of an author's whole body of work. This periodical is published four times a year and can be obtained through APS Publications in New York (*see* Appendix B). It is one of the most stimulating periodicals for the serious student of children's literature.

Sometimes it is possible to obtain authors or illustrators as speakers for programs, book fairs, or teachers' meetings. At such a time, an author may autograph library copies of his book. One school prepared for a visit by Louis Slobodkin by reading all of his works and interpreting them through art activities. The children contributed to a large notebook of pictures and essays, which was presented to their guest. Slobodkin was welcomed by a huge newspaper displayed in the hall. The headline announced his arrival, and all articles were related to his books (*see* p. 601).

Children may write letters to authors and illustrators to express their appreciation and enjoyment of their books. These should be sent in

An author visits with children and autographs her book for them.

Worthington Hills School, Worthington, Ohio, Janet Hickman, author.

care of the publisher. Some groups might even suggest sequels to a book. One 9-year-old child wrote and illustrated another chapter for E. B. White's *Stuart Little* because she was dissatisfied with his ending! Children may send their own illustrations along with their letters. Occasionally, letters may request clarification, further information, or biographical material. Children should be taught the value of the author's or illustrator's time, however, and their letters should not require time-consuming answers. All authors and illustrators are delighted to receive letters that indicate a child's real interest and enjoyment of a book. They are less than pleased with those which make demands or ask such cliché questions as: "Where do you get your ideas for books?" or "Please send us a picture and biography of you by next week." Requests such as the latter should be directed to the publishing house, not the author.

Filmed and taped interviews of authors and illustrators are available (*see* "Non-print Materials" in this chapter). One 6-year-old in telling the story of *Whistle for Willie* mixed up that story with the film interview of Ezra Jack Keats. After describing where Keats lived, as seen in the film, the boy said: "I go to visit Mr. Keats often, he's my friend and Peter's you know." Somehow children should feel that authors and illustrators are people and friends.

THE READING PROGRAM

One of the best-kept secrets in education is that children learn to read by reading. Most teachers overteach the skills of reading to the detriment of reading practice and enjoyment. Many primary-grade teachers spend over half of their day teaching children to learn how to read without ever giving them an opportunity for reading. How many teachers have told their students that they may read a book *after* they have finished all their other work? Thus, good students are rewarded with the opportunity to read and become better students; while the slower student is denied this chance. Instructional reading materials may teach a child to become literate, but no one ever learned to love reading except by reading a complete book. Programmed materials will hardly produce a book-lover. Reading from one blue card to a purple one may produce an adult who can read a popular magazine, but it will certainly not develop a lifetime reader. Many schools still require all children to plod through all the basal texts, regardless of whether they need to do so. The time has come to free children so that they can select their own books and discover the joy in reading.

Some approaches to reading have built-in the satisfactions of self-selection and time to read real books. The language experience approach begins with the child's creation of his own stories. Recognizing that reading grows out of much opportunity for talk, the child is given rich experiences which will stimulate real communication. He hears many stories and is encouraged to interpret them through some kind of creative activity. Gradually, he comes to understand that his talk can be written down and that others can then read it. One day, after spending many hours listening to the teacher "chat" about the words and letters that she writes for him, he begins to write. Soon he is writing and then reading his own stories. The next step is to read what others have written. He is ready for books.

With the number and variety of trade books, both hardback and paperback, available today there is really no reason why all children must read from the same textbooks. If teachers really understand the process of teaching reading, then a book or the back of a cereal box can be used!

One school prepared for an author's visit by making an enormous newspaper heralding his arrival.

Maryland Avenue School, Bexley, Ohio. Used by permission of Sue Scatterday, principal, and Judith Rosenfeld, librarian.

Children do not have to use basal texts for beginning reading. There are many trade books available today with enjoyable stories that have been written with simplified vocabularies which are easy to read. These are interesting stories written by imaginative authors; they offer far more challenge than most pre-primers.

Another approach to reading, which gives children an opportunity to read trade books of their own selection, has been called SSR or Sustained Silent Reading. This approach is based on the premise that children learn to read by reading. Its proponents have laid down hard-and-fast rules for initiating SSR,[4] but many variations are being tried successfully. In general, this plan suggests that all children in a class (some schools arrange for all the students in a school) read silently from a book of their own choosing for a particular length of time. It is suggested that the teacher use a timer, beginning with five or ten minutes. The teacher must read also and no interruptions should be allowed. In some schools, where they have tried this approach, the teachers agreed to read children's literature as a way of becoming acquainted with the children's favorite books. Each day the period is lengthened slightly until the children can sustain their reading for thirty minutes or longer. Usually at the end of the period, the children are told they may continue reading as long as they desire, but they are free to stop now if they wish. This approach does have the advantage of assuring every child a quiet time during the day when he can read a book of his own choosing. It also provides an example of an adult model who is reading and enjoying it. Children must have access to a wide variety of materials if the plan is to be successful.

SSR does have some artificial aspects to it. One wonders if all children have to read at the same time, or if they couldn't select their time for reading, as well as their books. However, it does stress the importance of reading practice, and it does recognize the value of giving every child a chance to read some time every day. Certainly it provides children with a rich opportunity to develop the habit of reading and to *become* readers—persons who not only know how to read but do read.

Increasingly, trade books have become an important resource in remedial reading classes. Daniel Fader's well-known research was reported in his book *Hooked on Books.* He was given a class of high-school-age boys, most of whom did not know how to read. For one year Fader allowed them to read anything they wished—comics and many adult and juvenile paperbacks. His findings showed that given the time, freedom of selection, and accessibility of interesting books, the students not only read but improved dramatically in their reading ability.[5] Another school received money for a remedial reading teacher, but they preferred to use the money to hire a teacher whom they called a "Reading Motivator." This person met with reluctant readers, children who could read at grade level but were not reading. They met with her every day for some forty-five minutes at a time in mixed-age level groups of some eight to ten children. Sometimes they read a book together and then discussed it. They compared two biographies of a single person and wrote their evaluations of the books. They dramatized books, wrote about their favorite authors, and did many of the activities listed in Chapters 11 and 12 of this book. The reading test scores showed a significant gain for these children and for the school as a whole.[6]

Even more exciting than the test scores was the reaction of the children who at last had discovered the joy of reading. All too frequently reading test scores measure children's mastery of the mechanics of reading, rather than their reading behavior. No reading test will tell *if* a child reads, what he reads, or how much he reads. So far, no reading tests have been devised that will measure enthusiasm or register boredom.

Whatever reading method is used, whatever commercially-produced materials have been adopted, if teachers want children to become readers they must provide them with exciting, well-written books at their reading level and give them time to read and discuss them.

[4] Robert A. McCracken and Marlene McCracken. *Reading Is Only The Tiger's Tail* (San Rafael, Calif.: Leswing Press, 1972).

[5] Daniel Fader and Elton B. McNeil. *Hooked on Books: Program and Proof* (New York: Berkeley), 1968.
[6] Martin Luther King, Jr., Laboratory School, Evanston Public Schools, Evanston, Ill.

The School Library Media Center

CHANGING NAMES, CHANGING FUNCTIONS

The confusing array of names for what used to be called "the library" reflects the expansion of services and materials now expected of that institution. Once a school was proud if it could boast of its own library and trained librarian. Now, however, the emphasis is upon a media center for each school which contains books; films, tapes, slides, art prints, and transparencies; instamatic cameras, both still and movie; duplicating machines; listening centers and viewing centers; and realia, including pets and artifacts. Such centers have been variously called The Instructional Materials Center, The Instructional Media Center, The Learning Center, The Media Center, and The Library Media Center. The term "media specialist" is often substituted for the older term "librarian." Arguments and justifications for the use of each of these terms have been delineated and debated. Each name carries certain connotations and limitations. Some feel that the terms "instructional" or "learning" centers imply that teachers may teach in their classrooms, but real learning or instruction takes place in the center! Others object to the term "instructional"—must all materials be instructional? What about the books which are read for sheer pleasure? Should children think that only the center has resources for instruction? The term "media" is the plural of "medium," which Webster's Seventh Dictionary defines as "a channel of communication," an all-encompassing term that describes the purpose of print, speech, film, art, music, and so on. However, in many persons' minds media primarily means "mass media"—TV, newspapers, and films. Many, including The American Library Association, would opt for the best of both worlds by using the term Library Media Center or just Library. Children, parents, and teachers know the meaning of the term "library." Public libraries have added many audiovisual materials to their collections and instituted some amazing new services while still maintaining their original names of "library."

The name is not as important as the materials and services. For the purposes of this text the term "library media center" will be used to designate the place where teachers, children, and parents may expect to find a rich collection of carefully selected and arranged materials of communication, and a staff of experts who know these materials and their potential for use with children. The primary purpose of this center, regardless of its name, is to provide the best services and materials to facilitate real learning for children.

Increasingly, new school library media centers have become the focal point of many schools, with classrooms radiating out from them. The space should be as flexible and fluid as possible to allow for growth and change. The environment should encourage free access to materials at all times. In fact, in schools which are both physically and philosophically open, it is sometimes difficult to tell where the media center begins and ends. Children flow in and out, doing projects, finding resources, making their own books, producing films. As the library media center becomes more closely identified with the total instructional program, it becomes more integrated into the total school environment.

STANDARDS FOR SCHOOL LIBRARY MEDIA CENTERS

The *Standards for Media Programs* jointly published in 1969 by The American Association of School Librarians (AASL) and the National Education Association (NEA) Department of Audiovisual Instruction (DAVI) were very specific in their recommendations as to the number of books, filmstrips, films, and recordings that should be available for schools of 250 students or over. These recommendations made a tremendous impact upon school libraries. They came at a time when school libraries were receiving substantial federal monies through NDEA and ESEA programs, and for this reason, the standards could be readily implemented. Certainly, they provided the impetus for the establishment of many media centers in which books and audiovisual aids were unified in an instructional center.

The application of these standards to all schools seemed too prescriptive, in that they did not allow for individual variations and needs. Such factors as differences in curricula and student abilities require certain variations in the collections. For example, a school which emphasizes individ-

A beautifully designed school library media center can become the focal point of the school.
Davenport Ridge School, Stamford, Connecticut. Photographed by Martin Tornallyay; from *School Media Quarterly*.

ualized instruction would have to have a different media program than a school operating more conventionally. Thus, a joint committee of The American Association of School Libraries (AASL) and The Association for Educational Communication and Technology (AECT, formerly DAVI) met to make more flexible general recommendations for balanced collections in both building and district school media programs. These joint recommendations were published in 1975 by the American Library Association under the title of *Media Programs: District and School.* The base recommendation was that a school with 500 or fewer students have a minimum collection of 20,000 items or 40 per student. An item is defined as a book (casebound or paperback), film, videotape, filmstrip, transparency, slide, periodical subscription, kit, or any other form of material or associated equipment. Some of the 1975 recommendations for a school of 500 students or less are:

Books: 8,000 to 12,000 volumes, or 16 to 24 per user
Periodicals: 50 to 175 titles

Filmstrips: 500 to 2,000 items, or 1 to 4 per user
Films: Access to 3,000 titles of 16 mm. films; 500 to 1,000 titles of 8 mm. films
Slides and Transparencies: 2,000 to 6,000 items, or 4 to 12 per user
Tapes, Cassettes, Discs, and Audio Cards: 1,500 to 2,000 items, or 3 to 4 per user
Games and Toys: 400 to 750 items
Models and Sculpture: 200 to 500 items
Specimens: 200 to 400 items.

These standards also recommend one full-time media specialist for every 250 students, and a support staff of one media technician and one media aide per specialist.

BOOKS IN THE CENTER

Trade Books

Regardless of how varied the materials, books will continue to be important sources of information and recreation. There can be no question about the impact of the school library on children's reading behavior. Gaver studied the pattern of reading in schools that had centralized libraries, compared with those schools that had only classroom collections, and found that the amount of reading was definitely related to the nature of the library provided. Children who had continuous access to a good school library staffed by qualified personnel generally read two or three times as many books as those who had only a classroom collection or were served by a central collection for the entire school system. Those students who had access to their own school library also read a greater variety of reading materials.[7] Now that media centers have become established in many of our schools, we need to have definitive research as to the impact of continuous exposure to multi-media.

Paperbacks

Paperbacks have found their place on the bookshelves in elementary-school classrooms and the library media center. In many instances children will select a paperback in preference to a hardbound copy of the same title. The relatively low cost of paperbacks makes it possible to use multiple copies of a title for in-depth literature discussions with five or six students. It has been found that paperbacks are durable and last for approximately four to ten readings.[8] They are lightweight and easily carried to and from home.

Juvenile departments of publishing houses have begun to publish their own quality line of paperbacks, usually those titles that have been their best-sellers, such as the *Little House* books by Laura Ingalls Wilder or *Charlotte's Web* by E. B. White. Increasingly, however, publishing houses are issuing juvenile titles in both hardback and paperback, as they do in adult literature. The paperback explosion can only increase children's interests in reading.

Many schools have made it possible for children to purchase paperbacks through book clubs or paperback bookstores. Pride of ownership motivates wide reading and encourages the reading of books. Children learn to make choices as they select books from attractive displays.

Parents may help set up a paperback bookstore and so become aware of the many quality books that are available to children at reasonable prices. In one school the parents and children created the "Book Nook," a tiny paperback bookstore literally made from a broom closet. They decorated it with Maurice Sendak posters, a charming hanging lamp, and even turned the old sink into a "trading pot" where children could place a "used" paperback and exchange it for another. The whole school takes justifiable pride in this paperback bookstore. In another school the parents made a large wooden case on wheels that can be opened to create a bookstore anywhere in the building. Closed, it can be pushed flat against a wall. Parents will need help in getting such bookstores started and assuming responsibility for their operation. The librarian, a teacher who knows books, parents, and one or two children could serve as the selection committee to order new books. If teachers and parents are supportive of the store in the beginning, it will sustain itself once children know its regular hours and can find the books they want to buy and read.

MEDIA

Collections of quality media can be rich resources for extending and enriching the literature program, as well as other areas of the curriculum. Films, filmstrips, filmloops, discs, cassette tapes, and slides may be used to introduce a book or poem to develop meaning, to provide background, or to present literature in another form. The school media center should make these materials easily accessible to children and to teachers. Only a few of the many materials can be reviewed in this volume. Catalogues of audiovisual materials and recommended lists of professional organizations should be consulted (*see* Appendix B).

Selection of the type of media to be used should be made on the basis of the material that most effectively conveys the content. Materials should be considered on the basis of overall purposes, quality of production, and authenticity of presentation. Faithfulness to the story and interpretation of theme should also be considered.

---

[7] Mary Virginia Gaver. "Research on Elementary School Libraries," *ALA Bulletin* (February 1962), p. 121.

[8] Max Bogart. *Paperback Books in New Jersey Schools* (Trenton, N.J.: Department of Instruction, 1965), p. 34.

A converted broom closet becomes a busy paperback bookstore.

Martin Luther King, Jr., Laboratory School, Evanston, Illinois. Photographed by Fred P. Wilken.

Since many of the films, filmstrips, and recordings are based upon traditional literature, there is probably no exact version, but the characters and theme should be faithful to familiar interpretations. For example, The Society for Visual Education filmstrip and record of *Little Red Riding Hood* moralizes at the conclusion when Red Riding Hood says it was wrong to wander from the path, and now she would always mind her mother. This ending does not provide the justice of the traditional tale nor leave the moral to the listener. An inquisitive neighbor is an additional character added to the filmstrip, *The Elves and the Shoemaker,* also by SVE, presenting a different theme from many other versions. In *King Midas,* an EBEC (Encyclopedia Britannica Educational Corporation) filmstrip, the familiar character, Marigold, is not included. The EBEC version of *The Pied Piper* shows the Mayor of Hamelin keeping the money for himself; neither the usual version of the legend nor Browning's poem includes this incident.

The language of captions and recordings, as well as the voice quality, should be evaluated before using the materials. The coordination of the narrator's text with the illustration and the pacing of the narration are important criteria to assess. The use of non-print material should extend an experience or provide a value not obtained by the use of the printed book. Media, when carefully evaluated and used optimally, should contribute to the development of children's thinking and attitudes, as well as enhancing their esthetic experience.

Some caution should be given concerning the misuse of multi-media. At no time should media simply fulfill a "school-keeping" or custodial function. There is no excuse for showing three films to all children in an elementary school on Friday afternoon! Nor is there any reason for children to see the same film three and four times in one year. The use of multi-media in schools should serve educational purposes, not primarily entertainment ones. Consistently, all research studies on children's TV-viewing habits reveal that boys and girls watch TV some 3 to 5 hours per day. Teachers and librarians need to ask how their use of multi-media differs from that which the child views at home. If children are plugged in in the morning and unplugged in the after-

noon, only to go home and sit passively viewing TV for three hours, then McLuhan's dire predictions of a non-print world have come true. If, however, children have an opportunity to discuss what they are seeing, if the media leads them back to a book, if it extends their knowledge of a particular subject, then it has served a worthwhile purpose.

Filmstrips

Filmstrips can be viewed by one child using an individual viewer, by small interest groups, or by an entire class interested in literature-related materials. Many filmstrips are accompanied by a record or cassette tape. Filmstrips are particularly helpful for individual use by children of all ages. Captions can be read or the pictures can be used without the captions. The SVE sound filmstrip, *The Little Engine that Could,* includes easy-to-read captions within the frame, and the record presents the story with clear, crisp diction. Interesting sound effects do not overpower the story. Children could use a filmstrip and tape record their telling of the story, or they could tell the story as the frames are moved at their own pace. Children can also make their own filmstrips (*see* Chapter 12).

Filmstrips need to be evaluated as carefully as

A young child prepares to view a filmstrip.
Martin Luther King, Jr., Laboratory School, Evanston, Illinois.

books. In an excellent review[9] of the usefulness of filmstrips, Ethel Heins complains of a double standard that allows teachers and librarians to accept shoddy art work and abridged texts in filmstrips that would be totally unacceptable in books.

Many filmstrips are based on drawings that resemble cartoons. Disney cartoons are the basis of an EBEC series, *Fantasy Stories*. These filmstrips—including such titles as *Cinderella, Ben and Me, Alice in Wonderland,* and *Ferdinand the Bull*—might be used effectively for critical comparison of the text and film versions. Adapted from Disney motion pictures, these and several other series with Disney versions should be carefully evaluated.

Two filmstrips by SVE, *Three Billy Goats Gruff* and *The Town Mouse and the Country Mouse,* are delightfully illustrated by Burridge and Smith, respectively. The productions are not in cartoon style, and the text is well written. Details of the house, cupboard, and costumes in the SVE *The Elves and the Shoemaker* provide an authentic old German setting for this tale by Grimm. Dutch artists created the drawings for the EBEC series that includes *The Lady of Staveren, The Wild Swans,* and *Gulliver among the Lilliputians.* In *The Wild Swans* an effect of tapestry is created, with interesting details of flowers and foliage in a pleasing design.

A cartoon style is used for the illustrations in an SVE series of Hans Christian Andersen stories. The coarse features of *The Little Match Girl* and the almost grotesque appearance of the child in *The Emperor's New Clothes* are examples of art work that should be compared to rich illustrations available in fine books (*see* Chapter 4). However, Danish artists Helga Neergaard and Beate Neergaard created interesting figures and settings with colláge techniques for the Andersen stories by EBEC. Each story is summarized at the beginning of the filmstrip, and the children are urged to "tell the story ourselves while looking at the pictures." This would be a good filmstrip to follow the reading of Andersen's fairy tales.

Tall tales from the United States have been done and "overdone" in filmstrips. Many of them present stereotyped comic-book characters—Paul Bunyan in his checked shirt with a garish bright blue ox; John Henry, a fat black baby with a hammer in his hand; and Johnny Appleseed with his saucepan hat and Bible under his arm. Coronet's set, *Tall Tales in American Folklore,* has departed from these cliché pictures in their presentations of Big Moose, Davy Crockett, Febold Feboldson, Johnny Appleseed, Stormalong, and Tony Beaver. The set contains six sound filmstrips with three records or tape cassettes, plus the usual teacher's guide. Appropriate sound effects provide lively music and narration. The narrator's voice is flexible enough to keep the stories moving.

African Legends and Folktales (CCM Films) is a set of six filmstrips with narration by the actor Moses Gunn. The illustrations feature animals, natural beauty, and tribal customs which provide general background on the heritage of Afro-Americans. Stories included are "The Tortoise's Secret," "The Fox Fools Anansi," "Anansi Fools the Elephant," "Why the Ashanti Raise Yams," "Why the Turtle Has a Hard Shell," and "The Talking Yam." A Nigerian folktale, *Tayo,* has been produced by Guidance Associates. Bold, stylized woodcuts and vibrant paintings convey the feeling of African design in this fanciful tale.

Chiquitin and the Devil: A Puerto Rican Folktale is a retelling of the popular story, *Oté: A Puerto Rican Folktale* by Pura Belpré. This is the tale of a young boy who outwits a nearsighted devil and saves his family from starvation. Actress Rita Moreno effectively narrates this Guidance Associates filmstrip. A Latin background is created by colorful art work and appropriate music.

Children's Storybook Theatre (ACI Films, Inc.) features filmstrip stories from around the world. Included in the set are "Joanjo," a Portuguese tale of a little boy from a fishing family whose dream of an exciting life takes an unusual twist; "The Old Sheepdog," a Czechoslovakian tale of an elderly sheepdog who earns his way out of "forced retirement" through an heroic act; and "The Stolen Necklace," a tale from India of a humble gardener who returns a valuable necklace to a princess.

Some of the thirty-six filmstrips that make up the McGraw-Hill Films set, *Children's Literature Series,* are disappointing. New art work was cre-

---

[9] Ethel L. Heins. "Literature Bedeviled: A Searching Look at Filmstrips," *The Horn Book Magazine* (June 1974), pp. 306–313.

ated for the Caldecott Award-winner *Many Moons* and for the very popular *Evan's Corner* (*see* Chapter 3). Color was added to Barbara Cooney's crisp black-and-white scratchboard illustrations for *Peter's Long Walk,* which somehow cheapened that attractive book. However, some books were faithfully rendered with their original art work; one example is *A Pair of Red Clogs.* This, then, is an ambitious project that has met with only partial success.

One of the few sets of filmstrips on mythology that is well done throughout is titled *The Great Myths of Greece* (EBEC). The first strip provides a general introduction to Greek mythology, showing pictures of Greek art and architecture, and finishing with the story of Narcissus. The three other strips include the stories of Demeter and Persephone, Phaeton, and Orpheus and Eurydice. Stylized illustrations by John Fleming are excellent, making use of subtle colors and shadings.

All of the Newbery Award-winning books have been made into filmstrips in a rather ambitious project attempted by Miller-Brody Productions. It is of course very difficult to reduce a long, well-written book such as *Call It Courage* or *Mrs. Frisby and the Rats of NIMH* to some sixty frames. Only a very condensed version of the story can be presented in the manner of a re-written classic, thus destroying the quality of the writing for which the book received its award! The child may learn something of the plot and characters in the story, but he will have been deprived of the greatness of the book.

The *Meet the Newbery Author Series,* also done by Miller-Brody Productions, provides a unique introduction to such authors and their works. The one on Lloyd Alexander pictures this author in his Philadelphia home. His love of cats, Mozart, and the epic hero make him seem very human indeed. Jean Craighead George's passion for nature is emphasized in the filmstrip about her. This series is available with kits, which include hardbound copies of the award-winning books, plus paperbacks of some of the authors' other works. The filmstrips with just the records or cassettes are available also.

Ann Grifalconi discusses *How a Book Is Made* in a filmstrip produced by Media Plus. Using a book she illustrated, *The Ballad of the Burglar of Babylon* by Elizabeth Bishop, the narrator details the planning and executing of the art work in Part I; Part II shows the actual printing; and Part III discusses the binding. This particular filmstrip is useful for a class in children's literature; for children studying book-making; or for comparing with the film, *The Story of a Book,* by Waterman Films.

Ann Grifalconi's picture book *The Toy Trumpet* has also been made into a filmstrip by Media Plus. This is the delightful story of a small Mexican boy who is determined to have a trumpet. The strip expands the book's illustrations, but since Ann Grifalconi did the art work for both, consistency is maintained. The narration is in English or Spanish and is accompanied by lively guitar music. The filmstrip is particularly useful in a bilingual situation.

Some fine picture-book filmstrips have also been produced by Miller-Brody Productions. One series titled the *Famous Authors/Illustrators Filmstrip Series* includes three color sound filmstrips based upon the well-known picture books *The Judge* by Harve Zemach, *Amos and Boris* by William Steig, and *All upon a Stone* by Jean George. In most instances original art work from the books has been used.

The pictures and sound quality are excellent for the Viking Press filmstrip/cassette, *The Village Tree* by Taro Yashima. The striking, impressionistic watercolors recall the author's childhood in a Japanese village. Viking's filmstrip of *Obadiah the Bold* faithfully reproduces the popular story by Brinton Turkle of the little Quaker boy who longs to go to sea as a fearless pirate.

Morton Schindel, founder of Weston Woods, was the first to realize the importance of producing book-based audiovisual materials that preserved the integrity of the text and the original art work. The name Weston Woods has become synonymous with quality productions of children's literature. Their picture book sets include four filmstrips, four records or cassettes, and four text booklets. One such set includes *Hide and Seek Fog* by Tresselt, *A Kiss for Little Bear* by Minarik, *The Little House* by Burton, and *Whose Mouse Are You?* by Kraus. Fine narration and superior musical accompaniment remain faithful to the feeling of these stories. The *Weston Woods Catalog* lists all of these picture-book sets.

Scholastic has also made a major contribution in providing filmstrips based upon picture books. Their multi-media kits include filmstrips, records, and paperback books. The very popular set of Bridwell's, *Clifford the Big Red Dog,* is one such example. It includes the title story plus *Clifford Gets a Job, Clifford Takes a Trip,* and *Clifford's Tricks*—all by Norman Bridwell.

As filmstrips come into their own and more and more companies begin to look to the filmstrip potential within their own publishing lists, we may expect to see an improvement in art work and production. Hopefully the good, the authentic will drive out the poor and shoddy. Teachers and media specialists need to be as discriminating in their selection of filmstrips as they are about books. They need to be equally judicious about the use of filmstrips.

Films

CRITERIA FOR SELECTION

Increasingly, films have become an ordinary part of both school and public library service. So many are now available that it is beyond the scope of this book to review all of them, particularly the instructional film for classroom use. However, there is a wealth of excellent art films and filmed interpretations of children's books that can make a rich contribution to the literature program. By suggesting criteria for the evaluation of these films and by describing some of the best of them, it is hoped that teachers and librarians will develop their own standards of taste and selectivity in this rapidly growing area.

A film selected for viewing should be evaluated in terms of the integrity of the treatment, the authenticity, originality, sensitive narration, and appeal to the age and interest of the intended audience. Stories translated from book to film should retain the spirit of the original story, and, at the same time, do well that which the film medium can do but which print cannot. In addition, the film must be judged as a unique art form and meet such criteria of technical excellence as clarity, good print quality, clear sound, and creative photography.

Many of today's films do provide a visual experience through technical processes—such as time-lapse photography, for example—that

would be impossible for the ordinary human to experience. A film should offer the child a valid esthetic experience. Film viewing should be more than a passive experience; it should allow for dynamic interaction and involvement. A film, like a book, should promote some kind of creative response. Children could discuss the film, but a project that was implemented by the Center for Understanding Media found that "children's responses to movies were best understood through something they can express in an active, creative, uninhibited way—something they can paint about, dance about, dramatize, tell a story about."[10]

Four kinds of films are useful in the literature program. These include:

1. Art films which are complementary to the literature experience.
2. Informational films that can extend or serve as a background for particular books.
3. Film versions of stories (for poetry, *see* Chapter 6).
4. Films about authors, illustrators, and literature.

Examples of each of these will be discussed below.

THE ART FILM

Many short art films provide a sensitive, imaginative experience which complements the literary experience. Some of these films heighten sensory awareness; others create a mood or feeling; while still others may carry a narrative line without words or with very few words.

The Searching Eye is a superb film by Pyramid which heightens awareness to the natural beauty around us. It is a simple story of a 10-year-old boy exploring a beach, but in telling the story the filmmaker utilizes every known film technique—close-up, underwater, time lapse, high-speed, and aerial photography. The viewer is led to observe the wonders of nature in a way in which he has never seen them before. This film could be used in conjunction with Tana Hoban's remarkable book *Look Again!* or Scheffer's beautiful book *The Seeing Eye.* Many short art films

[10]Susan Rice. *Films Kids Like* (Chicago, Ill.: The American Library Association, 1973), p. 17.

provide a kind of visual poetry. *Leaf* by Pyramid is a delicate non-verbal experience of a leaf that falls from a branch dancing along thermal currents to its implicit fate in a stream. Another film by Pyramid, *T Is for Tumbleweed*, depicts the expedition of a tumbleweed from the day it was blown from its place of origin to its final resting place. The tumbleweed is personified and children are delighted with its many adventures. *Moods of Surfing* (Pyramid) is a lyrical film that catches the varied experiences of surfing—the power of the waves, the delight of the participants, the challenge of humans against the sea. The vivid musical soundtrack helps create the crashing noise of the awesome waves and the peace of the little ones.

Dunes (Pyramid) is a short poetic film about sand dunes and the animal life in this environment. Characters in the film are a scorpion, a sidewinder snake, a lizard, and a tarantula. They are all shown finding shelter to protect them when a storm arises. *Rainshower* (Churchill) first shows the effect of the threat of rain on domestic animals in the barnyard, and then proceeds to show its effect on the people in town. After the narrator introduces the film, there is no further sound except that of the rain. Children might make tape recordings of appropriate poems to accompany the beautifully photographed rainshower. Through time-lapse photography Contemporary-McGraw-Hill Films has produced a splendid film on the life of the *Sky*. In a very short period of time the viewer sees sunrise, cloud formations, and sunset.

Many films, like wordless picture books, convey narration with few, if any words. *Corral* produced by Contemporary-McGraw-Hill Films shows a cowboy in Alberta, Canada, breaking a wild horse. The roping and riding of the spirited horse is photographed against a background of the wide expanse of prairies and sharp-rising grandeur of mountains. A classic film about taming a wild horse is *White Mane* (Macmillan). Photographed in the Carmargue marsh region of France, it is the moving story of a boy and his love for the white stallion that he tamed. Pursued by rustlers, the boy rides his horse into the sea.

A superb film in which the pursuers become the pursued is *Still Waters* (Contemporary-McGraw-Hill). Using beautiful underwater photography the story is told from the point of view of the fish who are happily catching frogs and ducklings until a motorboat approaches and, then, the fish are caught. This film might be used with *Swimmy* or *Fish Is Fish*, both by Lionni, or it could be contrasted with the wordless book, *What Whiskers Did* by Carroll, which has a similar theme.

The Golden Fish (Contemporary-McGraw-Hill) is told from two points of view. In the first part of the story we see how a little Chinese boy living in Paris obtains a goldfish at a local carnival. The point of view shifts in the second part of the film when the boy leaves for school. Now the filmmaker shows us a joyous ballet with the canary bird dancing in its cage and the fish flipping around in its shallow bowl. With one disastrous flip, it lands outside the bowl. A stray cat comes in through the fire escape and picks up the fish. Interrupted by the return of the boy, the cat drops it back in the fish bowl. The film returns to the point of view of the boy who, knowing nothing of what has occurred before his arrival, puts an artificial flower in the fish bowl and sits gazing at his wondrous fish. Children love the gentle suspense of this film. And the open ending allows for much discussion of what they think happens the next day.

String Bean (Contemporary-McGraw-Hill) is a poignant story of an old lady living in a shabby apartment, who tends a string bean plant with loving care. The plant soon reaches the point where it must be transplanted outside. When she plants it in one of the city's formal gardens she encounters difficulties. The themes of loneliness, reverence for life, and hope are conveyed in this moving story through the effective use of both black-and-white and color photography. Children could relate the film to *Maxie* by Kantrowitz and *Joseph's Yard* by Keeping.

BACKGROUND FILMS

Some films can be used to provide background information or enriching visual experiences related to literature. Children can see the film *Pigs* (Churchill) while they are enjoying E. B. White's well-loved story *Charlotte's Web*. This film shows a day in the life of pigs beginning with the little piglets nursing their mother, wallowing in the mud, fighting, or just walking in the meadow.

Filled with sensory appeal, the children squeal right along with the pigs during the mud scene. Children are helped to really see pigs; to be observant of varieties of ears, snouts, and tails in a way they would never do when visiting the barnyard. Younger children can relate the film to *Pig Tale* by Helen Oxenbury, or see how many nursery rhymes they know about pigs.

Death of a Legend (National Film Board of Canada) relates real facts about wolves, a wildlife species that is threatened with extinction. The film contains beautiful shots of wolves and other animals of Canada's north, including caribou, deer, and moose. This film would be a rich resource to show after a class had enjoyed hearing *Julie of the Wolves* by Jean George. Another excellent film that could link children's interest in *Julie of the Wolves* to Eskimo myths and legends is *The Eskimo in Life and Legend* by EBEC. The film opens with a scene inside an igloo where a storyteller is relating a tale in the native language. The narrator interposes an English translation. The film continues as a man makes a stone carving of the sea goddess, who keeps all the seals at the bottom of the sea. A boy's first catch, tribal customs, and a dance show modern life, as well as the myths of the people. Superb photography makes this film excellent in itself, but it would also enrich the literature about Eskimo life.

The Loon's Necklace (Encyclopedia Britannica) uses authentic masks of the Indians of British Columbia to tell the legend of how the loon received his distinguishing neckband. Eerie sound effects and dramatic close-ups of the masks are used to show how the Indians feared their gods. This popular film could serve as an introduction to the study of myth and legend with 10-, 11-, and 12-year-olds.

FILM VERSIONS OF STORIES

Many films are based upon traditional folk tales, fables and legends, or modern picture books. Puppets and animated toys are frequently used in the folk tales. Both animation and iconographic techniques are utilized to make picture books into movies. Animation is the process in which an illusion of movement is given by filming hundreds of static pictures in sequence. It is the technique used to create animated cartoons. In the iconographic technique the still pictures

in a book appear to move through the subtle movements of the camera, zooming in to photograph a small portion of a picture, pulling back to pan an entire page, slowly moving the lens up a hill to give the effect of climbing. Both of these techniques make use of the actual pictures in the book, and so present a very authentic version of the story.

Under the direction of Morton Schindel, the Weston Woods Studio has utilized the iconographic technique to produce many outstanding films based upon picture books. The camera is used skillfully to focus on part of the picture as the narrator reads the story. For example, in *The Camel Who Took a Walk*, the viewer feels that he is walking down the path as the camera "pans" slowly over the page. When the tiger's eyes are described, there is a good close-up; and when the bird is mentioned, the camera eye moves up the tree to the bird. Schindel combined the use of both animation and the iconographic techniques in producing Ezra Jack Keats' beautiful book, *The Snowy Day*. *Rosie's Walk* by Hutchins is also animated to the appropriate tune of "Turkey in the Straw." Rosie is stalked by a fox whom she unwittingly leads from one disaster to another. *Curious George Rides a Bike* presents another adventure of this mischievous monkey first created by H. A. Rey. *The Five Chinese Brothers*, adapted from the well-loved tale by Clare Bishop, is the story of these remarkable brothers each of whom has a special skill. The Caldecott Award-winning book by Gail E. Haley, *A Story, A Story*, has been made into an animated color film by Weston Woods. It is the African folktale of how Anansi the Spider Man bought all the stories belonging to the Sky God. The style of the film is animation and iconograph. Such films make it possible for all children to see the pictures easily, and their attention can be focused upon the particular object or character being discussed. The text is read clearly, with excellent timing. Other titles of picture-book films from Weston Woods include *Harold and the Purple Crayon; Drummer Hoff; Leopold, the See-through Crumbpicker; Blueberries for Sal; Crow Boy;* and *The Three Robbers*.

Some films that are based upon picture books include an animated version of *Swimmy* (Connecticut), the little fish who outsmarted the brawnier ones. Optical effects and a musical background produce an aquatic setting for this favorite story. Connecticut Films also produced *Frederick,* based on another picture book by Leo Lionni. This is the story of the poetic mouse who stores up sun, color, and words instead of food for the winter. The light-hearted music and the three-dimensional quality of this animated film enhance its warmth. Lionni's abstract art for his well-known story, *Little Blue and Little Yellow,* was easily adapted for animation. Its color theme, which may be interpreted both in the racial sense and the chromatic sense, is made comprehensible for children. This film is distributed by Contemporary-McGraw-Hill Films.

Macmillan has produced a delightful animated version of *Madeline's Rescue.* This is the ingenious story of Madeline's adoption of a stray dog. The background pictures are faithful to the original illustrations by Bemelmans. Animation is also used to tell the longer modern fairy tale of *Many Moons* (Macmillan) based upon James Thurber's story of the little princess who demanded the moon. When neither the king nor the wise man can obtain it for her, the Court Jester ingeniously fulfills her wish.

Many folk tales made into films use animation to convey their age-old stories. Gerald McDermott's story *Anansi* (Texture Films) utilizes animation and brilliant graphic techniques. This film of the mischievous adventures of the spider folk hero of the Ashanti people of Ghana is a great favorite of children. *The Magic Tree* (Texture), also created by McDermott, is an African folk tale from the Congo. The story is narrated by Athmani Magoma against a sound track of rhythmic drumbeats. Deep, rich blues serve as an effective background for silhouetted characters, whose faces resemble masks. This is a beautiful film with a more complex story than the popular tale of Anansi. McDermott has also created an exciting Pueblo Indian legend, *Arrow to the Sun* (Texture), using the same techniques. *Why the Sun and the Moon Live in the Sky* (ACI Productions) is told with animated cardboard cutouts made by Blair Lent, who illustrated the book by this title. This legend of Eastern Nigeria is well narrated by the storyteller, Spencer Shaw. The musical background is based upon African rhythms. *The Rug Maker* (Learning Corporation of America), another African folk tale from the

book *When the Stones Were Soft* by Eleanor B. Heady, is presented in bold, colorful animation. It is the somewhat moralistic tale of the chief's son who wishes to marry a beautiful maiden, who will only consent if he promises to learn a useful trade. He learns to weave rugs, a skill which later enables him to escape bondage from an enemy tribe.

The well-known Norse tale of *The Fisherman and His Wife* uses hand manipulated puppets in silhouette against backgrounds of old engravings and architectural drawings. This twenty-minute color film was produced in Stockholm for Weston Woods Studios. Delicate animated puppets tell the old Russian folk tale, *Snow Girl,* the snow child who comes alive much to the delight of the old couple who first made her and then adopt her. Every summer she melts and disappears. A combination of classical music and jazz provides an unusual soundtrack for this colorful film, which was produced in Poland and is distributed by Contemporary-McGraw-Hill Films.

Charming animated toys bring to life the well-known fairy tale by Hans Christian Andersen, *The Steadfast Tin Soldier.* Made in Denmark, this fine film is distributed through Macmillan. Animated dolls also dramatize the beloved Grimm fairy tale, *Sleeping Beauty, Brier Rose,* the story of the princess who is cursed by an evil witch and doomed to sleep for one hundred years until she is awakened by her prince. The addition of the thirteenth wise woman in the form of a raven and a three-headed dragon is an unnecessary intrusion into what is otherwise an exceptionally beautiful film. This version was made in Germany and is distributed by BFA.

Hans Christian Andersen's tale of *The Ugly Duckling* (Coronet) is presented through a color film of live animals in the Danish countryside. The "duckling" encounters the other animals, enters a charming thatched-roof cottage, and leaves when the cat and hen seem to communicate their disgust. Winter scenes do not include the growing swan, so he does not appear until he sees his own reflected beauty in a pond. This film would provide an excellent introduction to the story, or enrich children's experiences with it. Live bears are also used in the Coronet film, *Goldilocks and the Three Bears.* A little girl dreams that a cabin in the woods becomes a "real bear's house," and she becomes Goldilocks. Kindergarten and first-grade children will enjoy the bears who sit in storybook chairs, eat steaming porridge when they return to the house, and amble gently toward Goldilocks. Unfortunately, the child actress appears overdramatic. The fable, *The Hare and the Tortoise*, is presented by EBEC with live animals shown as they move through the woods, over stones, around roots. The narration tells the story in excellent style.

Using live actors and animals, Weston Woods has produced the story of *Zlateh the Goat* from the collection of Jewish folk tales of the same name by Singer. This is a survival tale of a boy and his goat who are caught in a three-day blizzard and must burrow into a haystack for protection. Unlike the written story, there is little conversation between the boy and his beloved goat. However, the sound track of music and blizzard reminds one of the adult film, *Dr. Zhivago*. The photography of the family's peasant hut, the storm, the countryside, and inside the haystack is superb.

Sound films of stories may enrich a child's experience with the book. Weston Woods has produced *The Doughnuts*, recreating one of the most amusing episodes from *Homer Price* by Robert McCloskey. By using real children in integrated scenes, a thirty-five-year-old doughnut machine, and some 12,000 doughnuts, the film adheres faithfully to the original text. *Evan's Corner*, produced by BFA Educational Media, is taken from Elizabeth Starr Hill's book about a boy who decides he needs his own corner to be alone in; with his mother's consent he picks one and sets out to furnish it in his own way with a picture, furniture, a flower, and a live fish. The actors who recreate this warm story of a black family are very believable.

Originally created for CBS television by Gordon Parks, *J.T.* is the story of a black boy's attempts to save a wounded alley cat. J.T. steals a radio, is threatened by neighborhood toughs, and is helped back to understanding by his worried mother and grandmother and a compassionate neighborhood grocer. The book *J.T.* by Jane Wagner was taken from the film. A book was also made after the filming of the classic, *The Red Balloon* by Lamorisse, distributed by Macmillan. This is the story of a little French boy who befriends a magic red balloon, which assumes dimensions of human personality. The boy tries unsuccessfully to escape a gang of boys who want to destroy his red balloon. This film fantasy has no narration, and needs none.

The National Film Board of Canada has produced a beautifully colored film based on Holling's book, *Paddle-to-the-Sea*, distributed by Contemporary Films. This is the odyssey of a tiny carved Indian in a toy canoe which journeys from the North Woods, through the Great Lakes, down the St. Lawrence River, and out into the sea.

Full-length films based on literature are difficult to obtain and expensive to buy or rent. Titles that are available include *Misty*, *Johnny Tremain*, *Island of the Blue Dolphins*, and *My Side of the Mountain*. Hopefully, *Sounder*, the fine film based on the Newbery Award-winning book by William H. Armstrong, will be available to schools soon. Some of these films may be shown in school and library programs with certain restrictions placed on advertising and the size of the audience.

FILMS ABOUT AUTHORS, ILLUSTRATORS AND LITERATURE

Films can give information about book production and introduce authors and illustrators to children. *The Story of a Book* by Waterman Films, for example, shows how H. C. Holling, author of *Pagoo*, did research in a library and made observations of ocean life before illustrating his story about a tiny hermit crab. *Ezra Jack Keats* by Weston Woods shows his audience how he paints the world he knows into his books for children. The audience visits his studio where he demonstrates the making of the marbleized papers which he uses for the background of many of his colláges. The film concludes with an iconographic motion-picture rendition of *A Letter to Amy*. Weston Woods has also visited the home and studio of *James Daugherty*, the noted author-illustrator-historian who has written books about Lincoln, Thoreau, and Daniel Boone.

Connecticut Films have produced two short filmed interviews of British authors, *Alan Garner* and *Leon Garfield*. Garner shows us his very ancient house near Cheshire and the ring of old stones that was the setting for his book *The Weirdstone of Brisingamen*. A young boy asks questions of Garfield and the author describes his style of working. Both films give insight into these authors and are particularly useful in college classes of children's literature.

The Lively Art of Picture Books (Weston Woods) is a long film that is more appropriate for classes in children's literature and library science than for children. One section deals with various artists' interpretations of life and a story; for example, many different illustrations of trees, villages, and cats are shown. Another part of the film shows Barbara Cooney, Robert McCloskey, and Maurice Sendak in their homes and in their studios as they discuss their work in a very informal manner. A third part of the film presents the book *Time of Wonder.* Parts of this longer film have been made into short, separate films that children would enjoy. These film clips show interviews with *Robert McCloskey* in his barn studio and with *Maurice Sendak* in the tiny New York studio where he formerly lived and worked.

E. P. Dutton has produced a long documentary film titled *Mr. Shepard and Mr. Milne,* distributed by Weston Woods. This motion picture was filmed on location at the late A. A. Milne's London and Sussex homes and at Ernest Shepard's early home and studio in Surrey. Shepard was in his alert nineties when the film was made, and it shows him talking about his experiences with Milne. A middle-aged Christopher Robin Milne reads his father's words and selections from *Winnie the Pooh.* Various visits are made to the locales of some of the stories and poems: the London Zoo, where Christopher Robin fed buns to the elephants; Buckingham Palace, where Christopher Robin watched the changing of the Guard with Alice; and the fields and forests surrounding Cotchford Farm, Milne's Sussex home. The film seems most appropriate for students of children's literature and avid Pooh fans in the middle grades.

Connecticut Films' *There's Something about a Story* presents the viewpoints of ten different storytellers concerning the art of storytelling. They discuss the values, choices of material, and techniques for learning and telling stories. The film shows the telling of three complete stories and parts of seven others to groups of children. Another film, *The Pleasure Is Mutual: How to Conduct Effective Picture Book Programs,* shows excerpts from actual programs conducted by librarians and volunteers in libraries, schools, and playgrounds. Joanna Foster has written a handbook by the same title to use in conjunction with this film, which is available from the Children's Book Council. *Libraries Are Kids' Stuff* was filmed at the Myers Elementary School Library in Tucson, Arizona, and is available through Weston Woods. This film shows how the librarian, teachers, and the students use a school media program. All of these films would be useful in pre-service and in-service education and in working with library aides and parents.

Recordings and Cassettes

CRITERIA FOR SELECTION

The wide range of recordings (phonodiscs) and cassette tapes based upon children's literature available today makes it essential to select the best. Both the content and the presentation of the material should be evaluated. The narrator should possess a pleasant, natural voice and speak distinctly so as to be able to be understood without strain. Every word and name should be properly pronounced. Voice quality should be free of harshness, breathiness, or nasal tone. Variation in voice tone is also necessary. The story should be well paced for the understanding and the interest level of the age group for which it is intended. Beware of a too saccharine rendition or any condescension toward "little children" in the presentation. Overdramatization, modern colloquialisms, or overemphasis upon sound also limit the literary worth of a recording. Technical excellence in cutting the record or recording the tape should be expected. Consistent volume level should be maintained, and there should be no extraneous background noise.

Many record producers use adapted or abridged versions of children's stories to shorten them or provide more dialogue to create interest. This would not be acceptable in a book, but does seem to be one of the necessary evils of recording stories, particularly longer books. The adaptation should retain the flavor and mood of the original text, however, and the abridgments should be done with care. Many literary recordings have a musical background or include sound effects, such as the sound of the ocean in the Newbery Award Record of *Call It Courage* by Sperry. These additions should not overpower the story but be an integral part of it, creating the mood or the emotional impact of the tale.

SHORT STORIES ON RECORD

The school library media center will want to have several types of literature records or tapes available for all the various age levels and interest levels in the school. Mother Goose is available in many forms. A gay, rollicking Caedmon disc of *Mother Goose* verse has been made by Celeste Holm, Cyril Ritchard, and Boris Karloff. The music enriches the setting of this record, and the variation of voices and excellent pacing maintain interest. Weston Woods has produced a filmstrip and a disc or cassette of rhymes from *The Mother Goose Treasury* by Raymond Briggs. These happy verses are sung by Buffy Allen and Randy Peyton. Many of the fine picture-book renditions of books and filmstrips produced by Weston Woods are now available on cassettes. Approximately three to four stories appear on one cassette; for example, *Whose Mouse Are You?*, *The Little House*, *A Kiss for Little Bear*, and *Hide and Seek Fog*. The narration for these stories is excellent and the music and fine sound effects add to the telling. Containing inaudible signals for automatically advancing filmstrip projectors, these cassettes, like the original phonodiscs, can be used with or without the filmstrips of the same titles.

Several companies have recorded the well-loved stories of Beatrix Potter. John Cunningham narrates *The Tale of Benjamin Bunny* along with three other Potter tales for Weston Woods; while Claire Bloom reads the tales of *Peter Rabbit*, *Benjamin Bunny*, *Mr. Jeremy Fisher*, *Mrs. Tiggy-Winkle*, and *Two Bad Mice* for Caedmon. *Peter Rabbit and His Friends: The Favorite Tales of Beatrix Potter* has been beautifully narrated by Elinor Basescu for CMS Records, Inc.

Children enjoy listening to Claire Bloom as she recounts the story of *Goldilocks and the Three Bears*; *Little One Eye, Little Two Eyes and Little Three Eyes*; *The Brave Little Tailor*; and *The Babes in the Woods* for Caedmon Records. Her British accent gives a lift to the story-telling but does not interfere with children's understanding. Caedmon has also recorded Douglas Fairbanks, Jr., reading three fairy tales from the Andrew Lang Collections—*Beauty and the Beast*, *The Boy Who Kept a Secret*, and *The Princess on the Glass Hill*. His voice is pleasing and well-modulated. Three longer tales from Andrew Lang's *Blue Fairy Book* and *The Red Fairy Book* were recorded by Glynis Johns. While children are familiar with these stories, they may be surprised by some of the unusual twists in these versions. For example, in "The True History of Little Golden-Hood" (Red-Riding Hood) not only is the color of the hood different but the grandmother herself arrives to give the wolf his proper punishment. Children will be interested in comparing this version with the more familiar one. Other tales on this record are "Snow White and Rose-Red" and "East of the Sun and West of the Moon." The narrator's lilting voice and her enthusiasm for the stories make this a very lively recording. Andrew Lang's prose version of *The Pied Piper and Other Stories* is beautifully told by Keith Baxter for Caedmon. The other fairy tales include the well-loved "Thumbelina" and "Colony of Cats." This latter story might be heard prior to Boris Karloff's reading of Browning's poem *The Pied Piper*, also for Caedmon. Michael Redgrave's reading of *Tales of Hans Christian Andersen* is appropriate to the fine style of the Keigwin translation. This Caedmon recording includes "The Tinder Box," "The Emperor's New Clothes," and "The Emperor's Nightingale."

Eve Watkinson and Christopher Casson maintain the traditional style in their Spoken Arts recordings, *Best Loved Fairy Tales by Perrault* and *Grimms' Fairy Tales*. Harp music, the cries of seagulls, and the sound of waves contribute to the effect of "The Fisherman and His Wife." In "The Goose Girl" the verse of the horse, Falada, is sung to a haunting melody.

Listening to well-told stories can be a pleasurable experience for children and an enlightening one for the teacher or librarian who wishes to become a better storyteller. A series produced by Weston Woods features such well-known persons as *Ruth Sawyer, Storyteller* and *Frances Clarke Sayers, Storyteller*. Ruth Sawyer tells "The Voyage of the Wee Red Cap," a story she is known for; while Frances Clarke Sayers tells several Hans Christian Andersen tales. The British Broadcasting Corporation released a series of

Folk Tales and Legends from Great Britain through CMS Records. Four charming folk tales, one each from England, Ireland, Scotland, and Wales are told by excellent storytellers. Lee Montague tells the English story, "Cap of Rushes"; Maureen Potter gives an excellent rendition of the Irish tale, "The Giant's Wife"; Magnus Magnusson adds much character to the Scottish story, "The Faery Flag of Dunvegan"; and Ray Smith tells the Welsh story of "Where Arthur Sleeps." The authentic background music sets the mood for each of these tales. Highlights of the *Second John Masefield Storytelling Festival* and the *Third John Masefield Storytelling Festival* are available from the Toronto Public Library. The *Second Festival* record includes the stories "Uncle Bouqui Rents a Horse" And "Anansi and the Crabs" from *Anansi the Spider Man* by Philip Sherlock, "The Wondersmith and His Son," "The Three Sillies," and "Lady Isabel and the Elf Knight." The stories from the *Third Festival* are "How the Wasp Got His Sting" from the *West Indian Folktales* by Lucille Iremonger, "Damon and Pythias" from *Long Ago and Many Lands* by Sophia Fahs, and "Kate Crackernuts" from *English Folk and Fairy Tales* by Joseph Jacobs. The stories are varied in character, but each one represents the teller's individual style and personality.

Harold Courlander brings wit and humor to the Folkways record, *Folk Tales from West Africa.* This includes the perceptive tales of "The Cow-tail Switch" and "Younde Goes to Town" and the amusing tales of "Talk," "Throw Mountain," and "Don't Shake Hands with Everyone." Courlander has also recorded some of his other tales for Folkways/Scholastic, including *Folk Tales from Indonesia* and *Ashanti Folk Tales from Ghana.* The well-known storyteller and former head of Children's Work at the New York Public Library, Augusta Baker, has recorded three tales from Courlander's book *Uncle Bouqui of Haiti* for Folk-ways/Scholastic Records. Anne Pellowski's smooth style, effective pauses, and authentic phrasing are evident in her CMS series of recordings from around the world, which include *English Folk and Fairy Tales; Folk Tales and Legends of Eastern Europe; European Folk and Fairy Tales; Norse Folk and Fairy Tales;* and *Folk Tales, Legends, Proverbs and Riddles of the Pacific Islands.* CMS also uses the fine story-telling skills of Christine Price

for *Japanese Folk and Fairy Tales.* She tells the well-known tales of "Momotaro, Son of the Peach"; "Urashima"; and "The Miraculous Tea Kettle." Ruth Sawyer's *Joy to the World* is a beautiful album of Christmas legends recorded by Weston Woods. Unusual tales from Arabia, Serbia, and Ireland are told in Sawyer's inimitable style.

Jack Moyles reads four selections from Courlander's book *People of the Short Blue Corn.* These *Hopi Tales* are told with vividness for Folkways/Scholastic Records. Diane Wolkstein reads some *Tales of the Hopi Indians* for Spoken Arts Records. Her presentation is beautifully clear, and her imitation of animal sounds adds to the pleasure of listening to these stories. Dorothy Reid tells seven stories from her book, *Tales of Nanabozho,* the great change artist of the Ojibwa. This record was made for the Ontario Department of Education and is available through the Provincial Library Services in Toronto, Canada. *Richard Chase Tells Three "Jack Tales" from the Southern Appalachians* for Folk-Legacy Records. Some of these same Jack tales are told and sung by Billy Edd Wheeler on phonodisc or cassettes under the title *Some Mountain Tales about Jack* (Spoken Arts). Wheeler introduces the mountaineer version of the hero Jack taken from "Jack and the Beanstalk," and then tells four adventure stories about him. Told to the accompaniment of his guitar, children will recognize some of the original sources of these exaggerated tales.

RECORDS OF LONGER STORIES

Longer stories may be presented effectively by recording selections from the story or by narrating a part and then dramatizing some of it. Peter Ustinov provides a fine dramatic reading of Thurber's *Many Moons* and *The Great Quillow* for Caedmon Records. By changing his vocal quality, pitch, and diction, Ustinov recreates characters as diverse as princesses, wizards, and bakers. The Boris Karloff interpretation of *Many Moons* (Caedmon) is equally well done. Karloff's reading of *The Jungle Book* and *Just-So Stories* (Caedmon) is excellent also. The sound effects of the animals, recorded at the Dublin Zoo, and the Indian music enrich, but do not overwhelm, the story "Rikki-Tikki-Tavi" of *The Jungle Book* recorded by Spoken Arts and narrated by Christopher Casson and Eve Watkinson. Two excellent British actors, George Rose and Carole Shelley, do all the voices and narration for a CMS recording of Lewis Carroll's *Alice in Wonderland.* Shelley plays the role of Alice, while Rose does literally dozens of voices for the other mad characters in this well-loved story. No musical background or sound effects detract from the amusing and satirical dialogue of this fantastic tale.

Two recordings of *The Wind in the Willows* might be compared before a purchase is made. The London recording by Toby Robertson keeps much of the original text, yet the dialogue is presented by several voices. Sound effects of the river add to the realism, and they sing such songs as the "Ducks Ditty." Pathways of Sound presents two chapters from *The Wind in the Willows*—"Dulce Domum" and "The Piper at the Gates of Dawn." Robert Brooks, Hume Cronyn, and Jessica Tandy read each chapter. Their pacing, intonation, and fine interpretation provide an excellent model of oral reading. The first record would serve well as an introduction to the book, while the latter album would be an excellent source for children and teachers to hear after part of the book had been read and discussed in school.

Luckily, Caedmon recorded Randall Jarrell reading his delightful story *The Bat-Poet* before Jarrell's death. This is the allegorical tale of the little bat who is different from all the other bats in that he remains awake during the day so that he can see the world and write his "bat poems." While the three poems in the story are mostly for adults, middle-graders love the story and capture some of the lyrical quality of the poetry. Other recordings of poets reading their own work, or of selections from poetry have been discussed in Chapter 6.

Fine recordings of selections from full-length books will not deter children from reading them; in fact, these records usually generate interest in the stories and send children to the books. Certainly this is true of the series of Newbery Award Records and Cassettes distributed by Miller-Brody Productions. Jean George's story, *Julie of the Wolves,* for example, successfully combines narration with dramatization to relate this survival story of an Eskimo girl lost on the Arctic tundra. A few authentically recorded wolf calls

and Eskimo music lend color and interest to the presentation. Numerous sound effects and the singing of Negro spirituals add to the moving dramatization of the story of *Amos Fortune, Free Man* by Elizabeth Yates. *The Wheel on the School,* also part of the Newbery Award Series, presents a lively dramatization of DeJong's book. The clear dialogue will help children pronounce difficult Dutch names. The text and characterizations are true to the original story. Sound effects include such appropriate details as the cries of seagulls and the sound of wooden shoes, church bells, and stork calls. Some of the Newbery Honor Books have also been recorded in this series. These include such titles as Fred Gipson's *Old Yeller,* the well-known story of a boy and his dog. Narrated by Bob Kaliban, who speaks with an authentic Texas accent, the recording vividly recreates life as it was lived in Texas during the mid-1860s. Other fine titles in this record series include the amusing story *From the Mixed-up Files of Mrs. Basil E. Frankweiler,* based on the book by E. L. Konigsburg; *The Cricket in Times Square* by George Selden; and the moving story of *Sounder* by William H. Armstrong.

Miller-Brody has also produced a record and/or cassette titled *Eli Wallach Reads Isaac Bashevis Singer.* Included on this recording are some of the most popular Jewish stories from two of Singer's books, *Zlateh the Goat and Other Stories* and *When Shlemiel Went to Warsaw and Other Stories.* These stories range from comedy to fantasy to parable, and they are a delight to hear. A set of four records are sold by Miller-Brody under the title *E. B. White Reads Charlotte's Web.* Children would enjoy hearing this famous author reading his favorite selections from this most popular fantasy. Another favorite fantasy, A. A. Milne's *Winnie the Pooh* comes alive with Maurice Evans' lively recording, also from Miller-Brody.

Viking Press has dramatized some of its award-winning books, including *Blue Willow* by Doris Gates, *Queenie Peavy* by Robert Burch, *Summer of the Swans* by Betsy Byars, and *Rabbit Hill* by Robert Lawson. These dramatizations are not up to the quality of most of the Newbery Award Series, but they do provide creditable performances. The dialogue and text are authentic, with some cutting of course. The High Tor Repertory Players were responsible for the dramatizations.

Ruby Dee and Ossie Davis assume the voices of various persons telling their personal stories about slavery in narratives derived from the book by Julius Lester titled *To Be a Slave*. Lester himself provides the connecting passages in this moving account of the real meaning of slavery. Selections from this Caedmon record might be used to introduce Paula Fox's Newbery Award-winning book, *The Slave Dancer*.

Julie Harris gives a dramatic reading of thirty-one entries from *Anne Frank: The Diary of a Young Girl* for Spoken Arts. She reads the diary not as a young girl trying to imitate the voice of Anne, but as literature. When she comes to the last band of the record containing an epilogue stating what happened to the Frank family, the Van Daans, Mr. Dussel, and Anne after their secret hiding place was found by the Nazis, Julie Harris dramatically breaks down and must begin the sentence again. Students who have read *The Upstairs Room* by Johanna Reiss or *The Endless Steppe* by Esther Hautzig could compare the experiences of those two girls with Anne Frank.

Tape recordings of interviews with authors, produced by Eloise Norton, are available from the University of Michigan. Authors answer questions written by children. Among the tapes available are interviews with Rebecca Caudill and Marguerite de Angeli. The authors tell how they get ideas for books, how they write, and give glimpses into their personal lives.

Pathways to Children's Literature have a series of interviews with authors available on cassette tapes. These include *Barbara Wersba* discussing her book *The Dream Watcher*; *Arna Bontemps* talking about his love of poetry, his friendship with Langston Hughes, and reading two of his own poems; and *Ann Petry* relating how she came to write *Tituba of Salem Village*. *June Jordan* discusses her book *Who Look at Me* on a Crowell Author Conversation Record distributed by Pathways Educational Programs.

Miller-Brody has developed a unique series titled *Meet the Newbery Author*. Addressed to children, these tapes introduce such interesting authors as *Eleanor Estes, Lloyd Alexander,* and *Jean Craighead George*. Unfortunately, these are available as Multi-Media Kits, which means they are sold with filmstrips, records or cassettes, and a set of eighteen of the author's books or twenty-

four paperbacks. Sets without the books may be purchased, but individual records or cassettes cannot be ordered. While most schools will want the filmstrip and records, many children's literature classes or individual teachers might want to hear the interviews alone.

Increasingly, multi-media sets are being produced. Weston Woods has many available containing filmstrips, records, and books. Scholastic and Miller-Brody also have many kits for use with literature. SVE includes four prints and four cloth hand puppets in their kit, *How Talu the Elephant Got His Farm Back: A West African Folktale*. The media specialist will have to weigh the price of the kits against the materials it includes. Questions such as the following need to be asked:

> Do we need special puppets for this book? Wouldn't it be better to have children make their own?
> Do we need twenty-four paperback copies of Lloyd Alexander's books or do we already have most of them?
> Can these items be purchased individually? How much more does the kit cost?
> Is each item in the kit of equal quality?
> Is the set in a format that can be easily shelved and stored together?
> Is the packaging durable and attractive?

These are hard questions which must be answered individually for each kit on the market.

Television

The amount of time that children spend viewing television is excessive. By the time a child finishes high school he has spent 11,000 hours in classrooms but has logged over 15,000 hours watching television. There are many children who spend as much as five or six hours before the television screen, and the average viewing by children is three hours a day. Children reach their peak period of viewing at ages 10 to 12; the very time when they used to reach their peak period of reading. Good readers consistently register less viewing time than poor readers. In a study on the characteristics of active readers, as compared to children of comparable ability but who read less, Judith Sostarich found that active sixth-grade readers reported spending 38 percent more time reading than did others, while the other readers reported watching television for 23 percent more time than active readers.[11]

The amount of time that children spend viewing television is significant; but of equal importance is the impact of that viewing. Obviously, that amount of viewing cuts into the time that children formerly spent in playing and in reading. It is difficult to measure the impact of the content of television, although Evelyn Kaye reports that some studies show a definite relationship between televised violence and aggressive behavior in children.[12] Kaye also quotes from a recent study of Saturday morning children's television, showing that 71 percent of the stories included at least one example of human violence. The National Association for Better Broadcasting has been successful in dramatizing the amount of violence on television through their monitoring study, which resulted in the loss of a license renewal for one Los Angeles station.

Television programs have a further effect on children in that they create a demand for exciting, stimulating books. Everything must be fast-paced. Rare, indeed, is the child who can sustain interest in such leisurely moving plots as that of *The Wind in the Willows*. Television has also played a part in the increased sophistication of children. Since they regularly view many adult programs, they grow up and grow out of many children's books at an earlier and earlier age.

However, television is not all bad, and some programs have dramatically increased children's demands for particular books. Following the televised versions of Norton's *The Borrowers*, Barrie's *Peter Pan*, Baum's *The Wizard of Oz*, Alcott's *Little Women*, *The 18th Emergency* by Byars, and many more, children eagerly asked to read those books or parts of them. The *Little House on the Prairie* television series has generated renewed interest in all the Laura Ingalls Wilder books by both boys and girls.

Nancy Larrick[13] suggests that television may serve as a bridge to reading. She recommends that parents and teachers link particular books with television. If children watch the weather report every night, they might be interested in reading Schneider's *Everyday Weather and How It Works*. Certainly, children would be interested in reading the diary of Laura Ingalls Wilder published after her death titled *On the Way Home*. Older children might be introduced to Rose Wilder Lane's novel, *Let the Hurricane Roar*, which was based on her mother's life. A teacher may capitalize on this interest in frontier life by suggesting other pioneer stories, such as *Carolina's Courage* by Elizabeth Yates or *The Cabin Faced West* by Jean Fritz.

Teachers and librarians also need to alert children to particular programs that they shouldn't miss viewing in the evenings or over weekends. *Scholastic Magazine* provides posters of interesting forthcoming programs and teleguides to help teachers and librarians prepare children for a broadcast and they give suggestions for following up the program. An excellent guide was developed for the telecast of *The Borrowers* by Mary Norton, for example. Suggestions were made for displaying other books about imaginary people in a corner of the room designated as "Little People—Big Story." An explanation was given of "image transformation," the special technique which enabled tiny people to be juxtaposed with normal-sized people on the screen. Five interesting suggestions were given for follow-up activities, including writing about the Borrowers moving into the classroom or making a model of what their home might look like. All these activities would enrich and extend children's experience of the television program.

Advance descriptions of a program, such as "The Autobiography of Miss Jane Pittman," suggest the opportunity for sharing books about that period in time, as well as reading excerpts from the book itself. This kind of superior television production can serve as the impetus for selecting books, poems, or records around the same theme. Teachers and librarians will want to notify children when the Cousteau specials and the

[11] Judith Sostarich. "A Study of the Reading Behavior of Sixth-Graders: Comparison of Active and Other Readers" (Unpublished Dissertation, The Ohio State University, 1974), p. 137.

[12] Evelyn Kaye. *The Family Guide to Children's Television* (New York: Pantheon, 1974).

[13] Nancy Larrick. *A Parent's Guide to Children's Reading,* 3rd ed. (New York: Simon & Schuster, 1969), p. 109.

"America" programs which are now syndicated will be on. Special documentaries also need to be called to children's attention.

A follow-up discussion the next morning of a particularly interesting program may extend its meaning for children. The teacher can read parts of the story that had been dramatized, and children might compare versions. Even the most dreadful commercials can be analyzed in class. Children might be asked to determine the specific appeal of a commercial. Were the sponsors hoping to transfer the notion that if parents really cared for their children they'd buy the best-smelling peanut butter? Children today are fairly sophisticated in understanding the skewed reasoning behind advertising, although their purchasing behavior indicates that they are still "taken in." Discussions of television in the classroom are important.

Knowing that children view television an average of some three hours a day, a staff should think very carefully before they extend that time for viewing at school. In many schools *all* primary-grade children see *The Electric Company* program whether the content is appropriate to their instructional needs or not. Such indiscriminate viewing does not set an example for becoming selective in television-viewing behavior. Children need to learn to make choices, in school as well as at home. Perhaps television could be set up in the media center and only those children who wanted to see a particular program go. Others might want to stay in their room and paint or read or even write their own stories! In brief, television programs—like films, filmstrips, and records—should do more than fulfill a school-keeping function.

There are some excellent television programs which children should see in school. Some educational television channels schedule specific programs focused on literature—sometimes in the format of story-telling, dramatizations or book discussions. One excellent program, *Cover to Cover,* highlights books on similar themes or discusses a specific book in depth. Schools with closed-circuit television facilities can retrieve these programs for use at appropriate times.

Teachers and librarians should assume responsibility for educating children to the intelligent use of television. We need to help children become more discriminating viewers of television by alerting them to programs of quality, as well as by extending the experience after a telecast.

THE LIBRARY MEDIA SPECIALIST AND THE MEDIA PROGRAM

The library media specialist[14] plays a very important role in the quality of learning and living that takes place in the library media center, the school, and the community. Serving as a full-time contributing faculty member, the librarian works with children, teachers, parents, and volunteer and professional aides. Specialized training provides background knowledge of children's books and all media for instruction, library media procedures, knowledge of children's development and behavior, understanding of various teaching methods, and knowledge of school curriculum needs and organization. Increasingly, the library media specialist is called upon to give leadership not only in providing the materials for instruction but in shaping the curriculum itself.

The library media center should be open all day and before school and after school for children, teachers, and parents to use. While certain events must be scheduled and arranged for—such as a story time for a group of primary-grade children, the showing of a special film, or the visit of an author or artist—these can usually take place in a special listening or viewing area of the center and not interfere with its ongoing use. Individuals, groups, or even complete classes should feel free to come to the library media center whenever a need or desire arises, without making previous arrangements. In addition, the library media specialist will set aside certain periods each week to conduct special activities—such as book introductions, a group study of myths and legends, or story hours for those teachers requesting them. Both teachers and the library media specialist should be involved in the initiation of learning and the extension of that learning. Ideally, interests and learning will flow

[14] The terms library media specialist and librarian will be used interchangeably to denote that person who is responsible for directing the school library media program. It is assumed that such a director would have had training as a school librarian, a media specialist, and in many instances would also have a teaching certificate.

from the classroom to the center and from the center to the classroom.

In giving the School Library Media Program of the Year Award—sponsored by the American Association of School Librarians and Encyclopedia Britannica, Inc.—the Selection Committee developed the following generalizations regarding positive characteristics of modern elementary school library media programs.

They are unified programs, providing printed and audiovisual materials and equipment.

The emphasis is on learning and learners, and on providing a learning environment to attract and assist children and their teachers.

There is much attention in these programs to individualized instruction; recognizing the differences in children's interests, abilities, and needs; requiring a rich collection of media, and guidance in finding and using them.

There is much concern for making the materials and equipment easily accessible to children and to teachers, so that media can be used in classrooms or at home as well as in the library media center.

There is a continuing emphasis on the importance of reading for children, recognizing that schools must be concerned about reading habits, attitudes, and relevant reading experiences, as well as reading skills, if children are to develop into lifetime readers.

There is emphasis on visual literacy in the modern world, and programming to encourage children to become more discriminating as they choose and use media in all formats.

There is growing recognition of the importance of involving teachers and children in building a collection of media to insure that it is appropriate in a given situation, and to encourage its fullest use.

There is widespread concern for helping children to "learn to learn" so they become expert in finding and using information and develop good study skills and habits.[15]

These characteristics suggest the development of a broad base for school library media programs; a variety of print and non-print materials, great

[15] *School Media Quarterly*, Vol. 1 (Spring 1973), p. 233.

accessibility, broad responsibility for helping children and teachers in their use of the center, and emphasis upon individualization and personalization of services. The following description of a day in a school library media center suggests how these characteristics can be translated into an action program.

One Day in a School Library Media Center

BEFORE SCHOOL ACTIVITIES

The library media specialist works with a middle-grade teacher and the professional library aide to list the kinds of materials that might go into a kit or Jackdaw on the history of their community. Copies of old newspapers and photographs, tapes of senior citizens, potential places to make rubbings, possible field trips, and copies of *The Foxfire Book* are all considered as possibilities.

Some of the 9- and 10-year-olds are spending the day at a creek in the area. The teacher stops by the center to pick up a microscope; several Instamatic cameras; a tape recorder; and field guides on birds, bugs, and plants. He had previously sent in a request, so all materials were laid out waiting for him.

The children come in and out of the center returning books; filmstrip projectors; tape recorders and cassettes; art prints; and Butterscotch, the center's peripatetic guinea pig. Parent volunteers and two 12-year-old children help with the reshelving of media and books.

Two members of the Chess Club are busy having a preschool game in the story-telling area.

One girl is carefully arranging her collection of stones in a special display case. Children are encouraged to share their hobbies and display their collections here.

MORNING CONTACTS

Two 10-year-olds want information on E. L. Konigsburg, their favorite author. The librarian directs them to Hopkins' book *More Books by More People* and the reference series *Something about the Author.* The vertical file contains information from the publisher and a copy of a letter written by the author to another child.

Four primary-grade children go to the listening area to see a filmstrip and record presentation of *Blueberries for Sal.* They will compare the Weston Woods presentation with the book.

The library media specialist goes to a primary-grade classroom for a sharing period about dragons. She listens to a program about dragon characters in books, including *Mr. Drackle and His Dragons, The Dragon of an Ordinary Family,* and *The Popcorn Dragon.* Three children share a box movie with the class that they had made of *The Reluctant Dragon.* Many pictures and papier-mâché dragons attest to their reading of *The 14th Dragon.* The librarian had first introduced these children to the subject "Dragons in Literature."

A committee from the intermediate unit comes to preview filmstrips on life in the sea. The clerk gives them viewers—each sees a filmstrip and takes notes. The committee will discuss important points to bring out when they show the filmstrips to their classmates.

The 6- and 7-year-olds have been invited to a multi-media program based on the theme "Being Yourself." The librarian shares Helen Oxenbury's story *Pig Tale* with them. A student-teacher tells a flannelboard story of *The Little Rabbit Who Wanted Red Wings,* and they see the Viking sound filmstrip of *Dandelion.* The librarian leads the discussion on what was similar about these three stories.

Several 9-year-olds ask for help with bookbinding. They have been studying folk tales in their classroom and some of them have written their own folk tales. These are completed and ready for binding. The parent volunteer lets them choose cloth material for the covers and helps them follow the printed directions given in the book-binding corner.

The library media specialist meets with a group of six 8-year-olds for a planned lesson on the use of the card catalogue. The lesson is reinforced with programmed materials. Children demonstrate their learnings by finding an informational book or filmstrip or recording using the call number from the card.

The drama consultant comes in to listen to records of authentic Indian chants which she wants to use as background music for a dramatization by a group of 7-year-olds. The librarian shows her the Indian poetry section and the beautiful pictures of *The Trees Stand Shining* by Jones.

The librarian has a luncheon meeting with a parent committee and the public librarian to plan a program on books for children.

AFTERNOON CONTACTS

The librarian sees the principal and reports on the luncheon meeting concerning the book program. They discuss ways in which the whole school may be involved and the best times to schedule talks for the author/illustrator who has been invited to attend.

Several children from the class that were studying folk tales come in to find variants of the story of "Rumpelstiltskin," while others compared various illustrated versions of "Cinderella" and "Rapunzel."

A group of well-read youngsters from the middle grades continue their work on developing an "authors" game based on books actually in the library.

The librarian has scheduled "book talks" on some of the new books that have been nominated for the Newbery Award. The middle-graders who have read them will form a Newbery Committee and make their own award.

AFTER SCHOOL ACTIVITIES

The field trip group returns from their day at the creek. They are dirty, exhausted, and exhilarated. They bring back the equipment they had borrowed, but want books about pond life, crayfish, dams, and ecology to take home to study. The library media specialist suggests to their teacher that they might want to see the art film *Still Waters* after they have finished their research.

Children wander in to check out books before the school bus leaves. One 6-year-old's mother comes for Butterscotch, the guinea pig, a pre-arranged check-out for a week. Two 7-year-olds borrow art prints and cameras. Their teacher had read *Evan's Corner* to them and now they are each fixing up their own special places at home and taking pictures of them.

Two student teachers talk with the librarian about their project for a university class in children's literature. One wants to borrow the tape recorder and have an in-depth discussion with a 12-year-old who has been reading LeGuin's *A Wizard of Earthsea*. The other is doing a unit on the theme of freedom and wants the librarian's suggestions about how to proceed.

Two librarians and two teachers from other schools in the system come for their monthly meeting to discuss new books. This month they have all agreed to read the Newbery nominations, and there is a lively discussion about these books. While they can't agree on a winner, many books are recommended for purchase.

Special Services of the Library Media Specialist

Increasingly, the library media specialist is asked to become a teacher of teachers, parents, and children. As more and more teachers abandon the single textbook approach, they feel the need to have an in-service program or workshop on the many materials available today. The teachers and the administration may ask the library media specialist to conduct such a course. Or it may be that a small group of teachers are just interested in getting together informally—say, once a week before school—to discuss new books or related materials. Interested teachers and librarians in the district might be responsible for preparing a bulletin on new and exciting books or films, filmstrips, or records that they have read, seen, or heard. Suggested activities to further children's interest in the library media center might be included in this bulletin.

Many school media programs are reaching out to the pre-school child and to parents. After all, these children will soon be enrolled in school and anything that can be done to enrich their formative years should prove beneficial in the near future. Some schools conduct a weekly story hour for pre-schoolers. Following the presentation, children and their mothers are encouraged to take books home to share. One school plans family nights in the school library media center. Students from one or two classes write invitations to their parents asking them to come to the school center to spend an evening. There is no planned program, no food, no cost involved. The librarian is there to help when needed. Parents look at books and magazines, see filmstrips, listen to tapes and recordings—just enjoy an evening at the library with their children. Another school librarian organized a weekly class in the evenings where middle-graders and their parents read the same books and then met to discuss them. Parents were impressed with both the quality of the books they read and the high level of the discussion. They found they enjoyed reading the books themselves, but even more, they enjoyed exchanging ideas with their own children and others.

Librarians may work with children in special ways, also, for they have the unique opportunity of serving the same children for some six to seven years. Each year the child meets a new teacher (although some schools utilize family groupings where children stay with the same teacher for as long as three years), but the librarian remains as a familiar friend. The librarian can see each child's developing interests, abilities, and needs, and personalize the selection of materials to meet them. When new books or cassette tapes come across the librarian's desk, individuals who would enjoy them are called.

The librarian media specialist also plans activities for special-interest groups. Some middle-graders are interested in reading or telling stories to younger children. They may be thinking of becoming teachers or librarians themselves, or perhaps they wish to add to their skills as baby sitters or recreational leaders. The librarian can help them make wise selections, practice reading the stories aloud, or telling them. They may tape record the stories and then play them for individual or group evaluations. Some 10- and 11-year-olds have enjoyed making flannelboard stories or using the overhead projector to show home-made transparencies. It is important that these students be prepared for their story-telling sessions with younger children, or they may contribute to the development of negative attitudes toward books rather than positive ones.

Some librarians have established book clubs for particularly interested readers. Such a club can provide opportunities for enthusiastic readers from several age levels to participate in stimulating "book talk." Special-interest groups may be formed to read and discuss books on sports or how to play chess; or "sci-fi" fans may share the latest science-fiction books. Some librarians have worked with such groups in furthering interest in literature through children's writing and illustrating their own books. In several schools parent volunteers regularly help children with the binding of these books. Once finished, they are placed in the library for others to check out and read. These books are very popular and are of genuine interest to children. Drama groups have also been initiated in the media center. Middle-graders have videotaped their plays and shown them to others. Boys and girls regularly borrow Instamatic cameras from the media center to record field trips and different school-related activities. With proper guidance, some children have been successful in making their own films and documentaries.

These are just some of the many ways that the library media specialist can make a unique contribution to the lives of children. It seems obvious that a school library media center with a professional library media specialist is the key to quality education at all levels.

Child-created books are a popular addition to the library collection.

Martin Luther King, Jr., Laboratory School, Evanston, Illinois. Photographed by Fred P. Wilken.

Many library media specialists have had real concern for extending their services to include Saturdays and vacation periods. Some school library media centers[16] have been very successful in doing this, but most of them have been funded under ESEA Title III and so have had an adequate professional staff. Increasingly, this should be a goal for all school library media centers. It does not make good sense to have materials worth thousands of dollars standing unused at the very time when children are most free to use them. Schools of the future will certainly make better use of their resources.

Children's Services of the Public Library

The programs of the school library media center and the children's services of the public library do not duplicate each other but rather complement each others' work. Traditionally, the public library has provided activities for children during periods when they were not involved in school, such as Saturday morning story hours or

[16]One example is the Meyers Demonstration Library in the Meyers Elementary School, Tucson, Arizona.

vacation reading clubs. In the past few years emphasis has been placed upon "outreach programs," bringing library services to those children who have not been reached before—such as pre-schoolers, the poor, migrant children, and hospitalized children. Today there is a new vitality, a willingness to experiment and try new approaches which is reflected in much of the work of the children's services in public libraries. It is probably too early to measure the effect of these programs upon children, but there is much that teachers and school librarians may learn by a careful look at some of these innovations.

STORY HOURS AND OTHER ACTIVITIES

The children's room of most public libraries has traditionally conducted story hours on Saturday mornings and after school for the school-age child and during the week for pre-schoolers. In some libraries the ritual of lighting the story hour

Public libraries have reached out to the pre-school child. Youngsters are entranced as they listen to the librarian.
Mary Wilson Branch, Orange County Free Library, California, Oakley Stephens, librarian.

candle began the story and it was blown out at the end of the tale. But other innovations have brought new light to the story-hour period.

Many libraries have initiated "Sleepy-time Story Hours" or "P.J. Stories," where young children are encouraged to come to the library in their pajamas, listen to several stories, hear a lullaby, and go home and pop into bed. It's different; it's fun; and the hope is to re-emphasize the importance of the bedtime story hour. Parents are given lists of appropriate books to read for naps or bedtime at home.

Several public libraries have installed a "dial-a-story" program. Every day a different poem or short story of interest to pre-school children is recorded and presented over the phone. The Erie, Pennsylvania, and San Francisco public libraries are two of the many offering this service. A similar service proved so popular in Pittsburgh, Pennsylvania, that after one week the library and telephone company had to discontinue it because regular telephone service was being severely disrupted!

Attendance at the story hour at the Schlow Memorial Library[17] increased from an average of ten children to an average of 120 children with many Saturdays reaching nearly 200. This was the result of a cooperative program presented by students in children's literature classes at Pennsylvania State University working with the public library to produce "The Book Magic Hour." Revolving around a theme usually selected from *The Calendar* (a Children's Book Council publication), students plan a multi-media program that might include demonstrations, music, puppet plays or a flannelboard story, story-telling, and a short film. A culminating activity always involves some participation by the children either in art work, a science experiment, or drama. Books related to the program's theme are selected and displayed, and children are encouraged to take them out.

Many story hours include mime, drama, or puppets. Increasingly, multi-media programs schedule films and filmstrips along with story-telling. Children are encouraged to participate in creative dramatics, crafts groups, sing-along sessions, and poetry-writing clubs.

Young adult groups have their special library programs also. The Wilmette Public Library in Illinois conducts a "Book-Rap for Junior High," in which this age group may discuss the contemporary novels and problems of young people once a week.

Vacation Reading Clubs continue to be a popular service of the public library. Most research on the effectiveness of these clubs indicates that they tend to attract those children who are already readers.[18] Many of these clubs utilize extrinsic motivational devices, which are awarded to children for reading a certain number of books. It has been argued that since the clubs are voluntary, no one *has* to compete in them who does not wish to do so. However, one would wish that the joy of reading a book might be its own reward, and that club activities—such as dramatizing books, doing art work, seeing films, and just sharing books—would be motivation enough.

OUTREACH PROGRAMS OF PUBLIC LIBRARIES

Some of the most interesting innovations in library service have been in the area of early-childhood projects. For example, a special Media Library for Pre-schoolers was developed in Erie, Pennsylvania, under a federal grant (Library Services and Construction Act Title I). Library cards are issued to any child who has not yet entered first grade. The library is open every day, except Wednesday and Thursday, from 10:00 A.M. to 8:00 P.M., from 10:00 to 5:00 P.M. on Saturdays, and from noon until 4:00 P.M. on Sundays. Children may borrow books, cassettes, filmstrips, toys, animals (including cage and food), puppets, games, and surprise boxes. The Media Library is not a baby-sitting service; adults must accompany the child. There is a so-called "Adult Play Pen" that houses books for adults. Also, there are planned parent programs that run concurrently with activities for the children. Some of

[17]McCune, Brenda, and Jane M. Singh. "It Happens the Year 'Round," *Top of the News*, American Library Association, Vol. 28 (April 1972), pp. 254–261.

[18]Goldhor, Herbert. "An Exploratory Study of the Effect of a Public Summer Reading Club on Reading Skills," *Library Quarterly*, Vol. 36 (January 1966), pp. 14–24.

Many public libraries have extended their resources for children to include animals, artifacts, and toys.

Warwick Public Library, Rhode Island. Alice Forsstrom, Children's Librarian. Photographed by Joan Glazer.

these classes are concerned with choosing books for children, terrarium-making, cooking with a child, how to give explicit and positive directions to a child, and selection of toys for tots. Parents are also encouraged to get on the floor with the children and learn to play with them. Based on the premise that before children ever acquire skill in reading, they must have talking skill, the center provides many activities that will stimulate language. Often, children have only heard language that tells them what *not* to do. Therefore, the center encourages parents to tell stories, talk with children, and read aloud. Young children are given many things to talk about and observe. They may play with the rabbits on the floor while a professional aide talks about the color of the rabbits, their different sizes, how their ears twitch, and how they eat. As they hold the rabbits, a spontaneous story time might develop; for example, the aide might tell the story of *The Little Rabbit Who Wanted Red Wings.* However, the story is not forced, and if children are not interested, they may do other things. Certainly, this is a program that could serve as an excellent model to be incorporated into other library programs.

Other pre-school programs plan regularly scheduled story hours in various homes throughout an area in an attempt to reach children who do not come to the library. In this way the library is brought to the child. Story-tellers from the public libraries will frequently go to day-care centers to tell stories and, incidentally, provide

the center with a good model for story-telling and lists of appropriate stories.

The Children's Department of the Orlando, Florida, library decided to saturate children with books and stories. In three years they held workshops with some 10,000 Girl Scout leaders, Sunday school teachers, day-care aides, playground directors, Head-Start assistants, and baby-sitters. Their goal was to be sure that every child in the community heard stories and learned to love books. They felt that children who have had this experience learn to communicate and read more easily than those deprived of stories and books in their formative years. They produced a fifteen-minute color film, *Sharing Literature with Children,* which was used in their workshop sessions.

Many public librarians provide a story hour for hospitalized children or teach volunteers to do so. Some public libraries are placing children's books in pediatricians' and orthodontists' offices. The Children's Services Roundtable of the Michigan Library Association has published a "Wiggler's List," paperbacks and magazines for use by physicians, dentists, osteopaths, chiropractors, medical clinics, or any other groups who have waiting rooms for children. The list was distributed at the state association meetings of these groups.

Another group of children that education has frequently bypassed are the children of migrant workers. While for a past decade or so special summer-school programs have been set up for these children which provide remedial instruction, medical attention, food, and clothing, it is usually too little and too late. The average adult migrant worker has the equivalent of only a third-grade education. In Wicomico County, Maryland, the public library had provided paperbacks for these children and for their parents.[19] However, they noticed that very few of them had been read, although the juvenile paperbacks were the most popular. Then they received funds from the Department of Compensatory, Urban and Supplementary Education to rent a Children's Caravan Media-mobile from Weston Woods. With two full-time staff members, the Caravan

[19]Daphine Thompson. "Curious George in the Tomato Field," *Top of the News,* Vol. 30 (June 1974), pp. 420–424.

visited each summer school once a week, where they usually stayed all day. The staffers conducted programs that always involved singing and listening to records, as this was the favorite activity. The music was followed by a story, film, or filmstrips. The Caravan was stocked with over 2,500 juvenile paperbacks, some 150 of them in Spanish. These were taken home regularly and were read. Children did not have to officially check them out and over one-half of them were never returned. Previously, when the books had been given to the children, they were not read. Now the programs so stimulated children to read that they wanted to keep the books.

The emphasis in all these programs is to bring children and books together. By providing animals, toys, multi-media programs, and books, librarians hope to broaden the base of their services and encourage more youngsters to use libraries. The outreach programs of many libraries are now serving children who have never before been affected. One study found that three-quarters of the youngest library patrons will develop a life-long reading habit by being brought to an interest in books. This same study[20] of the Baltimore program maintains that a child brought up in a home where reading is a major activity is three times more likely to use the public library. It is the old hen-and-egg story, it is hard to tell which comes first, the reading habit or the library. Certainly, the two are closely linked.

Working with the Community

What is valued in a community will be cultivated there. Teachers, librarians, both public and school, and concerned parents will want to work together to make theirs a community which shows that it respects every child's right to read by providing the books and the motivation for reading. A question which every community must answer is: Are we really as interested in every child's learning to read—as much as his or her learning to play games? If the answer is yes, then parents must ask if their libraries are

as adequate as their football fields; if they give as much time to family reading as to the Little League; if their children receive books for presents as well as skates and bikes. Obviously, the question should not be an either-or choice, but we make the comparison for value clarification. If yours is a sports community rather than a reading community, what can be done to educate parents as to the value of both?

WORKING WITH PARENTS

The Parents' Role

Teachers and librarians have a responsibility to provide parent education wherever it will help children. Parent education is an integral part of the many pre-school projects described in the last section of this book; however, parents of children of all age levels need to be alerted to the value of good books and to their role in guiding their children's reading.

Parents often are not aware of the value of building the child's own library. Space should be provided in the home for each child's books. Book gifts should be encouraged among family and friends; and children should enjoy making lists of books they would like to own. Money received for a birthday or Christmas gift can be taken by the child to the bookstore, where he can select volumes for his personal library. No birthday or Christmas should be complete without at least one book as a present. Teachers can encourage children to buy the good paperbacks that are available through school paperback book clubs. Parents need to know how these clubs operate—that primarily this is an opportunity for their children to buy good books at reasonable prices. A display of some of these books, contrasted with the books bought at the supermarket or airport, would make an interesting P.T.A. book talk addition. As stated before in this chapter, every elementary school should have a paperback bookstore where children can select their own books for purchase. Parents have been very cooperative in helping to operate such bookstores.

In a busy family life it is difficult for parents to find time for family reading activities. However, if parents are informed of the value of reading aloud in terms of their children's beginning

[20]Martin, Lowell A. *Baltimore Reaches Out, Library Service to Disadvantaged.* No. 3 in the Deiches Fund Studies of Public Library Service, Baltimore Enoch Pratt Free Library, 1967.

interest in reading (*see* Chapter 1), they may be more willing to find the time. Once started, it is hoped that they will discover the joys of family reading, of making literature a part of family activities. One father, for example, always read the story of Eeyore's birthday party from *Winnie the Pooh* on his birthday. It became his private indulgence, but his children never forgot the story! Other families have taken appropriate books along with them on vacations. While exploring the Southwest for the first time, one family with three girls under 12, took Byrd Baylor's *When Clay Sings* and *One Small Blue Bead* by Schweitzer; Miles' lovely Indian story *Annie and the Old One;* and several informational books, such as *Secrets in Stones* by Wyler and Ames and *Strange Lizards* by Earle. Teachers or librarians who know children are going to take special trips can send appropriate books home, or at least make up a personalized list of titles. Parents might also be alerted to places they might go that are connected with books. In driving West they could easily make a stop at the home of Laura Ingalls Wilder, which is now maintained as a museum in Mansfield, Missouri. Children who have read her Little House books and seen the television series would love to see where this author lived and wrote her many books. A teacher thoroughly enjoyed visiting East Jaffrey, New Hampshire, where she made a rubbing of Amos Fortune's tombstone to share with the children in her class. With overseas travel becoming increasingly common, even for children, a trip to Beatrix Potter's lovely old farmhouse at Near Sawrey in England's Lake District is an experience for young and old alike. Joan Bodger has written a delightful account of a book-loving family's trip through the British Isles looking for the sources of children's books. Titled *How the Heather Looks,*[21] this book describes the family's journey through Caldecott Country—long walks along the riverbanks of the setting for *The Wind in the Willows* and their delightful visit to Beatrix Potter's house. Linking the journey with the books, this was certainly an imaginatively planned motor trip. Teachers, librarians, or families could do the same, or plan equally exciting trips in the United States. Photographs, figurines,

and brochures will create further interest in these books upon returning home.

Book Lists for Parents

Librarians and teachers may help parents guide children's reading by providing interesting book lists. Many libraries have lists of "Cuddle Books" or "lap books" for reading aloud to preschoolers. The Children's Service Division of the American Library Association prepared "Mother Hubbard's Cupboard," an annotated bibliography of books and records for pre-school play and activity. For older children there are lists of good mysteries—always in demand—exciting animal stories, or books on particular hobbies such as craft books. A list of inexpensive paperbacks can be sent home with children as suggestions for personal libraries. As the class becomes involved in a particular unit of study, the teacher can send home a brief note explaining the study and suggesting books to read. Books for Christmas and other holidays may be listed in the school news bulletin for parents. A particularly worthwhile list is one sent home before summer vacation recommending good books to read. Some librarians have children help prepare these lists, which makes them even more valuable.

Many school libraries provide a special bookshelf for parents with helpful books on child guidance. Among these books parents should find Nancy Larrick's useful paperback, *A Parent's Guide to Children's Reading,* Virginia Reid's *Reading Ladders for Human Relations,* and Arbuthnot's *Children's Reading in the Home* (*see* Appendix B). Such volumes will provide additional suggestions to guide selection of books for children. A competent speaker or study-group consultant can help parents consider the criteria of good literature for children. Children's book editors, the local librarian, and managers of bookstores also may serve as resource people for parent-study programs. Several innovative bookstores have arranged "book parties" in homes, describing new books and making them available for purchase.

EXTENDING COMMUNITY INTERESTS

Book Fairs

Parents may also become interested in children's books by participating in planning for a children's community book fair. This is a display

---

[21]Joan Bodger. *How the Heather Looks* (New York: Viking, 1959).

of new children's books that is usually a representative sampling from several publishing firms and is sent out on a loan basis. Book fairs may be organized by the local bookseller, but more frequently they are the result of widespread community participation. Planning may be initiated by a state or public library, the school, or other agency. It is especially important that librarians or teachers work with the parent committees in selecting books. Unaware of the need for quality, some parents have accepted the selections of book jobbers, only to find few good books available for display. Books may be purchased or ordered, and the sponsoring group usually receives a small percentage of the profits. Groups of children can visit the fair and make lists of the books most desired. Frequently, authors or illustrators can be persuaded to visit a book fair to talk with the children and autograph their books.

Every year the Children's Book Council sponsors the Children's Book Showcase. The purpose of this Showcase is to select the best-designed and/or illustrated children's books that have been published in the United States during the previous year, and to prepare a catalogue of pertinent information about the production and design elements of these books. Four well-known persons judge the books of the previous year, and select those that they deem worthy of being placed in the Showcase. Various cities and institutions, such as public libraries and universities, have sponsored the annual Showcase. This is always an exciting event in the children's book world as the authors, illustrators, publishers, and designers get together to talk about the creation of the books. After the first Showcase of the year when the books are displayed, any school, university, or library may replicate the show, sell the catalogue, and create real appreciation in their communities for quality art in children's books. Further information on how one can have such a Showcase is available from the Children's Book Council (*see* Appendix D for the address).

Resource People

It is not true that all authors or illustrators live in New York or California. Almost every city has one or two local authors or poets who might be willing to come to talk with children. Be sure the children have read something these authors have written before they come, so that there is a basis for the interview. It may be possible to videotape the session, so that it can be used another time.

Also, every community has people with interesting backgrounds, hobbies, or talents who can share their accomplishments with school children. Frequently such people can serve to promote further interest in children's literature. The fabric of our children's literary heritage is woven with strands from many countries. If a community is fortunate enough to have someone who can recall the tales of his native country, children will enjoy hearing them. The local community may have a chapter of the National Story League. Its members tell stories in community centers, libraries, and at parties. Some citizens will have hobbies that may be connected with children's literature. In one community a woman who collected dolls had many that were replicas of well-known storybook characters displayed in the school library. An archeologist shared some of his early relics and small digging tools with children for a book display on early civilizations. Teachers and librarians might cooperate with parent groups in setting up a file of resource people in the community who will share their interests with children.

Utilizing Community Resources

Concern for the development of lifetime reading habits is not the sole responsibility of the school or library. The interest of one individual might make all the difference as to whether a child really *becomes* a reader. Virginia Lightner in Marion, Ohio, was concerned that more children have an opportunity to read quality literature. Working with her local church, she helped to establish a church library for children that contained all kinds of exciting, well-written books, including fantasy, historical fiction, contemporary fiction, and informational books. Frequently, memorial contributions are given to the library and appropriate books are purchased. The library is open Sunday mornings before and after church services. On a larger scale, Margaret C. McNamara founded the "Reading is FUN-damental" Organization.[22] Serving as a reading

---

[22]James Daniel. "A Reading Program that Works," *Readers Digest,* Vol. 104 (February 1974), pp. 43–48. Or write to "Reading is FUN-damental," Smithsonian Institution, Washington, D.C. 20560, for further information.

aide in the Washington, D.C., schools, she was appalled at the lack of really interesting books for boys and girls to read. With a Ford Foundation grant of $5,000 for a pilot program, Mrs. McNamara began distributing quality paperbacks to children in sixty-one D.C. schools whose family income averaged under $5,000. For some children this was the first book they had ever owned. Gradually the RIF plan spread to other cities. With national advertising, this non-profit organization will help any interested school to get started. Beginning with the approval of the principal, organizers enlist the aid of local parents, labor groups, service clubs, and businesspeople to help raise funds. The RIF headquarters will send a list of good children's paperbacks, which cost them an average of fifty cents per book. Different sponsors have worked out different plans. Many of them utilize the rule of "read five and keep one." In Pittsburgh, the Urban League and Chatham College pioneered the idea that even poor children have some money to spend for books. They give the children one free book and charge ten cents each for three more. RIF is now operating in 176 cities and towns and has given four million books to over 800,000 children. Children are reading dramatically more in schools where the plan is in operation. Currently, an effort is being made to evaluate the total impact of RIF in measurable terms. The purpose of the plan is not to teach reading, however, but to motivate the reading of books. Certainly, Mrs. McNamara's plan has been successful in meeting that goal.

Every community has someone who is vitally interested in seeing that children have an opportunity to read good books. As a teacher, librarian, or principal, search for them and work with them. Frequently a university or college with a creative teacher of children's literature can increase the community's awareness of good books. Professor Joel West of Limestone College in South Carolina and his class celebrated the fiftieth anniversary of the publication of A. A. Milne's *Winnie the Pooh* with a "Pooh-Do" for 110 third-grade children. The children were first greeted in the "100 Aker Wood" by the class, and then taken on a "North Pole Expotition" to see the adventures of Winnie the Pooh. The children heard the story of how Pooh got stuck in rabbit's door after eating too much honey, while they saw a live dramatization portraying this episode. After seeing a puppet show of the time Eeyore lost his tail, the children played "Pin the Tail on Eeyore." A scavenger Pooh Hunt was organized so that each child searched for the honey pot. The "Expotition" ended at the North Pole where honey sandwiches, gingerbread Pooh cookies, Pooh suckers, and lemonade were served. Each child received a copy of the recipes and a list of all of A. A. Milne's books and other good books to read. Both children and college students learned in the process of having a very enjoyable afternoon.

Some bookstores which feature children's books have sponsored novel autograph parties that children may attend to meet the authors or illustrators and purchase their books. An exciting bookstore to visit is the Children's Book Centre in London, which is a bookstore devoted entirely to children's books. Unfortunately, in this country, outside of the largest cities, it has become increasingly difficult to find bookstores that carry good children's books. Many department stores now have jobbers who place slick picture-book flats, Disney books, and rows of series books on the shelves, much as the delivery man piles bread up in the supermarkets. Some smaller stores that still do their own ordering may have quality books for children. However, unlike European countries that count on selling their books in bookstores, some 80 percent of the children's trade books in this country are sold directly to libraries. As a result our bookstores have dried up like deserts. Contrasting the commercial climate for books in various countries is one way to determine what is valued in those countries.

Educating for the Future

Increasingly, high-school students and students in community colleges are taking courses titled "Educating for Parenthood" or "Child Development" or even "Children's Literature" itself. All these courses stress the importance of reading quality literature to children from an early age. Students learn the criteria for selecting good books. Many of them are asked to read a story aloud or tell a story to a class or during a library story hour, while other students record the responses of the group. A most interesting read-aloud program, "Project Promise,"[23] was conducted and reported by Jane Porter. This was a program in which black high-school juniors visited a middle-grade classroom twice a week and spent approximately forty-five minutes reading aloud and discussing prose and poetry. Its purpose was twofold; namely the recruitment of black high-school students who might be interested in teaching as a profession, and the improvement of reading achievement and increased interest in reading of middle-grade students from the inner city. A weekly seminar on the Ohio State University campus helped the high-schoolers learn about appropriate books and activities

to try in the elementary schools. Twenty-one high-school students participated and there were no dropouts during the entire year. Significant gains were made in reading achievement of both the elementary students and the high-school students who read to them. Another interesting aspect of this study was the fact that it involved every level of education—elementary, high school, and the university working cooperatively to make books exciting for boys and girls. When these young students become parents perhaps they will be more concerned for the intellectual climate of their community, working to improve their schools and their libraries. It is hoped that the day will come when everyone—at home, school, and community—will work cooperatively to create an effective reading environment for all children.

[23]E. Jane Porter. "'Project Promise,' Recruiting High School Students for Teaching in City Schools," *Elementary English,* Vol. 48 (March 1971), pp. 336–340.

SUGGESTED LEARNING EXPERIENCES

1. Spend a day in an elementary school. Focus on the environment for learning, the physical environment, the intellectual climate, the emotional climate. Describe the quality of living and learning in that school. Support your descriptions with careful observations.
2. Visit an elementary school and focus on the provisions for a literature program. Does the teacher read to the children? What is read? What are the children reading? What books are available for them to read? How often are these books changed?
3. Spend a day in a school library media center. What does the librarian do? What questions do the children ask? Compare your description with the account of a day in the media center given in this chapter.
4. Diagram the kind of a classroom you would hope to have as a teacher. Plan the reading center and list what you would have in it.
5. Visit the children's room of several different libraries and compare what you see. What books are children reading, taking home? May they check out non-print materials? Talk with children's librarians. What innovative practices have they initiated, what plans for the future do they have?
6. Prepare a plan for introducing an author or illustrator to one elementary-school class. You might write a publisher for information, read speeches or articles on the author or illustrator, and use biographical references.
7. Preview some of the films and filmstrips related to children's literature. Plan the introductory and follow-up activities for one of them.
8. Listen to several records or cassettes based upon children's books. Compare them with the original text.
9. Plan a section of a bulletin for parents of pre-schoolers, giving suggestions of what they should read to their children and how to do so.
10. Your class, or a committee, may want to plan a special program based on one book or around a theme for a group of children. If possible, invite the children and give the program.

RELATED READINGS

1. Barber, Raymond W., ed. "Media Services in Open-Education Schools," *Drexel Library Quarterly,* Vol. 9, July 1973.

A special issue devoted to articles about the role of the school library media center in open schools. The articles give an excellent overview of the purposes and goals of a media center, and would be useful to all librarians who wish to improve their services.

2. Davies, Ruth Ann. *The School Library Media Center: A Force for Excellence,* 2nd ed. New York: R. R. Bowker, 1974.

An updating of a very comprehensive book on the school media program. The author includes a thorough discussion on the new standards for media programs. Chapters on how the library media program supports the teaching of English, social studies, science, mathematics, and the humanities are useful.

3. Gillespie, John T., and Diana L. Spirt. *Creating a School Media Program.* New York: R. R. Bowker, 1973.

Primarily concerned with the administration of school media centers and programs, the book includes useful chapters on budgets, staff, facilities, media selection, and acquisition and organization.

4. Greene, Ellin, and Madalynne Schoenfeld. *A Multimedia Approach to Children's Literature.* Chicago, Ill.: American Library Association, 1972.

This paperback is designed as a buying guide to a quality collection of book-related non-print materials for use with children from pre-school to grade 8. Suggestions for using these materials are given in the introduction.

5. Heins, Ethel L. "Literature Bedeviled: A Searching Look at Filmstrips," Vol. 50, *The Horn Book Magazine,* June 1974.

A splendid critical analysis of the quality of literature filmstrips today. The author gives many examples and develops her criteria implicitly through her analyses.

6. Hill, Janet. *Children Are People: The Librarian in the Community.* London, England: Hamish Hamilton, 1973.

An English librarian describes her outreach program in the London Borough of Lambeth. She believes that a librarian's job is to bring books to children wherever they may be—in park play groups, sports centers, or welfare housing. This is an excellent picture of a committed librarian's work in another country.

7. Hopkins, Lee Bennett. *Books Are by People.* New York: Citation Press, 1969.
———. *More Books by More People.* New York: Citation Press, 1974.

The first book provides fresh human-interest accounts of some 104 interviews with persons who make books for young children; while the second contains 65 interviews with authors of books for middle-graders. Children can read these interviews themselves.

8. Iarusso, Marilyn, and Mary Nicholaou. *Recordings for Children,* 3rd ed. New York: New York Library Association, 1972.

Using sound criteria for evaluation, a committee developed this selected list of recordings and cassettes. Brief annotations are given.

9. *The Junior Book of Authors,* Stanley Kunitz and Howard Haycraft, eds. 1951.
More Junior Authors, Muriel Fuller, ed., 1963.
Third Book of Junior Authors, Doris De Montreville and Donna Hill, eds., 1972.

This series of reference books are all published by H. W. Wilson. Authors or artists write their own brief biographies. The books contain photographs of each person and a guide to the pronunciation of some names. Other references are also cited.

10. Kaye, Evelyn. *The Family Guide to Children's Television.* New York: Pantheon, 1974.

A paperback television guide that suggests ways of evaluating television, how to discuss programs and commercials with children, and ways of changing and improving television programming of children's shows.

11. Larrick, Nancy. *A Parent's Guide to Children's Reading,* 4th ed. New York: Doubleday, 1975. (Paperback edition by Bantam.)

This guide to children's reading includes suggestions for reading to the very young up to what the teenager will read. A clear, sensible explanation is given to parents on how reading is taught today and the part that trade books can play in it. Provides a useful list of favorite books of boys and girls.

12. McCracken, Robert A., and Marlene McCracken. *Reading Is Only the Tiger's Tail.* San Rafael, Calif.: Leswing, 1972.

This is a very practical book on how to teach reading using children's trade books. The McCrackens combine the Language Experience method of teaching with the use of Sustained Silent Reading. Teachers will find this paperback text extremely useful.

13. National Association for Better Broadcasting. *Better Radio and Television*, Box 130, Topanga, Calif.

This bulletin is published four times a year. It regularly publishes its objective evaluations of television series—both commercial children's shows and commercial prime-time series that children watch.

14. Rice, Susan. *Films Kids Like*. Chicago, Ill.: American Library Association, 1973.

A brief description of the Children's Film Theatre Project, plus an annotated list of films and children's reactions to them.

15. Schoenfeld, Madalynne, Chairman of the Committee. *Films for Children: A Selected List*, 3rd ed. New York: New York Library Association.

A carefully selected list of recommended films for children. Annotations reveal the criteria used for selection.

16. *Something about the Author*, Anne Commire, ed. Detroit, Mich.: Gale Research Company. Vol. 1, 1971; Vol. 2, 1971; Vol. 3, 1972; Vol. 4, 1973; Vol. 5, 1973; Vol. 6, 1974; Vol. 7, 1975.

These reference books provide biographies and photos of authors and artists; quotes and pictures from their books are also included. Children and adults would find these books very useful.

17. Walck *Monographs*. New York: Walck.

A biographical series about well-known writers of children's books, including *Walter de la Mare* (1961), *Beatrix Potter* (1961), *E. Nesbit* (1964), *Kenneth Grahame* (1963), *R. L. Stevenson* (1966), and others. Information about the author's life, quotations from diaries and letters, and critical comments about the works of the author are given.

18. Wintle, Justin, and Emma Fisher. *The Pied Pipers*. New York: Two Continents Publishing Group, 1975.

Provides transcripts of some twenty-four in-depth interviews with authors and illustrators of children's books. Critical analysis of their work precedes each interview, allowing the reader to see the relationship between the writing and experience.

RECOMMENDED REFERENCES[24]

BOOKS

Alcott, Louisa. *Little Women*, illustrated by Barbara Cooney. Crowell, 1955 (1868).

Armstrong, William H. *Sounder*, illustrated by James Barkley. Harper & Row, 1969.

Bailey, Carolyn S. *The Little Rabbit Who Wanted Red Wings*, illustrated by Dorothy Grider. Platt & Munk, 1970 (1945).

Barrie, J. M. *Peter Pan*, illustrated by Nora Unwin. Scribner, 1950 (1904).

Baum, L. Frank. *The Wizard of Oz*. World, 1972 (1900).

Baylor, Byrd. *When Clay Sings*, illustrated by Tom Bahti. Scribner, 1972.

Belpré, Pura. *Oté: A Puerto Rican Folk Tale*, illustrated by Paul Galdone. Pantheon, 1969.

Bemelmans, Ludwig. *Madeline's Rescue*. Viking, 1953.

Bishop, Claire Huchet. *The Five Chinese Brothers*, illustrated by Kurt Wiese. Coward-McCann, 1938.

Bishop, Elizabeth. *The Ballad of the Burglar of Babylon*, illustrated by Ann Grifalconi. Farrar, Straus, 1968.

Blume, Judy. *Are You There God? It's Me, Margaret*. Bradbury, 1970.

Bridwell, Norman. *Clifford Gets a Job*. Scholastic, 1972.

———. *Clifford Takes a Trip*. Scholastic, 1969.

———. *Clifford the Big Red Dog*. Scholastic, 1969.

———. *Clifford's Tricks*. Scholastic, 1971.

[24] All books listed at the end of this chapter are recommended subject to the qualifications noted in the text. *See* Appendix D for publishers' complete addresses.

Briggs, Raymond. *The Mother Goose Treasury.* Coward-McCann, 1966.

Burch, Robert. *Queenie Peavy,* illustrated by Jerry Lazare. Viking, 1966.

Burton, Virginia Lee. *The Little House.* Houghton Mifflin, 1942.

Byars, Betsy. *The 18th Emergency,* illustrated by Robert Grossman. Viking, 1973.

———. *Summer of the Swans,* illustrated by Ted Coconis. Viking, 1970.

Carroll, Ruth. *What Whiskers Did.* Walck, 1965.

Courlander, Harold. *People of the Short Blue Corn: Tales and Legends of the Hopi Indians,* illustrated by Enrico Arno. Harcourt Brace Jovanovich, 1970.

Dayrell, Elphinstone. *Why the Sun and the Moon Live in the Sky,* illustrated by Blair Lent. Houghton Mifflin, 1968.

DeJong, Meindert. *The Wheel on the School,* illustrated by Maurice Sendak. Harper & Row, 1954.

Dowden, Anne O. *Wild Green Things in the City: A Book of Weeds.* Crowell, 1972.

Earle, Olive L. *Strange Lizards.* Morrow, 1964.

Emberley, Barbara. *Drummer Hoff,* illustrated by Ed Emberley. Prentice-Hall, 1967.

Flora, James. *Leopold, the See-through Crumbpicker.* Harcourt Brace Jovanovich, 1961.

Forbes, Esther. *Johnny Tremain,* illustrated by Lynd Ward. Houghton Mifflin, 1946.

Fox, Paula. *The Slave Dancer,* illustrated by Eros Keith. Bradbury, 1973.

Frank, Anne. *Anne Frank: The Diary of a Young Girl.* Doubleday, 1967.

Freeman, Don. *Dandelion.* Viking, 1964.

Fritz, Jean. *The Cabin Faced West,* illustrated by Feodor Rojankovsky. Coward-McCann 1958.

Froman, Elizabeth. *Mr. Drackle and His Dragons,* illustrated by David McKee. F. Watts, 1971.

Garner, Alan. *The Weirdstone of Brisingamen.* Walck, 1969.

Gates, Doris. *Blue Willow,* illustrated by Paul Lantz. Viking, 1940.

George, Jean C. *All upon a Stone,* illustrated by Don Bolognese. Crowell, 1971.

———. *Julie of the Wolves,* illustrated by John Schoenherr. Harper & Row, 1972.

———. *My Side of the Mountain.* Dutton, 1959.

Gipson, Fred. *Old Yeller,* illustrated by Carl Burger. Harper & Row, 1956.

Glubok, Shirley. *The Art of the Eskimo.* Harper & Row, 1964.

Grahame, Kenneth. *The Wind in the Willows,* illustrated by E. H. Shepard. Scribner, 1908.

Grifalconi, Ann. *The Toy Trumpet.* Bobbs-Merrill, 1967.

Haley, Gail E. *A Story, A Story.* Atheneum, 1970.

Hautzig, Esther. *The Endless Steppe: Growing Up in Siberia.* Crowell, 1968.

Heady, Eleanor B. *When the Stones Were Soft, East African Fireside Tales,* illustrated by Tom Feelings. Funk & Wagnalls, 1968.

Henry, Marguerite. *Misty of Chincoteague,* illustrated by Wesley Dennis. Rand McNally, 1947.

Hill, Elizabeth Starr. *Evan's Corner,* illustrated by Nancy Grossman. Holt, Rinehart and Winston, 1967.

Hoban, Tana. *Look Again!* Macmillan, 1971.

Holling, Holling C. *Paddle-to-the-Sea.* Houghton Mifflin, 1941.

———. *Pagoo.* Houghton Mifflin, 1957.

Holm, Anne. *North to Freedom,* translated by L. W. Kingsland. Harcourt Brace Jovanovich, 1965.

Houston, James. *Tiktá Liktak: An Eskimo Legend.* Harcourt Brace Jovanovich, 1965.

Hutchins, Pat. *Rosie's Walk.* Macmillan, 1968.

Jacobs, Joseph. *English Folk and Fairy Tales,* 3rd rev. ed., illustrated by John D. Batten. Putnam (1892).

Jarrell, Randall. *The Bat-Poet,* illustrated by Maurice Sendak. Macmillan, 1964.

Johnson, Crockett. *Harold and the Purple Crayon.* Harper & Row, 1958.

Jones, Hettie. *The Trees Stand Shining,* illustrated by Robert Andrew Parker. Dial, 1971.

Jordan, June. *Who Look at Me.* Crowell, 1969.

Kantrowitz, Mildred. *Maxie,* illustrated by Emily McCully. Parents', 1970.

Keats, Ezra Jack. *A Letter to Amy.* Harper & Row, 1968.

———. *The Snowy Day.* Viking, 1962.

———. *Whistle for Willie.* Viking, 1964.

Keeping, Charles. *Joseph's Yard.* F. Watts, 1969.

Kingman, Lee. *Peter's Long Walk,* illustrated by Barbara Cooney. Doubleday, 1953.

Kipling, Rudyard. *The Jungle Books,* illustrated by Robert Shore. Macmillan, 1964 (1894–1895).

———. *Just-So Stories,* illustrated by Etienne Delessert. Doubleday, 1972 (1902).

Konigsburg, E. L. *From the Mixed-up Files of Mrs. Basil E. Frankweiler.* Atheneum, 1967.

Kraus, Robert. *Whose Mouse Are You?,* illustrated by Jose Aruego. Macmillan, 1970.

Lamorisse, Albert. *The Red Balloon.* Doubleday, 1956.

Lane, Rose Wilder. *Let the Hurricane Roar.* McKay, 1933.

Lang, Andrew. *The Blue Fairy Book,* illustrated by Reisie Lonette. Random House, 1959 (1889).

———. *The Red Fairy Book.* Random House, 1960 (1890).

Lawson, Robert. *Ben and Me.* Little, Brown, 1939.

———. *Rabbit Hill.* Viking, 1944.

Leaf, Munro. *The Story of Ferdinand,* illustrated by Robert Lawson. Viking, 1936.

LeGuin, Ursula K. *A Wizard of Earthsea,* illustrated by Ruth Robbins. Parnassus, 1968.

Lenski, Lois. *Cotton in My Sack.* Lippincott, 1949.

Lester, Julius. *To Be a Slave,* illustrated by Tom Feelings. Dial, 1968.

Lionni, Leo. *Fish Is Fish.* Pantheon, 1970.

———. *Frederick.* Pantheon, 1967.

———. *Little Blue and Little Yellow.* Astor-Honor, 1959.

———. *Swimmy.* Pantheon, 1963.

McCloskey, Robert. *Blueberries for Sal.* Viking, 1948.

———. *Homer Price.* Viking, 1943.

———. *Make Way for Ducklings.* Viking, 1941.

———. *Time of Wonder.* Viking, 1957.

McDermott, Gerald. *Anansi the Spider.* Holt, Rinehart and Winston, 1972.

———. *Arrow to the Sun.* Viking, 1974.

———. *The Magic Tree, A Tale from the Congo.* Holt, Rinehart and Winston, 1973.

Mahy, Margaret. *The Dragon of an Ordinary Family,* illustrated by Helen Oxenbury. F. Watts, 1969.

Matsuno, Masako. *A Pair of Red Clogs,* illustrated by Kazue Mizumura. World, 1960.

Miles, Miska. *Annie and the Old One,* illustrated by Peter Parnall. Little, Brown, 1971.

Milne, A. A. *Winnie the Pooh,* illustrated by Ernest H. Shepard. Dutton, 1926.

Minarik, Else Holmelund. *A Kiss for Little Bear,* illustrated by Maurice Sendak. Harper & Row, 1968.

Norton, Mary. *The Borrowers,* illustrated by Beth Krush and Joe Krush. Harcourt Brace Jovanovich, 1953.

O'Brien, Robert C. *Mrs. Frisby and the Rats of NIMH,* illustrated by Zena Bernstein. Atheneum, 1971.

O'Dell, Scott. *Island of the Blue Dolphins.* Houghton Mifflin, 1960.

O'Neill, Mary. *Hailstones and Halibut Bones,* illustrated by Leonard Weisgard. Doubleday, 1961.

Oxenbury, Helen. *Pig Tale.* Morrow, 1973.

Petry, Ann. *Harriet Tubman: Conductor on the Underground Railway.* Crowell, 1955.

———. *Tituba of Salem Village.* Crowell, 1964.

Piper, Watty. *The Little Engine that Could,* illustrated by George Hauman and Doris Hauman. Platt & Munk, 1954 (1930).

Potter, Beatrix. *The Tale of Benjamin Bunny.* Warne, 1904.

———. *The Tale of Mr. Jeremy Fisher.* Warne, 1906.

———. *The Tale of Mrs. Tiggy-Winkle.* Warne, 1905.

———. *The Tale of Peter Rabbit.* Warne, 1902.

———. *The Tale of Two Bad Mice.* Warne, 1904.

Raboff, Ernest. *Pablo Picasso.* Doubleday, 1968.

Reid, Dorothy N. *Tales of Nanabozho,* illustrated by Donald Grant. Walck, 1963.

Reiss, Johanna. *The Upstairs Room.* Crowell, 1972.

Rey, H. A. *Curious George Rides a Bike.* Houghton Mifflin, 1952.

Scheffer, Victor B. *The Seeing Eye.* Scribner, 1971.

Schneider, Herman. *Everyday Weather and How It Works*, rev. ed., illustrated by Jeanne Bendick. McGraw-Hill, 1961.

Schweitzer, Byrd Baylor. *One Small Blue Bead*, illustrated by Symeon Shimin. Macmillan, 1965.

Seidelman, James E., and Grace Mintoyne. *The 14th Dragon*. Harlan Quist, 1968.

Selden, George. *The Cricket in Times Square*, illustrated by Garth Williams. Farrar, Straus, 1960.

Sherlock, Philip M. *Anansi the Spider Man, Jamaican Folk Tales*, illustrated by Marcia Brown. Crowell, 1954.

Singer, Isaac Bashevis. *When Shlemiel Went to Warsaw*, translated by the author and Elizabeth Shub, illustrated by Margot Zemach. Farrar, Straus, 1968.

———. *Zlateh the Goat and Other Stories*, translated by the author and Elizabeth Shub, illustrated by Maurice Sendak. Harper & Row, 1966.

Sperry, Armstrong. *Call It Courage*. Macmillan, 1940.

Steig, William. *Amos and Boris*. Farrar, Straus, 1971.

Thayer, Jane. *The Popcorn Dragon*, illustrated by Jay Barnum. Morrow, 1953.

Thurber, James. *The Great Quillow*, illustrated by Doris Lee. Harcourt Brace Jovanovich, 1944.

———. *Many Moons*, illustrated by Louis Slobodkin. Harcourt Brace Jovanovich, 1943.

Tresselt, Alvin. *Hide and Seek Fog*, illustrated by Roger Duvoisin. Lothrop, 1965.

Turkle, Brinton. *Obadiah the Bold*. Viking, 1965.

Tworkov, Jack. *The Camel Who Took a Walk*, illustrated by Roger Duvoisin. Dutton, 1951.

Ungerer, Tomi. *The Three Robbers*. Atheneum, 1962.

Wagner, Jane. *J. T.*, photographs by Gordon Parks. Van Nostrand, 1969.

Wersba, Barbara. *The Dream Watcher*. Atheneum, 1968.

White, E. B. *Charlotte's Web*, illustrated by Garth Williams. Harper & Row, 1952.

———. *Stuart Little*, illustrated by Garth Williams. Harper & Row, 1945.

Wier, Ester. *The Loner*, illustrated by Christine Price. McKay, 1963.

Wilder, Laura Ingalls. The *Little House* Series, illustrated by Garth Williams. Harper & Row, 1953.

> *By the Shores of Silver Lake* (1939)
> *Little House in the Big Woods* (1932)
> *Little House on the Prairie* (1935)
> *Little Town on the Prairie* (1941)
> *The Long Winter* (1940)
> *On the Banks of Plum Creek* (1937)
> *These Happy Golden Years* (1943)

———. *On the Way Home*, edited by Rose Wilder Lane. Harper & Row, 1962.

Williams, Margery. *The Velveteen Rabbit*, illustrated by William Nicholson. Doubleday, 1958 (1922).

Wyler, Rose, and Gerald Ames. *Secrets in Stones*. Four Winds, 1971.

Yashima, Taro, *pseud.* (Jun Iwamatsu). *Crow Boy*. Viking, 1955.

———. *The Village Tree*. Viking, 1953.

Yates, Elizabeth. *Amos Fortune, Free Man*, illustrated by Nora Unwin. Dutton, 1950.

———. *Carolina's Courage*, illustrated by Nora S. Unwin. Dutton, 1964.

Zemach, Harve. *The Judge*, illustrated by Margot Zemach. Farrar, Straus, 1969.

FILMS

Alan Garner. Connecticut Films.

Anansi. Texture Films.

Arrow to the Sun. Texture Films.

Blueberries for Sal. Weston Woods.

The Camel Who Took a Walk. Weston Woods.

Corral. Contemporary (McGraw-Hill).

Crow Boy. Weston Woods.

Curious George Rides a Bike. Weston Woods.

Death of a Legend. National Film Board of Canada.
The Doughnuts. Weston Woods.
Drummer Hoff. Weston Woods.
Dunes. Pyramid.
The Eskimo in Life and Legend. Encyclopedia Britannica Educational Corporation.
Evan's Corner. BFA Educational Media.
Ezra Jack Keats. Weston Woods.
The Fisherman and His Wife. Weston Woods.
The Five Chinese Brothers. Weston Woods.
Frederick. Connecticut Films.
The Golden Fish. Contemporary (McGraw-Hill).
Goldilocks and the Three Bears. Coronet.
The Hare and the Tortoise. Encyclopedia Britannica Educational Corporation.
Harold and the Purple Crayon. Weston Woods.
Island of the Blue Dolphins. Universal-International.
J. T. Columbia Broadcasting System (Carousel Films).
James Daugherty. Weston Woods.
Johnny Tremain. Buena Vista (Walt Disney Productions).
Leaf. Pyramid.
Leon Garfield. Connecticut Films.
Leopold the See-through Crumbpicker. Weston Woods.
Libraries Are Kids' Stuff. Weston Woods.
Little Blue and Little Yellow. Contemporary (McGraw-Hill).
The Lively Art of Picture Books. Weston Woods.
The Loon's Necklace. Encyclopedia Britannica Educational Corporation.
Madeline's Rescue. Macmillan.
Many Moons. Macmillan.
The Magic Tree. Texture Films.
Maurice Sendak. Weston Woods.
Misty. 20th-Century Fox.
Moods of Surfing. Pyramid.
Mr. Shepard and Mr. Milne. Dutton (Weston Woods).
My Side of the Mountain. Paramount.
Paddle-to-the-Sea. National Film Board of Canada (Contemporary Films).
Pigs. Churchill.
The Pleasure Is Mutual: How to Conduct Effective Picture Book Programs. Children's Book Council.
Rainshower. Churchill.
The Red Balloon. Macmillan.
Robert McCloskey. Weston Woods.
Rosie's Walk. Weston Woods.
The Rug Maker. Learning Corporation of America.
The Searching Eye. Pyramid.
Sharing Literature with Children. Children's Department; Orlando, Florida, Public Library.
Sky. Contemporary Films (McGraw-Hill).
Sleeping Beauty, Brier Rose. BFA Educational Media.
Snow Girl. Contemporary (McGraw-Hill).
The Snowy Day. Weston Woods.
The Steadfast Tin Soldier. Macmillan.
Still Waters. Contemporary (McGraw-Hill).
A Story, A Story. Weston Woods.
The Story of a Book. Waterman Films (Newenhouse-Novo).
String Bean. Contemporary (McGraw-Hill).
Swimmy. Connecticut Films.
T Is for Tumbleweed. Pyramid.

There's Something About a Story. Connecticut Films.
The Three Robbers. Weston Woods.
The Ugly Duckling. Coronet.
White Mane. Macmillan.
Why the Sun and the Moon Live in the Sky. ACI Productions.
Zlateh the Goat. Weston Woods.

FILMSTRIPS

African Legends and Folk Tales (six titles). CCM Films.
Alice in Wonderland (*Fantasy Stories*). Encyclopedia Britannica Educational Corporation.
All upon a Stone (*Famous Authors/Illustrators Filmstrip Series*). Miller-Brody.
Amos and Boris (*Famous Authors/Illustrators Filmstrip Series*). Miller-Brody.
Ben and Me (*Fantasy Stories*). Encyclopedia Britannica Educational Corporation.
Blueberries for Sal. Weston Woods.
Call It Courage (*Newbery Award Winning Books*). Miller-Brody.
Chiquitin and the Devil: A Puerto Rican Folktale. Guidance Associates.
Cinderella (*Fantasy Stories*). Encyclopedia Britannica Educational Corporation.
Clifford the Big Red Dog, Clifford Gets a Job, Clifford Takes a Trip, Clifford's Tricks (Set includes records and books). Scholastic.
Dandelion. Viking.
The Elves and the Shoemaker. Society for Visual Education.
The Emperor's New Clothes. Society for Visual Education.
Evan's Corner (*Children's Literature Series*). McGraw-Hill.
Ferdinand the Bull (*Fantasy Series*). Encyclopedia Britannica Educational Corporation.
The Great Myths of Greece. Encyclopedia Britannica Educational Corporation.
Gulliver among the Lilliputians. Encyclopedia Britannica Educational Corporation.
Hide and Seek Fog, A Kiss for Little Bear, The Little House, Whose Mouse Are You? (Set includes records or cassettes and text booklets). Weston Woods.
How a Book Is Made (Parts I, II, and III). Media Plus.
Jean Craighead George (*Meet the Newbery Author Series.* Kit available). Miller-Brody.
Joanjo (*Children's Storybook Theater*). ACI Films, Inc.
The Judge (*Famous Authors/Illustrators Filmstrip Series*). Miller-Brody.
King Midas. Encyclopedia Britannica Educational Corporation.
The Lady of Staveren. Encyclopedia Britannica Educational Corporation.
The Little Engine that Could. Society for Visual Education.
The Little Match Girl. Society for Visual Education.
Little Red Riding Hood. Society for Visual Education.
Lloyd Alexander (*Meet the Newbery Author Series.* Kit available). Miller-Brody.
Many Moons (*Children's Literature Series*). McGraw-Hill.
Mrs. Frisby and the Rats of NIMH (*Newbery Award Winning Books*). Miller-Brody.
Obadiah the Bold. Viking.
The Old Sheepdog (*Children's Storybook Theater*). ACI Films, Inc.
A Pair of Red Clogs (*Children's Literature Series*). McGraw-Hill.
Peter's Long Walk (*Children's Literature Series*). McGraw-Hill.
The Pied Piper. Encyclopedia Britannica Educational Corporation.
The Stolen Necklace (*Children's Storybook Theater*). ACI Films, Inc.
Tall Tales in American Folklore (six titles). Coronet.
Tayo. Guidance Associates.
Three Billy Goats Gruff. Society for Visual Education.
The Town Mouse and the Country Mouse. Society for Visual Education.
The Toy Trumpet. Media Plus.
The Village Tree. Viking.
The Wild Swans. Encyclopedia Britannica Educational Corpration.

RECORDINGS

Alice in Wonderland (three discs). CMS Records.
Amos Fortune, Free Man (dramatization). Newbery Award Records (Miller-Brody).
Ann Petry. Pathways to Children's Literature.
Anne Frank: The Diary of a Young Girl. Spoken Arts.
Arna Bontemps. Pathways to Children's Literature.
Ashanti Folk Tales from Ghana. Folkways/Scholastic.
Barbara Wersba. Pathways to Children's Literature.
The Bat-Poet. Caedmon.
Beauty and the Beast and Other Stories. Caedmon.
Best Loved Fairy Tales by Perrault. Spoken Arts.
Blue Willow (dramatization). Viking.
Call It Courage. Newbery Award Records (Miller-Brody).
The Cricket in Times Square (dramatization). Newbery Award Records (Miller-Brody).
E. B. White Reads Charlotte's Web. Miller-Brody.
Eleanor Estes (*Meet the Newbery Author Series.* Kit available) Miller-Brody.
Eli Wallach Reads Isaac Bashevis Singer. Miller-Brody.
English Folk and Fairy Tales. CMS Records.
European Folk and Fairy Tales. CMS Records.
Folk Tales and Legends from Great Britain. British Broadcasting Company (CMS Records).
Folk Tales and Legends of Eastern Europe. CMS Records.
Folk Tales from Indonesia. Folkways/Scholastic.
Folk Tales from West Africa. Folkways/Scholastic.
Folk Tales, Legends, Proverbs and Riddles of the Pacific Islands. CMS Records.
Frances Clarke Sayers, Storyteller (two discs). Weston Woods.
From the Mixed-up Files of Mrs. Basil E. Frankweiler (dramatization). Newbery Award Records
   (Miller-Brody).
Goldilocks and the Three Bears and Other Stories. Caedmon.
The Great Quillow. Caedmon.
Grimms' Fairy Tales. Spoken Arts.
Hopi Tales. Folkways.
Japanese Folk and Fairy Tales. CMS Records.
Jean Craighead George (*Meet the Newbery Author Series.* Kit available) Miller-Brody.
Joy to the World. Weston Woods.
Julie of the Wolves (dramatization). Newbery Award Records (Miller-Brody).
June Jordan. Pathways Educational Programs (A Crowell Author Conversation Record).
The Jungle Book: Mowgli's Brothers (side 2: *Just-So Stories*). Caedmon.
The Jungle Books by Rudyard Kipling (vol. 1). Spoken Arts.
Lloyd Alexander (*Meet the Newbery Author Series.* Kit available) Miller-Brody.
Many Moons. Caedmon.
Marguerite de Angeli (tape only). University of Michigan Audio-Visual Education Center.
Mother Goose. Caedmon.
The Mother Goose Treasury. Weston Woods.
Norse Folk and Fairy Tales. CMS Records.
Old Yeller. Newbery Award Records (Miller-Brody).
Peter Rabbit and His Friends: The Favorite Tales of Beatrix Potter. CMS Records.
Queenie Peavy (dramatization). Viking.
The Pied Piper (side 2: "The Hunting of the Snark"). Caedmon.
The Pied Piper and Other Stories. Caedmon.
Rabbit Hill (dramatization). Viking.
Rebecca Caudill (tape only). University of Michigan Audio-Visual Education Center.
Richard Chase Tells Three "Jack Tales" from the Southern Appalachians. Folk-Legacy Records.
Ruth Sawyer, Storyteller (two discs). Weston Woods.
Second John Masefield Storytelling Festival. Toronto Public Library.

Snow-White and Rose-Red and Other Andrew Lang Fairy Tales. Caedmon.
Some Mountain Tales about Jack. Spoken Arts.
Sounder (dramatization). Newbery Award Records (Miller-Brody).
Summer of the Swans (dramatization). Viking.
The Tale of Benjamin Bunny. Weston Woods.
The Tale of Peter Rabbit. Caedmon.
Tales of Hans Christian Andersen. Caedmon.
Tales of Nanabozho. Ontario Department of Education, Provincial Library Service.
Tales of the Hopi Indians. Spoken Arts.
Third John Masefield Storytelling Festival. Toronto Public Library.
To Be a Slave. Caedmon.
Uncle Bouqui of Haiti. Folkways/Scholastic.
The Wheel on the School (dramatization). Newbery Award Records (Miller-Brody).
The Wind in the Willows. (vols. 1–4). Pathways of Sound.
The Wind in the Willows. London.
Winnie the Pooh (four discs). Miller-Brody.

11 Extending Literature through Creative Activities

I hear, and I forget
I see, and I remember
I do, and I understand.
                    Chinese Proverb

Time and again in Piaget's writing he emphasizes the active role that the child plays in his own learning and the role of activity in that learning. "Knowledge is derived from action," he maintains. "To know an object is to act upon and to transform it. . . . To know is therefore to assimilate reality into structures of transformation, and these are the structures that intelligence constructs as a direct extension of our actions." [1]

Children learn more about books if they have an opportunity to interpret them in ways that are meaningful to them—through art or music activities, drama, talk, writing, or creating games. To act upon the book is to know it, to make it a memorable experience.

Just as children should be given a choice of books to read, so, too, should they be given a choice of various ways to interpret a book. Not all children should have to write a letter to the author or give an oral book report, or create a diorama. Many more options should be open to the child to find a satisfying way for him to share a book he has enjoyed. Children should also be allowed the option of *not* sharing their reading. Some stories or poems are too special, too personal to be shared. The child may want to savor them, to read them again and again in order to hold their thoughts close to him. A teacher should know the children in the class well enough to know what will help each student have memorable experiences with books. A teacher should encourage those activities that will enhance children's delight in books, make them want to read more and better books, and at the same time discourage any requirements, such as the weekly book report, that will make children actually dislike reading. The activities suggested in this chapter are planned to increase children's enjoyment and appreciation of books.

---

[1] Jean Piaget. *Science of Education and the Psychology of the Child* (New York: Orion, 1970), pp. 28–29.

Extending Literature through Art and Media

Exciting stories, sensitive descriptions of beauty, and vivid characterizations are the "stuff" of the creative environment that motivates children's responses in writing, creative dramatics, and art activities. Children of all ages should have the opportunity to express their feelings and reactions to books through varied art activities and media. Artistic interpretation requires the reader to evaluate the most exciting or interesting parts of the book and to select those details which seem vital and necessary, deleting those which are unimportant. To interpret a book through making a colláge, a mural, or a three-dimensional construction is a synthesizing process requiring much thought and selection. It may prove far more illuminating than the typical book report. More important is the fact that the child will have acted upon the book, becoming involved in interpreting it and making it a memorable experience for him.

FLAT PICTURES AND COLLÁGE

Too frequently, children are given crayons and manila paper and told to make a picture of any story they like. This vague direction, coupled with a lack of interesting and varied materials, will produce nothing but dull sterile pictures. Children must be "filled to overflowing" before they can create. They should have many materials, constantly and freely available to them—including chalk, paint, colored tissue papers, scrap materials, yarn, steel wool, buttons, clay, junk for construction work, and papier mâché. The teacher's role is to design a rich environment for creativity by providing materials and by challenging children's thinking. Librarians and teachers can help children think about their stories or poems by asking such focusing questions as:

What would be the most appropriate material for you to use for your picture?

What colors do you see when you think of this story?

How will you portray the main character? How old is he or she? What does he or she wear?

Where does the story take place? When did it take place? How will you convey the setting of this story?

How much time elapses in this tale? In what time of year does it take place?

What do you think is the most exciting, the funniest, the saddest incident?

Does the story make you think of anything in your life? (For example, do you have a secret hiding place as in *The Secret Garden* by Burnett or the poem "Keziah" by Brooks [from *Bronzeville Boys and Girls*])?

What do you think happened after the end of the story?

Children should be encouraged to go beyond the literal representation of a scene or character to create a new esthetic visual form. Wide variety, seen in the photograph of different interpretations of *Leopold the See-through Crumbpicker*, was produced by the availability of interesting material and the fact that the teacher interrupted the reading of this funny story by James Flora just at the point when Minerva started to paint Leopold in order to make him visible. The children's pictures reveal their highly imaginative interpretations. A similar approach could be used with *Lion* by DuBois or the story, *The Four Fur Feet* by Margaret Wise Brown, in which the reader sees only the little black feet of the animal who walks around the world. In Seidelman's story, *The 14th Dragon*, which is unfortunately out of print but still obtainable in libraries, thirteen artists have drawn or painted their conceptions of a dragon, inviting the reader to create the fourteenth one.

Experimentation with certain media is stimulated by some book illustrations. For example, in *The 14th Dragon* one of the dragons has been created by blowing on a blot of ink with a straw. After seeing *Swimmy* by Leo Lionni, one group of primary-grade children printed with lacepaper doilies and potato prints to create similar underwater effects. After sharing Keats' *The Snowy Day*, *Peter's Chair*, or *Hi, Cat!* children enjoyed making their own colláge pictures. *Jennie's Hat* by Keats suggests the use of ribbons, valentines, gift wrapping paper, and pictures of flowers from seed catalogues. In the filmed interview of Ezra Jack Keats by Weston Woods (*see* Chapter 10), he demonstrates how he makes the marbleized paper backgrounds for his book, *Dreams*, and the poetry book, *In a Spring Garden*, edited by Richard Lewis. Following the showing of the film,

Collàge and crayon were used by fourth-graders as they visualized *Leopold, The See-through Crumbpicker* by Flora. Evanston, Illinois Public Schools, Barbara Friedberg, teacher.

children will want to create their own marbleized paper. This is easily done by filling throw-away aluminum foil cake pans with water and then dropping oil-based paint (leftover cans of house paint) onto the water and stirring slightly with a stick to make interesting patterns. Place a piece of paper face down on the water and paint and gently lift it up. Acrylic paints are more expensive to use, but they also give more vibrant color to the marbleized paper. Be sure to have turpentine or paint cleaner in readiness to clean hands after this activity. Let the paper dry, and then it can be used for book-binding material or as background for cutout silhouettes as *In a Spring Garden* (Lewis), or as collàge material itself (*see Dreams* by Keats).

Children's appreciation for the amount of work involved in creating pictures for books would be increased if they had the opportunity to make their own scratchboard illustrations. Some of the best examples of scratchboard are seen in the illustrations that Frans Haacken did for *Peter and the Wolf* (Prokofieff) and those of Barbara Cooney for *The Little Juggler* and *Chanticleer and the Fox*. While the colors in these books are the result of using color separations during the printing process, children should crayon very heavily on cardboard, then apply India ink on top with a ball of cotton, allow this to dry, and use scissors or pins to scratch in a design. It is generally better to use a small piece of cardboard, as the scratching process can be tedious. For this reason, the technique is more appropriate for children 8 and older.

Middle-grade children also enjoy creating their own cardboard cuts. This technique has been used successfully by Blair Lent for his illustrations of *The Wave* (Hodges) and his own *John*

Seven-year-olds create a colláge interpretation of *Hi, Cat!* by Ezra Jack Keats. Notice the use of rich material.
Barrington Road School, Upper Arlington Public Schools, Ohio, Marlene Herbert, teacher.

Resplendent down to his blue-cellophane scales, a friendly dragon is constructed out of rolled newspapers, egg cartons, and papier mâché.
Susan Lee, graduate student, The Ohio State University.

Tabor's Ride. In this process the picture is built up by glueing pieces of cardboard, screening, or textured materials to a heavier piece of cardboard. Then, using a brayer and water-soluble printers' ink, children can make prints from their pictures. The end result resembles a linoleum block print, but the cardboard cut does not involve the use of sharp linoleum-cutting tools, which can be dangerous.

Prints can also be taken from styrofoam meat trays. Designs may easily be pressed in with a pencil or scissors. Water-soluble inks or tempera paints can be put on the design with a brayer and a print made.

CONSTRUCTION

Unless the teacher wants to give children the opportunity to work in the same medium as a book, it is frequently better to suggest that they use a different medium for their interpretations. For example, rather than draw some of the zany animals of Dr. Seuss, one group of 7-year-olds constructed their own "Seuss animals" out of boxes, paper tubes, cloth, buttons, and paint. A 9-year-old group wrote and illustrated their own book titled "On Beyond Dr. Seuss," which followed the idea established in *On Beyond Zebra.* They used scraps of various kinds of cloth to create their absurd animals, which included such characters as an "Elephant Goat."

A small group of 7- and 8-year-olds read books on dragons, including *The 14th Dragon, Mr. Drackle and His Dragons* by Froman, *The Dragon of an Ordinary Family* by Mahy, and *The Reluctant Dragon* by Grahame. Some of the children's dragons were made of egg cartons (the dividers make fine spiny backs) and papier mâché; while others were of pieces of wood, spools, and rope. Egg cartons can be cut apart and used to construct other animals. The penguins from the Atwaters' *Mr. Popper's Penguins* can be made from the individual dividers of egg cartons.

A group of primary-grade children read Blair Lent's *From King Boggen's Hall to Nothing-at-All,* which is an interesting collection of nursery rhymes about such strange and curious houses as a coal-scuttle house; a Jack-in-the-Pulpit house; and Peter, Peter's pumpkin house. The children then designed their own houses out of various kinds of materials. Some of their creations were big enough for them to crawl into, while others were only suitable for the house of a mouse.

Children also enjoy constructing their own special places to read. Following the reading of *Evan's Corner* by Hill, groups of 6- and 7-year-olds made their own special corners out of cardboard cartons. These had little doors and windows, pillows for comfortable reading, and signs on the doors. Older children have made special reading rooms out of old refrigerator boxes. The notion of having a quiet place for reading—whether it be a "cubbie" made from bookshelves (*see* second color section), a two-story book house, or a cardboard retreat—intrigues children and seems to increase their desire to read.

Children are fascinated with monsters and robots these days. One group of 8-year-olds created a huge monster out of discarded boxes, corrugated paper, mailing tubes, wooden clothespins, buttons, and other found objects. Detergent soap has to be added to tempera paint in order to make it adhere to the glossy surfaces of many cardboard boxes. Such stories as *The Judge* (Zemach), *Where the Wild Things Are* (Sendak), and *Monstrous Glisson Glop* (Massie) inspired the children's creation of their own monsters. Other books that lend themselves to box sculpture or construction might be *The Little House* by Burton, *You Look Ridiculous* by Waber, and *The Old Woman Who Lived in a Vinegar Bottle* by Godden.

DIORAMAS AND TABLE DISPLAYS

A diorama is a three-dimensional setting made by arranging objects or figures in front of a scenic background. Frequently used in museums to illustrate habitat groups, the technique can be adapted for children's illustration of scenes from literature. A large cardboard carton placed on one side can serve as a background for the setting. Clay or papier-mâché models or paper cutouts can be placed in the foreground. Lights can be added at the back. Plastic wrap, placed over the open side, will protect the scene. Children have constructed dioramas of such books as Heyward's *The Country Bunny and the Little Gold Shoes, The Old Woman Who Lived in a Vinegar Bottle* by

Following the reading of Blair Lent's *From King Boggen's Hall to Nothing at All,* primary-grade children construct their own unique houses. Notice the "mouse house" in the picture in the upper left-hand corner.

Martin Luther King, Jr., Laboratory School, Evanston, Illinois, JoAnn Wilkin, teacher. Photographed by Fred Wilkin.

Godden, and Wilder's *Little House in the Big Woods.* A sequence of events can be shown by dividing the diorama into two or more sections. For example, *The Little House* by Burton could be shown in the country and after the city "mushroomed" around it. One diorama built by a student who had enjoyed Norton's *The Borrowers* illustrated the materials "borrowed" by the tiny Clock family to furnish their home. The following description was used to create this diorama:

> Homily was proud of her sitting room: the walls had been papered with scraps of old letters out of wastepaper baskets, and Homily had arranged the handwriting sideways in vertical strips which ran from floor to ceiling. On the walls . . . hung several portraits of Queen Victoria as a girl; these were postage stamps, . . . a chest of drawers made of match boxes. There was a round table with a red velvet cloth, which Pod had made from the wooden bottom of a pill box supported on the carved pedestal of a knight from the chess set. . . . The floor of the sitting room was carpeted with deep red blotting paper. . .[2]

[2]Mary Norton. *The Borrowers,* illustrated by Beth Krush and Joe Krush (New York: Harcourt Brace Jovanovich, 1953), p. 15.

Older children enjoy constructing peep shows in shoe boxes. A miniature scene representing an incident or book setting is arranged in the box. Light can be admitted through a narrow opening cut across the box lid and covered with tissue paper. At the end of the box a peephole is cut for viewing the scene. *Beauty and the Beast*, or *Tom's Midnight Garden* by Pearce, *Mary Poppins* by Travers, and numerous other books can be interpreted in this way. Poems and nursery rhymes can also be represented by peep shows. "The Old Woman in the Shoe," Fyleman's "The Best Game the Fairies Play," and De la Mare's "The Old Stone House" are examples of poems that are suitable for this treatment.

Guessing boxes can be made by constructing a peep show and then covering the open side. Questions or words on the outside serve as clues to the title of the book. For "Book Week," peep shows may be numbered, but not titled. As children throughout the school view the displays, they can write titles on numbered sheets. Each child can check his responses against an answer sheet posted nearby.

Table scenes and models help children recall incidents in books; for example, the Pilgrim homes described by Meadowcroft's *The First Year* can be built in miniature. The schoolroom scene or "Ellen's room" in *Shaw's Fortune: The Picture Story of a Colonial Plantation* by Edwin Tunis would make excellent table scenes or models. A group of 7-year-olds arranged figures for the scene from McCloskey's *Make Way for Ducklings*, depicting the swan boats on the pond in the Boston Public Garden. Michael, the policeman, was shown blowing his whistle as Mrs. Mallard and her ducklings crossed Beacon Street.

One group of 8-year-olds made papier mâché whales, while several others made models of the good ship *Rodent* as described in the humorous fable, *Amos and Boris* by William Steig. *The Enormous Egg* (Butterworth) was also made by shaping papier mâché over an inflated balloon. When it was cut open, the figures of Nate Twitchell and his famous dinosaur were placed inside of it.

In creating dioramas and table displays every part should be made by children. Commercial figurines or objects tend to cheapen the display and certainly lessen the involvement of children. The actual exhibit is not nearly as important as

Dioramas that illustrate two popular children's books.

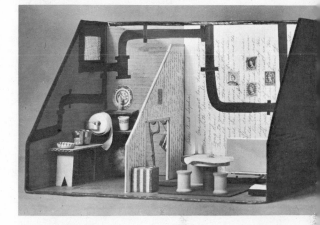

The Borrowers' kitchen and living room are illustrated in a diorama that shows the pipes, wallpaper made from a letter, postage-stamp pictures, bottlecap dishes, thimble pails, gauze hand towels, half of a manicure scissors used to cut raw potato, and a supply of pins used by Pod for climbing.

Constructed by Phyllis Morales, student, The Ohio State University.

The use of natural materials is appropriate for a diorama of *My Side of the Mountain* by Jean George.

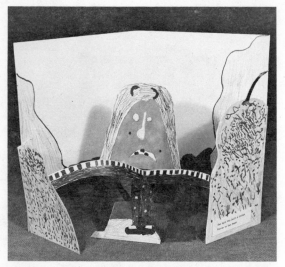

A pop-up picture of the Japanese folk tale, "The Ogre Who Built the Bridge," makes an interesting table display.

Dan Pazak, student, Annehurst School, Westerville, Ohio, Cathy Hart, media specialist.

the process of making it and its effect on children's understanding and interest in books.

TIME LINES AND MAPS

Time concepts are difficult for children to grasp until sometime near the end of the concrete-operational stage of thinking or the beginning of formal operations (ages 9–11). During this time of consolidation it may be helpful for them to prepare a calendar of the major events of one person's life. Some boys and girls enjoy making a time-line with real string or twine from which descriptive markers may be strung. This activity is particularly appropriate in conjunction with biography or books of historical fiction.

Children can construct a chart of the major world events occurring during the lifetime of one person. This might be motivated by reading any of Genevieve Foster's *The World of* _____ books. A chart might be made, for example, for the lifetime of Benjamin Franklin. Major events can be indicated by single years or decades. Another approach would be to focus on the events of a particular year. Again, following the model presented by Genevieve Foster in her "year" books (see *Year of the Pilgrims: 1620*), all of the events of the American Revolution of 1776 might be presented on a time line.

A similar kind of composite time-line can be devised for a group of leaders who lived during the same period. Taking 1700–1800, it would be interesting to mark the lives of various Revolutionary War leaders. Children could see that Benjamin Franklin was 26 years old when George Washington was born; but that he died only nine years before Washington died. Who else lived during this time? How old were they when the Revolution began? Such a time-line might be developed into a mural with representative pictures for each leader.

Children can also be encouraged to construct maps of the setting or action of particular books. Seven- and 8-year-olds could construct a pictorial map of the action in *One Fine Day* by Hogrogian. Starting in the forest, they could depict the various encounters of the fox, including his meeting with the old woman, a cow; his request to the field for grass; his plea to the stream for water; his meetings with the fair maiden, the peddler, the hen, the miller; and his eventual return to the old woman who then sewed his tail in place! The various trips that Johnny made to try to lose his pet, *The Biggest Bear* (Ward), could also be charted on a map. Even *Rosie's Walk* (Hutchins) could be depicted on a map of the barnyard.

Children can illustrate the many settings for the series of *Little House* books by Laura Ingalls Wilder on an actual map of the United States. A map of the regional stories of this country could be made; or the various settings for such tall tales as Paul Bunyan, Pecos Bill, John Henry, or Mike Fink (*see* "Chart of Tall-tale Heroes," Chapter 4) could be located. Similarly, a map of the many folk tales of the world could be created, showing the origins of such characters as Cinderella, The Three Billy Goats Gruff, Vasilisa, Anansi, Monotaro, Glooscap, Tony Di Moany, Kantjil, and many others (*see* "Chart on Cross-cultural Study of Folk Tales," Chapter 4).

Maps for such famous "countries of the mind" as Prydain, Earthsea, and Narnia would be intriguing to devise. *Journey Outside* by Mary Steele also suggests interesting possibilities for mapping, beginning with Dilar's journey from the underground river of the Raft People.

The value of mapping the action of story settings is that it sends the reader back to the book for sequence and verification. It helps the child to visualize the action of the story. Mapping

"Folk Tales of the World" or "Regional Stories" helps the student see and appreciate the cultural diversity of literature.

MURALS

Theme, characters, and settings of favorite books may provide the impetus for the creation of cooperatively planned murals. After selecting the theme, the children and teacher should discuss the scenes or characters to be portrayed in the mural. Each child may make a sketch of one part, or small groups may meet to plan one section. These preliminary drawings may be fastened to the chalkboard with masking tape or pinned to the bulletin board so that they can be easily moved as children plan the total effect of the mural. Help children see that the overlapping of some figures gives depth to the mural.

A variety of material can be used for murals. Crayon drawings may be cut out, pinned in place, and then glued or stapled to a large sheet of wrapping paper. This type of assembled mural is made easily and quickly. Chalk or tempera paint is effective in creating large murals. Older children may enjoy using small bits of paper to produce a mosaic design. A mural of paper sculpture creates an interesting three-dimensional effect when the figures or objects are fastened to the mural with small wads of masking tape. Two-sided figures may be stuffed with

Eight-year-olds interpret Steig's *Amos and Boris* through pictures, poetry, models of the ship *Rodent,* and papier mâché whales.

Barrington Road School, Upper Arlington Public Schools, Ohio, Carolyn Fahrbach, teacher. Photographed by Roy Wilson.

The Enormous Egg was made by shaping papier mâché over an inflated balloon. The figures of Nate Twitchell and his famous dinosaur were placed inside.

newspapers and stapled together before being attached to the mural. One group of 6- and 7-year-olds depicted McCloskey's story, *Make Way for Ducklings*. The ducks stood out beautifully as they tried to cross the streets of Boston. Chalk, paint, crayon, and other materials may also be combined in making murals. A colláge mural can be made of yarn, various scraps of papers, seeds, twigs, cloth, bits of sponge for trees, wire, ribbons, and so forth.

Planning these murals provides the children with the opportunity for discussing themes, characters, types of illustrations, and kinds of books. Through such discussions, children grow in their appreciation of literature and in their ability to solve problems of construction and organization.

The events in one story may be illustrated in a mural. Children in kindergarten can easily make a mural of *The Three Bears* (Galdone). A group of 6-, 7-, and 8-year-olds made a series of five large murals to illustrate Browning's well-known poem, "The Pied Piper of Hamelin." The first picture showed the townspeople, and the second depicted the objectionable rats. The third one showed the mayor making the agreement with the piper; the fourth pictured the piper and the children; while the last one showed "The Joyous Land" where the piper had promised to take them. Done with colláge materials and shiny bits of foil mosaic for the joyous land, these were outstanding pictures. The effect was of a continuous picture.

A mural might also represent a synthesis of children's favorite characters in animal fantasy, including Charlotte, Wilbur, and Templeton; Winnie the Pooh and his friends; Stuart Little; Louis and his trumpet; Chester, the cricket who finds himself in Times Square with Harry the Cat and Tucker the Mouse; Walter, the Lazy Mouse; and those famous friends of the English countryside, Mr. Toad, Mole, Rat, and Badger. The identification of their favorite character would be revealing of the students' previous backgrounds in literature.

A study of fables might inspire children to create a mural depicting their favorites. They could write the morals in balloon blurbs, similar to the pictures made by the Provensens for *Aesop's Fables* (edited by Untermeyer; *see* illustration on p. 215). Another group made a colláge mural of their favorite characters from folk tales,

Fifth-graders painted a mural of the fearsome tropical island of the man-eaters and captured an exciting moment in *Call It Courage*.

Bexley, Ohio, Public Schools, Cornelia Downs, teacher.

including *Anansi the Spider* (McDermott); *Zomo the Rabbit* (Sturton); *The Crane Maiden* (Matsutani); *The Five Chinese Brothers* (Bishop); "The Bremen Town Musicians," "The Frog Prince," and "Rumpelstiltskin" (Grimm); *Jack and the Beanstalk* (Stobbs); and others. The synthesizing of various stories or even nursery rhymes is a more challenging task than the mere representation of a single story (*see* "Chart on Levels and Types of Questions," Chapter 12).

CONSTRUCTING BOX MOVIES

A simple box movie may be constructed by attaching dowel rods or pieces of broom handles for rollers at either side of a suit box, carton, or wooden fruit box. An old window shade or a strip of shelf paper can be used for the children's illustrations of the sequence of events in the story. Each end of the strip is fastened to a roller. One child rolls the paper by turning the rod as the narrator relates the story. If window shades are not available, edging shelf paper with masking tape will make the "film strip" more durable.

If children have made individual pictures of certain scenes, it is a good idea to mount them on the window shade or roller sheet of paper and then secure their edges with masking tape. This prevents the pictures from tearing or catching on the roller. It is easier for a group of children to work on a box movie if the scenes are rolled from side to side rather than from top to bottom. In making a horizontal movie the entire roller may be pinned to a bulletin board or taped to the chalkboard and several children can work at once. Remember, the first picture or frame should be placed farthest to the right, the next scene following on the left in reverse order. For example, assuming the children had drawn ten scenes, they should be glued and taped to the roller strip in countdown fashion, beginning at the left (Scene 10, 9, 8, 7, 6, 5, 4, 3, 2, 1). Then the series can be rolled from left to right in proper order for viewing. Children need to remember this if they are drawing directly on the roller sheet.

The same principle can be carried out with older children who wish to make individual "movies." Drawings or pictures in a series can be made on a strip of adding-machine tape and pulled through slits cut in a heavy paper envelope.

Some good stories for box movies for primary-grade children include Sendak's *Pierre*, Flack's *Ask Mr. Bear*, *One Fine Day* by Hogrogian, and any of the folktales—such as "Jack and the Beanstalk," "The Three Billy Goats Gruff," and some of the Anansi stories. Older children can depict such myths as the stories of Icarus, Pegasus, Demeter and Persephone, Maui, or Thor and his hammer. Tall tales also lend themselves well to sequencing for a box movie.

FLANNELBOARD STORIES

After the teacher presents a flannelboard story, children often love to create their own. Small groups can plan and construct figures to portray the story. If the number of children in a group is limited to three or four, the storytellers will not block the view of the audience, and each child can present his own character.

Stories may also be taped, leaving the children free to manipulate their figures. However, some of the spontaneity for the telling is lost in this process.

Young children love to retell their favorite folk tales, such as *The Three Bears* or *The Three Little Pigs* (Galdone). Some of Leo Lionni's stories—such as *Little Blue and Little Yellow* or *Frederick*—can be adapted for retelling as flannelboard stories. An 8-year-old boy easily held the attention of his classmates as he related the story of *The Five Chinese Brothers* by Bishop, and manipulated the figures on the flannelboard. Another student had a wonderful time showing *Impossible, Possum* by Conford on a flannelboard. This is the story of Randolph, who cannot hang from his tail as other possums do, and must use sticky sap from the tree as glue. When the sap dries up, his sister tricks him by giving him water and telling him it is sap. Then Randolph realizes that he has at last learned to hang by his tail. The girl pictured in the photograph on page 656 is entertaining a group of 6-year-olds with the old folk tale adapted by Hirsh, *Could Anything Be Worse?*. (*See* Chapter 12 for a list of titles that are particularly suited to telling as flannelboard stories.)

Some informational books can be portrayed graphically using a flannelboard. The animals that live in *The Hole in the Tree* by George could be drawn and placed on the flannelboard to present information about their habits. Stories with

An older child has made a felt story of Hirsh's *Could Anything Be Worse?*, which she shares with a group of primary-grade children.

Worthington Hills School, Worthington, Ohio, Mary Karrer, Librarian.

an ecological theme—such as *The Last Free Bird* by A. Harris Stone or *The Mountain* by Peter Parnall—can also be depicted on a flannelboard.

Children develop language skills as they tell stories using the feltboard or flannelboard. A shy child may tell a felt story with confidence because attention is focused upon the figures he manipulates, and these tangibles help him to recall the sequence of events.

BULLETIN BOARDS

Children should have the opportunity to plan their own bulletin-board displays depicting their favorite books. Their paintings, colláges, and murals will be shown in the classroom where literature is used to widen and deepen interests and understandings. But a bulletin board placed in the hall or library can be seen by the whole school.

A "participation" bulletin board is fun to create, and provides a kind of game activity for all. For example, a group of 9-year-olds drew and mounted pictures of their favorite book characters. Brief descriptions were written on cards and placed in an envelope pocket at the lower right-hand corner of the bulletin board. The cards contained such statements as: "I started a dough-nut machine and couldn't get it stopped." "I wanted the moon to wear on a chain around my neck." "My tail was used as a bell-pull." When a child played the game, he fastened the correct statement card beside the matching picture. The teacher or a member of the group that made the display checked his responses before the cards were returned to the envelope for the next player.

Story sequences can also be utilized for a participation bulletin board. Pictures can be matched to written descriptions numbered in order. Children may arrange pictures illustrating events in the proper order, or they may arrange both caption and picture according to sequence. Such activities help children become more aware of plot development. For example, events in *Journey Cake, Ho!* by Sawyer were illustrated by a group of 6-year-olds. Mounted on oak tag, the pictures were stacked in random order on a shelf near the bulletin board. During work time a child could choose to arrange the pictures in sequential order on the bulletin board.

Children may also participate in the planning and arranging of special bulletin boards. Books for seasons of the year; books related to certain subjects, such as sports stories, or books written by one author can form the theme. One group of 11-year-olds designed a "haunted house" display of mystery stories. Children who are studying their state may make an outline map of yarn and place appropriate book jackets around it. Some third-graders in one school displayed their favorite animal stories under the caption "Tales of Tails." Seasonal themes may be utilized for literature bulletin boards. For example, "A Fall of Favorites," might show leaves and acorns with appropriate book titles. The caption, "Right Down Your Line" could be illustrated by favorite book jackets strung on a clothes line. Children will enjoy thinking of other intriguing possibilities. Bulletin-board space should also be provided for children's advertisements and recommendations of favorite books.

MOBILES

To make a mobile, cutouts or objects representing a book theme or characters are balanced and suspended on thread or fine wire attached to rods. The objects or figures must be hung so that they move freely. Wire coat hangers can be cut with tin shears or pliers for the balancing rods. Black thread, attached to each end with airplane glue, will suspend the next figure or rod. Very simple mobiles can be made by hanging objects from the cut branch of a tree or from a coat hanger. Since mobiles turn freely, the figures should be painted on both sides. If figures are drawn and cut out of oak-tag paper and then painted with "dope" (airplane modeling paint), they will be bright and durable.

Individuals or groups of three or four children can plan a mobile. Guidance by the teacher or librarian is essential in developing appreciation of literature, as boys and girls participate in this activity. The values of children's creative efforts in planning and constructing *their own* mobiles far

Real objects can be used in a mobile. Authentic Pennsylvania Dutch designs were painted on egg shells to illustrate *The Egg Tree* by Milhous.

Constructed by Barbara Glancy, student, The Ohio State University.

outweigh the artistic effect of those produced commercially.

Almost any story may be represented by a mobile, but one that seems particularly well-suited is *Attic of the Wind* by Lund. This is a poetic tale of all the things that are blown away, only to be discovered in the "attic of the wind." Children can make a mobile of feathers, balloons, old letters, and hats that they think might be found in the "attic of the wind." A group of children interested in creating "found poetry" (*see* Chapter 6) could make a "found objects" mobile. Using the book *See What I Found* by Livingston, children could display their own collections, which might include keys, pebbles, buttons, and so on. After making their mobiles of "found objects," they could describe them using Myra Cohn Livingston's book as a model.

Individual nursery rhymes—such as the "Old Woman Who Lived in the Shoe" or "Little Bo Peep"—make interesting mobiles. Favorite animal characters or fantasy characters can form the theme of a mobile. Using the books of one author or illustrator is another way of creating a mobile.

As children consider themes of books and poems and ways to symbolize them for a mobile, they are extending their understandings of the meaning and significance of those stories and poems. Not all children will want to make mobiles, nor should they have to do so. No teacher wants her room to look like a mobile jungle! Children should always have the option of interpreting their reading in a variety of ways.

CREATING SLIDES AND FILMSTRIPS

Slides

Children enjoy retelling a story by way of a series of slides that they have made. Since slides are only 2″ × 2″, they require very small drawings similar to the squares of favorite cartoons. This accounts for some of the appeal of making slides, but it does limit the activity to children above 8 who can do such fine work.

By using a ditto sheet of 2″ × 2″ boxes, children can plan and draw their slides, first deter-

mining just how many slides they will need to convey the sequence of the story. Unnecessary pictures can be crossed off on the master sheet or story board. When the child is satisfied with his series, he then places a black image positive transparency over the dittoed planning sheet and runs it through a thermofax machine. He may decide to make his slides in black and white or to color them. Permanent-colored marking pens provide a good source of color. The final step in the process is to cut out the slides and mount them into 2″ × 2″ ready-mount frames. The child may tell the story as the pictures are projected, or he may tape record the story. Complete directions for this process follow:

SLIDE-MAKING

1. Make a ditto of a series of 2″ × 2″ boxes. Let your children use several sheets to plan their pictures. On the final drawings, be sure that your children use a *lead* pencil and outline *everything* they want to have show up, including the frame of the picture.

2. Using a black image positive transparency (3 M Co.) run the ditto and the transparency through a thermofax machine. This process transfers the image from the ditto to the transparency.

3. Children may then use permanent colored marking pens to complete their illustrations. One particularly well lasting and bright brand

Creating
the Learning
Environment

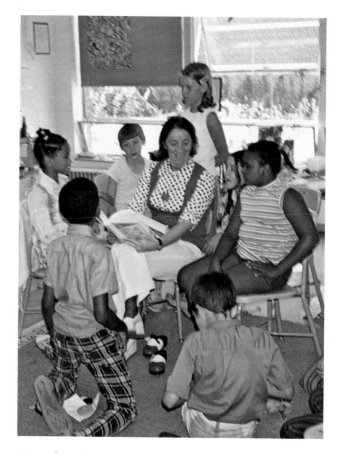

A teacher shares poetry with a small group of children.
Ohio State University Workshop, Moler School, Columbus, Ohio.
Barbara Friedberg, teacher.

A quiet comfortable place to read.
Ohio State University Workshop, Moler School, Columbus, Ohio. Joetta Beaver, teacher.

An inviting reading center at the end of the corridor in an old school.
Brunswick Park School, London, England. Wendla Kernig, Headmistress.

Boys share their excitement about a book.
Ohio State University Workshop. Gay Dunn, teacher.

Six- and -7 -year-olds made and decorated their own "Book Cubbies."
Martin Luther King, Jr., Laboratory School, Evanston, Illinois. JoAnn Wilkins, teacher.

Children Interpret Books Through Art Activities

Three children made rich use of material in this felt wall-hanging of the *Light Princess*. Hillside Public Library, New Hyde Park, New York. Marcia Posner, librarian.

Six-year-olds created their own twelve-headed trolls in a chalk mural following the reading of the *D'Aulaire's Trolls*.

Avondale Elementary School, Columbus, Ohio. Charlane Ellis, teacher.

Eight-, 9-, and 10-year-olds extend their knowledge of mythology by creating stories and pictures of their own mythological creatures.

Martin Luther King, Jr., Laboratory School, Evanston, Illinois. Barbara Friedberg, teacher.

An 8-year-old's interpretation of "You Look Ridiculous," Said the Rhinoceros to the Hippopotamus by Bernard Waber.

Columbus Summer School, Columbus, Ohio. Marilyn Parker, teacher.

A 9-year-old boy's papier-mâché interpretation of *Leopold, The See-through Crumb Picker* by James Flora.

London City Public Schools, London, Ohio. Laura P. Weisel, teacher.

A 9-year-old girl made an exquisite colláge of Anansi using colored tissue paper, felt, and yarn.

Martin Luther King, Jr., Laboratory School, Evanston, Illinois. Barbara Friedberg, teacher.

Moptop

Moptop likes his hair like a mop, because he said it look pretty. Moptop's Mother said, "You need a haircut. Then he went to get a haircut. Then his birthday came. The kids said, "Your hair looks good, Moptop

Through Art and Written Language

A 6-year-old boy retells Freeman's story of *Mop Top* in his own words and picture. Kent School, Columbus, Ohio. Elise Schilder, teacher.

After many experiences with folk tales, 8-year-olds created their own stories and colláges.

Greensview School, Upper Arlington, Ohio. Susan Lee, teacher.

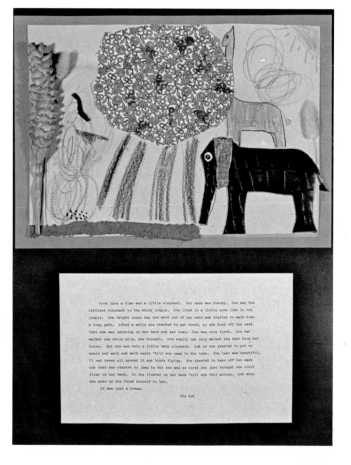

Through Oral Activities

Paper-bag puppets provide an opportunity for telling the story of *Pippi Longstocking.* Ohio State University Workshop. Barbara Friedberg, teacher.

A group of 7-year-olds dance "The Wild Rumpus" after hearing Sendak's *Where the Wild Things Are.*   West Lafayette Public Schools, Indiana. Nancy Sawrey, teacher.

is Staedtler Lumocolor #317 permanent, available at art supply stores.

4. After the illustrations are completed and cut to the 2″ × 2″ size, they may be fastened into a slide frame (Kodak Ready Mount B 207, 2″ × 2″, 100/box . . . at camera stores). Once the slide is in position, it may be held securely with scotch or masking tape on the three open sides.

Almost any story is appropriate for a slide presentation. Some that seem particularly well-suited are the well-known folk tales, "Cinderella"; "The Little Red Hen"; some of the Anansi tales; *The Turnip* (Domanska); and such modern tales as *Petunia* (Duvoisin); *Harry, the Dirty Dog* (Zion); *The Camel Who Took a Walk* (Tworkov); and longer tales—such as *James and the Giant Peach* (Dahl); some of the escapades of *The Mouse and the Motorcycle* (Cleary); and that lovable resident of London, *A Bear Called Paddington* (Bond).

Other ways to make slides include photographing them. Younger children's pictures may be photographed and made into a slide show. Older children could illustrate their favorite poems by taking appropriate photos. This requires them to think through the theme of the poem and demands a high level of ability to take effective pictures. For those schools that have a 35mm. camera for the use of children, such an activity would be very worthwhile and would extend children's interest in both poetry and photography.

Another way to make slides is to lift an image from a color or black-and-white picture on clay-coated paper. The steps involved in this process are:

MAKING SLIDES FROM MAGAZINE PICTURES

Materials

Clear contact paper (available from hardware and housewares stores).
2″ × 2″ color transparency frame
Magazines with slick, colored pictures (clay base)
Small pan of water; drop of liquid detergent
Iron
Spoon
Clear plastic spray

Procedures

Pull contact paper from its adhesive backing
Apply contact paper to 2″ × 2″ clay-base picture
Rub contact paper with spoon over entire picture, making sure there are no air bubbles
Cut out
Place in warm soapy water and in 2 or 3 minutes peel off the back and let transparency dry
Place between slide frames
Iron just the edges of the frame closed
May be sprayed with plastic spray

Since it is difficult to find such very small pictures, children can create a mood with different colors and textures without using an actual picture. Magazines that provide successful picture transfers include *National Geographic, Saturday Review, Better Homes and Gardens, Newsweek, Sports Illustrated,* and others.

Filmstrips

Children enjoy creating stories on old filmstrips. Take any filmstrip that is about to be discarded and recycle it by dipping it in a small pan of bleach, such as Clorox. This removes the emulsion and makes the strip blank. The filmstrip should then be washed under clear water and dried with a soft cloth. It can be clamped to a clothes line overnight to be sure it is dry. Children can then draw their own pictures, using every four sprocket holes as one frame. They may write their caption in the next frame. They do need to allow for a "leader" at the beginning and end of their stories. Temporary filmstrips may be made using non-permanent magic markers, typewriters, and in some cases pen or pencil. These may be made permanent by spraying the strip with a plastic spray. Permanent marking pens, acrylic inks, and paints may be used with care. If spilled, the spots cannot be removed.

Children can also create a series of pictures and captions and then take photographs of these with a 35 mm. camera. A normal thirty-six-exposure roll of 35 mm. film can result in a strip of thirty double frames or sixty-six single frames, leaving a few frames for leader and trailer.

Filmstrips have the advantage of being compact and easily handled. They are always in sequence. Slides, however, give more flexibility in arrangement and are more easily made. The creation of both media fascinates children.

FILM-MAKING

Increasingly, children are being given the opportunity to create their own films. Some of the most successful ones for elementary-school students involve the creation of an animated film from their own paintings and drawings. A detailed description of this approach is given in Yvonne Andersen's informative book, *Making Your Own Animated Movies.* In this book the au-

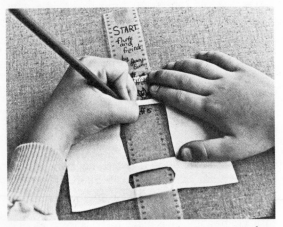

A child creates his own filmstrip by using a mask to guide the spacing.

With permission of the Institute for Development of Educational Activities, Inc., an affiliate of the Charles F. Kettering Foundation, Dayton, Ohio.

thor describes working with children from 5 to 18 years in creating films. Another useful book is *Making Your Own Movies* by Harry Helfman. This author gives some hints on how to operate a simple, inexpensive movie camera and presents some basic techniques for shooting a film. A description of panning a picture book is given, along with ways to vary the length of the shot.

Movie-making is not easy but it does offer a real challenge to children from age 8 and up. It should be done under the direction of a knowledgeable teacher or media specialist.

Extending Literature through Sewing and Cooking

CREATIVE STITCHERY AND WALL HANGINGS

"Creative stitchery" is a very old form of art that has recently been revived. Once children have learned some simple basic stitches they may want to create scenes or characters from their favorite books. Virginia Lee Burton's *The Little House* could be depicted during four seasons. A map of the settings for the Wilder books might be done on burlap in outline stitch. Boys and girls who are studying a unit on the pioneers might want to make samplers of their own. Storybook quilts could also be created. Certainly, there are many possibilities of ways to extend children's interest in books through creative stitchery.

Wall hangings may be sewn, or figures may be ironed or glued on to the cloth. Scenes from *Charlotte's Web* by White are always favorite children's topics. Animals or characters may be padded with strips of cloth or pieces of foam rubber before they are sewn to the background. This gives them a slightly rounded, three-dimensional look. Varied materials, such as old sheets and colored or natural burlap, can be used as background for figures and objects that represent book characters, titles, books by one author, poetry, or Mother Goose rhymes. Felt, pieces of printed cotton, buttons, rickrack, lace, sequins, and found objects should be available for making the figures and scenery. The wall hanging of *The Light Princess* by MacDonald that is pictured in the second color section was created by three children of various ages. They each made scenes from the story on squares of dark blue denim,

Children's wall hangings of their favorite books, depicting Rabbit from *Winnie the Pooh* and the two worlds of Narnia as portrayed in *The Lion, the Witch and the Wardrobe*.
Martin Luther King, Jr., Laboratory School, Evanston, Illinois, Barbara Friedberg, teacher.

and then the librarian sewed the squares together. A close look at this wall hanging shows a rich use of sequins, buttons, ribbons, and felt. When the hanging is finished a dowel rod, flat stick, or hanger can serve to support the hanging.

Other sewing activities might include making pillows with favorite characters on them for the reading center. One group of 9-year-olds designed a Winnie the Pooh rug and then hooked it. They liked it so much that it was decided to hang it rather than use it as a rug. Another group of 9-year-olds each made tiny book characters out of felt for Christmas tree ornaments. These included Frederick, Winnie the Pooh, the Three Little Pigs, Petunia, and Charlotte and Wilbur. The figures were proudly displayed on their literary tree.

DOLLS

It is far better for children to create their own figures for dioramas and displays than to use commercial toys. Small figures may be made from pipe cleaners, clothespins, or modeled in clay; larger dolls can be made from socks. Char-

acters from books should be portrayed authentically.

Children also enjoy making animal dolls—such as characters from *Winnie the Pooh* by Milne, *The Cricket in Times Square* by Selden, or *The Wind in the Willows* by Grahame. The well-loved story of *The Velveteen Rabbit* by Williams suggests the creation of dolls, as does that sprightly New England tale of *Miss Hickory* by Bailey. One class of 9-year-olds created Miss Hickory out of twigs and also made her corncob house. Children will suggest other storybook characters that might make interesting dolls.

COOKING

Teachers have once again recognized the many values inherent in cooking in the classroom—the math concepts of measuring, the reading skills involved in following a recipe exactly, the social skills of working cooperatively, not to mention children's delight in really making something good for everyone to share. Literature may be enriched through cooking. *The Pooh Cook Book* by Virginia Ellison includes many recipes—such as

The figure of Karana was made of a stocking body with clay head and limbs. This authentic doll combined interest in reading and doll-making.

"Haycorn Squash," "Cottleston Pie," and "Hipy Papy Bthuthdth Thuthda Bthuthday Cake"—which would add to the enjoyment of the Winnie the Pooh stories and might even suggest a Pooh Party to the class.

Young children, after hearing the story of *Bread and Jam for Frances* (Hoban), could make bread-and-jam sandwiches for a surprise party for another class. Then, while they were eating the sandwiches, someone might read or tell that particular "Frances" story. Other children, hearing the story of *Sam* (Scott), said they had never eaten raspberry tarts. The next day their teacher brought in a recipe and the ingredients, and they made enough so that everyone could have a tart for lunch.

Middle-grade children who were studying the life of George Washington Carver experimented with making peanut butter in a blender. A group of 10-year-olds became very excited about trying some of the recipes in *My Side of the Mountain* by Jean George. They found they could boil water in a skunk cabbage leaf, and that it is possible to make flour from acorns. They even made acorn pancakes. Since Jean George is a well-known naturalist, and has attested to the accuracy of the recipes given in her book, it seemed safe to try some of them. Certainly, the experiments enriched children's appreciation of the book, and those who had not read *My Side of the Mountain* promptly did so.

Two 9-year-old girls made a box of chocolate turtles, which they gave to their class to eat while one of them read aloud Chapter 10, "Dribble" from *Tales of a Fourth Grade Nothing* by Blume. This is a very funny episode in which Fudge eats his older brother's pet turtle!

Another group of middle-graders cooked home-made doughnuts in preparation for a "Homer Price Party" that they gave for the rest of the middle-grade classes. They had scheduled the Weston Woods film, "The Doughnuts," based on McCloskey's *Homer Price,* and gave out their doughnuts at the end of the showing.

An activity that involves both cooking and art is the making of baking-dough model figures. A group of 10-year-olds used the following recipe to model their favorite storybook characters in order to decorate a literary Christmas tree for the library media center:

BAKING-DOUGH MODELED FIGURES

Mix 4 cups flour with 1 cup of salt.
Add approximately 1½ cups warm water.
Food coloring may be added.
Knead thoroughly for 5 minutes or until it is smooth.
Model on aluminum foil.
Make flat or standing figures, using toothpicks, wires, or pipe cleaners to attach small parts.
Insert a circle of wire or string for hanger.
Moisten slightly when sticking small pieces together.
Put foil on baking sheet and bake for one hour at 350°.
If dough is left white, figures may be painted after baking with model enamel. (However, the natural look of cookie dough with no coloring or paint is very attractive.)
Store leftover dough in a plastic bag in an airtight container; this clay will keep a long time.

Children using the dough made well-known nursery-rhyme figures—such as the Old Woman in the Shoe, Jack Sprat and his wife, Humpty Dumpty; folk tale characters—including the

Favorite storybook characters are modeled out of baking dough.

Students in EPIC (Educational Programs for Informal Classrooms), The Ohio State University.

Three Pigs, the Musicians of Bremen; and such well-known characters as Peter Rabbit, the monsters from *Where the Wild Things Are*, and Frederick.

Once cooking and making characters from play dough has been initiated, children will be quick to think of other "party situations" which may call for these activities. They might plan the kind of a party *Pippi Longstocking* (Lindgren) or *Amelia Bedelia* (Parish) would give. Certainly, both would be unconventional and stretch children's imaginations. Response to books may take as many forms as creative teachers and children can devise.

Extending Literature through Music and Movement

PICTURE-BOOK EDITIONS OF SINGLE SONGS

In recent years there has been an increasing number of fine picture-book interpretations of single songs. These include the well-known Caldecott Honor Books, such as Spier's beautifully illustrated *The Fox Went Out on a Chilly Night* and the Emberleys' *One Wide River to Cross*. Unfortunately, the music is not provided for the picture interpretations of *Mommy, Buy Me a China Doll* by the Zemachs and *Waltzing Matilda*, the well-known Australian song illustrated by A. B. Paterson. Children thoroughly enjoy the silly cumulative Ozark tale of how Eliza Lou suggests ways her family can obtain money in order to buy her a doll. Teachers or children might compose their own song to go along with the rhythm of the text. Fortunately, the tune to *Waltzing Matilda* is well-known and so perhaps not needed for the book. The pictures do help to explain the meaning of such Australian terms as "Swagman," "Billabong," and "Jumbuck." A resourceful Aunt Rhody makes good use of the dead goose in the spirited folk song *Go Tell Aunt Rhody*. Charming pictures by Aliki add much to the humor of this American folk song. The music is included. New verses were created by children for one of their favorite songs, *Oh, A-Hunting We Will Go*. John Langstaff selected some of the most popular verses, such as "We'll catch a bear/and put him in underwear," and incorporated them into a book under the song's title. Nancy Parker drew the amusing pictures. Children will be sure to want to create their own additions to this song when they hear these verses.

Students may want to identify their favorite songs or carols and make picture books for them. The Bicentennial would suggest illustrating "Yankee Doodle," "America," or "Home on the Range." Peter Spier's authentic and exciting pictures for *The Star Spangled Banner* or *The Erie Canal* might serve as fine examples. Certainly, literature, art, and music would be served by this activity.

FINDING BACKGROUND MUSIC

The process of identifying appropriate background music for prose selections and poetry would help children appreciate the mood and changes in mood in books. A second-grade group discussed the kind of music that would portray the action of *Where the Wild Things Are* by Sendak. They recognized the increasing tempo and volume, and the quiet conclusion of the story. Older children might enjoy reading De la Mare's poem "Silver" or Tennyson's "The Charge of the Light Brigade" to music of their own choosing. One middle-grade child appropriately chose the music of Blood, Sweat, and Tears' "Variations on a Theme" by Eric Satic to provide the background for his taping of the poem "Loneliness" by Brooks Jenkins in *Reflections on a Gift of a Watermelon Pickle* (Dunning). Selecting such background music requires real sensitivity to the tone of the poem as well as a knowledge of music. Other suggestions were given in Chapter 6, "Poetry."

COMPOSING MUSIC

Poetry may be set to music as children create melody and identify the rhythmical elements. One group of talented 7-year-olds wrote their own sad tale of a princess who was captured during a battle and taken from her palace. Her knight-in-arms wandered the lonely countryside in search of her, while the poor princess grieved in her prison tower for him. The children made up a theme for each of the main characters, which they repeated during the various movements of their composition. The story was first told to their classmates and then the song was played on the autoharp and Glockenspiel.

Literature can be the inspiration for children's composition of songs. Both literature and children's appreciation for music will be enriched in the process.

MOVEMENT AND LITERATURE

Increasing attention has been given to a child's thinking control over his own body movements. The relationship between thought and movement has received much attention, particularly in England. Basic rhythmical movements might be introduced through Mother Goose rhymes. For example, children could walk to "Tommy Snooks and Bessie Brooks," gallop to "Ride a Cock Horse," jump to "Jack Be Nimble," and run to "Wee Willie Winkie." Nursery rhymes could also motivate dramatic action with such verses as "Hickory Dickory Dock," "Three Blind Mice," and "Jack and Jill."

As children learn basic movements, they can use them in different areas of space, at different levels, and at different tempos. Swinging, bending, stretching, twisting, bouncing, and shaking are the kinds of body movements that may be made by standing tall, at a middle position, or by stooping low. For example, "A Swing Song" by Allingham could be interpreted by swinging, pushing motions that vary in speed according to

the words in the poem. Other poetry that suggests movement includes "The Merry-Go-Round" by Baruch, "The Giant Shoes" by Fallis, "The African Dance" by Hughes, and "The Potatoes' Dance" by Lindsay.

Children who have had this kind of experience are ready to create a rhythmical interpretation of a longer story. *May I Bring a Friend?* by De Regniers, *Where the Wild Things Are* by Sendak, *The Moon Jumpers* by Udry, and *Ma nDA La* by Adoff are all examples of books that are appropriate for rhythmic activity.

Extending Literature through Drama

FORMS OF DRAMA

Books become more real to children as they identify with the characters through creative drama. Young children begin this identification with others through dramatic play. A 5-year-old engaged in impromptu play may become an airplane zooming to the airport built of blocks; another assumes the role of mother in the play house; others take the parts of delivery people. Sometimes children of this age will play a very familiar story without adult direction. For example, "The Three Billy Goats Gruff" is often a favorite. Dramatic play represents this free response of children as they interpret experience.

Dramatic improvisation is very similar to dramatic play in that it is characterized by spontaneous dialogue and action. Younger children usually require some givens—such as puppets, props (a stethoscope to suggest a doctor), bits of costume (a long skirt for grandmother). With slightly older children, situations, time, and setting may be determined with the children's help. When working with a group of 8-year-olds, Dorothy Heathcote[3] asked the students three questions: whom they wanted their play to be about, when it took place, and what their central problem was. The students decided their story was going to be about a king who lived in the "olden days." Their problem was that their king

---

[3]Dorothy Heathcote. In a workshop for the In-Service Language Arts Project at The Ohio State University, Columbus, Ohio, Spring 1971.

was dying; in fact, he was "dying of death" (almost always fatal!) Because Heathcote took their suggestions very seriously, these children worked out a moving scene in which six of them carried their dying king to a kind of ceremonial spot (which was the teacher's desk) to determine the future of the tribe. These 8-year-olds believed in the story they had improvised; they attended to their king with proper concern. No longer third-graders, they were chieftains of long ago and their king was dying.

Working with a group of high-schoolers, Heathcote provided even less direction. The students decided that they had just arrived on an unknown planet. Heathcote said: "Very well, you have my note of instructions (imaginary), now when I walk to the door, you shall begin." And begin they did! They explored their planet cautiously, took hands so they would not be lost in the mist, and determined that the planet was uninhabited. They then sat down to draw up a set of rules that they would use to govern themselves until they could once again make contact with headquarters. While both these plays were reminiscent of folk tales or television plays, they were completely spontaneous for the groups playing them. Questions from the teacher forced them to make decisions and commitments about their situations; the rest came from their imaginations.

Creative drama is structured and cooperatively-planned playmaking. It is usually developed from a simple story, folk tale, poem, or scenes from a long book. It goes beyond dramatic play or simple improvisation in that it has a form with a beginning, middle, and an end. The dialogue is always created by the players, whether the content is taken from a story, poem, or chapter of a book. Occasionally, children may create an original story based upon such familiar characters as those in the *Little House* series by Laura Ingalls Wilder. Perhaps they would like to imagine the kind of a birthday party that would be given for *Curious George* (Rey). While these are creative experiences, some structure is known about the characters or the situation. Most teachers and some children prefer the security of the story structure to complete improvisation.

Pantomime is a useful form in beginning creative drama. In preparation for acting out Leo Lionni's story *Frederick*, a group of 6-, 7-, and 8-year-olds pantomimed the role of the mice. They scurried and scuttled about the room busily gathering their winter supplies. Later, the role of Frederick was added, and again all the rest of the children played at being mice. Only after the children had thought about their roles as mice was dialogue included. Children may also pantomime small portions of a scene in order to understand and feel a character more deeply. For example, a group of 9-year-olds pretended they were the evil witch from "Snow White." They pantomimed waking up in the morning and then standing before a mirror to ask the well-known question of who was the fairest in the land. Several children pantomimed the scene in which Goldilocks comes into the bears' house and samples the porridge. Pantomime is almost always an essential step in the development of believable creative drama with children.

Moving from pantomime to the extemporaneous dialogue of creative drama is an easy transition. Scenes should be kept quite short. Many children should have an opportunity to "play" the scene, which will vary slightly each time. Staging is simple; props are negligible; and additional characters may be added as the play is developed. After playing each scene the children are guided by the teacher in evaluating the characterization and plot development. A new cast is chosen and the scene is played again.

Children play out the story as if they "believe" in the roles they assume. The teacher's major concern is with the process and values for the children involved. While occasionally a play developed creatively may be shared with another classroom, the value of creative drama lies in the *process of playing* and does not require an audience. A more formal production may grow out of creative dramatics, but then its primary purpose becomes entertainment, not expression. For such a production children plan more elaborate settings, acquire props, and wear costumes. Although the lines may become "finalized" as the scenes are rehearsed, they are neither written nor memorized.

Formal plays requiring memorization of written scripts have no place in the elementary school. When the child is limited by preplanned dialogue, there is little or no opportunity for him to think through the reactions of the character to the situation. Creativity is further limited when elementary-school children attempt to write scripts. Usually their writing skill is not equal to the task of natural dialogue. Also, the length of time required to compose scripts often becomes so frustratingly long that interest in the play is killed.

Even when formal productions are developed creatively, there are several cautions to be considered. The child may have developed a sincere belief in his role, but when costumed, he may become overly concerned with the trappings of his part. The regal queen who gracefully mounted the throne during a creative rehearsal may remain a chubby 9-year-old fussing with her mother's long skirt in an audience situation. Rehearsing for a perfect play on a P.T.A. program produces tense teachers and tense children. There is real danger of exploiting children when the teacher decides to "put on" the perfect play for parents and guests. It would be far better to educate parents as to the values of creative drama and let them enjoy the spontaneity of a childlike performance.

VALUES OF CREATIVE DRAMA

The many values of creative drama suggest its significance for the elementary-school curriculum. The child broadens living and learning experiences by playing the roles of people in the past, in other places, and in different situations. In creating plays children obtain information and utilize their understandings from social studies and science classes. Language skills are developed through this form of creative expression. Tensions may be released and emotional and social adjustments can be fostered through creative dramatics. For example, the child who consistently seeks attention through "show off" behavior, may gain attention legitimately in creative drama. The child who identifies with characters who are alone, or cold, or scorned gains new insights and understandings of human behavior and becomes more sensitive to the needs of others. Since there is no written script in creative drama, the player is forced to "think on his feet" and draw on his inner resources. Skills for democratic living are developed through cooperative planning of action and characterization. Devel-

oping the ability to accept and give criticism in the informal evaluation period, which should follow each playing, is an important concomitant of learning. The greatest value of creative drama lies in the process of doing it, the experience itself. Finally, interpretation of literature through drama brings children joy and zest in learning and living.

DRAMATIZING STORIES

The first step in dramatizing narratives is the selection of a good story to read or tell to children. Many teachers and librarians have their favorite stories for dramatizing. However, some titles will be suggested here as particularly good starters.

Very young children of 3 through 5 will become involved in dramatic play, but they usually do not have the sustained attention to act out a complete story. They may play a part of a favorite folk tale (for example, "The Three Billy Goats Gruff" crossing the bridge), but they seldom will complete a whole story. And no one should expect them to do so.

Primary-grade children enjoy playing simple stories such as *Caps for Sale* by Slobodkina, *Ask Mr. Bear* by Flack, or Elkin's *Six Foolish Fishermen*. The teacher or librarian might read *Caps for Sale* while half the class pretends to be the peddler and the rest of the class are the monkeys. The action of the peddler and the monkeys can be pantomimed, while the story is read aloud. Next, a small group of children can be asked to play the story while improvising the dialogue.

Folk-tales are also a rich source of dramatization. They are usually short, have plenty of action, a quick plot, and interesting characters. A favorite is *Stone Soup* by Marcia Brown. This is the story of three jovial French soldiers who trick an entire village into providing them with the ingredients for soup, which the soldiers claim to have made from three large stones. The story naturally divides into three parts—the first scene with the soldiers approaching the village; the making of the soup with the villagers' help, of course; and the last scene when the soldiers leave. Children can decide which scenes they want to play first. Usually they like to play the part where the stone soup is made. With some preliminary discussion of the characters of the soldiers and the villagers, the children may decide who will provide certain ingredients for the soup. Discourage them from actually bringing carrots or barley; instead, ask them to describe their contributions so others can almost smell and taste them. If the action lags, the teacher may enter the play and add a particularly nice morsel of beef, for example, telling how she just happened to have found one piece stored in the cellar. The playing may stop at an agreed-upon signal such as: "I never thought I'd live to see the day when you could make soup out of stones," and the soldiers reply: "It's all in knowing how!" Following the evaluation period in which the teacher points out some of the good features of the playing (for example the children stayed in character—"Ann really acted greedy"; "I could almost smell the onion that Jim put in the soup"; and so on), the teacher can ask children to tell what they liked about individual interpretations. What could be added to the playing can be discussed, and then the play is tried again with another group. It is also interesting to dramatize *Nail Soup* by the Zemachs, for the children become very interested in different versions of the same folk tale. In fact, in one class of 8-year-olds, half the class worked with *Stone Soup*, while the other half worked with the student-teacher on *Nail Soup*; and then they played them to surprise each other.

Other folk tales that children enjoy dramatizing include *The Three Wishes* (Galdone). This is the well-known story of the couple who were granted three wishes. While dreaming and planning how they will use their wishes, the husband foolishly wastes one of his. His wife becomes so angry at him that she wishes a link of sausage will stick to the end of his nose. After much pulling and struggling, they have to use their last wish to correct the second wish, and all their wishes are used up! This can be a lively story, and children love to play it. Another very funny one is the tale titled, "Who Will Wash the Pot?", in the book *The Lazies* by Ginsburg. In this story the couple argue all day over who is going to wash the pot after they had eaten the cereal. They agree that the first one who speaks will have to wash it. The villagers come thinking they are ill, but it is the mayor who knows how to get them to talk!

Stories from myths—such as Prometheus or Pandora's Box or *The Golden Touch* (Hawthorne) are fine material for 9, 10, or 11-year-olds to dramatize. They also enjoy doing parts of such stories as *The Courage of Sarah Noble* by Dalgliesh or *Sarah Somebody* by Florence Slodbodkin. Scenes from some of the children's favorite stories—such as "Piglet Meets a Heffalump" or "Eeyore Has a Birthday" from *Winnie the Pooh* (Milne), or the scene from *Charlotte's Web* (White) where Wilbur first meets Charlotte—lend themselves well to dramatization. Scenes from modern stories—such as the encounter between Mrs. Andrews and Annabel's teacher and principal in *Freaky Friday* (Rodgers)—delight middle-graders. Each teacher will want to experiment with new and exciting material that will capture the imagination of the class.

An illustration of children's interpretation of a book through creative dramatics is included here to clarify purposes and methods. The *marginal* notes identify the teacher's role as well as the procedural steps that are to be used in presenting the material.

AN ACCOUNT OF CREATIVE DRAMATICS

Class Development

Mrs. Stein read the Thurber story, *Many Moons*, to a group of 9-year olds. The main character is a little princess who becomes ill of a "surfeit of raspberry tarts." When she is ill the Princess Lenore demands the moon to wear around her neck. The Lord Chamberlain, the Royal Wizard, and the Royal Mathematician are unable to agree on the facts about the moon or a method of ob-

Identification of Teaching Techniques

The story selected for creative dramatics should have action, tight plot, and natural, interesting characters. A quick, satisfying ending, and sufficient dialogue are essential.

The teacher reads the story with enthusiasm and dramatic emphasis.

taining it for her. Only the Court Jester discovers her ideas and is wise enough to solve the problem.

On the day following the teacher's reading, the children participated in retelling the story. The teacher's questions led them to a clear delineation of character:

> What kind of a little girl is Lenore?
> How does she treat the servants?
> Why does she behave in this way?

Children are involved in summarizing the story.

All the children pantomimed Lenore entering the throne room. After developing the character of the King and his three wise men, small groups pantomimed their movements and suggested a few phrases of greeting for the king. These questions guided the pantomime:

> How does the old Mathematician walk?
> What does he carry?
> What does he do when he approaches the king?
> How does he greet the King?

Teacher's questions guide children's understanding of the characters and setting.

The use of pantomime in the initial stages encourages children to use their bodies and helps them develop belief in the characters. It avoids mere verbalization.

In the third class session, the children listed the major events in sequence and selected one incident they wanted to play.

This was the scene in which the worried King calls for his advisors to solve the problem of getting the moon for Lenore.

The total class is involved in character development. Each child participates. The teacher may select a few children to demonstrate their interpretation of character. The teacher's questions stimulate creative responses.

> *Mrs. Stein:* Whom does the King call first?
> *Children:* The Lord High Chamberlain.
> *Mrs. Stein:* Let's talk about the Chamberlain. What kind of man is he?
> *Bill:* He is short and fat.
> *Sally:* And he wears thick glasses.
> *Jerry:* He thinks he knows more than anyone else.
> *Mrs. Stein:* What are some of the things he has done for the King?
> *Children:* He has brought ivory, peacocks, pink elephants, blue poodles and—and—
> *Mrs. Stein:* Perhaps we should hear the list again. Why does the Lord Chamberlain say he can't get the Moon?
> *Anne:* It is made of melted metal of some kind and 30,000 miles away.
> *Bruce:* Melted copper!

[*The teacher leads a similar discussion of the Royal Wizard and the Royal Mathematician.*]

The addition of one or two lines of conversation makes it possible to evaluate brief units of action. Also, many children can participate before an entire scene is planned.

It is not necessary to begin with the first scene in the story—children may choose to first "play" the most exciting scene or the one with the most characters. This process often strengthens the introductory scene if the entire story is to be developed as a play.

The teacher directs attention to sequence of events in the scene.

Characterization is reviewed. Physical characteristics and personality patterns are discussed. Children may want to return to the word pictures in the text and look at the illustrations as they imagine the appearances of the major characters.

The teacher suggests the setting by mapping areas necessary to the action. Only a few pieces of furniture are used. In the beginning, no props

Mrs. Stein: (*Placing two chairs in front of the room.*) Here is the throne—it has a high back—is covered with soft red velvet. Who would like to play King? All right, Mike. (*She then selects the other characters for the scene.*)

Mrs. Stein: King—where are you sitting? Royal Advisors—take your places.

Audience—remember, we will talk about the scene *after* our imaginary curtain comes down. Be ready to tell how to make the scene better.

Mrs. Stein: When the scene opens, who is the first person to speak? Do you know what you are going to say, King? All ready, places! Curtain! [*The children play the scene which ends when the teacher says, "Cut."*]

Mrs. Stein: What did you especially like about this scene?

Hank: The Lord Chamberlain and all the others really bowed down to the King.

Mary: They forgot all the things they had done for the King.

Mrs. Stein: We'll come to that suggestion later, Mary. Let's talk about the things we liked first.

Tom: I liked it when the Chamberlain pretended to read his grocery list.

are needed. Later, such simple items as crown and scepter may be added if the children suggest them.

In selecting volunteers for the first playing, it is wise to choose children who will "carry the scene." Avoid typing characters. The fat boy usually should *not* play the part of the fat chamberlain, for example. Some child other than the dainty little blond in the class could play the part of Princess Lenore.

Sometimes children may suggest having a child play the part of an animal or tree. Unless the animal is personified with human qualities of character, this is not recommended. There is little value in pretending to be a tree.

In creating the mood and giving directions, the teacher uses the name of the character rather than the name of the child playing that character.

The teacher emphasizes the responsibility of the audience for the evaluation. When beginning creative dramatics, it should be stressed that the audience does not participate during the scene.

The teacher briefly reviews the action before giving an agreed upon stage direction for beginning play.

Although she may be tempted to add comments or suggestions, the teacher joins the audience and refrains from giving any stage directions until the scene has been played. If the players are "floundering," it may be necessary to stop the action and replan. In case one player resorts to buffoonery, the teacher may temporarily halt the action and quietly but firmly assign another child to the part.

The scene is ended when the teacher gives an agreed upon terminating phrase. "Curtain," "finish," or "cut" are words that might be used.

The players return to their seats for the evaluation period.

The evaluation period begins with positive comments.

Children and teacher continue to refer to names of characters instead of using the name of the child who played the part.

Negative comments are accepted, but held in abeyance for the suggestion period.

Suzy: The Royal Wizard really seemed old and fussy.

Bill: I didn't know when to come in.

Mrs. Stein: How could we help the advisers know when to appear?

Mike: The King could tell the palace guard to send them in.

Children: That's neat—good idea!

Mrs. Stein: What other suggestions do you have for improving the scene? Mary, you were concerned about remembering what the advisers had done for the King.

Bill: Well, I was the Mathematician and I couldn't remember all that stuff.

Mary: Mrs. Stein, couldn't we just write those funny things on a sheet of paper like they do in the story?

Mrs. Stein: Yes, I think that would help. We would want to use Thurber's exact words because they are so funny.

Larry: I thought the Court Jester was really funny.

Mrs. Stein: Yes, he was. What things did he do that we enjoyed?

Larry: He made silly faces and he imitated the fat old Chamberlain.

Bruce: He did too much—I thought it was too silly.

Mrs. Stein: Would a Court Jester do anything to try to make the King laugh while he was talking to one of his advisers?

Marilyn: I don't think so. He's supposed to help. The King wouldn't like being interrupted.

Mrs. Stein: When would the Jester try to entertain the King? What would he do? Yes, Jim, he could imitate them as they leave the throne room. This illustration in the book shows him playing his lute.

Suzy: The Royal Wizard turned his back to the audience and we couldn't hear him.

Mrs. Stein: Is there another way to arrange the furniture on the stage so this won't happen?

Suzy: If we put the throne at the side of the stage the advisers wouldn't have to turn their backs.

Mrs. Stein: Good idea! Let's try it that way. Let's play the scene again now. We've added the palace guard. Who would like to be King? [*She continues to select a new cast.*]

The players themselves recognize difficulties.

Rather than giving answers, the teacher asks leading questions to guide children in solving the problem.

The teacher encourages the children to suggest ways to improve the play.

In certain circumstances, a part of the story could actually be read.

All comments are accepted. If the teacher withholds her views for a time, more perceptive children will usually recognize distracting elements and inadequate character portrayal.

Further questions help the children discover relationships between characters and predict behavior in the existing situation. They recognize inadequacies in the first playing, and plan for improvements.

The book is used to aid in planning.

Stage techniques receive less emphasis than plot and character development. However, such suggestions are accepted. The teacher's questions will lead children to improve stage techniques.

Whenever possible, children's ideas are tried out.

Children indicate their willingness to participate in many ways. A hand tentatively extended, or

Mrs. Stein: [*Aware of need for guidance.*] Let's remember the suggestions we've made. The King is really worried about Lenore's illness. He orders the guard to summon his advisers. Tomorrow the advisers can read from a list. For this time, just remember as many items as you can. The Jester will do funny things only after each adviser leaves. All right, let's play! Be ready to evaluate as soon as the scene is ended. Curtain!

In later sessions, the same techniques were used to develop the next scenes. One scene was created to explain why the Princess was sick. The children decided she had been greedy at her own birthday party. This new scene made it possible to add a number of characters as the guests who came to the royal birthday party. The children planned ways in which the Princess would further reveal her selfish character when she opened her gifts. For example, one gift was a mirror. The princess vainly exclaimed how pretty she was.

Some scenes were telescoped in order to preserve continuity of the plot.

shining eyes may reveal a desire for a part. Try to give parts so children will experience a measure of success. A shy child cannot be expected to play the part of an aggressive King in the initial playing.

The teacher's descriptive phrases continuously emphasize characterization.

Once again, the teacher summarizes suggestions and the play begins.

New scenes may be created. Other characters may be added. Every opportunity to develop creativity is utilized.

The play might end with the development of only one scene. If the entire story is dramatized, the scenes are planned and played over a longer period of time. When the playing no longer produces creative responses, it is time to try another story.

DRAMATIZATION THROUGH PUPPETRY

Puppetry is another form of play-making that provides experiences in interpreting literature. Beginning in the kindergarten with the construction of paper-bag puppets or simple stick puppets, this activity can give pleasure to children throughout the elementary school. Materials and types of puppets will range from the simple to the complex, depending upon age and the child.

The techniques of creative dramatics should be followed as puppet plays are created cooperatively by children and teachers. It is highly recommended that children "play out" stories prior to using their puppets. Written scripts are not necessary and may prove very limiting. Playing the story creatively will allow the child to identify with the characters before becoming involved with the mechanical manipulation of the puppet.

Values of Puppetry

Many children will "lose themselves" in the characterization of a puppet while hidden behind a puppet stage, although they may hesitate to express ideas and feelings in front of the class. Through puppetry, children learn to project their voices and develop facility in varying voice quality to portray different characters. For example, a rather quiet, shy child may use a booming voice as he becomes the giant in "Jack and the Beanstalk." Puppetry also facilitates the development of skills in arts and crafts. Problems of stage construction, backdrops for scenery, and the modeling of characters provide opportunities for the development of creative thinking. There is a danger, however, that children will spend so much time on the creation of their puppets that they will not give enough attention to dramatizing the actual story. This is why the playing of the story without puppets is essential to a smooth playing of the tale with puppets. A well-played puppet show will extend children's appreciation of the stories and make literature a more memorable experience for them.

Selecting Stories for Puppetry

The techniques of puppetry are most appropriate for certain stories. For example, a group of 7-year-olds presented a puppet show based on Rudyard Kipling's *The Elephant's Child*. At the appropriate moment the crocodile pulled the elephant's short, stocking nose into the familiar elongated trunk. Such action would be nearly impossible for live actors to portray. Another group of 10-year-olds used marionettes to capture the hilarious action of the laughing-gas birthday party described in Travers' *Mary Pop-*

pins. This scene would be difficult to portray in any other dramatic form. Other stories that lend themselves to interpretation through puppetry are *The Fat Cat* (Kent), the "Gingerbread Boy" in Haviland's *The Fairytale Treasury, Rosie's Walk* (Hutchins), *Frederick* and *Alexander and the Wind-up Mouse* (both by Lionni).

Constructing Puppets and Marionettes

Numerous books are available that tell children how to make puppets, marionettes, and stages. Young children enjoy making simple cardboard figures that can be stapled to sticks or to tongue depressors. Paper bags stuffed with old stockings or newspaper may be tied to represent a puppet head and body. Ears, hair, aprons, and so on may be attached to create animals or people. By placing his hand in a sock or paper

Students enjoy producing and watching a puppet show.
Courtesy of Elnora M. Portteus, Director of School Libraries, Cleveland, Ohio, Public Schools.

The tale of "The Three Little Pigs" is effectively told through the use of shadow puppets.
Summer workshop, The Ohio State University.

bag, the child can make the puppet appear to talk by moving his fingers and thumb.

A very simple puppet may be created by using a pingpong ball for a head and a plain handkerchief. The index finger can be inserted in a hole in the ball; the handkerchief is then slit and slipped over the puppeteer's hand. Two rubber bands secure the handkerchief to the thumb and second finger, thereby making the arms of the puppet. Children can be taught to move their fingers and the puppet's head. Puppets that are somewhat more complex to construct may have heads of papier mâché, potatoes, styrofoam balls, or other materials. Cloth bodies can be cut and sewn by the children. Cardboard cylinders and small boxes can be used to create animal puppets. Yarn, fuzzy cloth, or old mittens make good cover materials for animals.

Marionettes require a degree of skill usually possessed by older elementary-school children. These figures are manipulated by moving strings attached to parts of the body and a board held aloft to which the strings are attached. A clothesline marionette is one of the simplest to make. Loops of clothesline form the framework of the body. Limbs and body may be covered with papier mâché. Two strings fastened to screw eyes placed on either side of the head can be used to move the figure. Arms and legs are made to move by attaching other strings to the elbow and knee joints. A marionette body can also be made by stuffing the foot of a sock and cutting and sewing arms and legs. One group of 9-year-olds made animal marionettes by folding strips of paper into springs for the legs and body. A special string on the giraffe made him stretch his neck in a most believable fashion. Wooden marionettes can be made by children who are able to remain interested for a long period of time while they construct the complex figures.

Most books on puppetry give directions for constructing stages. A simple stage for stick or hand puppets can be made by turning a table on its side. The puppeteer sits or kneels behind the table top. Another simple stage can be made by hanging curtains so they cover the lower and upper parts of a doorway. A table, cardboard, or side of a large box can also be placed in a doorway. This type of stage is particularly good because children waiting their turns at the side of the stage are hidden from view. Older children can construct a framework for more durable puppet stages. Permanent stages that can be moved from room to room should be available in the school. This is a way of involving parents in school activities. Screens or hinged wings may be placed at the side of such a puppet stage. Cloth, paper, or old window shades can be used for background material. The educational values of planning and creating a puppet show far outweigh the time and effort that is required to produce it.

Literature and Writing

Children's writing will grow out of exciting and rich sensory experiences that bring a depth of feeling about people, places, and things. Exposure to much fine literature of increasing complexity will provide children with a cafeteria of forms and examples from which they may choose models for their own writing. Creative writing does not develop in a vacuum. A child must have something that he wants to write about and then be able to select the appropriate form for his message.

James Moffett maintains that the child's natural mode of discourse is narrative:

> They [children] utter themselves almost entirely through stories—real or invented—and they apprehend what others say through story. . . . The monologues they write most easily are stories, of course, which follow a chronological continuity. But they do not make up stories easily without stimulants and prompters, and when they do, the stories are seldom original.[4]

Literature may serve as a stimulant for children's writing and provide them with a variety of forms. In fact, children's writing regularly re-

veals their previous exposure to literature in the use of vocabulary, form, and content. (*See* "Response to Literature", Chapter 12.)

DEVELOPING SENSITIVITY TO LANGUAGE

Children's appreciation of the writing of others increases as they listen to many fine stories, read widely themselves, and have many opportunities to create their own stories and poems. Skill in descriptive writing may be developed by helping children to become aware of the power of words in conveying sensory images. After a story has been finished, the teacher and children may reread and relish particularly enjoyable words, phrases, or paragraphs.

Creative writing requires many first-hand experiences of touching and feeling and savoring textures, sounds, colors, shapes, rhythms, and patterns. Literature, too, can sharpen sensitivity to nature, people, and relationships. Rich sensory imagery helps children "see" the world around them in new perspectives. For example, in *A Fresh Look at Night*, Jeanne Bendick presents various night scenes in lovely descriptive language a child can understand:

> A city full of lights and windows is like frozen fireworks on the Fourth of July.

> Rainy nights are like silk and satin. Snowy nights are like feathers and fur.[5]

Children's delight in a fog-shrouded village has been captured by Tresselt in *Hide and Seek Fog*. Vivid imagery characterizes his descriptions. For example, he sees the children as they:

> . . . spoddled in the lazy lapping waves on the beach . . . But out of doors the fog twisted about the cottages like slow-motion smoke. It dulled the rusty scraping of the beach grass. It muffled the chattery talk of the low tide waves. And it hung wet and dripping, from the bathing suits and towels on the clothesline.[6]

A group of 8-year-olds heard the story of *Amos and Boris* by William Steig. They decided to write a diary such as Amos, the whale, might have written; or one that Boris, the mouse, might have

---

[4]James Moffett. *Teaching the Universe of Discourse* (New York: Houghton Mifflin, 1968), pp. 49, 56.

[5]Jeanne Bendick. *A Fresh Look at Night* (New York: F. Watts, 1963), unpaged.
[6]Alvin Tresselt. *Hide and Seek Fog*, illustrated by Roger Duvoisin (New York: Lothrop, 1965), unpaged.

kept. After the children had written their first entries, the university supervisor for the class discussed the rich use of language in *Amos and Boris.* He had copied his favorite expressions from the book on cards and he shared these with the group. They included:

He loved to hear the surf sounds . . .
   the bursting breakers
   the backwashes with rolling pebbles.

In a few minutes Boris was already in the water, with waves washing at him, and he was feeling the wonderful wetness.

"Amos help me," said the mountain of a whale to the mote of a mouse.[7]

The children then wrote the second entry in their diaries. The contrast between their first writing and their second shows the influence of simply calling attention to Steig's rich use of language. The amount of writing also increased. A sample of a first and second entry by a child appear below:

Dear Diary,
   It was Tuesday two days after I saved Amos. We are just starting to be getting acquainted.
   Amos told me all about land, how I wish I could live on land.
   I wish we could meet sometime again.
                                       By Boris

Dear Diary,
   Well its Tuesday and Amos built a ladder down the great tunnel, well, at least that's what Amos calls it. It really is my spout.
   One day we had a feast. We had a fat juicy lobster, some plump juicy sea cucumbers, some meaty clams and some sand-breaded fish. After that we were so full and tired we talked and talked and finally we went to sleep happy.
                                       Well, Bye
                                       Boris (Chris ——)

Barrington Road School
Upper Arlington, Ohio
Carolyn Fahrbach, Teacher
Roy Wilson, Ohio State University Supervisor

[7]William Steig. *Amos and Boris* (New York: Farrar, Straus, 1971), unpaged.

All of the students showed a richer use of language in their second entries. They used such words from the book as "sand breaded" and "sounded," but they used them in ways meaningful to their entries.

The sequence of this writing is also important to note. On the first day nothing much was said to call children's attention to Steig's use of language. It was suggested that they might want to retell the story from the point of view of one of the characters and in diary form. This recasting of the story appeared to be enough of a challenge for their first attempts. The following day, however, after they had mastered the diary form, attention was given to the rich use of language, and this was directly reflected in their second entries.

Another teacher copied down children's favorite expressions from particular folk tales. Then she put them on a chart making two columns—"What the Author Says" and "What We Say"—encouraging children to add their own descriptions. An example follows:

SPEAKING OF WITCHES

What the Author Says	What We Say
". . . Her wild hair waved about her face. Her nose, that looked like a rainspout, quivered and sniffed at the clearing . . ." From *Baba Yaba* by Ernest Small	"Witches are mean and skinny with long crooked fingers." "They boil kids in stew." "They got fur on their ears." "They talk funny."

SPEAKING OF SIMPLETONS

What the Author Says	What We Say
"Donkey-brains!" "Tony-de-Moany was so simple-minded that anybody could have dumped soup on his head and he wouldn't have noticed." From *Bungling Pedro* by Alexander Mehdevi	"Dummy," "stupid" Brainless "Ding-bat"

Cuningham

Barbara

Someday when I have nothing to do, I'm going to read a book instead of watch T.V.

Two 7-year-olds interpret the story *Someday* differently. Which one caught the irony in the book?

A similar chart might be developed after sharing Eve Merriam's poem, "A Cliché," with middle-graders. A column could be made for each of the overworked expressions that the author describes as clichés in her poem. Children could then think of ways to describe "warm" other than saying "warm as toast," or a better description for "quiet" than "quiet as a mouse." They could add to the list of clichés and create fresh new metaphors for them. One group of 9-year-olds made the following comparisons:

Slow as a six week spelling test
Slow as a moving glacier
Lonely as an ant in orbit

> Martin Luther King, Jr., Laboratory School
> Evanston, Illinois
> Barbara Friedberg, Teacher

Younger children may be encouraged to explore various dimensions of feeling or various functions of an object. After one group of 6-year-olds had heard the story, *Some Things Are Scary* by Florence Heide, they made up their own ideas of scary situations and dictated them:

Stepping on something squishy when you are in your barefeet is SCARY.

Holding onto someone's hand that isn't your mother's when you thought it was is SCARY.

> Barrington Road School
> Upper Arlington, Ohio
> Barbara Sommers, Teacher

See What I Found by Myra Cohn Livingston explores the various possibilities or functions of a single object. When a child hears the lines about a key, his imagination may open doors with "a silver key to secret places." Creative uses of a rubber band, a piece of clay, a little bug, or a seashell may be discovered by sharing this book in class. The teacher should be sure to have a collection of objects—such as old keys, shells, buttons, ribbons, feathers, paper clips, tacks, pencils, and so on, and let children select an object to hold and feel while they think of various new and inventive uses for it.

An individual or class notebook of interesting passages and descriptive phrases provides another way to develop awareness of language. One group of 12-year-olds each chose a particular theme—such as hope, love, fear, courage—for a whole year, and kept a section in their notebooks of appropriate passages. The selections for "fear" included these quotes:

Someday I'm going to be a policeman so I can help people cross the streets.

Columbus Public Schools, Ohio, Annie Roseboro, teacher.

Still I believe I know what courage is: it is to smile when fear has locked all smiles within your breast.

If you have learned to be alone without fear, then no man can call you weak. . . . Many a strong man trembles when night has made him a small island in the ocean of darkness and the hooting owl is heard.[8]

. . . fear isn't necessarily a bad thing. It's a result of aiming high.[9]

LITERATURE AS MODEL

Story Starters

Ideally, we would hope that children would write out of their own experiences and emotions about the things that matter to them. Unless children have been in schools that care about this kind of writing and have been encouraged to do much personal writing from the very beginning of school, many children will need some kind of prompters or story starters. Once children feel confident in their ability to express themselves, the flow of writing will increase.

[8]Erik Haugaard. *Hakon of Rogen's Saga,* illustrated by Leo Dillon and Diane Dillon (Boston, Mass.: Houghton Mifflin, 1963), pp. 37, 79.
[9]Sylvia Louise Engdahl. *Enchantress from the Stars,* illustrated by Rodney Shackell (New York: Atheneum, 1970), p. 72.

Some teachers have found particular books, stories, or poems useful for getting children started. For example, younger children enjoy relating events that might happen on their streets after they have heard the zany story by Dr. Seuss, *And to Think that I Saw It on Mulberry Street.* The pattern of the book *Someday* by Zolotow inspired several 7-year-olds to think of their "someday" hopes and desires. Some of the children were not mature enough to catch the irony of this story, and simply drew pictures and dictated stories of what they hoped to be "someday." Others recognized that the wishes were highly improbable. One girl's telling statement has a message for all of us who are interested in bringing children and books together. She wrote simply:

Someday when I have
nothing to do, I'm
going to read a book
instead of watch T.V.

Columbus Schools, Ohio
Annie Roseboro, Teacher

Seven-year-olds wrote and illustrated additional verses about the kinds of friends they would invite to visit the king and the queen after they had heard the story *May I Bring A Friend?* by De Regniers. These included such funny situations as:

When I introduced my friends
  the snakes.
The queen said,
  "For Heaven's Sakes!"

  Heidi Hoff

When I introduced
  My friend the bear.
The queen said
  "I ran out of silverware!"

  Phillip Bokovay
  West Lafayette Indiana Public Schools
  Nancy Sawrey, Teacher

Primary-school children enjoy making booklets about their wishes. A teacher might read several stories or poems about wishes; for example, the poem, "I Keep Three Wishes Ready" by Annette Wynne; or the folk tales *The Three Wishes*, illustrated by Paul Galdone, *The Old Woman Who Lived in a Vinegar Bottle* by Rumer Godden, or the modern tale of *The Seven Wishes of Joanna Peabody* by Gray, which tells of a special television spirit who grants a child in a tenement family her seven wishes. Children might discuss wise and foolish wishes, and then create their own "Wish Books."

The pattern of the book *Fortunately* by Remy Charlip stimulated two 8-year-old girls to write their own "fortunate" and "unfortunate" incidents:

GOING TO SCHOOL

One day unfortunately, I woke up.
Fortunately I got dressed.
Unfortunately I was tired.
Fortunately I went downstairs to eat breakfast.
Unfortunately my Mom wasn't there.
Fortunately my breakfast was on the table.
Unfortunately my breakfast was cold.
Fortunately I wasn't hungry.
Unfortunately I was late for school.
Fortunately I could ride my bike.
Unfortunately my bike tire popped.
Fortunately I could run.
Unfortunately I skinned my knee and it held me
  back.

Fortunately I finally got to school.
Unfortunately it was Saturday.
Fortunately I went back to bed.
  The End

  Paige Perman and Kristy Klein
  Barrington Road School
  Upper Arlington, Ohio
  Sherrie Goubeaux, Teacher

Joan Lexau's book *That's Good, That's Bad* follows this same pattern, and could also be used to motivate children's creations of "good and bad situations."

Another book which is an excellent story starter is *Alexander and the Terrible, Horrible, No Good, Very Bad Day* by Judith Viorst. Children in the middle grades delight in detailing their terrible, horrible, very bad days. One child gave a new creative twist to this pattern as she wrote about "The Wonderful Magnificent Day."

New incidents may be created in relation to a particular theme. After hearing several of Kipling's *Just So Stories*, young authors can experiment with animal stories entitled "How the

Three 9-year-olds wrote and illustrated their own Anansi tale (*see* page 680).
Martin Luther King, Jr., Laboratory School, Evanston, Illinois, Barbara Friedberg, teacher.

iment with animal stories entitled "How the Giraffe Got Its Long Neck," "Why a Cat Has Nine Lives," or "How the Skunk Got Its Smell." In all instances teachers will want to encourage originality by suggesting that the Kipling stories be used as a springboard for fresh new stories that the children create.

Occasionally, children will like a particular story or characters so well that they will want to create further adventures for the book. Near Christmas one primary-grade teacher read the quiet story of the little Swedish elf called *The Tomten* (Lindgren) to her students. Then each of the children wrote and illustrated their stories of what the Tomten might do if he came to their houses.

Knowing the characteristics of *Pippi Longstocking* (Lindgren)—her frankness, her amazing strength, and her straightforward logic—children might want to create new adventures which would feature Pippi in such situations as planning a birthday party. What strange characters would Pippi be apt to invite? Where would she have the party? What would they eat? Would she give children rides on her horse and let them play with her monkey? Children might suppose her long lost father showed up, or the pirates. Discussion with children before they write will help them recall details of a character's personality and put them in the mood for writing. Children should always be given a choice of several possibilities for writing, plus the option of choosing a subject that no one has suggested. Remember these are only story-starters. If children can start on their own with no extrinsic motivation, so much the better; then they are on their way to becoming real writers who are truly self-motivated. This should be every teacher's ultimate goal for children's writing.

Forms of Literature as Model

As children are exposed to a wide variety of literature—including folk tales, fables, myths, and poetry—they enjoy using some of these forms in their own writing. One group of 8- and 9-year-olds read many folk tales. Their teacher shared some of her favorites with them. They discussed such characteristics as talking animals, use of repetition, magic, and enchantment. Children voluntarily began writing their own folk tales. Three girls worked together and wrote and illustrated the following original Anansi story:

THE END OF ANANSI

A long time ago in a village of Eastern Africa there lived a spider named Anansi. Everyone in the village was married—all except Anansi. His father was very disappointed. "Why aren't you married like everyone else?" his father asked one day, and Anansi said nothing.

Years passed and Anansi was getting old. His father had died. Anansi kept remembering what his father had said again and again, "Why aren't you married like everyone else?"

One day as Anansi hobbled along the road he saw some animals moving out of their house. The next week he hobbled past the same house and saw an old, beautiful spider carrying some suitcases. Just at that moment he got a tingle—he had fallen madly in love with her.

Anansi couldn't sleep at all that night. He couldn't stop thinking about the beautiful spider. He had to find out her name. He had to see her so he would go tomorrow morning.

The next morning he went over to her house. When she opened the door, she said, "Hello." He said, "I've come to greet you a hello. I'm your next door neighbor."

"Hi it's nice to meet you—oh, I just wanted to meet you. My name is Arta. What's yours?"

"Anansi."

"Please come in."

"Thank you," said Anansi.

"Would you like some yams fresh from my garden and some tea?"

"Yes, please."

"Fine," said Arta.

When Arta was in the kitchen, Anansi was thinking what his father had said. It kept going through his mind, "Why can't you be married like everyone else," Anansi thought.

Arta came back from the kitchen. Anansi tasted the tea. It was good. Anansi tasted the yams; they were good, too. Anansi said, "How do you grow such fine yams?"

"My uncle is a very good farmer and he helped me plant them."

"Oh, that's nice. I think I'd better be going now. Thank you very much for having me over. You'll have to come over to my house some time."

They did quite a bit of going over to each other's houses. They had been going together for two and one-half years. Anansi thought it was time. One night Anansi asked Arta over for dinner. As it got far into the night, Anansi finally asked Arta to marry him. Arta refused. Arta grabbed her coat and ran far out into the night. Anansi's heart was broken. He couldn't eat or sleep because of Arta whom he loved more than anything in the world. Two weeks later he died from starvation.

The moral of this story is: Don't wait too long.
The End

Amy Wadsworth, Kathy Cunningham, and Janice Goldblat
Martin Luther King, Jr., Laboratory School
Evanston Public Schools, Illinois
Barbara Friedberg, Teacher

This story incorporates the folk tale style of the Anansi stories and ends with the usual moral of the fable. The influence of the Anansi stories is reflected in the repetition, the use of interior monologue, and the subtle humor of the tale. The illustrations are as humorous as the story. In one picture the girls have placed the conversation in a balloon form similar to that in the comics. The story then becomes a synthesis of their implicit knowledge of both traditional and modern folklore.

Teachers can capitalize on children's interest in comic books by encouraging them to make comics out of their favorite stories. One boy made a "Pooh Fun Book" that included original adventures of Pooh, a "Pooh Crossword Puzzle," Christopher Robin's Diary, Pooh's Jokes, and numbered directions for drawing Pooh, plus other kinds of written discourse.

Many children enjoy creating their own fables using a cartoon style. They call them "Fable Funnies." The Provensens' illustrations for *Aesop's Fables* can be a useful model for this kind of writing and illustrating activity. Sendak's amusing illustrations for *King Grisly-Beard: A Tale from the Brothers Grimm* also presents a comic-book twist to an old folk tale.

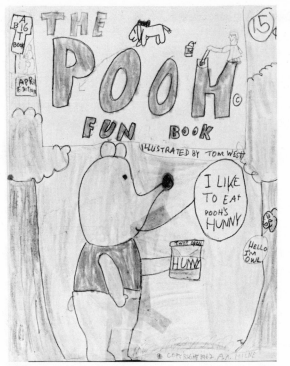

A Pooh fun book created by a 9-year-old child includes original adventures of Pooh, crossword puzzles, Pooh jokes, and a Christopher Robin diary.

Martin Luther King, Jr., Laboratory School, Evanston, Illinois, Barbara Friedberg, teacher.

One group of 12-year-olds decided to create some modern versions of fables. They thought of appropriate stories for such well-known morals as "beauty is only skin deep," "slow but sure wins the race," and "don't cry wolf unless you mean it." This story was written to illustrate a modern application of the moral: "Don't count your chickens before they hatch."

One day my mother told me to go to the store to get a gallon of milk. It cost 96 cents. She gave me a dollar and said that I could keep the money that was left over.

While I was riding down to the store, I told myself what I was going to buy: a 4-cent candy bar, then I would sell it for 5 cents, buy a pack of gum, trade it for some Cracker Jacks, and at last I would trade it for a 40-cent bag of M & M Fruit Chewies.

When I put the milk on the counter the clerk said, "96 cents, 4 cents tax, that will be one dollar." Don't count your chickens before they hatch.

Craig Leichner
Allaire Stuart, Teacher
Boulder Public Schools, Colorado

Middle-graders have also enjoyed retelling a familiar folk tale in a modern setting. Cinderella becomes a younger sister who has to baby-sit while her older sisters go to a rock concert. Hansel and Gretel are taken as hostages by an escaped prisoner and devise a way to push him in the radar oven! A very funny story to use as a starter for writing modern fairy tales is *Jim and the Beanstalk* by Raymond Briggs. This is a modern version of "Jack and the Beanstalk" in which the giant is a pitiful old man who used to like fried boy, but now needs false teeth, glasses, and a wig. Jim is so successful in restoring the giant's lost youth that he has to run for the beanstalk when the giant's appetite returns. The pictures of Jim carrying the giant's false teeth and wig are very funny indeed.

Other forms of prose—such as the tall tale, myth, or autobiography—may serve as models for children's writing. It is essential that many examples of different literary forms be shared and discussed with children so that they may understand pattern and elements. Concrete poetry, or even drawing a shape around a poem to reinforce its content, intrigues children. One 8-year-old was motivated by the poems in *Hailstones and Halibut Bones* by Mary O'Neill to write her own description of the color "gray." Her poem started with: "Gray is a mouse with a squeaky voice," so she enclosed the whole poem in the shape of a mouse (*see* the picture on page 682).

Since limericks are one of children's favorite forms of poetry, they should be encouraged to try writing some limericks about their friends. After sharing many of the limericks by Lear, the teacher could read David McCord's limerick on how to write a limerick!

The limerick's lively to write:
Five lines to it—all nice and tight.

Winter is

Winter is,
Ice skating,
Numb fingers,
Time for warmer clothes,
Everyone playing out in the snow,
Rabbits turning white,

Ice cold water,
Snow!

by,
Mary Ann
Hauck

Gray is a mouse
with a squeaky voice
It's the feeling when
You're getting old
Gray is grandma's curls.
Gray is lonely

ANN

A class poetry book includes poems that are expressed in both visual and written form.
Greensview School, Upper Arlington Public Schools, Ohio, Susan Lee, teacher.

Two long ones, two trick
Little short ones; then quick
As a flash here's the last one in sight.[10]

Haiku is another form of poetry that older children may enjoy composing. Its simplicity of form masks its complexity and hidden meanings. For this reason it is best to begin with other forms of poetry. Further suggestions for ways to encourage children to write all forms of poetry can be found in Chapter 6 of this book.

[10] David McCord. "Write Me a Verse," in *Take Sky* (Boston, Mass.: Little, Brown, 1962), p. 55.

EXTENDING FORMS OF WRITTEN DISCOURSE

While it is true that children first start by writing stories, they should be given many opportunities to write other kinds of discourse as soon as they are developmentally ready to do so. When children can comfortably take the point of view of another person, they can be encouraged to report the story from a different perspective. They can write diaries or logs of particular characters, or have several characters carry on imaginary correspondence. Factual reporting of what happened in a story can be translated into a newspaper article. Skill in persuasive writing can be developed by writing advertisements for books or preparing lost-and-found items. All kinds of writing may be motivated by literature. Teachers need to see the opportunities that are available, and then help children have experiences with many forms of written discourse.

Logs, Diaries, and Imaginary Correspondence

Once children can assume a different point of view, they enjoy retelling a story in the first person using the form of a log or diary. Rather than retell an entire story, they might write one or two entries as the children did when writing about *Amos and Boris* by Steig (*see* page 675).

The teacher might read aloud *My Side of the Mountain* by George, a story that includes both entries from Sam Gribley's diary and newspaper articles describing the "Wild Boy Seen in the Woods." Ann Hamilton in *The Cabin Faced West* (Fritz) kept a diary, and also wrote letters to her cousin Margaret back east in Gettysburg. Children might continue this correspondence or write the kind of diary that Ann's friend, Andy, might have kept. *Harriet the Spy* (Fitzhugh) kept a notebook that was the cause of much trouble when her classmates discovered it. Children might want to establish a "spy route" for one week and keep their own notebooks.

Logs or diaries can be created for characters who never kept them. David, who escaped from a concentration camp and made his way *North to Freedom* (Holm), might well have kept a record of his trip. Children could write some of his entries. Karana, who lived all alone on the *Island of the Blue Dolphins* (O'Dell), could have written a diary. What would she have said about the death of her brother, the taming of her dog, the visit of the Aleut girl? How would she have decorated the cover of her journal? Manolo in *Shadow of a Bull* (Wojciechowska) could have kept a secret diary reflecting his thoughts and fears concerning bull-fighting. Some child might want to be his voice and write what he might have thought and said.

Children might also enjoy assuming the voice of an inanimate object and telling its story. Carolina's doll, Lydia-Lou, might give her account of the long trek across the country in a covered wagon. And only Lydia-Lou could tell what eventually happened to her after the little Indian girl made the trade for her Indian doll in the story of *Carolina's Courage* by Yates. One teacher of 9-year-olds had a set of the Winnie the Pooh stuffed animals. Each weekend a child could borrow one of his or her favorites for a visit home, provided they kept an account of Piglet's experiences or Pooh's escapades. These were frequently written in the form of "Pooh's Diary" or "Piglet's Doings" or "The Events of Eeyore."

Using Robert Lawson's device of telling a story from the viewpoint of an animal, as seen in *Ben and Me*, children might report the story of the surrender at Appomattox as told by Traveller, Robert E. Lee's horse. This would require much research into that particular event. An easier story to tell might be Macaroon's tale of his taming of the spoiled child, Erika, in the Cunningham story of a little raccoon called *Macaroon*.

Children might also write imaginary correspondence between several characters. This would require a good understanding of each character and the ability to be flexible enough to capture different points of view. Seven- and 8-year-olds might write a letter to *Stevie* (Steptoe) from Robert. They could speculate as to whether Robert would tell Stevie that he missed him. Some could then assume the role of Stevie and answer the letter. Older children might write the American boy's answers to the Canadian boy's *Letter on the Tree* (Carlson). Irene Hunt's story *Across Five Aprils* includes many letters from the Illinois farm boys involved in the Civil War, but none from Jethro, the 9-year-old boy who is left home alone. Children might compose a packet of the letters Jethro might have written to his brothers and to his beloved schoolteacher.

Letters written and sent to authors and illustrators expressing appreciation for their work can also be encouraged by the teacher or librarian. These can be addressed to the author or illustrator in care of their publishing houses. The set of reference books titled *Something about the Author* (*see* Appendix B) frequently includes the home address of authors. In writing to these persons, teachers should be certain that children have read their books or know their illustrations and have a genuine reason to correspond with them. Requests for pictures or biographical information should be directed to publishers, not authors.

This letter from a 10-year-old indicates a real interest in the book *America's Abraham Lincoln,* and the response by May McNeer reflects her delight in the letter:

Dear May McNeer:

I've read your book called *America's Abraham Lincoln* and think it's wonderful. I like to read about Lincoln very much. I have read all the books in our school library on him. I think your book is the best one because it tells information without being a bore. I also think the colored pictures are

Older children may want to create their own logs or diaries.

From *How to Make Your Own Books* by Harvey Weiss. Copyright © 1974 by Harvey Weiss, with permission of Thomas Y. Crowell Company, Inc., publisher.

beautiful. I would like very much to get a letter from you.

Sincerely yours,
Jeannie G.

February 6, 1962

Dear Jeannie:

Thank you for your very nice letter. It was a pleasure to learn that you like our *America's Abraham Lincoln* so much. We take it as a real compliment that one who has read so much on Lincoln should like our book best. Lincoln is a great subject, and one that provides a continual enjoyment as you go from junior books into such wonderful volumes as those by Carl Sandburg and others.

We had a rewarding experience in doing that book. Together we went to Springfield and New Salem Village and then my husband went to Kentucky and made sketches of the original home site. Now we are working on *America's Mark Twain,* and my husband is finishing a large number of pictures on the life and books of Sam Clemens. It is to be published next fall.

Thank you again for writing to us. We wish you many fine hours of reading all sorts of books in the future. I can tell from your letter that you are a real reader.

Sincerely,
May McNeer
[signature]

Newspapers and Advertisements

Imagining themselves reporters for a local paper, children can prepare news articles based upon events in literature. An interview with a professor who just returned from a trip in his twenty-one-balloon flying ship might be reported after reading *The Twenty-one Balloons* by DuBois. A series of news accounts of Merrill's *The Push-cart War* could present the amusing battles between mighty trucks and puny pushcarts in New York City. A report could be made of the discovery of oil at the Amory home by General De Gaulle, the mole hero of *Mr. Twigg's Mistake* by Lawson. Charlie's day in the chocolate factory, as related by Dahl, would make interesting "news copy." By pretending they are witnesses to a famous historical event, children can write an "I was there" story. Such a story can be motivated by reading historical fiction or biography.

An entire group could contribute ideas for a class newspaper based upon events related to literature. The paper could include news stories, editorials on book reading, and announcements of book awards. For example, a headline might herald the arrival of *The Cricket in Times Square;* the society column could give a report of Eeyore's birthday party, and describe Cinderella at the Prince's ball; the sports page could report the results of the race between the hare and the tortoise, and the race for the silver skates of Hans Brinker; the death of Charlotte, the spider, could be recorded in the obituary column. The "Lost and Found Column" could contain an ad for Candy, the little lost dog of *Hurry Home, Candy* (DeJong), Little Bo Peep's sheep, and Lucy Locket's pocketbook.

Another kind of newspaper that requires much more research is one created for a particular day in the past. Capitalizing on the current interest in the television series "Little House on the Prairie," children could compose a weekly newspaper describing the day of the storm, for example. They would have to determine the date, write accurate ads for food and clothing, check the price of commodities, and do some research on Laura Ingalls Wilder herself. The teacher could obtain a copy of a local paper for a similar time, and children could check format, national news of the period, and types of editorials and advertisements.

Surveys, Directions, and Other Types of Writing

Teachers will find that books may provide the motivation for much expository writing. Writing directions helps children think through a sequence, to write clearly and with economy of words. The children who created the collàge pictures in this chapter, described how they made a collàge and why they made it. They defined "collàge," and said that it was the way Ezra Jack Keats frequently made his pictures. Other children wrote on how to make cardboard cuts and vegetable print pictures.

Creating and writing the directions for playing literary games provides children with an opportunity to write clear directions. They may check the clarity of their writing by asking two friends to play the game following their directions. Then they can record the questions asked, and change the directions accordingly.

Writing clues for a literary treasure hunt or a "Mystery Title Hunt" requires knowledge of the books and the ability to provide hints but not give away the answers. Again, this calls for a special skill in writing.

Teachers have frequently used favorite books or reading behavior as a subject for children's surveys. Students can determine the favorite books of the class, for example. Then they can prepare a survey based upon the five top titles, determining which is the most popular book in the class. Other surveys have been made concerning teachers' favorite books, how frequently and how long each teacher in the building reads aloud to the class, which books are checked out most frequently from the library, where and when are children's favorite places and times to read. Children doing such research will learn much about books and conducting and organiz-

ing the results of a survey. Their questions must be well-stated so that the answers can be categorized and counted. The results of the survey should be charted and shared with the class.

A radio script about books can be written and given during Book Week. Questions for interviewing an author or illustrator could be written before the interview. Book commercials might also be developed for the program.

The possibilities for writing all kinds of discourse related to books are infinite. Teachers will want to provide children with many opportunities to write across the whole spectrum of discourse.

BOOK-MAKING AND ILLUSTRATING

Nothing motivates children to write more than the opportunity to create a book, to bind it, and illustrate it. Teachers should learn how to bind books themselves, and then teach children. Materials for book-binding should be constantly and freely available. Ask parents for leftover pieces of material, explaining what they are wanted for.

After hearing Ruth Krauss' book, *This Thumbprint*, a 9-year-old created her own version.

Moler School, Columbus, Ohio, Public Schools, Joetta Beaver, teacher.

Small scraps may be put in the colláge box, but larger pieces should be saved for book-binding. Contact paper can be substituted for cloth, but it is somehow not as satisfying to most people.

Since binding books does involve time and some expense, it should be reserved for the carefully written and illustrated story. Children should look at the beautiful picture books that are available today; notice the various media that are used; the carefully designed endpapers, title page, and so on. Children can be encouraged to illustrate their books with care. Pictures may be colored with felt pens or paints, or made from cardboard cuts or vegetable prints, as colláge pictures, or as anything which is a variation of the usual hastily sketched pencil or crayon illustrations. Marbleized paper may be created for the endpapers, or a bright piece of colored paper that blends with the cover. Children should decide how many illustrations they want for their stories or poems, and how they will place the printed matter on the page. They may look at some of the carefully designed title pages of printed books and think about ways they can capture the theme of their stories when making their own books. Many older children enjoy writing a dedication page or including a copyright date. As children create their own books, they learn much about the care and design that has gone into the books they read.

Many librarians have provided a special shelf for books made by children. Again, when children realize that others are going to read the stories they have created, they take special care that the story is an enjoyable one and that the book itself is attractive and readable. Librarians report that these child-created books are some of the most popular in the library. Certainly the child derives much pleasure in having created a book that others enjoy reading.

The directions for binding books are included here:

HOW TO MAKE A BOOK

1. Decide what size your book should be. Then, cut paper for the pages that is twice the width and the same height as the size you want. Cut half as many pieces as pages you need. Remember to allow for end pages and title pages.

2. Fold these papers to form pages and either hand or machine stitch up the center.

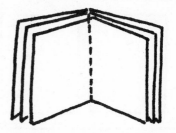

3. Place the open pages on the material that you will use for the cover. This material can be fabric, wallpaper, or contact type paper. Cut the material to a size approximately one inch larger on all sides than the open pages.

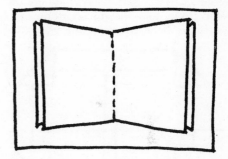

4. Cut two pieces of cardboard, each just slightly larger than a single book page. These will form the support for the cover.
5. Cut four large pieces of Dry Mounting Tissue (Eastman Kodak Company, available at camera stores). Make two pieces the size of the cardboard and two pieces the size of a single page. Also, cut several small strips of Dry Mounting Tissue approximately 2″ × 1/2″.[11]
6. Place the cover material on a flat surface face down. Position the Dry Mounting Tissue (cardboard size) on the material. Now place the cardboard pieces on top. Leave a space

---

[11] Although the Dry Mounting Tissue process produces the most satisfactory book, a solution of Metylan Paste (available from Henkle Incorporated, Teaneck, New Jersey, 07666) and water or white glue and water, brushed on, can be substituted and is less expensive.

between the cardboard pieces to allow for the pages and for the book to open and close.

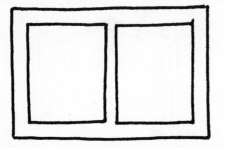

7. With an iron, set on low, carefully press the cardboard. This will mount the material to the cardboard. Never place iron directly on the Dry Mount, as it will stick.
8. Place the small pieces of Dry Mounting Tissue between the cardboard and the material at the corners. Use the iron again to adhere the two. Repeat and fold the top, bottom and sides until your book cover is completed!

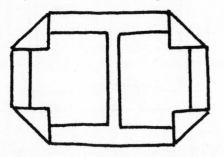

9. Place the two remaining pieces of Dry Mounting Tissue on the cardboard side of the book cover. Position the sewn pages in the middle. Press the first and last pages down to form end papers. Use the iron to mount the pages to the cover. Now, fill the pages with your story!

Extending Literature through Games

Games provide another means for extending children's knowledge of books and authors. The planning and creation of games by children provide many opportunities for problem-solving, for reinforcing the interpretation of the story, and for creative expression. Games capitalize upon the child's natural inclination for play, and bring teacher and child together in the mutual enjoyment of books.

GUESSING GAMES AND RIDDLES

Children enjoy "acting out" real-life situations and scenes from books. Many guessing games utilize pantomime in some form. Young children may try to guess the Mother Goose or folk-tale character being pantomimed. Beginning with 7- and 8-year-olds, guessing games can be performed in small groups with teacher-written directions. As proficiency increases, older children can determine the particular characters or titles to be acted out. One group might choose to portray a title by actions representing words or syllables. The first audience group that guesses the title correctly has the privilege of presenting the next charade. In another version of this game two teams alternate in presenting timed charades. The team that names the most dramatized books in the shortest time wins the game. Teams may pantomime characters and scenes from stories, as well as book titles. Charades and guessing games differ from pantomime in that the games both require an audience. Charades are more complex and sophisticated than guessing games in that they require the audience to guess words or syllables all during the play rather than at the end of a scene. They also require more interchange between the player and the audience than guessing games do.

Riddles are fun for all ages. They can be based upon several types of questions. Samples of types of riddles follow:

WHO AM I?

I rescued the big ocean liner. Who am I? (*Answer: Little Toot*)

I am a house painter who longs to go exploring. I keep penguins in the ice box. Who am I? (*Answer:* Mr. Popper of *Mr. Popper's Penguins*)

My ability to write saved a pig from death. Who am I? (*Answer:* Charlotte in *Charlotte's Web*)

WHO LIVED HERE?

Who lived on a boat in the Yangtze River? (*Answer:* Ping in *The Story about Ping*)

Who lived neither in the Highlands of Scotland nor the Lowlands, but halfway between? (*Answer:* Wee Gillis)

Who lived in a school with eleven other little girls? (*Answer:* Madeline)

WHAT IS IT?

What did *Little Leo* take to Italy? (*Answer:* His Indian suit)

With what did Pecos Bill capture lightning? (*Answer:* A tornado)

What one thing did Janey Larkin cherish on all of her moves? (*Answer:* Her *Blue Willow* plate)

"Find the Missing Color" is a game that can be played by writing the correct color word from the titles of stories the children have read. The game might include:

Island of the _____ *Dolphins* (*Answer:* Blue)
The _____ *Stallion* (*Answer:* Black)
The Children of _____ *Knowe* (*Answer:* Green)
The Little Rabbit Who Wanted _____ *Wings* (*Answer:* Red)
_____ *Willow* (*Answer:* Blue)
Hans Brinker or the _____ *Skates* (*Answer:* Silver)
The _____ *Bow* (*Answer:* Bronze)

Similarly, with words representing foods, such titles as the following could be given in a game called "What Food?":

_____ *Girl* (*Answer:* Strawberry)
On the Banks of _____ *Creek* (*Answer:* Plum)
Space Ship under the _____ *Tree* (*Answer:* Apple)
The _____ *Trick* (*Answer:* Lemonade)
The Enormous _____ (*Answer:* Egg)
_____ *John* (*Answer:* Onion)
Wonderful Flight to the _____ *Planet* (*Answer:* Mushroom)
Miracles on _____ *Hill* (*Answer:* Maple)

Children can be given samples of all these different types of riddles and, working in groups, they can create their own. Some of the 8- and 9-year-olds might want to make their own books of riddles. One class could exchange riddles with another. A new book-riddle could be displayed on the library bulletin board each week, or printed in the classroom newspaper. Children can make "Guess Who?" games and puzzles that can be duplicated for individual use.

Literary crossword puzzles devised by children in the middle grades are another means of extending literature. Children should be instructed to ask questions concerning stories that are known to almost everyone in the class. It is better to make easy crossword puzzles at first. The sample one on "folk tales" (p. 690) was devised for a middle-grade group of children who had been studying folklore. Crossword puzzles may be enclosed in an appropriate shape, such as a book or a picture of a covered wagon for historical fiction or a space ship for science-fiction titles or characters. A teacher or librarian can make a sample crossword puzzle to show children how, but the real value is in the construction itself, which children can easily do.

Older children have fun writing sets of clues on paper shaped like footprints for the game, "Book Detective." Different groups could compose four clues for each book numbered in order of their difficulty. If the group cannot guess the name of the book with the first clue, the children can ask the leader for another clue. The group that identifies the most books with the fewest footprint clues wins the game.

"Twenty Questions" is a game that can be played by small groups or the entire class. For example, in one room five 9-year-olds might be questioning a classmate who is thinking of a book. The questions can be answered only by responding "yes" or "no." Children quickly learn to ask categorical questions. Some of the questions may include:

Is it a fairy tale?
Does it take place in modern times?
Is it an animal book?
Do the animals actually exist?
Are they farm animals?

The questioning continues until all twenty questions are asked or the book title is guessed.

FOLK TALE CROSSWORD PUZZLE[12]

Across

1. And they all lived happily ever _____.
2. "Oh fish in the sea
Come listen to _____."
3. A French tale about a cat is _____ in Boots.
4. The second name of the princess who was the fairest of them all.
5. Tom _____ Tot spun five skeins each day.
6. Jack sold his cow for a handful of _____.
7. "Who's afraid of the big, bad _____?"
8. The color of Miss Riding Hood's hood.
9. Many folk tales begin, "Once upon a _____"

Down

6. The name of Paul Bunyan's ox.
8. Cinderella's coachman was made from the largest of these.
10. What Congo Boy wanted most of all.
11. The first name of the princess who was the fairest of them all.
12. The Russian Cinderella.
13. The Japanese wise man burned the _____ fields so all the villagers would climb the mountain.
14. This is a very special kind of soup, made to fool the greedy villagers.

Children who have watched "Hollywood Squares" on television will have no difficulty in playing "Literature Tic Tac Toe." Literature categories may be written on the board. With the guidance of the teacher, the children will have previously submitted appropriate questions for each category. These will be written on cards and placed in labeled envelopes. There are two players in this game. The first player chooses the category with which he would like to start; for example, science books. He then draws a question from the envelope pertaining to his category.

[12] Constructed by Ellen Esrick, Reading Motivator, Martin Luther King, Jr., Laboratory School, Evanston, Illinois Public Schools.

If he answers the question correctly, he may place his mark in the square. The players continue in the usual tic-tac-toe fashion until one player or "the cat" wins.

"Book Baseball" is another way of utilizing children's knowledge of literature. Four bases are designated in the room. The teacher "pitches" questions based on authors, titles, or characters to each player in turn. If the question is answered correctly, "the batter" moves to first base; if not, he makes an out. The player progresses from base to base as other teammates answer correctly. Following baseball rules, the opposing team takes its turn "at bat" when the other team makes three outs.

A book version of "Hot Potato" is played with any number of children sitting in a circle. The leader, who stands in the center, gives a book to a player and calls, "Book." By the count of five the player must give the title of a book and return the "hot book" to the leader or be eliminated. The game may be varied by calling for an author, a poem, or a favorite character.

BOARD GAMES

Children in the middle grades can be encouraged to construct board or table games based upon knowledge of popular books, authors, or characters. The basic patterns may be designed for two or four players, who move numbers or figures along marked spaces in a pathway or channel to reach a desired goal. A player can move forward by selecting a question card from a pile and giving the correct answer. The game may be made more interesting by adding chance cards, which would govern the number of question cards to be drawn or spaces to be moved forward.

Using similar procedures, a table game can be devised that uses the characters and events in one book. "Courage"[13] was based on Sperry's *Call It Courage.* The game is played by throwing dice in order to move markers around a course. When the marker stops on certain squares, the player must draw a card from the center pack. Cards of courage, with such labels as "Direction pointed by Kivi the Albatross" or "Mafatu's

[13]Game created by Sharlene Polk, student, The Ohio State University.

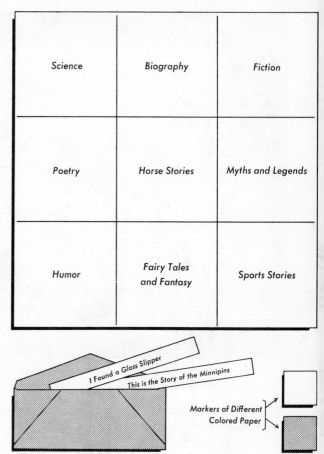

Science	Biography	Fiction
Poetry	Horse Stories	Myths and Legends
Humor	Fairy Tales and Fantasy	Sports Stories

I Found a Glass Slipper

This is the Story of the Minnipins

Markers of Different Colored Paper

"Literature Tic Tac Toe," with the categories written on the board.

knife," give the player ten additional points. The player loses ten points if he draws a card of fear, with such titles as "Mast and sail broken by typhoon" or "Noise from eater-of-men's drums." The game continues until one player accumulates 100 points, taking Mafatu back to the island of Hikueri.

A group of 9- and 10-year-olds created a board game for Merrill's *The Pushcart War.* The players were divided into two teams: the "Mighty Mammoth Truckers" and the "Pushcart Peddlers." The board was divided into a road with squares marked on it. Played with a spinner, everyone could move his truck or pushcart as

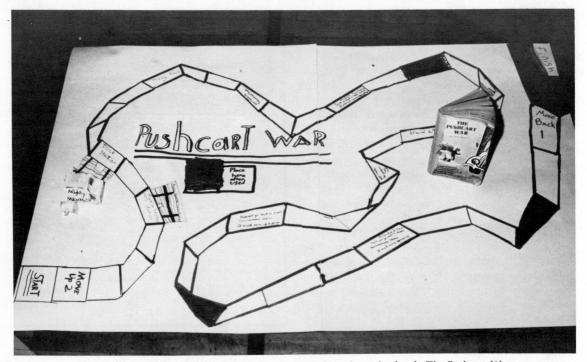

Two 9-year-old boys constructed a board game based on the book *The Pushcart War*.
Martin Luther King, Jr., Laboratory School, Evanston, Illinois, Barbara Friedberg, teacher.

many spaces ahead as the spin showed. If a player landed on a square marked "The Pea Shooter Campaign," he could advance five spaces if the player were a peddler; however, the truckers had to go back five spaces. Construction of the game sent children back to the book for an accurate description of both sides of this amusing battle in New York City.

Another group of children created a "Charlotte's Web Game" that they played with large artificial spiders. A "Freaky Friday" game, based on the book by that title by Mary Rodgers, would be fun to devise. All of the mad escapades of Annabel on the day she turned into her mother could be incorporated. Children will think of many books that might lend themselves to use as games. The only requirement is that they should be well-known books so that the clues, rewards, or penalties will be understood by all players.

Children can develop an awareness of types of books by playing a game in which it is necessary to classify titles. In a game entitled "Katy-No-Pockets," a board is constructed by folding plastic-coated paper so that each player has twelve pockets. Forty-eight cards of one color are labeled with titles of books; five to eight category cards are placed in the center. Title cards are dealt to the players who place them in the pockets. Each child in turn draws a category card. Suppose he draws the category card *Horse Stories*. If he has title cards of *King of the Wind* and *The Black Stallion*, he removes these cards from the pockets and replaces the category card at the bottom of the center pile. The game ends when a player removes all his cards from the pockets.

The game of *Authors*, always popular with children, may be made by using familiar book titles and well-known authors of children's literature. Cards can be designed so that there are four title cards for each author selected. Children take turns "calling" or "drawing" for cards until they complete their "books" of four title cards. The following authors and titles of books can be used for sets of cards:

LLOYD ALEXANDER

The Book of Three
The Black Cauldron
The Cat Who Wished to Be a Man
Time Cat, The Remarkable Journeys

JUDY BLUME

Are You There God? It's Me, Margaret
Blubber
Otherwise Known as Sheila the Great
Tales of a Fourth-Grade Nothing

CAROLYN HAYWOOD

"B" Is for Betsy
Betsy's Busy Summer
Eddie and His Big Deals
Little Eddie

MARGUERITE HENRY

Brighty of the Grand Canyon
King of the Wind
Misty of Chincoteague
White Stallion of Lipizza

MEINDERT DEJONG

Far Out the Long Canal
The House of Sixty Fathers
Hurry Home, Candy
The Wheel on the School

DR. SEUSS

The 500 Hats of Bartholomew Cubbins
And to Think that I Saw It on Mulberry Street
Horton Hatches the Egg
The Cat in the Hat

ROBERT McCLOSKEY

Burt Dow, Deep-Water Man
Centerburg Tales
Homer Price
Lentil

BEVERLY CLEARY

Beezus and Ramona
Henry Huggins

The Mouse and the Motorcycle
Ribsy

LAURA INGALLS WILDER

Little House in the Big Woods
The Long Winter
On the Banks of Plum Creek
These Happy Golden Years

Children can also make variations of lotto and bingo games based upon literature. Titles, authors, characters, and places in children's literature are written on "Book-O" cards. A caller reads matching identification cards, and the players place markers over the proper squares. A winner is declared when a player has one horizontal, diagonal, or vertical row covered. The game can also be played until a winner has all squares on his card covered. Each card in the set must be different. Old calendars with large squares marked for each month can be saved to make "Book-O" cards.

Commercially prepared games are also available for activities related to children's literature. However, children derive many values through the process of constructing their own games. When boys and girls plan puzzles, riddles, and games, they recall characters from literature, titles, authors, and situations. If the complete group is to enjoy the games, each child needs to read widely. It is important to remember that the purpose of these games is to stimulate reading, not to master isolated details of children's literature. Increasingly, educators have come to recognize the values of both playing and constructing games.

Through games, pantomime, creative dramatics, creative-writing activities, and the use of varied art media, children interpret and extend their understandings of children's literature. Valuable in their own right, these activities lead to deeper insights and lasting appreciations.

SUGGESTED LEARNING EXPERIENCES

1. Working in pairs, select a book or poem and extend it through one of the activities suggested in the sections on "Art and Media," "Sewing and Cooking," or "Games." Plan to bring your finished project to class and describe the planning which you had to do.
2. Pantomime Mother Goose rhymes or favorite folk tales for your class. You might work in groups and play charades using these verses and tales.

3. Work with a group of children or your peers to dramatize a scene from children's literature. If possible, ask an observer to record your directions and evaluation. Share these in class.

4. Work with a small group of children 8 years old or older in developing a puppet play. Have them make and dress their puppets and plan the story they are going to tell. Someone else could record the process with a camera and show slides of the sequence.

5. Following the directions for drawing and coloring slides or filmstrips, create your own story and present it to your classmates.

6. Write your own version of "A terrible, horrible, no-good, very bad day." Plan to illustrate it and bind it into a book.

7. Visit a middle-grade classroom and observe the variety of written discourse in the room and the quality of the content. Plan ways to vary the form and improve the quality of the writing.

8. Make and tell a flannelboard story to a group of primary-grade children in school or during a library story hour. Write your evaluation of the experience. How attentive were the children? What would you do differently another time?

9. Working in small groups of two or three, select a children's book that you like very much and list all the appropriate activities that could extend children's understanding and appreciation of that book.

RELATED READINGS

1. Anderson, Yvonne. *Making Your Own Animated Movies.* Boston, Mass.: Little, Brown, 1974.
   Anderson describes her actual work with children from 5 to 18 in creating their own films.

2. Barlin, Ann, and Paul Barlin. *The Art of Learning through Movement.* New York: Ritchie Ward Press, 1971.
   Clear and succinct, this book offers simple techniques that reflect the author's wide experiences in public-school teaching.

3. Bauer, Caroline Feller. *Getting It Together with Books.* Oregon Educational and Public Broadcasting Service, A Division of the Oregon State System of Higher Education, 1974.
   A teletext based upon an educational television program designed for librarians and teachers. Many practical suggestions for sample story hours and library programs are included.

4. Carlson, Ruth Kearney. *Enrichment Ideas.* Dubuque, Iowa: Wm. C. Brown, 1970.
   This little booklet contains a wealth of creative activities that have been motivated by literature. One chapter suggests ways of helping children write different forms of poetry.

5. Clegg, A. B. *The Excitement of Writing.* New York: Schocken, 1972.
   Formerly head of the West Riding Schools in Yorkshire, England, Sir Alex Clegg reports on the writing activities in these schools. The author includes many samples of children's writing and suggests the kinds of experiencing and environment from which they were derived. This book presents a sharp contrast to many "gimmicky" books on ways to motivate children's writing.

6. Helfman, Harry. *Making Your Own Movies.* New York: Morrow, 1970.
   A useful book for teachers and children. The author presents some basic techniques of film-making. A description of panning a picture book to create the illusion of movement is given.

7. Linderman, Earl W., and Donald W. Herberholz. *Developing Artistic and Perceptual Awareness,* 3rd ed. Dubuque, Iowa: Wm. C. Brown, 1974.
   A unique book on art methods in the elementary school that emphasizes the development of awareness and flexibility in children's thinking and creating. Contains many practical suggestions for helping children use a variety of materials in their art work.

8. McCaslin, Nellie. *Creative Dramatics in the Classroom,* 2nd ed. New York: McKay, 1974.
   A useful and sound book on creative drama that moves from pantomime to improvisation to building plays from stories and poems. A unique chapter provides suggestions for creative dramatics in special education.

9. Moffett, James. *Teaching the Universe of Discourse.* Boston, Mass.: Houghton Mifflin, 1968.

    A sound rationale for a language-arts program that is attuned to children's needs and development. Chapter Two discusses the kinds and orders of written and oral discourse that teachers should try to encourage in their classes.

10. Siks, Geraldine Brain. *Creative Dramatics, An Art for Children.* New York: Harper & Row, 1958.

    The elementary-school teacher can obtain a thorough understanding of creative dramatics through this excellent book. Many examples and questions to be used in setting the stage, interpreting the story, and planning the dramatization illustrate creative dramatics at its best. Specific helps are presented by relating stories, motivation, and development to the interests and needs of different age levels. An annotated list of poems and stories to dramatize will be especially useful.

11. Stewig, John W. *Spontaneous Drama: A Language Art,* Columbus, Ohio: Charles Merrill, 1973.

    A practical "how-to-do-it" book on improvisation. Teachers will find this very useful.

12. Wachowiak, Frank, and Theodore Ramsay. *Emphasis: Art,* 2nd ed. Scranton, Penna.: Intext, 1971.

    An invaluable book for the teacher who wants specific directions for helping children make a mural, use tempera batik, tissue paper colláge, vegetable prints, box sculpture, and so on. Illustrated with many colored pictures of children's art work.

13. Weiss, Harvey. *How to Make Your Own Books.* New York: Crowell, 1974.

    Both teachers and children in the middle grades will want to use this book, which gives instructions for making travel journals, diaries, photo albums, scrapbooks, scrolls, and so on. Clear directions are given for different ways of binding a variety of books.

14. Whitehead, Robert. *Children's Literature: Strategies of Teaching.* Englewood Cliffs, N.J.: Prentice-Hall, 1968.

    Gives many suggestions and techniques for motivating children to read and to interpret their reading through creative activities. Some of the motivational devices are contrary to what has been suggested in this text; other activities will prove very useful.

RECOMMENDED REFERENCES[14]

Adoff, Arnold. *Ma nDA La,* illustrated by Emily McCully. Harper & Row, 1971.

Aesop. *Aesop's Fables,* selected and adapted by Louis Untermeyer, illustrated by Alice Provensen and Martin Provensen. Golden Press, 1966.

Alexander, Lloyd. *The Black Cauldron.* Holt, Rinehart and Winston, 1965.

———. *The Book of Three.* Holt, Rinehart and Winston, 1964.

———. *The Cat Who Wished to Be a Man.* Dutton, 1973.

———. *Time Cat, The Remarkable Journeys,* illustrated by Bill Sokol. Holt, Rinehart and Winston, 1963.

Aliki, pseud. (Aliki Brandenberg). *Go Tell Aunt Rhody.* Macmillan, 1974.

Allingham, William. "A Swing Song," in *Favorite Poems Old and New,* Helen Ferris, ed., illustrated by Leonard Weisgard. Doubleday, 1957.

Atwater, Richard, and Florence Atwater. *Mr. Popper's Penguins,* illustrated by Robert Lawson. Little, Brown, 1938.

Bailey, Carolyn S. *The Little Rabbit Who Wanted Red Wings,* illustrated by Dorothy Grider. Platt & Munk, 1970 (1945).

———. *Miss Hickory,* illustrated by Ruth Gannett. Viking, 1962 (1946).

Baruch, Dorothy. "The Merry-Go-Round," in *Time for Poetry,* May Hill Arbuthnot and Shelton Root, eds. Scott, Foresman, 1968.

Bemelmans, Ludwig. *Madeline.* Viking, 1939.

Bendick, Jeanne. *A Fresh Look at Night.* F. Watts, 1963.

---

[14] All books listed at the end of this chapter are recommended subject to the qualifications noted in the text. See Appendix D for publishers' complete addresses.

Bishop, Claire Huchet. *The Five Chinese Brothers*, illustrated by Kurt Wiese. Coward-McCann, 1938.

Blume, Judy. *Are You There God? It's Me, Margaret*. Bradbury, 1970.

———. *Blubber*. Bradbury, 1974.

———. *Otherwise Known as Sheila the Great*. Dutton, 1972.

———. *Tales of a Fourth Grade Nothing*, illustrated by Roy Doty. Dutton, 1972.

Bond, Michael. *A Bear Called Paddington*, illustrated by Peggy Fortnum. Houghton Mifflin, 1960.

Boston, L. M. *The Children of Green Knowe*, illustrated by Peter Boston. Harcourt Brace Jovanovich, 1955.

Briggs, Raymond. *Jim and the Beanstalk*. Coward-McCann, 1970.

Brooks, Gwendolyn. *Bronzeville Boys and Girls*, illustrated by Ronni Solbert. Harper & Row, 1965.

Brown, Marcia. *Stone Soup*. Scribner, 1947.

Brown, Margaret Wise. *Four Fur Feet*, illustrated by Remy Charlip. Young Scott Books, 1961.

Browning, Robert. *The Pied Piper of Hamelin*, illustrated by Harold Jones. F. Watts, 1962.

Burnett, Frances Hodgson. *The Secret Garden*, illustrated by Tasha Tudor. Lippincott, 1962 (1910).

Burton, Virginia Lee. *The Little House*. Houghton Mifflin, 1942.

Butterworth, Oliver. *The Enormous Egg*, illustrated by Louis Darling. Little, Brown, 1956.

Cameron, Eleanor. *The Wonderful Flight to the Mushroom Planet*, illustrated by Robert Henneberger. Little, Brown, 1954.

Carlson, Natalie S. *The Letter on the Tree*, illustrated by John Kaufmann. Harper & Row, 1964.

Carroll, Lewis, pseud. (Charles L. Dodgson). *Alice's Adventures in Wonderland*, illustrated by John Tenniel. Macmillan, 1963 (1865).

Charlip, Remy. *Fortunately*. Parents', 1964.

Cleary, Beverly. *Beezus and Ramona*, illustrated by Louis Darling. Morrow, 1955.

———. *Henry Huggins*, illustrated by Louis Darling. Morrow, 1950.

———. *The Mouse and the Motorcycle*, illustrated by Louis Darling. Morrow, 1965.

———. *Ribsy*, illustrated by Louis Darling. Morrow, 1964.

Conford, Ellen. *Impossible, Possum*, illustrated by Rosemary Wells. Little, Brown, 1971.

Cooney, Barbara. *Chanticleer and the Fox*. Crowell, 1958.

———. *The Little Juggler*. Hastings House, 1961.

Corbett, Scott. *The Lemonade Trick*. Little, Brown, 1960.

Cunningham, Julia. *Macaroon*, illustrated by Evaline Ness. Pantheon, 1962.

Dahl, Roald. *Charlie and the Chocolate Factory*, illustrated by Joseph Schindelman. Knopf, 1964.

———. *James and the Giant Peach*, illustrated by Nancy Burkert. Knopf, 1961.

Dalgliesh, Alice. *The Courage of Sarah Noble*, illustrated by Leonard Weisgard. Scribner, 1954.

DeJong, Meindert. *Far Out the Long Canal*, illustrated by Nancy Grossman. Harper & Row, 1964.

———. *The House of Sixty Fathers*, illustrated by Maurice Sendak. Harper & Row, 1956.

———. *Hurry Home, Candy*, illustrated by Maurice Sendak. Harper & Row, 1953.

———. *The Wheel on the School*, illustrated by Maurice Sendak. Harper & Row, 1954.

De la Mare, Walter. "The Old Stone House" in *Rhymes and Verses: Collected Poems for Young People*, illustrated by Elinore Blaisdill. Holt, Rinehart and Winston, 1947.

———. "Silver" in *Time for Poetry*, May Hill Arbuthnot and Shelton Root, eds. Scott, Foresman, 1968.

De Regniers, Beatrice Schenk. *May I Bring a Friend?*, illustrated by Beni Montresor. Atheneum, 1964.

Dodge, Mary Mapes. *Hans Brinker, or the Silver Skates*, illustrated by George Wharton Edwards. Scribner, 1915 (1865).

Domanska, Janina. *The Turnip*. Macmillan, 1969.

Du Bois, William Pène. *Lion*. Viking, 1956.

———. *The Twenty-one Balloons*. Viking, 1947.

Dunning, Stephen, *et al. Reflections on a Gift of Watermelon Pickle and Other Modern Verse*. Lothrop, 1967.

Duvoisin, Roger. *Petunia.* Knopf, 1950.

Elkin, Benjamin. *Six Foolish Fishermen,* illustrated by Katherine Evans. Children's Press, 1957.

Ellison, Virginia. *The Pooh Cook Book,* illustrated by Ernest H. Shepard. Dutton, 1969.

Emberley, Barbara. *One Wide River to Cross,* illustrated by Ed Emberley. Prentice-Hall, 1966.

Engdahl, Sylvia Louise. *Enchantress from the Stars,* illustrated by Rodney Shackell. Atheneum, 1970.

Estes, Eleanor. *The Hundred Dresses,* illustrated by Louis Slobodkin. Harcourt Brace Jovanovich, 1944.

Fallis, Edwina. "The Giant Shoes," in *Let's Read Together Poems* (Book 3), Helen A. Brown and Harry J. Helt, eds. Harper & Row, 1954.

Farley, Walter. *The Black Stallion,* illustrated by Keith Ward. Random House, 1944.

Fitzhugh, Louise. *Harriet the Spy.* Harper & Row, 1964.

Flack, Marjorie. *Ask Mr. Bear.* Macmillan, 1932.

———. *The Story about Ping,* illustrated by Kurt Wiese. Viking, 1933.

Flora, James. *Leopold, the See-through Crumbpicker.* Harcourt Brace Jovanovich, 1961.

Foster, Genevieve. *The World of Captain John Smith.* Scribner, 1959.

———. *The World of Columbus & Sons.* Scribner, 1965.

———. *Year of the Pilgrims: 1620.* Scribner, 1969.

Fritz, Jean. *The Cabin Faced West,* illustrated by Feodor Rojankovsky. Coward-McCann, 1958.

Froman, Elizabeth. *Mr. Drackle and His Dragons,* illustrated by David McKee. F. Watts, 1971.

Fyleman, Rose. "The Best Game the Fairies Play" in *Time for Poetry,* May Hill Arbuthnot and Shelton Root, eds. Scott, Foresman, 1968.

Galdone, Paul. *The Three Bears.* Seabury, 1972.

———. *The Three Little Pigs.* Seabury, 1970.

———. *The Three Wishes.* McGraw-Hill, 1961.

Gates, Doris. *Blue Willow,* illustrated by Paul Lantz. Viking, 1940.

George, Jean. *The Hole in the Tree.* Dutton, 1957.

———. *My Side of the Mountain.* Dutton, 1959.

Ginsburg, Mirra. *The Lazies, Tales of the Peoples of Russia.* Macmillan, 1973.

Godden, Rumer. *Impunity Jane,* illustrated by Adrienne Adams. Viking, 1954.

———. *The Old Woman Who Lived in a Vinegar Bottle,* illustrated by Mairi Hedderwick. Viking, 1972.

Grahame, Kenneth. *The Reluctant Dragon,* illustrated by Ernest H. Shepard. Holiday, 1938.

———. *The Wind in the Willows,* illustrated by E. H. Shepard. Scribner, 1908.

Gramatky, Hardie. *Little Toot.* Putnam, 1939.

Gray, Genevieve. *The Seven Wishes of Joanna Peabody,* illustrated by Elton Fax. Lothrop, 1972.

Grimm Brothers. "The Bremen Town Musicians," "The Frog Prince," and "Rumpelstiltskin" in *Grimm's Fairy Tales,* introduction by Frances Clark Sayers. Follett. 1968.

———. *King Grisly-Beard: A Tale from the Brothers Grimm,* translated by Edgar Taylor, illustrated by Maurice Sendak. Farrar, Straus, 1973.

Haugaard, Erik Christian. *Hakon of Rogen's Saga,* illustrated by Leo Dillon and Diane Dillon. Houghton Mifflin, 1963.

Haviland, Virginia, ed. *The Fairy Tale Treasury,* illustrated by Raymond Briggs. Coward-McCann, 1972.

Hawthorne, Nathaniel. *The Golden Touch,* illustrated by Paul Galdone. McGraw-Hill, 1959.

Haywood, Carolyn. *"B" Is for Betsy.* Harcourt Brace Jovanovich, 1939.

———. *Betsy's Busy Summer.* Harcourt Brace Jovanovich, 1956.

———. *Eddie and His Big Deals.* Morrow, 1955.

———. *Little Eddie.* Morrow, 1947.

Heide, Florence P. *Some Things Are Scary,* illustrated by Osburn. Scholastic, 1971.

Henry, Marguerite. *Brighty of the Grand Canyon,* illustrated by Wesley Dennis. Rand McNally, 1953.

———. *King of the Wind,* illustrated by Wesley Dennis. Rand McNally, 1948.

———. *Misty of Chincoteague,* illustrated by Wesley Dennis. Rand McNally, 1947.

———. *White Stallion of Lipizza,* illustrated by Wesley Dennis. Rand McNally, 1964.

Heyward, DuBose. *The Country Bunny and the Little Gold Shoes*, illustrated by Marjorie Flack. Houghton Mifflin, 1939.

Hill, Elizabeth Starr. *Evan's Corner*, illustrated by Nancy Grossman. Holt, Rinehart and Winston, 1967.

Hirsh, Marilyn. *Could Anything Be Worse?* Holiday, 1974.

Hoban, Russell. *Bread and Jam for Frances*, illustrated by Lillian Hoban. Harper & Row, 1964.

Hodges, Margaret. *The Wave*, illustrated by Blair Lent. Houghton Mifflin, 1964.

Hogrogian, Nonny. *One Fine Day*. Macmillan, 1971.

Holm, Anne. *North to Freedom*, translated by L. W. Kingsland. Harcourt Brace Jovanovich, 1965.

Hughes, Langston. "The African Dance," in *Favorite Poems Old and New*, Helen Ferris, ed., illustrated by Leonard Weisgard. Doubleday, 1957.

Hunt, Irene. *Across Five Aprils*. Follett, 1964.

Hutchins, Pat. *Rosie's Walk*. Macmillan, 1968.

Keats, Ezra Jack. *Dreams*. Macmillan, 1974.

———. *Hi, Cat!* Macmillan, 1970.

———. *Jennie's Hat*. Harper & Row, 1966.

———. *Peter's Chair*. Harper & Row, 1967.

———. *The Snowy Day*. Viking, 1962.

Kent, Jack. *The Fat Cat, A Danish Folktale*. Parents', 1971.

Kipling, Rudyard. *The Elephant's Child*, illustrated by Leonard Weisgard. Walker, 1970.

———. *Just-So Stories*, illustrated by Etienne Delessert. Doubleday, 1972 (1902).

Krauss, Ruth. *This Thumbprint*. Harper & Row, 1967.

Krumgold, Joseph. *. . . And Now Miguel*, illustrated by Jean Charlot. Crowell, 1953.

———. *Onion John*, illustrated by Symeon Shimin. Crowell, 1959.

Langstaff, John. *Oh, A-Hunting We Will Go*, illustrated by Nancy Winslow Parker. Atheneum, 1974.

Lawson, Robert. *Ben and Me*. Little, Brown, 1939.

———. *Mr. Twigg's Mistake*. Little, Brown, 1947.

Leaf, Munro. *Wee Gillis*, illustrated by Robert Lawson. Viking, 1938.

Lenski, Lois. *Strawberry Girl*. Lippincott, 1945.

Lent, Blair. *From King Boggen's Hall to Nothing-at-All*. Little, Brown, 1967.

———. *John Tabor's Ride*. Little, Brown, 1966.

Lewis, Richard, compiler. *In a Spring Garden*, illustrated by Ezra Jack Keats. Dial, 1965.

Lexau, Joan. *That's Good, That's Bad*, illustrated by Aliki. Dial, 1963.

Lindgren, Astrid. *Pippi Longstocking*, illustrated by Louis Glanzman. Viking, 1950.

———. *The Tomten*, adapted from a poem by Viktor Rydberg, illustrated by Harald Wiberg. Coward-McCann, 1961.

Lindsay, Vachel. "The Potatoes' Dance," in *Favorite Poems Old and New*, Helen Ferris, ed., illustrated by Leonard Weisgard. Doubleday, 1957.

Lionni, Leo. *Alexander and the Wind-up Mouse*. Pantheon, 1969.

———. *Frederick*. Pantheon, 1967.

———. *Little Blue and Little Yellow*. Astor-Honor, 1959.

———. *Swimmy*. Pantheon, 1963.

Livingston, Myra Cohn. *See What I Found*, illustrated by Erik Blegvad. Harcourt Brace Jovanovich, 1962.

Lund, Doris. *Attic of the Wind*, illustrated by Ati Forberg. Parents', 1966.

McCloskey, Robert. *Burt Dow, Deep-Water Man*. Viking, 1963.

———. *Centerburg Tales*. Viking, 1951.

———. *Homer Price*. Viking, 1943.

———. *Lentil*. Viking, 1940.

———. *Make Way for Ducklings*. Viking, 1941.

McCord, David. *Take Sky*, illustrated by Henry B. Kane. Little, Brown, 1962.

McDermott, Gerald. *Anansi the Spider*. Holt, Rinehart and Winston, 1972.

MacDonald, George. *The Light Princess*, illustrated by Maurice Sendak. Farrar, Straus, 1969.

McNeer, May. *America's Abraham Lincoln*, illustrated by Lynd Ward. Houghton Mifflin, 1957.

————. *America's Mark Twain*, illustrated by Lynd Ward. Houghton Mifflin, 1962.

Mahy, Margaret. *The Dragon of an Ordinary Family*, illustrated by Helen Oxenbury. F. Watts, 1969.

Massie, Diane. *Monstrous Glisson Glop.* Parents', 1970.

Matsutani, Miyoko. *The Crane Maiden*, English version by Alvin Tresselt, illustrated by Chihiro Iwasaki. Parents', 1968.

Meadowcroft, Enid. *The First Year*, illustrated by Grace Paull. Crowell, 1946.

Mehdevi, Alexander. *Bungling Pedro and Other Majorcan Tales*, illustrated by Isabel Bodor. Knopf, 1970.

Merriam, Eve. "A Cliché," in *It Doesn't Always Have to Rhyme*, illustrated by Malcolm Spooner. Atheneum, 1964.

Merrill, Jean. *The Pushcart War*, illustrated by Ronni Solbert. Scott, 1964.

Milne, A. A. *Winnie the Pooh*, illustrated by Ernest H. Shepard. Dutton, 1926.

Norton, Mary. *The Borrowers*, illustrated by Beth Krush and Joe Krush. Harcourt Brace Jovanovich, 1953.

O'Dell, Scott. *Island of the Blue Dolphins.* Houghton Mifflin, 1960.

O'Neill, Mary. *Hailstones and Halibut Bones*, illustrated by Leonard Weisgard. Doubleday, 1961.

Parish, Peggy. *Amelia Bedelia*, illustrated by Fritz Siebel. Harper & Row, 1963.

Parnall, Peter. *The Mountain.* Doubleday, 1971.

Paterson, A. B. *Waltzing Matilda.* Holt, Rinehart and Winston, 1972.

Pearce, Philippa, reteller. *Beauty and the Beast*, illustrated by Alan Barnett. Crowell, 1972.

————. *Tom's Midnight Garden*, illustrated by Susan Einzig. Lippincott, 1959.

Politi, Leo. *Little Leo.* Scribner, 1951.

Prokofieff, Serge. *Peter and the Wolf*, illustrated by Frans Haacken. Watts, 1961.

Rey, H. A. *Curious George.* Houghton Mifflin, 1941.

Rodgers, Mary. *Freaky Friday.* Harper & Row, 1972.

Sawyer, Ruth. *Journey Cake, Ho!*, illustrated by Robert McCloskey. Viking, 1953.

Scott, Ann Herbert. *Sam*, illustrated by Symeon Shimin. McGraw-Hill, 1967.

Seidelman, James E., and Grace Mintoyne. *The 14th Dragon.* Harlan Quist, 1968.

Selden, George. *The Cricket in Times Square*, illustrated by Garth Williams. Farrar, Straus, 1960.

Sendak, Maurice. *Pierre.* Harper & Row, 1962.

————. *Where the Wild Things Are.* Harper & Row, 1963.

Seuss, Dr., pseud. (Theodor S. Geisel). *And to Think that I Saw It on Mulberry Street.* Vanguard, 1937.

————. *The Cat in the Hat.* Random House, 1957.

————. *The 500 Hats of Bartholomew Cubbins.* Vanguard, 1938.

————. *Horton Hatches the Egg.* Random House, 1940.

————. *On Beyond Zebra.* Random House, 1955.

Slobodkin, Florence. *Sarah Somebody*, illustrated by Louis Slobodkin. Vanguard, 1969.

Slobodkin, Louis. *The Space Ship under the Apple Tree.* Macmillan, 1952.

Slobodkina, Esphyr. *Caps for Sale.* Scott, 1947.

Small, Ernest. *Baba Yaga*, illustrated by Blair Lent. Houghton Mifflin, 1966.

Sorensen, Virginia. *Miracles on Maple Hill*, illustrated by Beth Krush and Joe Krush. Harcourt Brace Jovanovich, 1956.

Speare, Elizabeth George. *The Bronze Bow.* Houghton Mifflin, 1961.

Sperry, Armstrong. *Call It Courage.* Macmillan, 1940.

Spier, Peter. *The Erie Canal.* Doubleday, 1970.

————. *The Fox Went Out on a Chilly Night.* Doubleday, 1961.

————. *The Star Spangled Banner.* Doubleday, 1973.

Spyri, Johanna. *Heidi*, illustrated by Greta Elgaard. Macmillan, 1962 (1884).

Steele, Mary Q. *Journey Outside*, illustrated by Rocco Negri. Viking, 1969.

Steig, William. *Amos and Boris.* Farrar, Straus, 1971.

Steptoe, John. *Stevie.* Harper & Row, 1969.

Stobbs, William. *Jack and the Beanstalk.* Delacorte, 1969.

Stone, A. Harris. *The Last Free Bird*, illustrated by Sheila Heins. Prentice-Hall, 1967.

Sturton, Hugh. *Zomo the Rabbit*, illustrated by Peter Warner. Atheneum, 1966.

Tennyson, Alfred, Lord. *The Charge of the Light Brigade*, illustrated by Alice Provensen and Martin Provensen. Golden Press, 1964.

Thurber, James. *Many Moons*, illustrated by Louis Slobodkin. Harcourt Brace Jovanovich, 1943.

Travers, P. L. *Mary Poppins*, illustrated by Mary Shepard. Harcourt Brace Jovanovich, 1934.

Tresselt, Alvin. *Hide and Seek Fog*, illustrated by Roger Duvoisin. Lothrop, 1965.

Tunis, Edwin. *Shaw's Fortune: The Picture Story of a Colonial Plantation.* World, 1966.

Tworkov, Jack. *The Camel Who Took a Walk*, illustrated by Roger Duvoisin. Dutton, 1951.

Udry, Janice May. *The Moon Jumpers*, illustrated by Maurice Sendak. Harper & Row, 1959.

Viorst, Judith. *Alexander and the Terrible, Horrible, No Good, Very Bad Day*, illustrated by Ray Cruz. Atheneum, 1972.

Waber, Bernard. *"You Look Ridiculous," Said the Rhinoceros to the Hippopotamus.* Houghton Mifflin, 1966.

Ward, Lynd. *The Biggest Bear.* Houghton Mifflin, 1952.

White, E. B. *Charlotte's Web*, illustrated by Garth Williams. Harper & Row, 1952.

Wilder, Laura Ingalls. The *Little House* Series, illustrated by Garth Williams. Harper & Row, 1953.
By the Shores of Silver Lake (1939)
Little House in the Big Woods (1932)
Little House on the Prairie (1935)
Little Town on the Prairie (1941)
The Long Winter (1940)
On the Banks of Plum Creek (1937)
These Happy Golden Years (1943)

Williams, Margery. *The Velveteen Rabbit*, illustrated by William Nicholson. Doubleday, 1958 (1922).

Wojciechowska, Maia. *Shadow of a Bull*, illustrated by Alvin Smith. Atheneum, 1964.

Wynne, Annette. *"I Keep Three Wishes Ready,"* in *Time for Poetry*, May Hill Arbuthnot and Shelton Root, eds. Scott, Foresman, 1968.

Yates, Elizabeth. *Carolina's Courage*, illustrated by Nora S. Unwin. Dutton, 1964.

Zemach, Harve. *The Judge*, illustrated by Margot Zemach. Farrar, Straus, 1969.

————. *Mommy, Buy Me a China Doll*, illustrated by Margot Zemach. Follett, 1966.

————. *Nail Soup*, adapted from the text by Nils Djurklo, illustrated by Margot Zemach. Follett, 1964.

Zion, Gene. *Harry, the Dirty Dog*, illustrated by Margaret Bloy Graham. Harper & Row, 1956.

Zolotow, Charlotte. *Someday*, illustrated by Arnold Lobel. Harper & Row, 1964.

12 The Literature Program

A student participant from a university was sharing Yashima's *Crow Boy* with a
class of 9- and 10-year-olds in an inner city school. When she finished reading
the book she told the children that the story took place in Japan and asked them
if they knew where Japan was. There was a mad dash for the globe to see who
could be the first to locate Japan. Then the participant went on to ask what
Japan was, finally eliciting the answer she wanted—"an island." Next she asked
what appeared to be a very unrelated question: "Why did Chibi have a rice ball
wrapped in a radish leaf for his lunch instead of a hamburger?" The children
were as baffled as the supervisor sitting in the back of the room. Finally, the
participant gave them a brief but erroneous geography lesson in which she told
them that since Japan was an island it was very wet and flat so the Japanese
people could only raise rice, not beef for hamburgers! And there the matter was
left—a miserable geography lesson which had somehow moved from Japan to
growing rice, but had lost Crow Boy and the class along the way.

The supervisor could no longer refrain from entering the discussion. She told
the children that they had just heard one of her favorite stories and she wondered if she could ask them some questions. She asked them to recall how Chibi
had felt at the very beginning of that story. They looked once again at the first
picture that showed a frightened Chibi hiding beneath the schoolhouse and the
second one that pictured him cowering away from the schoolmaster. Then she
reread the last two pages that told of a grown-up, but still shy Crow Boy, shopping in the village for his family and then setting off for his mountain home,
straightening his shoulders and imitating the cry of a happy crow. The supervisor asked the children to compare how the boy felt at the beginning of the
story with the way he felt at the end. The children discussed what they thought
had made Chibi change. Then, looking at the endpapers of the book, the supervisor asked the children why Taro Yashima might have chosen to paint a butterfly and a flowering peach branch against a dark background to represent this
story. There was no response, and so the supervisor tried one last question; she
asked: "What is a butterfly before it becomes a butterfly?" Three boys bran-
dished their hands wildly and one of them said: "It's a caterpillar, and it
changes, it *changes* just like Crow Boy changed!"

This anecdote actually happened very much as it is recorded here. It provides
an excellent example of what should *not* be done in discussing a work of fiction,
and an alternative approach that can be used. If the participating student had

wanted to present facts about Japan, as her questions indicated, then she should have used an informational book. The supervisor, on the other hand, emphasized the feelings of Chibi and what had happened to him to make him change from a frightened little boy to a happy, responsible youth. She was not certain that the children were ready for the question concerning the way the artist had captured meaning in his pictures for the endpapers—and some of them were not. However, three or four children did develop some insight into how an author-artist can convey meaning in both words and pictures. And all of the children derived a fuller understanding of some of the causes of personality development.

The first approach to sharing *Crow Boy* with a class can serve as an example of how literature has been used and misused in elementary schools in the United States. For years, teachers have used literature to teach something else—to motivate reading; to enrich the social studies; to increase children's vocabularies; to inculcate manners, morals, and safety rules. An examination of the curriculum guides for many elementary schools reveals very few devoted to literature, although there may be a section on literature within the language-arts guide or the reading guide. Not until students reach junior high school or, more frequently, high school does literature receive much attention. The majority of the elementary schools in the United States have no planned literature programs.

Most of what a child studies at school is concerned with learning skills or facts; only literature is concerned with thought and feelings. Literature helps a child develop an understanding of what it means to become fully human. A young child loves and hates, knows fear and courage, sadness and joy, disappointments and hope. He needs to know that these are not unique feelings, that he is not alone. Literature will help him find validity in his experience, extend his insights, and develop new ones. It can enlarge and deepen compassion and help him to develop his "humanness" and understand others.

It does not make good sense to postpone children's experience of literature until the junior high school. Bloom maintains that children have obtained at least 75 percent of their total general achievement by the time they have reached 13. He points out that "the first period of elementary schools (grades one through three) is probably the most crucial period available to the public

schools for the development of general learning patterns."[1] And yet during this crucial period of education we have allowed the teaching of literature to be almost incidental, depending upon the interest and whim of the teacher.

The first National Assessment of Literature indicated that less than half of the 13-year-olds (43 percent) in the United States agreed with the statement that it was important to study literature in school, in contrast with some 99 percent of the 17-year-olds who attested to its importance.[2] This is understandable, since many of the 13-year-olds were just *beginning* their study of literature, while the 17-year-olds had had experience with it. The 13-year-olds probably had had exposure to literature, but they thought of it as reading or story hour, not literature. They also did not see literature as having intrinsic value in their lives. When asked to give reasons for the importance of literature, some 70 percent of the 13-year-olds gave only utilitarian reasons, such as it improves grammar or speech or "it helps you get into college."

Even researchers have measured the impact of a literature program when it is introduced into the elementary curriculum in terms of growth in other areas. Cazden[3] recommends reading aloud to the pre-schooler for its effect on his language development. Cohen's study of the impact of a read-aloud program on 7-year-olds was measured by the growth in children's reading com-

[1] Benjamin Bloom. *Stability and Change in Human Characteristics* (New York: Wiley, 1964), p. 110.
[2] *Highlights of the First National Assessment* (Denver, Col.: National Assessment of Educational Progress, November 1972), p. 1.
[3] Courtney Cazden. *Child's Language and Education* (New York: Holt, Rinehart and Winston, 1972).

prehension and vocabulary.[4] The Nebraska Literature Curriculum was first developed as a way of providing proper models for children's writing.[5] And advocates of the Sustained Silent Reading approach[6] do not care what children read as long as they read. Is it any wonder that 13-year-olds see only a utilitarian value for literature? During the most important years of their educational lives, their teachers always value literature for what it does to improve other skills or enrich other subjects. For too long now, literature in the elementary school has been a handmaiden for reading, language arts, and the social studies. The time has come to recognize what the experience of literature, as literature, may do for the child.

What Literature Does for Children

PROVIDES ENJOYMENT

First and foremost, literature provides enjoyment. Four- and 5-year-olds laugh out loud at the Barretts' funny book *Animals Should Definitely Not Wear Clothing*. They thoroughly enjoy the verses and the cartoonlike little pictures of *Father Fox's Pennyrhymes* by the Watsons. Like Max, they enjoy being frightened by the monsters in Sendak's *Where the Wild Things Are*, provided they can tame them and return home to the comfort of a warm supper. They respond to the repetition of the Troll's cry of "Who's that tripping over my bridge?" and eagerly anticipate what is going to happen when the Big Billy Goat crosses the bridge. The primary-school child delights in the bobbing rhythm of "Mrs. Peck-Pigeon/Is picking for bread" by Farjeon or the sound of "The pickety fence/The pickety fence/Give it a lick it's/The pickety fence" by McCord. He laughs at the funny antics of Lobel's *Frog and Toad*

Are Friends and empathizes with the little boy in Alexander's story *Nobody Asked Me If I Wanted a Baby Sister.*

All children and adults have lived through a day like Alexander's in *Alexander and the Terrible, Horrible, No Good, Very Bad Day* by Judith Viorst. This is a book that never fails to connect with today's child. The laughter that follows the reading of *The Shrinking of Treehorn* by Heide is more sophisticated and brittle. Yet children enjoy the irony of this commentary on a suburban family.

Judy Blume's book *Are You There God? It's Me, Margaret* is so popular with girls in the middle grades that there is usually a waiting list for it. Girls also identify with Gold's *Amelia Quackenbush*, with her different but loving family, and her difficult adjustment to a new school. Sad books bring a kind of enjoyment, as all children who have read Armstrong's *Sounder* will tell you. Many older children enjoy being frightened, too, and they delight in the suspense of *Blackbriar* by William Sleator or the horror of living through the Leningrad siege as described in *Boris* by Jaap ter Haar.

The list of books that children enjoy can go on and on. There are so many fine ones—and so many that children won't find unless teachers, librarians, and parents lead the way. A literature program in a school would assure children the opportunity to know some of these books. It would intensify and expand the child's enjoyment of many more.

DEVELOPS IMAGINATION

Literature develops children's imagination and helps them to consider nature, people, experiences, or ideas in new ways. Tana Hoban's exciting photographic puzzle, *Look Again!*, gives children a rich visual experience and helps them to see a sunflower, or a snail, or a zebra from a new perspective. Janina Domanska's *What Do You See?* is a simple tale of the limited viewpoint of a bat who sees the world as dark, a frog who sees it as wet, while for the fly it's dry, and for the fern it's green. Only the lark flying high can see that all viewpoints are correct. Beautiful designs and lush colors provide children with different perspectives in this kind of pre-schooler's variation of "The Blind Men and the Elephant."

---

[4] Dorothy Cohen. "The Effect of Literature on Vocabulary and Reading Achievement," *Elementary English,* Vol. 45 (February 1968), pp. 209–213, 217).

[5] Evertts, Eldonna, *et al. Nebraska Study of the Syntax of Children's Writing, 1964–1965, I* (Lincoln, Neb.: University of Nebraska Press, 1967).

[6] Robert A. McCracken and Marlene J. McCracken. *Reading Is Only the Tiger's Tail* (San Rafael, Cal.: Leswing, 1972).

Good writing will pique curiosity and question if children have "ever thought of a hill, or a mouse, or a relationship in this way?" The title of Ciardi's poem, "The River Is a Piece of Sky" may give the child a new way of looking at a reflection in the water. In concluding the poem Ciardi separates his metaphor with the idea that the river has splashes, but that the sky doesn't. Literature helps children entertain ideas that had never occurred to them before. Saint-Exupéry's *The Little Prince* is dejected when he finds out that his rose is not the only rose in the world. The fox, however, tells him that it is his love for his rose that makes it unique to him.

In the "Foreword" to Robert Frost's poems, *You Come Too,* Hyde Cox describes the way a question by Frost made him see education in a new light:

> "How many things have to happen to you," he [Frost] asks his young friends, "before something occurs to you?" Things that happen to you, of course, are only events. Things that occur to you are ideas; and he is saying that ideas are more important. That is the kind of question he asks that I would not have thought to ask myself, and it leads to one of the best things he ever taught me: to entertain ideas. We all speak of having ideas but entertaining them is an art. You have to invite them in and make them feel at home—as you do company—while you get to know them, to see if you want to know them better. Entertaining ideas is almost the heart of education.[7]

Literature opens windows for children that they never knew existed; it helps them to entertain new ideas, to see the world from a new perspective, and to develop their imaginations.

GIVES VICARIOUS EXPERIENCE

New perspectives are derived as the child has vicarious experiences through literature. Good writing may transport the reader to other places and other periods of time, and expand his life space. Identification with others is experienced as the reader enters an imaginary situation with his

[7]Hyde Cox. "Foreword" of *You Come Too, Favorite Poems for Young Readers* by Robert Frost, with wood engravings by Thomas W. Nason (New York: Holt, Rinehart and Winston, 1959), p. 9.

emotions tuned to those of the story. He may feel he *is* Ishi as he reads Kroeber's *Ishi, Last of His Tribe,* and actually sense some of the pain that gripped this Indian who was the lone survivor of his tribe. The young reader sits tensely as he imagines he is bumping along in a covered wagon by the side of Carolina in *Carolina's Courage* (Yates). He does not need to be told that slavery is wrong in Paula Fox's *The Slave Dancer;* instead, the author shows him the devastation that it wrecks upon slave and master. A history textbook tells; a quality piece of imaginative writing has the power to make the reader feel, to transport him to the deck of a slave ship and force him into the hold until he chokes on the very horror of it.

Literature provides vicarious experiences of adventure, excitement, and struggle against the elements or other obstacles. In fantasy, Will Stanton, seventh son of a seventh son, must do battle against the forces of evil, the power of the dark, and the unbelievably intense cold before he can complete the circle of the old ones. The strength of this fantasy, *The Dark Is Rising* by Susan Cooper, is the degree to which she involves the reader in Will's struggle. In *Banner in the Sky* by Ullman, Rudi meets many dangers, but must choose between responsibility to others and his consuming desire to scale the mountain peak where his father died. Often the adventure of the spirit is found in biography, such as is portrayed in Simon's story of Albert Schweitzer, *All Men Are Brothers.* Whether his reading takes him to another land, another time period, or an imaginative country of the mind, the young reader will return home enriched by these vicarious experiences. He will then see himself and his immediate world in a new way. Reading gets us out of our own time and place, out of ourselves; but in the end it will return us to ourselves, a little different, a little changed by this experience.

DEVELOPS INSIGHT INTO HUMAN BEHAVIOR

Literature reflects life; yet no book can contain all of living. By its very organizing properties literature has the power to shape and give coherence to human experience. It may focus on one aspect of life, one period of time in an individual's life, and so enable a reader to see and understand relationships that he had never considered. In *A Figure of Speech*, Norma Mazer makes us see one family's mistreatment of their 83-year-old grandfather through the eyes of Jenny, his adoring granddaughter. Each action that the family takes is done for "Grandpa's good," but the reader sees Grandpa stripped of his dignity and self-worth. Jenny herself contributes to the downfall of the old man when she sobbingly reveals her parents' plan to put him in an old folk's home. The reader can see the entire chain of events that eventually leads to tragedy. He realizes that behavior is caused; that the more the family treats Grandpa like a doddering old man, the more feeble he becomes. The author makes you feel Jenny's frustration and disillusionment with her self-seeking family. The reader's compassion for the elderly may be deepened by experiencing this book. For the first time a 10- or 12-year-old might consider what it would be like to grow old. The child reading this story can't help but develop a greater appreciation for the worth of each individual, old or young.

Every story contains the potential for many stories. Mary Stolz helps children understand this when she tells the same story from two different points of view. *A Dog on Barkham Street* is Edward's story of his desire for a dog and his difficulty in keeping it, once he gets it. *The Bully of Barkham Street* is told from the point of view of Martin, who caused most of Edward's problems. Children can understand the two viewpoints and gain real insight into human behavior by comparing these two books.

A child may derive an understanding of the strengths and weaknesses of human nature from a picture book, as well as a junior novel, from fantasy as well as realism, from historical fiction as easily as contemporary fiction. Don Freeman's lovable *Dandelion* is able to laugh at himself for becoming such a "dandy lion" that even his own friends don't recognize him. The thirst for power drove King Morgant to try to misuse *The Black Cauldron* in Lloyd Alexander's Prydain Series. But Gwydion forgave him, remembering a time when he was a fearless and noble lord. When Taran asked him how there could be any honor for a man who had betrayed them, Gwydion replied:

"It is easy to judge evil unmixed. . . . But, alas, in most of us good and bad are closely woven as the threads on a loom; greater wisdom than mine is needed for the judging."[8]

Present-day knowledge of psychology would easily explain Stephen de Beauville's fear of dogs by relating it to the time when he was bitten as a fifteen-month-old child. However, in fourteenth-century England he is branded a coward. Some twelve years later when he tells his friend, Sir Pagan, that he is a coward, Sir Pagan answers him with cheerful conviction:

"Only a coward can be truly brave. . . . One's valour is in proportion to one's fear. The man who is always entirely unafraid can never be brave. He has nothing to be brave about. One can only show real courage if one is afraid. The coward, therefore, being afraid of nearly everything, is alone capable of the highest courage."[9]

Literature can show children how others have lived and "become," no matter what the time or place. As children gain increased awareness of the lives of others, as they vicariously try out other roles, they may develop a better understanding of themselves and those around them. Through wide reading as well as living, the child acquires his perceptions of literature and life.

PRESENTS THE UNIVERSALITY OF EXPERIENCE

Literature continues to ask universal questions about the meaning of life and human relationships with nature and other people. Literature helps children toward a fuller understanding of the common bonds of humanity. By comparing the stories of *Stevie* by Steptoe and *Thy Friend, Obadiah* by Turkle, they discover the universal truth that we seldom know how much we like a person (or even a pet gull) until we've lost him. The theme of *Warrior Scarlet* by Rosemary Sutcliff is far more than the attainment of manhood; it is the story of every runt in every litter.

The story of Max leaving home to go to the island of *Where the Wild Things Are* follows the ancient pattern of Homer's *The Iliad* and *The Odyssey*. It is repeated again and again in myth

[8]Lloyd Alexander. *The Black Cauldron* (New York: Holt, Rinehart and Winston, 1965), p. 217.
[9]Barbara Leonie Picard. *One Is One* (New York: Holt, Rinehart and Winston, 1965), p. 139.

and legend and seen in such widely divergent modern stories as *Sounder* by Armstrong, *Julie of the Wolves* by Jean George, *Call it Courage* by Sperry, and *A Wrinkle in Time* by Madeleine L'Engle. These are all stories of a person's journey through terror and hardship and his eventual return home. It is the story of everyman's journey through life.

War stories frequently portray people's many acts of humanness in the midst of inhumanity. *Boris* by Jaap ter Haar, *The Upstairs Room* by Reiss, *To Fight in Silence* by Wuorio—all tell of the uncommon bravery of common people to do what they can to fight a wrong. The first story ever recorded by man was the story of *Gilgamesh* (retold by Bryson), the story of a friendship. Children's literature is replete with other stories of such true friendships as is seen in *Knight's Fee* by Sutcliff, E. B. White's *Charlotte's Web*, and LeGuin's *A Wizard of Earthsea*. There is also the terrible renunciation of friendship in *Friedrich* by Richter. Literature illumines all of life; it casts its light on all that is good in human life, but it may also spotlight that which is dark and debasing in the human experience.

Literature enables us to live many lives and to begin to see the universality of human experience. It provides a record of all that people have ever thought or dreamed of throughout the ages. Nearly 150 years ago, Sir John Herschel, in an address at the opening of a library at Eton, had this to say about the value of literature:

> Give a man a taste for reading and the means of gratifying it, and you cannot fail to make him a happy, as well as a better man. You place him in contact with the best minds in every period of history, with the wisest and the wittiest, the tenderest and the bravest, those who really adorned humanity. You make him a citizen of all nations and a contemporary of all ages.

Purposes of the Literature Program

Each school staff will want to develop its own literature program in terms of the background and abilities of the children it serves. The five values of literature identified in the last section may be derived from reading any quality litera-

ture. Teachers need to know their children, the potential of their material, and have an understanding of the structure of literature; then they will be free to make the right match between child and book. This chapter can suggest guidelines and give examples, but it can not prescribe *the* literature program that would work with all children. The four purposes for a literature program—discovering delight in books, interpreting literature, developing literary awareness, and developing appreciation—can be achieved through varied methods and materials.

DISCOVERING DELIGHT IN BOOKS

One of the major purposes of any literature program is to provide children with the opportunity to experience literature, to enter into and become involved in a book. The title of *Hooked on Books* (*see* "Related Readings") by Fader and McNeil comes close to describing this goal. A literature program must get children excited about reading, turned on to books, tuned into literature.

One of the best ways to interest children in books is to surround them with many of the finest, as described in Chapter 10 of this book in the section "Creating the Learning Environment." Give them time to read and a teacher who regularly reads to them. Expose them to a wide variety of literature—prose and poetry, realism and fantasy, contemporary and historical fiction, traditional and modern. Provide time for children to talk about books, to share them with others, and to interpret them through various creative activities. Let them see that adults enjoy books too. One 6-year-old and his teacher were reading Lobel's *Frog and Toad Are Friends* together. When they came to the part where Toad is experiencing his "sad time of day" (waiting for the mail that he never receives), the teacher burst out laughing. The 6-year-old looked up at her and said: "I didn't know grown-ups liked books!" If children are to like books they must be with adults who delight in them.

The first step in any literature program is to discover delight in books. This should be the major purpose of the literature program in the elementary school and should not be hurried or bypassed. Delight in books only comes about through long and loving experiences with them.

INTERPRETING LITERATURE

Wide reading is necessary for creating interest in books, but children need to have an opportunity to have in-depth experiences with books if they are to grow in their responses to literature. The teacher and child can talk about the personal meaning that a story has for his life. In the anecdote described at the beginning of this chapter, children could have been encouraged to discuss the times they may have felt as frightened as Crow Boy. In exploring the personal and social values of the story, they might have considered ways in which the other children could have helped Chibi be less frightened of school. The point is not to conduct a moralizing lesson but to help children interpret various roles in the story and consider the alternative choices that are open to the characters. As children respond to the book in this fashion they begin to see the interrelationship of the characters, the effect one life may have on another. They may even develop some self-understanding of their relations with others. As children relate what they are reading to their background of experience, they internalize the meaning of the story. Louise Rosenblatt was one of the first to remind us that the reader counts as much as the work that he is reading. "The literary experience," she says, "must be phased as a transaction between the reader and the text."[10]

With elementary-school-age children, we almost always begin with their personal response to the story. Only if the question appears to be appropriate for the background of the children would the teacher ask how the author or the artist created meaning. In the discussion of *Crow Boy*, the supervisor asked about the significance of the endpaper designs *after* the children had talked about the ways Chibi had changed. The children's recognition of the symbolic nature of the art could only follow from a discussion of the meaning of the story. Then, understanding reinforced the meaning of the story. The literary or artistic craft of a book is not as important as its message.

Another way that children can show their response to a book is through interpretative activi-

ties. It would require a high degree of sophistication and understanding to dramatize the story of *Crow Boy*, for example. Children might prefer to retell the story by making slides. Others might want to read other books by Yashima and compare them with *Crow Boy*. These creative activities would all add to the interpretation of the book and deepen the child's response to it.

DEVELOPING LITERARY AWARENESS

Children in the elementary school can't help but develop some literary awareness. However, knowledge about literature should be secondary to children's wide experiencing of literature. Too frequently, we have substituted the study of literary criticism for the experience of literature itself. Attention to content should precede consideration of form. However, some literary understanding increases children's enjoyment of books. Some 8- and 9-year-olds are excited to discover the different variants of "Cinderella," for example. They enjoy comparing the various beginnings and endings of folk tales and like to write their own. Obviously some of this delight has been derived from knowledge of folklore. Teachers need to know something of the structure of literature in order to provide children with a frame of reference to direct their insights. Children, however, should be led to discover these literary elements gradually, and only as these elements shed light on the children's understanding of the meaning of the story or poem. Knowledge of the structure of a discipline frees a teacher to be unstructured in her approach to teaching. Knowing literature, she may tune in to where the children are and extend their thinking and understandings. The teacher does not have to rely upon the questions in a literary reader; she is free to ask her own questions directly related to the needs of the children she teaches.

Types of Literature

During the time the child is in the elementary school he will develop some understandings about types of literature or various genre. The primary-school child can usually differentiate between prose and poetry, between fiction and nonfiction. He may not use those words, nor is it important for him to do so. He'll probably tell you that McCloskey's *Make Way for Ducklings*

[10]Louise M. Rosenblatt. *Literature as Exploration* (Appleton-Century, 1938, Noble and Noble, 1968), p. 35.

tells a story; while *Ducks Don't Get Wet* by Goldin "just tells you about ducks." However, he is making a beginning at a useful classification system for himself. Later, he will discover that within the classification of fiction are books whose content may be described as realism or fantasy. As he looks up information in the school media center, he will learn that nonfiction includes informational books and biography. He finds that poetry and traditional literature—including folk tales, legends, and myths—have their own classifications.

Children should not be required to memorize all of these classifications. An understanding of the various types of literature will develop as teachers and librarians introduce a variety of books to children. When children have had free access to the school library media center for six or seven years, they will surely have discovered the various types of books and their classifications. A framework for thinking about literature will develop gradually as children consider what kinds of stories they particularly like, or what kinds of information they need for a particular purpose. Such knowledge will also be useful when children begin evaluating books. Then they discover, for example, that the characters in fairy tales are usually flat, two-dimensional characters because they represent goodness (the fairy godmother) or wickedness (the stepmother). These are seen in sharp relief to the characters in realistic fiction, who grow and change and are a mixture of good and bad. Again, this kind of understanding is developed over a period of time with much experiencing of a wide range of literature.

Elements of Literature

Knowledge of the components of literature—such as the traditional constants of plot, characterization, theme, style, setting, and point of view of the author—comes about gradually. Some children are intrigued with knowing about such literary devices as symbols, metaphors, imagery, use of flashbacks, and so on. Such knowledge can be forced, taught superficially without children really understanding the relationship between the use of the device and the author's meaning. This is the kind of knowledge which is better known by the teacher who can ask the appropriate questions which might help children discover meaning. Focus should be primarily on the personal meaning of the content. Discussion of literary form should only be introduced where it leads to a richer understanding of a book, and then only after children have had time to respond to it personally.

The Place of Classics

Some literature programs (The Nebraska Curriculum) have recommended particular books for study at each age level. It is the position of this writer that there is no one book, or twenty books, or one hundred books that should be read by all children. There are many books that it would be unfortunate if children missed, but none that should be required of all. Knowledge of certain literary classics of childhood—such as *Alice's Adventures in Wonderland* or *The Wind in the Willows*—is enriching, but not absolutely essential to one's development. What is important is that we give children rich experiencing of literature at various stages of development.

Knowledge of time-tested works of prose and poetry—such as Mother Goose rhymes, fables, myths, and Bible stories—does provide a background for understanding many literary allusions. "Don't count your chicks before they hatch," "a matter of sour grapes," "dog in the manger," "the Midas touch," "the voice of Cassandra" are all examples of often-used expressions derived from literature. However, the reason they continue to be used is that their meanings have significance for today's living. Teachers who know literature will share appropriate literary classics with children because they are still *good stories,* not because they are the source of literary allusions. If children are not ready "to connect" with these stories, then such stories would have little meaning for them and would serve an inappropriate literature experience. So much depends upon the teacher's understanding of children and knowledge of literature.

Authors and Illustrators

Study of the works of particular authors has characterized the teaching of literature at the secondary level more frequently than at the elementary school. Children enjoy knowing something about authors and illustrators as they read their books. Teachers and librarians will always want to tell children the name of the author and illustrator of a book as they introduce it. They may ask children if they know any other books that this particular person has illustrated or written. Some children delight in being able to recognize the art work of Ezra Jack Keats or Leo Lionni or Taro Yashima. They are beginning to recognize the style of an artist's work and this should be encouraged. Middle-grade children frequently discover favorite authors. They want another book by Jean Little, another Judy Blume, or another William Steele. They may be reading series books, and so they ask for another one of the Narnia series (C. S. Lewis), the Prydain series (Alexander), or the Little House books (Wilder). Some children develop special interests in sports stories, mysteries, or biographies. These are all ways that children categorize books. They show that children are developing a framework for literature, a way of thinking about books. This should be encouraged but not taught. One certain way to kill interest in a particular book or author would be to have everyone in the class study that author's books—Kenneth Grahame or *The Wind in the Willows* could be destroyed in this way. The elementary school need not repeat the *Silas Marner* syndrome of the secondary school.

Knowledge about particular books, authors, and the craft of writing will come about as children find increasing satisfaction in a range and diversity of works. Such knowledge should not be the primary focus of the literature program. It will occur as a natural result of real experiencing of books.

DEVELOPING APPRECIATION

The long-term goal of a literature program is the development of a lifetime pattern of preference for reading quality literature. Appreciation for literature develops gradually as a result of many fulfilling experiences with literature.

Margaret Early[11] has suggested that there may be three developmental and sequential stages in the growth of appreciation:

1. The stage of unconscious enjoyment.
2. The stage of self-conscious appreciation.
3. The stage of conscious delight.

The first stage is similar to the notion of dis-

covering delight in literature, becoming engaged with it. At this level children read or the teacher reads to them for their enjoyment. They seldom touch on the way the author has created meaning. The reader in the second stage is interested in more than plot; he asks why. He is willing to look below the surface of a story for deeper meanings. He enjoys exploring the story to see how the author, poet, or artist has reinforced his meaning by his language or art. The third stage describes the mature reader who finds delight in many kinds of literature from many periods of time, appreciating the best of each genre and author. Obviously, not even college students or many adults ever reach this level of conscious delight.

A literature program for the elementary school should focus on the first stage of unconscious enjoyment. If all children could be given the opportunity to find enjoyment in literature, they would be building a firm foundation for literary appreciation. As children are encouraged to interpret the meaning of the story or poem, through discussion or creative activities, some of them may be entering the second stage of self-conscious appreciation. As children respond to literature, discuss how they feel about the story and what it means to them, they may be ready to deal with the "whys" of their feelings and the ways the author or artist created those feelings. Children will need guidance from teachers and librarians as they begin to refine their understandings and become more discriminating readers.

In summary, the literature program in the elementary school will give children experiences that will contribute to these four purposes:

1. Discovering delight in books
2. Interpreting literature
3. Developing literary awareness
4. Developing appreciation

The first two purposes should receive the greatest emphasis in the elementary school.

Sharing Literature with Children

From the time of the earliest primitive fire circle to the Middle Ages—when minne-singers and troubadours sang their ballads—to the modern age of television, people have found delight in hearing stories and poems. Since literature

[11]Margaret Early. "Stages of Growth in Literary Appreciation" in *The English Journal*, Vol. 49 (March 1960), pp. 161–166.

serves many educational purposes in addition to entertainment and enjoyment, teachers should place a high priority on sharing literature with children. Boys and girls of all ages should have the opportunity to hear good literature every day.

READING TO CHILDREN

One of the best ways to interest children in books is to read to them frequently from the time they are able to listen. Pre-schoolers and kindergarten children should have an opportunity to listen to stories two or three times a day. Parent volunteers, high-school students, college participants—all can be encouraged to read to small groups of children throughout the day. Children should have a chance to hear their favorite stories over and over again at a listening center. The child from a book-loving family may have heard over one thousand bedtime stories before he ever comes to kindergarten; while some children may never have heard one. Equal opportunity should be readily available for all.

Teachers accept the idea of reading a story at least once a day to the primary-grade child. Increasingly, the daily story hour is advocated by almost all authorities in reading. The research done by Cohen[12] and replicated by Cullinan, Jaggar, and Strickland would support this practice.

Unfortunately, the practice of a daily story in the middle grades is not as common as in the primary grades. Chow Loy Tom found that less than 40 percent of the middle-grade teachers in the nation read aloud to their students once a day.[13] This percentage decreased in grades five and six to 27 percent and 26 percent. The most frequent reason that the teachers checked for not reading aloud was that they did not have enough time. Frequently, respondents expressed guilt over taking time to read in an overcrowded curriculum:

> I feel guilty in a way, when I let the curriculum slide—and "steal" time for reading. Yet enjoyment and interest . . . and discussion later is much higher here.[14]

[12]*See* Chapter 1, p. 25.
[13]Chow Loy Tom. "What Teachers Read to Pupils in the Middle Grades" (Unpublished Dissertation, The Ohio State University, Columbus, Ohio 1969), p. 174.
[14]*Ibid.*, p. 163.

Obviously, many of these teachers equate reading aloud to children with entertainment rather than education. We know that the two most important motivating factors in helping children become readers are:

1. Time for reading books of their choosing.
2. Hearing good books read aloud by an enthusiastic teacher.

In these middle grades many children still do not have the ability to read the books in which they are interested. Most modern television-reared children have developed interests and appreciation levels above their reading-ability levels. Once a child has heard a good book read aloud, he can hardly wait to savor it again. Reading aloud thus generates further interest in books. Good oral reading should develop a taste for fine literature.

Selecting Books to Read Aloud

Teachers and librarians will want to select books to read aloud in terms of the children's interests, background in literature, and the quality of the writing. Usually, the teachers will not select books that children in the group are reading avidly on their own. The story hour is the time to stretch their imaginations, to extend interests, and to develop appreciation of fine writing. If children have not had much experience in listening to stories, begin where they are. Appreciation for literature appears to be developmental and sequential. Eight- and 9-year-olds who have had little exposure to literature still delight in such stories as *Harry the Dirty Dog* by Zion, *Mike Mulligan and His Steam Shovel* by Burton, and *Stevie* by Steptoe. Other children of this same age who have had much experience with literature are ready for longer stories—such as *James and the Giant Peach* by Dahl, *The Bears' House* by Sachs, or *The 18th Emergency* by Byars.

In the writer's experience, children tend to enjoy fantasies if they are read aloud. The subtle humor of Milne's *Winnie the Pooh* may be completely lost when the child is reading alone; when shared by an appreciative teacher-reader, the awkward but well-meaning Pooh and the dismal Eeyore become real personages to 8- and 9-year-olds. The quiet but moving story of *The Mousewife* by Rumer Godden becomes more meaningful if read aloud and discussed with children. Its theme of the importance of freedom and vision (if only in a little mousewife) needs to be shared with children.

There is a real place for sharing some of the beautiful picture books with older children as well as younger ones. *Dawn* by Uri Shulevitz creates the same feeling visually as one of Emily Dickinson's clear, rarefied poems. It is a visual experience for all ages, but particularly for anyone who has felt "at oneness" with the world before the sunrise. Keeping's unusual story of what a city child views *Through the Window* is only appropriate for children in the middle grades. They will respond to its stunning artwork and its somber overtones.

Many of the folk tales and myths and legends have been beautifully illustrated as single tales and should be shared with 8-, 9-, 10-, and 11-year-olds. The exquisite details of Nancy Burkert's illustrations for *Snow-White* by Jarrell might be lost upon young children. The complex Russian folktales of *The Firebird* illustrated by Bogdanovic, and Uri Shulevitz's *The Fool of the World and the Flying Ship* and *Soldier and Tsar in the Forest* would all make a rich contribution to the literature program in the middle grades. Marcia Brown's fable *Once a Mouse* and Barbara Cooney's *Chanticleer and the Fox* are more appropriately shared with older children. Tomaino's *Persephone, Bringer of Spring,* with its stunning illustrations by Ati Forberg, would make an excellent introduction to a study of Greek myths. Most of these books are "too good for children to miss" and need to be shared with them.

The teacher should strive for balance in what is read aloud to children. Children tend to like what they know. As they are introduced to a variety of types of books, they will broaden their base of appreciation. If 12-year-olds are all reading contemporary fiction, the teacher might read *Enchantress from the Stars* by Engdahl or *The Nargun and the Stars* by Wrightson to extend children's interest to fantasy. A study of the American Revolution could be enriched by the teacher reading the story of *Johnny Tremain* by Forbes or *Early Thunder* by Jean Fritz. However, there is a real danger that middle-grade teachers will choose to read aloud only those books which will support the social studies program. Chow

Loy Tom[15] found this to be the case in her national study of what middle-grade teachers read aloud to their students. Some 70 percent of the teachers who did read aloud reported that they chose titles that would correlate with social studies. This practice can destroy the whole notion of broadening children's interests in a variety of types of literature and providing a kind of balance in the selection of materials shared with children.

Primary-grade teachers will read many books to their children, certainly a minimum of one a day. Middle-grade teachers may present parts of many books to their students during book talks or as teasers to interest children in reading the books. But how many books will teachers read in their entirety? An educated guess might be that starting with 8-year-olds—when teachers begin to read longer, continuous stories to boys and girls—an average of some four to five books are read aloud during the year. This means that for the next four years, when children are reaching the peak of their interest in reading, they may hear no more than twenty books read by their teachers! Certainly those books must be selected with care in terms of their relevance for the particular groups of boys and girls and for the quality of their writing. A suggested list of books to read aloud is included in this chapter to serve as a possible guide to selection. Notice that the age groups overlap deliberately. There is no such thing as a book for 5-year-olds or 10-year-olds. It is important to stress that. Only a teacher who knows the children, their interests, and their background of experience can *truly* select appropriate books for a particular class.

Teachers should keep a record of the books that they have shared with the children they teach, and a brief notation of the reaction of the class to each title. This would enable teachers to see what kind of balance is being achieved, and what the particular favorites of the class are. Such a record would provide future teachers with information as to the likes and dislikes of the class and their background of exposure to literature. It also might prevent the situation that was discovered by a survey of one school in which every teacher in the school, with the exception of the

[15] Chow Loy Tom, *Ibid.*

kindergarten and the second-grade teachers, had read *Charlotte's Web* aloud to the class! *Charlotte's Web* is a great book, but not for every class. Perhaps teachers in a school need to agree on what is the most appropriate time for reading particular favorites. Teachers and librarians should be encouraged to try reading new books to children, instead of always reading the same ones. But some self-indulgence should be allowed every teacher who truly loves a particular book, for that enthusiasm can't help but rub off on children.

100 BOOKS TO READ ALOUD

3-, 4-, and 5-year Olds

Asbjornsen, P. C., and Jorgen E. Moe. *The Three Billy Goats Gruff,* illustrated by Marcia Brown. Harcourt Brace Jovanovich, 1957.

Brown, Margaret Wise. *Goodnight Moon,* illustrated by Clement Hurd. Harper & Row, 1947.

———. *The Runaway Bunny,* Illustrated by Clement Hurd. Harper & Row, 1972 (1942).

Burningham, John. *Mr. Gumpy's Outing.* Holt, Rinehart and Winston, 1971.

Carle, Eric. *The Very Hungry Caterpillar.* World, 1970.

Galdone, Paul. *The Little Red Hen.* Seabury, 1973.

———. *The Three Bears.* Seabury, 1972.

Hutchins, Pat. *Rosie's Walk.* Macmillan, 1968.

Keats, Ezra Jack. *The Snowy Day.* Viking, 1962.

Krauss, Ruth. *The Carrot Seed,* illustrated by Crockett Johnson. Harper & Row, 1945.

Minarik, Else. *Little Bear,* illustrated by Maurice Sendak. Harper & Row, 1957.

Munari, Bruno. *Who's There? Open the Door!* World, 1957.

Piper, Watty. *The Little Engine that Could,* illustrated by George Hauman and Doris Hauman. Platt & Munk, 1954 (1930).

Potter, Beatrix. *The Tale of Peter Rabbit.* Warne, 1902.

Preston, Edna Mitchell. *Squawk to the Moon, Little Goose,* illustrated by Barbara Cooney. Viking, 1974.

Slobodkina, Esphyr. *Caps for Sale.* Scott, 1947.

Spier, Peter. *To Market, to Market.* Doubleday, 1967.

Tolstoy, Alexei. *The Great Big Enormous Turnip,* illustrated by Helen Oxenbury. F. Watts, 1969.

Watson, Clyde. *Father Fox's Pennyrhymes,* illustrated by Wendy Watson. Crowell, 1971.

Wildsmith, Brian. *Brian Wildsmith's Mother Goose.* F. Watts, 1963.

5-, 6-, and 7-year Olds

Burton, Virginia Lee. *The Little House.* Houghton Mifflin, 1942.

Caudill, Rebecca. *A Pocketful of Cricket,* illustrated by Evaline Ness. Holt, Rinehart and Winston, 1964.

Duvoisin, Roger. *Petunia.* Knopf, 1950.

Freeman, Don. *Dandelion.* Viking, 1964.

Gág, Wanda. *Millions of Cats.* Coward-McCann, 1928.

Hoban, Russell. *A Baby Sister for Frances,* illustrated by Lillian Hoban. Harper & Row, 1964.

Keats, Ezra Jack. *Peter's Chair.* Harper & Row, 1967.

Lionni, Leo. *Little Blue and Little Yellow.* Astor-Honor, 1959.

———. *Swimmy.* Pantheon, 1963.

Lobel, Arnold. *Frog and Toad Are Friends.* Harper & Row, 1970.

McCloskey, Robert. *Blueberries for Sal.* Viking, 1948.

———. *Make Way for Ducklings.* Viking, 1941.

———. *One Morning in Maine.* Viking, 1952.

Scott, Ann Herbert. *Sam,* illustrated by Symeon Shimin. McGraw-Hill, 1967.

Sendak, Maurice. *Where the Wild Things Are.* Harper & Row, 1963.

Seuss, Dr., *pseud.* (Theodor S. Geisel). *And to Think that I Saw It on Mulberry Street.* Vanguard, 1937.

Udry, Janice May. *Let's Be Enemies,* illustrated by Maurice Sendak. Harper & Row, 1961.

Ward, Lynd. *The Biggest Bear.* Houghton Mifflin, 1952.

Zion, Gene. *Harry the Dirty Dog,* illustrated by Margaret Bloy Graham. Harper & Row, 1956.

Zolotow, Charlotte. *Mr. Rabbit and the Lovely Present,* illustrated by Maurice Sendak. Harper & Row, 1962.

7-, 8-, and 9-year Olds

Aesop's Fables, selected and adapted by Louis Untermeyer, illustrated by A. Provensen and M. Provensen. Golden Press, 1966.

Brown, Marcia. *Once a Mouse.* Scribner, 1961.

Dalgliesh, Alice. *The Courage of Sarah Noble,* illustrated by Leonard Weisgard. Scribner, 1954.

Grimm, The Brothers. *Snow-White and the Seven Dwarfs,* trans-

Schweitzer, Byrd Baylor. *One Small Blue Bead,* illustrated by Symeon Shimin. Macmillan, 1965.

Shulevitz, Uri. *Dawn.* Farrar, Straus, 1974.

Slobodkin, Florence. *Sarah Somebody,* illustrated by Louis Slobodkin. Vanguard, 1969.

Steig, William. *Amos and Boris.* Farrar, Straus, 1971.

Steptoe, John. *Stevie.* Harper & Row, 1969.

7-, 8-, and 9-year Olds (*Continued*)

lated by Randall Jarrell, illustrated by Nancy Ekholm Burkert. Farrar, Straus, 1972.

Hill, Elizabeth Starr. *Evan's Corner*, illustrated by Nancy Grossman. Holt, Rinehart and Winston, 1967.

Kipling, Rudyard. *The Elephant's Child*, illustrated by Leonard Weisgard. Walker, 1970.

Lionni, Leo. *Frederick*. Pantheon, 1967.

Miles, Miska. *Annie and the Old One*, illustrated by Peter Parnall. Little, Brown, 1971.

Ness, Evaline. *Sam, Bangs and Moonshine*. Holt, Rinehart and Winston, 1966.

Turkle, Brinton. *Thy Friend, Obadiah*. Viking, 1969.

Viorst, Judith. *Alexander and the Terrible, Horrible, No Good, Very Bad Day*, illustrated by Ray Cruz. Atheneum, 1972.

White, E. B. *Charlotte's Web*, illustrated by Garth Williams. Harper & Row, 1952.

Wilder, Laura Ingalls. *Little House in the Big Woods*, illustrated by Garth Williams. Harper & Row, 1953 (1932).

Yashima, Taro, *pseud.* (Jun Iwamatsu). *Crow Boy*. Viking, 1955.

Zemach, Harve. *Duffy and the Devil*, illustrated by Margot Zemach. Farrar, Straus, 1973.

9-, 10-, and 11-year Olds

Andersen, Hans Christian. *The Nightingale*, translated by Eva LeGallienne, illustrated by Nancy Ekholm Burkert. Harper & Row, 1965.

Armstrong, William H. *Sounder*, illustrated by James Barkley. Harper & Row, 1969.

Burch, Robert. *Queenie Peavy*, illustrated by Jerry Lazare. Viking, 1966.

Byars, Betsy. *The 18th Emergency*, illustrated by Robert Grossman. Viking, 1973.

DeJong, Meindert. *Hurry Home, Candy*, illustrated by Maurice Sendak. Harper & Row, 1953.

Fritz, Jean. *The Cabin Faced West*, illustrated by Feodor Rojankovsky. Coward-McCann, 1958.

Haugaard, Erik Christian. *Hakon of Rogen's Saga*, illustrated by Leo Dillon and Diane Dillon. Houghton Mifflin, 1963.

Konigsburg, E. L. *From the Mixed-up Files of Mrs. Basil E. Frankweiler*. Atheneum, 1967.

L'Engle, Madeleine. *A Wrinkle in Time*. Farrar, Straus, 1962.

Lewis, C. S. *The Lion, the Witch, and the Wardrobe*, illustrated by Pauline Baynes. Macmillan, 1950.

Merrill, Jean. *The Pushcart War*, illustrated by Ronni Solbert. Scott, 1964.

Milne, A. A. *Winnie the Pooh*, illustrated by Ernest H. Shepard. Dutton, 1926.

Neville, Emily C. *Berries Goodman*. Harper & Row, 1965.

O'Brien, Robert C. *Mrs. Frisby and the Rats of NIMH*, illustrated by Zena Bernstein. Atheneum, 1971.

O'Dell, Scott. *Island of the Blue Dolphins*. Houghton Mifflin, 1960.

Pearce, Philippa. *Tom's Midnight Garden*, illustrated by Susan Einzig. Lippincott, 1959.

Peare, Catherine Owens. *The Helen Keller Story*. Crowell, 1959.

Sleator, William. *Blackbriar*. Dutton, 1972.

Ullman, James R. *Banner in the Sky*. Lippincott, 1954.

Yates, Elizabeth. *Amos Fortune, Free Man*, illustrated by Nora Unwin. Dutton, 1950.

11-, 12-, and 13-year Olds

Alexander, Lloyd. *The Black Cauldron*. Holt, Rinehart and Winston, 1965.

Behn, Harry. *The Faraway Lurs*. World, 1963.

Cleaver, Vera, and Bill Cleaver. *Where the Lilies Bloom*, illustrated by Jim Spanfeller. Lippincott, 1969.

Cooper, Susan. *The Dark Is Rising*, illustrated by Alan E. Cober. Atheneum, 1973.

Cunningham, Julia. *Dorp Dead*, illustrated by James Spanfeller. Pantheon, 1965.

Engdahl, Sylvia. *Enchantress from the Stars*, illustrated by Rodney Shackell. Atheneum, 1970.

Forbes, Esther. *Johnny Tremain*, illustrated by Lynd Ward. Houghton Mifflin, 1946.

Gates, Doris. *Two Queens of Heaven*, illustrated by Trina Schart Hyman. Viking, 1974.

George, Jean. *Julie of the Wolves*, illustrated by John Schoenherr. Harper & Row, 1972.

Hautzig, Esther. *The Endless Steppe: Growing Up in Siberia*. Crowell, 1968.

Jones, Weyman. *Edge of Two Worlds*, illustrated by J. C. Kocsis. Dial, 1968.

LeGuin, Ursula K. *A Wizard of Earthsea*, illustrated by Ruth Robbins. Parnassus, 1968.

Picard, Barbara. *One Is One*. Holt, Rinehart and Winston, 1965.

Southall, Ivan. *Ash Road*, illustrated by Clem Seale. St. Martin, 1965.

Speare, Elizabeth George. *The Witch of Blackbird Pond*. Houghton Mifflin, 1958.

Sperry, Armstrong. *Call It Courage*. Macmillan, 1940.

Steele, Mary Q. *Journey Outside*, illustrated by Rocco Negri. Viking, 1969.

Sutcliff, Rosemary. *Warrior Scarlet*, illustrated by Charles Keeping, Walck, 1958.

Watson, Jane Werner. *The Iliad and the Odyssey*, illustrated by Alice Provensen and Martin Provensen. Golden, 1956.

Wojciechowska, Maia. *Shadow of a Bull*, illustrated by Alvin Smith. Atheneum, 1964.

Techniques of Reading Aloud

Effective oral reading by the teacher is an important factor in capturing children's interests. Generally, children like to be seated close to the teacher so that all can see the pictures easily and enjoy the twinkle in the teacher's eye. If children are seated on a rug or chairs pulled close to each other, they seem to identify more easily with the characters and action of the story. Proximity to friends who suppress giggles or hold their breaths in anticipation enhances enjoyment.

A picture book should be held so the children can see the pictures at all times. If the teacher knows the text, the book may be held directly in front of the body. When reading the book, it is easier to hold it perpendicularly at one side and turn the head sufficiently to read the words. The book should be held at the children's eye level and moved slowly so that all children will have an opportunity to see the pictures. Also, eye contact with children should be maintained by looking away from the book at frequent intervals.

The teacher's voice is an instrument for communicating the author's meanings and moods. Distinct articulation is one essential for effective oral reading. Another important element is the voice tone and pitch. Conversation should be read naturally, and volume should be varied with the content of the story. Humor, mystery, disgust, and other feelings can be communicated through the voice.

Anyone reading a story to children should be familiar with the story and should have reread it in preparation for sharing it orally. In this way the reader can emphasize particularly well-written passages, read dialogue as conversation, anticipate the timing of amusing remarks, and be able to look up from the book more frequently to see children's reactions.

An introduction to the selection will set the stage for enjoyment and appreciation. The dust jacket of a book may be displayed; and the children can discuss the author, possible meanings of the title, and predictions about the story. From the very beginning of the school years the author and illustrator should be noted. Only very unusual words need to be explained before reading. For example, in the old English folktale, *The Three Wishes* (Joseph Jacobs), sausage is referred to as a link of "black pudding." Children might understand how a sausage could stick to the end of a man's nose, but they would be confused by the term "pudding," unless they were told this was the original name for sausage. Paul Galdone's lively pictures also clarify the meaning. It is wise to keep introductions as brief as possible and move quickly into reading the selection itself.

The length of the unit selected for reading should vary with age level. Usually stories for children under the age of 7 should be short, so that they may be completed in one reading period. Middle-grade children enjoy continued stories, but an incident or chapter should be completed at one time. Older children will accept the fact that a story might have to be interrupted in the middle of events, but whenever possible it is best to stop at an appropriate breaking point.

If children have not had an opportunity to hear many stories, the teacher or librarian may have to plan very short read-aloud sessions. Gradually, however, these periods can be lengthened to as long as twenty minutes for primary-grade children and one-half hour or longer for middle-graders. Younger children might do better to listen two or three times a day for shorter periods until they can sustain attention.

Instead of interrupting the continuity of the story, discussion should follow the reading of one chapter or incident or entire poem. Frequently it is helpful if a poem is read twice. After completing a story, the teacher or librarian may solicit children's reactions (*see* the section on "Guiding Discussion of Books" in this chapter). The teacher can lead children to discover additional contributions to the story by the illustrator, the theme of the story, the language of the tale—whatever is the strength of the particular story. Children might be helped to compare the story with another one with a similar theme. Discussion should be brief, however.

If the teacher has made a poor selection for this class, there should be no embarrassment about saying so. Suggest that the book will be put on the reading table for those who wish to finish it, and that another book will be selected for the next story hour. If for any reason teachers or librarians do not like a particular book, they should not share it. Dislike of a book can be as easily communicated as enthusiasm. As teachers free themselves to read naturally with joy and honest delight, children will find increasing satisfaction in books.

STORY-TELLING

A 5-year-old said to his teacher: "Tell the story from your face." His preference for the story *told* by the teacher or librarian instead of the story that is read directly from the book is echoed by boys and girls everywhere. The art of story-telling is frequently neglected in the elementary school today. There are many beautiful books, and our harried life allows little time for learning stories. Yet children should not be denied the opportunity to hear well-told stories. Through story-telling, the teacher helps transmit the literary heritage.

Story-telling provides for intimate contact and rapport with the children. No book separates the teacher from the audience. The story may be modified to fit group needs. A difficult word or phrase can be explained in context. For example, in telling a Mexican folk tale, the meaning of the word *mesa* may be interpolated. Stories can be personalized for very young children by substituting their names for those of the characters. Such a phrase as "and, David, if you had been there you would have seen the biggest Billy Goat Gruff. . . ." will redirect the child whose interest has wandered. The pace of the story can be adapted to the children's interests and age levels.

Guides for Telling Stories

From the time of the early minstrels, story-telling has been considered an art. For this reason many teachers have been afraid to attempt it. However, the classroom teacher is an artist in working with children and should have no fear in telling stories to them. Enjoyment of the tale and knowledge of children will help to convey enthusiasm and appreciation for the story. All life experiences enrich the interpretation of the story. Sensitivity to textures, line, pattern, color, and rhythm helps the storyteller to convey details and images. Skill in story-telling requires a rich vocabulary and enjoyment of words and language patterns. The teacher must be able to identify with the setting and characters of the story in order to communicate the spirit and feelings expressed in the tale.

If the teacher knows and enjoys the story, techniques will come naturally. The story, however, should be carefully prepared. The teacher needs to be thoroughly familiar with its plot, characters, and the flavor of its language; but it need not be memorized. In fact, memorization often results in a stilted, artificial presentation. There is the added danger of being completely confused when a line is forgotten. The storyteller should first visualize the setting; imagine the appearance of characters, their age and costume; and plan an introduction that will set the mood of the story. It may be wise to learn the pattern of some introductions such as, "Once there was, and once there wasn't. . . ." If there are repeated chants or songs, these should be memorized. Outline the sequence of events, including major incidents, the climax, and conclusion. Good diction and a pleasant, natural voice are important. Sincerity rather than an artificial, condescending manner is essential.

The good storyteller does not call attention to himself, but to the story. Voice and, perhaps, a few gestures transport children to storyland. Many storytellers believe sound effects should be omitted. If the lion roars, the narrator should not attempt an imitation of a roar, but the idea can be conveyed as the word "roared" is given a deeper tone and increased volume. The *r* sound may be exaggerated so the lion "urroarrd." Writers and such well-known storytellers as Ruth Sawyer and Gudrun Thorne-Thomsen suggest variations in pitch, tone, and volume of voice in accordance with the mood of the story to make it more effective. Well-timed pauses may help listeners anticipate a climax. No amount of study of these techniques will substitute for actual practice. With experience comes assurance and a willingness to experiment. Tape recordings can be made to evaluate story-telling skills. These tapes can be compared with the recordings of such artists as Sawyer, Thorne-Thomsen, and Harold Courlander. By learning a few stories at first, and adding to the repertoire each year, the teacher and the librarian will soon have a rich resource for literature.

Selecting Stories

Stories that are to be told should be selected with care. Stories worth the telling have special characteristics that include a quick beginning, action, a definite climax, natural dialogue, and a satisfying conclusion. It is best to select stories with only three or four speaking characters. Such folk tales as "The Three Billy Goats Gruff," "Chicken Little," and "Cinderella" are particular favorites of younger children. The repetitive pattern of these tales makes them easy to tell. Originally passed down from generation to generation by word of mouth, these tales were polished and embellished with each retelling. *Gone Is Gone* by Gág, *Ask Mr. Bear* by Flack, and "Elsie Piddock Skips in Her Sleep" from Colwell's collection, *A Storyteller's Choice,* exemplify other favorite tales to tell. Middle-grade children will enjoy folk tales from other lands, such as Batchelor's *A Cap for Mul Chand,* Babbitt's *Jataka Tales, The Cow Tail Switch* collected by Courlander and Herzog, and *Heather and Broom* by Sorche Nic Leodhas. Incidents from biographies and longer books may be adapted for story-telling. Stories of such American folk heroes as Paul Bunyan, Pecos Bill, and John Henry delight 8- to 12-year-olds.

If the exact words are necessary to convey the humor or mood, the story should be read rather than told. Kipling's story of *The Elephant's Child* would lose much of its charm without the inclusion of such phrases as "the great grey-green, greasy, Limpopo River all set about with fever-trees" or "the bicolored python rock snake with its scalesome flailsome tail." Since these phrases require memorization, it is recommended that the teacher read this story.

Just as books with rich language should be read to children, so should picture books in which the illustrations form an integral part of the whole. The pictures of *Madeline* by Bemelmans add much humor and delight to this story, and children should not be denied the beauty and charm of Burton's rhythmical illustrations of *The Little House.*

Feltboard Stories

Story-telling may be varied by using a flannel- or feltboard. To tell a feltboard story, the scenery or characters of a story may be made of flannel, felt, pellon, or paper. As the story is told, the figures are placed in the proper positions on the board. If the figures are made of paper, strips of flannel attached to the reverse side will cause them to adhere to the feltboard. Glueing felt to the inside of an artist's cardboard portfolio and trimming it with tape is an easy way to make

a feltboard. Felt is more durable for the board than flannel. Feltboards may also be purchased commercially. Hook and loop boards which use velcro enable the teacher to hang larger objects on the board. Unfortunately, velcro, which is a fabric that comes in two parts (one part sticks to the other), is still rather expensive. Boards already constructed can be ordered, or the material can be purchased for a home-made one. Magnetic boards can also be used to tell visual stories.

Some tales are more suitable for feltboard presentation than others. The stories should be simple and have few characters. Not every incident or scene in the story needs to be included. Detailed settings are too difficult to recreate. While some rapid changes can be portrayed on a feltboard, most physical action is better dramatized. The cumulative tale, or one in which elements are added, is usually quite appropriate for a felt-story presentation. For example, in what better way could Gág's *Nothing at All* complete his metamorphosis from a round ball to the shape of a dog to a live dog with spots, tongue, ears, and tail that wags? Similarly, children delight in watching the appearance and disappearance of the red wings on the rabbit in Bailey's *The Little Rabbit Who Wanted Red Wings.* The old folk tale, *No Room* by Rose Dobbs, or as retold by Hirsh in *Could Anything Be Worse?,* lends itself well to telling on a feltboard. This is the tale of the man who complains that his house is too small and so he goes to the rabbi to ask for advice. The rabbi suggests he invite the chickens into the house, then the cow, then his wife's relatives, and so on. When the man can no longer stand it, the rabbi suggests he take them out one by one. When they are at last alone, both the man and his wife appreciate all the room they now have in their house! This story can be easily shown by making a simple outline of the house, adding all the animals, and then taking them out again! (*see* the picture in Chapter 11, p. 656).

One of the advantages to the storyteller in using a feltboard is that the figures can be arranged in sequence and thus serve as cues for the story. It is essential to *tell* the feltboard story. If the teller tries to read it and manipulate the figures, he is helplessly lost in a tangle of pages

The story, *The Man Who Didn't Wash His Dishes*, is told by adding figures and objects to the flannelboard.
Demonstrated by Sheila Johnston, Purdue University student.

and felt characters. While telling a feltboard story, remember to look at the children rather than the board.

The feltboard story is an attention-getting device. Children are intrigued to see what will appear next. As soon as the storyteller is finished, children like to retell the story again in their own words. This is an excellent language experience and should be encouraged. Children also like to make and tell their own stories.

Try to keep all the pieces of a feltboard story together in a plastic bag clearly marked with the title of the story. If possible, also put a paperback copy of the book or story in the bag to keep the memory of it fresh and to share with the children after the story has been told. If teachers or librar-

ians just make two feltboard stories a year, they will soon build a collection of tales to share. These are fun to make and even more fun to share with an enthusiastic audience. Storytellers have their own favorites, but the ones listed below seem particularly well suited for a feltboard presentation. Each one includes some magical change which would be hard to dramatize in another way.

SUGGESTED STORIES FOR THE FELTBOARD

Bailey, Carolyn Sherwin. *The Little Rabbit Who Wanted Red Wings*, illustrated by Dorothy Grider. Platt & Munk, 1945.

Dobbs, Rose. *No Room, An Old Story Retold*, illustrated by Fritz Eichenberg. McKay, 1944.

Duvoisin, Roger. *House of Four Seasons*. Lothrop, 1956.

———. *Petunia.* Knopf, 1950.

Freeman, Don. *Dandelion.* Viking, 1964.

Gág, Wanda. *Nothing at All.* Coward-McCann, 1928.

Galdone, Paul. *The Three Wishes.* McGraw-Hill, 1961.

Ginsburg, Mirra. *Mushroom in the Rain,* illustrated by Jose Aruego and Ariane Dewey. Macmillan, 1974.

———. *Three Kittens,* illustrated by Giulio Maestro. Crown, 1973.

Hirsh, Marilyn. *Could Anything Be Worse?* Holiday, 1974.

Krasilovsky, Phyllis. *The Man Who Didn't Wash His Dishes,* illustrated by Barbara Cooney. Doubleday, 1950.

Lawson, Robert. *Robbut, A Tale of Tails.* Viking, 1949.

Lionni, Leo. *Frederick.* Pantheon, 1967.

———. *Little Blue and Little Yellow.* Astor-Honor, 1959.

Nic Leodhas, Sorche. *Always Room for One More,* illustrated by Nonny Hogrogian. Holt, Rinehart and Winston, 1965.

Seuss, Dr. pseud. (Theodor Geisel). *The 500 Hats of Bartholomew Cubbins.* Vanguard, 1938.

Tresselt, Alvin. *The Mitten,* illustrated by Yaroslava. Lothrop, 1964.

Waber, Bernard. *"You Look Ridiculous," Said the Rhinoceros to the Hippopotamus.* Houghton Mifflin, 1966.

Zion, Gene. *Harry the Dirty Dog,* illustrated by Margaret Bloy Graham. Harper & Row, 1956.

Projecting Figures

Flannelboard figures may be placed on the overhead projector to create a story in silhouettes. The figures can also be cut from cardboard or heavy paper. By attaching a thin wire to the cardboard, or even straws to the paper, the figures can be moved without a hand showing. If the story is to appear in color, take sheets of colored acetate and cut them in the form of story characters and place them on the lighted overhead table.

Story-telling Devices

Frequently the attention of young children is captured by the use of real objects as story-telling devices. For example, a "story bag" might contain appropriate objects. As the teacher begins the story of *The Gingerbread Boy* by Galdone, a gingerbread cookie could be taken from the story bag. An Indian arrowhead, a live cricket in a jar, an apple and some beans might be pulled out at the appropriate times for Caudill's delightful story of *A Pocketful of Cricket.* In telling Flack's *Ask Mr. Bear,* an egg, a feather, wool, and a butter carton could be drawn from the bag. These objects can symbolize the suggestions made by the animals in the story for Danny's birthday present

to his mother. When telling the story of *Jennie's Hat* by Ezra Jack Keats, Caroline Bauer[16] suggests in her teletext, *Storytelling,* that someone in the audience can act as Jennie. As the story is told, the different objects that Jennie first tried as hats—a basket, flowerpot, saucepan—might be tried on by the audience "Jennie." When the birds bring objects to decorate Jennie's hat, the real hat may be decorated too, with eggs, flowers, and greeting cards—a kind of living collage. A hat with miniature objects on it also could be used to introduce the West African folk tales in *Tales from the Story Hat* by Aardema. Librarians and teachers will think of other objects that could be used as story-telling devices.

A hand puppet may be used to announce story time, or the puppet may become the protagonist of the story. A Cinderella puppet might relate her own story. Antique dolls could be used to tell the stories of *Hitty* by Field or *Impunity Jane* by Godden. A tiny artificial Christmas tree might relate Andersen's tale of *The Fir Tree.*

One teacher interested a primary-grade group in *Appolonia's Valentine* by showing examples of the cut-paper valentines described by Milhous. Appolonia's story came alive as the children saw the intricately cut Pennsylvania Dutch designs.

Whether or not one uses devices, it is the enthusiasm of the story-teller that captures children's attention and develops appreciation of literature.

Book Talks

Librarians and teachers frequently make use of a book talk as a way of introducing books to children from age 8 and upward. The primary purpose of a book talk is to interest children in reading the book themselves. Rather than reveal the whole story, the book talk should tell just enough about the book to entice others to read it. A book talk may be about one title; it may be about several unrelated books that would have wide appeal; or it may revolve around several books which have a similar theme, such as "getting along in the family" or "courage" or "survival stories."

---

[16]Caroline Feller Bauer. *Storytelling* (Portland, Ore.: Oregon Educational and Public Broadcasting Service, Oregon State System of Higher Education, 1974), p. 167.

The book talk should begin with a recounting of an amusing episode or the telling about an exciting moment in the book. The narrator might want to assume the role of a character in a book, such as Julie in *Julie of the Wolves* by Jean George, and tell of her experience of being lost without food or a compass on the North Slope of Alaska. The speaker should stop before the crisis is over or the mystery solved. Details should be specific. It is better to let the story stand on its own than to characterize it as a "terribly funny" story or the "most exciting" book you've ever read. Enthusiasm for the book will convey the speaker's opinion of it. This is one reason why book talks should be given only about stories the speaker genuinely likes. Children will then come to trust this evaluation. It is best if the book is on hand as it is discussed, so that the children can check it out as soon as the book talk is finished.

A good book talk takes time to prepare, yet it is well worth the preparation if children are drawn into reading the book. Some teachers and librarians find it is helpful to tape their book talks in order to listen to and evaluate them. Children who missed the talk might be encouraged to listen to the tape. A list of the books included in the book talk can be made available to children following the talk, so they can remember the names of the titles. Remember, the effectiveness of a book talk is judged by the number of children who want to borrow the books after they have been introduced.

Guiding Discussion of Books ³

PLANNING THE POSSIBILITIES

Every book has multiple possibilities for discussion, yet certain books have greater potential than others. A teacher or librarian needs to be completely familiar with the content, the relevancy, and the literary strengths of a particular book prior to discussing it with an individual child or a group. The more planning that is done to discover all the possibilities in a book, the freer the teacher will be to follow children's interests and extend their understandings. Rather than being restricted to a single lesson plan, which might not meet the needs of the particular group being taught, the leader who has thought through

the potential of a particular book may explore as many aspects as seem worthwhile for the developmental level of the children. A way of planning for the various directions a discussion might take, or the possibilities for interpretations, or extended reading can be shown in a diagram called "a web." No teacher or librarian would ever want to have a class pursue all these possibilities, for fear of destroying a book with too much attention! But the very fact of having mapped the possibilities enables the teacher to link knowledge of the potential of the book with children's interests, past experience, and growing abilities.

The two webs shown indicate planning for discussion of the picture book *Crow Boy* by Yashima and the adventure tale *Call It Courage* by Sperry. Again, no teacher will want to explore *all* these avenues with children; but having mapped the possibilities, the teacher may select the most appropriate direction for a particular group of children.

DEVELOPING QUESTIONS

Ideally, teachers and librarians should listen more to children's responses to books, and question less. Listen to a tape of a teacher and a group of children discussing a book and you will prob-

The school librarian leads an in-depth book discussion.

Worthington Hills School, Worthington, Ohio, Mary Karrer, librarian.

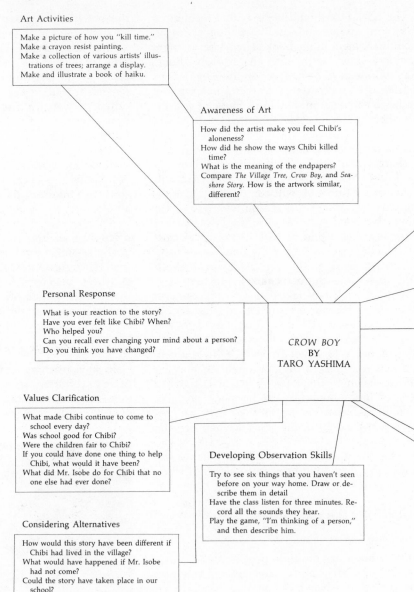

Art Activities

Make a picture of how you "kill time."
Make a crayon resist painting.
Make a collection of various artists' illustrations of trees; arrange a display.
Make and illustrate a book of haiku.

Awareness of Art

How did the artist make you feel Chibi's aloneness?
How did he show the ways Chibi killed time?
What is the meaning of the endpapers?
Compare *The Village Tree, Crow Boy,* and *Seashore Story.* How is the artwork similar, different?

Personal Response

What is your reaction to the story?
Have you ever felt like Chibi? When?
Who helped you?
Can you recall ever changing your mind about a person?
Do you think you have changed?

CROW BOY
BY
TARO YASHIMA

Values Clarification

What made Chibi continue to come to school every day?
Was school good for Chibi?
Were the children fair to Chibi?
If you could have done one thing to help Chibi, what would it have been?
What did Mr. Isobe do for Chibi that no one else had ever done?

Developing Observation Skills

Try to see six things that you haven't seen before on your way home. Draw or describe them in detail
Have the class listen for three minutes. Record all the sounds they hear.
Play the game, "I'm thinking of a person," and then describe him.

Considering Alternatives

How would this story have been different if Chibi had lived in the village?
What would have happened if Mr. Isobe had not come?
Could the story have taken place in our school?

ably hear more teacher talk than child talk. This inverse ratio should change as children become more interested in books and are given more opportunity to discuss them freely, rather than to report on them.

Some children do need guidance in thinking about a book, however. Sometimes only one question—such as "What did this book make you think about?"—is enough to help a child put the book into some kind of perspective. A teacher or librarian may help a child begin to formulate a frame of reference for books with such questions as "Can you show me another book that Leo Lionni has illustrated?" Or "Which

Literary Awareness

Character Development
    What made Chibi become Crow Boy?
    Did the other children change?

Point of View
    What did the other children think about
      Chibi?
    What did the adults think of him?
    What did Mr. Isobe think of him?

Drama

Dramatize the children at play when Chibi
  comes along. What do they say? Do?
Be one of the parents who had heard Crow
  Boy's imitations of crows. Tell your husband about the event.
Interview an adult Crow Boy about his memories of school, or Mr. Isobe. What would
  he say? How would he say it?

Related Literature

Compare and contrast with
    Pocketful of Cricket by Caudill
Other books by Yashima
    The Village Tree
    Youngest One
    Umbrella
    Seashore Story
Other books with themes of peer alienation
    The Hundred Dresses by Estes
    How Many Miles to Babylon? by Fox
    The Greyhound by Griffiths
    The Summer Birds by Farmer
Japanese folk tales
    The Crane Maiden by Matsutani
    The Golden Crane by Yamaguchi
    The Wave by Hodges
    The Funny Little Woman by Mosel

Poetry

In a Spring Garden by Lewis
Haiku-The Mood of Earth by Atwood
Don't Tell the Scarecrow by Issa, et al.
"To Look at Anything" by Moffitt
"Unfolding Bud" by Koriyama
"Crows" by McCord

Writing

Suppose Chibi kept a diary; write some of
  his entries.
You may want to write about a time you felt
  like Chibi.
You may want to write your response to the
  book.
You could try writing your own Haiku.

do you like the best, the Prydain series or the Narnia series? Why?" It is possible to ask too many questions about one book and so kill the child's interest in it. On the other hand, some superficial questions may simply become routine and not extend the child's thinking or sharpen his observations.

Purpose of Questioning

Questions will vary according to the purpose that the teacher has in mind. For example, after planning the web of *Call it Courage*, the teacher may decide to try to relate the story to children's living today. The questions would then focus

Art Interpretation

Make a model of Mafatu's boat.
Create a diorama of the Marae or Sacred
place.
Symbolize Mafatu's seven tests.
Create a mural of the story.

Drama

Dramatize the different groups talking about
Mafatu.
Select a character of today
Dramatize what his peers think about
him.
Dramatize how his family sees him.
Dramatize how his teachers see him.

Values Clarification

What takes the greatest courage?
Admit a wrong.
Take a stand against a popular
belief.
Stand up for your rights.
Which would you rather be and
why?
A mountain climber.
A policeman.
A surgeon.
What if Mafatu had decided not to
go?

Personal Response

Do you have any hidden fears?
Have you ever felt as rejected as
Mafatu? When?
What tests of physical courage are
available to children of today?

Tests of Courage Today

The Bears' House by Sachs
Rosa Parks by Greenfield
Mustang, Wild Spirit of the West by Henry
Dag Hammarskjold by Simon
Profiles in Courage by Kennedy

Incredible Journeys

James and the Giant Peach by Dahl
A Wrinkle in Time by L'Engle
A Wind in the Door by L'Engle
North to Freedom by Holm
Journey Outside by Steele
The Farthest Shore by LeGuin

upon current situations that require a person's utmost courage. The students might identify the kinds of courage that are demanded in certain crises and discover that some of them may require more psychological fortitude than physical courage. This could send them back to the book to analyze the various meanings of the seven tests which Mafatu had to undergo.

If, on the other hand, a teacher of young children wanted to look at children's developmental levels in relation to their ability to perceive a humorous situation, she might share Barrett's *Animals Should Definitely Not Wear Clothing* and note which of the children can explain what is humorous about the last picture in which a large woman is dressed identically to a larger elephant. In this instance a simple "Tell me what's funny about this picture" would be all that is needed.

Some teachers might utilize a book for values clarification with students. For example, in discussing the book *A Figure of Speech* by Norma Mazer, students might try telling the story from Jenny's point of view, her mother's, or Jenny's older brother and wife. Each of them would see the problem of the aging grandfather in a very different light. The discussion might consider what alternatives were open to the family, other than putting Grandpa away in an old people's home. They could role play the family conference that could have occurred if everyone had been willing to be honest and open with each other. Questions which would lead to this kind of discussion would be very different from those which might focus on some literary aspect of this book.

There is a place for questions concerning the literary strengths of a book or poem, provided

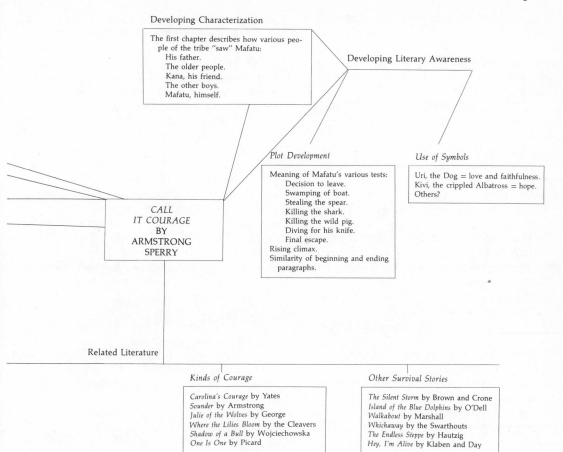

Developing Characterization

The first chapter describes how various people of the tribe "saw" Mafatu:
His father.
The older people.
Kana, his friend.
The other boys.
Mafatu, himself.

Developing Literary Awareness

Plot Development

Meaning of Mafatu's various tests:
Decision to leave.
Swamping of boat.
Stealing the spear.
Killing the shark.
Killing the wild pig.
Diving for his knife.
Final escape.
Rising climax.
Similarity of beginning and ending paragraphs.

Use of Symbols

Uri, the Dog = love and faithfulness.
Kivi, the crippled Albatross = hope.
Others?

*CALL
IT COURAGE
BY
ARMSTRONG
SPERRY*

Related Literature

Kinds of Courage

Carolina's Courage by Yates
Sounder by Armstrong
Julie of the Wolves by George
Where the Lilies Bloom by the Cleavers
Shadow of a Bull by Wojciechowska
One Is One by Picard

Other Survival Stories

The Silent Storm by Brown and Crone
Island of the Blue Dolphins by O'Dell
Walkabout by Marshall
Whichaway by the Swarthouts
The Endless Steppe by Hautzig
Hey, I'm Alive by Klaben and Day

the questions are geared to the developmental level of the children. After reading *The Cabin Faced West* by Jean Fritz, one group of 8- and 9-year-olds examined the significance of the title, the meaning of "the road," the recurring use of the words "some day," and Ann's longing to set a proper table with her mother's lavender-flowered dishes. The children realized that all these objects symbolized Ann's homesickness for her former "cultured life" in Gettysburg, in contrast to living in a windowless log cabin that her father had even faced toward the West. The children then talked about the things they might miss if they were among the first settlers on the moon, for example. In all these instances teachers' questions were related to the purposes of developing personal and literary responses from children.

Levels of Questions

Questions also need to be evaluated in terms of the levels of thought that they require from the respondent. Teachers can be taught to ask questions which demand a higher level of thought than simple recall or yes/no answers. The following categorization[17] of questioning may prove useful to the teacher or librarian who wishes to become more skillful in question-asking:

[17]These categories have been derived from Benjamin S. Bloom, ed. *Taxonomy of Educational Objectives* (New York: Longmans, Green, 1956); Norris Sanders. *Classroom Questions: What Kinds?* (New York: Harper & Row, 1966); and Willavene Wolf, Charlotte S. Huck, and Martha L. King. "Critical Reading Ability of Elementary School Children," USOE Report, Project No. 5-1040, Contract No. OE-4-10-187 (1967).

1. MEMORY (Literal Comprehension). Involves simple recall of story, naming of characters, describing the setting. Questions require only that the student responds with facts or ideas found in the story or poem. This category includes many "who _____," "what _____," and "when _____" kinds of questions.

Examples:

A. *Context of Question.* Teacher has just finished reading *The Elephant's Child* by Kipling.

Questions:

1. What was the name of the snake in this story?
2. How did the Crocodile change the elephant's nose?
3. Who wrote this story?

B. *Context of Question.* Middle-graders are responding to a book-report form.

1. Give the title of the book.
2. Give the name of the author and illustrator.
3. State the name of the publisher and date of publication.
4. Identify the characters in the story.
5. Where did the story take place?
6. Describe the most exciting incident in the story.

2. TRANSLATION. Requires the student to recast an idea into another mode or form of communication, such as moving from the printed word to the oral or the pictorial or graphic. Includes such forms as drama; or making a model, diagram, or map of the setting. The child is not asked to elaborate or interpret the idea, just present it in a different form.

Examples:

A. *Context of Question.* A group of primary-grade children have just finished seeing a sound filmstrip of *The Little Red Hen* by Galdone.

Questions:

1. Fold a piece of paper into four and draw a picture of the four characters—the little hen, the cat, the dog, and the mouse.
2. Retell this story in your own words.

B. Following the picture in the book a 9-year-old boy decides to make his own model of the Kon-Tiki.

C. Using the description given by the author, Mary Norton, of *The Borrowers'* kitchen, two 9-year-old girls make a detailed diorama of it.

3. INTERPRETATION. Several kinds of thinking are represented in this category, including seeing relationships among characters, determining the reasons (or cause and effect) for certain behavior or events in a story, comparing and contrasting variants of a folk tale or books with similar themes, forming generalizations concerning books of a certain type or by a certain author. Interpretation questions ask a child to go beyond the information given in the book, to begin to put it in a frame of reference useful to the child.

Examples:

A. *Context of the Question.* Primary children have just heard their teacher read the story of *Stevie* by John Steptoe.

Questions:

1. How does Robert feel about Stevie? How do you know?
2. How do you suppose that Stevie feels about Robert?

B. *Context of the Question.* Comparing books of a similar theme—*Dandelion* by Freeman and *Harry the Dirty Dog* by Zion.

Questions:

1. Dandelion says that he will never try to be anything but himself in the end of his story. What do you think about Harry? Has he reformed? Give reasons for your answers.

C. *Context of the Question.* Eight-year-olds are looking at Marcia Brown's book *Once a Mouse.*

Questions:

1. Look at the shape of the hill in this picture. How is it like the action occurring on the page?
2. Look at the shadow of the tiger; what is it? What do you think the artist was trying to say by creating the shadow of a dog instead of a tiger?
3. What can you discover about Marcia Brown's use of color in this book?

D. *Context of the Question.* A 12-year-old is discussing the books of Madeleine L'Engle with her teacher. She has just finished reading *A Wind in the Door.*

Questions:
1. This story is a sequel to *A Wrinkle in Time.* How is it like that story? How is it different?
2. You've also read *Meet the Austins* by the same author. Do you see any similarities in this story to the other two?
3. What do you think is the major theme that Madeleine L'Engle is stating in all these stories?

4. APPLICATION. These questions expect the student to make direct application of knowledge, skills, or criteria learned previously to a new situation in life, another book, or another poem. It frequently involves identifying and solving a problem.

Examples:

A. *Context of the Situation.* Teacher had read the 7-year-olds in her class the story of *The Courage of Sarah Noble* by Dalgleish.
1. No questions were asked in this situation.
2. At noon one of the children came running in and announced that she had been frightened by a large dog but she had just pretended she was Sarah Noble and walked by him saying, "Keep up your courage, Jennie Lou, keep up your courage."
3. Primary-grade teachers may look for other examples of children's application of their knowledge of literature as they play out the story of "The Three Bears" in the play corner, or write stories that contain such expressions as "Alas, said the King!"

B. *Context of the Question.* A teacher of 12-year-olds had just finished sharing *Edge of Two Worlds* by Jones with the class.
1. How many different edges of two worlds are suggested in this book? (Students identified the world between Indians and whites, adolescence and adulthood, youth and age, trust and fear, decision and indecision.)
2. What are the edges of the worlds in which you live today? Are they the unhappy places that Sequoyah suggested?

C. *Context of the Question.* Students had looked at the way poets compared two objects

(metaphor) in such poems as "Steam Shovel" by Malam, "The Toaster" by Jay Williams, and "Apartment House" by Raftery in *Reflections on a Gift of Watermelon Pickle* edited by Dunning and others.
Questions:
1. Can you find examples of other poems that describe one object in terms of another?
2. Can you find pictures that compare two different objects?

5. ANALYSIS. Analysis questions emphasize elements, form, and organization of the story or poem. In the critical reading of expository writing—such as is found in informational books, editorials, and advertisements—a student will be asked to use deductive and inductive reasoning, noting fallacies and inaccuracies. Children who have not achieved the level of formal operations in their thinking (usually age 12 and up) have difficulty with many analysis questions.

Examples:

A. *Context of Question.* A group of 10-year-olds were reading *The Door in the Wall* by De Angeli.
Questions:
1. What is the meaning of the title of this book?
2. What other "doors" did Robin finally open? What is the symbolic meaning of each of them?

B. *Context of Questions.* Students have discussed ways in which authors reveal character. A group of them have read *Call It Courage* by Sperry.
Questions:
1. How did Armstrong Sperry tell about Mafatu in the first chapter?
2. Why is it helpful to see a character from so many different points of view?

6. SYNTHESIS. These questions require the student to put together elements and parts of poems and literature in such a way as to create a unified, unique structure. Many of the activities suggested in Chapter 11 call for synthesis on the part of the student.

Examples:

A. *Context of the Question.* Primary-grade children have just heard the story of *Rosie's Walk* by Pat Hutchins.

Questions:
1. Can you retell this story from the point of view of the fox?
2. What sound effects can you create for taping your story?

B. *Context of the Question.* Middle-graders have just finished conducting a survey of their favorite characters in books.
   1. They are going to make a mural of these characters and must solve the problem of how to relate them. How can they portray *Harriet the Spy,* on the same mural as *Charlotte's Web* and *Are You There God? It's Me, Margaret?*

C. *Context of the Question.* The teacher has just read *The Tiniest Sound* by Mel Evans to a class of 9-year-olds.
   Questions:
   1. Could you write a similar story about "The Softest Touch," "The Loudest Noise," or "The Sweetest Taste"?
   2. How could the format of your book reflect its theme?

7. EVALUATIVE. These questions require a judgment of the value or quality of the writing based upon established criteria. The criteria are either known or developed first; then books, poems, art, films, and so on are judged on how closely they meet the criteria.
   Examples:
   A. *Context of the Question.* A group of 8-year-olds have been studying folk tales. Their teacher gives them four copies of *Cinderella*—one illustrated by Marcia Brown, one by LeCain, one by Nola Langner, and *Walt Disney's Cinderella.*
      Questions:
      1. How are these versions alike? Different?
      2. Can you order them from one through four (one being the highest) on the basis of their illustrations? Give your reasons.
      3. Can you order them on the basis of the quality of the language? Which would you place first? Second? And so on. Why?
   B. *Context of the Question.* The teacher has read *Enchantress from the Stars* by Engdahl to a group of 12-year-olds.
      Questions:
      1. Which characters in this book are the best developed by the author?

2. Which ones do you know the least about?
3. Which one would you like to be if you were given a choice? Why?

C. *Context of the Question.* The class has been reading books on the theme of "survival," including *Julie of the Wolves* and *My Side of the Mountain* by Jean George, *Call It Courage* by Armstrong Sperry, and *The Endless Steppe* by Esther Hautzig.
   Questions:
   1. Which of these stories seems the most believable to you? Why?
   2. Order these stories on the basis of which required the greatest courage to which required the least. Why did you put them in that order?
   3. Order these books according to the experience you would most like to have participated in, to the one you would have least liked to have undergone. Again, give your reasons.

Types of Questions

Questions may also be classified as broad or narrow, or convergent or divergent. The con-

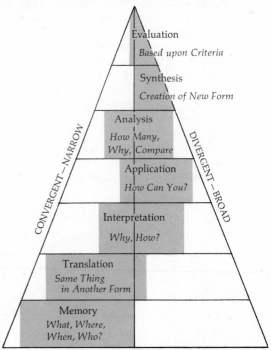

LEVELS AND TYPES OF QUESTIONS

vergent questions seek one "best" or "right" answer, while divergent questions suggest more than one acceptable response. Both types of questions may be asked to produce all levels of thinking, but convergent questions tend to focus on the memory and simple recall, while divergent questions promote higher levels of original thinking. Unfortunately, teachers usually ask more convergent than divergent questions. Such questions take less time for the child's response and they are easier to evaluate. However, the child's response to literature depends as much on what he brings to the active reading of a story or poem as to the content itself. The more divergent questions allow the child to link into this background of experience and give varied interpretations of the story. Imaginative writing is always open to a variety of interpretations, in contrast to scientific or mathematical problems which may be seeking *the* correct answer.

Most convergent questions can be rewritten in such a way as to provide for divergent thinking. For example, the following questions might be asked about *White Bird* by Clyde Bulla. The first question asks for a convergent answer, while the second seeks divergent responses:

1. In searching for his white bird, how many different experiences did John Thomas have? What were they?
2. What do you think John Thomas learned in his search for his white bird?

The first question depends upon *direct recall* from the book, while the second asks the reader to *interpret* the effect of his various experiences on John Thomas. The teacher could ask students to predict how Luke would receive John Thomas when he returned home, based upon children's *analysis* of Luke's character. Then the ending of the story could be read, and they could check the accuracy of their predictions (*applications*). This question allows for various interpretations and some diversity, yet it does make a child think about the consistency of a character. A question that requires *synthesis* might be to ask students to rewrite the story from the point of view of Luke, perhaps in the form of Luke's diary. An *evaluative* question might ask them to compare *White Bird* with *The Loner* by Ester Wier, looking for similarities and differences between Luke in the one book and "the Boss" in the second, and,

finally, determining which character is more fully developed or more believable.

Other kinds of questions might include a very open-ended one that would weigh alternative kinds of behaviors. Students might speculate on what would have happened to both John Thomas and Luke if John Thomas had decided not to return. They could also clarify their own values by considering how they would have behaved if they had been John Thomas—would they have returned home or would they have run away? What other alternatives were open to John Thomas? To Luke?

No one has ever determined a correct sequencing of questions for literature—if there is such a thing. Generally, it is recommended that the teacher ask questions that lead children back to the book rather than away from it, at least at first. Discussions that speculate about what might have happened or use the book as a springboard for value clarification seem to be more appropriate for the end of a discussion rather than the beginning. It is very difficult to get young children back to responding to the book if they are busy retelling a different version or relating the story to the time that they were as angry as John Thomas. Ideally, the teacher would hope that children might want to ask questions about a book they had read or simply share their responses to a book without any prodding. When adults read a book that excites them, they invariably talk about it with their friends. Children should be encouraged to do the same.

PLANNING IN-DEPTH DISCUSSIONS

After the teacher or librarian has planned a web of possibilities for a particular book, specific lessons might be developed for an in-depth discussion of the strengths of a story or poem. Even after careful planning the teacher will want to remain flexible enough to adjust these plans to the response of the group. It is best to work with small groups of five to six children when exploring literature in depth.

An In-depth Look at a Picture Book

WHERE THE WILD THINGS ARE
BY MAURICE SENDAK

Most primary-grade children love this particular book and ask to have it read again and again. A teacher might well increase children's enjoyment of this story by helping them to discover the layers of meaning in it and how the author-illustrator conveyed these meanings. After reading the story and sharing the awesome pictures, the following questions might guide children's discoveries about this book:

What kind of story is this?

Children will probably respond with such expressions as "funny," "scary," "make-believe."

Could this story really happen? Where?

Most of the action in this story took place in Max's imagination. While it is a make-believe story or fantasy, children might well say that it could have happened in Max's mind, but not in "real life."

What kind of boy is Max? How do you know? Is he like other children you know?

Children will give their varied impressions. Some will think he is naughty, others that he has a vivid imagination and a good sense of humor. One child may call attention to the expression on Max's face in the fifth picture in the book. Another may point out that Max is enjoying making up this story.

How did Max treat the Wild Beasts? Why do you suppose he treated them this way?

Children will remember that Max tamed the wild beasts by "the magic trick of staring into all their yellow eyes without blinking," and then led them in their "wild rumpus." Finally, he sent them off to bed without their suppers. Children will recognize that Max did to the Wild Beasts the very same things that had been done to him.

Was Max happy with the Wild Beasts?

The Wild Beasts all went to sleep and Max became lonely. Most of all he "wanted to be where someone loved him best of all," so he went home.

What did Max find waiting for him in his room? Who brought it? What did the supper tell us about Max's mother?

Most children infer that Max's mother brought him his supper, but they do not always see that by this action, she is conveying her love and forgiveness. Actually, the warm supper symbolizes her continuing love.

What did you notice about the size of the pictures in this story?

Why do you think the illustrator made them this way? What happens to the size of the pictures after Max returns to his room?

Children may notice that the pictures become larger and larger as Max's dream becomes more fantastic. They become smaller after Max returns home, but never as small as the first pictures; just as Max will never be quite the same little boy after his fantasy.

What did you notice about the color of the pictures? Why do you suppose Sendak used these colors?

Most of the colors used are greens and blues. Children may decide these convey the idea of a jungle, or a dream, or night.

The teacher will want to summarize or have a child summarize the important learnings that they discovered by discussing this story. Some observations might be the way the author-illustrator paints his pictures to convey characterization and exaggeration in this story. They might include the fact that authors sometimes use one object to represent something of greater importance than the object itself; namely, that a warm supper can stand for a mother's love. The discussion could conclude with these questions:

Have you ever felt like being a wild thing? What made you feel this way?

Children will want to tell their individual experiences.

Would you like to dance your own "wild rumpus" right here? What kind of music should be played? What kind of monsters are you going to be?

Comparing Picture Storybooks

DANDELION BY DON FREEMAN
HARRY THE DIRTY DOG BY GENE ZION,
    ILLUSTRATED BY MARGARET BLOY GRAHAM

These two books have a similar theme; that is, the importance of being true to one's own nature. Their plots are quite different, however. *Dandelion* is the story of a lion who is invited to a party. To prepare for the party he does, in fact, become a "dandy lion"—having his mane curled, buying a new checked sports coat, new cap, and even a bouquet of dandelions for his hostess. He dresses up so much that Miss Giraffe does not recognize him and refuses to let him into the party.

Harry the Dirty Dog is quite the opposite of *Dandelion,* as one might suspect from the title. Harry is a white dog with black spots who gets so dirty that he becomes a black dog with white spots, and his family doesn't recognize him. When

Harry digs up the scrubbing brush that he had carefully buried, takes it upstairs, and jumps in the bathtub, the children get his message, give him a bath, and discover their dog!

After a violent wind and rainstorm unfurl Dandelion's curls and soak his new sports jacket so he must take it off to dry, Dandelion once again tries to go to Miss Giraffe's party; and, this time, he is recognized. Dandelion laughs at himself and promises never to turn himself into a dandy again: "From now on I'll always be just plain me."

Harry, however, does not reform so completely. For a while, he is glad to be clean so that his family recognizes him. The last page pictures him clean and asleep, but the scrubbing brush is hidden under his pillow!

After the teacher has read these two books to the children, the plots and themes can be compared by asking such questions as:

How are these two stories alike?

Both have animals as characters. As a result of foolish behavior, both main characters are not recognized by their families and friends. Dandelion and Harry decide they'll never act that way again, although the reader is less sure of Harry's reformation.

How are these stories different?

Dandelion is bathed and dressed in fine clothes to go to a party.

Harry gets very dirty playing by himself.

What is the big idea (or theme) that the authors are telling in both these stories?

You are happier being yourself. You shouldn't try to be something you are not.

Do people ever act as Harry or Dandelion did? Have you ever acted this way?

Children will give examples from their experience.

Have you read any other books that have this same theme?

Children may remember reading or having heard *Pig Tale* by Helen Oxenbury; *Just the Thing for Geraldine* by Ellen Conford; *The Unhappy Hippopotamus* by Nancy Moore; *Veronica* by Roger Duvoisin; *Robbut, A Tale of Tails* by Lawson; *The Little Rabbit Who Wanted Red Wings* by Bailey; *The Whingdingdilly* by Bill Peet; or *"You Look Ridiculous"* by Waber. All these books have similar themes. They could be displayed on a special table in the classroom and the children could be encouraged to read as many of them as possible.

After they had read these books, children could be asked to make up a story with a plot different from *Dandelion* or *Harry the Dirty Dog,* but utilizing the same theme.

Comparing Different Versions of the Same Tale

Seven-, 8-, and 9-year-olds enjoy comparing different editions of the same folk tale. They can be encouraged to contrast the illustrations, the differences in plot, and the variations in language. A teacher or librarian might give them four picture-book versions of *Cinderella,* such as the Perrault edition illustrated by Errol LeCain or Marcia Brown. These could be compared with the extended story by C. S. Evans, illustrated by Arthur Rackham. In turn, all three of these Cinderellas could be contrasted with *Walt Disney's Cinderella.* Different children in the group might read the following descriptions of Cinderella's flight from the ball at the stroke of midnight:

Then she sprang up and fled as lightly as a deer. The prince followed her, but he couldn't catch up with her. However, she lost one of her glass slippers and he picked it up very carefully.

Cinderella arrived home out of breath, without a coach, without footmen, in her old clothes; nothing remained of her splendor but one of her little slippers; the twin of the one she had lost.[18]

The accompanying picture shows a running Cinderella transforming from a richly dressed lady into a simply dressed French peasant girl in an apron, while the stars have all become clock faces registering midnight.

The longer edition of *Cinderella,* as told by C. S. Evans, is illustrated with Rackham's well-known black silhouettes. Evans describes the same scene in this way:

With a cry of alarm she sprang to her feet, and without even pausing to say good-bye, rushed out of the ballroom, down the steps of the terrace and into the palace garden. So great was her haste that one of her glass slippers came off and she did not even notice her loss.

Four, five, six! chimed the clock, and Cinderella ran as she had never run before. She lost herself

---

[18]Charles Perrault. *Cinderella,* illustrated by Errol LeCain (Scarsdale, N.Y.: Bradbury, 1972), unpaged.

Clock stars register midnight as a richly dressed Cinderella is transformed back into a French peasant girl.

Copyright © Errol LeCain. Illustration copyrighted © 1972 by Errol LeCain. First published in the United States by Bradbury Press.

in the shrubberies, and found her way out again, blundered among the flower beds and snapped the roses from their stalks in the speed of her flight.

Seven, eight, nine!

She crossed a lawn and found herself on a wide drive bordered by trees, which she knew must lead to the palace gates.

Ten, eleven, twelve!

And on the stroke of twelve her beautiful gown changed into the ragged dress of a kitchen-maid.[19]

The text for *Walt Disney's Cinderella* introduces new characters to this traditional tale. It also provides a new incident in which mice rescue Cinderella from the locked tower where her stepmother has imprisoned her.

—Bong! Bong! the clock struck.

"Oh!" cried Cinderella. The magic was about to end.

Without a word she ran from the ballroom, down the long palace hall, and out the door. One of her little glass slippers flew off, but she could not stop.

She leaped into her coach and away they raced home. But as they rounded the first corner, the clock finished its strokes. The spell was broken. And there in the street stood an old horse, a dog, and a ragged girl, staring at a small round pumpkin. About them some mice ran chattering.

"Glass slipper!" the mice cried. "Glass slipper!" And Cinderella looked down. Sure enough, there was a glass slipper on the pavement.

"Oh, thank you, Godmother!" she said.[20]

[19]C. S. Evans. *Cinderella*, illustrated by Authur Rackham (Viking, 1972), p. 84 (1919).

[20]Jane Werner, adaptor, *Walt Disney's Cinderella*, illustrations by the Walt Disney Studio adapted from the Walt Disney Motion Picture "Cinderella" (Racine, Wis.: Golden Press, 1950).

This selection is accompanied by two pictures, one a blonde, chic Cinderella racing down the palace stairs; and another showing the Walt Disney castle in the background, while Cinderella, now a pretty peasant girl with one patch on her apron, examines a sparkling shoe while a dog and horse and little dressed mice look on.

After the children have heard these selections and been given ample time to look at the illustrations, the following questions might be asked:

Which of these versions make you feel the urgency of Cinderella's flight? Why do you think this is so?

Which story told you how the Prince felt about the glass slipper?

Which version included talking animals? Why do you suppose they were added to the story?

Why do you suppose Walt Disney made the old horse the coachman and the dog the footman, instead of the traditional large rat and lizards?

Which story tells you the magic was about to end? Did you need to be told? How did you know about this in the other versions?

Looking at the illustrations, which story looks as if it could take place today? Which tale makes you feel that it takes place in another country?

Where was the story of Cinderella first told? Which conveys a feeling for the origin of the story?

Which illustrations show transformations? How has the artist done this?

Compare *Walt Disney's Cinderella* to *Walt Disney's Snow White.* Except for the color of the hair, how are these heroines different? Alike?

Which selection gives you the clearest picture of Cinderella's flight?

Which pictures do you like the best? Why?

Identifying Form and Setting

Using the opening paragraphs from the following three books, upper-grade children can be helped to surmise the form of the literature and determine the time or place setting for each selection:

He was called "Smith" and was twelve years old. Which in itself was a marvel: for it seemed as if the smallpox, the consumption, brainfever, jailfever, and even the hangman's rope had given him a wide berth for fear of catching something. . . . Smith was rather a sooty spirit of the violent and ramshackle town, and inhabited the tumbledown mazes about fat St. Paul's like the strong smells and jaundiced air itself.[21]

Once upon a time and a long time ago the tiger was king of the forest. At evening when all the animals sat together in a circle and talked and laughed together, Snake would ask, "Who is the strongest of us all?"
"Tiger is the strongest," cried the dog. "When Tiger whispers the trees listen. When Tiger is angry and cries out, the trees tremble."[22]

Claudia knew that she could never pull off the old-fashioned kind of running away. That is, running away in the heat of anger with a knapsack on her back. She didn't like discomfort; even picnics were untidy and inconvenient: all those insects and the sun melting the icing on the cupcakes. Therefore, she decided that her leaving home would not be just running from somewhere but would be running to somewhere. To a large place, a comfortable place, an indoor place, and preferably a beautiful place. And that's why she decided upon the Metropolitan Museum of Art in New York City.[23]

What kind of stories do children anticipate from these opening paragraphs? The following questions might be used to guide children's comparisons of these selections:

In the first selection, what clues do you have concerning the time and setting of the story?

When would it have seemed a marvel to live until 12?

What kind of a book do you think this will be? How do you know?

---

[21] Leon Garfield. *Smith,* illustrated by Antony Maitland (New York: Pantheon, 1967), p. 3.
[22] Philip M. Sherlock. *Anansi the Spider Man, Jamaican Folk Tales,* illustrated by Marcia Brown (Crowell, 1954), pp. 3–4.
[23] E. L. Konigsburg. *From the Mixed-up Files of Mrs. Basil E. Frankweiler* (Atheneum, 1967), p. 5.

Mafatu has conquered his fear of Moana, the sea god, and triumphantly returns home.

Reprinted with permission of Macmillan Publishing Co., Inc. from *Call It Courage* by Armstrong Sperry. Copyright 1940 by Macmillan Publishing Co., Inc., renewed 1968 by Armstrong Sperry.

What kind of a story is the second one? (Folk tale)

What clues helped you to decide? (The traditional beginning, talking animals, language patterns)

When and where does the last story take place?

What do you know about Claudia?

Could this story really happen? How can you find out?

Students may discover other contrasts among these selections. Generally, they should be helped to see that different kinds of literature use different forms. A folk tale can be readily differ-entiated from historical fiction or realistic fiction. The setting will provide the clue to helping children distinguish between historical and realistic fiction. While the word *fiction* indicates that the stories are not true, they could conceivably happen. Historical fiction must be true to its time and place in history, just as today's realistic fiction should present a believable slice of actuality.

In-depth Study of Characterization

CALL IT COURAGE BY ARMSTRONG SPERRY

After children have enjoyed this well-written and exciting story, the teacher could plan a literature lesson to identify ways in which the author revealed the character of Mafatu. In the first chapter the reader learns that Mafatu fears the sea, and the reason for this fear. He is told what the older members of the tribe think about Mafatu, and particularly how his father feels about him. Mafatu is taunted and jeered at by the boys and laughed at by the girls. The text explains what Mafatu thinks, and what he is finally forced to do. Seldom does an author use as many different ways to reveal character as Sperry does in this chapter. A sixth-grade teacher planned the following in-depth study of techniques of character development:

INTRODUCTION

Ask the children how they get to know a person. Have them imagine that a new pupil comes to class. How would they find out about him?

List suggestions on the board. Possible responses might be: "Look at him, describe him"; "listen to what he says"; "notice how he talks"; "ask somebody about him"; "see how he plays"; "find out how he treats you."

Help children realize the limitations of surface impressions. Children will recognize that you need to see a person in many situations over a period of time to really know him.

Ask children how an author might reveal character to the reader.

PROCEDURE

Use paperback books of *Call It Courage*. Ask children to read Chapter 1 and find passages in which the character of Mafatu is described. Number each passage by writing lightly in the book. On a separate sheet of paper indicate the various ways the author helps the reader see Mafatu.

The following passages are illustrative of what the children might identify:

1. "It was the sea that Mafatu feared. He had been surrounded by it ever since he was born. The thunder of it filled his ears; the crash of it upon the reef, the mutter of it at sunset, the threat and fury of its storms—on every hand, wherever he turned—the sea." (p. 2)
   [*Telling about the character and his one fear.*]

2. "They worshipped courage, those early Polynesians. The spirit which had urged them across the Pacific in their sailing canoes, before the dawn of recorded history, not knowing where they were going nor caring what their fate might be, still sang its song of danger in their blood. There was only courage. A man who was afraid—what place had he in their midst? And the boy Mafatu—son of Tavana Nui, the Great Chief of Hikueri—always had been afraid." (p. 1)
   [*Describing the character in his surroundings.*]

3. "'That will be fun, won't it?' Kana insisted, watching Mafatu closely. But the boy made no answer. Kana started to speak; he stopped, turned impatiently, and walked away. Mafatu wanted to cry out after him: 'Wait, Kana! I'll go! I'll try'—But the words would not come. Kana had gone." (p. 9)
   [*Letting the character talk; showing what others say to the character.*]

4. "He knew in that instant what he must do: he must prove his courage to himself, and to the others, or he could no longer live in their midst. He must face Moana, the Sea God—face him and conquer him. He must." (p. 11)
   [*Revealing the character's thoughts.*]

5. "Mafatu, standing tense in the shadows, heard a scornful laugh. 'Not all of us will go,' he heard Kana scoff. 'Not Mafatu!'
   "'Ha! He is afraid.'
   "'He makes good spears,' offered Viri generously.
   "'Ho! That is woman's work. Mafatu is afraid of the sea. He will never be a warrior.' Kana laughed again, and the scorn of his voice was like a spear thrust through Mafatu's heart.
   "'Aia!' Kana was saying. 'I have tried to be friendly with him. But he is good only for making spears. Mafatu is a coward.'" (pp. 10, 11)
   [*Showing what others say about the character and how that makes Mafatu feel.*]

6. "The older people were not unkind to the boy, for they believed that it was all the fault of the tupapau—the ghost-spirit which possesses every child at birth. But the girls laughed at him, and the boys failed to include him in their games ... Mafatu's stepmother knew small sympathy for him, and his stepbrothers treated him with open scorn. ... The boy learned to turn these jibes aside, but his father's silence shamed him. He tried with all his might to overcome his terror of the sea." (p. 6)
   [*Showing the reactions of his family to Mafatu.*]

7. "The boy's hands tightened on his paddle. Behind him lay safety, security from the sea. What matter if they jeered? For a second he almost turned back. Then he heard Kana's voice once more saying: 'Mafatu is a coward.'
   "The canoe entered the race formed by the ebbing tide. It caught up the small craft in its churn, swept it forward like a chip on a millrace. No turning back now. . . ." (p. 13)
   [*Showing the character in action.*]

In a later lesson students might look at the character *development* of Mafatu. The following questions could be used to guide this discussion:

How did Mafatu change? (He overcame fear.)
What were events that caused Mafatu to develop courage? (Left home, faced storm, defied tabu, fought shark, killed pig, overcame octopus, escaped man-eaters.)
How did Mafatu feel toward Uri? How do you know? (He loved Uri and saved his life.)
When does Mafatu finally begin to have some confidence in himself? What gave this to him? (When he had forced himself to take the spear from the *tabu* platform.)
The story ends with the same paragraph with which it begins, with the exception of one line. How does the omission of that line show the change in Mafatu's character?
Do you know anyone whose character has changed?
Do you know the reasons for that change?

Values Clarification through Literature

Literature is a rich source for helping children begin to clarify their own values, for understanding themselves and seeing their relationships within this world. In using a book as a vehicle for values clarification, the teacher could ask divergent questions which would help a child gain insight into his own values. The process of values clarification never imposes values; instead it encourages the child to consider the values he holds. Not a moralistic or didactic approach, values clarification simply helps the student develop a better understanding of what he really stands for and believes in.

In their book *Values and Teaching,* the authors define what they call the *process of valuing*.[24] They maintain that for a value to result, children must be involved in three processes: choosing, prizing, and acting. Values-clarification questions would focus upon choosing from among alternatives after thoughtful consideration of the consequences of each; prizing and cherishing particular values; affirming them and being willing to act upon these values.

Literature suggests alternative experiences in living, and can provide the stimulus for thoughtful clarification of the reader's values. Many books can be used for values clarification, but the following questions are based upon *The Bears' House* by Marilyn Sachs.

Primarily, this is the story of Fran Ellen who is 10 years old and still sucks her thumb. The girls in her class tease her and tell her that she is dirty and smells. Fran Ellen retreats into a fantasy world by doing her work at school quickly so she can play with "The Bears' House," an old doll's house that belonged to her teacher when she was a child. The Bears' House becomes a real house in Fran Ellen's fantasies. Here Mama Bear cooks and cleans and gives Fran Ellen a beautiful dress; and Papa Bear holds her on his lap whenever she is unhappy. Fran Ellen's fantasy world contrasts sharply with her real world, where her father has deserted the family, her mother is sick, and Fran Ellen is trying desperately to take care of her baby sister, Flora, whom she adores. No one except the author and reader is aware of Fran Ellen's two worlds.

THE BEARS' HOUSE BY MARILYN SACHS

When Fran Ellen's mother becomes ill and can no longer look after the baby, the older brother, Fletcher, tells the family that they have three choices, and also suggests what the consequences of these choices might be:

1. They can write to their uncle in Alabama, who would probably want them to come down there to live. They think he is a mean man and don't want to go there.
2. They can tell one of the neighbors, but they don't know them well; Fletcher thinks they would report them to the police.
3. They can just not tell anyone that their father has left them and that their mother has spent the day in bed crying. Somehow they can share the work, take care of the baby, and cope.

The children chose the last alternative. Do you think they made a wise decision? Why or why not?

What other alternatives were there?
    Children will think of others but the following alternatives might be considered: (a.) Fletcher could have told his principal and at the same time express concern for keeping the family together. (b.) He could have been honest with the welfare woman, who did know the family. (c.) Others?
How could Fran Ellen have kept Susan and Jennifer from teasing her?
Why do you think children tease other children? How did it make Susan and Jennifer feel? Fran Ellen?
Whose fault was it that Fran Ellen was dirty and smelly?
Why did Fran Ellen suck her thumb?
Why did Fran Ellen like The Bears' House so well?
What things do you do when you can't solve a problem?
Where do you go when you are unhappy?
If you are going to write a final chapter to this story, how would you have things work out?
What might have happened if Miss Thompson hadn't come home with Fran Ellen?
Are some problems too big for children to handle? What kinds of problems?

If the class were studying the theme "Getting along with Others," different groups might want to read *Blubber* by Judy Blume, *The Hundred Dresses* by Eleanor Estes, *The Summer Birds* by Penelope Farmer, or *The Greyhound* by Helen Griffiths.

[24]Louis E. Raths, Merrill Harmin, and Sidney B. Simon. *Values and Teaching* (Columbus, Ohio: Charles E. Merrill, 1966), pp. 28–29.

Fran Ellen sucks her thumb and retreats into her fantasy of living in *The Bears' House.*

Illustration from *The Bears' House* by Marilyn Sachs, illustrated by Louis Glanzman. Copyright © 1971 by Marilyn Sachs. Reproduced by permission of Doubleday & Company, Inc.

The real danger in any form of values clarification is that the teacher may turn the discussion into a moralistic session. The primary purpose of values clarification is always to help the child think about his own values, to give him an opportunity to generate alternatives in a situation, and then to choose from among them. Children and youth of today are confronted with many more choices than in previous generations. They need help in looking at a problem from different perspectives and in weighing the alternatives. Literature frequently shows how characters have developed their values. As children read books and discuss them, they learn something about the *process of valuing*, how it happens, what makes people hold certain beliefs and behave in a certain manner.

Children Share Their Reading

ALTERNATIVES TO ORAL BOOK REPORTS

For years teachers have devised various extrinsic methods to motivate children to read. Book worms, book trees, book charts, and required weekly book reports have been used to stimulate children's reading behavior. *A gold star by any other name still tarnishes!* Too frequently these motivational devices have brought about results that were in conflict with the desired purposes of well-meaning teachers. Competent readers may come to enjoy the smug satisfaction of winning competitions rather than finding long-lasting pleasure in books for their own sakes. They may select five "thin" books in order to achieve more rockets placed after their names, instead of one book that challenges their reading ability. Meanwhile, a slow reader feels defeated before he begins, and turns away from books as sources of pleasure and information. When competition is stressed, emphasis is placed on the quantity of books read rather than on the quality of the reading experience.

A child once defined a book report as "when a kid tells a story poorer than the author!" Unfortunately, that is a very apt description of most oral book reports. When child after child stands up and follows a "prescribed method" of reporting, such as: "The author of this book is . . . , the story is about . . . , the characters are . . . , I liked it because . . ."—most children and the teacher are eventually bored to death. Certainly, no interest has been generated in the book, and the teacher has not learned anything about what the child's real response to that book is. What then has transpired? A child has been required to read a book in order to report on it. The rest of the class is required to listen to a report of a book in which they may have no interest. Some teachers require a written or oral report for every book the child reads which, for most children, amounts to punishment for reading! If our ultimate goal is sharing books with children, and in having them share them with each other, is to develop an interest in and love for literature, there has got to be a better way to do it than the required, deadly dull book report!

If a child reads a book in which he becomes really involved and is enthusiastic about it, his first inclination is to tell someone about this book. This should be encouraged. He may discuss it with his teacher in a conference; he may share it informally with a small group who have either read the book or would like to read it; he may make a display, create a picture, write about it, or follow any of the activities suggested in

Chapter 11. All these methods would involve some interpretation and analysis of the book, helping him to think about what seemed important to him in the story.

A child should also have the option of *not* sharing his book. Occasionally, a book may make such an impact on a child that he does not want to discuss it; he only wants to experience it again. One 9-year-old girl was observed in a classroom reading a book for some forty-five minutes. She was completely absorbed in her reading and oblivious to all the other activities going on around her. Finally, she closed her book and put it back on the shelf. When asked if she wasn't going to finish it, she responded: "Oh, I don't have to, it's my very favorite book and I've read it three times so I know how it ends. I was just rereading my special parts." (The book was the well-loved *The Secret Garden* by Burnett.) No teacher should require a book report from this child to prove she was reading! Casual observation would tell one that. A discussion with the child about what she particularly liked in the "special parts" might prove illuminating, but it could also be an invasion of her private world. A sensitive teacher would know whether to talk with the child or not.

Time for informal sharing of books should be provided during the school day. Children might place their names on the chalkboard or on a bulletin board if they have a book to share. Before dividing the class into groups for such a book-sharing period, the teacher could say: "Today we have three persons who want to share their books. You may decide which group you wish to join. Who would like to hear a story of a modern girl who rode a horse clear across Montana to get help for her grandfather? (*The Long Journey* by Barbara Corcoran.) Who would like to hear about a freaky television set that shows everything one day in advance? (*A Billion for Boris* by Mary Rodgers.) Who would like to hear another story about the characters from *A Wrinkle in Time? (A Wind in the Door* by Madeleine L'Engle.)" Children can then make choices according to interest in the content of the story, rather than the individual popularity of the person sharing the book. The children can meet in small groups in various parts of the room or hall; and the teacher can circulate from one group to another to listen to the discussions. Children may also tape record their discussions, which the teacher can play later in order to listen to children's responses.

Another day all the children who had read one particular book could meet to share their impressions of it. Or a group of children might share books by the same author—such as *Where the Lilies Bloom, Grover, The Mimosa Tree*, and others by the Cleavers. This kind of discussion would need guidance by the teacher if children were to compare themes and discuss styles of writing.

One day each child might have an opportunity to share a favorite book in a small group of five or six children. One very enthusiastic 9-year-old boy was overheard as he started to share his favorite story, *Island of the Blue Dolphins* by O'Dell. He first polled his group to see how many had read the book. Since none of them had, he began with this introduction:

> "You might think it odd that I'd like a story with a picture of a girl on the cover. But this book just isn't like any story I've ever read. It tells the story of Karana who lived for eighteen years on an island in the Pacific all by herself." Then, because his audience didn't seem too impressed, he said again, "Eighteen years—do you realize how long that would be?"

His enthusiasm sold the other boys on reading the book!

Other alternatives to the deadly dull book report might include these more creative approaches:

1. Select and read an interesting or unusual part of the story.
2. Interview a character from a story, such as Elana (*Enchantress from the Stars* by Engdahl), when she returned to the Federation's Anthropological Center.
3. Several children could share their knowledge of an author and his books by one of them playing the role of the author and the others doing an interview.
4. Children could role play a portion of a story (*see* Chapter 11).
5. Children could play the roles of the various mothers in *Berries Goodman* by Neville and pretend to meet at a P.T.A. session.
6. Stories can be retold from a different character's point of view. For example, the story of *Blubber* by Judy Blume would be a very different story if told by Linda (Blubber) herself.

However children choose to share their stories, the activity should create interest in the book and extend children's thinking about the story.

CREATIVE BOOK REVIEWS

The written book report is also an anathema to most children and is seen as punishment for reading a book. Teachers and children should explore the possibilities of writing more creative reports that will extend children's thinking about the book, rather than just retell the story.

Teachers also should consider the child's developmental skill in writing before asking him to prepare a written account of his reading. If young children are required to write book reports before they have achieved a measure of writing facility, their interest in reading may be permanently damaged. Children in kindergarten and the primary grades can develop group lists of favorite books. Reporting may be extended as they dictate captions for illustrations or brief summaries for storybook murals. After hearing the teacher read *A Very Special House* by Krauss, one primary-school group dictated a book review on an experience chart shaped like a house. Another group retold the story of *Stone Soup* by Brown, and added their illustrations of the soldiers and the villagers who were tricked into providing the ingredients for the soup made of stones.

Periodically, children in the middle grades may develop lists of their favorite books. A group list of class favorites might be compiled and sent home as a possible Christmas list, or exchanged with other classes for purposes of comparison. Where schools have established paperback bookstores, brief book reviews can announce the arrival of new books. One school puts out the "Book Nook News," in which children write about their favorite paperbacks and list new titles.

Some classes write brief reactions to books on 3 × 5 cards, which are then filed in a box by author so that others can read them. These cards clearly state the reader's feelings:

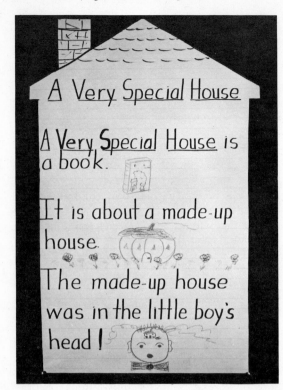

A group of primary-grade children dictated a book review on an experience chart shaped like a house.
Clarfield School, Columbus, Ohio, Public Schools, Virginia Kessler, teacher.

A group of 6-year-olds retold and illustrated the story of *Stone Soup*.

Hammond, Indiana, Public Schools, Sandra Isolampi, student teacher.

Butler, Beverly. *Light a Single Candle*

I liked this book because it gives you a feeling of empathy and warmth for the girl who gets blind. In fact while I was reading it, I felt like I was her.

> Written by Suzy Muslin
> Evanston Public Schools

Foul

The reason I liked *Foul* is because its about Connie Halkins and how he lived in the ghetto and how he became the great basketball player he is today. Personally I think it is very sad and yet at times it can be happy. I also liked it because Connie was weak and his brothers were strong. Connie was never good at anything until he started playing basketball.

> Written by Norman Atkins
> Evanston Public Schools

One teacher in the middle grades encouraged students to select a quotation from a book and then write of a moment in their own lives that reminded them of the quote. Following the reading aloud of *Banner in the Sky* by Ullman, the teacher asked the 11- and 12-year-olds to write about their goals, and to mention if their parents' goals for them were the same or different. If they didn't want to write about themselves, they could create an imaginary person to write about. Here is one boy's story:

> I chose not to write about someone else. But about myself because I think that my situation is similar to Rudi's.
>
> For instance Rudi wants to climb the Citadel. I am not sure what I want to do. Rudi's mother has her own ideas about what he should do. Which happens to be working in a hotel. My mother has her own idea also. She wants me to go into law.
>
> Rudi's problems are different yet the same. We both have a parent or parents that have different ideas about what we should do.

The one big difference is that he keeps trying to do what he wants and I don't. Also Rudi is able to live out his dream. At least he can try. Of course he would never get his mother's approval. But he tries anyway. I can try with my mother's approval. That is she would say it was alright but I don't think she would mean it.

Rudi's mother doesn't want him to climb the Citadel because her husband was killed on it. I don't know why my mother wants me to go into law. I think I probably want to be an electric engineer but don't really know.

Dave F.
The Sidwell Friends School
Washington, D.C.
Judith Rosenfeld, Teacher

Children may also write character sketches. After reaching Chapter 5 in *Berries Goodman* by Emily Neville, the teacher asked a small group of 12-year-olds to consider whether they would like any of the mothers in the story for their mothers. The two sample answers show remarkable understanding of the characters and the students' own criteria for motherhood. They also represent an example of values clarification, since the students were asked to choose a particular mother whom they could accept.

Mrs. Goodman

Mrs. Goodman seems to be a mother that I would like to have. She isn't strict and she really doesn't hastle Berries and tries to understand Berries. Yet she doesn't like Berries around her so much.

Mrs. Graham

Mrs. G. is a very strict mother. She seems to be a bad influence on Sandra. I can't really say anything good for Mrs. G. But I know one thing. She sure is prejudiced against Jews and if I were a Jew I would be prejudiced against her.

Mrs. Fine

Mrs. Fine is the kind that is over protective of her child. She seems to be nice but not the mother I would like to have. She loves her child but she doesn't let him be alone or have fun on his own without her help.

Pilar

Mrs. Graham, Mrs. Fine, Mrs. Goodman

Mrs. Graham is a very strict mother. Sandra her daughter must play outside unless it is raining. She is prejudiced against Jews, and calls them names. She tries to act sweet and makes a lovely first appearance no matter how she feels. She has a very loud deep voice which is often used on Sandra. (I would not like her for a mother).

Mrs. Fine is a very sweet mother. She over protects her son Sidney though. She expects her son to be grown up and not to play boy games. She lets him have a lot of things like brownies before dinner. (I might like her as a mother.)

Mrs. Goodman doesn't pay much attention to her son. She just likes to lock herself in a room and relax. She worries about him sometimes and can get pretty upset. (I wouldn't like her, I need a mother I can talk to. I think of all 3 mothers, I would like to have Mrs. Fine.)

Clare

Sidwell Friends School
Judith Rosenfeld, Librarian

Other suggestions for writing about books might include writing a letter of appreciation to the author telling why the child liked the book or making any suggestions for improvement— but this should be done with caution. Children might be encouraged to write their own stories of what happened after the story ended. One 8-year-old did rewrite the ending to *Stuart Little*, illustrating and binding it.

Book reviews can be printed in a room newspaper, a school magazine, put on a bulletin-board display or in a class file or notebook. Riddles, advertisements, and dust jackets with summaries are other forms that may be utilized in writing about books. Suggestions in Chapter 11 provide further opportunities for creative writing about books. Teachers will want to encourage children to try a variety of ways of sharing their interest in a book with others.

Children's Response to Books

One of the most exciting developments in the teaching of literature is the emphasis upon studying children's responses to books. Rather than imposing upon the child our concepts of the value of a particular book, we should listen to the child's response to that book as a clue to his thinking and feeling. Louise Rosenblatt[25] maintains that the reader recreates the text within his mind. If we believe this transactional theory—that the reader interacts with the author and reconstructs the story—then it is important to tap in and see what the reader is making of it. The process of the interpretation is more important than the interpretation itself; both are of greater value than the content of the book or the craft of the writing.

There has been little or no research on young children's unsolicited responses to literature. However, James Britton, in his working paper for the Dartmouth Conference titled "Response to Literature,"[26] lays the groundwork for this approach with children. He maintains that "our aim should be to refine and develop responses that children are already making—to fairy stories, folk songs, pop songs, television serials, their own games and rhymes and so on. Development can best be defined as an increasing sense of form."[27]

RESPONSE THROUGH PLAY AND ART

Listen to children's play as they spontaneously act out "Goldilocks and the Three Bears" in the playhouse corner; or as a girl sees a basket and announces to her companions that she is going to be "Little Red Riding Hood" and go pick flowers for her grandmother. Someone is found to play the wolf and they are all engrossed in a matter of minutes. No one arranged or suggested the idea of playing these roles; they just happened, growing naturally out of the previous experience of these children with folk tales. Children's play is filled with such references to the literature of childhood. They indicate how well children have assimilated these favorite tales and accommodated them into their spontaneous play.

Children's art work will reflect their knowledge and enjoyment of literature. One group of 6-year-olds talked about all the spooky, scary things they could think of. Most of their references were to Halloween symbols of spookiness—ghosts, witches, and demons. Their teacher then read them *D'Aulaires' Trolls.* They were excited by these new concepts of spooky creatures and immediately wanted to draw them. The chalk mural that they made of "six-headed trolls" and "trolls with bugs in their hair" is pictured in the second color section of this book. The idea of "spookiness" for these children had been enlarged to incorporate a cross-cultural concept of what was scary in another country.

One teacher of 6- and 7-year-olds determined their level of understanding of the story *Fish Is Fish* by Leo Lionni. This is the tale of a tadpole turned frog, who returns to his pond and tells his friend, the fish, about all the strange creatures he has seen on land. The fish sees them all in his mind as "fish people" or "fish birds" or "fish cows." When the teacher finished reading the story to three of the children she said: "Now let's imagine that the frog described one other creature that he had seen on land to the fish. Suppose he told him all about a furry little black kitten. How do you suppose the fish would see it? Could you draw me a picture of what the fish would see?" One little girl carefully drew a picture of a black furry kitten. Another child started her picture by saying: "Now let's see, I think he'd see the whiskers as gills, so I'll make them stick out like gills." She then went on to draw a "fish-cat." The third went off on his own creative tangent and told a long story about the cat falling in the water so the fish really did see him as a cat! All of these children had heard the same story at the same time, but their responses as shown in their art work suggested different levels of understanding.

The pictures on page 743 show two children's responses to the story, *The Biggest House in the World* also by Lionni. After reading this book, the children were asked to choose any animal and grant it the same wish as the little snail had; namely, that it could change itself in any way. The girl (Lisa, age 8) chose a bird, and she made his tail large, more elaborate, and more colorful. The boy (David, age 10) also drew a bird. He used the vocabulary of the story saying: "The bird twitched his tongue in order to make his beak bigger so he could eat more." Finally, his

[25]Louise Rosenblatt. *Literature as Exploration* (Noble and Noble, 1968), p. 35. (1938).
[26]James R. Squire, ed. *Response to Literature* (Champaign, Ill.: National Council of Teachers of English, 1968).
[27]*Ibid.,* p. 4.

beak becomes so heavy that he can't see over it or lift it up. The boy's comment was: "He'll have to get a derrick to lift it up now." This 10-year-old got the notion of the bird becoming the cause of his own self-destruction, as in the story of the snail, whereas the 8-year-old girl saw only the change of size and the elaboration of color. Both had translated the story into their own crea-

tive drawings, but one child appeared to have a fuller understanding of the meaning of the story.

A group of first-graders responded to *The Biggest House in the World* through a variety of media and math activities. They took surveys of children's preferences for color, kind, and size of house (one story, two story, or three story). Their concept of the word "house" was enlarged to

When asked to replicate the action in the story *The Biggest House in the World* by Lionni, an 8-year-old girl confined her change to elaboration and color, while a 10-year-old boy included the aspect of self-destruction.
Tremont Elementary School, Upper Arlington, Ohio, Jill Boyd, teacher.

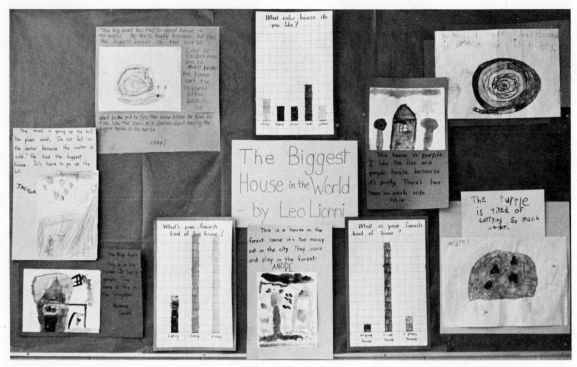

A first-grade group responded to Lionni's book by making pictures and surveys of their favorite colors, sizes, and kinds of houses.

Barrington Road School, Upper Arlington Public Schools, Laurie Mahla, EPIC Student Teacher, The Ohio State University.

include the "houses" of a snail and turtle (shells). The bulletin board in the picture displays the creative results of this extension of one book.

RESPONSE THROUGH TALK

The young child shows his delight in being read to in many ways; he joins in on the refrain of a story; he anticipates what is coming on the next page; he points to various items in a picture and names them; and he listens intently during the exciting places. In brief, he responds joyously and with his whole being.

In the classroom most children listen to the story hour with the same kind of active interest. They may interrupt with an: "Oh, he's going to get it when he comes home," or "we slept on an island once," or "my sister has bunk beds just like those." Britton tells us that the child is experiencing literature in the role of a spectator.[28]

He is connecting his experience with someone else's. Moreover, he can experience this pleasure again and again as he hears that story or enjoys others.

The following transcript[29] shows the various talk reactions of a 5-year-old, a 7-year-old, a 9-year-old, and an 11-year-old to the picture story of *Little Blue and Little Yellow* by Lionni. Despite the fact that little blue and little yellow are simply torn pieces of paper, all children automatically assumed that they are boys, even though the teacher has made no references to gender. This is an interesting commentary on our cultural values. The children's recorded comments follow:

Page 1 introduces Little Blue.

5-year-old: "Hello, Blue!" [Shows automatic acceptance and wants to participate in the story.]

[28] James Britton. *Language and Learning* (London, England: Penguin, 1970), pp. 108–109.

[29] Recorded by Marianne Kubat, student, The Ohio State University.

Page 2 shows Little Blue at home with his mother and father.

7-year-old: The tall one is papa and the fat one is mama. [Attempts to categorize the abstract shapes.]

Page 3 shows Little Blue's friends.

9-year-old: "They're all different colors."

11-year-old: Those are black and yellow children and the red one is an Indian and they are all together. [Deeper analysis, recognizing symbolism.]

Page 4 states that of all the children Little Yellow is Little Blue's best friend.

5-year-old: "My best friend is . . ." [At this point all the children had something to say about their best friends!]

Page 5 shows where Little Yellow lives.

7-year-old: "The big brown thing is their house, huh?" [The 5-year-old just accepted it as their house; 7-year-old needed reassurance.]

Page 6 shows the children playing hide-and-seek and Ring-a-Ring-o-Roses.

9-year-old: "That's supposed to be Ring around the Rosies."

Page 7 pictures them at school seated in neat rows.

11-year-old: "Yuch!"

Page 8 shows them playing after school.

7-year-old: "See the red one is way up in the air."

Page 9—Mama Blue goes shopping and tells Little Blue to stay home, but he goes out to find Little Yellow.

5-year-old: "Oh, oh." [Anticipating punishment.]

7-year-old: "Awwwww." [Tattling tone.]

11-year-old: "He's too little to be left alone."

Page 10—The house is empty.

5-year-old: "They moved away in the middle of the night 'cause his mommy couldn't pay for stuff." [Drawing on his own experience or knowledge of others.]

Page 11 shows Little Blue looking for his friend.

9-year-old: Looking at dark background: "That's outside and that's an old dark building." [Wanting to give meaning to abstract picture.]

Page 12—Suddenly he sees Little Yellow.

7-year-old: "Yeah!"

Page 13—They hug each other until they become green!

7-year-old: "Oh, oh I know what would happen if I went home green." [Anticipates action and consequences.]

Pages 14 and 15—The friends play.
[No comments.]

Page 16—They chase Little Orange.

11-year-old: "Orange looks scared." [Orange, like all the other colors, is a torn circle of paper.]

Page 17—They climb a mountain
[No comments.]

Page 18—They become tired and go home.

7-year-old: "See he's sitting down now." [Green circle is shown near the bottom of the page.]

Page 19—Mama and Papa Blue do not recognize Little Green as their child.

5-year-old: "They are too!" [Defiant.]

7-year-old: "Poor Little Blue and Little Yellow." [Sympathetic.]

9-year-old: "They didn't even know their own kids?" [Incomprehensible.]

11-year-old: "Man, they don't know who their kids are!" [Disgust.]

Page 20—Then Little Blue and Little Yellow began to cry blue and yellow tears.

5-year-old: "Is cry really that color?"

7-year-old: "The blue and yellow is coming out."

Page 21—They pull themselves together and once again they are Little Blue and Little Yellow.

11-year-old: "Ya mean, they got it together?"

Page 22—The Blues were very happy.

5-year-old: [Giggled.]

7-year-old: [Clapped.]

Page 23—They hugged and kissed their son and also Little Yellow—then they became green.

5-year-old: "Oh, no, not again!" [Puts his hand to his forehead.]

Page 24—Now at last they understood what had happened, so they went across the street to tell the Yellows.

7-year-old: I think Little Blue and Little Yellow have their arms around each other. [Child is interpreting the picture through her understanding of the theme.]

Last page—"They all hugged each other with joy and the children played until supper time."

5-year-old: "And they lived happily ever after." [Wants the security of the traditional ending.]

Looking at the *endpapers* after reading the story.

7-year-old: "The black is at darktime and the white is at daytime."

9-year-old: "Black is when they're sad and white is when he's home again."

In the discussion that followed, the 9- and 11-year-olds saw larger meanings in the story than did the 5- and 7-year-olds:

9-year-old: "It just means that these two kids liked each other so much that they became just alike."

11-year-old: "Everybody knows that blue and yellow make green; their parents should have known that."

9-year-old: "I think their parents understood how two people can be real good friends and get a whole lot like each other, but I'd feel awful bad if my parents didn't know who I was."

11-year-old: "The kids don't care what anybody looks like or what color you are. It's grownups that hassle you about it. The kids taught the parents that it doesn't matter what color you are, just that you like each other."

From this discussion, it is easy to see the child's growing understanding of complexity and meaning. The 5-year-old puts himself into the story true to his egocentric nature. He compared parts of the story to his own experiences. He enjoyed the illustrations and began to talk to them rather than about them. He seemed to be quite concerned when the child was left alone and when the parents didn't recognize the children. He never tried to analyze the abstract shapes, but just accepted them on a literal level. *Little Blue and Little Yellow* left him with no real message or moral, just the good feeling of having heard a story with a happy ending.

The 7-year-old seemed just right for this story. She comprehended the simple abstract pictures and frequently took on the role of narrator by explaining the pictures in her comments. Her comments also showed a developing empathy for the characters.

The 9-year-old was able to see the story in terms of symbolic meanings. He asked if all the different colors signified the races of the world. The others agreed on this theme. He also made the astute observation that persons become very much alike when they are such close friends. His attitude toward the parents not recognizing their own children was one of disgust at their stupidity!

The 11-year-old's responses revealed the greatest maturity in thinking. He readily identified the theme of friendship and saw the various shapes as different types of people, instead of just representations of races. He imposed different emotions on the pictures—such as "scared," "hurt," "sad," "excited," and so on. He saw the story as a kind of puzzle that he enjoyed "psyching out."

This transcript illustrates Britton's point that:

A sense of literary form increases as we find satisfaction in a greater range and diversity of works, and particularly as we find satisfaction in works which, by their complexity or the subtlety of their distinctions, their scope or their unexpectedness, make greater and greater demands on us.[30]

On one level, *Little Blue and Little Yellow* appears to be a simple picture book based upon the age-old theme of loss and recovery. On a higher level, however, it moves to the theme of friendship and getting along with those who may be different from you.

Each age level responded to the story on their own terms of understanding. It would have done little good (and could be destructive of enjoyment of literature) if the younger children were pushed to try to formulate the abstractions achieved by more mature ones. However, Britton maintains that teachers may refine and develop the responses that children are already making, by gradually exposing them to stories with increasingly complex patterns of events.[31]

The consistent sharing of good literature will

[30]James Britton, *Response to Literature*, James R. Squire, ed. (Champaign, Ill.: National Council of Teachers of English, 1968), p. 5.

[31]James Britton, *Ibid.*, p. 4.

result in children's increasing sense of form. Teachers need to listen to children's responses to literature. It will reveal far more of the child's thinking—what he *personally* makes of the story— than a book report will ever tell.

A teacher-librarian[32] from England talked with one of his students (a boy, 11 years old) about *The Farthest Shore* by LeGuin. Their talk could well be the conversation of two adults who are utterly intrigued with a story. Here are some extracts in which the student discusses the theme of the book:

> I think it's got the advantage of most books of its kind, as it has the chance to describe another world. But this book does a lot more; some books tend to stick on the "other world" theme, but you just took that fact for granted in this book, and went on from there.

> I don't think it was an adventure story, with lots of big, exciting action. It was replaced by something that to me was more interesting.

> It had a great many good ideas instead. It made you think. And all the ideas connected together. Everything seemed to be based on the idea of "Balance" and "Equilibrium."

> 'Balance' is the Balance of Nature, and if things act naturally they act within the balance. . . . That's why this person who defies death, Cob, was against the balance and so upsets everything. That was what the book was mainly about.

The discussion of theme continues and then moves to an equally fine understanding of the interrelationship of the two main characters:

> I think that the relationship of the two main characters, Ged and Arren, is one of the most interesting things in the book, especially as after a while I began to realize that the person who was leading the quest was not who I thought.

> No, Arren is the main person in this book really, although you think Ged will be, because he was in *The Wizard of Earthsea*. But you in fact see things much more through the eyes of Arren.

> You follow Arren and the development of his character very closely, from the hero-worshipping

[32] Peter Nixon. "The Best Read of 1973," *Children's Literature in Education*, Vol. 14 (1974), pp. 18–20. Used by permission.

of Ged, at the beginning of the book, and through his doubts in the middle when he keeps saying, "Sparrowhawk is only taking me to my death. I don't want to die."

> This was to show that the loss of power was affecting them too, that they weren't Superman and beyond it. . . . What Sparrowhawk was doing was giving Arren as much experience as he could to make him a wise king. It is clear that though Ged was leader before he's now handing over to someone else.

Finally, the student thoughtfully considers the function of fantasy and its relationship to reality:

> This is much more a realistic book than a fantasy— just because it's another world doesn't make it less realistic.

> Why do you think it was put in another world, then, rather than dealing with those themes in this world?

> You'd need to work pretty hard to put something of that nature into this world. You'd have to solve out all the complexities and problems here, and it would take ten or twenty times as long. Actually most of the things in that book are from this world, transplanted, but the author has taken only the basic themes she needs. The whole of Earthsea is more basic and open than our world.

Most of the teacher's comments have been eliminated in these extracts from a conversation which lasted for nearly one hour! Such depth of understanding could only have been achieved by a student who had developed a real love and appreciation for fine books. The fact that he could talk for one hour to an equally appreciative adult may partially account for his insightful comments. A thoughtful discussion of a book helps to organize and clarify one's personal response to it.

Response through Writing

Children will show their beginning understanding of literary form by spontaneously choosing to use various written forms for their stories. Just as a child may choose to create a picture with paint or colláge or scratchboard; so, too, may he choose a folk tale, a fable, or a poem as the best form for what he wishes to write. This is the young child's way of indicating that he has assimilated the idea of form and can accommodate his writing to create it. For example, when a group of 6-year-olds had heard the stories of "The Sleeping Beauty" and "Snow White," they composed a story, "The Sleeping Prince," in which a witch casts a spell on a birthday cake to win the friendship of the princess who had not been invited to the party. One bite of the cake causes Prince Jonathan to sleep for ten years. The spell is broken when the witch breaks her bottle of witchcraft and dies. The story ends:

As soon as the witch was dead, the spell came off the Prince. He sat up in bed and stretched. He ran to his Mother and Father. They were so happy that they planned a party for the whole kingdom. The Queen herself made a beautiful white cake for the big party. The cake had ten layers and was covered with pink flowers. The King and Queen invited Princess Alice and Jonathan and the Princess be-

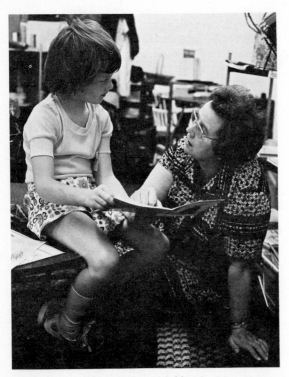

Teachers need to listen to children's responses to literature.

The Ohio State University Workshop, Moira McKenzie, visiting teacher.

came friends again. Prince Jonathan grew up to be King and lived happily ever after.

Suzanne Heinmiller, Teacher
Columbus Public Schools, Ohio

Few folk tales include ten-layered birthday cakes with flowers, but the jealousy, the witch, and the overcoming of evil are all a part of traditional literature, as is the "happily ever after" ending.

After hearing several of Kipling's *Just-So Stories* one 11-year-old decided to write her interpretation of the origin of the lion:

HOW THE LION GOT BIG

One day many years ago in southern India there came through the jungle a kitten. It was the smallest kitten you could ever imagine. This made the kitten very upset. All the animals in India had heard about the poor, poor, poor little tinsy, tinesy kitten, and all of them were laughing hysterically.

Once someone laughed at him and he decided that it was the last time he was going to be laughed at. He set out to see the cruel world in which he thought he lived. At that time, to him, the world was cruel. He was walking along a trail seldom used. He was crying so very, very pitifully, that if you'd been there, you just couldn't have stood it. Then suddenly he noticed what he was walking in. At first he thought it was powder (which is just what it was) but then he changed his mind. It couldn't possibly be snow. Or could it? You see he had never seen any really, real live snow in his life. But no it couldn't be that. Could a falling star have whisked by? No, it wouldn't have. Well then what was it?

"It is fairy powder," said a small voice. "I just couldn't stand there and listen to you cry like that. If you'd listen to yourself you'd see how impossible it is."

"I'm sorry if I disturbed you," said the little kitten. "But if you were me you'd be crying, too."

"Well, what reason would you have for crying so much?" asked the fairy.

"Me, just me, me, me," cried the little kitten, and started crying all over again.

"Why, what's supposed to be wrong with you?" she asked.

"I'm little," he said.

"Well so am I," said the fairy.

"But you're supposed to be," he said, starting to cry again.

"Very well, if you'll stop crying, you can be very, very big."

"Really," asked the kitten, sniffing back the tears.

"Certainly," she said. And with a wave of her magic wand, he was as big as a full grown lion, today. . . .

That's why today we say that the kitten is related to the lion. And that's how we came to have lions. He and his descendants were the lions.

> Patricia Derby
> Columbus Public Schools, Ohio

Older children have also been quick to grasp the pattern of such books as *The Tiniest Sound* by Mel Evans, or the poems of *Hailstones and Halibut Bones* by Mary O'Neill, or *Prayers from the Ark* by De Gasztold—and they enjoy creating their own versions (*see* Chapter 11).

Margaret Spencer suggests that when children move from writing their own stories to writing or reporting on books, they have much less to say, even though they thoroughly enjoyed the book.[33] Moffett[34] also makes the point that fictionalizing and reporting are very different modes of discourse. A comparison of the following brief reviews, in contrast to the previous long narrative, would support these observations. In describing her favorite book, one 10-year-old writes:

> My favorite book is *King of the Wind*. I think it has a lot of feeling. A boy loves his horse, the horse that the stable master thought was worthless. The boy won't part from it and stayed with him at all the races he went to. When the horse died the boy was all alone. I think the author showed how the boy felt, not only the horse.
>
> Armit Singh
> Evanston Public Schools, Illinois
> Barbara Friedberg, Teacher

Another girl from the same school writes:

> My favorite book is *Charlotte's Web*. The reason it is my favorite book is that it is both sad and happy. . . . The part in *Charlotte's Web* that I like best is the part where Charlotte spins those words about Wilbur in her web and how everyone was puzzled. Also (how could I forget) the part when they got to the fair and met that real fat pig. Also the part when Fern always comes to visit. Really I like the whole book!
>
> Ilene Lippitz
> Evanston Public Schools
> Barbara Friedberg, Teacher

In evaluating children's responses to books we would need to look at the way literature had influenced children's writing, at the same time that we looked at their written responses to books.

The unsolicited response of children to books as revealed in their play, their art, and their writing may be of far greater importance than the solicited response. We need, however, to study both kinds. Unfortunately, the research on children's response to books is very slim, as has been noted. Much has been done at the high-school and college levels, particularly the study of James Squire[35] and that by Alan Purves and Victoria Rippere.[36] As elementary-school teachers become more aware of the way they can tune in to children's responses to literature, they will see the value of examining the nature of children's thinking about it. While we all believe that literature is important for children, we do not truly know what difference it makes in a child's life, if any. An in-depth study of children's responses to books is just as important, if not more important, than the studies of children's interests in books. We should explore the developmental nature of response and conduct longitudinal studies of a child's responses over the years. As teachers and librarians, we need to be still and listen to what the children are telling us about their involvement with books and what it means to them.

---

[33] Margaret Spencer. "Stories and Storytelling" in *Children Using Language*, Anthony Jones and Jeremy Mulford, eds. (London, England: Oxford University Press, 1971), p. 140.

[34] James Moffett. *Teaching the Universe of Discourse.* (Houghton Mifflin, 1968), Chapter Two.

[35] James Squire. *The Responses of Adolescents while Reading Four Short Stories* (Champaign, Ill.: National Council of Teachers of English, 1964).

[36] Alan C. Purves and Victoria Rippere. *Elements of Writing about a Literary Work: A Study of Response to Literature.* NCTE Research Report, No. 9 (Champaign, Ill.: National Council of Teachers of English, 1968).

Planning a Literature Program

There is no one literature program that is appropriate for all children, just as there is no one book that must be read by all children. What is essential is that all children have a rich experience of literature with teachers and librarians who understand and appreciate it.

Good literature programs in the elementary school do not happen without real planning and commitment by all the faculty. One teacher may be very enthusiastic about literature and provide a rich program in his or her classroom. However, children need a long and loving exposure to literature over a period of years, if it is to become a life-long pleasure for them. Each faculty needs to develop a literature program based upon their knowledge of the values of literature for children, the needs and characteristics of children, knowledge of the learning process, and a thorough understanding of literature.

In the beginning of this chapter it was suggested that the major purposes or objectives of a literature program were four:

1. Discovering delight in books
2. Interpreting literature
3. Developing literary awareness
4. Developing appreciation for literature.

The major emphasis in the elementary school should be on the first two purposes. Young children should have many opportunities to experience and enjoy literature. Teachers should not view literature as a content subject to be taught but as an experience which will broaden and deepen the child's living. As children explore various patterns, relationships, and modes of living in literature they will come to a better understanding of themselves, and at the same time enlarge their own life spaces.

DETERMINING CHILDREN'S BACKGROUND IN LITERATURE

The maxim of beginning where children are applies to literature as well as any other area. In planning a literature program a staff must first consider what has been the children's previous experience with literature. Has the child been fortunate enough to have come from a home that values reading, that has many books; has he been read to regularly? Or is school apt to be the child's first introduction to books and story hours? How much have other teachers read aloud to these children? What experiences with literature do they have in common?

Teachers may want to take an informal survey or inventory of their children's backgrounds in literature. They may construct their own or use those which have already been published.[37] These inventories are not tests of children's literary knowledge but simply what their name implies—an informal survey to see what kind of exposure children have had to literature. They may be given informally to younger children or duplicated and read aloud to middle-grade children. The results of these inventories would provide the teacher with some base for knowing the literary background of the students. Identifying some of the gaps in children's exposure to literature would be helpful in planning a literature program for them. For example, if children showed little knowledge of some of the well-known folk tales, teachers might want to conduct a folk-tale unit, since these stories appear to please many age groups. If a middle-grade group did not know Scott O'Dell's story, *Island of the Blue Dolphins*, their teacher might decide to read it aloud to them.

Appreciation for literature appears to be developmental. If children have not had the opportunity to laugh at the antics of *Harry the Dirty Dog* by Zion when they are 5 or 6, they need the experience at 7 and 8. We need research on the sequential stages of appreciating literature, but we have some evidence to show that children must go through the "picture-storybook stage," the "nonsense-poetry" stage, even the "series-book stage" if they are to become active, involved readers. This, then, is the value of finding what children's exposure to literature has been.

ORGANIZING THE CURRICULUM

Each faculty should be free to plan their own literature programs. However, they will want to

[37] *See* Charlotte S. Huck. "An Inventory of Children's Literary Background" in the Guidebook to *Ventures*, Book 4; "An Inventory of Students' Literary Backgrounds" in the Skill Book for *Dimensions*, Grade 7 (Glenview, Ill.: Scott, Foresman, 1966).

A first-grader reveals an exposure to folk tales in his illustrations and writing.
Barrington Road School, Upper Arlington Public Schools, Columbus, Ohio, Carolyn Whipps, teacher.

provide for a balance in literature between the old and the new, prose and poetry, fiction and nonfiction, realism and fantasy, and fiction with historical and contemporary settings. In planning the curriculum some agreement should be made by the teachers and librarians concerning a basic list of materials that provides these balances. An important consideration is to find literature which is relevant to children's lives, books which interest them now and in which they can find delight.

There should also be a balance between opportunities for wide reading and for small-group, in-depth reading. Not all children in one group or grade level must read the same books, but all children should have experienced literature in a way that has excited and fulfilled them. Children should be free to explore a variety of ways in which to interpret what they have read—through art, music, creative drama, movement, talk, or writing.

Throughout the school year there will be experiences emphasizing enjoyment and experiences designed to extend children's understandings. It is hoped that increased understanding will develop enjoyment. Literary awareness may be developed gradually by both incidental and planned instruction. Discussion of the craft of writing should be secondary to the child's personal responses to the selection and consideration of the book's meaning for his own life.

The study of literature may be organized around authors, genres, content, or themes. Young children enjoy being able to recognize a Brian Wildsmith book or an Ezra Jack Keats title or a Leo Lionni volume. If the teacher is knowledgeable about books, other unifying ways of looking at them can be suggested, such as finding books with surprise endings, or finding books about dolls, or discovering books that are set at a time many years ago. Young children can discover a variety of ways to categorize and think about books.

Eight- and 9-year-olds enjoy learning about folk tales. Using the charts in Chapter 4 of this book, a teacher can organize groups to study folk tales from different countries or to look at the many variants of a single folk tale. Children may then want to write and create their own folk tales or fables. Children also often become interested in studying myths. They enjoy finding the mythological stories behind the names of the planets, in the space program, and in advertising. Creation of their own myths and mythological beasts adds greatly to their interest in this unit (*see* the second color section).

Another way of organizing the literature curriculum is through a thematic approach. One group of 7-year-olds studied the theme of "Big and Little" using such books as *Once a Mouse* by Marcia Brown, *The Lion and the Rat* by La Fontaine, *Amos and Boris* by Steig, *Big Sister and Little Sister* and *Big Brother* both by Zolotow. Another group of 8- and 9-year-olds concentrated on the theme of "Friendship," introduced by the teacher reading the first recorded story of *Gilgamesh* (Bryson). Other stories about friends included the classic Greek tale of Damon and Pythias; such tales of animal friendships as are found in *Winnie the Pooh* (A. A. Milne), *Charlotte's Web* (E. B. White), and *The Cricket in Times Square* (Selden); and modern tales of friendship (both good and bad) as in *Kate* (Little), *The Noonday Friends* (Stolz), *Amelia Quackenbush* (Gold), and *Harriet the Spy* (Fitzhugh). The theme of "Journeys" focused the

reading of one 9- and 10-year-old group, who read of such incredible journeys as *The Twenty-one Balloons* (Du Bois); *The Fabulous Flight* (Lawson); *James and the Giant Peach* (Dahl); *A Wrinkle in Time* and *A Wind in the Door* (both by L'Engle); and *The Lion, the Witch and the Wardrobe* (Lewis). Some read of real journeys, such as *Kon-Tiki* (Heyerdahl), *I Sailed on the Mayflower* (Pilkington), and *Charles A. Lindbergh* (Wise). Fictional journeys also included *The Freewheeling of Joshua Cobb* (Hodges), *The Long Journey* (Corcoran), and *Julie of the Wolves* (George). The children then planned actual trips they would like to make, including cost and pretend booking of plane and hotel accommodations. Some wrote stories of incredible journeys; others kept diaries or made maps of their intended trips. The thematic approach to literature gives children a choice of books and poems and incorporates many genre, while providing some shape and form for reading and exploration.

EVALUATING THE LITERATURE PROGRAM

It is as easy to identify a school in which literature is an integral part of the curriculum as it is to recognize a home where books are loved and valued. However, since this text has not recommended any body of content that all children must learn, but rather has suggested that each school should plan its own literature program, the questions on pages 753–754 might serve as guidelines in both the planning and the evaluation stages.

The best evaluation of the impact of a literature program for today's children will be their reading habits as adults. One of the challenges of education is to teach skills, attitudes, and appreciations so that children will continue to make reading an integral part of their lives. It lies within the power of every teacher and librarian to give children a rich experience with literature. We must do more than teach children *to read;* we must help them to *become readers,* to find a lifetime of pleasure in the reading of good books. To the teacher is granted the opportunity to become the piper who leads children into the world of books. It is exciting and deeply satisfying to become such a piper, "piping down the valleys wild."

Availability of Books and Other Media

1. Is there a school library media center in each elementary-school building? Does it meet American Library Association standards for books and other media?
2. Is there a professionally trained librarian and adequate support staff in each building?
3. Does every classroom contain several hundred paperbacks and a changing collection of hardbacks?
4. Are reference books easily accessible to each classroom?
5. May children purchase books in a school-run paperback bookstore?
6. Do teachers encourage children to order books through various school book clubs?
7. May children take books and some media home?
8. Has the school board made some provision for keeping library media centers functioning during vacation periods?
9. Are children made aware of the program of the public library?

Time for Literature

10. Do all children have time to read books of their own choosing every day?
11. Do all teachers read to the children at least once a day?
12. Do children have time to discuss their books with an interested adult or with other children every week?
13. Are children allowed time to interpret books through art, drama, music, or writing?

Stimulating Interest

14. Do teachers show their enthusiasm for books by sharing new ones with children, reading parts of their favorite ones, discussing them, and so on?
15. Do classroom and library displays call attention to particular books?
16. Are children encouraged to set up book displays in the media center, the halls, and their classrooms?
17. Does the media specialist plan special events—such as story hours, book talks, sharing films, working with book clubs?
18. Do teachers and librarians work with parents to stimulate children's reading?
19. Are special bibliographies prepared by the librarians or groups of children on topics of special interest—such as mysteries, animal stories, science fiction, fantasy, and so on?
20. Are opportunities planned for contacts with authors and illustrators to kindle interest and enthusiasm for reading?

Balances in the Curriculum

21. Do teachers and librarians try to introduce children to a wide variety of genre and to different authors when reading aloud?
22. Do teachers share poetry as frequently as prose?
23. Do children read both fiction and nonfiction?
24. Are children exposed to new books and contemporary poems as frequently as some of the old favorites of both prose and poetry?
25. Do children have a balance of wide reading experiences with small-group, in-depth discussion of books?

Evaluating Growth of Children

26. Are children encouraged to keep records of their own reading?
27. Do these records go into the child's cumulative file so that the next teacher knows what he has read?
28. Do teachers give children an "Inventory on Literature" to determine their background of exposure to books?
29. Do teachers record examples of children's unsolicited responses to literature, as seen in their play, talk, art, or writing?
30. Do children seem attentive and involved, as they listen to stories? Do they have favorites which they ask to have reread?
31. Are children allowed to respond to books in a variety of ways (art, drama, writing), rather than by required book reports?
32. Is depth of understanding emphasized, rather than the number of books read?
33. Are children responding to a greater range and complexity of work?
34. Are children relating literature to their own lives?
35. Are children voluntarily reading more at school?
36. Do parents report an increase in reading at home?
37. What percentage of the children can be described as active readers? Has this percentage increased?
38. Are some children beginning to see literature as a source of life-long pleasure?

A GUIDE FOR EVALUATING A LITERATURE PROGRAM (*Continued*)

Evaluating the Professional Growth of Teachers

39. Are teachers increasing their knowledge of children's literature?

40. What percentage of the staff have taken a course in children's literature in the past five years?

41. Are some staff meetings devoted to ways of improving the use of literature in the curriculum?

42. Do teachers attend professional meetings that feature programs on children's literature?

43. Are in-service programs in literature made available on a regular basis?

44. Are such professional journals as *Language Arts* (formerly *Elementary English*), *The Horn Book*, and *Children's Literature in Education* available in every teachers' lounge?

45. Are professional books on children's literature available in each elementary school?

46. Have the teachers and librarians had a share in planning their literature programs?

47. Do teachers feel responsible not only for teaching children to read but for helping children find joy in reading?

SUGGESTED LEARNING EXPERIENCES

1. Record the responses of a small group of children of various age levels to one story. Analyze their responses in terms of their stages of development.

2. Make a web for outlining the potential uses of a picture book, a poem, and a book for older children. Present one of the selections to children and be prepared to follow up on several of the suggestions.

3. Plan a lesson on a particular book and try writing questions of every type described in the chart on questions in this chapter.

4. Develop a list of books and poems around a particular theme for either primary- or intermediate-age children. Plan some possible extending activities for them.

5. Give a literature inventory to a group of children, and draw some conclusions about their previous exposure to literature. Plan what you think might be a rich literature program for them.

6. Examine literature readers, sample kits of literature, and published units on literature. Note the purposes, content, plans of organization, and activities. Analyze the types of questions that have been prepared.

7. Look at several state and local curriculum guides for the elementary school and see what suggestions they give for teaching literature. Literature may be included in the guides for reading or language arts.

8. Survey a local school to see how much time teachers devote to reading aloud and what titles they have read.

9. Make a tape recording of a group discussion of a book read by you and several of your peers. Analyze the discussion to discover the factors that were considered.

10. Using "The Guide for Evaluating a Literature Program," visit an elementary school and evaluate their program. Certain members of the class could be responsible for finding the answers to certain sections of the Guide. Combine your findings in a report and make recommendations concerning the literature program of that school.

RELATED READINGS

1. Britton, James. *Language and Learning.* London, England: Penguin, 1970.

In Chapter Three of this book the author stresses the difference between two kinds of language-using behaviors: the participant role and the spectator role. Literature, he maintains, belongs to the spectator role, where we use language to contemplate what has happened to us or others.

2. Fader, Daniel, and Elton B. McNeil. *Hooked on Books.* New York: Berkeley, 1966.

A well-known study of the impact of a free reading program on the improvement in reading and attitude toward reading by a group of adolescent boys in a training school.

3. Purves, Alan C. *Literature Education in Ten Countries.* New York: Wiley, 1973.

   A report of a literature survey in ten countries by the International Literature Committee. The response of two age groups was the focus, ages 14 and 18. Differences in the literature curriculums and the preferred modes of response for the children were established.

4. Purves, Alan C., and Richard Beach. *Literature and the Reader: Research in Response to Literature Reading Interests, and the Teaching of Literature.* Urbana, Ill.: National Council of Teachers of English, 1972.

   A comprehensive report of the research on students' interests in reading and their responses to their reading. Both elementary- and secondary-school studies are represented.

5. Raths, Louis E., Merrill Harmin, and Sidney B. Simon. *Values and Teaching.* Columbus, Ohio: Merrill, 1966.

   One of the first books—and still one of the best—to delineate the role of values clarification. This book combines the theory with many practical suggestions for the classroom teacher.

6. Rosenblatt, Louise. *Literature as Exploration.* New York: Noble and Noble, 1968 (1938).

   Rosenblatt was one of the first persons to recognize the transactional relationship between the reader and the book. She emphasizes that the reader and his response to a book is every bit as important as the book itself.

7. Sawyer, Ruth. *The Way of the Storyteller,* rev. ed. New York: Viking, 1962.

   A great storyteller shares her experiences and pictures story-telling as an art. A classic in the field, the book includes helpful advice on selection, and eleven stories often told by the author. Weston Woods Studios has produced a record album entitled *Ruth Sawyer, Storyteller,* which includes her comments on story-telling and her rendition of four stories.

8. Spencer, Margaret. "Stories and Storytelling," in *Children Using Language,* Anthony Jones and Jeremy Mulford, eds., National Association for the Teaching of English. London, England: Oxford University Press, 1971.

   Spencer has identified an interesting way of looking at the impact of literature on children; namely, by examining children's writing of their own stories. This is a fine example of a study employing an "unsolicited response" to literature.

9. Squire, James R. *The Responses of Adolescents while Reading Four Short Stories,* NCTE Research Report No. 2. Urbana, Ill.: National Council of Teachers of English, 1964.

   A classic study of the oral responses of some fifty-two high-school students to four short stories. Response patterns were categorized into six different types. Student responses during the reading of a story were found to differ from those following the conclusion of the story.

10. Squire, James R., ed. *Response to Literature.* Urbana, Ill.: National Council of Teachers of English, 1968.

    A report of the Literature Study Group at the Anglo-American Seminar at Dartmouth. This bulletin brings together several important papers on response; particularly, James Britton's "Response to Literature" and Benjamin DeMott's "Reading, Writing, Reality, Unreality."

11. University of Nebraska. *A Curriculum for English.* Lincoln, Neb.: University of Nebraska Press, 1966.

    An analysis of children's literature is included in this description of an integrated literature composition program for the elementary grades. Six bulletins (one for each grade level) contain many units for literary study. Another bulletin, *Poetry for the Elementary Grades,* gives many suggestions for teaching poetry.

12. Wisconsin English Language Arts Curriculum Project. *English Language Arts in Wisconsin.* Madison, Wis.: Department of Public Instruction, 1968.

    An example of a sequential curriculum in the language arts for kindergarten through grade twelve. The first section is on the literature program. One of the strengths of this curriculum guide is that teachers have described some of their actual classroom practices.

RECOMMENDED REFERENCES[38]

Aardema, Verna. *Tales from the Story Hat,* illustrated by Elton Fax. Coward-McCann, 1960.

Alexander, Lloyd. *The Black Cauldron.* Holt, Rinehart and Winston, 1965.

———. *The Book of Three.* Holt, Rinehart and Winston, 1964.

———. *The Castle of Llyr.* Holt, Rinehart and Winston, 1966.

———. *The High King.* Holt, Rinehart and Winston, 1968.

———. *Taran Wanderer.* Holt, Rinehart and Winston, 1967.

Alexander, Martha. *Nobody Asked Me If I Wanted a Baby Sister.* Dial, 1971.

Andersen, Hans Christian. *The Fir Tree,* illustrated by Nancy Ekholm Burkert. Harper & Row, 1970.

Armstrong, William H. *Sounder,* illustrated by James Barkley. Harper & Row, 1969.

Atwood, Ann. *Haiku: The Mood of Earth.* Scribner, 1971.

D'Aulaire, Ingri, and Edgar D'Aulaire. *D'Aulaires' Trolls.* Doubleday, 1972.

Babbitt, Ellen. *Jataka Tales,* illustrated by Ellsworth Young. Appleton (1912).

Bailey, Carolyn S. *The Little Rabbit Who Wanted Red Wings,* illustrated by Dorothy Grider. Platt & Munk, 1970 (1945).

Barrett, Judi. *Animals Should Definitely Not Wear Clothing,* illustrated by Ron Barrett. Atheneum, 1970.

Batchelor, Julie F. *A Cap for Mul Chand,* illustrated by Corrine Dillon. Harcourt Brace Jovanovich, 1950.

Bemelmans, Ludwig. *Madeline.* Viking, 1939.

Blume, Judy. *Are You There God? It's Me, Margaret.* Bradbury, 1970.

———. *Blubber.* Bradbury, 1974.

Bogdanovic, Toma (illustrator). *The Fire Bird.* Scroll Press, 1972.

Brown, Marcia. *Once a Mouse.* Scribner, 1961.

———. *Stone Soup.* Scribner, 1947.

Brown, Marion, and Ruth Crone. *The Silent Storm,* illustrated by Fritz Kredel. Abingdon, 1963.

Bryson, Bernarda. *Gilgamesh, Man's First Story.* Holt, Rinehart and Winston, 1967.

Bulla, Clyde R. *White Bird,* illustrated by Leonard Weisgard. Crowell, 1966.

Burnett, Frances Hodgson. *The Secret Garden,* illustrated by Tasha Tudor. Lippincott, 1962 (1910).

Burton, Virginia Lee. *The Little House.* Houghton Mifflin, 1942.

———. *Mike Mulligan and His Steam Shovel.* Houghton Mifflin, 1939.

Butler, Beverly. *Light a Single Candle.* Dodd, 1962.

Byars, Betsy. *The 18th Emergency,* illustrated by Robert Grossman. Viking, 1973.

Carroll, Lewis, pseud. (Charles L. Dodgson). *Alice's Adventures in Wonderland,* illustrated by John Tenniel. Macmillan, 1963 (1865).

Caudill, Rebecca. *A Pocketful of Cricket,* illustrated by Evaline Ness. Holt, Rinehart and Winston, 1964.

Ciardi, John. "The River Is a Piece of Sky," in *The Reason for the Pelican.* Lippincott, 1959.

Cleaver, Vera, and Bill Cleaver. *Grover,* illustrated by Frederic Marvin. Lippincott, 1970.

———. *The Mimosa Tree.* Lippincott, 1970.

———. *Where the Lilies Bloom,* illustrated by James Spanfeller. Lippincott, 1969.

Colwell, Eileen. *A Storyteller's Choice,* illustrated by Carol Barker. Walck, 1963.

Conford, Ellen. *Just the Thing for Geraldine,* illustrated by John Larrecq. Little, Brown, 1974.

Cooney, Barbara. *Chanticleer and the Fox.* Crowell, 1958.

Cooper, Susan. *The Dark Is Rising,* illustrated by Alan E. Cober. Atheneum, 1973.

Corcoran, Barbara. *The Long Journey,* illustrated by Charles Robinson. Atheneum, 1970.

Courlander, Harold, and George Herzog. *The Cow Tail Switch and Other West African Stories,* illustrated by Madye Lee Chastain. Holt, Rinehart and Winston, 1947.

Cunningham, Julia. *Dorp Dead,* illustrated by James Spanfeller. Pantheon, 1965.

———. *Onion Journey,* illustrated by L. Cooley. Pantheon, 1967.

[38] All books listed at the end of this chapter are recommended subject to the qualifications noted in the text. *See* Appendix D for publishers' complete addresses.

————. *Viollet,* illustrated by Alan E. Cober. Pantheon, 1966.

Dahl, Roald. *James and the Giant Peach,* illustrated by Nancy Burkert. Knopf, 1961.

Dalgliesh, Alice. *The Courage of Sarah Noble,* illustrated by Leonard Weisgard. Scribner, 1954.

De Angeli, Marguerite. *The Door in the Wall.* Doubleday, 1949.

Dobbs, Rose. *No Room, An Old Story Retold,* illustrated by Fritz Eichenberg. McKay, 1944.

Domanska, Janina. *What Do You See?* Macmillan, 1974.

Du Bois, William Pène. *The Twenty-one Balloons.* Viking, 1947.

Dunning, Stephen, *et al. Reflections on a Gift of Watermelon Pickle and Other Modern Verse.* Lothrop, 1967.

Duvoisin, Roger. *Petunia.* Knopf, 1950.

————. *Veronica.* Knopf, 1961.

Engdahl, Sylvia. *Enchantress from the Stars,* illustrated by Rodney Shackell. Atheneum, 1970.

Estes, Eleanor. *The Hundred Dresses,* illustrated by Louis Slobodkin. Harcourt Brace Jovanovich, 1944.

Evans, C. S. *Cinderella,* illustrated by Arthur Rackham. Viking, 1972 (1919).

Evans, Mel. *The Tiniest Sound,* illustrated by Ed Young. Doubleday, 1969.

Farjeon, Eleanor. "Mrs. Peck-Pigeon," in *Poems for Children.* Lippincott, 1938.

Farmer, Penelope. *The Summer Birds,* illustrated by James Spanfeller. Harcourt Brace Jovanovich, 1962.

Field, Rachel. *Hitty, Her First Hundred Years,* illustrated by Dorothy Lathrop. Macmillan, 1937.

Fitzhugh, Louise. *Harriet the Spy.* Harper & Row, 1964.

Flack, Marjorie. *Ask Mr. Bear.* Macmillan, 1932.

Forbes, Esther. *Johnny Tremain,* illustrated by Lynd Ward. Houghton Mifflin, 1946.

Fox, Paula. *How Many Miles to Babylon?,* illustrated by Paul Giovanopoulos. D. White, 1967.

————. *The Slave Dancer,* illustrated by Eros Keith. Bradbury, 1973.

Freeman, Don. *Dandelion.* Viking, 1964.

Fritz, Jean. *The Cabin Faced West,* illustrated by Feodor Rojankovsky. Coward-McCann, 1958.

————. *Early Thunder,* illustrated by Lynd Ward. Coward-McCann, 1967.

Frost, Robert. *You Come Too,* illustrated by Thomas W. Nason. Holt, Rinehart and Winston, 1959.

Gág, Wanda. *Gone Is Gone.* Coward-McCann, 1936.

————. *Nothing at All.* Coward-McCann, 1928.

Galdone, Paul. *The Gingerbread Boy.* Seabury, 1975.

————. *The Little Red Hen.* Seabury, 1973.

Garfield, Leon. *Smith,* illustrated by Antony Maitland. Pantheon, 1967.

Gasztold, Carmen Bernos de. *Prayers from the Ark,* translated by Rumer Godden, illustrated by Jean Primrose. Viking, 1962.

George, Jean. *Julie of the Wolves,* illustrated by John Schoenherr. Harper & Row, 1972.

————. *My Side of the Mountain.* Dutton, 1959.

Godden, Rumer. *Impunity Jane,* illustrated by Adrienne Adams. Viking, 1954.

————. *The Mousewife,* illustrated by William Pène Du Bois. Viking, 1951.

Gold, Sharlya. *Amelia Quackenbush.* Seabury, 1973.

Goldin, Augusta R. *Ducks Don't Get Wet,* illustrated by Leonard Kessler. Crowell, 1965.

Grahame, Kenneth. *The Wind in the Willows,* illustrated by E. H. Shepard. Scribner, 1908.

Greenfield, Eloise. *Rosa Parks,* illustrated by Moneta Barnett. Crowell, 1973.

Griffiths, Helen. *The Greyhound,* illustrated by Victor Ambrus. Doubleday, 1964.

Grimm, The Brothers. *Snow-White and the Seven Dwarfs,* translated by Randall Jarrell, illustrated by Nancy Ekholm Burkert. Farrar, Straus, 1972.

Haar, Jaap ter. *Boris,* translated by Martha Mearns, illustrated by Rien Poortvliet. Delacorte, 1970.

Hautzig, Esther. *The Endless Steppe: Growing Up in Siberia.* Crowell, 1968.

Heide, Florence P. *The Shrinking of Treehorn,* illustrated by Edward Gorey. Holiday, 1971.

Henry, Marguerite. *King of the Wind,* illustrated by Wesley Dennis. Rand McNally, 1948.

————. *Mustang, Wild Spirit of the West,* illustrated by Robert Lougheed. Rand McNally, 1971.

Heyerdahl, Thor. *Kon-Tiki.* Rand McNally, 1960.

Hirsh, Marilyn. *Could Anything Be Worse?* Holiday, 1974.

Hoban, Tana. *Look Again!* Macmillan, 1971.

Hodges, Margaret. *The Freewheeling of Joshua Cobb*, illustrated by Richard Cuffari. Farrar, Straus, 1974.

————. *The Wave*, illustrated by Blair Lent. Houghton Mifflin, 1964.

Holm, Anne. *North to Freedom*, translated by L. W. Kingsland. Harcourt Brace Jovanovich, 1965.

Hutchins, Pat. *Rosie's Walk*. Macmillan, 1968.

Issa, *et al. Don't Tell the Scarecrow and Other Japanese Poems*, illustrated by Talivaldis Stubis. Four Winds, 1970.

Jacobs, Joseph. *The Three Wishes*, illustrated by Paul Galdone, McGraw-Hill, 1961.

Jones, Weyman. *Edge of Two Worlds*, illustrated by J. C. Kocsis. Dial, 1968.

Keats, Ezra Jack. *Jennie's Hat*. Harper & Row, 1966.

Keeping, Charles. *Through the Window*. F. Watts, 1970.

Kennedy, John F. *Profiles in Courage*, Young Readers Memorial Edition. Harper & Row, 1964.

Kipling, Rudyard. *The Elephant's Child*, illustrated by Leonard Weisgard. Walker, 1970.

————. *Just-So Stories*, illustrated by Etienne Delessert. Doubleday, 1972 (1902).

Klaben, Helen, and Beth Day. *Hey, I'm Alive!* McGraw-Hill, 1964.

Konigsburg, E. L. *From the Mixed-up Files of Mrs. Basil E. Frankweiler*. Atheneum, 1967.

Koriyama, Naoshi. "Unfolding Bud," in *Reflections on a Gift of Watermelon Pickle and Other Modern Verse*, Stephen Dunning, *et al.*, eds. Lothrop, 1967.

Krauss, Ruth. *A Very Special House*, illustrated by Maurice Sendak. Harper & Row, 1953.

Kroeber, Theodora. *Ishi, Last of His Tribe*, illustrated by Ruth Robbins. Parnassus, 1964.

La Fontaine. *The Lion and the Rat*, illustrated by Brian Wildsmith. F. Watts, 1963.

Langner, Nola. *Cinderella*. Retold and illustrated. Scholastic, 1972.

Lawson, Robert. *The Fabulous Flight*. Little, Brown, 1949.

————. *Robbut, A Tale of Tails*. Viking, 1949.

LeGuin, Ursula K. *The Farthest Shore*, illustrated by Gail Garraty. Atheneum, 1972.

————. *A Wizard of Earthsea*, illustrated by Ruth Robbins. Parnassus, 1968.

L'Engle, Madeleine. *Meet the Austins*. Vanguard, 1960.

————. *A Wind in the Door*. Farrar, Straus, 1973.

————. *A Wrinkle in Time*. Farrar, Straus, 1962.

Lewis, C. S. *The Horse and His Boy*, illustrated by Pauline Baynes. Macmillan, 1962.

————. *The Last Battle*, illustrated by Pauline Baynes. Macmillan, 1964.

————. *The Lion, the Witch, and the Wardrobe*, illustrated by Pauline Baynes. Macmillan, 1950.

————. *The Magician's Nephew*, illustrated by Pauline Baynes. Macmillan, 1964.

————. *Prince Caspian, the Return to Narnia*, illustrated by Pauline Baynes. Macmillan, 1964.

————. *The Silver Chair*, illustrated by Pauline Baynes. Macmillan, 1962.

————. *The Voyage of the "Dawn Treader,"* illustrated by Pauline Baynes. Macmillan, 1962.

Lewis, Richard, compiler. *In a Spring Garden*, illustrated by Ezra Jack Keats. Dial, 1965.

Lionni, Leo. *The Biggest House in the World*. Pantheon, 1968.

————. *Fish Is Fish*. Pantheon, 1970.

————. *Little Blue and Little Yellow*. Astor-Honor, 1959.

Little, Jean. *Kate*. Harper & Row, 1971.

Lobel, Arnold. *Frog and Toad Are Friends*. Harper & Row, 1970.

McCloskey, Robert. *Make Way for Ducklings*. Viking, 1941.

McCord, David. "Crows," in *Far and Few*. Little, Brown, 1925.

————. "The Pickety Fence," in *Every Time I Climb a Tree*, illustrated by Marc Simont. Little, Brown, 1967.

Marshall, James Vance. *Walkabout*, illustrated by Noela Young. Doubleday, 1961.

Matsutani, Miyoko. *The Crane Maiden*, English version by Alvin Tresselt, illustrated by Chihiro Iwasaki. Parents', 1968.

Mazer, Norma Fox. *A Figure of Speech*. Delacorte, 1973.

Milhous, Katherine. *Appolonia's Valentine*. Scribner, 1954.

Milne, A. A. *Winnie the Pooh*, illustrated by Ernest H. Shepard. Dutton, 1926.

Moffitt, John. "To Look at Anything," in *Reflections on a Gift of Watermelon Pickle and Other Modern Verse*, Stephen Dunning, et al., eds. Lothrop, 1967.

Moore, Nancy. *The Unhappy Hippopotamus*, illustrated by Edward Leight. Vanguard, 1957.

Mosel, Arlene. *The Funny Little Woman*, illustrated by Blair Lent. Dutton, 1972.

Neville, Emily C. *Berries Goodman*. Harper & Row, 1965.

Nic Leodhas, Sorche. *Heather and Broom: Tales of the Scottish Highlands*, illustrated by Consuelo Joerns. Holt, Rinehart and Winston, 1960.

Norton, Mary. *The Borrowers*, illustrated by Beth Krush and Joe Krush. Harcourt Brace Jovanovich, 1953.

O'Dell, Scott. *Island of the Blue Dolphins*. Houghton Mifflin, 1960.

O'Neill, Mary. *Hailstones and Halibut Bones*, illustrated by Leonard Weisgard. Doubleday, 1961.

Oxenbury, Helen. *Pig Tale*. Morrow, 1973.

Peet, Bill. *The Whingdingdilly*. Houghton Mifflin, 1970.

Perrault, Charles. *Cinderella*, illustrated by Marcia Brown. Scribner, 1954.

———. *Cinderella*, illustrated by Errol LeCain. Bradbury, 1972.

Picard, Barbara. *One Is One*. Holt, Rinehart and Winston, 1965.

Pilkington, Roger. *I Sailed on the Mayflower*, illustrated by D. Bissett. St. Martin, 1966.

Ransome, Arthur. *The Fool of the World and the Flying Ship*, illustrated by Uri Shulevitz. Farrar, Straus, 1968.

Reiss, Johanna. *The Upstairs Room*. Crowell, 1972.

Richter, Hans Peter. *Friedrich*, translated by Edite Kroll. Holt, Rinehart and Winston, 1970.

Rodgers, Mary. *A Billion for Boris*. Harper & Row, 1974.

Sachs, Marilyn. *The Bears' House*, illustrated by Louis Glanzman. Doubleday, 1971.

Saint-Exupéry, Antoine de. *The Little Prince*, translated by Katherine Woods. Harcourt Brace Jovanovich, 1943.

Selden, George. *The Cricket in Times Square*, illustrated by Garth Williams. Farrar, Straus, 1960.

Sendak, Maurice. *Where the Wild Things Are*. Harper & Row, 1963.

Sherlock, Philip M. *Anansi the Spider Man, Jamaican Folk Tales*, illustrated by Marcia Brown. Crowell, 1954.

Shulevitz, Uri. *Dawn*. Farrar, Straus, 1974.

———. *Soldier and Tsar in the Forest: A Russian Tale*, translated by Richard Lourie. Farrar, Straus, 1972.

Simon, Charlie M. *All Men Are Brothers: A Portrait of Albert Schweitzer*, photos by Erica Anderson. Dutton, 1956.

———. *Dag Hammarskjold*. Dutton, 1967.

Sleator, William. *Blackbriar*. Dutton, 1972.

Sperry, Armstrong. *Call It Courage*. Macmillan, 1940.

Steele, Mary Q. *Journey Outside*, illustrated by Rocco Negri. Viking, 1969.

Steig, William. *Amos and Boris*. Farrar, Straus, 1971.

Steptoe, John. *Stevie*. Harper & Row, 1969.

Stolz, Mary. *The Bully of Barkham Street*, illustrated by Leonard Shortall. Harper & Row, 1963.

———. *A Dog on Barkham Street*, illustrated by Leonard Shortall. Harper & Row, 1960.

———. *The Noonday Friends*, illustrated by Louis Glanzman. Harper & Row, 1965.

Sutcliff, Rosemary. *Knight's Fee*, illustrated by Charles Keeping. Walck, 1960.

———. *Warrior Scarlet*, illustrated by Charles Keeping. Walck, 1958.

Swarthout, Glendon, and Kathryn Swarthout. *Whichaway*, illustrated by R. M. Powers. Random House, 1966.

Tomaino, Sarah F. *Persephone, Bringer of Spring*, illustrated by Ati Forberg. Crowell, 1971.

Turkle, Brinton. *Thy Friend, Obadiah*. Viking, 1969.

Ullman, James. *Banner in the Sky*. Lippincott, 1954.

Viorst, Judith. *Alexander and the Terrible, Horrible, No Good, Very Bad Day*, illustrated by Ray Cruz. Atheneum, 1972.

Waber, Bernard. *"You Look Ridiculous," Said the Rhinoceros to the Hippopotamus*. Houghton Mifflin, 1966.

Watson, Clyde. *Father Fox's Pennyrhymes,* illustrated by Wendy Watson. Crowell, 1971.

Watson, Jane Werner. *The Iliad and the Odyssey,* illustrated by Alice Provensen and Martin Provensen. Golden, 1956.

White, E. B. *Charlotte's Web,* illustrated by Garth Williams. Harper & Row, 1952.

————. *Stuart Little,* illustrated by Garth Williams. Harper & Row, 1945.

Wier, Ester. *The Loner,* illustrated by Christine Price. McKay, 1963.

Wilder, Laura Ingalls. *The Little House Series,* illustrated by Garth Williams. Harper & Row, 1953.

>   *By the Shores of Silver Lake* (1939).
>   *Little House in the Big Woods* (1932).
>   *Little House on the Prairie* (1935).
>   *Little Town on the Prairie* (1941).
>   *The Long Winter* (1940).
>   *On the Banks of Plum Creek* (1937).
>   *These Happy Golden Years* (1943).

Wise, William. *Charles A. Lindbergh,* illustrated by Paul Sagsoorian. Putnam, 1970.

Wojciechowska, Maia. *Shadow of a Bull,* illustrated by Alvin Smith. Atheneum, 1964.

Wrightson, Patricia. *The Nargun and the Stars.* Atheneum, 1974.

Wuorio, Eva-Lis. *To Fight in Silence.* Holt, Rinehart and Winston, 1973.

Yamaguchi, Tohr. *The Golden Crane,* illustrated by Marianne Yamaguchi. Holt, Rinehart and Winston, 1963.

Yashima, Taro, *pseud.* (Jun Iwamatsu). *Crow Boy.* Viking, 1955.

————. *Seashore Story.* Viking, 1967.

————. *Umbrella.* Viking, 1958.

————. *The Village Tree.* Viking, 1953.

————. *Youngest One.* Viking, 1962.

Yates, Elizabeth. *Carolina's Courage,* illustrated by Nora S. Unwin. Dutton, 1964.

Zion, Gene. *Harry the Dirty Dog,* illustrated by Margaret Bloy Graham. Harper & Row, 1956.

Zolotow, Charlotte. *Big Brother,* illustrated by Mary Chalmers. Harper & Row, 1960.

————. *Big Sister and Little Sister,* illustrated by Martha Alexander. Harper & Row, 1966.

The John Newbery Medal is named in honor of John Newbery, a British publisher and bookseller of the eighteenth century. He has frequently been called the father of children's literature, since he was the first to conceive the idea of publishing books expressly for children.

The Award is presented each year to "the author of the most distinguished contribution to American literature for children." To be eligible for the award, the author must be an American citizen or a permanent resident of the United States. The selection of the winner is made by a committee of the Children's Services Division of the American Library Association. There are twenty-three members on this committee. The winning author is presented with a bronze medal designed by René Paul Chambellan and donated by Frederick G. Melcher. The announcement is made in January. Later, at the summer conference of the American Library Association, a banquet is given in honor of the Award winners.

The following list of books includes the Award winners (capitalized and listed first) and the runners-up, or Honor Books, for each year. The date on the left indicates the year in which the Award was conferred. All books were necessarily published the preceding year. The name of the present publisher, if not the same as when the book was originally issued, is given in parentheses.

1922 THE STORY OF MANKIND by Hendrik Van Loon. Boni & Liveright (Liveright).
The Great Quest by Charles Boardman Hawes. Little, Brown.
Cedric the Forester by Bernard G. Marshall. Appleton.
The Old Tobacco Shop by William Bowen. Macmillan.
The Golden Fleece by Padraic Colum. Macmillan.
Windy Hill by Cornelia Meigs. Macmillan.

1923 THE VOYAGES OF DOCTOR DOLITTLE by Hugh Lofting. Stokes (Lippincott).
[No record of the runners-up.]

1924 THE DARK FRIGATE by Charles Boardman Hawes. Little, Brown.
[No record of the runners-up.]

1925 TALES FROM SILVER LANDS by Charles J. Finger. Illustrated by Paul Honoré. Doubleday.
Nicholas by Anne Carroll Moore. Putnam.
Dream Coach by Anne and Dillwyn Parrish. Macmillan.

1926 SHEN OF THE SEA by Arthur Bowie Chrisman. Illustrated by Else Hasselriis. Dutton.
The Voyagers by Padraic Colum. Macmillan.

1927 SMOKY, THE COWHORSE by Will James. Scribner.
[No record of the runners-up.]

1928 GAY NECK by Dhan Gopal Mukerji. Illustrated by Boris Artzybasheff. Dutton.
The Wonder-Smith and His Son by Ella Young. Longmans, Green (McKay).
Downright Dencey by Caroline Dale Snedeker. Doubleday.

1929 TRUMPETER OF KRAKOW by Eric P. Kelly. Illustrated by Angela Pruszynska. Macmillan.
The Pigtail of Ah Lee Ben Loo by John Bennett. Longmans, Green (McKay).
Millions of Cats by Wanda Gág. Coward-McCann.
The Boy Who Was by Grace T. Hallock. Dutton.
Clearing Weather by Cornelia Meigs. Little, Brown.
The Runaway Papoose by Grace P. Moon. Doubleday.
Tod of the Fens by Eleanor Whitney. Macmillan.

1930 HITTY, HER FIRST HUNDRED YEARS by Rachel Field. Illustrated by Dorothy P. Lathrop. Macmillan.
Pran of Albania by Elizabeth C. Miller. Doubleday.
The Jumping-Off Place by Marian Hurd McNeely. Longmans, Green (McKay).
A Daughter of the Seine by Jeanette Eaton. Harper (Harper & Row).

1931 THE CAT WHO WENT TO HEAVEN by Elizabeth Coatsworth. Illustrated by Lynd Ward. Macmillan.
Floating Island by Anne Parrish. Harper (Harper & Row).
The Dark Star of Itza by Alida Malkus. Harcourt.
Queer Person by Ralph Hubbard. Doubleday.
Mountains Are Free by Julia Davis Adams. Dutton.
Spice and the Devil's Cave by Agnes D. Hewes. Knopf.
Meggy McIntosh by Elizabeth Janet Gray. Doubleday.

1932 WATERLESS MOUNTAIN by Laura Adams Armer. Illustrated by Sidney Armer and the author. Longmans, Green (McKay).
The Fairy Circus by Dorothy Lathrop. Macmillan.
Calico Bush by Rachel Field. Macmillan.
Boy of the South Seas by Eunice Tietjens. Coward-McCann.
Out of the Flame by Eloise Lounsbery. Longmans, Green (McKay).
Jane's Island by Marjorie Hill Alee. Houghton Mifflin.
Truce of the Wolf by Mary Gould Davis. Harcourt.

1933 YOUNG FU OF THE UPPER YANGTZE by Elizabeth Foreman Lewis. Illustrated by Kurt Wiese. Winston (Holt, Rinehart and Winston).
Hepatica Hawks by Rachel Field. Macmillan.
Romantic Rebel by Hildegarde Hawthorne. Appleton.
Auntie by Maude and Miska Petersham. Doubleday.
Tirra Lirra by Laura E. Richards. Little, Brown.
Little House in the Big Woods by Laura Ingalls Wilder. Harper (Harper & Row).

1934 INVINCIBLE LOUISA by Cornelia Meigs. Little, Brown.
Forgotten Daughter by Caroline Dale Snedeker. Doubleday.
Swords of Steel by Elsie Singmaster. Houghton Mifflin.
ABC Bunny by Wanda Gág. Coward-McCann.
Winged Girl of Knossos by Erick Berry. Appleton.
New Land by Sarah L. Schmidt. McBride.
Apprentices of Florence by Anne Kyle. Houghton Mifflin.

1935 DOBRY by Monica Shannon. Illustrated by Atanas Katchamakoff. Viking.

The Pageant of Chinese History by Elizabeth Seeger. Longmans, Green (McKay).

Davy Crockett by Constance Rourke. Harcourt.

A Day on Skates by Hilda Van Stockum. Harper (Harper & Row).

1936 CADDIE WOODLAWN by Carol Ryrie Brink. Illustrated by Kate Seredy. Macmillan.

Honk the Moose by Phil Stong. Dodd, Mead.

The Good Master by Kate Seredy. Viking.

Young Walter Scott Elizabeth Janet Gray. Viking.

All Sail Set by Armstrong Sperry. Winston (Holt, Rinehart and Winston).

1937 ROLLER SKATES by Ruth Sawyer. Illustrated by Valenti Angelo. Viking.

Phoebe Fairchild: Her Book by Lois Lenski. Stokes (Lippincott).

Whistler's Van by Idwal Jones. Viking.

The Golden Basket by Ludwig Bemelmans. Viking.

Winterbound by Margery Bianco. Viking.

Audubon by Constance Rourke. Harcourt.

The Codfish Musket by Agnes D. Hewes. Doubleday.

1938 THE WHITE STAG by Kate Seredy. Viking.

Bright Island by Mabel L. Robinson. Random House.

Pecos Bill by James Cloyd Bowman. Whitman.

On the Banks of Plum Creek by Laura Ingalls Wilder. Harper (Harper & Row).

1939 THIMBLE SUMMER by Elizabeth Enright. Farrar & Rinehart (Holt, Rinehart and Winston).

Leader by Destiny by Jeanette Eaton. Harcourt.

Penn by Elizabeth Janet Gray. Viking.

Nino by Valenti Angelo. Viking.

"Hello, the Boat!" by Phyllis Crawford. Holt (Holt, Rinehart and Winston).

Mr. Popper's Penguins by Richard and Florence Atwater. Little, Brown.

1940 DANIEL BOONE by James H. Daugherty. Viking.

The Singing Tree by Kate Seredy. Viking.

Runner of the Mountain Tops by Mabel L. Robinson. Random House.

By the Shores of Silver Lake by Laura Ingalls Wilder. Harper (Harper & Row).

Boy with a Pack by Stephen W. Meader. Harcourt.

1941 CALL IT COURAGE by Armstrong Sperry. Macmillan.

Blue Willow by Doris Gates. Viking.

Young Mac of Fort Vancouver by Mary Jane Carr. Crowell.

The Long Winter by Laura Ingalls Wilder. Harper (Harper & Row).

Nansen by Anna Gertrude Hall. Viking.

1942 THE MATCHLOCK GUN by Walter D. Edmonds. Illustrated by Paul Lantz. Dodd, Mead.

Little Town on the Prairie by Laura Ingalls Wilder. Harper (Harper & Row).

George Washington's World by G. Foster. Scribner.

Indian Captive by Lois Lenski. Stokes (Lippincott).

Down Ryton Water by E. R. Gaggin. Viking.

1943 ADAM OF THE ROAD by Elizabeth Janet Gray. Illustrated by Robert Lawson. Viking.

The Middle Moffat by Eleanor Estes. Harcourt.

"Have You Seen Tom Thumb?" by Mabel Leigh Hunt. Stokes (Lippincott).

1944 JOHNNY TREMAIN by Esther Forbes. Illustrated by Lynd Ward. Houghton Mifflin.

These Happy Golden Years by Laura Ingalls Wilder. Harper (Harper & Row).

Fog Magic by Julia L. Sauer. Viking.

Rufus M. by Eleanor Estes. Harcourt.

Mountain Born by Elizabeth Yates. Coward-McCann.

1945 RABBIT HILL by Robert Lawson. Viking.

The Hundred Dresses by Eleanor Estes. Harcourt.

The Silver Pencil by Alice Dalgliesh. Scribner.

Abraham Lincoln's World by Genevieve Foster. Scribner.

Lone Journey by Jeanette Eaton. Harcourt.

1946 STRAWBERRY GIRL by Lois Lenski. Lippincott.

Justin Morgan Had a Horse by Marguerite Henry. Wilcox & Follett (Follett).

The Moved-Outers by Florence Crannell Means. Houghton Mifflin.

Bhimsa, the Dancing Bear by Christine Weston. Scribner.

New Found World by Katherine B. Shippen. Viking.

1947 MISS HICKORY by Carolyn Sherwin Bailey. Illustrated by Ruth Gannett. Viking.

The Wonderful Year by Nancy Barnes. Messner.

Big Tree by Mary Buff and Conrad Buff. Viking.

The Heavenly Tenants by William Maxwell. Harper (Harper & Row).

The Avion My Uncle Flew by Cyrus Fisher. Appleton.

The Hidden Treasure of Glaston by Eleanore M. Jewett. Viking.

1948 THE TWENTY-ONE BALLOONS by William Pène du Bois. Viking.

Pancakes-Paris by Claire Huchet Bishop. Viking.

Li Lun, Lad of Courage by Carolyn Treffinger. Abingdon-Cokesbury (Abingdon).

The Quaint and Curious Quest of Johnny Longfoot by Catherine Besterman. Bobbs-Merrill.

The Cow-Tail Switch by Harold Courlander and George Herzog. Holt (Holt, Rinehart and Winston).

Misty of Chincoteague by Marguerite Henry. Rand McNally.

1949 KING OF THE WIND by Marguerite Henry. Illustrated by Wesley Dennis. Rand McNally.

Seabird by Holling Clancy Holling. Houghton Mifflin.

Daughter of the Mountains by Louise Rankin. Viking.

My Father's Dragon by Ruth S. Gannett. Random House.

Story of the Negro by Arna Bontemps. Knopf.

1950 THE DOOR IN THE WALL by Marguerite de Angeli. Doubleday.

Tree of Freedom by Rebecca Caudill. Viking.

Blue Cat of Castle Town by Catherine Coblentz. Longmans, Green (McKay).

Kildee House by Rutherford Montgomery. Doubleday.

George Washington by Genevieve Foster. Scribner.

Song of the Pines by Walter Havighurst and Marion Havighurst. Winston (Holt, Rinehart and Winston).

1951 AMOS FORTUNE, FREE MAN by Elizabeth Yates. Illustrated by Nora Unwin. Aladdin (Dutton).
Better Known as Johnny Appleseed by Mabel Leigh Hunt. Lippincott.
Gandhi, Fighter without a Sword by Jeanette Eaton. Morrow.
Abraham Lincoln, Friend of the People by Clara I. Judson. Wilcox & Follett (Follett).
The Story of Appleby Capple by Anne Parrish. Harper (Harper & Row).

1952 GINGER PYE by Eleanor Estes. Harcourt.
Americans before Columbus by Elizabeth Chesley Baity. Viking.
Minn of the Mississippi by Holling Clancy Holling. Houghton Mifflin.
The Defender by Nicholas Kalashnikoff. Scribner.
The Light at Tern Rock by Julia L. Sauer. Viking.
The Apple and the Arrow by Mary Buff. Houghton Mifflin.

1953 SECRET OF THE ANDES by Ann Nolan Clark. Illustrated by Jean Charlot. Viking.
Charlotte's Web by E. B. White. Harper (Harper and Row).
Moccasin Trail by Eloise J. McGraw. Coward-McCann.
Red Sails for Capri by Ann Weil. Viking.
The Bears on Hemlock Mountain by Alice Dalgliesh. Scribner.
Birthdays of Freedom by Genevieve Foster. Scribner.

1954 AND NOW MIGUEL by Joseph Krumgold. Illustrated by Jean Charlot. Crowell.
All Alone by Clarie Huchet Bishop. Viking.
Shadrach by Meindert DeJong. Harper (Harper & Row).
Hurry Home, Candy by Meindert DeJong. Harper (Harper & Row).
Theodore Roosevelt, Fighting Patriot by Clara I. Judson. Follett.
Magic Maize by Mary Buff. Houghton Mifflin.

1955 THE WHEEL ON THE SCHOOL by Meindert DeJong. Illustrated by Maurice Sendak. Harper (Harper & Row).
The Courage of Sarah Noble by Alice Dalgliesh. Scribner.
Banner in the Sky by James Ramsey Ullman. Lippincott.

1956 CARRY ON, MR. BOWDITCH by Jean Lee Latham. Houghton Mifflin.
The Golden Name Day by Jennie D. Lindquist. Harper (Harper & Row).
The Secret River by Marjorie Kinnan Rawlings. Scribner.
Men, Microscopes, and Living Things by Katherine B. Shippen. Viking.

1957 MIRACLES ON MAPLE HILL by Virginia Sorensen. Illustrated by Beth Krush and Joe Krush. Harcourt.
Old Yeller by Fred Gipson. Harper (Harper & Row).
The House of Sixty Fathers by Meindert DeJong. Harper (Harper & Row).
Mr. Justice Holmes by Clara I. Judson. Follett.
The Corn Grows Ripe by Dorothy Rhoads. Viking.

The Black Fox of Lorne by Marguerite de Angeli. Doubleday.

1958 RIFLES FOR WATIE by Harold Keith. Illustrated by Peter Burchard. Crowell.
The Horsecatcher by Mari Sandoz. Westminster.
Gone-away Lake by Elizabeth Enright. Harcourt.
The Great Wheel by Robert Lawson. Viking.
Tom Paine, Freedom's Apostle by Leo Gurko. Crowell.

1959 THE WITCH OF BLACKBIRD POND by Elizabeth George Speare. Houghton Mifflin.
The Family under the Bridge by Natalie S. Carlson. Harper (Harper & Row).
Along Came a Dog by Meindert DeJong. Harper (Harper & Row).
Chucaro by Francis Kalnay. Harcourt.
The Perilous Road by William O. Steele. Harcourt.

1960 ONION JOHN by Joseph Krumgold. Illustrated by Symeon Shimin. Crowell.
My Side of the Mountain by Jean George. Dutton.
America Is Born by Gerald Johnson. Morrow.
The Gammage Cup by Carol Kendall. Harcourt.

1961 ISLAND OF THE BLUE DOLPHINS by Scott O'Dell. Houghton Mifflin.
America Moves Forward by Gerald Johnson. Morrow.
Old Ramon by Jack Schaefer. Houghton Mifflin.
The Cricket in Times Square by George Selden. Farrar (Farrar, Straus).

1962 THE BRONZE BOW by Elizabeth George Speare. Houghton Mifflin.
Frontier Living by Edwin Tunis. World Publishing.
The Golden Goblet by Eloise J. McGraw. Coward-McCann.
Belling the Tiger by Mary Stolz. Harper & Row.

1963 A WRINKLE IN TIME by Madeleine L'Engle. Farrar (Farrar, Straus).
Thistle and Thyme by Sorche Nic Leodhas. Holt, Rinehart and Winston.
Men of Athens by Olivia Coolidge. Houghton Mifflin.

1964 IT'S LIKE THIS, CAT by Emily Neville. Illustrated by Emil Weiss. Harper & Row.
Rascal by Sterling North. Dutton.
The Loner by Ester Wier. McKay.

1965 SHADOW OF A BULL by Maia Wojciechowska. Illustrated by Alvin Smith. Atheneum.
Across Five Aprils by Irene Hunt. Follett.

1966 I, JUAN DE PAREJA by Elizabeth Borten de Treviño. Farrar, Straus.
The Black Cauldron by Lloyd Alexander. Holt, Rinehart and Winston.
The Animal Family by Randall Jarrell. Pantheon.
The Noonday Friends by Mary Stolz. Harper & Row.

1967 UP A ROAD SLOWLY by Irene Hunt. Follett.
The King's Fifth by Scott O'Dell. Houghton Mifflin.
Zlateh the Goat and Other Stories by Isaac Bashevis Singer. Harper & Row.
The Jazz Man by Mary Hays Weik. Atheneum.

1968 FROM THE MIXED-UP FILES OF MRS. BASIL E. FRANKWEILER by E. L. Konigsburg. Atheneum.

Jennifer, Hecate, Macbeth, William McKinley, and Me, Elizabeth by E. L. Konigsburg. Atheneum.

The Black Pearl by Scott O'Dell. Houghton Mifflin.

The Fearsome Inn by Isaac Bashevis Singer. Scribner.

The Egypt Game by Zilpha Keatley Snyder. Atheneum.

1969 THE HIGH KING by Lloyd Alexander. Holt, Rinehart and Winston.

To Be a Slave by Julius Lester. Dial.

When Shlemiel Went to Warsaw and Other Stories by Isaac Bashevis Singer. Farrar, Straus.

1970 SOUNDER by William H. Armstrong. Harper & Row.

Our Eddie by Sulamith Ish-Kishor. Pantheon.

The Many Ways of Seeing: An Introduction to the Pleasures of Art by Janet Gaylord Moore. World.

Journey Outside by Mary Q. Steele. Viking.

1971 SUMMER OF THE SWANS by Betsy Byars. Viking.

Kneeknock Rise by Natalie Babbitt. Farrar, Straus.

Enchantress from the Stars by Sylvia Louise Engdahl. Atheneum.

Sing Down the Moon by Scott O'Dell. Houghton Mifflin.

1972 MRS. FRISBY AND THE RATS OF NIMH by Robert C. O'Brien. Atheneum.

Incident at Hawk's Hill by Allan W. Eckert. Little, Brown.

The Planet of Junior Brown by Virginia Hamilton. Macmillan.

The Tombs of Atuan by Ursula K. LeGuin. Atheneum.

Annie and the Old One by Miska Miles. Atlantic-Little, Brown.

The Headless Cupid by Zilpha Keatley Snyder. Atheneum.

1973 JULIE OF THE WOLVES by Jean Craighead George. Harper & Row.

Frog and Toad Together by Arnold Lobel. Harper & Row.

The Upstairs Room by Johanna Reiss. Crowell.

The Witches of Worm by Zilpha Keatley Snyder. Atheneum.

1974 THE SLAVE DANCER by Paula Fox. Bradbury.

The Dark Is Rising by Susan Cooper. Atheneum.

1975 M. C. HIGGINS THE GREAT by Virginia Hamilton. Macmillan.

My Brother Sam Is Dead by James Collier and Christopher Collier. Four Winds.

Philip Hall Likes Me. I Reckon Maybe. by Bette Greene. Dial.

The Perilous Gard by Elizabeth Pope. Houghton Mifflin.

Figgs & Phantoms by Ellen Raskin. Dutton.

The Caldecott Medal is named in honor of Randolph Caldecott, a prominent English illustrator of children's books during the nineteenth century. This Award is presented each year to "the artist of the most distinguished American picture book for children." The winner is selected by the same committee that chooses the Newbery winner.

The following list of books includes the Award winners (capitalized and listed first) and the runners-up, or Honor Books, for each year. The date on the left indicates the year

in which the Award was conferred. If the illustrator's name is not cited, it means the author illustrated the book. The Caldecott Award is given to the illustrator, not to the author of these books.

1938 ANIMALS OF THE BIBLE, A PICTURE BOOK. Text selected from the King James Bible by Helen Dean Fish. Illustrated by Dorothy O. Lathrop. Stokes (Lippincott).

Seven Simeons by Boris Artzybasheff. Viking.

Four and Twenty Blackbirds compiled by Helen Dean Fish. Illustrated by Robert Lawson. Stokes (Lippincott).

1939 MEI LI by Thomas Handforth. Doubleday.

The Forest Pool by Laura Adams Armer. Longmans, Green (McKay).

Wee Gillis by Munro Leaf. Illustrated by Robert Lawson. Viking.

Snow White and the Seven Dwarfs translated and illustrated by Wanda Gág. Coward-McCann.

Barkis by Clare Turlay Newberry. Harper (Harper & Row).

Andy and the Lion by James Daugherty. Viking.

1940 ABRAHAM LINCOLN by Ingri d'Aulaire and Edgar Parin d'Aulaire. Doubleday.

Cock-a-Doodle-Doo by Berta Hader and Elmer Hader. Macmillan.

Madeline by Ludwig Bemelmans. Simon and Schuster.

The Ageless Story by Lauren Ford. Dodd, Mead.

1941 THEY WERE STRONG AND GOOD by Robert Lawson. Viking.

April's Kittens by Clare Turlay Newberry. Harper (Harper & Row).

1942 MAKE WAY FOR DUCKLINGS by Robert McCloskey. Viking.

An American ABC by Maud Petersham and Miska Petersham. Macmillan.

In My Mother's House by Ann Nolan Clark. Illustrated by Velino Herrera. Viking.

Paddle-to-the-Sea by Holling Clancy Holling. Houghton Mifflin.

Nothing at All by Wanda Gág. Coward-McCann.

1943 THE LITTLE HOUSE by Virginia Lee Burton. Houghton Mifflin.

Dash and Dart by Mary Buff and Conrad Buff. Viking.

Marshmallow by Clare Turlay Newberry. Harper (Harper & Row).

1944 MANY MOONS by James Thurber. Illustrated by Louis Slobodkin. Harcourt.

Small Rain. Text arranged from the Bible by Jessie Orton Jones. Illustrated by Elizabeth Orton Jones. Viking.

Pierre Pidgeon by Lee Kingman. Illustrated by Arnold Edwin Bare. Houghton Mifflin.

Good-Luck Horse by Chih-Yi Chan. Illustrated by Plato Chan. Whittlesey.

Mighty Hunter by Berta Hader and Elmer Hader. Macmillan.

A Child's Good Night Book by Margaret Wise Brown. Illustrated by Jean Charlot. W. R. Scott.

1945 PRAYER FOR A CHILD by Rachel Field. Pictures by Elizabeth Orton Jones. Macmillan.

Mother Goose. Compiled and illustrated by Tasha Tudor. Oxford.

In the Forest by Marie Hall Ets. Viking.

Yonie Wondernose by Marguerite de Angeli. Doubleday.

The Christmas Anna Angel by Ruth Sawyer. Illustrated by Kate Seredy. Viking.

1946 THE ROOSTER CROWS by Maud Petersham and Miska Petersham. Macmillan.

Little Lost Lamb by Margaret Wise Brown. Illustrated by Leonard Weisgard. Doubleday.

Sing Mother Goose. Music by Opal Wheeler. Illustrated by Marjorie Torrey. Dutton.

My Mother Is the Most Beautiful Woman in the World by Becky Reyher. Illustrated by Ruth C. Gannett. Lothrop.

You Can Write Chinese by Kurt Wiese. Viking.

1947 THE LITTLE ISLAND by Golden MacDonald. Illustrated by Leonard Weisgard. Doubleday.

Rain Drop Splash by Alvin R. Tresselt. Illustrated by Leonard Weisgard. Lothrop.

Boats on the River by Marjorie Flack. Illustrated by Jay Hyde Barnum. Viking.

Timothy Turtle by Al Graham. Illustrated by Tony Palazzo. Robert Welch (Viking).

Pedro, Angel of Olvera Street by Leo Politi. Scribner.

Sing in Praise by Opal Wheeler. Illustrated by Marjorie Torrey. Dutton.

1948 WHITE SNOW, BRIGHT SNOW by Alvin Tresselt. Illustrated by Roger Duvoisin. Lothrop.

Stone Soup. Told and illustrated by Marcia Brown. Scribner.

McElligot's Pool by Theodor S. Geisel (Dr. Seuss). Random House.

Bambino the Clown by George Schreiber. Viking.

Roger and the Fox by Lavinia R. Davis. Illustrated by Hildegard Woodward. Doubleday.

Song of Robin Hood. Anne Malcolmson, ed. Illustrated by Virginia Lee Burton. Houghton Mifflin.

1949 THE BIG SNOW by Berta Hader and Elmer Hader. Macmillan.

Blueberries for Sal by Robert McCloskey. Viking.

All around the Town by Phyllis McGinley. Illustrated by Helen Stone. Lippincott.

Juanita by Leo Politi. Scribner.

Fish in the Air by Kurt Wiese. Viking.

1950 SONG OF THE SWALLOWS by Leo Politi. Scribner.

America's Ethan Allen by Stewart Holbrook. Illustrated by Lynd Ward. Houghton Mifflin.

The Wild Birthday Cake by Lavinia R. Davis. Illustrated by Hildegard Woodward. Doubleday.

Happy Day by Ruth Krauss. Illustrated by Marc Simont. Harper (Harper & Row).

Henry-Fisherman by Marcia Brown. Scribner.

Bartholomew and the Oobleck by Theodor S. Geisel (Dr. Seuss). Random House.

1951 THE EGG TREE by Katherine Milhous. Scribner.

Dick Whittington and His Cat told and illustrated by Marcia Brown. Scribner.

The Two Reds by Will (William Lipkind). Illustrated by Nicolas (Mordvinoff). Harcourt.

If I Ran the Zoo by Theodor S. Geisel (Dr. Seuss). Random House.

T-Bone the Baby-Sitter by Clare Turlay Newberry. Harper (Harper & Row).

The Most Wonderful Doll in the World by Phyllis McGinley. Illustrated by Helen Stone. Lippincott.

1952 FINDERS KEEPERS by Will (William Lipkind). Illustrated by Nicolas (Mordvinoff). Harcourt.

Mr. T. W. Anthony Woo by Marie Hall Ets. Viking.

Skipper John's Cook by Marcia Brown. Scribner.

All Falling Down by Gene Zion. Illustrated by Margaret Bloy Graham. Harper (Harper & Row).

Bear Party by William Pène du Bois. Viking.

Feather Mountain by Elizabeth Olds. Houghton Mifflin.

1953 THE BIGGEST BEAR by Lynd Ward. Houghton Mifflin.

Puss in Boots. Told and illustrated by Marcia Brown. Scribner.

One Morning in Maine by Robert McCloskey. Viking.

Ape in a Cape by Fritz Eichenberg. Harcourt.

The Storm Book by Charlotte Zolotow. Illustrated by Margaret Bloy Graham. Harper (Harper & Row).

Five Little Monkeys by Juliet Kepes. Houghton Mifflin.

1954 MADELINE'S RESCUE by Ludwig Bemelmans. Viking.

Journey Cake, Ho! by Ruth Sawyer. Illustrated by Robert McCloskey. Viking.

When Will the World Be Mine? by Miriam Schlein. Illustrated by Jean Charlot. W. R. Scott.

The Steadfast Tin Soldier translated by M. R. James. Adapted from Hans Christian Andersen. Illustrated by Marcia Brown. Scribner.

A Very Special House by Ruth Krauss. Illustrated by Maurice Sendak. Harper (Harper & Row).

Green Eyes by Abe Birnbaum. Capitol.

1955 CINDERELLA by Charles Perrault. Illustrated by Marcia Brown. Harper (Harper & Row).

Book of Nursery and Mother Goose Rhymes. Compiled and illustrated by Marguerite de Angeli. Doubleday.

Wheel on the Chimney by Margaret Wise Brown. Illustrated by Tibor Gergely. Lippincott.

1956 FROG WENT A-COURTIN' by John Langstaff. Illustrated by Feodor Rojankovsky. Harcourt.

Play with Me by Marie Hall Ets. Viking.

Crow Boy by Taro Yashima. Viking.

1957 A TREE IS NICE by Janice May Udry. Illustrated by Marc Simont. Harper (Harper & Row).

Mr. Penny's Race Horse by Marie Hall Ets. Viking.

1 Is One by Tasha Tudor. Oxford (Walck).

Anatole by Eve Titus. Illustrated by Paul Galdone. Whittlesey (McGraw).

Gillespie and the Guards by Benjamin Elkin. Illustrated by James Daugherty. Viking.

Lion by William Pène du Bois. Viking.

1958 TIME OF WONDER by Robert McCloskey. Viking.
Fly High, Fly Low by Don Freeman. Viking.
Anatole and the Cat by Eve Titus. Illustrated by Paul Galdone. Whittlesey (McGraw).

1959 CHANTICLEER AND THE FOX. Edited and illustrated by Barbara Cooney. Crowell.
The House That Jack Built by Antonio Frasconi. Crowell.
What Do You Say, Dear? by Sesyle Joslin. Illustrated by Maurice Sendak. W. R. Scott.
Umbrella by Taro Yashima. Viking.

1960 NINE DAYS TO CHRISTMAS by Marie Hall Ets and Aurora Labastida. Viking.
Houses from the Sea by Alice E. Goudey. Illustrated by Adrienne Adams. Scribner.
The Moon Jumpers by Janice May Udry. Illustrated by Maurice Sendak. Harper (Harper & Row).

1961 BABOUSHKA AND THE THREE KINGS by Ruth Robbins. Illustrated by Nicolas Sidjakov. Parnassus.
Inch by Inch by Leo Lionni. Obolensky.

1962 ONCE A MOUSE by Marcia Brown. Scribner.
The Fox Went Out on a Chilly Night by Peter Spier. Doubleday.
Little Bear's Visit by Else Minarik. Illustrated by Maurice Sendak. Harper (Harper & Row).
The Day We Saw the Sun Come Up by Alice Goudey. Illustrated by Adrienne Adams. Scribner.

1963 THE SNOWY DAY by Ezra Jack Keats. Viking.
The Sun Is a Golden Earring by Natalia Belting. Illustrated by Bernarda Bryson. Holt, Rinehart and Winston.
Mr. Rabbit and the Lovely Present by Charlotte Zolotow. Illustrated by Maurice Sendak. Harper & Row.

1964 WHERE THE WILD THINGS ARE by Maurice Sendak. Harper & Row.
Swimmy by Leo Lionni. Pantheon.
All in the Morning Early by Sorche Nic Leodhas. Illustrated by Evaline Ness. Holt, Rinehart and Winston.
Mother Goose and Nursery Rhymes by Philip Reed. Atheneum.

1965 MAY I BRING A FRIEND? by Beatrice Schenk de Regniers. Illustrated by Beni Montresor. Atheneum.
Rain Makes Applesauce by Julian Scheer. Illustrated by Marvin Bileck. Holiday.
The Wave by Margaret Hodges. Illustrated by Blair Lent. Houghton Mifflin.
A Pocketful of Cricket by Rebecca Caudill. Illustrated by Evaline Ness. Holt, Rinehart and Winston.

1966 ALWAYS ROOM FOR ONE MORE by Sorche Nic Leodhas. Illustrated by Nonny Hogrogian. Holt, Rinehart and Winston.
Hide and Seek Fog by Alvin Tresselt. Illustrated by Roger Duvoisin. Lothrop.
Just Me by Marie Hall Ets. Viking.
Tom Tit Tot. Joseph Jacobs, ed. Illustrated by Evaline Ness. Scribner.

1967 SAM, BANGS AND MOONSHINE by Evaline Ness. Holt, Rinehart and Winston.

One Wide River to Cross by Barbara Emberley. Illustrated by Ed Emberley. Prentice-Hall.

1968 DRUMMER HOFF by Barbara Emberley. Illustrated by Ed Emberley. Prentice-Hall.
Frederick by Leo Lionni. Pantheon.
Seashore Story by Taro Yashima. Viking.
The Emperor and the Kite by Jane Yolen. Illustrated by Ed Young. World Publishing.

1969 THE FOOL OF THE WORLD AND THE FLYING SHIP by Arthur Ransome. Illustrated by Uri Shulevitz. Farrar, Straus.
Why the Sun and the Moon Live in the Sky by Elphinstone Dayrell. Illustrated by Blair Lent. Houghton Mifflin.

1970 SYLVESTER AND THE MAGIC PEBBLE by William Steig. Windmill/Simon and Schuster.
Goggles by Ezra Jack Keats. Macmillan.
Alexander and the Wind-up Mouse by Leo Lionni. Pantheon.
Pop Corn and Ma Goodness by Edna Mitchell Preston. Illustrated by Robert Andrew Parker. Viking.
Thy Friend, Obadiah by Brinton Turkle. Viking.
The Judge by Harve Zemach. Illustrated by Margot Zemach. Farrar, Straus.

1971 A STORY, A STORY by Gail E. Haley. Atheneum.
The Angry Moon by William Sleator. Illustrated by Blair Lent. Atlantic-Little, Brown.
Frog and Toad Are Friends by Arnold Lobel. Harper & Row.
In the Night Kitchen by Maurice Sendak. Harper & Row.

1972 ONE FINE DAY by Nonny Hogrogian. Macmillan.
If All the Seas Were One Sea by Janina Domanska. Macmillan.
Moja Means One: Swahili Counting Book by Muriel Feelings. Illustrated by Tom Feelings. Dial.
Hildilid's Night by Cheli Duran Ryan. Illustrated by Arnold Lobel. Macmillan.

1973 THE FUNNY LITTLE WOMAN by Arlene Mosel. Illustrated by Blair Lent. Dutton.
Hosie's Alphabet by Hosea Baskin, Tobias Baskin, and Lisa Baskin. Illustrated by Leonard Baskin. Viking.
When Clay Sings by Byrd Baylor. Illustrated by Tom Bahti. Scribner.
Snow-White and the Seven Dwarfs by the Brothers Grimm, translated by Randall Jarrell. Illustrated by Nancy Ekholm Burkert. Farrar, Straus.
Anansi the Spider by Gerald McDermott. Holt, Rinehart and Winston.

1974 DUFFY AND THE DEVIL by Harve Zemach. Illustrated by Margot Zemach. Farrar, Straus.
The Three Jovial Huntsmen by Susan Jeffers. Bradbury.
Cathedral by David Macaulay. Houghton Mifflin.

1975 ARROW TO THE SUN. Adapted and illustrated by Gerald McDermott. Viking.
Jambo Means Hello: Swahili Alphabet Book by Muriel Feelings. Illustrated by Tom Feelings. Dial.

National Book Award, Children's Book Category was presented for the first time in March 1969. A panel of judges chooses a book considered to be the most distinguished juvenile of the preceding year written by an American author and published in the United States. The cash award of $1,000 is contributed by Children's Book Council and administered by the National Book Committee.

1969 JOURNEY FROM PEPPERMINT STREET by Meindert DeJong. Harper & Row.

1970 A DAY OF PLEASURE: STORIES OF A BOY GROWING UP IN WARSAW by Isaac Bashevis Singer. Farrar, Straus.

1971 THE MARVELOUS MISADVENTURES OF SEBASTIAN by Lloyd Alexander. Dutton.

1972 THE SLIGHTLY IRREGULAR FIRE ENGINE by Donald Barthelme. Farrar, Straus.

1973 THE FARTHEST SHORE by Ursula K. LeGuin. Atheneum.

1974 THE COURT OF THE STONE CHILDREN by Eleanor Cameron. Dutton.

1975 M. C. HIGGINS THE GREAT by Virginia Hamilton. Macmillan.

The Laura Ingalls Wilder Award is given "to an author or illustrator whose books published in the United States, have over a period of years made a substantial and lasting contribution to literature for children." This award was established in 1954 by the Children's Services Division of the American Library Association, and was presented first to Laura Ingalls Wilder herself, for her well-loved "Little House" books. A committee of six determines the winner of this award, which is given every five years. A medal designed by Garth Williams has been presented to these authors:

1954 Laura Ingalls Wilder
1960 Clara Ingram Judson
1965 Ruth Sawyer
1970 E. B. White
1975 Beverly Cleary

The Hans Christian Andersen Prize, the first international children's book award, was established in 1956 by the International Board on Books for Young People. Given every two years, the Award medal has, since 1960, recognized the winner's entire body of work for children. In 1966 the award was expanded to honor an illustrator as well as an author. A committee of five, each from a different country, judges the selections recommended by the board or library association in each country. The following have won the Hans Christian Andersen Prize:

1956 Eleanor Farjeon for THE LITTLE BOOKROOM. Oxford (Walck).

1958 Astrid Lindgren for RASMUS PA LUFFEN. Rabén and Sjögren (Viking; titled RASMUS AND THE VAGABOND).

1960 Erich Kästner. Germany.

1962 Meindert DeJong. United States.

1964 René Guillot. France.

1966 Tove Jansson (author). Finland.
Alois Carigiet (illustrator). Switzerland.

1968 James Krüss (author). Germany.
Jose Maria Sanchez-Silva (author). Spain.
Jiri Trnka (illustrator). Czechoslovakia.

1970 Gianni Rodari (author). Italy.
Maurice Sendak (illustrator). United States.

1972 Scott O'Dell (author). United States.
Ib Spang Olsen (illustrator). Denmark.

1974 Maria Gripe (author). Sweden.
Farshid Mesghali (illustrator). Iran.

GENERAL AWARDS

AIGA CHILDREN'S BOOK SHOW
American Institute of Graphic Arts, 1059 Third Ave., New York, N.Y. 10021. Exhibition of 100–150 books selected for excellence of graphic design (alternate years).

AIGA FIFTY BOOKS OF THE YEAR
American Institute of Graphic Arts, 1059 Third Ave., New York, N.Y. 10021. Selected for excellence of design and manufacture; includes varying number of children's books.

MILDRED L. BATCHELDER AWARD
Children's Services Division, American Library Association, 50 East Huron St., Chicago, Ill. 60611. For most outstanding book originally published in a foreign language in another country.

IRMA SIMONTON BLACK AWARD
Bank Street College of Education, 610 West 112th St., New York, N.Y. 10025. For an outstanding book for young children.

BOOK WORLD CHILDREN'S SPRING BOOK FESTIVAL AWARDS
Book World, *The Chicago Tribune*, Tribune Tower, Chicago, Ill. 60611. For outstanding books published during first six months of the award year, in three categories: Picture Books, Middle Ages, Older Children.

BOSTON GLOBE-HORN BOOK AWARDS
The Boston Globe, Boston, Mass. 02107, and *The Horn Book Magazine*, 585 Boylston St., Boston, Mass. 02116. Two awards, one each for outstanding text and illustration.

THE BROOKLYN ART BOOKS FOR CHILDREN CITATIONS
Brooklyn Museum, 188 Eastern Parkway, Brooklyn, N.Y. 11238, and Brooklyn Public Library, Grand Army Plaza, Brooklyn, N.Y. 11238. Given to recognize a number of "currently available" books which are both good literature and works of art.

LEWIS CARROLL SHELF AWARD
University of Wisconsin, Wisconsin Book Conference, School of Education, Madison, Wis. 53706. Chosen from books nominated by publishers as worthy "to sit on the shelf with *Alice in Wonderland.*"

CHILDREN'S BOOK SHOWCASE
Children's Book Council, 67 Irving Place, New York, N.Y. 10003. A varying number of books selected to exemplify "the highest graphic standards."

NEW YORK TIMES BEST ILLUSTRATED CHILDREN'S BOOKS OF THE YEAR
The New York Times, 229 West 43rd St., New York, N.Y. 10036. Ten books selected for excellence of illustration.

AWARDS BASED ON SPECIAL CONTENT

JANE ADDAMS BOOK AWARD
Women's International League for Peace and Freedom and

Jane Addams Peace Association, 345 East 46th St., New York, N.Y. 10017. For a book with literary merit that stresses themes of dignity, equality, peace, and social justice.

CHILD STUDY ASSOCIATION OF AMERICA/WEL-MET CHILDREN'S BOOK AWARD

Child Study Association, 50 Madison Ave., New York, N.Y. 10010. For a distinguished book for children or young people that deals realistically with their problems.

CHRISTOPHER AWARD, CHILDREN'S BOOK CATEGORY

The Christophers, 12 East 48th St., New York, N.Y. 10017. Books for various age levels that reflect a high level of human and spiritual values.

COUNCIL ON INTERRACIAL BOOKS FOR CHILDREN AWARD

Council on Interracial Books for Children, 23 West 15th St., New York, N.Y. 10011. Prizes for unpublished manuscripts by writers from minority ethnic groups.

JEWISH BOOK COUNCIL, CHARLES AND BERTIE G. SCHWARTZ JUVENILE AWARD

Jewish Book Council of the National Jewish Welfare Board, 15 East 26th St., New York, N.Y. 10010. For best children's book on a Jewish theme or for cumulative contributions to Jewish juvenile literature.

CORETTA SCOTT KING AWARD

Johnson Publishing Company, Encyclopedia Britannica, Combined Book Publishers Group, Xerox Publishing Corp., and Englewood, N.J. Library Council (Awards Chairman: Mrs. Glyndon F. Greer, Englewood Middle School, Tryon and Liberty Rd., Englewood, N.J. 07631). For a book that promotes "better understanding and appreciation of the culture and contribution of all peoples to the American dream."

NEW YORK ACADEMY OF SCIENCES CHILDREN'S SCIENCE BOOK AWARD

New York Academy of Sciences, 2 East 63rd St., New York, N.Y. 10021. For books of high quality in the field of science for children; in two cateogires: Younger Children and Older Children.

EDGAR ALLEN POE AWARD

Mystery Writers of America, 105 East 19th St., New York, N.Y. 10003. For best juvenile mystery.

GEORGE C. STONE CENTER FOR CHILDREN'S BOOKS RECOGNITION OF MERIT AWARDS

Claremont Reading Conference, Claremont Graduate School, Claremont, Cal. 91711. For a children's book that arouses "awareness of the beauty and complexity of their expanding universe."

WESTERN HERITAGE JUVENILE BOOK AWARD

National Cowboy Hall of Fame and Western Heritage Center, 1700 N.E. 63rd St., Oklahoma City, Okla. 73111. For a juvenile best portraying the authentic American West.

WESTERN WRITERS OF AMERICA SPUR AWARDS

Western Writers of America, Inc., 1505 West D St., North Platt, Neb. 69101. For best western juvenile in two categories: Fiction and Nonfiction.

WOODWARD SCHOOL ANNUAL BOOK AWARD

Woodward School, 321 Clinton Ave., Brooklyn, N.Y.

11205. For a children's book which best demonstrates good human relations.

REGIONAL AND STATE AWARDS

CHILDREN'S READING ROUND TABLE AWARD

Chicago Chapter, Children's Reading Round Table, Caroline Rubin, ed., 1321 East 56th St., Chicago, Ill. 60637. Given to a Midwesterner for oustanding achievements in children's literature.

COMMONWEALTH CLUB OF CALIFORNIA LITERATURE AWARD

Commonwealth Club of California, Monadnock Arcade, 681 Market St., San Francisco, Cal. 94105. Given to best juvenile book by a Californian.

INDIANA AUTHORS' DAY AWARDS

Indiana University Writers' Conference, 464 Ballantine Hall, Bloomington, Ind. 47401. Given to most distinguished juvenile books by Indiana authors for three categories: Young Children, Children, Young Adults.

NEWARK COLLEGE OF ENGINEERING'S NEW JERSEY AUTHOR CITATIONS

Newark College of Engineering, Dr. Herman A. Estrin, Department of Humanities, 323 High St., Newark, N.J. 07102. Given to notable authors of children's books who are New Jersey natives or residents.

NORTH CAROLINA DIVISION AMERICAN ASSOCIATION OF UNIVERSITY WOMEN'S AWARD IN JUVENILE LITERATURE

North Carolina Literary and Historical Association, 109 East Jones St., Raleigh, N.C. 27611. Given to best children's book by a North Carolina resident.

OHIOANA BOOK AWARD

Ohioana Library Association, 1109 Ohio Departments Building, Columbus, Ohio 43215. Given to an Ohio author for an outstanding children's book.

RUTGERS AWARD

Graduate School of Library Service, Rutgers University, New Brunswick, N.J. 08903. Given at irregular intervals to New Jersey residents for "distinguished contribution to literature for children."

LASTING CONTRIBUTIONS TO CHILDREN'S LITERATURE

REGINA MEDAL

Catholic Library Association, 461 West Lancaster Ave., Haverford, Penna. 19041. For "continued distinguished contribution to children's literature."

UNIVERSITY OF SOUTHERN MISSISSIPPI CHILDREN'S COLLECTION MEDALLION

University of Southern Mississippi Book Festival, USM Library, Hattiesburg, Miss. 39401. For writer or illustrator who has made an "outstanding contribution to the field of children's literature."

AWARDS BASED ON CHILDREN'S CHOICES

DOROTHY CANFIELD FISHER CHILDREN'S BOOK AWARD

Vermont State PTA and State Department of Libraries, Janice J. Byington, Award Chairman, Craftsbury Common,

Vt. 05827. Chosen by Vermont school children from a list of thirty titles.

College of Education, University of Georgia, Athens, Ga. 30601. Chosen by Georgia school children voting from a list of twenty titles.

SUE HEFLEY AWARD
Louisiana Association of School Librarians, P.O. Box 131, Baton Rouge, La. 70821. Chosen by Louisiana school children in Grades 4–8, voting from a master list.

NENE AWARD
Children's Section of Hawaii Library Association and Hawaii Association of School Librarians. Chosen by vote of Hawaii school children.

NEW ENGLAND ROUND TABLE OF CHILDREN'S LIBRARIANS AWARD
New England Round Table of Children's Librarians, Mrs. Ann A. Flowers, Wayland Public Library, Wayland, Mass. 01778. Chosen by children's votes from a master list of books which have been consistently popular.

PACIFIC NORTHWEST YOUNG READERS CHOICE AWARD
Pacific Northwest Library Association. Chosen by vote of children in Grades 4–8 in Washington, Oregon, Montana, Idaho, and British Columbia from a list of fifteen titles.

SEQUOYAH CHILDREN'S BOOK AWARD
Oklahoma Library Association. Chosen by Oklahoma children in Grades 4–8, voting from a master list.

CHARLIE MAY SIMON CHILDREN'S BOOK AWARD
Elementary School Council, Department of Education, Little Rock, Ark. 72201. Chosen by Arkansas school children in Grades 4–6, voting from a master list.

WILLIAM ALLEN WHITE CHILDREN'S BOOK AWARD
William Allen White Memorial Library, Kansas State Teachers College, Emporia, Kans. 66801. Chosen by Kansas school children in Grades 4–8, voting from a master list.

OTHER ENGLISH-SPEAKING COUNTRIES

IBBY HONOR LIST
International Board on Books for Young People (through Children's Book Council, 67 Irving Place, New York, N.Y. 10003). Two books from each National Section of IBBY, representing the best in children's literature from each country (chosen every two years).

Australia
AUSTRALIAN BOOK OF THE YEAR AWARD
Australian Children's Book Council. Awards in two categories: Picture Book and Book of the Year.

Canada
CANADIAN LIBRARY AWARDS BOOK OF THE YEAR FOR CHILDREN
Canadian Library Association, 151 Sparks St., Ottawa KIP 5E3, Canada. Awards in two categories: English Language, and French.

AMELIA FRANCES HOWARD-GIBBON MEDAL
Canadian Library Association, 151 Sparks St., Ottawa KIP 5E3, Canada. For outstanding illustration in Canadian children's books.

England
CARNEGIE MEDAL
British Library Association, 7 Ridgmount St., Store St., London W.C.1, England. For a children's book of outstanding merit.

ELEANOR FARJEON AWARD
Children's Book Circle. Given to an individual "for distinguished services to children's books."

THE GUARDIAN AWARD FOR CHILDREN'S FICTION
The Guardian, 164 Deansgate, Manchester, England. For an outstanding work of fiction for children.

KATE GREENAWAY MEDAL
British Library Association, 7 Ridgmount St., Store St., London W.C.1, England. For the most distinguished work in the illustration of children's books.

THE TIMES EDUCATIONAL SUPPLEMENT INFORMATION BOOK AWARD
Times Newspaper Ltd., Printing House Square, London E.C.4, England. For a distinguished book of nonfiction for children.

WHITBREAD AWARD FOR CHILDREN'S BOOKS
Booksellers Association of Great Britain and Ireland, 154 Buckingham Palace Road, London 5W1W, 9TZ, England. For a book for children age 7 and older.

For more information about these and other awards, including lists of the prize winners, see *Children's Books: Awards and Prizes*, published biennially by The Children's Book Council, Inc., 67 Irving Place, New York, N.Y. 10003.

Appendix B Book Selection Aids*

GUIDES TO OPERATING THE SCHOOL LIBRARY MEDIA CENTER

1. *Book and Non-book Media: Annotated Guide to Selection Aids for Educational Materials.* Flossie L. Perkins. National Council of Teachers of English, 1111

*Prices subject to change.

Kenyon Road, Urbana, Ill. 61801. 1972. 298 pp. $4.95.

This revised and expanded version of *Book Selection Media* contains guides to more than 250 selection aids for books, pamphlets, films, and records for all ages. Includes references to specific subject matter, such as Mexico and Mexican-Americans, and educators guide to free materials. Indexed for special interest and age groups, this bulletin is well-organized and includes all bibliographic materials, costs, addresses, and evaluation of specific book selection aids.

2. *Children Are Centers for Understanding Media.* Susan Rice and Rose Mukerji, eds. Association for Childhood Educational International, 3615 Wisconsin Avenue, N.W., Washington, D.C. 20016. 1973. 89 pp. $3.95.

   The editors define literature as perceiving, creating, and communicating with greater awareness of the world and one's own identity. Thirteen specialists suggest ways to help children become "literate" in sight and sound technology. Also includes bibliographies and sources of films, equipment, and supplies.

3. *Creating a School Media Program.* John T. Gillespie and Diana L. Spirt. R. R. Bowker Company, Bowker Order Department, P.O. Box 1807, Ann Arbor, Mich. 48106. 1973. 237 pp. $11.50.

   A "how to" guide for initiating and organizing a media center in a school. Chapters on staff tasks, evaluation, developing objectives, and converting a traditional school library to a media center. Appendices include criteria for selecting educational media and audiovisual equipment.

4. *Educational Media Yearbook.* James W. Brown, ed. R. R. Bowker, Bowker Order Department, P. O. Box 1807, Ann Arbor, Mich. 48106. 1973. 453 pp. $19.75.

   Forty-one articles, surveys, and reports covering such subjects as multimedia publishing, university film rental libraries, and graduate training of media personnel. A multimedia resources directory lists some 1,200 print and nonprint items dealing with AV. Lists of organizations, foundations, and federal funding agencies are included.

5. *Issues in Children's Book Selection.* R. R. Bowker Company, P.O. Box 1807, Ann Arbor, Mich. 48106. 1973. 225 pp. $9.95.

   A collection of twenty-nine articles which were originally published in the *School Library Journal* and *Library Journal* between March 1968 and May 1973. The articles share a basic theme: the need for more respect for the intelligence and sophistication of children. They cover a range of topics from censorship to ethnic images.

6. *Media Programs.* The American Association of School Librarians, ALA, and The Association for Educational Communications and Technology, NEA. The American Library Association, 50 East Huron Street, Chicago, Ill. 60611. 1975. 128 pp. $2.95.

Presents the new official standards for school library media programs jointly established by these two associations. An essential for every elementary and secondary school library.

7. *A Multimedia Approach to Children's Literature.* Ellin Greene and Madalynne Schoenfeld, comps. The American Library Association, 50 East Huron Street, Chicago, Ill. 60611. 1972. 288 pp. $3.75.

   A selective list of films, filmstrips, and recordings based on books for children from preschool to Grade 8. Entries are indexed by author, subject, film, and recordings. A directory of distributors, along with buying information, is included. This is a useful guide for anyone working with children.

8. *Problems in School Media Management: Bowker Series in Problem-Centered Approaches to Librarianship.* Peggy Sullivan. R. R. Bowker, Bowker Order Department, P.O. Box 1807, Ann Arbor, Mich. 48106. 1971. 245 pp. $10.75.

   Outlining a series of thirty case studies based on actual situations, the author discusses such issues as conflicts between librarians and other school personnel and attempts at censorship by the community.

9. *The School Library Media Center: A Force for Educational Excellence,* 2nd ed. Ruth Ann Davis. R. R. Bowker, Bowker Order Department, P.O. Box 1807, Ann Arbor, Mich. 48106. 1974. 476 pp. $12.50.

   Focuses on the interdependency of the school library media program and the total instructional program of the school. Includes discussions of the role of the media specialist, guidelines for selecting materials, development of library programs for curriculum areas, mini-units, book evaluation guidelines, and an extensive bibliography.

10. *Steps to Service. A Handbook of Procedures for the School Library Media Center.* Mildred L. Nickel. The American Library Association, 50 East Huron Street, Chicago, Ill. 60611. 1975.

    A practical manual of recommended procedures for the maintenance of a school library media center. The author considers such basic concerns as budget, evaluation and selection of materials, use of media, and the challenge of censors.

Reference Books

1. *Books for Elementary School Libraries: An Initial Collection.* Elizabeth D. Hodges, comp. and ed. The American Library Association, 50 East Huron Street, Chicago, Ill. 60611. 1969. 321 pp. $7.50.

   Over 3,000 books appropriate for children in grades K-8 are annotated. Books are selected to reflect children's interests and to support curricular demands. This list is recommended by the editor as a first-year collection in a new school library.

2. *Children's Books: Awards and Prizes.* Children's Book Council, Inc., 67 Irving Place, New York, N.Y. 10003. 1975. 176 pp. $4.95.

Revised periodically, this paperback lists over sixty U.S. children's book awards; awards given in Australia, Canada, Great Britain, and New Zealand are included as well. Each award is preceded by a brief history that includes sponsor, criteria, and the form in which recognition is given. An invaluable reference source.

3. *Children's Books in Print.* R. R. Bowker, Bowker Order Department, P.O. Box 1807, Ann Arbor, Mich. 48106. 1974. $20.00.

Including almost every children's book in print from K-12, the 41,000 titles are arranged alphabetically in author, title, and illustrator indexes. A fourth index provides addresses for ordering books from some 500 publishers. Published annually.

4. *Children's Catalog,* 12th ed. Rachel Fidell and Estelle A. Fidell, eds. The H. W. Wilson Company, 950 University Avenue, Bronx, N.Y. 10452. 1971. 1,156 pp. $25.00.

A new edition every five years, kept up-to-date by four annual paper supplements, this is one of the most useful and comprehensive lists in the field of children's literature. It contains some 5,119 titles. Part 1 is a classified list giving author, title, publisher, date, price, approximate grade level, and brief synopsis. Part 2 is an alphabetical author, title, and subject index to all the books. A directory of publishers and distributors is included in Part 3. The intent is to list "the best books for children in the fields of fiction and nonfiction."

5. *Children's Literature: A Guide to Reference Sources.* Virginia Haviland, *et al.,* comp. Library of Congress, Superintendent of Documents, U.S. Government Printing Office, Washington, D.C. 20402. 1966. 341 pp. $2.50.
First Supplement, 1972. Compiled with the assistance of Margaret N. Coughlan. 316 pp. $3.00.

A comprehensive guide to many reference sources in children's literature, this annotated bibliography describes books, articles, and pamphlets concerned with the study of children's books in this country and throughout the world. It has an especially useful section on the historical development of children's books. The supplement lists 746 titles with analytical annotations. It has two new sections, "Publishing and Promotion" and "Teaching Children's Literature." An invaluable bibliography for the serious student of children's literature.

6. *Choosing a Child's Book.* Children's Book Council, 67 Irving Place, New York, N.Y. 10003. Newly revised, 1973. Single copies available free for a stamped self-addressed envelope; 50 copies for $2.00.

This CBC pamphlet has been distributed to over a million adults in libraries, at book fairs, and in bookstores.

7. *The Elementary School Library Collection,* 8th ed. Mary Virginia Gaver, *et. al.,* eds. The Bro-Dart Foundation, 124 Church Street, New Brunswick, N.J. 08901. Approximately 830 pp. $19.50 each, or, two years at $33.00.

This work is designed as a guide for the acquisition of a balanced elementary school collection of good quality. Phase 1 represents a minimum collection for the smallest school library. Phases 2 and 3 include professional and audiovisual materials, as well as children's books. Arranged in Dewey Decimal call number sequence, entries consist of a reproduction of an actual catalogue card for each title in the collection. The eighth edition contains over 10,000 listings. New material as well as listings from previous editions have been reviewed and compared.

8. *Folklore: An Annotated Bibliography and Index to Single Editions.* Elsie B. Ziegler. F. W. Faxon Company, Westwood, Mass. 1973. 213 pp. $12.00.

A helpful bibliography for teachers and librarians interested in locating appropriate folklore for story hours, study units, and research. Entries are annotated and indexed by title, subject, motif, country, type of folklore and illustrator. Increased interest in single editions of favorite old tales makes this a particularly needed index.

9. *Index to Fairy Tales, 1949–1972, Including Folklore, Legends and Myths in Collections.* Norma Olin Ireland. F. W. Faxon Company. Westwood, Mass. 1973. 779 pp. $18.00.

Covering some 400 collections, this index lists author, editor or compiler, subject (location, character, and so on) of individual tales; as well as titles. The completeness of subject entries and the clarity of format make this book a useful reference source for teachers and librarians.

10. *Index to Poetry for Children and Young People: 1964–1969.* 1972 ed. John E. Brewton, Sara W. Brewton, and G. Meredith, comps. Blackburn, Ill. The H. W. Wilson Company, 950 University Avenue, Bronx, N.Y. 10452. $20.00.

This new edition is in effect an extension of the three previous volumes titled *Index to Children's Poetry.* This volume indexes some 117 collections of poems for children and young people with title, subject, author, and first-line entries. More than 11,000 poems are classified under some 2,000 subjects.

11. *Index to Young Reader's Collective Biographies,* 2nd ed. Judith Silverman, ed. R. R. Bowker, Bowker Order Department, P.O. Box 1807, Ann Arbor, Mich. 48106. 1975. 322 pp. $14.95.

Indexes by individual and subject 5,833 biographies in 720 collections of biographies which are suitable for students at the elementary through junior high school levels.

12. *Junior High School Library Catalog,* 2nd ed. The H. W. Wilson Company, 950 University Avenue, Bronx, N.Y. 10452. 1970. $30.00. Supplements free.

Includes four annual supplements listing titles of fiction and nonfiction appropriate for use at the junior high school level. Full bibliographic information is given, along with descriptive and critical annotations. Elementary teachers and librarians need to know this reference book, since some mature readers in the elementary school will be ready for titles on this list.

13. *Paperback Books for Young People: An Annotated Guide to Publishers and Distributors.* John T. Gillespie and Diana L. Spirt. American Library Association, 50 East Huron Street, Chicago, Ill. 60611. 1972. 186 pp. $5.00.

Approximately 100 of the most prominent paperback publishers are listed and described. Distributors of paperbacks in the United States, arranged by state, are listed, and indications of their services are given. An annotated listing of selection aids for paperback books is also featured. Indispensable for setting up a school paperback bookstore.

14. *Periodicals for School Libraries: A Guide to Magazines, Newspapers, and Periodical Indexes,* rev. ed. Marian H. Scott, comp. and ed. The American Library Association, 50 East Huron Street, Chicago, Ill. 60611. 1973. 292 pp. $4.95.

Over 500 periodicals for children from kindergarten through Grade 12 are evaluated. Items are selected to meet standards and to correspond to a wide range of interests, reading levels, and curricular demands. The titles are coded to indicate suitability for various grade levels. Included are key foreign and ethnic periodicals.

15. *Subject Guide to Children's Books in Print.* R. R. Bowker, Bowker Order Department, P.O. Box 1807, Ann Arbor, Mich. 48106. 1974. $20.00.

Arranges the same titles as *Children's Books in Print* under 7,000 subject categories based on the tenth edition of the Sears Catalog and the Library of Congress cataloging information. A valuable aid for enriching subject collections or helping readers find more books on favorite topics. Published each year.

General Booklists

1. *Adventuring with Books: 2,400 Titles for Pre-K-Grade 8,* 2nd ed. Shelton L. Root, Jr., and a Committee of the Council, comps. National Council of Teachers of English. Citation Press, Education Services Division, Scholastic Magazines, Inc., 904 Sylvan Avenue, Englewood Cliffs, N.J. 07632. 1973. 402 pp. $1.95.

A classified bibliography of old favorites and books of recent publication. Most titles have been published since 1967. Books are briefly annotated; price, date, and age levels are included. Listings are arranged by fourteen broad subjects, with author and title indexes. Revised periodically.

2. *The Best in Children's Books: The University of Chicago Guide to Children's Literature 1966-1972.* Zena Sutherland, ed. University of Chicago, The University of Chicago Press, Chicago, Ill. 60637. 1973. 484 pp. $9.95.

Included are 1,400 comprehensive reviews which have been selected from *The Bulletin of the Center for Children's Books.* Titles are alphabetically arranged by author and indexed by title, developmental values, curricular use, reading level, subject matter, and type of literature. Publication and buying information is also included. A useful guide to literature of quality for children.

3. *Bibliography of Books for Children.* Sylvia Sunderlin, ed. The Association for Childhood Education International, 3615 Wisconsin Avenue, N.W., Washington, D.C. 20016. 1974. 128 pp. $2.75. Revised every three years.

Presents the best books reviewed by *Childhood Education* during the preceding two years. It covers a wide range of interests and reading abilities. Includes over 1,500 entries that are annotated, priced, and grouped by age levels. This booklist is well indexed, and cross-references are included.

4. *Children and Books,* 4th ed. May Hill Arbuthnot and Zena Sutherland. Scott, Foresman and Co., 1900 East Lake Avenue, Gleview, Ill. 60025. 1972. 836 pp. $12.25.

This well-known textbook on children's literature includes extensive bibliographies of children's books which have been expanded and updated from previous editions. This edition also contains information on the media center, minorities, censorship, and television.

5. *Children's Books.* Virginia Haviland and Lois B. Watt, comps. Superintendent of Documents, U.S. Government Printing Office, Washington, D.C. 20402. 1974. 16 pp. 15¢.

An annual list which contains about 200 annotations of outstanding books for preschool through junior high school. Books are arranged by subject; age group and reading levels are indicated. Earlier lists are available.

6. *Children's Books of International Interest: A Selection from Four Decades of American Publishing.* Virginia Haviland, ed. American Library Association, 50 East Huron Street, Chicago, Ill. 60611. 1972. 69 pp. $2.50.

Selection of over 300 titles which have been

individually re-evaluated for literary value and universality of interest. This list encompasses over forty years of children's book productions and was published in the hope of stimulating an exchange of children's literature over international borders.

7. *Children's Books of the Year.* The Child Study Association of America, eds. 50 Madison Avenue, New York, N.Y. 10010. 42 pp. $2.50 plus 35¢ postage.

   Compiled annually, this is a classified, annotated bibliography of about 600 books. Titles are grouped by age, from preschool through early teens, and subdivided into categories such as "Fantasy,," "Children in Other Lands," "Easy to Read," "Adventure and Mystery," "Sports," "Mostly about Animals," "Science Fiction." Title index.

8. *Children's Books Too Good to Miss,* 6th ed. May Hill Arbuthnot, *et. al.* Western Reserve University Press, 11000 Cedar Road, Cleveland, Ohio 44106. 1971. 97 pp. $2.95.

   A small, but excellent, booklist of almost 300 titles that includes the "classics" of today and yesterday. The annotations are well done, as is a fine section on "The Artist and Children's Books." Entries are classified by age groups and within age groups by type of book.

9. *Fanfare: The Horn Book's Honor List, 1966–1970.* The Horn Book Committee, eds. *The Horn Book Magazine,* 585 Boylston Street, Boston, Mass. 02116. 1971. 15¢.

   A classified list of books for preschool-twelfth grade, chosen by the reviewing editors for *The Horn Book Magazine* as the best books for this five-year period.

10. *Growing Up with Books.* R. R. Bowker Company, eds. 1180 Avenue of the Americas, New York, N.Y. 10036. 1975. 32 pp. Revised annually. 100 copies for $11.00.

    Lists about 200 books in a pocket-sized paperback. Entries are classified by age and interest, and include brief annotations. Prepared for quantity distribution to PTA's, libraries, bookstores, and civic clubs.

11. *Growing Up with Paperbacks.* R. R. Bowker Company, eds. 1180 Avenue of the Americas, New York, N.Y. 10036. 1975. 32 pp. Revised biennially. 100 copies for $11.00.

    Lists about 200 paperback books. Titles are arranged by age levels and by interest, and are briefly annotated. Prepared for quantity distribution to PTA's, libraries, bookstores, and civic clubs.

12. *Let's Read Together: Books for Family Enjoyment,* 3rd ed. Committee of National Congress of Parents and Teachers, and Children's Services Division, American Library Association, eds. ALA, 50 East Huron Street, Chicago, Ill. 60611. 1969. 116 pp. $2.00.

An annotated bibliography of over 550 books for children from the youngest to 15 years old. Arranged by categories of reader interest and age level. Intended as an aid to parents in selecting books for their children, for family reading aloud, individual reading, and a child's own library.

13. *Notable Children's Books, 1940–1959.* American Library Association, 50 East Huron Street, Chicago, Ill. 60611. 1966. 48 pp. $1.50.

    The annual Notable Children's Books lists provide the basis for this selection of nearly 300 children's books. Each of the titles has been re-evaluated after at least a five-year period of use. Those of enduring worth and interest to children are included in this twenty-year reappraisal.

14. *Notable Children's Books.* Compiled annually by the Book Evaluation Committee, Children's Services Division, American Library Association, 50 East Huron Street, Chicago, Ill. 60611. 1974. One copy free when accompanied by self-addressed envelope and 20¢ in stamps; quantity rates.

    Each year an ALA committee selects what it considers to be the distinctive books of the preceding year. The list first appears in the April issue of the ALA Bulletin. It contains brief annotations in a leaflet format. Good distribution pieces to help stimulate interest in current books.

15. *Paperback Books for Children.* The Committee on Paperback Lists for Elementary School of the American Library Association, comps. Citation Press, Education Services Division, Scholastic Magazines, Inc., 904 Sylvan Avenue, Englewood Cliffs, N.J. 07632. 1972. 130 pp. 95¢.

    Classified list of 700 titles. Brief annotations and general grade levels are given. Useful in setting up a paperback bookstore in the school.

16. *A Parent's Guide to Children's Reading,* 4th ed. Nancy Larrick. Bantam Books, Inc., 666 Fifth Avenue, New York, N.Y. 10019. 1975. 374 pp. $1.95.

    This well-known handbook for parents suggests appropriate titles for children's reading at each stage of their development. Special chapters on television, language development, poetry, and paperbacks are particularly useful. A section on how reading is taught today will answer many parental questions.

17. *Reading Ladders for Human Relations,* 5th ed. Virginia M. Reid and a Committee from the National Council of Teachers of English, eds. The American Council on Education, 1785 Massachusetts Avenue, N.W., Washington, D.C. 20036. 1972. 346 pp. $3.95.

    A classified, annotated bibliography of nearly 1,500 titles for kindergarten through Grade 12. Titles are grouped under four headings: "Creating a Positive Self-Image," "Living with Others," "Appreciating Different Cultures," and "Coping with Change." Under each thematic heading books are arranged in order of difficulty, providing the "reading ladders." Instructional strategies are suggested to increase the sensitivities of young readers. This is a unique bibliography that emphasizes values in books.

18. *The Wide World of Children's Books: An Exhibition for International Book Year*. Virginia Haviland, comp. Library of Congress, Washington, D.C., Superintendent of Documents, U.S. Government Printing Office. 1972. 84 pp. 50¢.

Lists and annotates 138 titles which represent thirty-eight countries. These books were chosen to honor UNESCO's designation of 1972 as International Book Year, and were selected for attractiveness, intrinsic excellence, and importance within a national body of literature.

Specialized Book Lists

1. *AAAS Science Book List for Children*. Hilary J. Deason, comp. American Association for the Advancement of Science, 1515 Massachusetts Avenue, N.W., Washington, D.C. 20005. 1972. 253 pp. $1.50.

This is the third edition of an annotated list of over 1,500 science and mathematics trade books for children in the elementary school.

2. *About 100 Books: A Gateway to Better Intergroup Understanding*. Ann G. Wolfe. The American Jewish Committee, 165 East 56th Street, New York, N.Y. 10022. 1972. 75¢.

This is the seventh edition of an annotated list of children's books that reflect events and problems in intergroup relations. Many of these books would be useful for values clarification.

3. *American History in Juvenile Books: A Chronological Guide*. Seymour Metzner, ed. The H. W. Wilson Company, 950 University Avenue, Bronx, N.Y. 10452. 1966. 329 pp. $10.00.

A graded bibliography which is arranged chronologically, beginning with Grade 3 and continuing through Grade 7. Over 2,000 titles of juvenile trade books relating to American history are included. A useful reference.

4. *Behavior Patterns in Children's Books: A Bibliography*. Clara J. Kircher, comp. Catholic University Press of America, Washington, D.C. 1966. 132 pp. $1.95.

This annotated bibliography of over 500 books is organized under twenty-two different headings—such as "Honesty," "Facing Up to One's Fears," "Understanding Those Who Are Different." The chapter "From Tomboy to Young Woman" perpetuates prescribed sex roles. The books mentioned in some sections would be useful for values clarification.

5. *The Best of the Best*. Walter Scherf, ed. Catalogs of the International Youth Library: R. R. Bowker Company. Bowker Order Department, Box 1807, Ann Arbor, Mich. 48106. 1971. 189 pp. $9.50 in U.S. and Canada.

A bilingual catalogue which provides information on about 1,500 children's books representing fifty-seven countries or languages. Titles were selected by librarians of the International Youth Library in collaboration with book experts from individual countries. Countries are alphabetically arranged, and titles are given in the major language of the country, with English and German translations. The entries are not annotated and no publication dates are given.

6. *Best-selling Children's Books*. Jean Spealman Kujoth. Scarecrow Press, Inc., 52 Liberty Street, Metuchen, N.J. 08840. 1973. 305 pp. $7.50.

Identifies and describes 958 books now in print which have sold 100,000 copies or more since publication. Information is provided as to number of copies sold, type of book, year of publication, author, title, illustrator, subject-category, and age level.

7. *The Black American in Books for Children: Readings in Racism*. With an introduction by Donnarae MacCann. MacCann and Gloria Woodard, eds. The Scarecrow Press, Inc., 52 Liberty Street, Metuchen, N.J. 08840. 1972. 223 pp.

The whole issue of racism in books for children is explored in this collection of articles. Many books are cited as examples of varying points of view.

8. *The Black Experience in Children's Books*. Barbara Rollock, selector. New York Public Library, Office of Branch Libraries, 8 East 40th Street, New York, N.Y. 10016. 1974. 128 pp. $2.50.

An updating of the very popular list first selected by Augusta Baker. It includes an annotated list of more than 900 titles of books that present the black experience in the United States, South and Central America, the Caribbean, Africa, and England. The introduction clearly states the criteria which were used in the selection of these books.

9. *Books for Friendship*, 3rd ed. Mary Ester McWhirter, ed. American Friends Service Committee and Anti-Defamation leage of B'nai B'rith. 1962. 63 pp. *1968 Supplement*. American Friends Service Committee, 160 North 15th Street, Philadelphia, Penna. 19102. 1968. $1.25.

A classified, annotated bibliography of books for ages 6–15. Supplement updates the original list.

10. *British Children's Books in the Twentieth Century*. Frank Eyre, ed. E. P. Dutton and Co., Inc., 201 Park Avenue South, New York, N.Y. 10003. 1973. 153 pp. $7.95.

A revised and enlarged edition of a book published in England as *20th Century Children's Books*. The present edition is a critical study of the British contribution to modern children's literature. The appendices contain a brief acknowledgment of writing for children that has come from Australia, Canada, and so on.

11. *Children and Poetry, A Selective, Annotated Bibliography.* Virginia Haviland and William Jay Smith, comps. Library of Congress, Superintendent of Documents, U.S. Government Printing Office, Washington, D.C. 20402. 1970. 67 pp. 75¢.

   This bibliography includes five sections: "Rhymes," "Poetry of the Past," "Twentieth Century Poetry," "Anthologies," and "World Poetry." The items are annotated, and illustrations are reproduced from the books listed. Some fine anthologies, such as Nancy Larrick's *On City Streets*, are not included, however.

12. *Children's Book Showcase.* The Children's Book Council, eds. 67 Irving Place. New York, N.Y. 10003. 1975. 64 pp. $5.95.

   Lists the titles which have been selected as the best designed/illustrated children's books published in the U.S. during the previous year. Judges' critiques are included, along with bibliographic and design information and a small black-and-white two-page illustration. This is the catalogue for "The Showcase Exhibit." One is produced every year by the Children's Book Council.

13. *Children's Books and Recordings Suggested as Holiday Gifts.* New York Public Library Committee, eds. Office of Branch Libraries, 8 East 40th Street, New York, N.Y. 10016. Annual. $2.00.

   Each year during November and December an exhibition of children's books suggested as holiday gifts has been held in the central Children's Room of the New York Public Library. A catalogue of annotated titles is available.

14. *Films Kids Like.* Susan Rice, ed., Published for the Center for Understanding Media. American Library Association, 50 East Huron Street, Chicago, Ill. 60611. 1973. 150 pp. $5.50.

   A selected, annotated list of approximately 225 "child-tested" short films. Gives children's responses and reproductions of pictures that children drew of some of the films.

15. *Folklore of the North American Indians: An Annotated Bibliography.* Judith C. Ullom, comp., with a foreword by Virginia Haviland. Library of Congress, Superintendent of Documents, U.S. Government Printing Office, Washington, D.C. 20402. 1969. 126 pp. $2.25.

   This bibliography contains 152 annotated items which range from early collections to current retellings of American Indian stories. Introductions with folklore background are included for each section representing one of the eleven North American culture areas.

16. *Good and Inexpensive Books for Children.* The Associa-

tion for Childhood Education International, ed. 3615 Wisconsin Avenue, N.W., Washington, D.C. 20016. 1972. 62 pp. $2.00. Formerly titled *Children's Books . . . for $1.50 or less.*

   This revision lists about 500 worthwhile but inexpensive books for children through Grade 6. Arranged alphabetically, classified, and briefly annotated.

17. *Good Reading for the Disadvantaged Reader: Multiethnic Resources.* George D. Spache. Garrard, 2 Overhill Road, Scarsdale, N.Y. 10583. 1970. 212 pp. $4.25.

   This volume contains materials on how to build a positive self-concept, and lists books by age levels for use with various minorities, including Puerto Ricans and Eskimos. It also lists books for adult literacy programs.

18. *Good Reading for Poor Readers,* rev. ed. George Spache, comp. Garrard, 2 Overhill Road, Scarsdale, N.Y. 10583. 1972. $4.95.

   A list of easy books for the reluctant reader in the elementary school. Each title is annotated and graded, and a special reading level is given for each book. Includes trade books, series, magazines, newspapers, programmed materials, and textual materials. Especially useful for teachers of Grades 4 through 7.

19. *Growing Up with Science Books,* 9th ed. R. R. Bowker Company, ed. 1180 Avenue of the Americas, New York, N.Y. 10036. 1974. 36 pp. 100 copies for $11.00.

   Lists about 200 titles that are of interest for today's child with scientific interests. Similar to the booklet *Growing Up with Books,* the entries are annotated, priced, and classified within five different age groupings. They are excellent for distribution by PTA's, libraries, or booksellers.

20. *I Read, You Read, We Read; I See, You See, We See; I Hear, You Hear, We Hear; I Learn, You Learn, We Learn.* Children's Services Division, American Library Association, 50 East Huron Street, Chicago, Ill. 60611. 1971. 112 pp. $2.00.

   A guide to materials for volunteers and others working with the culturally different child. It includes books to read, films to see, records and tapes to hear.

21. *Image of the Black in Children's Fiction.* Dorothy Broderick. R. R. Bowker Company, Bowker Order Department, Box 1807, Ann Arbor, Mich. 48106. 1973. 215 pp. $13.50.

   This study examines stereotypes and racism in children's literature, and considers historical developments. It includes bibliographies, indexes, and references to standard selection tools.

22. *Introducing Books: A Guide for the Middle Grades.* John T. Gillespie and Diana L. Lembo. R. R. Bowker, Bowker Order Department, P.O. Box 1807, Ann Arbor, Mich. 48106. 1970. 318 pp. $10.95.

Plot summaries of eighty-eight books for 9–14-year-olds are given in this companion volume to *Juniorplots*. Selections are organized around eleven developmental themes which are stressed in the middle-grade curriculum. Related books and audiovisual materials are suggested.

23. *Juniorplots: A Book Talk Manual for Teachers and Librarians.* John T. Gillespie and Diana L. Lembo. R. R. Bowker, Bowker Order Department, P.O. Box 1807, Ann Arbor, Mich. 48106. 1967. 222 pp. $9.95.

Plot summaries of eighty books arranged according to eight basic behavioral themes are included in this publication. Books have been selected for readers from 9–16 years. The introduction provides a guide to preparing and delivering book talks.

24. *Literature by and about the American Indian.* Anna Lee Stensland. National Council of Teachers of English, 1111 Kenyon Road, Urbana, Ill. 61801. 1973. 208 pp. $4.75.

An annotated bibliography for junior and senior high school students. Annotations include brief summaries, suggestions as to good and bad points of the book, and information about the author. Selections range from myths and legends to fiction, history, and anthropology. Study guides to selected books are also included.

25. *Little Miss Muffet Fights Back*, rev. ed. Feminists on Children's Media, comps. Feminist Book Mart, 162–11 Ninth Avenue, Whitestone, N.Y. 11357. 1974. 62 pp. $1.00.

A bibliography of recommended nonsexist books about girls. Books were chosen for this list because they portray girls and women as active, vital human beings, or because they further understanding of social conditions and the choices which are related to them. The annotations range from picture books to books for older readers. Also includes an annotated list of recommended readings on sexism in children's books and education.

26. *Matters of Fact: Aspects of Non-fiction for Children.* Margery Fisher. Thomas Y. Crowell, 201 Park Avenue, S., New York, N.Y. 10003. 1972. 488 pp. $11.95.

This critical discussion by a noted British writer is a valuable resource for aid in selecting and evaluating nonfiction for children. Although many of the books discussed are British, some familiar U.S. titles are included. Criteria established may be applied to all informational books.

27. *Music Books for the Elementary School Library.* Peggy Flanagan Baird, comp. Music Educators National Conference, 1201 16th Street, N.W., Washington, D.C. 20036. 1972. 48 pp. $3.00.

The author has reviewed and annotated this list of about 200 books. Illustrations, grade level, appeal to children, and educational value are discussed.

28. *Picture Books for Children.* Patricia Jean Cianciolo and members of Elementary Booklist Committee of the National Council of Teachers of English, eds. American Library Association, 50 East Huron Street, Chicago, Ill. 60611. 1973. 159 pp. $6.50.

This bibliography of over 375 items presents picture books for children from preschool to high school. Listings provide this information: author, title, illustrator, publisher, year, retail price, age recommendation, and annotation. Particular attention is given to the artistic impact of these books.

29. *Reading, Children's Books and Our Pluralistic Society.* Harold Tanyzer and Jean Karl, comps. and eds. Perspectives in Reading, No. 16, International Reading Association, Box 695, Newark, Del. 19711. 1972. 89 pp. $3.00 to members; $3.50 to nonmembers.

Contains many articles on ethnic literature for children, along with an annotated listing of recent (since 1967) bibliographies on ethnic materials for people of all ages.

30. *Reading with Your Child Through Age 5.* Prepared by the Children's Book Committee of the Child Study Association in cooperation with the staff of the Child-Study-Project Head Start. The Child Study Press, 50 Madison Avenue, New York, N.Y. 10010. 1972. 40 pp. $1.50.

This bulletin starts with an excellent introduction on the values and times to read aloud to your child. It provides an annotated list of 227 favorite books of preschool children, including hard-cover and paperback prices.

31. *Reference and Subscription Books Reviews 1972–74.* Reprinted from *The Booklist*, Vols. 69–70 (September 1, 1972 to July 15, 1974). Prepared by The American Library Association Reference and Subscription Books Review Committee. American Library Association, 50 East Huron Street, Chicago, Ill. 60611. 1975.

Includes 137 reviews of reference books first published in *The Booklist*. Useful to teachers, parents, and librarians as a buyers' and consumer's guide to reference books. Reviews are arranged alphabetically and reprinted in their entirety. Revised periodically.

32. *RIF's Guide to Book Selection.* Reading Is Fundamental, Room 2407 Arts and Industries Building, Smithsonian Institute, Washington, D.C. 20560. 1973. 91 pp. Free.

A briefly annotated list of 1,850 paperbacks for children from preschool through the elementary grades. Includes special lists of books for black, Spanish-speaking, and American Indian children.

33. *Starting Out Right.* Bettye I. Latimer, ed. Children's Literature Review Board. Produced through the

Office of Equal Educational Opportunity, Civil Rights Act (1964), Title IV. Wisconsin Department of Public Instruction. Madison, Wis. 53705. 1972.

This bibliography is a guide for choosing books about black people for children from preschool through Grade 3. Titles are accompanied by a commentary which indicates books which are recommended and those which are not. The editors' concern is in assessing the overall quality of these books and the kinds of images of black people which are conveyed to the reader.

34. *Stories*. Ellin Greene, comp. New York Public Library. Office of Branch Libraries, 8 East 40th Street, New York, N.Y. 10016. 1972. $1.00.

A revised edition of *A List of Stories to Tell and to Read Aloud!* This bulletin suggests proven stories and poems to tell to children. Entries are briefly annotated; age level is not suggested.

35. *Thirty Mid-century Children's Books Every Adult Should Know*. Ethel Heins, rev. *The Horn Book*, Inc., 585 Boylston Street, Boston, Mass. 02116. 1973. 10¢ each or .08¢ for orders of 100 or more. (Send a self-addressed stamped envelope for single copies.)

This collection is a revision of Ruth Hill Viguers' *Thirty Twentieth-century Children's Books Every Adult Should Know*. Annotations of all books appear on the front and back of a single sheet of paper. Fine for handouts at PTA's, civic groups, or classes in children's literature.

36. *We Build Together, A Reader's Guide to Negro Life and Literature for Elementary and High School Use*, 3rd rev. Charlemae Rollins, ed. National Council of Teachers of English, 1111 Kenyon Road, Urbana, Ill. 61801. 1967. 77 pp. $1.65.

This volume contains perceptive and complete annotations of children's books that portray black culture. Shows the changing role of the black person in literature, and discusses stereotypes and language.

37. *Young People's Literature in Series: Fiction, an Annotated Bibliographical Guide*. Judith K. Rosenberg and Kenyon C. Rosenberg, eds. Libraries Unlimited, Inc., Box 263, Littleton, Colo. 80120. 1972. 176 pp. $7.50.

This list describes 1,400 books for children of ages 8–14. Titles listed have been published since 1955. Evaluative annotations are included, and indexes are provided by title and series.

Periodicals

1. *Appraisal: Children's Science Books*. Children's Science Book Review Committee, Longfellow Hall, 13 Appian Way, Cambridge, Mass. 02138. Published three times a year. $4.00 per year. Single copies $1.50.

Each issue contains reviews of about seventy-five children's science books. Two reviews are included for each title—one by a children's librarian and one by a specialist. A useful publication for anyone ordering or recommending science books for children.

2. *Book Review Digest*. The H. W. Wilson Company, 950 University Avenue, Bronx, N.Y. 10452. Published monthly, except February and July. Service basis rate quoted on request.

Evaluates about 4,000 adult and children's books each year. Provides for comparison, as several reviews of a book are listed in one source. Reviews are taken from English and U.S. periodicals devoted to reviewing current literature.

3. *Bookbird*. A quarterly published by the International Board on Books for Young People. Richard Bamberger, ed. U.S. Subscriptions: Package Library of Foreign Children's Books, Inc., 119 Fifth Avenue, New York, N.Y. 10003. $5.00.

An international periodical on literature for children and young people. Includes papers about books and authors in many countries, prize-winning books, and books recommended for translation.

4. *The Booklist*. American Library Association, 50 East Huron Street, Chicago, Ill. 60611. Published twice a month through July and once in August. $20.00 per year.

Reviews both adult and juvenile books, some before publication. The comprehensive reviews are annotated and graded by age levels and grades. Includes reviews of encyclopedias and reference books, along with special topic bibliographies on such subjects as career education, women's liberation, drug education, black Americans. It frequently includes reviews of audiovisual materials, and suggests the kind of library for which the books are recommended. It is the library profession's own reviewing medium, and is a recognized authority in the field.

5. *Book World*. 230 41st Street, New York, N.Y. 10036. Published weekly.

Children's books are reviewed each week in this magazine supplement to the *Washington Post* and *The Chicago Tribune*. Zena Sutherland is editor of the column on children's books. During "Book Week' in the fall and again in the spring a large special edition of the book section features children's books.

6. *The Bulletin of the Center for Children's Books*. Graduate Library School, University of Chicago Press, 5801 Ellis Avenue, Chicago, Ill. 60637. Issued monthly except August. $8.00 per year.

An authoritative reviewing service concerned with critical evaluation of current juvenile books. Reviews include adverse, as well as favorable comments. Each entry is graded and fully annotated with heavy emphasis on the curricular use of the book, developmental values, and literary merit.

7. *The Calendar.* Children's Book Council, 67 Irving Place, New York, N.Y. 10003. A one-time only handling charge of $5.00; no annual fee.

A semi-annual newsletter full of information about children's books, special events, articles, and free and inexpensive materials available from publishers. Titles of prize-winning books and upcoming television programs that are based on children's books are noted. An amazing amout of useful information is provided.

8. *Childhood Education.* Association for Childhood Education International, 3615 Wisconsin Avenue, N.W., Washington, D.C. 20016. Published six times a year in October, November, January, February, March, and May. $12.00 per year (includes membership).

This professional magazine includes a column on children's books that contains annotations for some twenty-five books each issue. The reviews are written by a committee of librarians and subject specialists and are edited by the chairperson. Most reviews are incorporated into successive editions of *Bibliography of Books for Children,* published every three years by the Association.

9. *Children's Literature.* Temple University Press, Philadelphia, Penn. 19122. Published annually. Paperback edition $4.95.

This annual may be purchased separately, or is included in the membership fee of the Children's Literature Association. The contributors to the annual represent many disciplines, including psychology, folklore, sociology, and comparative literature. The content of the articles emphasizes criticism, not teaching techniques.

10. *Children's Literature in Education.* APS Publications, Inc., 150 Fifth Ave., New York, N.Y. 10011. Published four times a year. $15.00 a year.

A British publication devoted to serious criticism of children's literature, and commentary on the role of literature in education. Contributors present varying viewpoints; most of the authors whose work is discussed are familiar to both England and the U.S.

11. *Cricket Magazine.* Open Court Publishing Company, 1058 Eighth Street, LaSalle, Ill. 61301. Published monthly. $13.00 for 12 issues.

This literary magazine for elementary school children includes serializations and excerpts from favorite books, as well as new stories and poems by well-known authors. Regular features are "Meet Your Author"; "Cricket's Bookshelf," with child-oriented reviews; and the "Cricket League," for children's own writing. One of the very few magazines of quality for children.

12. *The Horn Book Magazine.* Horn Book, Inc., 585 Boylston Street, Boston, Mass. 02116. Published six times yearly. $10.50 per year.

Devoted wholly to children's books and reading, this magazine includes detailed reviews of current children's books. Emphasis is placed on the literary quality of the books. Entries are classified by subject and age level. Articles about authors, illustrators, award books, and the history of children's literature are frequently featured. Acceptance papers by the winners of the Newbery and Caldecott Medals, together with biographical pieces about the winners, appear in the August issue each year. In October there is a "Fanfare" list of outstanding books of the preceding year.

13. *The Instructor.* Instructor Publications, Inc., Instructor Park, Dansville, N.Y. 14437. Published monthly with combined August/September and June/July issues. $8.00 per year.

This popular magazine for teachers has a section devoted to books for children that includes annotations, grades, and priced entries. Occasionally, articles concerning children's literature are featured.

14. *Interracial Books for Children.* Council on Interracial Books for Children, Inc., 1841 Broadway, New York, N.Y. 10023. Published eight times per year. $8.00.

This bulletin has many interesting articles related to eradicating racist and sexist materials in both the literature for children and in instructional texts.

15. *Language Arts* (formerly *Elementary English*). National Council of Teachers of English, 1111 Kenyon Road, Urbana, Ill. 61801. Issued monthly, September through May (November/December combined issue). $15.00 per year (including membership in NCTE).

As the official journal of the Elementary Section of the National Council of Teachers of English, this periodical regularly reviews children's books in their "Books for Children" section. Articles about teaching literature in the elementary school; about authors, illustrators, children's reading interests, and research in literature are frequent features of this professional journal.

16. *Media and Methods.* North American Publishing Company, 134 N. 13th Street, Philadelphia, Penna. 19107. Published nine times per year, September through May. $9.00 for one year.

Concerned with the wide use of media in the classroom and contemporary teaching techniques. Geared more to the middle school and high school teacher, it provides useful articles on upcoming television shows, new films and filmstrips, and teaching techniques.

17. *The New York Times Book Review.* New York Times Co., Times Square, New York, N.Y. Published weekly. $13.00 per year.

Book reviews of the latest children's books are

presented each week in a special column of the New York *Times* entitled "For Younger Readers." During "Book Week" in the fall and in mid-May, a special section, the *Book Review*, is devoted to children's books. In the November issue a jury of art experts selects its choices of the ten best-illustrated children's books of the year. Before Christmas the editor's choice of "100 Outstanding Books" is included.

18. *Phaedrus: A Journal of Children's Literature Research.* Phaedrus, Inc., 14 Beacon Street, Boston, Mass. 02108. Published twice a year. $9.00 per year.

A reference tool for those involved in theoretical inquiry and research in children's literature. Each issue contains sections on selected dissertations; periodical literature; antiquarian and new booksellers; and recent bibliographies, catalogues, and studies.

19. *Previews.* R. R. Bowker Company, 1180 Avenue of the Americas, New York, N.Y. 10036. Published nine times per year. $5.00 per year.

A useful selection aid for librarians, media specialists, and all who select nonprint media and equipment for educational use. Contains reviews of audiovisual materials, new listings, and evaluations of equipment needed.

20. *Publishers' Weekly,* "Children's Book Number." R. R. Bowker and Company, 1180 Avenue of the Americas, New York, N.Y. 10036. $20.00 per year.

Twice a year (spring and fall) this "Publisher's Bible" devotes huge issues to children's books. It lists juveniles of all types for all ages and tastes, and includes an index of children's books by author, title, and illustrator. Dates of publication, including forthcoming books, are indicated. Feature articles on children's books are always included in these special issues.

21. *School Library Journal.* R. R. Bowker and Company, 1180 Avenue of the Americas, New York, N.Y. 10036. Issued monthly from September through May. $10.80.

This periodical tries to evaluate every new children's book published each year, covering more than 85 percent of each year's new books for children. It carries over 2,000 critical reviews written by practicing school and public librarians and teachers. Single stars indicate a book's excellence in relation to others of its kind. Entries are arranged by grade levels and subject categories. Articles on current issues in publishing and teaching—such as sexism in children's books and censorship—are regular features of this journal. Each December the editors make their selection of the "Best Books" of the previous year.

22. *School Media Quarterly.* American Association of School Librarians, American Library Association, 50 East Huron Street, Chicago, Ill. 60611. Published four times a year in fall, winter, spring, and summer. AASL membership required. Subscription price of $1.25 a year included in membership dues.

The official journal of the AASL. Many of its articles are relevant to book evaluation and selection processes. Issues on censorship, new standards for media programs, and other concerns of school librarians are discussed.

23. *Science Books.* A Quarterly Review. American Association for the Advancement of Science, 1515 Massachusetts Avenue, N.W., Washington, D.C. 20005. Published quarterly. $10.00 per year.

Reviews trade books, textbooks, and reference works in the pure and applied sciences for students in elementary, junior high, secondary schools, and college, and for those in professional work. About 200 titles are reviewed in each issue. Three levels are given for elementary; very simple, intermediate, and advanced; double-starred books are highly recommended. Each book is reviewed by a qualified specialist. The published annotations are prepared by the editorial staff from notes and comments of the reviewers.

24. *Science and Children.* National Science Teachers Association, 1201 Sixteenth Street, N.W., Washington, D.C. 20036. $5.00 per year. Free to members.

Includes a monthly column that reviews recent science books and audiovisual materials.

25. *Teacher.* (formerly *Grade Teacher*). Macmillan Professional Magazines, Inc., 22 West Putnam Avenue, Greenwich, Conn. 06830. Published monthly, September through June; May–June issue combined. $8.00 per year.

Children's books are regularly reviewed in a "Books for Children" column each month. Occasional articles about children's literature are included.

26. *Top of the News.* Children's Services Division and the Young Adult Services Division of American Library Association. Publication Office, 1201–05 Bluff Street, Fulton, Mo. 65251. Published November, January, April, and June. $7.50 per year, included in membership dues; $15.00 per year to nonmembers.

This quarterly journal contains interesting articles on issues in children's literature, news of international publishing, the May Hill Arbuthnot honor lecture, and many other features of interest to librarians and teachers of children's literature.

27. *Wilson Library Bulletin.* The H. W. Wilson Company, 950 University Avenue, Bronx, N.Y. 10452. Issued monthly, September–June. $11.00 per year. Single copies $1.00.

This bulletin includes discussions and reviews of all types of books, adult and children's. Features include a monthly review of current library reference books, news of literary awards, biographical sketches of authors, and a section devoted to displays of the month. The October issue is devoted to children's books.

Information about Authors and Illustrators

1. *Authors and Illustrators of Children's Books.* Miriam S. Hoffman and Eva A. Samuels, eds. R. R. Bowker Company, Bowker Order Department, P.O. Box 1807, Ann Arbor, Mich. 48106. 1972. 447 pp. $14.95.

   Reprints some fifty articles published between 1950 and 1971 on various artists and illustrators. A biographical sketch of the subject, bibliography of works, and a list of awards and honors follow each essay.

2. *Books Are by People: Interviews with 104 Authors and Illustrators of Books for Young Children.* Lee Bennett Hopkins. Citation Press, Education Services Division, Scholastic Magazines, Inc., 904 Sylvan Avenue, Englewood Cliffs, N.J. 07632. 1969. 349 pp. $6.95 hardback; $4.50, paperback.

   Authors and illustrators of books for young children are interviewed in their homes. Although no attempt is made to write full biographies, enough facts are given to satisfy the casual reader and to provide interesting information for children. Authors are asked questions about their books, and about their working habits and life styles.

3. *The Junior Book of Authors.* Stanley Kunitz and Howard Haycraft, eds. 1951. 309 pp. $10.00.
   More Junior Authors. Muriel Fuller, ed., 1963. 235 pp. $10.00.
   Third Book of Junior Authors. Doris DeMontreville and Donna Hill, eds. 1972. 320 pp. $12.00.
   All published by the H. W. Wilson Company, 950 University Avenue, Bronx, N.Y. 10454.

   In this series of reference books the authors and artists of children's books write their own brief biographies. Contains photographs of each person, and a guide to the pronunciation of some names. Other references are also cited.

4. *More Books by More People: Interviews with Sixty-five Authors of Books for Children.* Lee Bennett Hopkins. Citation Press, Education Services Division, Scholastic Magazines, Inc., 904 Sylvan Avenue, Engle-

wood Cliffs, N.J. 07632. 1974. 410 pp. Paperback, $4.95.

   Written in the same style as *Books Are by People,* this volume introduces sixty-five more authors and illustrators of children's books. Most of these authors write for middle-grade children. Special attention has been given to the author's way of working.

5. *The Pied Pipers.* Justin Wintle and Emma Fisher. The Two Continents Publishing Group, 30 East 42nd Street, New York, N.Y. 10017. 1975. $10.95.

   Fascinating in-depth interviews of twenty-four writers of children's books. Fourteen of the writers are British, the rest but one are U.S., and the other French. These interviews reveal exciting insights into children's literature and the men and women who write it.

6. *A Sense of Story: Essay on Contemporary Writers for Children.* John Rowe Townsend. J. B. Lippincott Company, East Washington Square, Philadelphia, Penna. 19105. 1971. 216 pp. $6.50.

   Considers the work of nineteen British, U.S. and Australian writers in literary terms, and gives biographical and bibliographical details. It is difficult for one author to analyze the work of other authors without reflecting his own personal bias, however.

7. *Something about the Author,* Vols. 1–8. Anne Commire. Gale Research Book Tower, Detroit, Mich. 48226. $22.50 each.

   These volumes contain information about contemporary authors and illustrators of books for young people. Pictures of the authors, as well as reproductions of illustrations from books accompany the text; and information is presented in a clear and interesting way. Middle-grade children would find these brief biographies very useful.

8. *The Who's Who of Children's Literature.* Brian Doyle, comp. and ed. Schocken Books, 67 Park Avenue, New York, N.Y. 10016. 1968. 380 pp. $3.95.

   This guide to the most notable authors and illustrators of children's books (nineteenth century to present) is intended to provide basic information as well as enjoyable reading. Few contemporary U.S. authors or illustrators are represented in this British publication.

Appendix C   Pronunciation Guide

Names of authors and illustrators often cause difficulties in pronunciation. Some of those most likely to be troublesome will be found in the following guide. For other names,

one helpful source is the series titled *Something about the Author* (*see* Appendix B, "Information about Authors and Illustrators").

Aliki	ah *lee* ki
Ardizzone, Edward	ar dit *zoh* nee
Asbjørnsen, P. C.	*ahs* byern sen
Asimov, Isaac	*az* i mov
D'Aulaire, Edgar and Ingri	doh *lair*
Behn, Harry	bane
Benét, Rosemary and Stephen	ben *ay* ·
Bolognese, Don	boh loh *nay* zee
Bontemps, Arna	*bon* tomp
Brunhoff, Jean de	zhahn duh *broo* noff
Carigiet, Alois	al *wah* cah ree *jyay*
Caudill, Rebecca	*kaw* d'l
Charlip, Remy	*reh* mee *shar* lip
Chönz, Selina	se *lee* nah shoonz
Ciardi, John	*char* dee
Colum, Padraic	*paw* drig *cawl* um
Dahl, Roald	roo all doll
De Angeli, Marguerite	dee *an* jel ee
De Gasztold, Carmen	duh *gaz* tol
DeJong, Meindert	*mine* dert de *yung*
De la Mare, Walter	duh lah mair
De Regniers, Beatrice	duh *rayn* yay
Du Bois, William Pène	pane doo *bwah*
Duvoisin, Roger	dyoo vwah zahn
Farjeon, Eleanor	*far* zhun
Francoise	frahn *swahz*
Friis-Bastaad, Babbis	*bah* bis freez *baw* stahd
Gág, Wanda	gahg
Geisel, Theodor Seuss	*guy* zel
Goudey, Alice	*gou* dee (ou as in loud)
Grifalconi, Ann	*gree* fal koh nee
Gripe, Maria	*gree* puh
Haugaard, Erik	*how* gard
Hautzig, Esther	*how* tzig
Hogrogian, Nonny	ha *groh* gee an
Jansson, Tove	*toh* vay *yahn* son
Jarrell, Randall	juh *rell*
Kjelgaard, Jim	*kel* gard
Krasilovksy, Phyllis	kraz uh *love* ski
Lexau, Joan	*lex* oh
Lionni, Leo	lee *oh* nee
Lobel, Arnold	*loh* bel
Minarik, Else	*min* ah rik
Montresor, Beni	*bay* nee *mohn* tre sor
Munari, Bruno	moo *nah* ree
Nic Leodhas, Sorche	*sore* kuh nik lee *oh* das
Oechsli, Kelly	*ox* ley
Orgel, Doris	or *gel*
Perrault, Charles	pair *oh*
Piatti, Celestino	chel ess *tee* noh pee *ah* tee
Politi, Leo	poh *lee* tee
Roethke, Theodor	*ret* kee
Saint Exupéry, Antoine de	an *twahn* duh san tag zoe pay ree
Sasek, Miroslav	*meer* oh slahf *sah* sek
Schoenherr, John	*show*en hair
Seredy, Kate	*shair* uh dee
Serraillier, Ian	*ee* an ser *ail* yay
Shimin, Symeon	*sim* ee un *shi* min
Shulevitz, Uri	*oo* ree *shool* uh vitz
Sidjakov, Nicolas	*sid* juh koff
Simont, Marc	si *mahnt*
Slobodkin, Louis	sloh *bod* kin
Slobodkina, Esphyr	ess fer sloh bod *keen* ah
Solbert, Ronni	*soll* bert
Syme, Ronald	sime
Tashjian, Virginia	*tas* jun
Tenniel, Sir John	ten yel
Tolkien, J. R. R.	*tohl* keen
Tresselt, Alvin	*treh* selt
Uchida, Yoshiko	yoh shee koh oo *chee* dah
Udry, Janice	*yoo* dri
Ungerer, Tomi	*toh* mee *ung* ger er
Van Iterson, Siny	*see* nee vahn *ee* ter son
Waber, Bernard	*way* ber
Weisgard, Leonard	*wise* gard
Wier, Ester	weer
Wiese, Kurt	*vee* zuh
Wojciechowska, Maia	*my* ah voy che *hov* skah
Wuorio, Eva-Lis	*ay* vuh lis *woor* yoh
Yashima, Taro	tar oh yah shee mah
Ylla	*eel* ah
Zemach, Margot	zee mock
Zolotow, Charlotte	*zol* uh tow (rhymes with how)

Appendix D Publishers' Addresses

BOOK PUBLISHERS

ABELARD-SCHUMAN, LTD.; 257 Park Ave. S.; New York, N.Y. 10010.

ABINGDON PRESS; 201 Eighth Ave. S.; Nashville, Tenn. 37202.

ADDISON-WESLEY PUBLISHING CO., INC.; Reading, Mass. 01867.

ALLYN & BACON, INC.; 470 Atlantic Ave.; Boston, Mass. 02210.

AMERICAN EDUCATION PUBLICATIONS (*see* Xerox Education Publications).

ATHENEUM PUBLISHERS; 122 East 42nd St.; New York, N.Y. 10017.

A. S. BARNES & CO., INC.; Forsgate Dr.; Cranbury, N.J. 08512.

BEACON PRESS; 25 Beacon St.; Boston, Mass. 02108.

THE BOBBS-MERRILL CO., INC.; 4300 West 62nd St.; Indianapolis, Ind. 46268.

BOWMAR; Box 3623; Glendale, Calif. 91201.

BRADBURY PRESS, INC.; 2 Overhill Rd.; Scarsdale, N.Y. 10583.

GEORGE BRAZILLER, INC.; One Park Ave.; New York, N.Y. 10016.

CHANDLER & SHARP PUBLISHERS, INC.; 5609 Paradise Dr.; Corte Madera, Calif. 94925.

CHILDRENS PRESS; 1224 West Van Buren St.; Chicago, Ill. 60607.

CHILTON BOOK CO.; Chilton Way; Radnor, Pa. 19089.

CITATION PRESS (see Scholastic Book Services).

WILLIAM COLLINS + WORLD PUBLISHING CO., INC.; 2080 West 117th St.; Cleveland, Ohio 44111.

COWARD, MCCANN AND GEOGHEGAN, INC.; 200 Madison Ave.; New York, N.Y. 10016.

CREATIVE EDUCATIONAL SOCIETY; 123 S. Broad St.; Mankato, Minn. 56001.

CRITERION BOOKS; 257 Park Ave. S.; New York, N.Y. 10010.

CROWELL-COLLIER (see Macmillan Publishing Co.).

THOMAS Y. CROWELL CO.; 666 Fifth Ave.; New York, N.Y. 10019.

CROWN PUBLISHERS, INC.; 419 Park Ave. S.; New York, N.Y. 10016.

DELACORTE PRESS; DELL PUBLISHING CO., INC.; 1 Dag Hammarskjold Plaza; 245 E. 47th St.; New York, N.Y. 10017.

THE DIAL PRESS; 1 Dag Hammarskjold Plaza; 245 E. 47th St.; New York, N.Y. 10017.

DODD, MEAD & CO.; 79 Madison Avenue; New York, N.Y. 10016.

DOUBLEDAY & CO., INC.; 277 Park Ave.; New York, N.Y. 10017.

DOVER PUBLICATIONS, INC.; 180 Varick St.; New York, N.Y. 10014.

DUFOUR EDITIONS, INC.; Chester Springs, Pa. 19425.

E. P. DUTTON & CO., INC.; 201 Park Ave. S.; New York, N.Y. 10003.

M. EVANS AND CO., INC.; 216 E. 49th St.; New York, N.Y. 10017

FARRAR, STRAUS & GIROUX, INC.; 19 Union Square W.; New York, N.Y. 10003.

FOLLETT PUBLISHING COMPANY; Div. of Follett Corp. 1010 W. Washington Blvd.; Chicago, Ill. 60607.

FOUR WINDS PRESS; 50 W. 44th St.; New York, N.Y. 10036.

FUNK & WAGNALLS INC.; 55 E. 77 Street; New York, N.Y. 10021.

GARRARD PUBLISHING CO.; 1607 N. Market St.; Champaign, Ill. 61820.

GOLDEN GATE JUNIOR BOOKS; 6922 Hollywood Blvd.; Los Angeles, Calif. 90028.

GOLDEN PRESS (see Western Publishing Co.).

GREENWILLOW BOOKS (see William Morrow and Co., Inc.).

GROSSET & DUNLAP, INC.; 51 Madison Ave.; New York, N.Y. 10010.

GROSSMAN PUBLISHERS; 625 Madison Ave.; New York, N.Y. 10022.

HARCOURT BRACE JOVANOVICH, INC.; 757 Third Ave.; New York, N.Y. 10017.

HARPER & ROW, PUBLISHERS; 10 E. 53rd St.; New York, N.Y. 10022.

HARVEY HOUSE, INC., PUBLISHERS; 20 Waterside Plaza; New York, N.Y. 10010.

HASTINGS HOUSE PUBLISHERS, LTD.; 10 E. 40th St.; New York, N.Y. 10016.

HAWTHORN BOOKS, INC.; 260 Madison Ave.; New York, N.Y. 10016.

HILL & WANG; 19 Union Sq. W.; New York, N.Y. 10003.

HOLIDAY HOUSE, INC.; 18 E. 56th St.; New York, N.Y. 10022.

HOLT, RINEHART AND WINSTON, INC.; 383 Madison Ave.; New York, N.Y. 10017.

HOUGHTON MIFFLIN CO.; 2 Park St.; Boston, Mass. 02107.

ISLAND HERITAGE, LTD.; 1020 Auahi St., Bldg. 3; Honolulu Hawaii 96814.

ALFRED A. KNOPF, INC.; 201 E. 50th St.; New York, N.Y. 10022.

LERNER PUBLICATIONS CO.; 241 First Ave. N.: Minneapolis, Minn. 55401.

LION BOOKS; 111 E. 39th St.; New York, N.Y. 10018.

J. B. LIPPINCOTT CO.; E. Washington Sq.; Philadelphia, Pa. 19105.

LITTLE, BROWN AND CO.; 34 Beacon St.; Boston, Mass. 02106.

LIVERIGHT; 386 Park Ave. S.; New York, N.Y. 10016.

LOTHROP, LEE & SHEPARD CO.; 105 Madison Ave.; New York, N.Y. 10016.

MCGRAW-HILL BOOK CO.; 1221 Ave. of the Americas; New York, N.Y. 10020.

DAVID MCKAY CO., INC.; 750 Third Ave.; New York, N.Y. 10017.

MACMILLAN PUBLISHING CO., INC.; 866 Third Ave.; New York, N.Y. 10022.

JULIAN MESSNER; 1 West 39th St.; New York, N.Y. 10018.

WILLIAM MORROW AND CO., INC.; 105 Madison Ave.; New York, N.Y. 10016.

THE NATURAL HISTORY PRESS; 277 Park Ave.; New York, N.Y. 10017.

THOMAS NELSON, INC.; 407 Seventh Ave., S.; Nashville, Tenn. 37203.

THE NEW AMERICAN LIBRARY, INC.; 1301 Ave. of the Americas; New York, N.Y. 10019.

W. W. NORTON CO., INC.; 500 Fifth Ave.; New York, N.Y. 10036.

OXFORD UNIVERSITY PRESS, INC.; 200 Madison Ave.; New York, N.Y. 10016.

PANTHEON BOOKS; 201 E. 50th St.; New York, N.Y. 10022.

PARENTS' MAGAZINE PRESS; 52 Vanderbilt Ave.; New York, N.Y. 10017.

PARNASSUS PRESS; 2721 Parker St.; Berkeley, Calif. 94704.

PENGUIN BOOKS, INC.; 7110 Ambassador Rd.; Baltimore, Md. 21207.

PETER PAUPER PRESS; 629 MacQuesten Pkwy.; Mt. Vernon, N.Y. 10552.

S. G. PHILLIPS, INC.; 305 W. 86th St.; New York, N.Y. 10024.

PLATT & MUNK; 1055 Bronx River Ave.; Bronx, N.Y. 10472.

PRENTICE-HALL, INC.; Englewood Cliffs, N.J. 07632.

G. P. PUTNAM'S SONS; 200 Madison Ave.; New York, N.Y. 10016.

HARLAN QUIST BOOKS; 192 East 75th St.; New York, N.Y. 10021.

RAND MCNALLY & CO.; Box 7600; Chicago, Ill. 60680.

RANDOM HOUSE, INC.; 201 E. 50th St.; New York, N.Y. 10022.

REILLY & LEE; HENRY REGNERY CO.; 180 N. Michigan Ave.; Chicago, Ill. 60601.

ST. MARTIN'S PRESS, INC.; 175 Fifth Ave.; New York, N.Y. 10010.

SCHOCKEN BOOKS, INC.; 200 Madison Ave.; New York, N.Y. 10016.

SCHOLASTIC BOOK SERVICES; Scholastic Magazines, Inc.; 50 W. 44th St.; New York, N.Y. 10036.

SCOTT, FORESMAN AND CO.; 1900 E. Lake Ave., Glenview, Ill. 60025.

CHARLES SCRIBNER'S SONS; 597 Fifth Ave.; New York, N.Y. 10017.

SCROLL PRESS, INC.; 129 E. 94th St.; New York, N.Y. 10028.

THE SEABURY PRESS, INC.; 815 Second Ave.; New York, N.Y. 10017.

SIMON & SCHUSTER, INC.; Rockefeller Center; 630 Fifth Ave.; New York, N.Y. 10020.

STACKPOLE BOOKS; Cameron and Kelker Sts.; Harrisburg, Pa. 17105.

STERLING PUBLISHING COMPANY, INC.; 419 Park Avenue S.; New York, N.Y. 10016.

TIME-LIFE BOOKS; Time & Life Bldg.; Rockefeller Center; New York, N.Y. 10020.

TUDOR PUBLISHING CO.; 221 Park Ave. S.; New York, N.Y. 10003.

CHARLES E. TUTTLE COMPANY, INC.; 28 East Main St.; Rutland, Vt. 05701.

VAN NOSTRAND REINHOLD CO.; 450 W. 33rd St.; New York, N.Y. 10001.

VANGUARD PRESS, INC.; 424 Madison Ave.; New York, N.Y. 10017.

THE VIKING PRESS; 625 Madison Ave.; New York, N.Y. 10022.

HENRY Z. WALCK, INC.; 750 Third Ave.; New York, N.Y. 10017.

WALKER AND CO.; 720 Fifth Ave.; New York, N.Y. 10019.

FREDERICK WARNE & CO., INC.; 101 Fifth Ave.; New York, N.Y. 10003.

WASHINGTON SQUARE PRESS (see Simon & Schuster, Inc.)

FRANKLIN WATTS, INC.; 730 Fifth Ave.; New York, N.Y. 10019.

WESTERN PUBLISHING CO.; 1220 Mound Ave.; Racine, Wis. 53404.

THE WESTMINSTER PRESS; Witherspoon Bldg.; Philadelphia, Pa. 19107.

DAVID WHITE CO.; 60 E. 55th St.; New York, N.Y. 10022.

ALBERT WHITMAN & CO.; 560 West Lake St.; Chicago, Ill. 60606.

WINDMILL BOOKS, INC.; 201 Park Ave. S.; New York, N.Y. 10010.

WORLD PUBLISHING COMPANY (see William Collins + World).

XEROX EDUCATION PUBLICATIONS; Education Ctr.; Columbus, Ohio 43216.

YALE UNIVERSITY PRESS; 302 Temple St.; New Haven, Conn. 06511.

YOUNG SCOTT BOOKS (see Addison-Wesley Publishing Co.).

MEDIA SOURCES

ACI FILMS, INC.; 35 W. 45th St.; New York, N.Y. 10036.

AMERICAN LIBRARY ASSOC.; 50 E. Huron St.; Chicago, Ill. 60611.

BFA EDUCATIONAL MEDIA; Division of CBS; 2211 Michigan Ave.; Santa Monica, Calif. 90404.

CAEDMON RECORDS; D. C. Heath and Co.; 2700 N. Richardt Ave.; Indianapolis, Ind. 46219.

CAPITOL RECORDS, INC.; 1750 N. Vine St.; Hollywood, Calif. 90028.

CAROUSEL FILMS, INC., 1501 Broadway; New York, N.Y. 10036.

CCM FILMS; CROWELL-COLLIER-MACMILLAN SCHOOL AND LIBRARY SERVICES; 866 Third Ave.; New York, N.Y. 10022.

CHILDREN'S BOOK COUNCIL, INC.; 67 Irving Pl.; New York, N.Y. 10003.

CHURCHILL FILMS; 662 N. Robertson Blvd.; Los Angeles, Calif. 90069.

CMS RECORDS, INC.; 14 Warren St.; New York, N.Y. 10007.

CONNECTICUT FILMS, INC.; 6 Cobble Hill Rd.; Westport, Conn. 06880.

CORONET INSTRUCTIONAL FILMS; 65 East South Water St.; Chicago, Ill. 60601.

WALT DISNEY PRODUCTIONS; Educational Film Div.; 477 Madison Ave., New York, N.Y. 10022.

ENCYCLOPEDIA BRITANNICA EDUCATIONAL CORP.; 425 N. Michigan Ave.; Chicago, Ill. 60611.

FOLK-LEGACY RECORDS, INC.; Sharon, Conn. 06069.

FOLKWAYS; 701 Seventh Ave.; New York, N.Y. 10036.

FOLKWAYS/SCHOLASTIC; 906 Sylvan Ave.; Englewood Cliffs, N.J. 07632.

GUIDANCE ASSOCIATES; 41 Washington Ave.; Pleasantville, N.Y. 10570.

LEARNING CORPORATION OF AMERICA; Subsidiary of Columbia Pictures Industries, Inc.; 711 Fifth Ave.; New York, N.Y. 10022.

LONDON RECORDS, INC.; 539 W. 25th St.; New York, N.Y. 10001.

LYCEUM PRODUCTIONS; Box 1226; Laguna Beach, Calif. 92652.

MCGRAW-HILL FILMS; 1221 Ave. of the Americas; New York, N.Y. 10020.

MEDIA PLUS, INC.; 60 Riverside Dr.; New York, N.Y. 10024.

MILLER-BRODY PROD.; 342 Madison Ave.; New York, N.Y. 10017.

NATIONAL FILM BOARD OF CANADA; 680 Fifth Ave.; New York, N.Y. 10019.

NEWBERY AWARD RECORDS, INC.; 342 Madison Ave.; New York, N.Y. 10017.

NEWENHOUSE-NOVO; 1825 Willow Rd.; Northfield, Ill. 60093.

ONTARIO DEPARTMENT OF EDUCATION; Mrs. Dorothy Reid; Provincial Library Service; 14th Fl. Mowat Bldg.; Government of Ontario; Toronto 5, Canada.

PATHWAYS EDUCATIONAL PROGRAMS, INC.; 1075 Central Park Ave.; Scarsdale, N.Y. 10582.

PATHWAYS OF SOUND, INC.; 102 Mount Auburn St.; Cambridge, Mass. 02138.

PYRAMID FILMS; Box 1048; Santa Monica, Calif. 90406.

REMBRANDT FILMS; 59 E. 54th St.; New York, N.Y. 10022.

SCHOLASTIC MAGAZINES, INC.; 50 W. 44th St.; New York, N.Y. 10036.

SPOKEN ARTS, INC.; 310 North Ave.; New Rochelle, N.Y. 10801.

STERLING EDUCATIONAL FILMS; Div. of the Walter Reade Organization; 241 E. 34th St.; New York, N.Y. 10016.

SVE; SOCIETY FOR VISUAL EDUCATION, INC.; 1345 Diversey Pkwy.; Chicago, Ill. 60614.

TEXTURE FILMS, INC.; 1600 Broadway; New York, N. Y. 10019.

THE UNIV. OF MICH.; Audio-Visual Education Center; Frieze Bldg.; 720 E. Huron; Ann Arbor, Mich. 48104.

THE VIKING PRESS; 625 Madison Ave.; New York, N.Y. 10022.

WATERMAN FILMS (see Newenhouse-Novo).

WESTON WOODS STUDIOS, INC.; Weston, Conn. 06880.

SUBJECT INDEX

AUTHOR, ILLUSTRATOR, TITLE INDEX

Numbers in bold type indicate the page where a selection is discussed at length; starred numbers indicate a quoted poem. The abbreviation "il." marks pages where an illustration is reproduced in the text. The letters "F" indicate a film, "FS" a filmstrip, "R" a recording. Color Section I is found between pages 114 and 115.

791

Charlotte S. Huck

After graduating from Northwestern University, Charlotte S. Huck joined the faculty of Early and Middle Childhood Education at The Ohio State University, where she recently won the Distinguished Teaching Award. Before Dr. Huck became Professor of Education at Ohio State, she had been an elementary school teacher for seven years in both Missouri and Illinois. She has served the National Council of Teachers of English in many capacities, including as a member of the editorial board, as chair of the Elementary Section, and as a member of the executive committee. She is the current president of NCTE, and has functioned on its Literature Commission. Dr. Huck was a member of the Newbery-Caldecott Award Committee of the American Library Association. Her pervading concern with children's literature is evidenced as well by Dr. Huck's work on the Second World Congress of Reading, held in Copenhagen, and her co-chairing of Commission 3 of the International Conference on Language and Learning in York, England. She has been a Visiting Professor at both the University of Denver and the University of Hawaii, and has published many articles in such periodicals as *Reading Teacher* and *Language Arts*.